Business Administration Books

of

WEST PUBLISHING COMPANY

St. Paul, Minnesota 55102

DOWER AND VIHON'S CASES ON LEGAL PROBLEMS OF BUSINESS IN A FREE SOCIETY

Harry A. Dower
Adjunct Professor of Law, Lehigh University.

Charles F. Vihon
Professor of Law, Lehigh University.

The book is designed as a classroom text and covers the following subjects by chapter: Introduction; Freedom of Choice of Location and Form of the Business Enterprise-Mobility of Capital Products; Fair Taxation of Business Enterprises; Stockholder Agreements and Internal Controls; Sales and Transfers of Securities; Business Acquisitions and Divisions; Distribution of Goods and Services; Administrative Agencies; Relations with Employees; Dealing with Local Government; The Business in Financial Difficulty. Table of Cases and Index included.

Approximately 725 pages-1973

FISHER'S INTRODUCTION TO THE LEGAL SYSTEM—THEORY—OVERVIEW— BUSINESS APPLICATIONS

Bruce D. Fisher
Professor of Business Administration, University of Tennessee.

The book is designed as a classroom text and covers the following subject matter by chapter: Definition and Nature of Law; Sources of Law; Legal Machinery; Legal Reasoning; An Overview of Substantive Law; White Collar Crimes; White Collar Torts; Contract Remedies; Types of Enforceable Promises; The Agreement; Commitment to the Bargain; Problems with the Agreement; Federal Antitrust Laws; Labor Law; Protection of Business Ideas. Table of Cases and Index included. Teacher's manual and test manual available.

621 pages-1972

KEETON'S CPCU SELECTIONS FROM PROGRAMMED PROBLEMS IN INSURANCE LAW

Robert E. Keeton
Professor of Law, Harvard University.

The book is designed as a classroom text for a CPCU course—CPCU Part IV— Insurance and Business Law. It contains problems and their answers and is keyed to Keeton's Basic Text on Insurance Law for more extensive study.

Paperback, 124 pages-1972

KEETON'S PROGRAMMED PROBLEMS IN INSURANCE LAW

Robert E. Keeton
Professor of Law, Harvard Univerity.

The book is designed as a classroom text for an elementary course and contains problems on insurance law and their answers. It is also keyed to Keeton's Basic Text on Insurance Law for more intensive study.

Paperback, 243 pages-1972

I

BUSINESS ADMINISTRATION BOOKS

KEMPIN AND WIESEN'S CASES AND MATERIALS ON LEGAL ASPECTS OF THE MANAGEMENT PROCESS

Frederick G. Kempin, Jr.
Vice-Dean and Professor of Business Law, the Wharton School of Finance and Commerce, University of Pennsylvania.

Jeremy L. Wiesen
Former Professor of Business Law, Columbia University.

The book is designed as a classroom text and covers the following subjects by chapter: Corporate Personality; Joint Stock and Stockholders; Limited Liability; History and Development of the Business Corporation; The Partnership Concept; Internal Partnership Management-Policy Decisions; Interlude on the Authority of Agents; Power of a Partner to Act for the Partnership; Partner's Torts and Crimes, Dissolution of the Partnership; Powers of Directors; Powers of Officers; Ultra Vires, and Corporate Torts and Crimes; Dividends; Management's Duties to the Corporation; Enforcement of Management's Duties to Corporate Creditors; The Duty of Care; Management's Duties to the Shareholders; Judicial Control of Management— The Power to Dissolve; Management's Duties to the Public. Table of Cases and Index included.

732 pages-1969

LAKIN AND BERGER'S CPA LAW EXAMINATION REVIEW—MATERIALS—QUESTIONS—ANSWERS

Leonard Lakin
Professor of Business Law, Bernard M. Baruch College, City University of New York.

Howard J. Berger
Professor of Business Law, Bernard M. Baruch College, City University of New York.

The book is designed as a classroom text and covers the following subject matter by chapter: How to Successfully Take the CPA Business Law Examination; An Analysis of the CPA Business, Law Examination; Laws of Accountants Legal Responsibility; Accountant's Legal Responsibility; Agency; Anti-trust; Bankruptcy; Commercial Paper; Contracts; Corporations; Federal Securities Regulations; Insurance; Partnerships; Property; Regulation of the Employer and Employee Relationship; Sales; Secured Transactions; Suretyship; Wills and Estates and Trusts.

410 pages-1972

McNULTY'S FEDERAL INCOME TAXATION OF INDIVIDUALS IN A NUTSHELL

John K. McNulty
Professor of Law, University of California, Berkeley.

The book can be used as a classroom text or collateral reading source and covers the following subjects by chapter: What is Income: Statutory Inclusion and Exclusion from Gross Income; What Is Deductible: Profit Related Deductions; Mixed (Personal and Profit Seeking) Deductions; Personal Deductions; Annual Accounting: When Is Income Taxable; To Whom is Income Taxable; How Is Income Taxable. Table of Cases and Index included.

Paperback, 322 pages-1972

OBERER AND HANSLOWE'S COLLECTIVE BARGAINING AND THE LAW—AN OVERVIEW

Walter E. Oberer
Professor of Law and Professor of Industrial and Labor Relations, Cornell University.

Kurt L. Hanslowe
Professor of Law and Professor of Industrial and Labor Relations, Cornell University.

The book is designed as a classroom text and covers the following subject matter by chapter: Labor as a Commodity: The Rise and Decline of the Double Standard; Paternal Protection: of Law, Collective Bargaining, and Social Therapy; The Need for Balance: Government as Umpire. Table of Cases and Index included.

Paperback, 202 pages-1972

PAUST AND UPP'S BUSINESS LAW

Jordan L. Paust
Law Department Chairman, Los Angeles City College.

Robert D. Upp
Professor of Law, Los Angeles City College.

The book is designed as a classroom text for a one-semester course and covers the following subjects by part: The Law and the Courts; The Law of Contracts; The Law of Sales; Bailments; Agency; Partnerships; Corporations; Negotiable Instruments; Appendices covering The Uniform Commercial Code, Uniform Partnership Act, and Dictionary of Legal Terms. Table of Cases and Index included. Teacher's manual and student workbook available.

750 pages-1969

SMITH AND ROBERSON'S BUSINESS LAW, UNIFORM COMMERCIAL CODE, 3rd EDITION

Len Young Smith
Department of Business Law Chairman Emeritus, Northwestern University.

G. Gale Roberson
Professorial Lecturer in Business Law, Northwestern University.

The book is designed as a classroom text containing cases and problems and covers the following subjects by part: Introduction to Law-Contracts; Agency; Bailments and Carriers; Sales; Commercial Paper; Partnership; Corporations; Unfair Competition, Bankruptcy, Secured Transactions; Property; Trusts, Mortgages, Insurance, Wills; Appendices covering The Uniform Commercial Code, Uniform Partnership Act, Uniform Limited Partnership Act, Model Business Corporation Act and Dictionary of Legal Terms. Table of Cases and Index included. Teacher's manual and student workbook available.

1464 pages-1971

WALTON SERIES—AMERICAN BUSINESS LAW—VOLUME I, 2nd EDITION

Len Young Smith
Department of Business Law Chairman Emeritus, Northwestern University.

G. Gale Roberson
Professorial Lecturer in Business Law, Northwestern University.

The book is an exact reprint of chapters 1 to 28 of Smith and Roberson's Business Law, U.C.C., 1971, 3rd edition and is designed as a classroom text containing cases and problems covering the following subjects by part: Introduction to Law-Contracts; Agency; Bailments and Carriers; Sales; Commercial Paper.

748 pages-1971

*

LEGAL PROBLEMS

OF

BUSINESS

IN A

FREE SOCIETY

by

HARRY A. DOWER
Adjunct Professsor of Law

and

CHARLES F. VIHON
Assistant Professor of Law
both of the
Graduate School, College of Business & Economics
Lehigh University

ST. PAUL, MINN.
WEST PUBLISHING CO.
1973

COPYRIGHT © 1973

By

WEST PUBLISHING CO.

Library of Congress Catalog Card Number: 73–75063

To Marion Clark Dower, for her devotion to freedom
and justice and for her patience.

*

PREFACE

This is a book for students and teachers. It is a book for a survey course which considers the legal problems which a business faces in a free society. As such it is not a work of scholarly research and is not exhaustive of any of the topics considered. It is not a display of our erudition. It does not contain copious footnotes or citations to authorities for the statements made because in our experience students in a survey course do not have the time to examine each individual statement of fact (or fancy) and it has been our purpose to use the available space in a manner that will be more helpful to students. We have a deep and continuing interest in the works of scholarship, and we ourselves are engaged in research on several of the topics covered in this book which we hope when produced will merit the recognition of other scholars.

We did not want to produce just another casebook. The literature abounds with collections of cases and author's comments which are much like many others; newer ones are distinguished from older ones only because they carry more current cases. We both believe in the law as an instrument of freedom and justice and it occurred to us that stating our views of the function of the law of business in a free society would be a most appropriate theme for a new casebook. Our students for several years have responded with enthusiasm to this approach and these materials.

We assume that students using this book will previously have studied subjects relating to the structure of corporations, as well as economics and finance, and will have some understanding of the development of the common law. The book has been designed for those students who will find a survey course useful in approaching that part of their education which is concerned with the law as it relates to business transactions. It can be used by students who will later seek advanced courses in each of the topics covered in the book, as well as by those students who will emphasize some other branch of the law in their education. The book also will be useful for students pursuing an education in business administration.

We apologize to those purists who believe that the entire report of a case, including concurring and dissenting opinions, should be printed. Our own inclination has been to do this but limitations of space have compelled us to excise large parts of many of the cases. Also, we are quite aware that many other topics could have been selected for study; our own experiences as both teachers and practitioners of the law have inclined us to select the topics which are included. Many other cases could have been used within the topics covered but here our only apology is for our vanity: we have used some of the cases in which we ourselves have been counsel. To those persons who will maintain that many of the cases are too long we would only reply that in our view part of the intellectual exercise of studying material of this kind is to acquire the skill of digesting a complex problem so that the digest will be meaningful to the student. Regretfully we have had to eliminate most of the dissenting opinions although many of the cases we selected have been rather controversial. For the more enquiring students we recommend studying the full reports of many of the cases. Also, we have listed at the end of each chapter one or two standard reference works which cover the material generally under consideration in that chapter as well as a reference to the Index of Legal Periodicals where additional law journal articles can be found and which can be selected by the student from the journals available to him. We would also note that the Practicing Law Institute (PLI), 1133 Avenue of the Americas, New York, N. Y. 10036, and the American Law Institute—American Bar Association (ALI–ABA) Joint Committee on Continuing Legal Education, 4025 Chestnut Street, Philadelphia, Pa., 19104, have a number of publications covering these subjects; since these are frequently revised with current material we have not referred to any of them specifically. These publications are more "practical" than this book. They nonetheless are generally of high quality and are helpful in providing additional information about these topics for one who is not a specialist in each of the fields. A request addressed either to PLI or to ALI–ABA for a current list of its publications will always be promptly answered.

Following each chapter we have included suggested reference sources. These sources, texts, treatises, loose-leaf services, periodicals and the categories under which law review and other journal articles pertinent to the subject matter of the chapter may be found, are meant to be neither exhaustive nor quality-judged. The essential criterion here has been source material most likely to be available to the student and which tends most frequently to be used in practice. Clearly a bibliography of the subjects of these chapters would in itself be a volume of size comparable to this one, the presentation of which in a book of this character would be wholly out of context.

With specific respect to the Index of Legal Periodicals to which topic headings are referenced at the end of each chapter, for those readers who may be unfamiliar with legal research tools, the Index contains references to virtually all English-language periodicals whose subject is law or some aspect thereof. Contained in these periodicals will be articles, mostly of a scholarly bent, both descriptive and explicative of virtually every facet of the law and, therefore, of the subjects contained in this book.

We have eliminated the footnotes in nearly all of the cases, again as a means of reducing the length of the cases. In those few instances where we have retained the footnotes we have used our own numbers

PREFACE

for them but have noted at the end of each footnote the number of the Court's footnote.

We do not believe that anyone who prepares a book can ever give adequate recognition to all those persons who contributed to the ideas of the authors, and since the theme of this book is our own, we decline to embarrass those of our mentors who directly or indirectly stimulated us into organizing these materials and into thinking and expressing ourselves as we have done in the book; we will not face the risk of their denial. However, we would like to note our appreciation of the efforts of Linda D. Renick for her help in preparing the final draft of the manuscript.

H.A.D.
C.F.V.

March, 1973

*

SUMMARY OF CONTENTS

SUMMARY OF CONTENTS

TABLE OF CONTENTS

TABLE OF CONTENTS

TABLE OF CONTENTS

TABLE OF CONTENTS

TABLE OF CONTENTS

TABLE OF CONTENTS

TABLE OF CONTENTS

*

TABLE OF CASES

References are to Pages

TABLE OF CASES

"The life of the law has not been logic; it has been experience. The felt necessities of the time, the prevalent moral and political theories, intuitions of public policy, avowed or unconscious, even the prejudices which judges share with their fellow-men, have had a good deal more to do than the syllogism in determining the rules by which men should be governed."

Holmes, *The Common Law*, p. 1.

The Eleven Federal Judicial Circuits

See 28 U.S.C.A. § 41

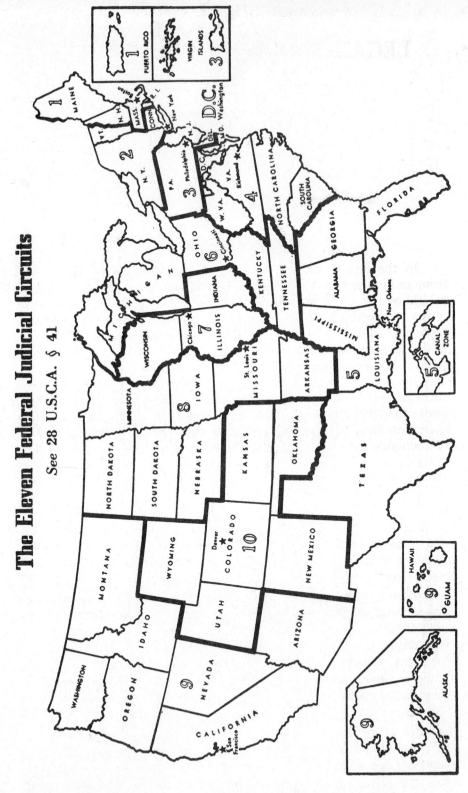

LEGAL PROBLEMS OF BUSINESS
in a
FREE SOCIETY

Chapter I

INTRODUCTION

In the last five hundred years the Western world has moved from an agrarian to a mercantile to an industrial economy. In medieval times the principal economic activity was agriculture and most forms of wealth were measured in terms of land and agricultural products. Most certainly there were other kinds of economic activity because people had to be clothed and housed then as well as today. Whether people then spent more time than today in religious activity or some other form of diversion from the immediate pressures of everyday life is probably difficult to measure, but it is generally thought that people have more leisure time today, that is, they spend less time in economic activity. Also, there is a greater variety of economic activity today and fewer and fewer people are engaged in agriculture to the point where less than 10% of the population of the United States is engaged in producing food for the rest of the people in the country and for people in other parts of the world. Man has expanded his productive capacity through the use of machines, both in agriculture and other economic enterprises, so that the number of people now involved in agriculture with machines and other products of science are able to produce the food for an ever increasing number of consumers. Machines have increased the capacity of people to provide goods and services (and to make war) so that more and more of the people in the Western world are now engaged in manufacturing or in providing services of an infinite variety to people who desire them. Unquestionably a richer material life is available for many people in modern society; until it is available for all people, however, many problems will have to be solved and much improvement in the system will have to be accomplished.

While the foundations of our legal system are drawn from a number of ancient societies and religions, and by no means arrived as a full-blown body of jurisprudence coming out of the heavens or suddenly communicated by some diety to a peculiarly perceptive person, the principles of the legal system relating to modern business (that is, to the modern Western economic system) have most of their origins in the Middle Ages, in an agrarian society and economy. Our concepts of the law of private property and the legal problems involved in moving products from factory to market and from market to consumer reach back to the agrarian society of the Middle Ages. The roots of this system go back in history much further. Most certainly the concept of private ownership of property evolved thousands of years before recorded history. One can readily observe an attitude of exclusivity of domain practiced by lower animals, particularly by those with any degree of domestication. Possessiveness and dominion over property within certain boundaries have evolved along with the biological development of man, and the more sophisticated his organic structure has become the more sophisticated his concepts of property. Whether this is the consequence of sexual drives or other reasons has been examined by others. Also, in Western society concepts of state ownership (or non-private ownership) have existed from unrecorded times and exist to a greater or lesser degree today throughout the Western world. Those societies that we think of, or aspire to be considered, as democratic societies have a greater degree of private ownership of property than those that we think of as being authoritarian which have a much lesser degree of private ownership. This distinction is by no means precise. The United Kingdom, certainly one of the freer societies of the world, is pursuing a policy of state ownership of major industrial, transportation and communication properties; the exclusive right to occupy a dwelling, an aspect of private property, is known and practiced throughout the entire world, in both democratic and authoritarian societies. Various forms of cooperative ownership and control of dwellings and production and marketing facilities exist in democratic societies as well as in authoritarian societies. The fact that there is no clear delineation between private and non-private ownership of property in various societies is noted only as an example of the continuing change which occurs in the history of human affairs.

Every society and every economy has evolved methods of arranging for the distribution or allocation of resources and products within the society. Western society has placed a much greater emphasis on the private ownership of property than upon state ownership as a means of arranging for this distribution. Yet the ownership of the largest industries, disseminated through hundreds of thousands of participating owners called shareholders, is totally unlike the ownership enjoyed by the fifteenth century English gentleman who held his country estates more or less free of royal (that is, governmental) control. The thoroughly widespread ownership of the large business concerns in modern Western society when compared with the medieval practice of a single owner of an economic unit is clearly more like public (that is, non-private) ownership than anything else. This is true of the large industrial, transportation, communications, and financial corporations, and apparently is becoming true of agricultural enterprises too.

The concentration of productive capacity and other forms of wealth that has occurred in the twentieth century was almost unknown to medieval society. One can imagine that the Duke of Norfolk, or the Duke of Burgundy, or several royal families owned tremendous agricultural enterprises in the Middle Ages. But these few examples were really exceptional instances of concentrated economic power when compared with the great number of large corporations operating on an international scale in modern Western society. One concern, American Telephone and Telegraph Company, employs more people (directly or indirectly through subsidiaries which it controls) than the total population of many medieval countries. The amount of wealth assembled in many modern large corporations is so vast that it is totally beyond the capacity of any one person or family or even groups of families to own in the sense that an English gentleman owned his farms in the Middle Ages.

Control of these modern enterprises is another matter. Many persons have noted that within the last century, and particularly within the last five decades, the medieval concept of private ownership of property has almost disappeared. This concept was a combination of the power to control property, as well as to enjoy the benefits and the products of the property (the profits), and the right to transfer the property; ownership of a share in a large corporation continues to mean the almost unlimited right to transfer it (absent any fraudulent or deceptive practices), but it also means the diminishing right to enjoy the profits of the property, and almost no control at all over the basic productive property. Again this is a highly imprecise statement; again it is noted only to indicate the trend of the changes which are appearing in Western society. Also, in reference to control, from an objective viewpoint the holder of a bond issued by a large industrial enterprise is really not much different from the holder of a share of stock issued by the same enterprise; the bondholder may have certain prior rights to the product of the enterprise, in this case called "interest", with no voice at all in the management or control of the enterprise (although in many instances a trustee for him has the power to restrict certain transactions), while the shareholder has a right to a different kind of product of the enterprise, a "dividend" (generally a management-determined portion of the profit), but in practical effect no control.

Periodically a shareholder of a large corporation goes through a ritual in which the managers of the enterprise pretend to seek his approval and consent to their continuation in office. While the faces change in the management group, nearly every large corporation is controlled by the same management group year in year out in the same manner that bureaucracies have controlled governmental agencies for centuries. They are really self-perpetuating and instead of depending upon divine right, or primogeniture or some other form of inheritance, they use the modern equivalent called a "proxy", which is really just as effective.

But democracy does not exist everywhere that private ownership of property exists or everywhere that non-state control of production exists. In the first half of the twentieth century three highly authoritarian systems of government developed, one each in the Soviet Union, Italy and Germany, and in the latter two private ownership of property continued while in the first (the Soviet Union) insofar as productive enterprises were concerned private ownership has been almost entirely discontinued. And in both Fascist Italy and Nazi German a substantial degree of governmental control was imposed on the business system. While the economy was almost totally state controlled in Fascist Italy and Nazi Germany, the right to the profits of the system and the right to transfer this benefit continued to belong to individual owners; in the Soviet Union both of these rights were and are rights of the state, which in one sense may mean that they are widely disseminated throughout the entire society. Further, in times of great national stress, such as the conduct of a large scale war, societies which accord to individuals the right of ownership of property and the control of production take from the individuals some of the freedom to operate or control the productive facility and instead direct it from a state agency. However, even under these circumstances, the right to the profits of the property continues to belong to individuals although there may be some limitations imposed by the government directly through price control or indirectly through additional taxation; the right to transfer the property has generally remained unimpeded at all times.

Private ownership of property has not and does not mean that the society in which this system occurs is a democratic society. Throughout much of the world where private ownership does exist the limitations on individual freedoms are so severe that it cannot be said that those societies are democratic. The clearest example of this for most Americans is the system of slavery which existed in the Southern States from colonial times to the Civil War, where even human beings were the private property of others. Anybody who has served in the military forces of any country will know what an authoritarian system is. And many, if not all, of the societies today which are predominantly agrarian or pastoral which recognize private property can hardly be said to be democratic. While the outright ownership of human beings is nearly everywhere forbidden by law, other subtler forms of bondage continue and no civil liberties exist. That is, freedom of speech and thought, freedom of worship, freedom of association, freedom from oppression by the government or large land owners do not exist, frequently even for those with property. They have no freedom of contract and have no guarantees of being dealt with fairly or equally under the law.

The principal differences between a democratic and an authoritarian economic system are related to ownership and control of property; in a democracy ownership is private and control is accomplished by a minimum of direction from the state, that is, by freedom of contract. Whether the business enterprise be large or small, be owned by hundreds of thousands of shareholders, or by a sole proprietor, or anything between, in a democratic system initiative to operate the productive enterprise remains in the hands of private individuals rather than in a state agency. As small as any sole proprietorship may be, or as large as any giant industrial corporation may be, there is no state agency directing either of them to produce certain products and not others, to sell in certain markets and not in others, to employ certain people and not others (although there may be prohibitions against several kinds of discrimination in employment) and except in unusual times there is no state agency fixing prices or determining quality or quantity of production. There is no state agency planning for the production of a given number of motor vehicles, for example, or determining the size or horsepower of those vehicles, or their color or decoration, or their prices or the markets in which they may be sold, or which productive enterprises may produce them, or if more than one enterprise is to be engaged in producing them which one may produce which vehicles, etc. We accord to individuals, as distinguished from the state, the right to make these determinations, and depend upon a number of fundamental legal principles and a market place as the means of regulating the production of these enterprises, always in an indirect manner rather than by government decree.

In democratic societies the initiative to make contracts as a manager or an employee or a customer or a supplier or an investor in an enterprise has remained in the hands of individuals. No government makes these choices for others. Centuries ago, much as today, subject to the vagaries of nature and climate, a farmer could plow such fields as he chose, plant and harvest such crops as he chose, market them as he chose at such prices as he chose, all without interference from the king or other form of government. Our ancestors wrested from the king, not only in the dramatic moments at Runnymede in 1215 but slowly through the centuries, the right to produce and buy and sell and work and invest as they chose. This liberty, this freedom of contract, this mobility of labor and product and capital, this freedom of choice evolved in a society which denied control of these matters to the sovereign, and came to require him or the government to protect it against the government itself in these endeavors in the vague expression "due process of law."

But this freedom was never unlimited. Restraints of trade and monopolies were abhorred at common law in the Middle Ages as well as by modern statute. Freedom of contract never did permit a farmer or a merchant to combine with someone else to fix the price of a commodity, or to limit its production, or to allocate markets. To the extent that monopolies were permitted or tolerated they were the prerogative of the sovereign or of persons designated by the sovereign for this purpose; remnants of this practice still exist in the patent system and the designation of certain retail establishments as being purveyors of a product to the reigning sovereign, and to public utilities which have been granted a monopoly to provide a service or a product within a prescribed territory. Freedom of contract does not permit fraud or deceptive practices in selling or buying goods or land. After centuries, the transfer of land became permissible aside from rigid lines of descent, and when contracts were made for this purpose certain restrictions developed relating to the free transferability of the property (the rule against perpetuities) and the accumulation of income from the property. But the laws in this respect, that is the activities of government, were always limitations or prohibitions on the kinds of contracts to be made or some aspect of a transaction, not a direction as to whom the contract should be made with or as to the property which should be dealt with. The individual or the property owner or the manager of an enterprise was not directed by the state to produce any product, to work for some employer, to sell in a given market, to transfer property to a specified person, etc. As noted above, initiative, enterprise, remained with the individual. Further, as this system flourished, and its benefits became appreciated, the state itself discontinued participation in the economic system in competition with privately owned enterprises.

In the modern Western world those enterprises which have not been granted a state monopoly, even though widely owned but controlled by a small group, enjoy this freedom of contract. While several governmental agencies exist to assemble data, available for both government and private business, concerning the structure of the economy, information about the demand for existing and new products, the availability of plants and equipment to supply them, etc., very little planning for the entire economy is done by the government We rely on the market place, the entry into it and the exit from it generally without restrictions by the government, and the initiative of the managers of business units, both large and small, to provide the planning. We have chosen a multiplicity of planning units, one in each enterprise to do the planning in our economy. Three or four motor manufacturers, perhaps a dozen steel manufacturers, three or four electrical equipment manufacturers, three or four aircraft manufacturers, a half dozen chemical manufacturers, three or four tire manufacturers, several dozen retail food chain stores, tens of thousands of retail clothing stores, and so on throughout our entire economy, are the units which do the planning. With it all, however, and counter to our early history, there is a substantial amount of central planning and governmental direction in agriculture, although again the controls are largely negative controls rather than directions to plant certain crops or raise certain cattle.

The concept of freedom of contract was more frequently articulated in the United States in the nineteenth and early twentieth century than it has been recently. Laissez-faire, another expression of the concept, became a term of opprobrium because of the manner in which this concept was applied by courts and large property owners. The freedom to make such contracts as a person chose had been held by the courts to be immune from any kind of governmental regulation because of the concept of due process of law then current. An ever

growing groundswell of opposition to the practice of courts in rejecting (holding unconstitutional) measures adopted by federal and state
legislative bodies designed to improve the lot of large numbers of people, and to improve the working of the business system, on the basis
of freedom of contract, led to the adoption of much of the New Deal
legislation in the 1930's and to a reversal of form by the courts. While
this led the courts to interpret the Constitution to permit Congress
to enact all kinds of remedial legislation and new programs, the emotions which had been generated in favor of these programs and against
the old legal concepts led to the abandonment of the term "freedom
of contract" and nothing was provided in its place. Because the
phrase is currently out of favor does not mean that the practice no
longer continues. Rarely has there been any legislation in this country providing for state agencies empowered to issue mandates to produce, to buy, to sell, to invest, to hire, or to serve (except as a remedy
for some infraction of the law); there have been a number of prohibitions, but this legislation did not take the initiative away from individuals and grant it to the state. There is a vast difference between
setting a price as a result of cost and competition in recognition of
prohibitions against combining with other producers to fix prices, on
the one hand, and being directed by the state to sell at a given price,
on the other. This vast difference is the difference between democracy
and authoritarianism in a business system.

Consider what Chief Justice Hughes had to say about freedom of
contract in West Coast Hotel Co. v. Parrish, 300 U.S. 379, 57 S.Ct.
578, 81 L.Ed. 703 (1937) when the Court upheld a minimum wage
statute of the State of Washington and overruled its earlier decision
in Adkins v. Children's Hospital, 261 U.S. 525, 43 S.Ct. 394, 67 L.Ed.
785 (1923). The owner of the West Coast Hotel Co. argued that a
statute fixing minimum wages interfered with his freedom of contract and therefore deprived him of liberty without due process of
law. In part, this is what the Court said:

> The principle which must control our decision is not in doubt.
> The constitutional provision invoked is the due process clause of
> the Fourteenth Amendment governing the States, as the due
> process clause invoked in the Adkins Case governed Congress.
> In each case the violation alleged by those attacking minimum
> wage regulation for women is deprivation of freedom of contract.
> What is this freedom? The Constitution does not speak of freedom
> of contract. It speaks of liberty and prohibits the deprivation of
> liberty without due process of law. In prohibiting that deprivation
> the Constitution does not recognize an absolute and uncontrollable
> liberty. Liberty in each of its phases has its history and connota-
> tion. But the liberty safeguarded is liberty in a social organiza-
> tion which requires the protection of law against the evils which
> menace the health, safety, morals and welfare of the people. Lib-
> erty under the Constitution is thus necessarily subject to the re-
> straints of due process, and regulation which is reasonable in rela-
> tion to its subject and is adopted in the interests of the community
> is due process.

This essential limitation of liberty in general governs freedom of contract in particular. More than twenty-five years ago we set forth the applicable principle in these words, after referring to the cases where the liberty guaranteed by the Fourteenth Amendment had been broadly described.

"But it was recognized in the cases cited, as in many others, that freedom of contract is a qualified and not an absolute right. There is no absolute freedom to do as one wills or to contract as one chooses. The guaranty of liberty does not withdraw from legislative supervision that wide department of activity which consists of the making of contracts, or deny to government the power to provide restrictive safeguards. Liberty implies the absence of arbitrary restraint, not immunity from reasonable regulations and prohibitions imposed in the interests of the community." Chicago, B. & Q. R. Co. v. McGuire, 219 U.S. 549.

This power under the Constitution to restrict freedom of contract has had many illustrations. That it may be exercised in the public interest with respect to contracts between employer and employee is undeniable. Thus statutes have been sustained limiting employment in underground mines and smelters to eight hours a day (Holden v. Hardy, 169 U.S. 366); in requiring redemption in cash of store orders or other evidences of indebtedness issued in the payment of wages (Knoxville Iron Co. v. Harbison, 183 U.S. 13); in forbidding the payment of seamen's wages in advance (Patterson v. The Eudora, 190 U.S. 169); in making it unlawful to contract to pay miners employed at quantity rates upon the basis of screened coal instead of the weight of the coal as originally produced in the mine (McLean v. Arkansas, 211 U.S. 539); in prohibiting contracts limiting liability for injuries to employees (Chicago, B. & Q. R. Co. v. McGuire, 219 U.S. 549); in limiting hours of work of employees in manufacturing establishments (Bunting v. Oregon, 243 U.S. 426); and in maintaining workmen's compensation laws (New York C. R. Co. v. White, 243 U.S. 188).

It should be noted that in each example of a restriction of freedom of contract given by the Court that private initiative in making the contract had been exercised. The restriction in each case related to a term or a condition of a contract of employment—in no case was there a mandate to employ or to serve. The restriction applied in each case after the parties had agreed to the employment and then only to the terms of the employment; both parties were free to make the contract or not as they chose with the legislated restriction in mind, but the legislation did not compel them to make the contract of employment. While the government may "provide restrictive safeguards" it may not impose "arbitrary restraints." It may establish "reasonable regulations and prohibitions imposed in the interests of the community" and what is "reasonable" and what is "in the interests of the community" are ideas and concepts which change with the times. (Does anyone seriously question in the last half of the twentieth century the "reasonableness" of workmen's compensation laws? They were vigorously opposed in the first decade of the century as being "unreasonable.") As the Court said, "There is no absolute freedom to do as one wills or to contract as one chooses." *But*

there is an absolute freedom to initiate a contract in a democracy.
The limitations, restrictions, prohibitions, safeguards, and restraints
on the contract to be made are a large part of the inquiry made in
this book.

A second aspect of private ownership of property, noted above,
is the individual owner's participation in the profits of the property.
Most of the Western world, particularly the United States and the
United Kingdom, has developed a system of taxation based largely on
incomes derived either from economic units, or from one's own services. Aside from recurring outcries of confiscatory taxation, the profits of the economic system belong to the individuals who either by
their efforts have produced them or by their ownership of the enterprise have become entitled to them or to a share of them. When the
profits of the system, or the payments for the services rendered, have
exceeded the needs of the recipient for his living (no matter what
the scale) the excess has remained for investment and reinvestment.
Frequently the profits have been invested directly by the economic
enterprise which has produced them, rather than being distributed
in full to the owners. This has been a consequence of centralized control in place of owner control, and so long as the managers of the
large enterprises have distributed a sufficient amount of the profits
of the system to the owners the latter have remained largely quiescent.
In authoritarian systems no problems exist as to the method of allocating or distributing the profits of the economic system, at least no individual is permitted to make his choice in this regard as an individual. State agencies determine how much of it shall be reinvested in
the enterprise, how much shall go to defense, how much shall be ap-
propriated for other governmental purposes, and how much shall be
directed into other enterprises. Centralized control, centralized direction for the entire economy is the system used. Not so in the
democratic society. The state intervenes in the distribution of profits
only in the form of the tax collector, and in this connection we have
certain notions of fairness of taxation. (Fairness is demonstrably
imperfect when the very wealthy are able to avoid, by law, a substantial portion of the tax burden.) Also, the reinvestment of the
profits of the system is done entirely on a voluntary basis and the
only limitation placed upon this process by the government is an insistence that there be a full and fair disclosure by the issuers and by
the sellers and buyers of securities.

The freedom to transfer property, whether it be the product of
an enterprise, or the productive facility itself, continues unimpeded
much as it has for several recent centuries. Actually, a system which
accords to individuals the private ownership of property must as a
part of that system provide for some means of transfering the ownership. The goods and services produced by the economic system, particularly where specialized kinds of production have become common,
must be transferable to the ultimate consumer or user. In a simple
agrarian economy one might conceivably produce all that he needs,
and no more, and consume all of that and have nothing for transfer.

But once human activity becomes more specialized than this, the product of human activity must be transferable from the producer to the consumer and exchangeable for other goods and services. Conceivably the state could collect all such production, and allocate it in such fashion as the managers of the government should deem appropriate. Or we could permit this to be done by individual volition, buying and selling as we choose. Obviously, the latter is the system chosen by the Western world. And this is accomplished through a market, which is more or less a free market. Since not all persons or enterprises have equal bargaining power, the market is subject to the influences, sometimes not very subtle, of powerful economic units, generally to their own advantage and to the detriment of the public. Because of this, we insist upon free competition and we attempt to prohibit combinations of persons who seek to prevent the operation of a free market. Also, we demand fairness in trading and dealing. This led to the enactment of our antitrust and trade regulation laws.

Not only must the products of the economy be freely transferable, but also productive units within the economic system must be transferable. These concepts arose in a system of private ownership, because human mortality being what it is, some system for the devolution of property upon the owner's death had to exist. Centuries ago this system was primogeniture, which has since been followed by the use of trusts and by the ability to make a will which permits the disposition of property almost entirely as one wishes (aside from a few provisions which one must make for a surviving spouse). We have also arranged for the transfer of productive enterprises during one's lifetime, again almost without limit, so long as this is done fairly and not to persons or other productive units which would result in a combination in restraint of trade. This has been accomplished largely through the transfer of shares of stock on securities exchanges under which exceedingly small parts of the ownership of an enterprise are transferred. Occasionally an entire unit of production is transferred; this has led, in part, in recent years to the peculiar economic unit called a "conglomerate" which may not survive a vigorous attack under the existing antitrust laws if one should ever be brought. Again, however, the state does not direct the manner in which the transfer is to be made, or by whom, or to whom, or when; our laws provide only that under certain circumstances it may not be done to certain transferees, or it may not be done in an unfair, fraudulent or deceptive manner, or that ownership may not be tied up in perpetuity. Initiative again remains with the owner of the property.

Bankruptcy or insolvency is another aspect of the private ownership of property and the necessity of providing for its transfer. In a system where government corporations never fail there is no need for a legal system to be concerned about bankruptcy. But where private persons own an enterprise which has the freedom to fail, and private persons have the freedom to do business with an enterprise which can fail, some system must be evolved to distribute the pieces. In the United States we have a Bankruptcy Act for this purpose, and again the system is one which relies to a large extent on private initiative. There is no government agency looking into the solvency of businesses and determining which have enough resources to continue and which do not. Individual creditors and debtors do this. If the government were to make this determination the possibility of oppression is so enormous that we find it difficult to contemplate. We have no government administrator of bankrupt enterprises arbitrarily determining who and how much shall be paid; instead we have enacted into law a system of priorities of payment and within that system certain kinds of equality of distribution. Without private ownership of property, none of this would be necessary.

In the United States we either are or aspire to be a democracy. We have the political system and institutions for a representative democracy, we have a system of personal freedoms articulated in the Bill of Rights, and an economic system which is based upon the principles of private property and freedom of contract. The method used in this volume of examining the legal problems of business in a democratic society is not dependent upon comparing the democratic institutions and systems with those of an authoritarian society; the comparison is used only as a technique to illustrate the manner in which laws have developed in a democratic business system. If we had a different system we would have a different set of legal problems. Also, within our democratic system itself if we were to do some things differently we would have a different set of legal problems. For example, the price of a commodity could be determined by a committee composed of members chosen from the public, from the industry which typically produces the commodity, from employees generally as well as those within the industry, and from representatives of a consumer organization. If so, we could do away with most of the antitrust laws, and then have a whole new body of laws relating to the manner in which the price commission should operate, what kind of price increases would be permissible, what quality of product would be required, and the terms under which the product could be distributed to various wholesalers and retailers, etc. In short, each form of economic activity could have its own regulatory body much as a public utility commission. Our experience with this type of system, regulated by a Federal agency, during World War II led us to abandon it as soon as possible and caused many people to yearn for a return to the free market place and to suffer with the antitrust laws. A similar system, with less detailed regulation, was instituted in 1971; its results are unclear but the frustrations it has engendered are widely reported.

The laws we have are the consequence of the system we have chosen, and our experience with it. With a different system and a different experience we would have different laws. And if the experiences we have with our laws do not lead us to achieve our democratic goals, we will have new and different laws.

Chapter II

FREEDOM OF CHOICE OF LOCATION AND FORM OF THE BUSINESS ENTERPRISE—MOBILITY OF CAPITAL AND PRODUCTS

A. INTRODUCTORY NOTE

Several of the characteristics of the operation of a business system in a democratic society are the privileges which entrepreneurs have of (1) choosing the organization form of their enterprise, (2) operating from such base or bases and, (3) selling such products in such areas as they please. There are a few limitations on this; for example, many of the learned professions may not operate in the corporate form (at least not to the same extent as the usual business enterprise), and zoning and land planning regulations will not permit the location of a factory in a residential area. However, these are the exceptions which prove the rule.

A business enterprise may operate as a sole proprietorship, as a partnership, as a corporation, or any one of a number of variations of these forms, and no governmental agency requires that one form or another be used. Again, there are a few exceptions to this; most banks, insurance companies, and public utilities, for example, are required by particular regulatory statutes to be incorporated. Until recently a self-imposed industry limitation required securities brokers to be partnerships, or at least not to be incorporated.

The owners or managers of a business enterprise may choose the city, state, or country as the location of their business enterprise which suits them, and they may exercise any means of selection that suits them, rational or irrational, in duplication of existing enterprises or in territory with no competition. They may choose the products to be produced by the enterprise and they may send them into such markets as they choose with no governmental restraint; and, in fact, our system demands that there not be any private restraints. Of course there are a few limitations such as a public utility being given a "franchise area" in which to operate and sometimes certain agricultural products must be marketed within a governmentally defined marketing area. But by and large initiative remains with the private individual.

One of the fundamentals of our economic and legal system of doing business is that we may choose how we shall conduct a business and where we shall sell our goods and services. And within our Federal system one state may not by its own legislation exclude goods or services produced in another state, since only Congress may regulate interstate commerce. The United States Supreme Court has frequently held that one state may not establish an economic barrier against competition with goods and services produced in another state. "[T]his principle that our economic unit is the Nation, which alone has the gamut of powers necessary to control of the economy, including the vital power of erecting customs barriers against foreign competition, has as its corollary that the states are not separable economic units. * * * Our system, fostered by the Commerce Clause, is that every farmer and every craftsman shall be encouraged to produce by the certainty that he will have free access to every market in the Nation, that no home embargoes will withhold his export, and no foreign state will by customs duties or regulations exclude them. Likewise, every consumer may look to the free competition from every producing area in the Nation to protect him from exploitation by any. Such was the vision of the Founders; such has been the doctrine of this Court which has given it reality." Hood & Sons v. Du Mond, 336 U.S. 525, 69 S.Ct. 657, 93 L.Ed. 865 (1949).

The freedom to choose the form of a business enterprise does not lead to many legal problems. In practice most of the problems are tax problems as discussed below and in Chapter III. (1) As long as there are graduated income tax rates taxing personal incomes at a higher rate than the maximum rate at which corporate income is taxed, there will be the decision to be made whether a business enterprise should be conducted as a sole proprietorship or a corporation (or a partnership, which as a separate entity is not taxed since the income allocable to the individual partners is taxed to them as their personal income). (2) At one time the possibility of limited liability for a small business enterprise would substantially influence the choice of the form of the enterprise but for many years no small, close corporation could obtain any substantial amounts of credit for borrowed money without having the individual stockholders personally guarantee or assume the obligation of the corporation to repay the money. On the other hand, no large business enterprise can be operated without a system of centralized management and without the principle of limited liability so that nearly all of such enterprises are corporations. (There are a few large enterprises which technically are not corporations but nonetheless have all of the characteristics of a corporation.)

Further, the legal problems involved in forming a corporation have largely been solved, since this has been reduced to a routine. In a small business corporation not enough persons use the advantages which are provided by Section 1244 of the Internal Revenue Code, 26 U.S.C.A. § 1244, but this will come in time. Most of the problems concerning the formation of a corporation which related to whether a corporation was a *de facto* or a *de jure* corporation as a practical matter no longer exist. Lawyers engaged by businessmen to handle the incorporation of a business enterprise now uniformly pay more attention to the necessary formalities and advise their clients that they must observe them before beginning business. Also, there are several highly specialized businesses which are able to perform the task of incorporation in any of the United States. All lawyers are aware of their identity and for one reason or another prefer one over another of these companies. However, the services of a lawyer are still needed by the businessman even though the incorporation services are to be performed by one of these service companies; every active business is going to need the services of a lawyer sooner or later and one should be consulted at the outset.

A corporation is considered to be a separate legal person, a separate legal entity, by all states. It is entitled to nearly all the rights and privileges of an individual person except those things which can be done only by a natural person. For example, it cannot vote in a public election, but it is entitled to due process of law, equal protection of the laws, and generally to all of the same rights and privileges as an individual businessman in the conduct of its business.

The creation of this separate legal entity, endowed with its distinctive attributes, is exclusively a function of each individual state. Until recently much of this was accomplished by a ritual that was almost as ridiculous as implications to the moon to increase the fertility of the women of a primitive tribe. Some of this still goes on today. If the corporation is being formed in a law office, a junior member of the law firm will perform the ritual and one to three persons (varying with the amount of ritual required by the corporation statute of the state of incorporation) will affix their signatures to several papers which in turn will be filed with an agency of the state of incorporation and in due course articles of incorporation or a charter will be issued attesting to the formation of the corporation. If the incorporation is done in the offices of one of the service companies, the same ritual will be performed but this time by a layman and not by a junior member of a law firm.

While many states will require the names and addresses of the incorporators the true identity of the persons to become active in the corporation is hardly ever revealed. Also, in the past the general purpose or nature of the business of the corporation was required to be disclosed with some definiteness but now a business corporation may be formed with a charter which permits it to engage in almost every business activity not otherwise prohibited by law.

The large corporation, whose securities are listed on a securities exchange, or even a corporation with more than $1,000,000 in assets and 500 shareholders, is now required to file rather detailed information with the Securities and Exchange Commission under several provisions of the Securities Exchange Act of 1934, 15 U.S.C.A. § 78a et seq., but this does not apply to several hundred thousand small business corporations; yet none of the publicly held corporations is required to disclose this information at the time of incorporation.

The problems relating to the formation of the corporation fall into two general categories depending on the size of the business venture. If the enterprise is a small one which will operate entirely within one state, almost without reference to the number of its shareholders, then it will usually be incorporated in that state. The advantages of incorporating in Delaware (referred to below) will hardly apply to it since it will be able to accomplish nearly all of its corporate actions by the unanimous written consent of its shareholders and directors. It will have to pay the same corporate taxes (in the state in which it does business) regardless of whether or not it is incorporated in that state, and may very well avoid paying taxes to the state of incorporation if it does no business there.

As noted above, many business enterprises turn to the corporate form because of a potential saving in Federal income taxes. Frequently, the possibility of having a portion of the earnings of the enterprise taxed at the lowest corporate rate (presently 22%) instead of the higher rates levied on individuals will in itself be one reason for incorporating.

Because many small corporations do not pay dividends to their shareholders, these earnings may be accumulated and under many circumstances later be distributed to the shareholders as capital gains. If all of the corporate attributes are desired by the businessman operating the enterprise, except the burden of Federal income taxation, the provisions of Subchapter S of the Internal Revenue Code, Sections 1371 to 1379, inclusive, 26 U.S.C.A. §§ 1371–1379, and Section 1244 of the Internal Revenue Code 26 U.S.C.A. § 1244, may well be considered. (See Chapter III below.) Briefly, under Subchapter S no Federal income taxes will be levied at the corporate level, although the problem of the imposition of state taxes at the corporate level will probably continue.

For these corporations the problem of choosing a state of incorporation is not much of a problem; as indicated above, the state where it will do its business will probably be its state of incorporation. Under the provisions of Section 1244 of the Internal Revenue Code any loss which may be incurred by the original individual shareholders on the disposition of their stock in the small business (Subchapter S) corporation will permit them to obtain the tax advantage of having their loss fully deductible from their ordinary income instead of being limited to a capital loss under which generally they realize only one-half of the tax-saving as a consequence of the loss.

The large corporation which is going to operate on an interstate basis more and more will look to Delaware as the state of its incorporation. Delaware has become a popular place of incorporation and many interstate corporations are incorporated there; as a consequence, more and more corporate advisors, not only lawyers, are becoming familiar with the corporation law of the state of Delaware. The high level of predictability (if not certainty) of the solutions to legal problems at the corporate level resulting from incorporation in Delaware make this choice a popular one. Shareholders throughout the rest of the United States, or their advisors, who give any thought to the matter will have a preference for Delaware corporation law because of their developing familiarity with it. In turn, this makes the marketing of the securities of Delaware corporations a simpler job.

Aside from the advantages of familiarity and some certainty, there are other advantages to incorporation in Delaware, most of which are advantages to management. Cumulative voting is permitted but not required in Delaware as it is in many states; that is, in the election of the board of directors of the corporation the shareholder does not have a number of votes equal to the number of directors to be elected times the number of shares he holds. The shareholder cannot lump all of his votes together and vote for one director in order to seek minority representation on the board of directors. The group of candidates as a whole slate which receives the most number of votes becomes the board of directors. Thus, management can have a board which is composed exclusively of persons friendly to each other and to management. Occasionally the owner of a large minority block of stock is able to "muscle" his way onto a board of directors but this is rather uncommon.

Other attributes of Delaware incorporation, thought to be advantageous to management, include rights of indemnification for directors and officers (see Chapter IV below), the ability to pay dividends out of current earnings even though the corporation may be in a deficit position, lower state taxes at the time of incorporation and during the period of operation, no laws regulating the sale of securities in Delaware ("blue-sky" laws) and a method of merging, consolidating, and transferring the assets of the corporation easier than is found in many states. Also, there is an intangible and hard to assess factor that is probably as important as any other, a generally favorable or benign attitude toward business and corporations in the Legislature and Courts of Delaware and which attitude business management anticipates will continue into the foreseeable future.

Delaware does not impose a tax on dividends received by a corporation. Many other states also do not impose such a tax. Delaware does not impose a tax on a capital gain realized by a corporation on the sale of stock in another corporation. Many other states do. Thus, if a Delaware corporation for one reason or another owns shares of stock of another corporation, which it then sells at a profit, Delaware will not impose a tax on the profit. If, however, the corporation were incorporated in any one of many other states a substantial tax on the profit would be levied even though the state of incorporation had no connection with the transaction except the fact that the selling corporation was incorporated in that state. Delaware, therefore, becomes the state of incorporation of many businesses holding the stock of other corporations, whether they be investment companies as such, or parent companies holding the stock of subsidiaries which may or may not be incorporated in other states. Attempts are then made to have the holding company conduct its business only in Delaware.

A technique is growing whereby a business operating on an interstate basis will have a parent corporation incorporated in Delaware and, where any substantial volume of business is conducted in any other state, a separate corporation to operate in that state incorporated there as a subsidiary of the parent. Each subsidiary will then file its state corporate tax returns with the state in which it has been incorporated, this being the state in which the subsidiary operates, while the parent and every other subsidiary will not have registered to do business in that state and will file no reports or tax returns with that state. (Most states find it difficult to reach beyond their territorial jurisdiction to compel these out-of-state corporations to report to them.) Not all national corporations, by any means, are doing this. But those national corporations which do are finding that corporate management becomes the body which allocates income and expenses among its various subsidiaries and thus to some extent these corporations are able to determine the transactions which are to be taxed at the state level; this makes it possible for them to determine the amount of state taxes which the corporation will pay. This has led to problems at the state level which largely remain unresolved at this time.

Two cases reported below, Superior Oil Co. v. Franchise Tax Bd., 60 Cal.2d 406, 34 Cal.Rptr. 545, 386 P.2d 33 (1963) and Skelly Oil Co. v. Minnesota, 269 Minn. 351, 131 N.W.2d 632 (1964) illustrate some of the problems of state taxation of a fair share of a national corporation's income. They also illustrate how two different states can view, for tax purposes, almost identical transactions in two different ways.

In the *Superior Oil* and *Skelly Oil* cases there was no dispute about California or Minnesota having the power to levy taxes on these companies; it was only the portion of their business attributable to each state that was to be taxed. In International Shoe Co. v. State of Washington, 326 U.S. 310, 66 S.Ct. 154, 90 L.Ed. 95 (1945) the fundamental question raised was under what circumstances does a state have jurisdiction over a foreign corporation which is selling its products in that state. A state may levy a tax on a corporation only if it has jurisdiction over it; but it should be noted that jurisdiction for tax purposes does not mean jurisdiction for all purposes. The case of Southern Machine Co., Inc. v. Mohasco Industries, Inc., 401 F.2d 374 (6th Cir. 1968), reported below, illustrates some of the problems relating to the circumstances under which a corporation can be sued in the courts of a state where it is selling its products (in this case licensing the use of a patent) even though it may not be maintaining an office in that state.

These cases illustrate some of the legal problems encountered by a business which expands its operations beyond its home community. None of these would exist if we did not permit this kind of initiative. Most of the problems would not exist if we did not have a Federal system with a multiplicity of governments (sometimes called sovereigns) each insisting or having the power to insist on being able to prescribe the manner in which business shall be conducted or taxed within its borders. If we did not allow mobility of capital and products of a business, and if we did not have a Federal system we would not have these problems.

B.   IMPACT OF STATE TAXATION

SUPERIOR OIL COMPANY v. FRANCHISE TAX BOARD OF THE STATE OF CALIFORNIA

Supreme Court of California, 1963.
34 Cal.Rptr. 545, 60 Cal.2d 406, 386 P.2d 33.

PEEK, Justice.   The defendant Franchise Tax Board appeals from a judgment awarding to the plaintiff Superior Oil Company a tax refund of $502,645.48 including interest, claimed to constitute an excess levy of the corporate franchise tax for the company's fiscal year ending August 31, 1952.

The franchise tax is impressed annually on corporations for the privilege of exercising the corporate franchise within California. (Rev. & Tax.Code, § 23151.)

The measure of the tax is limited to income reasonably attributable to sources in California.   Section 24301 of the Revenue and Taxation Code * as it read in part during the taxable year in question, provided as follows: "When the income of a taxpayer subject to the tax imposed under this part is derived from or attributable to sources both within and without the State, the tax shall be measured by the net income derived from or attributable to sources within this State. Such income shall be determined by an allocation upon the basis of sales, purchases, expenses of manufacture, payroll, value and situs of tangible property or by reference to any of these or other factors or by such other method of allocation as is fairly calculated to determine the net income derived from or attributable to sources within this State. * * *"

The issue presented both to the trial court and on this appeal is whether the plaintiff's operations in several jurisdictions, including California, are unitary in nature and thus subject to local taxation on a basis which allocates a portion of the over-all net income to this state (Rev. & Tax.Code, § 24301) or whether, on the other hand, the local operations are sufficiently separate to justify local taxation on the net income derived from such separate, local operations.

Plaintiff takes the position that its operations are unitary with the result that the local allocated net income and taxes thereon are lesser amounts than the corresponding amounts which the Board contends properly result from the claimed separate, local operations.   It is conceded that if Superior is entitled to use an allocation formula on the basis that its over-all operations are unitary, then the particular allocation of income which it urges, and determination of tax due therefrom, are correct.

The essential facts have been stipulated and are not in dispute.

* Now Revenue and Taxation Code, § 25101.

Plaintiff is a California corporation with its principal place of business in Los Angeles. The franchise tax here involved is that for the tax year ending August 31, 1952 based on plaintiff's earnings for its tax year ending August 31, 1951. During that period plaintiff's principal income was derived from the production and sale of petroleum and petroleum products in more than a score of states, including California, and in foreign countries. Other income was produced from a realty subdivision in California, from gains made on the sale of capital assets both within and without this state, and from dividends on stock investments.

In a true sense plaintiff is not an integrated oil company. That is, it refined and processed only a minor portion of its production. Generally, its raw petroleum was sold at the well site to other companies. All production in California was sold in California, and all out of state production was sold outside of California.

Plaintiff's income producing activities were centrally controlled from its executive offices in Los Angeles, as well as were many administrative functions such as accounting, purchasing of equipment, supplies and insurance.

Personnel were moved frequently throughout the several states where plaintiff operated. At any given time only twenty per cent, more or less, of plaintiff's employees were employed primarily in California.

For the income year here involved plaintiff was required to file returns reporting its net income in eight other states, in addition to California. With respect to the returns filed in seven of such other states, and pursuant to the local requirements thereof, it computed its income by the use of the separate accounting method, deducting from the gross receipts derived from the production and sale of petroleum products in each state the expenses attributable thereto including a fixed share of the common overhead expenses. Losses from such operations ranged from $9,397.69 in Arkansas to $3,410,381.90 in Louisiana and only in one state, Mississippi, was a profit ($942,395.68) reported. In the eighth state, Kentucky, plaintiff employed a formula method which allocated a nominal portion of the integrated over-all net income to that state. The method of computation in each of the several states was dependent only on local requirements, and was in no way affected by that employed in any other state.

In reporting its income during the year ending on August 31, 1951, petitioner employed the separate accounting method for those purely intrastate activities—the real estate subdivision project, sale of capital assets in California, and income from dividends. The allocation formula which it utilized as to its petroleum operations required that it total all receipts from those operations in all the states and countries involved, deducting therefrom the aggregate expenses in all the states and countries, and apportioning the remaining net income based upon the pro rata distribution within California of property, payroll and sales factors. This resulted in a net income attributable to the production and sale of petroleum products in California of $756,533.16, and a total net income from all sources attributable to California of $1,135,060.68.

By its separate accounting method the board determined that the net income from California sources was $10,637,633.46, subject to some minor statutory adjustments not in issue. Accordingly, it imposed an additional tax assessment of $381,250.99, representing the differential in the tax calculated pursuant to the disputed accounting methods. Eventually the additional assessment was paid, under protest, and the instant action was instituted to recover the same.

It might be noted that the circumstances surrounding Superior's particular income record vividly point up the effect of the accounting method to be utilized, not only as to the California tax, but also as to the gross tax payable in all of the various taxing states involved. For the tax year in question Superior had over-all net earnings of, roughly, $3,200,000. If an allocation arrangement were employed in each taxing state involved, Superior would pay taxes to each of the various states based on such state's pro rata share of that amount, which shares could not exceed 100% of the amount. On the other hand, if the separate accounting method were used in each state involved, then in six of the nine taxing states no tax would be paid (other than some nominal minimum), as losses were sustained in such states. In the other three states, including California, profits of $11,500,000 were realized and taxes in each such state would be payable on individual bases, the total of which bases would equal that amount. The unitary accounting method employing an allocation formula then, if applied uniformly, would result in a substantially smaller over-all tax liability, as the total taxable basis would be substantially less, neglecting for the moment the differing rates and exemptions in the several states.

It would be of still greater benefit to Superior if it could employ a separate accounting method in the states wherein it suffered losses, which method it apparently has employed in six of the seven states wherein there were losses, and an allocation method in the taxing state or states where it has realized large profits, as in California. Superior's over-all tax liability would be greatest if it were required to employ an allocation method in the states where losses were sustained, and a separate accounting method in the profit-making states. In any event it is Superior's contention that the board seeks to impose a tax on claimed separate earnings in California which are more than three times greater than its actual over-all earnings, and that such imposition is inequitable and improper under the California law. Of course, we are not concerned in this proceeding with the propriety of the methods used to determine taxable income in the other states.

The narrow issue herein, in terms of the statute, is whether Superior's income is "derived from or attributable to sources both within and without the State." (Rev. & Tax.Code, § 24301.) If such income can be so categorized then an allocation of total net income would naturally follow from the mandatory language of section 24301, and a separate accounting, as sought by the board, could not be approved.

Previously this court has had occasion to determine when separate accounting was proper. In Butler Brothers v. McColgan, 17 Cal. 2d 664, the Franchise Tax Board assessed an additional tax based, in that case, on an allocation formula following a return by Butler Brothers on a separate accounting basis. The taxpayer paid and sought to recover. Judgment was for the board on a finding that the business was unitary in nature.

Butler Brothers was a corporation engaged in a wholesale merchandising business with outlets in several states, including California. Each outlet operated independently, including the purchase and sale of goods, but each was subjected to central executive control from the corporation's principal office in Chicago. The outlets shared in corporate overhead, executive salaries, central advertising, and the expenses of maintaining a central buying division, although the cost of each purchase and the expense incurred therein were chargeable to the individual outlets concerned. During the year in question the California operations suffered a loss, whereas the overall operations realized a profit. The corporation's separate return of its California business included the apportioned share of the common administrative expenses.

In affirming the judgment, this court stated 17 Cal.2d at pages 667 and 668: "It is only if its business within this state is truly separate and distinct from its business without this state, so that the segregation of income may be made clearly and accurately, that the separate accounting method may properly be used. Where, however, interstate operations are carried on and that portion of the corporation's business done within the state cannot be clearly segregated from that done outside the state, the unit rule of assessment is employed as a device for allocating to the state for taxation its fair share of the taxable values of the taxpayer. * * * If there is any evidence to sustain a finding that the operations of appellant in California during the year 1935 contributed to the net income derived from its entire operations in the United States, then the entire business of appellant is so clearly unitary as to require a fair system of apportionment by the formula method in order to prevent overtaxation to the corporation or undertaxation by the state."

At page 678, of 17 Cal.2d the court concluded: "In accordance with the foregoing analysis it is our opinion that the unitary nature of appellant's business is definitely established by the presence of the following circumstances: (1) unity of ownership; (2) unity of operation as evidenced by central purchasing, advertising, accounting and management divisions; and (3) unity of use in its centralized executive force and general system of operation."

The foregoing three unities were described as the "elements of a unitary business" in Edison California Stores v. McColgan, 30 Cal.2d 472. In that case a situation similar to that in the Butler Brothers case prevailed, except that the retail business in each state was separately incorporated. The court concluded that the elements of central management, purchasing, distribution, store operations, and administrative factors were sufficient to hold that the operation was unitary in spite of the separate legal entities, and stated 30 Cal.2d at page 481, 183 P.2d at page 21: "If the operation of the portion of the business done within the state is dependent upon or contributes to the operation of the business without the state, the operations are unitary * * *" (See also John Deere Plow Co. of Moline v. Franchise Tax Board, 38 Cal.2d 214.)

On the evidence submitted in the instant case and, as stated, not controverted, the trial court made extensive findings of fact, including a finding that "California business operations contributed substantially to the out-of-state portion" of its business in areas relating to executive policy making, administrative control, coordination of exploration activities, well production and land acquisition, training of technical personnel, specific scientific and technical development and testing laboratories, drilling operations and drilling equipment, manufacturing and sales, accounting, tax returns, personnel, insurance and purchasing.

The court also found that "Superior's California operations were substantially dependent upon the out-of-state operations" in areas relating to the borrowing of substantial funds on assets located outside of California in order to finance projects within California, the transfer of company funds from sources outside of California to finance projects within California, legal counseling provided by the chief counsel located in Texas and other attorneys in Washington, D. C., the supplying and control of tubular materials from Superior's Texas office and transfer of other materials to California from company sources outside of California, fiscal control from Superior's Texas office for half of the year in question, geophysical technical information and services supplied to California from the company's Texas laboratories, certain landlease controls supplied by offices in Texas, the transfer of valuable drilling equipment from out-of-state for California operations, the transfer of skilled personnel from out-of-state for purposes of performing services in California, and the supply, on a daily basis, of technical and other information to the company's California offices in order that executive and policy decisions could be made and over-all control exercised.

In addition the court expressly found that the unities of ownership, operation and use existed in connection with Superior's over-all business and that "[t]he business done by plaintiff within the State of California was not separate or distinct from its business done without this state."

Without setting forth in greater detail the very extensive record bearing on the foregoing findings, it will suffice to say that while the agreed factual statement furnishes some basis for controversy the record substantially supports the essential findings. Moreover, the board does not contend otherwise.

In view of the findings and the law applicable thereto as set forth in the excerpts from the prior decisions of this court it would appear to follow that the judgment herein must be affirmed. The board, however, asserts that the test is not one of determining the existence of the three unities, but instead that the court must first determine that in order for the operations within the state to be an integral portion of a unitary business carried on within and without the state, it must appear that the operations within and without the state are "necessary and essential" to each other and to the functioning of the business as a whole. It then argues that only in those cases where the foregoing situation exists does it become impossible to make the computations necessary for a separate accounting for individual state tax purposes, and hence justify the employment of an allocation formula. In other words the argument appears to be that the employment of an allocation formula is justified only when the various local operations are so essential to the over-all operations that it is impossible to make separate accounting computations. After so arguing the board then takes a somewhat inconsistent position and states that the issue herein is "whether Superior's income from its California petroleum producing activities *can reasonably be computed separately* from its petroleum producing activities outside the state." (Emphasis added.)

It is obvious that the elements of necessity and essentiality upon which defendant's contention is predicated did not appear in the Butler Brothers and Edison California Stores cases, even to as great an extent as they appear herein. Defendant, however, relies upon language in the Edison California Stores case, 30 Cal.2d at page 479, where it is said, in making reference to the opinion of the United States Supreme Court in affirming the decision in the Butler Brothers case, 315 U.S. 501: "It was there declared that since all the factors in the conduct of the Butler Brothers business were *essential* to the realization of profits, the business was properly treated as unitary." (Emphasis added.)

The use of the term "essential" in the foregoing excerpt was unfortunate and did not fairly describe the Supreme Court's views in the Butler Brothers case. That court did not state or hold that the business was unitary because the various local factors were essential to the over-all operations, as defendant would have us believe. In fact the term "essential" was not used at any place in the opinion. The holding of the court that "California was justified in assuming that the San Francisco branch *contributed its aliquot share* to the advantages of centralized management of this unitary enterprise and to the net income earned." (315 U.S. at page 509.) (Emphasis added.) Primarily the Supreme Court was concerned with whether the allocation method taxed extra-territorial value or otherwise infringed upon the Fourteenth Amendment. It concluded that there was no infringement. In its view the test was not one based on essential activities, but rather one based on contributing activities, and this court arrived at a similar result in Edison California Stores v. McColgan, supra, 30 Cal.2d 472, at page 481, wherein it concluded that operations are unitary if the business done within the state "is dependent upon or contributes to" the over-all operations.

The board would next distinguish the instant case from other cases wherein unitary businesses were held to exist, on the basis of the interstate businesses involved. We may agree that there is room for the distinction which it urges, but such distinction is one without substance. In its argument in the Butler Brothers and California Edison Stores cases the board points out that the product with which the taxpayers dealt moved in interstate traffic, whereas in the instant case the petroleum products moved only in intrastate traffic; that both in and out of California the products produced were sold where produced. No contention is made that Superior is not engaged in interstate business, but only that its products did not move in interstate traffic before being disposed of by Superior.

It is true that in Butler Brothers the goods sold in California were acquired from sources both from without and from within California but this was only a factor in determining that the business was unitary. None of the three unities announced in that case as determinative necessarily require the interstate movement of products. These, as stated, are unity of ownership, unity of operation as evidenced by central management and administration, and unity of use of its executive force and operational systems. Also in Butler Brothers the court further clarified the nature of the essential unities when it distinguished the modern judicial concept thereof in the following language 17 Cal.2d at page 668: "In the early cases in which the unit rule first made its hesitating appearance there was always a physical link, a palpable unity of substance * * *. Then in Adams Express Co. v. Ohio State Auditor, 1897, supra [Adams Express Co. v. Ohio State Auditor, 165 U.S. 194], the standard unity of substance was openly replaced by one of unity of use and management. This decision clearly recognized that in assessing tangible property for taxation, its value-producing qualities in connection with other pieces of tangible property outside the state must be considered."

Superior's business primarily is the production and sale of petroleum products. Like Butler Brothers it sells its products locally. The difference, if any, therefore must relate to the manner of acquisition of such products. Butler Brothers was able to purchase its products in interstate trade. Superior however, because of the character of its business, cannot so acquire its product. It is only through a multitude of individual operations which precede and make possible the outflow of petroleum at a producing well that Superior is able to obtain possession of a product which it can market. While the actual recovery and sale of the crude oil are, perhaps, local activities, nevertheless very extensive interstate transactions are theretofore involved in the other individual operations which make such production possible. The evidence here reveals that such essential factors as land acquisition, exploration, technology, testing, availability of equipment and personnel, financing and many others are definitely interstate in character. It must also be considered that each producing well in a particular state is the end product of interstate activities which may involve many other unproductive wells in many other states. Superior's products are thus acquired for the local market only as the result of interstate transactions to no less extent than were Butler Brothers' products made available at its local markets. It was not deemed necessary that Butler Brothers' goods be sold on an interstate basis for the unit rule to apply in that case, and the sale of Superior's products on the local market is likewise not determinative.

It appears to be the whole substance of the position urged by the board that we should no longer seek out a set of circumstances which, if found to exist, *require* by statutory mandate the application of an allocation formula. Instead, the board proposes that we declare a different set of circumstances which, if satisfied, would then require separate accounting. This is manifest by its insistence that if separate accounting is reasonably possible, it must prevail even if those circumstances which heretofore have been held to require an allocation formula are also present. Such a position is inconsistent with that previously urged by the board and adopted by this court in the Butler Brothers and Edison California Stores cases. No reason is suggested for departing from the established tests, other than that such departure will best serve the board's present purposes although there is no reason to believe that it will always work to the board's advantage. But regardless of the relative merits of a new and different test we are nevertheless directed by the Legislature, insofar as is discernible, to apply tests which are consistent with those heretofore established.

Section 24301 of the Revenue and Taxation Code instructs us as to the circumstances which require an allocation, rather than the contrary circumstances which, the board urges, require separate, accounting. Thus it directs that income attributable to sources within the state "shall be determined by an allocation" when the income of a taxpayer "is derived from or attributable to sources both within and without the State," rather than that such income be determined by a separate accounting method when "California petroleum producing activities can reasonably be computed separately from its petroleum producing activities outside the state," as urged by the board. The context of the statutory language is mandatory. Under the circumstances prevailing we would be required to conclude, even as a matter of law, that the income of the taxpayer was "derived from or attributable to sources both within and without the State," and that separate accounting could not be employed.

The judgment is affirmed.

* * *

SKELLY OIL COMPANY v. COMMISSIONER
OF TAXATION

Supreme Court of Minnesota, 1964.
269 Minn. 351, 131 N.W.2d 632.

NELSON, Justice. Certiorari upon the relation of the commissioner of taxation and Skelly Oil Company, hereinafter referred to as Skelly, to review an order of the Board of Tax Appeals. Skelly contends that said order was in error and not in conformity with law in the following respects: (1) In including in its income apportionable to and subject to tax in Minnesota, a portion of its production income for the years 1951 to 1955; (2) in failing to make provision for deduction of the full amount of Federal income taxes paid by it on the class of income assignable to Minnesota.

Skelly is a Delaware corporation with its principal offices in Tulsa, Oklahoma. It is qualified to transact business in this state and files tax returns here as required by Minn.St. c. 290. Its Minnesota corporate income and franchise tax returns are completed according to the accrual method of accounting, that being the method employed in keeping the taxpayer's books.

The company is engaged principally in the production and sale of crude oil and natural gas, both of which are carried on wholly outside Minnesota, and in the refining of crude oil and the marketing of the resulting refined products and of related accessories, appliances, and products such as tires, batteries, and liquid petroleum gas. Its activities in this state related only to such refining and marketing, which are carried on partly within and partly without this state. This was true during the years 1951 to 1955.

Skelly is organized internally on a departmental basis with operating departments and service or administrative departments. The operating departments are known as Lands and Leases, Geology and Geophysics, Oil and Gas Production, Manufacturing, and Marketing— each under a vice president—and also a Pipeline Department which is connected with the Manufacturing Department and is supervised by a manager. The first three departments are concerned only with the company's production activities. The latter three are concerned only with refining and marketing.

There are four administrative departments—Accounting, Purchasing, Law, and Secretary-Treasurer. These departments provide services to the several operating departments and also to Skelly's president and executive vice president and their assistants.

Skelly has carried on the manufacture of refined petroleum products during the times herein mentioned at three widely separated refineries—one at El Dorado, Kansas, a second at Longview, Texas, and the third at Denver, Colorado. The first two refineries have each been served by pipelines owned and operated by the taxpayer for the transportation of crude oil from adjacent production areas. Skelly also has a pipeline in Velma, in southern Oklahoma, but this line has no connection with any Skelly refinery. It is actually a field-gathering system connected with production rather than a pipeline for purposes of transportation and is so far from any Skelly refinery that transportation costs would make it uneconomical to use it for transportation of oil to the company's refineries. The Kansas pipeline is substantially larger than the other two and services about 4,000 wells as against 400 by the Velma line and 75 by the Longview line. (The latter was sold subsequent to the years here in issue.)

When decisions are made as to where, when, and in what volume Skelly's production of crude oil and natural gas shall be carried on, they are made without participation by the Manufacturing or Marketing Departments and without regard to whether Skelly has refineries, or to the needs of such refineries, although they are subject to the control exercised by state regulatory authorities. Such decisions lie wholly within the hands of the three departments having to do with production, namely, Lands and Leases, Geology and Geophysics, and Oil and Gas Production. The job of the Department of Geology and Geophysics is to search and explore for likely producing areas and to make recommendations when evidence favors their acquisition. These recommendations go to Lands and Leases, which secures the necessary drilling and production rights, usually through leases but occasionally by the purchase of fee title, and makes other necessary arrangements including agreements with other producers which will facilitate drilling and exploration.

The Departments of Geology and Geophysics and Lands and Leases make the decision with respect to the drilling of the first well on acquired acreage, the Department of Oil and Gas Production participating only in decisions with respect to the drilling of additional wells on the same acreage. The Manufacturing and Marketing Departments are not consulted in the making of production decisions even though there may be a Skelly refinery nearby. Lands and Leases and Geology and Geophysics work closely together and share joint offices, at strategic points from Bismarck, North Dakota, to Shreveport, Louisiana. The record is clear that no such office has ever been maintained in Minnesota and that Skelly has never done any geological work in Minnesota nor had any oil or gas leases, refinery, wells, or pipelines in the state, its activities here being limited to marketing.

The operation of the producing wells is the sole responsibility of the Oil and Gas Production Department. The gas produced is sold in its natural state at the well to connecting transmission companies. If there is any condensate drawn off at the gas wells, this is also sold to third parties at the point of production and customarily removed by tank trucks.

Oil obtained from the wells is run directly into one or more storage tanks which the production department maintains on the producing leasehold, the number of tanks varying with the number and productivity of the wells and the size of the property. With two exceptions, the oil is then sold to outside pipeline companies operating in the area, with delivery to the pipeline at the tanks if direct connection has been made, or, if not, by trucking to a point of delivery elsewhere. The exceptions noted are that about 60 percent of the taxpayer's production in Kansas is transported to its refinery at El Dorado for manufacture there, and about 10 percent of its east Texas production to its refinery at Longview for like purpose.

Skelly's production in the vicinity of Velma, Oklahoma, is sold to outside interests, delivery to the purchaser being made at a central storage point to which Skelly moves the oil through its Velma gathering system. Skelly also buys the oil of other producers in this area and moves it together with its own production to the storage point, where it is all sold to buyers who transport it through connecting pipelines to refineries in the area. The cost of transportation to Skelly's refineries would be prohibitive.

All sales of Skelly crude production to third parties are made at what is called the "posted field price" or, if the sale is made at a point elsewhere than at the producing premises, that price plus cost of transportation to such point. The posted field price is the announced price being paid currently by purhasers of the crude oil at the well-head in a specific area for crude petroleum of the kind and quality there available. All large buyers "post" such prices, and they do so by circulation of printed bulletins. During the years here involved Skelly posted field prices in areas where it was a buyer of crude oil, namely, Kansas, where the El Dorado refinery is situated; southern Oklahoma, where purchased oil is carried along with Skelly production in the Velma gathering system; and in eastern Texas, where crude oil was then being purchased for the Longview refinery.

Posted field prices control the amounts at which crude oil passes from hand to hand in the fields to which they relate. They are bona fide competitive prices, not subject to manipulation or rigging, for the reason, aside from others, that their maintenance is effectively policed by state regulatory bodies and also by state and Federal taxing authorities in connection with enforcement of taxing statutes.

The posted field prices control not only what Skelly pays for production bought from others, but also what it gets for its own production sold to others. This is the case with respect both to the purchase of crude oil for its own refineries and the purchase of crude oil which it later resells to others. For example, in the Velma area neither Skelly's own production nor the crude oil purchased from other producers goes to the taxpayer's own refineries. The sales to others are at the posted field price plus transportation costs.

The production of crude oil in Kansas and in eastern Texas going to the El Dorado and Longview refineries was transferred or "sold" by the Oil and Gas Production Department to the Manufacturing Department precisely as is done when the sale is made to outside parties. The production department was credited with the sale and the Manufacturing Department charged with the purchase in this amount. About 15 percent of the taxpayer's purchase of crude oil is made under what are called buy-and-sell agreements, usually with other refineries, whereby each party agrees to sell to the other a specified quantity of oil from a particular area at the posted field price in effect on the date of delivery, plus a flat additional amount to cover transportation costs if delivery is elsewhere than at the place of production. Such arrangements are not of advantage to production operations on the production departments, but only to the Manufacturing and Marketing Departments. An occasional objective is the earning of a transportation profit which is included in the earnings of Manufacturing and Marketing Departments but never in the earnings or the profits of the production departments. The agreements are advantageous to the Manufacturing Department also in minimizing refinery production costs by permitting the purchase of crude oil stored near the refinery and the sale of crude oil stored at a distance. Such agreements also help in maintaining adequate refinery inventories and facilitate in obtaining the particular grades of crude oil needed for current operations.

Not all producers of crude oil are also refiners. (In that respect those producers of crude oil are unlike Skelly.) Nonrefining producers are numerous and include some of the major producers. There are also nonproducing refiners, some of them in the oil-producing states and some in other states. Minnesota, for example, has at least two refineries operated within its borders by non-producers. Enterprises which both produce and refine sometimes separate the two operations legally by incorporating one or the other, or both, as subsidiaries. Examples are the Standard Oil Company of Indiana and the Barnsdahl Oil Company. It appears that the production and refining of crude oil involve differing skills. They each can be and are carried on profitably as separate enterprises. Refiners and producers have separate trade associations. Refinery employees and production employees each have separate union contracts even when there is but one employer, as in Skelly's case.

During the taxable years here involved, Skelly produced crude oil in not less than 15 midcontinent states. In all but 2 of the 15 states, and also in Canada, beginning in 1957, every barrel of oil and gas produced was sold to outside interests. In most of these areas there was neither intent nor prospect that it would be otherwise. This was so even in Colorado where Skelly has a refinery as well as production operations. Acquisition of the Denver refinery had no relation to the existence of production properties in Colorado, and in 1955, for example, of the 1,128,575 barrels of crude oil produced in that state not a single barrel was refined in the Denver refinery, all being sold to outside interests.

On an overall basis, during none of the taxable years was there ever as much as 10 percent of Skelly's annual production of crude oil even delivered to the pipelines serving its own refineries, and when account is taken of the fact that of the quantity so delivered a portion was thereafter sold to outside parties, the percentage that found its way into Skelly's own refineries was never as high as 9 percent. In computing net income from Skelly's production operations on the one hand and from its manufacturing and marketing operations on the other, all profits derived from operation of the company's lease gathering systems are credited to the Oil and Gas Production Department and all derived from the operation of the pipeline gathering systems are carried into manufacturing profits, notwithstanding that in the latter case a substantial part of the crude oil transported is sold to outside interests. General and administrative or overhead expenses, such as the expenses incurred by the several administrative or service departments and the executive offices, are divided between the departments on the basis of comparative direct operating expenses. This is the basis which must be observed in computing the deduction for percentage depletion allowed for Federal tax purposes. The record is thus clear that Skelly's refining and marketing operations do not serve to increase the amount of the company's production income, which is fully earned at the point where the crude oil is available for sale. Where the production operations cease, the value of the crude oil produced is always represented by the posted field price.

In all producing states which impose income taxes Skelly is required to pay taxes on the whole of its production income, measured by the posted field prices, derived within the taxing state's borders. Such prices are also taken as determinative of fair market value for purposes of state severance or production taxes, in computing allowable depletion deductions under the Internal Revenue Code, and in determining the production shares of royalty owners.

In its Minnesota returns Skelly included an income apportionable to Minnesota under Minn.St. 290.17(4) only such income as was derived from its manufacturing and marketing operations. The commissioner of taxation filed orders determining that additional taxes were owing, based mainly on increasing the reported income by adding thereto a portion of the taxpayer's production income. The parties are agreed that, except in respect of the amount of the deduction allowed for Federal income taxes paid, these orders were based on correct computations, both of the taxpayer's production income and of its apportionable income derived from manufacturing and marketing.

The commissioner in apportioning a part of Skelly's production income to this state on the basis of the statutory three-factor formula made a determination of the extent to which the taxpayer's sales, tangible property, and payroll related to production and that ratio which these amounts were of the taxpayer's total sales, tangible property, and payroll. This ratio, it will be observed, is very substantially different from the ratio which production income is of the total income. For example, in 1955, a representative year, sales, tangible property, and payroll relating to production averaged only 37 percent of the total sales, tangible property, and payroll, yet production accounted for 74 percent of the company's total profit. In contrast, manufacturing and marketing, which, on an average, was represented by 63 percent of the total sales, tangible property, and payroll, accounted for a mere 26 percent of the total profit. Skelly contends, and the record so discloses, that the part of its production income which the commissioner added to the reported apportionable income was that percentage of the production income which the crude oil sales made by Skelly's Oil and Gas Production Department to its Manufacturing Department was of the total of the taxpayer's production and its purchases of crude oil. In other words, the part excluded was the percentage which taxpayer's crude oil sales to others was of its total production and purchases. The percentage included was approximately 40 and that excluded approximately 60.

The Board of Tax Appeals found that the inclusion of 40 percent of production income in the apportionable income "resulted in attributing to Minnesota a percentage of income out of all proportion to the business transacted by taxpayer in Minnesota." The board was of the opinion, also, as was contended by Skelly, that the taxpayer was engaged in two separate businesses, that of "producing" and that of "marketing." Somehow the board nevertheless concluded that the two should be treated as one "[t]o the extent that production goes into marketing activities," on the theory that to this extent the businesses are "integrated." The board concluded further that "the extent that production goes into marketing activities" is measured by the percentage of the taxpayer's own crude oil production which entered pipelines serving the taxpayer's refineries (which it found ranged between a low of 7.49 percent in 1955 and a high of 9.32 percent in 1951) and thus held, contrary to the taxpayer's contention, that this percentage of production income is includible in apportionable income and that when so limited the inclusion does not result in a denial of due process.

Skelly assigns as error: (1) The holding of the board that Minnesota's taxing statutes permit apportionment to this state of a part of the income derived from the production of crude oil, a separate business conducted wholly without this state; (2) the holding of the board that such apportionment does not deprive Skelly of its property without due process of law, contrary to U.S.Const. Amend. XIV and Minn. Const. art. 1, § 7.

The taxpayer contends that since none of its business of producing and selling crude oil is conducted within Minnesota taxation by this state of any of its income from that business would deprive it of its property without due process of law.

* * *

The Board of Tax Appeals found that the actual percentage of Skelly's crude oil production entering its own pipeline amounted to 9.32 percent for 1951; 7.93 percent for 1952; 8.02 percent for 1953; 8.89 percent for 1954; and 7.49 percent for 1955. The board's findings of fact are accepted by Skelly as correct.

The board further found that in applying the three-factor formula prescribed by § 290.19, to obtain the percentage of income subject to tax in Minnesota, the commissioner excluded from the total sales factor of the denominator 100 percent of the sales attributable to production operations, but did include 40 percent of the property and payroll factors attributable thereto. The board further found that the failure to include in the denominator of the fraction the same percent of production sales as property and payroll resulted in overstating taxable income by $40,066.82 in 1951; $93,700.34 in 1952; $95,434.18 in 1953; $81,632.85 in 1954; and $91,168.39 in 1955. Thus, the board found that the addition of 40 percent of production income to apportionable income and the application thereto of the formula used by the commissioner resulted in attributing to Minnesota a percentage of income out of all appropriate proportion to the business transacted by the taxpayer in Minnesota.

The board in the memorandum attached to its decision makes the following statement:

*   *   *

"The proof presented here by taxpayer by way of expert testimony and exhibits, that the business of producing is separate from that of marketing, was conclusive. This is also the view adopted by courts in oil producing states." (Italics supplied.)

The board then refers in its memorandum to taxpayer's contention that because it operates two businesses the entire income of the one which does no business in Minnesota must therefore be exempt from taxation in Minnesota even though a portion of production in the instant case goes into marketing and refining, the business which is subject to taxation in Minnesota.

The board then cites definitions of "unitary business" found in Western Auto Supply Co. v. Commr. of Taxation, 245 Minn. 346, and states that "[i]t seems apparent to the board that under the assumed circumstances, income from both production and marketing would come within the above definitions, even though technically each might be a separate business." The board expresses the view that the meaning of the two words "unitary" as used in the Western Auto case and the statutory word "integral" as used in allocation cases is the same. They do, however, stress the fact that in this case they are faced with a vastly different situation than that involved in the Western Auto case. The board goes on to say:

" *   *   *   Instead of 100% of production going into marketing activities, we have something under 10% for each of the years involved. To the extent that production goes into marketing activities we believe the businesses are integrated, and to the extent that production income in this same percentage is used for apportionment, Minnesota can subject the same to a tax without violating the due process clauses."

The board then cites the Western Auto Supply case; Marshall-Wells Co. v. Commr. of Taxation, 220 Minn. 458, and Butler Brothers v. McColgan, 315 U.S. 501, suggesting that nothing has been said in these cases which would lead to any different conclusion. The board fails to discuss or refer to the fact that Skelly's refining and marketing operations do not serve to increase the amount of the company's production income, which is fully earned at the point where the crude oil is available for sale, that it is there that production operations cease, and that the value of the crude oil produced is represented by the posted field price, a bona fide competitive price. Neither the commissioner, the board, nor anyone else disputes that Skelly is required, in all oil-producing states which impose income taxes, to pay such taxes on the whole of its production income, measured by the posted field prices, derived within each taxing state's borders and that such prices are also taken as determinative of fair market value for purposes of state severance or production taxes, in computing allowable depletion deductions under the Internal Revenue Code, and in determining the production shares of royalty owners.

Under the circumstances the Board of Tax Appeals was clearly justified upon the record in finding that the taxpayer was engaged in two separate businesses; that the business of producing was in no way dependent upon the business of marketing; that each business could be operated entirely independent of each other; and that all producing income is fully earned at the well-head and is not increased or affected by Skelly's manufacturing and marketing activities. The board admitted in its memorandum that the proof presented by Skelly that the business of producing is separate from that of marketing was conclusive. It further stated that this view is also the view adopted by courts in oil-producing states.

*   *   *

If Skelly's production operations are in fact a business separate from its marketing operations under § 290.17(3), as found by the board, all income produced by those operations is assignable to other states. Of course, if that were not the case, and if the production operations and the manufacturing and marketing operations constituted a single business, then under § 290.17(4), subject only to the requirements of due process, the income of the two together would be apportionable within and without Minnesota in accordance with whatever method is appropriate under § 290.19. However, since the production operations are carried on wholly outside of Minnesota and since the income they produce is fully earned at the point of production, it must necessarily follow that § 290.17(3) is applicable only to Skelly's marketing operations income and that none of its production income is apportionable to Minnesota.

1.   The record is clear that the board has bypassed its own finding that the two businesses were separate. Its conclusions that any of the production income is apportionable to Minnesota have no support in the findings and neither the record nor the evidence reasonably sustains such a determination. Skelly's production income was already subject to being taxed in full at the point of production. While taxation of the same income more than once may not be unlawful, depending upon circumstances, Cream of Wheat Co. v. County of Grand Forks, 253 U.S. 325, 330, it is nevertheless offensive to common concepts of what constitutes fairness, particularly when it is multiple taxation of the sort the board's unsupported conclusion produces in the instant case.

*   *   *

3. We think that the board reached manifestly sound and inescapable conclusions in determining that the taxpayer's production operations and its manufacturing and marketing operations constitute separate businesses and that paragraphs (3) and (4) of § 290.17 require that where a taxpayer has more than one nonpersonal service business each must be dealt with separately and the income from each assigned or apportioned to Minnesota only if that particular business is conducted in Minnesota, either in whole or in part. The board's abrupt disregard of these conclusions by the application of any formula under § 290.19 is plainly contrary to the legislative mandate embodied in § 290.17(3, 4). There is no basis under the board's findings or the statute for adding to Skelly's marketing income any percentage of its production income in view of the undisputed facts that its production operations are carried on wholly outside of Minnesota and its income therefrom fully earned at the point of production.

* * *

The commissioner has cited Butler Brothers v. McColgan, supra; Bass, Ratcliff & Gretton, Ltd. v. State Tax Comm., 266 U.S. 271; and Underwood Typewriter Co. v. Chamberlain, 254 U.S. 113, as authority for the immunity of the apportionment formulas from attack. The Supreme Court of the United States said in the Hans Rees' Sons case (283 U.S. 134):

"* * * When, as in this case, there are different taxing jurisdictions, each competent to lay a tax with respect to what lies within, and is done within, its own borders, and the question is necessarily one of apportionment, evidence may always be received which tends to show that a state has applied a method, which, albeit fair on its face, operates so as to reach profits which are in no just sense attributable to transactions within its jurisdiction."

Under attack in that case was the validity of a statutory method of apportionment applied by North Carolina to income derived from operations carried on both within and without that state. The state court had held that because the operations constituted what is characterized as a "single business enterprise"—"a unitary business"—the statutory method was immune to attack. The Supreme Court disagreed. It said that evidence lacking in the Underwood and Bass cases was present and that this evidence showed that (283 U.S. 135):

"* * * the statutory method, as applied to the appellant's business for the years in question operated unreasonably and arbitrarily, in attributing to North Carolina a percentage of income out of all appropriate proportion to the business transacted by the appellant in that state. In this view, the taxes as laid were beyond the state's authority."

No other conclusion is permissible here if production income, no matter what the percentage, is included in apportionable income because of the fact that Skelly's sole activity in Minnesota has been and is the marketing of finished products. Under the circumstances, Minnesota may include in the measure of its income tax only such income as is attributable to that activity. It may not include any production-operations income if it does not appear that the included portion is fairly attributable to the marketing operations reaching into this state.

The United States Supreme Court said in Butler Brothers v. Mc-Colgan, 315 U.S. 501, 507, that the test is whether the state is taxing only income "created by business within its borders." * * * Clearly, the fact that Skelly's production income is fully earned at the point where the crude oil is produced and is neither more nor less than what it would be if Skelly had no refineries, distinguishes the situation here from that case. Skelly's sole activity in Minnesota is the marketing of finished products, as the proof clearly shows. The only permissible conclusion is that taxes based on the inclusion of production income, no matter what the percentage, in apportionable income are beyond the state's authority. Minnesota may include in the apportionable income subject to its tax only income attributable to Skelly's marketing activity. See, Northwestern States Portland Cement Co. v. Minnesota, 358 U.S. 450, 79 S.Ct. 357, 3 L.Ed.2d 421, 67 A.L.R.2d 1292.

The commissioner cites Superior Oil Co. v. Franchise Tax Bd., 60 Cal.2d 406, and Honolulu Oil Corp. v. Franchise Tax Bd., 60 Cal.2d 417, a companion case, as involving corporations carrying on operations similar to Skelly's and appears to place considerable reliance on these cases. The corporations apparently explored for and produced crude oil but did not refine and market the resulting products (as does Skelly). The sole issue as we see it in both cases was whether the portion of income from the taxpayers' interstate production operations which was taxable in California should be computed on the basis of a statutory apportionment formula similar to that which the commissioner applied to Skelly's interstate refining and marketing income or whether it should be computed on the basis of a separate accounting. The apportionment formula was held controlling in each instance on the ground (contrary to the contention of the Franchise Tax Board in the Honolulu case) that the *taxpayer's production business* was a "unitary business." Neither of those cases, however, gives any support to the commissioner's contention that Skelly's production operations and its refining and marketing operations are a single business and should be treated as such for purposes of § 290.17.

4. Since we have reached the conclusion that there must be a reversal on the grounds that the provisions of § 290.19 are not applicable, other questions raised on this appeal need not be discussed. The Board of Tax Appeals has found conclusively that Skelly's production operations and marketing operations constitute separate, independent businesses; that only the marketing operations are carried on within the borders of Minnesota; and that the income of each business has been determined correctly and is independent of that of the other. Under the circumstances, only § 290.17(3) applies as the governing tax statute, so far as concerns income from taxpayer's separate production business.

The taxpayer is entitled to exclusion of income derived from production and sale of crude oil outside Minnesota from taxable income subject to apportionment under §§ 290.17(4) and 290.19. Its marketing operations remain subject to § 290.17(4) for taxing purposes.

Reversed and remanded.

* * *

———

Efforts have been made from time to time to have Congress adopt legislation which would alleviate, if not solve, the problem of allocating income of an interstate business among the several states in which it does business on a fair basis; that is, fair to the states as well as to the interstate business. The most recent effort in this respect has been the Interstate Taxation Act which has passed the House of Representatives several times, but so far has not been passed by the Senate. In fact, no hearings have ever been held by any Senate Committee, although the bill has been introduced at several Sessions. One purpose of the bill would be to establish uniform jurisdictional rules for state taxes of all kinds. For state income tax purposes, an interstate corporation would be subject to tax only in those states in which it has a business location in the state during the taxable year and in which it owns or leases property, has one or more employees, and maintains a stock of its products for sale in the ordinary course of business. Mere sales solicitation, without the foregoing factors, would not be sufficient to give the state or locality jurisdiction to levy a tax. State income taxes could be imposed on an interstate corporation only by apportioning on a pro rata basis the income earned within the state as compared with the entire income earned by the corporation, where the apportionment formula is determined (1) on the basis of property owned within the state as compared with all property owned, and (2) payroll paid within the state as compared with the entire payroll paid by the corporation. If adopted, and if the Act were to withstand a challenge as to its constitutionality, it would provide a definite method of allocating income among the states in which an interstate corporation does business. Presumably it would permit each state to determine the rate of taxation it would levy upon its pro rata portion of that corporation's business. As a consequence, one offshoot of the system would be a disclosure as to whether any one state were really a "tax-haven" for new business locations. In any event, it is most likely that interstate corporations would be paying taxes at the state level on no more than 100% of their income. Many corporate treasurers will testify that today because of the application of various allocation formulas their corporation must pay taxes at the state level on more than 100% of their earned income. Whether corporate management would be in a position to shift transactions from one state to another which has a lower rate of taxation remains to be seen. One attribute of the Interstate Taxation Act is that it provides for continued examination by appropriate committees of the Congress in resolving the problems arising from state taxation of interstate commerce, and if unsatisfactory progress is made then the Act provides that a report shall be made to Congress to recommend new legislation "in the national interest."

C.   DOING BUSINESS IN OTHER STATES

INTERNATIONAL SHOE CO. v. STATE OF WASHINGTON, OFFICE OF UNEMPLOYMENT COMPENSATION AND PLACEMENT

Supreme Court of the United States, 1945.
326 U.S. 310, 66 S.Ct. 154, 90 L.Ed. 95.

Mr. Chief Justice STONE delivered the opinion of the Court.

The questions for decision are (1) whether, within the limitations of the due process clause of the Fourteenth Amendment, appellant, a Delaware corporation, has by its activities in the State of Washington rendered itself amenable to proceedings in the courts of that state to recover unpaid contributions to the state unemployment compensation fund exacted by state statutes, Washington Unemployment Compensation Act, Washington Revised Statutes, § 9998—103a through § 9998—123a, 1941 Supp., and (2) whether the state can exact those contributions consistently with the due process clause of the Fourteenth Amendment.

The statutes in question set up a comprehensive scheme of unemployment compensation, the costs of which are defrayed by contributions required to be made by employers to a state unemployment compensation fund.

The contributions are a specified percentage of the wages payable annually by each employer for his employees' services in the state. The assessment and collection of the contributions and the fund are administered by respondents.   Section 14(c) of the Act, Wash.Rev. Stat.1941 Supp., § 9998—14c, authorizes respondent Commissioner to issue an order and notice of assessment of delinquent contributions upon prescribed personal service of the notice upon the employer if found within the state, or, if not so found, by mailing the notice to the employer by registered mail at his last known address.   That section also authorizes the Commissioner to collect the assessment by distraint if it is not paid within ten days after service of the notice.   By §§ 14(e) and 6(b) the order of assessment may be administratively reviewed by an appeal tribunal within the office of unemployment upon petition of the employer, and this determination is by § 6(i) made subject to judicial review on questions of law by the state Superior Court, with further right of appeal in the state Supreme Court as in other civil cases.

In this case notice of assessment for the years in question was personally served upon a sales solicitor employed by appellant in the State of Washington, and a copy of the notice was mailed by registered mail to appellant at its address in St. Louis, Missouri. Appellant appeared specially before the office of unemployment and moved to set aside the order and notice of assessment on the ground that the service upon appellant's salesman was not proper service upon appellant; that appellant was not a corporation of the State of Washington and was not doing business within the state; that it had no agent within the state upon whom service could be made; and that appellant is not an employer and does not furnish employment within the meaning of the statute.

The motion was heard on evidence and a stipulation of facts by the appeal tribunal which denied the motion and ruled that respondent Commissioner was entitled to recover the unpaid contributions. That action was affirmed by the Commissioner; both the Superior Court and the Supreme Court affirmed. 154 P.2d 801. Appellant in each of these courts assailed the statute as applied, as a violation of the due process clause of the Fourteenth Amendment, and as imposing a constitutionally prohibited burden on interstate commerce. The cause comes here on appeal under § 237(a) of the Judicial Code, 28 U.S.C.A. § 344(a), appellant assigning as error that the challenged statutes as applied infringe the due process clause of the Fourteenth Amendment and the commerce clause.

The facts as found by the appeal tribunal and accepted by the state Superior Court and Supreme Court, are not in dispute. Appellant is a Delaware corporation, having its principal place of business in St. Louis, Missouri, and is engaged in the manufacture and sale of shoes and other footwear. It maintains places of business in several states, other than Washington, at which its manufacturing is carried on and from which its merchandise is distributed interstate through several sales units or branches located outside the State of Washington.

Appellant has no office in Washington and makes no contracts either for sale or purchase of merchandise there. It maintains no stock of merchandise in that state and makes there no deliveries of goods in intrastate commerce. During the years from 1937 to 1940, now in question, appellant employed eleven to thirteen salesmen under direct supervision and control of sales managers located in St. Louis. These salesmen resided in Washington; their principal activities were confined to that state; and they were compensated by commissions based upon the amount of their sales. The commissions for each year totaled more than $31,000. Appellant supplies its salesmen with a line of samples, each consisting of one shoe of a pair, which they display to prospective purchasers. On occasion they rent permanent sample rooms, for exhibiting samples, in business buildings, or rent rooms in hotels or business buildings temporarily for that purpose. The cost of such rentals is reimbursed by appellant.

The authority of the salesmen is limited to exhibiting their samples and soliciting orders from prospective buyers, at prices and on terms fixed by appellant. The salesmen transmit the orders to appellant's office in St. Louis for acceptance or rejection, and when accepted the merchandise for filling the orders is shipped f. o. b. from points outside Washington to the purchasers within the state. All the merchandise shipped into Washington is invoiced at the place of shipment from which collections are made. No salesman has authority to enter into contracts or to make collections.

The Supreme Court of Washington was of opinion that the regular and systematic solicitation of orders in the state by appellant's salesmen, resulting in a continuous flow of appellant's product into the state, was sufficient to constitute doing business in the state so as to make appellant amenable to suit in its courts. But it was also of opinion that there were sufficient additional activities shown to bring the case within the rule frequently stated, that solicitation within a state by the agents of a foreign corporation plus some additional activities there are sufficient to render the corporation amenable to suit brought in the courts of the state to enforce an obligation arising out of its activities there. * * * The court found such additional activities in the salesmen's display of samples sometimes in permanent display rooms, and the salesmen's residence within the state, continued over a period of years, all resulting in a substantial volume of merchandise regularly shipped by appellant to purchasers within the state. The court also held that the statute as applied did not invade the constitutional power of Congress to regulate interstate commerce and did not impose a prohibited burden on such commerce.

Appellant's argument, renewed here, that the statute imposes an unconstitutional burden on interstate commerce need not detain us. For 53 Stat. 1391, 26 U.S.C.A. § 1606(a), provides that "No person required under a State law to make payments to an unemployment fund shall be relieved from compliance therewith on the ground that he is engaged in interstate or foreign commerce, or that the State law does not distinguish between employees engaged in interstate or foreign commerce and those engaged in intrastate commerce." It is no longer debatable that Congress, in the exercise of the commerce power, may authorize the states, in specified ways, to regulate interstate commerce or impose burdens upon it. * * *

Appellant also insists that its activities within the state were not sufficient to manifest its "presence" there and that in its absence the state courts were without jurisdiction, that consequently it was a denial of due process for the state to subject appellant to suit. It refers to those cases in which it was said that the mere solicitation of orders for the purchase of goods within a state, to be accepted without the state and filled by shipment of the purchased goods interstate, does not render the corporation seller amenable to suit within the state. See Green v. Chicago, Burlington & Quincy R. Co., 205 U.S. 530. * * * And appellant further argues that since it was not present within the state, it is a denial of due process to subject it to taxation or other money exaction. It thus denies the power of the state to lay the tax or to subject appellant to a suit for its collection.

Historically the jurisdiction of courts to render judgment in personam is grounded on their de facto power over the defendant's person. Hence his presence within the territorial jurisdiction of a court was prerequisite to its rendition of a judgment personally binding him. Pennoyer v. Neff, 95 U.S. 714. But now that the capias ad respondendum has given way to personal service of summons or other form of notice, due process requires only that in order to subject a defendant to a judgment in personam, if he be not present within the territory of the forum, he have certain minimum contacts with it such that the maintenance of the suit does not offend "traditional notions of fair play and substantial justice." Milliken v. Meyer, 311 U.S. 457. * * *

Since the corporate personality is a fiction, although a fiction intended to be acted upon as though it were a fact, Klein v. Board of Tax Supervisors, 282 U.S. 19, 24, it is clear that unlike an individual its "presence" without, as well as within, the state of its origin can be manifested only by activities carried on in its behalf by those who are authorized to act for it. To say that the corporation is so far "present" there as to satisfy due process requirements, for purposes of taxation or the maintenance of suits against it in the courts of the state, is to beg the question to be decided. For the terms "present" or "presence" are used merely to symbolize those activities of the corporation's agent within the state which courts will deem to be sufficient to satisfy the demands of due process. L. Hand, J., in Hutchinson v. Chase & Gilbert, 2 Cir., 45 F.2d 139, 141. Those demands may be met by such contacts of the corporation with the state of the forum as make it reasonable, in the context of our federal system of government, to require the corporation to defend the particular suit which is brought there. An "estimate of the inconveniences" which would result to the corporation from a trial away from its "home" or principal place of business is relevant in this connection. Hutchinson v. Chase & Gilbert, supra, 45 F.2d 141.

"Presence" in the state in this sense has never been doubted when the activities of the corporation there have not only been continuous and systematic, but also give rise to the liabilities sued on, even though no consent to be sued or authorization to an agent to accept service of process has been given. St. Clair v. Cox, 106 U.S. 350, 355. * * * Conversely it has been generally recognized that the casual presence of the corporate agent or even his conduct of single or isolated items of activities in a state in the corporation's behalf are not enough to subject it to suit on causes of action unconnected with the activities there. * * * To require the corporation in such circumstances to defend the suit away from its home or other jurisdiction where it carries on more substantial activities has been thought to lay too great and unreasonable a burden on the corporation to comport with due process.

While it has been held in cases on which appellant relies that continuous activity of some sorts within a state is not enough to support the demand that the corporation be amenable to suits unrelated to that activity, * * * there have been instances in which the continuous corporate operations within a state were thought so substantial and of such a nature as to justify suit against it on causes of action arising from dealings entirely distinct from those activities. * * *

Finally, although the commission of some single or occasional acts of the corporate agent in a state sufficient to impose an obligation or liability on the corporation has not been thought to confer upon the state authority to enforce it, Rosenberg Bros. & Co. v. Curtis Brown Co., 260 U.S. 516, other such acts, because of their nature and quality and the circumstances of their commission, may be deemed sufficient to render the corporation liable to suit. * * * True, some of the decisions holding the corporation amenable to suit have been supported by resort to the legal fiction that it has given its consent to service and suit, consent being implied from its presence in the state through the acts of its authorized agents. * * * But more realistically it may be said that those authorized acts were of such a nature as to justify the fiction. * * *

It is evident that the criteria by which we mark the boundary line between those activities which justify the subjection of a corporation to suit, and those which do not, cannot be simply mechanical or quantitative. The test is not merely, as has sometimes been suggested, whether the activity, which the corporation has seen fit to procure through its agents in another state, is a little more or a little less. * * * Whether due process is satisfied must depend rather upon the quality and nature of the activity in relation to the fair and orderly administration of the laws which it was the purpose of the due process clause to insure. That clause does not contemplate that a state may make binding a judgment in personam against an individual or corporate defendant with which the state has no contacts, ties, or relations. Cf. Pennoyer v. Neff, supra; Minnesota Commercial Men's Ass'n v. Benn, 261 U.S. 140.

But to the extent that a corporation exercises the privilege of conducting activities within a state, it enjoys the benefits and protection of the laws of that state. The exercise of that privilege may give rise to obligations; and, so far as those obligations arise out of or are connected with the activities within the state, a procedure which requires the corporation to respond to a suit brought to enforce them can, in most instances, hardly be said to be undue. * * *

Applying these standards, the activities carried on in behalf of appellant in the State of Washington were neither irregular nor casual. They were systematic and continuous throughout the years in question. They resulted in a large volume of interstate business, in the course of which appellant received the benefits and protection of the laws of the state, including the right to resort to the courts for the enforcement of its rights. The obligation which is here sued upon arose out of those very activities. It is evident that these operations establish sufficient contacts or ties with the state of the forum to make it reasonable and just according to our traditional conception of fair play and substantial justice to permit the state to enforce the obligations which appellant has incurred there. Hence we cannot say that the maintenance of the present suit in the State of Washington involves an unreasonable or undue procedure.

We are likewise unable to conclude that the service of the process within the state upon an agent whose activities establish appellant's "presence" there was not sufficient notice of the suit, or that the suit was so unrelated to those activities as to make the agent an inappropriate vehicle for communicating the notice. It is enough that appellant has established such contacts with the state that the particular form of substituted service adopted there gives reasonable assurance that the notice will be actual. * * * Nor can we say that the mailing of the notice of suit to appellant by registered mail at its home office was not reasonably calculated to apprise appellant of the suit. * * *

Only a word need be said of appellant's liability for the demanded contributions of the state unemployment fund. The Supreme Court of Washington, construing and applying the statute, has held that it imposes a tax on the privilege of employing appellant's salesmen within the state measured by a percentage of the wages, here the commissions payable to the salesmen. This construction we accept for purposes of determining the constitutional validity of the statute. The right to employ labor has been deemed an appropriate subject of taxation in this country and England, both before and since the adoption of the Constitution. * * * And such a tax imposed upon the employer for unemployment benefits is within the constitutional power of the states. * * *

Appellant having rendered itself amenable to suit upon obligations arising out of the activities of its salesmen in Washington, the state may maintain the present suit in personam to collect the tax laid upon the exercise of the privilege of employing appellant's salesmen within the state. For Washington has made one of those activities, which taken together establish appellant's "presence" there for purposes of suit, the taxable event by which the state brings appellant within the reach of its taxing power. The state thus has constitutional power to lay the tax and to subject appellant to a suit to recover it. The activities which establish its "presence" subject it alike to taxation by the state and to suit to recover the tax. * * *

Affirmed.

Mr. Justice JACKSON took no part in the consideration or decision of this case.

Mr. Justice BLACK concurred. (Opinion omitted.)

* * *

SOUTHERN MACHINE COMPANY v. MOHASCO INDUSTRIES, INC.

United States Court of Appeals, Sixth Circuit (1968).
401 F.2d 374.

CELEBREZZE, Circuit Judge.   This declaratory judgment action arose out of a licensing agreement between Southern Machine Company, Inc., (hereinafter "Southern Machine") Plaintiff-Appellant, and Mohasco Industries, Inc., (hereinafter "Mohasco") Defendant-Appellee.   Southern Machine brought the action in the United States District Court for the Eastern District of Tennessee pursuant to 28 U.S.C. A. § 2201 joining as parties defendant Mohasco and Louisa Carpet Mills, Inc., (hereinafter "Louisa").   Upon the motion of Mohasco, the District Court quashed service of process and dismissed the action as to it for lack of in personam jurisdiction.   Since jurisdiction over Mohasco is indispensable for the full declaratory relief sought, Southern Machine has appealed the granting of Mohasco's motion.   We reverse.

Service of process was made on Mohasco outside the State of Tennessee through the Secretary of State of Tennessee; but no question is raised concerning the adequacy of the notice or the opportunity to be heard or the compliance with the service provisions of the applicable statute, T.C.A. § 20–236.   The questions raised by this appeal relate solely to the power of a Tennessee court to bind Mohasco by a judgment *in personam:* (1) Has the Tennessee legislature extended the jurisdictional reach of its courts to non-resident defendants in the position of Mohasco?   (2) Can the jurisdictional reach of Tennessee courts, consistently with due process, be extended to non-residents in the position of Mohasco?   The two questions merge into one if the Tennessee legislature has authorized Tennessee courts to reach to the full constitutional limits in pursuit of non-resident defendants.

In 1965 the Tennessee legislature enacted a "long arm" statute, which, among other provisions, purports to give Tennessee courts jurisdiction over non-residents who engage in the transaction of any business in Tennessee as to "any action or claim for relief" arising out of that business transaction.   T.C.A. § 20–235(a).   In considering this Act, we can put to one side cases where the activities of a corporation are sufficient to justify the assumption of jurisdiction even for causes of action arising outside the forum state.   Cf. Perkins v. Benquet Consolidated Mining Co., 342 U.S. 437 (1952).   The Tennessee Long Arm Statute is a "single act" statute by which the State only purports to assume jurisdiction over causes of action arising out of the defendant's activities in the State.   Since the old "doing business" statute, T.C.A. § 20–220, contains the same limitation, however, some question has been raised whether the "transaction of any business" provision of the "long arm" statute extended the jurisdiction of Tennessee courts any further than the former Act; no authoritative Tennessee State court has yet interpreted the "long arm" statute.   We think it is clear that for causes of action arising out of a non-resident defendant's business activities in the State, the Tennessee legislature intended to extend the jurisdiction of Tennessee courts over a non-resident to the full extent permitted by the Fourteenth Amendment.

First, the federal district courts that have interpreted the statute have unanimously found that the statute comprehends the full jurisdiction allowable under the Fourteenth Amendment. Hamilton National Bank of Chattanooga v. Russell, 261 F.Supp. 145 (E.D.Tenn. 1966). * * * Second, the Tennessee Act is substantially the same as the Illinois Long Arm Statute, Ill.Rev.Stat. c. 110, § 17, which had been interpreted as extending jurisdiction to the constitutional limits long before enactment of the Tennessee statute. See Nelson v. Miller, 11 Ill.2d 378, 143 N.E.2d 673 (1957). * * * Third, as was well noted in Temco, Inc. v. General Screw Products, Inc., 261 F.Supp. 793 (M.D.Tenn.1966), " * * * [a] new statute would not have been needed had not an expanded interpretation been desired." 261 F.Supp. at 797. Finally, the Tennessee legislature specifically provided that the "long arm" statute was remedial legislation and was to be liberally construed. T.C.A. § 20–240.

Having found that the Tennessee courts are authorized to reach as far as the Constitution will permit, our sole problem is determining the limits that the Fourteenth Amendment places upon a state's extraterritorial exercise of in personam jurisdiction. In approaching that problem, a pedantic quibbling with the wording of the statute is inappropriate. The language is general and was intended to cover any business activity that has a substantial enough contact with the state to satisfy constitutional requirements.

With the issue thus narrowed, we turn to the facts of the instant case. In May, 1962, Mohasco and Southern Machine entered into a license agreement by which Southern Machine was authorized to manufacture and sell various tufting machine attachments on which Mohasco held the patent or licensing rights. The agreement contains the usual patent licensing provisions, disavowing any representation by Mohasco as to the validity and enforceability of the patents and prohibiting Southern Machine from attacking the validity of the patents, and also contains some provisions peculiar to Mohasco's licensing plan.

* * *

Affidavits submitted by officers of the two corporations are in conflict concerning the nature of the negotiations leading to the execution of the agreement. But the assertion is uncontested that at the time the agreement was executed Southern Machine, a Tennessee corporation, had only one manufacturing plant, which was located in Chattanooga, Tennessee. Southern Machine says that the negotiations were primarily by long distance telephone between Tennessee and New York, while Mohasco contends that the negotiations occurred at its office in Amsterdam, New York in March, 1962. In any event, the agreement provides that it is to be construed as having been made in New York and in accordance with the law of New York; and both parties acknowledge that the agreement was drawn up by Mohasco, signed by Southern Machine in Chattanooga, and then finally executed by Mohasco in New York.

   * * *

Although Mohasco is a New York corporation with its principal offices in Amsterdam, New York, it has divisions located in other states. Nevertheless, Mohasco has no office and neither owns nor leases any property in Tennessee. Nor has Mohasco qualified to do business in Tennessee or appointed the Secretary of State of Tennessee or any other person as agent for the service of process in that State. On the other hand, Mohasco has apparently managed to derive a profit from the commerce of Tennessee. A regional sales representative calls about six times a year on an independent Memphis distributor of Mohawk products. Also three salesmen, one of whom is a resident of Tennessee, solicit orders from retailers in the State; and one of Mohasco's divisions solicits orders by mail in the State. All orders from Tennessee, however, from whatever source, are mailed to the New York office for acceptance or rejection there, and all merchandise that is shipped into Tennessee is shipped from outside the State to the customer, presumably by common carrier.

The present controversy concerns the licensing agreement outlined above and a contract between Louisa Carpet Mills, Inc., a Kentucky corporation, and Southern Machine for the manufacture and delivery of certain machines, including some of the patented attachments. When the contract between Louisa and Southern Machine had been executed, Mohasco, pursuant to its agreement, approved Louisa for a use license. After delivery of one machine and preparation of the rest of the order, however, Louisa refused to take a use license because the patents covered by the license agreement had been held invalid by the United States District Court for the Northern District of Georgia. Mohasco Industries, Inc. v. E. T. Barwick Mills, Inc., 221 F.Supp. 191 (N.D.Ga.1963). Aff'd 340 F.2d 319 reh. denied 342 F.2d 431 (5th Cir. 1965) cert. denied 382 U.S. 847 (1965). If Southern Machine would not deliver, Louisa threatened to obtain the machines elsewhere; and it is alleged in the complaint without contradiction that other manufacturers without licenses from Mohasco have been manufacturing and selling the patented attachments " * * * with impunity and without any apparent or effective action on the part of Mohasco to stop or prevent such manufacturing or sales. * * * " Upon being advised of the circumstances, Mohasco, nevertheless, refused to waive the use licensing requirement for Louisa. Southern Machine then brought this action against Mohasco and Louisa to have its rights declared under both the licensing agreement and its contract with Louisa.

The nature and quality of a person's contact with a state that will serve as the basis for the exercise of *in personam* jurisdiction over that person by the state is not a subject of easy description. We have come a long way since the simplistic rule of Pennoyer v. Neff, 95 U.S. 714, 24 L.Ed. 565 (1878), that " * * * [p]rocess from * * * one state cannot run into another state * * *." 95 U.S. at 727. Presence of the defendant in the forum state at the time process is served is no longer required. Our courts have moved "away from the bias favoring the defendant toward [a policy] permitting the plaintiff to insist that the defendant come to him" when a sufficient basis exists for such insistence. In early attempts to pay lip service to the dogma of *Pennoyer* while still sustaining jurisdiction over non-residents, the court tried to define that sufficient basis by fictionalized approaches, such as "implied consent," "presence," and "doing business." But those approaches failed to " * * * [put] the real question * * * " and in International Shoe Co. v. State of Washington, 326 U.S. 310, 66 S.Ct. 154, 90 L.Ed. 95 (1945), the United States Supreme Court broke with the past and established a new test:

"* * * due process requires only that in order to subject a defendant to a judgment *in personam*, if he be not present within the territory of the forum, he have certain minimum contacts with it such that the maintenance of the suit does not offend 'traditional notions of fair play and substantial justice' " 326 U.S. at 316, 66 S.Ct. at 158. Today, it can no longer be doubted, if it ever was, that the doing of an act or the causing of a consequence in the forum state by the defendant can satisfy the requirements of the "minimum contacts" test.

But "traditional notions of fair play and substantial justice" is hardly a precise and definitive standard; it gives us no more basis for judging than the highly amorphous and ultimately subjective standard of reasonableness. As we have noted before, application of the test "* * * must * * * be worked out with reference to the facts of a particular case * * * " Velandra v. Regie Nationale Des Usines Renault, 336 F.2d 292, 295 (6th Cir. 1964). On the other hand, the test does at least state the real issue; and after twenty-three years of application, it can no longer be considered an unknown quantity. Although the test can never be stated as a dogmatic principle *à la Pennoyer,* a general outline of its present outermost limits can be derived from pertinent Supreme Court opinions, and decisions of the other federal courts will aid in applying the rule thus derived to particular facts.

When considering a single act as the basis of *in personam* jurisdiction, the two most pertinent Supreme Court cases after *International Shoe* are McGee v. International Life Insurance Company, 355 U.S. 220 (1957), and Hanson v. Denckla, 357 U.S. 235 (1958). In *McGee*, the only contacts of a Texas insurance company with California were the mailing of a reinsurance certificate and premium notices into the State and the receiving of the signed certificate and premium payments by mail from the State on only one policy insuring a California resident. Upholding the jurisdiction of a California court over the Texas insurance company in a suit by a California beneficiary of the policy, the Supreme Court said: "It is sufficient for purposes of due process that the suit was based on a contract which had substantial connection with that State." 355 U.S. at 223, 78 S.Ct. at 201.

Hanson v. Denckla, supra served notice, however, that an interest in the plaintiff or an interest in the cause of action are not by themselves sufficient to justify a state issuing process beyond its borders.

In that case, the Court held that Florida could not assume *in personam* jurisdiction over a Delaware trustee of a trust that was executed in Pennsylvania by a domicile of Pennsylvania who later moved to Florida. Noting the trend toward expanding personal jurisdiction over non-residents, the Court cautioned that to satisfy the requirements of due process " * * * it is essential in each case that there be some act by which the defendant purposefully avails itself of the privilege of conducting activities within the forum state, thus invoking the benefits and protections of its laws." 357 U.S. at 253.

From these two cases, three criteria emerge for determining the present outerlimits of *in personam* jurisdiction based on a single act. First, the defendant must purposefully avail himself of the privilege of acting in the forum state or causing a consequence in the forum state. Second, the cause of action must arise from the defendant's activities there. Finally, the acts of the defendant or consequences caused by the defendant must have a substantial enough connection with the forum state to make the exercise of jurisdiction over the defendant reasonable.

Applying these criteria to the instant case, we first approach the *sine qua non* for *in personam* jurisdiction: Has Mohasco purposefully availed itself of the privilege of transacting business in Tennessee? In considering this question, we can first dispose of those matters that are immaterial. For example, Mohasco has denied that any of its agents have been physically present in Tennessee concerning any matter related to the licensing agreement. Physical presence of an agent is not necessary, however, for the transaction of business in a state. The soliciting of insurance by mail, the transmission of radio broadcasts into a state, and the sending of magazines and newspapers into a state to be sold there by independent contractors are all accomplished without the physical presence of an agent; yet all have been held to constitute the transaction of business in a state. Similarly, the contention that Southern Machine solicited the license agreement from Mohasco is immaterial. Shealy v. Challenger Manufacturing Company, 304 F.2d 102 (4th Cir. 1962). Mohasco chose to deal with Southern Machine; and as Judge Sobeloff noted in *Shealy*, it cannot diminish the purposefulness of Mohasco's choice that " * * * [Mohasco,] like the maker of the better mousetrap, is fortunate enough to get the business without active solicitation * * *." 304 F.2d at 104. Likewise, the technicalities of the execution of the contract and the contractual provision that the contract was made in New York and was to be interpreted according to the law of New York cannot change the business realities of the transaction. * * * Legal principles designed for choice of law purposes or for the purpose of interpreting a contract are not sufficient guides for measuring the power of a state to issue process beyond its borders. Hanson v. Denckla, 357 U.S. 235, 253 (1958).

We are applying a constitutional standard defined in the broadest terms of "general fairness" to the defendant. * * * For the purposes of that standard, business is transacted in a state when obligations created by the defendant or business operations set in motion by the defendant have a realistic impact on the commerce of that state; and the defendant has purposefully availed himself of the opportunity of acting there if he should have reasonably foreseen that the transaction would have consequences in that state. There can be little doubt that both of these tests are satisfied in this case.

Mohasco dealt directly with a Tennessee corporation whose only manufacturing plant was located in Chattanooga. The subject of the transaction was a licensing agreement that called for the manufacture of tufting machines at that plant and that contemplated the marketing of the tufting machines in Tennessee as well as other states. Machines manufactured under the agreement have in fact been sold or leased in Tennessee to E'Con Carpet Mills, Inc., and Mohasco has presumably obtained royalties from that buyer or lessee. The license agreement's direct impact on the commerce of Tennessee can hardly be denied, and it can also hardly be denied that the parties contemplated such an impact at the time the license agreement was executed.

So it is clear that Mohasco has purposely availed itself of the privilege of transacting business in Tennessee; therefore, we can proceed to the second inquiry: Does the cause of action arise from the business transacted in the State? This question can be disposed of shortly. Although Mohasco argues that this controversy arises from Louisa's refusal to perform under its contract with Southern Machine, that argument misses the gist of the declaratory relief sought and ignores the business realities of the licensing agreement. Southern Machine was licensed by Mohasco to manufacture attachments, the manufacturing of which was allegedly protected by Mohasco's exclusive power to license. When it entered into the agreement, Southern Machine probably could reasonably assume that Mohasco would place restrictions on other manufacturers similar to those placed on Southern Machine and, thus, that it would be able to effectively compete in the sale of the attachments. Presumably, Southern Machine went to some expense in producing and marketing the attachments. Since the patents covering the attachments have been held invalid in one Circuit, Southern Machine's continuing rights and obligations under the license agreement have a questionable status.

* * *

Since it is clear that this cause of action arises from the licensing agreement, we must confront the final question: Does the licensing agreement have a substantial enough connection with Tennessee to make it reasonable to compel Mohasco to come to Tennessee to defend this suit? We think it does.

Ultimately, our decision must depend upon a determination of whether Tennessee has an interest in resolving the conflict at issue; but, once the first two questions have been answered affirmatively, resolution of the third involves merely ferreting out the unusual cases where that interest cannot be found. In this case, we are aided somewhat in that determination by the Tennessee legislators, who have declared that State's interest in any cause of action arising from any business transaction in Tennessee. As Judge Friendly noted in Buckley v. New York Post Corporation, 373 F.2d 175 (2d Cir. 1967):

> "Once we free our minds from traditional thinking that the plaintiff must inevitably seek out the defendant, such a doctrine would not seem to violate basic notions of fair play; any view that it does must rest on an inarticulate premise, which a legislature is free to question, that plaintiffs are much more given to making unjust claims than defendants are to not paying just ones." 373 F.2d at 181.

We should be careful not to subvert the expressed interest of Tennessee by a too grudging interpretation of the long arm statute or a too restrictive view of the requirements of due process.

That interest of the State cannot be measured by "a little more or a little less," International Shoe Co. v. State of Washington, 326 U.S. 310, 319, 66 S.Ct. 154, 159, 90 L.Ed. 95 (1945); it is not diminished simply because only one contract is relied upon as the basis of jurisdiction. * * * And when the contract is with a resident of Tennessee, the State's interest in resolving a suit based on the contract and brought by that resident cannot be doubted. * * * Besides this contract is not a one-shot affair. Mohasco has retained substantial control over the manufacture and marketing of the attachments, and it is of no legal significance whether Mohasco has in fact exercised those powers. * * * The agreement contemplates a long continuing relationship between Mohasco and Southern Machine. Mohasco apparently thought that it could profit from such an arrangement, and it has in fact received a return from the agreement. * * * Tennessee has a continuing interest in this continuing relationship, and apparently Mohasco has a continuing interest in profiting from the Tennessee market. It cannot complain if along with the profits from the Tennessee market it must also accept the process from the Tennessee courts.

Throughout the opinion, this Court has taken the uncontested facts in the complaint and affidavits as true and from those facts has drawn reasonable inferences pertinent to the issues of *in personam* jurisdiction. In so doing, this Court expresses no view as to the probable outcome of the suit in a trial on the merits. The judgment of the District Court is reversed and the case is remanded for further proceedings consistent with this opinion.

———

In an age of instant inter-planetary electronic communications, do we really need to be concerned about adequate notice to a defendant that it is being sued? Are not all the old concepts of fair notice to a defendant, as a matter of due process of law, really concerned with giving it an adequate opportunity to defend itself before a default judgment is entered against it? If "forum-shopping" is involved (the practice of casting about for a court or jurisdiction where it is anticipated that one's cause will be better received) this can be dealt with under other legal concepts. Under certain circumstances a defendant may "remove" a suit against it from a state court to a Federal court in the same district, which a defendant may do for any reasons sufficient to it which may include an attempt to overcome local prejudice, greater convenience to the defendant or its lawyers, a more efficient system of court procedures or even the desire to prolong the litigation because the dockets of Federal courts are frequently more crowded than those of the state courts. But aside from these factors, if either the plaintiff or the defendant has some connection with the jurisdiction in which the suit is brought, do we really need have any more concern? Is not the possibility of being sued one of the calculations a business should make in expanding into a new territory with a new plant or entering a new market? With communications being so efficient, must a plaintiff seek out a defendant in a jurisdiction where the defendant has some substantial contacts?

D. INDEPENDENT NATURE OF THE BUSINESS ENTITY

On "Piercing The Corporate Veil"

Much has been written and studied elsewhere in connection with the problems involved in using a corporation for illegal, wrongful, or sometimes immoral purposes. In nearly every case a corporation will be treated as an independent entity, one separate and apart from its shareholders so long as the corporation is not being used as a vehicle to accomplish a transaction which the persons who control the corporation themselves could not or would not do. But in nearly every situation where there is a substantial amount of dealing between the corporation and either the persons who control it or other corporations controlled by them, the situation will be looked upon rather unfavorably by the courts as to the corporation and its controlling persons, and rather favorably to outsiders. If the dealings have not been at "arms length" and other persons including the tax collector are harmed or dealt wtih unfairly in this matter, there is a laudable tendency on the part of the courts, the tax collectors, and other interested persons to view the interposition of a corporate charter between the principal persons entering into the transaction as a sham, and therefore to be disregarded. The freedom of choice of the legal form of the business enterprise is thus restricted. Note once again that in this situation even though the corporate entity should be disregarded, there is no direction by the state or by any other party to do business in a corporate form or some other manner; so long as the persons who control the corporation cause it to deal fairly (admittedly a poorly defined concept) with other persons, including the government, there will be no legal restraint in using the corporate form. But we have learned by experience that we cannot tolerate having the persons who dominate a corporation causing it to deal on less than fair terms with others. As a consequence from time to time we have cases like Yacker v. Weiner, 109 N.J.Super. 351, 263 A.2d 188 (1970), aff'd 114 N.J.Super. 526, 277 A.2d 417 (1971), reported below.

YACKER v. WEINER

Superior Court of New Jersey, Chancery Division, 1970.
109 N.J.Super. 351, 263 A.2d 188.

LANE, J. S. C. Plaintiff, the receiver of Mar Building Co., Inc. (improperly referred to in the title as Mar Building, Inc.; referred to herein as Mar), an insolvent construction corporation, seeks to recover monies diverted from the corporation by Markus Weiner (Weiner) and Martin Blashinsky (Blashinsky), its former officers, and to pierce the corporate veil of Mar so as to hold Middlesex Apts., Inc. (Middlesex), the owner of the realty, responsible for obligations due from Mar to certain creditors. The matter is before the court on final hearing.

Middlesex was formed January 26, 1965. The incorporators were Weiner, Blashinsky and Sarah Bernstein, each of whom subscribed to 60 shares of stock, and Julius and Estelle Greenman who together subscribed to 30 shares. Mar was incorporated January 28, 1965. The incorporators, with equal shares of stock, were Blashinsky, Weiner and Bernstein. The same attorney incorporated both corporations.

Middlesex acquired title to land in Matawan, New Jersey, upon which Mar was to construct an apartment project. A contract was entered into between Mar and Middlesex on March 3, 1965 under which Mar was to do the construction for $680,000. Middlesex obtained from The Dime Savings Bank of Brooklyn a construction and permanent loan in the amount of $825,000. It was the intention of Blashinsky and Weiner to mortgage out the entire job, including the cost of the land, using none of their own money.

The amount paid by Middlesex for the land and other items exclusive of construction was $148,571.20. The total cost of the land and buildings to date was $968,939.42.

As of 1968 the cost of the building had been $806,000. There were, however, $141,153.01 of claims asserted by contractors against Mar for work done in the construction. With the exception of three creditors, these claims have been settled by Middlesex on the basis of 25 cents on the dollar. The three creditors who refused to settle are the receiver of Charles J. Rooney Plumbing & Heating, Inc., Ace-Manzo, Inc. and Manzo Contracting Co., Inc. At the trial of this case defendants not only denied liability but also vigorously contested the validity and amount of the claims of the three creditors.

The theory upon which plaintiff proceeds against Middlesex is that a fraud was committed at the time the contract was signed with Mar for the construction of the buildings. It is contended that Blashinsky and Weiner, the active principals of Middlesex, must have known that the buildings could not possibly have been built for $680,-000. Testimony was given by a well-qualified builder that anyone computing the probable cost for the construction of the buildings in 1965 would have arrived at a figure in the neighborhood of $900,000. Defendants sought to counteract that testimony by offering testimony of their own building expert. He testified that $703,000 ($23,000 over the contract price) would have been a valid estimate of costs. That figure, however, did not include anything for organization expenses, legal fees, temporary heat, electricity, salaries, or profit to the corporation. Testimony was also offered by defendants from an accountant who represented one of the investors in Middlesex and Mar and also Middlesex itself. He testified that from his examination of the contracts entered into and estimates that he saw for certain supplies such as lumber, masonry and hardware, the total cost was to have been $680,170. However, in such computation one of the contracts (Weiner Electric Co.) was taken at $10,000 less than its actual figure, and the amounts estimated for some of the suppliers were unreasonably low. Again no consideration was given to organization expenses, legal fees, temporary heat, electricity, salaries, or profit to the corporation. It is perfectly clear to the court that the contract price of $680,000 had no relationship to what the actual cost of construction was going to be. The court discounts the effect of the accountant's testimony because most of the contracts were entered into well after the contract between Middlesex and Mar and therefore they could not have been in Blashinsky's and Weiner's contemplation when the $680,000 contract price was arrived at.

The case presents a situation that all too often is seen. One or more persons organize a corporation to buy land and another corporation to enter into a construction contract which has little or no relationship to estimated costs of the work to be performed. That contract provides that no stop notices will be filed. The construction company, completely controlled by the people who own the real estate holding company, then enters into subcontracts for a major portion of the work. If the construction company can get away with it, its subcontracts prohibit any recourse to the Mechanics Lien Law. The amount of the general contract is grossly inadequate, the incorporators of the two corporations keeping from the mortgage funds the costs of the land, interest to be paid on the mortgage, organization costs of the landowning corporation and a profit to the incorporators. Inevitably, the construction company becomes insolvent the subcontractors are not paid, and the incorporators grow fat on the work, labor and materials put in the project by the subcontractors who end with a claim against the insolvent construction corporation.

It is fundamental that a corporation is an entity wholly separate and distinct from the individuals who compose and control it, but the corporate cloak may not be utilized as a subterfuge to justify wrong or perpetuate fraud. Frank v. Franks Inc., 9 N.J. 218, 223–224.
* * *

In Irving Investment Corp. v. Gordon, 3 N.J. 217, 223, 69 A.2d 725, 728 (1949), the court said:

"It is where the corporate form is used as a shield behind which injustice is sought to be done by those who have the control of it that equity penetrates the veil."

That statement connotes merely that there must be equitable fraud present to permit of such action. Fraud, in the sense of a court of equity, includes all acts, omissions or concealments which involve a breach of a legal or equitable duty, trust or confidence justly reposed, and are injurious to another, or by which an undue or unconscientious advantage is taken of another. * * * Plainly, the facts sustain the conclusion that the use of the corporate form is here fraudulent in the above sense.

The subcontractors who entered into contracts with Mar were justified in assuming that the general contract was for an amount which reasonably could be expected to cover the cost of the construction of the buildings. Although the Middlesex-Mar contract was filed it is unreasonable to expect each subcontractor and supplier to compute the cost of the whole job to determine if the general contract price was adequate. In forming Mar and in causing it to enter into a contract for a sum that could not possibly have covered the cost of the construction, Weiner and Blashinsky perpetrated a fraud upon the subcontractors and caused their corporation, Middlesex, to participate in the fraud. An undue and unconscionable advantage was taken by Middlesex of such subcontractors. Middlesex itself apparently recognizes its responsibility. $20,000 was loaned to Mar during the course of the construction by or through the attorney who organized the corporations. This amount was repaid by Middlesex. Middlesex undertook to negotiate with Mar's creditors and, in fact, settled with them for 25 cents on the dollar except the ones involved in this suit. There will be a judgment in favor of the receiver against Middlesex for the amount of the claims of the three creditors involved in this action.

* * *

The claim against Blashinsky and Weiner individually by the receiver is rested upon a different basis. They are charged with wasting Mar's assets and mismanaging its business. See Knepper, Liability of Corporate Officers and Directors (1969), § 8.13, at 153.

In Cole v. Brandle, 127 N.J.Eq. 31, the Court of Errors and Appeals adopted the opinion of the vice-chancellor who stated:

* * * Here, defendants as officers of Investment Co. were trustees of corporate assets and as such were bound to administer such trust faithfully for the benefit of creditors as well as stockholders and they are charged with having been unfaithful to their trust in that they misapplied such assets wilfully, in fraud of creditors. * * * [at 37].

* * *

Plaintiff contends that Blashinsky and Weiner, as the controlling officers of Mar, caused it to make improper payments. Among the improper payments were loans made to themselves. Such loans were prohibited by the statute in effect at the time, N.J.S.A. 14:8–10. Other expenditures that were made by Mar included $30,000 paid to Blashinsky and Weiner for another building project in which they were interested. A payment of $5,000 was made to the attorney who incorporated Mar. Such payment was clearly excessive for legal services in forming the corporation. The formation of the corporation was rudimentary. The minutes of the first meeting of incorporators were not even complete. It is significant that in the checkbook the stub for the $5,000 check has $450 which is crossed out. Also, through this attorney Mar received a loan of $20,000. Whether the $5,000 is for a legal fee or for a bonus, its payment was gross mismanagement.

Although, as noted above, no figure was considered for salaries in the Middlesex-Mar contract, salaries were in fact taken by Blashinsky and Weiner. Since even under Blashinsky's and Weiner's attempted justification of the $680,000 contract figure, no consideration was given to salaries, the taking of salaries by them constituted waste and mismanagement. It is clear that they treated the assets of Mar as though they were their own personal property. There was no attempt to safeguard the assets or capital for the legitimate purposes of the corporation.

As to the withdrawal of $30,000 for the other building corporation, an attempt was made to show that $30,000 had been loaned by three individuals, all of whom were interested in Middlesex, to Weiner for use in the other construction project, but that Weiner improperly devoted the money to Mar, so that the withdrawal of $30,000 from Mar to the other construction project was merely an exchange. During the early part of the construction an accountant by the name of Samuel Fogel maintained the books of Mar. The general ledger was maintained through March 31, 1966. The cash receipts and disbursement book was maintained through November 1, 1966. Testimony offered by defendants as to the $30,000 transaction was at variance with the books. Although Fogel is alive, he was not produced at the trial nor was there any explanation given as to the failure to produce him. Although his office is in New York, he was subject to having his deposition taken. The failure to produce Fogel even though the court had expressed its expectation that he would be produced raises an inference that defendants feared exposure of facts which would be unfavorable to them. State v. Clawans, 38 N.J. 162, 170. Defendants did offer the testimony of the accountant for Middlesex and for one of the investors in Mar. He had examined Mar's books in January of 1966. Notwithstanding the fact that he attempted to support the $30,000 alleged "exchange transaction," he had done nothing about having corrective entries made in Mar's books. The court accepts as true what is shown by the general ledger and the cash receipts and disbursements book of Mar, as opposed to the self-serving testimony given at the trial on defendants' behalf. The $30,000 expenditure is carried on the general ledger of Mar as a loan to the other construction project. There is no corresponding entry to show that it was an exchange.

The general ledger shows that the capital stock account of Mar totaled $37,300 made up as follows:

June 1965	$ 9,000	Sarah Bernstein
July 1965	10,000	not traceable
Sept. 1965	8,000	not traceable
Oct. 1965	300	(Markus) Weiner
	5,000	Unger
	5,000	Fenster
Total	$37,300	

There is also contained in the general ledger an entry for a loan in the amount of $20,000 to Mar by Fenster. Withdrawals from Mar for loans total $39,131.50. Thus, the entire capital was withdrawn.

In Kleinberg v. Schwartz, 87 N.J.Super. 216 (App.Div.1965), aff'd o. b. 46 N.J. 2 (1965), the Court stated:

* * * The capital of a corporation is a "trust fund" and the directors, as trustees thereof, may not dispose of it to the prejudice of creditors without an equivalent consideration, and no stockholder is entitled to any share of it until all the debts are paid. * * * [at 223].

The improper payments total $56,821.31 as appears by Schedule A attached hereto. [Schedule A is not printed. It lists the following categories: Salaries to officers, $9,941.98; Loans to officers, $4,500.00; Payments to or on behalf of Middlesex, $1,747.35; Attorney's fee, $5,000.00; Payments to other construction projects in which Weiner and Blashinsky had an interest, $34,119.00; Miscellaneous improper expenditures, $1,512.98.]

The fact that the claims of the three creditors in suit do not total $56,821.31 does not lessen the liability of Blashinsky and Weiner to the corporation. There undoubtedly are at least claims against Mar for taxes by both the United States and the State of New Jersey as well as the expenses of the receivership proceedings. After the payment of the remaining creditors, the balance of the assets of the insolvent corporation in the hands of the receiver will be distributed in accordance with N.J.S.A. 14:13–8.

There will be a judgment in favor of the plaintiff and against Blashinsky and Weiner individually, jointly and severally, in the amount of $56,821.31 with interest at 6% from September 9, 1966, the date of the last improper withdrawal with costs. There will be a judgment against Middlesex for the amount of the Rooney, Ace-Manzo, Inc. and Manzo Contracting Co., claims with costs. The primary fund from which these three claims are to be paid is the proceeds of the judgment against Blashinsky and Weiner. The plaintiff, however, may proceed against Middlesex without first exhausting its remedies against Blashinsky and Weiner. To the extent that Middlesex pays the plaintiff under this judgment, it will be subrogated to the plaintiff's judgment against Blashinsky and Weiner.

The attorney for the plaintiff will submit a judgment embodying the views set forth herein within 10 days in accordance with R. 4:42–1.

QUESTIONS

1.   Ought we to have a national corporation law to deal with corporations that operate on an interstate basis?   One enacted by Congress?   And continue to have state corporation laws to deal with those that operate only within one state?   Should we consider adopting the Model Business Corporation Act as a Federal statute?   Or as a Uniform Act proposed for adoption by all states?   Should it be proposed as an addition to the Uniform Commercial Code?   Should the Uniform Commercial Code be made an Act of Congress?   Should we provide by appropriate Federal legislation a maximum rate of taxation which may be imposed by states on interstate businesses?   With or without the Interstate Taxation Act?

2.   What about regional or local differences in reference to incorporation statutes?   Should a state in which the predominant economic activity is some form of agriculture be permitted to authorize the incorporation of a bank with a substantially smaller amount of capital than a bank which is to be centered in a large metropolitan area?   Or should all banks be required to have very substantial capitalizations?   Even beyond the capacity of a local community to contribute?   Or beyond the desires of local business to deal with?   Or is the safety of a depositor's money, protected by Federal Deposit Insurance, more important?

3.   Is the corporation law of Delaware a good substitute for a national law?   Should the Delaware Legislature, or the people of Delaware, have this extra-territorial power?   Is the Delaware statute itself satisfactory from the viewpoint of shareholders?   Of managers?   Of creditors?   Should the citizens of a West Coast state be content to permit the citizens of the state of Delaware to determine for them the basic law relating to their relationship as shareholders to a corporation?   Are shareholders and investors, particularly those from out of the state of Delaware, adequately protected by Delaware corporation law?   Or, are the Federal Securities Acts of 1933 and 1934 adequate protection?

4.   Is freedom of choice to select the state of incorporation desirable?   Is it necessary in a democracy?   What is the difference between this and a governmentally mandated system providing for the location of production plants?

5.   What should be the minimum contacts with a state before a corporation from out of the state would be subject to its jurisdiction?   For tax purposes?   For service of process, that is, to be sued?   Should we have a central office, managed by the Federal Government under which persons wishing to sue a corporation chartered by some other state would be required to file their notice of intention to sue in a given state, and if the defendant were to dispute this have the gov-

ernmental agency determine which is the appropriate forum in which the suit should be brought? Should we have a national court for this purpose? To determine jurisdiction or to determine the merits of the controversy?

6.　Should we require all business enterprises to be incorporated? How much freedom of choice in determining the location and form of the business enterprise is necessary to maintain mobility of capital and mobility of product? How necessary to 20th century society is our Federal system of one national government and 50 state governments? Is it necessary to maintain Federalism to permit each state to determine the kind of taxes it will impose upon interstate business? Or should we tax interstate business at the national level only and local business at the local level only? If we had a national forum for the determination of all of these questions, what fundamental policies should be articulated for it? Should we continue to permit freedom of choice of location and form of the business enterprise? Or should be have a national agency to direct each economic unit how these things should be done?

Suggested Reference Sources

Texts and Treatises

Bittker & Eustis, *Federal Income Taxation of Corporations and Share-holders*. Federal Tax Press, New York City.

Cavitch, *Business Organizations with Tax Planning*. Matthew Bender & Company, Albany, N. Y.

Corporation Trust Company, *What Constitutes Doing Business*. New York City.

Fletcher, *Cyclopedia of the Law of Private Corporations*. Callaghan & Company, Mundelein, Illinois.

Rabkin & Johnson, *Federal Income, Gift and Estate Taxation*. Matthew Bender & Company, Albany, N. Y.

Loose-Leaf Services

Commerce Clearing House, State Tax Guide. Chicago, Illinois.

Topic Headings in the Index to Legal Periodicals

Business
Corporations: Foreign
Taxation (subdivision by jurisdiction)

Chapter III

FAIR TAXATION OF BUSINESS ENTERPRISES

A. INTRODUCTORY NOTE—SUBSTANCE OVER FORM

The principal feature of a democratic system of taxation is that persons in equal positions shall be taxed equally. This concept of equality is stated or implied in several places in the Federal Constitution. Article I, Sec. 8, clause 1 provides: "[T]he Congress shall have Power To lay and collect Taxes, Duties, Imposts and Excises, . . . but all Duties, Imposts and Excises shall be uniform throughout the United States." Further, Article I, Sec. 9, clause 4 provides that no direct taxes shall be laid unless they are laid in proportion to the census. The XVIth Amendment changed this slightly by providing "[T]he Congress shall have power to lay and collect taxes on incomes, from whatever source derived, without apportionment among the several states, and without regard to any census or enumeration." Conceptually uniformity still prevails because income taxes imposed at graduated rates are still imposed on all persons who have the same income in the same manner.

Corporations are taxed differently from individuals, although "Small Business Corporations" (whose characteristics are noted below) by the election of their shareholders are not taxed as corporations by the United States government. As a consequence of the way corporate income tax rates are stated it can be said that as a practical matter corporations have two rates of tax; the first rate presently at 22% on the first $25,000 of its income, and the second rate, presently at 48%, on its income in excess of $25,000. These rates have changed from time to time in the past and will undoubtedly change again in the future but the concept seems to be well established that there shall be only two rates of tax on corporate incomes. (Those corporations which unreasonably accumulate their income, or those which operate as personal holding companies (incorporated investment portfolios), are required to pay penalty taxes measured by the amount of their undistributed current income.)

Individuals, however, are taxed at increasing rates which currently run from 14% to 70% of taxable income; in the past this has run as high as 90% of taxable income. Because of the difference in tax rates imposed on individuals and corporations many business enterprises in the past were operated either as sole proprietorships, on the one hand, or as corporations on the other. The decision as to the form of the business entity was frequently dictated by considerations relating almost entirely to the tax impact of the projected income from the business enterprise. Tax publications are full of suggestions as to tax savings which can be accomplished by choosing one form of business entity over another. However, in 1958, Congress amended the Internal Revenue Code by adopting Subchapter S (Secs. 1371–1379 (26 U.S.C.A. §§ 1371–1379) [1] one purpose of which was to eliminate the impact of Federal income taxation in determining whether or not the business enterprise should be incorporated. In many respects, but not all, it permitted qualifying small business corporations to be treated for tax purposes much as a partnership, that is, not to be taxed at all and to have its income flow through the corporation to the shareholders while the income retained most of its tax characteristics as received by the corporation. Ordinary income as well as capital gains pass through the corporation to its shareholders and both are included in the shareholders' own personal income tax returns with the same characteristics as though the individual shareholders had received or realized the income themselves. Tax free interest on municipal bonds does not pass through the corporation to the shareholders as tax-free income.

Long term capital gains are taxed at a more advantageous rate than other kinds of taxable income. With a few exceptions, individuals are permitted to treat one-half of a long term capital gain as not subject to tax and the other one-half to be added to the rest of their income and taxed as ordinary income; however, for many years prior to January 1, 1970, by a special computation, the maximum effective rate of tax on a long term capital gain was 25% of the gain. In 1970 and 1971 the maximum rate (with some exceptions) were increased in two steps to $29\frac{1}{2}\%$ and $32\frac{1}{2}\%$ respectively. For all taxable years beginning in 1972 (again, with some exceptions), it may be said that there will be no more alternative tax computations on long term capital gains because starting in 1972, 50% of a long term capital gain will be deductible by the individual taxpayer and the other 50% will be added to his other income and taxed as ordinary income. With a maximum individual tax rate of 70% this would put a ceiling of 35% on the taxes on long term capital gains; however, if the individual rates should be increased to more than 70%, then the maximum tax on a long term capital gain would be one-half of the maximum rate on other income. Corporations also have had the option of using an alternative rate to compute the tax due on capital gains realized by them. Without going into details, before January 1, 1970, the rate was 25%. With a few exceptions which will be eliminated in 1975, the rate in 1970 was changed to 28%, and for 1971 and thereafter the rate was changed to 30%.

This difference in the rate of tax imposed on the excess of net long term capital gains over net short term capital losses is what has led to great amounts of both tax planning and tax litigation. No matter how one views the matter, taxation is a cost of doing business; a variable cost, undoubtedly, but nonetheless a cost which is added to other

1. In this Introductory Note all references to sections of the Internal Revenue Code may be found in sections with a corresponding number in Title 26 of the United States Code (26 U.S.C.A.)

costs of producing goods and services. While a business enterprise may not pay any income taxes while it is operating at a loss, when it does operate at a profit, as every business enterprise is designed to do, then it must pay a tax which is measured by its profits. (Excise taxes imposed on the sales price of commodities, and import duties imposed on the value of commodities, are imposed whether or not the business is operating at a profit.) But income taxes which are a variable cost are nonetheless costs which must be included in the price of the goods or charges for the services. Thus the desire to minimize this variable cost, recognized as being a proper desire, has led to many plans and arrangements to reduce taxes. Corporations have been formed, or not formed, plans have been utilized or abandoned, elections under Subchapter S of the Internal Revenue Code have been made or not made, dividends have been paid or not paid, or if paid, then paid in stock, income has been deflected to or from the business enterprise, corporations have been merged or not merged, dissolved or not dissolved, capitalized with common stock only or with some combination of common stock and debt securities, all with the idea of minimizing income taxes; and in many cases the object of selecting one form of a transaction over another has been a desire to achieve either a tax-free transaction or a long term capital gain either presently or some time in the future. By and large where these transactions have had some economic substance, other than solely minimizing or eliminating income taxes, they have been treated for tax purposes in the manner chosen by the taxpayer; on the contrary, where minimizing or eliminating income taxes was the only purpose of the transaction, while for non-tax law purposes the transaction was still recognized, for tax purposes it has been ignored.

The Treasury is greatly in need of funds. The demands made on government at all levels for more goods and services to be provided at public expense constantly exceed the willingness of the public to pay for them. Except to the extent that the amount of the public debt is expanded by the Federal Government, all significant amounts of money received by the Treasury must come from taxation. And all taxes in one way or another are imposed on the business system. Tax revenues come not only from the direct payments by business enterprises, such as income taxes, excise taxes, real estate taxes, etc., but revenues also come from the tax payments made by employees on their wages and salaries and taxes paid by shareholders and bondholders on the dividends and interest they receive, and taxes paid by professionals and other persons engaged in service enterprises. All of these must come from economic activity, from the business system.

In a democratic society one of our concepts of fairness is that the burden of taxation shall be distributed equally among all taxpayers who are in equal positions. What is "equal" and what is an "equal position" are matters of policy to be determined from time to time, usually by the legislature. However, the tax collectors and the courts in considering the fair application of the tax system to taxpayers keep this fundamental premise in mind at all times. Tax litigation does not arise until the administrators of the tax system (the Internal Revenue Service at the Federal level) come across a transaction viewed differently by them from the manner in which it was viewed by the taxpayer, a transaction which is either subject to taxation in their view under the terms of the taxing statute, or does not adhere to the fundamental principle of equality and fairness even though it may have been a perfectly proper non-tax law transaction. Thus the law has evolved various concepts, either by doctrines developed by the courts, or specific provisions of the Internal Revenue Code to deal with this problem. These include many concepts which are explained in the cases contained in this Chapter and Chapter VI as well as by provisions in the Internal Revenue Code. While in practice most of the concepts operate in favor of the government, taxpayers too have many opportunities to consider the economic realities of their transactions for tax purposes. Briefly, some of the sections of the Internal Revenue Code which permit the government to ignore the form of the transaction conducted by the business enterprise and treat the matter in its economic substance are:

(a) Section 269 which provides that if control of a corporation was acquired for the principal purpose of tax avoidance, then certain tax credits, deductions, and other types of benefits are to be disallowed to the acquirers;

(b) Section 318 which provides under a number of circumstances, but not all, that stock which is owned by members of a family group or by persons who are closely affiliated with each other either in a trust, estate, partnership, or other corporation shall be attributed to (deemed to be owned by) others within the same group;

(c) Section 531 which provides for a penalty tax on a corporation which fails to pay dividends where it accumulates its earnings beyond the reasonable needs of the business;

(d) Section 541 which provides for a penalty tax on the undistributed investment income and certain types of personal service income received by a corporation where a limited number of persons hold the controlling stock of the corporation;

(e) Section 382 which provides that a net operating loss may not be carried over from one corporation to another where 50% of the first corporation's stock changes ownership in a two year period and the first corporation's business is changed;

(f) Section 482 which provides that the Commissioner of Internal Revenue may reallocate income, deductions, credits, or other allowances between related taxpayers to reflect their respective incomes clearly, thus preventing the distortion of income among taxpayers under common control.

On the other hand, these provisions of the Internal Revenue Code permit the taxpayer to treat his transactions in the form of their economic substance:

(a) Section 351 which provides for the non-recognition of gain or loss on the transfer of property to a corporation solely in exchange for its stock or securities if the former property owners, the transferors, control the corporation immediately after the transfer, thus permitting the tax-free transfer of property to a corporation by individuals at the time of incorporation as well as many other types of transactions;

(b) Section 354 which provides for the non-recognition of gain or loss on the exchange of stock of one corporation for the stock of another where the two corporations are parties to a plan of reorganization as that term is defined in Sec. 368 of the Internal Revenue Code (which contemplates mergers, consolidations, recapitalizations, changes of state of incorporation, etc., rather than the financial rehabilitation of a bankrupt enterprise);

(c) Section 361 which provides for non-recognition of gain or loss between corporations which are parties to a plan of reorganization on the exchange of property among them;

(d) Section 381 which permits certain tax attributes of one corporation to be transferred to a successor corporation in certain reorganizations, also under specified limitations;

(e) Subchapter S, Sections 1371–1379, which provides for the non-taxability of small business corporations where under limited circumstances the shareholders have elected not to have their corporation taxed;

(f) Section 1501 which provides for the filing of consolidated income tax returns by corporations which are members of an affiliated group, entirely at the election of the management of the parent or controlling corporation.

The above references are by no means all of the occasions in the Internal Revenue Code where the tax law looks to the substance of a transaction rather than its legalistic form. However, those references along with the cases which follow do illustrate the policy of the law in a democratic society of taxing persons equally who are in equal situations. Our experience has been that the failure to practice equality in this regard is a form of intolerable oppression—a situation which led in part to the American Revolution. Suppose for example that a satisfactory system could be developed to make fair determinations relating to the relative degrees of prosperity of the 50 states in the United States, and that all of the citizens from the most prosperous state would be taxed at a higher rate on their income than the citizens of any other state, and all those in the second most prosperous, second highest rate, and so on, and all those in the poorest state either no taxes or the lowest rate, all without regard to the incomes of the individuals in each state and assume that the system included a prohibition against moving from one state to another. The burden would be intolerable on the poorest persons in the most prosperous state as compared with the light burden on the wealthiest persons in the least prosperous state. How long before another revolution? Or suppose that wealthy persons because of the size or complexity of their affairs could arrange to use or be advised as how to use legal concepts such as corporations, trusts, assignments, reorganizations, etc., in such fashion as to reduce or eliminate the amount of taxes they otherwise would pay while a wage-earner would be deprived of the use of any of these devices, not only because his affairs were relatively simple but because his taxes were withheld from his wages before he even got them. In a democracy we would not and will not tolerate this either; this is what we mean by fairness and equality in taxation.

The doctrine to accomplish this goal of fairness and equality which has been evolved by our laws, is "substance over form", a doctrine largely developed by the courts. We look to the substance of a transaction, its economic reality, its impact upon the taxpayer, and if he is an individual then also the impact upon members of his family, and if a corporation then upon other entities which either control it or which it controls, to determine whether in substance there has been any shifting of the tax burden to a lower bracket taxpayer or making a transaction appear to be tax-free when in reality it is not, or ought not to be. The principal case in this regard, and outside of the Internal Revenue Code itself, in many respects the foundation of all Federal income tax law, is Gregory v. Helvering, 293 U.S. 465, 55 S.Ct. 266, 79 L.Ed. 596 (1935), reported below. Its enunciation of the principle of substance over form has been repeated in many tax cases over the years. While other cases decided before it, some reported below, adhered to this principle, it illustrates the point and articulates the principle better than any of the others. It should be noted that the same theme, although stated differently, runs through all of the law relating to business in a democratic society. The *Gregory* case involved a transaction called a "spin-off" and while the case was in litigation Congress changed the tax law eliminating tax-free spin-offs. The 1954 Internal Revenue Code re-established tax-free spin-offs (Sec. 355) under detailed rules and also restated the terms of corporate reorganizations (which are discussed in Chapter VI below), so that the precise terms of the statute interpreted in the *Gregory* case no longer exist. But anyone assuming to have any knowledge of Federal income tax law must know the *Gregory* case. The manner in which "substance over form" is applied is covered in the other cases reported below.

GREGORY v. HELVERING

Supreme Court of the United States, 1935.
293 U.S. 465, 55 S.Ct. 266, 79 L.Ed. 596.

Justice SUTHERLAND delivered the opinion of the Court.

Petitioner in 1928 was the owner of all the stock of United Mortgage Corporation. That corporation held among its assets 1,000 shares of the Monitor Securities Corporation. For the sole purpose of procuring a transfer of these shares to herself in order to sell them for her individual profit, and, at the same time, diminish the amount of income tax which would result from a direct transfer by way of dividend, she sought to bring about a "reorganization" under section 112(g) of the Revenue Act of 1928, set forth later in this opinion. To that end, she caused the Averill Corporation to be organized under the laws of Delaware on September 18, 1928. Three days later, the United Mortgage Corporation transferred to the Averill Corporation the 1,000 shares of Monitor stock, for which all the shares of the Averill Corporation were issued to the petitioner. On September 24, the Averill Corporation was dissolved, and liquidated by distributing all its assets, namely, the Monitor shares, to the petitioner. No other business was ever transacted, or intended to be transacted, by that company. Petitioner immediately sold the Monitor shares for $133,-333.33. She returned for taxation, as capital net gain, the sum of $76,007.88, based upon an apportioned cost of $57,325.45. Further details are unnecessary. It is not disputed that if the interposition of the so-called reorganization was ineffective, petitioner became liable for a much larger tax as a result of the transaction.

The Commissioner of Internal Revenue, being of opinion that the reorganization attempted was without substance and must be disregarded, held that petitioner was liable for a tax as though the United corporation had paid her a dividend consisting of the amount realized from the sale of the Monitor shares. In a proceeding before the Board of Tax Appeals, that body rejected the commissioner's view and upheld that of petitioner. 27 B.T.A. 223. Upon a review of the latter decision, the Circuit Court of Appeals sustained the commissioner and reversed the board, holding that there had been no "reorganization" within the meaning of the statute. 69 F.2d 809. Petitioner applied to this court for a writ of certiorari, which the government, considering the question one of importance, did not oppose. We granted the writ.

Section 112 of the Revenue Act of 1928 deals with the subject of gain or loss resulting from the sale or exchange of property. Such gain or loss is to be recognized in computing the tax, except as provided in that section. The provisions of the section, so far as they are pertinent to the question here presented, follow:

"Sec. 112. * * * (g) *Distribution of Stock on Reorganization.* If there is distributed, in pursuance of a plan of reorganization, to a shareholder in a corporation a party to the reorganization, stock or securities in such corporation or in another corporation a party to the reorganization, without the surrender by such shareholder of stock or securities in such a corporation, no gain to the distributee from the receipt of such stock or securities shall be recognized. * * *

"(i) *Definition of Reorganization.* As used in this section * * *

"(1) The term 'reorganization' means * * * (B) a transfer by a corporation of all or a part of its assets to another corporation if immediately after the transfer the transferor or its stockholders or both are in control of the corporation to which the assets are transferred. * * * "

It is earnestly contended on behalf of the taxpayer that since every element required by the foregoing subdivision (B) is to be found in what was done, a statutory reorganization was effected; and that the motive of the taxpayer thereby to escape payment of a tax will not alter the result or make unlawful what the statute allows. It is quite true that if a reorganization in reality was effected within the meaning of subdivision (B), the ulterior purpose mentioned will be disregarded. The legal right of a taxpayer to decrease the amount of what otherwise would be his taxes, or altogether avoid them, by means which the law permits, cannot be doubted. United States v. Isham, 17 Wall. 496; Superior Oil Co. v. Mississippi, 280 U.S. 390; Jones v. Helvering, 71 F.2d 214. But the question for determination is whether what was done, apart from the tax motive, was the thing which the statute intended. The reasoning of the court below in justification of a negative answer leaves little to be said.

When subdivision (B) speaks of a transfer of assets by one corporation to another, it means a transfer made "in pursuance of a plan of reorganization" (section 112(g)) of corporate business; and not a transfer of assets by one corporation to another in pursuance of a plan having no relation to the business of either, as plainly is the case here. Putting aside, then, the question of motive in respect of taxation altogether, and fixing the character of the proceeding by what actually occurred, what do we find? Simply an operation having no business or corporate purpose—a mere device which put on the form of a corporate reorganization as a disguise for concealing its real character, and the sole object and accomplishment of which was the consummation of a preconceived plan, not to reorganize a business or any part of a business, but to transfer a parcel of corporate shares to the petitioner. No doubt, a new and valid corporation was created. But that corporation was nothing more than a contrivance to the end last described. It was brought into existence for no other purpose; it performed, as it was intended from the beginning it should perform, no other function. When that limited function had been exercised, it immediately was put to death.

In these circumstances, the facts speak for themselves and are susceptible of but one interpretation. The whole undertaking, though conducted according to the terms of subdivision (B), was in fact an elaborate and devious form of conveyance masquerading as a corporate reorganization, and nothing else. The rule which excludes from consideration the motive of tax avoidance is not pertinent to the situation, because the transaction upon its face lies outside the plain intent of the statute. To hold otherwise would be to exalt artifice above reality and to deprive the statutory provision in question of all serious purpose.

Judgment affirmed.

LUCAS v. EARL

Supreme Court of the United States, 1930.
281 U.S. 111, 50 S.Ct. 241, 74 L.Ed. 731.

Justice HOLMES delivered the opinion of the Court.

This case presents the question whether the respondent, Earl, could be taxed for the whole of the salary and attorney's fees earned by him in the years 1920 and 1921, or should be taxed for only a half of them in view of a contract with his wife which we shall mention. The Commissioner of Internal Revenue and the Board of Tax Appeals imposed a tax upon the whole, but their decision was reversed by the Circuit Court of Appeals, 30 F.2d 898. A writ of certiorari was granted by this court.

By the contract, made in 1901, Earl and his wife agreed "that any property either of us now has or may hereafter acquire * * * in any way, either by earnings (including salaries, fees, etc.), or any rights by contract or otherwise, during the existence of our marriage, or which we or either of us may receive by gift, bequest, devise, or inheritance, and all the proceeds, issues, and profits of any and all such property shall be treated and considered, and hereby is declared to be received, held, taken, and owned by us as joint tenants, and not otherwise, with the right of survivorship." The validity of the contract is not questioned, and we assume it to be unquestionable under the law of the State of California, in which the parties lived. Nevertheless we are of opinion that the Commissioner and Board of Tax Appeals were right.

The Revenue Act of 1918 approved February 24, 1919, c. 18, §§ 210, 211, 212(a), 213(a), imposes a tax upon the net income of every individual including "income derived from salaries, wages, or compensation for personal service * * * of whatever kind and in whatever form paid," § 213(a). The provisions of the Revenue Act of 1921, in sections bearing the same numbers are similar to those of the above. A very forcible argument is presented to the effect that the statute seeks to tax only income beneficially received, and that taking the question more technically the salary and fees became the joint property of Earl and his wife on the very first instant on which they were received. We well might hesitate upon the latter proposition, because however the matter might stand between husband and wife he was the only party to the contracts by which the salary and fees were earned, and it is somewhat hard to say that the last step in the performance of those contracts could be taken by anyone but himself alone. But this case is not to be decided by attenuated subtleties. It turns on the import and reasonable construction of the taxing act. There is no doubt that the statute could tax salaries to those who earned them and provide that the tax could not be escaped by anticipatory arrangements and contracts however skilfully devised to prevent the salary when paid from vesting even for a second in the man who earned it. That seems to us the import of the statute before us and we think that no distinction can be taken according to the motives leading to the arrangement by which the fruits are attributed to a different tree from that on which they grew.

Judgment reversed.

* * *

MORRISSEY v. COMMISSIONER

Supreme Court of the United States, 1935.
296 U.S. 344, 56 S.Ct. 289, 80 L.Ed. 263.

Chief Justice HUGHES delivered the opinion of the Court.

Petitioners, the trustees of an express trust, contest income taxes for the years 1924 to 1926, inclusive, upon the ground that the trust has been illegally treated as an "association." The Circuit Court of Appeals affirmed the decision of the Board of Tax Appeals which sustained the ruling of the Commissioner of Internal Revenue. 74 F.2d 803. We granted certiorari because of a conflict of decisions as to the distinction between an "association" and a "pure trust," the decisions being described in one of the cases as "seemingly in a hopeless state of confusion." Coleman-Gilbert Associates v. Commissioner of Internal Revenue (C.C.A.) 76 F.2d 191, 193.

The facts were stipulated. In the year 1921 petitioners made a declaration of trust of real estate in Los Angeles. They were to be designated in "their collective capacity" as "Western Avenue Golf Club." The trustees were authorized to add to their number and to choose their successors; to purchase, encumber, sell, lease, and operate the "described or other lands"; to construct and operate golf courses, club houses, etc.; to receive the rents, profits, and income; to make loans and investments; to make regulations; and generally to manage the trust estate as if the trustees were its absolute owners. The trustees were declared to be without power to bind the beneficiaries personally by "any act, neglect or default," and the beneficiaries and all persons dealing with the trustees were required to look for payment or indemnity to the trust property. The beneficial interests were to be evidenced solely by transferable certificates for shares which were divided into 2,000 preferred shares of the par value of $100 each, and 2,000 common shares of no par value, and the rights of the respective shareholders in the surplus, profits, and capital assets were defined. "Share ledgers" showing the names and addresses of shareholders were to be kept.

The trustees might convene the shareholders in meeting for the purpose of making reports or considering recommendations, but the votes of the shareholders were to be advisory only. The death of a trustee or of a beneficiary was not to end the trust, which was to continue for twenty-five years unless sooner terminated by the trustees.

During the years 1921 and 1922, the trustees sold beneficial interests and paid commissions on the sales. About 42 acres (of the 155 acres described by the declaration of trust) were plotted into lots which were sold during the years 1921 to 1923, most of the sales being on the installment basis.   On the remaining property a golf course and club house were constructed, and in 1923 this property with the improvements was conveyed to Western Avenue Golf Club, Inc., a California corporation, in exchange for its stock.   Under a lease from the corporation petitioners continued the operation of the golf course until January 12, 1924.   After that date petitioners' activities were confined to collections of installments of principal and interest on contracts of purchase, the receipt of interest on bank balances and of fees on assignments by holders of purchase contracts, the execution of conveyances to purchasers, the receipt of dividends from the incorporated club, and the distribution of moneys to the holders of beneficial interests.   On December 31, 1923, the total number of outstanding beneficial interests was 3,016 held by 920 persons; by December 31, 1926, the number of interests had been gradually decreased to 2,172, held by 275 persons. The holdings by the trustees ranged approximately from 16 to 29 per cent.

Petitioners contend that they are trustees "of property held in trust," within section 219 of the Revenue Acts of 1924 and 1926, and are taxable accordingly and not as an "association."   They urge that, to constitute an association, the applicable test requires "a quasi corporate organization in which the beneficiaries, whether or not certificate holders, have some voice in the management and some control over the trustees and have an opportunity to exercise such control through the right to vote at meetings"; and that, in any event, the activities in which petitioners were engaged, during the tax years under consideration, did not constitute "a carrying on of business" within the rule applied by this court.

The government insists that the distinction between associations and the trusts taxed under section 219 is between "business trusts on the one side" and other trusts "which are engaged merely in collecting the income and conserving the property against the day when it is to be distributed to the beneficiaries"; that Congress intended that all "business trusts" should be taxed as associations.

1.   The Revenue Acts of 1924 and 1926 provided:

"The term 'corporation' includes associations, joint-stock companies, and insurance companies."   Revenue Act 1924, § 2(a) (2); Revenue Act 1926, § 2(a) (2).

* * *

The Corporation Tax Act of 1909 which imposed an excise tax upon the privilege of doing business in a corporate capacity, embraced associations having a capital stock represented by shares and "organized under the laws of the United States or of any state or territory." Flint v. Stone Tracy Co., 220 U.S. 107; Eliot v. Freeman, 220 U.S. 178. The Income Tax Act of 1913, taxed the net income of "every corporation, joint-stock company or association, and every insurance company, organized in the United States, no matter how created or organized, not including partnerships." * * *

       * * *

The question is not one of the power of Congress to impose this tax upon petitioners but is simply one of statutory construction— whether Congress has imposed it. See Burk-Waggoner Oil Association v. Hopkins, 269 U.S. 110. The difficulty with the regulations as an exposition was that they themselves required explication; that they left many questions open with respect both to their application to particular enterprises and to their validity as applied. The so-called "control test" had led to much litigation, and the change in the regulations after the decision in Hecht v. Malley, 265 U.S. 144, caused increased uncertainty. That situation is put in a strong light by the action of Congress, in order to afford relief to taxpayers, in enacting section 704 of the Revenue Act of 1928 as a "retroactive" provision applicable, as stated, to trust returns which had been filed for a taxable year prior to 1925 under previous regulations and rulings, and also by giving an option to a trustee, in specified circumstances, in relation to the Revenue Act of 1926 and prior acts. While it is impossible in the nature of things to translate the statutory concept of "association" into a particularity of detail that would fix the status of every sort of enterprise or organization which ingenuity may create, the recurring disputes emphasize the need of a further examination of the congressional intent.

    3. "Association" implies associates. It implies the entering into a joint enterprise, and, as the applicable regulation imports, an enterprise for the transaction of business. This is not the characteristic of an ordinary trust—whether created by will, deed, or declaration—by which particular property is conveyed to a trustee or is to be held by the settlor, on specified trusts, for the benefit of named or described persons. Such beneficiaries do not ordinarily, and as mere cestuis que trust, plan a common effort or enter into a combination for the conduct of a business enterprise. Undoubtedly the terms of an association may make the taking or acquiring of shares or interests sufficient to constitute participation, and may leave the management, or even control of the enterprise, to designated persons. But the nature and purpose of the co-operative undertaking will differentiate it from an ordinary trust. In what are called "business trusts" the object is not to hold and conserve particular property, with incidental powers, as in the traditional type of trusts, but to provide a medium for the conduct of a business and sharing its gains. Thus a trust may be created as a convenient method by which persons become associated for dealings in real estate, the development of tracts of land, the construction of improvements, and the purchase, management, and sale of properties; or for dealings in securities or other personal property; or for the production, or manufacture, and sale of commodities; or for commerce, or other sorts of business; where those who become beneficially interested, either by joining in the plan at the outset, or by later participa-

tion according to the terms of the arrangement, seek to share the advantages of a union of their interests in the common enterprise.

The government contends that such an organized community of effort for the doing of business presents the essential features of an association. Petitioners stress the significance of, and the limitations said to be implied in, the provision classifying associations with corporations.

4. The inclusion of associations with corporations implies resemblance; but it is resemblance and not identity. The resemblance points to features distinguishing associations from partnerships as well as from ordinary trusts. As we have seen, the classification cannot be said to require organization under a statute, or with statutory privileges. The term embraces associations as they may exist at common law. Hecht v. Malley, supra. We have already referred to the definitions, quoted in that case, showing the ordinary meaning of the term as applicable to a body of persons united without a charter "but upon the methods and forms used by incorporated bodies for the prosecution of some common enterprise." These definitions, while helpful, are not to be pressed so far as to make mere formal procedure a controlling test. The provision itself negatives such a construction. Thus unincorporated joint-stock companies have generally been regarded as bearing the closest resemblance to corporations. But, in the Revenue Acts, associations are mentioned separately and are not to be treated as limited to "joint-stock companies," although belonging to the same group. While the use of corporate forms may furnish persuasive evidence of the existence of an association, the absence of particular forms, or of the usual terminology of corporations, cannot be regarded as decisive. Thus an association may not have "directors" or "officers," but the "trustees" may function "in much the same manner as the directors in a corporation" for the purpose of carrying on the enterprise. The regulatory provisions of the trust instrument may take the place of "by-laws." And as there may be, under the reasoning in the Hecht Case, an absence of control by beneficiaries such as is commonly exercised by stockholders in a business corporation, it cannot be considered to be essential to the existence of an association that those beneficially interested should hold meetings or elect their representatives. Again, while the faculty of transferring the interests of members without affecting the continuity of the enterprise may be deemed to be characteristic, the test of an association is not to be found in the mere formal evidence of interests or in a particular method of transfer.

What, then, are the salient features of a trust—when created and maintained as a medium for the carrying on of a business enterprise and sharing its gains—which may be regarded as making it analogous to a corporate organization? A corporation, as an entity, holds the title to the property embarked in the corporate undertaking. Trustees, as a continuing body with provision for succession, may afford a corresponding advantage during the existence of the trust. Corporate organization furnishes the opportunity for a centralized management through representatives of the members of the corporation. The designation of trustees, who are charged with the conduct of an enterprise, who act "in much the same manner as directors," may provide a similar scheme, with corresponding effectiveness. Whether the trustees are named in the trust instrument with power to select successors, so as to constitute a self-perpetuating body, or are selected by, or with the advice of, those beneficially interested in the undertaking, centralization of management analogous to that of corporate activities may be achieved. An enterprise carried on by means of a trust may be secure from termination or interruption by the death of owners of beneficial interests and in this respect their interests are distinguished from those of partners and are akin to the interests of members of a corporation. And the trust type of organization facilitates, as does corporate organization, the transfer of beneficial interests without affecting the continuity of the enterprise, and also the introduction of large numbers of participants. The trust method also permits the limitation of the personal liability of participants to the property embarked in the undertaking.

It is no answer to say that these advantages flow from the very nature of trusts. For the question has arisen because of the use and adaptation of the trust mechanism. The suggestion ignores the postulate that we are considering those trusts which have the distinctive feature of being created to enable the participants to carry on a business and divide the gains which accrue from their common undertaking, trusts that thus satisfy the primary conception of association and have the attributes to which we have referred, distinguishing them from partnerships. In such a case, we think that these attributes make the trust sufficiently analogous to corporate organization to justify the conclusion that Congress intended that the income of the enterprise should be taxed in the same manner as that of corporations.

5. Applying these principles to the instant case, we are of the opinion that the trust constituted an association. The trust was created for the development of a tract of land through the construction and operation of golf courses, club houses, etc., and the conduct of incidental businesses, with broad powers for the purchase, operation, and sale of properties. Provision was made for the issue of shares of beneficial interests, with described rights and priorities. There were to be preferred shares of the value of $100 each and common shares of no par value. Thus those who took beneficial interests became shareholders in the common undertaking to be conducted for their profit according to the terms of the arrangement. They were not the less associated in that undertaking because the arrangement vested the management and control in the trustees. And the contemplated development of the tract of land held at the outset, even if other properties were not acquired, involved what was essentially a business enterprise. The arrangement provided for centralized control, continuity, and limited liability, and the analogy to corporate organization was carried still further by the provision for the issue of transferable certificates.

Under the trust, a considerable portion of the property was surveyed and subdivided into lots which were sold and, to facilitate the sales, the subdivided property was improved by the construction of streets, sidewalks, and curbs. The fact that these sales were made before the beginning of the tax years here in question, and that the remaining property was conveyed to a corporation in exchange for its stock, did not alter the character of the organization. Its character was determined by the terms of the trust instrument. It was not a liquidating trust; it was still an organization for profit, and the profits were still coming in. The powers conferred on the trustees continued and could be exercised for such activities as the instrument authorized.

* * *

The judgment is affirmed.

EISNER v. MACOMBER

Supreme Court of the United States, 1920.
252 U.S. 189, 40 S.Ct. 189, 64 L.Ed. 521.

Justice PITNEY delivered the opinion of the Court.

This case presents the question whether, by virtue of the Sixteenth Amendment, Congress has the power to tax, as income of the stockholder and without apportionment, a stock dividend made lawfully and in good faith against profits accumulated by the corporation since March 1, 1913.

It arises under the Revenue Act of September 8, 1916, which, in our opinion (notwithstanding a contention of the government that will be noticed), plainly evinces the purpose of Congress to tax stock dividends as income.

The facts, in outline, are as follows:

On January 1, 1916, the Standard Oil Company of California, a corporation of that state, out of an authorized capital stock of $100,-000,000, had shares of stock outstanding, par value $100 each, amounting in round figures to $50,000,000. In addition, it had surplus and undivided profits invested in plant, property, and business and required for the purposes of the corporation, amounting to about $45,000,000, of which about $20,000,000 had been earned prior to March 1, 1913, the balance thereafter. In January, 1916, in order to readjust the capitalization, the board of directors decided to issue additional shares sufficient to constitute a stock dividend of 50 per cent. of the outstanding stock, and to transfer from surplus account to capital stock account an amount equivalent to such issue. Appropriate resolutions were adopted, an amount equivalent to the par value of the proposed new stock was transferred accordingly, and the new stock duly issued against it and divided among the stockholders.

Defendant in error, being the owner of 2,200 shares of the old stock, received certificates for 1,100 additional shares, of which 18.07 per cent., or 198.77 shares, par value $19,877, were treated as representing surplus earned between March 1, 1913, and January 1, 1916. She was called upon to pay, and did pay under protest, a tax imposed under the Revenue Act of 1916, based upon a supposed income of $19,877 because of the new shares; and an appeal to the Commissioner of Internal Revenue having been disallowed, she brought action against the Collector to recover the tax. In her complaint she alleged the above facts, and contended that in imposing such a tax the Revenue Act of 1916 violated article 1, § 2, cl. 3, and article 1, § 9, cl. 4, of the Constitution of the United States, requiring direct taxes to be apportioned according to population, and that the stock dividend was not income within the meaning of the Sixteenth Amendment. A general demurrer to the complaint was overruled upon the authority of Towne v. Eisner, 245 U.S. 418; and, defendant having failed to plead further, final judgment went against him. To review it, the present writ of error is prosecuted.

The case was argued at the last term, and reargued at the present term, both orally and by additional briefs.

We are constrained to hold that the judgment of the District Court must be affirmed: First, because the question at issue is controlled by Towne v. Eisner, supra; secondly, because a re-examination of the question with the additional light thrown upon it by elaborate arguments, has confirmed the view that the underlying ground of that decision is sound, that it disposes of the question here presented, and that other fundamental considerations lead to the same result.

In Towne v. Eisner, the question was whether a stock dividend made in 1914 against surplus earned prior to January 1, 1913, was taxable against the stockholder under the Act of October 3, 1913 (38 Stat. 114, 166, c. 16), which provided (section B, p. 167) that net income should include "dividends," and also "gains or profits and income derived from any source whatever." Suit having been brought by a stockholder to recover the tax assessed against him by reason of the dividend, the District Court sustained a demurrer to the complaint. 242 Fed. 702. The court treated the construction of the act as inseparable from the interpretation of the Sixteenth Amendment; and, having referred to Pollock v. Farmers' Loan & Trust Co., 158 U.S. 601, and quoted the Amendment, proceeded very properly to say (242 Fed. 704):

"It is manifest that the stock dividend in question cannot be reached by the Income Tax Act and could not, even though Congress expressly declared it to be taxable as income, unless it is in fact income."

* * *

The Sixteenth Amendment must be construed in connection with the taxing clauses of the original Constitution and the effect attributed to them before the amendment was adopted. In Pollock v. Farmers' Loan & Trust Co., 158 U.S. 601, under the Act of August 27, 1894, it was held that taxes upon rents and profits of real estate and upon returns from investments of personal property were in effect direct taxes upon the property from which such income arose, imposed by reason of ownership; and that Congress could not impose such taxes without apportioning them among the states according to population, as required by article 1, § 2, cl. 3, and section 9, cl. 4, of the original Constitution.

Afterwards, and evidently in recognition of the limitation upon the taxing power of Congress thus determined, the Sixteenth Amendment was adopted, in words lucidly expressing the object to be accomplished:

"The Congress shall have power to lay and collect taxes on incomes, from whatever source derived, without apportionment among the several states and without regard to any census or enumeration."

As repeatedly held, this did not extend the taxing power to new subjects, but merely removed the necessity which otherwise might exist for an apportionment among the states of taxes laid on income. Brushaber v. Union Pacific R. R. Co., 240 U.S. 1. * * *

A proper regard for its genesis, as well as its very clear language, requires also that this amendment shall not be extended by loose construction, so as to repeal or modify, except as applied to income, those provisions of the Constitution that require an apportionment according to population for direct taxes upon property, real and personal. This limitation still has an appropriate and important function, and is not to be overridden by Congress or disregarded by the courts.

In order, therefore, that the clauses cited from article 1 of the Constitution may have proper force and effect, save only as modified by the amendment, and that the latter also may have proper effect, it becomes essential to distinguish between what is and what is not "income," as the term is there used, and to apply the distinction, as cases arise, according to truth and substance, without regard to form. Congress cannot by any definition it may adopt conclude the matter, since it cannot by legislation alter the Constitution, from which alone it derives its power to legislate, and within whose limitations alone that power can be lawfully exercised.

The fundamental relation of "capital" to "income" has been much discussed by economists, the former being likened to the tree or the land, the latter to the fruit or the crop; the former depicted as a reservoir supplied from springs, the latter as the outlet stream, to be measured by its flow during a period of time. For the present purpose we require only a clear definition of the term "income," as used in common speech, in order to determine its meaning in the amendment, and, having formed also a correct judgment as to the nature of a stock dividend, we shall find it easy to decide the matter at issue.

After examining dictionaries in common use (Bouv.L.D.; Standard Dict.; Webster's Internat. Dict.; Century Dict.), we find little to add to the succinct definition adopted in two cases arising under the Corporation Tax Act of 1909 (Stratton's Independence v. Howbert, 231 U.S. 399; Doyle v. Mitchell Bros. Co., 247 U.S. 179), "Income may be defined as the gain derived from capital, from labor, or from both combined," provided it be understood to include profit gained through a sale or conversion of capital assets, to which it was applied in the Doyle Case, 247 U.S. 183.

Brief as it is, it indicates the characteristic and distinguishing attribute of income essential for a correct solution of the present controversy. The government, although basing its argument upon the definition as quoted, placed chief emphasis upon the word "gain," which was extended to include a variety of meanings; while the significance of the next three words was either overlooked or misconceived. *"Derived—from—capital"; "the gain—derived—from—capital,"* etc. Here we have the essential matter: *not* a gain *accruing to* capital; not a *growth* or *increment* of value *in* the investment; but a gain, a profit, something of exchangeable value, *proceeding from* the property, *severed from* the capital, however invested or employed, and *coming in,* being *"derived"*—that is, *received* or *drawn by* the recipient (the taxpayer) for his *separate* use, benefit and disposal— *that* is income derived from property. Nothing else answers the description.

The same fundamental conception is clearly set forth in the Sixteenth Amendment—"incomes, *from* whatever *source derived"*—the essential thought being expressed with a conciseness and lucidity entirely in harmony with the form and style of the Constitution.

Can a stock dividend, considering its essential character, be brought within the definition? To answer this, regard must be had to the nature of a corporation and the stockholder's relation to it. We refer, of course, to a corporation such as the one in the case at bar, organized for profit, and having a capital stock divided into shares to which a nominal or par value is attributed.

* * *

A "stock dividend" shows that the company's accumulated profits have been capitalized, instead of distributed to the stockholders or retained as surplus available for distribution in money or in kind should opportunity offer. Far from being a realization of profits of the stockholder, it tends rather to postpone such realization, in that the fund represented by the new stock has been transferred from surplus to capital, and no longer is available for actual distribution.

The essential and controlling fact is that the stockholder has received nothing out of the company's assets for his separate use and benefit; on the contrary, every dollar of his original investment, together with whatever accretions and accumulations have resulted from employment of his money and that the other stockholders in the business of the company, still remains the property of the company, and subject to business risks which may result in wiping out the entire investment. Having regard to the very truth of the matter, to substance and not to form, he has received nothing that answers the definition of income within the meaning of the Sixteenth Amendment.

* * *

We are clear that not only does a stock dividend really take nothing from the property of the corporation and add nothing to that of the shareholder, but that the antecedent accumulation of profits evidenced thereby, while indicating that the shareholder is the richer because of an increase of his capital, at the same time shows he has not realized or received any income in the transaction.

It is said that a stockholder may sell the new shares acquired in the stock dividend; and so he may, if he can find a buyer. It is equally true that if he does sell, and in doing so realizes a profit, such profit, like any other, is income, and so far as it may have arisen since the Sixteenth Amendment is taxable by Congress without apportionment. The same would be true were he to sell some of his original shares at a profit. But if a shareholder sells dividend stock he necessarily disposes of a part of his capital interest, just as if he should sell a part of his old stock, either before or after the dividend. What he retains no longer entitles him to the same proportion of future dividends as before the sale. His part in the control of the company likewise is diminished. Thus, if one holding $60,000 out of a total $100,000 of the capital stock of a corporation should receive in common with other stockholders a 50 per cent. stock dividend, and should sell his part, he thereby would be reduced from a majority to a minority stockholder, having six-fifteenths instead of six-tenths of the total stock outstanding. A corresponding and proportionate decrease in capital interest and in voting power would befall a minority holder should he sell dividend stock; it being in the nature of things impossible for one to dispose of any part of such an issue without a proportionate disturbance of the distribution of the entire capital stock, and a like diminution of the seller's comparative voting power—that "right preservative of rights" in the control of a corporation. Yet, without selling, the shareholder, unless possessed of other resources, has not the wherewithal to pay an income tax upon the dividend stock. Nothing could more clearly show that to tax a stock dividend is to tax a capital increase, and not income, than this demonstration that in the nature of things it requires conversion of capital in order to pay the tax.

* * *

We have no doubt of the power or duty of a court to look through the form of the corporation and determine the question of the stockholder's right, in order to ascertain whether he has received income taxable by Congress without apportionment. But, looking through the form, we cannot disregard the essential truth disclosed, ignore the substantial difference between corporation and stockholder, treat the entire organization as unreal, look upon stockholders as partners, when they are not such, treat them as having in equity a right to a partition of the corporate assets, when they have none, and indulge the fiction that they have received and realized a share of the profits of the company which in truth they have neither received nor realized. We must treat the corporation as a substantial entity separate from the stockholder, not only because such is the practical fact but because it is only by recognizing such separateness that any dividend—

even one paid in money or property—can be regarded as income of the stockholder. Did we regard corporation and stockholders as altogether identical, there would be no income except as the corporation acquired it; and while this would be taxable against the corporation as income under appropriate provisions of law, the individual stockholders could not be separately and additionally taxed with respect to their several shares even when divided, since if there were entire identity between them and the company they could not be regarded as receiving anything from it, any more than if one's money were to be removed from one pocket to another.

Conceding that the mere issue of a stock dividend makes the recipient no richer than before, the government nevertheless contends that the new certificates measure the extent to which the gains accumulated by the corporation have made him the richer. There are two inseparable difficulties with this: In the first place, it would depend upon how long he had held the stock whether the stock dividend indicated the extent to which he had been enriched by the operations of the company; unless he had held it throughout such operations the measure would not hold true. Secondly, and more important for present purposes, enrichment through increase in value of capital investment is not income in any proper meaning of the term.

     *   *   *

Thus, from every point of view we are brought irresistibly to the conclusion that neither under the Sixteenth Amendment nor otherwise has Congress power to tax without apportionment a true stock dividend made lawfully and in good faith, or the accumulated profits behind it, as income of the stockholder. The Revenue Act of 1916, in so far as it imposes a tax upon the stockholder because of such dividend, contravenes the provisions of article 1, § 2, cl. 3, and article 1, § 9, cl. 4, of the Constitution, and to this extent is invalid, notwithstanding the Sixteenth Amendment.

Judgment affirmed.

Justices HOLMES, BRANDEIS, CLARKE and DAY dissented.

     *   *   *

BORGE v. COMMISSIONER OF INTERNAL REVENUE

United States Court of Appeals, Second Circuit, 1968.
405 F.2d 673.

HAYS, Circuit Judge. Petitioners seek review of a decision of the Tax Court sustaining the Commissioner's determination of deficiencies in their income tax payments for the years 1958 through 1962, inclusive. The Tax Court upheld both the Commissioner's allocation to Borge [1] under Section 482 of the Internal Revenue Code of 1954, 26

---

1. "Borge" refers herein to Victor Borge. His wife has been included as a party to the action solely because of the filing of joint returns. (Court's footnote 1.)

U.S.C.A. § 482 (1964), of a portion of the compensation received by Danica Enterprises, Inc., Borge's wholly owned corporation, for services performed by Borge as an entertainer, and the Commissioner's disallowance, under Section 269 of the Internal Revenue Code of 1954, 26 U.S.C.A. § 269 (1964), of Danica's deduction of losses from its rock cornish hen business in excess of $50,000 per year, and of its loss carryovers. We affirm.

From April 1952 through February 28, 1959, Borge conducted a poultry business on a 400-acre farm in Connecticut under the name of ViBo Farms. The farm business centered on and pioneered in the development and commercial sale of processed, quality chickens called rock cornish hens.

Borge incurred substantial losses in his poultry business.[2] For each of the years 1954 through 1957 the poultry losses exceeded $50,-000. In the first two months of 1958 the poultry losses amounted to $23,133, and market conditions were unfavorable. Borge's tax consultant advised him that if the poultry losses for 1958 exceeded $50,-000 the Commissioner would probably recompute Borge's taxes for each year that the losses had exceeded $50,000, pursuant to Section 270 of the Internal Revenue Code of 1954, 26 U.S.C.A. § 270 (1964).[3] In an effort to avoid the application of Section 270, Borge organized Danica, and, on March 1, 1958, transferred to the corporation, in exchange for all of its stock and a loan payable, the assets of the poultry business (except the farm real property).

Borge is a well-known professional entertainer. During the years preceding the organization of Danica he made large sums from television, stage and motion picture engagements.

Since Danica had no means of meeting the expected losses from the poultry business, Borge and Danica entered into a contract at the time of the organization of the corporation under which Borge agreed to perform entertainment and promotional services for the corporation for a 5-year period for compensation from Danica of $50,000 per

2. Borge's net losses from the poultry business were as follows:

Calendar Year	Net Loss
1953	$ 26,665
1954	62,159
1955	79,486
1956	345,879
1957	220,146
1958(through February 28)	23,133

(Court's footnote 3.)

3. § 270. Limitation on deductions allowable to individuals in certain cases.

(a) Recomputation of taxable income.

If the deductions allowed by this chapter * * * and attributable to a trade or business carried on by him for 5 consecutive taxable years have, in each of such years * * *, exceeded by more than $50,000 the gross income derived from such trade or business, the taxable income * * * of such individual for each of such years shall be recomputed. For the purpose of such recomputation in the case of any such taxable year, such deductions shall be allowed only to the extent of $50,000 plus the gross income attributable to such trade or business, except that the net operating loss deduction, to the extent attributable to such trade or business, shall not be allowed.

(Court's footnote 4.)

year. Danica offset the poultry losses [4] against the entertainment profits, which far exceeded the $50,000 per year it had contracted to pay Borge.[5] Borge obviously would not have entered into such a contract with an unrelated party.

Danica did nothing to aid Borge in his entertainment business. Those who contracted with Danica for Borge's entertainment services required Borge personally to guarantee the contracts. Danica's entertainment earnings were attributable solely to the services of Borge, and Danica's only profits were from the entertainment business.

The only year during the period in dispute in which Danica actually paid Borge anything for his services was 1962, when Borge was paid the full $50,000.

The issues in controversy are (1) whether the Commissioner, acting under Section 482 of the Internal Revenue Code of 1954, 26 U.S.C.A. § 482 (1964), properly allocated to Borge from Danica $75,000 per year from 1958 through 1961 and $25,000 for 1962, and (2) whether the Commissioner, acting under Section 269 of the Internal Revenue Code of 1954, 26 U.S.C.A. § 269 (1964), properly disallowed Danica's loss deductions in excess of $50,000 per year for fiscal years 1959 through 1961 and its net loss carryovers for fiscal years 1960 through 1962.

I.

When two or more organizations, trades or businesses, whether or not incorporated, are owned or controlled by the same interests, Section 482 of the Internal Revenue Code of 1954, 26 U.S.C.A. § 482 (1964), authorizes the Commissioner to apportion gross income between or among such organizations, trades or businesses if he deems that apportionment is necessary clearly to reflect income or to prevent evasion of tax.[6] We conclude that the Commissioner could properly

---

4. Danica's net poultry losses for the tax years here in dispute were as follows:

Fiscal Year (ending February 28)	Net Loss
1959	$309,557
1960	194,346
1961	69,473
1962	29,797
1963	57,586

(Court's footnote 5.)

5. Danica's net entertainment income for the years in dispute, before deducting Borge's salary, averaged $166,465. The annual net entertainment income was as follows:

Fiscal Year (ending February 28)	Net Entertainment Income
1959	$141,441
1960	146,402
1961	143,826
1962	283,315
1963	117,340

(Court's footnote 6.)

6. § 482. Allocation of income and deductions among taxpayers.

In any case of two or more organizations, trades, or businesses (whether or not incorporated, whether or not organized in the United States, and whether or not affiliated) owned or controlled directly or indirectly by the same interests, the Secretary or his delegate may distribute, apportion, or allocate gross income, deductions, credits, or allowances between or among such organizations, trades, or businesses, if he determines that such distribution, apportionment, or allocation is necessary in order to prevent evasion of taxes or clearly to reflect the income of any such organizations, trades, or businesses.

(Court's footnote 7.)

have found that for purposes of Section 482 Borge owned or controlled two businesses, an entertainment business and a poultry business, and that the allocation to Borge of part of the entertainment compensation paid to the corporation was not error.

We accept, as supported by the record, the Tax Court's finding: that Borge operated an entertainment business and merely assigned to Danica a portion of his income from that business; that Danica did nothing to earn or to assist in the earning of the entertainment income; that Borge would not have contracted for $50,000 per year with an unrelated party to perform the services referred to in his contract with Danica. Thus Borge was correctly held to be in the entertainment business.

At the same time Danica, Borge's wholly owned corporation, was in the poultry business.

Petitioners, relying primarily on Whipple v. Commissioner, 373 U.S. 193, argue that Borge is not an "organization, trade or business" and that Section 482 is therefore inapposite.

In *Whipple* the Supreme Court held only that where one renders services to a corporation as an investment, he is not engaging in a trade or business:

"Devoting one's time and energies to the affairs of a corporation is not of itself, and without more, a trade or business of the person so engaged. Though such activities may produce income, profit or gain in the form of dividends or enhancement in the value of an investment, this return is distinctive to the process of investing and is generated by the successful operation of the corporation's business as distinguished from the trade or business of the taxpayer himself. When the only return is that of an investor, the taxpayer has not satisfied his burden of demonstrating that he is engaged in a trade or business since investing is not a trade or business and the return to the taxpayer, though substantially the product of his services, legally arises not from his own trade or business but from that of the corporation." 373 U.S. at 202, 83 S.Ct. at 1174.

Here, however, Borge was in the business of entertaining. He was not devoting his time and energies to the corporation; he was carrying on his career as an entertainer, and merely channeling a part of his entertainment income through the corporation.

Moreover, in *Whipple* petitioner was devoting his time and energies to a corporation in the hope of realizing capital gains treatment from the sale of appreciated stock. When the hoped-for appreciation did not materalize he attempted to deduct his losses as ordinary losses. The Court decided that where one stands to achieve capital gains through an investment, any losses incurred in connection with the investment are capital losses. Borge is clearly earning ordinary income; the only question is who should pay the taxes on it. Thus, *Whipple* is not apposite.

For somewhat similar reasons we find Commissioner v. Gross, 236 F.2d 612 (2d Cir. 1956), on which petitioner also seeks to rely, also inapposite.

Nor do we consider the other cases cited by petitioners persuasive. The Commissioner is not arguing here, as he did, for example, in Charles Laughton, 40 B.T.A. 101 (1939), remanded, 113 F.2d 103 (9th Cir. 1940), that the taxpayer should be taxed on the entire amount paid into the wholly owned corporation, i. e. that the corporation should be ignored. See also Pat O'Brien, 25 T.C. 376 (1955); Fontaine Fox, 37 B.T.A. 271 (1938). Instead he recognizes the existence of the corporation, but under Section 482 allocates a portion of its income to its sole shareholder who alone was responsible for the production of such income.

Petitioner contends that the Congress, in enacting the personal holding company and collapsible corporation provisions of the Code, precluded the Commissioner's action in this case under Section 482. We do not read those provisions, however, as the only available methods for dealing with the situations there involved. As the Third Circuit said in National Sec. Corp. v. Commissioner, 137 F.2d 600, 602 (3d Cir.), cert. denied, 320 U.S. 794,

"In every case in which [Section 482] is applied its application will necessarily result in an apparent conflict with the literal requirements of some other provision of the [Internal Revenue Code]. If this were not so Section [482] would be wholly superfluous."

The fact that similar, but not identical, factual situations have been dealt with by legislation does not mean that this situation, because it was not also specifically dealt with by legislation, cannot be reached even by a general code provision.

We thus conclude that the Tax Court was correct in upholding the Commissioner's ruling that Borge controlled two separate businesses. See Pauline W. Ach, 42 T.C. 114 (1964), aff'd, 358 F.2d 342 (6th Cir.), cert. denied, 385 U.S. 899.

The Commissioner's action in allocating a part of Danica's income to Borge was based upon his conclusion that such allocation was necessary in order clearly to reflect the income of the two businesses under Borge's common control. The Commissioner's allocation has received the approval of the Tax Court. As this Court held in dealing with the predecessor of Section 482, "Whether the Tax Court, was correct in allocating income to the petitioner under § 45 [of the Internal Revenue Code of 1939] is essentially one of fact and the decision below must be affirmed if supported by substantial evidence." Advance Mach. Exch. v. Commissioner, 196 F.2d 1006, 1007–08 (2d Cir.), cert. denied, 344 U.S. 835. Here the determination of the Commissioner and the decision of the Tax Court are supported by substantial evidence that the income of Borge's two businesses has been distorted through Borge's having arranged for Danica to receive a large part of his entertainment income although Danica did nothing to earn that income, and the sole purpose of the arrangement was to permit Danica to offset losses from the poultry business with income from the entertainment business. The amount allocated by the Commissioner ($75,000 per year) was entirely reasonable—indeed, generous—in view of the fact that Danica's annual net income from Borge's entertainment services averaged $166,465 during the years in question.

II.

Section 269 of the Internal Revenue Code of 1954, 26 U.S.C.A. § 269 (1964), provides that where any person acquires control of a corporation for the principal purpose of evading or avoiding federal income taxes by securing the benefit of a deduction or other allowance not otherwise available, the Commissioner may disallow the deduction or allowance.

As we have pointed out above Borge organized Danica in order to avoid the recomputation of taxes authorized by Section 270 of the Internal Revenue Code of 1954, 26 U.S.C.A. § 270 (1964). The Tax Court found that "the Commissioner had reason to hold that 'the principal purpose for which [Borge acquired control of Danica]' was evasion of Federal income tax within the meaning of section 269 * * *." That finding is not clearly erroneous and must, therefore, be accepted. Whipple v. Commissioner, supra, * * * Indeed, petitioners do not challenge the finding.

Since Borge's purpose in organizing Danica was avoidance of the $50,000 per year loss limitation of Section 270, the Commissioner did not act unreasonably in disallowing, under Section 269, deductions for subsequent years in excess of $50,000—deductions which Borge would have been denied if Danica had not been organized.

We find no merit in petitioner's contention that, because Section 270 applies only to deductions "allowable to an individual," Section 269 cannot be used to disallow a deduction claimed by Danica. Section 269 is a general provision. It was "designed to put an end promptly to any market for, or dealings in, interests in corporations or property which have as their objective the reduction through artifice of the income or excess profits tax liability." * * *

It is argued that Danica's deductions should be allowed because Section 270 does not limit a corporation's deductions to $50,000 regardless of how many years it loses more than that amount. The fact that Danica might have been allowed an unlimited loss deduction had it run the poultry business from its inception in no way tends to contradict the finding that Danica was incorporated with the purpose of evading or avoiding federal income taxes. There is no reason for giving taxpayers the benefit of an incorporation which they did not themselves undertake.

Petitioner also argues that Section 269 may not be used to disallow any but built-in losses of the corporation. Nothing in the language of the statute suggests any such limitation on the deductions that may be disallowed. The only requirement is that the deduction be one that the taxpayer would not enjoy but for incorporation. Both the House and the Senate reports specifically state that "anticipated" or "prospective" losses were among those that the Commissioner could disallow as deductions under Section 269. * * * While there is authority to the contrary (Herculite Protective Fabrics Corp. v. Commisssioner, 387 F.2d 475 (3d Cir. 1968); Zanesville Inv. Co. v. Commissioner, 335 F.2d 507 (6th Cir. 1964)) the better view permits the disallowance of deductions for post-acquisition losses of an acquired corporation where those deductions were a part of the purpose for which the corporation was acquired. Luke v. Commissioner, 351 F.2d 568 (7th Cir. 1965) * * *

Petitioners' final argument is that there could have been no attempt to avoid or evade the application of Section 270 because there were no five consecutive years in which the poultry business' deductions exceeded its gross income by $50,000. It is sufficient to dispose of that contention to note that the parties stipulated to the contrary.

Affirmed as modified and remanded for recomputation of the deficiency.

IRVING R. KAUFMAN, Circuit Judge (dissented in part).

* * *

MURPHY LOGGING CO. v. UNITED STATES

United States Court of Appeals, Ninth Circuit, 1967.
378 F.2d 222.

CHAMBERS, Circuit Judge. Harry, Edward and Peter Murphy know the logging business pretty well. But in their apparent quest for federal income tax savings, they have collided with the internal revenue service.

The Brothers Murphy have operated as loggers in the timber lands of Oregon for some time. Today considerable equipment is usually required in that sort of business.

Before the tax years in controversy, the Murphy brothers operated for a long time as a partnership. In 1958 they added a corporation. The partnership was called Murphy Timber Co. and the corporation was called Murphy Logging Co. Hereafter we shall refer to them as the Murphy partnership and Logging, Inc. A valuable intangible of the Murphys was their ability to get contracts for cutting timber from the Crown-Zellerbach Corporation.

Murphy partnership was owned 53⅓% by Harry, 33⅓% by Edward and 13⅓% by Peter, the disparities conformed in some respect to the age of the brothers. Harry seems to have been the lead man in the enterprises.

The ratio of ownership in Logging, Inc., was equal. Logging, Inc., after it was organized, did the business for the brothers with others and it was the operator in the field on logging contracts. Murphy partnership owned the logging equipment and leased it to Logging, Inc., for about the amount of the annual depreciation.

From April, 1958, to April, 1959, the Zellerbach contract was with Logging, Inc. for logging near Grand Ronde, Oregon. In the fall of 1958, Logging, Inc., added another logging contract 100 miles away at Santiam, Oregon, with the Santiam Lumber Co. This required more machinery, and Logging, Inc. purchased it from Santiam for that operation.

In the spring of 1959, the time was approaching for a new annual contract with Zellerbach. The Murphy brothers decided they should have a new company to do business with Zellerbach, leaving Logging, Inc., as the operator of the Santiam contract. So they incorporated Murphy Timber Co. (hereafter Timber, Inc.).

One Murphy setup was as good as another for Zellerbach. In April, 1959, Murphy Timber, Inc., obtained a new one year Zellerbach contract to be performed in the Grand Ronde area as before. The concept of forming Timber, Inc., was that the Murphy partnership would sell its logging equipment to Timber, Inc., for a price to be later determined by an independent appraiser. There would be no more leasing from the partnership. (Each of the three brothers subscribed and paid for a nominal amount of stock of Timber, Inc.: $500 each. No other stock was issued.)

The agreement to sell the equipment was made shortly after Murphy Timber, Inc., was formed. In the fall of 1959 the appraisement was made. And the value of the equipment was fixed at $238,-150. (Parenthetically we find the appraiser's testimony quite amusing as he relates how he was coaxed by the oldest brother to keep the value up and by the youngest to keep it down. This represents a struggle by Peter, the youngest, to get on a parity with his brothers at the earliest date possible.)

Obviously, $1,500 received from the issuance of stock would not pay for the equipment. It may be assumed that someone advised the Murphys that taxwise it was dangerous to have the Murphy partnership wait until Timber, Inc. earned enough profit from operations to pay the debt, either in installments or all at once. "Thin capitalization," we assume, was sought to be avoided by having the corporation borrow the money from a third party: The First National Bank of Oregon.

It would appear that the equipment sold to Timber, Inc. by the partnership had either greatly appreciated in value or had been depreciated faster than its useful life was expiring. Clearly one motivation for the new setup must have been to get a new tax basis on the machinery to start depreciating again. Tax reduction is not evil if you do not do it evilly. Often an inefficient operator, wise as to taxes, can do better than an efficient operator who is stupid about his taxes.

When the revenue agents looked at the lush new depreciation of Timber, Inc., they decided to go after the company and the Murphys individually. They discovered that when Timber, Inc., borrowed $240,-000 about December 31, 1959, for immediate payment of the debt to the Murphy partnership, that the Murphy brothers had individually guaranteed the note.

The collectors recast the transaction as a tax free exchange between the partnership and Timber, Inc., disallowed the stepped up depreciation base of Timber, Inc. on the equipment. And, further, they held the payment with money borrowed from the bank for the equipment to be a constructive dividend to the partners.

The Murphys elected to pay the asserted deficiency and sue for it back. The district court sustained the internal revenue service. On this appeal, we disagree.

When taxpayers have used pure gimmicks of form to shield the real essence of a transaction, we have not hesitated to approve or order recasting for tax purposes of a transaction. See Estate of Starr v. Commissioner, 9 Cir., 274 F.2d 294, and our Oesterreich cases: Oesterreich v. Commissioner, 9 Cir., 226 F.2d 798; Commissioner v. Wilshire Holding Corp., 9 Cir., 244 F.2d 905, 262 F.2d 51, and 288 F.2d 799.

The cases on "thin" capitalization are quite varied as to facts and therefore conversion of what went into a corporation into equity capital by the commissioner must be considered on a case to case basis. At the time of trial at least, the government conceded that this was the first case of its type. The government called it indirect borrowing by the Murphys.

As we read the trial transcript, if the Murphys individually had been worthless (instead of affluent in personal assets) and the bank had still made the loan, then the taxpayer might have been better off in contesting with the agents in so far as the obligation to the bank was concerned, but we do not think that they should be penalized here for responsibility. Also, we find it an oversimplification to look only to the nominal stated capital of Timber, Inc. in determining the value of the Murphys' equity investment. Estate of Miller v. C. I. R., 9 Cir., 239 F.2d 729; United States v. Cornish, 9 Cir., 348 F.2d 175. In addition to putting $1,500 into the new operation, the Murphys also contributed the expectancy of future custom from Zellerbach as well as their own integrity and reputation for getting things done. These latter assets are extremely important in the logging business generally. Here they may well have been more valuable than the tangible machinery. In any case, we hold that they were adequate to prevent the corporation from being treated as "thinly" capitalized.

Thus, we are unwilling to collapse the transaction by saying that the bank loan of $240,000 to the corporation was really to the individual stockholders. And, so we are unable to go on and say the sale of the machinery to Timber, Inc., was a tax free contribution of equity capital by the Murphy partnership to Timber, Inc. under Sec. 351 of the Internal Revenue Code of 1954. Without the assumptions we have rejected, there is no basis for denying Timber, Inc. its interest charges paid to the bank and depreciation on the new basis; and, so the payments for the equipment by Timber, Inc., to the Murphy partners should not be constructive dividends.

The judgment is reversed.

LOWNDES v. UNITED STATES

United States District Court, District of Maryland, 1966.
258 F.Supp. 193.
Aff'd 384 F.2d 635 (1967).

WINTER, Circuit Judge (by designation).   This suit for refund of income taxes raises the questions of whether plaintiff Anne W. Lowndes received income taxable as long term capital gains or as ordinary income on the dates that four corporations, all of the issued and outstanding stock of which she had acquired, were liquidated and assets distributed, or whether she received income taxable as ordinary income on the dates that she acquired the stock of those corporations. Suit was filed by her and her husband because they filed joint income tax returns for the years in question.   The transactions by which she acquired the stock were conducted in her name, but were negotiated by her husband; her only participation was to execute various documents to carry out the transactions which he arranged.

Concerned are the tax years 1957, 1959 and 1960.   In 1957 Mrs. Lowndes acquired all of the outstanding stock of two corporations which were liquidated later in that year, but six months after the date of acquisition of stock.   In 1959 Mrs. Lowndes acquired all of the outstanding stock of two more corporations, which were liquidated in 1960, again six months after the date of acquisition of stock.   She and Mr. Lowndes treated the gains which she realized as long term capital gains, realized on the respective dates of liquidation.   The Commissioner, however, treated the gains as ordinary income, realized on the dates of stock acquisition, or alternatively on the dates of liquidation, and assessed additional income taxes with interest thereon.   It is stipulated that all of the additional assessments have been paid in full, demand for repayment refused, and the jurisdiction of this Court under 28 U.S.C.A. § 1346(a) (1) properly invoked.   The parties have further stipulated that if plaintiffs are entitled to judgment, they will agree upon the amount of judgment to be entered.

The stock of all four corporations was acquired from subsidiaries of three subsidiaries of Bethlehem Steel Company, viz., Bethlehem Steel Company, Bethlehem-Cuba Iron Mines Company and Bethlehem Limestone Company (hereinafter individually as well as collectively called "Bethlehem").   The stock acquired in 1957 was that of American Well and Prospecting Company (hereinafter called "American Well") and Bethlehem Quarry Company (hereinafter called "Bethlehem Quarry").   The 1959 acquisitions were the stock of Indian Coal Company (hereinafter called "Indian Coal") and Maryland Century Coal Company (hereinafter called "Maryland Century").   The acquisitions came about when Bethlehem, which had theretofore acquired these companies but had ceased to operate them for a number of years, decided to dispose of them because they were no longer useful to Bethlehem and Bethlehem desired to simplify its corporate structure. Bethlehem caused all of their assets to be reduced to cash and paid all of their liabilities, including liabilities for taxes.   Bethlehem had a loss in each of the companies but, by a quirk in the federal income tax laws, Bethlehem could gain no tax advantage from its loss if it undertook to dissolve the corporations and distribute the cash, which was in the form of bank accounts, to itself. Rather, Bethlehem was obliged, if it was to realize a loss for tax purposes, to sell the stock in an arm's length transaction to a third party. The only condition Bethlehem imposed on such sales was that they be for a price agreeable to it, payable in cash.

The sale of the stock of American Well is typical of each of the four transactions. By bill of sale dated April 17, 1957 Bethlehem sold all of the stock of American Well (1,000 shares) to Mrs. Lowndes at and for the price of $93,000.00. At the time of the sale American Well's sole net asset was a bank account in the amount of $100,000.00; it had no liabilities; and Bethlehem warranted that it had no tax or contingent liabilities. Immediately prior to the sale, American Well closed out its checking account theretofore existing and opened a new checking account at the Union Trust Company of Maryland (hereinafter called "Union Trust"). This was done in conformity with one of the conditions fixed by Union Trust for making a loan to Mrs. Lowndes. On April 17, 1957, Mrs. Lowndes borrowed $93,000.00 from Union Trust on her demand note bearing interest at 4½% and pledged as security for the loan the 1,000 shares of American Well. Simultaneously, the theretofore officers and directors of American Well resigned, Mr. and Mrs. Lowndes and another person were elected as directors, and Mr. and Mrs. Lowndes were elected officers of American Well, as well as two individuals who were also officers of Union Trust. American Well adopted bank resolutions which limited withdrawals from its checking account at Union Trust to checks signed by Mr. or Mrs. Lowndes *and* one of the two individuals who was an officer of Union Trust. On the same date American Well instructed Union Trust to convert the checking accounts to time deposit accounts for a six month period bearing interest at 2½%, representing that it would make no withdrawals for a period of six months.

On October 22, 1957 Mrs. Lowndes, as the sole stockholder of American Well, instructed its board of directors to liquidate and dissolve the company and distribute its assets to her. A partial liquidating dividend of $99,000.00 was paid October 24, 1957. A final liquidating dividend was paid after November 1, 1957. Payment of the Union Trust loan was accomplished by use of the time deposit of American Well. For the year 1957 American Well reported and paid income tax on the interest earned on the time deposit and, for the same year, taxpayers claimed a tax deduction for the interest paid by Mrs. Lowndes to Union Trust on the loan.

The transactions in regard to the three other companies were identical. The stock of Bethlehem Quarry, consisting of 1,709 shares, was also acquired April 17, 1957. The purchase price was $169,789.15. Bethlehem Quarry had no liabilities, except a reserve for federal income tax in the amount of $2,534.00, and its sole asset was cash in bank in the amount of $179,346.00. Mrs. Lowndes borrowed $169,-789.15 from Union Trust on a 4½% demand note, secured by a pledge of 1,709 shares of Bethlehem Quarry. New directors and officers were elected for Bethlehem Quarry. Shortly before settlement, Bethlehem Quarry had theretofore established a new demand account at Union Trust; it adopted new bank resolutions limiting the persons who could sign on the checking account to Mr. or Mrs. Lowndes and one of the bank officers; and on the date of settlement with Mrs. Lowndes converted the checking account to a time account bearing interest at 2½%, again representing that there would be no withdrawals for six months. On October 22, Mrs. Lowndes directed Bethlehem Quarry's board of directors to liquidate and dissolve that company and to distribute its assets to her. A partial liquidating dividend, in the amount of $179,000.00, was paid October 24, 1957 and, on November 1, 1957, a final liquidating dividend was authorized. Payment of Mrs. Lowndes' loan from Union Trust was made from funds from Bethlehem Quarry's time deposit. No additional distribution was made to Mrs. Lowndes, because there were insufficient funds to pay the expenses incident to liquidation and dissolution of Bethlehem Quarry, so that Mrs. Lowndes refunded $947.35 to Bethlehem Quarry, thus reducing the total net liquidating proceeds received by her to $178,-052.65. For 1957 Bethlehem Quarry reported as taxable income the interest earned on its time deposit and paid the tax thereon. Taxpayers claimed as a tax deduction the interest Mrs. Lowndes paid on the loan from Union Trust.

From the standpoint of Bethlehem and the taxpayers these transactions were so satisfactory that, in 1959, when Bethlehem undertook to sell 1,000 shares of Indian Coal, which had no liabilities and a single asset of $100,000.00 cash in bank, and 3,000 shares of Maryland Century, which had no liabilities and a single asset of cash in bank of $300,000.00, Mrs. Lowndes undertook to buy them for $95,500.00 and $286,500.00, respectively. Again, prior to settlement, these companies closed their existing bank accounts, opened demand accounts at Union Trust and deposited all their funds therein; Mrs. Lowndes borrowed the purchase prices in full from Union Trust on demand notes bearing interest at 5%; new officers and directors were elected; new bank resolutions adopted restricting signatories on the account to Mr. or Mrs. Lowndes *and* a bank officer; and Indian Coal and Maryland Century gave Union Trust written instructions to convert the demand accounts to time accounts bearing interest at 3%, representing that no withdrawals would be made for six months. On May 26, 1960 Mrs. Lowndes, as the sole stockholder of Indian Coal and Maryland Century, instructed the directors thereof to liquidate the companies and distribute their assets to her. Liquidating dividends were paid her on May 26, 1960 and June 6, 1960. Mrs. Lowndes' loans from Union Trust were repaid from corporate funds. Mr. and Mrs. Lowndes claimed as tax deductions the interest paid by Mrs. Lowndes to Union Trust on the latter two loans, and both corporations paid income tax on their interest income.

Other than the testimony which established that the transactions between Bethlehem and Mrs. Lowndes were negotiated at arm's length, the only testimony offered was that of Mr. Lowndes, who testified by deposition. He testified that when he had learned that Bethlehem " * * * had a couple of corporations that they wanted to liquidate for sale" and inquired "whether or not I would be interested in buying them," he went to see "Charlie Hoff, who was President of the Union Trust Company at that time." Mr. Hoff agreed to lend the money for Mrs. Lowndes to purchase the stock on condition that the loan be in existence for six months, so that the bank "would have a chance to make some money off of it," that the bank accounts be converted into six month certificates of deposit, and that two of his officers would be officers of the corporation. According to Mr. Lowndes, "in other words, what he was doing was locking us in. You can see what I mean. We couldn't touch any of the money without one of his officers signing the withdrawal."

Mr. Hoff also required Mrs. Lowndes to require the companies she was about to purchase to move their accounts to Union Trust a week or so before settlement in order to collect funds.

When first questioned, Mr. Lowndes claimed that he went to Union Trust because he didn't know how else to finance the purchase. He claimed that it "never occurred to me" to finance the purchases out of the bank accounts of the corporations whose stock was being purchased. He also claimed that the reason why financing of this type never occurred to him was because "I was thinking about putting the money to work. I wanted to put the money to work." He explained that "putting the money to work" meant converting it into a certificate of deposit which earned interest. *Mr. Lowndes was unequivocal that he never had any thought of reactivating the business of any of the four companies,* and he reiterated that he did not consider liquidating the corporations on the days of settlement, because he wanted to put the money to work in the form of certificates of deposit. He admitted that when the corporations were ultimately liquidated the funds derived from them were used to repay the Union Trust loans made by Mrs. Lowndes which had been created to purchase the stock. Because of the restrictive bank resolutions, this must have been done with the acquiescence of Union Trust.

On cross examination, Mr. Lowndes disclaimed that Bethlehem imposed any restrictions on what might be done with the corporations after Mrs. Lowndes purchased their stock. Mr. Lowndes claimed that the moneys on deposit at Union Trust in a demand account were converted to a time account *at the instance of the bank,* although from his other testimony, this condition was not unacceptable to him. He admitted that he was aware that a taxpayer could obtain more favorable tax treatment of the sale of securities which he held for more than six months. Indeed, as an officer of two banks and one business corporation, as well as a director of another bank and four other business corporations, Mr. Lowndes could be presumed to have a reasonable familiarity with the long term capital gains provisions of the Federal Income Tax laws. When asked if the rule regarding taxation of long term capital gains did not make it more beneficial for Mrs. Lowndes to defer liquidation of the corporations, all of the stock of which she had purchased from Bethlehem, his initial reply was, "I had no need for the money at that time." When pressed, Mr. Lowndes finally admitted that "one of the reasons" why the corporations were not liquidated immediately was to gain the benefit of capital gains treatment of the income realized by Mrs. Lowndes. He then added that it was Union Trust which had insisted that the loan made by Mrs. Lowndes exist for six months, and that Union Trust wanted the use of the money on deposit for at least that period.

Taxpayers argue that Mrs. Lowndes did not receive income taxable as ordinary income on April 17, 1957, when she acquired the stock of American Well and Bethlehem Quarry, and on November 23, 1959, when she acquired the stock of Indian Coal and Maryland Century. Their argument is two-fold. First, they argue that the existence of these corporate entities insulated Mrs. Lowndes from tax liability until the dates of liquidation thereof. Second, they argue that even if these entities are disregarded, Mrs. Lowndes acquired only bank accounts, a species of capital asset. The government argues vigorously to the contrary. This Court need not decide the asserted second legal question because, if the corporate entities are disregarded, as a matter of fact Mrs. Lowndes purchased cash. Prior to the closing of each of the transactions involving these corporations, the corporations, at the instance of Mrs. Lowndes (whom Mr. Lowndes claims was so directed by Union Trust), closed their respective bank accounts in the banks in which they had theretofore existed and opened new accounts at Union Trust. Of course, in modern day banking practice this transaction was accomplished by a transfer of credits reflected in a series of bookkeeping operations by a clearing house, correspondent bank or federal reserve bank; but in fact and in law, the withdrawal of funds from one bank and redeposit in another constitutes a conversion of credits in the first bank into cash and deposit of the cash thus obtained in the second bank. More significantly, once the accounts had been opened at Union Trust they were again converted into cash *on the very date that control of them was obtained by Mrs. Lowndes.* Union Trust was instructed to convert demand accounts to a "time deposit basis." Again in modern banking practice, Union Trust would achieve this by an internal bookkeeping operation, but legally the effect of the bookkeeping entries was to constitute a withdrawal of cash from a demand account and a redeposit in a time account or, alternatively, a cash purchase of a certificate of deposit.

Thus, the determinative question is whether, under the facts and circumstances established by the evidence and applicable rules of law, the corporate entities should be disregarded for income tax purposes.

Ordinarily an individual and a corporation are for purposes of taxation separate juridical entities. The fact that Mrs. Lowndes owned all of the stock of each of the four corporations, standing alone, is irrelevant. Disregard of a corporate entity for purposes of taxation has been approved, however, on at least two distinct reciprocal grounds. In New Colonial Ice Co., Inc. v. Helvering, 292 U.S. 435, the Court recognized that disregard of the corporate entity is the exception, rather than the rule, but stated that disregard is proper where failure to disregard " * * * otherwise would present an obstacle to the due protection or enforcement of public or private rights." Id. p. 442. Gregory v. Helvering, 293 U.S. 465, is another example of the application of the rule stated in the New Colonial Ice case, but is important also for articulation of the doctrine that the presence of a motive to avoid taxes is not sufficient basis to justify disregarding a corporate entity if there is also a business purpose for the entity. Id. p. 469.

While the New Colonial Ice case stated a reason for disregard of a corporate entity in negative terms, Moline Properties, Inc. v. Commissioner of Internal Revenue, 319 U.S. 463, enunciated the affirmative test that a corporate entity should be recognized for tax purposes so long as the purpose of its being " * * * is the equivalent of business activity or is followed by the carrying on of business by the corporation * * *." Id. pp. 438–439. Absent such a "business purpose," a corporate entity may be disregarded. Shaw Construction Co. v. C. I. R., 323 F.2d 316 (9 Cir. 1963). * * *

Another line of Supreme Court cases, overlapping in part those to which reference has already been made, must also be considered. The starting point of this line is Commissioner of Internal Revenue v. Court Holding Co., 324 U.S. 331, which firmly established the doctrine that the incidence of taxation depends upon the substance of a transaction and not upon its form. "To permit the true nature of a transaction to be disguised by mere formalisms, which exist solely to alter tax liabilities, would seriously impair the effective administration of the tax policies of Congress." Id. p. 334. * * *

Taxpayers do not dispute the validity of these authorities, but argue most strenuously, that the substance of Mrs. Lowndes' transaction was a bona fide long term capital gains transaction, because she held her investment in each corporation for six months before causing each corporation's cash to be distributed to her, and that for a period of six months after Mrs. Lowndes' acquisition of their stock, each of the corporations had a business purpose, i. e., investment of its funds in income-producing time deposit certificates, with partial control thereof vested in outsiders. While superficially appealing, these arguments do not withstand close scrutiny.

In the ownership of Bethlehem, each of the corporations lacked any remaining business purpose. Bethlehem's sole motive in disposing of them was to dispose of them under the most favorable tax circumstances to Bethlehem. As previously mentioned, Mr. Lowndes was candid in admitting that he had no thought of reactivating any corporate purpose of any one of them and, in fact, they engaged in no business enterprise except to place cash which they owned on a time deposit interest bearing basis. Business purpose, if any, must exist in earning interest on corporate funds.

It is difficult to believe that Union Trust would insist that cash in its bank be retained on an interest bearing basis where retention of the cash would cost Union Trust an interest expense, particularly when Union Trust had an effective veto over any withdrawal from a non-interest bearing demand account. But such is the testimony of Mr. Lowndes; Mr. Hoff who is said to have exacted this condition is deceased; and no other representative of Union Trust testified in corroboration or contradiction of Mr. Lowndes. If Mr. Lowndes is believed, the conclusion, nevertheless, follows that the investment of corporate funds was not a business purpose of any one of the four corporations Mrs. Lowndes controlled, but was a condition precedent to the making of a loan for the accommodation of Mrs. Lowndes, exacted from each of the corporations. This asserted business activity of the corporations after their stock was purchased is purely illusory.

More broadly considered, Mrs. Lowndes' transactions were nothing more than the immediate purchase of cash at a discount. That the bank accounts were converted to cash twice as part of the transactions has been shown. While the fact that Mrs. Lowndes could have financed the purchases by immediate liquidation and dissolution of the corporations and use of their funds is not conclusive, it is a fact which sheds much light on the true nature of the transaction, because when liquidation and dissolution were ultimately effected, the record shows that it was the funds of the corporations which were employed to repay Union Trust and not separate funds of Mrs. Lowndes. What, then, was the purpose of investing the corporations' funds in interest bearing time deposits? If not to serve a business purpose of Union Trust, as previously discussed, the inevitable answer is that the purpose was to reduce the effective interest cost to Mrs. Lowndes, of the loans made her by Union Trust, even below the partial reduction achieved by her in claiming the interest as deductions in her joint income tax returns. The manner in which the transactions were carried out and the means by which the Union Trust loans were repaid lead the Court to conclude that, although formally cast in other forms, Mrs. Lowndes purchased cash, at a discount, paying for it with the cash she had purchased, and incurring only a theoretical liability on the notes to Union Trust she made, because those notes in turn were secured by the very cash which had been purchased. It was her ability to treat the cash as her own on the date of purchase that enabled her to effect the purchase. Delay in full realization of the fruits of the purchases for six months cannot be justified by any discernible business reason. Thus, the substance of the transaction was that Mrs. Lowndes realized income on the two dates that she purchased all of the stock of the four corporations, and that income should be taxed to her as ordinary income on those dates.

Counsel may agree upon the amount of judgment to be entered.

B. THE SUBCHAPTER S CORPORATION

In 1958 the Internal Revenue Code was amended by adding Subchapter S to it in order to permit small business corporations not to be taxed and to have the pro rata share of each shareholder's income taxed to him much as though the corporation were a partnership. A small business corporation was defined as one with no more than ten shareholders, with no more than one class of stock, and all of whose shareholders were either individuals or estates. It must be remembered that in every other aspect of the law these corporations are corporations and nothing else, and the fact that they are exempted from paying Federal income taxes does not alter this circumstance. In order to distinguish them from other corporations which are required to pay a tax various names have been devised for these corporations by persons who write about taxation, some of which do such violence to the English language that they will not be reported here. Nonetheless, it must be kept in mind that these business enterprises are corporations at all times.

One of the purposes of the enactment of Subchapter S of the Internal Revenue Code was to permit small businesses to select the legal form of their business without being unduly influenced by income taxes. Various safeguards to assure that this technique would not be manipulated to avoid taxation beyond the purpose which Congress intended were included in the provisions of Subchapter S. There has been little litigation involving the use of this technique, and perhaps it should then be concluded that the system has worked well. The cases which are reported below are two of the very few cases which have arisen. They also illustrate the point that taxpayers are presumed to have intended the consequence of the arrangements which they have made and that without specific statutory authorization the concept of substance over form is applied almost exclusively for the benefit of the government. While taxpayers may organize their affairs in order to reduce to a minimum the taxes which they are properly required to pay, sometimes described as the "great American indoor sport", they are "[n]ot bound to choose that pattern which will best pay the Treasury; there is not even a patriotic duty to increase one's taxes." (Judge Learned Hand in Helvering v. Gregory, 69 F.2d 809 (2d Cir.1934) when that case was decided by the Second Circuit Court of Appeals prior to being appealed to the United States Supreme Court.) Because one of our basic freedoms permits taxpayers to take the initiative in arranging their affairs and reporting them for tax purposes (our self-assessment system) our concept of fairness to other taxpayers, to be enforced by the government, requires the policy that taxpayers be taxed on the basis of their having intended the consequences of the transactions they have undertaken subject to the power of the government to review them in the light of "substance over form."

BARNES MOTOR & PARTS COMPANY v. UNITED STATES

United States District Court, E. D. North Carolina, Wilson Division, 1970.
309 F.Supp. 298.

LARKINS, District Judge.   The issues in this action relate to the statutory limitations on the availability of Subchapter S (Title 26 U.S.C.A. §§ 1371 through 1377) elections to small business corporations, specifically, the one-class-of-stock and the affiliated-group requirements, and the applicability of the laches principle to the conduct of government agents.   The action was filed by the plaintiff on March 25, 1969, as a suit to recover Internal Revenue taxes paid for the years 1963 through 1966.   This Court has jurisdiction of the subject matter under Title 28 U.S.C.A. § 1346(a) (1).   The issues are before the Court upon the parties' cross motions for summary judgment filed with appropriate exhibits and affidavits pursuant to the provisions of Rule 56 of the Federal Rules of Civil Procedure.   This Court is of the opinion that the plaintiff is not entitled to any recovery for the reasons given in this opinion.

FINDINGS OF FACT

The plaintiff is a North Carolina corporation with its principal place of business in Wilson, North Carolina.   During all of the taxable years in question, the plaintiff was an accrual-basis taxpayer, filed its federal income tax returns in Greensboro with the District Director of Internal Revenue for the District of North Carolina and used a taxable year ending December 31.

The plaintiff was organized on February 16, 1925, under the name of Barnes Motor Company with an authorized capital of $50,000 consisting of 500 shares of capital stock with a par value of $100 per share.   On January 3, 1928, its Articles of Incorporation were amended to change the name of the corporation to Barnes Motor & Parts Company.   On January 2, 1941, the Articles of Incorporation were again amended to increase the authorized capital to $100,000 and to provide for 300 shares of $100 par value preferred stocks and 200 shares of $100 par value "Class A Non-voting Common Stock" in addition to the previously authorized 500 shares of $100 par value common stock. The corporate charter shows that the "Class A" common differs from the original voting common only as to the voting rights of the shareholders.   The plaintiff has never issued any of its authorized preferred stock.

Subsequent to January 2, 1941, the plaintiff issued the following certificates for 180 shares of its "Class A" common stock:

Certificate Number	Name of Shareholder	Number of Shares
16	R. E. Kirkland	50
17	R. E. Kirkland	50
18	R. E. Kirkland	20
21	R. E. Kirkland	20
19	K. M. Banks	20
20	Sarah N. Harrell	20

The certificates evidencing the shares came from the plaintiff's regular common stock book and differed from the voting common stock certificates in that the words "Class A" were written in ink on the faces of the certificates. On September 18, 1944, K. M. Banks sold his 20 shares to R. E. Kirkland. A new certificate issued upon the transfer of these 20 shares came from the plaintiff's common stock book and had the words "Class A" written on the certificate in ink.

The plaintiff alleges that since the transfer of Banks' shares to R. E. Kirkland in 1944, all 180 shares of the "Class A" stock have been treated as voting common stock for all purposes. The six certificates originally having the words "Class A" written on their faces have been cancelled, the first on December 16, 1952, two more in January, 1953, and the remaining three on October 28, 1964, and the stock certificates issued in their places were the plaintiff's regular common stock certificates without the "Class A" designations. It is the plaintiff's contention that even if shares of the "Class A" non-voting common stock were ever validly issued, such shares were converted to voting common stock in 1944 or shortly thereafter.

In 1955, Barnes Motor & Parts Company of Raleigh, Inc. (the Raleigh Corporation) was organized as a subsidiary of the plaintiff to carry on the activities formerly carried on by the Raleigh branch of the plaintiff. Upon the organization of the Raleigh Corporation, its manager purchased $12\frac{1}{2}\%$ of the stock, and the remaining $87\frac{1}{2}\%$ was purchased by the plaintiff. The plaintiff owned $87\frac{1}{2}\%$ of the Raleigh Corporation from July 1, 1955, until December 31, 1959. On that date the plaintiff acquired the remaining $12\frac{1}{2}\%$ of the outstanding stock. It held 100% of the stock from December 31, 1959, until September 29, 1961, at which time it transferred 60% of the outstanding stock in the Raleigh Corporation to its stockholders. It transferred the remaining 40% of the stock to that corporation's new manager on or about June 25, 1962. Therefore, since June 25, 1962, the stockholders of the plaintiff have owned 60% of the outstanding stock of the Raleigh Corporation and its manager has owned the remaining 40%.

Following the enactment of the Small Business Corporations Act in 1958, the plaintiff decided to file an election under Subchapter S of the Internal Revenue Code. Prior to filing such an election, the plaintiff and its stockholders conferred with their accountant, who advised them that the plaintiff could properly make the Subchapter S election. The plaintiff then made a timely election to be treated as a small business corporation beginning with the taxable year 1958.

On or about February 18, 1963, R. E. Kirkland, one of the plaintiff's stockholders, died. Thereafter, on or about March 18, 1963, within the time prescribed by the Federal Tax Regulations, the executor of the estate of R. E. Kirkland filed with the office of the District Director of Internal Revenue in Greensboro a "Statement of Consent to Election by New Shareholders," whereby he consented to the corporation's election to be treated as a small business corporation. The remaining stockholders did not file a consent to the election in

1963 because they believed that the election made by the plaintiff for 1958 and subsequent years, to which they had already consented, constituted a valid and proper election and that no further action was necessary.

In 1964, the plaintiff organized another subsidiary corporation, Barnes Motor & Parts Company of Smithfield, Inc. (the Smithfield Corporation). Upon incorporation, the manager of the new subsidiary purchased 100 shares of stock, and the plaintiff purchased 350 shares. The manager's employment was terminated after about 1½ years, and, at this point, it was determined that the Smithfield Corporation should be liquidated as of the end of the calendar year 1965. Therefore, pursuant to a plan of liquidation, the plaintiff purchased the manager's stock on October 6, 1965. The assets of the Smithfield Corporation were transferred to the plaintiff, and Articles of Dissolution of the Smithfield Corporation were filed as of December 31, 1965.

The plaintiff has filed an information return, Form 1120–S, each year since 1958, and the returns have been accepted by the Internal Revenue Service until an audit in 1967. The stockholders reported their respective pro rata portions of the taxable income of the plaintiff on their individual federal income tax returns for each of the years after 1958 and paid the appropriate income tax thereon.

After examining the plaintiff's federal income tax returns for the taxable years ended December 31, 1963, December 31, 1964, December 31, 1965, and December 31, 1966, the Commissioner of Internal Revenue determined that the plaintiff's election in 1958 to be treated as a small business corporation under Subchapter S had not been a valid election because of the plaintiff's failure to meet the statutory requirements and that consequently the plaintiff was not entitled to be treated as a small business corporation for any of the taxable years under examination. Therefore, on or about April 12, 1968, deficiencies were assessed against the plaintiff in the following amounts:

Year	Income Tax	Interest	Total
1963	$20,076.84	$4,910.85	$24,987.69
1964	17,663.50	3,260.73	20,924.23
1965	26,814.03	3,341.10	30,155.13
1966	26,850.26	1,734.60	28,584.86
	$91,404.63	$13,247.28	$104,651.91

The plaintiff paid the assessed deficiencies and the interest on or about April 22, 1968, and, on or about August 12, 1968, within two years after payment of the assessments, filed a timely claim for refund of the amounts paid. On November 27, 1968, the Commissioner of Internal Revenue notified the plaintiff that all of the claim for refund had been disallowed in full. As a result of the Commissioner's denial of the claim for a refund, this action was brought to recover the deficiencies and interest paid in April 1968.

CONCLUSIONS OF LAW

Subchapter S of the Internal Revenue Code (26 U.S.C.A. §§ 1371 through 1377) was passed by Congress in 1958 to enable individuals operating a small business to minimize the importance of tax considerations in choosing a form of business organization. The statute does this by permitting certain small corporations to avoid the corporate tax and elect to "pass through" their earnings or net operating losses to shareholders, who in turn report the earnings or losses on their individual returns.

To prevent complexities in attributing the corporate distributions to the various shareholders, Congress placed several limitations on the electing small business corporations, one of which is that a Subchapter S corporation must have only one class of stock.[1] This requirement was inserted in the statute because holders of preferred stock have certain preferences in distribution rights over holders of common stock, voting stock is worth more than non-voting stock, and the government, if forced to account for these value differences, would have a difficult time in allocating the proper proportion of earnings or losses to each individual shareholder. The Commissioner, adopting this reasoning in promulgating his Federal Tax Regulations, declared that treasury or unissued stock of a separate class would not disqualify a corporation but that the existence of outstanding shares not identical with respect to a number of rights, including voting rights, would prevent a corporation from being entitled to Subchapter S status.

The plaintiff's contention is that it had only one class of stock outstanding when it elected in 1958 to be taxed as a small business corporation under Subchapter S. The plaintiff points out that none of the authorized preferred stock was ever issued but does concede that the "Class A" non-voting common was issued in 1941 to give its Raleigh manager ownership of the corporation without any control. However, argues the plaintiff, in 1944 the "Class A" stock was transferred to the holders of the original common, and the record shows that since 1945 all outstanding shares of the "Class A" stock have been treated as voting common, that all of the shares did vote at all stockholders' meetings at which their owners were present in person or represented by proxy and that no distinction as to class was made in the corporate records after 1945. The plaintiff contends that even though some of the "Class A" certificates were still outstanding between 1958 and 1964, the certificates were not the thing owned but were only representative of the rights of the certificate-holders. Since the holders of these certificates actually had voting rights, then the "Class A" non-voting common should be treated as identical to the regular voting

---

1. Title 26 U.S.C.A. § 1371(a) states: * * * the term "small business corporation" means a domestic corporation which is not a member of an affiliated group (as defined in section 1504) and which does not—

(1) have more than 10 shareholders;

(2) have as a shareholder a person (other than an estate) who is not an individual;

(3) have a nonresident alien as a shareholder; and

(4) have more than one class of stock.

common and therefore the corporation should be presumed to have only one class of stock for purposes of Subchapter S.

As additional argument, the plaintiff contends that the "Class A" stock is *de facto* voting common because the corporation replaced all "Class A" shares canceled after 1958 with regular certificates that did not have the "Class A" designation on their faces. Although there was no technical cancellation, this was obviously the intent of the corporation and the shareholders, and its informal action at the expense of technical accuracy should not deprive the plaintiff of Subchapter S status. The plaintiff also attacks the Commissioner's regulation, which defines a second class of stock as one which differs in voting rights, on the grounds that it is not related to limiting complexities of distribution, the original reason for the one-class-of-stock requirement.

Despite the persuasiveness of the plaintiff's substance-over-form argument, this Court feels impelled to conclude that the statute should be strictly construed and that the existence of the "Class A" stock should preclude the plaintiff from electing to be taxed under Subchapter S. The plaintiff concedes that it did issue 180 shares of the "Class A" non-voting common stock in 1941 and that the last certificate representing those shares was not canceled until a corporate reorganization in 1967. Therefore, a second class of stock with a difference in voting rights did exist on the records at the time of the election in 1958. Although the statute itself does not define a second class of stock in terms of voting rights, the Treasury Regulation which does so is reinforced by the legislative history of the statute. Therefore, this Court must hold, simply on the basis of the language of the statute and the regulation, that the existence of an outstanding class of stock with a difference in voting rights will disqualify a corporation from being treated as a small business corporation under Subchapter S. Pollack v. Commissioner of Internal Revenue, 392 F.2d 409 (5th Cir., 1968).

The Court must also take exception to the plaintiff's *de facto* argument, that it changed the "Class A" stock to voting common but simply failed to change the certificates. If the plaintiff's failure had been simply a bookkeeping omission, its case would be much stronger. Here, however, until the corporate reorganization in 1967, the corporate charter authorized the issuance of only 500 shares of voting common stock; and yet, as of 1946, there were 760 shares outstanding. An amendment to the charter authorizing cancellation of the non-voting "Class A" shares was not made until 1967. If this Court accepted the plaintiff's argument that the "Class A" shares were actually voting common, it would not only violate the designations on the certificates but also the specific language of the plaintiff's charter.

The plaintiff's contention that the "Class A" shares were actually voted after 1945 is not demonstrated by the record. The minutes of the stockholders' meetings do show the number of outstanding shares and list the "Class A" shares as part of the outstanding stock. However, there is no breakdown on how or whether the particular blocks of shares were voted because all matters were apparently decided unanimously. To say that the "Class A" shares would have been considered voting shares in any dispute which may have arisen is mere speculation.

A second question raised by the contentions of the parties is whether the plaintiff fails to qualify for Subchapter S status because it was a member of an affiliated group. Section 1371(a) defines "affiliated group" in terms of the section 1504 definition which includes parent-subsidiary arrangements in which the parent owns 80% of the voting stock of the subsidiary. Again, the apparent reasoning behind the affiliated-group requirement, like the one-class-of-stock requirement is that Congress intended to limit the availability of Subchapter S to those corporations whose distributions to shareholders do not create difficult computations and who are conducting primarily a small and simple business operation.

The plaintiff's ownership of $87\frac{1}{2}\%$ of its Raleigh subsidiary at the time of its election in 1958 is undisputed. The plaintiff argues, however, that this Court should disregard the affiliated-group requirement in this case because the plaintiff eliminated this disability on September 29, 1961, when it transferred 60% of the subsidiary's stock to its shareholders, because it relied on the advice of its accountant and therefore made the election in good faith and because the government should not be permitted to question plaintiff's election after accepting its returns for nine years after the election and for six years after the disqualifying factor had disappeared. The defendant, again requesting a strict construction of the statute, suggests that the election was void from its inception since the plaintiff failed to meet the statutory requirements; and again the Court must agree.

Even if the Court were to overlook the disqualifying aspect of the 80% ownership at the time of the election because the defect was removed before the taxable years in question, the plaintiff again violated the requirements of the statute by owning more than 80% of its Smithfield subsidiary between October 6 and December 31, 1965, an interval which was during the taxable period in question. Although the ownership of the subsidiary was merely a temporary arrangement which was part of a plan of liquidation, the plaintiff carried out the plan apparently without consideration for the consequences it might have on the Subchapter S election. The Court therefore feels that such manipulation offers further grounds to support the finding that the plaintiff did not meet the statute's affiliated-group requirement.

The third and final issue in this action is whether the principle of laches should bar the government from challenging the plaintiff's 1958 election. The essence of the plaintiff's argument is that if the taxpayer met all the requirements for a properly electing small business corporation in the years under examination and made an election which was proper on its face during a year which is now barred by the statute of limitations, then the Commissioner of Internal Revenue should not now be permitted to look at the barred years to determine whether the election was properly made. The plaintiff shows by affidavit that the information necessary to discover the disqualifying characteristics was available to the government at the time of the election and that the government's failure to thoroughly investigate the election then should bar it from challenging the election now.

The plaintiff's argument is not acceptable. The form on which the 1958 election was made, No. 2553, entitled "Election by Small Business Corporation," does not disclose that the plaintiff owned $87\frac{1}{2}\%$ of its Raleigh subsidiary, nor does it disclose that the plaintiff issued a non-voting class of stock in 1941. Moreover, the information return, No. 1120–S, filed each year after 1958, also does not show the disqualifying features of the corporation. Therefore, the government had no notice until the audit in 1967 that the plaintiff was not entitled to be treated as a small business corporation under Subchapter S. In such a situation, where the plaintiff did not rely on the assertions of a particular agent but merely on the government's inaction, and where the facts constituting the disability were peculiarly within the knowledge of plaintiff's officers, stockholders and tax advisor, the law appears to be well-settled that the rights of the government are not affected by the laches or inaction of its agents and that the government is not now estopped from going back to question the plaintiff's 1958 election under Subchapter S. McComb v. Homeworker's Handicraft Cooperative et al., 176 F.2d 633 (4th Cir., 1949). * * *

On the basis of the foregoing and after a careful examination of the record and a due consideration of the contentions of the parties, this Court is of the opinion that the plaintiff did not meet the requirements of section 1371(a) and is therefore not entitled to be taxed as a small business corporation under Subchapter S. See Fulk & Needham, Inc. v. United States, 411 F.2d 1403 (4th Cir., 1969). Therefore, the plaintiff is entitled to no relief.

ORDER

Now therefore, in accordance with the foregoing, it is:

Ordered that the plaintiff's motion for summary judgment be, and the same hereby is, denied;

Further ordered that the defendant's motion for summary judgment be, and the same hereby is, allowed;

Further ordered that the Clerk shall serve copies of this opinion and order upon all counsel of record.

Let this order be entered forthwith.

BENDEROFF v. UNITED STATES

United States District Court, S. D. Iowa, Central Division, 1967.
270 F.Supp. 87.*

STEPHENSON, Chief Judge.   This action is brought by plaintiff taxpayers who are attempting to recover taxes, interest and penalties which were assessed against them for the calendar year 1959.   Jurisdiction exists under 28 U.S.C.A. § 1346(a) (1).

During the fiscal years ending March 31, 1959 and March 31, 1960, the plaintiff taxpayers were stockholders of V. C. Benderoff Company, a duly qualified subchapter "S" corporation.   The proportionate share of the income of V. C. Benderoff Company therefore must be included in computing the income of the individual shareholders for the calendar year 1959 in accordance with the statute set forth below.[1]   There are two basic issues involved in this action: (1) Was the distribution by V. C. Benderoff Company to its shareholders during May, 1959 taxable? (2) If the distribution was taxable, is the Internal Revenue Service barred by the applicable statute of limitations from assessing the tax against plaintiff taxpayers?

At the close of its fiscal year on March 31, 1959, V. C. Benderoff Company had earnings and profits of $48,688.29.   This amount was treated as income to the shareholders and their proportionate share was properly included as income on their income tax returns for the calendar year 1959.   During May 1959, the corporation made a distribution of $45,207.88 to its shareholders.   Plaintiff taxpayers urge that this was a distribution of earnings of the previous fiscal year and, as such, were not subject to another tax.   The government contends that unless the distribution exceeds the earnings of the corporation for the fiscal year ending March 31, 1960, the distribution is taxable to the stockholder for the calendar year during which it is made.   The statute

---

* This case was reversed on appeal. See explanatory note which follows the Opinion.

1. Title 26 U.S.C. § 1373, [as amended by Sec. 64(a), Technical Amendments Act of 1958, P.L. 85–866, 72 Stat. 1606] CORPORATION UNDISTRIBUTED TAXABLE INCOME TAXED TO SHAREHOLDERS.

(a) *General Rule.*—The undistributed taxable income of an electing small business corporation for any taxable year shall be included in the gross income of the shareholders of such corporation in the manner and to the extent set forth in this section.

(b) *Amount Included in Gross Income.*—Each person who is a shareholder of an electing small business corporation on the last day of a taxable year of such corporation shall include in his gross income, for his taxable year in which or with which the taxable year

of the corporation ends, the amount he would have received as a dividend, if on such last day there had been distributed pro rata to its shareholders by such corporation an amount equal to the corporation's undistributed taxable income for the corporation's taxable year. For purposes of this chapter, the amount so included shall be treated as an amount distributed as a dividend on the last day of the taxable year of the corporation.

(c) *Undistributed Taxable Income Defined.*—For purposes of this section, the term "undistributed taxable income" means taxable income (computed as provided in subsection (d)) minus the amount of money distributed as dividends during the taxable year, to the extent that any such amount is a distribution out of earnings and profits of the taxable year as specified in section 316(a) (2). (26 U.S.C. 1964 ed., Sec. 1373.) (Court's footnote 2) governing the question is 26 U.S.C. § 1373(b). A treasury regulation interpreting this statute provides as follows:

> (b) *Source of distribution.* Except as provided in paragraph (c) of this section, any actual distribution of money by an electing small business corporation to a shareholder which but for the operation of this section, would be a dividend out of accumulated earnings and profits shall be considered a distribution of previously taxed income to the extent of the shareholder's net share of previously taxed income immediately before the distribution. Thus, a distribution of property other than money or a distribution in exchange for stock, or a constructive distribution under section 1373(b), is never a distribution of previously taxed income. Since current earnings and profits are first applied to distributions of money which are not in exchange for stock (see paragraph (d) and (e) of § 1.373–1), a distribution of previously taxed income may occur only if during its taxable year the corporation makes such money distributions in excess of its earnings and profits for such taxable year. (26 C.F.R., Sec. 1.1375–4.)

It appears to the Court that the May distribution by the corporation would be nontaxable to the shareholders for the calendar year 1959 only to the extent that the distribution exceeded the earnings and profits of the corporation for the fiscal year ending March 31, 1960. Since the earnings and profits of the corporation for that fiscal year were $50,945.40 and the May 1959 distribution was only $45,207.88, the entire May distribution was taxable to the shareholders for the calendar year 1959. Although the plaintiff taxpayers could possibly have avoided the dilemma they now find themselves in if the corporate distribution had been made at another time,[2] the tax law places some weight and significance on form and the choice of one alternative rather than another for achieving a desired end is often critical and may be determinative of the tax effect of a certain transaction. In this instance, the choice of the taxpayer resulted in a corporate distribution which was taxable to the shareholders for the calendar year 1959.

Even though the May, 1959 corporate distribution was a taxable distribution, plaintiff taxpayers urge that Section 6501(e) (1) (A) (ii) of the Internal Revenue Code of 1954 barred the collection and assessment of the additional tax resulting from the classification of the distribution as a taxable one. The applicable portion of 26 U.S.C. § 6501 is set forth below:

> (a) *General Rule.*—Except as otherwise provided in this section, the amount of any tax imposed by this title shall be assessed

2. Congress amended this portion of the tax law by the Act of April 14, 1966 Pub.L. 89–389, 80 Stat. 111. This amendment provides that distributions made within two and one-half months of the end of a corporation's taxable year shall be considered a distribution of previously taxed income. Although plaintiff taxpayers herein could have elected under this amendment to have their May 1959 corporate distribution considered as a distribution of previously taxed income, such an election was not made because of the adverse tax consequences it would have had on other years. (Court's footnote 5.)

within 3 years after the return was filed (whether or not such return was filed on or after the date prescribed) or, if the tax is payable by stamp, within 3 years after such tax became due, and no proceeding in court without assessment for the collection of such tax shall be begun after the expiration of such period.

(b) Time Return Deemed Filed.—

(1) *Early return.*—For purposes of this section, a return of tax imposed by this title, except tax imposed by chapter 21 or 24, filed before the last day prescribed by law or by regulations promulgated pursuant to law for the filing thereof, shall be considered as filed on such last day.

*   *   *   *   *   *   *   *   *   *

(e) *Omission From Gross Income.*—Except as otherwise provided in subsection (c)—

(1) *Income taxes.*—In the case of any tax imposed by subtitle A—

(A) *General rule.*—If the taxpayer omits from gross income an amount properly includible therein which is in excess of 25 percent of the amount of gross income stated in the return, the tax may be assessed, or a proceeding in court for the collection of such tax may be begun without assessment, at any time within 6 years after the return was filed. For purposes of this subparagraph—

(i) In the case of a trade or business, the term "gross income" means the total of the amounts received or accrued from the sale of goods or services (if such amounts are required to be shown on the return) prior to diminution by the cost of such sales or services; and

(ii) In determining the amount omitted from gross income, there shall not be taken into account any amount which is omitted from gross income stated in the return if such amount is disclosed in the return, or in a statement attached to the return, in a manner adequate to apprise the Secretary or his delegate of the nature and amount of such item. (26 U.S.C. 1964 ed., Sec. 6501.)

The Internal Revenue Service did not attempt to impose additional assessments upon plaintiff taxpayers for the calendar year 1959 until April 1964. The assessments would thus be barred unless they fall within subsection (e) of the statute set forth above. Plaintiff taxpayers contend that the May, 1959 distribution may not be considered in determining whether an amount in excess of 25 per cent of the gross income stated in the return was improperly excluded from their returns. This contention is based upon the premise that information regarding the May, 1959 distribution was contained in the returns in such a manner so as to apprise adequately the Secretary of the Treasury or his delegate of the nature and amount of that item. Plaintiffs contend that the Balance Sheet attached to V. C. Benderoff Company's return for the fiscal year ending March 31, 1960 disclosed that a distribution had been made during the year since the beginning balance in the "Undistributed Income Taxable to Stockholders" account was $45,207.88 and the balance at the end of the year was $49,782.90 (the same amount as was reported as taxable income for that fiscal year). If no distribution had been made, the account would have contained an amount equivalent to the beginning balance plus the taxable income for the fiscal year. Plaintiff therefore concludes that the corporation's return adequately disclosed the distribution, that the six-year statute of limitations is inapplicable and that the three-year statute of limitations bars additional assessments against the plaintiff for the calendar year 1959. The Court disagrees.

Schedule K of V. C. Benderoff Company's return provides for the reporting of distributions of previously undistributed taxable income. This schedule contains a column for listing nondividend distributions. This is precisely what the plaintiffs contend was the nature of the May, 1959 distribution. However, the nondividend distributions column of schedule K of the corporations return does not list the May, 1959 distribution but merely contains dashes which seemingly indicate that no such distributions were made during the fiscal year ending March 31, 1959. Plaintiff taxpayers cannot expect the Internal Revenue Service to discover the omission through an examination of the corporate financial statements attached to the return. Neither the nature nor the amount of the May, 1959 distribution was adequately disclosed in the corporate return or in those of the plaintiff taxpayers, and, therefore the distribution may be considered in determining whether an amount in excess of 25 per cent of the gross income was excluded from the return. The assessments against the plaintiff taxpayers for the calendar year 1959 were properly made in that they were governed by the six-year rather than the three-year statute of limitations.

The foregoing shall constitute the Court's finding of fact and conclusions of law. Judgment will be entered in favor of the defendant at plaintiffs' cost.

[The *Benderoff* case was reversed on appeal by the U. S. Court of Appeals, Eighth Circuit (398 F.2d 132 (1968)) in an opinion written by Chief Judge Van Oosterhout. The taxpayers, on appeal, did not challenge the District Court's finding that the May 1959 distribution of $45,207.88 as well as the $48,688.29 earned by the corporation and "passed through" to them as of March 31, 1959 were both taxable in 1959. They abandoned this point and appealed only on the ground that the assessment of the deficiency when made in 1964 was barred by the general three-year statute of limitations. The government argued that the tax returns of the individual taxpayers understated their income by more than 25% and that this was not otherwise disclosed and that therefore the six-year statute should apply. But the Court of Appeals held that there was sufficient information attached to the return of the corporation to alert the government to the fact that the May distribution had been made and that therefore the three-year statute should apply. Because the assessment was admittedly made in the fourth year after the return was filed, the Court held that this was too late and therefore reversed the District Court.]

C. NOTE ON TAX PROCEDURES

The American system of Federal income taxation is a system of self-assessment; that is, the taxpayer files an income tax return (on a prescribed form) showing a summary of the transactions he has entered into in the twelve months which make up his fiscal period. This self-assessment system is a marvel to the rest of the world. In spite of the criticism that many Americans apparently prefer entertainment which honors lawlessness, when it comes to paying income taxes the great preponderance of American taxpayers are honest with their government. This is not to say that many of them do not give themselves the benefit of every doubt which is possible, since the primary activity of tax planners is to seek to apply "legitimate" means of tax savings. Nearly every business and every lawyer and accountant is bombarded daily with offers of books, brochures and pamphlets, nearly all of which are to be accompanied by periodic supplements, on the subject of taxes and how to live with less of them or even without them. Too often the authors of this printed material have had too little professional training or experience to write with authority on their chosen subject. Frequently their treatment of the subject under discussion is superficial for the reason that no branch of the law is a specialty all of its own and the concepts and doctrines of every branch of the law cut across tax law, as well as every other branch of the law.

While ignorance, poor advice and ineptitude of both the taxpayer and his advisors lead to many tax disputes, a genuine difference of opinion as to the propriety of, or the interpretation of, a particular provision of the Internal Revenue Code also gives rise to tax disputes. For example, an honest difference of opinion can (and frequently) does exist in reference to the useful life of a capital asset (a machine tool, for example) in determining the depreciation allowance which is to be used by the taxpayer. All of the cases dealt with in this Chapter are cases where an honest dispute did exist, and in a few of them one must assume either ignorance or ineptitude also led to the dispute.

Tax disputes start with an audit of an income tax return prepared by an officer of the Internal Revenue Service, called a Revenue Agent. Many business tax returns will be selected for audit, particularly those of large corporations. Many small business enterprises may not have their income tax returns audited for many years. There is a basis for selection which changes from time to time but once a return has been selected for audit the Revenue Agent will make an initial study of the return in his office and schedule an appointment with the taxpayer, or if the return shows it was prepared by an accountant or an attorney, the Revenue Agent will contact that person. As soon as an appointment can be made the Revenue Agent will meet with the taxpayer and his representatives, usually at the principal office of the business, to go over the details of the return. Many items making up the total figures in the return will be reviewed and frequently these will be adjusted by agreement between the Revenue Agent and the taxpayer or his representative. It is only when such an agreement cannot be made that a tax dispute commences.

If there are any issues which would cause a substantial change in the tax from the amount shown on the return, the Revenue Agent will consider the matter in his office and discuss the matter with his supervisors, and if the Internal Revenue Service desires to pursue the matter an "RAR" (Revenue Agent's Report) will be sent to the taxpayer with the proposed adjustments described briefly, along with a sheet showing the recalculation of the taxes as proposed by the Internal Revenue Service. The taxpayer may agree at that point and if so, a form will be supplied to him for this purpose. If he disagrees, he will be notified that he has 30 days in which to "Protest" the findings of the Revenue Agent in writing. (This is called "the 30 day letter," taking its name from the period of time in which the taxpayer is given to respond.)

If the taxpayer does protest the Revenue Agent's findings, his protest will be reviewed in the District Director's Office and some attempt will be made to arrive at a settlement of the disputed issues again. If they are not settled, and the taxpayer has requested a conference with the Appellate Division of the Regional Commissioner's Office, in a short time (30 days or longer depending on how busy the particular staff of the Appellate Division is at the time) the taxpayer will receive a letter requesting that a conference be scheduled in his office. The Internal Revenue Service is organized into seven Regions and each region is headed by a Regional Commissioner. In addition to the Appellate Division, his staff includes a group of attorneys who are called Regional Counsel who will conduct the litigation if the matter continues beyond the level of the Appellate Division.

The staff of the Appellate Division is composed of skilled career officers. These persons are highly trained and dedicated to the excellent performance of their jobs. They are skilled negotiators and almost without exception are polite and in turn are responsive to courteous treatment. When a conference is held they will know their case thoroughly and will have reviewed it independently with an idea of a fair settlement of the case. Their job is to negotiate settlements, being fair both to the government and to the taxpayer.

If a taxpayer cannot reach a settlement at the level of the Appellate Division then a Statutory Notice of Deficiency in income taxes will be issued to the taxpayer. If nothing further is done within the next 90 days, the assessment becomes final and the Internal Revenue Service through another Division will proceed to collect the tax. If the taxpayer disputes the findings set forth in the notice, then he has 90 days from the date of the notice to do either of two things: (a) file a Petition with the United States Tax Court in Washington, D. C. or (b) pay the tax when he receives a bill for it and later file a claim for a refund with a view of litigating the claim for a refund in the District Court of the United States in the District in which he resides.

The advantage to the taxpayer of proceeding in the United States Tax Court is that he does not have to pay the tax before litigating the question. On the other hand, interest charges continue to run on the amount of tax which is finally determined to be due so that a taxpayer who desires to avoid the interest charge may pay the tax and then sue for a refund. His payment stops the running of interest chargeable to him, and if he is later successful on the claim for a refund he will receive 6% interest on the amount of money paid to the government during the period of time between payment and the refund. Also, some issues are better received by the District Courts than by the Tax Court, or vice versa, so that a taxpayer may choose his forum depending upon where he or his advisors are of the opinion that the case will be best received.

If the taxpayer proceeds in the Tax Court the matter is conducted much like any other law suit except that a judge of the Tax Court sits alone (that is, without a jury) and hears the evidence. The usual practice in the Tax Court is for the taxpayer and the Internal Revenue Service to get together beforehand and to arrive at an agreement on the facts in the case in order to eliminate the hearing in the Tax Court, or at least to shorten it substantially. The judges of the Tax Court insist that this be done. The case is then submitted to the judges of the Tax Court and generally the judge who has heard the case will write the decision in the matter.

If the taxpayer and his advisors or the Internal Revenue Service are of the opinion that the decision of the United States Tax Court is incorrect as a matter of law then either party may appeal the case to the United States Circuit Court of Appeals for the Circuit in which the taxpayer resides. As in all appellate practice, no issues of fact may be retried; only issues of law may be contested. A fair number of cases upon appeal to a Court of Appeals from the Tax Court are reversed. Sometimes, two different Circuit Courts of Appeal will reach opposite results on the same legal issue which has arisen in different cases, and then this provides the most common basis for obtaining a writ of certiorari from the Supreme Court of the United States to have that Court consider the legal issues.

Most trials in the United States District Courts are trials in which the parties have waived a trial by jury. This is also true of tax cases. If a suit for a refund is decided by the District Court in a manner in which either of the parties believes to be wrong, then an appeal to the Circuit Court of Appeals may be taken in the same manner as any other case. Also, a taxpayer who has paid the tax in dispute, and filed a claim for a refund, may sue for the refund in the United States Court of Claims which sits only in Washington, D. C. If the parties do not submit a case to the Court of Claims in which all the facts are agreed (contesting only the legal issues) then a Commissioner of the Court of Claims will hear the testimony of the parties, and write a report which will form the basis of deciding the issues of fact so that the Court of Claims need consider only the disputed legal issues. Again either party may seek a writ of certiorari from the Supreme Court.

While the government and the taxpayer have several forums in which tax disputes may be litigated most of the litigation occurs in the United States Tax Court. But most tax disputes are not litigated; they are settled at the level of the District Director's Office. Most of those which are not settled in this manner are settled at the Appellate Division. Even after cases are docketed in the Tax Court they frequently will be settled before going to trial. Litigation of this kind is highly technical and rarely, if ever, are there any dramatic or emotional incidents occurring in these hearings such as occur in common law courts, particularly in the trial of criminal cases.

QUESTIONS

1. If all businesses were state-owned, would there need to be any tax laws as such? Or would all income from the business system be state revenue? Would there be any merit in having any form of local taxation? Why are municipally owned businesses such as water systems exempt from taxation? Are the customers of those municipally-owned businesses being subsidized by privately owned businesses or the customers of privately owned businesses? If the national government owned all business would it be necessary to have a system of laws which would require each business unit to provide a portion of its revenues to the national treasury? Whether or not it had any net income?

2. Since the manner of determining income is subject to wide interpretation, should the national government require the use of a uniform system of accounting, at least for tax purposes? How could this be designed if we were to adhere to the fundamental principle of "substance over form?" Would it be simpler to levy a "value added" tax, that is a tax on the value added to a product at each level in the production cycle? Is this anything more than a national sales tax to be paid by each business, the cost of which would be added to its product? Would a national sales tax be a fairer means of raising national revenue than a tax on incomes? Why?

3. Is "substance over form" a fair doctrine? Is it fair if it is applied only in favor of the government? Should a taxpayer be permitted to apply "substance over form" in our system of self assessment of taxes? Why not let him use hindsight if the government has the equal opportunity? Is this necessary in a democratic system which relies on freedom of choice, and the use of initiative by the individual?

4. Should the net earnings of every corporation be taxed to the shareholders whether or not paid out as dividends? Whether or not the corporation pays any income taxes? Should every corporation, regardless of its size, be permitted to make the election under Subchapter S? Should this be subject to majority control in each corpo-

ration, thus binding the nonelecting shareholders to the choice of the majority? Why?

5. Should any distinction in taxation be made between capital gains and ordinary income? Why tax only one-half of the long term gain? Could some averaging system be developed whereby the gain would be spread over the period of time that the stockholder held the stock, and require him to recompute his taxes for the prior years and pay them in the year in which the gain is realized? (This system is used in part in several other situations, particularly relating to trusts where the income has been accumulated for several years.) Or, should a taxpayer be permitted or required to adjust his income each year by the increase or decrease in the value of his capital whether or not realized? Is failing to tax one-half of long term capital gains fair to the wage-earner who has one hundred percent of his income taxable to him? If capital gains were to be taxed in full what would happen to the free transferability of property in our system of private ownership of property?

Suggested Reference Sources

Texts and Treatises

Bittker & Eustis, *Federal Income Taxation of Corporations and Shareholders.* Federal Tax Press, New York City.

Mertens, *Law of Federal Income Taxation.* Callaghan & Company, Mundelein, Illinois.

Rabkin & Johnson, *Federal Income, Gift and Estate Taxation.* Matthew Bender & Company, Albany, N. Y.

Loose-Leaf Services

Commerce Clearing House, Federal Tax Reports, Chicago, Illinois

Prentice Hall, Federal Taxes, Englewood Heights, N. J.

Periodicals

Journal of Taxation, N. Y.

Tax Law Review, New York University School of Law

Topic Headings in the Index to Legal Periodicals

Taxation

Income Taxes

Chapter IV

STOCKHOLDER AGREEMENTS AND INTERNAL CONTROLS

A. INTRODUCTORY NOTE

When a group of people assemble to conduct a business enterprise experience has shown that it is necessary to have some person or a committee to provide leadership and direction to the enterprise. This is true even in a two-man partnership where one can normally expect one of the partners to exert more direction over the enterprise than the other. In a corporation this is presumably done by the board of directors, yet in practice the board is frequently dominated by a small group (sometimes formalized and given the title of "Executive Committee"), particularly where the board consists of more than five to seven directors. Or, as frequently happens in close corporations the founder or principal stockholder will dominate the entire enterprise and may consult or meet with the directors only infrequently. But we have also learned by experience that large or small investors in the enterprise who are not active in the management must have their rights protected.

In a legal system where the state owns all business enterprises and there are no minority shareholders, no internal controls are necessary. This is also true in the United States where there are many publicly owned business enterprises such as the Tennessee Vally Authority, the Port of New York Authority, the Pennsylvania Turnpike Commission, innumerable municipally owned water companies, etc. While legislation is frequently designed to provide some protection of the public interest in the investment which it has made in these enterprises, this is usually accomplished by statutes particularly relating to the individual enterprise itself or as to classes of similarly publicly owned enterprises. But there are no minority stockholders whose rights can be impinged upon by management and thus this kind of legal problem of a business enterprise does not exist as to them. The problems discussed in this Chapter arise only in a system where there is private ownership, divided into shares of stock, in a business enterprise, a situation which occurs in those societies we think of as being democratic.

The system of internal controls that we have evolved is patterned after our political system of representative government. The stockholders elect a policy making body, the board of directors, which is charged with the responsibility of operating the business for the benefit of the stockholders. The board of directors in turn elects a group of officers who are charged with the execution of the policies

110

adopted by the directors and the day to day management of the business. In many corporations all the principal officers will also be members of the board of directors; in close corporations the officers, directors, and shareholders may be identical with the possible exception that a lawyer may serve as a director without being an officer or shareholder. In large publicly owned corporations typically two or three principal officers serve on the board, and the rest of the directors come from other business enterprises. At least in theory this is the way it is designed.

Insofar as considering the rights of minority shareholders is concerned nearly every close corporation operates as though it were no corporation at all. And why not? If the stockholders, directors, and officers are all the same people there are no minority stockholders for them to account to for their actions in managing the business. An annual ritual is performed by the lawyer for the corporation who will draw minutes showing that the directors and officers have been elected and at some convenient time either a waiver of notice of holding the meeting or a unanimous consent to the action taken will be appended to the minutes and all statutory requirements will have been satisfied. This is not to say that all goes peacefully in close corporations; many complaints are made, sometimes ending in litigation, by one stockholder out of a total of three against the other two. The stockholders in closely held corporations also have problems among themselves relating to the transfer (and sometimes voting) of their stock which do not exist in the publicly held corporations; there is no market for their stock and upon their withdrawal from the business enterprise or their death some means of providing a market for their stock is generally necessary. These problems are dealt with below.

In the publicly held corporation where the very existence of large numbers of stockholders makes it impossible to have a consensus on all matters, or to assemble a voting trust agreement of a majority of shares, some means of protecting the interests of the minority stockholder is necessary. Cumulative voting, referred to in Chapter II above, is sometimes thought of as a part of the answer to this problem because it theoretically makes it possible for minority representation on the board of directors, but it is hardly effective. Assume a board of seventeen directors of a large corporation; how could one possibly assemble proxies for one-seventeenth of the outstanding stock in order to assure the election of one director out of seventeen? Further, in those corporations subject to the statutory requirements of cumulative voting, one does not notice that the rights of minority shareholders are dealt with any better than in those corporations which are not subject to the requirement. Also, the quality of directors does not seem to vary in any manner between those business enterprises which have been incorporated in states which require cumulative voting and those which do not.

Thus the stockholder's derivative suit is the method we have developed for the protection of minority interests. In a democratic society this is done not by a governmental agency but by individuals seeking to protect and enforce their rights as well as the rights of other shareholders. The government does not enter into this process in any manner except to provide courts as the forum for the adjudication of these disputes. The Securities and Exchange Commission does not enter into these suits, although under the provisions of Section 14 of the Securities Exchange Act of 1934, 15 U.S.C.A. § 78n, the Commission does supervise the proxy material which is sent to shareholders by the management of a company, but this is the performance of its obligations under the general policy of the Federal Securities Acts which require full and fair disclosure by a company to its investors. Also, in a very limited manner the Securities and Exchange Commission will, under the provisions of the Investment Company Act of 1940, 15 U.S.C.A. § 80a–1, et seq., prevent overreaching by a management company in entering into an investment advisory contract with the nearly always captive mutual fund which it manages. But the rights of minority stockholders if protected at all are protected by law suits brought against the directors and officers of a corporation for their mismanagement of, or sometimes for their fraudulent dealing with, the corporation.

Two cases reported below Smith v. Brown Borhek Co., 414 Pa. 325, 200 A.2d 398 (1964), and Selheimer v. Manganese Corporation of America, 423 Pa. 563, 224 A.2d 634 (1966), illustrate the vagaries of the law in this regard. Directors contemplating their duties and minority stockholders attempting to enforce their rights cannot be helped much by either of these cases which are typical of many jurisdictions. (Also see the cases under Chapter VI below.)

If a minority stockholder suit is successful, the judgment of the court will frequently require the directors jointly and severally to pay to the corporation the loss which it has been demonstrated the corporation has suffered as a consequence of their mismanagement. Since this can run into very substantial sums of money, undoubtedly frequently in excess of the individual resources of many of the directors, and because even the successful defense of a minority stockholder's suit can be tremendously expensive, two techniques have been developed in recent times. The corporation laws of a number of states, including Delaware (General Corporation Law, 8 Del.Code § 145), now permit the by-laws of a corporation to provide for the indemnification of directors and officers for any expenses which they incur in the successful defense of the suit. The case of Merritt-Chapman & Scott Corporation v. Wolfson et al., 264 A.2d 358 (Del.Super. 1970), reported below, deals with this problem. Also, directors and officers may be similarly indemnified even though the suit has been lost if by an independent evaluation they were found to have exercised only poor business judgment but not actual fraud. The second technique is the purchase of officer's and director's liability insurance from one of a small number of casualty insurance companies which have just begun to underwrite this kind of insurance. The insurance policy generally provides that the insurance company will defend the claim, that the first part of the loss, for example, $20,000, shall be borne by the individual officers and directors, and that the insurance company will pay a substantial part of the excess (for example 95%), all in exchange for a very substantial premium. The size of the premium will vary with the size and activity of the corporation. Premiums of $100,000 per year or more are not uncommon.

B.   MINORITY STOCKHOLDER'S SUITS

SMITH v. BROWN–BORHEK COMPANY

Supreme Court of Pennsylvania, 1964.
414 Pa. 325, 200 A.2d 398.

BELL, Chief Justice. Plaintiff owns 516 out of a total of 8,000 shares of stock (outstanding) in the Brown-Borhek Company. He brought this stockholder's derivative suit on October 23, 1962, to recover for the corporation $605,507.00, the amount of the loss allegedly resulting from negligent mismanagement by the individual defendants, who are, or were at the relevant times, officers and directors. The defendants filed an answer denying plaintiff's material allegations and set up new matter alleging ratification of the acts in issue. Plaintiff filed a reply to the new matter in which he admitted that the stockholders ratified defendants' challenged actions, but denied the legal effect of this ratification and the legality of many of the votes which were cast for ratification. The Court of Common Pleas granted defendants' motion for judgment on the pleadings and this appeal followed.

The transactions complained of are a series of sales on credit by Brown-Borhek Company to a large customer, Raydel Homes Corp., throughout 1960 and 1961, and an eventual compromise of the latter's indebtedness in 1962. In 1960 Brown-Borhek's sales to Raydel totaled $550,562, or 37% of all sales. On December 31, 1960, Brown-Borhek carried an account receivable from Raydel of $262,010, which amounted to 60% of Brown-Borhek's receivables and 29% of all its assets. In 1961, Brown-Borhek's sales to Raydel amounted to approximately $1,050,290, 50% of all sales. On December 31, 1961, Raydel's account receivable with Brown-Borhek was $653,994.00; this represented 80% of its receivables and 63% of all its assets.

Raydel's indebtedness of $605,507 owing to Brown-Borhek as of November 30, 1961, was compromised on February 7, 1962, by an agreement under which Brown-Borhek received $363,300 worth of Raydel 5% noncumulative preferred stock with a par value of $10.00 a share and a promissory note for $242,207, with interest at 6% payable December 31, 1962. In defendants' new matter, they aver that this transaction was *part* of a composition by Raydel with its major creditors and that in addition Raydel made a cash payment to Brown-Borhek of $50,000. This cash payment was admitted by plaintiff in his reply. Brown-Borhek's President stated at the annual stockholders' meeting that Raydel is presently in bankruptcy, and that nothing of value has been realized as yet from the preferred stock or from the promissory note.

Plaintiff does not aver fraud nor personal profit by the defendants but alleges that the above transactions occurred *when* the individual defendants knew or should have known (a) that Raydel's liabilities greatly exceeded its assets and (b) that it was unable to meet its current obligations, and (c) that defendants had no reasonable expectation that the indebtedness would be paid. Furthermore, plaintiff alleges that the Raydel stock and promissory note were worthless at the time of receipt. All of these allegations were specifically or substantially denied by defendants, who suffered far greater financial losses from this Raydel account than did the plaintiff. Both sides agree that the defendants set credit limits on sales to Raydel which they subsequently did not adhere to, and that Raydel's receivables were carried on the average for a longer period than those of other customers. Finally, plaintiff alleges that during the last half of 1961 the President of Brown-Borhek spent his full time campaigning for the office of Mayor of Bethlehem and that its Vice President was similarly engaged in the management of the United Gas Improvement Company. Defendants aver that these outside activities did not prevent these officers from attending to their respective duties and particularly to this Raydel account and furthermore that the vice presidency had always been only a part time job. Defendants admitted that the directors failed to remove these officers, but denied that this failure was due to negligence on their part.

Defendants, in addition to a denial of plaintiff's importantly relevant material averments, set up new matter, viz., ratification by the stockholders of Brown-Borhek at their annual meeting on April 10 1963. This ratification was made by and pursuant to the following resolution:

"WHEREAS, in accordance with the notice of this meeting the chairman has reviewed the handling of the Raydel account and the questions concerning it raised in a suit by Leland E. Smith, NOW THEREFORE

"BE IT RESOLVED that the actions of the officers and directors in connection with the Raydel account be and hereby are ratified and confirmed and made the actions of this Corporation."

This resolution was carried by a vote of 6,693 to 405. Plaintiff's shares were not voted, but counsel for plaintiff was present at this stockholders' meeting.

The lower Court gave judgment for the defendants on the basis of this ratification. Plaintiff contends (1) that the aforesaid transactions could not be ratified under the law and (2) that even if ratification were permitted by law, (a) the transactions could not be ratified by less than all of the Brown-Borhek stockholders and (b) that the vote itself was legally defective because defendants voted their own shares and the proxies of other stockholders in favor of the resolution. We find no merit in any of these contentions.

The rule regarding judgment on the pleadings is well settled.

In Poole v. Great American Insurance Co., 407 Pa. 652, the Court, quoting from Ross v. Metropolitan Life Insurance Co., 403 Pa. 135, said: " 'A motion for judgment on the pleadings, like preliminary objections, is the equivalent of the old statutory demurrer and admits all facts which are well pleaded [but not the pleader's conclusions or averments of law.]   *   *   *   Such a motion should be granted and judgment should be entered only in a case which is clear and free from doubt [cases supra.]' "   *   *   *

We must therefore assume that defendants were aware of Raydel's precarious financial condition and took a business risk which turned out disastrously for all the stockholders of Brown-Borhek Company.

I.   *Could the Actions of Defendants be Ratified?*

In Chambers v. Beaver-Advance Corp., 392 Pa. 481, the Court said:

"The general rule is well established that stockholders can ratify any action of the Board of Directors [or officers] which they themselves could have lawfully authorized. Russell v. Henry C. Patterson Co., 232 Pa. 113.   *   *   *   This general rule is 'subject, however, to the limitation   *   *   *   "the majority stockholder may not, as against the corporation and minority stockholder, dissipate or waste its funds, or fraudulently dispose of them in any way, either by ratifying the action of the board of directors in voting themselves illegal salaries or by any other [similar] act." ' : Lowman v. Harvey R. Pierce Co., 276 Pa. 382, 386."   *   *   *

We repeat; nowhere in his complaint does the plaintiff allege that there has been fraud, self-dealing, personal profit or intentional dissipation or waste of corporate funds. In the last analysis plaintiff bases his case on the alleged failure of the officers and directors to devote their full time to the management of the business and particularly to a prudent consideration of the Raydel account and failure to exercise "that diligence, care and skill which ordinarily prudent men would exercise under similar circumstances in their personal business affairs". This prudent man rule is the standard set forth in the Business Corporation Law of May 5, 1933, P.L. 364, Article 4, Section 408, 15 P.S. § 2852–408.

Plaintiff in his oral argument before this Court repeatedly emphasized that the alleged mismanagement by defendants consisted of *their negligent failure to exercise their duties*, and not of affirmative negligence or the deliberate exercise of bad judgment or intentional wrongdoing. We believe that plaintiff portrays defendants' alleged failure to act as he would have had them do, as a failure to exercise wise business judgment in the light of the disastrous business transaction from which they suffered far greater losses than he.   The meaning and application of the "prudent man rule" (a) in the field of a testamentary or inter vivos trust, containing relatively few securities and (b) in the business or banking world are very different.   For example, in the banking business bad loans or sour investments or unsuccessful business transactions are part and parcel of that business and are charged off every year, either voluntarily or on directions from the Pennsylvania Department of Banking or from the Comptroller of the Currency or the Federal Reserve Board or the Federal Deposit Insurance Corporation.   In the business world of profit and loss, which is often popularly described as the profit system, it is too often forgotten that all businesses do not flourish, nearly every business has some losses and some bad accounts, and many insolvencies and bankruptcies frequently occur even in these prosperous times.   If the test of negligence which is applicable in the field of torts or in the Estate field were similarly applicable in the business or banking field, it would *realistically* be very difficult if not almost impossible to secure the services of *able and experienced* corporate directors.   Such persons would rarely ever accept a directorship if they could be held liable for every "bad" account or every mistake of judgment.   From an early date this Court has consistently and realistically recognized the danger of subjecting corporate directors to liability whenever any of the transactions of the company did not meet with success.   *   *   *

As Justice Linn pertinently observed in Hunt v. Aufderheide, 330 Pa. 362:

"*   *   *   Most all business   *   *   *   involves speculative elements.   The fiduciary character of the directors' relation to the corporation and the measure of their responsibility are quite different from those of a trustee under a will or a deed; such a trustee must preserve the principal for the benefit of remaindermen, and at the same time, within the restricted field of investment   *   *   *,   obtain income for parties presently entitled.   But the assets of a business corporation are held in a lighter grasp; shares of stock are taken with notice that the assets shall be employed in making a profit, and that *it is customary to take business risks.*"

Furthermore, plaintiff's allegation of complete inactivity and inattention on the part of defendants is belied by his own pleadings.   It is clear that defendants gave considerable effort to preserving Raydel as a functioning business enterprise, hopeful of its success.   In extending credit and in further extensions of credit they had to balance (a) the outlet for their merchandise and (b) the opportunity for repayment in full, against (c) a very substantial reduction of their market and (d) a fractional payment of their claim out of insolvency or the wreck of bankruptcy.   We make this observation not to condone or approve any of the defendants' acts but in support of a legitimate inference that they were indeed managing, as opposed to ignoring, the affairs of their corporation or the Raydel account.

Plaintiff-appellant further contends that these transactions could not legally be ratified, as in fact they were, after this suit challenging their legality had been commenced. We find no merit in this contention. In Chambers v. Beaver-Advance Corporation, 392 Pa. 481, we noted (in a footnote on page 490) that in Hornsby v. Lohmeyer, 364 Pa. 271, a ratification after suit was brought was held effective. In that case, the Court pertinently said:

"Courts are reluctant to interfere in the internal management of a corporation, since *that is a matter for the discretion and judgment of the directors and stockholders, unless a minority stockholder's rights are jeopardized or injured by fraud or waste of company assets, or an overreaching, actual or legal* [citing numerous cases]." Prompt ratification after suit brought provides a salutary method for the resolving of differences within the corporation without the expense, delay and corporate paralysis that often result from a protracted derivative suit. Accord, Fletcher on Corporations, Volume 2, Chapter 11, Section 766, pages 1113–1114; Putnam v. Juvenile Shoe Corporation, 307 Mo. 74; Kerbs v. California Eastern Airways, Inc., 33 Del.Ch. 69, 90 A.2d 652.

In the Kerbs case, the Supreme Court of Delaware recently held that ratification, otherwise unobjectionable, is not invalid even *after trial* and while appeal is pending.

It is clear that defendants' aforesaid actions as directors and officers of Brown-Borhek Company could be legally ratified, even after suit had been brought.

II. *Were the Challenged Actions of the Directors and Officers Legally Ratified?*

Plaintiff attacks (a) the right of the directors to vote their own stock and (b) their right to vote proxy stock and (c) the adequacy of the proxy statement for the Annual Meeting of Brown-Borhek Company at which the Resolution of Ratification was carried. We shall consider these related questions together.

It is well settled that directors acting for themselves as stockholders are entitled to vote their stock in their own self interest and for their own benefit so long as there is no fraud, overreaching or attempt to intentionally dissipate the corporation's assets. Chambers v. Beaver-Advance Corp., 392 Pa., supra, page 488 and ten cases cited therein.
* * *

Plaintiff in his reply to defendants' answer raised a further issue, namely, that two of the interested defendants held the proxies of "a substantial majority of the stockholders," and that as interested parties these defendants could not vote the proxies in favor of the exonerating ratification resolution.

The vote of a proxy is binding on the stockholder who gives it, provided it is not exercised in bad faith. Lowman v. Harvey R. Pierce, 276 Pa. 382; Fletcher on Corporations, Vol. 5, § 2060, pp. 232–3. Fletcher thus aptly states the law: "As a rule where a proxy is duly constituted, and the power to vote thereby conferred is unlimited, a vote by the proxy binds the stockholder to the same extent as if cast by the stockholder in person, and this is generally held to be true even though the power conferred is exercised against the interest of the corporation, or of the stockholder, unless the vote was the result of fraud or collusion by the proxy and others against the giver of it, or the vote is so contrary to the stockholder's interest as to show that the proxy must have acted in bad faith."

In the instant case the stockholders were fairly and fully informed that, because of Smith's pending suit, the actions of the officers and directors in connection with the Raydel Account were to come before the annual meeting for consideration and approval. There was no fraud or concealment.

The notice of the Annual Meeting included the following paragraph among the matters to be considered:

"2. To review in detail the manner in which the officers and directors of the Company handled the account of Raydel Homes Corporation and its predecessor companies (which matter is the subject of a stockholders' suit filed in the Court of Common Pleas of Lehigh County, Pennsylvania, by Leland E. Smith), and to entertain any resolutions which might be offered concerning this matter."

The proxy did not contain—as required by the rules of the Securities & Exchange Commission with reference to securities listed on the Exchange—a provision permitting or directing the proxy to vote *for or against* management's conduct of the Raydel matters. This was not necessary, since the stockholders were on notice that this question and an appropriate resolution would be presented at the meeting.

At the meeting itself, the President made an extended statement of all the transactions involving Raydel and management's reasons therefor. This was made a part of the record by defendants' answer, and in important matters, relevant herein, was not denied in plaintiff's reply. Even if we do not accept at face value every statement and explanation made by the President and contained in defendants' answer, it is clear that a full disclosure was made to the stockholders. Plaintiff complains in essence and in effect that the President presented the facts in a light favorable to management and very unfavorable to plaintiff's theory of this case.

If, as here, the directors could properly vote their own stock in favor of ratification and exoneration, they similarly could properly vote the stock of other shareholders who before they signed a proxy were fairly informed of the issues which were to be considered and voted upon.

Moreover, if the 3,858 shares held in trust for certain individual defendants were not entitled to vote and if the 867 shares which the officers and directors own individually are subtracted from the vote in favor of the resolution, the resolution still carried by 1,968 to 405.

We find no merit in any of plaintiff's contentions.

Judgment affirmed.

COHEN, J., files a dissenting opinion; EAGEN, J., concurs in the result; ROBERTS, J., files a concurring opinion.

JONES, J., absent.

ROBERTS, Justice (concurring). I concur with the majority in affirming the judgment of the court below. However, since the majority find no impropriety—by way of negligence or otherwise—in the conduct or actions of the board of directors, I see no reason or need, on this record and under the circumstances recited in the majority opinion, to consider or rule on the question of ratification by the shareholders. It is an issue not necessary to the proper disposition of the case.

COHEN, Justice (dissenting).

The majority agrees that the general rule which permits shareholder's ratification is subject to the limitation that:

" '* * * *the majority stockholder may not*, as against the corporation and minority stockholder, dissipate or waste its funds, or fraudulently dispose of them in any way, either by ratifying the action of the board of directors * * * or by any other [similar] act.' Lowman v. Harvey R. Pierce Co., 276 Pa. 382, 120 A. 404." (Emphasis supplied).

The Court of Chancery of the State of Delaware, a sophisticated jurisdiction in the determination of corporate issues, has held that:

> "Plaintiffs correctly state the well-settled rule to be that a waste of corporate assets is incapable of ratification without unanimous stockholder consent." Saxe v. Brady, 184 A. 2d 602 (1962).

Fletcher Cyclopedia Corporations comments that "ratification does not relieve the directors from the legal consequences of their alleged wrongful acts." Vol. 2, Ch. 11, § 764 (Revised Volume 1954).

The Federal Court of Appeals for the Second Circuit has gone so far as to say that a shareholder's vote cannot prevent the institution of a derivative suit or annul one once it has been brought. Gottesman v. General Motors Corporation, 268 F.2d 194, 197 (2d Cir. 1959).

Here the majority brushes aside plaintiff's complaint as portraying "defendants' alleged failure to act as [plaintiff] would have had them do, as a failure to exercise wise business judgment." By this statement the majority finds the conduct, which by defendants' own admission constituted negligence and mismanagement, innocuous. Further, the majority holds that plaintiff does not allege any intentional dissipation or waste of corporate funds. I do not so read the complaint. The complaint alleges that the officers and directors of the defendant corporation did not manage the corporation as required by the Act of May 5, 1933, P.L. 364, Art. 4, § 401, 15 P.S. § 2852–401, as amended. Plaintiff complains that defendants did not exercise any business judgment, good or bad; that there was no action taken by the board of directors or officers, but a complete abdication of their obligation to manage and supervise the corporate affairs. The complaint clearly alleges a failure to act, a non-feasance on the part of the directors, and a resulting loss, waste and dissipation of corporate assets. I would consider these allegations, together with the loss of $650,000, representing 63% of the corporate assets, to be clearly indicative of waste of an aggravated nature.

The majority's determination severely erodes the policy of Section 408 of the Business Corporation Law, 15 P.S. § 2852–408. In reality, by virtue of the majority's determination, ratification by the shareholders of the actions of the officers and directors is rendered nothing more than an exculpation in which the shareholders assume the role of a board of pardons. The result of the majority opinion is to approve the failure on the part of the officers and directors to manage the business—not their failure to properly manage the business but their failure to even consider the problems of the business—and to relieve the directors of their responsibilities as fiduciaries and to exonerate them from all wrongdoing. This determination illustrates the extreme in the breakdown of democratic processes in Pennsylvania corporations and makes the ownership of a minority interest in a Pennsylvania corporation a most hazardous venture.

I dissent.

SELHEIMER v. MANGANESE CORPORATION OF AMERICA

Supreme Court of Pennsylvania, 1966.
423 Pa. 563, 224 A.2d 634.

JONES, J. These appeals stem from a stockholders' derivative suit in equity instituted by certain stockholders of Manganese Corporation of America [Manganese] against Manganese and Ernest F. Pie, Albert W. Himfar, Nelson Kusner and Charles A. Gillan, Jr., who, at various times, were the officers and managing majority directors of Manganese. After the commencement of this suit in the Court of Common Pleas No. 3 of Philadelphia County, Perry N. Selheimer, a director of Manganese throughout the time the corporation was engaged in business activity, was severed as a party plaintiff and joined as an additional defendant.

The thrust of this action is that the four defendants, as officers and majority directors of Manganese, so mismanaged the affairs of the corporation as to result in a wasting of the corporation's assets with a resultant loss to the corporation of approximately $400,000. The case was tried before Judge Maurice W. Sporkin of the Court of Common Pleas No. 2 of Philadelphia County, sitting as chancellor, who held the original defendants "guilty of such negligence in recklessly mismanaging the business affairs of [Manganese], wasting its assets and causing its insolvency, as to be legally responsible for its loss and damage totalling $382,537.30   *   *   *" and directed that the defendants reimburse the court-appointed receiver of Manganese in that amount. Defendants filed exceptions to numerous findings of fact, conclusions of law and the decree of the chancellor. These exceptions were argued before a court en banc—consisting of the chancellor, Judges Ethan Allen Doty and Bernard J. Kelley—which sustained (with Judge Sporkin dissenting) defendants' exceptions both to the chancellor's conclusion of law that defendants were liable for the loss suffered by Manganese and to the decree nisi and decreed that Manganese's complaint be dismissed. Manganese has appealed from this decree * * * and Charles A. Gillan, Jr., has appealed from that portion of the decree dismissing the original defendants' complaint against the additional defendant Selheimer.

A review of the factual background of this controversy is essential. In March, 1958, the defendants Himfar and Kusner formed a corporation known as Mangamex, Inc. [Mangamex] for the purpose of producing manganese oxide at a plant located in Paterson, New Jersey. All Mangamex's capital stock was issued to Himfar and Kusner, Pie and Gillan becoming stockholders at a later date.

In January, 1959, Pie, Gillan, Himfar and Kusner, through nominees, incorporated Manganese as a Pennsylvania corporation. Manganese's capital structure consisted of authorized capital stock consisting of (a) 400,000 shares, Class A stock, having a par value of $2.00 per share and (b) 200,000 shares, Class B stock, having a par value of 20¢ per share. Of the seven directors authorized, Class B stockholders were entitled to elect four persons as majority directors and Class A stockholders to elect three persons as minority directors. In Manganese's articles of incorporation Pie, Gillan, Himfar and Kusner were designated as its first directors. On January 19, 1959—Manganese's first regular directors' meeting—the directors authorized the purchase from Mangamex of all its assets—evaluated in the agreement at $91,500—which consisted of the lease and *that portion* of the equipment of the Paterson plant which it had purchased six months previously from Eastern. The consideration for this purchase by Manganese was the transfer to Mangamex of *all* Manganese's Class B stock—200,000 shares—and an assumption of all Mangamex's outstanding indebtedness amounting to $10,000. Subsequent to the completion of this sale and purchase, Mangamex distributed *all* the Class B stock of Manganese to its four stockholders, Himfar, Gillan, Kusner and Pie, each receiving 50,000 shares.

At the same meeting on January 19, 1959, each of the Class B stockholders became an officer of Manganese and an executive committee—to which Pie and Gillan, president and vice-president in charge of operations, respectively, were appointed—was created with authority to exercise all the board of directors' power when the board was not in session.

At the first stockholders' meeting—February 19, 1959—the four defendants were elected majority directors by Class B stockholders and Selheimer, the additional defendant, was elected a minority director by Class A stockholders.

The four defendants, as Manganese's officers, then entered into an agreement with First Securities Commission, Inc., [First Securities], a licensed dealer in securities of which Selheimer was president, for the public offering and sale by the latter of up to 200,000 shares of Class A stock of Manganese at an offering price of $3.00 per share. This agreement provided for a commission to First Securities of $.45 per share sold as well as $.10 per share for expenses; Manganese was thus to receive $2.45 for every share of Class A stock sold. In order to show cash on hand in Manganese at its inception, the first 40,000 shares of Class A stock were issued to Pie, or his nominees, at their par value of $1.00 per share. The public offering and sale of Class A stock by Manganese was accomplished *without first registering the issue with the Federal Securities Exchange Commission,* under a procedure made possible by virtue of an exemption provided by the federal "Securities Act of 1933". Such exemption was available if the entire issue of stock would be sold only to Pennsylvania residents *and* if Manganese, incorporated in Pennsylvania, was *actually* "doing business" in Pennsylvania. The total net proceeds realized by Manganese from the sale of Class A stock was $412,914.50. The prospectus and the circulars which accompanied this Class A stock public offering, prepared by and at the direction of Manganese's officers and directors, stated that Manganese proposed to erect and operate a plant in Pennsylvania wherein substantial operating activities would be centered and that Manganese had arranged for the purchase for $100,000 of an ideally located plant at Colwyn, Pa., which would enable Manganese to operate at advantageous freight rates and under other felicitous conditions.

Subsequent to the formal organization of Manganese and prior to the formulation of plans concerning an operating plant, the four defendants, without authorization at a directors' meeting, proceeded to pay themselves salaries out of the proceeds of the sale of the Class A stock. In June 1959—upon a resolution submitted by Selheimer, the additional defendant,—the board of directors voted to discontinue the payment of these salaries and repay that which had been paid. Up to the date of the decree in the court below the amount of the salaries paid prior to the June, 1959, meeting was never paid back.

On March 13, 1959, Manganese entered into an agreement to purchase for $100,000 a property in Colwyn, Pennsylvania; $10,000 was given as a down payment with final settlement to be consummated on or before September 1, 1959. The Colwyn plant was far better suited and superior to the Paterson plant for the commercial production contemplated by Manganese. The Paterson plant lacked a railroad siding, a proper storage area, and its equipment was "out of phase" or improperly arranged for profitable commercial production. Some of its inadequacies were known by defendants for Pie, in a letter to corporation counsel dated January 21, 1959, stated: "It is mandatory that we leave the plant in N. J. because it has no siding which creates a very expensive operation in the handling of ore to and from the plant." It is beyond explanation, why, in the face of such knowledge of the unsuitability of the Paterson plant for profitable production, the defendants continued to pour corporate money into and to utilize the Paterson plant. The testimony of defendants is to the effect that they had planned to use the Paterson plant as a "testing" or a "pilot" plant designed particularly for operations in a stage intermediate between research and full-scale production and that to accomplish this it would take the expenditure of approximately $30,000 to $40,000. However, by the time the Paterson plant finally was made ready for production in May 1959, over $158,000 had been expended for equipment and the productivity of that plant had been seriously handicapped by the improper arrangement of the equipment purchased. The production at the Paterson plant never exceeded a "token" rate; as of August 31, 1959, the Paterson plant had sustained an operating loss of $104,000 while the total sales of Manganese's products produced up to that date at that plant amounted to $2,000.

When the settlement of the Colwyn property finally took place in August 1959, only $55,000 of the $412,000 realized from the sale of Class A stock, *which in the public offering of such stock had been earmarked for the Colwyn plant*, remained and this amount was patently insufficient to establish the originally projected plant in Colwyn. *The Colwyn plant was never utilized during its ownership by Manganese.* Moreover, even though defendants were fully advised by corporate counsel of the necessity of establishing operations in Pennsylvania in accordance with the SEC exemption, such advice was ignored. When Manganese went into bankruptcy in October 1960 the receiver salvaged approximately $30,000 from the sale of the corporate assets. The record is clear beyond question that the failure of the defendants to utilize the Colwyn plant, where profitable production was possible, and the pouring of Manganese's money into the Paterson plant, which defendants knew could not result in profitable production and which their actual experience in the Paterson plant made so evident, resulted in the ultimate insolvency of Manganese.

The record further reveals that, when, prior to the formation of Manganese, a portion of the equipment at the Paterson plant was acquired by the defendants acting for Mangamex, such acquisition was through *direct* dealings with Eastern which at the time owned all the "in place" equipment at the Paterson plant. However, subsequent to the formation of Manganese, all purchases of additional "in place" equipment from Eastern were made through an intermediary or "middle man", one Alan Savitt, a personal friend of one of defendants, Himfar. Moreover, two pieces of equipment, thus acquired, for which approximately $4,000 was paid neither appeared on Manganese's inventories nor have they been accounted for. Satisfactory explanation for this conduct does not appear on this record. The chancellor found that the use of the intermediary to purchase the equipment created a "reasonable inference of wilful misconduct and a pattern of self-enrichment by the managing defendants, to the prejudice of Manganese and its stockholders, and militates against their good faith and fair dealing."

The chancellor found that the conduct of all four defendants could be portrayed "if not as fraudulent, then assuredly as imprudent beyond explanation", and that the "actions of the managing defendants were palpably careless, reckless and wanting in that diligence and skill of reasonably prudent men and not the result of judgment or acts of ineptitude * * *. The acts and omissions * * * are ample * * * to fasten inescapable responsibility on the four defendants who actually had charge of management and conducted the corporation's affairs."

The chancellor further found that Selheimer was not negligent in his duty to exercise care in the conduct of the affairs of Manganese. The record reveals that Selheimer, at various times, expressed concern over the corporation's financial condition and lack of production and that he protested the management of the corporation, threatened legal action and finally organized the Stockholder's Protective Committee.

The majority of the court en banc agreed with the conclusions of the chancellor that the actions of defendants were "imprudent", "wasteful", "careless" and negligent. Our reading of the opinion of the court en banc indicates that its decree was predicated upon its interpretation of our recent ruling in Smith v. Brown-Borhek Co., 414 Pa. 325, an interpretation under which, absent proof of fraud, self-dealing or personal profit or wanton misconduct, directors of a business corporation would not be subject to personal liability, even though their actions were "imprudent", "wasteful", "careless" and "negligent". In our view, the court en banc has misinterpreted Smith v. Brown-Borhek Co., supra.

The yardstick by which the actions of directors of a business corporation is to be measured and the relationship of such directors vis-a-vis the corporation has been mandated by the legislature.

Section 408, art. IV of the Business Corporation Law of 1933 provides: "Officers and directors shall be deemed to stand in a fiduciary relation to the corporation, and shall discharge the duties of their respective positions in good faith and with that diligence, care and skill which ordinarily prudent men would exercise under similar circumstances in their personal business affairs." This statute mandates a standard of care for directors much more stringent and harsh than the standard enunciated by our courts prior to the passage of the statute. Our case law prior to the statute taught that the directors of corporations—whether business, banking, or otherwise—were held simply to a standard of ordinary care and diligence and that, absent fraud or gross negligence amounting to fraud, such directors would not be personally liable for their actions. The standard prior to Section 408 might well be stated as that care, skill and diligence which the ordinary prudent man would exercise *in similar circumstances*.

The leading case in this area is Spering's Appeal, 71 Pa. 11 (1872). In *Spering,* Mr. Justice (later Chief Justice) Sharswood stated that directors ought not be judged by the same strict standard as the agent or trustee of a private estate and " * * * while directors are personally responsible to the stockholders for any losses resulting from fraud, embezzlement or wilful misconduct or breach of trust for their own benefit and not for the benefit of the stockholders, for gross inattention and negligence by which such fraud or misconduct has been perpetrated by agents, officers or co-directors, yet they are not liable for mistakes of judgment, even though they may be so gross as to appear to us absured and ridiculous, provided they are honest and provided they are fairly within the scope of the powers and discretion confided to the managing body" (at p. 24). In Swentzel v. Penn Bank, 147 Pa. 140 (1892), creditors of a bank sued to hold its officers and directors liable for losses resulting from the bank's failure. The charge in *Swentzel* was that the officers and directors were negligent in their management of the bank's affairs and that the corporate losses had occurred by reason of that negligence. The Court there held that the care owed by the director of a bank is not the same ordinary care that he takes in his own affairs (at p. 150), stating the rule of ordinary care is not that "ordinary care which a man takes of his own business, but the ordinary care of a bank director in the business of a bank. Negligence is the want of care according to the circumstances, and the circumstances are everything in considering this question." (at p. 150). The Court held that directors, whom the court termed "gratuitous mandatories", are only liable for fraud or for such gross negligence as amounts to fraud.

In Hunt v. Aufderheide, et al., 330 Pa. 362, we reiterated that, in the period prior to the enactment of Section 408, the directors of a corporation (bank) were held simply to "the care, skill and diligence which the ordinary prudent man would exercise in similar circumstances" (at p. 366).

In the period subsequent to the statute our attention is directed to only two decisions, Smith v. Brown-Borhek Co., 414 Pa. 325, and Otis & Co. v. Pennsylvania R. Co., 61 F.Supp. 905 (E.D.Pa.) (1945). We shall discuss, infra, the former. In *Otis*, the Court stated that, while the extent to which Section 408 of the Business Corporation Law changed the prior law was "uncertain", however, "the test of liability can hardly be different from that applied in Hunt v. Aufderheide, et al., 1938, 330 Pa. 362," i. e., directors are held to the degree of care "which an ordinary prudent man would exercise in similar circumstances" (61 F.Supp. pp. 910, 911).

To what, if any, extent has Section 408 changed the law prior to its passage? An examination of Section 408 reveals two significant facts: (a) that the relationship between directors and officers vis-à-vis the corporation is termed a "fiduciary relation"; (b) that the standard of care mandated is that directors act in good faith *and* exercise such care as the "ordinarily prudent man" would exercise under similar circumstances *in their personal affairs*.

While our own case law is not marked with outstanding clarity on the general subject, it is clear beyond question that "[t]he fiduciary character of the directors' relation to the corporation and the measure of their responsibility are quite different from those of a trustee under a will or a deed; * * *:" Hunt v. Aufderheide, et al., supra, 330 Pa. pp. 376, 377; Smith v. Brown-Borhek Co., supra, 414 Pa. p. 333. The "fiduciary relation" contemplated by Section 408, supra, would seem to equate that concept well-expressed in Schaffhauser v. Arnholt & Schafer Brewing Co., 218 Pa. 298 (1907): "While it may not be legally accurate to say that a director of a corporation is a trustee for the entire body of stockholders, within the exact meaning of that term, there can be no doubt he does occupy such a fiduciary relation as to imperatively demand, both in good morals and sound law, that he shall manage the business of the company in such manner as to promote, not his own interests, but the common interests of all the shareholders." * * *

In construing Section 408 we bear in mind certain background: (1) the phrase "in their personal affairs" was not to be found in the Uniform Model Business Corporation Act (9 U.L.A. p. 186, et seq.) but was inserted in Section 408 at the suggestion of a committee of the Pennsylvania Bar Association "Pennsylvania Banking and Building and Loan Law", Segal, Vol. I, § 402, p. 362; (2) prior to the adoption of Section 408, our case law had rejected the standard of care expressly provided in Section 408; (3) the standard of care in Section 408 does not represent the majority view (see, for example, Briggs v. Spaulding, 141 U.S. 132; * * * (4) Section 408 imposes on a director of a *business* corporation a much *higher* degree of care than the law imposes on a director of a banking corporation or a director of a building and loan corporation.

In recent years, with one exception, this Court has not been called upon to squarely meet the issue of the standard of due care imposed in Section 408. The wording of Section 408 is clear and unequivocal and the test therein imposed in evaluating the business corporation directors' actions is mandated by the legislature. The rule is harsh and strict and it may well render unattractive positions as directors of business corporations. Nevertheless, the legislature has spoken on the subject and we are bound to follow the legislative direction, regardless of our own doubts as to the wisdom of the rule. Any change must emanate from the legislature and not the judiciary.

In our view, however, regardless of whether we follow the statutory rule or the rule enunciated in our case law prior to the statute, the same result follows in the case at bar.

In view of the emphasis placed by a majority of the court en banc on Smith v. Brown-Borhek Co., 414 Pa. 325, and its conclusions that *Smith* compelled a finding that the defendants could not be held personally liable, we must analyse *Smith*.

In *Smith*—decided solely on the pleadings—a minority stockholder of a business corporation instituted a derivative action against the officers and directors of the corporation to recover a corporate loss, allegedly resulting from negligent mismanagement. The particular conduct of which complaint was made was that the defendants, over a two year period, had extended credit to a customer whom the defendants knew or should have known was not a good credit risk, that the customer went bankrupt and that a loss was sustained by the corporation. Subsequent to the institution of suit, a stockholders' annual meeting was held and, at that meeting, the stockholders, by a vote approximately in the ratio of 15–1, ratified the actions of defendants in handling the customer's account. As a reading of *Smith* clearly indicates two questions were raised: (1) whether the actions of defendant directors *could be* ratified; (2) whether such actions were *legally* ratified. In determining the first issue, the Court noted that there was no allegation of "fraud, self-dealing, personal profit or intentional dissipation or waste of corporate funds" nor any charge or "affirmative negligence or the deliberate exercise of bad judgment or intentional wrong doing" but simply a charge that defendants negligently failed to exercise their duties, i. e., passive negligence. Under such circumstances, the Court held that the defendants' actions could be ratified, as they were, by the stockholders. The discussion of the second issue, i. e., the legality of the ratification, is completely inapposite to the case at bar since herein ratification was neither alleged nor proven. A study of *Smith* completely negatives the conclusion of the majority of the court en banc that "the present case is controlled by Smith v. Brown-Borhek, supra."

Returning to the findings in the court below, the chancellor found that the losses of Manganese and its insolvency "were the result of imprudent, wasteful, careless, negligent and wanton acts of omission and commission by all [four defendants] in their management of the affairs of Manganese." The court en banc, even though it disagreed with the chancellor's findings of "wanton acts of omission and commission" and even though it found no fraud, self-dealing or personal profit gained, *expressly approved* the chancellor's findings that the defendants' actions were "imprudent", "wasteful", "careless" and "negligent" and added that there "is no question that the officers were unwise and imprudent in many respects". The question is squarely raised: in the absence of fraud, self-dealing, or proof of personal profit or wanton acts of omission and commission, are the directors of a business corporation, who have been imprudent, wasteful, careless and negligent, personally liable, under either the common law or Section 408, where such actions have resulted in corporate losses resulting in the insolvency of the corporation? An affirmative answer is self-evident.

The rule is well settled that "[c]ourts are reluctant to interfere in the internal management of a corporation, since that is a matter for the discretion and judgment of the directors and stockholders, unless a minority stockholder's rights are jeopardized or injured by fraud or *waste of* company assets, or an overreaching, actual or legal: [citing authorities].": Chambers v. Beaver-Advance Corp., 392 Pa. 481 (1958) (Emphasis supplied); Bowman v. Gum, Inc., 327 Pa. 403 (1937).

In determining the personal liability of the directors in the case at bar we bear in mind certain well established principles: (a) the directors of a business corporation are not insurers that their actions will result in pecuniary profit and they are, in the course of their duties, called upon to undertake certain calculated "business risks"; (b) for errors in judgment, exercised in good faith, the directors of a corporation should not be penalized; (c) "what may be negligence in one case may not be want of ordinary care in another, and the question of negligence is therefore ultimately a question of fact, *to be determined under all the circumstances"*: Briggs v. Spaulding, 141 U.S. 132, 152 (Emphasis supplied). Cf: Bowerman v. Hamner, 250 U.S. 504.

* * *

From creation to bankruptcy, the corporate life of Manganese spanned less than two years and, within that short period of time, its assets shrunk from over $400,000 to $30,000. Of course, this short span of corporate life and shrinkage of assets do not *per se* justify a conclusion that these defendants were guilty of any misconduct or negligence. However, a careful study of this record convinces us that the destruction of Manganese was due to the gross mismanagement of the corporation by the director-officer defendants.

Prior to Manganese's formation, these four defendants, then in sole and absolute control of Mangamex, had had the experience of operating the Paterson plant; from that experience, they knew, and had every reason to know, that the Paterson plant,—because of a lack of railroad siding, proper storage areas and other factors—could not be operated profitably. The Paterson plant operation was feasible only as a "testing" or "pilot" plant and not for full scale production. To secure additional funds, the defendants formed Manganese with a capital structure so devised that the public, the Class A stock purchasers, would put up these additional funds and the defendants, sole owners of the Class B stock, would completely dominate Manganese's affairs.

The manner in which the Class A stock was offered to the public is significant when viewed in the light of subsequent events. First, the offering of such stock to the public was effected by taking advantage of an exemption provided by the Securities Act, supra, an exemption which was *legally* available only if Manganese was "doing business" in Pennsylvania, yet, despite the sound advice of corporate counsel given to these defendants, Manganese never did business in Pennsylvania and our reading of this record indicates that they intended, at best, only a "token" compliance with the federal statutory requirement. Second, the public which purchased the Class A stock did so in reliance upon the defendants' representations that Manganese planned that its "substantial operating activities" would be centered at the Colwyn, Pa. plant about to be purchased again, through the medium of the purchase of this plant by a small down payment of ten (10%) per cent of the purchase price, defendants simply rendered "lip service" to their respesentations to the stock-purchasing public and they then proceeded to deplete Manganese's assets to such an extent that it became impossible to place the Colwyn plant on any productive basis.

In their representations to the stock-purchasing public, defendants stated the rate of production at the Colwyn plant would be 24 tons daily, or 480 tons per month, of manganese oxide. After eight months of Manganese operation of the Colwyn plant, a total of only 70 tons had been produced "with forty four tons in progress, and seven thousand pounds of copper carbonate." Despite their experience with operation of this plant under Mangamex and Manganese, defendants continued to expend corporate funds on the Paterson plant and to take no action to place the Colwyn plant on a productive basis.

Defendants' actions in respect to the Colwyn plant were not the result of errors in judgment or a calculated business risk nor can such actions be classified as mere negligence. With the knowledge which defendants had of the unsuitability of the Paterson plant for profitable production, the pouring of Manganese's funds into this plant defies explanation; in fact, the defendants have failed to give any satisfactory explanation or advance any justification for such expenditures.

The chancellor found—although, apparently, the majority of the court en banc disagreed—and the record, in our view, fully supports such findings that "the unexplained use of   *   *   *   an intermediary to purchase equipment for Paterson from [Eastern] creates a reasonable inference of wilful misconduct and a pattern of self-enrichment by the managing defendants, to the prejudice of Manganese and its stockholders and militates against their good faith and fair dealing.", that "[i]n the unauthorized payment of salaries to themselves,   *   *   *, the officers, defendants, acted in violation of their duties," and that the "purchase of equipment in behalf of Manganese from Industrial Power and Equipment Co., a firm owned by Pie and Gillan, [without either approval by the board of directors or a full disclosure of the facts to the stockholders], was improper."

This record indicates clearly that these defendants, as the controlling directors and officers, wasted and dissipated Manganese's assets. Their actions constituted negligence such as was inimical to the corporation and the other stockholders of this corporation. Whether their conduct as directors and officers be measured by the yardstick provided in Section 408 of the Business Corporation Law, supra, or by common law, their conduct offended their fiduciary relationship to this corporation in such manner as to justify the imposition upon them of personal liability for such conduct.

As to the liability of Selheimer, the additional defendant, we agree with the chancellor's conclusion and disagree with the conclusion of the majority of the court en banc. A review of this record reveals no basis for the imposition upon him of personal liability for his conduct. Selheimer not only protested against defendants' conduct but his protests were crystallized into actions. Selheimer disassociated himself from defendants' waste of the corporate funds and their other misconduct. Bearing in mind the weakness of his minority position and the strength of the defendants' majority positions, Selheimer did all that he could have done to divert defendants from their course of conduct.

The chancellor directed that defendants reimburse Manganese for its losses. Defendants were directed to make reimbursement in the sum of $382,537.30 which represents the difference between the amount realized from the public sale of the Class A stock ($412,914.50) and the amount which the receiver of Manganese realized from the sale of Manganese remaining assets ($30,377.20). In adopting this measure of damages—tantamount to attributing *all* Manganese's losses to defendants' conduct—we believe the chancellor erred. The duty of reimbursement should be limited to those losses which were proximately caused by the negligent and wasteful conduct of defendants. As this Court said in Hunt v. Aufderheide et al., 330 Pa. at page 368: " * * * the value of its [the corporation's] *diverted* assets marks the maximum of its recovery." (Emphasis supplied). The record does not substantiate a finding that *all* Manganese losses were attributable to the defendants' misconduct. The nexus between Manganese's losses and defendants' negligent and wasteful actions must act as the basis for reimbursement. To establish such relationship the matter must be remanded to the court below.

Decree reversed. The matter is remanded to the court below to proceed in a manner consistent with this opinion.

BELL, C. J., absent.

C. DIRECTOR'S AND OFFICER'S INDEMNIFICATION

MERRITT–CHAPMAN & SCOTT CORPORATION
v. WOLFSON

Superior Court of Delaware, New Castle, 1970.
264 A.2d 358.

STIFTEL, President Judge. Merritt-Chapman & Scott Corporation seeks a declaratory judgment determining that the three defendants are not entitled to indemnification for legal fees under Delaware's indemnification statutes. Defendants filed a counterclaim for indemnification and both sides moved for summary judgment. The issue is whether or not the defendants are entitled to be indemnified by the plaintiff corporation for attorneys' fees and expenses incurred in the defense of a criminal action brought against them by virtue of their positions within the structure and operations of the plaintiff corporation.

The criminal action was brought in the Federal District Court for the Southern District of New York. Defendants Louis Wolfson and

Elkin Gerbert were directors and managing officers of Merritt-Chapman & Scott Corporation during the time period pertinent to the criminal litigation. Defendant Joseph Kosow was neither a director nor officer of Merritt-Chapman & Scott but during the same period of time, was chairman of the board and president of Industrial Finance Corporation, a subsidiary of Merritt-Chapman & Scott, serving at the request of and pursuant to an employment agreement with the parent corporation, entered into on July 26, 1962.

In August, 1966, a Federal Grand Jury in the Southern District of New York returned an indictment against these defendants, among others, in an action entitled United States of America v. Wolfson et al., No. 66 Cr.A. 832. The indictment contained five separate counts and at the conclusion of the criminal trial in 1968, defendant Wolfson was found guilty of Counts One, Three, Four and Five, defendant Gerbert was convicted under Counts One, Three, Four and Five, and defendant Kosow was found guilty under Count One. Defendants seek indemnity for expenses incurred in the defense of a portion of Count One of the indictment.

Count One charged the defendants with conspiracy. The specific acts charged in furtherance of that conspiracy were perjury, subornation of perjury, filing false statements with the SEC, obstruction of justice, and fraud upon the corporate shareholders in violation of SEC Rule 10b–5. At the close of the government's case, the court removed the 10b–5 fraud element from Count One of the indictment. In dismissing this element of the conspiracy charge, the court made the following statement:

"The conduct of the defendants in the context of a civil case could, arguably, come within the purview of the rule and the case law interpreting it. This is not, however, a civil case, and the standards applicable to penal statutes must apply". (Tr. 4637).

"The underlying principle [to define a criminal standard] is that no person shall be held criminally responsible for conduct which he could not reasonably understand to be proscribed. Jordan v. DeGeorge, 341 U.S. 233 (1951). While the rule can be constitutionally applied in the criminal context to certain conduct, see United States v. Re, 336 F.2d 306, decided by the Second Circuit in 1964, the fact remains that in the context of the facts adduced in the government's case, the requirement of definiteness has not been fulfilled since it cannot be said that this rule provides *a person of ordinary intelligence* with fair notice that his contemplated conduct, that is, the conduct delineated by the government's evidence, was forbidden by its terms. See United States v. Harriss, 347 U.S. 612 (1964)." (Emphasis supplied). (Tr. 4641).

The jury returned verdicts of guilty on all counts, as charged, including the Count One conspiracy charge, although the fraud part (10b–5) of the conspiracy count was dismissed, and each defendant was sentenced under Count One to a term in prison and a $10,000 fine.

The indemnification statute upon which defendants rely is 8 Del. Code § 145(c), as follows:

"(c) To the extent that a director, officer, employee or agent of a corporation has been successful on the merits or otherwise in defense of any action, suit or proceeding referred to in subsections (a) and (b), or in defense of any claim, issue or matter therein, he shall be indemnified against expenses (including attorneys' fees) actually and reasonably incurred by him in connection therewith."

Assuming, without deciding, that defendants are otherwise qualified under 8 Del.Code § 145, they will be entitled to indemnification for expenses incurred in their criminal defense only if and to the extent that this court determines that they were "successful on the merits or otherwise".

It is the position of the defendants that because the fraud portion of the conspiracy count was removed at the close of the government's case, such removal constituted a success on the merits, and to the extent that their defense involved this portion of Count One of the indictment, they are entitled to reimbursement for legal expenses attributable to this part of the defense. There is no dispute as to the reasonableness of the amount of the expenses sought to be recovered. Defendants argue that criminal fraud was the essence of the government's case against them and that when the conspiracy objective to violate SEC Rule 10b–5 was removed, the major portion of the case was dismissed, *ergo* successfully defended "on the merits or otherwise". I find this argument unacceptable.

Count One of the Criminal indictment did not charge any of the defendants with criminal fraud. They were charged with conspiracy. One of several objectives of the conspiracy was to violate Rule 10b–5, a regulation designed to protect the investing public from fraud. Defendants were convicted under Count One of *conspiracy*, although the alleged violations of Rule 10b–5 were removed from the count. In dismissing the 10b–5 charge, the court made the following observation:

"The dismissal of this *part of the conspiracy* count does not, however, require the dismissal of the entire count. The count charges, in addition to a conspiracy to violate Rule 10b–5, that the defendants conspired to obstruct justice, 18 U.S.C. § 1621, and to suborn perjury, 18 U.S.C. § 1622. *The fact that one of the objects of the conspiracy is removed does not invalidate the entire conspiracy charge.*" Emphasis added.)   (Tr. 4642–43.)

Under Count One, the defendants were charged with conspiracy and they were found guilty of conspiracy. It is difficult to understand how they can claim "success on the merits or otherwise" after they were charged and convicted of Count One of the indictment.

No common law right to indemnification existed. 40 Calif.L.Rev. 104 (1952). Indemnification statutes were enacted in Delaware, and elsewhere, to induce capable and responsible businessmen to accept positions in corporate management. See Mooney v. Willys-Overland Motors, Inc., 204 F.2d 888 (3rd Cir., 1953). 8 Del.Code § 145 is a new statute, enacted to clarify its predecessor, 8 Del.Code § 122(10), and to give vindicated directors and others involved in corporate affairs a judicially enforcible right to indemnification.

It would be anomalous, indeed, and diametrically opposed to the spirit and purpose of the statute and sound public policy to extend the benefits of indemnification to these defendants under the facts and circumstances of this case. Accordingly, defendants' motion for summary judgment is denied. Plaintiff's motion is granted.

It is so ordered.

D.   VOTING TRUSTS

Frequently a corporation will have a fair number of shareholders but not enough for the securities of the corporation to be traded over the counter let alone be listed on any securities exchange. There will not be enough activity in the securities of the corporation for any brokerage firm to be interested in providing a market place for persons to buy or sell the securities of the corporation; that is, there will be no over the counter trading. Yet the management group will be desirous of maintaining control of the corporation and protecting against the disaffection of any friendly shareholders or preventing the acquisition of stock of other shareholders by some person who is or potentially may be antagonistic to management. One way to do this is through the use of a voting trust. These are generally permitted by the corporation statutes of most states and generally provide that the term of the trust may not exceed ten years. The purpose of this limitation is to guard against any perpetuity, thus providing for the free transferability of the shares of stock at some date in the future; in the meantime, management may protect its position by designating one or a small group of the management personnel as the voting trustees. Those persons who desire to participate in the voting trust, which is always done on a voluntary basis, cause their shares of stock in the corporation to be transferred to the voting trustee or trustees on the books of the corporation, and receive in exchange a voting trust certificate from the trustees. Generally these voting certificates are transferable but once the stock of the corporation has been transferred to the trustees it cannot be removed from the trust without the consent of the parties to the trust agreement. These voting trusts are generally looked upon with disfavor by the courts because they sometimes permit the voting control of the corporation to be concealed from nonparticipating shareholders or from creditors and because the voting trustees rarely act in any fiduciary manner, that is they generally vote for themselves for directors of the corporation. As noted above these voting trust agreements are entered into on a voluntary basis. The state does not provide which persons shall be the directors of a corporation nor limit their means of providing for the continuation of the management of the corporation. If we did not have private control of the business enterprise, and if we did not have freedom of contract, and if we did not require some means of transfering privately owned property, we would not have these problems. Our system has been to limit the kind of voting trust agreement which may be entered into rather than to prohibit them.

ABERCROMBIE v. DAVIES

Supreme Court of Delaware, 1957.
36 Del.Ch. 371, 130 A.2d 338.

SOUTHERLAND, Chief Justice. The pertinent facts are as follows:

American Independent Oil Company ("American") is a Delaware corporation. It was formed to develop an oil concession in the Kuwait-Saudi Arabian neutral zone. The organizers were James S. Abercrombie, Sunray Oil Corporation ("Sunray"), Phillips Petroleum Company ("Phillips"), Ralph K. Davies, Signal Oil and Gas Company ("Signal"), The Hancock Oil Company ("Hancock"), The Globe Oil and Refining Company ("Globe"), Lario Oil and Gas Company ("Lario"), Ashland Oil & Refining Company ("Ashland"), Deep Rock Oil Corporation ("Deep Rock"), and Allied Oil Company (later acquired by Ashland). The organizers subscribed in varying proportions to American's original issue of stock. Additional stock was later issued, and there are now outstanding 150,000 shares.

The organization agreement provided that the Board of Directors of American should consist of one director for each 5,000 shares held, and that the directors should be elected by cumulative voting. In effect, each stockholder has been permitted to name the director or directors to represent on the board his or its interests. Davies represents his own interest and is president of the corporation. At all times the number of directors has been fifteen. No one stockholder holds a majority of stock, and no one stockholder is represented by more than four directors. Obviously, smooth functioning of such a board was dependent either upon substantial harmony among the interests represented on it or upon an effective coalition of the interests of a majority.

On March 30, 1950, six of the stockholders took steps to form such a coalition. On that date an agreement was executed between eight individuals designated "Agents", and the six stockholders—Davies, Ashland, Globe, Lario, Hancock and Signal. These stockholders hold about 54½% of the shares. They are represented on the board by eight of the fifteen directors. The Agents named in the agreement were at the time the eight directors representing these six stockholders.

The obvious purpose of the agreement was to achieve effective control of the board and thus control of corporate policy. The motive for the agreement, according to the defendants, was to prevent acquisition of control by Phillips, which was the largest single stockholder, holding about one-third of the stock. In the view we take of the case, only the purpose is material.

The Agents' Agreement is an unusual one. In effect, it transfers voting control of the stock of the six stockholders to the eight Agents for a period of ten years (subject to termination by seven of the Agents). The Agents are to be, as far as possible, identical with the directors. The agreement of seven of the eight is required to vote the stock and elaborate provisions are added for the choice of an arbitrator to resolve disagreements. Somewhat similar provisions attempt to control the action of the directors. A more detailed examination of the agreement will later be made. At the moment we note that the majority of the board secured by this agreement (eight of the fifteen) comprised Davies, the two Signal directors, the two Hancock directors, the director representing Globe and Lario, and the two Ashland directors.

The effective control thus sought to be achieved apparently lasted until December 9, 1954. On that date a meeting of the Board of Directors was held in Chicago. A resolution was adopted calling a special meeting of the board for December 16, to consider and take action upon certain amendments to the by-laws and other matters. This resolution was adopted by a vote of nine to six. This majority consisted of Abercrombie, the four Phillips directors, the Sunray director, the Deep Rock director, and the two Ashland directors. The minority consisted of Davies and the Globe, Lario, Hancock and Signal directors. The nature of the action to be considered at the proposed meeting was such as to indicate to the minority that the control of the board set up by the Agents' Agreement was seriously threatened. The Ashland directors, it was charged, had violated the Agents' Agreement. Counter moves were made by Davies. Litigation was instituted in California by Davies, Signal, Hancock, Globe and Lario against Ashland and its two directors. American, named as a defendant, was preliminarily enjoined from recognizing any action taken at a board meeting of December 16, and Ashland was enjoined from violating the Agents' Agreement.

In the meantime, the suit below was filed by Abercrombie, Phillips and Sunray against the other shareholders and the Agents. Davies, Signal, Hancock, Lario, Globe and six of the Agents appeared and answered. Plaintiffs filed a motion for summary judgment. Several contentions arose out of the hearings on this motion. The Chancellor made the following rulings of law:

(1) Certain provisions of the Agents' Agreement attempting to control directorate action are invalid on their face;

(2) The agreement is not a voting trust;

(3) The provisions respecting stockholder action are severable from the illegal provisions, and constitute a valid stockholders' pooling agreement.

Both sides appeal. All of the issues argued below have been presented here.

We turn to an analysis of the Agents' Agreement.

Paragraph 1 provides in part:

"Upon the signing of this Agreement, or as soon thereafter as it may be possible for them to do so, by those whose certificates may be pledged or deposited, as hereinafter referred to, the Shareholders will deliver to the Agents the certificate or certificates representing all the shares of American Independent Oil Company now owned or controlled by them, said certificates to be endorsed in blank or attached to a stock power endorsed in blank. Said Agents will give to each depositing Shareholder a proper receipt for all certificates so delivered."

The certificates and stock powers are to be deposited in escrow in a bank or trust company, subject to withdrawal at any time by any seven of the agents.

Paragraph 2 sets forth a method of dealing with a possible increase in the number of Agents "(or in case a Voting Trust shall have been created, the number of Trustees)".

Paragraph 3 provides in part:

"During the term of this Agreement the Agents or their successors shall have the sole and exclusive voting power of the stock subject to this Agreement. The Shareholders shall deliver to the Agents and shall keep in effect during the life of this Agreement proxies giving said Agents or their successors jointly and each of them severally, with full power of substitution to any or all of them, the power to vote the stock at all regular and special meetings of the stockholders and to vote for, do or assent or consent to any act or proceeding which the Shareholders of said corporation might or could vote for, do or assent or consent to."

Paragraph 3 also provides:

"The vote of the Agents shall always be exercised as a unit, on any matter on which a vote of the stockholders is called for, as any seven of said Agents shall direct and determine. If any seven Agents fail to agree on any such matter, then the question in disagreement shall be submitted for arbitration to some disinterested person (i. e., one having no financial interest in American Independent Oil Company), chosen by the affirmative vote of seven of the Agents, as sole arbitrator."

Then follow provisions for the choice of an arbitrator if seven Agents fail to agree upon the matter, and for the enforcement of his decision.

Then follow two paragraphs dealing with control of directorate action. These are the provisions held invalid by the Chancellor as an unlawful attempt to strip the directors of their statutory right and duty to manage the corporate affairs.

Paragraph 3 then concludes:

"In the event a Voting Trust is established as provided in Paragraph 7 hereof, the provisions of the two preceding subparagraphs shall remain in effect, substituting the words "Trustee" or "Trustees" for the words "Agent" or "Agents" wherever those words occur in said two subparagraphs."

Paragraph 4 provides for filling a vacancy in the position of Agent. As to the corporate shareholders, the successor is to be named by the shareholder that the Agent was representing. As to Davies, his successor is to be named by the majority of the remaining Agents. Each corporate shareholder has the right to remove its Agent or Agents at any time without cause.

Paragraphs 6 and 7 provide:

"6. Except as herein otherwise provided, the proxies to be given hereunder shall not be revoked and the powers herein delegated to said Agents shall be irrevocable during a period of ten years from and after the date of said Agreement. This Agreement, however, shall terminate if any seven of the Agents hereunder declare in writing that the Agreement is terminated. Unless the Agents by unanimous vote otherwise determine, this Agreement shall also terminate if and when less than 50% of the outstanding shares of American Independent Oil Company remain subject to this Agreement. Upon the termination of said Agreement the certificates representing all of the shares so held under this Agreement and then remaining in escrow or in the hands of said Agents or their successors shall be returned or assigned to the parties then entitled thereto, upon surrender to said Agents of the receipts given for said certificates.

"7. Any seven of said Agents may at any time withdraw said stock certificates from escrow and transfer said stock to the persons then acting as Agents, as trustees to be held under a voting trust. The parties agree, upon the written request of seven of said Agents to execute a voting trust agreement substantially in the form attached hereto marked Exhibit "A", the persons then acting as Agents to be Trustees, and the Shareholders parties hereto to be Beneficiaries thereunder. The parties do hereby constitute any one of said Agents their attorney in fact to execute said voting trust agreement for them and in their names, in the event any of them should be unable, or should fail or refuse to sign said voting trust agreement upon the written request of seven of said Agents. Upon the execution of said voting trust agreement the Shareholders will surrender to said Agents the receipts given for said certificates."

This agreement, plaintiffs assert, is invalid on its face. Among other contentions they say that in substance, though not in form, it is a voting trust, and that it is void because it does not comply with the provisions of our voting trust statute. Defendants reply that it is not, and was not intended to be, a voting trust, and is a mere pooling agreement of the kind recognized as legal in Delaware by the decision in

Ringling Bros.-Barnum & Bailey Combined Shows v. Ringling, 29 Del. Ch. 610.

The General Corporation Law, 8 Del.Code § 218, provides in part:

"(a) One or more stockholders may by agreement in writing deposit capital stock of an original issue with or transfer capital stock to any person or persons, or corporation or corporations authorized to act as trustee, for the purpose of vesting in such person or persons, corporation or corporations, who may be designated voting trustee or voting trustees, the right to vote thereon for any period of time determined by such agreement, not exceeding ten years, upon the terms and conditions stated in such agreement. Such agreement may contain any other lawful provisions not inconsistent with said purpose. After the filing of a copy of such agreement in the principal office of the corporation in the State of Delaware, which copy shall be open to the inspection of any stockholder of the corporation or any beneficiary of the trust under said agreement daily during business hours, certificates of stock shall be issued to the voting trustees to represent any stock of an original issue so deposited with them, and any certificates of stock so transferred to the voting trustees shall be surrendered and cancelled and new certificates therefor shall be issued to the voting trustees, and in the certificates so issued it shall appear that they are issued pursuant to such agreement, and in the entry of such voting trustees as owners of such stock in the proper books of the issuing corporation that fact shall also be noted. The voting trustees may vote upon the stock so issued or transferred during the period in such agreement specified."

This statute was enacted in 1925. 34 Del.L. c. 112, § 6. Prior to its passage there was no Delaware decision declaring that voting trusts were lawful at common law—a question upon which the decisions in other states were in disagreement. See 5 Fletcher, Cyclopedia Corporations, § 2078. In Perry v. Missouri-Kansas Pipe Line Co., 22 Del.Ch. 33, it was determined that in Delaware, as in New York, voting trusts derive their validity solely from the statute. *"The test of validity is the rule of the statute. When the field was entered by the Legislature it was fully occupied and no place was left for other voting trusts."* Quoted by the Chancellor with approval from Matter of Morse, 247 N.Y. 290. The statute lays down for voting trusts "the law of their life"; compliance with its provisions is mandatory. Voting trusts not so complying are illegal. * * *

The correctness of the holding in the Missouri-Kansas case has never been questioned in Delaware, so far as we know. It has a direct bearing upon the instant case. If any stockholders' agreement provided for joint or concerted voting is so drawn as in effect to occupy the field reserved for the statutory voting trust, it is illegal, whatever mechanics may be devised to attain the result. The provisions of the instrument determine its legal effect, and if they clearly create a voting trust, any intention of the parties to the contrary is immaterial. Aldridge v. Franco-Wyoming Oil Co., 24 Del.Ch. 126.

A review of the Delaware decisions upon the subject of voting trusts shows that our courts have indicated that one essential feature that characterizes a voting trust is the separation of the voting rights of the stock from the other attributes of ownership. In Peyton v. William C. Peyton Corporation, 22 Del.Ch. 187, Chancellor Wolcott said:

"A voting trust as commonly understood is a device whereby two or more persons owning stock with voting powers, divorce the voting rights thereof from the ownership, retaining to all intents and purposes the latter in themselves and transferring the former to trustees in whom the voting rights of all the depositors in the trust are pooled."

* * *

When we apply these tests to the Agents' Agreement we find: (1) that the voting rights of the pooled stock have been divorced from the beneficial ownership, which is retained by the stockholders; (2) that the voting rights have been transferred to fiduciaries denominated Agents; (3) that the transfer of such rights is, through the medium of irrevocable proxies, effective for a period of ten years; (4) that all voting rights in respect of all the stock are pooled in the Agents as a group, through the device of proxies running to the agents jointly and severally, and no stockholder retains the right to vote his or its shares; and (5) that on its face the agreement has for its principal object voting control of American.

These elements, under our decisions, are the elements of a voting trust.

We find one other significant circumstance.

Paragraph 7 of the Agents' Agreement gives any seven of the eight agents the power to withdraw the stock from escrow and to transform the Agreement into a formal voting trust. Any one of the agents is authorized to sign the voting trust agreement for any shareholder who fails to do so upon the request of any seven of the agents. A form of a voting trust agreement is attached as an exhibit to the Agents' Agreement. A comparison of this form with the provisions of the Agents' Agreement shows that upon the execution of the Voting Trust Agreement the scheme of control functions just as it functions under the Agents' Agreement. Without pausing for a detailed analysis, we note that Paragraphs 2, 4, 5 and 6 of the Agents' Agreement are paralleled (in some cases almost verbatim) by Paragraphs 2, 5, 8 and 10, respectively, of the Voting Trust Agreement. Paragraph 3 of the Agents' Agreement is paralleled in part by Paragraph 3 of the Voting Trust Agreement. The provisions of Paragraph 3 of the Agents' Agreement controlling directorate action remain in effect as part of the Voting Trust Agreement.

Thus the only significant changes made in transforming the Agents' Agreement into a Voting Trust Agreement are the provisions formalizing the trust, viz.: (1) the Agents become Trustees—a change of name and nothing more; (2) the stock with irrevocable stock powers running to the Agents becomes stock registered in their names as

Trustees; and (3) voting trust certificates instead of receipts are issued to the stockholders.

To sum up: the substance of the voting trust already existed; the transformation added only the special mechanics that the statute requires.

Now, the provisions of the statute that were not complied with are the requirement that the shares be transferred on the books and the requirement that a copy of the agreement shall be filed in the corporation's principal office in Delaware. The effect was to create a secret voting trust. The provision respecting the filing of a copy in the principal office in Delaware "open to the inspection of any stockholder * * * or any beneficiary of the trust" is a provision obviously for the benefit of all stockholders and of all beneficiaries of the trust, who are entitled to know where voting control of a corporation resides. And the provision for transfer of the stock on the corporate books necessarily serves, though perhaps only incidentally, a similar purpose with respect to the officers and directors. If the validity of a stockholders' pooling agreement of the kind here presented were to be sustained, the way is clear for the creation of secret voting trusts. The statute clearly forbids them.

The Chancellor took the contrary view. He held the Agents' Agreement not to be a voting trust because (1) title to the stock did not pass to the Agents, and (2) because the Agents are in fact the agents and are subject to the directions of their principals.

The failure to transfer the stock on the books is not a sufficient reason in this case for holding the Agents' Agreement not a voting trust. It is an indication that the parties did not intend to create a voting trust; but that subjective intention is unimportant. The stock here was endorsed in blank and delivered to the agents for deposit in escrow with irrevocable proxies. Transfer of the stock on the books is not essential to effect an irrevocable transfer of voting rights to fiduciaries, divorced from the other attributes of the stock, in order to secure voting control, as the Agents' Agreement demonstrates. It is such a transfer that is the characteristic feature of a voting trust.

The fact that the Agents are subject to control by their respective principals does not prevent the agreement from constituting a voting trust. The stock is voted by the Agents as a group. No one stockholder retains complete control over the voting of its stock. It cannot vote its own stock directly; all it can do is to direct its Agent how to vote on a decision to be made by the Agents as a group. The stock of any corporate stockholder may at any time be voted against its will by the vote of the seven other agents. The control of the agents rests upon the provisions that they are severally chosen by the respective stockholders and each may be removed and replaced by the stockholder he represents. In effect, these provisions come to this: that each corporate stockholder participating in the agreement reserves the right to name and remove the fiduciary or fiduciaries representing him. Such a provision is not inconsistent with a voting trust. In fact, the scheme is carried forward to the voting trust set out as "Exhibit A" to the Agents' Agreement. See Paragraphs 3 and 5, paralleling Paragraphs 3 and 4 of the Agents' Agreement. And the alleged continuing control of the Agent by the stockholder clearly would not exist in the event of the death, removal or resignation of Davies in his capacity of Agent. In that case his successor, whether Agent or Trustee, is named by a majority of the remaining Agents or Trustees, as the case may be, and his estate has no control whatever over the Agent so named.

Defendants stress the contention that the parties to the Agents' Agreement did not intend to create a voting trust. As above noted, the intent that governs is the intent derived from the instrument itself. A desire to avoid the legal consequences of the language used is immaterial. Additional arguments (1) that the fiduciaries vested with voting rights are called agents instead of trustees, and (2) that title to the stock did not pass to the agents, have already been noticed.

In support of their argument that the Agents' Agreement creates only a stockholders' pooling agreement and not a voting trust, defendants lean heavily on the decision of this Court in Ringling Bros.-Barnum & Bailey Combined Shows v. Ringling, 29 Del.Ch. 610. That case involved a true pooling agreement, far short of a voting trust. Two stockholders agreed to act jointly in exercising their voting rights. There was no deposit of the stock with irrevocable stock powers conferring upon a group of fiduciaries exclusive voting powers over the pooled stock. Indeed, the Supreme Court (modifying the decision below) held that the agreement did not provide, either expressly or impliedly, for a proxy to either stockholder to vote the other's shares. The Ringling case is clearly distinguishable on the facts.

And although the case recognizes the validity of various forms of pooling agreements, it does not announce, as defendants appear to think, an unrestricted and uncritical approval of all agreements between stockholders relating to the voting of their stock. Not all pooling agreements are lawful. Cf. Smith v. Biggs Boiler Works Co., 32 Del.Ch. 147.

Defendants would push the general statements of the Ringling case to unwarranted lengths. They quote extensively from that part of the opinion which deals with the scope of the voting trust statute. Among other things, the Court said [29 Del.Ch. 610]:

"But the statute does not purport to deal with agreements whereby stockholders attempt to bind each other as to how they shall vote their shares."

We gather that defendants go so far as to say that a pooling agreement may assume any form whatever without running afoul of the voting trust statute. Thus, if we understand defendants' argument, a pooling agreement may, through the medium of fiduciaries with exclusive voting powers, lawfully accomplish substantially the same purposes as a voting trust and thus avoid compliance with § 218. We disagree. Obviously, as a pooling agreement in substance and purpose approaches more and more nearly the substance and purpose of the statute, there comes a point at which, if the statute is not complied with, the agreement is illegal. A pooling agreement may not escape the statutory controls by calling the trustees agents and giving to the stockholders receipts instead of voting trust certificates. If this were not so, stockholders could, through the device of an agreement such as the one before us, accept for themselves the chief benefits of the statute: unified voting control through fiduciaries for an appreciable period of time; and escape its burdens: the requirements for making an open record of the matter, and the limitations in respect of time. If the agreement before us is upheld, what is there to prevent a similar agreement for 15 years—or 25 years?

Although the general language of the Ringling case, if read literally, may seem to lend some support to the position of the defendants, we do not think that it should be carried so far as to permit the result urged by them in this case.

Defendants also rely on the decision of the Chancellor in Aldridge v. Franco-Wyoming Oil Co., supra. In that case an agreement provided for the deposit of shares with a trustee and the issuance of "bearer certificates" to the depositing stockholder. It was held not to be a voting trust, because under the agreement each stockholder retained full control of his stock. He could withdraw the stock from the trust at any time, or, as long as it remained in the trust, he could obtain a proxy to vote it at any time. The Aldridge case is not in point.

For the foregoing reasons, we are compelled to disagree with the holding of the Chancellor upon the question discussed. We are of opinion that the Agents' Agreement is void as an illegal voting trust.

Our conclusion upon this question makes it unnecessary to discuss any of the other questions raised on the appeal.

The cause is remanded to the Court of Chancery of New Castle County, with instructions to vacate paragraphs (2) to (5) inclusive of the order of October 24, 1956, and to enter a further order consistent with this opinion, with such provisions for injunctive relief, if any, as the Chancellor may determine to be appropriate.

E. BUY–SELL AGREEMENTS AND STOCK REDEMPTIONS

1. INTRODUCTORY NOTE

As noted above, there is no market for the stock in a close corporation. Any legal system, such as that in the United States, which contemplates the private ownership of property must concomitantly provide for the transferability of the property. (See Chapter VI below, for a further discussion of this problem.) But where no established public market exists for the securities of a business enterprise, either a market must be established or some means for the transfer of the securities must be designed, particularly in the event of the death of one of the security holders. Because of the nature of the close corporation, one much like a partnership in which new participants in the ownership of the enterprise are not welcome or wanted without the general consent of the existing owners, a public or limited public offering of the securities is not satisfactory. The owners of the securities of the enterprise are also the managers of the enterprise who have been accustomed to working with each other and frequently do not want to be bothered with the problem of adjusting to a new participant in the business not selected or acceptable to them. Thus, in many cases formal written agreements exist among the stockholders of a close corporation limiting the transfer of the stock in the corporation held by them either to each other or to the corporation itself. Even without a written agreement of this kind it is unlikely that any stranger would want to purchase the stock of a close corporation unless he knew in advance that he were acceptable to the other participants in the business; this is particularly true if the purchase of a minority interest were being considered.

Small corporations rarely pay dividends, in spite of the potential threat of Section 531 of the Internal Revenue Code, 26 U.S.C.A. § 531, which imposes a penalty tax on the corporation on the accumulation of its earnings beyond the reasonable needs of the business. Small business corporations, with adequate advice, can nearly always find appropriate and reasonable needs for the earnings of the business. In contrast to the large publicly held corporation where the shareholders invest to obtain a dividend, in small close corporations many substitutes for a return on the investment are found for those who are manager-owners of the business. These may include substantial salaries, pension plans, profit-sharing plans, medical expense reimbursement plans, group life, hospital and surgical benefit, health and accident insurance plans, travel and entertainment expense allowances, prepaid expenses to attend business conventions at far-off exotic places, extended vacations and frequent holidays, and the use of company-owned facilities for transportation or business-related recreation purposes. The expense of some or many of these benefits may be disallowed for income tax purposes to the business and may be taxed as additional income to the manager-owner, but since the tax never runs to 100% of the cost of these things, the manager-owner still derives a benefit from them. And even though additional taxes may have to be paid by the corporation and him because of some of these benefits, this penalty does not result in an equivalent benefit to a stockholder of the enterprise who is not participating in its management and does not receive these company paid management "fringes." Further, a minority stockholder suit complaining about the foregoing benefits to the management will be expensive to conduct, will probably result in only a limited success at best, and to the extent successful will result in a judgment requiring repayment of some of the benefits to the corporation; this does not put any payment into the hands of the dissenting stockholder. In short, in most close corporations the stock is held by the managers and the corporations are operated in a manner as though there were no minority stockholders, which, incidentally, is constantly destructive of any possibility of a transfer of its securities to a purchaser outside of the manager-owner group.

Thus the only market for the securities of a close corporation is limited to the existing shareholders or to the corporation itself. Generally the problem arises only when a manager-owner dies, or decides to withdraw from the business either because he has reached retirement age, or ill health or he has decided to engage in some other business activity. The first situation is the one dealt with most frequently because life insurance agents and trust departments of banks have done a fairly good job of educating manager-owners of the difficulties that would be faced by their estates or the survivors in the business if some means had not previously been prepared for the purchase of their securities in the close corporation upon the death of one of them. Much life insurance is sold in this manner, and many buy-sell agreements are prepared because life insurance is being sold. These are contracts which a person makes during his lifetime in reference to business property which he owns and are enforceable by or against his estate in all jurisdictions. This is another aspect of freedom of contract, of private ownership of property, which are characteristics of a democratic legal system. Once more, if we did not have this system, if all business property were owned by the state, or if it all were to pass to the state upon death, or if the state were to designate successor owners, or if there were no death taxes, then we would not have these legal problems; undoubtedly, we would have others.

The buy-sell agreement, accompanied by life insurance, may take several forms. Each has its own advantages and disadvantages. An agreement between two shareholders requiring the survivor of them to purchase the stock from the estate of the first to die is the simplest; if accompanied by life insurance (and it should be noted that there is no necessity of having life insurance to enforce one of these agreements) the survivor will normally have paid the premiums on the life insurance policy on his fellow stockholder and will have been made the beneficiary of the policy; the survivor will thus collect the proceeds upon the death of his fellow stockholder. It is customary to have the buy-sell agreement provide some formula for the evaluation of the stock upon the death of one of the shareholders, and in this manner a price is predetermined. The price is paid to the decedent's estate upon the transfer of the stock to the survivor; the estate then has money and the survivor is the sole owner of the business.

Another form of buy-sell agreement is one in which the corporation is a party to the agreement along with the shareholders, and in this form the corporation is obligated to buy the stock of a deceased stockholder upon his death. Under this type of agreement the corporation generally will have paid the premiums on the life insurance and will receive the proceeds of the policy upon the death of the shareholder and thus will have the cash to purchase his stock from his estate. Again the agreement will have the usual provisions which are found in the type of agreement made between stockholders, but this type of agreement is not necessarily enforceable by the decedent's estate against the corporation. If the corporation is in a deficit position at the time of the death of the stockholder, when the proceeds of the life insurance are received, it is possible that under the law of the state of its incorporation it may not be permitted to use any of its assets to redeem (that is, purchase from a stockholder) any of its stock. Cash received by a corporation from the proceeds of life insurance is just another asset of the corporation to which the creditors of the corporation can look for the payment of their claims. Sometimes, in contemplation of this problem, the buy-sell agreement will be made with a trustee who will receive the life insurance proceeds, use the proceeds to purchase the stock from the decedent's estate, and pursuant to the trust agreement transfer the stock to the corporation for cancellation. It is believed that this type of an arrangement would not withstand a vigorous challenge brought by creditors of a corporation in financial difficulty.

The payment of the premiums for the life insurance used in the buy-sell agreement creates many problems. If the agreement is one between stockholders alone, either they must have the resources to pay the premiums themselves, or if the premiums are paid by the corporation, then they must be prepared to have the premium payment treated as taxable income to them; if perchance they should have received this money as a bonus, that is, as additional compensation, it may be deductible to the corporation as a salary expense under the provisions of Section 162 of the Internal Revenue Code. But if it is not allowed as salary, then it will be treated as a dividend and the corporation will receive no deduction for income taxes at all. If the corporation is the owner and beneficiary of the policy, and pays the premium, the corporation will not receive any deduction for the payment of the premiums under the provisions of Section 264(a) (1) of the Internal Revenue Code, and at present it is thought that the stockholders will not be taxable in any manner as a consequence of the payment of the premium. However, it is clearly demonstrable that the stockholders receive a benefit from this type of transaction, and it should not be assumed for all time that the payment of the premium by the corporation will not in any manner be taxable to the shareholders. One thing is generally clear; under the provisions of Section 101(a) of the Internal Revenue Code amounts received under a life insurance contract paid by reason of the death of the insured are excluded from gross income and thus are not subject to an income tax whether received by the corporation or by a surviving stockholder. (This may not be true if the life insurance policy of which the proceeds have been paid was a pre-existing policy which was purchased for a valuable consideration by the surviving stockholder or the corporation under the above arrangements.)

The most difficult problems in this area, however, are still tax problems. Frequently shareholders will not have sufficient resources to be able to purchase the stock of a deceased or retiring stockholder. Or, they may have such a large portion of their resources already committed to the business enterprise that in good sound financial planning they are reluctant to raise the additional money (by sale of other assets or by borrowing upon them) to purchase the additional stock. Further, they may not have sufficient income or resources to pay the premiums on the policies of life insurance necessary to provide the funds to purchase the stock of a decedent, or to use the cash values in the policies as a source of funds to buy the stock of a retiring stockholder. Thus they are almost compelled to plan on using the arrangement whereby the corporation will purchase the stock of a retiring or deceased stockholder. When a corporation buys its stock this transaction for tax purposes is called a "redemption," whether or not the stock so acquired is cancelled, retired, or held as treasury stock. (§ 317(b), Internal Revenue Code, 26 U.S.C.A.)

Stock redemptions cause tax trouble. A distribution of money or other property "[m]ade by a corporation to a shareholder with respect to its stock * * *" if made out of current or accumulated earnings and profits is taxable as a dividend, that is, as ordinary income. (Internal Revenue Code §§ 301(a), 301(c), 316(a), and 317 (a), 26 U.S.C.A.). If, however, a corporation redeems its stock in a limited number of ways as provided in Section 302(b) of the Internal Revenue Code, then the payment made on the redemption instead of being taxed as a dividend, will be taxed as part or full payment in exchange for the stock, that is, as a capital gain, and if the stock has been held for six months or more, then as a long term capital gain. (Internal Revenue Code § 302(a), 26 U.S.C.A.). But only those redemptions which satisfy the requirements of Internal Revenue Code, Section 302(b) will qualify for the capital gain treatment. Where stock in a corporation forms a substantial part of a decedent's estate, a redemption from the estate of an amount of that stock sufficient to pay death taxes and funeral and administration expenses, although it does not comply with Section 302(b) will not be taxed as a dividend. (§ 303(a), Internal Revenue Code, 26 U.S.C.A.). It will be treated as a capital transaction, and frequently, because of other provisions of the Internal Revenue Code not relevant here, it will not be taxable at all. All other redemptions which do not qualify under Section 302(b) or Section 303(a) are taxable dividends. (Internal Revenue Code § 302(d), 26 U.S.C.A.).

The language of most statutes is rather difficult (although see Sections 1 and 2 of the Sherman Anti-Trust Act, 15 U.S.C.A. §§ 1 and 2, referred to in Chapter VII below, and selected sections of the Bankruptcy Act in Chapter XI below). The Internal Revenue Code, even to those persons who work with it professionally a great deal of time, is very difficult reading. The Regulations adopted under the Internal Revenue Code are more easily read, although these also often have the effect of a soporific. Revenue Rulings generally are easier reading although few laymen would consider them "vacation" or "hospital" type reading.

Congress has enacted the Internal Revenue Code. The Regulations have been adopted pursuant to the provisions of the Administrative Procedure Act, 5 U.S.C.A. § 551, et seq., (See Chapter VIII below). This means that the Treasury Department will have drafted the Regulations after much study, and proposed them to the public by advertising them in the *Federal Register,* and inviting comments concerning the proposals. Tax practitioners, industry groups, and other lobbyists generally, will respond to this invitation, and frequently this results in a revision in the Proposed Regulations. In any event, the Regulations become final only after a great amount of consideration has been given to them by government and the public. As a consequence they are given great weight by the courts in deciding tax matters. Revenue Rulings, on the other hand, are announcements of policy positions taken by the Internal Revenue Service, generally in reference to a specific problem, and are published in the *Internal Revenue Bulletin* each week. These are available for the guidance of the taxpaying public as well as by Internal Revenue Service personnel; they are nearly always followed by the courts. Rev.Rul. 56–103, reported below, is a typical example of a Revenue Ruling.

U. S. v. Maclin P. Davis, 397 U.S. 301, 90 S.Ct. 1041, 25 L.Ed.2d 323 (1970) deals with some of the difficult problems involved in stock redemptions of close corporations. Note also how the principle of "substance over form" is applied in this situation. The conflict between fair taxation and maintaining free transferability of property, both attributes of a democratic business system, is not easily resolved, and in most cases the conflict is won by the taxing authorities. Perhaps people should arrange their affairs with a long-term consideration of the tax impact upon them; it would not be impossible.

26 CFR 1.302–2: REDEMPTIONS NOT TAXABLE AS DIVIDENDS

Rev.Rul. 56–103.

Where a majority shareholder is also a beneficiary of his father's estate, a redemption by a corporation of that part of its capital stock held by the estate constitutes a distribution essentially equivalent to a dividend under the provisions of section 302(d) of the Internal Revenue Code of 1954, regardless of the fact that a part of such redemption is pursuant to a contract between the decedent and the corporation.

Advice has been requested relative to the Federal income tax consequences of a redemption by a corporation of a part of its common stock held by an estate.

Corporation *A* had only common stock outstanding of which 27 percent of the shares were owned by the estate of *B*, 48 percent by the decedent's son, and the remaining 25 percent by employees of the corporation who are unrelated to the decedent. The value of the estate of B is estimated at $250x$ dollars, including the 27 percent stock interest in corporation A. The sole beneficiary of the estate was the decedent's son.

In 1947 corporation A entered into an agreement with B, now deceased, which provided that the corporation would in the event of death purchase from his estate as many shares of its stock as could be purchased for $75x$ dollars. The purchase price per share of the stock was set at the book value as of the date of death. Under this contract the corporation was obligated to purchase 13 percent of the stock of corporation A from the estate.

The estate of B and the minority shareholders of corporation A desired to have the corporation acquire all of its stock owned by the estate. Accordingly, the corporation redeemed 13 percent of its stock from the estate for $75x$ dollars as provided in the contract, and, in addition, redeemed the remaining shares (14 percent) of stock held by the estate at the same price.

Section 302 of the Internal Revenue Code of 1954 relating to distributions in redemption of stock, provides in part:

> (a) GENERAL RULE.—If a corporation redeems its stock * * * and if paragraph (1), (2), (3), or (4) of subsection (b) applies, such redemption shall be treated as a distribution in part or full payment in exchange for the stock.

Section 318(a) of the Code applies in determining the ownership of stock for purposes of section 302(b). Insofar as is pertinent, stock owned by a beneficiary of an estate is considered as being owned by the estate within the purview of section 318(a) (2) (A) of the Code.

In the instant case, the estate of B, for the purposes of section 302, is considered to own all of the stock owned by the sole beneficiary of the estate. Therefore, the estate owned 75 percent (27 percent plus 48 percent) of the shares of the corporation's stock. Hence, such a redemption did not qualify as a termination of a shareholder's interest or as a substantially disproportionate redemption under section 302 (b) (2) and (3) of the Code.

Section 302(b) (1) of the Code with respect to redemptions treated as exchanges reads as follows:

> * * * REDEMPTIONS NOT EQUIVALENT TO DIVIDENDS.
> —Subsection (a) shall apply if the redemption is not essentially equivalent to a dividend.

In determining whether a distribution in redemption is essentially equivalent to a dividend, each case must be decided upon its own particular circumstances. The courts have held in many cases that whether a redemption of stock is essentially equivalent to a dividend depends primarily upon the net effect of the distribution rather than the motives and plans of the shareholders or the corporation. See

M. A. Flanagan et al. v. Helvering, 116 Fed. (2d) 937; James H. Boyle v. Commissioner, 187 Fed. (2d) 557, certiorari denied, 342 U.S. 817; Joshua E. Smith v. United States, 121 Fed. (2d) 692. The absence of a plan to avoid taxation is not controlling. A redemption of stock which does not as a practical matter change the essential relationship between the stockholders and the corporation is generally considered equivalent to a dividend. See John T. Roberts et al. v. Commissioner, 203 Fed. (2d) 304.

As the relative stock interest of the principal shareholder was not materially changed by the redemption, the distribution to him is equivalent to a dividend. J. Natwick v. Commissioner, 36 B.T.A. 866; W. & K. Holding Co. v. Commissioner, 38 B.T.A. 830. The fact that the redemption is pursuant to a contract between the corporation and the decedent does not appear to be significant for this purpose.

Accordingly, it is held that (except to the extent that the distribution may qualify under the provisions of section 303 of the Code as a redemption of stock to pay death taxes) the redemption by the corporation of a part of its stock from the estate constituted a distribution essentially equivalent to a dividend. Such redemption is treated as a distribution of property to which section 301 applies as provided in section 302(d) of the Code, and is taxable as a dividend to the extent of earnings and profits of the corporation as defined in section 316 of the Code.

UNITED STATES v. DAVIS

Supreme Court of the United States, 1970.
397 U.S. 301, 90 S.Ct. 1041, 25 L.Ed.2d 323.

Mr. Justice MARSHALL delivered the opinion of the Court.

In 1945, taxpayer and E. B. Bradley organized a corporation. In exchange for property transferred to the new company, Bradley received 500 shares of common stock, and taxpayer and his wife similarly each received 250 such shares. Shortly thereafter, taxpayer made an additional contribution to the corporation, purchasing 1,000 shares of preferred stock at a par value of $25 per share.

The purpose of this latter transaction was to increase the company's working capital and thereby to qualify for a loan previously negotiated through the Reconstruction Finance Corporation. It was understood that the corporation would redeem the preferred stock when the RFC loan had been repaid. Although in the interim taxpayer bought Bradley's 500 shares and divided them between his son and daughter, the total capitalization of the company remained the same until 1963. That year, after the loan was fully repaid and in accordance with the original understanding, the company redeemed taxpayer's preferred stock.

In his 1963 personal income tax return taxpayer did not report the $25,000 received by him upon the redemption of his preferred stock as income.   Rather, taxpayer considered the redemption as a sale of his preferred stock to the company—a capital gains transaction under § 302 of the Internal Revenue Code of 1954 resulting in no tax since taxpayer's basis in the stock equaled the amount he received for it.   The Commissioner of Internal Revenue, however, did not approve this tax treatment.   According to the Commissioner, the redemption of taxpayer's stock was essentially equivalent to a dividend and was thus taxable as ordinary income under §§ 301 and 316 of the Code. Taxpayer paid the resulting deficiency and brought this suit for a refund.   The District Court ruled in his favor, 274 F.Supp. 466 (D.C. M.D.Tenn.1967), and on appeal the Court of Appeals affirmed.   408 F.2d 1139 (C.A.6th Cir. 1969).

The Court of Appeals held that the $25,000 received by taxpayer was "not essentially equivalent to a dividend" within the meaning of that phrase in § 302(b) (1) of the Code because the redemption was the final step in a course of action that had a legitimate business (as opposed to tax avoidance) purpose.   That holding represents only one of a variety of treatments accorded similar transactions under § 302 (b) (1) in the circuit courts of appeals.   We granted certiorari, 396 U.S. 815 (1969), in order to resolve this recurring tax question involving stock redemptions by closely held corporations.   We reverse.

I

The Internal Revenue Code of 1954 provides generally in §§ 301 and 316 for the tax treatment of distributions by a corporation to its shareholders; under those provisions, a distribution is includible in a taxpayer's gross income as a dividend out of earnings and profits to the extent such earnings exist.   There are exceptions to the application of these general provisions, however, and among them are those found in § 302 involving certain distributions for redeemed stock. The basic question in this case is whether the $25,000 distribution by the corporation to taxpayer falls under that section—more specifically, whether its legitimate business motivation qualifies the distribution under § 302(b) (1) of the Code.   Preliminarily, however, we must consider the relationship between § 302(b) (1) and the rules regarding the attribution of stock ownership found in § 318(a) of the Code.

Under subsection (a) of § 302, a distribution is treated as "payment in exchange for the stock," thus qualifying for capital gains rather than ordinary income treatment, if the conditions contained in any one of the four paragraphs of subsection (b) are met.   In addition to paragraph (1)'s "not essentially equivalent to a dividend" test, capital gains treatment is available where (2) the taxpayer's voting strength is substantially diminished, (3) his interest in the company is completely terminated, or (4) certain railroad stock is redeemed. Paragraph (4) is not involved here, and taxpayer admits that paragraphs (2) and (3) do not apply.   Moreover, taxpayer agrees that for the purposes of §§ 302(b) (2) and (3) the attribution rules of § 318(a) apply and he is considered to own the 750 outstanding shares of common stock held by his wife and children in addition to the 250 shares in his own name.[1]

Taxpayer, however, argues that the attribution rules do not apply in considering whether a distribution is essentially equivalent to a dividend under § 302(b) (1). According to taxpayer, he should thus be considered to own only 25 percent of the corporation's common stock, and the distribution would then qualify under § 302(b) (1) since it was not pro rata or proportionate to his stock interest, the fundamental test of dividend equivalency. See Treas.Reg. 1.302–2(b). However, the plain language of the statute compels rejection of the argument. In subsection (c) of § 302, the attribution rules are made specifically applicable "in determining the ownership of stock for purposes of this section." Applying this language, both courts below held that § 318(a) applies to all of § 302, including § 302(b) (1)—a view in accord with the decisions of the other courts of appeals, a longstanding treasury regulation, and the opinion of the leading commentators.

Against this weight of authority, taxpayer argues that the result under paragraph (1) should be different because there is no explicit reference to stock ownership as there is in paragraphs (2) and (3). Neither that fact, however, nor the purpose and history of § 302(b) (1) support taxpayer's argument. The attribution rules—designed to provide a clear answer to what would otherwise be a difficult tax question—formed part of the tax bill that was subsequently enacted as the 1954 Code. As is discussed further, infra, the bill as passed by the House of Representatives contained no provision comparable to § 302 (b) (1). When that provision was added in the Senate, no purpose was evidenced to restrict the applicability of § 318(a). Rather, the attribution rules continued to be made specifically applicable to the entire section, and we believe that Congress intended that they be taken into account wherever ownership of stock was relevant.

Indeed, it was necessary that the attribution rules apply to § 302 (b) (1) unless they were to be effectively eliminated from consideration with regard to §§ 302(b) (2) and (3) also. For if a transaction failed to qualify under one of those sections solely because of the attribution rules, it would according to taxpayer's argument nonetheless qualify under § 302(b) (1). We cannot agree that Congress intended so to nullify its explicit directive. We conclude, therefore, that the attribution rules of § 318(a) do apply; and, for the purposes of deciding whether a distribution is "not essentially equivalent to a dividend"

---

1. Section 318(a) provides in relevant part as follows:
"General rules.—For purposes of those provisions of this subchapter to which the rules contained in this section are expressly made applicable—
"(1) Members of family.—
"(A) In general.—An individual shall be considered as owning the stock owned, directly, or indirectly, by or for—

"(i) his spouse (other than spouse who is legally separated from the individual under a decree of divorce or separate maintenance), and
"(ii) his children, grandchildren, and parents."
In § 318(b) the rules contained in subsection (a) are made specifically applicable to "section 302 (relating to the redemption of stock)." (Court's footnote 4.)

under § 302(b) (1), taxpayer must be deemed the owner of all 1,000 shares of the company's common stock.

II

After application of the stock ownership attribution rules, this case viewed most simply involves a sole stockholder who causes part of his shares to be redeemed by the corporation. We conclude that such a redemption is always "essentially equivalent to a dividend" within the meaning of that phrase in § 302(b) (1) [2] and therefore do not reach the Government's alternative argument that in any event the distribution should not on the facts of this case qualify for capital gains treatment.

* * *

By the time of the general revision resulting in the Internal Revenue Code of 1954, the draftsmen were faced with what has aptly been described as "the morass created by the decisions." Ballenger v. United States, 301 F.2d 192, 196 (C.A.4th Cir. 1962). In an effort to eliminate "the considerable confusion which exists in this area" and thereby to facilitate tax planning, H.R.Rep.No.1337, 83d Cong., 2d Sess., at 35, the authors of the new Code sought to provide objective tests to govern the tax consequences of stock redemptions. Thus, the tax bill passed by the House of Representatives contained no "essentially equivalent" language. Rather, it provided for "safe harbors" where capital gains treatment would be accorded to corporate redemptions that met the conditions now found in §§ 302(b) (2) and (3) of the Code.

It was in the Senate Finance Committee's consideration of the tax bill that § 302(b) (1) was added, and Congress thereby provided that capital gains treatment should be available "if the redemption is not essentially equivalent to a dividend." Taxpayer argues that the purpose was to continue "existing law," and there is support in the legislative history that § 302(b) (1) reverted "in part" or "in general" to the "essentially equivalent" provision of § 115(g) (1) of the 1939 Code. According to the Government, even under the old law it would have been improper for the Court of Appeals to rely on "a business purpose for the redemption" and "an absence of the proscribed tax avoidance purpose to bail out dividends at favorable tax rates." * * * However, we need not decide that question, for we find from the history of the 1954 revisions and the purpose of § 302(b) (1) that Congress intended more than merely to re-enact the prior law.

In explaining the reason for adding the "substantially equivalent" test, the Senate Committee stated that the House provisions "appeared unnecessarily restrictive, particularly, in the case of redemptions of preferred stock which might be called by the corporation without the shareholder having any control over when the redemption may take

2. Of course, this just means that a distribution in redemption to a sole shareholder will be treated under the general provisions of § 301, and it will only be taxed as a dividend under § 316 to the extent that there are earnings and profits. (Court's footnote 8.)

place." S.Rep.No.1622, 83d Cong., 2d Sess., at 44. This explanation gives no indication that the purpose behind the redemption should affect the result. Rather, in its more detailed technical evaluation of § 302(b) (1), the Senate Committee reported as follows:

> The test intended to be incorporated in the interpretation of paragraph (1) is in general that currently employed under section 115(g) (1) of the 1939 Code. Your committee further intends that in applying this test for the future that the inquiry will be devoted solely to the question of whether or not the transaction by its nature may properly be characterized as a sale of stock by the redeeming shareholder to the corporation. For this purpose the presence or absence of earnings and profits of the corporation is not material. Example: X, the sole shareholder of a corporation having no earnings or profits causes the corporation to redeem half of its stock. Paragraph (1) does not apply to such redemption notwithstanding the absence of earnings and profits. S.Rep. No.1622, *supra*, at 234.

The intended scope of § 302(b) (1) as revealed by this legislative history is certainly not free from doubt. However, we agree with the Government that by making the sole inquiry relevant for the future the narrow one whether the redemption could be characterized as a sale, Congress was apparently rejecting past court decisions that had also considered factors indicating the presence or absence of a tax avoidance motive. At least that is the implication of the example given. Congress clearly mandated that pro rata distributions be treated under the general rules laid down in §§ 301 and 316 rather than under § 302, and nothing suggests that there should be a different result if there were a "business purpose" for the redemption. Indeed, just the opposite inference must be drawn since there would not likely be a tax avoidance purpose in a situation where there were no earnings or profits. We conclude that the Court of Appeals was therefore wrong in looking for a business purpose and considering it in deciding whether the redemption was equivalent to a dividend. Rather, we agree with the Court of Appeals for the Second Circuit that: "the business purpose of a transaction is irrelevant in determining dividend equivalency" under § 302(b) (1). Hasbrook v. United States, 343 F. 2d 811 (1965).

Taxpayer strongly argues that to treat the redemption involved here as essentially equivalent to a dividend is to elevate form over substance. Thus, taxpayer argues, had he not bought Bradley's shares or had he made a subordinated loan to the company instead of buying preferred stock, he could have gotten back his $25,000 with favorable tax treatment. However, the difference between form and substance in the tax law is largely problematical, and taxpayer's complaints have little to do with whether a business purpose is relevant under § 302(b) (1). It was clearly proper for Congress to treat distributions generally as taxable dividends when made out of earnings and profits and then to prevent avoidance of that result without regard to motivation where the distribution is in exchange for redeemed stock.

We conclude that that is what Congress did when enacting § 302 (b) (1). If a corporation distributes property as a simple dividend, the effect is to transfer the property from the company to its shareholders without a change in the relative economic interests or rights of the stockholders. Where a redemption has that same effect, it cannot be said to have satisfied the "not essentially equivalent to a dividend" requirement of § 302(b) (1). Rather, to qualify for preferred treatment under that section, a redemption must result in a meaningful reduction of the shareholder's proportionate interest in the corporation. Clearly, taxpayer here, who (after application of the attribution rules) was the sole shareholder of the corporation both before and after the redemption, did not qualify under this test. The decision of the Court of Appeals must therefore be reversed and the case remanded to the District Court for dismissal of the complaint.

It is so ordered.

Mr. Justice DOUGLAS, with whom THE CHIEF JUSTICE and Mr. Justice BRENNAN concur, dissenting.

F. MINORITY PROPOSALS

SEC v. MEDICAL COMMITTEE FOR HUMAN RIGHTS

Supreme Court of the United States, 1972.
404 U.S. 403, 92 S.Ct. 577, 39 L.Ed.2d 560.

Mr. Justice MARSHALL delivered the opinion of the Court.

The Medical Committee for Human Rights acquired by gift five shares of stock in Dow Chemical Co. In March 1968, the Committee's national chairman wrote a letter to the company expressing concern over its policy with respect to the production and sale of napalm. The letter also requested that there be included in the company's proxy statement for 1968 a proposal to amend Dow's Certificate of Incorporation to prohibit the sale of napalm unless the purchaser gives reasonable assurance that the napalm will not be used against human beings. Dow replied that the proposal was too late for inclusion in the 1968 proxy statement and for discussion at that year's annual meeting, but that it would be reconsidered the following year.

In an exchange of letters with Dow in 1969, the Committee indicated its belief that it had a right under Rule 14a–8 of the Securities and Exchange Commission, 17 CFR § 240.14a–8 (1970) (promulgated pursuant to § 14(a) of the Securities-Exchange Act of 1934, 48 Stat. 895, as amended, 15 U.S.C.A. § 78n(a)), to have its proposal included in the company's proxy statement for consideration by all shareholders. On February 7, 1969, Dow responded that it intended to omit the proposal from the 1969 statement under the authority of subsections of the SEC Rule relied on by the Committee which permitted omission of shareholder proposals under two sets of circumstances:

§ (c) (2)—"If it clearly appears that the proposal is submitted by the security holder primarily for the purpose of enforcing a personal claim or redressing a personal grievance against the issuer or its management, or primarily for the purpose of promoting general economic, political, racial, religious, social or similar causes"; or

§ (c) (5)—"If the proposal consists of a recommendation or request that the management take action with respect to a matter relating to the conduct of the ordinary business operations of the issuer."

Dow requested that its decision be reviewed by the Division of Corporation Finance of the SEC. On February 18, 1969, the Chief Counsel for the Division wrote both Dow and the Committee to inform them that "this Division will not recommend any action to the Commission if this proposal is omitted from the management's proxy material." App., at 21. The SEC Commissioners granted a request by the Committee that they review the Division's decision and affirmed it. App., at 43. The Committee then sought and obtained review of the Commission's decision in the United States Court of Appeals for the District of Columbia.

On July 8, 1970, the Court of Appeals held that the decision of the SEC was reviewable under § 25(a) of the Securities-Exchange Act of 1934, 15 U.S.C.A. § 78(y) (a); that while review of Dow's decision was clearly available in District Court, review of the SEC's decision could also be obtained in a Court of Appeals; that the validity of the Commission's determination was extremely dubious, especially in light of its failure to state reasons supporting its conclusions; and that the case should be remanded to the Commission for reconsideration and a statement of reasons. 139 U.S.App.D.C. 226, 432 F.2d 659. The Commission petitioned for review here, and we granted certiorari on March 22, 1971. 401 U.S. 973.

Events have taken place, subsequent to the decision by the court below, and some subsequent to our decision to grant certiorari, which require that we dismiss this case on the ground that it has now become moot. In January 1971, the Medical Committee again submitted its napalm resolution for inclusion in Dow's 1971 proxy statement. This time Dow acquiesced in the Committee's request and included the proposal. At the annual stockholder's meeting in May 1971, Dow's shareholders voted on the Committee's proposal. Less than 3% of all voting shareholders supported it, and pursuant to Rule 14a–8(c) (4) (i), 17 CFR § 240.14a–8(c) (4) (i), Dow may exclude the same or substantially the same proposal from its proxy materials for the next three years. We find that this series of events has mooted the controversy.

Respondent argues that it will continue to urge the adoption of the proposal and its inclusion in proxy statements, and that it is likely that Dow will reject inclusion in the future as it has in the past. It is true that in permitting the proposal to be included in the 1971 proxy statement Dow stated that it adhered to its opinion that the proposal might properly be omitted and that its inclusion was without prejudice to future exclusion. However, this does not create the controversy that is necessary for us to retain jurisdiction to decide the merits. Whether or not the Committee will actually resubmit its proposal or a similar one in 1974 is purely a matter of conjecture at this point, as is whether or not Dow will accept it. If Dow were likely to repeat its allegedly illegal conduct, the case would not be moot. See Walling v. Helmerich & Payne, Inc., 323 U.S. 37, 43; United States v. W. T. Grant Co., 345 U.S. 629, 632–633 (1953). However, in light of the meager support the proposal attracted, we can only speculate that Dow will continue to include the proposal when it again becomes eligible for inclusion, rather than to repeat this litigation. Thus, we find that "the allegedly wrongful behavior could not reasonably be expected to recur." United States v. Phosphate Export Association, 393 U.S. 199 (1968). The case is therefore moot.

"[I]t is well settled that federal courts may act only in the context of a justiciable case or controversy." Benton v. Maryland, 395 U.S. 784, 788, 23 L.Ed.2d 707, 712, 89 S.Ct. 2056 (1969). "Our lack of jurisdiction to review moot cases derives from the requirement of Article III of the Constitution under which the exercise of judicial power depends upon the existence of a case or controversy." Liner v. Jafco, Inc., 375 U.S. 301, 306 n. 3; cf. Doremus v. Board of Education, 342 U.S. 429, 434 (1952).

Accordingly, the judgment of the Court of Appeals is vacated and the case is remanded to that court for dismissal.

Mr. Justice POWELL and Mr. Justice REHNQUIST took no part in the consideration or decision of this case.

SEPARATE OPINION

Mr. Justice DOUGLAS, dissenting.

With all respect, I must dissent from the judgment of the Court that this case has become moot because the Dow Chemical Company acquiesced in the decision of the Court of Appeals below. The underlying dispute in this case is essentially a private one, between Dow and the Medical Committee for Human Rights, though it has large public overtones. In 1969, Dow refused to submit to its shareholders the Medical Committee's proposal that Dow amend its corporate charter to forbid the manufacture of napalm. Dow refused again in 1970. Only in 1971, after the decision of the Court of Appeals now under review, did Dow permit such a proposal to be submitted for a vote. In doing so, however, Dow resolutely affirmed its right to reject the proposal at any future time.

This gratuitous conduct did not, in my view, moot the controversy. "Mere voluntary cessation of allegedly illegal conduct does not moot a case." United States v. Concentrated Phosphate Export Ass'n., 393 U.S. 199. If it could, then a defendant would always be "free to return to his old ways." United States v. W. T. Grant Co., 345 U.S. 629, 632.

But it is said that because of the poor showing made by the proposal when finally submitted, Dow could refuse to resubmit it for three years under SEC proxy rules not at issue in this case. Ante, p. 406. The Court suggests that it is "purely a matter of conjecture" that the proposal will again be submitted at the expiration of this period, and that Dow will attempt again to reject it. The Court seems to think that Dow's best strategy, given the proposal's poor showing, is to let it go to a vote, rather than undertake protracted litigation. Ante, p. 406.

This assumption, however, is not only baseless, it is irrelevant. In Grant, supra, an antitrust violation was charged because of an interlocking directorate. In response to the suits, the interlocking directors resigned, and defendant companies represented to the court their intention not to revive the interlock. We disposed of this argument in summary fashion. "Such a profession does not suffice to make a case moot." Id., at 633. Here, Dow has not even made the minimal representation we rejected in Grant, nor is it likely to do so.

This is not a controversy that could not arise again for decades, Golden v. Zwickler, 394 U.S. 103, or a controversy whose decision could have no possible future effect on the parties, Atherton Mills v. Johnston, 259 U.S. 13. Dow has for the past four years fought tooth and nail its obligation to include this shareholder proposal. While "[a] case might become moot if subsequent events made it absolutely clear that the allegedly wrongful behavior could not reasonably be expected to recur," Concentrated Phosphate, supra, at 203, that is hardly the situation here.

While this litigation is not formally between Dow and the Medical Committee, but between the SEC and the Medical Committee, it does involve a whole panoply of substantive and procedural rights in connection with a corporation's obligation to include shareholder proposals in proxy materials. The modern super-corporations, of which Dow is one, wield immense, virtually unchecked power. Some say that they are "private governments," whose decisions affect the lives of us all. The philosophy of our times, I think, requires that such enterprises be held to a higher standard than that of the "morals of the marketplace" which exalts a single-minded, myopic determination to maximize profits as the traditional be-all and end-all of corporate concern. The "public interest in having the legality of the practices settled militates against a mootness conclusion." Grant, supra, at 632, 97 L.Ed. at 1309.

There is no reason to assume Dow's antipathy to the inclusion of this shareholder proposal will be any less in 1974 than it is today.

Perhaps Dow will adopt the advice given to it by the Court. But it is just as likely to decide its superior financial position makes continued litigation the preferable alternative, which may now be conducted under proxy rules more favorable to corporate management than are the present rules.

This case now joins a growing list of monuments to the present Court's abdication of its constitutional responsibility to decide cases properly within its jurisdiction. See, e. g., Picard v. Connor, 404 U.S. 270, (Douglas, J., dissenting); North Carolina v. Rice, 404 U.S. 244, (Douglas, J., dissenting); McClanahan v. Morauer & Hartzell, Inc., 404 U.S. 16, (Douglas, J., dissenting). Once again, I dissent.

QUESTIONS

1. If the state owned or controlled all business units, would there be any necessity for any internal controls within a business? How would the managers be required to account to the owners, that is, the government, for their operations? Would criminal laws be appropriate? Or some system of civil penalties? If so, where would the managers get the money to pay the penalties? In a privately owned system, where the managers control other people's property should they be required to account to the owners in the same fashion as the trustees of a family trust? If so, what effect would this have on the initiative of the managers? Or should the trustees of family trusts be permitted (if not required) to use more initiative? Or should we determine by some national law what standard of conduct we expect from managers of interstate corporations whose stockholders reside in more than one state? Should we require all states to adopt the same standards?

2. Should we rely on minority stockholder's suits to maintain the rights of the owners against management or should we establish a governmental agency for this purpose? How diffuse was the ownership of corporations when the body of law relating to officer's and director's liability for mismanagement developed? Were Federal regulatory agencies developed in part as a consequence of this diffusion of ownership? Is this system of minority stockholder's suits working well enough to require the managers of corporations to deal fairly with stockholders?

3. Should officers and directors of a corporation be permitted to be indemnified against judgments which may be rendered against them for their mismanagement? With or without fraudulent activity on their part? If not, is it possible that only a few people would serve as directors of large enterprises? How do the military services obtain generals and admirals to manage large military enterprises? Do they have a system of indemnification? Do the rules of the club immunize them from liability for their mismanagement? Should the law require that evidence of mismanagement be produced in the same manner that evidence of malpractice by a physician is produced, that is by

the testimony of other physicians who state that in their opinion the defendant did less than is customary in the profession? If this were the rule of evidence, would a new type of lodge of corporate managers be created, dedicated to secrecy in these matters?

4. In what manner do the tax laws in reference to stock redemptions contribute to the concentration of economic power? Does the inability to sell stock in a corporation to that corporation result in small corporations being sold to larger ones? Should some other means of providing for the transferability of stock in small business enterprises be developed? If so, how? Would the elimination of the favorable tax treatment of long term capital gains make any difference in this problem?

5. Should we permit corporate management to solicit proxies from the shareholders of their corporation? If so, should we permit this to be done at corporate expense? If not at corporate expense, would it not mean that the compensation to be paid to directors and officers would have to be increased in an amount sufficient to pay for the cost of proxy solicitations? Should we require that minority stockholders be permitted to solicit proxies at corporate expense? If so, how large a group should be required before this could be done at corporate expense? Is the SEC exercising its powers adequately in reference to the proxy solicitation rules it has established? In enforcing the rules which it has established? Should the law be changed in reference to the manner of proxy solicitations? How?

Suggested Reference Sources

Texts and Treatises

Aranow & Einhorn, *Proxy Contests For Corporate Control.* Columbia University Press, New York City.

Fletcher, *Cyclopedia of the Law of Private Corporations.* Callaghan & Company, Mundelein, Illinois.

Washington & Bishop, *Indemnifying The Corporate Executive, Business, Legal And Tax Aspects of Reimbursement For Personal Liability.* Ronald Press, New York City.

Topic Headings in the Index to Legal Periodicals

Corporations: Stockholders
Corporations: Voting

Chapter V

SALE AND TRANSFER OF SECURITIES

A. SALE OF NEW STOCK—SECURITIES ACT OF 1933

INTRODUCTORY NOTE—FULL AND FAIR DISCLOSURE

A democratic society, like every other society, is concerned with the manner in which the profits of its economic system are invested and reinvested. The products of the economy remaining after current consumption are called profits, and the profits of the economy as a whole are available for investment. Every economy has evolved a system of equating its production and property in terms of monetary units, and in the United States we refer to the profits of our economy as a given sum of dollars per year. In an economy with a gross national product of more than $1,000,000,000,000 per year and profits or savings amounting to more than $50,000,000,000 or 5% of the gross national product, some system must exist to provide for the investment and reinvestment of this huge sum. When we talk of savings of this amount we also mean investment and reinvestment of this amount because investment cannot exist without savings. Savings equal investment; investment equals savings. This relatively simple formula lies at the bottom of economic progress. There can be no economic progress without profits and there can be no funds available for investment unless there are profits and as the profits are saved they also must be invested. The legal problems involved in the manner in which this is done in a democratic society are the subject of inquiry in this Chapter.

In an authoritarian society the channeling of profits of the economy into new investment is generally performed by a government planning office and by government decree. If the current production plan established by the government calls for additional agricultural production, a decision to put 100,000,000 units of the currency of the country into a new plant to build tractors will be done as a consequence of various governmental orders. In a free society (admittedly a relative phrase) the decision to invest in a new tractor plant will be made almost entirely without government orders. Tax and fiscal policies of the government can, of course, and do, make substantial differences in the timing of the investment but no governmental directives relating to making investments will be issued. Existing tractor manufacturers will consider the reinvestment of some of the earnings of their enterprises in expanded facilities; competitors in similar lines of business considering the possibility of entering into the tractor manufacturing business will do a substantial amount of planning and research (inquiries which may possibly be similar to those made in governmental bureaus in authoritarian societies) and will consider the extent of the capital requirements to expand into a new line of business, and new groups made up of persons who may not be experienced in the production of tractors will contemplate the formation of a new enterprise for this purpose and of obtaining capital from outside sources to develop a new unit in the tractor manufacturing industry. The additional capital thus will come either from undistributed earnings of an existing enterprise or from outside sources. The manner in which this is done within an existing enterprise is not covered in this volume; obtaining capital for the expansion of an existing enterprise or for a new enterprise from outside sources is the subject of this examination. We have used the system of capital markets in our society for this purpose. Corporations in need of capital offer their securities in this market to suppliers of capital. Sometimes the market is as highly organized as a stock exchange, sometimes the clientele of a single or group of investment banking firms, and sometimes only a single investor such as a life insurance company. But in each case individuals as free men on behalf of themselves or their investment institution will make the investment decision; no government agency will compel them to invest or not invest.

The suppliers of capital, that is, investors, in the United States consist of a number of different types of institutions and organizations as well as individuals. While commercial banks provide substantial amounts of capital, primarily for short term loans, they are not organized to provide permanent capital (such as an investment in common stock) for business enterprises. It is true that they frequently lend money on the security of a mortgage on an industrial plant, or buy large quantities of corporate bonds, yet their primary function is commercial lending, that is, short term lending. Mortgages and bonds must be repaid and thus are not included in the term "permanent" capital. Life insurance companies, pension funds, mutual funds, and large personal trusts (established either under the terms of a will or an inter vivos trust agreement) are the institutions which provide substantial amounts of capital to the business system. Frequently they will do this by a so-called "direct placement" under which they will purchase all the securities being offered by a business enterprise under terms negotiated between them and the issuer. At other times, they will participate with a limited number of investors in what is called a "non-public offering" which is exempt from any of the Federal securities statutes and regulations (see S.E.C. Release No. 4552, Non-public Offering Exemption, reported below). However, all these institutions will frequently purchase securities along with individual persons in a "public offering" and this type of transaction is the principal concern of this Chapter.

By and large the institutional investor is able to fend for itself in determining whether or not to invest in any business enterprise. Its investment officers are normally skilled and sophisticated persons, trained in examining into a business enterprise and assessing the risks involved, and comparing them with other types of investments available to the institution at any time. The flow of funds, in a life insurance company, for example, from policy holders to the insurance company, and from the insurance company into the capital market is deemed to be adequately protected by the expertise of the investment officers of the life insurance company. (It should be noted that large life insurance companies from the viewpoint of the flow of cash through the company are primarily investment institutions as can be seen from an examination of the annual report of any large life insurance company.) If the individual persons who are the policy holders were solicited directly to make a personal investment in an amount equal to that portion of their annual premium which is to be channeled into investment making this payment as an investor and not as a policy-holder, we would not permit this kind of solicitation because we have determined that the free flow of funds into the capital markets can best be accomplished by providing some kind of legal protection to investors. We do not find it necessary to provide the same kind of legal protection when the investment is made by the informed and sophisticated investment officers of the life insurance company. The same is true of employee participants in pension funds in relation to the investment officers of their funds, and shareholders in mutual funds and the investment officers of their funds. When a public offering of securities is made, the informed export is entitled to the benefits of securities legislation just as much as any individual investor. The distinction is that a private offering can be made to the informed expert while it rarely can be made to the unsophisticated investor. What constitutes a private offering as distinguished from a public offering under the Federal Securities Act of 1933, 15 U.S.C.A. § 77a et seq. is not dependent upon any arbitrary division according to numbers in any class (such as is found in many state securities statutes) but turns on "[w]hether the particular class of persons affected need the protection of the Act." S. E. C. v. Ralston Purina Co., 346 U.S. 119, 73 S.Ct. 981, 97 L.Ed. 1494 (1953), reported below and S. E. C. Release No. 4552, referred to above. If the person being offered the investment is able to "fend for himself," then this will qualify as a private offering; conversely, if the offering is made to a large or small group of people who are not able to "fend for themselves" then this will very probably be a transaction covered by the provisions of the Securities Act of 1933. It is sometimes said that a private offering can be made to the treasurers of 100 life insurance companies, but not to three widows. One has yet to see a decision on either of those cases but this does suggest the nature of the regulation of the sale of new securities.

Under Section 5 of the Securities Act of 1933, 15 U.S.C.A. § 77e a security (a term which is very broadly defined) may be sold through the mails or through the instrumentalities of interstate commerce only if a registration statement is in effect as to the security. An "instrumentality of interstate commerce" is broadly construed; it has been suggested that using a telephone to call within one city, or delivering a check which is then sent through a clearing house, are both covered by this phrase. A registration statement is a document filed with the Securities and Exchange Commission which carries detailed information about the issuing company and the manner in which the securities are being offered and sold to the public. The prospectus which must be delivered to a person to whom the security is being offered is made a part of, and comprises the bulk of, the registration statement. The prospectus contains the actual offer by the issuing company to the prospective investor for the sale of the security to him. No representations may be made in connection with the offering and sale of the security except those which are contained in the prospectus.

Historically, we have conducted sales in our business system under the rule of *caveat emptor*—let the buyer beware. While we have made some changes in this practice through the centuries, particularly in reference to the sale of securities, Section 11 of the Securities Act of 1933 changed this substantially by permitting investors to recover their loss where the registration statement either has contained a false statement, or has omitted to state a fact when it should have been stated to avoid having the registration statement be misleading. In either case the fact must have been "material" which means a matter which an average prudent investor needs to know before he can make an investment decision, a decision as to whether or not to buy the security. This approaches the concept of *caveat venditor*—let the seller beware, because no longer does an investor who has suffered a loss on his investment have to show "scienter" (knowledge of the falsity of a statement by the person making it) as was required at common law; he need only show that he was misled by a material untrue statement or in a further departure from the common law, that he was misled by the omission to state a material fact. At common law, except under situations where one person was in a fiduciary position as to another, the omission to state a material fact was not fraud; stating something false, not just omitting it, had to be proved. These principles are well illustrated by the now celebrated case of Escott v. BarChris Construction Corp., 283 F.Supp. 643 (D.C.N.Y.1968), reported below.

Much of the legislation adopted in our society from time to time is the consequence of excesses in some given practice when the excesses have occurred a few years prior to the legislation. These excesses are frequently real, but sometimes only imagined. The Securities Act of 1933, referred to above, was adopted as a consequence of the very real excesses in the investment industry which occurred in the late 1920s. It became obvious that the system of channeling savings into investment in a democratic system was seriously in need of reform. The common law concepts of fraud and deceit were found to be clearly inadequate to protect the public on a large scale. Our constitutional concepts of due process of law have prevented our having a system of directing the investment of funds into a specific enterprise by a government bureau. Similarly, the fundamental premise of our economic system, freedom of contract or freedom of choice, eliminated any suggestion of granting a government bureau the power to pass upon the quality of any proposed investment. In order to have the system continue to work, the Securities Act of 1933, referred to above, was adopted. Its preamble states its purpose to be: "[t]o provide full and fair disclosure of the character of the securities sold in interstate and foreign commerce and through the mails, and to prevent frauds in the sale thereof." Full and fair disclosure is the technique adopted by our democratic society.

The system has obviously worked well. While there have been some failures of brokerage firms or investment banking houses, generally as a consequence of poor business practices, since the adoption of the Securities Act of 1933 there has been little fraud or deceit in the sale of the securities in any major amount and there has been no collapse of nay major corporation shortly after having filed a registration statement in connection with a public offering of its securities. Many small companies have registered their securities with the Securities and Exchange Commission and have failed shortly thereafter, but these were nearly all companies in which the risk of the investment was clearly disclosed.

SECURITIES AND EXCHANGE COMMISSION v. RALSTON PURINA CO.

Supreme Court of the United States, 1953.
346 U.S. 119, 73 S.Ct. 981, 97 L.Ed. 1494.

Mr. Justice CLARK, delivered the opinion of the Court.

Section 4(1) of the Securities Act of 1933 exempts "transactions by an issuer not involving any public offering" [1] from the registration requirements of § 5.[2] We must decide whether Ralston Purina's offerings of treasury stock to its "key employees" are within this exemption. On a complaint brought by the Commission under § 20(b) of the Act seeking to enjoin respondent's unregistered offerings, the District Court held the exemption applicable and dismissed the suit. The Court of Appeals affirmed. The question has arisen many times since the Act was passed; an apparent need to define the scope of the private offering exemption prompted certiorari.

1. 48 Stat. 77, as amended, 48 Stat. 906, 15 U.S.C.A. § 77d. (Court's footnote 1.)

2. "Sec. 5. (a) Unless a registration statement is in effect as to a security, it shall be unlawful for any person, directly or indirectly—
"(1) to make use of any means or instruments of transportation or communication in interstate commerce or of the mails to sell or offer to buy such security through the use or medium of any prospectus or otherwise; or
"(2) to carry or cause to be carried through the mails or in interstate commerce, by any means or instruments of transportation, any such security for the purpose of sale or for delivery after sale. * * *" 48 Stat. 77, 15 U.S.C.A. § 77e. (Court's footnote 2.)

Ralston Purina manufactures and distributes various feed and cereal products. Its processing and distribution facilities are scattered throughout the United States and Canada, staffed by some 7,000 employees. At least since 1911 the company has had a policy of encouraging stock ownership among its employees; more particularly, since 1942 it has made authorized but unissued common shares available to some of them. Between 1947 and 1951, the period covered by the record in this case, Ralston Purina sold nearly $2,000,000 of stock to employees without registration and in so doing made use of the mails.

In each of these years, a corporate resolution authorized the sale of common stock "to employees   *   *   *   who shall, without any solicitation by the Company or its officers or employees, inquire of any of them as to how to purchase common stock of Ralston Purina Company." A memorandum sent to branch and store managers after the resolution was adopted, advised that "The only employees to whom this stock will be available will be those who take the initiative and are interested in buying stock at present market prices." Among those responding to these offers were employees with the duties of artist, bakeshop foreman, chow loading foreman, clerical assistant, copywriter, electrician, stock clerk, mill office clerk, order credit trainee, production trainee, stenographer, and veterinarian. The buyers lived in over fifty widely separated communities scattered from Garland, Texas, to Nashua, New Hampshire and Visalia, California. The lowest salary bracket of those purchasing was $2,700 in 1949, $2,435 in 1950 and $3,107 in 1951. The record shows that in 1947, 243 employees bought stock, 20 in 1948, 414 in 1949, 411 in 1950, and the 1951 offer, interrupted by this litigation, produced 165 applications to purchase. No records were kept of those to whom the offers were made; the estimated number in 1951 was 500.

The company bottoms its exemption claim on the classification of all offerees as "key employees" in its organization. Its position on trial was that "A key employee   *   *   *   is not confined to an organization chart. It would include an individual who is eligible for promotion, an individual who especially influences others or who advises others, a person whom the employees look to in some special way, an individual, of course, who carries some special responsibility, who is sympathetic to management and who is ambitious and who the management feels is likely to be promoted to a greater responsibility." That an offering to all of its employees would be public is conceded.

The Securities Act nowhere defines the scope of § 4(1)'s private offering exemption. Nor is the legislative history of much help in staking out its boundaries. The problem was first dealt with in § 4(1) of the House Bill, H.R. 5480, 73d Cong., 1st Sess., which exempted "transactions by an issuer not with or through an underwriter; * * *." The bill, as reported by the House Committee, added "and not involving any public offering." H.R.Rep.No.85, 73d Cong., 1st Sess. 1. This was thought to be one of those transactions "where there is no practical need for   *   *   *   [the bill's] application or where the public benefits are too remote." The exemption as thus delimited became law. It assumed its present shape with the deletion of "not with or through an underwriter" by § 203(a) of the Securities Exchange Act of 1934, a change regarded as the elimination of superfluous language. H.R.Rep. No.1838, 73d Cong., 2d Sess. 41.

Decisions under comparable exemptions in the English Companies Acts and state "blue sky" laws, the statutory antecedents of federal securities legislation have made one thing clear—to be public, an offer need not be open to the whole world. In Securities and Exchange Comm. v. Sunbeam Gold Mines Co., 9 Cir., 1938, 95 F.2d 699, this point was made in dealing with an offering to the stockholders of two corporations about to be merged. Judge Denman observed that:

"In its broadest meaning the term 'public' distinguishes the populace at large from groups of individual members of the public segregated because of some common interest or characteristic. Yet such a distinction is inadequate for practical purposes; manifestly, an offering of securities to all redheaded men, to all residents of Chicago or San Francisco, to all existing stockholders of the General Motors Corporation or the American Telephone & Telegraph Company, is no less 'public', in every realistic sense of the word, than an unrestricted offering to the world at large. Such an offering, though not open to everyone who may choose to apply, is none the less 'public' in character, for the means used to select the particular individuals to whom the offering is to be made bear no sensible relation to the purposes for which the selection is made. * * * To determine the distinction between 'public' and 'private' in any particular context, it is essential to examine the circumstances under which the distinction is sought to be established and to consider the purposes sought to be achieved by such distinction."

The courts below purported to apply this test. The District Court held, in the language of the Sunbeam decision, that "The purpose of the selection bears a 'sensible relation' to the class chosen," finding that "The sole purpose of the 'selection' is to keep part stock ownership of the business within the operating personnel of the business and to spread ownership throughout all departments and activities of the business." The Court of Appeals treated the case as involving "an offering, without solicitation, of common stock to a selected group of key employees of the issuer, most of whom are already stockholders when the offering is made, with the sole purpose of enabling them to secure a proprietary interest in the company or to increase the interest already held by them."

Exemption from the registration requirements of the Securities Act is the question. The design of the statute is to protect investors by promoting full disclosure of information thought necessary to informed investment decisions. The natural way to interpret the private offering exemption is in light of the statutory purpose. Since exempt transactions are those as to which "there is no practical need for * * [the bill's] application," the applicability of § 4(1) should turn on whether the particular class of persons affected need the protection of the Act.   An offering to those who are shown to be able to fend for themselves is a transaction "not involving any public offering."

The Commission would have us go one step further and hold that "an offering to a substantial number of the public" is not exempt under § 4(1).   We are advised that "whatever the special circumstances, the Commission has consistently interpreted the exemption as being inapplicable when a large number of offerees is involved."   But the statute would seem to apply to a "public offering" whether to few or many. It may well be that offerings to a substantial number of persons would rarely be exempt.   Indeed nothing prevents the commission, in enforcing the statute, from using some kind of numerical test in deciding when to investigate particular exemption claims.   But there is no warrant for superimposing a quantity limit on private offerings as a matter of statutory interpretation.

The exemption, as we construe it, does not deprive corporate employees, as a class, of the safeguards of the Act.   We agree that some employee offerings may come within § 4(1), *e. g.*, one made to executive personnel who because of their position have access to the same kind of information that the act would make available in the form of a registration statement.   Absent such a showing of special circumstances, employees are just as much members of the investing "public" as any of their neighbors in the community.   Although we do not rely on it, the rejection in 1934 of an amendment which would have specifically exempted employee stock offerings supports this conclusion.   The House Managers, commenting on the Conference Report, said that "the participants in employees' stock-investment plans may be in as great need of the protection afforded by availability of information concerning the issuer for which they work as are most other members of the public."   H.R.Rep.No.1838, 73d Cong., 2d Sess. 41.

Keeping in mind the broadly remedial purposes of federal securities legislation, imposition of the burden of proof on an issuer who would plead the exemption seems to us fair and reasonable.   * * * Agreeing, the court below thought the burden met primarily because of the respondent's purpose in singling out its key employees for stock offerings.   But once it is seen that the exemption question turns on the knowledge of the offerees, the issuer's motives, laudable though they may be, fade into irrelevance.   The focus of inquiry should be on the need of the offerees for the protections afforded by registration.   The employees here were not shown to have access to the kind of information which registration would disclose.   The obvious opportunities for pressure and imposition make it advisable that they be entitled to compliance with § 5.

Reversed.

ESCOTT v. BARCHRIS CONSTRUCTION CORPORATION

United States District Court, S. D. New York, 1968.
283 F.Supp. 643.

McLEAN, District Judge. This is an action by purchasers of 5½ per cent convertible subordinated fifteen year debentures of BarChris Construction Corporation (BarChris). * * *

The action is brought under Section 11 of the Securities Act of 1933 (15 U.S.C.A. § 77k). Plaintiffs allege that the registration statement with respect to these debentures filed with the Securities and Exchange Commission, which became effective on May 16, 1961, contained material false statements and material omissions.

Defendants fall into three categories: (1) the persons who signed the registration statement; (2) the underwriters, consisting of eight investment banking firms, led by Drexel & Co. (Drexel); and (3) Bar-Chris's auditors, Peat, Marwick, Mitchell & Co. (Peat, Marwick).

The signers, in addition to BarChris itself, were the nine directors of BarChris, plus its controller, defendant Trilling, who was not a director. Of the nine directors, five were officers of BarChris, i. e., defendants Vitolo, president; Russo, executive vice president; Pugliese, vice president; Kircher, treasurer; and Birnbaum, secretary. Of the remaining four, defendant Grant was a member of the firm of Perkins, Daniels, McCormack & Collins, BarChris's attorneys. He became a director in October 1960. Defendant Coleman, a partner in Drexel, became a director on April 17, 1961, as did the other two, Auslander and Rose, who were not otherwise connected with BarChris.

Defendants, in addition to denying that the registration statement was false, have pleaded the defenses open to them under Section 11 of the Act, plus certain additional defenses, including the statute of limitations. Defendants have also asserted cross-claims against each other, seeking to hold one another liable for any sums for which the respective defendants may be held liable to plaintiffs.

This opinion will not concern itself with the cross-claims or with issues peculiar to any particular plaintiff. These matters are reserved for later decision. On the main issue of liability, the questions to be decided are (1) did the registration statement contain false statements of fact, or did it omit to state facts which should have been stated in order to prevent it from being misleading; (2) if so, were the facts which were falsely stated or omitted "material" within the meaning of the Act; (3) if so, have defendants established their affirmative defenses?

Before discussing these questions, some background facts should be mentioned. At the time relevant here, BarChris was engaged primarily in the construction of bowling alleys, somewhat euphemistically referred to as "bowling centers." These were rather elaborate affairs. They contained not only a number of alleys or "lanes," but also, in most cases, bar and restaurant facilities.

BarChris was an outgrowth of a business started as a partnership by Vitolo and Pugliese in 1946. The business was incorporated in New York in 1955 under the name of B & C Bowling Alley Builders, Inc. Its name was subsequently changed to BarChris Construction Corporation.

The introduction of automatic pin setting machines in 1952 gave a marked stimulus to bowling. It rapidly became a popular sport, with the result that "bowling centers" began to appear throughout the country in rapidly increasing numbers. BarChris benefited from this increased interest in bowling. Its construction operations expanded rapidly. It is estimated that in 1960 BarChris installed approximately three per cent of all lanes built in the United States. It was thus a significant factor in the industry, although two large established companies, American Machine & Foundry Company and Brunswick, were much larger factors. These two companies manufactured bowling equipment, which BarChris did not. They also built most of the bowling alleys, 97 per cent of the total, according to some of the testimony.

BarChris's sales increased dramatically from 1956 to 1960. According to the prospectus, net sales, in round figures, in 1956 were some $800,000, in 1957 $1,300,000, in 1958 $1,700,000. In 1959 they increased to over $3,300,000, and by 1960 they had leaped to over $9,-165,000.

For some years the business had exceeded the managerial capacity of its founders. Vitolo and Pugliese are each men of limited education. Vitolo did not get beyond high school. Pugliese ended his schooling in seventh grade. Pugliese devoted his time to supervising the actual construction work. Vitolo was concerned primarily with obtaining new business. Neither was equipped to handle financial matters.

Rather early in their career they enlisted the aid of Russo, who was trained as an accountant. He first joined them in the days of the partnership, left for a time, and returned as an officer and director of B & C Bowling Alley Builders, Inc. in 1958. He eventually became executive vice president of BarChris. In that capacity he handled many of the transactions which figure in this case.

In 1959 BarChris hired Kircher, a certified public accountant who had been employed by Peat, Marwick. He started as controller and became treasurer in 1960. In October of that year, another ex-Peat, Marwick employee, Trilling, succeeded Kircher as controller. At approximately the same time Birnbaum, a young attorney, was hired as house counsel. He became secretary on April 17, 1961.

* * *

In 1960 BarChris began a practice which has been referred to throughout this case as the "alternative method of financing." In substance this was a sale and leaseback arrangement. It involved a distinction between the "interior" of a building and the building itself, i. e., the outer shell. In instances in which this method applied, BarChris would build and install what it referred to as the "interior package." Actually this amounted to constructing and installing the equipment in a building. When it was completed, it would sell the interior to a factor, James Talcott Inc. (Talcott), who would pay BarChris the full contract price therefor. The factor then proceeded to lease the interior either directly to BarChris's customer or back to a subsidiary of BarChris. In the latter case, the subsidiary in turn would lease it to the customer.

* * *

By early 1961, BarChris needed additional working capital. The proceeds of the sale of the debentures involved in this action were to be devoted, in part at least, to fill that need.

The registration statement of the debentures, in preliminary form, was filed with the Securities and Exchange Commission on March 30, 1961. A first amendment was filed on May 11 and a second on May 16. The registration statement became effective on May 16. The closing of the financing took place on May 24. On that day BarChris received the net proceeds of the financing.

By that time BarChris was experiencing difficulties in collecting amounts due from some of its customers. Some of them were in arrears in payments due to factors on their discounted notes. As time went on those difficulties increased. Although BarChris continued to build alleys in 1961 and 1962, it became increasingly apparent that the industry was overbuilt. Operators of alleys, often inadequately financed, began to fail. Precisely when the tide turned is a matter of dispute, but at any rate, it was painfully apparent in 1962.

In May of that year BarChris made an abortive attempt to raise more money by the sale of common stock. It filed with the Securities and Exchange Commission a registration statement for the stock issue which it later withdrew. In October 1962 BarChris came to the end of the road. On October 29, 1962, it filed in this court a petition for an arrangement under Chapter XI of the Bankruptcy Act. BarChris defaulted in the payment of the interest due on November 1, 1962 on the debentures.

The Debenture Registration Statement

In preparing the registration statement for the debentures, Grant acted for BarChris. He had previously represented BarChris in preparing the registration statement for the common stock issue. In connection with the sale of common stock, BarChris had issued purchase warrants. In January 1961 a second registration statement was filed in order to update the information pertaining to these warrants. Grant had prepared that statement as well.

Some of the basic information needed for the debenture registration statement was contained in the registration statements previously filed with respect to the common stock and warrants. Grant used these old registration statements as a model in preparing the new one, making the changes which he considered necessary in order to meet the new situation.

The underwriters were represented by the Philadelphia law firm of Drinker, Biddle & Reath. John A. Ballard, a member of that firm, was in charge of that work, assisted by a young associate named Stanton.

Peat, Marwick, BarChris's auditors, who had previously audited BarChris's annual balance sheet and earnings figures for 1958 and 1959, did the same for 1960. These figures were set forth in the registration statement. In addition, Peat, Marwick undertook a so-called "S–1 review," the proper scope of which is one of the matters debated here.

The registration statement in its final form contained a prospectus as well as other information. Plaintiffs' claims of falsities and omissions pertain solely to the prospectus, not to the additional data.

The prospectus contained, among other things, a description of BarChris's business, a description of its real property, some material pertaining to certain of its subsidiaries, and remarks about various other aspects of its affairs. It also contained financial information. It included a consolidated balance sheet as of December 31, 1960, with elaborate explanatory notes. These figures had been audited by Peat, Marwick. It also contained unaudited figures as to net sales, gross profit and net earnings for the first quarter ended March 31, 1961, as compared with the similar quarter for 1960. In addition, it set forth figures as to the company's backlog of unfilled orders as of March 31, 1961, as compared with March 31, 1960, and figures as to BarChris's contingent liability, as of April 30, 1961, on customers' notes discounted and its contingent liability under the so-called alternative method of financing.

Plaintiffs challenge the accuracy of a number of these figures. They also charge that the text of the prospectus, apart from the figures, was false in a number of respects, and that material information was omitted.   *   *   *

[The Court at this point digested over 6,500 pages of stenographic notes of testimony taken at the trial. The digest alone was over 25 pages of the original opinion in the case. Briefly, sales figures were overstated, work in process was overestimated, bowling alleys which had been built for others and in one manner or another were taken over by BarChris had been operated by it without disclosure of this fact. BarChris obtained a release of $147,466.80 in cash from the factor (Talcott) on December 22, 1960, to swell its cash balance at year end but was required to return it to Talcott not later than January 16, 1961. Other items of current assets were overstated. Notes received from customers were discounted with Talcott and BarChris remained contingently liable on these notes; the extent of this contingent liability was understated in the amount of $375,795. As a consequence of these matters, and others, net earnings and earnings per share were overstated. The Prospectus stated that the backlog of unfilled orders was $6,905,000 on March 31, 1961, approximately $4,000,000 higher than a year earlier; the Court found that nine bowling interiors were erroneously included in this computation, resulting in an overstatement of work to be performed of $4,490,000. Thus the backlog was actually less than a year earlier. Russo, Vitolo, and Pugliese had loaned the company $386,615 which remained unpaid when the Registration statement became effective (May 16, 1961) but the Prospectus said that all such advances had been repaid. The Prospectus stated that since 1955 the company had been required to repurchase less than ½ of 1% of the notes it had taken from customers and discounted with unaffiliated financial institutions; however, one month before the effective date BarChris knew it might have to repurchase more than $1,350,000 of such notes from customers, some of whom later also became bankrupt. And because of repossession of bowling alleys, the company had begun to operate them; the Prospectus made no reference to this activity. A summary of these details, as prepared by the Court, follows.]

Summary

For convenience, the various falsities and omissions which I have discussed in the preceding pages are recapitulated here. They were as follows:

1. 1960 Earnings

    (a) Sales

As per prospectus	$9,165,320
Correct figure	8,511,420
Overstatement	$ 653.900

    (b) Net Operating Income

As per prospectus	$1,742,801
Correct figure	1,496,196
Overstatement	$ 246,605

    (c) Earnings per Share

As per prospectus	$ .75
Correct figure	.65
Overstatement	$ .10

2. 1960 Balance Sheet

    Current Assets

As per prospectus	$4,524,021
Correct figure	3,914,332
Overstatement	$ 609,689

3. Contingent Liabilities as of December 31, 1960 on Alternative Method of Financing

As per prospectus	$ 750,000
Correct figure	1,125,795
Understatement	$ 375,795
Capitol Lanes should have been shown as a direct liability	$ 325,000

4. Contingent Liabilities as of April 30, 1961

As per prospectus	$ 825,000
Correct figure	1,443,853
Understatement	$ 618,853
Capitol Lanes should have been shown as a direct liability	$ 314,166

5. Earnings Figures for Quarter ending March 31, 1961

  (a) Sales

As per prospectus	$2,138,455
Correct figure	1,618,645
Overstatement	$ 519,810

  (b) Gross Profit

As per prospectus	$ 483,121
Correct figure	252,366
Overstatement	$ 230,755

6. Backlog as of March 31, 1961

As per prospectus	$6,905,000
Correct figure	2,415,000
Overstatement	$4,490,000

7. Failure to Disclose Officers' Loans Outstanding and Unpaid on May 16, 1961 $ 386,615

8. Failure to Disclose Use of Proceeds in Manner not Revealed in Prospectus

  Approximately $1,160,000

9. Failure to Disclose Customers' Delinquencies in May 1961 and BarChris's Potential Liability with Respect Thereto

    Over $1,350,000

10. Failure to Disclose the Fact that BarChris was Already Engaged, and was about to be More Heavily Engaged, in the Operation of Bowling Alleys

Materiality

It is a prerequisite to liability under Section 11 of the Act that the fact which is falsely stated in a registration statement, or the fact that is omitted when it should have been stated to avoid misleading, be "material." The regulations of the Securities and Exchange Commission pertaining to the registration of securities define the word as follows (17 C.F.R. § 230.405 (*l*)) :

"The term 'material', when used to qualify a requirement for the furnishing of information as to any subject, limits the information required to those matters as to which an average prudent investor ought reasonably to be informed before purchasing the security registered."

What are "matters as to which an average prudent investor ought reasonably to be informed"? It seems obvious that they are matters which such an investor needs to know before he can make an intelligent, informed decision whether or not to buy the security.

Early in the history of the Act, a definition of materiality was given in Matter of Charles A. Howard, 1 S.E.C. 6, 8 (1934), which is still valid today. A material fact was there defined as:

" * * * a fact which if it had been correctly stated or disclosed would have deterred or tended to deter the average prudent investor from purchasing the securities in question."

Cf. List v. Fashion Park, Inc., 340 F.2d 457, 462 (2d Cir. 1965), cert. denied, 382 U.S. 811 (1965) (Securities Exchange Act of 1934 § 10 (b)) ; Restatement of Torts § 538(2) (a) (1938) ; Restatement (Second) of Torts § 402B comment g (1965)

The average prudent investor is not concerned with minor inaccuracies or with errors as to matters which are of no interest to him. The facts which tend to deter him from purchasing a security are facts which have an important bearing upon the nature or condition of the issuing corporation or its business.

Judged by this test, there is no doubt that many of the misstatements and omissions in this prospectus were material. This is true of all of them which relate to the state of affairs in 1961, i. e., the overstatement of sales and gross profit for the first quarter, the understatement of contingent liabilities as of April 30, the overstatement of orders on hand and the failure to disclose the true facts with respect to officers' loans, customers' delinquencies, application of proceeds and the prospective operation of several alleys.

The misstatements and omissions pertaining to BarChris's status as of December 31, 1960, however, present a much closer question. The 1960 earnings figures, the 1960 balance sheet and the contingent liabilities as of December 31, 1960 were not nearly as erroneous as plaintiffs have claimed. But they were wrong to some extent, as we have seen. Would it have deterred the average prudent investor from purchasing these debentures if he had been informed that the 1960 sales were $8,511,420 rather than $9,165,320, that the net operating income was $1,496,196 rather than $1,742,801 and that the earnings per share in 1960 were approximately 65¢ rather than 75¢? According to the unchallenged figures, sales in 1959 were $3,320,121, net operating income was $441,103, and earnings per share were 33¢. Would it have made a difference to an average prudent investor if he had known that in 1960 sales were only 256 per cent of 1959 sales, not

276 per cent; that net operating income was up by only $1,055,093, not by $1,301,698, and that earnings per share, while still approximately twice those of 1959, were not something more than twice?

These debentures were rated "B" by the investment rating services. They were thus characterized as speculative, as any prudent investor must have realized. It would seem that anyone interested in buying these convertible debentures would have been attracted primarily by the conversion feature, by the growth potential of the stock. The growth which the company enjoyed in 1960 over prior years was striking, even on the correct figures. It is hard to see how a prospective purchaser of this type of investment would have been deterred from buying if he had been advised of these comparatively minor errors in reporting 1960 sales and earnings.

Since no one knows what moves or does not move the mythical "average prudent investor," it comes down to a question of judgment, to be exercised by the trier of the fact as best he can in the light of all the circumstances. It is my best judgment that the average prudent investor would not have cared about these errors in the 1960 sales and earnings figures, regrettable though they may be. I therefore find that they were not material within the meaning of Section 11.

The same is true of the understatement of contingent liabilities in footnote 9 by approximately $375,000. As disclosed in that footnote, BarChris's contingent liability as of December 31, 1960 on notes discounted was $3,969,835 and, according to the footnote, on the alternative method of financing was $750,000, a total of $4,719,835. This was a huge amount for a company with total assets, as per balance sheet, of $61,101,085. Purchasers were necessarily made aware of this by the figures actually disclosed. If they were willing to buy the debentures in the face of this information, as they obviously were, I doubt that they would have been deterred if they had been told that the contingent liabilities were actually $375,000 higher.

This leaves for consideration the errors in the 1960 balance sheet figures which have previously been discussed in detail. Current assets were overstated by approximately $600,000. Liabilities were understated by approximately $325,000 by the failure to treat the liability on Capitol Lanes as a direct liability of BarChris on a consolidated basis. Of this $325,000 approximately $65,000, the amount payable on Capitol within one year, should have been treated as a current liability.

As per balance sheet, cash was $285,482. In fact, $145,000 of this had been borrowed temporarily from Talcott and was to be returned by January 16, 1961 so that realistically, cash was only $140,482. Trade accounts receivable were overstated by $150,000 by including Howard Lanes Annex, an alley which was not sold to an outside buyer.

As per balance sheet, total current assets were $4,524,021, and total current liabilities were $2,413,867, a ratio of approximately 1.9 to 1. This was bad enough, but on the true facts, the ratio was worse. As corrected, current assets, as near as one can tell, were approximately

$3,924,000, and current liabilities approximately $2,478,000, a ratio of approximately 1.6 to 1.

Would it have made any difference if a prospective purchaser of these debentures had been advised of these facts? There must be some point at which errors in disclosing a company's balance sheet position become material, even to a growth-oriented investor. On all the evidence I find that these balance sheet errors were material within the meaning of Section 11.

Since there was an abundance of material misstatements pertaining to 1961 affairs, whether or not the errors in the 1960 figures were material does not affect the outcome of this case except to the extent that it bears upon the liability of Peat, Marwick. That subject will be discussed hereinafter.

The "Due Diligence" Defenses

Section 11(b) of the Act provides that:

" * * * no person, other than the issuer, shall be liable * * * who shall sustain the burden of proof—

* * *

(3) that (A) as regards any part of the registration statement not purporting to be made on the authority of an expert * * * he had, after reasonable investigation, reasonable ground to believe and did believe, at the time such part of the registration statement became effective, that the statements therein were true and that there was no omission to state a material fact required to be stated therein or necessary to make the statements therein not misleading; * * * and (C) as regards any part of the registration statement purporting to be made on the authority of an expert (other than himself) * * * he had no reasonable ground to believe and did not believe, at the time such part of the registration statement became effective, that the statements therein were untrue or that there was an omission to state a material fact required to be stated therein or necessary to make the statements therein not misleading * * *."

Section 11(c) defines "reasonable investigation" as follows:

"In determining, for the purpose of paragraph (3) of subsection (b) of this section, what constitutes reasonable investigation and reasonable ground for belief, the standard of reasonableness shall be that required of a prudent man in the management of his own property."

Every defendant, except BarChris itself, to whom, as the issuer, these defenses are not available, and except Peat, Marwick, whose position rests on a different statutory provision, has pleaded these affirmative defenses. Each claims that (1) as to the part of the registration statement purporting to be made on the authority of an expert (which, for convenience, I shall refer to as the "expertised portion"), he had no reasonable ground to believe and did not believe that there were any untrue statements or material omissions, and (2) as to the other parts of the registration statement, he made a reasonable investigation, as a result of which he had reasonable ground to believe and did believe that the registration statement was true and that no material fact was omitted. As to each defendant, the question is whether he has sustained the burden of proving these defenses. Surprising enough, there is little or no judicial authority on this question. No decisions directly in point under Section 11 have been found.

Before considering the evidence, a preliminary matter should be disposed of. The defendants do not agree among themselves as to who the "experts" were or as to the parts of the registration statement which were expertised. Some defendants say that Peat, Marwick was the expert, others say that BarChris's attorneys, Perkins, Daniels, McCormack & Collins, and the underwriters' attorneys, Drinker, Biddle & Reath, were also the experts. On the first view, only those portions of the registration statement purporting to be made on Peat, Marwick's authority were expertised portions. On the other view, everything in the registration statement was within this category, because the two law firms were responsible for the entire document.

The first view is the correct one. To say that the entire registration statement is expertised because some lawyer prepared it would be an unreasonable construction of the statute. Neither the lawyer for the company nor the lawyer for the underwriters is an expert within the meaning of Section 11. The only expert, in the statutory sense, was Peat, Marwick, and the only parts of the registration statement which purported to be made upon the authority of an expert were the portions which purported to be made on Peat, Marwick's authority.

The parties also disagree as to what those portions were. Some defendants say that it was only the 1960 figures (and the figures for prior years, which are not in controversy here). Others say in substance that it was every figure in the prospectus. The plaintiffs take a somewhat intermediate view. They do not claim that Peat, Marwick expertised every figure, but they do maintain that Peat, Marwick is responsible for a portion of the text of the prospectus, i. e., that pertaining to "Methods of Operation," because a reference to it was made in footnote 9 to the balance sheet.

Here again, the more narrow view is the correct one. The registration statement contains a report of Peat, Marwick as independent public accountants dated February 23, 1961. This relates only to the consolidated balance sheet of BarChris and consolidated subsidiaries as of December 31, 1960, and the related statement of earnings and retained earnings for the five years then ended. This is all that Peat, Marwick purported to certify. It is perfectly clear that it did not purport to certify the 1961 figures, some of which are expressly stated in the prospectus to have been unaudited.

*   *   *

I turn now to the question of whether defendants have proved their due diligence defenses. The position of each defendant will be separately considered.

Russo

Russo was, to all intents and purposes, the chief executive officer of BarChris. He was a member of the executive committee. He was familiar with all aspects of the business. He was personally in charge of dealings with the factors. He acted on BarChris's behalf in making the financing agreements with Talcott and he handled the negotiations with Talcott in the spring of 1961. He talked with customers about their delinquencies.

Russo prepared the list of jobs which went into the backlog figure. He knew the status of those jobs. * * *

It was Russo who arranged for the temporary increase in Bar-Chris's cash in banks on December 31, 1960, a transaction which borders on the fraudulent. He was thoroughly aware of BarChris's stringent financial condition in May 1961. He had personally advanced large sums to BarChris of which $175,000 remained unpaid as of May 16.

In short, Russo knew all the relevant facts. He could not have believed that there were no untrue statements or material omissions in the prospectus. Russo has no due diligence defenses.

Vitolo and Pugliese

They were the founders of the business who stuck with it to the end. Vitolo was president and Pugliese was vice president. Despite their titles, their field of responsibility in the administration of Bar-Chris's affairs during the period in question seems to have been less all-embracing than Russo's. Pugliese in particular appears to have limited his activities to supervising the actual construction work.

Vitolo and Pugliese are each men of limited education. It is not hard to believe that for them the prospectus was difficult reading, if indeed they read it at all.

But whether it was or not is irrelevant. The liability of a director who signs a registration statement does not depend upon whether or not he read it or, if he did, whether or not he understood what he was reading.

And in any case, Vitolo and Pugliese were not as naive as they claim to be. They were members of BarChris's executive committee. At meetings of that committee BarChris's affairs were discussed at length. They must have known what was going on. Certainly they knew of the inadequacy of cash in 1961. They knew of their own large advances to the company which remained unpaid. They knew that they had agreed not to deposit their checks until the financing proceeds were received. They knew and intended that part of the proceeds were to be used to pay their own loans.

All in all, the position of Vitolo and Pugliese is not significantly different, for present purposes, from Russo's. They could not have believed that the registration statement was wholly true and that no material facts had been omitted. And in any case, there is nothing to show that they made any investigation of anything which they may not have known about or understood. They have not proved their due diligence defenses.

Kircher

Kircher was treasurer of BarChris and its chief financial officer. He is a certified public accountant and an intelligent man. He was throughly familiar with BarChris's financial affairs. He knew the terms of BarChris's agreements with Talcott. He knew of the customers' delinquency problem. He participated actively with Russo in May 1961 in the successful effort to hold Talcott off until the financing proceeds came in. He knew how the financing proceeds were to be applied and he saw to it that they were so applied. He arranged the officers' loans and he knew all the facts concerning them.

Moreover, as a member of the executive committee, Kircher was kept informed as to those branches of the business of which he did not have direct charge. He knew about the operation of alleys, present and prospective.   *   *   *

Kircher worked on the preparation of the registration statement. He conferred with Grant and on occasion with Ballard. He supplied information to them about the company's business. He read the prospectus and understood it. He knew what it said and what it did not say.

Kircher's contention is that he had never before dealt with a registration statement, that he did not know what it should contain, and that he relied wholly on Grant, Ballard and Peat, Marwick to guide him. He claims that it was their fault, not his, if there was anything wrong with it. He says that all the facts were recorded in BarChris's books where these "experts" could have seen them if they had looked. He says that he truthfully answered all their questions. In effect, he says that if they did not know enough to ask the right questions and to give him the proper instructions, that is not his responsibility.

There is an issue of credibility here. In fact, Kircher was not frank in dealing with Grant and Ballard. He withheld information \from them. But even if he had told them all the facts, this would not have constituted the due diligence contemplated by the statute. Knowing the facts, Kircher had reason to believe that the expertised portion of the prospectus, i. e., the 1960 figures, was in part incorrect. He could not shut his eyes to the facts and rely on Peat, Marwick for that portion.

As to the rest of the prospectus, knowing the facts, he did not have a reasonable ground to believe it to be true. On the contrary, he must have known that in part it was untrue. Under these circumstances, he was not entitled to sit back and place the blame on the lawyers for not advising him about it.

Kircher has not proved his due diligence defenses.

Trilling

Trilling's position is somewhat different from Kircher's. He was BarChris's controller. He signed the registration statement in that capacity, although he was not a director.

Trilling entered BarChris's employ in October 1960. He was Kircher's subordinate. When Kircher asked him for information, he furnished it. On at least one occasion he got it wrong.

Trilling was not a member of the executive committee. He was a comparatively minor figure in BarChris. The description of Bar-Chris's "management" on page 9 of the prospectus does not mention him. He was not considered to be an executive officer.

Trilling may well have been unaware of several of the inaccuracies in the prospectus. But he must have known of some of them. As a financial officer, he was familiar with BarChris's finances and with its books of account. He knew that part of the cash on deposit on December 31, 1960 had been procured temporarily by Russo for window dressing purposes. He knew that BarChris was operating Capitol Lanes in 1960. He should have known, although perhaps through carelessness he did not know at the time, that BarChris's contingent liability on Type B lease transactions was greater than the prospectus stated. In the light of these facts, I cannot find that Trilling believed the entire prospectus to be true.

But even if he did, he still did not establish his due diligence defenses. He did not prove that as to the parts of the prospectus expertised by Peat, Marwick he had no reasonable ground to believe that it was untrue. He also failed to prove, as to the parts of the prospectus not expertised by Peat, Marwick, that he made a reasonable investigation which afforded him a reasonable ground to believe that it was true. As far as appears, he made no investigation. He did what was asked of him and assumed that others would properly take care of supplying accurate data as to the other aspects of the company's business. This would have been well enough but for the fact that he signed the registration statement. As a signer, he could not avoid responsibility by leaving it up to others to make it accurate. Trilling did not sustain the burden of proving his due diligence defenses.

Birnbaum

Birnbaum was a young lawyer, admitted to the bar in 1957, who, after brief periods of employment by two different law firms and an equally brief period of practicing in his own firm, was employed by BarChris as house counsel and assistant secretary in October 1960. Unfortunately for him, he became secretary and a director of BarChris on April 17, 1961, after the first version of the registration statement had been filed with the Securities and Exchange Commission. He signed the later amendments, thereby becoming responsible for the accuracy of the prospectus in its final form.

Although the prospectus, in its description or "management," lists Birnbaum among the "executive officers" and devotes several sentences to a recital of his career, the fact seems to be that he was not an executive officer in any real sense. He did not participate in the management of the company. As house counsel, he attended to legal matters of a routine nature. Among other things, he incorporated subsidiaries, with which BarChris was plentifully supplied.

*   *   *

One of Birnbaum's more important duties, first as assistant secretary and later as full-fledged secretary, was to keep the corporate minutes of BarChris and its subsidiaries. This necessarily informed him to a considerable extent about the company's affairs. Birnbaum was not initially a member of the executive committee, however, and did not keep its minutes at the outset. According to the minutes, the first meeting which he attended, "upon invitation of the Committee," was on March 22, 1961. He became a member shortly thereafter and kept the minutes beginning with the meeting of April 24, 1961.

It seems probable that Birnbaum did not know of many of the inaccuracies in the prospectus. He must, however, have appreciated some of them. In any case, he made no investigation and relied on the others to get it right. Unlike Trilling, he was entitled to rely upon Peat, Marwick for the 1960 figures, for as far as appears, he had no personal knowledge of the company's books of account or financial transactions. But he was not entitled to rely upon Kircher, Grant and Ballard for the other portions of the prospectus. As a lawyer, he should have known his obligations under the statute. He should have known that he was required to make a reasonable investigation of the truth of all the statements in the unexpertised portion of the document which he signed. Having failed to make such an investigation, he did not have reasonable ground to believe that all these statements were true. Birnbaum has not established his due diligence defenses except as to the audited 1960 figures.

Auslander

Auslander was an "outside" director, i. e., one who was not an officer of BarChris. He was chairman of the board of Valley Stream National Bank in Valley Stream, Long Island. In February 1961 Vitolo asked him to become a director of BarChris. Vitolo gave him an enthusiastic account of BarChris's progress and prospects. As an inducement, Vitolo said that when BarChris received the proceeds of a forthcoming issue of securities, it would deposit $1,000,000 in Auslander's bank.

In February and early March 1961, before accepting Vitolo's invitation, Auslander made some investigation of BarChris. He obtained Dun & Bradstreet reports which contained sales and earnings figures for periods earlier than December 31, 1960. He caused inquiry to be made of certain of BarChris's banks and was advised that they regarded BarChris favorably. He was informed that inquiry of Talcott had also produced a favorable response.

On March 3, 1961, Auslander indicated his willingness to accept a place on the board. Shortly thereafter, on March 14, Kircher sent him a copy of BarChris's annual report for 1960. Auslander observed that BarChris's auditors were Peat, Marwick. They were also the auditors for the Valley Stream National Bank. He thought well of them.

Auslander was elected a director on April 17, 1961. The registration statement in its original form had already been filed, of course without his signature. On May 10, 1961, he signed a signature page for the first amendment to the registration statement which was filed on May 11, 1961. This was a separate sheet without any document attached. Auslander did not know that it was a signature page for a registration statement. He vaguely understood that it was something "for the SEC."

Auslander attended a meeting of BarChris's directors on May 15, 1961. At that meeting he, along with the other directors, signed the signature sheet for the second amendment which constituted the registration statement in its final form. Again, this was only a separate sheet without any document attached. Auslander never saw a copy of the registration statement in its final form.

At the May 15 directors' meeting, however, Auslander did realize that what he was signing was a signature sheet to a registration statement. This was the first time that he had appreciated that fact. A copy of the registration statement in its earlier form as amended on May 11, 1961 was passed around at the meeting. Auslander glanced at it briefly. He did not read it thoroughly.

At the May 15 meeting, Russo and Vitolo stated that everything was in order and that the prospectus was correct. Auslander believed this statement.

In considering Auslander's due diligence defenses, a distinction is to be drawn between the expertised and nonexpertised portions of the prospectus. As to the former, Auslander knew that Peat, Marwick had audited the 1960 figures. He believed them to be correct because he had confidence in Peat, Marwick. He had no reasonable ground to believe otherwise.

As to the non-expertised portions, however, Auslander is in a different position. He seems to have been under the impression that Peat, Marwick was responsible for all the figures. This impression was not correct, as he would have realized if he had read the prospectus carefully. Auslander made no investigation of the accuracy of the prospectus. He relied on the assurance of Vitolo and Russo, and upon the information he had received in answer to his inquiries back in February and early March. These inquiries were general ones, in the nature of a credit check. The information which he received in answer to them was also general, without specific reference to the statements in the prospectus, which was not prepared until some time thereafter.

It is true that Auslander became a director on the eve of the financing. He had little opportunity to familiarize himself with the company's affairs. The question is whether, under such circumstances, Auslander did enough to establish his due diligence defense with respect to the non-expertised portions of the prospectus.

* * *

Section 11 imposes liability in the first instance upon a director, no matter how new he is. He is presumed to know his responsibility when he becomes a director. He can escape liability only by using that reasonable care to investigate the facts which a prudent man would employ in the management of his own property. In my opinion, a prudent man would not act in an important matter without any knowledge of the relevant facts, in sole reliance upon representations of persons who are comparative strangers and upon general information which does not purport to cover the particular case. To say that such minimal conduct measures up to the statutory standard would, to all intents and purposes, absolve new directors from responsibility merely because they are new. This is not a sensible construction of Section 11, when one bears in mind its fundamental purpose of requiring full and truthful disclosure for the protection of investors.

I find and conclude that Auslander has not established his due diligence defense with respect to the misstatements and omissions in those portions of the prospectus other than the audited 1960 figures.

Rose

Rose, another "outside" director, is in a position comparable to Auslander's. He is a civil engineer. Peat, Marwick were the auditors for his firm and Kircher, when he was employed by Peat, Marwick, had worked on his firm's books in 1957 and 1958. Rose was favorably impressed by Kircher at that time.

* * *

Kircher sent Rose a copy of BarChris's annual report for 1960. Rose observed that Peat, Marwick were BarChris's auditors. Subsequently, in March, he inquired about BarChris of three different brokers. They informed him that BarChris was apparently well managed, that it had enjoyed a steady growth, and that its stock had gone up considerably, although it paid no dividends.

Rose visited BarChris's office in mid-March and was interested in the bowling exhibit on display there. He had dinner with Vitolo who explained BarChris's plans for expansion. The other officers talked to him in a similar vein.

Rose agreed to become a director and was elected on April 17, 1961, along with Auslander and the others. Rose was present at that meeting and there learned of the proposed financing for the first time. He read the first (March 30) version of the registration statement for "about ten minutes."

On May 10, Rose signed a separate signature sheet for the first amendment. Unlike Auslander, Rose did know that the signature sheet pertained to a registration statement.

Rose attended the directors' meeting on May 15. He signed the signature sheet for the registration statement in its final form. The entire document was not submitted to the meeting.

* * *

Up to May 16, Rose had not participated in BarChris's affairs. He made no investigation. He believed that the registration statement was true. The only basis for his belief was his reliance upon Peat, Marwick and upon the BarChris officers.

What has been said with respect to Auslander applies equally to Rose. He has not sustained the burden of proving his due diligence defense as to the portions of the registration statement other than the audited 1960 figures.

Grant

Grant became a director of BarChris in October 1960. His law firm was counsel to BarChris in matters pertaining to the registration of securities. Grant drafted the registration statement for the stock issue in 1959 and for the warrants in January 1961. He also drafted the registration statement for the debentures. In the preliminary division of work between him and Ballard, the underwriters' counsel, Grant took initial responsibility for preparing the registration statement, while Ballard devoted his efforts in the first instance to preparing the indenture.

Grant is sued as a director and as a signer of the registration statement. This is not an action against him for malpractice in his capacity as a lawyer. Nevertheless, in considering Grant's due diligence defenses, the unique position which he occupied cannot be disregarded. As the director most directly concerned with writing the registration statement and assuring its accuracy, more was required of him in the way of reasonable investigation than could fairly be expected of a director who had no connection with this work.

There is no valid basis for plaintiffs' accusation that Grant knew that the prospectus was false in some respects and incomplete and misleading in others. Having seen him testify at length, I am satisfied as to his integrity. I find that Grant honestly believed that the registration statement was true and that no material facts had been omitted from it.

In this belief he was mistaken, and the fact is that for all his work, he never discovered any of the errors or omissions which have been recounted at length in this opinion, * * *.

Grant contends that a finding that he did not make a reasonable investigation would be equivalent to a holding that a lawyer for an issuing company, in order to show due diligence, must make an independent audit of the figures supplied to him by his client. I do not consider this to be a realistic statement of the issue. There were errors and omissions here which could have been detected without an audit. The question is whether, despite his failure to detect them, Grant made a reasonable effort to that end.

Much of this registration statement is a scissors and paste-pot job. Grant lifted large portions from the earlier prospectuses, modifying them in some instances to the extent that he considered necessary. But BarChris's affairs had changed for the worse by May 1961. Statements that were accurate in January were no longer accurate in May. Grant never discovered this. He accepted the assurances of Kircher and Russo that any change which might have occurred had been for the better, rather than the contrary.

It is claimed that a lawyer is entitled to rely on the statements of his client and that to require him to verify their accuracy would set an unreasonably high standard. This is too broad a generalization. It is all a matter of degree. To require an audit would obviously be unreasonable. On the other hand, to require a check of matters easily verifiable is not unreasonable. Even honest clients can make mistakes. The statute imposes liability for untrue statements regardless of whether they are intentionally untrue. The way to prevent mistakes is to test oral information by examining the original written record.

* * *

As to the backlog figure, Grant appreciated that scheduled unfilled orders on the company's books meant firm commitments, but he never asked to see the contracts which, according to the prospectus, added up to $6,905,000. Thus, he did not know that this figure was overstated by some $4,490,000.

Grant was unaware of the fact that BarChris was about to operate Bridge and Yonkers.[1] He did not read the minutes of those subsidiaries which would have revealed that fact to him. On the subject of minutes, Grant knew that minutes of certain meetings of the BarChris executive committee held in 1961 had not been written up. Kircher, who had acted as secretary at those meetings, had complete notes of them. Kircher told Grant that there was no point in writing up the minutes because the matters discussed at those meetings were purely routine. Grant did not insist that the minutes be written up, nor did he look at Kircher's notes.   * * *

Grant knew that there had been loans from officers to BarChris in the past because that subject had been mentioned in the 1959 and January 1961 prospectuses. In March Grant prepared a questionnaire to be answered by officers and directors for the purpose of obtaining information to be used in the prospectus. The questionnaire did not inquire expressly about the existence of officers' loans. At approximately the same time, Grant prepared another questionnaire in order to obtain information on proxy statements for the annual stockholders' meeting. This questionnaire asked each officer to state whether he was indebted to BarChris, but it did not ask whether BarChris was indebted to him.

---

1. These were two of the bowling alleys
BarChris had built for others.

Despite the inadequacy of these written questionnaire's, Grant did, on March 16, 1961, orally inquire as to whether any officers' loans were outstanding. He was assured by Russo, Vitolo and Pugliese that all such loans had been repaid. Grant did not ask again. He was unaware of the new loans in April. He did know, however, that, at Kircher's request, a provision was inserted in the indenture which gave loans from individuals priority over the debentures. Kircher's insistence on this clause did not arouse his suspicions.

It is only fair to say that Grant was given to understand by Kircher that there were no new officers' loans and that there would not be any before May 16. It is still a close question, however, whether, under all the circumstances, Grant should have investigated further, perhaps by asking Peat, Marwick, in the course of its S–1 review, to look at the books on this particular point. I believe that a careful man would have checked.

There is more to the subject of due diligence than this, particularly with respect to the application of proceeds and customers' delinquencies.

The application of proceeds language in the prospectus was drafted by Kircher back in January. It may well have expressed his intent at that time, but his intent, and that of the other principal officers of BarChris, was very different in May. Grant did not appreciate that the earlier language was no longer appropriate. He never learned of the situation which the company faced in May. He knew that BarChris was short of cash, but he had no idea how short. He did not know that BarChris was withholding delivery of checks already drawn and signed because there was not enough money in the bank to pay them. He did not know that the officers of the company intended to use immediately approximately one-third of the financing proceeds in a manner not disclosed in the prospectus, including approximately $1,000,000 in paying old debts.

* * *

As far as customers' delinquencies is concerned, although Grant discussed this with Kircher, he again accepted the assurances of Kircher and Russo that no serious problem existed. He did not examine the records as to delinquencies, although BarChris maintained such a record. Any inquiry on his part of Talcott or an examination of BarChris's correspondence with Talcott in April and May 1961 would have apprised him of the true facts. It would have led him to appreciate that the statement in this prospectus, carried over from earlier prospectuses, to the effect that since 1955 BarChris had been required to repurchase less than one-half of one per cent of discounted customers' notes could no longer properly be made without further explanation.

Grant was entitled to rely on Peat, Marwick for the 1960 figures. He had no reasonable ground to believe them to be inaccurate. But the matters which I have mentioned were not within the expertised portion of the prospectus. As to this, Grant, was obliged to make a reasonable investigation. I am forced to find that he did not make one. After making all due allowances for the fact that BarChris's officers misled him, there are too many instances in which Grant failed to make an inquiry which he could easily have made which, if pursued, would have put him on his guard. In my opinion, this finding on the evidence in this case does not establish an unreasonably high standard in other cases for company counsel who are also directors. Each case must rest on its own facts. I conclude that Grant has not established his due diligence defenses except as to the audited 1960 figures.

The Underwriters and Coleman

The underwriters other than Drexel made no investigation of the accuracy of the prospectus. One of them, Peter Morgan, had underwritten the 1959 stock issue and had been a director of BarChris. He thus had some general familiarity with its affairs, but he knew no more than the other underwriters about the debenture prospectus. They all relied upon Drexel as the "lead" underwriter.

Drexel did make an investigation. The work was in charge of Coleman, a partner of the firm, assisted by Casperson, an associate. Drexel's attorneys acted as attorneys for the entire group of underwriters. Ballard did the work, assisted by Stanton.

On April 17, 1961 Coleman became a director of BarChris. He signed the first amendment to the registration statement filed on May 11 and the second amendment, constituting the registration statement in its final form, filed on May 16. He thereby assumed a responsibility as a director and signer in addition to his respoonsibility as an underwriter.

    *   *   *

On January 24, 1961, Coleman held a meeting with Ballard, Grant and Kircher, among others. By that time Coleman had about decided to go ahead with the financing, although Drexel's formal letter of intent was not delivered until February 9, 1961 (subsequently revised on March 7, 1961). At this meeting Coleman asked Kircher how Bar-Chris intended to use the proceeds of the financing. In reply to this inquiry, Kircher wrote a letter to Coleman dated January 30, 1961 outlining BarChris's plans. This eventually formed the basis of the application of proceeds section in the prospectus.

Coleman continued his general investigation. He obtained a Dun & Bradstreet report on BarChris on March 16, 1961. He read Bar-Chris's annual report for 1960 which was available in March.

    *   *   *

Coleman and Ballard asked pertinent questions and received answers which satisfied them.   *   *   *

After Coleman was elected a director on April 17, 1961, he made no further independent investigation of the accuracy of the prospectus. He assumed that Ballard was taking care of this on his behalf as well as on behalf of the underwriters.

In April 1961 Ballard instructed Stanton to examine BarChris's minutes for the past five years and also to look at "the major contracts of the company." Stanton went to BarChris's office for that purpose on April 24. He asked Birnbaum for the minute books. He read the minutes of the board of directors and discovered interleaved in them a few minutes of executive committee meetings in 1960. He asked Kircher is there were any others. Kircher said that there had been other executive committee meetings but that the minutes had not been written up.

Stanton read the minutes of a few BarChris subsidiaries. His testimony was vague as to which ones. * * *

As to the "major contracts," all that Stanton could remember seeing was an insurance policy. Birnbaum told him that there was no file of major contracts. Stanton did not examine the agreements with Talcott. He did not examine the contracts with customers. He did not look to see what contracts comprised the backlog figure. Stanton examined no accounting records of BarChris. His visit, which lasted one day, was devoted primarily to reading the directors' minutes.

On April 25 Ballard wrote to Grant about certain matters which Stanton had noted on his visit to BarChris the day before, none of which Ballard considered "very earth shaking." As far as relevant here, these were (1) Russo's remark as recorded in the executive committee minutes of November 3, 1960 to the effect that because of customers' defaults, BarChris might find itself in the business of operating alleys; * * *.

On May 9, 1961, Ballard came to New York and conferred with Grant and Kircher. They discussed the Securities and Exchange Commission's deficiency letter of May 4, 1961 which required the inclusion in the prospectus of certain additional information, notably net sales, gross profits and net earnings figures for the first quarter of 1961. They also discussed the points raised in Ballard's letter to Grant of April 25. As to the latter, most of the conversation related to what Russo had meant by his remark on November 3, 1960. Kircher said that the delinquency problem was less severe now than it had been back in November 1960, that no alleys had been repossessed, and that although he was "worried about one alley in Harlem" (Dreyfuss), that was a "special situation." Grant reported that Russo had told him that his statement on November 3, 1960 was "merely hypothetical." On the strength of this conversation, Ballard was satisfied that the one-half of one per cent figure in the prospectus did not need qualification or elaboration.

* * *

It must be remembered that this conference took place only one week before the registration statement became effective. Ballard did nothing else in the way of checking during that intervening week.

Ballard did not insist that the executive committee minutes be written up so that he could inspect them, although he testified that he knew from experience that executive committee minutes may be extremely important. If he had insisted, he would have found the minutes highly informative, as has previously been pointed out. Ballard did not ask to see BarChris's schedule of delinquencies or Talcott's notices of delinquencies, or BarChris's correspondence with Talcott.

Ballard did not examine BarChris's contracts with Talcott. He did not appreciate what Talcott's rights were under those financing agreements or how serious the effect would be upon BarChris of any exercise of those rights.

Ballard did not investigate the composition of the backlog figure to be sure that it was not "puffy." He made no inquiry after March about any new officers' loans, although he knew that Kircher had insisted on a provision in the indenture which gave loans from individuals priority over the debentures. He was unaware of the seriousness of BarChris's cash position and of how BarChris's officers intended to use a large part of the proceeds. He did not know that BarChris was operating [bowling alleys].

Like Grant, Ballard, without checking, relied on the information which he got from Kircher. He also relied on Grant who, as company counsel, presumably was familiar with its affairs.

The formal opinion which Ballard's firm rendered to the underwriters at the closing on May 24, 1961 made clear that this is what he had done. The opinion stated (underscoring supplied):

"In the course of the preparation of the Registration Statement and Prospectus by the Company, we have had numerous conferences with respresentatives of and counsel for the Company and with its auditors and we have raised many questions regarding the business of the Company. Satisfactory answers to such questions were in each case given us, and all other information and documents we requested have been supplied. We are of the opinion that the *data presented* to us are accurately reflected in the Registration Statement and Prospectus and that there has been omitted from the Registration Statement no material facts *included in such data*. Although *we have not otherwise verified* the completeness or accuracy of the information furnished to us, on the basis of the foregoing and with the exception of the financial statements and schedules (which this opinion does not pass upon), we have no reason to believe that the Registration Statement or Prospectus contains any untrue statement of any material fact or omits to state a material fact required to be stated therein or necessary in order to make the statements therein not misleading."

Coleman testified that Drexel had on understanding with its attorneys that "we expect them to inspect on our behalf the corporate records of the company including, but not limited to, the minutes of the corporation, the stockholders and the committees of the board authorized to act for the board." Ballard manifested his awareness of this understanding by sending Stanton to read the minutes and the major contracts. It is difficult to square this understanding with the formal opinion of Ballard's firm which expressly disclaimed any attempt to verify information supplied by the company and its counsel.

In any event, it is clear that no effectual attempt at verification was made. The question is whether due diligence required that it be made. Stated another way, is it sufficient to ask questions, to obtain answers which, if true, would be thought satisfactory, and to let it go at that, without seeking to ascertain from the records whether the answers in fact are true and complete?

I have already held that this procedure is not sufficient in Grant's case. Are underwriters in a different position, as far as due diligence is concerned?

The underwriters say that the prospectus is the company's prospectus, not theirs. Doubtless this is the way they customarily regard it. But the Securities Act makes no such distinction. The underwriters are just as responsible as the company if the prospectus is false. And prospective investors rely upon the reputation of the underwriters in deciding whether to purchase the securities.

There is no direct authority on this question, no judicial decision defining the degree of diligence which underwriters must exercise to establish their defense under Section 11.[2]

* * *

The purpose of Section 11 is to protect investors. To that end the underwriters are made responsible for the truth of the prospectus. If they may escape that responsibility by taking at face value representations made to them by the company's management, then the inclusion of underwriters among those liable under Section 11 affords the investors no additional protection. To effectuate the statute's purpose, the phrase "reasonable investigation" must be construed to require more effort on the part of the underwriters than the mere accurate reporting in the prospectus of "date presented" to them by the company. It should make no difference that this data is elicited by questions addressed to the company officers by the underwriters, or that the underwriters at the time believe that the company's officers are truthful and reliable. In order to make the underwriters' participation in this enterprise of any value to the investors, the underwriters must make some reasonable attempt to verify the data submitted to them. They may not rely solely on the company's officers or on the company's counsel. A prudent man in the management of his own property would not rely on them.

It is impossible to lay down a rigid rule suitable for every case defining the extent to which such verification must go. It is a question of degree, a matter of judgment in each case. In the present case,

2. There are at least two decisions of the Securities and Exchange Commission which indicate that it is the Commission's view that an underwriter must go beyond and behind the representations of management. Matter of Richmond Corp., [1962–1964 Decisions] CCH Sec.L.Rep. ¶ 76,904 (1963); Matter of Charles E. Bailey & Co., 35 S.E.C. 33 (1953). (Court's footnote 25.)

the underwriters' counsel made almost no attempt to verify management's representations. I hold that that was insufficient.

On the evidence in this case, I find that the underwriters' counsel did not make a reasonable investigation of the truth of those portions of the prospectus which were not made on the authority of Peat, Marwick as an expert. Drexel is bound by their failure. It is not a matter of relying upon counsel for legal advice. Here the attorneys were dealing with matters of fact. Drexel delegated to them, as its agent, the business of examining the corporate minutes and contracts. It must bear the consequences of their failure to make an adequate examination.

The other underwriters, who did nothing and relied solely on Drexel and on the lawyers, are also bound by it. It follows that although Drexel and the other underwriters believed that those portions of the prospectus were true, they had no reasonable ground for that belief, within the meaning of the statute. Hence, they have not established their due diligence defense, except as to the 1960 audited figures.

The same conclusions must apply to Coleman. Although he participated quite actively in the earlier stages of the preparation of the prospectus, and contributed questions and warnings of his own, in addition to the questions of counsel, the fact is that he stopped his participation toward the end of March 1961. He made no investigation after he became a director. When it came to verification, he relied upon his counsel to do it for him. Since counsel failed to do it, Coleman is bound by that failure. Consequently, in his case also, he has not established his due diligence defense except as to the audited 1960 figures.

Peat, Marwick

Section 11(b) provides:

"Notwithstanding the provisions of subsection (a) no person * * * shall be liable as provided therein who shall sustain the burden of proof—

* * *

"(3) that * * * (B) as regards any part of the registration statement purporting to be made upon his authority as an expert * * * (i) he had, after reasonable investigation, reasonable ground to believe and did believe, at the time such part of the registration statement became effective, that the statements therein were true and that there was no omission to state a material fact required to be stated therein or necessary to make the statements therein not misleading * * *."

This defines the due diligence defense for an expert. Peat, Marwick has pleaded it.

The part of the registration statement purporting to be made upon the authority of Peat, Marwick as an expert was, as we have seen, the 1960 figures. But because the statute requires the court to determine Peat, Marwick's belief, and the grounds thereof, "at the time such part of the registration statement became effective," for the purposes of this affirmative defense, the matter must be viewed as of May 16, 1961, and the question is whether at that time Peat, Marwick, after reasonable investigation, had reasonable ground to believe and did believe that the 1960 figures were true and that no material fact had been omitted from the registration statement which should have been included in order to make the 1960 figures not misleading. In deciding this issue, the court must consider not only what Peat, Marwick did in its 1960 audit, but also what it did in its subsequent "S–1 review." The proper scope of that review must also be determined.

It may be noted that we are concerned at this point only with the question of Peat, Marwick's liability to plaintiffs. At the closing on May 24, 1961, Peat, Marwick delivered a so-called "comfort letter" to the underwriters. This letter stated:

"It is understood that this letter is for the information of the underwriters and is not to be quoted or referred to, in whole or in part, in the Registration Statement or Prospectus or in any literature used in connection with the sale of securities."

Plaintiffs may not take advantage of any undertakings or representations in this letter. If they exceeded the normal scope of an S–1 review (a question which I do not now decide) that is a matter which relates only to the crossclaims which defendants have asserted against each other and which I have postponed for determination at a later date.

The 1960 Audit

Peat, Marwick's work was in general charge of a member of the firm, Cummings, and more immediately in charge of Peat, Marwick's manager, Logan. Most of the actual work was performed by a senior accountant, Berardi, who had junior assistants, one of whom was Kennedy.

Berardi was then about thirty years old. He was not yet a C.P.A. He had had no previous experience with the bowling industry. This was his first job as a senior accountant. He could hardly have been given a more difficult assignment.

After obtaining a little background information on BarChris by talking to Logan and reviewing Peat, Marwick's work papers on its 1959 audit, Berardi examined the results of test checks of BarChris's accounting procedures which one of the junior accountants had made, and he prepared an "internal control questionnaire" and an "audit program." Thereafter, for a few days subsequent to December 30, 1960, he inspected BarChris's inventories and examined certain alley construction. Finally, on January 13, 1961, he began his auditing work which he carried on substantially continuously until it was completed on February 24, 1961. Toward the close of the work, Logan reviewed it and made various comments and suggestions to Berardi.

It is unnecessary to recount everything that Berardi did in the course of the audit. We are concerned only with the evidence relating to what Berardi did or did not do with respect to those items which I have found to have been incorrectly reported in the 1960 figures in the prospectus.   *   *   *

[The Court then made a detailed analysis of several items which Berardi had omitted, such as his failure to learn that two bowling alleys had not been sold, failure to note that adequate reserves for uncollectible accounts had not been established and failure to note that reserves of $264,689 held by the factors were carried as a current asset of BarChris when part of the reserve would not be released within one year and some of it might not be released at all.]

The S–1 Review

The purpose of reviewing events subsequent to the date of a certified balance sheet (referred to as an S–1 review when made with reference to a registration statement) is to ascertain whether any material change has occurred in the company's financial position which should be disclosed in order to prevent the balance sheet figures from being misleading. The scope of such a review, under generally accepted auditing standards, is limited. It does not amount to a complete audit.

Peat, Marwick prepared a written program for such a review. I find that this program conformed to generally accepted auditing standards. Among other things, it required the following:

"1. Review minutes of stockholders, directors and committees. *   *   *

"2. Review latest interim financial statements and compare with corresponding statements of preceding year. Inquire regarding significant variations and changes.

*   *   *

"4. Review the more important financial records and inquire regarding material transactions not in the ordinary course of business and any other significant items.

*   *   *

"6. Inquire as to changes in material contracts   *   *   *.

*   *   *

"10. Inquire as to any significant bad debts or accounts in dispute for which provision has not been made.

*   *   *

"14. Inquire as to   *   *   *   newly discovered liabilities, direct or contingent   *   *   *."

Berardi made the S–1 review in May 1961. He devoted a little over two days to it, a total of 20½ hours. He did not discover any of the errors or omissions pertaining to the state of affairs in 1961 which I have previously discussed at length, all of which were material. The question is whether, despite his failure to find out anything, his investigation was reasonable within the meaning of the statute.

What Berardi did was to look at a consolidating trial balance as of March 31, 1961 which had been prepared by BarChris, compare it with the audited December 31, 1960 figures discuss with Trilling certain unfavorable developments which the comparison disclosed, and read certain minutes. He did not examine any "important financial records" other than the trial balance. As to minutes, he read only what minutes Birnbaum gave him, which consisted only of the board of directors' minutes of BarChris. He did not read such minutes as there were of the executive committee. He did not know that there was an executive committee, hence he did not discover that Kircher had notes of executive committee minutes which had not been written up. He did not read the minutes of any subsidiary.

In substance, what Berardi did is similar to what Grant and Ballard did. He asked questions, he got answers which he considered satisfactory, and he did nothing to verify them. For example, he obtained from Trilling a list of contracts. * * *

Berardi noticed that there had been an increase in notes payable by BarChris. Trilling admitted to him that BarChris was "a bit slow" in paying its bills. Berardi recorded in his notes of his review that BarChris was in a "tight cash position." Trilling's explanation was that BarChris was experiencing "some temporary difficulty."

Berardi had no conception of how tight the cash position was. He did not discover that BarChris was holding up checks in substantial amounts because there was no money in the bank to cover them. * * * Since he never read the prospectus, he was not even aware that there had ever been any problem about loans from officers.

During the 1960 audit Berardi had obtained some information from factors, not sufficiently detailed even then, as to delinquent notes. He made no inquiry of factors about this in his S–1 review. Since he knew nothing about Kircher's notes of the executive committee meetings, he did not learn that the delinquency situation had grown worse. He was content with Trilling's assurance that no liability theretofore contingent had become direct.

Apparently the only BarChris officer with whom Berardi communicated was Trilling. He could not recall making any inquiries of Russo, Vitolo or Pugliese. As to Kircher, Berardi's testimony was self-contradictory. At one point he said that he had inquired of Kircher and at another he said that he could not recall making any such inquiry.

There had been a material change for the worse in BarChris's financial position. That change was sufficiently serious so that the failure to disclose it made the 1960 figures misleading. Berardi did not discover it. As far as results were concerned, his S–1 review was useless.

Accountants should not be held to a standard higher than that recognized in their profession. I do not do so here. Berardi's review did not come up to that standard. He did not take some of the steps which Peat, Marwick's written program prescribed. He did not spend an adequate amount of time on a task of this magnitude. Most important of all, he was too easily satisfied with glib answers to his inquiries.

This is not to say that he should have made a complete audit. But there were enough danger signals in the materials which he did examine to require some further investigation on his part. Generally accepted accounting standards required such further investigation under these circumstances. It is not always sufficient merely to ask questions.

Here again, the burden of proof is on Peat, Marwick. I find that that burden has not been satisfied. I conclude that Peat, Marwick has not established its due diligence defense.

* * *

Defendants' motions to dismiss this action, upon which decision was reserved at the trial, are denied. Motions made at various times during the trial to strike certain testimony are also denied, except in so far as such motions pertain to evidence relating to the issues still undecided.

Pursuant to Rule 52(a), this opinion constitutes the court's findings of fact and conclusions of law with respect to the issues determined herein.

So ordered.

———

SECURITIES AND EXCHANGE COMMISSION v. GUILD FILMS COMPANY

United States Court of Appeals, Second Circuit, 1960.
279 F.2d 485.

MOORE, Circuit Judge. This is an appeal under 28 U.S.C.A. § 1292(a) from an order by the district court, 178 F.Supp. 418, granting a preliminary injunction to restrain the sale of 50,000 shares of Guild Films Company, Inc. common stock by two of the appellants, the Santa Monica Bank and The Southwest Bank of Inglewood. Pending a final determination of this action, the preliminary injunction was issued "unless and until" a registration statement should be filed under the Securities Act of 1933, 15 U.S.C.A. § 77a et seq.

Section 5 of the Act makes it unlawful for anyone, by any interstate communication or use of the mails, to sell or deliver any security unless a registration statement is in effect. Section 4 provides, however, that "the provisions of section 5 * * * shall not apply to * * * (1) Transactions by any person other than an issuer, underwriter, or dealer." The banks claim that they come within this exemption to the registration requirements. The district court rejected this claim, holding that the banks were "underwriters" within the meaning of the Act. While the issue involved can be simply stated, a rather complete discussion of the facts is necessary.

The Original Loans by the Banks and the Security Therefor

On September 17, 1958, the Santa Monica Bank and The Southwest Bank of Inglewood jointly agreed to loan Hal Roach, Jr., $120,000, represented by two notes. An unverified, undated financial statement submitted by Roach was relied upon in making the loan. The money was deposited in a joint checking account in the name of Roach and Charles H. Meacham. Roach's note for $60,000 to the Santa Monica Bank, which was to manage the loan for both banks, was dated September 17, 1958, and his note to The Southwest Bank for the same amount was dated September 25, 1958. Both notes were treated as due on December 15, 1958, although the note to The Southwest Bank was actually payable 18 days earlier.

The loans were initially secured by 34,475 shares of the Scranton Corp. (valued at $15 per share) and 2,000 shares of F. L. Jacobs Co. stock (valued at $8 per share). As agreed, this collateral was soon replaced by 30,000 shares of Jacobs stock. Roach had used a large part of the proceeds of the loans to purchase a substantial number of the 30,000 Jacobs shares put up as collateral.

The Jacobs Stock and the Renewal Notes

Roach was an officer, director, and the controlling shareholder of F. L. Jacobs Co., of which Alexander L. Guterma was president. This company controlled the Scranton Corp. which owned Hal Roach Studios, which in turn owned both W–R Corp. and Rabco T. V. Production, Inc.

W–R Corp. and Guild Films, Inc. had made an agreement on January 23, 1959, under which W–R Corp. was to obtain 400,000 shares of Guild Films common stock (the registration of 50,000 shares of this stock is herein dispute) and a number of promissory notes in exchange for certain film properties. The stock was not registered with the S. E. C., but Guild Films agreed to use its best efforts to obtain registration. However, seeking to come within an exemption provided in section 4 of the Securities Act, the parties provided the following in their agreement:

"Stock Taken for Investment: W–R warrants, represents and agrees that all of the said 400,000 shares of Guild's common stock being contemporaneously issued hereunder, whether registered in the name of W–R or in accordance with the instructions of W–R, are being acquired for investment only and not for the purpose or with the intention of distributing or reselling the same to others. Guild is relying on said warranty and representation in the issuance of said stock."

On February 5, 1959, for reasons discussed below, Roach directed that 100,000 shares of the Guild Films stock be issued in the name of W–R Corp. and 100,000 shares (represented by two 50,000 share certificates) in the name of Rabco. Meacham, the treasurer of Guild Films, directed that the transfer agent stamp this restriction on the stock certificates:

"The shares represented by this certificate have not been registered under the Securities Act of 1933. The shares have been acquired for investment and may not be sold, transferred, pledged or hypothecated in the absence of an effective registration statement for the shares under the Securities Act of 1933 or an opinion of counsel to the company that registration is not required under said Act."

The remaining 200,000 shares were not issued as the promised film properties were never transferred.

Although the Guild Films stock was issued "for investment only," the district court found that Roach "unquestionably" purchased it in order to have it resold. "In spite of the financial statement submitted by him to the Santa Monica Bank in September, 1958, Roach's financial position at that time was far from secure. A good part of the proceeds of the loan discussed below he had used to purchase Jacobs stock, in turn to post it as collateral for the loan and to fulfill other stock purchase commitments. Roach was financially pressed in December, 1958, when the Jacobs stock dropped to $5; he apparently had commitments to purchase more of this stock and no money with which to pay for it; he was indebted to the Pacific National Bank in the sum of $53,700 on a note which matured in March, 1959; he was unable to pay the Bank's notes as they matured. Although he sorely needed an extension of time in which to pay, he was unable to deliver sufficient collateral to accomplish this; he held his creditor at bay by promising additional collateral in the form of the Guild Films stock." These findings are uncontested.

On December 9, 1958, the Santa Monica Bank learned that the Jacobs stock had been suspended from trading on the New York Stock Exchange. That bank thereupon wrote to Roach asking him to liquidate the loan before December 15, 1958, because the Jacobs stock, which was then traded over-the-counter and had dropped in value to $5 per share, was "not now considered by our Loan Committee as acceptable collateral." After a number of conversations, the Santa Monica Bank agreed to renew Roach's note for 90 days upon deposit of 10,000 additional shares of Jacobs stock, or an equivalent in value in Scranton stock or upon payment of $30,000. A renewal note dated December 18, 1958 was sent to Meacham for Roach's signature, and interest on the matured note requested. The Santa Monica Bank agreed to renew on the same conditions. The notes were signed and returned, but Meacham requested "a few days in which to make up our minds" concerning the required additional collateral. Until the end of January, 1959, both banks were in constant communication with Roach, but no further collateral was deposited. On December 31, 1958, The Southwest Bank had informed him that its renewal would not be effective until additional security was supplied, and on January 28, 1959, it wrote to Roach demanding, by February 3, 1959, payment of the November 24, 1958 note, then more than six weeks overdue. On February 3, 1959, Roach telegraphed the Santa Monica Bank that he had "deposited $75,000 Guild Films, Inc. notes to your account at Chemical Corn Bank, New York. This best I can do till I return to Los Angeles next week." On the basis of this telegram,

The Southwest Bank wrote to Roach agreeing to defer action until February 10th.

The Guild Films Stock

On that date Roach wired The Southwest Bank that he had sent 50,000 shares of Guild Films stock to the Santa Monica Bank. By a divided vote the Loan Committee of The Southwest Bank decided to renew the note, making it payable "On 'Demand' if 'No Demand' then all due March 18, 1959." On February 12th, one of the 50,000 share Guild Films certificates in the name of Rabco T. V. Productions was received by the Santa Monica Bank. The restrictive legend quoted above was stamped on the face of the certificate. Upon receipt thereof, the Santa Monica Bank authorized the Chemical Corn Exchange Bank in New York to release the Guild Films notes.

Subsequent Attempts by the Banks to Sell the Guild Films Stock

On February 12th, the Santa Monica Bank and The Southwest Bank learned that the Jacobs stock had been suspended from all trading by the S. E. C. The Santa Monica Bank immediately telegraphed Roach demanding payment by February 16th, and stating that otherwise the stock would be sold to liquidate the loan. Roach failed to pay and the banks attempted to sell the securities through brokers on the American Stock Exchange.

The Guild Films transfer agent refused to transfer the stock to the banks because of the stamped restriction. The Santa Monica Bank then wired Guild Films that unless the stock was released or exchanged for unrestricted securities, the matter would be taken to the American Stock Exchange and the S. E. C. "for their assistance and release." Guild Films refused to act; it also refused an offer to exchange the 50,000 shares for 25,000 shares of unrestricted stock; and no application for registration was made to the S. E. C.

In August, 1959, the Santa Monica Bank brought an action against Guild Films in the New York Supreme Court to compel the transfer of the stock. On September 18, 1959, that court ordered the transfer of the stock to the bank. The court based its order on a referee's report which found that the stock was exempt from the Securities Act of 1933. The Santa Monica Bank thereupon ordered 9,500 shares of the Guild Films stock sold. The S. E. C. learned of the sale and notified the bank and Guild Films that the stock could not be sold without registration. The bank then sought a Commission ruling that the stock was exempt. Despite an adverse opinion by the Commission, the bank sold an additional 10,500 shares on September 24, 1959. At that point, the Commission filed this suit to restrain the delivery of these shares and the sale of the remainder of the stock. The district court granted a preliminary injunction against delivery and further sale.

The Securities Act of 1933 was primarily intended to "protect investors by requiring registration with the Commission of certain information concerning securities offered for sale." Gilligan Will & Co.

v. S. E. C., 2 Cir., 1959, 267 F.2d 461, 463. An exemption from the provisions of § 5 of the Act was provided by § 4(1) for "transactions by any person other than an issuer, underwriter or dealer" because it was felt that no protection was necessary in these situations. See H.R.Rep. No. 85, 73rd Cong., 1st Sess. (1933) at p. 15. The primary question involved in this case is: were appellants issuers, underwriters or dealers within this exemption?

An "underwriter" is defined in § 2(11), 15 U.S.C.A. § 77b(11), as "any person who has purchased from an issuer with a view to, or sells for an issuer in connection with, the distribution of any security, * * * or participates or has a participation in the direct or indirect underwriting of any such undertaking * * *." The burden of proof is on the one seeking an exemption. Gilligan, Will & Co. v. S. E. C., supra.

The banks cannot be exempted on the ground that they did not "purchase" within the meaning of § 2(11). The term, although not defined in the Act, should be interpreted in a manner complementary to "sale" which is defined in § 2(3) as including "every * * * disposition of * * * a security or interest in a security, for value * * *." In fact, a proposed provision of the Act which expressly exempted sales "by or for the account of a pledge holder or mortgagee selling or offering for sale or delivery in the ordinary course of business and not for the purpose of avoiding the provisions of the Act, to liquidate a bona fide debt, a security pledged in good faith as collateral for such debt," was not accepted by Congress. S. 875, 73rd Cong., 1st Sess. (1933) § 126. Cf. Throop & Lane, Some Problems of Exemption Under the Securities Act of 1933, 4 Law & Contemp.Prob. 89, 124 n. 103 (1937).

Nor is it a defense that the banks did not deal directly with Guild Films. This court has recently stated that "the underlying policy of the Act, that of protecting the investing public through the disclosure of adequate information, would be seriously impaired if we held that a dealer must have conventional or contractual privity with the issuer in order to be an 'underwriter'." S. E. C. v. Culpepper, 2 Cir., 1959, 270 F.2d 241, 246, following S. E. C. v. Chinese Consol. Benev. Ass'n, 2 Cir., 1941, 120 F.2d 738, certiorari denied, 1942, 314 U.S. 618. It was held in these two cases that § 4(1) "does not in terms or by fair implication protect those who are engaged in steps necessary to the distribution of a security issue. To give Section 4(1) the construction urged by the defendant would afford a ready method of thwarting the policy of the law and evading its provisions." S. E. C. v. Chinese Consol. Benev. Ass'n, supra, 120 F.2d at page 741.

The banks have contended that they were "bona fide pledgees" and therefore "entitled upon default to sell the stock free of restrictions." They assume that "good faith" in accepting the stock is a sufficient defense. See Loss, Securities Regulation, 346 (1951). But the statute does not impose such a "good faith" criterion. The exemption in § 4(1) was intended to permit private sales of unregistered securities to investors who are likely to have, or who are likely to obtain, such information as is ordinarily disclosed in registration statements. See S. E. C. v. Ralston Purina Co., 1953, 346 U.S. 119. The "good faith" of the banks is irrelevant to this purpose. It would be of little solace to purchasers of worthless stock to learn that the sellers had acted "in good faith." Regardless of good faith, the banks engaged in steps necessary to this public sale, and cannot be exempted.

Without imputing to the banks any participation in a preconceived scheme to use the pledge of these securities as a device for unlawful distribution, it may be noted that when the 50,000 shares of Guild Films stock were received on February 12, 1959, the banks knew that they had been given unregistered stock and that the issuer had specifically forbidden that the stock "be sold, transferred, pledged or hypothecated in the absence of an effective registration statement for the shares under the Securities Act of 1933 or an opinion of counsel to the company that registration is not required under said Act." Furthermore, from Roach's prior unfulfilled promises, the banks should have known that immediate sale was almost inevitable if they were to recoup their loans from the security received. On February 11, 1959, the day before the stock was received, the S. E. C. suspended trading in the Jacobs stock. And on the very day that the stock was received, appellants wired Roach that they would call the loan unless payment were made. For months the bank had threatened action but declined to act; circumstances finally required action. The banks cannot now claim that this possibility was unforeseeable. The district court properly enjoined the threatened violation.

Affirmed.

SECURITIES ACT OF 1933 RELEASE NO. 4552

Securities and Exchange Commission.
November 6, 1962.

NON–PUBLIC OFFERING EXEMPTION

The Commission today announced the issuance of a statement regarding the availability of the exemption from the registration requirements of Section 5 of the Securities Act of 1933 afforded by the second clause of Section 4(1) of the Act for "transactions by an issuer not involving any public offering," the so-called "private offering exemption." Traditionally, the second clause of Section 4(1) has been regarded as providing an exemption from registration for bank loans, private placements of securities with institutions, and the promotion of a business venture by a few closely related persons. However, an increasing tendency to rely upon the exemption for offerings of speculative issues to unrelated and uninformed persons prompts this statement to point out the limitations on its availability.

Whether a transaction is one not involving any public offering is essentially a question of fact and necessitates a consideration of all surrounding circumstances, including such factors as the relationship between the offerees and the issuer, the nature, scope, size, type and manner of the offering.

The Supreme Court in S. E. C. v. Ralston Purina Co., 346 U.S. 119, 124, 125 (1953), noted that the exemption must be interpreted in the light of the statutory purpose to "protect investors by promoting full disclosure of information thought necessary to informed investment decisions" and held that "the applicability of Section 4(1) should turn on whether the particular class of persons affected need the protection of the Act." The Court stated that the number of offerees is not conclusive as to the availability of the exemption, since the statute seems to apply to an offering "whether to few or many." [1] However, the Court indicated that "nothing prevents the Commission, in enforcing the statute, from using some kind of numerical test in deciding when to investigate particular exemption claims." It should be emphasized, therefore, that the number of persons to whom the offering is extended is relevant only to the question whether they have the requisite association with and knowledge of the issuer which make the exemption available.

Consideration must be given not only to the identity of the actual purchasers but also to the offerees. Negotiations or conversations with or general solicitations of an unrestricted and unrelated group of prospective purchasers for the purpose of ascertaining who would be willing to accept an offer of securities is inconsistent with a claim that the transaction does not involve a public offering even though ultimately there may only be a few knowledgeable purchasers.[2]

A question frequently arises in the context of an offering to an issuer's employees. Limitation of an offering to certain employees designated as key employees may not be a sufficient showing to qualify for the exemption. As the Supreme Court stated in the *Ralston Purina* case: "The exemption as we construe it, does not deprive corporate employees, as a class, of the safeguards of the Act. We agree that some employee offerings may come within Section 4(1), e. g., one made to executive personnel who because of their position have access to the same kind of information that the Act would make available in the form of a registration statement. Absent such a showing of special circumstances, employees are just as much members of the investing 'public' as any of their neighbors in the community." The Court's concept is that the exemption is necessarily

1. See, also, Gilligan, Will & Co. v. S. E.C., 267 F.2d 461, 467 (C.A. 2, 1959), cert. denied, 361 U.S. 896 (1960).

2. Reference is made to the so-called "investment clubs" which have been organized under claim of an exemption from the registration provisions of the Securities Act of 1933 as well as the Investment Company Act of 1940. It should not be assumed that so long as the investment club, which is an investment company within the meaning of the latter Act, does not *obtain* more than 100 members, a public offering of its securities, namely the memberships, will not be involved. An investment company may be exempt from the provisions of the Investment Company Act if its securities are owned by not more than 100 persons *and* it is not making and does not presently propose to make a public offering of its securities. (Section 3(c)(1)). Both elements must be considered in determining whether the exemption is available.

narrow. The exemption does not become available simply because offerees are voluntarily *furnished* information about the issuer. Such a construction would give each issuer the choice of registering or making its own voluntary disclosures without regard to the standards and sanctions of the Act.

The sale of stock to promoters who take the initiative in founding or organizing the business would come within the exemption. On the other hand, the transaction tends to become public when the promoters begin to bring in a diverse group of uninformed friends, neighbors and associates.

The size of the offering may also raise questions as to the probability that the offering will be completed within the strict confines of the exemption. An offering of millions of dollars to non-institutional and non-affiliated investors or one divided, or convertible, into many units would suggest that a public offering may be involved.

When the services of an investment banker, or other facility through which public distributions are normally effected, are used to place the securities, special care must be taken to avoid a public offering. If the investment banker places the securities with discretionary accounts and other customers without regard to the ability of such customers to meet the tests implicit in the *Ralston Purina* case, the exemption may be lost. Public advertising of the offerings would, of course, be incompatible with a claim of a private offering. Similarly, the use of the facilities of a securities exchange to place the securities necessarily involves an offering to the public.

An important factor to be considered is whether the securities offered have come to rest in the hands of the initial informed group or whether the purchasers are merely conduits for a wider distribution. Persons who act in this capacity, whether or not engaged in the securities business, are deemed to be "underwriters" within the meaning of Section 2(11) of the Act. If the purchasers do in fact acquire the securities with a view to public distribution, the seller assumes the risk of possible violation of the registration requirements of the Act and consequent civil liabilities.[3] This has led to the practice whereby the issuer secures from the initial purchasers representations that they have acquired the securities for investment. Sometimes a legend to this effect is placed on the stock certificates and stop-transfer instructions issued to the transfer agent. However, a statement by the initial purchaser, at the time of his acquisition, that the securities are taken for investment and not for distribution is necessarily self-serving and not conclusive as to his actual intent. Mere acceptance at face value of such assurances will not provide a basis for reliance on the exemption when inquiry would suggest to a reasonable person that these assurances are formal rather than real. The additional precautions of placing a legend on the security and issuing stop-transfer orders have proved in many cases to be an effective means of preventing illegal distributions. Nevertheless, these

3. See Release No. 33–4445.

are only precautions and are not to be regarded as a basis for exemption from registration. The nature of the purchaser's past investment and trading practices or the character and scope of his business may be inconsistent with the purchase of large blocks of securities for investment. In particular, purchases by persons engaged in the business of buying and selling securities require careful scrutiny for the purpose of determining whether such person may be acting as an underwriter for the issuer.

The view is occasionally expressed that, solely by reason of continued holding of a security for the six-month capital-gain period specified in the income-tax laws, or for a year from the date of purchase, the security may be sold without registration. There is no statutory basis for such assumption. Of course, the longer the period of retention, the more persuasive would be the argument that the resale is not at variance with an original investment intent, but the length of time between acquisition and resale is merely one evidentiary fact to be considered. The weight to be accorded this evidentiary fact must, of necessity, vary with the circumstances of each case. Further, a limitation upon resale for a stated period of time or under certain circumstances would tend to raise a question as to original intent even though such limitation might otherwise recommend itself as a policing device. There is no legal justification for the assumption that holding a security in an "investment account" rather than a "trading account," holding for a deferred sale, for a market rise, for sale if the market does not rise, or for a statutory escrow period, without more, establishes a valid basis for an exemption from registration under the Securities Act.[4]

An unforeseen change of circumstances since the date of purchase may be a basis for an opinion that the proposed resale is not inconsistent with an investment representation. However, such claim must be considered in the light of all of the relevant facts. Thus, an advance or decline in market price or a change in the issuer's operating results are normal investment risks and do not usually provide an acceptable basis for such claim of changed circumstances. Possible inability of the purchaser to pay off loans incurred in connection with the purchase of the stock would ordinarily not be deemed an unforeseeable change of circumstances. Further, in the case of securities pledged for a loan, the pledgee should not assume that he is free to distribute without registration. The Congressional mandate of disclosure to investors is not to be avoided to permit a public distribution of unregistered securities because the pledgee took the securities from a purchaser, subsequently delinquent.[5]

The view is sometimes expressed that investment companies and other institutional investors are not subject to any restrictions regarding disposition of securities stated to be taken for investment

4. See Release No. 33–3825 re The Crowell-Collier Publishing Company.

5. S.E.C. v. Guild Films Company, Inc. et al., 279 F.2d 486 (C.A.2, 1960), cert. denied sub nom., Santa Monica Bank v. S.E.C., 364 U.S. 819 (1960).

and that any securities so acquired may be sold by them whenever the investment decision to sell is made, no matter how brief the holding period. Institutional investors are, however, subject to the same restrictions on sale of securities acquired from an issuer or a person in a control relationship with an issuer insofar as compliance with the registration requirements of the Securities Act is concerned.

Integration of Offerings

A determination whether an offering is public or private would also include a consideration of the question whether it should be regarded as a part of a larger offering made or to be made. The following factors are relevant to such question of integration: whether (1) the different offerings are part of a single plan of financing, (2) the offerings involve issuance of the same class of security, (3) the offerings are made at or about the same time, (4) the same type of consideration is to be received, (5) the offerings are made for the same general purpose.

What may appear to be a separate offering to a properly limited group will not be so considered if it is one of a related series of offerings. A person may not separate parts of a series of related transactions, the sum total of which is really one offering, and claim that a particular part is a non-public transaction. Thus, in the case of offerings of fractional undivided interests in separate oil or gas properties where the promoters must constantly find new participants for each new venture, it would appear to be appropriate to consider the entire series of offerings to determine the scope of this solicitation.

As has been emphasized in other releases discussing exemptions from the registration and prospectus requirements of the Securities Act, the terms of an exemption are to be strictly construed against the claimant who also has the burden of proving its availability.[6] Moreover, persons receiving advice from the staff of the Commission that no action will be recommended if they proceed without registration in reliance upon the exemption should do so only with full realization that the tests so applied may not be proof against claims by purchasers of the security that registration should have been effected. Finally, Sections 12(2) and 17 of the Act, which provide civil liabilities and criminal sanctions for fraud in the sale of a security, are applicable to the transactions notwithstanding the availability of an exemption from registration.

NOTE ON STATE REGULATION OF SECURITY TRANSACTIONS

The Federal Securities Act of 1933, referred to above, was the first legislation adopted on a national level concerning the marketing

----

6. S.E.C. v. Sunbeam Gold Mining Co., 95 F.2d 699, 701 (C.A.9, 1938); Gilligan, Will & Co. v. S.E.C., 267 F.2d 461, 466 (C.A.2, 1959); S.E.C. v. Ralston Purina Co., 346 U.S. 119, 126 (1953); S.E.C. v. Culpepper et al., 270 F.2d 241, 246 (C.A.2, 1959).

of securities. By its terms it is limited in application to securities which are sold through the mail or through the instrumentalities of interstate commerce. Prior to this Act the regulation of the sale of securities, was accomplished, if at all, by the statutory schemes adopted by the several states and rather vague concepts of the common law. These statutes remain in effect, not only in the marketing of securities on an intrastate basis, but also as to those which are being sold on a nationwide basis. The fact that a security is registered with the Federal Securities and Exchange Commission (the SEC) does not eliminate the necessity of compliance with state laws on this subject, although generally if a security has been registered with the SEC the quantity of work to be done with the state agency is rather limited.

Each of the states (except Delaware which has no "blue sky laws") continues to regulate the sale of securities which are marketed entirely within one state (even though they may be sold through the mails) because of the intrastate offering exemption under Section 3(a) (11) of the Federal Securities Act, 15 U.S.C.A. § 77c(11); see S.E.C. Release No. 4434, Exemption for Local Offerings, reported below. It should be noted that this exemption is limited to the registration requirements of Section 5 of the Securities Act of 1933, 15 U.S.C.A. § 77e; the exemption does not apply to any other provisions of either that Act or the Securities Exchange Act of 1934, 15 U.S.C.A. § 78a et seq. Of particular importance is the application of Section 10b of the latter Act, 15 U.S.C.A. § 78j(b), and Rule 10b–5, 17 C.F.R. 240.10b–5. While Rule 10b–5 is litigated in the Federal Courts and this litigation nearly always applies to publicly held securities, there is no reason why it should not apply to any security transaction in a small corporation (one as small as three stockholders) in which an untrue statement of a material fact or the omission to state a material fact in connection with the purchase or sale of any security has led to a loss. One should expect more litigation in small corporations under the provisions of Rule 10b–5.

The various states have adopted three general types of security regulations: statutes providing for penalties for fraudulent practices in the sale of securities resulting in criminal prosecution or the suspension of trading, or both, in a proceeding brought by a state regulatory agency; the second type is a "dealer registration" method whereby persons engaged in the business of marketing or dealing in securities must register with a state regulatory agency and provide certain information in their registration statement; and the third type which includes elements of the other two plus an arrangement whereby securities may not be sold within the state unless the issue itself is registered. Some states may have a mixture of two or all three of these methods; no useful purpose would be served in this volume in attempting to detail the particular method used in all states or even in any one state. While the Federal Securities and Exchange Commission does not become involved in the assessment of the quality of a proposed issue of securities (instances of foot-dragging or peremptory rejection of a registration statement of securities deemed to be of little value are not unknown in times when the staff of the Commission is over-burdened with work) various state regulatory bodies have arrogated to themselves the power to make their own assessment of the quality of a proposed issue in determining whether or not they will give the required statutory approval to an application. It is difficult to see how a determination as subjective as this can satisfy the requirements of due process of law, but most issuers would rather not litigate this question in the courts and thus the practice generally goes unchallenged. It also provides the possibility of political favoritism.

In any event, state securities commissions or agencies do exist and generally provide a worthwhile service in regulating the marketing of securities. Many small enterprises must seek capital from a limited number of people and the expense of registering with the Federal Securities and Exchange Commission in terms of the total amount of money to be raised would be excessive. Generally raising capital for a local business from a group of local investors is accomplished under the provisions of state law. No one knows how often this is done without complying with state securities acts because most investors who have suffered a loss (as well as the issuer) are generally reluctant to make this known to the public by way of litigation or complaint to a state agency. Further, losses of this kind, where violations of either securities acts or the common law have occurred, are adjusted by negotiation and settlement by lawyers without any law suit and without the public ever knowing of the transaction. But the very existence of a body of law on this subject also makes the negotiations and settlements of disputes of this kind possible.

SECURITIES ACT OF 1933 RELEASE NO. 4434

Securities and Exchange Commission.
December 6, 1961.

SECTION 3(a) (11) EXEMPTION FOR LOCAL OFFERINGS

The meaning and application of the exemption from registration provided by Section 3(a) (11) of the Securities Act of 1933, as amended, have been the subject of court opinions, release of the Securities and Exchange Commission [Release Nos. 33–1459 (1937) and 33–4386 (1961)], and opinions and interpretations expressed by the staff of the Commission in response to specific inquiries. This release is published to provide in convenient and up-to-date form a restatement of the principles underlying Section 3(a) (11) as so expressed over the years and to facilitate an understanding of the meaning and application of the exemption.[1]

---

1. Since publication of the 1937 release, the Investment Company Act of 1940 was enacted, and under Section 24(d) thereof, the Section 3(a) (11) exemp- tion for an intrastate offering is not available for an investment company registered or required to be registered under the Investment Company Act.

General Nature of Exemption

Section 3(a)(11), as amended in 1954, exempts from the registration and prospectus requirements of the Act:

> "Any security which is a part of an issue offered and sold only to persons resident within a single State or Territory, where the issuer of such security is a person resident and doing business within, or, if a corporation, incorporated by and doing business within, such State or Territory."

The legislative history of the Securities Act clearly shows that this exemption was designed to apply only to local financing that may practically be consummated in its entirety within the State or Territory in which the issuer is both incorporated and doing business. As appears from the legislative history, by amendment to the Act in 1934, this exemption was removed from Section 5(c) and inserted in Section 3, relating to "Exempted Securities", in order to relieve dealers of an unintended restriction on trading activity.[2] This amendment was not intended to detract from its essential character as a transaction exemption.[3]

"Issue" Concept

A basic condition of the exemption is that the *entire issue* of securities be offered and sold exclusively to residents of the state in question. Consequently, an offer to a non-resident which is considered a part of the intrastate issue will render the exemption unavailable to the entire offering.

Whether an offering is "a part of an issue", that is, whether it is an integrated part of an offering previously made or proposed to be made, is a question of fact and depends essentially upon whether the offerings are a related part of a plan or program. Unity Gold Corporation, 3 S.E.C. 618, 625 (1938); Peoples Securities Company, SEC Release No. 6176, Feb. 10, 1960. Thus, the exemption should not be relied upon in combination with another exemption for the different parts of a single issue where a part is offered or sold to non-residents.

The determination of what constitutes an "issue" is not governed by state law. Shaw v. U. S., 131 F.2d 476, 480 (C.A.9, 1942). Any one or more of the following factors may be determinative of the question of integration: (1) are the offerings part of a single plan of financing; (2) do the offerings involve issuance of the same class of security; (3) are the offerings made at or about the same time; (4) is the same type

2. H.R. Report No. 1838, 73rd Cong., 2d Sess. (1934), p. 40.

3. See Report of the Securities and Exchange Commission to the Committee on Interstate and Foreign Commerce, dated August 7, 1941, on Proposals for Amendments to the Securities Act of 1933 and the Securities Exchange Act of 1934 where in referring to Sections 3(a)(1), 3(a)(9), 3(a)(10), 3(a)(11) and 3(b) of the Securities Act of 1933, it was said: " * * * Since these are in reality transaction exemptions the Commission proposes and representatives of the securities' industry agree that they should be redesignated as transaction exemptions and transferred to Section 4 * * *." (p. 24).

of consideration to be received, and (5) are the offerings made for the same general purpose.

Moreover, since the exemption is designed to cover only those security distributions, which, as a whole, are essentially local in character, it is clear that the phrase "sold only to persons resident" as used in Section 3(a)(11) cannot refer merely to the initial sales by the issuing corporation to its underwriters, or even the subsequent resales by the underwriters to distributing dealers. To give effect to the fundamental purpose of the exemption, it is necessary that the entire issue of securities shall be offered and sold to, and come to rest only in the hands of residents within the state. If any part of the issue is offered or sold to a non-resident, the exemption is unavailable not only for the securities so sold, but for all securities forming a part of the issue, including those sold to residents. Securities Act Release No. 201 (1934); Brooklyn Manhattan Transit Corporation; 1 S.E.C. 147 (1935); S. E. C. v. Hillsborough Investment Corp., 173 F.Supp. 86 (D.N.H.1958); Hillsborough Investment Corp. v. S. E. C., 276 F.2d 665 (C.A.1, 1960); S. E. C. v. Los Angeles Trust Deed & Mortgage Exchange, et al., 186 F. Supp. 830, 871 (S.D.Cal., 1960), aff'd 285 F.2d 162 (C.A.9, 1960). It is incumbent upon the issuer, underwriter, dealers and other persons connected with the offering to make sure that it does not become an interstate distribution through resales. It is understood to be customary for such persons to obtain assurances that purchases are not made with a view to resale to non-residents.

Doing Business Within the State

In view of the local character of the Section 3(a)(11) exemption, the requirement that the issuer be doing business in the state can only be satisfied by the performance of substantial operational activities in the state of incorporation. The doing business requirement is not met by functions in the particular state such as bookkeeping, stock record and similar activities or by offering securities in the state. Thus, the exemption would be unavailable to an offering by a company made in the state of its incorporation of undivided fractional oil and gas interests located in other states even though the company conducted other business in the state of its incorporation. While the person creating the fractional interests is technically the "issuer" as defined in Section 2(4) of the Act, the purchaser of such security obtains no interest in the issuer's separate business within the state. Similarly, an intrastate exemption would not be available to a "local" mortgage company offering interests in out-of-state mortgages which are sold under circumstances to constitute them investment contracts. Also, the same position has been taken of a sale of an interest, by a real estate syndicate organized in one state to the residents of that state, in property acquired under a sale and leaseback arrangement with another corporation organized and engaged in business in another state.

If the proceeds of the offering are to be used primarily for the purpose of a new business conducted outside of the state of incorporation and unrelated to some incidental business locally conducted, the exemption should not be relied upon. S. E. C. v. Truckee Showboat, Inc., 157 F.Supp. 824 (S.D.Cal.1957). So also, a Section 3(a)(11) exemption should not be relied upon for each of a series of corporations organized in different states where there is in fact and purpose a single business enterprise or financial venture whether or not it is planned to merge or consolidate the various corporations at a later date. S. E. C. v. Los Angeles Trust Deed & Mortgage Exchange et al., 186 F.Supp. 830, 871 (S.D.Cal.1960), aff'd 285 F.2d 162 (C.A.9, 1960).

Residence Within the State

Section 3(a)(11) requires that the entire issue be confined to a single state in which the issuer, the offerees and the purchasers are residents. Mere presence in the state is not sufficient to constitute residence as in the case of military personnel at a military post. S. E. C. v. Capital Funds, Inc. No. A46–60, D.Alaska, 1960. The mere obtaining of formal representations of residence and agreements not to resell to non-residents or agreements that sales are void if the purchaser is a non-resident should not be relied upon without more as establishing the availability of the exemption.

An offering may be so large that its success as a local offering appears doubtful from the outset. Also, reliance should not be placed on the exemption for an issue which includes warrants for the purchase of another security unless there can be assurance that the warrants will be exercised only by residents. With respect to convertible securities, a Section 3(a)(9) exemption may be available for the conversion.

A secondary offering by a controlling person in the issuer's state of incorporation may be made in reliance on a Section 3(a)(11) exemption provided the exemption would be available to the issuer for a primary offering in that state. It is not essential that the controlling person be a resident of the issuer's state of incorporation.

Resales

From these general principles it follows that if during the course of distribution any underwriter, any distributing dealer (whether or not a member of the formal selling or distributing group), or any dealer or other person purchasing securities from a distributing dealer for resale were to offer or sell such securities to a non-resident, the exemption would be defeated. In other words, Section 3(a)(11) contemplates that the exemption is applicable only if the entire issue is distributed pursuant to the statutory conditions. Consequently, any offers or sales to a non-resident in connection with the distribution of the issue would destroy the exemption as to all securities which are a part of that issue, including those sold to residents regardless of whether such sales are made directly to non-residents or indirectly through residents who as part of the distribution thereafter sell to non-residents. It would furthermore be immaterial that sales to non-residents are made without use of the mails or instruments of interstate commerce. Any such sales of part of the issue to non-residents, however few, would not be in compliance with the conditions of Section 3(a)(11), and would render the exemption unavailable for the entire offering including the sales to residents. Petersen Engine Co., Inc., 2 S.E.C. 893, 903 (1937); Professional Investors, 37 S.E.C. 173, 175 (1956); Universal Service, 37 S.E.C. 559, 563–564 (1957); S. E. C. v. Hillsborough Investment Corp., 173 F.Supp. 86 (D.N.H.1958); Hillsborough Investment Corp. v. S. E. C., 276 F.2d 665 (C.A.1, 1960).

This is not to suggest, however, that securities which have actually come to rest in the hands of resident investors, such as persons purchasing without a view to further distribution or resale to non-residents, may not in due course be resold by such persons, whether directly or through dealers or brokers, to non-residents without in any way affecting the exemption. The relevance of any such resales consists only of the evidentiary light which they might cast upon the factual question whether the securities had in fact come to rest in the hands of resident investors. If the securities are resold but a short time after their acquisition to a non-resident this fact, although not conclusive, might support an inference that the original offering had not come to rest in the state, and that the resale therefore constituted a part of the process of primary distribution; a stronger inference would arise if the purchaser involved were a security dealer. It may be noted that the non-residence of the underwriter or dealer is not pertinent so long as the ultimate distribution is solely to residents of the state.

Use of the Mails and Facilities of Interstate Commerce

The intrastate exemption is not dependent upon non-use of the mails or instruments of interstate commerce in the distribution. Securities issued in a transaction properly exempt under this provision may be offered and sold without registration through the mails or by use of any instruments of transportation or communication in interstate commerce, may be made the subject of general newspaper advertisement (provided the advertisement is appropriately limited to indicate that offers to purchase are solicited only from, and sales will be made only to, residents of the particular state involved), and may even be delivered by means of transportation and communication used in interstate commerce, to the purchasers. Similarly, securities issued in a transaction exempt under Section 3(a)(11) may be offered without compliance with the formal prospectus requirements applicable to registered securities. Exemption under Section 3(a)(11), if in fact available, removes the distribution from the operation of the registration and prospectus requirements of Section 5 of the Act. It should be emphasized, however, that the civil liability and anti-fraud provisions of Sections 12(2) and 17 of the Act nevertheless apply and may give rise to civil liabilities and to other sanctions applicable to violations of the statute.

Conclusion

In conclusion, the fact should be stressed that Section 3(a)(11) is designed to apply only to distributions genuinely local in character. From a practical point of view, the provisions of that section can exempt only issues which in reality represent local financing by local industries, carried out through local investment. Any distribution not of this type raises a serious question as to the availability of Section 3(a)(11). Consequently, any dealer proposing to participate in the distribution of an issue claimed to be exempt under Section 3(a)(11) should examine the character of the transaction and the proposed or actual manner of its execution by all persons concerned with it with the greatest care to satisfy himself that the distribution will not, or did not, exceed the limitations of the exemption. Otherwise the dealer, even though his own sales may be carefully confined to resident purchasers, may subject himself to serious risk of civil liability under Section 12(1) of the Act for selling without prior registration a security not in fact entitled to exemption from registration. In Release No. 4386, we noted that the quick commencement of trading and prompt resale of portions of the issue to non-residents raises a serious question whether the entire issue has, in fact, come to rest in the hands of investors resident in the state of the initial offering.

The Securities Act as a remedial statute, and the terms of an exemption must be strictly construed against one seeking to rely on it. S. E. C. v. Sunbeam Gold Mining Co., 95 F.2d 699, 701 (C.A.9, 1938). The courts have held that he has the burden of proving its availability. Gilligan, Will & Co. v. S. E. C., 267 F.2d 461, 466 (C.A.2, 1959); S. E. C. v. Ralston Purina Co., 346 U.S. 119, 126 (1954); S. E. C. v. Culpepper, 270 F.2d 241, 246 (C.A.2, 1959).

B. FAIR DEALING AND FAIR TRADING—SECURITIES EXCHANGE ACT OF 1934

The principal policy of the Securities Act of 1933, referred to above, is full and fair disclosure in the issuance of new securities. The Securities Exchange Act of 1934, 15 U.S.C.A. § 78a et seq., also has full and fair disclosure as its principal policy but this Act is concerned with the trading of securities, the regulation of securities exchanges and the registration of securities of corporations in which public investors have an interest. The 1933 Act is concerned with the distribution and marketing of new securities, while the 1934 Act is concerned with the transfer and trading of securities after they have been issued initially. Securities exchanges, such as the New York Stock Exchange and the American Stock Exchange, are required to register with the Securities and Exchange Commission. Further, all corporations that have listed their securities on a securities exchange and all other corporations which have 500 or more shareholders, and $1,000,000 or more in assets at book value, must register their securities with the Commission and must file periodic reports. Form 10, the annual report used for this purpose, is most comprehensive, and in 1970 was substantially revised. The information given to public investors by the management of a company is regulated (by the use of Forms 10–K and 8–K). Information used in the solicitation of proxies is also regulated. The trading of securities by insiders, and the use of information obtained by them as insiders, is limited and regulated. Manipulation of the prices of securities is prohibited.

Rule 10b–5, referred to above, adopted under the provisions of Section 10b of the 1934 Act contains almost the same wording as Section 17 of the 1933 Act, except that Rule 10b–5 applies to both a sale and a purchase of a security while Section 17 of the 1933 Act applies only to the sale of a new security. This difference permits a seller as well as a purchaser of an outstanding security who has been misled or defrauded to seek relief in the Federal Courts for his damages. In both cases the question of materiality is important and this problem has been discussed in Escott v. BarChris Construction Corp., referred to above. The penalties under Section 11 of the 1933 Act apply to the failure to make the prescribed full and fair disclosure in a registration statement, that is, in connection with newly issued securities; whereas the liabilities under Rule 10b–5 apply to the failure to make a full and fair disclosure of information about the outstanding security or about the company itself in a number of reports that are required under the Act or in other voluntary public announcements.

Registration under Section 12 of the 1934 Act, 15 U.S.C.A. § 78*l* requires that a corporation file with the Securities and Exchange Commission specified information about the company and the class of securities being registered. Also, the company is then required to comply with periodic reporting requirements and with the proxy solicitation requirements of the 1934 Act, and if any tender offers to the company's shareholders are to be made, then further compliance with the provisions of Sections 13 and 14 of the 1934 Act will also be required. Insiders (officers, directors and persons holding 10% or more of the stock of the company) are required to file with the Commission certain information in reference to their shareholdings and promptly to report any changes in the number of shares they hold. In addition any profit which any insider makes on purchases and sales of the securities of the company within a six month period must be remitted to the company, and if not, can be recovered for the company at the suit of a minority shareholder. Under the provisions of Sec. 14a of the 1934 Act a company must comply with the proxy solicitation rules of the Securities and Exchange Commission if it solicits any proxy, consent or authorization with respect to any security which is registered under Sec. 12. In this connection a case is reported below in Chapter VI: Mills v. Electric Auto-lite Co., 396 U.S. 375, 90 S.Ct. 616, 24 L.Ed.2d 593 (1970).

The Securities Exchange Act of 1934, referred to above, is concerned not only with the investment and reinvestment of savings in our society, but also with the necessity in a society in which there is private ownership of property for maintaining a system for the transfer of the property. While this latter problem is discussed more fully in Chapter VI below, it should be noted that concepts of private property and freedom of contract require that there shall be some means of transferring property from one private owner to another private owner on such terms as the parties may desire. We have no system whereby the government directs sellers to sell and buyers to buy, or to whom or from whom, or at what price; we find it most desirable to let the owners make these choices for themselves. Within this system we found that the transfer of securities was susceptible to so much fraud and deceit that we evolved the legal system of requiring full and fair disclosure as the means of controlling the marketplace. In order to make the system of private investment work in a democratic society private investors must have faith in the fairness of the market system under which they can acquire or dispose of their securities. As noted above, we have consciously chosen the requirement of full and fair disclosure of information about the issuing company, requirements which are in part enforced by a governmental agency and in part by private litigants, as the means of achieving this goal.

The cases reported in this chapter are by no means an exhaustive examination of Federal securities legislation nor of the work or the Rules of the Securities and Exchange Commission. The business of issuing, marketing and trading securities is one which fascinates most people with a little savings and our society has developed an exceedingly complex body of laws and rules to regulate this business. While it is difficult to find anyone who has been defrauded who himself did not have a little larceny in his heart when he entered into the transaction, the necessity of maintaining the highest reputation for integrity in the securities markets in order to provide a system for the investment of savings and the transfer of private property has led to the policy of full and fair disclosure in our securities laws. The cases which follow are designed to illustrate this point.

SECURITIES AND EXCHANGE COMMISSION v. TEXAS GULF SULPHUR CO.

United States Court of Appeals, Second Circuit, 1968.
401 F.2d 833.

WATERMAN, Circuit Judge. This action was commenced in the United States District Court for the Southern District of New York by the Securities and Exchange Commission (the SEC) pursuant to Sec. 21(e) of the Securities Exchange Act of 1934 (the Act), 15 U.S.C.A. § 78u(e), against Texas Gulf Sulphur Company (TGS) and several of its officers, directors and employees, to enjoin certain conduct by TGS and the individual defendants said to violate Section 10(b) of the Act, 15 U.S.C.A. § 78j(b), and Rule 10b–5 (17 CFR 240.10b–5) (the Rule), promulgated thereunder, and to compel the rescission by the individual defendants of securities transactions assertedly conducted contrary to law. The complaint alleged (1) that defendants Fogarty, Mollison, Darke, Murray, Huntington, O'Neill, Clayton, Crawford, and Coates had either personally or through agents purchased TGS stock or calls thereon from November 12, 1963 through April 16, 1964 on the basis of material inside information concerning the results of TGS drilling in Timmins, Ontario, while such information remained undisclosed to the investing public generally or to the particular sellers [1]; (2) that defendants Darke and Coates had divulged such information to others for use

1. The purchases by the parties during this period were:

Purchase Date	Purchaser	Shares Number	Shares Price	Calls Number	Calls Price
Hole K-55-1 Completed November 12, 1963					
1963					
Nov. 12	Fogarty	300	17¾-18		
15	Clayton	200	17¾		
15	Fogarty	700	17⅝-17⅞		
15	Mollison	100	17⅞		
19	Fogarty	500	18⅛		
26	Fogarty	200	17¾		
29	Holyk (Mrs.)	50	18		
Chemical Assays of Drill Core of K-55-1 Received December 9-13, 1963					
Dec. 10	Holyk (Mrs.)	100	20⅜		
12	Holyk (or wife)			200	21
13	Mollison	100	21⅛		
30	Fogarty	200	22		
31	Fogarty	100	23¼		
1964					
Jan. 6	Holyk (or wife)			100	23⅝
8	Murray			400	23¼
24	Holyk (or wife)			200	22¼-22⅜
Feb. 10	Fogarty	300	22⅛-22¼		
20	Darke	300	24⅛		
24	Clayton	400	23⅞		
24	Holyk (or wife)			200	24⅛
26	Holyk (or wife)			200	23⅜
26	Huntington	50	23¼		
27	Darke (Moran as nominee)			1000	22⅝-22¾
Mar. 2	Holyk (Mrs.)	200	22⅜		
3	Clayton	100	22¼		
16	Huntington			100	22⅜
16	Holyk (or wife)			300	23¼
17	Holyk (Mrs.)	100	23⅞		
23	Darke			1000	24¾
26	Clayton	200	25		
Land Acquisition Completed March 27, 1964					
Mar. 30	Darke			1000	25½
30	Holyk (Mrs.)	100	25⅞		
Core Drilling of Kidd Segment Resumed March 31, 1964					
April 1	Clayton	60	26½		
1	Fogarty	400	26½		
2	Clayton	100	26⅞		
6	Fogarty	400	28⅛-28⅞		
8	Mollison (Mrs.)	100	28⅛		
First Press Release Issued April 12, 1964					
April 15	Clayton	200	29⅜		
16	Crawford (and wife)	600	30⅛-30¼		
Second Press Release Issued 10:00-10:10 or 10:15 A.M., April 16, 1964					
1963					
April 16 (app. 10:20 A.M.)	Coates (for family trusts)	2000	31 31-31⅝		

(Court's footnote 2.)

in purchasing TGS stock or calls or recommended its purchase while the information was undisclosed to the public or to the sellers; [2] that defendants Stephens, Fogarty, Mollison, Holyk, and Kline had accepted options to purchase TGS stock on Feb. 20, 1964 without disclosing the material information as to the drilling progress to either the Stock Option Committee or the TGS Board of Directors; and (4) that TGS issued a deceptive press release on April 12, 1964. The case was tried at length before Judge Bonsal of the Southern District of New York, sitting without a jury. Judge Bonsal in a detailed opinion decided, *inter alia,* that the insider activity prior to April 9, 1964 was not illegal because the drilling results were not "material" until then; that Clayton and Crawford had traded in violation of law because they traded after that date; that Coates had committed no violation as he did not trade before disclosure was made; and that the

2. The purchases made by "tippees" during this period were:

Purchase Date	Purchaser	Shares Number	Price	Calls Number	Price
Chemicals Assays of K-55-1 Received Dec. 9-13, 1963					
1963					
Dec. 30	Caskey (Darke)			300	22¼
1964					
Jan. 16	Westreich (Darke)	2000	21¼-21¾		
Feb. 17	Atkinson (Darke)	50	23¼	200	23⅛
17	Westreich (Darke)	50	23¼	1000	23¼-23⅜
24	Miller (Darke)			200	23¾
25	Miller (Darke)			300	23⅜-23½
Mar. 3	E. W. Darke (Darke)			500	22½-22⅝
17	E. W. Darke (Darke)			200	23⅜
Land Acquisition Completed Mar. 27, 1964					
1964					
Mar. 30	Atkinson (Darke)			400	25¾-25⅞
	Caskey (Darke)	100	25⅞		
	E. W. Darke (Darke)			1000	25¾-25⅞
	Miller (Darke)			200	25½
	Westreich (Darke)	500	25¾		
30-31	Klotz (Darke)			2000	25½-26⅛
Second Press Release Issued April 16, 1964 (Reported over Dow Jones tape at 10:54 A.M.)					
April 16 (from 10:31 A.M.)					
	Haemisegger (Coates)	1500	31¼-35		

In this connection, we point out, that, though several of the Holyk purchases of shares and calls made between November 29, 1963 and March 30, 1964 were in the name of Mrs. Holyk or were in the names of both spouses, we have treated these purchases as if made in the name of defendant Holyk alone.

Defendant Mollison purchased 100 shares on November 15 in his name only and on April 8 100 shares were purchased in the name of Mrs. Mollison. We have made no distinction between those purchases.

Defendant Crawford ordered 300 shares about midnight on April 15 and 300 more shares the following morning, to be purchased for himself, and his wife, and these purchases are treated as having been made by the defendant Crawford.

In these particulars we have followed the lead of the court below. See the table at 258 F.Supp. 273-275 and the special references to the Holyk purchases at 273, and the Crawford purchases at 287. It would be unrealistic to include any of these purchases as having been made by other than the defendants, and unrealistic to include them as having been made by members of the general public receiving "tips" from insiders. (Court's footnote 4.)

issuance of the press release was not unlawful because it was not issued for the purpose of benefiting the corporation, there was no evidence that any insider used the release to his personal advantage and it was not "misleading, or deceptive on the basis of the facts then known," 258 F.Supp. 262, at 292–296 (S.D.N.Y.1966). Defendants Clayton and Crawford appeal from that part of the decision below which held that they had violated Sec. 10(b) and Rule 10b–5 and the SEC appeals from the remainder of the decision which dismissed the complaint against defendants TGS, Fogarty, Mollison, Holyk, Darke, Stephens, Kline, Murray, and Coates.

For reasons which appear below, we decide the various issues presented as follows:

(1) As to Clayton and Crawford, as purchasers of stock on April 15 and 16, 1964, we affirm the finding that they violated 15 U.S.C.A. § 78j(b) and Rule 10b–5 and remand, pursuant to the agreement by all the parties, for a determination of the appropriate remedy.

(2) As to Murray, we affirm the dismissal of the complaint.

(3) As to Mollison and Holyk, as recipients of certain stock options, we affirm the dismissal of the complaint.

(4) As to Stephens and Fogarty, as recipients of stock options, we reverse the dismissal of the complaint and remand for a further determination as to whether an injunction, in the exercise of the trial court's discretion, should issue.

(5) As to Kline, as a recipient of a stock option, we reverse the dismissal of the complaint and remand with directions to issue an order rescinding the option and for a determination of any other appropriate remedy in connection therewith.

(6) As to Fogarty, Mollison, Holyk, Darke, and Huntington, as purchasers of stock or calls thereon between November 12, 1963, and April 9, 1964, we reverse the dismissal of the complaint and find that they violated 15 U.S.C.A. § 78j(b) and Rule 10b–5, and remand, pursuant to the agreement of all the parties, for a determination of the appropriate remedy.

(7) As to Clayton, although the district judge did not specify that the complaint be dismissed with respect to his purchases of TGS stock before April 9, 1964, such a dismissal is implicit in his treatment of the individual appellees who acted similarly. Consequently, although Clayton is named only as an appellant our decision with respect to the materiality of K–55–1 renders it necessary to treat him also as an appellee. Thus, as to him, as one who purchased stock between November 12, 1963 and April 9, 1964, we reverse the implicit dismissal of the complaint, find that he violated § 78j(b) and Rule 10b–5, and remand pursuant to the agreement by all the parties, for a determination of the appropriate remedy.

(8) As to Darke, as one who passed on information to tippees, we reverse the dismissal of the complaint and remand, pursuant to the agreement by all the parties, for a determination of the appropriate remedy.

(9) As to Coates, as one who on April 16th purchased stock and gave information on which his son-in-law broker and the broker's customers purchased shares, we reverse the dismissal of the complaint, find that he violated 15 U.S.C.A. § 78j(b) and Rule 10b–5, and remand, pursuant to the agreement by all the parties, for a determination of the appropriate remedy.

(10) As to Texas Gulf Sulphur, we reverse the dismissal of the complaint and remand for a further determination by the district judge in the light of the approach taken in this opinion.

The occurrences out of which this litigation arose are not set forth hereafter in as detailed a manner as they are set out in the published opinion of the court below, but are stated sufficiently, we believe, for the exposition of the issues raised by the several appeals to us.

The Factual Setting

This action derives from the exploratory activities of TGS begun in 1957 on the Canadian Shield in eastern Canada. In March of 1959, aerial geophysical surveys were conducted over more than 15,000 square miles of this area by a group led by defendant Mollison, a mining engineer and a Vice President of TGS. The group included defendant Holyk, TGS's chief geologist, defendant Clayton, an electrical engineer and geophysicist, and defendant Darke, a geologist. These operations resulted in the detection of numerous anomalies, i. e., extraordinary variations in the conductivity of rocks, one of which was on the Kidd 55 segment of land located near Timmins, Ontario.

On October 29 and 30, 1963, Clayton conducted a ground geophysical survey on the northeast portion of the Kidd 55 segment which confirmed the presence of an anomaly and indicated the necessity of diamond core drilling for further evaluation. Drilling of the initial hole, K–55–1, at the strongest part of the anomaly was commenced on November 8 and terminated on November 12 at a depth of 655 feet. Visual estimates by Holyk of the core of K–55–1 indicated an average copper content of 1.15% and an average zinc content of 8.64% over a length of 599 feet. This visual estimate convinced TGS that it was desirable to acquire the remainder of the Kidd 55 segment, and in order to facilitate this acquisition TGS President Stephens instructed the exploration group to keep the results of K–55–1 confidential and undisclosed even as to other officers, directors, and employees of TGS. The hole was concealed and a barren core was intentionally drilled off the anomaly. Meanwhile, the core of K–55–1 had been shipped to Utah for chemical assay which, when received in early December, revealed an average mineral content of 1.18% copper, 8.26% zinc, and 3.94% ounces of silver per ton over a length of 602 feet. These results were so remarkable that neither Clayton, an experienced geophysicist, nor four other TGS expert witnesses, had ever seen or heard of a comparable initial exploratory drill hole in a base metal deposit. So, the trial court concluded, "There is no doubt that the drill core of K–55–1 was unusually good and that it excited the interest and speculation of those who knew about it." Id. at 282. By March 27, 1964, TGS decided that the land acquisition program had advanced to such a point that the company might well resume drilling, and drilling was resumed on March 31.

During this period, from November 12, 1963 when K–55–1 was completed, to March 31, 1964 when drilling was resumed, certain of the individual defendants listed in fn. 2, supra, and persons listed in fn. 4, supra, said to have received "tips" from them, purchased TGS stock or calls thereon. Prior to these transactions these persons had owned 1135 shares of TGS stock and possessed no calls; thereafter they owned a total of 8235 shares and possessed 12,300 calls.

On February 20, 1964, also during this period TGS issued stock options to 26 of its officers and employees whose salaries exceeded a specified amount, five of whom were the individual defendants Stephens, Fogarty, Mollison, Holyk, and Kline. Of these, only Kline was unaware of the detailed results of K–55–1, but he, too, knew that a hole containing favorable bodies of copper and zinc ore had been drilled in Timmins. At this time, neither the TGS Stock Option Committee nor its Board of Directors had been informed of the results of K–55–1, presumably because of the pending land acquisition program which required confidentiality. All of the foregoing defendants accepted the options granted them.

When drilling was resumed on March 31, hole K–55–3 was commenced 510 feet west of K–55–1 and was drilled easterly at a 45° angle so as to cross K–55–1 in a vertical plane. Daily progress reports of the drilling of this hole K–55–3 and of all subsequently drilled holes were sent to defendants Stephens and Fogarty (President and Executive Vice President of TGS) by Holyk and Mollison. Visual estimates of K–55–3 revealed an average mineral content of 1.12% copper and 7.93% zinc over 641 of the hole's 876-foot length. On April 7, drilling of a third hole, K–55–4, 200 feet south of and parallel to K–55–1 and westerly at a 45° angle, was commenced and mineralization was encountered over 366 of its 579-foot length. Visual estimates indicated an average content of 1.14% copper and 8.24% zinc. Like K–55–1, both K–55–3 and K–55–4 established substantial copper mineralization on the eastern edge of the anomaly. On the basis of these findings relative to the foregoing drilling results, the trial court concluded that the vertical plane created by the intersection of K–55–1 and K–55–3, which measured at least 350 feet wide by 500 feet deep extended southward 200 feet to its intersection with K–55–4, and that "There was real evidence that a body of commercially mineable ore might exist." Id. at 281–82.

On April 8 TGS began with a second drill rig to drill another hole, K–55–6, 300 feet easterly of K–55–1. This hole was drilled westerly at an angle of 60° and was intended to explore mineralization beneath K–55–1. While no visual estimates of its core were immediately available, it was readily apparent by the evening of April 10 that substantial copper mineralization had been encountered over the last 127 feet of the hole's 569-foot length. On April 10, a third drill rig commenced drilling yet another hole, K–55–5, 200 feet north of K–55–1, parallel to the prior holes, and slanted westerly at a 45° angle. By the evening of April 10 in this hole, too, substantial copper mineralization had been encountered over the last 42 feet of its 97-foot length.

Meanwhile, rumors that a major ore strike was in the making had been circulating throughout Canada. On the morning of Saturday, April 11, Stephens at his home in Greenwich, Conn. read in the New York Herald Tribune and in the New York Times unauthorized reports of the TGS drilling which seemed to infer a rich strike from the fact that the drill cores had been flown to the United States for chemical assay. Stephens immediately contacted Fogarty at his home in Rye, N. Y., who in turn telephoned and later that day visited Mollison at Mollison's home in Greenwich to obtain a current report and evaluation of the drilling progress. The following morning, Sunday, Fogarty again telephoned Mollison, inquiring whether Mollison had any further information and told him to return to Timmins with Holyk, the TGS Chief Geologist, as soon as possible "to move things along." With the aid of one Carroll, a public relations consultant, Fogarty drafted a press release designed to quell the rumors, which release, after having been channeled through Stephens and Huntington, a TGS attorney, was issued at 3:00 P.M. on Sunday, April 12, and which appeared in the morning newspapers of general circulation on Monday, April 13. It read in pertinent part as follows:

NEW YORK, April 12—The following statement was made today by Dr. Charles F. Fogarty, executive vice president of Texas Gulf Sulphur Company, in regard to the company's drilling operations near Timmins, Ontario, Canada. Dr. Fogarty said:

"During the past few days, the exploration activities of Texas Gulf Sulphur in the area of Timmins, Ontario, have been widely reported in the press, coupled with rumors of a substantial copper discovery there. These reports exaggerate the scale of operations, and mention plans and statistics of size and grade of ore that are without factual basis and have evidently originated by speculation of people not connected with TGS.

"The facts are as follows. TGS has been exploring in the Timmins area for six years as part of its overall search in Canada and elsewhere for various minerals—lead, copper, zinc, etc. During the course of this work, in Timmins as well as in Eastern Canada, TGS has conducted exploration entirely on its own, without the participation by others. Numerous prospects have been investigated by geophysical means and a large number of selected ones have been core-drilled. These cores are sent to the United States for assay and detailed examination as a matter of routine and on advice of expert Canadian legal counsel. No inferences as to grade can be drawn from this procedure.

"Most of the areas drilled in Eastern Canada have revealed either barren pyrite or graphite without value; a few have resulted in discoveries of small or marginal sulphide ore bodies.

"Recent drilling on one property near Timmins has led to preliminary indications that more drilling would be required for proper evaluation of this prospect. The drilling done to date has not been conclusive, but the statements made by many outside quarters are unreliable and include information and figures that are not available to TGS.

"The work done to date has not been sufficient to reach definite conclusions and any statement as to size and grade of ore would be premature and possibly misleading. When we have progressed to the point where reasonable and logical conclusions can be made, TGS will issue a definite statement to its stockholders and to the public in order to clarify the Timmins project."

* * * * * * * * * *

The release purported to give the Timmins drilling results as of the release date, April 12. From Mollison, Fogarty had been told of the developments through 7:00 P.M. on April 10, and of the remarkable discoveries made up to that time, detailed supra, which discoveries, according to the calculations of the experts who testified for the SEC at the hearing, demonstrated that TGS had already discovered 6.2 to 8.3 million tons of proven ore having gross assay values from $26 to $29 per ton. TGS experts, on the other hand, denied at the hearing that proven or probable ore could have been calculated on April 11 or 12 because there was then no assurance of continuity in the mineralized zone.

The evidence as to the effect of this release on the investing public was equivocal and less than abundant. On April 13 the New York Herald Tribune in an article head-noted "Copper Rumor Deflated" quoted from the TGS release of April 12 and backtracked from its original April 11 report of a major strike but nevertheless inferred from the TGS release that "recent mineral exploratory activity near Timmins, Ontario, has provided preliminary favorable results, sufficient at least to require a step-up in drilling operations." Some witnesses who testified at the hearing stated that they found the release encouraging. On the other hand, a Canadian mining security specialist, Roche, stated that "earlier in the week [before April 16] we had a Dow Jones saying that they [TGS] didn't have anything basically" and a TGS stock specialist for the Midwest Stock Exchange became concerned about his long position in the stock after reading the release. The trial court stated only that "While, in retrospect, the press release may appear gloomy or incomplete, this does not make it misleading or deceptive on the basis of the facts then known." Id. at 296.

Meanwhile, drilling operations continued. By morning of April 13, in K–55–5, the fifth drill hole, substantial copper mineralization had been encountered to the 580 foot mark, and the hole was subsequently drilled to a length of 757 feet without further results. Visual estimates revealed an average content of 0.82% copper and 4.2% zinc over a 525-foot section. Also by 7:00 A.M. on April 13, K–55–6 had found mineralization to the 946-foot mark. On April 12 a fourth drill rig began to drill K–55–7, which was drilled westerly at a 45° angle, at the eastern edge of the anomaly. The next morning the 137 foot mark had been reached, fifty feet of which showed mineralization. By 7:00 P.M. on April 15, the hole had been completed to a length of 707 feet but had only encountered additional mineralization during a 26-foot length between the 425 and 451-foot marks. A mill test hole, K–55–8, had been drilled and was complete by the evening of April 13 but its mineralization had not been reported upon prior to April 16. K–55–10 was drilled westerly at a 45° angle commencing April 14 and had encountered mineralization over 231 of its 249-foot length by the evening of April 15. It, too, was drilled at the anomaly's eastern edge.

While drilling activity ensued to completion TGS officials were taking steps toward ultimate disclosure of the discovery. On April 13, a previously-invited reporter for The Northern Miner, a Canadian mining industry journal, visited the drillsite, interviewed Mollison, Holyk and Darke, and prepared an article which confirmed a 10 million ton ore strike. This report, after having been submitted to Mollison and returned to the reporter unamended on April 15, was published in the April 16 issue. A statement relative to the extent of the discovery, in substantial part drafted by Mollison, was given to the Ontario Minister of Mines for release to the Canadian media. Mollison and Holyk expected it to be released over the airways at 11 P.M. on April 15th, but, for undisclosed reasons, it was not released until 9:40 A.M. on the 16th. An official detailed statement, announcing a strike of at least 25 million tons of ore, based on the drilling data set forth above, was read to representatives of American financial media from 10:00 A.M. to 10:10 or 10:15 A.M. on April 16, and appeared over Merrill Lynch's private wire at 10:29 A.M. and, somewhat later than expected, over the Dow Jones ticker tape at 10:54 A.M.

Between the time the first press release was issued on April 12 and the dissemination of the TGS official announcement on the morning of April 16, the only defendants before us on appeal who engaged in market activity were Clayton and Crawford and TGS director Coates. Clayton ordered 200 shares of TGS stock through his Canadian broker on April 15 and the order was executed that day over the Midwest Stock Exchange. Crawford ordered 300 shares at midnight on the 15th and another 300 shares at 8:30 A.M. the next day, and these orders were executed over the Midwest Exchange in Chicago at its opening on April 16. Coates left the TGS press conference and called his broker son-in-law Haemisegger shortly before 10:20 A.M. on the 16th and ordered 2,000 shares of TGS for family trust accounts of which Coates was a trustee but not a beneficiary; Haemisegger executed this order over the New York and Midwest Exchanges, and he and his customers purchased 1500 additional shares.

During the period of drilling in Timmins, the market price of TGS stock fluctuated but steadily gained overall. On Friday, November 8, when the drilling began, the stock closed at 17⅜; on Friday, November 15, after K–55–1 had been completed, it closed at 18. After a slight decline to 16⅜ by Friday, November 22, the price rose to 20⅞ by December 13, when the chemical assay results of K–55–1 were received, and closed at a high of 24⅛ on February 21, the day after the stock options had been issued. It had reached a price of 26 by March 31, after the land acquisition program had been completed and drilling had been resumed, and continued to ascend to 30⅛ by the close of trading on April 10, at which time the drilling progress up to then was evaluated for the April 12th press release. On April 13, the day on which the April 12 release was disseminated, TGS opened at 30⅛, rose immediately to a high of 32 and gradually tapered of to close at 30⅞. It closed at 30¼ the next day, and at 29⅜ on April 15. On April 16, the day of the official announcement of the Timmins discovery, the price climbed to a high of 37 and closed at 36⅜. By May 15, TGS stock was selling at 58¼.

I. The Individual Defendants

A. *Introductory*

Rule 10b–5, 17 CFR 240.10b–5, on which this action is predicated, provides:

> It shall be unlawful for any person, directly or indirectly, by the use of any means or instrumentality of interstate commerce, or of the mails, or of any facility of any national securities exchange,
>
> (1) to employ any device, scheme, or artifice to defraud,
>
> (2) to make any untrue statement of a material fact or to omit to state a material fact necessary in order to make the statements made, in the light of the circumstances under which they were made, not misleading, or
>
> (3) to engage in any act, practice, or course of business which operates or would operate as a fraud or deceit upon any person,
>
> in connection with the purchase or sale of any security.

Rule 10b–5 was promulgated pursuant to the grant of authority given the SEC by Congress in Section 10(b) of the Securities Exchange Act of 1934 (15 U.S.C.A. § 78j(b). By that Act Congress purposed to prevent inequitable and unfair practices and to insure fairness in securities transactions generally, whether conducted face-to-face, over the counter, or on exchanges, see 3 Loss, Securities Regulation 1455–56 (2d ed. 1961). The Act and the Rule apply to the transactions here, all of which were consummated on exchanges. See List v. Fashion Park, Inc., 340 F.2d 457, 461–62 (2 Cir.), cert. denied, 382 U.S. 811; Cochran v. Channing Corp., 211 F.Supp. 239, 243 (S.D.N.Y.1962). Whether predicated on traditional fiduciary concepts, see, e. g., Hotchkiss v. Fisher, 136 Kan. 530 (1932), or on the "special facts" doctrine, see, e. g., Strong v. Repide, 213 U.S. 419

(1909), the Rule is based in policy on the justifiable expectation of the securities marketplace that all investors trading on impersonal exchanges have relatively equal access to material information, see Cary, Insider Trading in Stocks, 21 Bus.Law. 1009, 1010 (1966). * * * The essence of the Rule is that anyone who, trading for his own account in the securities of a corporation has "access, directly or indirectly, to information intended to be available only for a corporate purpose and not for the personal benefit of anyone" may not take "advantage of such information knowing it is unavailable to those with whom he is dealing," i. e., the investing public. Matter of Cady, Roberts & Co., 40 SEC 907, 912 (1961). Insiders, as directors or management officers are, of course, by this Rule, precluded from so unfairly dealing, but the Rule is also applicable to one possessing the information who may not be strictly termed an "insider" within the meaning of Sec. 16(b) of the Act. Cady, Roberts, supra. Thus, anyone in possession of material inside information must either disclose it to the investing public, or, if he is disabled from disclosing it in order to protect a corporate confidence, or he chooses not to do so, must abstain from trading in or recommending the securities concerned while such inside information remains undisclosed. So, it is here no justification for insider activity that disclosure was forbidden by the legitimate corporate objective of acquiring options to purchase the land surrounding the exploration site; if the information was, as the SEC contends, material, its possessors should have kept out of the market until disclosure was accomplished. Cady, Roberts, supra at 911.

B. *Material Inside Information*

An insider is not, of course, always foreclosed from investing in his own company merely because he may be more familiar with company operations than are outside investors. An insider's duty to disclose information or his duty to abstain from dealing in his company's securities arises only in "those situations which are essentially extraordinary in nature and which are reasonably certain to have a substantial effect on the market price of the security if [the extraordinary situation is] disclosed." Fleischer, Securities Trading and Corporate Information Practices: The Implications of the Texas Gulf Sulphur Proceeding, 51 Va.L.Rev. 1271, 1289.

Nor is an insider obligated to confer upon outside investors the benefit of his superior financial or other expert analysis by disclosing his educated guesses or predictions. 3 Loss, op.cit. supra at 1463. The only regulatory objective is that access to material information be enjoyed equally, but this objective requires nothing more than the disclosure of basic facts so that outsiders may draw upon their own evaluative expertise in reaching their own investment decisions with knowledge equal to that of the insiders.

This is not to suggest, however, as did the trial court, that "the test of materiality must necessarily be a conservative one, particularly since many actions under Section 10(b) are brought on the basis of hindsight," 258 F.Supp. 262 at 280, in the sense that the materiality of facts is to be assessed solely by measuring the effect the knowledge of the facts would have upon prudent or conservative investors. As we stated in List v. Fashion Park, Inc., 340 F.2d 457, 462, "The basic test of materiality * * * is whether a *reasonable* man would attach importance * * * in determining his choice of action in the transaction in question. Restatement, Torts § 538(2) (a); accord Prosser, Torts 554–55; I Harper & James, Torts 565–66." (Emphasis supplied.) This, of course, encompasses any fact " * * * which in reasonable and objective contemplation *might* affect the value of the corporation's stock or securities * * *." List v. Fashion Park, Inc., supra at 462, quoting from Kohler v. Kohler Co., 319 F.2d 634, 642, (7 Cir. 1963). (Emphasis supplied.) Such a fact is a material fact and must be effectively disclosed to the investing public prior to the commencement of insider trading in the corporation's securities. The speculators and chartists of Wall and Bay Streets are also "reasonable" investors entitled to the same legal protection afforded conservative traders. Thus, material facts include not only information disclosing the earnings and distributions of a company but also those facts which affect the probable future of the company and those which may affect the desire of investors to buy, sell, or hold the company's securities.

In each case, then, whether facts are material within Rule 10b–5 when the facts relate to a particular event and are undisclosed by those persons who are knowledgeable thereof will depend at any given time upon a balancing of both the indicated probability that the event will occur and the anticipated magnitude of the event in light of the totality of the company activity. Here, notwithstanding the trial court's conclusion that the results of the first drill core, K–55–1, were "too 'remote' * * * to have had any significant impact on the market, i. e., to be deemed material," 258 F.Supp. at 283, knowledge of the possibility which surely was more than marginal, of the existence of a mine of the vast magnitude indicated by the remarkably rich drill core located rather close to the surface (suggesting mineability by the less expensive open-pit method) within the confines of a large anomaly (suggesting an extensive region of mineralization) might well have affected the price of TGS stock and would certainly have been an important fact to a reasonable, if speculative, investor in deciding whether he should buy, sell, or hold. After all, this first drill core was "unusually good and * * * excited the interest and speculation of those who knew about it." 258 F.Supp. at 282.

* * * Our survey of the facts found below conclusively establishes that knowledge of the results of the discovery hole, K–55–1, would have been important to a reasonable investor and might have affected the price of the stock.[3] * * *

3. We do not suggest that material facts must be disclosed immediately; the timing of disclosure is a matter for the business judgment of the corporate officers entrusted with the management of the corporation with-

Finally, a major factor in determining whether the K–55–1 discovery was a material fact is the importance attached to the drilling results by those who knew about it.   In view of other unrelated recent developments favorably affecting TGS, participation by an informed person in a regular stock-purchase program, or even sporadic trading by an informed person, might lend only nominal support to the inference of the materiality of the K–55–1 discovery; nevertheless, the timing by those who knew of it of their stock purchases and their purchases of *short-term* calls—purchases in some cases by individuals who had never before purchased calls or even TGS stock—virtually compels the inference that the insiders were influenced by the drilling results.   This insider trading activity, which surely constitutes highly pertinent evidence and the only truly objective evidence of the materiality of the K–55–1 discovery, was apparently disregarded by the court below in favor of the testimony of defendants' expert witnesses, all of whom "agreed that one drill core does not establish an ore body, much less a mine," 258 F.Supp. at 282–283.   Significantly, however, the court below, while relying upon what these defense experts said the defendant insiders *ought* to have thought about the worth to TGS of the K–55–1 discovery, and finding that from November 12, 1963 to April 6, 1964 Fogarty, Murray, Holyk and Darke spent more than $100,000 in purchasing TGS stock and calls on that stock, made no finding that the insiders were motivated by any factor other than the extraordinary K–55–1 discovery when they bought their stock and their calls.   *   *   *

The core of Rule 10b–5 is the implementation of the Congressional purpose that all investors should have equal access to the rewards of participation in securities transactions.   It was the intent of Congress that all members of the investing public should be subject to identical market risks,—which market risks include, of course the risk that one's evaluative capacity or one's capital available to put at risk may exceed another's capacity or capital.   The insiders here were not trading on an equal footing with the outside investors.   They alone were in a position to evaluate the probability and magnitude of what seemed from the outset to be a major ore strike; they alone could invest safely, secure in the expectation that the price of TGS stock would rise substantially in the event such a major strike should materialize, but would decline little, if at all, in the event of failure, for the public, ignorant at the outset of the favorable probabilities would likewise be unaware of the unproductive exploration, and the additional exploration costs would not significantly affect TGS market prices.   Such inequities based upon unequal access to knowledge should

in the affirmative disclosure requirements promulgated by the exchanges and by the SEC. Here, a valuable corporate purpose was served by delaying the publication of the K–55–1 discovery. We do intend to convey, however, that where a corporate purpose is thus served by withholding the news of a material fact, those persons who are thus quite properly true to their corporate trust must not during the period of non-disclosure deal personally in the corporation's securities or give to outsiders confidential information not generally available to all the corporations' stockholders and to the public at large. (Court's footnote 12.)

not be shrugged off as inevitable in our way of life, or, in view of the congressional concern in the area, remain uncorrected.

We hold, therefore, that all transactions in TGS stock or calls by individuals apprised of the drilling results of K–55–1 were made in violation of Rule 10b–5.   Inasmuch as the visual evaluation of that drill core (a generally reliable estimate though less accurate than a chemical assay) constituted material information, those advised of the results of the visual evaluation as well as those informed of the chemical assay traded in violation of law.   The geologist Darke possessed undisclosed material information and traded in TGS securities.   Therefore we reverse the dismissal of the action as to him and his personal transactions.   The trial court also found, 258 F.Supp. at 284, that Darke, after the drilling of K–55–1 had been completed and with detailed knowledge of the results thereof, told certain outside individuals that TGS "was a good buy."   These individuals thereafter acquired TGS stock and calls.   The trial court also found that later, as of March 30, 1964, Darke not only used his material knowledge for his own purchases but that the substantial amounts of TGS stock and calls purchased by these outside individuals on that day, see footnote 4, supra, was "strong circumstantial evidence that Darke must have passed the word to one or more of his 'tippees' that drilling on the Kidd 55 segment was about to be resumed."   258 F.Supp. at 284. Obviously if such a resumption were to have any meaning to such "tippees," they must have previously been told of K–55–1.

Unfortunately, however, there was no definitive resolution below of Darke's liability in these premises for the trial court held as to him, as it held as to all the other individual defendants, that this "undisclosed information" never became material until April 9.   As it is our holding that the information acquired after the drilling of K–55–1 was material, we, on the basis of the findings of direct and circumstantial evidence on the issue that the trial court has already expressed, hold that Darke violated Rule 10b–5(3) and Section 10(b) by "tipping" and we remand, pursuant to the agreement of the parties, for a determination of the appropriate remedy.   As Darke's "tippees" are not defendants in this action, we need not decide whether, if they acted with actual or constructive knowledge that the material information was undisclosed, their conduct is as equally violative of the Rule as the conduct of their insider source, though we note that it certainly could be equally reprehensible.

With reference to Huntington, the trial court found that he "had no detailed knowledge as to the work" on the Kidd–55 segment, 258 F.Supp. 281.   Nevertheless, the evidence shows that he knew about and participated in TGS's land acquisition program which followed the receipt of the K–55–1 drilling results, and that on February 26, 1964 he purchased 50 shares of TGS stock.   Later, on March 16, he helped prepare a letter for Dr. Holyk's signature in which TGS made a substantial offer for lands near K–55–1, and on the same day he, who had never before purchased calls on any stock, purchased a call on 100 shares of TGS stock.   We are satisfied that these purchases in

February and March, coupled with his readily inferable and probably reliable, understanding of the highly favorable nature of preliminary operations on the Kidd segment, demonstrate that Huntington possessed material inside information such as to make his purchase violative of the Rule and the Act.

C. *When May Insiders Act?*

Appellant Crawford, who ordered the purchase of TGS stock shortly before the TGS April 16 official announcement, and defendant Coates, who placed orders with and communicated the news to his broker immediately after the official announcement was read at the TGS-called press conference, concede that they were in possession of material information. They contend, however, that their purchases were not proscribed purchases for the news had already been effectively disclosed. We disagree.

Crawford telephoned his orders to his Chicago broker about midnight on April 15 and again at 8:30 in the morning of the 16th, with instructions to buy at the opening of the Midwest Stock Exchange that morning. The trial court's finding that "he sought to, and did, 'beat the news,' " 258 F.Supp. at 287, is well documented by the record. The rumors of a major ore strike which had been circulated in Canada and, to a lesser extent, in New York, had been disclaimed by the TGS press release of April 12, which significantly promised the public an official detailed announcement when possibilities had ripened into actualities. The abbreviated announcement to the Canadian press at 9:40 A.M. on the 16th by the Ontario Minister of Mines and the report carried by The Northern Miner, parts of which had sporadically reached New York on the morning of the 16th through reports from Canadian affiliates to a few New York investment firms, are assuredly not the equivalent of the official 10–15 minute announcement which was not released to the American financial press until after 10:00 A.M. Crawford's orders had been placed before that. Before insiders may act upon material information, such information must have been effectively disclosed in a manner sufficient to insure its availability to the investing public. Particularly here, where a formal announcement to the entire financial news media had been promised in a prior official release known to the media, all insider activity must await dissemination of the promised official announcement.

Coates was absolved by the court below because his telephone order was placed shortly before 10:20 A.M. on April 16, which was after the announcement had been made even though the news could not be considered already a matter of public information. 258 F.Supp. at 288. This result seems to have been predicated upon a misinterpretation of dicta in *Cady, Roberts,* where the SEC instructed insiders to "keep out of the market until the established procedures for public release of the information are *carried out* instead of hastening to execute transactions in advance of, and in frustration of, the objectives of the release," 40 SEC at 915 (emphasis supplied). The reading of a news release, which prompted Coates into action, is merely the first step in the process of dissemination required for compliance with the regulatory objective of providing all investors with an equal opportunity to make informed investment judgments. Assuming that the contents of the official release could instantaneously be acted upon, at the minimum Coates should have waited until the news could reasonably have been expected to appear over the media of widest circulation, the Dow Jones broad tape, rather than hastening to insure an advantage to himself and his broker son-in-law.

D.   *Is An Insider's Good Faith A Defense Under 10b–5?*

Coates, Crawford and Clayton, who ordered purchases before the news could be deemed disclosed, claim, nevertheless, that they were justified in doing so because they honestly believed that the news of the strike had become public at the time they placed their orders. However, whether the case before us is treated solely as an SEC enforcement proceeding or as a private action, proof of a specific intent to defraud is unnecessary. In an enforcement proceeding for equitable or prophylactic relief, the common law standard of deceptive conduct has been modified in the interests of broader protection for the investing public so that negligent insider conduct has become unlawful.   *   *   *

Absent any clear indication of a legislative intention to require a showing of specific fraudulent intent, see Note, 63 Mich.L.Rev. 1070, 1075, 1076 n. 29 (1965), the securities laws should be interpreted as an expansion of the common law both to effectuate the broad remedial design of Congress,   *   *   *   and to insure uniformity of enforcement.   *   *   *   Moreover, a review of other sections of the Act from which Rule 10b–5 seems to have been drawn suggests that the implementation of a standard of conduct that encompasses negligence as well as active fraud comports with the administrative and the legislative purposes underlying the Rule. Finally, we note that this position is not, as asserted by defendants, irreconcilable with previous language in this circuit because *"some form* of the traditional scienter requirement," Barnes v. Osofsky, 373 F.2d 269, 272 (2 Cir.1967), (emphasis supplied), sometimes defined as "fraud," Fischman v. Raytheon Mfg. Co., 9 F.R.D. 707 (SDNY 1949), rev'd on other grounds, 188 F.2d 783, 786 (2 Cir.1951) is preserved. This requirement, whether it be termed lack of diligence, constructive fraud, or unreasonable or negligent conduct, remains implicit in this standard, a standard that promotes the deterrence objective of the Rule.

Thus, the beliefs of Coates, Crawford and Clayton that the news of the ore strike was sufficiently public at the time of their purchase orders are to no avail if those beliefs were not reasonable under the circumstances.

*   *   *

Clayton, who was unaware of the April 16 disclosure announcement TGS was to make can, in support of his claim that the favorable news was public, rely only on the rumors and on the phone calls received by TGS prior to the placing of his order from those who seemed to have heard some version or rumors of the news. His awareness of the contents of the April 12 release renders unreasonable any claim that he believed the news was truly public.

Finally, Coates, * * * could not reasonably have expected the official release to have been disseminated when he placed his order before 10:20 for immediate execution nor were the Canadian disclosures relied on by Crawford sufficient to render the conduct of Coates permissible under the circumstances.[4]

E. *May Insiders Accept Stock Options Without Disclosing Material Information To The Issuer?*

On February 20, 1964, defendants Stephens, Fogarty, Mollison, Holyk and Kline accepted stock options issued to them and a number of other top officers of TGS, although not one of them had informed the Stock Option Committee of the Board of Directors or the Board of the results of K–55–1, which information we have held was then material. The SEC sought rescission of these options. The trial court, in addition to finding the knowledge of the results of the K–55 discovery to be immaterial, held that Kline had no detailed knowledge of the drilling progress and that Holyk and Mollison could reasonably assume that their superiors, Stephens and Fogarty, who were directors of the corporation, would report the results if that was advisable; indeed all employees had been instructed not to divulge this information pending completion of the land acquisition program, 258 F.Supp. at 291. Therefore, the court below concluded that only directors Stephens and Fogarty, of the top management, would have violated the Rule by accepting stock options without disclosure, but it also found that they had not acted improperly as the information in their possession was not material. 258 F.Supp. at 292. In view of our conclusion as to materiality we hold that Stephens and Fogarty violated the Rule by accepting them. However, as they have surrendered the options and the corporation has canceled them, * * * we find it unnecessary to order that the injunctions prayed for be actually issued. We point out, nevertheless, that the surrender of these options after the SEC commenced the case is not a satisfaction of the SEC claim, and a determination as to whether the issuance of injunctions against Stephens and Fogarty is advisable in order to prevent or deter future violations of regulatory provisions is remanded for the exercise of discretion by the trial court.

Contrary to the belief of the trial court that Kline had no duty to disclose his knowledge of the Kidd project before accepting the stock option offered him, we believe that he, a vice president, who had become the general counsel of TGS in January 1964, but who had been secretary of the corporation since January 1961, and was present in that capacity when the options were granted, and who was in charge

---

4. Coates's violations encompass not only his own purchases but also the purchases by his son-in-law and the customers of his son-in-law, to whom the material information was passed. * * * (Court's footnote 23.)

of the mechanics of issuance and acceptance of the options, was a member of top management and under a duty before accepting his option to disclose any material information he may have possessed, and, as he did not disclose such information to the Option Committee we direct rescission of the option he received. As to Holyk and Mollison, the SEC has not appealed the holding below that they, not being then members of top management (although Mollison was a vice president) had no duty to disclose their knowledge of the drilling before accepting their options. Therefore, the issue of whether, by accepting, they violated the Act, is not before us, and the holding below is undisturbed.

II. THE CORPORATE DEFENDANT

A. *Introductory*

At 3:00 P.M. on April 12, 1964, evidently believing it desirable to comment upon the rumors concerning the Timmins project, TGS issued the press release quoted in pertinent part in the text at page [219–220] supra. The SEC argued below and maintains on this appeal that this release painted a misleading and deceptive picture of the drilling progress at the time of its issuance, and hence violated Rule 10b–5(2). TGS relies on the holding of the court below that "The issuance of the release produced no unusual market action" and "In the absence of a showing that the purpose of the April 12 press release was to affect the market price of TGS stock to the advantage of TGS or its insiders, the issuance of the press release did not constitute a violation of Section 10(b) or Rule 10b–5 since it was not issued 'in connection with the purchase or sale of any security'" and, alternatively, "even if it had been established that the April 12 release was issued in connection with the purchase or sale of any security, the Commission has failed to demonstrate that it was false, misleading or deceptive." 258 F.Supp. at 294.

Before further discussing this matter it seems desirable to state exactly what the SEC claimed in its complaint and what it seeks. The specific SEC allegation in its complaint is that this April 12 press release "* * * was materially false and misleading and was known by certain of defendant Texas Gulf's officers and employees, including defendants Fogarty, Mollison, Holyk, Darke and Clayton, to be materially false and misleading."

The specific relief the SEC seeks is, pursuant to Section 21(e) of Securities Exchange Act of 1934, 15 U.S.C.A. § 78u(e), a permanent injunction restraining the issuance of any further materially false and misleading publicly distributed informative items.

B. *The "In Connection With * * *" Requirement*

In adjudicating upon the relationship of this phrase to the case before us it would appear that the court below used a standard that does not reflect the congressional purpose that prompted the passage of the Securities Exchange Act of 1934.

The dominant congressional purposes underlying the Securities Exchange Act of 1934 were to promote free and open public securities markets and to protect the investing public from suffering inequities in trading, including, specifically, inequities that follow from trading that has been stimulated by the publication of false or misleading corporate information releases. Commenting on the disclosure purposes of the House bill (H.R. 9323), the bill a Committee of Conference eventually integrated with a similar Senate bill (S. 3420) to make the bill passed by both Houses of Congress that became the Securities Exchange Act of 1934, the House Committee which reported out H.R. 9323 stated:

> The idea of a free and open public market is built upon the theory that competing judgments of buyers and sellers as to the fair price of a security brings about a situation where the market price reflects as nearly as possible a just price. Just as artificial manipulation tends to upset the true function of an open market, so the hiding and secreting of important information obstructs the operation of the markets as indices of real value. *There cannot be honest markets without honest publicity.* Manipulation and dishonest practices of the market place thrive upon mystery and secrecy. The disclosure of information materially important to investors may not instantaneously be reflected in market value, but despite the intricacies of security values truth does find relatively quick acceptance on the market. That is why in many cases it is so carefully guarded. Delayed, inaccurate, and misleading reports are the tools of the unconscionable market operator and the recreant corporate official who speculate on inside information. Despite the tug of conflicting interests and the influence of popular groups, responsible officials of the leading exchanges have unqualifiedly recognized in theory at least the vital importance of *true and accurate corporate reporting as an essential cog in the proper functioning of the public exchanges.* Their efforts to bring about more adequate and prompt publicity have been handicapped by the lack of legal power and by the failure of certain banking and business groups to appreciate that a business that gathers its capital from the investing public has not the same right to secrecy as a small privately owned and managed business. It is only a few decades since men believed that the disclosure of a balance sheet was a disclosure of a trade secret. Today few people would admit the right of any company to solicit public funds without the disclosure of a balance sheet. (Emphasis supplied.) H.R.Rep.No. 1383, 73rd Cong., 2d Sess. 11 (1934).

> *   *   *

Indeed, from its very inception, Section 10(b), and the proposed sections in H.R. 1383 and S. 3420 from which it was derived, have always been acknowledged as catchalls. See Bromberg, Securities Law: SEC Rule 10b–5, p. 19 (1967). In the House Committee hearings on the proposed House bill, Thomas G. Corcoran, Counsel with the Reconstruction Finance Corporation and a spokesman for the Roosevelt Administration, described the broad prohibitions contained in § 9(c), the section which corresponded to Section 10(b) of S. 3420 and eventually to Section 10(b) of the Act, as follows: "Subsection (c) says, 'Thou shalt not devise any other cunning devices' * * *. Of course subsection (c) is a catch-all clause to prevent manipulative devices. I do not think there is any objection to that kind of a clause. The Commission should have the authority to deal with new manipulative devices." * * *

Therefore it seems clear from the legislative purpose Congress expressed in the Act, and the legislative history of Section 10(b) that Congress when it used the phrase "in connection with the purchase or sale of any security" intended only that the device employed, whatever it might be, be of a sort that would cause reasonable investors to rely thereon, and, in connection therewith, so relying, cause them to purchase or sell a corporation's securities. There is no indication that Congress intended that the corporations or persons responsible for the issuance of a misleading statement would not violate the section unless they engaged in related securities transactions or otherwise acted with wrongful motives; indeed, the obvious purposes of the Act to protect the investing public and to secure fair dealing in the securities markets would be seriously undermined by applying such a gloss onto the legislative language. Absent a securities transaction by an insider it is almost impossible to prove that a wrongful purpose motivated the issuance of the misleading statement. The mere fact that an insider did not engage in securities transactions does not negate the possibility of wrongful purpose; perhaps the market did not react to the misleading statement as much as was anticipated or perhaps the wrongful purpose was something other than the desire to buy at a low price or sell at a high price. Of even greater relevance to the Congressional purpose of investor protection is the fact that the investing public may be injured as much by one's misleading statement containing inaccuracies caused by negligence as by a misleading statement published intentionally to further a wrongful purpose. We do not believe that Congress intended that the proscriptions of the Act would not be violated unless the makers of a misleading statement also participated in pertinent securities transactions in connection therewith, or unless it could be shown that the issuance of the statement was motivated by a plan to benefit the corporation or themselves at the expense of a duped investing public.

Nor is there anything about Rule 10b–5 which demonstrates that the SEC sought by the Rule not fully to implement the Congressional purpose and objectives underlying Section 10(b). See Securities Exchange Act of 1934, Release No. 3230 (May 21, 1942); 10 SEC Ann. Rep. 56–7 (1944); 8 SEC Ann.Rep. 10 (1942). To be sure, SEC official publicity accompanying the promulgation of the Rule emphasized the insider trading aspects of the Rule, particularly the prohibition against purchases by insiders, but this was emphasized because "the previously existing rules against fraud in the purchase of securities applied only to brokers and dealers," 8 SEC Ann.Rep. 10, and the Commission wished to make it emphatically clear that the Rule was expected, *inter alia*, to close this loophole.

The foregoing discussion demonstrates that Congress intended to protect the investing public in connection with their purchases or sales on Exchanges from being misled by misleading statements promulgated for or on behalf of corporations irrespective of whether the insiders contemporaneously trade in the securities of that corporation and irrespective of whether the corporation or its management have an ulterior purpose or purposes in making an official public release. Indeed, the Commission has been charged by Congress with the responsibility of policing all misleading corporate statements from those contained in an initial prospectus to those contained in a notice to stockholders relative to the need or desirability of terminating the existence of a corporation or of merging it with another. To render the Congressional purpose ineffective by inserting into the statutory words the need of proving, not only that the public may have been misled by the release, but also that those responsible were actuated by a wrongful purpose when they issued the release, is to handicap unreasonably the Commission in its work. * * *

As was pointed out by the trial court, 258 F.Supp. at 293, the intent of the Securities Exchange Act of 1934 is the protection of investors against fraud. Therefore, it would seem elementary that the Commission has a duty to police management so as to prevent corporate practices which are reasonably likely fraudulently to injure investors. And, of course, as we have already emphasized, a corporation's misleading material statement may injure an investor irrespective of whether the corporation itself, or those individuals managing it, are contemporaneously buying or selling the stock of the corporation. Therefore, when materially misleading corporate statements or deceptive insider activities have been uncovered, the courts, as they should, have broadly construed the statutory phrase "in connection with the purchase or sale of any security." * * * The court below found: "There is no evidence that TGS derived any direct benefit from the issuance of the press release or that any of the defendants who participated in its preparation used it to their personal advantage." 258 F. Supp. at 294. The requirement that a statement may not be found misleading unless its issuance is actuated by a "wrongful purpose" might well have the effect of permitting the issuers of misleading statements to seek an advantage but to escape liability if the advantage fails to materialize to the degree contemplated, or cannot be demonstrated.

More important, however, is the realization which we must again underscore at the risk of repetition, that the investing public is hurt by exposure to false or deceptive statements irrespective of the purpose underlying their issuance. It does not appear to be unfair to impose upon corporate management a duty to ascertain the truth of any statements the corporation releases to its shareholders or to the investing public at large. Accordingly, we hold that Rule 10b–5 is violated whenever assertions are made, as here, in a manner reasonably calculated to influence the investing public, e. g., by means of the financial media, * * * if such assertions are false or misleading or are so incomplete as to mislead irrespective of whether the issuance of the release was motivated by corporate officials for ulterior purposes. It seems clear, however, that if corporate management demonstrates that it was diligent in ascertaining that the information it published was the whole truth and that such diligently obtained information was disseminated in good faith, Rule 10b–5 would not have been violated.

C.   *Did the Issuance of the April 12 Release Violate Rule 10b–5?*

Turning first to the question of whether the release was misleading, i. e., whether it conveyed to the public a false impression of the drilling situation at the time of its issuance, we note initially that the trial court did not actually decide this question. Its conclusion that "the Commission has failed to demonstrate that it was false, misleading or deceptive," 258 F.Supp. at 294, seems to have derived from its views that "The defendants are to be judged *on the facts known to them* when the April 12 release was issued," 258 F.Supp. at 295 (emphasis supplied), that the draftsmen "exercised reasonable business judgment under the circumstances," 258 F.Supp. at 296, and that the release was not "misleading or deceptive *on the basis of the facts then known,*" 258 F.Supp. at 296 (emphasis supplied) rather than from an appropriate primary inquiry into the meaning of the statement to the reasonable investor and its relationship to truth. While we certainly agree with the trial court that "in retrospect, the press release may appear gloomy or incomplete," 258 F.Supp. at 296, we cannot, from the present record, by applying the standard Congress intended, definitively conclude that it was deceptive or misleading to the reasonable investor, or that he would have been misled by it. Certain newspaper accounts of the release viewed the release as confirming the existence of preliminary favorable developments, and this optimistic view was held by some brokers, so it could be that the reasonable investor would have read between the lines of what appears to us to be an inconclusive and negative statement and would have envisioned the actual situation at the Kidd segment on April 12. On the other hand, in view of the decline of the market price of TGS stock from a high of 32 on the morning of April 13 when the release was disseminated to 29⅜ by the close of trading on April 15, and the reaction to the release by other brokers, it is far from certain that the release was generally interpreted as a highly encouraging report or even encouraging at all. Accordingly, we remand this issue to the district court that took testimony and heard and saw the witnesses for a determination of the character of the release in the light of the facts existing at the time of the release, by applying the standard of whether the reasonable investor, in the exercise of due care, would have been misled by it.

* * *

We hold only that, in an action for injunctive relief, the district court has the discretionary power under Rule 10b–5 and Section 10(b) to issue an injunction, if the misleading statement resulted from a lack of due diligence on the part of TGS. The trial court did not find it necessary to decide whether TGS exercised such diligence and has not yet attempted to resolve this issue. While the trial court concluded that TGS had exercised "reasonable *business* judgment under the circumstances," 258 F.Supp. at 296 (emphasis supplied) it applied an incorrect *legal* standard in appraising whether TGS should have issued its April 12 release on the basis of the facts known to its draftsmen at the time of its preparation, 258 F.Supp. at 295, and in assuming that disclosure of the full underlying facts of the Timmins situation was not a viable alternative to the vague generalities which were asserted. 258 F.Supp. at 296.

It is not altogether certain from the present record that the draftsmen could, as the SEC suggests, have readily obtained current reports of the drilling progress over the weekend of April 10–12, but they certainly should have obtained them if at all possible for them to do so. However, even if it were not possible to evaluate and transmit current data in time to prepare the release on April 12, it would seem that TGS could have delayed the preparation a bit until an accurate report of a rapidly changing situation was possible. See 258 F.Supp. at 296. At the very least, if TGS felt compelled to respond to the spreading rumors of a spectacular discovery, it would have been more accurate to have stated that the situation was in flux and that the release was prepared as of April 10 information rather than purporting to report the progress "to date." Moreover, it would have obviously been better to have specifically described the known drilling progress as of April 10 by stating the basic facts. Such an explicit disclosure would have permitted the investing public to evaluate the "prospect" of a mine at Timmins without having to read between the lines to understand that preliminary indications were favorable—in itself an understatement.

The choice of an ambiguous general statement rather than a summary of the specific facts cannot reasonably be justified by any claimed urgency. The avoidance of liability for misrepresentation in the event that the Timmins project failed, a highly unlikely event as of April 12 or April 13, did not forbid the accurate and truthful divulgence of detailed results which need not, of course, have been accompanied by conclusory assertions of success. Nor is it any justification that such an explicit disclosure of the truth might have "encouraged the rumor mill which they were seeking to allay." 258 F. Supp. at 296.

We conclude, then, that, having established that the release was issued in a manner reasonably calculated to affect the market price of TGS stock and to influence the investing public, we must remand to the district court to decide whether the release was misleading to the reasonable investor and if found to be misleading, whether the court in its discretion should issue the injunction the SEC seeks.

CONCLUSION

In summary, therefore, we affirm the finding of the court below that appellants Richard H. Clayton and David M. Crawford have violated 15 U.S.C.A. § 78j(b) and Rule 10b–5; we reverse the judgment order entered below dismissing the complaint against appellees Charles F. Fogarty, Richard H. Clayton, Richard D. Mollison, Walter Holyk, Kenneth H. Darke, Earl L. Huntington, and Francis G. Coates, as we find that they have violated 15 U.S.C.A. § 78j(b) and Rule 10b–5. As to these eight individuals we remand so that in accordance with the agreement between the parties the Commission may notice a hearing before the court below to determine the remedies to be applied against them. We reverse the judgment order dismissing the complaint against Claude O. Stephens, Charles F. Fogarty, and Harold B. Kline as recipients of stock options, direct the district court to consider in its discretion whether to issue injunction orders against Stephens and Fogarty, and direct that an order issue rescinding the option granted Kline and that such further remedy be applied against him as may be proper by way of an order of restitution; and we reverse the judgment dismissing the complaint against Texas Gulf Sulphur Company, remand the cause as to it for a further determination below, in the light of the approach explicated by us in the foregoing opinion, as to whether, in the exercise of its discretion, the injunction against it which the Commission seeks should be ordered.

FRIENDLY, Circuit Judge (concurring). Agreeing with the result reached by the majority and with most of Judge Waterman's searching opinion, I take a rather different approach to two facets of the case.

I.

* * * The novel problem in the instant case is to define the responsibility of officers when a directors' committee administering a stock option plan proposes of its own initiative to make options available to them and others at a time when they know that the option price, geared to the market value of the stock, did not reflect a substantial increment likely to be realized in short order and was therefore unfair to the corporation.

A rule requiring a minor officer to reject an option so tendered would not comport with the realities either of human nature or of corporate life. * * *

II.

The second point, to me transcending in public importance all others in this important case, is the press release issued by TGS on April 12, 1964. This seems to me easier on the facts but harder on the law than it does to the majority.

No one has asserted, or reasonably could assert, that the purpose for issuing a release was anything but good. TGS felt it had a responsibility to protect would-be buyers of its shares from what it regarded as exaggerated rumors first in the Canadian and then in the New York City press, and none of the individual defendants sought to profit from the decline in the price of TGS stock caused by the release. I find it equally plain, as Judge Waterman's opinion convincingly demonstrates, that the release did not properly convey the information in the hands of the draftsmen on April 12, even granting, as I would, that in a case like this a court should not set the standard of care too high. To say that the drilling at Timmins had afforded only "preliminary indications that more drilling would be required for proper evaluation of this prospect," was a wholly insufficient statement of what TGS knew.   *   *   *

IRVING R. KAUFMAN, Circuit Judge (concurring). I concur in Judge Waterman's reasoned and thorough opinion and in the court's disposition of the instant appeal. I agree with Judge Friendly, however, that we should provide guidance to the District Courts with respect to pending private claims for damages based upon Rule 10(b) (5) arising out of the transactions now before us. And, I concur in as much as Part II of Judge Friendly's opinion as discusses the origins of the rule and the relevance of today's decision—involving only an application by the S.E.C. for an injunction—to private damage actions.

ANDERSON, Circuit Judge (concurring).

I concur in Judge Waterman's majority opinion and I concur in the discussion of law set forth in Part II of Judge Friendly's concurring opinion.

HAYS, Circuit Judge (concurring in part and dissenting in part).

I concur generally with Judge Waterman in his views as to the proper interpretation of Section 10(b) and Rule 10b–5 and as to the standards which are to be employed in the application of the statute and the rule.

With the exception of Stephens and Fogarty as recipients of stock options, I agree with the majority on the disposition of the cases involving individuals.

I do not agree on the remand of the issue with respect to Stephens and Fogarty as recipients of stock options. It seems to me clear that the injunction sought by the Commission should be granted.

The majority remand the case against the corporate defendant to the district court for a determination as to whether the April 12 press release was misleading and whether, if so, those responsible for the release used due diligence.

In my opinion the evidence establishes as a matter of law that the press release was misleading. Indeed, if the correct standard is applied, the finding of the trial court requires the conclusion that the press release was misleading:

"At 7:00 p. m. on April 9, those with knowledge of the drilling results had material information which it was reasonably certain, if disclosed, would have had a substantial impact on the market price of TGS's stock."

The evidence in the record in support of this finding is overwhelming.

Assuming arguendo that the corporation cannot be enjoined except on a showing of lack of due diligence, since Fogarty and those who assisted him in the preparation of the press release were aware of the drilling results to which the district court's finding refers, they obviously did not use due diligence in the preparation of the misleading press release.

I would grant the application for an injunction.

MOORE, Circuit Judge (dissenting) (with whom Chief Judge LUMBARD concurs):

* * *

Turning now to the hypothesis of disclosure: As previously stated, any announcement of the discovery of a remarkable mine would have been both false and misleading. The Commission, however, impliedly suggests for affirmative answer the question: "Whether the chances of imminent success, viewed in the light of the magnitude of the potential economic benefit to Texas Gulf" did not require disclosure by insiders of the status of the drilling [then only the first hole, K–55–1]? In the field of speculation, it would be interesting to know the position the Commission would have taken if TGS had announced that K–55–1 was "one of the most impressive drill holes completed in modern times" and that it "is just beyond your wildest imagination" (SEC Brief, p. 25). It requires no imagination to venture that such announcements might well have had the "wildest" impact on the market price of TGS stock.

* * *

Conclusion

In summary, the most disturbing aspect of the majority opinion is its utterly unrealistic approach to the problem of the corporate press release. If corporations were literally to follow its implications, every press release would have to have the same SEC clearance as a prospectus. Even this procedure would not suffice if future events should prove the facts to have been over or understated—or too gloomy or optimistic—because the courts will always be ready and available to substitute their judgment for that of the business executives responsible therefor. But vulnerable as the news release may be, what of the many daily developments in the Research and Development departments of giant corporations. When and how are promising results to be disclosed. If they are not disclosed, the corporation is concealing information; if disclosed and hoped-for results do not materialize, there will always be those with the advantage of hindsight to brand them as false or misleading. Nor is it consonant with reality to suggest, as does the majority, that corporate executives may be motivated in accepting employment by the opportunity to make "secret corporate compensation * * * derived at the expense of the uninformed public." Such thoughts can only arise from unfounded speculative imagination. And finally there is the sardonic anomaly that the very members of society which Congress has charged the SEC with protecting, i. e., the stockholders, will be the real victims of its misdirected zeal. May the Future, the Congress or possibly the SEC itself be able to bring some semblance of order by means of workable rules and regulations in this field so that the corporations and their stockholders may not be subjected to countless lawsuits at the whim of every purchaser, seller or potential purchaser who may claim he would have acted or refrained from acting had a news release been more comprehensive, less comprehensive or had it been adequately published in the news media of the 50 States.

UNITED STATES OF AMERICA
BEFORE THE
SECURITIES AND EXCHANGE COMMISSION

(Release Number 8459)

ADMINISTRATIVE PROCEEDING FILE NO. 3–1680
November 25, 1968.

In the Matters of

MERRILL LYNCH, PIERCE, FENNER
& SMITH, INC.
70 Pine Street
New York, New York

WINTHROP C. LENZ
JULIUS H. SEDLMAYR
GILLETTE K. MARTIN
DEAN S. WOODMAN
GEORGE L. SHINN
ARCHANGELO CATAPANO
EDWARD N. McMILLAN
PHILIP F. BILBAO
NORMAN H. HEINDEL, JR.
LEE W. IDLEMAN
LAWRENCE ZICKLIN
JAMES A. McCARTHY
ELIAS A. LAZOR
CHESTER T. SMITH, JR.

(8–7221)

Securities Exchange Act of 1934—
Sections 15(b), 15A and 19(a) (3)

Investment Advisers Act of 1940—
Section 203

FINDINGS,
OPINION
AND ORDER

BROKER-DEALER PROCEEDINGS

In these proceedings pursuant to Sections 15(b), 15A and 19(a) (3) of the Securities Exchange Act of 1934 ("Exchange Act") and

Section 203 of the Investment Advisers Act of 1940, an offer of settlement was submitted by Merrill Lynch, Pierce, Fenner & Smith, Inc. ("registrant"), a registered broker-dealer, and the above-named individual respondents, who were associated with registrant during the period covered by the order for proceedings. Under the terms of the offer, these respondents waived a hearing and post-hearing procedures and, solely for the purpose of these proceeding and without admitting the allegations in the order for proceedings, consented to findings of violations of anti-fraud provisions of the Securities Act of 1933 and the Exchange Act and rules thereunder by registrant and eight of the individual respondents as alleged in the order for proceedings, and that registrant, McMillan and Heindel failed to exercise reasonable supervision with a view to preventing such violations. Respondents further consented to the entry of an order imposing, in our discretion, certain sanctions as specified in the offer of settlement.

After due consideration of the offer of settlement and upon the recommendation of our staff, we have determined to accept such offer. On the basis of the order for proceedings, the answers filed thereto, and the offer of settlement, we make the findings set forth below.

Disclosure of Inside Information to Selected Customers

Between June 17 and 24, 1966, registrant, together with or willfully aided and abetted by the eight aforementioned individual respondents, willfully violated Section 17(a) of the Securities Act and Sections 10(b) and 15(c)(1) of the Exchange Act and Rules 10b-5 and 15c1-2 thereunder, and registrant, Heindel and McMillan failed reasonably to exercise supervision with a view to preventing such violations.

Registrant was named as managing underwriter in a registration statement filed with us on June 7, 1966, by Douglas Aircraft Co., Inc. ("Douglas") with respect to a proposed offering of $75,000,000 of convertible subordinated debentures. The registration statement contained an earnings report for the first five months of Douglas' fiscal year ending November 30, 1966, which indicated that Douglas had earned 85¢ per share for that period. Between June 17 and 22, because of registrant's position as managing underwriter, the registrant received material non-public information from Douglas' management with respect to its earnings which it in turn, between June 20 and 23, disclosed to certain of its institutional and other large customers.

That information was to the effect that Douglas would report earnings for the first six months of its 1966 fiscal year that were sharply lower than the 85¢ per share reported for the first five months, had sharply reduced its estimates of earnings for the 1966 fiscal year and was expecting to show little or no profit for the year, and had substantially reduced its projections of earnings for the following fiscal year. Thus, this information revealed a significant deterioration in the prospects of Douglas.

Some of the selected customers thereafter sold from existing positions and effected short sales of more than 190,000 shares of Douglas stock on the New York Stock Exchange and otherwise prior to public disclosure of the information and without any disclosure of such information being made to the purchasers. And in connection with such transactions by these customers, certain of whom did substantial brokerage business with registrant, registrant received commission or compensation in the form of customer-directed "give-ups." While this adverse information was being disclosed to various large customers, registrant did not disclose this information to other customers for whom it effected purchases of Douglas stock. On June 24, 1966, Douglas issued a news release which stated that its earnings for the first six months of its 1966 fiscal year were 12¢ per share and that in the opinion of management earnings for the entire fiscal year, if any, would be nominal.

The legal principles which govern the conduct of registrant described above have been set forth by us in Cady, Roberts & Co., (40 S.E.C. 907 (1961)) and more recently by the Court of Appeals for the Second Circuit in S.E.C. v. Texas Gulf Sulphur Co.

In *Cady, Roberts* a partner of a broker-dealer firm received material adverse information (a sizable dividend cut) concerning the issuer from a director who was also a registered representative of the broker-dealer firm. The partner acting on behalf of certain discretionary accounts and others sold stock of the issuer prior to public release of such information. We held that the partner was subject to the fiduciary responsibilities of a traditional corporate "insider," such as an officer, director or controlling person, with respect to the investing public and could not make advance use of the information. We noted that the relationship of the broker-dealer's employee to the issuer gave him access to information intended to be available only for a corporate purpose and not for the personal benefit of anyone, and that there is an inherent unfairness involved where one takes advantage of such information knowing it is unavailable to the investing public.

In *Texas Gulf* certain directors, officers and employees having possession of material favorable information (major developments in a mineral exploratory program) bought shares of the issuer, and recommended that others buy shares, before the information was publicly disseminated. The Court held that Section 10(b) of the Securities Exchange Act and Rule 10b-5 required persons having such access to information for a corporate purpose either to disclose it to public investors before acting on it for their personal benefit or to abstain from trading in or recommending the stock while the information remained undisclosed. The Court stated that Rule 10b-5 "is based in policy on the justifiable expectation of the securities market-place that all investors . . . have relatively equal access to material information." It further held that they violated that Rule not only by trading on the basis of inside information but also by "tipping" the information to others, since one who may not himself trade in securities without disclosing information known to him may not pass that information to others for their use in securities transactions.

Here a prospective managing underwriter was given material information (a substantial decline in recent earnings and downward revision of earnings estimates) by the issuer for use in connection with the proposed public offering. This highly significant information was entrusted to registrant by virtue of its business relationship with the issuer before it was publicly available. It was passed on by registrant to certain of its customers prior to its dissemination to the public. The principles enunciated in the *Cady, Roberts* and *Texas Gulf* cases prohibited the disclosure of such information by registrant to favored customers who might sell their holdings or sell short before appropriate public disclosure and thereby take advantage of the current market price before the expectable decline in such price upon public dissemination of the information.[1] And, aggravating the inherent unfairness of the disclosure to certain customers was the fact that, at the same time, registrant was effecting purchases of the stock for other customers to whom the adverse information was not available.

The information Douglas entrusted to registrant was of such importance that it could be expected to affect the judgment of investors whether to buy, sell, or hold Douglas stock. If generally known, such information could be expected to affect materially the market price of the stock. The advance disclosure of such information to a select group who could utilize it for their own benefit, and to the detriment of public investors to whom the information was not known, constituted an act, practice, or course of business which operated or would operate as a fraud or deceit upon such investors. We further conclude that registrant Heindel as manager of the New York Institutional Sales Office in which the five salesmen-respondents were employed, and McMillan as Director of the Institutional and Municipal Sales Division failed to take appropriate steps to prevent the conduct described above.

Public Interest

The offer of settlement provides that we may suspend the activities of registrant's New York Institutional Sales Office for up to 21 days, suspend the activities of registrant's West Coast Underwriting

---

1. It may be noted that on June 22, 1966, Douglas stock opened at a price of 90½. By the close of the following day the price had declined to 78¾, and it fell to 69 on June 27, the trad-ing day after the date of the news release. The price further declined to 61¾ by the end of that week. (Commission's footnote 7.)

Office for up to 15 days, direct that Catapano be dissociated from registrant for up to 60 days and censure him, direct that Bilbao, Idleman, Zicklin, McCarthy, Lazor, and Smith be so dissociated for all or part of the period of suspension of the New York Institutional Sales Office and censure them, and censure Woodman, Heindel, and McMillan. For the period of any dissociation no compensation is to be received from registrant. The offer further provides that our order imposing any of the above sanctions shall state that such sanctions shall not result in suspension of the membership or registration of any of the respondents in any national securities exchange or association.

In determining to accept the offer of settlement submitted by respondents we have taken into consideration registrant's undertaking to adopt, implement, and ensure compliance with, revised procedures to provide more effective protection against disclosure of confidential information, including but not limited to the procedures set forth in a Statement of Policy which is incorporated in the offer of settlement. The Statement of Policy prohibits disclosure by any member of the Underwriting Division of material information obtained from a corporation in connection with the consideration or negotiation of a public or private offering of its securities and not disclosed to the investing public by the corporation, except to senior executives of registrant, its legal department, persons directly involved with the underwriters in connection with the proposed offering, Research Division personnel whose views in connection with the proposed offering are sought by the Underwriting Division, and members of the buying departments of prospective co-underwriters for the purpose of enabling them to decide whether they will participate in the proposed offering. Any employee of registrant who receives such information is subject to the same restrictions as provided for members of the Underwriting Division.

As a matter of Commission policy, we do not, and indeed cannot, determine in advance that the Statement of Policy will prove adequate in all circumstances that may arise. Stringent measures will be required in order to avoid future violations. Obviously the prompt public dissemination of material information would be an effective preventive, and registrant has stated that it will use its best efforts to have the issuer make public any material information given to its Underwriting Division. We have also taken into account the substantial impact upon registrant, which is the largest brokerage firm in the country, of the suspension of activities of its New York Institutional Sales Office and West Coast Underwriting Office.

The offer of settlement does not include the imposition of statutory sanctions on Lenz, Sedlmayr, Martin and Shinn. These respondents had no supervisory responsibilities in the Institutional and Municipal Sales Division. Shinn did not assume his position as Director of the Research Division until shortly before the conduct in question. Martin has retired for reasons of health and is no longer associated with registrant. We have further noted that they as well as the other individual respondents have not previously been the subject of disciplinary action.

Under all the circumstances, and giving due consideration to the recommendations of our staff respecting the various aspects of the offer of settlement, we think it appropriate in the public interest to dispose of the proceedings as to the respondents who submitted the offer in accordance therewith and to impose the sanctions permitted by it.

Accordingly, IT IS ORDERED that the activities of registrant's New York Institutional Sales Office and registrant's West Coast Underwriting Office be, and they hereby are, suspended for 21 and 15 days, respectively, with the 21-day suspension commencing at the opening of business on December 5, 1968, and the 15-day suspension at the opening of business on December 11, 1968.

IT IS FURTHER ORDERED that Archangelo Catapano be, and he hereby is, censured and dissociated from registrant for 60 days; that Phillip F. Bilbao, Lee W. Idleman, Lawrence Zicklin, James A. McCarthy, Elias A. Lazor, and Chester T. Smith, Jr. be, and they hereby are, censured and dissociated from registrant for 21 days, such dissociations to commence at the opening of business on December 5, 1968, and no compensation to be received by them from registrant for the period of their dissociation.

IT IS FURTHER ORDERED that Dean S. Woodman, Edward N. McMillan, and Norman H. Heindel, Jr., be, and they hereby are, censured.

IT IS FURTHER ORDERED that the above sanctions shall not constitute a suspension of the membership or registration of any of the respondents in any national securities exchange or association.

By the Commission (Chairman COHEN and Commissioners OWENS, BUDGE, WHEAT and SMITH).

Orval L. DuBois
Secretary

HEIT v. WEITZEN

United States Court of Appeals, Second Circuit, 1968.
402 F.2d 909.

MEDINA, Circuit Judge. On this appeal from two judgments dismissing plaintiffs' complaints, we are presented with significant questions involving civil liability under Sections 10(b) and 18(a) of the Securities Exchange Act of 1934. Because the principal questions involved on these appeals have been under consideration by the active judges of this Court sitting *in banc* we have deferred decision until after the filing of the opinions in SEC v. Texas Gulf Sulphur Co., Docket No. 30882, 401 F.2d 833, on August 13, 1968.

There are three separate actions before us now, Heit v. Weitzen, et al., and Volk v. Weitzen, et al., originally consolidated by the District Court, and Howard v. Grant, et al., consolidated on appeal by this Court with *Heit* and *Volk*. The various complaints involve essentially the same operative facts as they all are based on the fact that Belock Instrument Corporation allegedly failed to disclose that a substantial amount of its income for the fiscal year 1964 was derived from various overcharges on government contracts. Thus, the consolidated amended complaint in *Heit* and *Volk* alleges that Heit on June 18, 1965 purchased $5,000 principal face amount of Belock's 6% convertible subordinated debentures at a price of 90% of face amount in reliance on various "materially false, misleading and untrue statements of Belock's net assets and past and prospective income," contained in Belock's Annual Report, and press releases, as well as documents filed by the individual defendants with the SEC and the American Stock Exchange. Volk allegedly purchased 100 shares of Belock common stock on April 22, 1965 and another 100 shares on April 27, 1965 in reliance on these same false statements. Heit and Volk seek to represent both themselves and the entire class of persons who purchased either common stock or debentures between April 30, 1964 and June 21, 1965, and who have either sold or continue to hold these investments at a loss. It is further alleged that the dissemination by defendants of these false statements had the effect of artificially inflating the market price of Belock's common stock and debentures and that defendants had knowledge or notice of the falsity of the statements. In addition to Belock Corporation, the individual defendants served in *Heit* and *Volk* include Weitzen, Tyminski, Fischer, and Grant, all directors of Belock Corporation, and Levy who was a vice president of the corporation.

In the *Howard* complaint it is alleged that plaintiff Helen Howard purchased a 6% convertible subordinated Belock Corporation debenture on June 16, 1965 at an artificially inflated price. The price inflation was allegedly caused by the circulation and dissemination by the defendants "through press statements to the investment community * * * of statements as to the purported earnings and income of Belock Instrument and forecasts with respect thereto which in fact were gross overstatements." Howard seeks to represent the entire class composed of persons who purchased Belock stock or debentures in the open market and who were either misled by the published false material or by the artificially inflated market price. The defendants in *Howard* who were served include, in addition to Belock Corporation, Tyminski and Grant, Carl M. Loeb, Rhoades & Co., who is Belock's controlling shareholder, and Lybrand, Ross Bros. & Montgomery, Belock's auditors.

In *Howard,* Judge Cooper granted defendants' motion to dismiss for failure to state a claim upon which relief could be granted, primarily because the alleged fraud did not occur "in connection with the purchase or sale of any security" as required by Rule 10b–5. Howard v. Levine, 262 F.Supp. 643 (S.D.N.Y.1965). Judge Sugarman, relying in part on Judge Cooper's opinion, similarly dismissed the Section 10 (b) claims in *Heit* and *Volk* for failure to satisfy the "in connection with" clause. Heit v. Weitzen, 260 F.Supp. 598 (S.D.N.Y.1966). Judge Sugarman also found that plaintiffs had failed to state a claim for relief under Section 18 of the 1934 Act since none of the reports upon which the claims were predicated were "filed" with the SEC as required by that Section. The motions to dismiss were granted without leave to replead. We also note that defendants in all the actions moved for summary judgment based on the fact that plaintiffs have suffered no damage since after the institution of these actions the price of both Belock's common stock and debentures has risen above the prices originally paid by plaintiffs. Neither of the judges below reached this question, nor do we.

I.

Rule 10b–5, 17 C.F.R. Section 240.10b–5, provides:

It shall be unlawful for any person, directly or indirectly, by the use of any means or instrumentality of interstate commerce, or of the mails or of any facility of any national securities exchange,

(a) To employ any device, scheme, or artifice to defraud,

(b) To make any untrue statement of a material fact or to omit to state a material fact necessary in order to make the statements made, in the light of the circumstances under which they were made, not misleading, or

(c) To engage in any act, practice, of course of business which operates or would operate as a fraud or deceit upon any person,

in connection with the purchase or sale of any security.

Each of the judges below referred to the fact that the basic fraudulent scheme alleged in the complaints was primarily directed toward the government "notwithstanding its possible incidental market impact." Thus, it was held that the concealment of the overcharges when the financial statements were released was for "the purpose of further defrauding the Government by not disclosing the original malfeasance and not for the purpose of perpetrating a 'misrepresentation or fraudulent practice usually associated with the sale or purchase of securities.'" Heit v. Weitzen, 260 F.Supp. 598 (S.D.N.Y.1966). Furthermore, as stated by Judge Cooper, since neither the corporate nor the individual defendants in the instant action were engaged in purchasing or selling Belock securities, he could see no basis for a finding that the alleged fraud occurred "in connection with the purchase or sale of any security."

However, we must now reassess the holdings below in light of the principles enunciated in SEC v. Texas Gulf Sulphur Co., Docket No. 30882, 401 F.2d 833. Judge Waterman writing for the Court in *Texas Gulf Sulphur* construed the "in connection with" requirement broadly and held that the clause was satisfied whenever a device was employed "of a sort that would cause reasonable investors to rely thereon, and, in connection therewith, so relying, cause them to purchase or sell a corporation's securities," SEC v. Texas Gulf Sulphur Co., at 860. There is no necessity for contemporaneous trading in securities by insiders or by the corporation itself. "Rule 10b–5 is violated whenever assertions are made * * * in a manner reasonably calculated to influence the investing public, e. g., by means of the financial media * * *, if such assertions are false or misleading or are so incomplete as to mislead irrespective of whether the issuance of the release was motivated by corporate officials for ulterior purposes." SEC v. Texas Gulf Sulphur Co.

Applying this rule, and accepting at face value plaintiffs' well pleaded allegations, as we must on a motion to dismiss for failure to state a claim, we conclude that plaintiffs have met the requirements of the "in connection with" clause. It is reasonable to assume that investors may very well rely on the material contained in false corporate financial statements which have been disseminated in the market place, and in so relying may subsequently purchase securities of the corporation. The "ulterior motive" present in the instant case—the concealment of the fraud from the government—is irrelevant, since the false information was circulated to a large segment of the investing public. It is impossible to isolate the particular "fraudulent" acts and consider them as directed toward the government alone.

As the "in connection with" clause has been satisfied, we must now deal with the question of the standard by which the conduct of the defendants is to be judged. Judge Waterman in the *Texas Gulf Sulphur* opinion held that proof of negligence was sufficient to sustain an action for injunctive relief under Rule 10b–5(2), but at the same time found it not necessary to decide whether negligence absent a showing of bad faith would suffice in a private suit for damages. SEC v. Texas Gulf Sulphur Co., at 863. However, no question of liability for damages was before the Court in *Texas Gulf Sulphur* and Judge Friendly, in a concurring opinion joined in part by other judges, intimated that the appropriate standard in a private damage action should embody a scienter requirement. SEC v. Texas Gulf Sulphur Co., supra. The question is troublesome. Compare Weber v. C. M. P. Corp., 242 F.Supp. 321 (S.D.N.Y.1965) with Royal Air Properties, Inc. v. Smith, 312 F.2d 210 (9th Cir. 1962). See also III Loss, Securities Regulation at 1785.

There is no occasion for us to enter this ticket now as we pass only upon the legal sufficiency of the complaints to allege a claim for relief. This each of the complaints fairly does. The charge that defendants "knew or should have known" adequately alleges actual knowledge of the falsity of the statements, and, alternatively, negligence or lack of diligence in failing to ascertain the true facts. If some form of scienter test is to be applied, as Judge Friendly seems to suggest in his concurring opinion in *Texas Gulf Sulphur,* we think the alternative allegation of actual knowledge of falsity is amply sufficient as a matter of pleading. And this would seem to be so whether the scienter test ultimately applied be strict or liberal. * * *

Therefore, as far as the claims under Rule 10b–5 are concerned we reverse the judgments appealed from and hold that each of the complaints is sufficient to withstand a motion to dismiss for failure to state a claim for relief.

II.

Section 18(a) of the 1934 Act, 15 U.S.C.A. Section 78r(a) provides:

> Any person who shall make or cause to be made any statement in any application, report, or document filed pursuant to this title or any rule or regulation thereunder or any undertaking contained in a registration statement as provided in subsection (d) of section 15 of this title, which statement was at the time and in the light of the circumstances under which it was made false or misleading with respect to any material fact, shall be liable to any person (not knowing that such statement was false or misleading) who, in reliance upon such statement, shall have purchased or sold a security at a price which was affected by such statement, for damages caused by such reliance, unless the person sued shall prove that he acted in good faith and had no knowledge that such statement was false or misleading. A person seeking to enforce such liability may sue at law or in equity in any court of competent jurisdiction. In any such suit the court may, in its discretion, require an undertaking for the payment of the costs of such suit, and assess reasonable costs, including reasonable attorneys' fees, against either party litigant.

Plaintiffs in *Heit* and *Volk* have contended that they relied on various documents which were "filed" within the meaning of Section 18. The documents in question are the "10K report" for the fiscal year ended October 31, 1964 [1] and Belock's annual report for the same year, which was filed with the American Stock Exchange.

Judge Sugarman correctly ruled that the copies of the annual report submitted to the SEC were not "filed" documents within the meaning of Section 18. Rule 14a–3(c), 17 C.F.R. Section 240.14a–3 (c), of the Regulations under the Securities Exchange Act of 1934, as

[1]. The "10K" report is a detailed document, similar to an annual report, which must be filed annually by all issuers of securities registered pursuant to Section 12 of the Securities Exchange Act of 1934 and by all registrants under the Securities Act of 1933 which are subject to Section 15 (d) of the Securities Exchange Act. Rule 13a–1, 17 C.F.R. Section 240.13a–1; Rule 15d–1, 17 C.F.R. Section 240.15d–1. The SEC has issued specific instructions outlining the material which must be contained in the "10K" report. When the "10K" report is filed with the SEC additional supplemental information must also accompany the report. This supplemental information consists of any annual report for the registrant's last fiscal year and every form of proxy soliciting material sent to more than ten of the registrant's stockholders with respect to any annual or other meeting of stockholders. 17 C.F.R. Section 249.310. * * * (Court's footnote 3.)

it read when the 1964 financial statements were issued on or about February 4, 1965 provided:

> Four copies of each annual report sent to security holders pursuant to this section shall be mailed to the Commission * * *. The annual report is not deemed to be "soliciting material" or to be "filed" with the Commission or subject to this regulation otherwise than as provided in this section, or to the liabilities of section 18 of the Act, except to the extent that the issuer specifically requests that it be treated as a part of the proxy soliciting material or incorporates it in the proxy statement by reference.

The above exemption provision, in addition to exempting the annual report filed with the SEC from the status of a "filed" document, also exempts the annual report filed with the American Stock Exchange from the coverage of Section 18. This result is required by the specific language of the second sentence of the above provision which contains several independent exemption clauses. Thus, the annual report is neither considered to be "filed with the Commission" nor subject to "the liabilities of section 18 of the Act." The latter phrase covers the alleged filing with the American Stock Exchange.

Although Fischman v. Raytheon, 188 F.2d 783 (2d Cir. 1951) held that Section 18(a) applied to "documents" filed with a national securities exchange, the effect of the above regulation is to withdraw annual reports from the category of "filed" documents. The SEC has the power to prescribe rules that "may be necessary for the execution of the functions vested in" it by the Securities Exchange Act, Section 23(a) Securities Exchange Act of 1934, 15 U.S.C.A. § 78w(a), and in the performance of this duty the Commission may properly determine which filings are to be deemed "filings" for the purposes of Section 18.

Therefore, the only possible "filed" document remaining is the "10K report" which is submitted to the SEC. We think it clear that the 10K report is a "filed" document within the meaning of Section 18. See Fischer v. Kletz, 266 F.Supp. 180 (S.D.N.Y.1967). The exemption provision contained in the SEC regulations relating to filing of the 10K report applies only to the copies of the annual report which accompany the 10K report and not the 10K report itself. Regulation 249.310 as it read when the Belock 10K report was allegedly filed provided:

> (i) Every registrant which files an annual report on this form [10K] shall furnish to the Commission for its information four copies of the following * * *
>
> (a) any annual report to stockholders covering the registrant's last fiscal year;
>
> *   *   *   *   *   *   *   *   *   *
>
> (ii) The foregoing material shall not be deemed to be "filed" with the Commission or otherwise subject to the liabilities of Section 18 of the Act, except to the extent that the registrant

specifically requests that it be treated as a part of its annual report on this form [10K] or incorporates it therein by reference.

The opinion of the District Court is unclear and we are unable to determine whether Judge Sugarman intended to hold that the 10K report was not a "filed" document. Appellees contend that Judge Sugarman ignored plaintiffs' claims based on form 10K simply because on oral argument appellants conceded that they could not allege or prove actual knowledge of and reliance upon any Belock 10K report. Appellants have denied making this concession. Reliance on the actual 10K report is an essential prerequisite for a Section 18 action and constructive reliance is not sufficient. Therefore, although under the liberal pleading provisions of the Federal Rules of Civil Procedure, the *Heit* and *Volk* complaints might well be considered broad enough to cover the allegation that they relied on misrepresentations contained in 10K reports, we believe it advisable to remand these cases to the District Court for a reconsideration of the question of leave to amend. Judge Sugarman may have relied on plaintiffs' alleged concession or he may have thought that the complaint was not broad enough to cover an allegation of reliance on a 10K report. On the other hand, he may have incorrectly assumed that a 10K report could not form the basis for a Section 18 action. Thus the interests of justice would seem to require a clear appraisal of the pros and cons.

Finally, although the complaint in *Howard* contains no Section 18 claim for relief, it is stated in appellants' brief that such allegations will be added to the *Howard* complaint "if leave to amend is granted." We leave this for the consideration of the District Court if, as and when such an application for leave to amend is addressed to that Court.

III.

The District Court did not rule on defendants' motions for summary judgment. We believe it would be inappropriate at this early stage in the proceedings to deal with the issue of damages raised by these motions. We agree with the SEC that questions relating to damages should be postponed until after the facts have been fully developed at the trial.

We wish to express our thanks to the SEC for submitting an *amicus curiae* brief at our request in this case.

Reversed and remanded for further proceedings consistent with this opinion.

Circuit Judge MOORE dissented.

FEDER v. MARTIN MARIETTA CORPORATION

United States Court of Appeals, Second Circuit, 1969.
406 F.2d 260.

WATERMAN, Circuit Judge. Plaintiff-appellant, a stockholder of the Sperry Rand Corporation ("Sperry") after having made the requisite demand upon Sperry which was not complied with, commenced this action pursuant to § 16(b) of the Securities Exchange Act of 1934, 15 U.S.C.A. § 78p(b) (1964), to recover for Sperry "short-swing" profits realized upon Sperry stock purchases and sales by the Martin Marietta Corporation ("Martin").[1] Plaintiff alleged that George M. Bunker, the President and Chief Executive of Martin Marietta, was deputized by, or represented, Martin Marietta when he served as a member of the Sperry Rand Board of Directors and therefore during his membership Martin Marietta was a "director" of Sperry Rand within the meaning of Section 16(b). The United States District Court for the Southern District of New York, Cooper, J., sitting without a jury, finding no deputization, dismissed plaintiff's action. 286 F.Supp. 937 (S.D. N.Y.1968). We hold to the contrary and reverse the judgment below.

The purpose of § 16(b) as succinctly expressed in the statute itself is to prevent "unfair use of information" by insiders and thereby to protect the public and outside stockholders. The only remedy which the framers of § 16(b) deemed effective to curb insider abuse of advance information was the imposition of a liability based upon an objective measure of proof, e. g., Smolowe v. Delendo Corp., 136 F.2d 231, 235 (2 Cir.), cert. denied, 320 U.S. 751 (1943). Thus, application of the act is not conditional upon proof of an insider's intent to profit from unfair use of information, e. g., Blau v. Lamb, 363 F.2d 507 (2 Cir. 1966), cert. denied, 385 U.S. 1002 (1967), or upon proof that the insider was privy to any confidential information, e. g., Ferraiolo v. Newman, 259 F.2d 342 (6 Cir. 1958), cert. denied, 359 U.S. 927 (1959). Rather, Section 16(b) liability is automatic, and liability attaches to any profit by an insider on any short-swing transaction embraced within the arbitrarily fixed time limits of the statute.

The judicial tendency, especially in this circuit, has been to interpret Section 16(b) in ways that are most consistent with the legislative purpose, even departing where necessary from the literal statutory language. See, e. g., cases cited in Blau v. Oppenheim, 250 F.Supp.

---

1. Section 16(b) provides:

(b) For the purpose of preventing the unfair use of information which may have been obtained by such beneficial owner, director, or officer by reason of his relationship to the issuer, any profit realized by him from any purchase and sale, or any sale and purchase, of any equity security of such issuer (other than an exempted security) within any period of less than six months, unless such security was acquired in good faith in connection with a debt previously contracted, shall inure to and be recoverable by the issuer, irrespective of any intention on the part of such beneficial owner, director, or officer in entering into such transaction of holding the security purchased or of not repurchasing the security sold for a period exceeding six months. Suit to recover such profit may be instituted at law or in equity in any court of competent jurisdiction by the issuer, or by the owner of any security of the issuer in the name and in behalf of the issuer if the issuer shall fail or refuse to bring such suit within sixty days after request or shall fail diligently to prosecute the same thereafter; but no such suit shall be brought more than two years after the date such profit was realized. This subsection shall not be construed to cover any transaction where such beneficial owner was not such both at the time of the purchase and sale, or the sale and purchase, of the security involved, or any transaction or transactions which the Commission by rules and regulations may exempt as not comprehended within the purpose of this subsection. (Court's footnote 1.)

881 (S.D.N.Y.1966). But the policy underlying the enactment of § 16
(b) does not permit an expansion of the statute's scope to persons
other than directors, officers, and 10% shareholders. Blau v. Lehman,
368 U.S. 403 (1962). Cf. Ellerin v. Massachusetts Mut. Life Ins. Co.,
270 F.2d 259 (2 Cir. 1959). Through the creation of a legal fiction,
however, our courts have managed to remain within the limits of
§ 16(b)'s literal language and yet have expanded the Act's reach.

In Rattner v. Lehman, 193 F.2d 564 (2 Cir. 1952), Judge Learned
Hand in his concurring opinion planted the seed for a utilization of the
theory of deputization upon which plaintiff here proceeds. In discussing the question whether a partnership is subject to Section 16(b) liability whenever a partner is a director of a corporation whose stock
the partnership traded, Judge Hand stated:

> I agree that § 16(b) does not go so far; but I wish to say
> nothing as to whether, if a firm deputed a partner to represent
> its interests as a director on the board, the other partners would
> not be liable. True, they would not even then be formally "direc-
> tors"; but I am not prepared to say that they could not be so
> considered; for some purposes the common law does treat a firm
> as a jural person. 193 F.2d at 567.

The Supreme Court in Blau v. Lehman, 368 U.S. 403 (1962), affirming 286 F.2d 786 (2 Cir. 1960), affirming 173 F.Supp. 590 (S.D.N.Y.
1959) more firmly established the possibility of an entity, such as a
partnership or a corporation, incurring Section 16(b) liability as a "director" through the deputization theory. Though the Court refused to
reverse the lower court decisions that had held no deputization, it
stated:

> Although admittedly not "literally designated" as one, it is con-
> tended that Lehman is a director. No doubt Lehman Brothers,
> though a partnership, could for purposes of § 16 be a "director"
> of Tide Water and function through a deputy * * *. 368 U.S.
> at 409.

In Marquette Cement Mfg. Co. v. Andreas, 239 F.Supp. 962, 967 (S.D.
N.Y.1965), relying upon Blau v. Lehman, the availability of the deputization theory to impose § 16(b) liability was again recognized. See
also Molybdenum Corp. of America v. International Mining Corp., 32
F.R.D. 415 (S.D.N.Y.1963).

In light of the above authorities, the validity of the deputization
theory, presumed to be valid here by the parties and by the district
court, is unquestionable. Nevertheless, the situations encompassed
by its application are not as clear. The Supreme Court in Blau v.
Lehman intimated that the issue of deputization is a question of fact
to be settled case by case and not a conclusion of law. See 368 U.S. at
408. Therefore, it is not enough for appellant to show us that inferences to support appellant's contentions should have been drawn from
the evidence. Id. at 409. Rather our review of the facts and inferences found by the court below is imprisoned by the "unless clearly erroneous" standard. Fed.R.Civ.P. 52(a). In the instant case, applying

that standard, though there is some evidence in the record to support the trial court's finding of no deputization, we, upon considering the entire evidence, are left with the definite and firm conviction that a mistake was committed. Guzman v. Pichirilo, 369 U.S. 698 (1962); United States v. United States Gypsum Co., 333 U.S. 364 (1948). Consequently, we reverse the result reached below.

Bunker served as a director of Sperry from April 29, 1963 to August 1, 1963, when he resigned. During the period December 14, 1962 through July 24, 1963, Martin Marietta accumulated 801,300 shares of Sperry stock of which 101,300 shares were purchased during Bunker's directorship. Between August 29, 1963 and September 6, 1963, Martin Marietta sold all of its Sperry stock. Plaintiff seeks to reach, on behalf of the Sperry Rand Corporation, the profits made by Martin Marietta from the 101,300 shares of stock acquired between April 29 and August 1, all of which, of course, were sold within six months after purchase.

The district court, in determining that Bunker was not a Martin deputy, made the following findings of fact to support its decision: (1) Sperry initially invited Bunker to join its Board two and a half months before Martin began its accumulation of Sperry stock; (2) Bunker turned down a second offer by Sperry at a time when Martin already held 400,000 shares of Sperry stock; (3) Sperry, not Martin, took the initiative to encourage Bunker to accept the directorship; (4) no other Martin man was ever mentioned for the position in the event Bunker absolutely declined; and (5) Bunker's fine reputation and engineering expertise was the prime motivation for Sperry's interest in him. In addition, the testimony of the only two witnesses who testified at trial, Mr. Bunker and a Mr. Norman Frost, a Sperry director and its chief counsel, were fully believed and accepted as truthful by the court. We assume all of the foregoing findings have a basis of fact in the evidence, but we find there was additional, more germane, uncontradicted evidence, overlooked or ignored by the district court, which we are firmly convinced require us to conclude that Martin Marietta was a "director" of Sperry Rand.

First and foremost is Bunkers' testimony that as chief executive of Martin Marietta he was "ultimately responsible for the total operation of the corporation" including personal approval of all the firm's financial investments, and, in particular, all of Martin's purchases of Sperry stock. As the district court aptly recognized, Bunker's control over Martin Marietta's investments, coupled with his position on the Board of Directors of Sperry Rand, placed him in a position where he could acquire inside information concerning Sperry and could utilize such data for Martin Marietta's benefit without disclosing this information to any other Martin Marietta personnel. Thus, the district court's findings that Bunker "never disclosed inside information relevant to investment decisions" and that the "information that he obtained while a director 'simply wasn't germane to that question at all' " are not significant. 286 F.Supp. at 946. Nor are these findings totally supported by the evidence. Bunker's testimony revealed that while he was a Sperry director three Sperry officials had furnished him with information relating to the "short-range outlook" at Sperry, and, in addition, Bunker admitted discussing Sperry's affairs with two officials at Martin Marietta and participating in sessions when Martin's investment in Sperry was reviewed. Moreover, an unsigned document concededly originating from the Martin Marietta files, entitled "Notes on Exploratory Investment in Sperry Rand Corporation," describing the Sperry management, evaluating their abilities, and analyzing the merit of Sperry's forecasts for the future, further indicates that Martin Marietta may have benefited, or intended to benefit, from Bunker's association with Sperry Rand.

In contrast, in Blau v. Lehman, supra, where Lehman Brothers was the alleged "director," the Lehman partner exercised no power of approval concerning the partnership's investment; was not consulted for advice; had no advance knowledge of Lehman Brothers' intention to purchase the stock of the corporation of which he was a member of the board of directors; and never discussed the operating details of that corporation's affairs with any member of Lehman Brothers. 368 U.S. at 406, 82 S.Ct. at 451. Similarly, in Rattner v. Lehman, supra, the court's decision was premised on the assumption that the defendant's purchases and sales were made without any advice or concurrence from the defendant's partner sitting on the Board of the company in whose stock the defendant traded.

It appears to us that a person in Bunker's unique position could act as a deputy for Martin Marietta even in the absence of factors indicating an intention or belief on the part of both companies that he was so acting. We do not hold that, without more, Bunker's control over Martin Marietta, see Marquette Cement Mfg. Co. v. Andreas, supra at 967, or the possibility that inside information was obtained or disclosed, mandates that Bunker was Martin's deputy. However, additional evidence detailed hereafter which indicates that the managements of Sperry Rand and of Martin Marietta intended that Bunker should act as Martin's deputy on the Sperry Board, and believed he was so acting, lends valuable support to our factual conclusion.

First, in Bunker's letter of resignation to General MacArthur, the Chairman of the Board of Directors of Sperry Rand, he stated:

> When I became a member of the Board in April, it appeared to your associates that the Martin Marietta ownership of a substantial number of shares of Sperry Rand should have representation on your Board. This representation does not seem to me really necessary and I prefer not to be involved in the affairs of Sperry Rand when there are so many other demands on my time
> * * *.

Martin Marietta urges that we should not read this letter to mean what it so clearly says. They would have us believe that this letter was so phrased because Bunker intended "to write a gentle letter of resignation to a great (but elderly) man whom he admired, in terms that he would understand." No matter how advanced in years the Chairman of the Sperry Board may have been, we are puzzled by defendant's contention that he, and only he, of all those on the Sperry Board, considered Bunker to be representing Martin's interests. Furthermore, if, throughout Bunker's service, the Chairman of the Board misunderstood the purpose of Bunker's directorship, why Bunker upon resignation would want this misunderstanding perpetuated is even more perplexing. Certainly the more logical inference from the wording of Bunker's letter of resignation is the inference that Bunker served on the Sperry Board as a representative of Martin Marietta so as to protect Martin's investment in Sperry.

Second, the Board of Directors of Martin Marietta formally consented to and approved Bunker's directorship of Sperry prior to Bunker's acceptance of the position. While Martin's organizational policy required that Bunker secure that Board's approval of any corporate directorship he were offered, the approval was not obtained until, significantly, the Board had been informed by Bunker that Martin had a 10 million dollar investment in Sperry stock at the time. Bunker testified that he "thought the Board would draw the inference that his presence on Sperry's Board would be to Martin's interest." Indeed, as noted by the district court, "the logic behind such an inference is obvious when we stop to consider that a directorship, by its very nature, carries with it potential access to information unavailable to the ordinary investor." 286 F.Supp. at 945. Surely such conduct by the Martin Board supports an inference that it deputized Bunker to represent its interests on Sperry's Board. The trial court's finding to the contrary leaves us with the definite and firm conviction that a mistake was indeed committed.

Finally, Bunker's testimony clearly established that the Martin Marietta Corporation had representatives or deputies who served on the boards of other corporations. The only distinctions drawn by the court below to differentiate Bunker's Sperry relationship from the relationship to Martin Marietta of other Martin Marietta deputies on other corporate boards were that Bunker had no duty to report back to Martin what was going on at Sperry and there was a lesser degree of supervision over Bunker's actions than over the actions of the others. Otherwise Bunker was a typical Martin deputy. In view of Bunker's position of almost absolute authority over Martin's affairs, such differences hardly suffice to refute the evidentiary value of the similarities between the functions of Bunker and those of Martin's representatives on other corporate boards.

In summary, it is our firm conviction that the district court erred in apportioning the weight to be accorded the evidence before it. The control possessed by Bunker, his letter of resignation, the approval by the Martin Board of Bunker's directorship with Sperry, and the functional similarity between Bunker's acts as a Sperry director and the acts of Martin's representatives on other boards, as opposed to the factors relied upon by the trial court, are all definite and concrete indicatives that Bunker, in fact, was a Martin deputy, and we find that indeed he was.

The trial court's disposition of the case obviated the need for it to determine whether § 16(b) liability could attach to the corporate director's short-swing profits realized after the corporation's deputy had ceased to be a member of the board of directors of the corporation whose stock had been so profitably traded in. It was not until after Bunker's resignation from the Sperry Board had become effective that Martin Marietta sold any Sperry stock. The issue is novel and until this case no court has ever considered the question. We hold that the congressional purpose dictates that Martin must disgorge all short-swing profits made from Sperry stock purchased during its Sperry directorship and sold after the termination thereof if sold within six months of purchase.

Relying upon the congressional objectives sought to be accomplished by the passage of § 16(b), this court, in Adler v. Klawans, 267 F.2d 840 (2 Cir. 1959), held that § 16(b) imposes liability to surrender his short-swing profits upon a person who is a director at the date of sale, whether or not he was a director at the date of purchase. The court explained:

> This [the language of § 16(b) itself] makes plain the intent of Congress to reach a "purchase and sale" or "sale and purchase" within a six month period by someone within one of the proscribed categories, i. e., one who was a director, officer or beneficial owner *at some time.*   *   *   *

It must be emphasized, of course, that the statute evidences a clear legislative intent to treat corporate directors and officers in one category of insiders and 10% shareholders in another. The act expressly sets forth that the liability of a 10% shareholder to surrender his short-swing profits is conditional upon his being such both at the time of purchase and at the time of sale but there is no such limitation in the case of officers and directors. 267 F.2d at 845; Blau v. Allen, 163 F.Supp. 702 (S.D.N.Y.1958). See also 2 Loss, Securities Regulation 1060 (2d ed. 1961).

Our decision in *Adler,* however, did not require us to consider the validity of Rule X–16A–10 of the Securities Exchange Commission, 17 C.F.R. § 240.16a–10, which reads:

> Any transaction which has been or shall be exempted by the Commission from the requirements of section 16(a) shall, in so far as it is otherwise subject to the provisions of section 16(b), be likewise exempted from section 16(b).

Section 16(a) of the Act provided, in 1963:

> Every person who is directly or indirectly the beneficial owner of more than 10 per centum of any class of any equity security (other than an exempted security) which is registered on a national securities exchange, or *who is a director* or an officer of the issuer of such security, shall file, at the time of the registration of such security or within ten days *after he becomes such beneficial owner, director, or officer,* a statement with the exchange (and a duplicate original thereof with the Commission) of

the amount of all equity securities of such issuer of which he is the beneficial owner, and within ten days after the close of each calendar month thereafter, if there has been any change in such ownership during such month, shall file with the exchange a statement (and a duplicate original thereof with the Commission) indicating his ownership at the close of the calendar month and such changes in his ownership as have occurred during such calendar month. 15 U.S.C.A. § 78p(a) (1964). (Emphasis supplied.)

On the form provided by the SEC for a director to file his statement of changes in stock ownership, the Commission further clarifies a director's obligation to report under § 16(a), as follows:

Form 4

1. Persons Required to File Statements.

Statements on this form are required to be filed by each of the following persons:

(a) Every person who at any time during any calendar month was (i) directly or indirectly the beneficial owner of more than 10 percent of any class of equity securities (other than exempt securities) listed and registered on a national securities exchange, or (ii) a director or officer of the company which is the issuer of such securities, and who during such month had any change in his beneficial ownership of any class of equity securities of such company * * *.

In *Adler,* this court read this last rule to require a director to report all "changes in his ownership" irrespective of whether the ownership was established "by a director while a director." 267 F.2d at 847. Indeed, § 16(a) itself expressly imposes its requirements on every person "who is a director" or who "becomes such * * * director." Thus, by finding that § 16(a)'s reporting rules extend to a director who became such after the acquisition of securities, we were able to avoid deciding whether Rule X–16A–10 constituted a proper exercise of the Commission's power.

* * *

To be sure, the congressional belief that inside information could be abused, the belief that prompted the prophylactic enactment of § 16(b), is just as germane to the situation when a person is a director only at the time of purchase as when he is a director only at the time of sale. For, in the case of a director who resigns his directorship before the sale it is possible for both the purchase and sale to have been unfairly motivated by insider knowledge; whereas if the purchase were made prior to the directorship only the sale could be motivated by inside information. Clearly, therefore, a "short swing" sale or purchase by a resigning director must be a transaction "comprehended within the purpose of" § 16(b), and to the extent Rule X–16A–10 exempts such a transaction from § 16(b) the Rule is invalid.

* * *

In view of the foregoing, we hold that § 16(b) applies to a sale of corporate stock by a former director of that corporation if the stock were purchased by him (or purchased by any jural person that had "deputized" him) during the time he was a director and the sale was made within six months after purchase.

Under the well-established rule, profits for § 16(b) purposes are computed by arbitrarily matching purchases with sales in order to obtain the maximum amount of profits. Gratz v. Claughton, 187 F.2d 46 (2 Cir. 1951); Smolowe v. Delendo Corporation, 136 F.2d 231 (2 Cir.), cert. denied, 320 U.S. 751 (1943). As the briefs do not agree as to the exact amount of the profits Martin Marietta made and do not give us all the relevant data for us to make a correct determination, and as, additionally, the trial court has discretion in connection with an award of interest in a § 16(b) suit, we remand the case to the district court with instructions to proceed with these determinations.

Reversed and remanded.

QUESTIONS

1. Is freedom of contract, the right to invest or not invest as one chooses, an adequate method of allocating savings for investment in our society? Do funds find their way to the most meritorious investment because of this system? Is a private decision as to the relative merit of an investment superior to one mandated by the government? What happens when socially useful enterprises in need of capital cannot compete adequately for funds with other units seeking capital? Is potential profit a satisfactory method of making this decision? In the short run or the long run? Should a non-profit enterprise, such as a hospital, be required to compete for capital with the profit-making manufacturer of a product which produces lung cancer? Is this the price we pay for freedom of contract? Or should we have a government agency allocating savings to enterprises which we find to be necessary even though no profit can be realized? Is this what we do with tax money? Should government invest in any profit-making organization?

2. Has "full and fair disclosure" of a company and its securities been an adequate method, along with freedom of contract, of channeling savings into investment? Is reliance on independent public accountants an adequate means of achieving full and fair disclosure? Should the SEC itself make the investigation of a company and its securities before allowing a registration statement to become effective? If so, should this investigation be limited to ascertaining that the requirements of government standards in reference to full and fair disclosure have been observed? How much do investors rely on the adequacy of financial statements prepared by independent public accountants? Would they have any greater reliance if the statements were prepared by the SEC? Would a prudent man place greater reliance on these statements?

3. Should the government be allowed to make a judgement about the quality of a security before allowing it to be offered or traded?

How much different would it be if the government were to do this instead of one of several privately owned investment rating services? Are the investment rating services accurate in their judgements? How many prudent investors rely upon their judgements? Should the rating services be required to disclose in full the basis of their rating? Should they be required to discuss this with the issuing company? Should they be prohibited from discussing this with the issuing company? Should the government establish standards for rating services to follow both in their internal operations as well as in making a judgement about a security?

4.   In reference to a registration statement prepared to accompany an offering of securities, should all directors of the corporation be held equally liable for inadequacies in the statement? Specifically, in the *BarChris* case, should Auslander and Rose, men who became directors on the eve of the effective date of the registration statement, have been equally liable with Russo? Did they have the chance to make a reasonable investigation of the "unexpertised" portion of the registration statement? Did the public investors know that they had made no investigation, reasonable or otherwise? If not, should the public investors have been notified that they did not? What would this have done to the offering of the securities? Would the underwriters have taken the issue if Auslander and Rose had said that they made no reasonable investigation of any portion of the registration statement? If not, why should the public investor be asked to buy the securities without this information? Should the underwriters be excused from liability where information is not given to them which could cause the investing public a loss? Should the Securities Act focus on benefiting the issuing company so it can market its securities rather than protecting the public investor? Suppose the purpose of the Act were completely reversed and the issuer could deceive the investor and the latter were prohibited from obtaining information; would savings be invested?

5.   Is it valid to assume that the securities markets must be maintained and operated for the primary benefit of the public investor? What other kinds of property are sold in our society with all of his solicitude? Consider the market for secondhand automobiles: is the manufacturer of the automobiles required by law to publish quarterly and annual reports about each of the automobiles (securities) which it has previously put into the market so that buyers and sellers of these automobiles will have full and fair disclosure about the company and its products? What is peculiar about securities that has led to the Securities Acts? Is it really much easier to practice fraud and deceit in the issuance, purchase and sales of securities than it is in other kinds of property? Aside from the fact that the land upon which Texas Gulf Sulphur made its fortunate mineral strike was in Canada, why did we require a fair press release concerning this information for the benefit of security holders but no similar disclosure to land holders from whom leases were being sought? Is there any greater potential for unfair dealing in securities than there is in other types of prop-

erty? Or is the necessity of maintaining public confidence in the securities markets, as a part of channeling savings into investments in our economy more important than maintaining confidence in the fairness of the market place for other kinds of property?

6.   Should an investment banking firm which is preparing for an underwriting be prohibited from executing any orders for the purchase or sale of securities of the issuer for any of its customers while it is preparing the registration statement? Should the underwriting and brokerage functions be completely separated? Should the information which a brokerage firm obtains in any manner be made immediately available to all customers of that brokerage firm? Or should it be concealed entirely, whether or not the firm is preparing to participate in an underwriting? How can an issuing company be protected against every idle rumor which comes to the attention of the brokerage firm? Could an effective distribution of new securities be made if underwriters were not able to have their normal brokerage customers available as potential purchasers of new issues? Is it really essential to the underwriting function for the firm to have continuing business in the form of brokerage commissions on the purchase and sale of existing securities? What would an underwriting firm do between offerings if it could not participate in the brokerage business?

7.   Are stockholders' derivative suits an adequate method of enforcing the rights of public shareholders to recover insiders' short-swing profits? Does the speculative nature of a substantial attorney's fee to be paid out of the amount recovered serve the public well? Should we devise some other method for recovering short-swing profits? Should the SEC be the sole body to seek recovery of short-swing profits? With the expense of this activity to come from the general revenues? Or should the realization of short-swing profits be made a criminal offense? To be enforced by the Justice Department? What about the constitutional prohibition against self-incrimination in reference to the periodic reports which must be filed by insiders? Is it better to have these reports than a potential criminal prosecution? Or should we prevent any officer or director from holding any of the securities of the company which he serves? Should we deny any shareholder the right to be a director or an officer of the corporation? Or deny him access to any information which is not available to the investing public generally? How can we improve the flow of information to the potential buyers and sellers of securities so that they will be making their investment decisions on the same basis as the person with whom they are dealing? Do many of the public investors really want this much information? Is full and fair disclosure really the answer to these problems in a free society? If not, should one substitute a government system of licensing to buy or to sell securities? If so, what would the conditions be upon which a license would be issued? What would this do to our traditional notions of the free transferability of private property?

8.   Do the securities markets exist only to make people rich? Brokers? Speculators? Issuers? Investors?

Suggested Reference Sources

Texts and Treatises

Fletcher, *Cyclopedia of the Law of Private Corporations.* Callaghan & Company, Mundelein, Illinois.

Israels & Guttman, *Modern Securities Transfers.* Warren, Gorham & Lamont, Boston, Massachusetts.

Loss, *Securities Regulation.* Little, Brown & Co., Boston, Massachusetts.

Loose-Leaf Services

Commerce Clearing House, Blue Sky Reporter. Chicago, Illinois

Commerce Clearing House, Federal Securities Law Reporter, Chicago, Illinois.

Prentice-Hall, Securities Regulation Service, Englewood Heights, N. J.

Topic Headings in the Index to Legal Periodicals

Securities

Stocks

Chapter VI

BUSINESS ACQUISITIONS AND DIVISIONS

A. PURCHASE AND SALE OF ASSETS

---

1. INTRODUCTORY NOTE

Freedom of contract, freedom of choice, allows a business enterprise to expand or contract as its owners or managers decide. Mobility into new territory has already been briefly discussed in Chapter II; this mobility can involve an expansion of the production facilities or a complete removal of them from one location to another. The expansion can also involve the acquisition of another business enterprise in the same, or a related, or a completely different business. Aside from the anti-trust laws (dealt with primarily in Chapter VII, below) our system permits individuals to expand in any manner they choose. There is no government agency directing any production unit to increase or decrease its capacity or sales or employees or investment, or directing it to establish additional production facilities in a new territory. Part of the freedom we cherish permits only private persons and institutions to make these decisions; we deny this power to the government. This system exists partly because of the due process of law provisions of the Vth and XIVth Amendments to the Federal Constitution and partly because we will not permit our elected representatives in Congress, as a political matter, to enact legislation which would change the system.

A democratic society as we know it provides for the private ownership of property. While there are undoubtedly many persons who hold that this is not a necessary attribute of a democracy, nonetheless it is one of the characteristics of those societies which do think of themselves as being democratic. It should be recognized that the development of resources and the production of goods had been accomplished under political and legal systems where the means of production (business property) have not been privately owned. But where business property is privately owned, some means of transferring the property must exist if the society is to continue to be viable. Many centuries ago the English common law evolved the concepts of prohibiting restraints on alienation (limitations on the transfer of property) and prohibiting perpetuities (tieing up the ownership of property perpetually). Both of these rules of law require that property must be transferable after a limited period of time, generally not exceeding the lifetime of some person who is alive at the time that the restrictions on its transfer are imposed. This was followed several centuries later by the development of the law of trusts which was later followed by the development of the law of wills, which together made it possible for an English gentleman to transfer property to members of his family other than his firstborn son; that is, the rule of primogeniture relating to the devolution of property was ended. This has resulted in our modern practice of freely transferable private property, transferable by its owners to any person at any price and under any terms and conditions that the parties may agree upon, a practice which has its roots as deep in our legal system as any other practice.

The needs of the government for revenue have been dealt with in other Chapters. Taxes on the transfers of property are a common method of taxation. Sales and use taxes on all kinds of property abound and in Western Europe are being called "value-added" taxes when imposed on business transactions. Taxes on capital gains are another form of taxes on the transfer of property, although they do not necessarily add to the cost of a product in the same manner as sales and use taxes. In order not to inhibit unduly the transfer of business properties our legal system, paralleling the modern growth of business, developed the concepts found in Sections 334(b) (2) and 337 of the Internal Revenue Code (26 U.S.C.A.), discussed infra, whereby the taxpayer does have some opportunity of relieving what otherwise would be a tax burden on the transfer of a business enterprise. Thus we attempt to continue to maintain our system of freedom of contract and freedom of choice whereby a business property may be transferred by its owners largely without governmental restraint; we have no governmental agency directing sellers to sell to specified purchasers, nor directing buyers to buy from specified sellers, whether buyers or sellers are private parties or governmental agencies.

If the managers of one business enterprise determine to expand the business by acquiring another business enterprise, the form of the acquisition will mainly be dependent upon the size of the business enterprise to be acquired. If it be a large one (admittedly a relative word) it will usually have had its financial statements prepared by a firm of independent public accountants who will have rendered their customary opinion relating to the information set forth in the financial statements. Further, periodic reports will have been filed with the Securities and Exchange Commission, again with certifications prepared by an independent public accounting firm. Great reliance is placed upon the authenticity of the information contained in these financial statements and reports. Frequently the public accounting firm will be one of eight or ten such firms with national and international reputations. Although a detailed and searching examination into the business and affairs of the enterprise to be acquired will be made by a purchaser, nonetheless with this information before it, the acquiring corporation can make an estimate of the value of the business to be acquired and thus enter into negotiations substantially well informed about the selling corporation. Because of this there is not much reluctance to buy the outstanding stock from the stockholders of the corporation to be acquired. Also, the transaction generally can be consummated more efficiently and quickly because the selling stockholders will have received a firm offer for their stock and can anticipate exactly how much money or securities they will receive for the sale of their stock; they will not need to be concerned with having their corporation sell its assets, pay all of its liabilities, and then distribute the balance to its stockholders in a liquidation of the selling corporation. Further, the directors of a liquidating corporation are generally reluctant to make distributions to shareholders until all the detailed steps required by the law of the state of incorporation relating to the liquidation of a corporation have been complied with, primarily the payment of all claims to creditors, some of which may not even be known. Directors may incur personal liability for the distribution of corporate assets to shareholders ahead of the payment of all liabilities of the corporation. Thus, a transaction of this kind from the viewpoint of the shareholder in the selling corporation may be drawn out for a year or more, whereas, the sale of his stock will normally result in payment within six to eight weeks, sometimes within seven to ten days, of an amount known precisely to him instead of some prospective amount to be paid to him at some indefinite time in the future in a corporate liquidation.

If the business to be acquired be a small (again a relative word) corporation, the acquiring corporation will nearly always want to purchase the assets of the seller. While financial statements will undoubtedly exist, they will frequently have been prepared by an accounting firm "without audit" and there will be no representation by any independent auditors as to the authenticity of the information contained in the financial statements. Under these circumstances the extent of the earnings as well as the liabilities of the selling corporation, both direct and contingent, may not be fully stated and again may not even be known to the managers and proprietors of the selling business. This failure to state fully all the liabilities of the selling corporation is hardly ever the consequence of intentional deceit; it frequently will arise because of the lack of knowledge or lack of sophistication of the managers and proprietors of the selling business as to the full extent of their contingent liabilities, or the delay in processing the income tax returns of the business enterprise by the Internal Revenue Service which may assess liabilities for additional taxes at any time within three years after the filing of a return (and under certain circumstances an even longer period), or the failure of the selling business to maintain a sufficient amount of liability insurance to cover claims against it for the product or services it has been producing which may not come to the surface for a period of two or more years. As to the potential income tax liability, a small business will frequently have been operated on the premise that the business and its managers are entitled to the benefit of every doubt which they can conceive in connection with stating the amount of tax liability of their enterprise; this frequently leads to an assessment of additional taxes when the returns of the business are audited.

In a large public corporation, where the controls of an independent auditing firm, and the requirement of full and fair disclosure in annual reports to stockholders and to the Securities and Exchange Commission exist, the margin of potential error in income tax liability is substantially reduced. The larger company will carry large amounts of liability insurance, or if the business be large enough, it will maintain adequate reserves for its liability of this kind (and be a so-called "self-insurer") and the potential exposure to claims of this kind will frequently be a very small fraction of the net worth of the selling business.

Further, an acquiring corporation most frequently will desire to buy the assets of a small corporation because of the potentially favorable tax treatment available in a transaction of this kind. The buyer and the seller can negotiate, item by item, the purchase price to be paid for the assets and unless the negotiated prices are grossly unrealistic, these prices will be recognized by the Internal Revenue Service and independent accounting firms as the cost or basis of the acquired assets in the hands of the purchaser. The amount paid for inventory, for example, will become the cost of this item when it is later sold in the normal course of business by the acquiring corporation; if a relatively high price has been paid for the inventory, the profit to be made by the acquirer on the resale will be smaller, and thus his income tax on the subsequent operation will be diminished. On the other hand, if a relatively low price is paid for the inventory, the subsequent resale will produce a higher profit, and, other things being equal, will produce both a higher net profit and a higher income tax on the subsequent transaction. In much the same manner, if tangible assets which are subject to depreciation are purchased at a relatively high price, the purchaser will have a higher base on which to charge depreciation against future operations, and thus diminish the income tax liability for future years; and the reverse is also true. Also, land is not subject to any depreciation allowance for income tax purposes and the acquirer's normal desire would be to negotiate as low a price as is possible for the land to be purchased thus not committing a greater amount of capital than is necessary to permanent investment in the enterprise without recapturing any part of it through a reduction in earnings and income taxes as a result of a depreciation allowance. In this respect, goodwill is also like land; it is not subject to any depreciation or amortization allowance for tax purposes although sound accounting practices may require that goodwill be amortized over a minimum period of years in order to state fairly the earnings of the business enterprise.

The acquiring corporation may have divergent interests in negotiating the purchase price of the individual assets of a business, or in allocating a lump sum purchase price on its books for those assets. As indicated above, if the managers of the acquiring corporation are interested in showing an early profit in the business acquired by them, their interest will be to allocate as much of the purchase price as feasibly can be done to assets which will not be subject to a depreciation or amortization allowance for income tax purposes, that is, to land and goodwill, even though this may result in a higher income tax liability in the immediate future. At the same time, their interest will be to allocate as little of the purchase price to inventory so that a quick profit can be made on the sale of this inventory in the period of operation immediately after the acquisition. In the same manner, but at a lower rate, less of the purchase price may be allocated to assets subject to a depreciation or amortization allowance because this will reduce the expense of future operations. It should be noted, however, that changing the rate of depreciation by extending it over a longer period of time could also have much the same effect without reducing the amount allocated to these particular assets.

Thus the acquiring corporation will nearly always want to buy the assets of a small business enterprise and not the stock from the stockholders. While an adequately drafted contract of sale will contain warranties and representations made by the selling corporation, as well as its principal stockholders, under which the authenticity of financial information (as well as other information) supplied by the latter to the acquiring corporation, will be warranted as being true and correct, after a transaction has been completed and errors in the information have been discovered, the remedies for breach of warranties available to the acquiring corporation are generally unsatisfactory. It will have a new business on its hands; it is impractical to think in terms of returning it to the sellers (either the selling corporation or its principal stockholders) because by the time the errors are discovered the selling corporation will most likely be in the process of dissolution or have been dissolved, and its directors and shareholders will no longer be able to return all the money (they will undoubtedly have paid a substantial amount of money in taxes), and the business itself will have undoubtedly changed its method of operation, its relationship with its customers, and its personnel and personnel policies. This frequently happens very quickly so that the business is no longer the same business as the one which was sold even a short time before. That is, a rescission of the transaction is not feasible because neither the buyer nor the seller can be restored to his position prior to the consummation of the transaction. Therefore, the negotiations for the acquisition must contemplate that it will be irreversible and that the buyer must seek other forms of protection for the performance of the obligations undertaken by the sellers in connection with the sale. If tangible assets have been purchased at their fair market value (about which reasonable minds can differ) the acquiring corporation will not have much cause for complaint. If a substantial sum of money has been paid for goodwill, and the earning capacity of the acquired business has been overstated or over-estimated as a consequence of errors in the financial statements provided to the buyer by the seller, then the buyer may consider negotiating some form of indemnity from the seller, perhaps to be secured by a portion of the purchase price which may be in the form of notes, debentures, or bonds of the buyer. At the same time the seller may resist this type of negotiation or resist having part of the payment of the purchase price deferred because it will complicate his tax problems (discussed below) or because he will have an aversion to any deferment.

If the acquiring corporation does purchase the stock from the shareholders of the selling corporation, whether it be a large or small business, the acquiring corporation can get some, but not all, of the tax advantages available when the transaction is cast as an acquisition of assets. Section 334(b) (2) of the Internal Revenue Code permits an acquiring corporation to use the price which it has paid for the stock of the acquired corporation as the basis for determining depreciation allowances to be used in the future, rather than the basis on the books of the acquired corporation of those assets which would be the normal method of treating this matter for income tax purposes. This may be done only if at least 80% of the stock of the acquired corporation was acquired by purchase within a twelve month period, and if the buying corporation later transferred the assets to itself pursuant to a plan of complete liquidation adopted within two years of the purchase of the stock. (It should be noted that the *plan* of liquidation must be adopted within the two year period; actually, under the provisions of Section 332(b) (3) the liquidation may be spread over a three year period following the adoption of the plan.) However, in this type of transaction the basis of the property acquired in the liquidation is allocated in direct proportion to the fair market value of the assets. There is no opportunity for the kind of "juggling" which is possible where the assets are purchased directly on a negotiated item by item basis. Section 334(b) (2) was adopted by Congress in the 1954 revision of the Internal Revenue Code as a consequence of the decision of the Tax Court in the leading case of Kimbell-Diamond Milling Co. v. Commissioner, 14 T.C. 74, aff'd per curiam, 187 F.2d 718 (5th Cir.1951), cert. denied, 342 U.S. 827 (1951), a case which is reported below.

From the viewpoint of the seller many, but not all, of the difficult tax problems occurring in the sale of a business have been eliminated. Section 337 of the Internal Revenue Code (26 U.S.C.A.), adopted in 1954, provides for the nonrecognition of gain or loss at the corporate level on the sale of corporate assets pursuant to a plan of liquidation where the liquidation is completed within twelve months of the date of the adoption of the plan. This has eliminated most of the tax problems of the seller where the transaction is cast in the terms of the sale of assets of the corporation. Briefly in this type of transaction the selling corporation arranges for the sale of its assets to a buyer and if it realizes a profit on the sale, there is no tax imposed on the corporation on this profit providing the requirements of Section 337 are met. While the sale of inventory in the normal course of business would result in ordinary income, and this applies if inventory is sold on a piece-meal basis in the ordinary course of business even if done under a plan of liquidation, nonetheless, if substantially all the inventory is sold in one transaction to one person, then under the provisions of Section 337(b) (2) this will qualify for the tax benefit noted above. There are other limitations to the non-recognition of gain which apply to installment obligations which have been received by the selling corporation in its normal business prior to the adoption of the plan of liquidation; the profit realized on the sale of these assets will be taxable, generally, as ordinary income received by the corporation.

Under the provisions of Section 337 a complete distribution of the assets of the corporation must be made to the shareholders within twelve months after the adoption of the plan of liquidation. What the shareholders receive in liquidation is then treated as a payment being made in exchange for their stock and in nearly every case will result in the transaction being taxed to them as a capital gain (or loss). (It is recognized that there are a few shareholders whose business is buying and selling stock for their own account, rather than for investment purposes, and as to these shareholders there is always the possibility that the transaction will be taxable as ordinary income.) Thus the net effect of Section 337 is that when a corporate business is to be sold, the corporation can sell its assets and not pay any tax on the profit, then pay all of its creditors, and distribute the balance of its money or other property received in connection with the sale to its shareholders in liquidation of the corporation. If the shareholders receive more in liquidation than the basis of their stock, and have held the stock for more than six months, then they will be taxed at long term capital gains rates; if they receive less, then they realize a long term capital loss which may or may not be useful to them in connection with other transactions affecting their taxation. Because this type of transaction most frequently occurs in a corporation with a limited number of shareholders, and because the directors themselves are frequently the principal shareholders, there is less reluctance on the part of the directors to make an interim distribution to the shareholders prior to the complete satisfaction of all the liabilities of the corporation. It is obvious that they will be able to recoup from themselves, if necessary, the amounts which would be needed to pay to creditors if the interim distribution has been paid in excess of the amount which is finally determined to be due to the shareholders. As noted above, directors of large public corporations would be most reluctant to make this kind of interim distribution; in fact, they should be advised against it.

But the sellers' problems are not always so simple. Sections 1245 and 1250 of the Internal Revenue Code impose taxes at ordinary income rates on the recapture of depreciation upon a sale of depreciated property at a price in excess of its adjusted basis, in both cases without reference to any other relief provisions of the Internal Revenue Code. This would mean that even though Section 337 provides for the non-recognition of gain to the selling corporation in a transaction which meets the requirements of that Section, the corporation will have to include as ordinary income the amount of the depreciation which it recaptures on a sale or any other disposition of personal property on which it had previously taken an allowance for depreciation, or as to real estate, on the amount of depreciation taken by it in excess of the straight line method of depreciation, so-called "additional depreciation." Further, even though an acquiring corporation, under the provisions of Section 334(b) (2), may use the price which it has paid for the stock of an acquired corporation as the basis for the assets of the acquired corporation which it later liquidates, ordinary income will be realized by the liquidating corporation (the acquired corporation) when this event occurs, measured by the amount of depreciation recaptured through the allocation of the purchase price over and above the basis of the assets on the books of the liquidating corporation. Many small business corporations are operated by their owner-managers on a policy of reducing income taxes of the business enterprise to a minimum level, but the same persons frequently find that they have not been operating their business with a view to its sale at a minimum tax cost. The taxes to be paid on the recapture of depreciation are a good example of this because many small enterprises will operate on the basis of using the most rapid method of depreciation allowed to them.

Section 1245 of the Internal Revenue Code (26 U.S.C.A.) imposes a tax at ordinary income rates on the recaptured depreciation which has previously been claimed on "Section 1245 property" which briefly is any personal property which has been the subject of a depreciation or amortization allowance, although there are some exceptions to this rule. Section 1250 similarly imposes a tax on the recapture of depreciation which has previously been claimed on real estate, although since 1970 there are rather complex rules relating to the method of computing the amount of depreciation which has been recaptured, where the depreciation has been claimed partly before January 1, 1970, and partly after that date. Reference must be made to this part of the income tax law to determine the taxability of the sale of real estate which has been the subject of a depreciation allowance. Prior to the adoption of these two provisions the amount received by a seller for a capital asset over its adjusted basis (its depreciated cost on its books) was taxed as a capital gain. The point of both of these sections is, however, that a sale, exchange, or other disposition of depreciable property at a price in excess of the adjusted basis of the property will result in ordinary income to the extent of the recapture of the depreciation on personal property or additional depreciation on real estate, even though the asset being sold is a capital asset. (Of course, the excess of the price being received over and above the original cost of the asset will be taxed as a capital gain.)

While tax problems are predominately the problems which must be dealt with on the purchase or sale of a small business enterprise they are not by any means the only ones. Some of the other problems are almost routine such as the applicability of Article VI of the Uniform Commercial Code relating to bulk sales where assets are being sold, or Article VIII relating to stock transfers where stock is being sold. If the acquiring corporation is at all prominent in its industry, then the impact of the anti-trust laws on the acquisition of another unit in that or a related industry must be considered. Also, in connection with the purchase of securities of publicly held companies, the Rules of the Securities and Exchange Commission and the rules of various stock exchanges must be considered. These problems are dealt with in the next section on the subject of mergers and reorganizations.

COMMISSIONER OF INTERNAL REVENUE v. COURT HOLDING CO.

Supreme Court of the United States, 1945.
324 U.S. 331, 65 S.Ct. 707, 89 L.Ed. 981.

Mr. Justice BLACK delivered the opinion of the Court.

An apartment house, which was the sole asset of the respondent corporation, was transferred in the form of a liquidating dividend to the corporation's two shareholders. They in turn formally conveyed it to a purchaser who had originally negotiated for the purchase from the corporation. The question is whether the Circuit Court of Appeals properly reversed the Tax Court's conclusion that the corporation was taxable under Section 22 of the Internal Revenue Code for the gain which accrued from the sale. The answer depends upon whether the findings of the Tax Court that the whole transaction showed a sale by the corporation rather than by the stockholders were final and binding upon the Circuit Court of Appeals.

It is unnecessary to set out in detail the evidence introduced before the Tax Court or its findings. Despite conflicting evidence, the following findings of the Tax Court are supported by the record:

The respondent corporation was organized in 1934 solely to buy and hold the apartment building which was the only property ever owned by it. All of its outstanding stock was owned by Minnie Miller and her husband. Between October 1, 1939 and February, 1940, while the corporation still had legal title to the property, negotiations for its sale took place. These negotiations were between the corporation and the lessees of the property, together with a sister and brother-in-law. An oral agreement was reached as to the terms and conditions of sale, and on February 22, 1940, the parties met to reduce the agreement to writing. The purchaser was then advised by the corporation's attorney that the sale could not be consummated because it would result in the imposition of a large income tax on the corporation. The next day, the corporation declared a "liquidating dividend", which involved complete liquidation of its assets, and surrender of all outstanding stock. Mrs. Miller and her husband surrendered their stock, and the building was deeded to them. A sale contract was then drawn, naming the Millers individually as vendors, and the lessees' sister as vendee, which embodied substantially the same terms and conditions previously agreed upon. One thousand dollars, which a month and a half earlier had been paid to the corporation by the lessees, was applied in part payment of the purchase price. Three days later, the property was conveyed to the lessees' sister.

The Tax Court concluded from these facts that, despite the declaration of a "liquidating dividend" followed by the transfers of legal title, the corporation had not abandoned the sales negotiations; that these were mere formalities designed "to make the transaction appear to be other than what it was", in order to avoid tax liability. The Circuit Court of Appeals drawing different inferences from the record, held that the corporation had "called off" the sale, and treated the stockholders' sale as unrelated to the prior negotiations.

There was evidence to support the findings of the Tax Court, and its findings must therefore be accepted by the courts. Dobson v. Commissioner of Internal Revenue, 320 U.S. 489; Commissioner of Internal Revenue v. Heininger, 320 U.S. 467; Commissioner of Internal Revenue v. Scottish American Investment Co., 323 U.S. 119. On the basis of these findings, the Tax Court was justified in attributing the gain from the sale to respondent corporation. The incidence of taxation depends upon the substance of a transaction. The tax consequences which arise from gains from a sale of property are not finally to be determined solely by the means employed to transfer legal title. Rather, the transaction must be viewed as a whole, and each step, from the commencement of negotiations to the consummation of the sale, is relevant. A sale by one person cannot be transformed for tax purposes into a sale by another by using the latter as a conduit through which to pass title. To permit the true nature of a transaction to be disguised by mere formalisms, which exist solely to alter tax liabilities, would seriously impair the effective administration of the tax policies of Congress.

It is urged that respondent corporation never executed a written agreement, and that an oral agreement to sell land cannot be enforced in Florida because of the Statute of Frauds, Comp.Gen.Laws of Florida, 1927, vol. 3, Sec. 5779, F.S.A. § 725.01. But the fact that respondent corporation itself never executed a written contract is unimportant, since the Tax Court found from the facts of the entire transaction that the executed sale was in substance the sale of the corporation. The decision of the Circuit Court of Appeals is reversed, and that of the Tax Court affirmed.

It is so ordered.

Reversed.

UNITED STATES v. CUMBERLAND PUBLIC SERVICE CO.

Supreme Court of the United States, 1950.
338 U.S. 451, 70 S.Ct. 280, 94 L.Ed. 251.

Mr. Justice BLACK delivered the opinion of the Court.

A corporation selling its physical properties is taxed on capital gains resulting from the sale. There is no corporate tax, however, on distribution of assets in kind to shareholders as part of a genuine liquidation. The respondent corporation transferred property to its shareholders as a liquidating dividend in kind. The shareholders transferred it to a purchaser. The question is whether, despite contrary findings by the Court of Claims, this record requires a holding that the transaction was in fact a sale by the corporation subjecting the corporation to a capital gains tax.

Details of the transaction are as follows. The respondent, a closely held corporation, was long engaged in the business of generating and distributing electric power in three Kentucky counties. In 1936 a local cooperative began to distribute Tennessee Valley Authority power in the area served by respondent. It soon became obvious that respondent's Diesel-generated power could not compete with TVA power, which respondent had been unable to obtain. Respondent's shareholders, realizing that the corporation must get out of the power business unless it obtained TVA power, accordingly offered to sell all the corporate stock to the cooperative, which was receiving such power. The cooperative refused to buy the stock, but countered with an offer to buy from the corporation its transmission and distribution equipment. The corporation rejected the offer because it would have been compelled to pay a heavy capital gains tax. At the same time the shareholders, desiring to save payment of the corporate capital gains tax, offered to acquire the transmission and distribution equipment and then sell to the cooperative. The cooperative accepted. The corporation transferred the transmission and distribution systems to its shareholders in partial liquidation. The remaining assets were sold and the corporation dissolved. The shareholders than executed the previously contemplated sale to the cooperative.

Upon this sale by the shareholders, the Commissioner assessed and collected a $17,000 tax from the corporation on the theory that the shareholders had been used as a mere conduit for effectuating what was really a corporate sale. Respondent corporation brought this action to recover the amount of the tax. The Court of Claims found that the method by which the stockholders disposed of the properties was avowedly chosen in order to reduce taxes, but that the liquidation and dissolution genuinely ended the corporation's activities and existence. The court also found that at no time did the corporation plan to make the sale itself. Accordingly it found as a fact that the sale was made by the shareholders rather than the corporation, and entered judgment for respondent. One judge dissented, believing that our opinion in Com'rs v. Court Holding Co., 324 U.S. 331, required a finding that the sale had been made by the corporation. Certiorari was granted, 338 U.S. 846, to clear up doubts arising out of the Court Holding Co. case.

Our Court Holding Co. decision rested on findings of fact by the Tax Court that a sale had been made and gains realized by the taxpayer corporation. There the corporation had negotiated for sale of its assets and had reached an oral agreement of sale. When the tax consequences of the corporate sale were belatedly recognized, the corporation purported to "call off" the sale at the last minute and distributed the physical properties in kind to the stockholders. They promptly conveyed these properties to the same persons who had negotiated with the corporation. The terms of purchase were substantially those of the previous oral agreement. One thousand dollars already paid to the corporation was applied as part payment of the purchase price. The Tax Court found that the corporation never really abandoned its sales negotiations, that it never did dissolve, and that the sole purpose of the so-called liquidation was to disguise a corporate sale through use of mere formalisms in order to avoid tax liability. The Circuit Court of Appeals took a different view of the evidence. In this Court the Government contended that whether a liquidation distribution was genuine or merely a sham was traditionally a question of fact. We agreed with this contention, and reinstated the Tax Court's findings and judgment. Discussing the evidence which supported the findings of fact, we went on to say that "the incidence of taxation depends upon the substance of a transaction" regardless of "mere formalisms," and that taxes on a corporate sale cannot be avoided by using the shareholders as a "conduit through which to pass title."

This language does not mean that a corporation can be taxed even when the sale has been made by its stockholders following a genuine liquidation and dissolution. While the distinction between sales by a corporation as compared with distribution in kind followed by shareholder sales may be particularly shadowy and artificial when the corporation is closely held, Congress has chosen to recognize such a distinction for tax purposes. The corporate tax is thus aimed primarily at the profits of a going concern. This is true despite the fact that gains realized from corporate sales are taxed, perhaps to prevent tax evasions, even where the cash proceeds are at once distributed in liquidation. But Congress has imposed no tax on liquidating distributions in kind or on dissolution, whatever may be the motive for such liquidation. Consequently, a corporation may liquidate or dissolve without subjecting itself to the corporate gains tax, even though a primary motive is to avoid the burden of corporate taxation.

Here, on the basis of adequate subsidiary findings, the Court of Claims has found that the sale in question was made by the stockholders rather than the corporation. The Government's argument that the shareholders acted as a mere "conduit" for a sale by respondent corporation must fall before this finding. The subsidiary finding that a major motive of the shareholders was to reduce taxes does not bar this conclusion. Whatever the motive and however relevant it may be in determining whether the transaction was real or a sham, sales of physical properties by shareholders following a genuine liquidation distribution cannot be attributed to the corporation for tax purposes.

The oddities in tax consequences that emerge from the tax provisions here controlling appear to be inherent in the present tax pattern. For a corporation is taxed if it sells all its physical properties and distributes the cash proceeds as liquidating dividends, yet is not taxed if that property is distributed in kind and is then sold by the shareholders. In both instances the interest of the shareholders in the business has been transferred to the purchaser. Again, if these stockholders had succeeded in their original effort to sell all their stock, their interest would have been transferred to the purchasers just as effectively. Yet on such a transaction the corporation would have realized no taxable gain.

Congress having determined that different tax consequences shall flow from different methods by which the shareholders of a closely held corporation may dispose of corporate property, we accept its mandate. It is for the trial court, upon consideration of an entire transaction, to determine the factual category in which a particular transaction belongs. Here as in the Court Holding Co. case we accept the ultimate findings of fact of the trial tribunal. Accordingly the judgment of the Court of Claims is affirmed.

Affirmed.

Mr. Justice DOUGLAS took no part in the consideration or decision of this case.

PRIDEMARK, INC. v. COMMISSIONER OF INTERNAL REVENUE

United States Court of Appeals, Fourth Circuit, 1965.
345 F.2d 35.

SOBELOFF, Circuit Judge. This petition for review principally challenges the determination of the Tax Court sustaining the Commissioner's application of the "reincorporation" doctrine, and his denial of an exemption from taxation to proceeds from the sale of certain sales contracts by liquidating corporations. The facts are fully set forth in Judge Pierce's opinion and we shall here state only those we deem essential.

Pridemark, Inc., one of the petitioners in this case, was incorporated in 1946 under the laws of Maryland, with a paid-in capital of $6,000 represented by 5,000 shares of common stock. From that date until February, 1958, Pridemark was the exclusive dealer for prefabricated homes resigned and manufactured by Golden Key Homes, Inc.

In 1950, Eugene Blitz, another petitioner, became president and sole shareholder of Pridemark. A new contract was signed with Golden Key whereby Pridemark was granted the exclusive right to sell Golden Key homes. Pridemark, in turn, was required to submit all contracts to Golden Key for approval and to purchase prefabricated homes solely from that manufacturer.

The second corporate petitioner, Pridemark, Inc. of Connecticut, was formed in 1952 by Eugene Blitz with a capital investment of $5,000 to act as Pridemark's selling agent in Connecticut. The two selling corporations maintained their principal offices at the same Baltimore location and were managed by the same personnel. They will be treated as one corporation for the purposes of this opinion.

The gross receipts of these petitioner corporations reached a peak of $3,178,042 in the fiscal year in 1956, then declined until gross receipts were only $1,791,266 in 1958. Less than $6,000 in total dividends was paid out during the 12 years of the corporation's existence preceding the year of liquidation.

As sales decreased the relationship between the petitioners and their supplier, Golden Key, steadily worsened. Controversies arose concerning the resale price at which the homes were to be sold and the emphasis to be placed in Pridemark's advertising campaigns on the respective trade names of the manufacturer and the dealer corporations. Several meetings were held during 1956 and 1957 to resolve these differences. In one of these conferences Eugene Blitz stated that he thought Pridemark would "do better" if it obtained another supplier. Finally, during a particularly heated discussion in the middle of 1957, Eugene Blitz suggested that the dealership be terminated so that another supplier could be obtained.

After several offers and counteroffers it was agreed that Golden Key would select and purchase those assets owned by Pridemark which the manufacturer thought valuable. Golden Key would then proceed to carry on its own selling operations. By an agreement dated February 3, 1958, Golden Key contracted to purchase all of Pridemark's customer contracts on which no deliveries had been made, leases on branch offices, customer lists and good will. Pridemark retained its Baltimore office and its corporate name because Golden Key did not think them worth purchasing. The purchase price was $174,866, $134,400 of which represented uncompleted contracts.

Before the sale, in January, 1958, the Board of Directors of Pridemark voted to dissolve the corporation. Eugene Blitz then held all the common stock as trustee for a voting trust of which he was an 80% beneficial owner. He also held all of the Class B preferred, with a par value of $100,000. Various employees held the Class A preferred, having a par value of $8,600. The A preferred was redeemed in July, 1958, and is not in issue here.

During the last half of 1958 approximately $108,000 was distributed to beneficiaries of the voting trust. The B preferred, held solely by Eugene Blitz, was redeemed in January, 1959, for $127,167, and the remaining assets, mostly uncollected accounts receivable, were conveyed directly to the five voting trust beneficiaries. They in turn reconveyed them to Eugene Blitz as trustee to dispose of as he saw fit. There was no testimony that the stockholders were under any legal or moral compulsion to reconvey their assets to Blitz. The only evidence indicates that this was done in order to enable him to collect the debts owed Pridemark.

Pridemark, Inc. of Connecticut, the common stock of which Eugene Blitz owned approximately 74%, was liquidated in the same manner.   Articles of dissolution for the two corporations were filed in Maryland and Connecticut.

I

If, when the individual petitioners dissolved Pridemark, they had permanently abandoned the selling of prefabricated homes it would have been clear that there had been a "complete liquidation" within the meaning of sections 331 and 337.[1]   The distributions to the shareholders would then be treated as a redemption of stock rather than a dividend, and sales of capital assets by the liquidating corporation would be tax exempt.   The shareholders of Pridemark, the old corporation, decided, however, in November, 1958, to form a new corporation to be called Pridemark Enterprises, Inc.   This corporation eventually signed a dealership contract with Hilco Homes, Inc., and began to sell prefabricated homes in the spring of 1959.   The formation of this new corporation, several months before the final dissolution of the old, prompted the Commissioner to invoke the "reincorporation" doctrine, thereby denying the tax exempt status of the corporate sales during the year of liquidation and taxing the distributions to the shareholders as dividends.   This approach, adopted by the Tax Court, is the subject of the present appeal.

Before considering the intricacies of the "reincorporation" doctrine it is necessary to elaborate upon the circumstances surrounding the death of the old corporation and the birth of the new.   The motivation of Eugene Blitz, the controlling shareholder of both corporations, in liquidating Pridemark is of particular relevance.   As we have seen, in late 1957 he expressed a desire to terminate business relations with Golden Key but still hoped to become agent for another manufacturer.   Efforts made at that time to find a suitable substitute for Golden Key were to no avail.   Decreasing sales and his own advancing age prompted Eugene Blitz to get out of the prefabricated home business and to plan investing in some new business to be conducted by his son.   Consequently, Pridemark sold all of its branch offices and customer lists to Golden Key in February, 1958.   As part of the transaction Golden Key was allowed to hire away any of Pridemark's personnel that it desired, Pridemark and its owners promising not to rehire any of these employees until a year had passed.   As a result Pridemark lost its entire sales force, some of whose members had been with the organization as long as 12 years.   The sales manager left to supervise Golden

---

1.   Int.Rev.Code of 1954, § 331:

"(a) General rule.—

"(1) Complete liquidations.—Amounts distributed in complete liquidation of a corporation shall be treated as in full payment in exchange for the stock."

Int.Rev.Code of 1954, § 337:

"(a) General rule.—If—

"(1) a corporation adopts a plan of complete liquidation on or after June 22, 1954, and

"(2) within the 12-month period beginning on the date of the adoption of such plan, all of the assets of the corporation are distributed in complete liquidation, less assets retained to meet claims, then no gain or loss shall be recognized to such corporation from the sale or exchange by it of property within such 12-month period." (Court's footnote 2.)

Key's selling activities. The business built up by Eugene Blitz was thereafter carried on by Golden Key without interruption.

The old corporation engaged in no active selling for the remainder of its corporate life. The inactivity continued from February, 1958, to the corporation's dissolution in February, 1959. During this period funds distributed to the shareholders were invested in companies manufacturing kitchen cabinets and "three-wheeled vehicles," and in several land development ventures. When these investments proved disappointing, the Blitzes, father and son, and the petitioners associated with them in the old corporation began to weigh the advisability of returning to the business they knew best, the retailing of prefabricated homes.

In October or November, 1958, a representative of Hilco Homes, Inc., a manufacturer of prefabricated homes, came to the head office of the old corporation on business unrelated to this case. In the course of his visit the possibility of Blitz representing Hilco was discussed. There is no indication in the record as to who broached this topic of conversation, but it was agreed that the subject should be explored at greater length at some future date. Negotiations followed in December, 1958, and finally, on February 9, 1959, a dealership arrangement was entered into between Hilco and Pridemark Enterprises, the new corporation.

In the meantime, the articles of the new corporation were executed on November 26, 1958, and it was incorporated under the laws of Maryland on January 2, 1959. Eugene Blitz, as trustee of the old corporate assets conveyed to him by the shareholders, transferred the lease on the Baltimore office and the right to use the name "Pridemark" to the new corporation. Both of these assets had been rejected by Golden Key the preceding year. During 1959, Eugene Blitz, still acting as trustee, contributed $39,000 in nine installments to the new corporation. Gershan Thiman, a petitioner here and an accountant for the old corporation, was made president of the new. Jules Blitz, son of Eugene, became treasurer in the new corporation as he had been in the old. Eugene Blitz, who had been president of the old corporation, was named secretary and Samuel Hoffman, an office worker in the old concern, vice-president. At various times after a year had passed from the sale to Golden Key four of the ten salesmen returned to work for the new corporation. The first returned in May, 1959, the last in February, 1962.

Eugene Blitz, owner of 80% of the old corporation's common stock, took a 61% interest in the new, and he signed stock options which, if exercised, would reduce his holdings to 44%. He associated with the new corporation in a purely advisory capacity, receiving no salary during the first two years of operation.

The remaining owners of the new corporation were Jules Blitz, Thiman, and McCaffrey (a salesman) who subscribed for 10% of the stock in the new company, compared to 5% in the old; and Perron and Hoffman, who had no common stock in the old company but took 5% and 4%, respectively, in the new.

Since the early years of the Internal Revenue Code taxpayers have devised many schemes in the hope of withdrawing corporate profits at capital gains rates without interrupting corporate business. The most obvious of these devices is that made possible by the liquidation provision of the Code, section 331(a)(1), which provides that:

"Amounts distributed in complete liquidation of a corporation shall be treated as in full payment in exchange for the stock."

Taxpayers soon attempted to attain the desired advantage by liquidating their corporations, distributing the assets to themselves as shareholders, then reconveying them to a new corporation in return for its stock. All this could be done in a lawyer's office without interruption of the corporation's business.

The Treasury chose to attack flagrant distortions of the underlying purpose of section 331 by describing such a transaction as a reorganization and treating the cash distributions as "boot" taxable at ordinary income rates. Int.Rev.Code of 1954, § 356(a). An apt description of the above type of transaction was found in section 112(g)(1)(C) of the 1934 Code, now known as a "D" reorganization. That section described as a reorganization:

"[A] transfer by a corporation of all or a part of its assets to another corporation if immediately after the transfer the transferor or its stockholders or both are in control of the corporation to which the assets are transferred."

The section was interpreted to include transfers through the shareholders, by way of liquidation, to the transferee corporation as well as transfers directly from the old corporation to the new.

The effectiveness of the "D" reorganization section of the Code in attacking "reincorporations" was considerably diminished by the Revenue Act of 1954 which, *inter alia*, added the requirement that there be a transfer of *substantially all* of the old corporation's assets to the new. Sections 368(a)(1)(D), 354(b)(1)(A). To understand the effect of this amendment it must be remembered that the reorganization section of the Code was originally adopted to protect against taxation on corporate transactions where no economic gain is actually realized. See Paul, Studies in Federal Taxation, Third Series (1940). The 1954 amendment was intended to withdraw beneficial reorganization treatment from transactions which Congress felt involved true economic gain. Its unintended result was to blunt an instrument highly useful in attacking "reincorporations."

The first effort designed to deal explicitly with the "reincorporation" problem was passed by the House in 1954, but rejected by the Senate. The Senate-House Conference Committee, also rejecting it, commented as follows:

"Liquidation followed by reincorporation.—The House bill in section 357 contained a provision dealing with a device whereby it has been attempted to withdraw corporate earnings at capital gains rates by distributing all the assets of a corporation in complete liquidation and promptly reincorporating the business assets. This provision gave rise to certain technical problems and it has not been retained in the bill as recommended by the accompanying conference report. It is the belief of the managers in the part of the House that, at the present time, the possibility of tax avoidance in this area is not sufficiently serious to require a special statutory provision. *It is believed that this possibility can appropriately be disposed of by judicial decision or by regulation within the framework of the other provisions of the bill.*" H. Conference Rep.No.2543, 83d Cong.2d Sess., p. 41 (3 U.S.C.Cong. & Adm.News (1954), pp. 5280, 5301). (Emphasis added.)

Just what force should be given to the italicized passage is unclear. Courts resort to congressional history for an explanation of changes incorporated in legislation. While a conference report cannot be used to make new law, it is clear here that the committee was aware of the problem and thought the present statutory scheme adequate to deal with it. We agree with the conferees' reading of the Code but hold that the facts of this case do not bring it within the "reincorporation" area because the transactions were not motivated by a desire to avoid the payment of taxes. The Commissioner attacks the transactions in two ways. First, he contends that there was no "complete liquidation" because the shareholders began selling prefabricated homes again through a new corporation before the old one was finally liquidated. Second, it is the Commissioner's position that the transactions, taken as a whole, constitute an "F" reorganization.

The Code provides no definition of "complete liquidation." We reject the simplistic argument of the taxpayer that the phrase refers only to the measures required by state law to terminate a corporation's legal existence. No reason is offered as to why the observance of such mechanical procedures would prompt Congress to treat as stock redemptions payments that are in reality dividends. A more convincing indication of what distributions are meant to be accorded favored treatment is found in an early report of the Senate Finance Committee. S. Rep.No.398, 68th Cong., 1st Sess. 12 (1924). There a distribution in complete liquidation was analogized to a sale of stock in that the shareholder "surrenders his interest in the corporation and receives money in place thereof." The corporation must have ceased to be a going corporate concern, or if the enterprise is continued in corporate form, the shareholder must have disassociated himself from it. See Regs. 1.332–2(c) (1955). If the liquidated business is not resumed by the new corporation as a continuation of a going concern, there is a "complete liquidation." This is what happened in the present case.

For over one year the principals stopped selling prefabricated homes. Every asset owned by the old corporation was offered to Golden Key. The salesmen, sales lists and sales offices, an organization built up over a 12-year period, were all transferred as a going business. Such a complete divestiture is not compatible with a purpose to revive the business at a later date. The new corporation cannot fairly be considered a continuation of the old business when in fact it has been continued, without interruption, by Golden Key.

The gross receipts of the old corporation in its last year of operation were $1,791,266. In its first year of operation the new corporation grossed less than $300,000, indicating plainly enough that a new business was being built up. Eugene Blitz, the president and controlling force of the old corporation, now acts in an advisory capacity only to the new. The assets transferred to the new corporation were a negligible proportion of the assets held by the old and much of the good will was in the name of Golden Key Homes rather than Pridemark. These facts compel a conclusion that there was, in fact, a complete liquidation of Pridemark.

The second approach pressed by the Commissioner, that of the "F" reorganization, is limited in scope. That section refers to "a mere change in identity, form, or place of organization, however effected." Int.Rev.Code of 1954, § 368(a) (1) (F). The section, though aged, has received almost no administrative or judicial attention until recently. Its application is limited to cases where the corporate enterprise continues uninterrupted, except perhaps for a distribution of some of its liquid assets. There is a mere change of corporate vehicles, the transferee being no more than the alter ego of the transferor. See Lane, "The Reincorporation Game: Have the Ground Rules Really Changed?," 77 Harv.L.Rev. 1218, 1247 (1964). Such was not the case here.

Since there is a complete liquidation of Pridemark, Inc., and Pridemark, Inc. of Connecticut, within the meaning of sections 331 and 337, the distributions to the shareholders are entitled to be treated as a redemption of stock and taxed as a capital gain.

II

Among the assets sold by the old corporation to Golden Key on February 3, 1958, were all of Pridemark's sales contracts upon which no deliveries had been made. There were 1,108 such contracts, 258 of which were described as "active" because it was anticipated that a substantial portion of them would be consummated by the final delivery of a house. A purchase price of $134,400 was agreed on by estimating the number of contracts in this active group that would result in final delivery (91) and multiplying it by the average purchase price of each house ($6,000). The agreed purchase price was 20% of this figure. The computation produced a figure of $109,200, to which was added $25,200 representing the possibility that eventually some of the remaining contracts might also be consummated. A total of $23,624 in deposits had been made by the customers in connection with these contracts.

Although the petitioners kept their books on an accrual basis they had not accrued, at any time prior to the sale, any amount with respect to these 1,108 uncompleted contracts. The taxpayers' position is that these contracts are "property" with the result that their sale during the year of complete liquidation is tax exempt under the terms of section 337(b). The Commissioner, on the other hand, contends that these uncompleted contracts are not "property," as that term is used in section 337, because they represent ordinary income earned by the performance of services. Before determining whether the gain should be recognized it is necessary to decide the nature of the gain that the Commissioner seeks to tax and the taxpayers seek to exempt.

The contracts were the product of Pridemark's sales activities carried on through its salesmen, sales offices, catalogues and other advertising. The contracts provided that neither Pridemark nor the customer was obligated to go through with the sale until the customer had met all of the following conditions: (1) obtain sufficient financing; (2) arrange for a contractor to erect the house; (3) secure a clear title to the building site; (4) arrange for compliance with local building and zoning ordinances. There was no duty on Pridemark's part to assist customers in fulfilling the contractual conditions, but the salesmen, to insure their eventual receipt of commissions, did give such assistance.

On the signing of a contract a deposit was required, varying in amount up to $500. This sum would later be applied against the cost of the house if a delivery was finally made. If no delivery was made the deposit would be forfeited to Pridemark or voluntarily returned depending on the particular circumstances.

Pridemark would accrue income from the contracts only when deliveries were begun. The Tax Court, on the other hand, held that the sale of the contracts constituted an anticipatory assignment of income and that the gain was therefore taxable as ordinary income.

Taxpayers insist that the contracts sold to Golden Key contained no "element of income," that they were mere "sales orders" which entitled Pridemark to no income until "all the services had been completed." We find this position untenable. When the contracts were signed and the deposits made the dealer corporation had entered into arrangements giving rise to ordinary income in a predictable number of instances. If customer payments gave rise to income as received, it follows that the consideration paid by Golden Key for the assignments should likewise be treated as ordinary income. Pridemark cannot be allowed to avoid such treatment by assigning the contracts before completion. The fact that arguably there were services still to be performed was relevant in determining the price Golden Key was willing to pay for the assignment, but it has no relevance to the present discussion.

Recent decisions have adopted two entirely compatible explanations in support of taxing as ordinary income amounts received in payment for the assignment of items similar to these contracts. Some courts have ruled that the right to earn ordinary income is not "property" for capital gain purposes under section 1221. Others have described the consideration so received as a lump sum substitute for future ordinary income. The two approaches reach essentially the same conclusion—that it was not the purpose of Congress to permit taxpayers to convert ordinary income into a capital gain by assigning the right to receive it to a third party.

The money paid to Pridemark represents the value of its efforts in securing the customer's signature on a contract and getting a deposit made on that contract. This was the dealer corporation's principal activity. While in some situations a distinction might be made between a legally enforceable right to earn future income and a mere expectancy that work done in the past may lead to such a right, that distinction may not be made here. The latter expectancy has been described as good will and taxed as a capital asset. Those cases are well summarized by the definition in Boe v. Commissioner of Internal Revenue, 307 F.2d 339, 343 (9th Cir. 1962), that "the essence of good will is the expectancy of continued patronage." In that case the taxpayers had contracted to be available to perform medical services as the need arose. These arrangements, it was hoped, would lead to contracts at some unspecified time in the future. Such was not the case here. The contracts sold to Golden Key were valuable, not for any hope for remote earning opportunity but for immediate or impending benefits. Golden Key was compensating Pridemark for its successful sales activities that had produced fruit ready to be picked.

As the capital gain provisions are an exception to the ordinary treatment accorded most income, they must be strictly construed. A capital gain represents an appreciation in value accruing over a prescribed period of time on the investment of money in property. The statutory sections dealing with such property are designed to lessen the hardship of taxing the appreciation in value of such property in any one tax year. It is clear that the contracts in question do not fall within this exception. They represent services rendered in obtaining the contracts rather than an enhancement of an income producing asset.

The taxpayer contends, however, that even if the sale price of the uncompleted contracts is an ordinary income item, it is nevertheless exempted from taxation by the provisions of section 337. That section exempts from taxation gains arising from the sale of "property" during the year of liquidation. The parties to the appeal offer contrasting definitions of "property." The taxpayers insist that the term embraces any asset other than those explicitly excluded. To this the Commissioner answers that it has the same meaning as when used in defining "capital asset" under section 1221. The Tax Court found it unnecessary to reach this issue, having decided that there was not complete liquidation.

Section 337 was embodied in the Internal Revenue Code of 1954 to allow liquidating corporations to avoid a double incidence of capital gains taxation—once when capital assets are sold by the corporation, and again on distribution of the proceeds to the shareholders. Congress, however, clearly indicated that it did not intend section 337 to be used as a device to avoid taxation on income generated by the normal operations of a business.[2] The taxpayers offer no explanation as to why Congress would wish to tax such income if received by the liquidating corporation directly from the customers but exempt it if it is received indirectly through a third party as consideration for an assignment before collection.

The heart of the definition of "property" in section 337 was taken almost verbatim from the definition of capital assets referred to above, now found in section 1221. Both sections are designed to give preferential tax treatment to sales of certain types of assets not held for sale in the ordinary course of business.[3] We interpret them as having the same meaning.

Thus, section 337 exempts the sale of capital assets only during the year of liquidation. The uncompleted sales contracts not being capital assets, the proceeds received for their assignment are to be taxed as ordinary income.

III

The remaining issues may be disposed of without extensive discussion.

For the reasons stated by the Tax Court we affirm its holding that deposits made on the "inactive" contracts must be included in Pridemark's income for the year in which those contracts were sold to Golden Key rather than in the year of final liquidation.

We reverse the Tax Court's decision that legal fees incurred in connection with the sale of assets to Golden Key are to be deducted from the gain realized on that sale. Its decision was predicated on the determination that there was no complete liquidation. Having found a liquidation, we approve Pridemark's deduction of these fees as ordinary and necessary business expenses incurred in liquidation. Pacific Coast Biscuit Co., 32 B.T.A. 39, 42 (1935); see Note, "Certain Tax Aspects of Organization, Reorganization, and Liquidation Costs," 10 Stan. L.Rev. 112, 118–19 (1957).

Finally, the Tax Court disallowed a deduction to Pridemark for the $30,000 paid to Eugene Blitz in 1959 as deferred compensation because, in part at least, the taxpayers had failed to sustain their burden of showing that the amount of compensation was reasonable. We affirm the disallowance on this ground. The Tax Court's resolution of this factual issue was in no sense arbitrary.

Affirmed in part and reversed in part.

2. "It is intended that, during the 12-month period, sales in the ordinary course of business shall result in ordinary gain to the corporation as if the corporation were not in the process of liquidating." S.Rep.No.1622, 83d Cong., 2d Sess. 259 (1954), U.S.Code Congressional and Administrative News 1954, p. 4897. (Court's footnote 14.)

3. See Note, "Tax Free Sales in Liquidation Under Section 337," 76 Harv.L. Rev. 780, 793 (1963). (Court's footnote 15.)

KIMBELL–DIAMOND MILLING COMPANY v. COMMISSIONER OF INTERNAL REVENUE

Tax Court of the United States.
14 T.C. 74, 1950.

BLACK, Judge: This proceeding involves deficiencies in income, declared value excess profits, and excess profits taxes for the fiscal years ended May 31, 1945 and 1946, in the following amounts:

Year ended—	Income tax	Declared value excess profits tax	Excess profits tax
May 31, 1945	$5,679.25	....	$7,055.55
May 31, 1946	....	$2,352.23	26,128.02

The deficiencies are primarily due to respondent's reduction of petitioner's basis in assets acquired by it in December, 1942, through the liquidation of another corporation known as Whaley Mill & Elevator Co. (sometimes hereinafter referred to as Whaley). By reason of this reduction respondent has adjusted petitioner's allowable depreciation and its excess profits tax credit based on equity invested capital. By appropriate assignments of error petitioner contests these adjustments. Other adjustments which respondent made have been conceded.

This leaves for our consideration the determination of petitioner's basis in the assets acquired from Whaley.

The facts have been stipulated and are adopted as our findings of fact. They may be summarized as follows:

Petitioner is a Texas corporation, engaged primarily in the business of milling, processing, and selling grain products, and has its principal office in Fort Worth, Texas. Petitioner maintained its books and records and filed its corporation tax returns on an accrual basis for fiscal years ended May 31 of each year. For the years ended May 31, 1945 and 1946, its returns were filed with the collector of internal revenue for the second collection district of Texas.

On or about August 13, 1942, petitioner sustained a fire casualty at its Wolfe City, Texas, plant which resulted in the destruction of its mill property at that location. The assets so destroyed, and the adjusted basis thereof, were as follows:

	Cost	Depreciation allowed or allowable	Adjusted basis
Mill building	$6,106.96	$2,967.50	$3,139.46
Elevator building	7,007.77	6,024.15	983.62
Machinery	24,785.70	16,840.85	7,944.85
Warehouse	13,984.79	9,076.52	4,908.27
Steel tank	4,886.48	2,940.78	1,945.70
Total	56,771.70	37,849.80	18,921.90

This property was covered by insurance, and on or about November 14, 1942, petitioner collected insurance in the amount of $124,551.10 ($118,200.16 as a reimbursement for the loss sustained by the fire and $6,350.94 as a premium refund). On December 26, 1942, petitioner's directors approved the transaction set forth in the minutes below:

That, Whereas, on or about August 1, 1942, the flour mill and milling plant of Kimbell-Diamond Milling Company located at Wolfe City, Texas was destroyed by fire; and

Whereas, Kimbell-Diamond Milling Company collected from the insurance companies carrying the insurance on the said destroyed properties the sum of $125,000.00 as indemnification for the loss sustained, which said insurance proceeds were by the proper officers of this corporation promptly deposited in a special account in the Fort Worth National Bank of Fort Worth, Texas, where they have since been kept intact in order to have the same available for replacing, as nearly as might be, the destroyed properties; and

Whereas, it has at all times been the intention and desire of Kimbell-Diamond Milling Company to replace its burned mill either by constructing a new mill or by purchasing facilities of substantially similar kind and use; and

Whereas, due to existing building restrictions and other causes, it has been found impractical and impossible to replace the destroyed facilities by new construction, but it has come to the attention of the officers of this corporation that the stock of Whaley Mill & Elevator Company, a Texas corporation, which, among its other assets, owns physical properties substantially comparable to the destroyed Wolfe City Milling plant, can be purchased;

Now, Therefore, Be It Resolved:

1. That the proper officers of Kimbell-Diamond Milling Company be, and they are hereby, authorized, empowered and directed to purchase the entire authorized, issued and outstanding capital stock of Whaley Mill & Elevator Company, a Texas corporation, consisting of 4,000 shares of the face or par value of $100.00 per share, for a sum not in excess of $210,000.00; that payment for the said stock of Whaley Mill & Elevator Company be made, to the extent possible, from the insurance proceeds deposited in a special account in the Fort Worth National Bank, and that the balance of the agreed consideration for the stock of Whaley Mill & Elevator Company be paid out of the general funds of Kimbell-Diamond Milling Company.

2. That as soon as practicable after the purchase of the Whaley Mill & Elevator Company stock hereby authorized has been consummated, all necessary steps be taken to completely

liquidate the said corporation by transferring its entire assets, particularly its mill and milling equipment, to Kimbell-Diamond Milling Company in cancellation and redemption of the entire issued and outstanding capital stock of Whaley Mill & Elevator Company, and that the charter of said corporation be forthwith surrendered and cancelled.

On December 26, 1942, petitioner acquired 100 per cent of the stock of Whaley Mill & Elevator Co. of Gainesville, Texas, paying therefor $210,000 in cash which payment, to the extent of $118,200.16, was made with the insurance proceeds received by petitioner as a result of the fire on or about August 13, 1942.

On December 29, 1942, the stockholders of Whaley assented to the dissolution and distribution of assets thereof. On the same date an "Agreement and Program of Complete Liquidation" was entered into between petitioner and Whaley, which provided, *inter alia:*

That, Whereas, Kimbell-Diamond owns the entire authorized issued and outstanding capital stock of Whaley, consisting of 4000 shares of a par value of $100.00 per share, which said stock was acquired by Kimbell-Diamond primarily for the purpose of enabling it to secure possession and ownership of the flour mill and milling plant owned by Whaley, the parties herewith agree that the said mill and milling plant shall forthwith be conveyed to Kimbell-Diamond by Whaley under the following program for the complete liquidation of Whaley viz:

(1) Kimbell-Diamond shall cause the 4000 shares of the capital stock of Whaley owned by it to be surrendered to Whaley for cancellation and retirement, whereupon Whaley shall forthwith convey, transfer and assign unto Kimbell-Diamond all property of every kind and character owned or claimed by it, particularly its flour mill and milling plant, located at Gainesville, Texas, and all machinery and equipment appurtenant thereto, or used in connection therewith, in full and complete liquidation of all of the outstanding stock of Whaley. The aforesaid distribution in complete liquidation shall be fully consummated by not later than midnight, December 31, 1942.

(2) When the entire assets of every kind and character, owned by Whaley, have been transferred to Kimbell-Diamond in full and complete liquidation of the capital stock of Whaley, owned by Kimbell-Diamond, Whaley shall forthwith make application to the Secretary of State of the State of Texas for its dissolution as a corporation and surrender its corporate charter.

On December 31, 1942, the Secretary of State of the State of Texas certified that the Whaley Mill & Elevator Co. was dissolved as of that date.

The assets so distributed to petitioner, the cost of same to Whaley, the depreciation sustained thereon while owned by Whaley, and

Whaley's adjusted basis therefor, as of December, 1942, were as follows:

	Cost to Whaley	Reserve for depreciation	Whaley's adjusted basis
Depreciable assets:			
Concrete elevator building	$24,666.59	$16,073.33	$8,593.26
Concrete mill building	68,871.95	30,033.22	38,838.73
Concrete tanks	25,753.30	9,741.05	16,012.25
Steel tanks	24,038.19	9,192.16	14,846.03
Brick office building	5,589.08	1,352.04	4,237.04
Machinery, mill	153,271.79	123,917.75	29,354.04
Machinery, elevator	17,682.61	12,428.12	5,254.49
Corn sheller	8,106.68	5,831.69	2,274.99
Country elevators	28,290.30	22,169.50	6,120.80
Garage	79.13	15.82	63.31
Warehouse	5,254.17	157.63	5,096.54
Laboratory equipment . . .	2,061.98	412.40	1,649.58
Furniture and fixtures . . .	1,088.47	167.91	920.56
Autos and trucks	11,207.92	4,947.92	6,260.00
Total	375,962.16	236,440.54	139,521.62
Land	. . . .		24,014.50
Other assets:			
Cash		211.13	
Receivables		44,672.61	
Inventory		118,981.85	
State warrants		992.88	
Deposits and prepaid		342.00	165,200.47
Total assets		. . . .	328,736.59
Liabilities:			
Accounts payable		4,136.75	
Accrued taxes		9,884.15	14,020.90
Net book value (to Whaley) of assets transferred to Kimbell-Diamond Milling Co. on liquidation of Whaley stock		. . . .	314,715.69

In filing its tax returns for the fiscal year ended May 31, 1943, petitioner did not include in net taxable income the amount of the insurance proceeds, less the adjusted basis of the destroyed assets, a net amount of $99,278.26. Respondent in his deficiency notice in Docket No. 10982 (involving the fiscal year ended May 31, 1943) determined that petitioner realized a gain of $99,278.26. In its petition in Docket No. 10982, petitioner alleged that it came within the provisions of section 112(f) of the Internal Revenue Code, pertaining to involuntary conversions, and realized no gain on the conversion of its assets. Prior to the hearing in Docket No. 10982, respondent filed an amended answer in which he affirmatively alleged that he had "erroneously determined that the petitioner took the assets of the Whaley Mill and Elevator Company at Whaley's adjusted basis of $328,736.59." Respondent alleged that, if petitioner had not complied with section 112(f), its basis in these assets would be $224,020.90, and if petitioner had complied with section 112(f) its basis would be $110,- 721.94. Respondent's allegations were based on the theory that what petitioner really acquired was not stock in Whaley, but rather the assets of Whaley. All allegations of fact in the amendment to answer were denied in the reply filed by petitioner.

In our decision in Docket No. 10982 we held that, since the affirmative allegations were made in the amendment to answer, the burden of proof was on respondent to sustain those allegations and that the burden thereon had not been met. We decided only the question of whether petitioner had complied with section 112(f), pertaining to involuntary conversions. On this question petitioner prevailed. As to the allegations contained in respondent's amendment to answer, we said (10 T.C. 7, 14):

> In this state of the record we prefer not to decide, in this proceeding, the legal question as to whether the purchase of shares in Whaley by the petitioner constitutes as a matter of law the acquisition of Whaley assets. We leave that question open for determination in any appropriate proceeding involving a later year, where a record presenting an adequate factual basis may be made. We shall let the present case rest on the issue raised in the petition and answer, founded on the determination as made by the Commissioner in the first instance.

There is no dispute that the petitioner's adjusted basis in its depreciable assets which were destroyed by fire was $18,921.90; nor that the depreciable assets which it received from Whaley had an adjusted basis in the hands of Whaley of $139,521.62. Petitioner, in the years herein involved, proceeded under the theory that it was entitled to Whaley's basis. Respondent takes the position that petitioner's cost is its basis in the assets acquired from Whaley. Respondent likewise asserts that for the purpose of computing excess profits credit we must use the actual cost to petitioner of the Whaley assets. The petitioner does not controvert the allocation of cost made by respondent to the various assets acquired from Whaley, both depreciable and nondepreciable property. As to the depreciable assets purchased to replace those involuntarily converted, respondent contends that petitioner's basis is limited by section 113(a) (9) of the Internal Revenue Code.

Petitioner takes two positions: The first is that the question of basis was decided in the prior proceeding, Docket No. 10982, Kimbell-Diamond Milling Co., 10 T.C. 7, and that consequently such decision is *res judicata* as to this proceeding; the second is that the transaction by which it acquired the assets of Whaley falls within the provisions of section 112(b) (6) of the Internal Revenue Code and petitioner's basis for the assets so taken over is governed by section 113 (a) (15) of the code.

We must first consider petitioner's contention that our decision in Docket No. 10982 estops respondent from contending that the basis of petitioner's assets acquired from Whaley is other than the basis in the hands of Whaley. Petitioner argues that collateral estoppel applies to these proceedings because the question of petitioner's basis in these same assets was in issue in the prior proceeding and that, because respondent failed in sustaining his burden of proof, the issue was, therefore, decided in favor of petitioner.

The principle of collateral estoppel was most recently discussed by the Supreme Court in Sunnen v. Commissioner, 333 U.S. 591, wherein it was said that "the prior judgment acts as a collateral estoppel only as to those matters in the second proceeding which were actually presented *and determined* in the first suit." (Emphasis supplied.) Examining our opinion in the first suit, it is clear that we did not determine the matter now before us, as we expressly stated that we were not deciding this issue; therefore, collateral estoppel is inapplicable.

Having decided the issue of *res judicata* against petitioner, we must now determine the question of petitioner's basis in Whaley's assets on the merits. Petitioner argues that the acquisition of Whaley's assets and the subsequent liquidation of Whaley brings petitioner within the provisions of section 112(b) (6) and, therefore, by reason of section 113(a) (15), petitioner's basis in these assets is the same as the basis in Whaley's hands. In so contending, petitioner asks that we treat the acquisition of Whaley's stock and the subsequent liquidation of Whaley as separate transactions. It is well settled that the incidence of taxation depends upon the substance of a transaction. Commissioner v. Court Holding Co., 324 U.S. 331. It is inescapable from petitioner's minutes set out above and from the "Agreement and Program of Complete Liquidation" entered into between petitioner and Whaley, that the only intention petitioner ever had was to acquire Whaley's assets.

We think that this proceeding is governed by the principles of Commissioner v. Ashland Oil & Refining Co., 99 F.2d 588, certiorari denied, 306 U.S. 661. In that case the stock was retained for almost a year before liquidation. Ruling on the question of whether the stock or the assets of the corporation were purchased, the court stated:

> The question remains, however, whether if the entire transaction, whatever its form, was essentially in intent, purpose and result, a purchase by Swiss of property, its several steps may be treated separately and each be given an effect for tax purposes as though each constituted a distinct transaction. * * * And without regard to whether the result is imposition or relief from taxation, the courts have recognized that where the essential nature of a transaction is the acquisition of property, it will be viewed as a whole, and closely related steps will not be separated

either at the instance of the taxpayer or the taxing authority. Prairie Oil & Gas Co. v. Motter, 10 Cir., 66 F.2d 309; Tulsa Tribune Co. v. Commissioner, 10 Cir., 58 F.2d 937, 940; Ahles Realty Corp. v. Commissioner, 2 Cir., 71 F.2d 150; Helvering v. Security Savings Bank, 4 Cir., 72 F.2d 874. * * *

See also Koppers Coal Co., 6 T.C. 1209 and cases there cited.

We hold that the purchase of Whaley's stock and its subsequent liquidation must be considered as one transaction, namely, the purchase of Whaley's assets which was petitioner's sole intention. This was not a reorganization within section 112(b) (6), and petitioner's basis in these assets, both depreciable and nondepreciable, is, therefore, its cost, or $110,721.74 ($18.921.90, the basis of petitioner's assets destroyed by fire, plus $91,799.84, the amount expended over the insurance proceeds). Since petitioner does not controvert respondent's allocation of cost to the individual assets acquired from Whaley, both depreciable and nondepreciable, respondent's allocation is sustained.

* * *

Decision will be entered for the Respondent.

---

26 U.S.C.A. (Internal Revenue Code)

§ 334. Basis of property received in liquidations

(a) **General rule.**—If property is received in a distribution in partial or complete liquidation (other than a distribution to which section 333 applies), and if gain or loss is recognized on receipt of such property, then the basis of the property in the hands of the distributee shall be the fair market value of such property at the time of the distribution.

(b) **Liquidation of subsidiary.**—

(1) **In general.**—If property is received by a corporation in a distribution in complete liquidation of another corporation (within the meaning of section 332(b)), then, except as provided in paragraph (2), the basis of the property in the hands of the distributee shall be the same as it would be in the hands of the transferor. If property is received by a corporation in a transfer to which section 332(c) applies, and if paragraph (2) of this subsection does not apply, then the basis of the property in the hands of the transferee shall be the same as it would be in the hands of the transferor.

(2) **Exception.**—If property is received by a corporation in a distribution in complete liquidation of another corporation (within the meaning of section 332(b)), and if—

(A) the distribution is pursuant to a plan of liquidation adopted—

(i) on or after June 22, 1954, and

(ii) not more than 2 years after the date of the transaction described in subparagraph (B) (or, in the case of a series of transactions, the date of the last such transaction); and

(B) stock of the distributing corporation possessing at least 80 percent of the total combined voting power of all classes of stock entitled to vote, and at least 80 percent of the total number of shares of all other classes of stock (except nonvoting stock which is limited and preferred as to dividends), was acquired by the distributee by purchase (as defined in paragraph (3)) during a 12-month period beginning with the earlier of—

(i) the date of the first acquisition by purchase of such stock, or

(ii) if any of such stock was acquired in an acquisition which is a purchase within the meaning of the second sentence of paragraph (3), the date on which the distributee is first considered under section 318(a) as owning stock owned by the corporation from which such acquisition was made,

then the basis of the property in the hands of the distributee shall be the adjusted basis of the stock with respect to which the distribution was made. For purposes of the preceding sentence, under regulations prescribed by the Secretary or his delegate, proper adjustment in the adjusted basis of any stock shall be made for any distribution made to the distributee with respect to such stock before the adoption of the plan of liquidation, for any money received, for any liabilities assumed or subject to which the property was received, and for other items.

(3) **Purchase defined.**—For purposes of paragraph (2) (B), the term "purchase" means any acquisition of stock, but only if—

(A) the basis of the stock in the hands of the distributee is not determined (i) in whole or in part by reference to the adjusted basis of such stock in the hands of the person from whom acquired, or (ii) under section 1014(a) (relating to property acquired from a decedent),

(B) the stock is not acquired in an exchange to which section 351 applies, and

(C) the stock is not acquired from a person the ownership of whose stock would, under section 318(a), be attributed to the person acquiring such stock.

Notwithstanding subparagraph (C) of this paragraph, for purposes of paragraph (2)(B), the term "purchase" also means an acquisition of stock from a corporation when ownership of such stock would be attributed under section 318(a) to the person acquiring such stock, if the stock of such corporation by reason of which such ownership would be attributed was acquired by purchase (within the meaning of the preceding sentence).

(4) **Distributee defined.**—For purposes of this subsection, the term "distributee" means only the corporation which meets the 80 percent stock ownership requirements specified in section 332(b).

(c) **Property received in liquidation under section 333.**—If—

(1) property was acquired by a shareholder in the liquidation of a corporation in cancellation or redemption of stock, and

(2) with respect to such acquisition—

(A) gain was realized, but

(B) as the result of an election made by the shareholder under section 333, the extent to which gain was recognized was determined under section 333,

then the basis shall be the same as the basis of such stock cancelled or redeemed in the liquidation, decreased in the amount of any money received by the shareholder, and increased in the amount of gain recognized to him. Aug. 16, 1954, c. 736, 68A Stat. 104; Nov. 13, 1966, Pub.L. 89–809, Title II, § 202(a), (b), 80 Stat 1576.

§ 337. Gain or loss on sales or exchanges in connection with certain liquidations

(a) General rule.—If—

(1) a corporation adopts a plan of complete liquidation on or after June 22, 1954, and

(2) within the 12-month period beginning on the date of the adoption of such plan, all of the assets of the corporation are distributed in complete liquidation, less assets retained to meet claims,

then no gain or loss shall be recognized to such corporation from the sale or exchange by it of property within such 12-month period.

(b) Property defined.—

(1) In general.—For purposes of subsection (a), the term "property" does not include—

(A) stock in trade of the corporation, or other property of a kind which would properly be included in the inventory of the corporation if on hand at the close of the taxable year, and property held by the corporation primarily for sale to customers in the ordinary course of its trade or business,

(B) installment obligations acquired in respect of the sale or exchange (without regard to whether such sale or exchange occurred before, on, or after the date of the adoption of the plan referred to in subsection (a)) of stock in trade or other property described in subparagraph (A) of this paragraph, and

(C) installment obligations acquired in respect of property (other than property described in subparagraph (A)) sold or exchanged before the date of the adoption of such plan of liquidation.

(2) Nonrecognition with respect to inventory in certain cases.— Notwithstanding paragraph (1) of this subsection, if substantially all of the property described in subparagraph (A) of such paragraph (1) which is attributable to a trade or business of the corporation is, in accordance with this section, sold or exchanged to one person in one transaction, then for purposes of subsection (a) the term "property" includes—

(A) such property so sold or exchanged, and

(B) installment obligations acquired in respect of such sale or exchange.

(c) Limitations.—

(1) Collapsible corporations and liquidations to which section 333 applies.—This section shall not apply to any sale or exchange—

(A) made by a collapsible corporation (as defined in section 341(b)), or

(B) following the adoption of a plan of complete liquidation, if section 333 applies with respect to such liquidation.

(2) Liquidations to which section 332 applies.—In the case of a sale or exchange following the adoption of a plan of complete liquidation, if section 332 applies with respect to such liquidation, then—

(A) if the basis of the property of the liquidating corporation in the hands of the distributee is determined under section 334(b)(1), this section shall not apply; or

(B) if the basis of the property of the liquidating corporation in the hands of the distributee is determined under section 334 (b)(2), this section shall apply only to that portion (if any) of the gain which is not greater than the excess of (i) that portion of the adjusted basis (adjusted for any adjustment required under the second sentence of section 334(b)(2)) of the stock of the liquidating corporation which is allocable, under regulations prescribed by the Secretary or his delegate, to the property sold or exchanged, over (ii) the adjusted basis, in the hands of the liquidating corporation, of the property sold or exchanged.

(d) Special rule for certain minority shareholders.—If a corporation adopts a plan of complete liquidation on or after January 1, 1958, and if subsection (a) does not apply to sales or exchanges of property by such corporation, solely by reason of the application of subsection (c)(2)(A), then for the first taxable year of any shareholder (other than a corporation which meets the 80 percent stock ownership requirement specified in section 32(b)(1), in which he receives a distribution in complete liquidation—

(1) the amount realized by such shareholder on the distribution shall be increased by his proportionate share of the amount by which the tax imposed by this subtitle on such corporation would have been reduced if subsection (c)(2)(A) had not been applicable, and

(2) for purposes of this title, such shareholder shall be deemed to have paid, on the last day prescribed by law for the payment of the tax imposed by this subtitle on such shareholder for such taxable year, an amount of tax equal to the amount of the increase described in paragraph (1).

Aug. 16, 1954, c. 736, 68A Stat. 106; Sept. 2, 1958, Pub.L. 85–866, Title I, § 19, 72 Stat. 1615.

B.   MERGERS AND REORGANIZATIONS

INTRODUCTORY NOTE

A business may also expand by acquiring another business through a merger or consolidation. While it is theoretically possible for two partnerships to merge with each other, this rarely happens in the legal sense, although it undoubtedly does occur in an economic sense. The legal arrangement following the merger of two partnerships as a practical matter is usually the formation of a new partnership. From the viewpoint of business corporation statutes, mergers and consolidations of corporations are thought of as being, in part, separate legal transactions, although in an economic sense as well as an income tax sense, they are much the same. A merger is a combination of two or more corporations into one of them, while a consolidation is the combination of two or more corporations into a new corporation. The effect of either of these transactions is that the several corporations which were parties to the merger or consolidation became a single corporation; in the case of a merger it will be the corporation which has been designated (generally in a "plan of merger") as the surviving corporation; in the case of a consolidation, it will be the new corporation designated in the "plan of consolidation." After the necessary papers have been filed with a state filing office, the separate existence of all of the corporations which were parties to either of the plans will terminate except for the corporation designated as the surviving corporation in the plan of merger, or the new corporation in the plan of consolidation. The surviving or new corporation will have all of the rights and privileges that any business corporation will have under the laws of the state of incorporation and will also have all of the rights and privileges that its predecessors had. The surviving or new corporation will accede to all of the property held by its predecessors, as well as all of their liabilities and thereafter will be responsible for their payment; the rights of creditors of the predecessor corporations are not impaired in any manner by the merger or consolidation.

None of these things can be one without the prior approval of the boards of directors of the corporations participating in either of the plans and without an affirmative vote of generally two-thirds of the stockholders. A small close corporation will have no difficulty complying with the provisions of the statute, whether it is the acquiring corporation or the one to be acquired; its shareholders and directors will probably operate by a unanimous written consent thus eliminating any necessity of going through the detailed mechanical steps otherwise required.

A large publicly held corporation will have a number of problems which it must consider. While the merger of a large corporation into a smaller one is not unknown (see Farris v. Glen Alden Corporation, 393 Pa. 427, 143 A.2d 25 (1958), reported below) it will be assumed for the purposes of this note that the acquiring corporation is the larger one. By necessity, because it cannot as a practical matter obtain unanimous written consent of its shareholders, it will have to comply with the provisions of its law of incorporation in regard to notice to shareholders of a meeting to consider the plan of merger. Generally a written notice must be mailed prior to such meeting and a copy of the plan of merger or consolidation must be included with the notice. The acquiring corporation which is going to issue its securities in the merger must consider whether it will be necessary to register the securities under the provisions of Section 5 of the Securities Act of 1933, 15 U.S.C.A. § 77e, or whether the provisions of Rule 133 of the Securities and Exchange Commission exempt the transaction from registration. However, it is likely that a proxy statement will be sent to the shareholders of the corporation which is being acquired and in some cases may also be sent to the shareholders of the acquiring corporation. Normally some publicity relating to the transaction will have occurred before the proxy statement is mailed to shareholders or filed with the Securities and Exchange Commission; under these circumstances the provisions of Section 14(a) of the Securities Exchange Act of 1934, 15 U.S.C.A. § 78n(a), and Rule 14a-9 issued by the Commission relating to disclosure requirements apply to the solicitation of proxies for this purpose. Some of these problems are illustrated by Mills v. The Electric Auto-Lite Co., 396 U.S. 375, 90 S. Ct. 616, 24 L.Ed. 593 (1970), reported below.

The impact of Section 7 of the Clayton Act, 15 U.S.C.A. § 18, as well as Section 5 of the Federal Trade Commission Act, 15 U.S.C.A. § 45, must also be considered. If the "[e]ffect of such acquisition may be substantially to lessen competition, or to tend to create a monopoly * * *", in the terms of Section 7 of the Clayton Act, or if the merger itself may be an "[u]nfair method of competition" in the terms of Section 5 of the Federal Trade Commission Act, then the merger may either be blocked by the Justice Department or be upset after it has taken place by litigation. The Internal Revenue Service and the Securities and Exchange Commission frequently will give advice in advance of a transaction, stating the attitude of the administrative agency concerning the proposal. Similarly, the Anti-Trust Division of the Department of Justice has adopted an informal "merger clearance" procedure under which it will inform an applicant of its present policy with respect to a proposed merger or acquisition, but will decline to adhere to this policy for all time in the future. The Federal Trade Commission has a similar program in operation.

FARRIS v. GLEN ALDEN CORPORATION

Supreme Court of Pennsylvania, 1958.
393 Pa. 427, 143 A.2d 25.

COHEN, Justice. We are required to determine on this appeal whether, as a result of a "Reorganization Agreement" executed by the officers of Glen Alden Corporation and List Industries Corporation, and approved by the shareholders of the former company, the rights and remedies of a dissenting shareholder accrue to the plaintiff.

Glen Alden is a Pennsylvania corporation engaged principally in the mining of anthracite coal and lately in the manufacture of air conditioning units and fire-fighting equipment. In recent years the company's operating revenue has declined substantially, and in fact, its coal operations have resulted in tax loss carryovers of approximately $14,000,000. In October 1957, List, a Delaware holding company owning interests in motion picture theaters, textile companies and real estate and to a lesser extent, in oil and gas operations, warehouses and aluminum piston manufacturing, purchased through a wholly owned subsidiary 38.5% of Glen Alden's outstanding stock. This acquisition enabled List to place three of its directors on the Glen Alden board.

On March 20, 1958, the two corporations entered into a "reorganization agreement," subject to stockholder approval, which contemplated the following actions:

1.   Glen Alden is to acquire all of the assets of List, excepting a small amount of cash reserved for the payment of List's expenses in connection with the transaction. These assets include over $8,000,000 in cash held chiefly in the treasuries of List's wholly owned subsidiaries.

2.   In consideration of the transfer, Glen Alden is to issue 3,621,-703 shares of stock to List. List in turn is to distribute the stock to its shareholders at a ratio of five shares of Glen Alden stock for each six shares of List stock. In order to accomplish the necessary distribution, Glen Alden is to increase the authorized number of its shares of capital stock from 2,500,000 shares to 7,500,000 shares without according preemptive rights to the present shareholders upon the issuance of any such shares.

3.   Further, Glen Alden is to assume all of List's liabilities including a $5,000,000 note incurred by List in order to purchase Glen Alden stock in 1957, outstanding stock options, incentive stock options plans, and pension obligations.

4.   Glen Alden is to change its corporate name from Glen Alden Corporation to List Alden Corporation.

5.   The present directors of both corporations are to become directors of List Alden.

6.   List is to be dissolved and List Alden is to then carry on the operations of both former corporations.

Two days after the agreement was executed notice of the annual meeting of Glen Alden to be held on April 11, 1958, was mailed to the shareholders together with a proxy statement analyzing the reorganization agreement and recommending its approval as well as approval of certain amendments to Glen Alden's articles of incorporation and bylaws necessary to implement the agreement. At this meeting the holders of a majority of the outstanding shares, (not incuding those owned by List), voted in favor of a resolution approving the reorganization agreement.

On the day of the shareholders' meeting, plaintiff, a shareholder of Glen Alden, filed a complaint in equity against the corporation and its officers seeking to enjoin them temporarily until final hearing, and perpetually thereafter, from executing and carrying out the agreement.

The gravamen of the complaint was that the notice of the anual shareholders' meeting did not conform to the requirements of the Business Corporation Law, 15 P.S. § 2852–1 et seq., in three respects: (1) It did not give notice to the shareholders that the true intent and purpose of the meeting was to effect a merger or consolidation of Glen Alden and List; (2) It failed to give notice to the shareholders of their right to dissent to the plan of merger or consolidation and claim fair value for their shares, and (3) It did not contain copies of the text of certain sections of the Business Corporation Law as required.

By reason of these omissions, plaintiff contended that the approval of the reorganization agreement by the shareholders at the annual meeting was invalid and unless the carrying out of the plan were enjoined, he would suffer irreparable loss by being deprived of substantial property rights.

The defendants answered admitting the material allegations of fact in the complaint but denying that they gave rise to a cause of action because the transaction complained of was a purchase of corporate assets as to which shareholders had no rights of dissent or appraisal. For these reasons the defendants then moved for judgment on the pleadings.

The court below concluded that the reorganization agreement entered into between the two corporations was a plan for a *de facto* merger, and that therefore the failure of the notice of the annual meeting to conform to the pertinent requirements of the merger provisions of the Business Corporation Law rendered the notice defective and all proceedings in furtherance of the agreement void. Wherefore, the court entered a final decree denying defendants' motion for judgment on the peladings, entering judgment upon plaintiff's complaint and granting the injunctive relief therein sought. This appeal followed.

When use of the corporate form of business organization first became widespread, it was relatively easy for courts to define a "merger" or a "sale of assets" and to label a particular transaction as one or the other. * * * But prompted by the desire to avoid the impact of adverse, and to obtain the benefits of favorable, government regulations, particularly federal tax laws, new accounting and legal techniques were developed by lawyers and accountants which interwove the elements characteristic of each, thereby creating hybrid forms of corporate amalgamation. Thus, it is no longer helpful to consider an individual transaction in the abstract and solely by reference to the various elements therein determine whether it is a "merger" or a "sale". Instead, to determine properly the nature of a corporate transaction, we must refer not only to all the provisions of the agreement, but also to the consequences of the transaction and to the purposes of the provisions of the corporation law said to be applicable. We shall apply this principle to the instant case.

Section 908, subd. A of the Pennsylvania Business Corporation Law provides: "If any shareholder of a domestic corporation which becomes a party to a plan of merger or consolidation shall object to such plan of merger or consolidation * * * such shareholder shall be entitled to * * * [the fair value of his shares upon surrender of the share certificate or certificates representing his shares]." Act of May 5, 1933, P.L. 364, as amended, 15 P.S. § 2852–908, subd. A.

This provision had its origin in the early decision of this Court in Lauman v. Lebanon Valley R. R. Co., 1858, 30 Pa. 42. There a shareholder who objected to the consolidation of his company with another was held to have a right in the absence of statute to treat the consolidation as a dissolution of his company and to receive the value of his shares upon their surrender.

The rationale of the Lauman case, and of the present section of the Business Corporation Law based thereon, is that when a corporation combines with another so as to lose its essential nature and alter the original fundamental relationships of the shareholders among themselves and to the corporation, a shareholder who does not wish to continue his membership therein may treat his membership in the original corporation as terminated and have the value of his shares paid to him. See Lauman v. Lebanon Valley R. R. Co., supra, 30 Pa. at pages 46–47. * * *

Does the combination outlined in the present "reorganization" agreement so fundamentally change the corporate character of Glen Alden and the interest of the plaintiff as a shareholder therein, that to refuse him the rights and remedies of a dissenting shareholder would in reality force him to give up his stock in one corporation and against his will accept shares in another? If so, the combination is a merger within the meaning of section 908, subd. A of the corporation law. * * *

If the reorganization agreement were consummated plaintiff would find that the "List Alden" resulting from the amalgamation would be quite a different corporation than the "Glen Alden" in which he is now a shareholder. Instead of continuing primarily as a coal mining company, Glen Alden would be transformed, after amendment of its articles of incorporation, into a diversified holding company whose interests would range from motion picture theaters to textile companies. Plaintiff would find himself a member of a company with assets of $169,000,000 and a long-term debt of $38,000,000 in lieu of a company one-half that size and with but one-seventh the long-term debt.

While the administration of the operations and properties of Glen Alden as well as List would be in the hands of management common to both companies, since all executives of List would be retained in List Alden, the control of Glen Alden would pass to the directors of List; for List would hold eleven of the seventeen directorships on the new board of directors.

As an aftermath of the transaction plaintiff's proportionate interest in Glen Alden would have been reduced to only two-fifths of what it presently is because of the issuance of an additional 3,621,703 shares to List which would not be subject to pre-emptive rights. In fact, ownership of Glen Alden would pass to the stockholders of List who would hold 76.5% of the outstanding shares as compared with but 23.5% retained by the present Glen Alden shareholders.

Perhaps the most important consequence to the plaintiff, if he were denied the right to have his shares redeemed at their fair value, would be the serious financial loss suffered upon consummation of the agreement. While the present book value of his stock is $38 a share after combination it would be worth only $21 a share. In contrast, the shareholders of List who presently hold stock with a total book value of $33,000,000 or $7.50 a share, would receive stock with a book value of $76,000,000 or $21 a share.

Under these circumstances it may well be said that if the proposed combination is allowed to take place without right of dissent, plaintiff would have his stock in Glen Alden taken away from him and the stock of a new company thrust upon him in its place. He would be projected against his will into a new enterprise under terms not of his own choosing. It was to protect dissident shareholders against just such a result that this Court one hundred years ago in the Lauman case, and the legislature thereafter in section 908, subd. A, granted the right of dissent. And it is to accord that protection to the plaintiff that we conclude that the combination proposed in the case at hand is a merger within the intendment of section 908, subd. A.

Nevertheless, defendants contend that the 1957 amendments to sections 311 and 908 of the corporation law preclude us from reaching this result and require the entry of judgment in their favor. Subsection F of section 311 dealing with the voluntary transfer of corporate assets provides: "The shareholders of a business corporation which acquires by sale, lease or exchange all or substantially all of the property of another corporation by the issuance of stock, securities or otherwise shall not be entitled to the rights and remedies of dissenting shareholders * * *." Act of July 11, 1957, P.L. 711, § 1, 15 P.S. § 2852–311, subd. F.

And the amendment to section 908 reads as follows: "The right of dissenting shareholders * * * shall not apply to the purchase by a corporation of assets whether or not the consideration therefor be money or property, real or personal, including shares or bonds or other evidences of indebtedness of such corporation. The shareholders of such corporaton shall have no right to dissent from any such purchase." Act of July 11, 1957, P.L. 711, § 1, 15 P.S. § 2852–908, subd. C.

Defendants view these amendments as abridging the right of shareholders to dissent to a transaction between two corporations which involves a transfer of assets for a consideration even though the transfer has all the legal incidents of a merger. They claim that only if the merger is accomplished in accordance with the prescribed statutory procedure does the right of dissent accrue. In support of this position they cite to us the comment on the amendments by the Committee on Corporation Law of the Pennsylvania Bar Association, the committee which originally drafted these provisions. The comment states that the provisions were intended to overrule cases which granted shareholders the right to dissent to a sale of assets when accompanied by the legal incidents of a merger. See 61 Ann.Rep.Pa.Bar Ass'n 277, 284 (1957). Whatever may have been the intent of the *committee,* there is no evidence to indicate that the *legislature* intended the 1957 amendments to have the effect contended for. But furthermore, the language of these two provisions does not support the opinion of the committee and is inapt to achieve any such purpose. The amendments of 1957 do not provide that a transaction between two corporations which has the effect of a merger but which includes a transfer of assets for consideration is to be exempt from the protective provisions of sections 908, subd. A and 515. They provide only that the shareholders of a corporation which acquires the property or purchases the assets of another corporation, *without more,* are not entitled to the right to dissent from the transaction. So, as in the present case, when as part of a transaction between two corporations, one corporation dissolves, its liabilities are assumed by the survivor, its executives and directors take over the management and control of the survivor, and, as consideration for the transfer, its stockholders acquire a majority of the shares of stock of the survivor, then the transaction is no longer simply a purchase of assets or acquisition of property to which sections 311, subd. F and 908, subd. C apply, but a merger governed by section 908, subd. A of the corporation law. To divest shareholders of their right of dissent under such circumstances would require express language which is absent from the 1957 amendments.

Even were we to assume that the combination provided for in the reorganization agreement is a "sale of assets" to which section 908, subd. A does not apply, it would avail the defendants nothing; we will not blind our eyes to the realities of the transaction. Despite the designation of the parties and the form employed, Glen Alden does not in fact acquire List, rather, List acquires Glen Alden, cf. Metropolitan Edison Co. v. Commissioner, 3 Cir., 1938, 98 F.2d 807, affirmed sub nom., Helvering v. Metropolitan Edison Co., 1939, 306 U.S. 522, and under section 311, subd. D the right of dissent would remain with the shareholders of Glen Alden.

We hold that the combination contemplated by the reorganization agreement, although consummated by contract rather than in accordance with the statutory procedure, is a merger within the protective purview of sections 908, subd. A and 515 of the corporation law. The shareholders of Glen Alden should have been notified accordingly and advised of their statutory rights of dissent and appraisal. The failure of the corporate officers to take these steps renders the stockholder approval of the agreement at the 1958 shareholders' meeting invalid. The lower court did not err in enjoining the officers and directors of Glen Alden from carrying out this agreement.

Decree affirmed at appellants' cost.

APPLICATION OF DELAWARE RACING ASSOCIATION

Supreme Court of Delaware, 1965.
213 A.2d 203.

WOLCOTT, Chief Justice. This is an appeal by stockholders of Delaware Steeplechase and Race Association (Steeplechase) from a judgment of the Vice Chancellor in an appraisal proceeding fixing the value of the Steeplechase stock.

Delaware Racing Association (Racing) filed a petition for an appraisal of the value of Steeplechase shares. Steeplechase, on July 31, 1963, under the provisions of 8 Del.C., § 253, had been merged into Racing. Stockholders of Steeplechase owning 77 common shares of the 1519 outstanding were determined to be entitled to an appraisal. The Vice Chancellor appointed an Appraiser who submitted a final report fixing the per share value of Steeplechase stock at $3,472.90. To this report both Racing and the stockholders filed exceptions. The Vice Chancellor fixed the per share value of Steeplechase at $2,321.30. This appeal followed.

A brief summary of the factual background is required. Steeplechase, between 1937 and July 31, 1963, owned and operated, with the exception of 1943, Delaware Park near Stanton, Delaware, a track for thoroughbred horse racing.   *   *   *

Steeplechase was organized and licensed and by 1938 had invested approximately $1,170,000 in fixed assets, of which only $15,-190.00 was supplied by the paid-in value of 1519 issued shares of $10 par common stock. The balance of the money invested by Steeplechase came from an issue of debentures and an issue of preferred stock. By 1945 the entire debenture issue had been redeemed, and by 1953 all of the preferred stock had been retired out of earnings, leaving as the sole corporate security outstanding 1519 shares of common stock. Meanwhile, from 1938 to July 31, 1963, the original investment of $1,170,000 in fixed assets had increased to $8,741,000.00. This increase had been financed out of earnings.

*   *   *

In April, 1962, William duPont, a director and large stockholder of Steeplechase, made an offer to all of Steeplechase's common stockholders to join with him in giving their shares to Delaware Park, Inc., a charitable corporation and sole owner of Racing, or, in the alternative, to sell their shares to him at a price of $1,530 per share, in which event he undertook to give such shares to Delaware Park, Inc. His offer was based upon an appraisal of Steeplechase stock made by Standard Research Consultants which fixed the fair market value of Steeplechase common stock as of December 31, 1962 at $1,530 per share. A summary of the appraisal report accompanied Mr. duPont's offer.

As a result of this offer a total of 1390 shares of Steeplechase was acquired by Delaware Park, Inc., either as a gift from Mr. duPont or as gifts from other registered shareholders of Steeplechase.

Delaware Park, Inc., thereupon, as the owner in excess of 90% of the shares of Steeplechase, caused Steeplechase to be merged into Racing pursuant to 8 Del.Code, § 253, the short-form merger statute.

Three questions are presented in this appeal:

* * *

2. Is the intrinsic value of a dissenting stockholder's stock in an appraisal proceeding resulting from a merger under 8 Del.Code, § 253, the liquidating rather than the going concern value of such shares?

3. Did the Vice Chancellor and the Appraiser err in their findings as to (a) asset value, (b) market value, (c) earnings value, (d) dividend value, and (e) the weight to be given each of these elements of value in appraising the Steeplechase stock?

* * *

Measure of Value

The stockholders argue that in an appraisal proceeding as a result of a short-form merger under 8 Del.Code, § 253, the value of minority stock is its liquidating rather than going concern value, as is the case with long-form mergers under 8 Del.Code, § 251.

The main thrust of the stockholders' argument for a different measure of value under § 253 from that under § 251 is that in mergers under § 251 a stockholder is free to continue in the going concern resulting from the merger or, in the alternative, is free to elect to withdraw from that enterprise and receive the value of his shares in cash. If he elects the latter, then it is proper, say the stockholders, to give him the going concern value of his stock, since he, himself, has chosen to withdraw from a going concern.

It is argued, however, that the same is not true with respect to short-form mergers under § 253 since the stockholder is given no election to continue his investment in the enterprise resulting from the merger, but is forced out and paid off in cash. Such being the case, it is said, he is entitled to be reimbursed for what has been taken from him, i. e., his aliquot interest in the assets of the corporation—in other words, the liquidating value of his shares.

We think, however, that there is no difference in the measure of value in appraisal proceedings growing out of a short-form merger under § 253 from the measure of value in appraisal proceedings growing out of a long-form merger under § 251.

In the first place, § 253(e) specifically provides that in the event a stockholder and the corporation fail to agree as to the value of the stock, either may petition for an appraisal as provided in 8 Del.Code, § 262(c), and that, thereafter, § 262(d) to (j) shall govern the rights and duties of the parties. Section 262 long preceded the enactment of § 253. It theretofore had applied only to long-form mergers and consolidations. A substantial line of decisions followed the enactment of § 262 to the effect that the dissenting stockholder was entitled to receive the value of his stock on a going concern basis. It must be presumed that the General Assembly in incorporating § 262 into § 253 did so with knowledge of the construction that had been placed upon § 262 by the Courts. Koeppel v. E. I. duPont de Nemours & Co., 8 W.W.Harr. 542; Crawford, Statutory Construction, § 224. We are of the opinion, therefore, that the General Assembly must have intended that the measure of value to be applied in appraisals under § 262 in short-form mergers under § 253 should be the same as the measure of value long applied in appraisals under § 262 with respect to long-form mergers under § 251.

The argument of the stockholders that the fact that they are being forced out of a going concern and being paid off in cash should lead to a measure of value which would give them that which they would have received in the event of dissolution, while perhaps superficially appealing, is more properly addressed to the General Assembly which enacted the law as we have found it.

Furthermore, we note that § 253 does not require, in all short-form mergers, that minority stockholders be forced out of the resulting corporation, for § 253(a) requires the parent corporation to state the terms and conditions of the merger "including the securities, cash or other consideration to be issued * * * upon surrender of each share of the subsidiary corporation * * * not owned by the parent corporation." Thus, conceivably, the parent corporation could if it wished permit the minority to remain in the resultant going enterprise. The fact that § 253 is designed to give the parent corporation, as we said in Stauffer v. Standard Brands, Del., 187 A.2d 78, "a means of eliminating the minority stockholders' interest in the enterprise" does not alter the result. The parent corporation at its election may adopt either method.

Since, therefore, the measure of value under § 253 is the same as the measure of value under § 251, it follows that these stockholders are entitled to be paid the intrinsic value of their shares determined on a going concern basis, which excludes a valuation based solely upon the liquidating value, or an aliquot share in the value of the assets of the merged corporation. Tri-Continental Corp. v. Battye, 31 Del. Ch. 523.

Asset Value

Both the Appraiser and the Vice Chancellor made findings as to the value of the assets of Steeplechase. The stockholders accept these findings but object to the deduction from the total asset value of 27% for obsolescence, to the refusal to include in the asset valuation a figure representing construction in progress and leasehold improvements, and to the deduction of a figure representing demolition costs from the value of the land.

Obsolescence

Delaware Park, the racing plant of Steeplechase, was built in 1937 when most of the patrons of the track arrived by railroad. At this time Delaware Park was favorably situated in close proximity to the tracks of the Pennsylvania and B. & O. Railroads. The establishment was laid out to take advantage of this then fortunate situation.

However, following the War, the pattern of transportation changed. Most, if not the greatly larger number of patrons now come to the track by automobile. The change in patron transportation habits was unfortunate from the point of view of Delaware Park. It now finds itself hemmed in by the railroad tracks which formerly served it so well.

Of primary concern are traffic and parking problems occasioned by the fact that the main entrance to the track for vehicular traffic is now an entrance across the racing oval from the grandstand and clubhouse. This causes traffic flow inside the park where none or little had been encountered before. In addition, the close proximity of the tracks to the rear of the grandstand has prevented the expansion of it to give more required space to accommodate the wagering public and for pari-mutuel ticket and money-handling problems. In addition, the change in traffic patterns has created problems in the supplying of facilities for animals and employees at the track.

The Appraiser found these items to be incurable functional and economic obsolescence, and concluded that a deduction for such obsolescence should be made. He concluded to apply the "age-life" method in order to determine what this deduction should be. This is one of the methods generally accepted for such purpose. The Appraisal of Real Estate, 212–213, 217–219.

The Appraiser's rationale in determining the percentage factor to be applied to determine obsolescence was that the racing facility had a life expectancy of $33\frac{1}{3}$ years which meant an age-life rate of 3% per year. He concluded that 1% of this was attributable to combined functional and economic obsolescence. Since the plant had been in existence for 27 years, he applied a 27% rate to the entire installation as an operational whole. This finding was approved by the Vice Chancellor.

The stockholders do not argue that no deduction should be made for obsolescence. They say, however, that the rate applied was far too high; that the rate should have been perhaps not more than 2%, and that in any event it should not have been applied in addition to depreciation to "equipment and personal property" and to the "newly refurbished clubhouse." They say that obsolescence is applicable only to the clubhouse and grandstand, and perhaps to the former main parking lot on Kirkwood Highway, not used at present to its former extent by reason of the change in transportation patterns.

We think, however, the stockholders misconceive what it was the Appraiser and the Vice Chancellor did. They concluded, and properly so we think upon this record, that the functional layout of Delaware Park was obsolete to a substantial degree because of the changes in the habits of the betting public, and because of the physical inability to adapt existing facilities to serve the public more efficiently.

This being so, they applied the obsolescence rate to the value of the plant as a whole, not to individual items as the stockholders would have them do. In so doing, we think they were correct for the test of the modernity of any facility to serve the public is its ability to do the job. If, by reason of the passage of time and the change of public habits, a racing plant, originally well designed for the purpose, has become less efficient to serve the purpose for which it is used, it has to some extent at least become obsolete as a whole—not merely the separate installations which together go to make up the whole plant.

We therefore affirm the ruling of the Appraiser and the Vice Chancellor that an obsolescence rate must be applied to the depreciated value of Steeplechase's racing plant as a whole. What that rate should be is a matter of judgment. The rate of 27% was determined in accordance with accepted theories and, in the judgment of both the Appraiser and Vice Chancellor, was proper. Since it is apparent that it was not arbitrarily determined, we will not disturb it.

We affirm the application of an obsolescence rate of 27% to the asset value of Steeplechase.

Construction in Progress and Leasehold Improvements

The stockholders object to the refusal of the Appraiser and the Vice Chancellor to include specifically in the assets of Steeplechase the sum of $192,607.00 which, apparently, was money paid for steel for future construction and for architects' fees. The difficulty with the argument made with respect to this is that at the hearing before him the Appraiser invited the stockholders to produce proof that the items in question were not included by the Appraiser in Current Assets as Deferred Charges. No such proof was offered and we think, therefore, the argument falls.

Deduction of Demolition Cost

The real estate appraiser for Steeplechase testified that the best possible use for its land was for residential purposes. The stockholders on the other hand produced witnesses who testified that probably the land would be used for industrial purposes and put a much higher value upon it. However, the Appraiser and the Vice Chancellor accepted the valuation of $2,754,000.00 based upon residential use as the more justified. The stockholders in this appeal do not take exception to this valuation.

They do, however, argue that it was improper to deduct from that valuation the sum of $457,000.00 representing the cost of demolition of existing structures in order to make the land available for residential use. They do not object to the amount estimated for demolition cost, but do object to any deduction at all for that purpose.

We think the stockholders are wrong. The land in question is being used, not for residential purposes, but for a racing plant. Since residential use is conceded to be the best possible use, presumably the land would be more valuable for that purpose than for any other.

Accordingly, a different use would necessarily discount the value of the land. Furthermore, it seems quite obvious to us that if the land were to be sold for residential use the purchaser in fixing the amount he was willing to pay would take into consideration the cost of demolishing existing structures in order to devote the land to the use intended.

It should be remembered, furthermore, that the value of the land to Steeplechase is its value as the location of a racing plant. Since we are concerned with a going concern value, we think the land value should reflect its value with respect to that going concern, and not with respect to a theoretical use. We accordingly affirm the deduction from land value of the cost of demolition of existing structures.

Market Value

The stockholders object to the Appraiser's finding, based upon the duPont offer to Steeplechase stockholders, of a market value of $1,530.00. They also object to the Vice Chancellor's use of the figure of $1,305.00 on the basis of a subsequent appraisal some year and a half after the fixing of the higher figure but reflecting the 1962 and 1963 earnings of Steeplechase. The stockholders take the position that there was no established market for Steeplechase shares and that the trading in the stock was so thin that none could be constructed.

It is, of course, axiomatic that if there is an established market for shares of a corporation the market value of such shares must be taken into consideration in an appraisal of their intrinsic value. Chicago Corporation v. Munds, 20 Del.Ch. 142. And if there is no reliable established market value for the shares a reconstructed market value, if one can be made, must be given consideration. Tri-Continental Corp. v. Battye, supra. It is, of course, equally axiomatic that market value, either actual or constructed, is not the sole element to be taken into consideration in the appraisal of stock.

The argument of the stockholders, we think, does not dispute this. They argue that market value is not an element to be considered in this appraisal because no reliable market existed, and none could be constructed.

The Appraiser found a market in the duPont offer to purchase Steeplechase shares at $1,530 and gave effect to this value in his ultimate appraisal. The stockholders attack this finding, citing in support Sporborg v. City Specialty Stores, 35 Del.Ch. 560. That case, however, is not apposite. It dealt with a situation in which a controlling stockholder for a period of almost two years prior to the merger had maintained a market in the stock. The use of a value based upon such an artificially maintained market was rejected because it was a market made only by one party in interest and which, consequently, was maintained at an artificially high level.

This is not the fact with respect to the duPont offer. He was not the controlling stockholder of Steeplechase. His offer was made, not on the basis of a so-called market figure, but was based on the true value of the stock as determined by a very exhaustive appraisal made by an independent appraiser. Under the circumstances, we think, a market value was established by the sale or gift of over 93% of Steeplechase stock over less than two years at a value of $1,530. Consequently, it was not error for the Appraiser to conclude that there was a market value at this amount.

The Vice Chancellor, however, did not accept this finding of the Appraiser. He preferred to adopt a "reconstructed market value" of $1,305 per share as of the date of the merger. The reconstructed market value as of the date of merger was made by the same appraisers who had, in February, 1962, fixed the market value of Steeplechase stock at $1,530 per share. The reason for the reduction in amount is that by the date of the merger the 1962 and 1963 earnings of Steeplechase were known. These earnings had declined and this fact led to a reduction in the figure representing market value.

We think it was proper for the Vice Chancellor to accept this reconstructed market value related precisely to the date of merger. Since value, particularly market value, is dependent to a large extent on earnings, it is proper to take into consideration a reduction in those earnings in constructing a market value. If this is a matter entering into the realm of judgment, as we think it probably is, we can find nothing in this record to indicate an erroneous exercise of judgment by the Vice Chancellor. We therefore affirm his finding as to market value.

Earnings Value

Using an average of the five-year period 1958–1962, the Appraiser fixed the earnings per share of Steeplechase stock at $182.13. The Vice Chancellor rejected this finding and using the five-year period 1959–1963 fixed the earnings per share of Steeplechase stock at $120.-19. The Appraiser in order to capitalize these earnings used a multiplier of 15.2, while the Vice Chancellor used a multiplier of 10. The stockholders except to the findings with respect to earnings value of both the Appraiser and the Vice Chancellor.

The main contention of the stockholders in this respect is a complaint against the use by Steeplechase of the sum-of-the-years digit method of depreciation which permitted Steeplechase to depreciate the major part of the cost of assets over the early years of their existence, thus reducing annual net income by a substantial amount. Accordingly, the stockholders' accountant divided Steeplechase's assets into those acquired prior to January 1, 1959 and those acquired or improved subsequent to that date. Depreciation on each of these assets was then recomputed on a basis which the accountant felt to be more proper. In so doing, the accountant materially increased the annual net earnings of Steeplechase.

Delaware law requires that earnings value be determined on the basis of historical earnings rather than on the basis of prospective earnings. Cottrell v. Pawcatuck Company, 36 Del.Ch. 169, 128 A.2d

225. Average earnings over the five-year period immediately preceding the merger have ordinarily been used as the basis for determining earnings value.

We therefore are of the opinion that the Vice Chancellor was correct in averaging earnings over the five years 1959–1963, since that was the period immediately preceding the merger. Even though the merger took place on July 31, 1963, the annual race meeting of that year had terminated by that time and all of Steeplechase's 1963 earnings had been made.

Furthermore, to start the period to be averaged with the year 1958 was to give a distorted effect to Steeplechase's earnings for the reason that 1958 was the first year of the so-called "long meeting," about 50 days, whereas theretofore meetings had been limited to 30 days. By reason of this, the earnings for 1958 were greatly increased. Furthermore, the new clubhouse had not been completed in 1958, although it was in progress, and there was no charge against 1958 earnings for this expense. All in all, we think it was more proper to take the five years 1959–1963 as the period to determine average earnings.

The argument of the stockholders based on the recalculation of depreciation by their accountant in reality comes down to nothing more than a disagreement among accountants as to what method should be followed in the depreciation of assets. The method of depreciation followed by Steeplechase was admittedly an acceptable accounting method and was accepted and approved by the Racing Commission and the Internal Revenue Service. This being so, we think the Appraiser and the Vice Chancellor did not err in accepting the method also.

Finally, the stockholders object to the use by the Vice Chancellor of a multiplier of 10 to fix the capitalized value of earnings. They argue that the multiplier of 15.2, that used by the Appraiser, should be applied. They point to the fact that Steeplechase is not an industrial-type business, not a retail store, nor a closed-end investment company. They liken it to a public utility as to which a proper multiplier is 15.2.

We think, however, that there are strong reasons why Steeplechase is not comparable to a public utility. In the first place, it is not a monopoly. It, in fact, operates in a field in which there is strong competition from other nearby tracks in neighboring states. In the second place, the State does not guarantee Steeplechase a fair return on its investment as it does with respect to public utilities. We think the two are not comparable. In fact, we believe Steeplechase to be unique.

In any event, the application of a multiplier to average earnings in order to capitalize them lies within the realm of judgment. There is no hard and fast rule to govern the selection. The multiplier of 10 used by the Vice Chancellor finds support in Dewing, The Financial Policies of Corporations (5th Ed.) 338–40, a book relied on in the past by the courts of this State. We cannot say, therefore, that reliance on this authority by the Vice Chancellor was improper. We affirm his use of a multiplier of 10.

Dividend Value

Both the Appraiser and the Vice Chancellor found that the dividend value of Steeplechase was zero and gave it 10% weight. The stockholders object to this and argue that dividend value should be given no independent weight whatsoever independent of earnings. Their reason for this is that earnings and dividends are so clearly related that they largely reflect the same value factor.

In Tri-Continental Corp. v. Battye, supra, we pointed out that the object of an appraisal was to give the dissenting stockholder the equivalent of that which he could expect to receive in one way or another if he had remained as a stockholder in the going concern. This means, of course, that dividends paid, or the possibility of them being paid in the future, is of especial significance in questions of valuation since receipt of dividends is ordinarily the most usual way for the stockholder to realize upon the value of his stock.

In the case of Steeplechase, no dividends have ever been paid on the common stock, and at the time of the merger it did not appear that the prospect of payment in the future was any brighter. This stemmed from the admittedly no-profit policy of the management, the restrictions imposed by the Racing Commission upon the payment of dividends on the common stock, and the plain fact that earnings in any substantial amount would not be available for the payment of dividends in the foreseeable future.

By reason of these facts, both the Appraiser and the Vice Chancellor gave the non-payment of dividends "substantial negative recognition." This conclusion is in accord with Adams v. R. C. Williams & Co., Del.Ch., 158 A.2d 797, in which the Chancellor referred back an appraisal proceeding to the Appraiser with instructions to give some weight to a negative dividend factor. On further hearing the Appraiser gave 40% weight to the zero earnings value, which was later affirmed by the Chancellor in an unreported opinion.

Since a negative dividend value clearly is pertinent in fixing the value of stock, we cannot say that the judgment of the Appraiser and the Vice Chancellor was in error in giving it a negative weighting. We affirm that decision.

Weighting

The Vice Chancellor reversed the weighting given by the Appraiser to the various elements of value and weighted those elements according to his own judgment. His weighting was as follows:

Asset Value	25%
Market Value	40%
Earnings Value	25%
Dividend Value	10%

In so doing the Vice Chancellor disagreed with the Appraiser who had weighted asset value at 40% and market value at 25%. The Vice Chancellor reduced the weight to be given asset value for the reason that there were no plans to liquidate the Steeplechase assets and, therefore, the assets would continue to be held for the purpose of future earnings.

Since the value of Steeplechase shares is not to be determined on the basis of a liquidation, we cannot say as a matter of law that the Vice Chancellor's judgment on this was clearly wrong.

The Vice Chancellor weighted market value at 40% because of his judgment that in the long run the most likely way in which an investor in Steeplechase stock, if permitted to continue in the resulting enterprise, could have realized on his investment was by way of a sale of his shares. This conclusion accords with the Tri-Continental case and, we think, is a proper reason for changing the weighting given this element by the Appraiser.

The question of what weight to give the various elements of value lies always within the realm of judgment. There is no precise criterion to apply to determine the question. It is a matter of discretion with the valuator. In the absence of a clear indication of a mistake of judgment, or a mistake of law, we think this Court should accept the reasoned exercise of judgment of the Vice Chancellor and not substitute its own guess as to what the proper weightings should be. Since there has been no showing of an improper or arbitrary exercise of judgment by the Vice Chancellor, we accept his findings in this respect.

By reason of the foregoing, the judgment of the Vice Chancellor fixing the value of the stockholders' stock in Steeplechase at $2,321.30 per share is affirmed.

Delaware General Corporation Law

§ 262(k)

(k) This section shall not apply to the shares of any class or series of a class of stock which, at the record date fixed to determine the stockholders entitled to receive notice of and to vote at the meeting of stockholders at which the agreement of merger or consolidation is to be acted on, were either (1) registered on a national securities exchange, or (2) held of record by not less than 2,000 stockholders, unless the certificate of incorporation of the corporation issuing such stock shall otherwise provide; nor shall this section apply to any of the shares of stock of the constituent corporation surviving a merger if the merger did not require for its approval the vote of the stockholders of the surviving corporation, as provided in subsection (f) of section 251 of this title. This subsection shall not be applicable to the holders of a class or series of a class of stock of a constituent corporation if under the terms of a merger or consolidation pursuant to sections 251 or 252 of this title such holders are required to accept for such stock anything except (a) stock or stock and cash in lieu of fractional shares, of the corporation surviving, or resulting from such merger or consolidation or (b) stock or stock and cash in lieu of fractional shares of any other corporation, which at the record date fixed to determine the stockholders entitled to receive notice of and to vote at the meeting of stockholders at which the agreement of merger or consolidation is to be acted on, were either (1) registered on a national securities exchange or (2) held of record by not less than 2,000 stockholders, or (c) a combination of stock or stock and cash in lieu of fractional shares as set forth in (a) and (b) of this subsection.

NOTE ON TAX PROBLEMS OF MERGERS AND REORGANIZATIONS

(Both Acquisitive and Divisive Reorganizations)

Section 368(a) (1) of the Internal Revenue Code (26 U.S.C.A. § 368(a) (1)) defines the term "reorganization" to mean many things for tax purposes, each of which is commonly designated as a "Type", and each Type takes its name from the subsection of Section 368(a) (1) in which it is described. Briefly they are as follows:

Type A, a statutory merger or consolidation;

Type B, the acquisition of stock in one corporation in exchange solely for voting stock of the acquiring corporation which must immediately after the acquisition have control of the acquired corporation;

Type C, the acquisition of substantially all of the assets of one corporation in exchange solely for voting stock of the acquiring corporation although liabilities of the acquired corporation may be assumed;

Type D, a transfer by a corporation of all or a part of its assets to another corporation which either it or its shareholders control immediately after the transfer, but only if, pursuant to the plan of reorganization, stock or securities of the acquired corporation are distributed in a transaction which qualifies as a tax free exchange or distribution;

Type E, a recapitalization; or

Type F, a mere change in identity, form or place of organization.

It can be readily seen that many of these transactions do not fit the common concept of a "reorganization"; yet all of them contemplate the continuation of the business enterprise in one form or another with the stockholders of the old business enterprise continuing to maintain a financial interest in it. The same is true of corporate divisions, which can take a variety of forms and are sometimes called "spin-offs", "split-offs", and "split-ups". In corporate divisions if the standards of Sec. 355 of the Internal Revenue Code are met a distribution of securities of a corporation to its shareholders of stock in a corporation controlled by it will not result in recognition of gain or loss to the distributee shareholders, that is, it will be tax-free to the shareholders. In acquisitions and divisions the key question is always whether the change in the form of ownership in the business enter-

312 BUSINESS ACQUISITIONS AND DIVISIONS   Ch. 6

prise held by the shareholder represents a distribution of assets to
him by his corporation reflecting its accumulated earnings and profits; if so, then the transaction will not be a tax-free transaction.   In
determining this question the courts have established several doctrines
which are as much a part of the tax law in reference to these problems
as anything written into the Internal Revenue Code itself by Congress.

In Gregory v. Helvering, 293 U.S. 465, 55 S.Ct. 266, 79 L.Ed. 596
(1935), reported in Chapter III above, the Supreme Court established
the "business purpose" doctrine in disallowing the tax-free distribution of certain shares of stock to the sole stockholder of the parent corporation because there was no "business purpose" to the transaction;
it was simply a plan of tax avoidance.   The concept of the *Gregory*
case pervades all tax law, as noted above.   This same doctrine applies
in corporate divisions, as can be seen from Helvering, Commissioner
v. Elkhorn Coal Co., 95 F.2d 752 (4th Cir.1937) cert. denied 305 U.S.
605, reported below.   Income Tax Regulations § 1.368–1(c) also emphasizes this point by stating, "[A] plan of reorganization must contemplate the bona fide execution of one of the transactions specifically described as a reorganization in Sec. 368(a) and for the bona fide
consumation of each of the requisite acts under which non-recognition
of gain is claimed.   *   *   *   A scheme, which involves an abrupt departure from normal reorganization procedure in connection with the
transaction on which the imposition of tax is imminent, such as a mere
device that puts on the form of a corporate reorganization as a disguise for concealing its real character, and the object and accomplishment of which is a consumation of a preconceived plan having no
business or corporate purpose, is not a plan of reorganization."

The continuity of the business enterprise is another court-deter-
mined requirement of a tax-free reorganization.   This actually takes
two forms, not only a continuity of the business itself, but equally important, a continuity of interest in the new corporation by the shareholders of the former corporation.   This distinction is drawn, and the
continuity requirements are well illustrated in U. S. v. Adkins-Phelps,
Inc., 400 F.2d 737 (8th Cir.1968), reported below.

All of the transactions leading up to the consummation of the
plan of reorganization, or the division of the corporation, are viewed
in their entirety by the courts.   This is called the "step-transaction"
doctrine.   If a reshuffling of corporate properties, or of stock in subsidiaries, occurs before the consummation of the plan of reorganization, particularly in such manner as to transfer assets to shareholders to give them something more than a change in the form of their
ownership of the corporation or its assets, then the courts will hold
that these steps are not a part of a plan or reorganization which qualifies as a tax-free transaction.   This is illustrated by two cases reported below, *Elkhorn Coal*, referred to above, which deals with both
a divisive and an acquisitive reorganization, and Commissioner v.
Gordon, 391 U.S. 83, 88 S.Ct. 1517, 20 L.Ed. 448 (1968), reported below.

HELVERING v. ELKHORN COAL CO.

United States Circuit Court of Appeals, Fourth Circuit, 1937.
95 F.2d 732.

PARKER, Circuit Judge. This is a petition to review a decision of the Board of Tax Appeals holding profit realized by the Elkhorn Coal & Coke Company upon a transfer of certain mining properties to the Mill Creek Coal & Coke Company to be nontaxable. The ground of the decision was that the transfer was made pursuant to a plan of reorganization within the meaning of section 203(h)(1)(A) of the Revenue Act of 1926, 44 Stat. 12. The facts were stipulated and are set forth at length in the findings of the Board which are reported with its opinion in Elkhorn Coal Co. v. Com'r, 34 B.T.A. 845.   *   *   *

[Early in December, 1925, Elkhorn Coal & Coke Company, hereafter referred to as the old company, formed a plan to transfer certain of its mining properties and equipment to a neighboring company, Mill Creek Coal & Coke Company. A majority of the directors of both corporations consisted of the same persons. The old company owned certain other assets which Mill Creek did not desire to acquire, so the old company formed a new company under the name of Elkhorn Coal Company, hereafter referred to as the new company. On December 18, 1925, the old company transferred to the new company the assets Mill Creek did not want in exchange for all of the stock of the new company, which was promptly distributed by the old company to its stockholders. This transaction today would be called a Type D reorganization under the provisions of Section 368(a)(1)(D) of the 1954 Internal Revenue Code, followed by a "spin-off", but would not be tax-free for several reasons. On December 31, 1925, the old company transferred the desired assets to Mill Creek in exchange for 1000 shares of the stock of Mill Creek, which number of shares was not sufficient to give the old company "control" (i. e. 80% voting control) of Mill Creek and therefore would not qualify as a tax-free exchange under several provisions of the Internal Revenue Code; however it was argued by the old company that the transfer on December 31, 1925 to Mill Creek was the transfer of all of its properties in exchange for Mill Creek stock and therefore came within the tax-free reorganization provisions of what under the 1954 Internal Revenue Code would be called a Type C reorganization, Section 368(a)(1)(C). On January 22, 1926, the new company exchanged additional shares of its stock with the stockholders of the old company, giving the stockholders in the old company the same interest in the new company that they had had in the old. In this exchange, the new company acquired all of the outstanding stock of the old company, making the old company the 100% owned subsidiary of the new company. The old company then transferred the 1000 shares of stock of Mill Creek (by this time its only asset) to its new corporate parent, the new company and the old company was dissolved. The Court concluded that, "[n]o reason appears for the organization of the new company except to provide a transferee to take over and hold the assets which were not to be transferred to the Mill Creek Company so that the transfer to that company when made would be a transfer of all the assets of the old company."]

The Board was of opinion that all of these transactions were carried through pursuant to prearranged plan, saying: "We do not doubt that before a single step was taken a plan had been formulated for regrouping the corporate assets"; and "The stipulated facts justify the inference that one of the motives which the stockholders of Elkhorn had in organizing the new corporation and causing the three corporations to adopt the several steps or plans of reorganization which were adopted and carried out, was to make the transfer of the mining properties from Elkhorn to Mill Creek without resulting tax liability to Elkhorn or to themselves." The Board thought, however, with five members dissenting, that because the transfers from the old company to the new were genuine and were separate and distinct from the transfer to the Mill Creek Company, the latter must be treated as a transfer of substantially all of the properties of the corporation within the meaning of the reorganization statute, summing up its conclusions as follows: "In our opinion, the facts show affirmatively that the transfer to Mill Creek was completely separate and distinct from the earlier transfer by Elkhorn to the new corporation. The transfer made on December 18 was complete within itself, regardless of what Elkhorn planned to do later, or did subsequently do. It was not a sham or a device intended to obscure the character of the transaction of December 31. The stipulated facts do not suggest other than a bona fide business move. The transfer made on December 31 was also complete within itself, and was made for reasons germane to the business of both corporations. This transfer falls within the terms of clause (A) of section 203(h) (1), whether or not Elkhorn was dissolved." [This provision is substantially similar to Sec. 368(a) (1) (C) of the 1954 Internal Revenue Code.]

A careful consideration of the evidentiary facts discloses no purpose which could have been served by the creation of the new company and the transfer of the assets to it, except to strip the old company of all of its properties which were not to be transferred to the Mill Creek Company, in anticipation of that transfer. The creation of the new company and its acquisition of the assets of the old was not a corporate reorganization, therefore, within the meaning of the statute or within any fair meaning of the term "reorganization." It did not involve any real transfer of assets by the business enterprise or any rearranging of corporate structure, but at most a mere shifting of charters, having no apparent purpose except the avoidance of taxes on the transfer to the Mill Creek Company which was in contemplation. To use in part the language of the Supreme Court in Gregory v. Helvering, 293 U.S. 465, it was "simply an operation having no business or corporate purpose—a mere device which put on the form of a corporate reorganization as a disguise for concealing its real character, and the sole object and accomplishment of which was the consummation of a preconceived plan, not to reorganize a business or any part of a business," but to give to the intended transfer to the Mill Creek Company the appearance of a transfer of all the corporate assets so as to bring it within the nonrecognition provision of section * * * [368(a) (1) (C) of the 1954 Internal Revenue Code].

Under such circumstances we think that the decision in Gregory v. Helvering, supra, is controlling. In that case, for the purpose of avoiding taxes on a liquidating dividend of shares of stock held by a corporation, a subsidiary was organized within the terms of the reorganization statute and the shares were transferred to it. The stock of the subsidiary was then delivered to the sole stockholder of the original corporation and shortly thereafter the subsidiary was dissolved and the shares which had been transferred to it were delivered to the stockholder. The court held that although the organization of the subsidiary came within the letter of the reorganization statute, such corporate manipulation would be ignored when it fulfilled no proper corporate function and was not in reality a reorganization within the meaning of the statute. The court said: "In these circumstances, the facts speak for themselves and are susceptible of but one interpretation. The whole undertaking, though conducted according to the terms of subdivision [D], was in fact an elaborate and devious form of conveyance masquerading as a corporate reorganization, and nothing else. The rule which excludes from consideration the motive of tax avoidance is not pertinent to the situation, because the transaction upon its face lies outside the plain intent of the statute. To hold otherwise would be to exalt artifice above reality and to deprive the statutory provision in question of all serious purpose."

We do not see how that case can be distinguished from this. If the property which was to be transferred to Mill Creek had been transferred to a new company created for the purpose and had been by that company transferred to Mill Creek, no one would contend that there was a distinction; and certainly there is no difference in principle between creating a subsidiary to take and convey the property to the intended transferee and creating a subsidiary to take over the other assets and having the old company make the transfer. In either case, the apparent reorganization is a mere artifice; and it can make no difference which of the affiliated corporations makes the transfer of assets which it is desired to bring within the nonrecognition provisions of the statute.

It is suggested in the opinion of the Board that the case before us is analogous to that which would have been presented if the old company, prior to the transfer to Mill Creek, had distributed to its stockholders all of the assets except those destined for such transfer; but the distinction is obvious. In the case supposed, the business enterprise would have definitely divested itself of the property distributed. Here it did not divest itself of the property at all, but merely made certain changes in the legal papers under which it enjoyed corporate existence. No rule is better settled than that in tax matters we must look to substance and not to form; and no one who looks to substance can see in the mere change of charters, which is all that we have here, any reason for permitting a transfer of a part of the corporate assets to escape the taxation to which it is subject under the statute.

Congress has seen fit to grant nonrecognition of profit in sale or exchange of assets only under certain conditions, one of which is that one corporation shall transfer "substantially all" of its properties for stock in another. If nonrecognition of profit can be secured by the plan adopted in this case, the exemption is broadened to cover all transfers of assets for stock, whether "substantially all" or not, if only the transferor will go to the slight trouble and expense of getting a new charter for his corporation and making the transfer of assets to the new corporation thus created in such way as to leave in the old only the assets to be transferred at the time the transfer is to be made. We do not think the statutory exemption may be thus broadened by such an artifice.

Having reached this conclusion, it is unnecessary to decide whether the unity of the plan under which the transfer was made brings it, without a unifying contract, within the principles laid down in Starr v. Commissioner (C.C.A.4th) 82 F.(2d) 964, wherein we said: "Where transfers are made pursuant to such a plan of reorganization, they are ordinarily parts of one transaction and should be so treated in application of the well-settled principle that, in applying income tax laws, the substance, and not the form, of the transaction shall control. * * * This is demanded also by the principle, equally well settled, that a single transaction may not be broken up into various elements to avoid a tax. * * * "

For the reasons stated, the decision of the Board will be reversed, and the cause will be remanded to it for further proceedings in accordance with this opinion.

Reversed.

HENRY H. WATKINS, District Judge, dissented.

UNITED STATES v. ADKINS–PHELPS, INCORPORATED

United States Court of Appeals, Eighth Circuit, 1968.
400 F.2d 737.

VAN OOSTERHOUT, Chief Judge. This is a timely appeal from final judgment of the District Court awarding Adkins-Phelps, Incorporated (taxpayer), $40,689.38 and interest as a refund of income tax of taxpayer for the fiscal year ending September 30, 1961, alleged to have been unlawfully assessed and collected. Adkins-Phelps, Incorporated, an Arkansas corporation, acquired the assets of J. F. Weinmann Milling Company (Weinmann), also an Arkansas corporation, through corporate reorganization procedures effected on November 11, 1959, which were admittedly in conformity with Arkansas law.

On the date of the reorganization, Weinmann had an unused net operating loss of $602,420.34. Taxpayer in its income tax return for the fiscal year ending September 30, 1961, absorbed its $88,825.73 income completely by off-setting pre-merger losses of Weinmann. The Commissioner disallowed the loss deduction, which resulted in the deficiency assessment of $40,689.38 here involved. The taxpayer, after paying such assessment, filed timely claim for refund which was disallowed, wereupon this action was commenced. Jurisdiction is established.

This case was tried before a jury. The only verdict returned by the jury was a response to a special interrogatory which was answered by the jury as follows: "That the plaintiff did not effect a merger with J. F. Weinmann Milling Company for the principal purpose of tax avoidance." * * * Upon the basis of the special verdict, the court on December 22, 1966, entered judgment for the taxpayer for the amount of the refund claimed.

    * * *

The Government upon this appeal asserts it is entitled to a reversal for the following reasons:

1. No corporate reorganization within the meaning of § 368(a) (1) (A), I.R.C.1954, (26 U.S.C.A. § 368(a) (1) (A)) exists because the continuity of interest requirement was not met.

    (a) The Adkins-Phelps stock acquired by Mrs. Weinmann pursuant to the merger agreement did not represent a substantial proprietary interest.

    (b) Insolvency of Weinmann completely wiped out all stockholders' equity in that corporation.

2. No § 368(a) (1) (A) reorganization exists because the continuity of business enterprise requirement was not met.

Section 381 provides that in the case of precisely defined types of corporate acquisition certain tax items of a transferor corporation as of the date of the transfer shall be taken into account by the acquiring corporation for income tax purposes. Among such items is the net operating loss carry-over, subject to the conditions imposed by § 381 (c) (1).

In order for a corporate acquisition to qualify for survival of loss carry-overs to the succeeding corporation, it must be one of the tax-free types set out in § 381(a). Included in the qualifying category is a transfer to which § 361 applies "but only if the transfer is in connection with the reorganization described in subparagraph (A) * * * of section 368(a) (1)." Section 368(a) (1) (A), primarily relied upon by taxpayer, includes in the definition of reorganization, "(A) a statutory merger or consolidation."

The Government does not contend that the Arkansas laws governing merger or consolidation have not been complied with. The parties agree that the compliance with state merger or consolidation statutes standing alone is not sufficient to satisfy the requirements of § 368(a) (1) (A). In addition, under the judicial gloss put upon the statute by the courts in light of the legislative history and purpose, a showing of continuity of interest is required. Such requirement is summarized in Southwest Natural Gas Co. v. Commissioner, 5 Cir., 189 F.2d 332, 334, as follows:

"(1) that the transferor corporation or its shareholders retained a substantial proprietary stake in the enterprise represented by a material interest in the affairs of the transferee corporation, and (2) that such retained interest represents a substantial part of the value of the property transferred."

* * *

The trial court, as a basis for its determination that the continuity of interest requirement has been met, states:

"The plan of reorganization called for an exchange of stock on a share-for-share basis between Adkins-Phelps and the stockholders of Weinmann.

The result of this exchange was that Mrs. Weinmann, who held 99% of the Weinmann stock, owned approximately one-sixth of the outstanding stock of Adkins-Phelps. In addition to being the principal shareholder, Mrs. Weinmann was also one of the largest creditors of Weinmann. We think, however, that it is immaterial whether Mrs. Weinmann occupied her position as an equity owner of Weinmann in her capacity as principal shareholder or as a creditor. The fact that she maintained a substantial equity interest in Adkins-Phelps subsequent to the merger we consider to be sufficient to meet the continuity of interest requirement, and we so hold."

Such finding and holding is supported by substantial evidence and is not clearly erroneous.

The Government does not seriously contend that a one-sixth stock interest would not be sufficient to establish continuity of interest. Principal reliance is placed upon a portion of the merger agreement reciting that the par value of Adkins-Phelps stock is $1.00 per share and the provision granting a stock option, which reads: "that for and as part of the consideration of the merger that the stockholders of the consolidated corporation, continuing under the name of Adkins-Phelps, Inc., bind themselves and agree that each stockholder will not transfer his, her or its capital stock in the Adkins-Phelps, Inc., corporation without first offering said stock to Adkins-Phelps, Inc., for par value."

The Government contends that by reason of the foregoing agreement all attributes of stock ownership are absent in the 997 shares of stock acquired by Mrs. Weinmann in the merger and that Mrs. Weinmann's stock interest could never be worth more than its $997 aggregate par value.

Such argument lacks validity for the reasons hereinafter set out:

1. Mrs. Weinmann, except for the sale restriction if valid, possessed all rights of a stockholder, including the right to vote the stock, the right to receive distribution of profits realized in the form of cash or stock dividends, preemptive rights to a proportionate share of any

new stock issued, and a right to pledge the stock as security. Such rights are substantial attributes of stock ownership.

2. The agreement placed Mrs. Weinmann under no obligation to sell the stock to the other shareholders. She had a complete right to continue to hold the stock. The Government contends that by reason of her age of 82 years, with a life expectancy of about 4 years, that Mrs. Weinmann or her heirs would soon have to sell all the stock for $997 under the agreement. The agreement does not fix a time period nor does it by its terms bind Mrs. Weinmann, her heirs or assigns, to sell the stock to any one at any time. Restrictions of this type are strictly construed and it is very doubtful whether the duty to sell would be binding upon Mrs. Weinmann's estate. * * *

The fact that Mrs. Weinmann improvidently, at her insistence and against contrary advice, sold her stock to Adkins-Phelps for $997 is not material to the issue here. The determination of the substantiality of the stock interest must be upon the basis of the situation existing at the time of the merger.

3. The purchase option agreement applied alike to all then existing stockholders and thus Mrs. Weinmann acquired the same purchase option with respect to other stockholders as she had given to them.

4. The fact that Arkansas by Article 2, Section 19 of its Constitution prohibits perpetuities, and the fact that the merger agreement option contains no time limitation and no provision for making it applicable to heirs or assigns, tend to support the view that the option right would expire upon the death of the grantor or the grantee of the option and would not pass to the heirs. See Roemhild v. Jones, 8 Cir., 239 F.2d 492, 495–497.

The Government makes the additional contention that Weinmann was insolvent prior to the merger and hence Mrs. Weinmann as a stockholder in that company had nothing to transfer to Adkins-Phelps in exchange for its stock. The value of the stock interest must be judged by the situation existing at the time of the merger. As of such time, the evidence does not compel a finding of insolvency of Weinmann in a bankruptcy sense. No adjudication of insolvency was ever made. The debts of Weinmann prior to the merger had been substantially reduced. $87,000 received as proceeds of a life insurance policy of a company officer was applied upon the bonded indebtedness. Mrs. Weinmann agreed that $89,000 of the indebtedness she claimed to be due her from the corporation could be treated as a contribution to capital. Concessions were made by the bondholders. It is established that Weinmann's real estate holdings were worth far more than the value attributed to the real estate by the company books.

The equity interest in a corporation remains in the shareholders until the creditors, by appropriate action, cut off such equity interest. See Palm Springs Holding Corp. v. Commissioner, 315 U.S. 185. * * *

No appropriate action has here been taken to divest the stock equity interest. The claims of all creditors have been adjusted and satisfied. An equity stock interest in the Weinmann stock has been established in Mrs. Weinmann and such interest which was exchanged for stock in Adkins-Phelps establishes the required continuity of interest.

In any event, Mrs. Weinmann was a substantial creditor of the corporation. The claims of other substantial creditors were satisfied. Thus it would seem to make little difference whether Mrs. Weinmann received her stock in Adkins-Phelps, Inc., as a stockholder or a creditor of the old corporation. See Seiberling Rubber Co. v. Commissioner, 6 Cir., 169 F.2d 595. * * *

Lastly, the Government urges that the continuity of business requirement has not been met. Such contention was properly rejected by the trial court. Upon this issue, the trial court states:

"Defendant approaches this issue in two ways. It first contends that under the rule of Libson Shops, Inc. v. Koehler, 353 U.S. 382 (1957), Adkins-Phelps may not deduct pre-merger losses incurred by Weinmann. Plaintiff contends, on the other hand, that *Libson Shops* case was decided under the 1939 Code, prior to the enactment of Sections 381 and 382 of the 1954 Code, and that the *Libson Shops* doctrine was superseded by the enactment of these sections. In support of this contention plaintiff cites the case of Maxwell Hardware Co. v. Commissioner, 343 F.2d 713 (9 Cir. 1965). This case held that by enacting Sections 381 and 382, Congress intended to substitute statutory rules for court-made law and the precedential value of the *Libson Shops* decision has been destroyed.

"We find the *Maxwell Hardware* case very persuasive in its argument and sound in its result. It seems clear to us that Sections 381 and 382 were designed to provide definite limitations upon the use to which operating loss carryovers may be put. Section 381 provides that a successor or transferee corporation may step into the 'tax shoes' of a transferor corporation, under certain circumstances, and take into account, among other things, the transferor's net operating loss carryovers. Section 382 sets out specific limitations on the right to take a net operating loss deduction where there has been a change in ownership of the corporate stock and a change in the corporation's trade or business.

"In connection with these new sections, and in light of the rationale of the *Maxwell Hardware* case, we cannot say that the *Libson Shops* case is still the law and that its requirements must be met before a net operating loss carryover may be taken."

It would appear from the trial court's opinion that the Government relied upon Libson Shops, Inc. v. Koehler, 353 U.S. 382. Maxwell Hardware Co. v. Commissioner, 9 Cir., 343 F.2d 713, relied upon by the trial court, clearly points out that *Libson Shops* arose under I.R.C. 1939 and that substantial changes were made by the Internal Revenue Code of 1954. As stated in *Maxwell,* the legislative history demonstrates that "it was the clearly expressed intention of Congress to attempt to bring some order out of chaos, and, in effect, to countenance 'trafficking' in operating loss carryovers except as affected by the special limitations of Section 382 and the general limitations of Section 381." 343 F.2d 713.

Revenue Ruling 63–29 discloses that the surviving corporation must engage in a business enterprise to qualify for the loss deduction but also makes clear that the surviving corporation "need not continue the activities conducted by its predecessor." All that is required in this respect is that the survivor continue to carry on some business activity. See Frederick Steel Co. v. Commissioner, 6 Cir., 375 F.2d 351; Bittker and Eustice, Federal Income Taxation of Corporations and Shareholders, § 12.19; Mertens Law of Federal Income Taxation § 20.54.

The Government, citing Pridemark, Inc. v. Commissioner, 4 Cir., 345 F.2d 35, urges that temporary cessation of business activities constitutes a break in the continuity of business requirement. *Pridemark* is readily distinguishable from our present case. In that case, all substantial assets including sales contracts and customer lists were sold to Golden Key and Golden Key was allowed to hire its personnel. The court found that there had been a complete liquidation of the corporation and that its business of selling prefabricated homes had been abandoned. In our present case, the temporary lull in business was caused by financial distress. Weinmann did not sell out substantially all the assets involved in its business operations. The business was resumed before the merger and as heretofore stated, the jury found the merger was not effected primarily for the purpose of tax avoidance. Weinmann's business had been very successful prior to Mr. Weinmann's death and its brand name products had wide acceptance in the West Memphis area where taxpayer operated. Under the facts presented by the record, we do not believe that the temporary suspension of taxpayer's business activities requires a determination that the continuity of business requirement has not been met. The trial court did not err in determining as a fact issue that the continuity of business requirement had been satisfied. Compare Clarksdale Rubber Co. v. Commissioner, 45 T.C. 234; H. F. Ramsey Co. v. Commissioner, 43 T.C. 500.

The judgment of the District Court is affirmed.

———

GREGORY v. HELVERING

Supreme Court of the United States, 1935.
293 U.S. 465, 55 S.Ct. 266, 79 L.Ed. 596.

(This case is reported in Chapter III at page 63.)

COMMISSIONER OF INTERNAL REVENUE v. GORDON

Supreme Court of the United States, 1968.
391 U.S. 83, 88 S.Ct. 1517, 20 L.Ed.2d 448.

Mr. Justice HARLAN delivered the opinion of the Court.

These cases, involving the interpretation of § 355 of the Internal Revenue Code of 1954, have an appropriately complex history.

American Telephone and Telegraph Company (hereafter A. T. & T.) conducts its local communications business through corporate subsidiaries. Prior to July 1, 1961, communications services in California, Oregon, Washington, and Idaho were provided by Pacific Telephone and Telegraph Company (hereafter Pacific). A. T. & T. held about 90% of the common stock of Pacific at all relevant times. The remainder was widely distributed.

Early in 1961, it was decided to divide Pacific into two separate corporate subsidiaries of A. T. & T. The plan was to create a new corporation, Pacific Northwest Bell Telephone Company (hereafter Northwest) to conduct telephone business in Oregon, Washington, and Idaho, leaving the conduct of the California business in the hands of Pacific. To this end, Pacific would transfer all its assets and liabilities in the first three States to Northwest, in return for Northwest common stock and debt paper. Then, Pacific would transfer sufficient Northwest stock to Pacific shareholders to pass control of Northwest to the parent company, A. T. & T.

Pacific had, however, objectives other than fission. It wanted to generate cash to pay off existing liabilities and meet needs for capital, but not to have excess cash left over. It also feared that a simple distribution of the Northwest stock would encounter obstacles under California corporation law. Consequently, the "Plan for Reorganization" submitted to Pacific's shareholders on February 27, 1961, had two special features. It provided that only about 56% of the Northwest common stock would be offered to Pacific shareholders immediately after the creation of Northwest. It also provided that, instead of simply distributing Northwest stock pro rata to shareholders, Pacific would distribute to its shareholders transferable rights entitling their holders to purchase Northwest common from Pacific at an amount to be specified by Pacific's Board of Directors, but expected to be below the fair market value of the Northwest common.

In its February 27 statement to shareholders, Pacific said that it was seeking a ruling from the Internal Revenue Service "with respect to the tax status of the rights to purchase which will be issued in connection with the offerings of capital stock of the New Company to shareholders of the Company. * * *"

The statement warned, however, that "[t]axable income to the holders of such shares may result with respect to such rights."

The plan was approved by Pacific's shareholders on March 24, 1961. Pacific transferred its assets and liabilities in Oregon, Washington, and Idaho to Northwest, and ceased business in those States on June 30, 1961. On September 29, 1961, Pacific issued to its common stockholders one right for each outstanding share of Pacific stock. These rights were exercisable until October 20, 1961. Six rights plus a payment of $16 were required to purchase one share of Northwest common. The rights issued in 1961 were sufficient to transfer about 57% of the Northwest stock.

By September 29, 1961, the Internal Revenue Service had ruled that shareholders who sold rights would realize ordinary income in the amount of the sales price, and that shareholders who exercised rights would realize ordinary income in the amount of the difference between $16 paid in and the fair market value, measured as of the date of exercise, of the Northwest common received. The prospectus accompanying the distributed rights informed Pacific shareholders of this ruling.

On June 12, 1963, the remaining 43% of the Northwest stock was offered to Pacific shareholders. This second offering was structured much as the first had been, except that eight rights plus $16 were required to purchase one share of Northwest.

The Gordons, respondents in No. 760, and the Baans, petitioners in No. 781, were minority shareholders of Pacific as of September 29, 1961. In the rights distribution that occurred that day the Gordons received 1,540 rights under the plan. They exercised 1,536 of the rights on October 5, 1961, paying $4,096 to obtain 256 shares of Northwest, at a price of $16 plus six rights per share. The average price of Northwest stock on the American Stock Exchange was $26 per share on October 5. On the same day, the Gordons sold the four odd rights for $6.36. The Baans received 600 rights on September 29, 1961. They exercised them all on October 11, 1961, receiving 100 shares of Northwest in return for their 600 rights and $1,600. On October 11, the agreed fair market value of one Northwest share was $26.94.

In their federal income tax returns for 1961, neither the Gordons nor the Baans reported any income upon the receipt of the rights or upon exercising them to obtain Northwest stock at less than its fair market value. The Gordons also did not report any income on the sale of the four rights. The Commissioner asserted deficiencies against both sets of taxpayers. He contended, in a joint proceeding in the Tax Court, that the taxpayers received ordinary income in the amount of the difference between the sum they paid in exercising their rights and the fair market value of the Northwest stock received. He contended further that the Gordons realized ordinary income in the amount of $6.36, the sales price, upon the sale of their four odd rights.

The Tax Court upheld the taxpayers' contention that the 1961 distribution of Northwest stock met the requirements of § 355 of the Code, with the result that no gain or loss should be recognized on the receipt by them or their exercise of the rights. The Tax Court held, however, that the Gordons' sale of the four odd rights resulted in ordinary income to them. The Commissioner appealed the *Baan* case to the Court of Appeals for the Ninth Circuit, and the *Gordon* case to the Court of Appeals for the Second Circuit; in the latter, the Gordons cross-appealed. The Ninth Circuit reversed the Tax Court, holding that the spread between $16 and fair market value was taxable as ordinary income to the Baans. The Second Circuit disagreed, sustaining the Tax Court on this point in the *Gordon* case, Judge Friendly dissenting. The Second Circuit went on to hold that the amount received by the Gordons for the four odd rights was taxable as a capital gain rather than as ordinary income, reversing the Tax Court on this point.

Because of the conflict, we granted certiorari. We affirm * * * the decision of the Court of Appeals for the Ninth Circuit, and reverse the decision of the Court of Appeals for the Second Circuit on both points.

Under §§ 301 and 316 of the Code, subject to specific exceptions and qualifications provided in the Code, any distribution of property by a corporation to its shareholders out of accumulated earnings and profits as a dividend taxable to the shareholders as ordinary income. Every distribution of corporate property, again except as otherwise specifically provided, "is made out of earnings and profits to the extent thereof." It is here agreed that on September 28, 1961, Pacific's accumulated earnings and profits were larger in extent than the total amount the Commissioner here contends was a dividend—the difference between the fair market value of all Northwest stock sold in 1961 and the total amount, at $16 per share, paid in by purchasers.

Whether the actual dividend occurs at the moment when valuable rights are distributed or at the moment when their value is realized through sale or exercise, it is clear that when a corporation sells corporate property to stockholders or their assignees at less than its fair market value, thus diminishing the net worth of the corporation, it is engaging in a "distribution of property" as that term is used in § 316. Such a sale thus results in a dividend to shareholders unless some specific exception or qualification applies. In particular, it is here agreed that the spread was taxable to the present taxpayers unless the distribution of Northwest stock by Pacific met the requirements for nonrecognition stated in § 355, or § 354, or § 346(b) of the Code. Since the Tax Court concluded that the requirements of § 355 had been met, it did not reach taxpayers' alternative contentions. Under the disposition that we make here upon the § 355 question, these alternative contentions remain open for further proceedings in the Tax Court.

Section 355 provides that certain distributions of securities of corporations controlled by the distributing corporation do not result in recognized gain or loss to the distributee shareholders. The requirements of the section are detailed and specific, and must be applied with precision. It is no doubt true, as the Second Circuit emphasized, that the general purpose of the section was to distinguish corporate fission from the distribution of earnings and profits. However, although a court may have reference to this purpose when there is a genuine question as to the meaning of one of the requirements Congress has imposed, a court is not free to disregard requirements simply because it considers them redundant or unsuited to achieving the general purpose in a particular case. Congress has abundant power to provide that a corporation wishing to spin off a subsidiary must, however bona fide its intentions, conform the details of a distribution to a particular set of rules.

The Commissioner contends that the 1961 distribution of Northwest stock failed to qualify under § 355 in several respects. We need, however, reach only one. Section 355(a) (1) (D) requires that, in order to qualify for nonrecognition of gain or loss to shareholders, the distribution must be such that "as part of the distribution, the distributing corporation distributes—

"(i) all of the stock and securities in the controlled corporation held by it immediately before the distribution, or

"(ii) an amount of stock in the controlled corporation constituting control within the meaning of section 368(c), and * * *."

Section 368(c) provides in relevant part that "the term 'control' means the ownership of stock possessing at least 80 percent of the total combined voting power of all classes of stock entitled to vote and at least 80 percent of the total number of shares of all other classes of stock of the corporation."

On September 28, 1961, the day before the first rights distribution, Pacific owned all of the common stock of Northwest, the only class of securities that company had issued. The 1961 rights offering contemplated transferring, and succeeded in transferring, about 57% of the Northwest common to Pacific shareholders. It therefore could not be clearer that this 1961 distribution did not transfer "all" of the stock of Northwest held by Pacific prior to it, and did not transfer "control" as that term is defined in § 368(c).

Nevertheless, taxpayers contend, and the Second Circuit agreed, that the requirements of subsection (a) (1) (D) were here met because Pacific distributed the remaining 43% of the Northwest stock in 1963. The court said that the purpose of the subsection "in no way requires a single distribution." The court apparently concluded that so long as it appears, at the time the issue arises, that the parent corporation has in fact distributed all of the stock of the subsidiary, the requirements of § (a) (1) (D) (i) have been satisfied.

We are forced to disagree. The Code requires that "the distribution" divest the controlling corporation of all of, or 80% control of, the controlled corporation. Clearly, if an initial transfer of less than a controlling interest in the controlled corporation is to be treated for tax purposes as a mere first step in the divestiture of control, it must at least be identifiable as such at the time it is made.

Absent other specific directions from Congress, Code provisions must be interpreted so as to conform to the basic premise of annual tax accounting. It would be wholly inconsistent with this premise to hold that the essential character of a transaction, and its tax impact, should remain not only undeterminable but unfixed for an indefinite and unlimited period in the future, awaiting events that might or might not happen. This requirement that the character of a transaction be determinable does not mean that the entire divestiture must necessarily occur within a single tax year. It does, however, mean that if one transaction is to be characterized as a "first step" there must be a binding commitment to take the later steps.

Here, it was little more than a fortuity that, by the time suit was brought alleging a deficiency in taxpayers' 1961 returns, Pacific had distributed the remainder of the stock. The plan for reorganization submitted to shareholders in 1961 promised that 56% of that stock would be distributed immediately. The plan went on,

"It is expected that within about three years after acquiring the stock of the New Company, the Company by one or more offerings will offer for sale the balance of such stock, following the procedures described in the preceding paragraph. The proceeds from such sales will be used by the Company to repay advances then outstanding and for general corporate purposes including expenditures for extensions, additions and improvements to its telephone plant.

"The prices at which the shares of the New Company will be offered pursuant to the offerings referred to * * * will be determined by the Board of Directors of the Company at the time of each offering."

It was further stated that such subsequent distributions would occur "[a]t a time or times related to its [Pacific's] need for new capital." Although there is other language in the plan that might be interpreted as preventing Pacific management from dealing with the Northwest stock in any way inconsistent with eventual sale to Pacific shareholders, there is obviously no promise to sell any particular amount of stock, at any particular time, at any particular price. If the 1961 distribution played a part in what later proved to be a total divestiture of the Northwest stock, it was not in 1961, either a total divestiture or a step in a plan of total divestiture.

Accordingly, we hold that the taxpayers, having exercised rights to purchase shares of Northwest from Pacific in 1961, must recognize ordinary income in that year in the amount of the difference between $16 per share and the fair market value of a share of Northwest common at the moment the rights were exercised.

The second question presented by the petition in No. 760, whether the $6.36 received by taxpayers Gordon upon the sale of four rights was taxable as ordinary income, as a capital gain, or not at all, does not require extended discussion in light of our view upon the first question. Since receipt and exercise of the rights would have produced ordinary income, receipt and sale of the rights, constituting merely an alternative route to realization, also produced income taxable at ordinary rates. * * *

The judgment of the Court of Appeals for the Second Circuit is reversed. The judgment of the Court of Appeals for the Ninth Circuit is affirmed. It is so ordered.

Mr. Justice MARSHALL took no part in the consideration or decision of these cases.

———

MILLS v. THE ELECTRIC AUTO–LITE COMPANY

Supreme Court of the United States, 1970.
396 U.S. 375, 90 S.Ct. 616, 24 L.Ed.2d 593.

Mr. Justice HARLAN delivered the opinion of the Court.

This case requires us to consider a basic aspect of the implied private right of action for violation of § 14(a) of the Securities Exchange Act of 1934 [15 U.S.C.A. § 78n(a)], recognized by this Court in J. I. Case Co. v. Borak, 377 U.S. 426. As in *Borak* the asserted wrong is that a corporate merger was accomplished through the use of a proxy statement that was materially false or misleading. The question with which we deal is what causal relationship must be shown between such a statement and the merger to establish a cause of action based on the violation of the Act.

I

Petitioners were shareholders of the Electric Auto-Lite Company until 1963, when it was merged into Mergenthaler Linotype Company. They brought suit on the day before the shareholders' meeting at which the vote was to take place on the merger against Auto-Lite, Mergenthaler, and a third company, American Manufacturing Company, Inc. The complaint sought an injunction against the voting by Auto-Lite's management of all proxies obtained by means of an allegedly misleading proxy solicitation; however, it did not seek a temporary restraining order, and the voting went ahead as scheduled the following day. Several months later petitioners filed an amended complaint, seeking to have the merger set aside and to obtain such other relief as might be proper.

In Count II of the amended complaint, which is the only count before us, petitioners predicated jurisdiction on § 27 of the 1934 Act, 15 U.S.C.A. § 78aa. They alleged that the proxy statement sent out by the Auto-Lite management to solicit shareholders' votes in favor of the merger was misleading, in violation of § 14(a) of the Act and SEC Rule 14a–9 thereunder. (17 CFR § 240.14a–9.) Petitioners recited that before the merger Mergenthaler owned over 50% of the outstanding shares of Auto-Lite common stock, and had been in control of Auto-Lite for two years. American Manufacturing in turn owned about one-third of the outstanding shares of Mergenthaler, and for two years had been in voting control of Mergenthaler and, through it,

328 BUSINESS ACQUISITIONS AND DIVISIONS Ch. 6

of Auto-Lite. Petitioners charged that in light of these circumstances the proxy statement was misleading in that it told Auto-Lite share-holders that their board of directors recommended approval of the merger without also informing them that all 11 of Auto-Lite's directors were nominees of Mergenthaler and were under the "control and domi-nation of Mergenthaler." Petitioners asserted the right to complain of this alleged violation both derivately on behalf of Auto-Lite and as representatives of the class of all its minority shareholders.

On petitioners' motion for summary judgment with respect to Count II, the District Court for the Northern District of Illinois ruled as a matter of law that the claimed defect in the proxy statement was, in light of the circumstances in which the statement was made, a ma-terial omission. The District Court concluded, from its reading of the *Borak* opinion, that it had to hold a hearing on the issue whether there was "a causal connection between the finding that there has been a violation of the disclosure requirements of § 14(a) and the alleged in-jury to the plaintiffs" before it could consider what remedies would be appropriate. * * *

After holding such a hearing, the court found that under the terms of the merger agreement, an affirmative vote of two-thirds of the Auto-Lite shares was required for approval of the merger, and that the respondent companies owned and controlled about 54% of the out-standing shares. Therefore, to obtain authorization of the merger, respondents had to secure the approval of a substantial number of the minority shareholders. At the stockholders' meeting, approximately 950,000 shares, out of 1,160,000 shares outstanding, were voted in favor of the merger. This included 317,000 votes obtained by proxy from the minority shareholders, votes that were "necessary and indispensa-ble to the approval of the merger." The District Court concluded that a causal relationship had thus been shown, and it granted an interlocu-tory judgment in favor of petitioners on the issue of liability, referring the case to a master for consideration of appropriate relief. * * *

The District Court made the certification required by 28 U.S.C. § 1292(b), and respondents took an interlocutory appeal to the Court of Appeals for the Seventh Circuit. That court affirmed the District Court's conclusion that the proxy statement was materially deficient, but reversed on the question of causation. The court acknowledged that, if an injunction had been sought a sufficient time before the stock-holders' meeting, "corrective measures would have been appropriate." 403 F.2d 429 (1968). However, since this suit was brought too late for preventive action, the courts had to determine "whether the mislead-ing statement and omission caused the submission of sufficient prox-ies," as a prerequisite to a determination of liability under the Act. If the respondents could show, "by a preponderance of probabilities, that the merger would have received a sufficient vote even if the proxy statement had not been misleading in the respect found," petitioners would be entitled to no relief of any kind.

The Court of Appeals acknowledged that this test corresponds to the common law fraud test of whether the injured party relied on the misrepresentation. However, rightly concluding that "[r]eliance by thousands of individuals, as here, can scarcely be inquired into" (*id.*, at 436 n. 10), the court ruled that the issue was to be determined by proof of the fairness of the terms of the merger. If respondents could show that the merger had merit and was fair to the minority shareholders, the trial court would be justified in concluding that a sufficient number of shareholders would have approved the merger had there been no deficiency in the proxy statement. In that case respondents would be entitled to a judgment in their favor.

Claiming that the Court of Appeals has construed this Court's decision in *Borak* in a manner that frustrates the statute's policy of enforcement through private litigation, the petitioners then sought review in this Court. We granted certiorari, * * * believing that resolution of this basic issue should be made at this stage of the litigation and not postponed until after a trial under the Court of Appeals' decision.

II

As we stressed in *Borak*, § 14(a) stemmed from a congressional belief that "[f]air corporate suffrage is an important right that should attach to every equity security bought on a public exchange." * * * The provision was intended to promote "the free exercise of the voting rights of stockholders" by ensuring that proxies would be solicited with "explanation to the stockholder of the real nature of the questions for which authority to cast his vote is sought." * * * The decision below, by permitting all liability to be foreclosed on the basis of a finding that the merger was fair, would allow the stockholders to be bypassed, at least where the only legal challenge to the merger is a suit for retrospective relief after the meeting has been held. A judicial appraisal of the merger's merits could be substituted for the actual and informed vote of the stockholders.

The result would be to insulate from private redress an entire category of proxy violations—those relating to matters other than the terms of the merger. Even outrageous misrepresentations in a proxy solicitation, if they did not relate to the terms of the transaction, would give rise to no cause of action under § 14(a). Particularly if carried over to enforcement actions by the Securities and Exchange Commission itself, such a result would subvert the congressional purpose of ensuring full and fair disclosure to shareholders.

Further, recognition of the fairness of the merger as a complete defense would confront small shareholders with an additional obstacle to making a successful challenge to a proposal recommended through a defective proxy statement. The risk that they would be unable to rebut the corporation's evidence of the fairness of the proposal, and thus to establish their cause of action, would be bound to discourage such shareholders from the private enforcement of the proxy rules that "provides a necessary supplement to Commission action." J. I. Case Co. v. Borak, 377 U.S., at 432.

Such a frustration of the congressional policy is not required by anything in the wording of the statute or in our opinion in the *Borak* case. Section 14(a) declares it "unlawful" to solicit proxies in contravention of Commission rules, and SEC Rule 14a-9 prohibits solicitations "containing any statement which * * * is false or misleading with respect to any material fact, or which omits to state any material fact necessary in order to make the statements therein not false or misleading * * *." Use of a solicitation that is materially misleading is itself a violation of law, as the Court of Appeals recognized in stating that injunctive relief would be available to remedy such a defect if sought prior to the stockholders' meeting. In *Borak*, which came to this Court on a dismissal of the complaint, the Court limited its inquiry to whether a violation of § 14(a) gives rise to "a federal cause of action for rescission or damages," 377 U.S., at 428. Referring to the argument made by petitioners there "that the merger can be dissolved only if it was fraudulent or non-beneficial, issues upon which the proxy material would not bear," the Court stated: "But the causal relationship of the proxy material and the merger are questions of fact to be resolved at trial, not here. We therefore do not discuss this point further." *Id.*, at 431. In the present case there has been a hearing specifically directed to the causation problem. The question before the Court is whether the facts found on the basis of that hearing are sufficient in law to establish petitioners' cause of action, and we conclude that they are.

Where the misstatement or omission in a proxy statement has been shown to be "material," as it was found to be here, that determination itself indubitably embodies a conclusion that the defect was of such a character that it might have been considered important by a reasonable shareholder who was in the process of deciding how to vote. This requirement that the defect have a significant *propensity* to affect the voting process is found in the express terms of Rule 14a-9, and it adequately serves the purpose of ensuring that a cause of action cannot be established by proof of a defect so trivial, or so unrelated to the transaction for which approval is sought, that correction of the defect or imposition of liability would not further the interests protected by § 14(a).

There is no need to supplement this requirement, as did the Court of Appeals, with a requirement of proof of whether the defect actually had a decisive effect on the voting. Where there has been a finding of materiality, a shareholder has made a sufficient showing of causal relationship between the violation and the injury for which he seeks redress if, as here, he proves that the proxy solicitation itself, rather than the particular defect in the solicitation materials, was an essential link in the accomplishment of the transaction. This objective test will avoid the impracticalities of determining how many votes were affected, and, by resolving doubts in favor of those the statute is designed to protect, will effectuate the congressional policy of ensuring that the shareholders are able to make an informed choice when they are consulted on corporate transactions.   *   *   *

III

Our conclusion that petitioners have established their case by showing that proxies necessary to approval of the merger were obtained by means of a materially misleading solicitation implies nothing about the form of relief to which they may be entitled.   We held in *Borak* that upon finding a violation the courts were "to be alert to provide such remedies as are necessary to make effective the congressional purpose," noting specifically that such remedies are not to be limited to prospective relief.   377 U.S., at 433.   In devising retrospective relief for violation of the proxy rules, the federal courts should consider the same factors that would govern the relief granted for any similar illegality or fraud.   One important factor may be the fairness of the terms of the merger.   Possible forms of relief will include setting aside the merger or granting other equitable relief, but, as the Court of Appeals below noted, nothing in the statutory policy "requires the court to unscramble a corporate transaction merely because a violation occurred."   403 F.2d, at 436.   In selecting a remedy the lower courts should exercise " 'the sound discretion which guides the determinations of courts of equity,' " keeping in mind the role of equity as "the instrument for nice adjustment and reconciliation between the public interest and private needs as well as between competing private claims."   *   *   *   Meredith v. Winter Haven, 320 U.S. 228, 235.

We do not read § 29(b) of the Act, which declares contracts made in violation of the Act or a rule thereunder "void   *   *   *   as regards the rights of" the violator and knowing successors in interest, as requiring that the merger be set aside simply because the merger agreement is a "void" contract.   This language establishes that the guilty party is precluded from enforcing the contract against an unwilling innocent party, but it does not compel the conclusion that the contract is a nullity, creating no enforceable rights even in a party innocent of the violation.   The lower federal courts have read § 29(b), which has counterparts in the Holding Company Act, the Investment Company Act, and the Investment Advisers Act, as rendering the contract merely voidable at the option of the innocent party.   *   *   *   This interpretation is eminently sensible.   The interests of the victim are sufficiently protected by giving him the right to rescind; to regard the contract as void where he has not invoked that right would only create the possibility of hardships to him or others without necessarily advancing the statutory policy of disclosure.

The United States, as *amicus curiae,* points out that as representatives of the minority shareholders, petitioners are not parties to the merger agreement and thus do not enjoy a statutory right under § 29 (b) to set it aside.   Furthermore, while they do have a derivative right to invoke Auto-Lite's status as a party to the agreement, a determination of what relief should be granted in Auto-Lite's name must hinge on whether setting aside the merger would be in the best interests of the shareholders as a whole. In short, in the context of a suit such as this one, § 29(b) leaves the matter of relief where it would be under *Borak* without specific statutory language—the merger should be set aside only if a court of equity concludes, from all the circumstances, that it would be equitable to do so. * * *

Monetary relief will, of course, also be a possibility. Where the defect in the proxy solicitation relates to the specific terms of the merger, the district court might appropriately order an accounting to ensure that the shareholders receive the value that was represented as coming to them. On the other hand, where, as here, the misleading aspect of the solicitation did not relate to terms of the merger, monetary relief might be afforded to the shareholders only if the merger resulted in a reduction of the earnings or earnings potential of their holdings. In short, damages should be recoverable only to the extent that they can be shown. If commingling of the assets and operations of the merged companies makes it impossible to establish direct injury from the merger, relief might be predicated on a determination of the fairness of the terms of the merger at the time it was approved. These questions, of course, are for decision in the first instance by the District Court on remand, and our singling out of some of the possibilities is not intended to exclude others.

IV

Although the question of relief must await further proceedings in the District Court, our conclusion that petitioners have established their cause of action indicates that the Court of Appeals should have affirmed the partial summary judgment on the issue of liability. The result would have been not only that respondents, rather than petitioners, would have borne the costs of the appeal, but also, we think, that petitioners would have been entitled to an interim award of litigation expenses and reasonable attorneys' fees. Cf. Highway Truck Drivers and Helpers Local 107 v. Cohen, 220 F.Supp. 735 (D.C.E.D.Pa.1963). We agree with the position taken by petitioners, and by the United States as *amicus*, that petitioners, who have established a violation of the securities laws by their corporation and its officials, should be reimbursed by the corporation or its survivor for the costs of establishing the violation.

The absence of express statutory authorization for an award of attorneys' fees in a suit under § 14(a) does not preclude such an award in cases of this type. In a suit by stockholders to recover short-swing profits for their corporation under § 16(b) of the 1934 Act, the Court of Appeals for the Second Circuit has awarded attorneys' fees despite the lack of any provision for them in § 16(b), "on the theory that the corporation which has received the benefit of the attorney's services should pay the reasonable value thereof." Smolowe v. Delendo Corp., 136 F.2d 231 (C.A.2d Cir. 1943). * * *

While the general American rule is that attorneys' fees are not ordinarily recoverable as costs, both the courts and Congress have developed exceptions to this rule for situations in which overriding considerations indicate the need for such a recovery. A primary judge-created exception has been to award expenses where a plaintiff has successfully maintained a suit, usually on behalf of a class, that benefits a group of others in the same manner as himself. See Fleischmann Corp. v. Maier Brewing Co., 386 U.S., at 718–719. To allow the others to obtain full benefit from the plaintiff's efforts without contributing equally to the litigation expenses would be to enrich the others unjustly at the plaintiff's expense. This suit presents such a situation. The dissemination of misleading proxy solicitations was a "deceit practiced on the stockholders as a group," J. I. Case Co. v. Borak, 377 U.S., at 432, and the expenses of petitioners' lawsuit have been incurred for the benefit of the corporation and the other shareholders.

* * *

For the foregoing reasons we conclude that the judgment of the Court of Appeals should be vacated and the case remanded to that court for further proceedings consistent with this opinion.

It is so ordered.

Judgment of Court of Appeals vacated and case remanded to that court.

Mr. Justice BLACK, concurring in part and dissenting in part.

I substantially agree with Parts II and III of the Court's opinion holding that these stockholders have sufficiently proved a violation of § 14(a) of the Securities Exchange Act of 1934 and are thus entitled to recover whatever damages they have suffered as a result of the misleading corporate statements, or perhaps to an equitable setting aside of the merger itself. I do not agree, however, to what appears to be the holding in Part IV that stockholders who hire lawyers to prosecute their claims in such a case can recover attorneys' fees in the absence of a valid contractual agreement so providing or an explicit statute creating such a right of recovery. The courts are interpreters, not creators, of legal rights to recover and if there is a need for recovery of attorneys' fees to effectuate the policies of the Act here involved, that need should in my judgment be met by Congress, not by this Court.

FEDERAL TRADE COMMISSION v. PROCTER & GAMBLE COMPANY

Supreme Court of the United States, 1967.
386 U.S. 568, 87 S.Ct. 1224, 18 L.Ed.2d 303.

(This case is reported in Chapter VII at page 390.)

QUESTIONS

1. In a system providing for the private ownership of property, is it really necessary to maintain free transferability of the property? Would it be possible to allocate the control of property to a person or a corporation for some given period of time and then require it to be surrendered to the government for reallocation? If so, how would the standards for this be established? What would be the effect on the "stewardship" of the property during that interim? Should ownership and control of property universally be limited to the lifetime of an individual? If so, how would this apply to the ownership of property by corporations which by law may exist in perpetuity?

2. How many of the problems relating to the acquisition and division of businesses are the consequence of our system of taxation which taxes only one half of the profit made on the transfer of a business? If the system of taxation were to be changed would the tax problems disappear? Or reappear in a different form a decade later? If the shareholders of corporations were taxed annually on their share of the distributed or undistributed earnings of the corporation, thus eliminating a future tax on the capital gain, would this inhibit the free transferability of the business unit as a separate property?

3. Should we provide for the tax-free exchange of property as is allowed in tax-free organizations? Does not the shareholder of a closely held corporation who exchanges his stock for a security of a large corporation really obtain something different from what he had before? Should not we expand our concept of "substance over form" (through legislation if necessary) to eliminate this tax-free exchange? Does the necessity of free transferability of property in our system really require that we allow for the tax-free exchange of property? If not, what would happen to those small business enterprises in need of capital for expansion which cannot compete for capital with larger units? Would investors generally think in terms of investing only in those corporations where a substantial market for the securities of the corporation already exists? How many business enterprises are started each year with the hope that they will expand to the full potential of its managers and its products? Would more and more business ventures be undertaken only by those large corporations which retain a substantial part of their earnings or have a ready and established market for their securities? How much of the desire for the free transferability of securities is behind the legislation which provides for the tax-free exchange of securities?

4. Is Section 337 of the Internal Revenue Code a satisfactory solution to the problems which appeared in the *Court Holding Company*

and *Cumberland Public Service Company* cases? Why require a liquidation in twelve months? Why not six months or eighteen months? Can most small corporations be liquidated in twelve months? Why should we allow the selling corporation to escape taxation on the profit it makes on the sale of its assets pursuant to a plan of liquidation? What public policy is involved in providing for the non-taxability of this transaction? Why do we do this when we tax the wage-earner on the profit he makes on the sale of his residence unless he reinvests the money in a new residence? Is business property more worthy of tax-free treatment than a residence? Is this fair? Has taxing the profit on the sale of a residence impeded the transfer of residences?

5. Should we allow the buyer and the seller of a business to determine the tax consequences of their transactoin by allowing them to allocate what is primarily a lump sum purchase price for a business among the several components of the business? Should we allow, for tax purposes if not otherwise, the buyer and the seller to allocate a portion of the total purchase price of a business for the inventory of the business which is higher than the seller's book cost (basis) of the inventory? Is this a way for the buyer to treat the purchase of goodwill for which he cannot get an income tax deduction at any time? If we allow this for inventory, why do we tax the amount of depreciation which has been recaptured on the sale of personal property? Or the amount of depreciation in excess of straight line depreciation which has been recaptured on the sale of real estate? Do the policies of freedom of contract and the free transferability of property require this privilege? In the long run, does it make any difference what price is allocated to inventory? Insofar as the parties themselves are concerned why should we not have the same standards of fairness in buying assets as occur in buying stock? Should we have a Rule 10(b)–5 for the sale of assets as we do for the sale of securities? Why not, particularly when Section 7 of the Clayton Act, which is the anti-merger statute, applies equally to the acquisition of assets as well as stock?

6. In an authoritarian system where the government owns all business property, how would a business be transferred? Would it be taken away from the persons who are authorized to manage it? Would it be thrust on another group of managers? Would it be split among many other businesses? All by government fiat? Who would make a decision to liquidate a business enterprise? What legal problems would exist in this system? Compare them with the legal problems in a free society. Do we have these legal problems because we have a free society?

7. In reference to the rights of minority stockholders in a merger, why should we allow a majority to override the minority? On the other hand, should we allow the minority to impede action? Or initiative? Isn't initiative the basis of the enterprise system? Do we allow private property to be taken away from private persons in any other context (except by government in exercising its right of eminent domain)? Do we allow this in any manner other than in a business cor-

poration? What is peculiar about stock that we allow this? Should we allow mergers at all?

8. In reference to fixing the valuation of the stock of a dissenting shareholder, are the daily market quotations of securities listed on a national securities exchange a satisfactory method of determining value? Are block transactions in securities ever made at prices substantially greater or less than the daily prices quoted on an exchange? Are the prices of securities on an exchange frequently subject to fluctuation by forces which have no relevance to the intrinsic value of the securities? By the assassination of a President? By the announcement of price controls? By the commencement of a war? By the negotiation of peace?

9. In reference to the solicitation of proxies by management to vote in favor of a merger, is it really necessary to have a detailed proxy solicitation statement? How much are these statements read? Is it possible to conceal information which ought to be disclosed by including it in a statement which discloses a mass of other information? Is the establishment of proxy solicitation rules for mergers, where the solicitation material is reviewed by a government agency, the SEC, a sufficient means of protecting the rights of minority stockholders? Is a minority stockholder suit, such as was brought in *Mills v. Electric Auto Lite Co.,* a sufficient means of protecting the minority stockholder? Or should we have a government agency, the SEC or the FTC or some other agency, review merger proposals, not only with reference to the impact on the securities markets or a competitive economy, but also with reference to the impact on minority stockholders? Because of the expense of litigation can a few stockholders dissenting from a merger hope to enforce their rights against management and the mass of the stockholders who have the corporate treasury at their disposal? Is this a contest between two equal parties of which a democracy can be proud? If not, what can we do to restore the balance? Would new laws help, or is this a situation inherent in owning stock?

———

Suggested Reference Sources

Texts and Treatises

Bittker & Eustis, *Federal Income Taxation of Corporations and Shareholders.* Federal Tax Press, New York City.

Loss, *Securities Regulation.* Little, Brown & Co., Boston, Massachusetts.

Fletcher, *Cyclopedia of the Law of Private Corporations.* Callaghan & Company, Mundelein, Illinois.

Scharf, *Techniques for Buying, Selling and Merging Businesses.* Prentice-Hall, Englewood Heights, N. J.

Topic Headings in the Index to Legal Periodicals

Consolidation and Merger

Corporate Reorganizations

Chapter VII

DISTRIBUTION OF GOODS AND SERVICES

A. THE ANTI–TRUST LAWS AND FREE COMPETITION

1. INTRODUCTORY NOTE

Every economy must have some system of providing for the distribution of the products of the economy. This could be accomplished in any number of ways including a governmental agency directing the distribution of goods and services to various consumers, perhaps by directing a producer to sell only to the consumers in his immediate vicinity, and by directing those consumers to buy only from him, or by allocating the goods and services to some distant group of consumers. The price of these products could be determined by a governmental agency which could have any rational or irrational basis for determining the price; it could fix the price at a uniform level throughout the reach of its mandate, or fix different prices within different markets or geographical areas, or even permit the producers to fix the price and have the governmental agency administer this price in such manner as the producers or the agency should determine. The agency also could determine which groups of persons could enter various productive fields, and which ones could leave it, what goods and services should be produced, at what quality, and in what quantity, and where all of this should be done. Or the government could permit groups of producers to make agreements to do any or all of the foregoing and through appropriate controls of either resources or capital or both, or by enlisting the aid of the government to compel compliance to achieve any of the foregoing.

In our society we have chosen freedom of contract as the means of achieving the distribution of goods and services. We permit, we want, individuals to determine for themselves what products they will produce, what they will sell, what prices they will charge and pay, and when and where they will do this. While we have various tax policies and government financed programs to stimulate some parts of the economy, policies and programs which change from time to time, we have no governmental agency allocating or distributing the products of our economy to various consumers or in various territories. We neither compel producers to distribute, nor consumers to acquire. Instead we have attempted to develop a free market where producers and consumers can choose for themselves what goods and services shall be exchanged among them, at what price and quality and in what quantities they choose. The laws we have developed to accomplish this result are the anti-trust laws.

We have placed our faith in an open market and free competition. This was no instant decision, obviously, but developed through centuries of experience both with state or private monopolies on the one hand, and laissez faire practices on the other. The political and economic system which we have evolved contemplates that only the government may have or grant a monopoly. We permit no cartels, no allocation of markets among private producers, no private treaties limiting the production of any goods. And where the government does grant a monopoly it is for a limited time, area, or purpose and generally is regulated by the government. A patent is a monopoly to "make, use, and vend" for seventeen years, the only monopoly we tolerate which is unregulated. We also have government-granted monopolies, sometimes called franchises, to provide certain kinds of goods and services, such as water, electricity, communications and transportation, but where these monopolies exist there is some plan by the government to control the price at which the goods and services are made available, and some compulsion to provide the services within the franchise area. But even within this limited area we generally demand some form of competition. Rail transportation must compete with motor transport, electricity with gas and coal and other forms of fuel, and we do not tolerate restraints of trade between groups of industries of this kind. Aside from this limited area, however, our economy depends on competition for its progress as well as for the development and distribution of the products of the economy. And our legal system reflects this arrangement.

As noted in Standard Oil Co. of N. J. v. U. S., 221 U.S. 1, 31 S.Ct. 502, 55 L.Ed. 619 (1911), reported below, the legislation enacted by Congress in this field was an outgrowth of the common law which for centuries held monopolies to be illegal, and on a case by case basis we evolved many of the concepts which existed prior to the advent of the Industrial Revolution. The rapid expansion of all forms of productive enterprises in the nineteenth century also led to many abuses in the marketplace. We found by experience that the common law courts and that state legislation were inadequate to deal with these problems and this led in 1890 to the enactment by Congress of the first and most important of all anti-trust laws, the Sherman Act, 15 U.S.C.A. § 1 et seq. In 1914 Congress enacted both the Federal Trade Commission Act, 15 U.S.C.A. § 44 et seq., and the Clayton Act, 15 U.S.C.A. § 12 et seq. The latter was amended in 1936 by the Robinson-Patman Act, 15 U.S.C.A. § 13, and in 1950 by the Celler-Kefauver Act, 15 U.S.C.A. § 18 (which is the present form of Section 7 of the Clayton Act).

The Sherman Act is the foundation of the law of free competition in our economy. Except for provisions relating to methods of enforcing anti-trust policies found in later statutes, it could probably have made all the other anticompetitive provisions of later legislation unnecessary. Section 1 of the Sherman Act provides, in part, "[E]very contract, combination * * *, or conspiracy in restraint of trade * * * is declared to be illegal." It provides further that any person who engages in any of the prohibited acts shall be guilty of a misdemeanor and subject to a fine not exceeding $50,000, or by imprisonment not exceeding one year, or both.   Section 2 of the Act, 15 U.S.C.A. § 2, provides in part, "[E]very person who shall monopolize, or attempt to monopolize, or combine or conspire with any other person or persons, to monopolize any part of the trade or commerce among the several States, or with foreign nations, shall be guilty of a misdemeanor * * *"   The same penalties as provided in Section 1 apply here.   The brevity of the statutory language has been commended (Appalachian Coals, Inc. v. U. S., 288 U.S. 344, 53 S.Ct. 471, 77 L.Ed. 825 (1933), reported below) and has made the interpretation of these statutes highly flexible.   Unlike the Internal Revenue Code, 26 U.S.C.A. § 1 et seq. or even the Clayton Act and its amendments, it does not go into great detail in proscribing anti-competitive activity. Whether more specific and detailed legislation in this area or more general legislation in other areas would be desirable is a question to ponder.   But there seems to be no indication that finely detailed provisions of the law in this area will be enacted by Congress or promulgated by any regulatory body.

The Federal Trade Commission Act, noted above, was adopted in 1914 to provide an administrative agency to enforce the anti-trust laws.   A non-partisan Commission, with a staff of experts, was created for this purpose.   Section 5 of the Act, 15 U.S.C.A. § 45, was amended in 1938 and now provides: "[U]nfair methods of competition in commerce, and unfair or deceptive acts or practices in commerce, are hereby declared unlawful."   The effect of this provision is that the Federal Trade Commission in serving the public interest proceeds against violations of the anti-trust laws, for the protection of competitors, as well as against unfair acts and practices for the protection of consumers.   One result has been that there has been a shift from the ancient practice of *caveat emptor* (let the buyer beware) to the beginning, at least, of *caveat venditor* (let the seller beware). Obviously this is an over-simplification but in a society with an increasingly complex technology and the mass distribution of its products on a world wide basis, a breakdown was becoming apparent in the old common law system of individual suits brought by a competitor seeking to halt the growth of a monopoly or by a single purchaser for damages arising from the purchase of a product which had been distributed by an unfair or deceptive trade practice.   It became increasingly apparent that individual law suits brought by individual persons would not protect the public interest sufficiently.

The Clayton Act, noted above, was also adopted in 1914.   One of its purposes was to prevent price discrimination which would diminish competition; this provision was amended by the Robinson-Patman Act of 1936, noted above.   Section 3 of the Clayton Act, 15 U.S.C.A. § 14, prohibits exclusive dealing arrangements and tying arrangements of commodities (but not services) under an agreement whereby the lessee or purchaser of the commodity "[s]hall not use or deal in the goods * * * of a competitor or competitors of the lessor or seller   *   *   * ”   where this practice may be “[t]o substantially lessen competition or tend to create a monopoly in any line of commerce.” The case of Standard Oil of Calif. v. United States, 337 U.S. 293, 69 S.Ct. 1051, 93 L.Ed. 1371 (1949) commonly referred to as the “Standard Stations” case, reported below, is an example of the kind of activity that is reached by Section 3 of the Clayton Act. It should be borne in mind that many of the practices which are made unlawful by the Clayton Act would also be unlawful under the Sherman Act.

Section 7 of the Clayton Act, 15 U.S.C.A. § 18, was amended in 1950 by the Celler-Kefauver Act. This section deals with mergers and acquisitions by corporations, and in this connection it should be noted that the technical, corporation statute concept of a “merger” is not the only thing that is prohibited. The Section prohibits the acquisition of “[t]he whole or any part of the stock or   *   *   *   the whole or any part of the assets of another corporation   *   *   * where in any line of commerce in any section of the country, the effect of such acquisition may be substantially to lessen competition or tend to create a monopoly.”

As noted above, the Robinson-Patman Act of 1936, was an amendment to Section 2 of the Clayton Act, 15 U.S.C.A. § 13. This statute has been roundly criticized since its enactment because of its vague language and because it can actually frustrate competition. Nonetheless, as a supplement to the anti-trust laws, it was designed to prohibit discrimination in price “[b]etween different purchasers of commodities of like grade and quality   *   *   *   where the effect of such discrimination may be substantially to lessen competition or tend to create a monopoly in any line of commerce, or to injure, destroy, or prevent competition   *   *   *.” Similar provisions apply to discriminatory practices (such as providing advertising allowances) unless they are made available on “proportionally equal terms” to all persons in competition in the distribution of the commodities. The Robinson-Patman Act was adopted as a means of protecting the small businessman from the ability of volume purchasers to demand and obtain price concessions which gave them unfair competitive advantages; the position of the individually owned corner grocery store in comparison with the large food chain stores is the example most commonly given. Yet price differentials are the essence of competition; while the Act does provide various defenses for price differentials, such as meeting the price of a competitor, the vagueness of the statute makes this defense a difficult one to maintain. A seller must meet his competitor’s prices in the marketplace, yet if he does he is in danger of being charged with a price-fixing conspiracy in violation of the Sherman Act. If he varies his prices in order to avoid suspicion under the Sherman Act, he may face a charge of discrimination under the Robinson-Patman Act. The failure to maintain this delicate balance has been the source of much litigation.

2. THE POLICY OF THE SHERMAN ACT

The case of Standard Oil Co. of N. J. v. U. S., 221 U.S. 1, 31 S.Ct. 502, 55 L.Ed. 619 (1911), reported below, added the "Rule of Reason" to the Sherman Act. The Court held that not every restraint of trade was prohibited by the statute; only those that were found to be "unreasonable." This has resulted in much litigation over the years in determining whether or not a particular combination or restraint of trade is "unreasonable." Appalachian Coals, Inc. v. U. S., 288 U.S. 344, 53 S.Ct. 471, 77 L.Ed. 825 (1933) reported below, is an example of what, from an objective viewpoint, can only be described as a combination in restraint of trade but nonetheless was found to be a "reasonable" one.

STANDARD OIL COMPANY OF NEW JERSEY v. UNITED STATES

Supreme Court of the United States, 1911.
221 U.S. 1, 31 S.Ct. 502, 55 L.Ed. 619.

Mr. Chief Justice WHITE delivered the opinion of the court:

The Standard Oil Company of New Jersey and thirty-three other corporations, John D. Rockefeller, William Rockefeller, and five other individual defendants, prosecute this appeal to reverse a decree of the court below. Such decree was entered upon a bill filed by the United States under authority of § 4 of the act of July 2, 1890, known as the anti-trust act, and had for its object the enforcement of the provisions of that act. The record is inordinately voluminous, consisting of twenty-three volumes of printed matter, aggregating about 12,000 pages, containing a vast amount of confusing and conflicting testimony relating to innumerable, complex, and varied business transactions, extending over a period of nearly forty years. In an effort to pave the way to reach the subjects which we are called upon to consider, we propose at the outset, following the order of the bill, to give the merest possible outline of its contents, to summarize the answer, to indicate the course of the trial, and point out briefly the decision below rendered.

The bill and exhibits, covering 170 pages of the printed record, was filed on November 15, 1906. Corporations known as Standard Oil Company of New Jersey, Standard Oil Company of California, Standard Oil Company of Indiana, Standard Oil Company of Iowa, Standard Oil Company of Kansas, Standard Oil Company of Kentucky, Standard Oil Company of Nebraska, Standard Oil Company of New York, Standard Oil Company of Ohio, and sixty-two other corporations and partnerships, as also seven individuals, were named as defendants. The bill was divided into thirty numbered sections, and sought relief upon the theory that the various defendants were engaged in conspiring "to restrain the trade and commerce in petroleum, commonly called 'crude oil,' in refined

oil, and in the other products of petroleum, among the several states
and territories of the United States and the District of Columbia
and with foreign nations, and to monopolize the said commerce."
The conspiracy was alleged to have been formed in or about the year
1870 by three of the individual defendants, *viz.*: John D. Rockefeller,
William Rockefeller, and Henry M. Flagler. The detailed averments
concerning the alleged conspiracy were arranged with reference to
three periods, the first from 1870 to 1882, the second from 1882 to
1899, and the third from 1899 to the time of the filing of the bill.

The general charge concerning the period from 1870 to 1882 was
as follows:

"That during said first period the said individual defendants, in
connection with the Standard Oil Company of Ohio, purchased and
obtained interests through stock ownership and otherwise in, and
entered into agreements with, various persons, firms, corporations,
and limited partnerships engaged in purchasing, shipping, refining,
and selling petroleum and its products among the various states, for
the purpose of fixing the price of crude and refined oil and the products thereof, limiting the production thereof, and controlling the transportation therein, and thereby restraining trade and commerce among
the several states, and monopolizing the said commerce."

To establish this charge it was averred that John D. and William
Rockefeller and several other named individuals, who, prior to 1870,
composed three separate partnerships engaged in the business of refining crude oil and shipping its products in interstate commerce,
organized in the year 1870 a corporation known as the Standard Oil
Company of Ohio, and transferred to that company the business of
the said partnerships, the members thereof becoming, in proportion
to their prior ownership, stockholders in the corporation. It was
averred that the other individual defendants soon afterwards became
participants in the illegal combination, and either transferred property to the corporation or to individuals, to be held for the benefit of
all parties in interest in proportion to their respective interests in
the combination; that is, in proportion to their stock ownership in
the Standard Oil Company of Ohio. By the means thus stated, it
was charged that by the year 1872, the combination had acquired substantially all but three or four of the thirty-five or forty oil refineries
located in Cleveland, Ohio. By reason of the power thus obtained,
and in further execution of the intent and purpose to restrain trade
and to monopolize the commerce, interstate as well as intrastate, in
petroleum and its products, the bill alleged that the combination and
its members obtained large preferential rates and rebates in many
and devious ways over their competitors from various railroad companies, and that by means of the advantage thus obtained many, if
not virtually all, competitors were forced either to become members
of the combination or were driven out of business; and thus, it was
alleged, during the period in question, the following results were
brought about: (a) That the combination, in addition to the refineries in Cleveland which it had acquired, as previously stated, and

which it had either dismantled to limit production, or continued to operate, also from time to time acquired a large number of refineries of crude petroleum, situated in New York, Pennsylvania, Ohio, and elsewhere. The properties thus acquired, like those previously obtained, although belonging to and being held for the benefit of the combination, were ostensibly divergently controlled, some of them being put in the name of the Standard Oil Company of Ohio, some in the name of corporations or limited partnerships affiliated therewith, or some being left in the name of the original owners, who had become stockholders in the Standard Oil Company of Ohio, and thus members of the alleged illegal combination. (b) That the combination had obtained control of the pipe lines available for transporting oil from the oil fields to the refineries in Cleveland, Pittsburg, Titusville, Philadelphia, New York and New Jersey. (c) That the combination during the period named had obtained a complete mastery over the oil industry, controlling 90 per cent of the business of producing, shipping, refining, and selling petroleum and its products, and thus was able to fix the price of crude and refined petroleum, and to restrain and monopolize all interstate commerce in those products.

The averments bearing upon the second period (1882 to 1899) had relation to the claim:

"That during the said second period of conspiracy the defendants entered into a contract and trust agreement, by which various independent firms, corporations, limited partnerships, and individuals engaged in purchasing, transporting, refining, shipping, and selling oil and the products thereof among the various states, turned over the management of their said business, corporations, and limited partnerships to nine trustees, composed chiefly of certain individuals defendant herein, which said trust agreement was in restraint of trade and commerce, and in violation of law, as hereinafter more particularly alleged."

The trust agreement thus referred to was set out in the bill. It was made in January, 1882. By its terms the stock of forty corporations, including the Standard Oil Company of Ohio, and a large quantity of various properties which had been previously acquired by the alleged combination, and which was held in diverse forms, as we have previously indicated, for the benefit of the members of the combination, was vested in the trustees and their successors, "to be held for all parties in interest jointly." In the body of the trust agreement was contained a list of the various individuals and corporations and limited partnerships whose stockholders and members, or a portion thereof, became parties to the agreement. This list is in the margin.[1]

* * *

1. 1st. All the stockholders and members of the following corporations and limited partnerships, to wit:
Acme Oil Company, New York.
Acme Oil Company, Pennsylvania.
Atlantic Refining Company of Philadelphia.
Bush & Company (Limited).
Camden Consolidated Oil Company.
Elizabethport Acid Works.

The agreement made provision for the method of controlling and managing the property by the trustees, for the formation of additional manufacturing, etc., corporations in various states, and the trust, unless terminated by a mode specified, was to continue "during the lives of the survivors and survivor of the trustees named in the agreement and for twenty-one years thereafter." The agreement provided for the issue of Standard Oil Trust certificates to represent the interest arising under the trust in the properties affected by the trust, which, of course, in view of the provisions of the agreement and the subject to which it related caused the interest in the certificates to be coincident with and the exact representative of the interest in the combination, that is, in the Standard Oil Company of Ohio. Soon afterwards it was alleged the trustees organized the Standard Oil Company of New Jersey and the Standard Oil Company of New York, the former having a capital stock of $3,000,000 and the latter a capital stock of

Imperial Refining Company (Limited).
Charles Pratt & Company.
Paine, Ablett, & Company.
Standard Oil Company, Ohio.
Standard Oil Company, Pittsburg.
Smith's Ferry Oil Transportation Company.
Solar Oil Company (Limited).
Stone & Fleming Manufacturing Company (Limited).
Also all the stockholders and members of such other corporations and limited partnerships as may hereafter join in this agreement at the request of the trustees herein provided for.
2d. The following individuals, to wit:
W. C. Andrews, John D. Archbold, Lide K. Arter, J. A. Bostwick, Benjamin Brewster, D. Bushnell, Thomas C. Bushnell, J. N. Camden, Henry L. Davis, H. M. Flagler, Mrs. H. M. Flagler, John Huntington, H. A. Hutchins, Charles F. G. Heye, A. B. Jennings, Charles Lockhart, A. M. McGregor, William H. Macy, William H. Macy, Jr., estate of Josiah Macy, William H. Macy, Jr., executor; O. H. Payne, A. J. Pouch, John D. Rockefeller, William Rockefeller, Henry H. Rogers, W. P. Thompson, J. J. Vandergrift, William T. Wardell, W. G. Warden, Joseph L. Warden, Warden Frew & Company, Louise C. Wheaton, H. M. Hanna, and George W. Chapin, D. M. Harkness, D. M. Harkness, trustee, S. V. Harkness, O. H. Payne, trustee; Charles Pratt, Horace A. Pratt, C. M. Pratt, Julia H. York, George H. Vilas, M. R. Keith, trustees, George F. Chester.
Also all such individuals as may hereafter join in the agreement at the re-

quest of the trustees herein provided for.
3d. A portion of the stockholders and members of the following corporations and limited partnerships, to wit:
American Lubricating Oil Company.
Baltimore United Oil Company.
Beacon Oil Company.
Bush & Denslow Manufacturing Company.
Central Refining Company of Pittsburg.
Chesebrough Manufacturing Company.
Chess Carley Company.
Consolidated Tank Line Company.
Inland Oil Company.
Keystone Refining Company.
Maverick Oil Company.
National Transit Company.
Portland Kerosene Oil Company.
Producers' Consolidated Land & Petroleum Company.
Signal Oil Works (Limited).
Thompson & Bedford Company (Limited).
Devoe Manufacturing Company.
Eclipse Lubricating Oil Company (Limited).
Empire Refining Company (Limited).
Franklin Pipe Company (Limited).
Galena Oil Works (Limited).
Galena Farm Oil Company (Limited).
Germania Mining Company.
Vacuum Oil Company.
H. C. Van Tine & Company (Limited).
Waters-Pierce Oil Company.
Also stockholders and members (not being all thereof) of other corporations and limited partnerships who may hereafter join in this agreement at the request of the trustees herein provided for.

$5,000,000, subsequently increased to $10,000,000 and $15,000,000, respectively. The bill alleged "that pursuant to said trust agreement the said trustees caused to be transferred to themselves the stocks of all corporations and limited partnerships named in said trust agreement, and caused various of the individuals and copartnerships who owned apparently independent refineries and other properties employed in the business of refining and transporting and selling oil in and among said various states and territories of the United States, as aforesaid, to transfer their property situated in said several states to the respective Standard Oil Companies of said states of New York, New Jersey, Pennsylvania, and Ohio, and other corporations organized or acquired by said trustees from time to time.   .   .   ." For the stocks and property so acquired the trustees issued trust certificates. It was alleged that in 1888 the trustees "unlawfully controlled the stock and ownership of various corporations and limited partnerships engaged in such purchase and transportation, refining, selling, and shipping of oil," as per a list which is excerpted in the margin.[2]

2.   List of Corporations the Stocks of Which Were Wholly or Partially Held by the Trustees of Standard Oil Trust.

	Capital Stock.	S. O. trust ownership.
New York state:		
Acme Oil Company, manufacturers of petroleum products	$ 300,000	Entire.
Atlas Refining Company, manufacturers of petroleum products	200,000	Do.
American Wick Manufacturing Company, manufacturers of lamp wicks	25,000	Do.
Bush & Denslow Manufacturing Company, manufacturers of petroleum products	300,000	50 per cent.
Chesebrough Manufacturing Company, manufacturers of petroleum	500,000	2,661–5,000
Central Refining Company (Limited), manufacturers of petroleum products	200,000	1–67.2 per cent.
Devoe Manufacturing Company, packers, manufacturers of petroleum	300,000	Entire.
Empire Refining Company (Limited), manufacturers of petroleum products	100,000	80 per cent.
Oswego Manufacturing Company, manufacturers of wood cases	100,000	Entire.
Pratt Manufacturing Company, manufacturers of petroleum products	500,000	Do.
Standard Oil Company of New York, manufacturers of petroleum products	5,000,000	Do.
Stone & Fleming Manufacturing Company (Limited), manufacturers of petroleum products	250,000	Do.
Thompson & Bedford Company (Limited), manufacturers of petroleum products	250,000	80 per cent.
Vacuum Oil Company, manufacturers of petroleum products	25,000	75 per cent.
New Jersey:		
Eagle Oil Company, manufacturers of petroleum products	350,000	Entire.
McKirgan Oil Company, jobbers of petroleum products	75,000	Do.
Standard Oil Company of New Jersey, manufacturers of petroleum products	3,000,000	Do.

The bill charged that during the second period quo warranto proceedings were commenced against the Standard Oil Company of Ohio, which resulted in the entry by the supreme court of Ohio, on March 2, 1892, of a decree adjudging the trust agreement to be void, not only because the Standard Oil Company of Ohio was a party to the same,

2. List of Corporations the Stocks of Which Were Wholly or Partially Held by the Trustees of Standard Oil Trust—Continued

	Capital Stock.	S. O. trust ownership.
Pennsylvania:		
Acme Oil Company, manufacturers of petroleum products	$ 300,000	Do.
Atlantic Refining Company, manufacturers of petroleum products	400,000	Do.
Galena Oil Works (Limited), manufacturers of petroleum products	150,000	86¼ per cent.
Imperial Refining Company (Limited), manufacturers of petroleum products	300,000	Entire.
Producers' Consolidated Land & Petroleum Company, producers of crude oil	1,000,000	65⁄132 per cent.
National Transit Company, transporters of crude oil	25,455,200	94 per cent.
Standard Oil Company, manufacturers of petroleum products	400,000	Entire.
Signal Oil Works (Limited), manufacturers of petroleum products	100,000	38¾ per cent.
Ohio:		
Consolidated Tank-Line Company, jobbers of petroleum products	1,000,000	57 per cent.
Inland Oil Company, jobbers of petroleum products	50,000	50 per cent.
Standard Oil Company, manufacturers of petroleum products	3,500,000	Entire.
Solar Refining Company, manufacturers of petroleum products	500,000	Do.
Kentucky:		
Standard Oil Company, jobbers of petroleum products	600,000	Do.
Maryland:		
Baltimore United Oil Company, manufacturers of petroleum products	600,000	5,059–6,000
West Virginia:		
Camden Consolidated Oil Company, manufacturers of petroleum products	200,000	51 per cent.
Minnesota:		
Standard Oil Company, jobbers of petroleum products	100,000	Entire.
Missouri:		
Waters-Pierce Oil Company, jobbers of petroleum products	400,000	50 per cent.
Massachusetts:		
Beacon Oil Company, jobbers of petroleum products	100,000	Entire.
Maverick Oil Company, jobbers of petroleum products	100,000	Do.
Maine:		
Portland Kerosene Oil Company, jobbers of petroleum products	200,000	Do.
Iowa:		
Standard Oil Company, jobbers of petroleum products	600,000	60 per cent.
Continental Oil Company, jobbers of petroleum products	300,000	62½ per cent.

but also because the agreement in and of itself was in restraint of trade and amounted to the creation of an unlawful monopoly. It was alleged that shortly after this decision, seemingly for the purpose of complying therewith, voluntary proceedings were had apparently to dissolve the trust, but that these proceedings were a subterfuge and a sham because they simply amounted to a transfer of the stock held by the trust in sixty-four of the companies which it controlled to some of the remaining twenty companies, it having controlled before the decree eighty-four in all, thereby, while seemingly in part giving up its dominion, yet in reality preserving the same by means of the control of the companies as to which it had retained complete authority. It was charged that especially was this the case, as the stock in the companies selected for transfer was virtually owned by the nine trustees or the members of their immediate families or associates. The bill further alleged that in 1897 the attorney general of Ohio instituted contempt proceedings in the quo warranto case, based upon the claim that the trust had not been dissolved as required by the decree in that case. About the same time, also, proceedings in quo warranto were commenced to forfeit the charter of a pipe line known as the Buckeye Pipe Line Company, an Ohio corporation, whose stock, it was alleged, was owned by the members of the combination, on the ground of its connection with the trust which had been held to be illegal.

The result of these proceedings, the bill charged, caused a resort to the alleged wrongful acts asserted to have been committed during the third period, as follows:

"That during the third period of said conspiracy, and in pursuance thereof, the said individual defendants operated through the Standard Oil Company of New Jersey, as a holding corporation, which corporation obtained and acquired the majority of the stocks of the various corporations engaged in purchasing, transporting, refining, shipping, and selling oil into and among the various states and territories of the United States and the District of Columbia and with foreign nations, and thereby managed and controlled the same, in violation of the laws of the United States, as hereinafter more particularly alleged."

It was alleged that in or about the month of January, 1899, the individual defendants caused the charter of the Standard Oil Company of New Jersey to be amended, "so that the business and objects of said company were stated as follows, to wit: 'To do all kinds of mining, manufacturing, and trading business; transporting goods and merchandise by land or water in any manner; to buy, sell, lease, and improve land; build houses, structures, vessels, cars, wharves, docks, and piers; to lay and operate pipe lines; to erect lines for conducting electricity; to enter into and carry out contracts of every kind pertaining to its business; to acquire, use, sell, and grant licenses under patent rights; to purchase or otherwise acquire, hold, sell, assign, and transfer shares of capital stock and bonds or other evidences of indebtedness of corporations, and to exercise all the privileges of ownership, including voting upon the stock so held; to carry on its business and have offices and agencies therefor in all parts of the world, and to hold, purchase, mortgage, and convey real estate and personal property outside the state of New Jersey.' "

The capital stock of the company—which, since March 19, 1892, had been $10,000,000—was increased to $110,000,000; and the individual defendants, as theretofore, continued to be a majority of the board of directors.

Without going into detail it suffices to say that it was alleged in the bill that shortly after these proceedings the trust came to an end, the stock of the various corporations which had been controlled by it being transferred by its holders to the Standard Oil Company of New Jersey, which corporation issued therefor certificates of its common stock to the amount of $97,250,000. The bill contained allegations referring to the development of new oil fields; for example, in California, southeastern Kansas, northern Indian territory, and nothern Oklahoma, and made reference to the building or otherwise acquiring by the combination of refineries and pipe lines in the new fields for the purpose of restraining and monopolizing the interstate trade in petroleum and its products.

Reiterating in substance the averments that both the Standard Oil Trust from 1882 to 1899, and the Standard Oil Company of New Jersey, since 1899, had monopolized and restrained interstate commerce in petroleum and its products, the bill at great length additionally set forth various means by which, during the second and third periods, in addition to the effect occasioned by the combination of alleged previously independent concerns, the monopoly and restraint complained of were continued. Without attempting to follow the elaborate averments on these subjects, spread over fifty-seven pages of the printed record, it suffices to say that such averments may properly be grouped under the following heads: Rebates, preferences, and other discriminatory practices in favor of the combination by railroad companies; restraint and monopolization by control of pipe lines, and unfair practices against competing pipe lines; contracts with competitors in restraint of trade; unfair methods of competition, such as local price cutting at the points where necessary to suppress competition; espionage of the business of competitors, the operation of bogus independent companies, and payment of rebates on oil, with the like intent; the division of the United States into districts, and the limiting the operations of the various subsidiary corporations as to such districts so that competition in the sale of petroleum products between such corporations had been entirely eliminated and destroyed; and finally reference was made to what was alleged to be the "enormous and unreasonable profits" earned by the Standard Oil Trust and the Standard Oil Company as a result of the alleged monopoly; which presumably was averred as a means of reflexly inferring the scope and power acquired by the alleged combination.

Coming to the prayer of the bill, it suffices to say that in general terms the substantial relief asked was, first, that the combination in restraint of interstate trade and commerce, and which had monopolized the same, as alleged in the bill, be found to have existence, and that the parties thereto be perpetually enjoined from doing any further act to give effect to it; second, that the transfer of the stocks of the various corporations to the Standard Oil Company of New Jersey, as alleged in the bill, be held to be in violation of the 1st and 2d sections of the anti-trust act, and that the Standard Oil Company of New Jersey be enjoined and restrained from in any manner continuing to exert control over the subsidiary corporations by means of ownership of said stock or otherwise; third, that specific relief by injunction be awarded against further violation of the statute by any of the acts specifically complained of in the bill. There was also a prayer for general relief.

* * *

First. The text of the act and its meaning.

We quote the text of the 1st and 2d sections of the act, as follows:

"Section 1. Every contract, combination in the form of trust or otherwise, or conspiracy, in restraint of trade or commerce among the several states or with foreign nations, is hereby declared to be illegal. Every person who shall make any such contract, or engage in any such combination or conspiracy, shall be deemed guilty of a misdemeanor, and, on conviction thereof, shall be punished by fine not exceeding $5,000, or by imprisonment not exceeding one year, or by both said punishments, in the discretion of the court.

"Sec. 2. Every person who shall monopolize, or attempt to monopolize, or combine or conspire with any other person or persons to monopolize, any part of the trade or commerce among the several states, or with foreign nations, shall be deemed guilty of a misdemeanor, and, on conviction thereof, shall be punished by fine not exceeding $5,000, or by imprisonment not exceeding one year, or by both said punishments, in the discretion of the court." [26 Stat. at L. 209, 15 U.S.C.A. §§ 1, 2.]

The debates show that doubt as to whether there was a common law of the United States which governed the subject in the absence of legislation was among the influences leading to the passage of the act. They conclusively show, however, that the main cause which led to the legislation was the thought that it was required by the economic condition of the times; that is, the vast accumulation of wealth in the hands of corporations and individuals, the enormous development of corporate organization, the facility for combination which such organizations afforded, the fact that the facility was being used, and that combinations known as trusts were being multiplied, and the widespread impression that their power had been and would be exerted to oppress individuals and injure the public generally. Although debates may not be used as a means for interpreting a statute (United States v. Trans-Missouri Freight Asso., 166 U.S. 318), that rule, in the nature of things, is not violated by resorting to debates as a means of ascertaining the environment at the time of the enactment of a particular law; that is, the history of the period when it was adopted.

There can be no doubt that the sole subject with which the 1st section deals is restraint of trade as therein contemplated, and that the attempt to monopolize and monopolization is the subject with which the 2d section is concerned. It is certain that those terms, at least in their rudimentary meaning, took their origin in the common law, and were also familiar in the law of this country prior to and at the time of the adoption of the act in question.

We shall endeavor, then first, to seek their meaning, not by indulging in an elaborate and learned analysis of the English law and of the law of this country, but by making a very brief reference to the elementary and indisputable conceptions of both the English and American law on the subject prior to the passage of the anti-trust act.

a. It is certain that at a very remote period the words "contract in restraint of trade" in England came to refer to some voluntary restraint put by contract by an individual on his right to carry on his trade or calling. Originally all such contracts were considered to be illegal, because it was deemed they were injurious to the public as well as to the individuals who made them. In the interest of the freedom of individuals to contract, this doctrine was modified so that it was only when a restraint by contract was so general as to be coterminus with the kingdom that it was treated as void. That is to say, if the restraint was partial in its operation, and was otherwise reasonable, the contract was held to be valid.

* * *

Let us consider the language of the 1st and 2d sections, guided by the principle that where words are employed in a statute which had at the time a well-known meaning at common law or in the law of this country, they are presumed to have been used in that sense unless the context compels to the contrary.

As to the 1st section, the words to be interpreted are: "Every contract, combination in the form of trust or otherwise, or conspiracy in restraint of trade or commerce * * * is hereby declared to be illegal." As there is no room for dispute that the statute was intended to formulate a rule for the regulation of interstate and foreign commerce, the question is, What was the rule which it adopted?

In view of the common law and the law in this country as to restraint of trade, which we have reviewed, and the illuminating effect which that history must have under the rule to which we have referred, we think it results:

a. That the context manifests that the statute was drawn in the light of the existing practical conception of the law of restraint of trade, because it groups as within that class, not only contracts which were in restraint of trade in the subjective sense, but all contracts or acts which theoretically were attempts to monopolize yet which in practice had come to be considered as in restraint of trade in a broad sense.

b.   That in view of the many new forms of contracts and combinations which were being evolved from existing economic conditions, it was deemed essential by an all-embracing enumeration to make sure that no form of contract or combination by which an undue restraint of interstate or foreign commerce was brought about could save such restraint from condemnation.   The statute under this view evidenced the intent not to restrain the right to make and enforce contracts, whether resulting from combinations or otherwise, which did not unduly restrain interstate or foreign commerce, but to protect that commerce from being restrained by methods, whether old or new, which would constitute an interference,—that is, an undue restraint.

c.   And as the contracts or acts embraced in the provision were not expressly defined, since the enumeration addressed itself simply to classes of acts, those classes being broad enough to embrace every conceivable contract or combination which could be made concerning trade or commerce or the subjects of such commerce, and thus caused any act done by any of the enumerated methods anywhere in the whole field of human activity to be illegal if in restraint of trade, it inevitably follows that the provision necessarily called for the exercise of judgment which required that some standard should be resorted to for the purpose of determining whether the prohibition contained in the statute had or had not in any given case been violated. Thus not specifying, but indubitably contemplating and requiring a standard, it follows that it was intended that the standard of reason which had been applied at the common law and in this country in dealing with subjects of the character embraced by the statute was intended to be the measure used for the purpose of determining whether, in a given case, a particular act had or had not brought about the wrong against which the statute provided.

And a consideration of the text of the 2d section serves to establish that it was intended to supplement the 1st, and to make sure that by no possible guise could the public policy embodied in the 1st section be frustrated or evaded.   The prohibition of the 2d embrace "every person who shall monopolize, or attempt to monopolize, or combine or conspire with any other person or persons to monopolize, any part of the trade or commerce among the several states or with foreign nations   *   *   *."   By reference to the terms of § 8 it is certain that the word "person" clearly implies a corporation as well as an individual.

The commerce referred to by the words "in part," construed in the light of the manifest purpose of the statute, has both a geographical and a distributive significance;   that is, it includes any portion of the United States and any one of the classes of things forming a part of interstate or foreign commerce.

Undoubtedly, the words "to monopolize" and "monopolize," as used in the section, reach every act bringing about the prohibited results.   The ambiguity, if any, is involved in determining what is intended by monopolize. But this ambiguity is readily dispelled in the light of the previous history of the law of restraint of trade to which we have referred and the indication which it gives of the practical evolution by which monopoly and the acts which produce the same result as monopoly, that is, an undue restraint of the course of trade, all came to be spoken of as, and to be indeed synonymous with, restraint of trade. In other words, having by the 1st section forbidden all means of monopolizing trade, that is, unduly restraining it by means of every contract, combination, etc., the 2d section seeks, if possible, to make the prohibitions of the act all the more complete and perfect by embracing all attempts to reach the end prohibited by the 1st section, that is, restraints of trade, by any attempt to monopolize, or monopolization thereof, even although the acts by which such results are attempted to be brought about or are brought about be not embraced within the general enumeration of the 1st section. And, of course, when the 2d section is thus harmonized with and made, as it was intended to be, the complement of the 1st, it becomes obvious that the criteria to be resorted to in any given case for the purpose of ascertaining whether violations of the section have been committed is the rule of reason guided by the established law and by the plain duty to enforce the prohibitions of the act, and thus the public policy which its restrictions were obviously enacted to subserve. And it is worthy of observation, as we have previously remarked concerning the common law, that although the statute, by the comprehensiveness of the enumerations embodied in both the 1st and 2d sections, makes it certain that its purpose was to prevent undue restraints of every kind or nature, nevertheless by the omission of any direct prohibition against monopoly in the concrete, it indicates a consciousness that the freedom of the individual right to contract, when not unduly or improperly exercised, was the most efficient means for the prevention of monopoly, since the operation of the centrifugal and centripetal forces resulting from the right to freely contract was the means by which monopoly would be inevitably prevented if no extraneous or sovereign power imposed it and no right to make unlawful contracts having a monopolistic tendency were permitted. In other words, that freedom to contract was the essence of freedom from undue restraint on the right to contract.

* * *

If the criterion by which it is to be determined in all cases whether every contract, combination, etc., is a restraint of trade within the intendment of the law, is the direct or indirect effect of the acts involved, then of course the rule of reason becomes the guide, and the construction which we have given the statute, instead of being refuted by the cases relied upon, is by those cases demonstrated to be correct. This is true, because the construction which we have deduced from the history of the act and the analysis of its text is simply that in every case where it is claimed that an act or acts are in violation of the statute, the rule of reason, in the light of the principles of law and the public policy which the act embodies, must be applied. From this it follows, since that rule and the result of the test as to direct or indirect, in their ultimate aspect, come to one and the same thing, that the difference between the two is therefore only that which obtains between things which do not differ at all.

* * *

Third.   The facts and the application of the statute to them.

Beyond dispute the proofs establish substantially as alleged in the bill the following facts:

1.   The creation of the Standard Oil Company of Ohio.

2.   The organization of the Standard Oil Trust of 1882, and also a previous one of 1879, not referred to in the bill, and the proceedings in the supreme court of Ohio, culminating in a decree based upon the finding that the company was unlawfully a party to that trust; the transfer by the trustees of stocks in certain of the companies; the contempt proceedings; and, finally, the increase of the capital of the Standard Oil Company of New Jersey and the acquisition by that company of the shares of the stock of the other corporations in exchange for its certificates.

The vast amount of property and the possibilities of far-reaching control which resulted from the facts last stated are shown by the statement which we have previously annexed concerning the parties to the trust agreement of 1882, and the corporations whose stock was held by the trustees under the trust, and which came therefore to be held by the New Jersey corporation.   But these statements do not with accuracy convey an appreciation of the situation as it existed at the time of the entry of the decree below, since, during the more than ten years which elapsed between the acquiring by the New Jersey corporation of the stock and other property which was formerly held by the trustees under the trust agreement, the situation, of course, had somewhat changed,—a change which, when analyzed in the light of the proof, we think establishes that the result of enlarging the capital stock of the New Jersey company and giving it the vast power to which we have referred produced its normal consequence; that is, it gave to the corporation, despite enormous dividends and despite the dropping out of certain corporations enumerated in the decree of the court below, an enlarged and more perfect sway and control over the trade and commerce in petroleum and its products. The ultimate situation referred to will be made manifest by an examination of §§ 2 and 4 of the decree below, which are excerpted in the margin.[3]

3.   Section 2.   That the defendants John D. Rockefeller, William Rockefeller, Henry H. Rogers, Henry M. Flagler, John D. Archbold, Oliver H. Payne, and Charles M. Pratt, hereafter called the seven individual defendants, united with the Standard Oil Company and other defendants to form and effectuate this combination, and since its formation have been and still are engaged in carrying it into effect and continuing it; that the defendants Anglo-American Oil Company (Limited), Atlantic Refining Company, Buckeye Pipe Line Company, Borne-Scrymser Company, Chesebrough Manufacturing Company, Consolidated, Cumberland Pipe Line Company, Colonial Oil Company, Continental Oil Company, Crescent Pipe Line Com-

Giving to the facts just stated the weight which it was deemed they were entitled to, in the light afforded by the proof of other cog-

pany, Henry C. Folger, Jr., and Calvin N. Payne, a copartnership doing business under the firm name and style of Corsicana Refining Company, Eureka Pipe Line Company, Galena Signal Oil Company, Indiana Pipe Line Company, Manhattan Oil Company, National Transit Company, New York Transit Company, Northern Pipe Line Company, Ohio Oil Company, Prairie Oil & Gas Company, Security Oil Company, Solar Refining Company, Southern Pipe Line Company, South Penn Oil Company, Southwest Pennsylvania Pipe Lines Company, Standard Oil Company of California, Standard Oil Company of Indiana, Standard Oil Company of Iowa, Standard Oil Company of Kansas, Standard Oil Company of Kentucky, Standard Oil Company of Nebraska, Standard Oil Company of New York, Standard Oil Company of Ohio, Swan & Finch Company, Union Tank Line Company, Vacuum Oil Company, Washington Oil Company, Waters-Pierce Oil Company,—have entered into and become parties to this combination, and are either actively operating or aiding in the operation of it; that by means of this combination the defendants named in this section have combined and conspired to monopolize, have monopolized, and are continuing to monopolize, a substantial part of the commerce among the states, in the territories, and with foreign nations, in violation of § 2 of the anti-trust act.

*   *   *   *   *   *   *   *   *   *   *   *   *

Section 4. That in the formation and execution of the combination or conspiracy the Standard Company has issued its stock to the amount of more than $90,000,000 in exchange for the stocks of other corporations which it holds, and it now owns and controls all of the capital stock of many corporations, a majority of the stock or controlling interests in some corporations, and stock in other corporations as follows:

Name of company.	Total capital stock.	Owned by Standard Oil Company.
Anglo-American Oil Company, Limited	£1,000,000	£999,740
Atlantic Refining Company	$ 5,000,000	$ 5,000,000
Borne-Scrymser Company	200,000	199,700
Buckeye Pipe Line Company	10,000,000	9,999,700
Chesebrough Manufacturing Company, Consolidated	500,000	277,700
Colonial Oil Company	250,000	249,300
Continental Oil Company	300,000	300,000
Crescent Pipe Line Company	3,000,000	3,000,000
Eureka Pipe Line Company	5,000,000	4,999,400
Galena-Signal Oil Company	10,000,000	7,079,500
Indiana Pipe Line Company	1,000,000	999,700
Lawrence Natural Gas Company	450,000	450,000
Mahoning Gas Fuel Company	150,000	149,900
Mountain State Gas Company	500,000	500,000
National Transit Company	25,455,200	25,451,650
New York Transit Company	5,000,000	5,000,000
Northern Pipe Line Company	4,000,000	4,000,000
Northwestern Ohio Natural Gas Company	2,775,250	1,649,450
Ohio Oil Company	10,000,000	9,999,850
People's Natural Gas Company	1,000,000	1,000,000
Pittsburg Natural Gas Company	310,000	310,000
Solar Refining Company	500,000	499,400
Southern Pipe Line Company	10,000,000	10,000,000
South Penn Oil Company	2,500,000	2,500,000
Southwest Pennsylvania Pipe Lines	3,500,000	3,500,000
Standard Oil Company (of California)	17,000,000	16,999,500
Standard Oil Company (of Indiana)	1,000,000	999,000
Standard Oil Company (of Iowa)	1,000,000	1,000,000
Standard Oil Company (of Kansas)	1,000,000	999,300
Standard Oil Company (of Kentucky)	1,000,000	997,200
Standard Oil Company (of Nebraska)	600,000	599,500
Standard Oil Company of New York	15,000,000	15,000,000

nate facts and circumstances, the court below held that the acts and dealings established by the proof operated to destroy the "potentiality of competition" which otherwise would have existed to such an extent as to cause the transfers of stock which were made to the New Jersey Corporation and the control which resulted over the many and various subsidiary corporations to be a combination or conspiracy in restraint of trade, in violation of the 1st section of the act, but also to be an attempt to monopolize and monopolization bringing about a perennial violation of the 2d section.

We see no cause to doubt the correctness of these conclusions, considering the subject from every aspect; that is, both in view of the facts established by the record and the necessary operation and effect

Name of company.	Total capital stock.	Owned by Standard Oil Company.
Standard Oil Company (of Ohio)	3,500,000	3,499,400
Swan & Finch Company	100,000	100,000
Union Tank Line Company	3,500,000	3,499,400
Vacuum Oil Company	2,500,000	2,500,000
Washington Oil Company	100,000	71,480
Waters-Pierce Oil Company	400,000	274,700

That the defendant National Transit Company, which is owned and controlled by the Standard Oil Company as aforesaid, owns and controls the amounts of the capital stocks of the following-named corporations and limited partnerships stated opposite each, respectively, as follows:

Name of company.	Total capital stock.	Owned by National Transit Company.
Connecting Gas Company	$ 825,000	$ 412,000
Cumberland Pipe Line Company	1,000,000	998,500
East Ohio Gas Company	6,000,000	5,999,500
Franklin Pipe Company, Limited	50,000	19,500
Prairie Oil & Gas Company	10,000,000	9,999,500

That the Standard Company has also acquired the control by the ownership of its stock or otherwise of the Security Oil Company, a corporation created under the laws of Texas, which owns a refinery at Beaumont in that state, and the Manhattan Oil Company, a corporation, which owns a pipe line situated in the states of Indiana and Ohio; that the Standard Company and the corporations and partnerships named in § 2 are engaged in the various branches of the business of producing, purchasing, and transporting petroleum in the principal oil-producing districts of the United States, in New York, Pennsylvania, West Virginia, Tennessee, Kentucky, Ohio, Indiana, Illinois, Kansas, Oklahoma, Louisiana, Texas, Colorado, and California, in shipping and transporting the oil through pipe lines owned or controlled by these companies from the various oil-producing districts into and through other states, in refining the petroleum and manufacturing it into various products, in shipping the petroleum and the products thereof into the states and territories of the United States, the District of Columbia, and to foreign nations, in shipping the petroleum and its products in tank cars owned or controlled by the subsidiary companies into various states and territories of the United States and into the District of Columbia, and in selling the petroleum and its products in various places in the states and territories of the United States, in the District of Columbia, and in foreign countries; that the Standard Company controls the subsidiary companies and directs the management thereof, so that none of the subsidiary companies competes with any other of those companies or with the Standard Company, but their trade is all managed as that of a single person.

of the law as we have construed it upon the inferences deducible from the facts, for the following reasons:

a.   Because the unification of power and control over petroleum and its products which was the inevitable result of the combining in the New Jersey corporation by the increase of its stock and the transfer to it of the stocks of so many other corporations, aggregating so vast a capital, gives rise, in and of itself, in the absence of countervailing circumstances, to say the least, to the prima facie presumption of intent and purpose to maintain the dominancy over the oil industry, not as a result of normal methods of industrial development, but by new means of combination which were resorted to in order that greater power might be added than would otherwise have arisen had normal methods been followed, the whole with the purpose of excluding others from the trade, and thus centralizing in the combination a perpetual control of the movements of petroleum and its products in the channels of interstate commerce.

b.   Because the prima facie presumption of intent to restrain trade, to monopolize and to bring about monopolization, resulting from the act of expanding the stock of the New Jersey corporation and vesting it with such vast control of the oil industry, is made conclusive by considering (1) the conduct of the persons or corporations who were mainly instrumental in bringing about the extension of power in the New Jersey corporation before the consummation of that result and prior to the formation of the trust agreements of 1879 and 1882; (2) by considering the proof as to what was done under those agreements and the acts which immediately preceded the vesting of power in the New Jersey corporation, as well as by weighing the modes in which the power vested in that corporation has been exerted and the results which have arisen from it.

Recurring to the acts done by the individuals or corporations who were mainly instrumental in bringing about the expansion of the New Jersey corporation during the period prior to the formation of the trust agreements of 1879 and 1882, including those agreements, not for the purpose of weighing the substantial merit of the numerous charges of wrongdoing made during such period, but solely as an aid for discovering intent and purpose, we think no disinterested mind can survey the period in question without being irresistibly driven to the conclusion that the very genius for commercial development and organization which it would seem was manifested from the beginning soon begot an intent and purpose to exclude others which was frequently manifested by acts and dealings wholly inconsistent with the theory that they were made with the single conception of advancing the development of business power by usual methods, but which, on the contrary, necessarily involved the intent to drive others from the field and to exclude them from their right to trade, and thus accomplish the mastery which was the end in view. And, considering the period from the date of the trust agreements of 1879 and 1882, up to the time of the expansion of the New Jersey corporation, the gradual extension of the power over the commerce in oil which ensued, the decision of the supreme court of Ohio, the tardiness or reluctance in conforming to the commands of that decision, the methods first adopted and that which finally culminated in the plan of the New Jersey corporation, all additionally serve to make manifest the continued existence of the intent which we have previously indicated, and which, among other things, impelled the expansion of the New Jersey corporation. The exercise of the power which resulted from that organization fortifies the foregoing conclusions, since the development which came, the acquisition here and there which ensued of every efficient means by which competition could have been asserted, the slow but resistless methods which followed by which means of transportation were absorbed and brought under control, the system of marketing which was adopted by which the country was divided into districts and the trade in each district in oil was turned over to a designated corporation within the combination, and all others were excluded, all lead the mind up to a conviction of a purpose and intent which we think is so certain as practically to cause the subject not to be within the domain of reasonable contention.

The inference that no attempt to monopolize could have been intended, and that no monopolization resulted from the acts complained of, since it is established that a very small percentage of the crude oil produced was controlled by the combination, is unwarranted. As substantial power over the crude product was the inevitable result of the absolute control which existed over the refined product, the monopolization of the one carried with it the power to control the other; and if the inferences which this situation suggests were developed, which we deem it unnecessary to do, they might well serve to add additional cogency to the presumption of intent to monopolize which we have found arises from the unquestioned proof on other subjects.

We are thus brought to the last subject which we are called upon to consider, *viz.*:

Fourth.   The remedy to be administered.

It may be conceded that ordinarily where it was found that acts had been done in violation of the statute, adequate measure of relief would result from restraining the doing of such acts in the future. Swift & Co. v. United States, 196 U.S. 375. But in a case like this, where the condition which has been brought about in violation of the statute, in and of itself is not only a continued attempt to monopolize, but also a monopolization, the duty to enforce the statute requires the application of broader and more controlling remedies. As penalties which are not authorized by law may not be inflicted by judicial authority, it follows that to meet the situation with which we are confronted the application of remedies two-fold in character becomes essential: 1st.   To forbid the doing in the future of acts like those which we have found to have been done in the past which would be violative of the statute. 2d.   The exertion of such measure of relief as will effectually dissolve the combination found to exist in violation of the statute, and thus neutralize the extension and continually operating force which the possession of the power unlawfully obtained has brought and will continue to bring about.

In applying remedies for this purpose, however, the fact must not be overlooked that injury to the public by the prevention of an undue restraint on, or the monopolization of, trade or commerce, is the foundation upon which the prohibitions of the statute rest, and moreover that one of the fundamental purposes of the statute is to protect, not to destroy, rights of property.

Let us, then, as a means of accurately determining what relief we are to afford, first come to consider what relief was afforded by the court below, in order to fix how far it is necessary to take from or add to that relief, to the end that the prohibitions of the statute may have complete and operative force.

The court below, by virtue of §§ 1, 2, and 4 of its decree, which we have in part previously excerpted in the margin, adjudged that the New Jersey corporation, in so far as it held the stock of the various corporations recited in §§ 2 and 4 of the decree, or controlled the same, was a combination in violation of the 1st section of the act, and an attempt to monopolize or a monopolization contrary to the 2d section of the act. It commanded the dissolution of the combination, and therefore in effect directed the transfer by the New Jersey corporation back to the stockholders of the various subsidiary corporations entitled to the same of the stock which had been turned over to the New Jersey company in exchange for its stock. To make this command effective § 5 of the decree forbade the New Jersey corporation from in any form or manner exercising any ownership or exerting any power directly or indirectly in virtue of its apparent title to the stocks of the subsidiary corporations, and prohibited those subsidiary corporations from paying any dividends to the New Jersey corporations, or doing any act which would recognize further power in that company, except to the extent that it was necessary to enable that company to transfer the stock. So far as the owners of the stock of the subsidiary corporations and the corporations themselves were concerned after the stock had been transferred, § 6 of the decree enjoined them from in any way conspiring or combining to violate the act, or to monopolize or attempt to monopolize in virtue of their ownership of the stock transferred to them, and prohibited all agreements between the subsidiary corporations or other stockholders in the future, tending to produce or bring about further violations of the act.

By § 7, pending the accomplishment of the dissolution of the combination by the transfer of stock, and until it was consummated, the defendants named in § 1, constituting all the corporations to which we have referred, were enjoined from engaging in or carrying on interstate commerce. And by § 9, among other things, a delay of thirty days was granted for the carrying into effect of the directions of the decree.

So far as the decree held that the ownership of the stock of the New Jersey corporation constituted a combination in violation of the

1st section and an attempt to create a monopoly or to monopolize under the 2d section, and commanded the dissolution of the combination, the decree was clearly appropriate. And this also is true of § 5 of the decree, which restrained both the New Jersey corporation and the subsidiary corporations from doing anything which would recognize or give effect to further ownership in the New Jersey corporation of the stocks which were ordered to be retransferred.

But the contention is that, in so far as the relief by way of injunction which was awarded by § 6 against the stockholders of the subsidiary corporations or the subsidiary corporations themselves after the transfer of stock by the New Jersey corporation was completed in conformity to the decree, that the relief awarded was too broad: a. Because it was not sufficiently specific, and tended to cause those who were within the embrace of the order to cease to be under the protection of the law of the land and required them to thereafter conduct their business under the jeopardy of punishments for contempt for violating a general injunction. New York, N. H. & H. R. Co. v. Interstate Commerce Commission, 200 U.S. 404. Besides it is said that the restraint imposed by § 6—even putting out of view the consideration just stated—was, moreover, calculated to do injury to the public, and it may be in and of itself to produce the very restraint on the due course of trade which it was intended to prevent. We say this since it does not necessarily follow because an illegal restraint of trade or an attempt to monopolize or a monopolization resulted from the combination and the transfer of the stocks of the subsidiary corporations to the New Jersey corporation that a like restraint or attempt to monopolize or monopolization would necessarily arise from agreements between one or more of the subsidiary corporations after the transfer of the stock by the New Jersey corporation. For illustration, take the pipe lines. By the effect of the transfer of the stock, the pipe lines would come under the control of various corporations instead of being subjected to a uniform control. If various corporations owning the lines determined in the public interests to so combine as to make a continuous line, such agreement or combination would not be repugnant to the act, and yet it might be restrained by the decree. As another example, take the Union Tank Line Company, one of the subsidiary corporations, the owner practically of all the tank cars in use by the combination. If no possibility existed of agreements for the distribution of these cars among the subsidiary corporations, the most serious detriment to the public interest might result. Conceding the merit, abstractly considered, of these contentions, they are irrelevant. We so think, since we construe the sixth paragraph of the decree, not as depriving the stockholders or the corporations, after the dissolution of the combination, of the power to make normal and lawful contracts or agreements, but as restraining them from, by any device whatever, recreating, directly or indirectly, the illegal combination which the decree dissolved. In other words, we construe the sixth paragraph of the decree, not as depriving the stockholders or corporations of the right to live under the law of the land, but as compelling obedience to that law.   As therefore the sixth paragraph as thus construed is not amenable to the criticism directed against it and cannot produce the harmful results which the arguments suggest, it was obviously right.   We think that, in view of the magnitude of the interests involved and their complexity, the delay of thirty days allowed for executing the decree was too short and should be extended so as to embrace a period of at least six months.   So also, in view of the possible serious injury to result to the public from an absolute cessation of interstate commerce in petroleum and its products by such vast agencies as are embraced in the combination, a result which might arise from that portion of the decree which enjoined carrying on of interstate commerce not only by the New Jersey corporation, but by all the subsidiary companies, until the dissolution of the combination by the transfer of the stocks in accordance with the decree, should not have been awarded.

Our conclusion is that the decree below was right and should be affirmed, except as to the minor matters concerning which we have indicated the decree should be modified.   Our order will therefore be one of affirmance, with directions, however, to modify the decree in accordance with this opinion.   The court below to retain jurisdiction to the extent necessary to compel compliance in every respect with its decree.

And it is so ordered.

APPALACHIAN COALS v. UNITED STATES

Supreme Court of the United States, 1933.
288 U.S. 344, 53 S.Ct. 471, 77 L.Ed. 825.

Mr. Chief Justice HUGHES delivered the opinion of the Court.

This suit was brought to enjoin a combination alleged to be in restraint of interstate commerce in bituminous coal and in attempted monopolization of part of that commerce, in violation of sections 1 and 2 of the Sherman Anti-Trust Act, 15 U.S.C.A. §§ 1, 2.   The District Court, composed of three Circuit Judges, made detailed findings of fact and entered final decree granting the injunction.   1 F.Supp. 339. The case comes here on appeal.   28 U.S.C.A. § 380.

Defendants, other than Appalachian Coals, Inc., are 137 producers of bituminous coal in eight districts (called for convenience Appalachian territory) lying in Virginia, West Virginia, Kentucky, and Tennessee.   These districts, described as the Southern High Volatile Field, form part of the coal bearing area stretching from central and western Pennsylvania through eastern Ohio, western Maryland, West Virginia, southwestern Virginia, eastern Kentucky, eastern Tennessee, and northeastern Alabama.   In 1929 (the last year for which complete statistics were available) the total production of bituminous coal east of the Mississippi river was 484,786,000 tons, of which defendants mined 58,011,367 tons, or 11.96 per cent.   In the so-called Appalachian territory and the immediately surrounding area, the total production was 107,008,209 tons, of which defendants' production was 54.21 per cent., or 64 per cent. if the output of "captive" mines (16,455,001 tons) be deducted. With a further deduction of 12,000,000 tons of coal produced in the immediately surrounding territory, which, however, is not essentially different from the particular area described in these proceedings as Appalachian territory, defendants' production in the latter region was found to amount to 74.4 per cent.

The challenged combination lies in the creation by the defendant producers of an exclusive selling agency. This agency is the defendant Appalachian Coals, Inc., which may be designated as the Company. Defendant producers own all its capital stock, their holdings being in proportion to their production. The majority of the common stock, which has exclusive voting right, is held by seventeen defendants. By uniform contracts, separately made, each defendant producer constitutes the Company an exclusive agent for the sale of all coal (with certain exceptions) which the producer mines in Appalachian territory. The Company agrees to establish standard classifications, to sell all the coal of all its principals at the best prices obtainable and, if all cannot be sold, to apportion orders upon a stated basis. The plan contemplates that prices are to be fixed by the officers of the Company at its central office, save that, upon contracts calling for future deliveries after sixty days, the Company must obtain the producer's consent. The Company is to be paid a commission of 10 per cent. of the gross selling prices f. o. b. at the mines, and guarantees accounts. In order to preserve their existing sales outlets, the producers may designate subagents, according to an agreed form of contract, who are to sell upon the terms and prices established by the Company and are to be allowed by the Company commissions of eight per cent. The Company has not yet begun to operate as selling agent; the contracts with it run to April 1, 1935, and from year to year thereafter unless terminated by either party on six months' notice.

The Government's contention, which the District Court sustained, is that the plan violates the Sherman Anti-Trust Act (15 U.S.C.A. §§ 1–7, 15 note)—in the view that it eliminates competition among the defendants themselves and also gives the selling agency power substantially to affect and control the price of bituminous coal in many interstate markets. On the latter point the District Court made the general finding that this elimination of competition and concerted action will affect market conditions, and have a tendency to stabilize prices and to raise prices to a higher level than would prevail under conditions of free competition. The court added that the selling agency will not have monopoly control of any market nor the power to fix monopoly prices.

Defendants insist that the primary purpose of the formation of the selling agency was to increase the sale, and thus the production, of Appalachian coal through better methods of distribution, intensive advertising and research, to achieve economies in marketing, and to eliminate abnormal, deceptive, and destructive trade practices. They disclaim any intent to restrain or monopolize interstate commerce, and in justification of their design they point to the statement of the District Court that "it is but due to defendants to say that the evidence in the case clearly shows that they have been acting fairly and openly, in an attempt to organize the coal industry and to relieve the deplorable conditions resulting from overexpansion, destructive competition, wasteful trade practices, and the inroads of competing industries." 1 F.Supp. page 341. Defendants contend that the evidence establishes that the selling agency will not have the power to dominate or fix the price of coal in any consuming market; that the price of coal will continue to be set in an open competitive market; and that their plan by increasing the sale of bituminous coal from Appalachian territory will promote, rather than restrain, interstate commerce.

First. There is no question as to the test to be applied in determining the legality of the defendants' conduct. The purpose of the Sherman Anti-Trust Act is to prevent undue restraints of interstate commerce, to maintain its appropriate freedom in the public interest, to afford protection from the subversive or coercive influences of monopolistic endeavor. As a charter of freedom, the act has a generality and adaptability comparable to that found to be desirable in constitutional provisions. It does not go into detailed definitions which might either work injury to legitimate enterprise or through particularization defeat its purposes by providing loopholes for escape. The restrictions the act imposes are not mechanical or artificial. Its general phrases, interpreted to attain its fundamental objects, set up the essential standard of reasonableness. They call for vigilance in the detection and frustration of all efforts unduly to restrain the free course of interstate commerce, but they do not seek to establish a mere delusive liberty either by making impossible the normal and fair expansion of that commerce or the adoption of reasonable measures to protect it from injurious and destructive practices and to promote competition upon a sound basis. The decisions establish, said this Court in Nash v. United States, 229 U.S. 373, "that only such contracts and combinations are within the act as, by reason of intent or the inherent nature of the contemplated acts, prejudice the public interests by unduly restricting competition or unduly obstructing the course of trade." * * *

In applying this test, a close and objective scrutiny of particular conditions and purposes is necessary in each case. Realities must dominate the judgment. The mere fact that the parties to an agreement eliminate competition between themselves is not enough to condemn it. "The legality of an agreement or regulation cannot be determined by so simple a test, as whether it restrains competition. Every agreement concerning trade, every regulation of trade, restrains." Chicago Board of Trade v. United States, 246 U.S. 231. The familiar illustrations of partnerships, and enterprises fairly integrated in the interest of the promotion of commerce, at once occur. The question of the application of the statute is one of intent and effect, and is not to be determined by arbitrary assumptions. It is therefore necessary in this instance to consider the economic conditions peculiar to the coal industry, the practices which have obtained, the nature of defendant's plan of making sales, the reasons which led to its adoption, and the probable consequences of the carrying out of that plan in relation to market prices and other matters affecting the public interest in interstate commerce in bituminous coal.

Second. The findings of the District Court, upon abundant evidence, leave no room for doubt as to the economic condition of the coal industry. That condition, as the District Court states, "for many years has been indeed deplorable." Due largely to the expansion under the stimulus of the Great War, "the bituminous mines of the country have a developed capacity exceeding 700,000,000 tons" to meet a demand "of less than 500,000,000 tons." In connection with this increase in surplus production, the consumption of coal in all the industries which are its largest users has shown a substantial relative decline. The actual decrease is partly due to the industrial condition but the relative decrease is progressing, due entirely to other causes. Coal has been losing markets to oil, natural gas and water power and has also been losing ground due to greater efficiency in the use of coal. The change has been more rapid during the last few years by reason of the developments of both oil and gas fields. The court below found that, based upon the assumption that bituminous coal would have maintained the upward trend prevailing between 1900 and 1915 in percentage of total energy supply in the United States, the total substitution between 1915 and 1930 has been equal to more than 200,000,000 tons per year. While proper allowance must be made for differences in consumption in different parts of the country, the adverse influence upon the coal industry, including the branch of it under review, of the use of substitute fuels and of improved methods is apparent.

This unfavorable condition has been aggravated by particular practices. One of these relates to what is called "distress coal." The greater part of the demand is for particular sizes of coal such as nut and slack, stove coal, egg coal, and lump coal. Any one size cannot be prepared without making several sizes. According to the finding of the court below, one of the chief problems of the industry is thus involved in the practice of producing different sizes of coal even though orders are on hand for only one size, and the necessity of marketing all sizes. Usually there are no storage facilities at the mines and the different sizes produced are placed in cars on the producer's tracks, which may become so congested that either production must be stopped or the cars must be moved regardless of demand. This leads to the practice of shipping unsold coal to billing points or on consignment to the producer or his agent in the consuming territory. If the coal is not sold by the time it reaches its destination, and is not unloaded promptly, it becames subject to demurrage charges which may exceed the amount obtainable for the coal unless it is sold quickly. The court found that this type of "distress coal" presses on the market at all times, includes all sizes and grades, and the total amount from all causes is of substantial quantity.

"Pyramiding" of coal is another "destructive practice." It occurs when a producer authorizes several persons to sell the same coal, and they may in turn offer it for sale to other dealers. In consequence "the coal competes with itself, thereby resulting in abnormal and destructive competition which depresses the price for all coals in the market." Again, there is misrepresentation by some producers in selling one size of coal and shipping another size which they happen to have on hand. "The lack of standardization of sizes and the misrepresentation as to sizes" are found to have been injurious to the coal industry as a whole. The court added, however, that the evidence did not show the existence of any trade war or widespread fraudulent conduct. The industry also suffers through "credit losses," which are due to the lack of agencies for the collection of comprehensive data with respect to the credits that can safely be extended.

In addition to these factors, the District Court found that organized buying agencies, and large consumers purchasing substantial tonnages, "constitute unfavorable forces." "The highly organized and concentrated buying power which they control and the great abundance of coal available have contributed to make the market for coal a buyers' market for many years past."

It also appears that the "unprofitable condition" of the industry has existed particularly in the Appalachian territory where there is little local consumption as the region is not industrialized. "The great bulk of the coal there produced is sold in the highly competitive region east of the Mississippi river and north of the Ohio river under an adverse freight rate which imposes an unfavorable differential from 35 cents to 50 cents per ton." And in a graphic summary of the economic situation, the court found that "numerous producing companies have gone into bankruptcy or into the hands of receivers, many mines have been shut down, the number of days of operation per week have been greatly curtailed, wages to labor have been substantially lessened, and the states in which coal producing companies are located have found it increasingly difficult to collect taxes."

Third. The findings also fully disclose the proceedings of the defendants in formulating their plan and the reasons for its adoption. The serious economic conditions had led to discussions among coal operators and state and national officials, seeking improvement of the industry. Governors of states had held meetings with coal producers. The limits of official authority were apparent. A general meeting of producers, sales agents and attorneys was held in New York in October, 1931, a committee was appointed and various suggestions were considered. At a second general meeting in December, 1931, there was further discussion and a report which recommended the organization of regional sales agencies, and was supported by the opinion of counsel as to the legality of proposed forms of contract, was approved. Committees to present the plan to producers were constituted for eighteen producing districts including the eight districts in Appalachian territory. Meetings of the representatives of the latter districts resulted in the organization of defendant Appalachian Coals,

Inc. It was agreed that a minimum of 70 per cent. and a maximum of 80 per cent. of the commercial tonnage of the territory should be secured before the plan should become effective. Approximately 73 per cent. was obtained. A resolution to fix the maximum at 90 per cent. was defeated. The maximum of 80 per cent. was adopted because a majority of the producers felt that an organization with a greater degree of control might unduly restrict competition in local markets. The minimum of 70 per cent. was fixed because it was agreed that the organization would not be effective without this degree of control. The court below also found that it was the expectation that similar agencies would be organized in other producing districts including those which were competitive with Appalachian coal, and that it was "the particular purpose of the defendants in the Appalachian territory to secure such degree of control therein as would eliminate competition among the 73 per cent. of the commercial production." But the court added: "However, the formation of Appalachian Coals was not made dependent upon the formation of other regional selling agencies and there is no evidence of a purpose, understanding or agreement among the defendants that in the event of the formation of other similar regional sales agencies there would be any understanding or agreement, direct or indirect, to divide the market territory between them or to limit production or to fix the price of coal in any market or to cooperate in any way." When, in January, 1932, the Department of Justice announced its adverse opinion, the producers outside Appalachian territory decided to hold their plans in abeyance pending the determination of the question by the courts. The District Court found that "the evidence tended to show that other selling agencies with a control of at least 70 per cent. of the production in their respective districts will be organized if the petition in this case is dismissed"; that in that event "there will result an organization in most of the districts whose coal is or may be competitive with Appalachian coal; but the testimony tends to show that there will still be substantial, active competition in the sale of coal in all markets in which Appalachian coal is sold."

Defendants refer to the statement of purposes in their published plan of organization—that it was intended to bring about "a better and more orderly marketing of the coals from the region to be served by this company (the selling agency) and better to enable the producers in this region, through the larger and more economic facilities of such selling agency, more equally to compete in the general markets for a fair share of the available coal business." The District Court found that among their purposes, defendants sought to remedy "the destructive practice of shipping coal on consignment without prior orders for the sale thereof, which results in the dumping of coal on the market irrespective of the demand"; "to eliminate the pyramiding of offers for the sale of coal"; to promote "the systematic study of the marketing and distribution of coal, the demand and the consumption and the kinds and grades of coal made and available for shipment by each producer in order to improve conditions"; to maintain an inspection and engineering department which would keep in constant contact with customers "in order to demonstrate the advantages and suitability of Appalachian coal in comparison with other competitive coals"; to promote an extensive advertising campaign which would show "the advantages of using coal as a fuel and the advantages of Appalachian coal particularly"; to provide a research department employing combustion engineers which would demonstrate "proper and efficient methods of burning coal in factories and in homes" and thus aid producers in their competition with substitute fuels; and to operate a credit department which would build up a record with respect to the "reliability of purchasers." The court also found that "defendants believe that the result of all these activities would be the more economical sale of coal, and the economies would be more fully realized as the organization of the selling agent is perfected and developed." But in view of the designation of subagents, economies in selling expenses would be attained "only after a year or so of operation."

No attempt was made to limit production. The producers decided that it could not legally be limited and, in any event, it could not be limited practically. The finding is that "it was designed that the producer should produce and the selling agent should sell as much coal as possible." The importance of increasing sales is said to lie in the fact that the cost of production is directly related to the actual running time of the mines.

Fourth. Voluminous evidence was received with respect to the effect of defendants' plan upon market prices. As the plan has not gone into operation, there are no actual results upon which to base conclusions. The question is necessarily one of prediction. The court below found that, as between defendants themselves, competition would be eliminated. This was deemed to be the necessary consequence of a common selling agency with power to fix the prices at which it would make sales for its principals. Defendants insist that the finding is too broad and that the differences in grades of coal of the same sizes and the market demands at different times would induce competition between the coals sold by the agency "depending upon the use and the quality of the coals."

The more serious question relates to the effect of the plan upon competition between defendants and other producers. As already noted, the District Court found that "the great bulk" of the coal produced in Appalachian territory is sold "in the highly competitive region east of the Mississippi river and north of the Ohio river under an adverse freight rate." Elaborate statistics were introduced with respect to the production and distribution of bituminous coal and the transportation rates from the different producing sections to the consuming markets, as bearing upon defendants' competitive position, together with evidence as to the requirements of various sections and consumers and the relative advantages possessed by reason of the different qualities and uses of the coals produced. It would be impossible to make even a condensed statement of this evidence (which has been carefully analyzed by both parties), but an examination of it fails to disclose an adequate basis for the conclusion that the operation of the defendants' plan would produce an injurious effect upon competitive conditions, in view of the vast volume of coal available, the conditions of production, and the network of transportation facilities at immediate command.   While strikes and interruptions of transportation may create temporary and abnormal dislocations, the bituminous coal industry under normal conditions affords most exceptional competitive opportunities.   Figures as to developed and potential productive capacity are impressive.   The court below found upon this point that the capacity of the mines in the Appalachian region operated by others than defendants is 82,660,760 tons, as against the capacity of defendants' mines of 86,628,880 tons, while the present yearly capacity of all mines in southern West Virginia, Virginia, eastern Kentucky, and Tennessee is 245,233,560 tons, based upon an eight-hour working day.   "This excess capacity over actual production," the court said, "could be brought into production at moderate expense and with reasonable promptness."   As to potential, undeveloped capacity in Appalachian territory, the court found that in the eight districts in this region not held by any operating, or by any captive, company, there are approximately 760,000 acres containing more than 4,300,000,000 tons of recoverable coal.   In addition, in the same territory "owned by captive companies and not being operated, or owned by operating companies who are using only a very small proportion of their holdings," there is an additional 860,000 acres, containing more than 4,600,-000,000 tons of coal.   Within the twenty-four counties in which defendants' mines are located, and immediately adjacent to them, on railroads already operating, "with the exception of short, feeder extensions," there are over 1,620,000 acres of coal bearing land, containing approximately 9,000,000,000 net tons of recoverable coal "comparable both in quality and mining conditions with the coal now being mined in that region."   "The opening up of this acreage would involve only the extension of short branch lines from the railroads and the building of mining plants.   The price of these lands at the present time would be less than half of the value of two or three years ago, and considerably less on a royalty basis.   Coal produced from these districts is available for any market in which Appalachian coal is sold.   Conditions in the coal industry are such that new companies are free to enter the business of producing and marketing coal in competition with existing companies."   In connection with this proof of developed and potential capacity, the "highly organized and concentrated buying power" that can be exerted must also have appropriate consideration.

Consumers testified that defendants' plan will be a benefit to the coal industry and will not restrain competition.   Testimony to that effect was given by representatives of the Louisville & Nashville Railroad, the Norfolk & Western Railroad, and the Chesapeake & Ohio Railroad, "the largest railroad users of coal operating in the Appalachian region," and by representatives of large utility companies and manufacturing concerns.   There was similar testimony by wholesale and retail dealers in coal.   There are 130 producers of coal other than defendants in Appalachian territory who sell coal commercially. There are also "a large number of mines that have been shut down and could be opened up by the owners on short notice." Competing producers testified that the operation of the selling agency, as proposed by defendants, would not restrain competition and would not hurt their business. Producers in western Pennsylvania, Alabama, Ohio, and Illinois testified to like effect. Referring to this testimony, the court below added, "The small coal producer can, to some extent, and for the purpose of producing and marketing coal, produce coal more cheaply than many of the larger companies and is not prevented by higher cost of operation from being a competitor in the market."

The Government criticizes the "opinion testimony" introduced by defendants as relating to a competitive situation not within the experience of the witnesses, and also animadverts upon their connections and interests, but the Government did not offer testimony of opposing opinions as to the effect upon prices of the operation of the selling agency. Consumers who testified for the Government explained their dependence upon coal from Appalachian territory.

The District Court commented upon the testimony of officers of the selling agency to the effect "that the organization would not be able to fix prices in an arbitrary way but, by the elimination of certain abuses, and by better advertising and sale organization, the producers would get more in the aggregate for their coal." "Other witnesses for the defendants" said the court, "indicated that there would be some tendency to raise the price but that the degree of increase would be affected by other competitors in the coal industry and by producers of coal substitutes."

Fifth. We think that the evidence requires the following conclusions:

1. With respect to defendant's purposes, we find no warrant for determining that they were other than those they declared. Good intentions will not save a plan otherwise objectionable, but knowledge of actual intent is an aid in the interpretation of facts and prediction of consequences. Chicago Board of Trade v. United States, supra. The evidence leaves no doubt of the existence of the evils at which defendants' plan was aimed. The industry was in distress. It suffered from overexpansion and from a serious relative decline through the growing use of substitute fuels. It was afflicted by injurious practices within itself—practices which demanded correction. If evil conditions could not be entirely cured, they at least might be alleviated. The unfortunate state of the industry would not justify any attempt unduly to restrain competition or to monopolize, but the existing situation prompted defendants to make, and the statute did not preclude them from making, an honest effort to remove abuses, to make competition fairer, and thus to promote the essential interests of commerce. The interests of producers and consumers are interlinked. When industry is grievously hurt, when producing concerns fail, when unemployment mounts and communities dependent upon profitable production are prostrated, the wells of commerce go dry. So far as actual purposes

are concerned, the conclusion of the court below was amply supported that defendants were engaged in a fair and open endeavor to aid the industry in a measurable recovery from its plight. The inquiry then, must be whether despite this objective the inherent nature of their plan was such as to create an undue restraint upon interstate commerce.

2. The question thus presented chiefly concerns the effect upon prices. The evidence as to the conditions of the production and distribution of bituminous coal, the available facilities for its transportation, the extent of developed mining capacity, and the vast potential undeveloped capacity, makes it impossible to conclude that defendants through the operation of their plan will be able to fix the price of coal in the consuming markets. The ultimate finding of the District Court is that the defendants "will not have monopoly control of any market, nor the power to fix monopoly prices"; and in its opinion the court stated that "the selling agency will not be able, we think, to fix the market price of coal." Defendants' coal will continue to be subject to active competition. In addition to the coal actually produced and seeking markets in competition with defendants' coal, enormous additional quantities will be within reach and can readily be turned into the channels of trade if an advance of price invites that course. While conditions are more favorable to the position of defendants' group in some markets than in others, we think that the proof clearly shows that, wherever their selling agency operates, it will find itself confronted by effective competition backed by virtually inexhaustive sources of supply, and will also be compelled to cope with the organized buying power of large consumers. The plan cannot be said either to contemplate or to involve the fixing of market prices.

The contention is, and the court below found, that while defendants could not fix market prices, the concerted action would "affect" them, that is, that it would have a tendency to stabilize market prices and to raise them to a higher level than would otherwise obtain. But the facts found do not establish, and the evidence fails to show, that any effect will be produced which in the circumstances of this industry will be detrimental to fair competition. A co-operative enterprise, otherwise free from objection, which carries with it no monopolistic menace, is not to be condemned as an undue restraint merely because it may effect a change in market conditions, where the change would be in mitigation of recognized evils and would not impair, but rather foster, fair competitive opportunities. Voluntary action to rescue and preserve these opportunities, and thus to aid in relieving a depressed industry and in reviving commerce by placing competition upon a sounder basis, may be more efficacious than an attempt to provide remedies through legal processes. The fact that the correction of abuses may tend to stabilize a business, or to produce fairer price levels, does not mean that the abuses should go uncorrected or that co-operative endeavor to correct them necessarily constitutes an unreasonable restraint of trade. The intelligent conduct of commerce through the acquisition of full information of all relevant facts may properly be sought by the co-operation of those engaged in trade, although stabilization of trade and more reasonable prices may be the result. Maple Flooring Association v. United States, supra; Cement Manufacturers' Association v. United States, 268 U.S. 588, 604. Putting an end to injurious practices, and the consequent improvement of the competitive position of a group of producers is not a less worthy aim and may be entirely consonant with the public interest, where the group must still meet effective competition in a fair market and neither seeks nor is able to effect a domination of prices.

Decisions cited in support of a contrary view were addressed to very different circumstances from those presented here. They dealt with combinations which on the particular facts were found to impose unreasonable restraints through the suppression of competition, and in actual operation had that effect. American Column & Lumber Co. v. United States, 257 U.S. 377. * * * In Addyston Pipe & Steel Company v. United States, 175 U.S. 211, the combination was effected by those who were in a position to deprive, and who sought to deprive, the public in a large territory of the advantages of fair competition and was for the actual purpose and had the result of enhancing prices—which in fact had been unreasonably increased. In United States v. Trenton Potteries Company, 273 U.S. 392, defendants, who controlled 82 per cent. of the business of manufacturing and distributing vitreous pottery in the United States, had combined to fix prices. It was found that they had the power to do this and had exerted it. The defense that the prices were reasonable was overruled, as the court held that the power to fix prices involved "power to control the market and to fix arbitrary and unreasonable prices," and that in such a case the difference between legal and illegal conduct could not "depend upon so uncertain a test" as whether the prices actually fixed were reasonable, a determination which could "be satisfactorily made only after a complete survey of our economic organization and a choice between rival philosophies." See United States v. L. Cohen Grocery Co., 255 U.S. 81. In the instant case there is, as we have seen, no intent or power to fix prices, abundant competitive opportunities will exist in all markets where defendants' coal is sold, and nothing has been shown to warrant the conclusion that defendants' plan will have an injurious effect upon competition in these markets.

3. The question remains whether, despite the foregoing conclusions, the fact that the defendants' plan eliminates competition between themselves is alone sufficient to condemn it. Emphasis is placed upon defendants' control of about 73 per cent. of the commercial production in Appalachian territory. But only a small percentage of that production is sold in that territory. The finding of the court below is that "these coals are mined in a region where there is very little consumption." Defendants must go elsewhere to dispose of their products, and the extent of their production is to be considered in the light of the market conditions already described. Even in Appalachian territory it appears that the developed and potential capacity of other producers will afford effective competition. Defendants insist that

on the evidence adduced as to their competitive position in the consuming markets, and in the absence of proof of actual operations showing an injurious effect upon competition, either through possession or abuse of power, no valid objection could have been interposed under the Sherman Act if the defendants had eliminated competition between themselves by a complete integration of their mining properties in a single ownership. United States v. United States Steel Corporation, 251 U.S. 417. * * * We agree that there is no ground for holding defendants' plan illegal merely because they have not integrated their properties and have chosen to maintain their independent plants, seeking not to limit but rather to facilitate production. We know of no public policy, and none is suggested by the terms of the Sherman Act, that in order to comply with the law those engaged in industry should be driven to unify their properties and businesses in order to correct abuses which may be corrected by less drastic measures. Public policy might indeed be deemed to point in a different direction. If the mere size of a single, embracing entity is not enough to bring a combination in corporate form within the statutory inhibition, the mere number and extent of the production of those engaged in a co-operative endeavor to remedy evils which may exist in an industry, and to improve competitive conditions, should not be regarded as producing illegality. The argument that integration may be considered a normal expansion of business, while a combination of independent producers in a common selling agency should be treated as abnormal—that one is a legitimate enterprise and the other is not—makes but an artificial distinction. The Anti-Trust Act aims at substance. Nothing in theory or experience indicates that the selection of a common selling agency to represent a number of producers should be deemed to be more abnormal than the formation of a huge corporation bringing various independent units into one ownership. Either may be prompted by business exigencies and the statute gives to neither a special privilege. The question in either case is whether there is an unreasonable restraint of trade or an attempt to monopolize. If there is, the combination cannot escape because it has chosen corporate form, and, if there is not, it is not to be condemned because of the absence of corporate integration. As we stated at the outset, the question under the act is not simply whether the parties have restrained competition between themselves but as to the nature and effect of that restraint. Chicago Board of Trade v. United States, supra. * * *

The fact that the suit is brought under the Sherman Act does not change the principles which govern the granting of equitable relief. There must be "a definite factual showing of illegality." Standard Oil Company v. United States, 283 U.S. page 179. We think that the Government has failed to show adequate grounds for an injunction in this case. We recognize, however, that the case has been tried in advance of the operation of defendants' plan, and that it has been necessary to test that plan with reference to purposes and anticipated consequences without the advantage of the demonstrations of experience. If in actual operation it should prove to be an undue restraint upon interstate commerce, if it should appear that the plan is used to the impairment of fair competitive opportunities, the decision upon the present record should not preclude the Government from seeking the remedy which would be suited to such a state of facts. We think also that in the event of future controversy arising from the actual operation of the plan the results of the labor of both parties in this litigation in presenting the voluminous evidence as to the industry, market conditions and transportation facilities and rates, should continue to be available, without the necessity of reproducing that evidence.

The decree will be reversed, and the cause will be remanded to the District Court with instructions to enter a decree dismissing the bill of complaint without prejudice and with the provision that the court shall retain jurisdiction of the cause and may set aside the decree and take further proceedings if future developments justify that course in the appropriate enforcement of the Anti-Trust Act.

It is so ordered.

---

3. PER SE VIOLATIONS

There are some trade practices which are held to be "per se violations" even though one might want to argue that the trade practice is a "reasonable" one. But reasonable or not, those practices which are said to be "per se violations" are forbidden. These include price fixing agreements, as shown by U. S. v. Trenton Potteries Co., 273 U. S. 392, 47 S.Ct. 377, 71 L.Ed. 700 (1927) ; refusals to deal with a customer as shown by U. S. v. General Motors Corp., 384 U.S. 127, 86 S. Ct. 1321, 16 L.Ed.2d 415 (1966); and group boycotts, as shown by Klor's Inc. v. Broadway-Hale Stores Inc., 359 U.S. 207, 79 S.Ct. 705, 3 L.Ed.2d 741 (1959). These three cases are reported below.

(a) Price Fixing Agreements

UNITED STATES v. TRENTON POTTERIES CO.

Supreme Court of the United States, 1927.
273 U.S. 392, 47 S.Ct. 377, 71 L.Ed. 700.

Mr. Justice STONE delivered the opinion of the Court.

Respondents, 20 individuals and 23 corporations, were convicted in the District Court for Southern New York of violating the Sherman Anti-Trust Law. Act July 2, 1890, c. 647. The indictment was in two counts. The first charged a combination to fix and maintain uniform prices for the sale of sanitary pottery, in restraint of interstate commerce; the second, a combination to restrain interstate commerce by limiting sales of pottery to a special group known to respondents as "legitimate jobbers."   On appeal, the Circuit Court of Appeals for the Second Circuit reversed the judgment of conviction on both counts on the ground that there were errors in the conduct of the trial. 300 F. 550. This court granted certiorari. 266 U.S. 597.

Respondents, engaged in the manufacture or distribution of 82 per cent. of the vitreous pottery fixtures produced in the United States for use in bathrooms and lavatories, were members of a trade organization known as the Sanitary Potters' Association.   Twelve of the corporate respondents had their factories and chief places of business in New Jersey, one was located in California, and the others were situated in Illinois, Michigan, West Virginia, Indiana, Ohio, and Pennsylvania.   Many of them sold and delivered their product within the Southern district of New York, and some maintained sales offices and agents there.

There is no contention here that the verdict was not supported by sufficient evidence that respondents, controlling some 82 per cent. of the business of manufacturing and distributing in the United States vitreous pottery of the type described, combined to fix prices and to limit sales in interstate commerce to jobbers.

The issues raised here by the government's specification of errors relate only to the decision of the Circuit Court of Appeals upon its review of certain rulings of the District Court made in the course of the trial.   It is urged that the court below erred in holding in effect (1) that the trial court should have submitted to the jury the question whether the price agreement complained of constituted an unreasonable restraint of trade; (2) that the trial court erred in failing to charge the jury correctly on the question of venue; and (3) that it erred also in the admission and exclusion of certain evidence.

Reasonableness of Restraint.

The trial court charged, in submitting the case to the jury that, if it found the agreements or combination complained of, it might return a verdict of guilty without regard to the reasonableness of the prices fixed, or the good intentions of the combining units, whether prices were actually lowered or raised or whether sales were restricted to the special jobbers, since both agreements of themselves were unreasonable restraints.   These instructions repeated in various forms applied to both counts of the indictment.   The trial court refused various requests to charge that both the agreement to fix prices and the agreement to limit sales to a particular group, if found, did not in themselves constitute violations of law, unless it was also found that they unreasonably restrained interstate commerce.   In particular the court refused the request to charge the following:

"The essence of the law is injury to the public.   It is not every restraint of competition and not every restraint of trade that works an injury to the public; it is only an undue and unreasonable restraint of trade that has such an effect and is deemed to be unlawful."

Other requests of similar purport were refused including a quotation from the opinion of this court in Chicago Board of Trade v. United States, 246 U.S. 231.

The court below held specifically that the trial court erred in refusing to charge as requested and held in effect that the charge as given on this branch of the case was erroneous. This determination was based upon the assumption that the charge and refusals could be attributed only to a mistaken view of the trial judge, expressed in denying a motion at the close of the case to quash and dismiss the indictment, that the "rule of reason" announced in Standard Oil Co. v. United States, 221 U.S. 1, and in American Tobacco Co. v. United States, 221 U.S. 106, which were suits for injunctions, had no application in a criminal prosecution. Compare Nash v. United States, 229 U.S. 373.

This disposition of the matter ignored the fact that the trial judge plainly and variously charged the jury that the combinations alleged in the indictment, if found, were violations of the statute as a matter of law, saying:

" * * * The law is clear that an agreement on the part of the members of a combination controlling a substantial part of an industry, upon the prices which the members are to charge for their commodity, is in itself an undue and unreasonable restraint of trade and commerce. * * * "

If the charge itself was correctly given and adequately covered the various aspects of the case, the refusal to charge in another correct form or to quote to the jury extracts from opinions of this court was not error, nor should the court below have been concerned with the wrong reasons that may have inspired the charge, if correctly given. The question therefore to be considered here is whether the trial judge correctly withdrew from the jury the consideration of the reasonableness of the particular restraints charged.

That only those restraints upon interstate commerce which are unreasonable are prohibited by the Sherman Law was the rule laid down by the opinions of this court in the Standard Oil and Tobacco Cases. But it does not follow that agreements to fix or maintain prices are reasonable restraints and therefore permitted by the statute, merely because the prices themselves are reasonable. Reasonableness is not a concept of definite and unchanging content. Its meaning necessarily varies in the different fields of the law, because it is used as a convenient summary of the dominant considerations which control in the application of legal doctrines. Our view of what is a reasonable restraint of commerce is controlled by the recognized purpose of the Sherman Law itself. Whether this type of restraint is reasonable or not must be judged in part at least, in the light of its effect on competition, for, whatever difference of opinion there may be among economists as to the social and economic desirability of an unrestrained competitive system, it cannot be doubted that the Sherman Law and the judicial decisions interpreting it are based upon the assumption that the public interest is best protected from the evils of monopoly and price control by the maintenance of competition. See United States v. Trans-Missouri Freight Association, 166 U.S. 290 * * *.

The aim and result of every price-fixing agreement, if effective, is the elimination of one form of competition. The power to fix prices, whether reasonably exercised or not, involves power to control the market and to fix arbitrary and unreasonable prices. The reasonable price fixed today may through economic and business changes become the unreasonable price of to-morrow. Once established, it may be maintained unchanged because of the absence of competition secured by the agreement for a price reasonable when fixed. Agreements which create such potential power may well be held to be in themselves unreasonable or unlawful restraints, without the necessity of minute inquiry whether a particular price is reasonable or unreasonable as fixed and without placing on the government in enforcing the Sherman Law the burden of ascertaining from day to day whether it has become unreasonable through the mere variation of economic conditions. Moreover, in the absence of express legislation requiring it, we should hesitate to adopt a construction making the difference between legal and illegal conduct in the field of business relations depend upon so uncertain a test as whether prices are reasonable—a determination which can be satisfactorily made only after a complete survey of our economic organization and a choice between rival philosophies. Compare United States v. Cohen Grocery Co., 255 U.S. 81 * * *. Thus viewed the Sherman Law is not only a prohibition against the infliction of a particular type of public injury. It "is a limitation of rights, * * * which may be pushed to evil consequences and therefore restrained." Standard Sanitary Mfg. Co. v. United States, 226 U.S. 20.

That such was the view of this court in deciding the Standard Oil and Tobacco Cases, and that such is the effect of its decisions both before and after those cases, does not seem fairly open to question. Beginning with United States v. Trans-Missouri Freight Association, supra, and United States v. Joint Traffic Association, 171 U.S. 505, where agreements for establishing reasonable and uniform freight rates by competing lines of railroad were held unlawful, it has since often been decided and always assumed that uniform price-fixing by those controlling in any substantial manner a trade or business in interstate commerce is prohibited by the Sherman Law, despite the reasonableness of the particular prices agreed upon. In Addyston Pipe & Steel Co. v. United States, 175 U.S. 211, a case involving a scheme for fixing prices, this court quoted with approval the following passage from the lower court's opinion ([C.C.A.] 85 F. 271):

"* * * The affiants say that in their opinion the prices at which pipe has been sold by defendants have been reasonable. We do not think the issue an important one, because, as already stated, we do not think that at common law there is any question of reasonableness open to the courts with reference to such a contract."

In Swift & Co. v. United States, 196 U.S. 375, this court approved and affirmed a decree which restrained the defendants "by combination, conspiracy or contract [from] raising or lowering prices or fixing uniform prices at which the said meats will be sold, either directly or through their respective agents." In Dr. Miles Medical Co. v. Park & Sons Co., 220 U.S. 373, decided at the same term of court as the Standard Oil and Tobacco Cases, contracts fixing reasonable resale prices were declared unenforcible upon the authority of cases involving price-fixing arrangements between competitors.

That the opinions in the Standard Oil and Tobacco Cases were not intended to affect this view of the illegality of price-fixing agreements affirmatively appears from the opinion in the Standard Oil Case, where, in considering the Freight Association Case, the court said (page 65):

"That as considering the contracts or agreements, their necessary effect and the character of the parties by whom they were made, they were clearly restraints of trade within the purview of the statute, they could not be taken out of that category by indulging in general reasoning as to the expediency or nonexpediency of having made the contracts or the wisdom or want of wisdom of the statute which prohibited their being made; that is to say, the cases but decided that the nature and character of the contracts, creating as they did a conclusive presumption which brought them within the statute, such result was not to be disregarded by the substitution of a judicial appreciation of what the law ought to be for the plain judicial duty of enforcing the law as it was made."

And in Thomsen v. Cayser, 243 U.S. 66, 84, it was specifically pointed out that the Standard Oil and Tobacco Cases did not overrule the earlier cases. The decisions in Maple Flooring Association v. United States, 268 U.S. 563, and in Cement Manufacturers' Protective Association v. United States, 268 U.S. 588, were made on the assumption that any agreement for price-fixing, if found, would have been illegal as a matter of law. In Federal Trade Commission v. Pacific States Paper Trade Association, 273 U.S. 52, we upheld orders of the Commission forbidding price-fixing and prohibiting the use of agreed price lists by wholesale dealers in interstate commerce, without regard to the reasonableness of the prices.

Cases in both the federal and state courts have generally proceeded on a like assumption, and in the second circuit the view maintained below that the reasonableness or unreasonableness of the prices fixed must be submitted to the jury has apparently been abandoned. See Poultry Dealers' Association v. United States (C.C.A.) 4 F.2d 840. While not necessarily controlling, the decisions of this court denying the validity of resale price agreements, regardless of the reasonableness of the price, are persuasive. * * *

Respondents rely upon Chicago Board of Trade v. United States, supra, in which an agreement by members of the Chicago Board of Trade controlling prices during certain hours of the day in a special class of grain contracts and affecting only a small proportion of the commerce in question was upheld. The purpose and effect of the agreement there was to maintain for a part of each business day the price which had been that day determined by open competition on the floor of the exchange. That decision, dealing as it did with a regulation of a board of trade, does not sanction a price agreement among competitors in an open market such as is presented here.

The charge of the trial court, viewed as a whole, fairly submitted to the jury the question whether a price-fixing agreement as described in the first count was entered into by the respondents. Whether the prices actually agreed upon were reasonable or unreasonable was immaterial in the circumstances charged in the indictment and necessarily found by the verdict. The requested charge which we have quoted, and others of similar tenor, while true as abstract propositions, were inapplicable to the case in hand and rightly refused.

The first count being sufficient and the case having been properly submitted to the jury, we may disregard certain like objections relating to the second count. The jury returned a verdict of guilty generally on both counts. Sentence was imposed in part on the first count and in part on both counts, to run concurrently. The combined sentence on both counts does not exceed that which could have been imposed on one alone. There is nothing in the record to suggest that the verdict of guilty on the first count was in any way induced by the introduction of evidence upon the second. In these circumstances the judgment must be sustained if either one of the two counts is sufficient to support it. Claassen v. United States, 142 U.S. 140, * * *

* * *

It follows that the judgment of the Circuit Court of Appeals must be reversed and the judgment of the District Court reinstated.

Reversed.

Mr. Justice VAN DEVANTER, Mr. Justice SUTHERLAND, and Mr. Justice BUTLER, dissent.

Mr. Justice BRANDEIS took no part in the consideration or decision of this case.

(b) Refusals to Deal

UNITED STATES v. GENERAL MOTORS CORPORATION

Supreme Court of the United States, 1966.
384 U.S. 127, 86 S.Ct. 1321, 16 L.Ed.2d 415.

Mr. Justice FORTAS delivered the opinion of the Court.

This is a civil action brought by the United States to enjoin the appellees from participating in an alleged conspiracy to restrain trade in violation of § 1 of the Sherman Act.[1] The United States District Court for the Southern District of California concluded that the proof failed to establish the alleged violation, and entered judgment for the defendants. The case is here on direct appeal under § 2 of the Expediting Act, 15 U.S.C. § 29 (1964 ed.). We reverse.

I.

The appellees are the General Motors Corporation, which manufactures, among other things, the Chevrolet line of cars and trucks, and three associations of Chevrolet dealers in and around Los Angeles, California. All of the Chevrolet dealers in the area belong to one or more of the appellee associations.

Chevrolets are ordinarily distributed by dealers operating under a franchise from General Motors. The dealers purchase the cars from the manufacturer, and then retail them to the public. The relationship between manufacturer and dealer is incorporated in a comprehensive uniform Dealer Selling Agreement. This agreement does not restrict or define those to whom the dealer may sell. Nor are there limitations as to the territory within which the dealer may sell. Compare White Motor Co. v. United States, 372 U.S. 253. The franchise agreement does, however, contain a clause (hereinafter referred to as the "location clause") which prohibits a dealer from moving to or establishing "a new or different location, branch sales office, branch service station, or place of business including any used car lot or location without the prior written approval of Chevrolet."

Beginning in the late 1950's, "discount houses' engaged in retailing consumer goods in the Los Angeles area and "referral services" began offering to sell new cars to the public at allegedly bargain prices. Their sources of supply were the franchised dealers. By 1960 a number of individual Chevrolet dealers, without authorization from General Motors, had developed working relationships with these establishments. A customer would enter one of these establishments and examine the literature and price lists for automobiles produced

---

1. The statute reads in relevant part: "Every contract, combination in the form of trust or otherwise, or conspiracy, in restraint of trade or commerce among the several States, or with foreign nations, is declared to be illegal. * * *" 26 Stat. 209, 15 U.S.C. § 1 (1964 ed.). (Court's footnote 1.)

by several manufacturers. In some instances, floor models were available for inspection. Some of the establishments negotiated with the customer for a trade-in of his old car, and provided financing for his new-car purchase.

The relationship with the franchised dealer took various forms. One arrangement was for the discounter to refer the customer to the dealer. The car would then be offered to him by the dealer at a price previously agreed upon between the dealer and the discounter. In 1960, a typical referral agreement concerning Chevrolets provided that the price to the customer was not to exceed $250 over the dealer's invoiced cost. For its part in supplying the customer, the discounter received $50 per sale.

Another common arrangement was for the discounter itself to negotiate the sale, the dealer's role being to furnish the car and to transfer title to the customer at the direction of the discounter. One dealer furnished Chevrolets under such an arrangement, charging the discounter $85 over its invoiced cost, with the discounter getting the best price it could from its customer.

These were the principal forms of trading involved in this case, although within each there were variations, and there were schemes which fit neither pattern. By 1960 these methods for retailing new cars had reached considerable dimensions. Of the 100,000 new Chevrolets sold in the Los Angeles area in that year, some 2,000 represented discount house or referral sales. One Chevrolet dealer attributed as much as 25% of its annual sales to participation in these arrangements, while another accounted for between 400 and 525 referral sales in a single year.

Approximately a dozen of the 85 Chevrolet dealers in the Los Angeles area were furnishing cars to discounters in 1960. As the volume of these sales grew, the nonparticipating Chevrolet dealers located near one or more of the discount outlets began to feel the pinch. Dealers lost sales because potential customers received, or thought they would receive, a more attractive deal from a discounter who obtained its Chevrolets from a distant dealer. The discounters vigorously advertised Chevrolets for sale, with alluring statements as to price savings. The discounters also advertised that all Chevrolet dealers were obligated to honor the new-car warranty and to provide the free services contemplated therein; and General Motors does indeed require Chevrolet dealers to service Chevrolet cars, wherever purchased, pursuant to the new-car warranty and service agreement. Accordingly, nonparticipating dealers were increasingly called upon to service, without compensation, Chevrolets purchased through discounters. Perhaps what grated most was the demand that they "precondition" cars so purchased—make the hopefully minor adjustments and do the body and paint work necessary to render a factory-fresh car both customer- and road-worthy.

On June 28, 1960, at a regular meeting of the appellee, Losor Chevrolet Dealers Association, member dealers discussed the problem and resolved to bring it to the attention of the Chevrolet Division's Los Angeles zone manager, Robert O'Connor. Shortly thereafter, a delegation from the association called upon O'Connor, presented evidence that some dealers were doing business with the discounters, and asked for his assistance. O'Connor promised he would speak to the offending dealers. When no help was forthcoming, Owen Keown, a director of Losor, took matters into his own hands. First, he spoke to Warren Biggs and Wilbur Newman, Chevrolet dealers who were then doing a substantial business with discounters. According to Keown's testimony, Newman told him that he would continue the practice "until * * * told not to by" Chevrolet, and that "when the Chevrolet Motor Division told him not to do it, he knew that they wouldn't let some other dealer carry on with it."

Keown then reported the foregoing events at the association's annual meeting in Honolulu on November 10, 1960. The member dealers present agreed immediately to flood General Motors and the Chevrolet Division with letters and telegrams asking for help. Salesmen, too, were to write.

Hundreds of letters and wires descended upon Detroit—with telling effect. Within a week Chevrolet's O'Connor was directed to furnish his superiors in Detroit with "a detailed report of the discount house operations * * * as well as what action we in the Zone are taking to curb such sales."

By mid-December General Motors had formulated its response. On December 15, James M. Roche, then an executive vice president of General Motors, wrote to some of the complaining dealers. He noted that the practices to which they were objecting *"in some instances* represent the establishment of a second and unauthorized sales outlet or location contrary to the provisions of the General Motors Dealers Selling Agreements." (Emphasis supplied.) Recipients of the letter were advised that General Motors personnel proposed to discuss that matter with each of the dealers. O'Connor in Los Angeles was apprised of the letter's content and instructed to carry on the personal discussions referred to therein. With respect to the offending dealers, he was to work with Roy Cash, regional manager for the Chevrolet Division. Cash had been briefed on the subject in Detroit on December 14.

General Motors personnel proceeded to telephone all area dealers, both to identify those associated with the discounters and to advise nonparticipants that General Motors had entered the lists. The principal offenders were treated to unprecedented individual confrontations with Cash, the regional manager. These brief meetings were wholly successful in obtaining from each dealer his agreement to abandon the practices in question. Some capitulated during the course of the four- or five-minute meeting, or immediately thereafter. One dealer, who met not with Cash but with the city sales manager for Chevrolet, put off decision for a week "to make sure that the other dealers, or most of them, had stopped their business dealings with discount houses."

There is evidence that unanimity was not obtained without reference to the ultimate power of General Motors. The testimony of dealer Wilbur Newman was that regional manager Cash related a story, the relevance of which was not lost upon him, that in handling children, "I can tell them to stop something. If they don't do it * * * I can knock their teeth down their throats."

By mid-January General Motors had elicited from each dealer a promise not to do business with the discounters. But such agreements would require policing—a fact which had been anticipated. General Motors earlier had initiated contacts with firms capable of performing such a function. This plan, unilaterally to police the agreements, was displaced, however, in favor of a joint effort between General Motors, the three appellee associations, and a number of individual dealers.

On December 15, 1960, representatives of the three appellee associations had met and appointed a joint committee to study the situation and to keep in touch with Chevrolet's O'Connor. Early in 1961, the three associations agreed jointly to finance the "shopping" of the discounters to assure that no Chevrolet dealer continued to supply them with cars. Each of the associations contributed $5,000, and a professional investigator was hired. He was instructed to try to purchase new Chevrolets from the proscribed outlets, to tape-record the transactions, if any, and to gather all the necessary documentary evidence—which the associations would then lay "at the doorstep of Chevrolet." These joint associational activities were both preceded and supplemented by similar "shopping" activities by individual dealers and by appellee Losor Chevrolet Dealers Association.

General Motors collaborated with these policing activities. There is evidence that zone manager O'Connor and a subordinate, Jere Faust, actively solicited the help of individual dealers in uncovering violations. Armed with information of such violations obtained from the dealers or their associations, O'Connor or members of his staff would ask the offending dealer to come in and talk. The dealer then was confronted with the car purchased by the "shopper," the documents of sale, and in most cases a tape recording of the transaction. In every instance, the embarrassed dealer repurchased the car, sometimes at a substantial loss, and promised to stop such sales. At the direction of O'Connor or a subordinate, the checks with which the cars were repurchased were made payable to an attorney acting jointly for the three defendant associations.

O'Connor testified that on no occasion did he "force" a dealer to repurchase; he merely made the opportunity available. But one dealer testified that when an assistant zone manager for the Chevrolet Division asked him to come in and talk about discount sales, "he specified a sum of money which I was to bring with me when I came down and saw him. * * * I kept the appointment and brought a cashier's check. I knew when I came down to Los Angeles that I was going to repurchase an automobile * * *." Another dealer testified that upon being confronted with evidence that one of his cars had been purchased through a referral service, he not only bought it back (without questioning the correctness of the price exacted) but also fired the employee responsible for the transaction—although the employee had been commended by the Chevrolet Division a few weeks earlier as the "number one fleet salesman" in the 11-state Pacific region.

By the spring of 1961, the campaign to eliminate the discounters from commerce in new Chevrolet cars was a success. Sales through the discount outlets seem to have come to a halt. Not until a federal grand jury commenced an inquiry into the matters which we have sketched does it appear that any Chevrolet dealer resumed its business association with the discounters.

II.

On these basic facts, the Government first proceeded criminally. A federal grand jury in the Southern District of California returned an indictment. After trial, the defendants were found not guilty. The present civil action, filed shortly after return of the indictment, was then brought to trial.

Both the Government and the appellees urge the importance, for purposes of decision, of the "location clause" in the Dealer Selling Agreement which prohibits a franchised dealer from moving to or establishing "a new or different location, branch sales office, branch service station, or place of business * * * without the prior written approval of Chevrolet." The appellees contend that this contractual provision is lawful, and that it justifies their actions. They argue that General Motors acted lawfully to prevent its dealers from violating the "location clause," that the described arrangements with discounters constitute the establishment of additional sales outlets in violation of the clause, and that the individual dealers—and their associations—have an interest in uniform compliance with the franchise agreement, which interest they lawfully sought to vindicate.

The Government invites us to join in the assumption, only for purposes of this case, that the "location clause" encompasses sales by dealers through the medium of discounters. But it urges us to hold that, so construed, the provision is unlawful as an unreasonable restraint of trade in violation of the Sherman Act.

We need not reach these questions concerning the meaning, effect, or validity of the "location clause" or of any other provision in the Dealer Selling Agreement, and we do not. We do not decide whether the "location clause" may be construed to prohibit a dealer, party to it, from selling through discounters, or whether General Motors could by unilateral action enforce the clause, so construed. We have here a classic conspiracy in restraint of trade: joint, collaborative action by dealers, the appellee associations, and General Motors to eliminate a class of competitors by terminating business dealings between them and a minority of Chevrolet dealers and to deprive franchised dealers of their freedom to deal through discounters if they so choose. Against this fact of unlawful combination, the "location clause" is of no avail. Whatever General Motors might or might not lawfully have done to enforce individual Dealer Selling Agreements by action within the borders of those agreements and the relationship which each defines, is beside the point. And, because the action taken constitutes a combination or conspiracy, it is not necessary to consider what might be the legitimate interest of a dealer in securing compliance by others with the "location clause," or the lawfulness of action a dealer might individually take to vindicate this interest.

The District Court decided otherwise. It concluded that the described events did not add up to a combination or conspiracy violative of the antitrust laws. But its conclusion cannot be squared with its own specific findings of fact. These findings include the essentials of a conspiracy within § 1 of the Sherman Act: That in the summer of 1960 the Losor Chevrolet Dealers Association, "through some of its dealer-members," complained to General Motors personnel about sales through discounters (Finding 34); that at a Losor meeting in November 1960 the dealers there present agreed to embark on a letter-writing campaign directed at enlisting the aid of General Motors (Finding 35); that in December and January General Motors personnel discussed the matter with every Chevrolet dealer in the Los Angeles area and elicited from each a promise not to do business with the discounters (Finding 39); that representatives of the three associations of Chevrolet dealers met on December 15, 1960, and created a joint investigating committee (Finding 40); that the three associations then undertook jointly to police the agreements obtained from each of the dealers by General Motors; that the associations supplied information to General Motors for use by it in bringing wayward dealers into line, and that Chevrolet's O'Connor asked the associations to do so (Findings 41 and 42); that as a result of this collaborative effort, a number of Chevrolet dealers were induced to repurchase cars they had sold through discounters and to promise to abjure such sales in future (Finding 42).

These findings by the trial judge compel the conclusion that a conspiracy to restrain trade was proved. The error of the trial court lies in its failure to apply the correct and established standard for ascertaining the existence of a combination or conspiracy under § 1 of the Sherman Act. See United States v. Parke, Davis & Co., 362 U.S. 29. The trial court attempted to justify its conclusion on the following reasoning: That each defendant and alleged co-conspirator acted to promote its own self-interest; that General Motors, as well as the defendant associations and their members, has a lawful interest in securing compliance with the "location clause" and in thus protecting the franchise system of distributing automobiles—business arrangements which the court deemed lawful and proper; and that in seeking to vindicate these interests the defendants and their alleged co-conspirators entered into no "agreements" among themselves, although they may have engaged in "parallel action."

These factors do not justify the result reached. It is of no consequence, for purposes of determining whether there has been a combination or conspiracy under § 1 of the Sherman Act, that each party acted in its own lawful interest. Nor is it of consequence for this purpose whether the "location clause" and franchise system are lawful of economically desirable. And although we regard as clearly erroneous and irreconcilable with its other findings the trial court's conclusory "finding" that there had been no "agreement" among the defendants and their alleged co-conspirators, it has long been settled that explicit agreement is not a necessary part of a Sherman Act conspiracy—certainly not where, as here, joint and collaborative action was pervasive in the initiation, execution, and fulfillment of the plan. United States v. Parke, Davis & Co., supra. * * *

Neither individual dealers nor the associations acted independently or separately. The dealers collaborated, through the associations and otherwise, among themselves and with General Motors, both to enlist the aid of General Motors and to enforce dealers' promises to forsake the discounters. The associations explicitly entered into a joint venture to assist General Motors in policing the dealers' promises, and their joint proffer of aid was accepted and utilized by General Motors.

Nor did General Motors confine its activities to the contractual boundaries of its relationships with individual dealers. As the trial court found (Finding 39), General Motors at no time announced that it would terminate the franchise of any dealer which furnished cars to the discounters. The evidence indicates that it had no intention of acting in this unilateral fashion. On the contrary, overriding corporate policy with respect to proper dealer relations dissuaded General Motors from engaging in this sort of wholly unilateral conduct, the validity of which under the antitrust laws was assumed, without being decided, in *Parke, Davis,* supra.

As Parke, Davis had done, General Motors sought to elicit from all the dealers agreements, substantially interrelated and interdependent, that none of them would do business with the discounters. These agreements were hammered out in meetings between nonconforming dealers and officials of General Motors' Chevrolet Division, and in telephone conversations with other dealers. It was acknowledged from the beginning that substantial unanimity would be essential if the agreements were to be forthcoming. And once the agreements were secured, General Motors both solicited and employed the assistance of its alleged co-conspirators in helping to police them. What resulted was a fabric interwoven by many strands of joint action to eliminate the discounters from participation in the market, to inhibit the free choice of franchised dealers to select their own methods of trade and to provide multilateral surveillance and enforcement. This process for achieving and enforcing the desired objection can by no stretch of the imagination be described as "unilateral" or merely "parallel." See *Parke, Davis,* supra, 362 U.S. at 46. * * *

There can be no doubt that the effect of the combination or conspiracy here was to restrain trade and commerce within the meaning of the Sherman Act. Elimination, by joint collaborative action, of discounters from access to the market is a *per se* violation of the Act.

In Klor's, Inc. v. Broadway-Hale Stores, Inc., 359 U.S. 207, the Court was confronted with the question whether "a group of powerful businessmen may act in concert to deprive a single merchant, like Klor, of the goods he needs to compete effectively." 359 U.S., at 210. The allegation was that manufacturers and distributors of electrical appliances had conspired among themselves and with a major retailer, Broadway-Hale, "either not to sell to Klor's [Broadway-Hale's next-door neighbor and competitor] or to sell to it only at discriminatory prices and highly unfavorable terms." 359 U.S., at 209. The Court concluded that the alleged group boycott of even a single trader violated the statute without regard to the reasonableness of the conduct in the circumstances. Group boycotts of a trader, said the Court, are among those "classes of restraints which from their 'nature or character' were unduly restrictive   *   *   *." 359 U.S., at 211. This was not new doctrine, for it had long been recognized that "there are certain agreements or practices which because of their pernicious effect on competition and lack of any redeeming virtue are conclusively presumed to be unreasonable and therefore illegal without elaborate inquiry as to the precise harm they have caused or the business excuse for their use," and that group boycotts are of this character. Northern Pac. R. Co. v. United States, 356 U.S. 1.   *   *   *

The principle of these cases is that where businessmen concert their actions in order to deprive others of access to merchandise which the latter wish to sell to the public, we need not inquire into the economic motivation underlying their conduct. See Barber, Refusals To Deal Under the Federal Antitrust Laws, 103 U.Pa.L.Rev. 847, 872–885 (1955). Exclusion of traders from the market by means of combination or conspiracy is so inconsistent with the free-market principles embodied in the Sherman Act that it is not to be saved by reference to the need for preserving the collaborators' profit margins or their system for distributing automobiles, any more than by reference to the allegedly tortious conduct against which a combination or conspiracy may be directed—as in Fashion Originators' Guild of America, Inc. v. Federal Trade Comm'n, supra, 312 U.S., at 468.

We note, moreover, that inherent in the success of the combination in this case was a substantial restraint upon price competition—a goal unlawful *per se* when sought to be effected by combination or conspiracy. E. g., United States v. Parke, Davis & Co., 362 U.S. 29.   *   *   * And the *per se* rule applies even when the effect upon prices is indirect. Simpson v. Union Oil Co., 377 U.S. 13.   *   *   *

There is in the record ample evidence that one of the purposes behind the concerted effort to eliminate sales of new Chevrolet cars by discounters was to protect franchised dealers from real or apparent price competition. The discounters advertised price savings.   *   *   *

Some purchasers found and others believed that discount prices were lower than those available through the franchised dealers. Certainly, * * * complaints about price competition were prominent in the letters and telegrams with which the individual dealers and salesmen bombarded General Motors in November 1960. (Finding 38.) And although the District Court found to the contrary, there is evidence in the record that General Motors itself was not unconcerned about the effect of discount sales upon general price levels.

The protection of price competition from conspiratorial restraint is an object of special solicitude under the anti-trust laws. We cannot respect that solicitude by closing our eyes to the effect upon price competition of the removal from the market, by combination or conspiracy, of a class of traders. Nor do we propose to construe the Sherman Act to prohibit conspiracies to fix prices at which competitors may sell, but to allow conspiracies or combinations to put competitors out of business entirely.

Accordingly, we reverse and remand to the United States District Court for the Southern District of California in order that it may fashion appropriate equitable relief. See United States v. Parke, Davis & Co., supra, 362 U.S., at 47–48. It is so ordered.

Reversed and remanded.

Mr. Justice HARLAN, concurring in the result.

Although I consider that United States v. Parke, Davis & Co., 362 U.S. 29, decided in 1960, represents basically unsound antitrust doctrine, see my dissenting opinion, 362 U.S., at 49, I see no escape from the conclusion that it controls this case. *Parke, Davis* held that a manufacturer cannot maintain resale prices by refusing to sell to those who do not follow his suggested prices if the refusal is attended by concerted action with his customers, even though he may unilaterally so conduct himself. See United States v. Colgate & Co., 250 U.S. 300. Although *Parke, Davis* related to alleged price-fixing, I have been unable to discern any tenable reason for differentiating it from a case involving, as here, alleged boycotting. The conclusion that *Parke, Davis* governs the present case is therefore unavoidable, given the undisputed evidence that General Motors acted in concert with its dealers in enforcing the location clause. In my opinion, however, General Motors is not precluded from enforcing the location clause by unilateral action, and I find nothing in the Court's opinion to the contrary.

On this basis I concur in the judgment of the Court.

(c) Group Boycotts

KLOR'S, INC. v. BROADWAY–HALE STORES, INC.

Supreme Court of the United States, 1959.
359 U.S. 207, 79 S.Ct. 705, 3 L.Ed.2d 741.

Mr. Justice BLACK delivered the opinion of the Court.

Klor's, Inc., operates a retail store on Mission Street, San Francisco, California; Broadway-Hale Stores, Inc., a chain of department stores, operates one of its stores next door. The two stores compete in the sale of radios, television sets, refrigerators and other household appliances. Claiming that Broadway-Hale and 10 national manufacturers and their distributors have conspired to restrain and monopolize commerce in violation of §§ 1 and 2 of the Sherman Act, 26 Stat. 209, as amended, 15 U.S.C. §§ 1, 2, 15 U.S.C.A. §§ 1, 2, Klor's brought this action for treble damages and injunction in the United States District Court.[1]

In support of its claim Klor's made the following allegations: George Klor started an appliance store some years before 1952 and has operated it ever since either individually or as Klor's, Inc. Klor's is as well equipped as Broadway-Hale to handle all brands of appliances. Nevertheless, manufacturers and distributors of such well-known brands as General Electric, RCA, Admiral, Zenith, Emerson and others have conspired among themselves and with Broadway-Hale either not to sell to Klor's or to sell to it only at discriminatory prices and highly unfavorable terms. Broadway-Hale has used its "monopolistic" buying power to bring about this situation. The business of manufacturing, distributing and selling household appliances is in interstate commerce. The concerted refusal to deal with Klor's has seriously handicapped its ability to compete and has already caused it a great loss of profits, goodwill, reputation and prestige.

The defendants did not dispute these allegations, but sought summary judgment and dismissal of the complaint for failure to state a cause of action. They submitted unchallenged affidavits which showed that there were hundreds of other household appliance retailers, some within a few blocks of Klor's who sold many competing brands of appliances, including those the defendants refused to sell to Klor's. From

---

1. Section 1 of the Sherman Act provides: "Every contract, combination in the form of trust or otherwise, or conspiracy, in restraint of trade or commerce among the several States, or with foreign nations, is declared to be illegal * * *." Section 2 of the Act reads, "Every person who shall monopolize, or attempt to monopolize, or combine or conspire with any other person or persons, to monopolize any part of the trade or commerce among the several States, or with foreign nations, shall be deemed guilty of a misdemeanor * * *." Section 4 of the Clayton Act, 38 Stat. 731, 15 U.S.C. § 15, 15 U.S.C.A. § 15, states, "Any person who shall be injured in his business or property by reason of anything forbidden in the antitrust laws may sue therefor * * * and shall recover threefold the damages by him sustained * * *." (Court's footnote 1.)

the allegations of the complaint, and from the affidavits supporting the motion for summary judgment, the District Court concluded that the controversy was a "purely private quarrel" between Klor's and Broadway-Hale, which did not amount to a "public wrong proscribed by the [Sherman] Act." On this ground the complaint was dismissed and summary judgment was entered for the defendants. The Court of Appeals for the Ninth Circuit affirmed the summary judgment. 255 F.2d 214. It stated that "a violation of the Sherman Act requires conduct of defendants by which the public is or conceivably may be ultimately injured." 255 F.2d at page 233. It held that here the required public injury was missing since "there was no charge or proof that by any act of defendants the price, quantity, or quality offered the public was affected, nor that there was any intent or purpose to effect a change in, or an influence on, prices, quantity, or quality * * *." Id., at page 230. The holding, if correct, means that unless the opportunities for customers to buy in a competitive market are reduced, a group of powerful businessmen may act in concert to deprive a single merchant, like Klor, of the goods he needs to compete effectively. We granted certiorari to consider this important question in the administration of the Sherman Act. 358 U.S. 809.

We think Klor's allegations clearly show one type of trade restraint and public harm the Sherman Act forbids, and that defendants' affidavits provide no defense to the charges. Section 1 of the Sherman Act makes illegal any contract, combination or conspiracy in restraint of trade, and § 2 forbids any person or combination from monopolizing or attempting to monopolize any part of interstate commerce. In the landmark case of Standard Oil Co. of New Jersey v. United States, 221 U.S. 1, this Court read § 1 to prohibit those classes of contracts or acts which the common law had deemed to be undue restraints of trade and those which new times and economic conditions would make unreasonable. Id., at pages 59–60. The Court construed § 2 as making "the prohibitions of the act all the more complete and perfect by embracing all attempts to reach the end prohibited by the 1st section, that is, restraints of trade, by any attempt to monopolize, or monopolization thereof * * *." Id., at page 61. The effect of both sections, the Court said, was to adopt the common-law proscription of all "contracts or acts which it was considered had a monopolistic tendency * * *" and which interfered with the "natural flow" of an appreciable amount of interstate commerce. Id., at pages 57, 61; Eastern States Retail Lumber Dealers' Ass'n v. United States, 234 U.S. 600. The Court recognized that there were some agreements whose validity depended on the surrounding circumstances. It emphasized, however, that there were classes of restraints which from their "nature or character" were unduly restrictive, and hence forbidden by both the common law and the statute. 221 U.S. at pages 58, 65. As to these classes of restraints, the Court noted, Congress had determined its own criteria of public harm and it was not for the courts to decide whether in an individual case injury had actually occurred. Id., at pages 63–68.

Group boycotts, or concerted refusals by traders to deal with other traders, have long been held to be in the forbidden category. They have not been saved by allegations that they were reasonable in the specific circumstances, nor by a failure to show that they "fixed or regulated prices, parcelled out or limited production, or brought about a deterioration in quality." Fashion Originators' Guild v. Federal Trade Commission, 312 U.S. 457. Cf. United States v. Trenton Potteries Co., 273 U.S. 392. Even when they operated to lower prices or temporarily to stimulate competition they were banned. For, as this Court said in Kiefer-Stewart Co. v. Joseph E. Seagram & Sons, 340 U.S. 211, "such agreements, no less than those to fix minimum prices, cripple the freedom of traders and thereby restrain their ability to sell in accordance with their own judgment." Cf. United States v. Patten, 226 U.S. 525.

Plainly the allegations of this complaint disclose such a boycott. This is not a case of a single trader refusing to deal with another, nor even of a manufacturer and a dealer agreeing to an exclusive distributorship. Alleged in this complaint is a wide combination consisting of manufacturers, distributors and a retailer. This combination takes from Klor's its freedom to buy appliances in an open competitive market and drives it out of business as a dealer in the defendants' products. It deprives the manufacturers and distributors of their freedom to sell to Klor's at the same prices and conditions made available to Broadway-Hale and in some instances forbids them from selling to it on any terms whatsoever. It interferes with the natural flow of interstate commerce. It clearly has, by its "nature" and "character," a "monopolistic tendency." As such it is not to be tolerated merely because the victim is just one merchant whose business is so small that his destruction makes little difference to the economy. Monopoly can as surely thrive by the elimination of such small businessmen, one at a time, as it can by driving them out in large groups. In recognition of this fact the Sherman Act has consistently been read to forbid all contracts and combinations "which 'tend to create a monopoly,'" whether "the tendency is a creeping one" or "one that proceeds at full gallop." International Salt Co. v. United States, 332 U.S. 392.

The judgment of the Court of Appeals is reversed and the cause is remanded to the District Court for trial.

Reversed.

---

4. MERGERS AND ACQUISITIONS

Much has been written (and undoubtedly more is to come) about the avalanche of business combinations which has occurred in the last several decades. This movement used to be called a "trend", and used to be described as moving at a "glacial" speed. But no more. Business combinations and "conglomerates" of all sizes developed in the period of 1945 to 1970, in spite of our traditional opposition to bigness.

The 1950 amendment to Section 7 of the Clayton Act, 15 U.S.C.A. § 18, failed to stop what has become an avalanche. Eventually it appears that the inability of one group of persons to manage an exceedingly large or complex group of businesses with different management problems may result in a reduction in size or dismemberment of some of the mergers or conglomerates. Perhaps, too, a national administration sufficiently independent of the political campaign financial support of large contributors from the business community, and with a will to proceed, can use the existing statutes to reverse the concentration of economic power and to reestablish a system of free entry into the market, of free price competition and of a multiplicity of producers so necessary to our system of distributing the products of our economy.

Two cases reported below illustrate some of these problems, F. T. C. v. Procter & Gamble Co., 386 U.S. 568, 87 S.Ct. 1224, 18 L.Ed. 2d 303 (1967), and U. S. v. Aluminum Co. of America, 377 U.S. 271, 84 S.Ct. 1283, 12 L.Ed.2d 314 (1964). These are by no means all of the problems. A large-scale attack on a large-scale conglomerate should be expected.

———

FEDERAL TRADE COMMISSION v. PROCTER & GAMBLE COMPANY

Supreme Court of the United States, 1967.
386 U.S. 568, 87 S.Ct. 1224, 18 L.Ed.2d 303.

Mr. Justice DOUGLAS delivered the opinion of the Court.

This is a proceeding initiated by the Federal Trade Commission charging that respondent, Procter & Gamble Co., had acquired the assets of Clorox Chemical Co. in violation of § 7 of the Clayton Act, 38 Stat. 731, as amended by the Celler-Kefauver Act, 64 Stat. 1125, 15 U.S.C.A. § 18.[1] The charge was that Procter's acquisition of Clorox might substantially lessen competition or tend to create a monopoly in the production and sale of household liquid bleaches.

Following evidentiary hearings, the hearing examiner rendered his decision in which he concluded that the acquisition was unlawful and ordered divestiture. On appeal, the Commission reversed, holding that the record as then constituted was inadequate, and remanded to the examiner for additional evidentiary hearings. 58 F.T.C. 1203. After the additional hearings, the examiner again held the acquisition unlawful and ordered divestiture. The Commission affirmed the examiner and ordered divestiture. The Court of Appeals for the Sixth

---

1. "No corporation engaged in commerce shall acquire, directly or indirectly, the whole or any part of the stock or other share capital and no corporation subject to the jurisdiction of the Federal Trade Commission shall acquire the whole or any part of the assets of another corporation engaged also in commerce, where in any line of commerce in any section of the country, the effect of such acquisition may be substantially to lessen competition, or to tend to create a monopoly." (Court's footnote 1.)

Circuit reversed and directed that the Commission's complaint be dismissed. 358 F.2d 74. We find that the Commission's findings were amply supported by the evidence, and that the Court of Appeals erred.

As indicated by the Commission in its painstaking and illuminating report, it does not particularly aid analysis to talk of this merger in conventional terms, namely, horizontal or verticle or conglomerate. This merger may most appropriately be described as a "product-extension merger," as the Commission stated. The facts are not disputed, and a summary will demonstrate the correctness of the Commission's decision.

At the time of the merger, in 1957, Clorox was the leading manufacturer in the heavily concentrated household liquid bleach industry. It is agreed that household liquid bleach is the relevant line of commerce. The product is used in the home as a germicide and disinfectant, and, more importantly, as a whitening agent in washing clothes and fabrics. It is a distinctive product with no close substitutes. Liquid bleach is a low-price, high-turnover consumer product sold mainly through grocery stores and supermarkets. The relevant geographical market is the Nation and a series of regional markets. Because of high shipping costs and low sales price, it is not feasible to ship the product more than 300 miles from its point of manufacture. Most manufacturers are limited to competition within a single region since they have but one plant. Clorox is the only firm selling nationally; it has 13 plants distributed throughout the Nation. Purex, Clorox's closest competitor in size, does not distribute its bleach in the northeast or mid-Atlantic States; in 1957, Purex's bleach was available in less than 50% of the national market.

At the time of the acquisition, Clorox was the leading manufacturer of household liquid bleach, with 48.8% of the national sales—annual sales of slightly less than $40,000,000. Its market share had been steadily increasing for the five years prior to the merger. Its nearest rival was Purex, which manufactures a number of products other than household liquid bleaches, including abrasive cleaners, toilet soap, and detergents. Purex accounted for 15.7% of the household liquid bleach market The industry is highly concentrated; in 1957, Clorox and Purex accounted for almost 65% of the Nation's household liquid bleach sales, and, together with four other firms, for almost 80%. The remaining 20% was divided among over 200 small producers. Clorox had total assets of $12,000,000; only eight producers had assets in excess of $1,000,000 and very few had assets of more than $75,000.

In light of the territorial limitations on distribution, national figures do not give an accurate picture of Clorox's dominance in the various regions. Thus, Clorox's seven principal competitors did no business in New England, the mid-Atlantic States, or metropolitan New York. Clorox's share of the sales in those areas was 56%, 72% and 64% respectively. Even in regions where its principal competitors were active, Clorox maintained a dominate position. Except in metropolitan Chicago and the west-central States Clorox accounted for at least 39%, and often a much higher percentage, of liquid bleach sales.

Since all liquid bleach is chemically identical, advertising and sales promotion are vital. In 1957 Clorox spent almost $3,700,000 on advertising, imprinting the value of its bleach in the mind of the consumer. In addition, it spent $1,700,000 for other promotional activities. The Commission found that these heavy expenditures went far to explain why Clorox maintained so high a market share despite the fact that its brand, though chemically indistinguishable from rival brands, retailed for a price equal to or, in many instances, higher than its competitors.

Procter is a large, diversified manufacturer of low-price, high-turnover household products sold through grocery, drug, and department stores. Prior to its acquisition of Clorox, it did not produce household liquid bleach. Its 1957 sales were in excess of $1,100,000,-000 from which it realized profits of more than $67,000,000; its assets were over $500,000,000. Procter has been marked by rapid growth and diversification. It has successfully developed and introduced a number of new products. Its primary activity is in the general area of soaps, detergents, and cleansers; in 1957, of total domestic sales, more than one-half (over $500,000,000) were in this field. Procter was the dominant factor in this area. It accounted for 54.4% of all packaged detergent sales. The industry is heavily concentrated—Procter and its nearest competitors, Colgate-Palmolive and Lever Brothers, account for 80% of the market.

In the marketing of soaps, detergents, and cleansers, as in the marketing of household liquid bleach, advertising and sales promotion are vital. In 1957, Procter was the Nation's largest advertiser, spending more than $80,000,000 on advertising and an additional $47,000,-000 on sales promotion. Due to its tremendous volume, Procter receives substantial discounts from the media. As a multi-product producer Procter enjoys substantial advantages in advertising and sales promotion. Thus, it can and does feature several products in its promotions, reducing the printing, mailing, and other costs for each product. It also purchases network programs on behalf of several products, enabling it to give each product network exposure at a fraction of the cost per product that a firm with only one product to advertise would incur.

Prior to the acquisition, Procter was in the course of diversifying into product lines related to its basic detergent-soap-cleanser business. Liquid bleach was a distinct possibility since packaged detergents—Procter's primary product line—and liquid bleach are used complementarily in washing clothes and fabrics, and in general household cleaning. As noted by the Commission:

"Packaged detergents—Procter's most important product category—and household liquid bleach are used complementarily, not only in the washing of clothes and fabrics, but also in general household cleaning, since liquid bleach is a germicide and disinfectant as well as a whitener.   From the consumer's viewpoint, then, packaged detergents and liquid bleach are closely related products.   But the area of relatedness between products of Procter and of Clorox is wider.   Household cleansing agents in general, like household liquid bleach, are low-cost, high-turnover household consumer goods marketed chiefly through grocery stores and pre-sold to the consumer by the manufacturer through mass advertising and sales promotions.   Since products of both parties to the merger are sold to the same customers, at the same stores, and by the same merchandising methods, the possibility arises of significant integration at both the marketing and distribution levels."   63 F.T.C. ——, ——.*

The decision to acquire Clorox was the result of a study conducted by Procter's promotion department designed to determine the advisability of entering the liquid bleach industry.   The initial report noted the ascendancy of liquid bleach in the large and expanding household bleach market, and recommended that Procter purchase Clorox rather than enter independently.   Since a large investment would be needed to obtain a satisfactory market share, acquisition of the industry's leading firm was attractive.   "Taking over the Clorox business   *   *   *   could be a way of achieving a dominant position in the liquid bleach market quickly, which would pay out reasonably well."   63 F.T.C., at ——.*   The initial report predicted that Procter's "sales, distribution and manufacturing setup" could increase Clorox's share of the markets in areas where it was low.   The final report confirmed the conclusions of the initial report and emphasized that Procter would make more effective use of Clorox's advertising budget and that the merger would facilitate advertising economies.   A few months later, Procter acquired the assets of Clorox in the name of a wholly owned subsidiary, the Clorox Company, in exchange for Procter stock.

The Commission found that the acquisition might substantially lessen competition.   The findings and reasoning of the Commission need be only briefly summarized.   The Commission found that the substitution of Procter with its huge assets and advertising advantages for the already dominant Clorox would dissuade new entrants and discourage active competition from the firms already in the industry due to fear of retaliation by Procter.   The Commission thought it relevant that retailers might be induced to give Clorox preferred shelf space since it would be manufactured by Procter, which also produced a number of other products marketed by the retailers.   There was also the danger that Procter might underprice Clorox in order to drive out competition, and subsidize the under-pricing with revenue from other products.   The Commission carefully reviewed the effect of the acquisition on the structure of the industry, noting that "[t]he practical tendency of the   *   *   *   merger   *   *   *   is to transform the liquid bleach industry into an arena of big business competition only, with the few small firms that have not disappeared through merger

* Full citation omitted from original.

eventually falling by the wayside, unable to compete with their giant rivals." 63 F.T.C., at ——.* Further, the merger would seriously diminish potential competition by eliminating Procter as a potential entrant into the industry. Prior to the merger, the Commission found, Procter was the most likely prospective entrant, and absent the merger would have remained on the periphery, restraining Clorox from exercising its market power. If Procter had actually entered, Clorox's dominant position would have been eroded and the concentration of the industry reduced. The Commission stated that it had not placed reliance on post-acquisition evidence in holding the merger unlawful.

The Court of Appeals said that the Commission's finding of illegality had been based on "treacherous conjecture," mere possibility and suspicion. 358 F.2d 74. It dismissed the fact that Clorox controlled almost 50% of the industry, that two firms controlled 65%, and that six firms controlled 80% with the observation that "[t]he fact that in addition to the six * * * producers sharing eighty per cent of the market, there were two hundred smaller producers * * * would not seem to indicate anything unhealthy about the market conditions." Id., at 80. It dismissed the finding that Procter, with its hugh resources and prowess, would have more leverage than Clorox with the statement that it was Clorox which had the "knowhow" in the industry, and that Clorox's finances were adequate for its purposes. Ibid. As for the possibility that Procter would use its tremendous advertising budget and volume discounts to push Clorox, the court found "it difficult to base a finding of illegality on discounts in advertising." 358 F.2d, at 81. It rejected the Commission's finding that the merger eliminated the potential competition of Procter because "[t]here was no reasonable probability that Procter would have entered the household liquid bleach market but for the merger." 358 F.2d, at 83. "There was no evidence tending to prove that Procter ever intended to enter this field on its own." 358 F.2d, at 82. Finally, "[t]here was no evidence that Procter at any time in the past engaged in predatory practices, or that it intended to do so in the future." Ibid.

The Court of Appeals also heavily relied on post-acquisition "evidence * * * to the effect that the other producers subsequent to the merger were selling more bleach for more money than ever before" (358 F.2d, at 80), and that "[t]here [had] been no significant change in Clorox's market share in the four years subsequent to the merger" (ibid.), and concluded that "[t]his evidence certainly does not prove anticompetitive effects of the merger." Id., at 82. The Court of Appeals, in our view, misapprehended the standards for its review and the standards applicable in a § 7 proceeding. Section 7 of the Clayton Act was intended to arrest the anticompetitive effects of market power in their incipiency. The core question is whether a merger may substantially lessen competition, and necessarily requires a prediction of the merger's impact on competition, present and future. See Brown Shoe Co. v. United States, 370 U.S. 294 * * * The sec-

* Full citation omitted from original.

tion can deal only with probabilities, not with certainties. Brown Shoe Co. v. United States, supra * * * And there is certainly no requirement that the anticompetitive power manifest itself in anticompetitive action before § 7 can be called into play. If the enforcement of § 7 turned on the existence of actual anticompetitive practices, the congressional policy of thwarting such practices in their incipiency would be frustrated.

All mergers are within the reach of § 7, and all must be tested by the same standard, whether they are classified as horizontal, vertical, conglomerate or other. As noted by the Commission, this merger is neither horizontal, vertical, nor conglomerate. Since the products of the acquired company are complementary to those of the acquiring company and may be produced with similar facilities, marketed through the same channels and in the same manner, and advertised by the same media, the Commission aptly called this acquisition a "product-extension merger".

* * *

The anticompetitive effects with which this product-extension merger is fraught can easily be seen: (1) the substitution of the powerful acquiring firm for the smaller, but already dominant, firm may substantially reduce the competitive structure of the industry by raising entry barriers and by dissuading the smaller firms from aggressively competing; (2) the acquisition eliminates the potential competition of the acquiring firm.

The liquid bleach industry was already oligopolistic before the acquisition, and price competition was certainly not as vigorous as it would have been if the industry were competitive. * * * There is every reason to assume that the smaller firms would become more cautious in competing due to their fear of retaliation by Procter. It is probable that Procter would become the price leader and that oligopoly would become more rigid.

The acquisition may also have the tendency of raising the barriers to new entry. The major competitive weapon in the successful marketing of bleach is advertising. Clorox was limited in this area by its relatively small budget and its inability to obtain substantial discounts. By contrast, Procter's budget was much larger; and, although it would not devote its entire budget to advertising Clorox, it could divert a large portion to meet the short-term threat of a new entrant. Procter would be able to use its volume discounts to advantage in advertising Clorox. Thus, a new entrant would be much more reluctant to face the giant Procter than it would have been to face the smaller Clorox. Possible economies cannot be used as a defense to illegality. Congress was aware that some mergers which lessen competition may also result in economies but it struck the balance in favor of protecting competition. See Brown Shoe Co. v. United States, supra.

The Commission also found that the acquisition of Clorox by Procter eliminated Procter as a potential competitor. The Court of Appeals declared that this finding was not supported by evidence because there was no evidence that Procter's management had ever intended to enter the industry independently and that Procter had never attempted to enter. The evidence, however, clearly shows that Procter was the most likely entrant. Procter had recently launched a new abrasive cleaner in an industry similar to the liquid bleach industry, and had wrested leadership from a brand that had enjoyed even a larger market share than had Clorox. Procter was engaged in a vigorous program of diversifying into product lines closely related to its basic products. Liquid bleach was a natural avenue of diversification since it is complementary to Procter's products, is sold to the same customers through the same channels, and is advertised and merchandised in the same manner. Procter had substantial advantages in advertising and sales promotion. * * *

It is clear that the existence of Procter at the edge of the industry exerted considerable influence on the market. First, the market behavior of the liquid bleach industry was influenced by each firm's predictions of the market behavior of its competitors, actual and potential. Second, the barriers to entry by a firm of Procter's size and with its advantages were not significant. There is no indication that the barriers were so high that the price Procter would have to charge would be above the price that would maximize the profits of the existing firms. Third, the number of potential entrants was not so large that the elimination of one would be insignificant. Few firms would have the temerity to challenge a firm as solidly entrenched as Clorox. Fourth, Procter was found by the Commission to be the most likely entrant. These findings of the Commission were amply supported by the evidence.

The judgment of the Court of Appeals is reversed and remanded with instructions to affirm and enforce the Commission's order.

It is so ordered.

Reversed and remanded.

Mr. Justice STEWART and Mr. Justice FORTAS took no part in the consideration or decision of this case.

Mr. Justice HARLAN, concurred.

UNITED STATES v. ALUMINUM COMPANY OF AMERICA

Supreme Court of the United States, 1964.
377 U.S. 271, 84 S.Ct. 1283, 12 L.Ed.2d 314.

Mr. Justice DOUGLAS delivered the opinion of the Court.

The question is whether the 1959 acquisition by the Aluminum Company of America (Alcoa) of the stock and assets of the Rome Cable Corporation (Rome) "may be substantially to lessen competition, or to tend to create a monopoly" in the production and sale of various wire and cable products and accessories within the meaning of

§ 7 of the Clayton Act.[1] The United States, claiming that § 7 had been violated, instituted this civil suit and prayed for divestiture. * * *

I.

The initial question concerns the identification of the "line of commerce," as the term is used in § 7.

Aluminum wire and cable (aluminum conductor) is a composite of bare aluminum wire and cable (bare aluminum conductor) and insulated or covered wire and cable (insulated aluminum conductor). These products are designed almost exclusively for use by electric utilities in carrying electric power from generating plants to consumers throughout the country. Copper conductor wire and cable (copper conductor) is the only other product utilized commercially for the same general purpose. Rome produced both copper conductor and aluminum conductor. In 1958—the year prior to the merger—it produced 0.3% of total industry production of bare aluminum conductor, 4.7% of insulated aluminum conductor, and 1.3% of the broader aluminum conductor line.

Alcoa produced no copper conductor. In 1958 it produced 32.5% of the bare aluminum conductor, 11.6% of insulated aluminum conductor, and 27.8% of aluminum conductor.

These products, as noted, are most often used by operating electrical utilities. Transmission and distribution lines are usually strung above ground, except in heavily congested areas, such as city centers, where they are run underground. Overhead, where the lines are bare or not heavily insulated, aluminum has virtually displaced copper, except in seacoast areas, as shown by the following table:

Percent of Aluminum Conductor in Gross Additions to Overhead Utility Lines.

	1950	1955	1959
Transmission Lines (All Bare Conductor) ...	74.4%	91.0%	94.4%
Distribution Lines:			
Bare Conductor	35.5	64.4	79.0
Insulated Conductor	6.5	51.6	77.2
Total, Transmission and Distribution Lines ..	25.0	60.9	80.1

Underground, where the conductor must be heavily insulated, copper is virtually the only conductor used. In sum, while aluminum con-

1. Section 7 of the Clayton Act, 38 Stat. 731, as amended by the Celler-Kefauver Antimerger Act, 64 Stat. 1125, 15 U.S.C.A. § 18, provides in relevant part:
"No corporation engaged in commerce shall acquire, directly or indirectly, the whole or any part of the stock or other share capital and no corporation subject to the jurisdiction of the Federal Trade Commission shall acquire the whole or any part of the assets of another corporation engaged also in commerce, where in any line of commerce in any section of the country, the effect of such acquisition may be substantially to lessen competition, or to end to create a monopoly."
(Court's footnote 1.)

ductor dominates the overhead field, copper remains virtually unrivaled in all other conductor applications.

The parties agree, and the District Court found, that bare aluminum conductor is a separate line of commerce. The District Court, however, denied that status to the broader aluminum conductor line because it found that insulated aluminum conductor is not an appropriate line of commerce separate and distinct from its copper counterpart. The court said the broad product group cannot result in a line of commerce, since a line of commerce cannot be composed of two parts, one of which independently qualifies as a line of commerce and one of which does not.

Admittedly, there is competition between insulated aluminum conductor and its copper counterpart, as the District Court found. Thus in 1959 insulated copper conductor comprised 22.8% of the gross additions to insulated overhead distribution lines. This is enough to justify grouping aluminum and copper conductors together in a single product market. Yet we conclude, contrary to the District Court, that that degree of competitiveness does not preclude their division for purposes of § 7 into separate submarkets * * *.

Insulated aluminum conductor is so intrinsically inferior to insulated copper conductor that in most applications it has little consumer acceptance. But in the field of overhead distribution it enjoys decisive advantages—its share of total annual installations increasing from 6.5% in 1950 to 77.2% in 1959. In the field of overhead distribution the competition of copper is rapidly decreasing. As the record shows, utilizing a high-cost metal, fabricators of insulated copper conductor are powerless to eliminate the price disadvantage under which they labor and thus can do little to make their product competitive, unless they enter the aluminum field. The price of most insulated aluminum conductors is indeed only 50% to 65% of the price of their copper counterparts; and the comparative installed costs are also generally less. As the District Court found, aluminum and copper conductor prices do not respond to one another.

Separation of insulated aluminum conductor from insulated copper conductor and placing it in another submarket is, therefore, proper. It is not inseparable from its copper equivalent though the class of customers is the same. The choice between copper and aluminum for overhead distribution does not usually turn on the quality of the respective products, for each does the job equally well. The vital factors are economic considerations. It is said, however, that we should put price aside and Brown Shoe, supra, is cited as authority. There the contention of the industry was that the District Court had delineated too broadly the relevant submarkets—men's shoes, women's shoes, and children's shoes—and should have subdivided them further. It was argued for example, that men's shoes selling below $8.99 were in a different product market from those selling above $9. We declined to make price, particularly such small price differentials, the determinative factor in that market. A purchaser of shoes buys with an eye to his budget, to style, and to quality as well as to price. But here, where insulated aluminum conductor pricewise stands so distinctly apart, to ignore price in determining the relevant line of commerce is to ignore the single, most important, practical factor in the business.

The combination of bare and insulated aluminum conductor products into one market or line of commerce seems to us proper. Both types are used for the purpose of conducting electricity and are sold to the same customers, electrical utilities. While the copper conductor does compete with aluminum conductor, each has developed distinctive end uses—aluminum as an overhead conductor and copper for underground and indoor wiring, applications in which aluminum's brittleness and larger size render it impractical. And, as we have seen, the price differential further sets them apart.

Thus, contrary to the District Court, we conclude (1) that aluminum conductor and copper conductor are separable for the purpose of analyzing the competitive effect of the merger and (2) that aluminum conductor (bare and insulated) is therefore a submarket and for purposes of § 7 a "line of commerce."

II.

Taking aluminum conductor as an appropriate "line of commerce" we conclude that the merger violated § 7.

Alcoa is a leader in markets in which economic power is highly concentrated. Prior to the end of World War II it was the sole producer of primary aluminum and the sole fabricator of aluminum conductor. It was held in 1945 to have monopolized the aluminum industry in violation of § 2 of the Sherman Act. See United States v. Aluminum Co., 2 Cir., 148 F.2d 416. Relief was deferred while the United States disposed of its wartime aluminum facilities under a congressional mandate to establish domestic competition in the aluminum industry. As a result of that policy and further federal financing and assistance, five additional companies entered the primary aluminum field so that by 1960 the primary producers showed the following capacity:

Aluminum Ingot Capacity Existing or Under Construction
at the End of 1960.
[SHORT TONS]

Company	Capacity	% of U. S.
Aluminum Company of America	1,025,250	38.6
Reynolds Metals Company	701,000	26.4
Kaiser Aluminum & Chemical Corp.	609,500	23.0
Ormet, Inc.	180,000	6.8
Harvey Aluminum	75,000	2.8
Anaconda Aluminum Company	65,000	2.4
United States total	2,655,750	100.0

In 1958—the year prior to the merger—Alcoa was the leading producer of aluminum conductor, with 27.8% of the market; in bare aluminum conductor, it also led the industry, with 32.5%. Alcoa plus Kaiser controlled 50% of the aluminum conductor market and, with its three leading competitors, more than 76%. Only nine concerns (including Rome with 1.3%) accounted for 95.7% of the output of aluminum conductor. In the narrower market of insulated aluminum conductor, Alcoa was third with 11.6% and Rome was eighth with 4.7%. Five companies controlled 65.4% and four smaller ones, including Rome, added another 22.8%.

In other words, the line of commerce showed highly concentrated markets, dominated by a few companies but served also by a small, though diminishing group of independents. Such decentralization as has occurred resulted from the establishment of a few new companies through federal intervention, not from normal, competitive decentralizing forces.

The proposition on which the present case turns was stated in United States v. Philadelphia National Bank, 374 U.S. 321:

"It is no answer that, among the three presently largest firms (First Pennsylvania, PNB, and Girard), there will be no increase in concentration. If this argument were valid, then once a market had become unduly concentrated, further concentration would be legally privileged. On the contrary, if concentration is already great, the importance of preventing even slight increases in concentration and so preserving the possibility of eventual deconcentration is correspondingly great."

The Committee Reports on § 7 show, as respects the Celler-Kefauver amendments in 1950, that the objective was to prevent accretions of power which "are individually so minute as to make it difficult to use the Sherman Act test against them." S.Rep.No.1775, 81st Cong., 2d Sess., p. 5. * * * As the Court stated in Brown Shoe Co. v. United States, 370 U.S. 294:

"Congress used the words 'may be substantially to lessen competition' (emphasis supplied), to indicate that its concern was with probabilities, not certainties. Statutes existed for dealing with clear-cut menaces to competition; no statute was sought for dealing with ephemeral possibilities. Mergers with a probable anticompetitive effect were to be proscribed by this Act." * * *

The acquisition of Rome added, it is said, only 1.3% to Alcoa's control of the aluminum conductor market. But in this setting that seems to us reasonably likely to produce a substantial lessening of competition within the meaning of § 7. It is the basic premise of that law that competition will be most vital "when there are many sellers, none of which has any significant market share." United States v. Philadelphia National Bank, 374 U.S., at 363. It would seem that the situation in the aluminum industry may be oligopolistic. As that condition develops, the greater is the likelihood that parallel policies of mutual advantage, not competition, will emerge. That tendency may well be thwarted by the presence of small but significant competitors. Though percentagewise Rome may have seemed small in the year prior to the merger, it ranked ninth among all companies and fourth among independents in the aluminum conductor market; and in the insulated aluminum field it ranked eighth and fourth respectively. Furthermore, in the aluminum conductor market, no more than a dozen companies could account for as much as 1% of industry production in any one of the five years (1955–1959) for which statistics appear in the record. Rome's competition was therefore substantial. The record shows indeed that Rome was an aggressive competitor. It was a pioneer in aluminum insulation and developed one of the most widely used insulated conductors. Rome had a broad line of high-quality copper wire and cable products in addition to its aluminum conductor business, a special aptitude and skill in insulation, and an active and efficient research and sales organization. The effectiveness of its marketing organization is shown by the fact that after the merger Alcoa made Rome the distributor of its entire conductor line. Preservation of Rome, rather than its absorption by one of the giants, will keep it "as an important competitive factor," to use the words of S.Rep.No.1775, supra, p. 3. Rome seems to us the prototype of the small independent that Congress aimed to preserve by § 7.

The judgment is reversed and since there must be divestiture, the case is remanded to the District Court for proceedings in conformity with this opinion.

Reversed and remanded.

Mr. Justice STEWART, whom Mr. Justice HARLAN and Mr. Justice GOLDBERG join, dissented.

B. FAIR TRADE PRACTICES

There is no fine line to be drawn between free competition and fair trade practices because the former cannot exist without the latter. It is thought that the Sherman Act could be construed to prohibit most of the trade practices which are proscribed by the Clayton Act and by Sec. 5 of the Federal Trade Commission Act. Exclusive dealing arrangements, tying arrangements, price discrimination, unfair and deceptive advertising, etc., all could be said to impinge upon free competition and therefore in themselves be a restraint of trade. But the thrust of the Sherman Act is against "combinations" of two or more persons in restraint of trade which is not necessarily the thrust of the other anti-trust legislation (as used here, also including the Federal Trade Commission Act). Further, the FTC is authorized to proceed against incipient methods of unfair competition and unfair or deceptive trade practices without awaiting the kind of case which could be proved in a court of law in a proceeding brought under the Sherman Act.

1. EXCLUSIVE DEALING ARRANGEMENTS

Section 3 of the Clayton Act provides that it shall be unlawful to sell (or lease) goods on the condition that the purchaser shall not use or deal in the goods of a competitor of the seller where the effect of such sale "[m]ay be to substantially lessen competition or tend to create a monopoly * * * ". The *Standard Stations* case, reported below, is a leading case concerning the interpretation of this section. The terms of the opinion are thought to be ambiguous in determining whether all tying, exclusive-dealing arrangements, and total-requirements contracts are prohibited. The case should be understood to mean that only those transactions of the kind described that would "substantially lessen competition" are those which are prohibited.

STANDARD OIL CO. OF CALIFORNIA AND STANDARD STATIONS, INC. v. UNITED STATES

Supreme Court of the United States, 1949.
337 U.S. 293, 69 S.Ct. 1051, 93 L.Ed. 1371.

Mr. Justice FRANKFURTER delivered the opinion of the Court.

This is an appeal to review a decree enjoining the Standard Oil Company of California and its wholly-owned subsidiary, Standard Stations, Inc., from enforcing or entering exclusive supply contracts with any independent dealer in petroleum products and automobile accessories. The use of such contracts was successfully assailed by the United States as violative of § 1 of the Sherman Act and § 3 of the Clayton Act.

The Standard Oil Company of California, a Delaware corporation, owns petroleum-producing resources and refining plants in California and sells petroleum products in what has been termed in these proceedings the "Western area"—Arizona, California, Idaho, Nevada, Oregon, Utah and Washington. It sells through its own service stations, to the operators of independent service stations, and to industrial users. It is the largest seller of gasoline in the area. In 1946 its combined sales amounted to 23% of the total taxable gallonage sold there in that year: sales by company-owned service stations constituted 6.8% of the total, sales under exclusive dealing contracts with independent service stations, 6.7% of the total; the remainder were sales to industrial users. Retail service-station sales by Standard's six leading competitors absorbed 42.5% of the total taxable gallonage; the remaining retail sales were divided between more than seventy small companies. It is undisputed that Standard's major competitors employ similar exclusive dealing arrangements. In 1948 only 1.6% of retail outlets were what is known as "split-pump" stations, that is, sold the gasoline of more than one supplier.

Exclusive supply contracts with Standard had been entered, as of March 12, 1947, by the operators of 5,937 independent stations, or 16% of the retail gasoline outlets in the Western area, which purchased from Standard in 1947 $57,646,233 worth of gasoline and $8,-200,089.21 worth of other products. Some outlets are covered by more than one contract so that in all about 8,000 exclusive supply contracts are here in issue. These are of several types, but a feature common to each is the dealer's undertaking to purchase from Standard all his requirements of one or more products. Two types, covering 2,777 outlets, bind the dealer to purchase of Standard all his requirements of gasoline and other petroleum products as well as tires, tubes, and batteries. The remaining written agreements, 4,368 in number, bind the dealer to purchase of Standard all his requirements of petroleum products only. It was also found that independent dealers had entered 742 oral contracts by which they agreed to sell only Standard's gasoline. In some instances dealers who contracted to purchase from Standard all their requirements of tires, tubes, and batteries, had also orally agreed to purchase of Standard their requirements of other automobile accessories. Of the written agreements, 2,712 were for varying specified terms; the rest were effective from year to year but terminable "at the end of the first 6 months of any contract year, or at the end of any such year, by giving to the other at least 30 days prior thereto written notice. * * * " Before 1934 Standard's sales of petroleum products through independent service stations were made pursuant to agency agreements, but in that year Standard adopted the first of its several requirements-purchase contract forms, and by 1938 requirements contracts had wholly superseded the agency method of distribution.

Between 1936 and 1946 Standard's sales of gasoline through independent dealers remained at a practically constant proportion of the area's total sales; its sales of lubricating oil declined slightly during that period from 6.2% to 5% of the total. Its proportionate sales of tires and batteries for 1946 were slightly higher than they were in 1936, though somewhat lower than for some intervening years; they have never, as to either of these products, exceeded 2% of the total sales in the Western area.

Since § 3 of the Clayton Act was directed to prohibiting specific practices even though not covered by the broad terms of the Sherman Act, it is appropriate to consider first whether the enjoined contracts fall within the prohibition of the narrower Act. The relevant provisions of § 3 are:

"It shall be unlawful for any person engaged in commerce, in the course of such commerce, to lease or make a sale or contract for sale of goods, wares, merchandise, machinery, supplies, or other commodities, whether patented or unpatented, for use, consumption, or resale within the United States * * * on the condition, agreement, or understanding that the lessee or purchaser thereof shall not use or deal in the goods * * * of a competitor or competitors of the * * * seller, where the effect of such lease, sale, or contract for sale or such condition, agreement, or understanding may be to substantially lessen competition or tend to create a monopoly in any line of commerce."

Obviously the contracts here at issue would be proscribed if § 3 stopped short of the qualifying clause beginning, "where the effect of such lease, sale, or contract for sale * * *." If effect is to be given that clause, however, it is by no means obvious, in view of Standard's minority share of the "line of commerce" involved, of the fact that that share has not recently increased, and of the claims of these contracts to economic utility, that the effect of the contracts may be to lessen competition or tend to create a monopoly. It is the qualifying clause, therefore, which must be construed.

* * *

The issue before us, therefore, is whether the requirement of showing that the effect of the agreements "may be to substantially lessen competition" may be met simply by proof that a substantial portion of commerce is affected or whether it must also be demonstrated that competitive activity has actually diminished or probably will diminish.

Since the Clayton Act became effective, this Court has passed on the applicability of § 3 in eight cases, in five of which it upheld determinations that the challenged agreement was violative of that Section. Three of these—United Shoe Machinery Corp. v. United States, 258 U.S. 451; International Business Machines Corp. v. United States, 298 U.S. 131; International Salt Co. v. United States, 332 U.S. 392 —involved contracts tying to the use of a patented article all purchases of an unpatented product used in connection with the patented article. The other two cases—Standard Fashion Co. v. Magrane-Houston Co., 258 U.S. 346; Fashion Originators' Guild v. Federal Trade Comm'n, 312 U.S. 457—involved requirements contracts not unlike those here in issue.

* * *

In the International Business Machines case, the defendants were the sole manufacturers of a patented tabulating machine requiring the use of unpatented cards. The lessees of the machines were bound by tying clauses to use in them only the cards supplied by the defendants, who, between them, divided the whole of the $3,000,000 annual gross of this business also. The Court concluded:

"These facts, and others, which we do not stop to enumerate, can leave no doubt that the fact of the condition in appellant's leases 'may be to substantially lessen competition,' and that it tends to create monopoly, and has in fact been an important and effective step in the creation of monopoly." 298 U.S. at page 136.

* * *

Two of the three cases decided by this Court which have held § 3 inapplicable also lend support to the view that such a showing is necessary. These are, Federal Trade Comm. v. Sinclair Co., 261 U.S. 463, and Pick Mfg. Co. v. General Motors Corp., 299 U.S. 3. The third —Federal Trade Comm. v. Curtis Pub. Co., 260 U.S. 568—went off on the ground that the contract involved was one of agency and so is of no present relevance. The Sinclair case involved the lease of gasoline pumps and storage tanks on condition that the dealer would use them only for Sinclair's gasoline, but Sinclair did not own patents on the pumps or tanks and evidently did not otherwise control their supply. Although the Trade Commission had found that few dealers needed more than one pump, the Court concluded that "the record does not show that the probable effect of the practise will be unduly to lessen competition." 261 U.S. at page 475. The basis of this conclusion was thus summarized:

"Many competitors seek to sell excellent brands of gasoline and no one of them is essential to the retail business. The lessee is free to buy wherever he chooses; he may freely accept and use as many pumps as he wishes and may discontinue any or all of them. He may carry on business as his judgment dictates and his means permit, save only that he cannot use the lessor's equipment for dispensing another's brand. By investing a comparatively small sum, he can buy an outfit and use it without hindrance. He can have respondent's gasoline, with the pump or without the pump, and many competitors seek to supply his needs." Id. at page 474. The present case differs of course in the fact that a dealer who has entered a requirements contract with Standard cannot consistently with that contract sell the petroleum products of a competitor of Standard's no matter how many pumps he has, but the case is significant for the importance it attaches, in the absence of a showing that the supplier dominated the market, to the practical effect of the contracts. The same is true of the Pick case, in which this Court affirmed in a brief per curiam opinion the finding of the District Court, concurred in by the Court of Appeals, that the effect of contracts by which dealers agreed not to sell other automobile parts than those manufactured by General Motors "had not been in any way substantially to lessen competition or to create a monopoly in any line of commerce." 299 U.S. at page 4.

* * *

Requirements contracts, on the other hand, may well be of economic advantage to buyers as well as to sellers, and thus indirectly of advantage to the consuming public. In the case of the buyer, they may assure supply, afford protection against rises in price, enable long-term planning on the basis of known costs, and obviate the expense and risk of storage in the quantity necessary for a commodity having a fluctuating demand. From the seller's point of view, requirements contracts may make possible the substantial reduction of selling expenses, give protection against price fluctuations, and—of particular advantage to a newcomer to the field to whom it is important to know what capital expenditures are justified—offer the possibility of a predictable market. * * * They may be useful, moreover, to a seller trying to establish a foothold against the counterattacks of entrenched competitors. * * * Since these advantages of requirements contracts may often be sufficient to account for their use, the coverage by such contracts of a substantial amount of business affords a weaker basis for the inference that competition may be lessened than would similar coverage by tying clauses, especially where use of the latter is combined with market control of the tying device. A patent, moreover, although in fact there may be many competing substitutes for the patented article, is at least prima facie evidence of such control. And so we could not dispose of this case merely by citing International Salt Co. v. United States, 332 U.S. 392.

* * *

We conclude, therefore, that the qualifying clause of § 3 is satisfied by proof that competition has been foreclosed in a substantial share of the line of commerce affected. It cannot be gainsaid that observance by a dealer of his requirements contract with Standard does effectively foreclose whatever opportunity there might be for competing suppliers to attract his patronage, and it is clear that the affected proportion of retail sales of petroleum products is substantial. In view of the widespread adoption of such contracts by Standard's competitors and the availability of alternative ways of obtaining an assured market, evidence that competitive activity has not actually declined is inconclusive. Standard's use of the contracts creates just such a potential clog on competition as it was the purpose of § 3 to remove wherever, were it to become actual, it would impede a substantial amount of competitive activity.

Since the decree below is sustained by our interpretation of § 3 of the Clayton Act, we need not go on to consider whether it might also be sustained by § 1 of the Sherman Act.

One last point remains to be disposed of. Appellant contends that its requirements contracts with California dealers, because nearly all the products sold to them are produced in California, do not substantially affect interstate commerce and therefore should have been exempted from the decree. It finds support for this contention in Addyston Pipe & Steel Co. v. United States, 175 U.S. 211. But the effect of appellant's requirements contracts with California retail dealers is to prevent them from dealing with suppliers from outside the State as well as within the State and is thus to lessen competition in both interstate and intrastate commerce. Appellant has not suggested that if these dealers were not bound by their contracts with it that they would continue to purchase only products originating within the State. The Addyston case, on the other hand, dealt not with the diminution of competition between suppliers brought about by the action of one at the expense of the rest, whether within or without the State, but a combination among them to restrain competition. Modification of the decree was required only to make clear that it did not reach a combination among the defendants doing business in a single State which was confined to transactions taking place within that same State.

The judgment below is affirmed.

Affirmed.

Mr. Justice JACKSON, with whom The CHIEF JUSTICE and Mr. Justice BURTON join, dissenting.

* * * It is indispensable to the Government's case to establish that either the actual or the probable effect of the accused arrangement is to substantially lessen competition or tend to create a monopoly.

I am unable to agree that this requirement was met. To be sure, the contracts cover "a substantial number of outlets and a substantial amount of products, whether considered comparatively or not." But that fact does not automatically bring the accused arrangement within the prohibitions of the statute. * * *

I should therefore vacate this decree and direct the court below to complete the case by hearing and weighing the Government's evidence and that of defendant as to the effects of this device.

* * *

It may be that the Government, if required to do so, could prove that this is a bad system and an illegal one. It may be that the defendant, if permitted to do so, can prove that it is, in its overall aspects, a good system and within the law. But on the present record the Government has not made a case.

If the courts are to apply the lash of the antitrust laws to the backs of businessmen to make them compete, we cannot in fairness also apply the lash whenever they hit upon a successful method of competing. That, insofar as I am permitted by the record to learn the facts, appears to be the case before us. I would reverse.

Mr. Justice DOUGLAS.

The economic theories which the Court has read into the Anti-Trust Laws have favored rather than discouraged monopoly. As a result of the big business philosophy underlying United States v. United Shoe Machinery Co., 247 U.S. 32; United States v. United States Steel Corp., 251 U.S. 417; United States v. International Harvester Co., 274 U.S. 693, big business has become bigger and bigger. Monopoly has flourished. Cartels have increased their hold on the nation. The trusts wax strong. There is less and less place for the independent.

The full force of the Anti-Trust Laws has not been felt on our economy. It has been deflected. Niggardly interpretations have robbed those laws of much of their efficacy. There are exceptions. Price fixing is illegal *per se*. The use of patents to obtain monopolies on unpatented articles is condemned. Monopoly that has been built as a result of unlawful tactics, e. g., through practices that are restraints of trade, is broken up. But when it comes to monopolies built in gentlemanly ways—by mergers, purchases of assets or control and the like—the teeth have largely been drawn from the Act.

We announced that the existence of monopoly power, coupled with the purpose or intent to monopolize, was unlawful. But to date that principle has not shown bright promise in application. Under the guise of increased efficiency big business has received approval for easy growth. United States v. Columbia Steel Co., 334 U.S. 495, represents the current attitude of the Court on this problem. In that case United States Steel—the giant of the industry—was allowed to fasten its tentacles tighter on the economy by acquiring the assets of a steel company in the Far West where competition was beginning to develop.

The increased concentration of industrial power in the hands of a few has changed habits of thought. A new age has been introduced. It is more and more an age of "monopoly competition." Monopoly competition is a regime of friendly alliances, of quick and easy accommodation of prices even without the benefit of trade associations, of what Brandeis said was euphemistically called "cooperation." While this is not true in all fields, it has become alarmingly apparent in many.

The lessons Brandeis taught on the curse of bigness have largely been forgotten in high places. Size is allowed to become a menace to existing and putative competitors. Price control is allowed to escape the influences of the competitive market and to gravitate into the hands of the few. But beyond all that there is the effect on the community when independents are swallowed up by the trusts and entrepreneurs become employees of absentee owners. Then there is a serious loss in citizenship. Local leadership is diluted. He who was a leader in the village becomes dependent on outsiders for his action and policy. Clerks responsible to a superior in a distant place take the place of resident proprietors beholden to no one. These are the prices which the nation pays for the almost ceaseless growth in bigness on the part of industry.

These problems may not appear on the surface to have relationship to the case before us. But they go to the very heart of the problem.

It is common knowledge that a host of filling stations in the country are locally owned and operated. Others are owned and operated by the big oil companies. This case involves directly only the former. It pertains to requirements contracts that the oil companies make with these independents. It is plain that a filling station owner who is tied to an oil company for his supply of products is not an available customer for the products of other suppliers. The same is true of a filling station owner who purchases his inventory a year in advance. His demand is withdrawn from the market for the duration of the contract in the one case and for a year in the other. The result in each case is to lessen competition if the standard is day-to-day purchases. Whether it is a substantial lessening of competition within the meaning of the Anti-Trust Laws is a question of degree and may vary from industry to industry.

The Court answers the question for the oil industry by a formula which under our decisions promises to wipe out large segments of independent filling station operators. The method of doing business under requirements contracts at least keeps the independents alive. They survive as small business units. The situation is not ideal from either their point of view or that of the nation. But the alternative which the Court offers is far worse from the point of view of both.

The elimination of these requirements contracts sets the stage for Standard and the other oil companies to build service-station empires of their own. The opinion of the Court does more than set the stage for that development. It is an advisory opinion as well, stating to the oil companies how they can with impunity build their empires. The formula suggested by the Court is either the use of the "agency" device, which in practical effect means control of filling stations by the oil companies, cf. Federal Trade Commission v. Curtis Co., 260 U.S. 568, or the outright acquisition of them by subsidiary corporations or otherwise. See United States v. Columbia Steel Co., supra. Under the approved judicial doctrine either of those devices means increasing the monopoly of the oil companies over the retail field.

When the choice is thus given, I dissent from the outlawry of the requirements contract on the present facts. The effect which it has on competition in this field is minor as compared to the damage which will flow from the judicially approved formula for the growth of bigness tendered by the Court as an alternative. Our choice must be made on the basis not of abstractions but of the realities of modern industrial life.

Today there is vigorous competition between the oil companies for the market. That competition has left some room for the survival of the independents. But when this inducement for their survival is taken away, we can expect that the oil companies will move in to supplant them with their own stations. There will still be competition between the oil companies. But there will be a tragic loss to the nation. The small, independent business man will be supplanted by clerks. Competition between suppliers of accessories (which is involved in this case) will diminish or cease altogether. The oil companies will command an increasingly larger share of both the wholesale and the retail markets.

That is the likely result of today's decision. The requirements contract which is displaced is relatively innocuous as compared with the virulent growth of monopoly power which the Court encourages. The Court does not act unwittingly. It consciously pushes the oil industry in that direction. The Court approves what the Anti-Trust Laws were designed to prevent. It helps remake America in the image of the cartels.

————

2. PRICE DISCRIMINATION

Section 2 of the Clayton Act was amended by the Robinson-Patman Act in 1936, as noted above. The Act generally provides that it shall be unlawful to discriminate in price between purchasers of commodities of like grade and quality where the effect of such discrimination may be substantially to lessen competition. There are several exceptions which do permit price differentials based upon a difference in cost of manufacture, sale or delivery, or as a consequence of the actual or imminent deterioration of perishable goods or obsolescence of seasonal goods, or a good faith effort to meet an equal price of a competitor. While the purpose of the antitrust laws is normally to provide for the distribution of goods of equal quality at the lowest price, it is interesting to note that the application of the Robinson-Patman Act can actually proscribe a price reduction where this would substantially lessen competition, as can be seen by the case which follows.

———

FEDERAL TRADE COMMISSION v. ANHEUSER–BUSCH, INC.

Supreme Court of the United States, 1960.
363 U.S. 536, 80 S.Ct. 1267, 4 L.Ed.2d 1385.

Mr. Chief Justice WARREN delivered the opinion of the Court.

The question presented is whether certain pricing activities of respondent, Anheuser-Busch, Inc., constituted price discrimination within the meaning of § 2(a) of the Clayton Act, 38 Stat. 730, as amended by the Robinson-Patman Act, 15 U.S.C.A. § 13(a).

Section 2(a) provides in pertinent part:

"That it shall be unlawful for any person engaged in commerce, in the course of such commerce, either directly or indirectly, to discriminate in price between different purchasers of commodities of like grade and quality, where either or any of the purchases involved in such discrimination are in commerce, where such commodities are sold for use, consumption, or resale within the United States or any Territory thereof or the District of Columbia or any insular possession or other place under the jurisdiction of the United States, and where the effect of such discrimination may be substantially to lessen competition or tend to create a monopoly in any line of commerce, or to injure, destroy, or prevent competition with any person who either grants or knowingly receives the benefit of such discrimination, or with customers of either of them   *   *   *."

This controversy had its genesis in a complaint issued by the Federal Trade Commission in 1955, which charged respondent, a beer producer, with a violation of § 2(a). The complaint alleged that respondent had "discriminated in price between different purchasers of its beer of like grade and quality by selling it to some of its customers at higher prices than to other[s]"; that, more specifically, respondent had lowered prices in the St. Louis, Missouri, market, without making similar price reductions in other markets; that this discrimination had already diverted substantial business from respondent's St. Louis competitors; that it was "sufficient" to have the same impact in the future; that there was a "reasonable probability" it would substantially lessen competition in respondent's line of commerce; and that it might also tend to create a monopoly or to injure, destroy, or prevent competition with respondent. Thus the complaint described a pricing pattern which had adverse effects only upon sellers' competition, commonly termed primary-line competition, and not upon buyers' competition, commonly termed secondary-line competition.

Both the hearing examiner and, on appeal, the Commission held that the evidence introduced at the hearing established a violation of § 2(a). The Commission found the facts to be as follows:

Respondent, a leading national brewer, sells a so-called premium beer, which is priced higher than the beers of regional and local breweries in the great majority of markets, although both the price of respondent's beer and the premium differential vary from market to market and from time to time. During the period relevant to this case, respondent had three principal competitors in the St. Louis area, all regional breweries: Falstaff Brewing Corporation, Griesedieck Western Brewing Company, and Griesedieck Brothers Brewery Company. In accord with the generally prevailing price structure, these breweries normally sold their products at a price substantially lower than respondent's.

In 1953, most of the national breweries, including respondent, granted their employees a wage increase, and on October 1, 1953, they put into effect a general price increase. Although many regional and local breweries throughout the country followed suit by raising their prices, Falstaff, Griesedieck Western, and Griesedieck Brothers maintained their pre-October price of $2.35 per standard case. Although respondent's sales in the St. Louis area did not decline, its national sales fell, along with industry sales in general.

On January 4, 1954, respondent lowered its price in the St. Louis market from $2.93 to $2.68 per case, thereby reducing the previous 58¢ differential to 33¢. A second price cut occurred on June 21, 1954, this time to $2.35, the same price charged by respondent's three competitors. On January 3, 1954, the day before the first price cut, respondent's price in the St. Louis market had been lower than its price in other markets,[1] and during the period of the price reductions in the St. Louis area, respondent made no similar price reductions in any other market. In March, 1955, respondent increased its St. Louis price 45¢ per case, and Falstaff, Griesedieck Western, and Griesedieck Brothers almost immediately raised their prices 15¢, which re-established a substantial differential. This ended the period of alleged price discrimination.

1. The following table discloses the degree of this price spread:

St. Louis, Mo.	$2.93	Washington, D. C.	$3.65
Chicago, Ill.	3.44	Detroit, Mich.	3.55
Cincinnati, Ohio	3.75	Boston, Mass.	3.69
Houston, Tex.	3.70	Kansas City, Mo.	3.15
Bronx, N. Y.	3.68	St. Paul, Minn.	3.53
Kearney, Nebr.	3.68	Sioux Falls, S. Dak.	3.50
St. Joseph, Mo.	3.17	Denver, Colo.	—
Buffalo, N. Y.	3.60	San Francisco, Calif.	3.79
Baltimore, Md.	3.62	Los Angeles, Calif.	3.80

(Court's Footnote 4.)

The Commission concluded:

"As a result of maintaining higher prices to all purchasers outside of the St. Louis area and charging the lower prices, as reduced in 1954, to only those customers in the St. Louis area, respondent discriminated in price as between purchasers differently located."

Since, as will appear, it is this aspect of the decision which concerns us, it is necessary only to sketch summarily the remaining elements in the Commission's decision. The Commission's finding of competitive injury was predicated to a substantial degree upon what it regarded as a demonstrated diversion of business to respondent from its St. Louis competitors during the period of price discrimination. For example, by comparing that period with a similar period during the previous year, the Commission determined that respondent's sales had risen 201.5%, Falstaff's sales had dropped slightly, Griesedieck Western's sales had fallen about 33%, and Griesedieck Brothers' sales had plummeted about 41%. In tabular form, the relative market positions of the St. Louis sellers were as follows:

	Dec. 31 1953	June 30 1954	Mar. 1 1955	July 31 1955
Respondent	12.5	16.55	39.3	21.03
Griesedieck Brothers	14.4	12.58	4.8	7.36
Falstaff	29.4	32.05	29.1	36.62
Griesedieck Western	38.9	33.	23.1	27.78
All others	4.8	5.82	3.94	7.21

The Commission rejected respondent's contention that its price reductions had been made in good faith to meet the equally low price of a competitor within the meaning of the proviso to § 2(b) of the Act, 15 U.S.C.A. § 13(b), and also found respondent's attack upon the examiner's cease-and-desist order to be meritless. The Commission thereupon adopted and issued that order, with only slight modification.

On review, the Court of Appeals set aside the order. 265 F.2d 677. We granted certiorari 361 U.S. 880, because a conflict had developed among the Courts of Appeals on a question of importance in the administration of the statute. See Atlas Building Products Co. v. Diamond Block & Gravel Co., 10 Cir., 269 F.2d 950.

* * *

A discussion of the import of the § 2(a) phrase "discriminate in price," in the context of this case, must begin with a consideration of the purpose of the statute with respect to primary-line competition. The Court of Appeals expressed some doubt that § 2(a) was designed to protect this competition at all, but respondent has not undertaken to defend that position here. This is entirely understandable. While "precision of expression is not an outstanding characteristic of the Robinson-Patman Act," Automatic Canteen Co. of America v. Federal Trade Comm., 346 U.S. 61, 65, it is certain at least that § 2(a) is violated where there is a price discrimination which deals the requisite injury to primary-line competition, even though secondary-line and tertiary-line competition are unaffected. The statute could hardly be read any other way, for it forbids price discriminations "where the effect * * * may be substantially to lessen competition or tend to create a monopoly *in any line of commerce,* or to injure, destroy, or prevent competition with any person *who either grants* or knowingly receives the benefit of such discrimination, or with customers of either of them." (Emphasis added.)

The legislative history of § 2(a) is equally plain. The section, when originally enacted as part of the Clayton Act in 1914, was born of a desire by Congress to curb the use by financially powerful corporations of localized price-cutting tactics which had gravely impaired the competitive position of other sellers. It is, of course, quite true— and too well known to require extensive exposition—that the 1936 Robinson-Patman amendments to the Clayton Act were motivated principally by congressional concern over the impact upon secondary-line competition of the burgeoning of mammoth purchasers, notably chain stores. However, the legislative history of these amendments leaves no doubt that Congress was intent upon strengthening the Clayton Act provisions, not weakening them, and that it was no part of Congress' purpose to curtail the pre-existing applicability of § 2(a) to price discriminations affecting primary-line competition.

> * * *

Thus neither the language of § 2(a), its legislative history, nor its judicial application countenances a construction of the statute which draws strength from even a lingering doubt as to its purpose of protecting primary-line competition. But the rationale of the Court of Appeals appears to have been shaped by precisely this type of doubt. The view of the Court of Appeals was that, before there can be a price discrimination within the meaning of § 2(a), "[t]here must be some relationship between the different purchasers which entitles them to comparable treatment." 265 F.2d, at page 681. Such a relationship would exist, the court reasoned, if different prices were being charged to *competing* purchasers. But the court observed that in this case all *competing* purchasers paid respondent the same price, so far as the record disclosed. Consequently, the court concluded that, even assuming the price cuts "were directed at [Anheuser-Busch's] local competitors, they were not *discriminatory*." Ibid.

> * * *

More important, however, is the incompatibility of the Circuit Court's rule with the purpose of § 2(a). The existence of competition among buyers who are charged different prices by a seller is obviously important in terms of adverse effect upon secondary-line competition, but it would be merely a fortuitous circumstance so far as injury to primary-line competition is concerned. Since, as we have indicated, in independent and important goal of § 2(a) is to extend protection to competitors of the discriminating seller, the limitation of that protection by the alien factor of competition among purchasers would constitute a debilitating graft upon the statute.

* * *

Respondent asserts that its view is supported by legislative history, court decisions, and reason. Respondent relies heavily, as did the Court of Appeals, upon a statement made during Congress' consideration of the Robinson-Patman legislation by Representative Utterback, a manager of the conference bill which became § 2(a). In this rather widely quoted exegesis of the section, Representative Utterback declared that "a discrimination is more than a mere difference," and exists only when there is "some relationship * * * between the parties to the discrimination which entitles them to equal treatment." Such a relationship would prevail among competing purchasers, according to the Congressman, and also "where * * * the price to one is so low as to involve a sacrifice of some part of the seller's necessary costs and profit," so that "it leaves that deficit inevitably to be made up in higher prices to his other customers." 80 Cong.Rec. 9416. * * * Finally, respondent argues that, unless its position is accepted, the law will impose rigid price uniformity upon the business world, contrary to sound economics and the policy of the antitrust laws.

The trouble with respondent's arguments is not that they are necessarily irrelevant in a § 2(a) proceeding, but that they are misdirected when the issue under consideration is solely whether there has been a price discrimination. We are convinced that, whatever may be said with respect to the rest of §§ 2(a) and 2(b)—and we say nothing here —there are no overtones of business buccaneering in the § 2(a) phrase "discriminate in price." Rather, a price discrimination within the meaning of that provision is merely a price difference.

* * *

These assumptions, we now conclude, were firmly rooted in the structure of the statute, for it is only by equating price discrimination with price differentiation that § 2(a) can be administered as Congress intended. As we read that provision, it proscribes price differences, subject to certain defined defenses, where the effect of the differences "may be substantially to lessen competition or tend to create a monopoly in any line of commerce, or to injure, destroy, or prevent competition with any person who either grants or knowingly receives the benefit" of the price differential, "or with customers of either of them." See Federal Trade Comm. v. Morton Salt Co., 334 U.S. 37. In other words, the statute itself spells out the conditions which make a price difference illegal or legal, and we would derange this integrated statutory scheme were we to read other conditions into the law by means of the nondirective phrase, "discriminate in price." Not only would such action be contrary to what we conceive to be the meaning of the statute, but, perhaps because of this, it would be thoroughly undesirable. As one commentator has succinctly put it, "Inevitably every legal controversy over any price difference would shift from the detailed governing provisions—'injury,' cost justification, 'meeting competition,' etc.—over into the 'discrimination' concept for *ad hoc* resolution divorced from specifically pertinent statutory text." Rowe, Price Differentials and Product Differentiation: The Issues Under the Robinson-Patman Act, 66 Yale L.J. 1, 38.

     * * *

What we have said makes it quite evident, we believe, that our decision does not raise the specter of a flat prohibition of price differentials, inasmuch as price differences constitute but one element of a § 2(a) violation. In fact, as we have indicated, respondent has vigorously contested this very case on the entirely separate grounds of insufficient injury to competition and good faith lowering of price to meet competition. Nor is it relevant that the Commission did not proceed upon the basis of the respondent's price differentials which existed prior to the period in question in this case. This choice is committed to the discretion of the Commission; and it may well be that the Commission did not believe the remaining statutory elements could be established with respect to other differentials. Our interest is solely with this case, and at this stage of the litigation that interest is confined exclusively to identifying and keeping distinct the various statutory standards which are part of the § 2(a) complex.

The judgment of the Court of Appeals is reversed and the case is remanded to that court for further proceedings not inconsistent with this opinion.

    Reversed.

----

3. UNFAIR METHODS OF COMPETITION

As noted above one of the functions of the Federal Trade Commission is to restrain trade practices which it finds to be unfair although they may not yet be fully developed violations of the Sherman Act. Also, the Commission is granted extensive powers to investigate an entire industry, as can be seen in reference to the *Cement Industry* case, reported below. This investigation was commenced in 1935 which led to a hearing before a Trial Examiner which lasted for three years and the record of which consisted of almost 100,000 pages, actually enough to line three walls from floor to ceiling of a medium sized office. The litigation involving this case was suspended during World War II (as was all anti-trust litigation) and was resumed after the end of the War and was finally concluded in 1948 with the opinion of the United States Supreme Court in FTC v. Cement Institute, 333 U.S. 683, 68 S.Ct. 793, 92 L.Ed. 1010 (1948), reported below.

Federal law is not the only law which prohibits unfair methods of competition. The case of Electrolux Corp. v. Val-Worth Inc., 6 N.Y. 2d 556, 190 N.Y.S.2d 977, 161 N.E.2d 197 (1959) which is reported below was brought under state law in a state court. It will be remembered from the *Standard Oil* case of 1911 that the Sherman Act was really an outgrowth of the common law; much the same could be said of all of the other anti-trust laws. Unfair competition is also unlawful under state law, either at common law or by statute, and occasionally a litigant will seek to enforce his rights in a state court rather than in a Federal court under one of the Federal statutes. There may be many reasons for this, one of which is that sometimes a remedy will be more expeditious in a state court than in a Federal court because the dockets of the former may not be so crowded as the dockets of the latter. Also, a common law remedy may be available where a private remedy under a Federal statute may not.

FEDERAL TRADE COMMISSION v. CEMENT INSTITUTE

Supreme Court of the United States, 1948.
333 U.S. 683, 68 S.Ct. 793, 92 L.Ed. 1010.

Mr. Justice BLACK delivered the opinion of the Court.

We granted certiorari to review the decree of the Circuit Court of Appeals which, with one judge dissenting, vacated and set aside a cease and desist order issued by the Federal Trade Commission against the respondents. 7 Cir., 157 F.2d 533. Those respondents are: The Cement Institute, an unincorporated trade association composed of 74 corporations which manufacture, sell and distribute cement; the 74 corporate members of the Institute, and 21 individuals who are associated with the Institute. It took three years for a trial examiner to hear the evidence which consists of about 49,000 pages of oral testimony and 50,000 pages of exhibits. Even the findings and conclusions of the Commission cover 176 pages. The briefs with accompanying appendixes submitted by the parties contain more than 4,000 pages. The legal questions raised by the Commission and by the different respondents are many and varied. Some contentions are urged by all respondents and can be jointly considered. Others require separate treatment. In order to keep our opinion within reasonable limits, we must restrict our record references to the minimum consistent with an adequate consideration of the legal questions we discuss.

The proceedings were begun by a Commission complaint of two counts. The first charged that certain alleged conduct set out at length constituted an unfair method of competition in violation of § 5 of the Federal Trade Commission Act. 15 U.S.C.A. § 45. The core of the charge was that the respondents had restrained and hindered competition in the sale and distribution of cement by means of a combination among themselves made effective through mutual understanding or agreement to employ a multiple basing point system of pricing. It was alleged that this system resulted in the quotation of identical terms of sale and identical prices for cement by the respondents at any given point in the United States. This system had worked so successfully, it was further charged, that for many years prior to the filing of the complaint, all cement buyers throughout the nation, with rare exceptions, had been unable to purchase cement for delivery in any given locality from any one of the respondents at a lower price or on more favorable terms than from any of the other respondents.

The second count of the complaint, resting chiefly on the same allegations of fact set out in Count I, charged that the multiple basing point system of sales resulted in systematic price discriminations between the customers of each respondent. These discriminations were made, it was alleged, with the purpose of destroying competition in price between the various respondents in violation of § 2 of the Clayton Act, 38 Stat. 730, as amended by the Robinson-Patman Act, 49 Stat. 1526. That section, with certain conditions which need not here be set out, makes it "unlawful for any person engaged in commerce, * * * either directly or indirectly, to discriminate in price between different purchasers of commodities of like grade and quality. * * *" 15 U.S.C.A. § 13.

Resting upon its findings, the Commission ordered that respondents cease and desist from "carrying out any planned common course of action, understanding, agreement, combination, or conspiracy" to do a number of things, 37 F.T.C. 97, 258–262, all of which things, the Commission argues, had to be restrained in order effectively to restore individual freedom of action among the separate units in the cement industry. Certain contentions with reference to the order will later require a more detailed discussion of its terms. For the present it is sufficient to say that, if the order stands, its terms are broad enough to bar respondents from acting in concert to sell cement on a basing point delivered price plan which so eliminates competition that respondents' prices are always identical at any given point in the United States.

We shall not now detail the numerous contentions urged against the order's validity. A statement of these contentions can best await the separate consideration we give them.

Jurisdiction.—At the very beginning we are met with a challenge to the Commission's jurisdiction to entertain the complaint and to act on it. This contention is pressed by respondent Marquette Cement Manufacturing Co. and is relied upon by other respondents. Count I of the complaint is drawn under the provision in § 5 of the Federal Trade Commission Act which declares that "Unfair methods of competition * * * are hereby declared unlawful." Marquette contends that the facts alleged in Count I do not constitute an "unfair method of competition" within the meaning of § 5. Its argument runs this way: Count I in reality charges a combination to restrain trade. Such a combination constitutes an offense under § 1 of the Sherman Act which outlaws "Every * * * combination * * * in restraint of trade." 15 U.S.C.A. § 1. Section 4 of the Sherman Act provides that the attorney general shall institute suits under the Act on behalf of the United States, and that the federal district courts shall have exclusive jurisdiction of such suits. Hence, continue respondents, the Commission, whose jurisdiction is limited to "unfair methods of competition," is without power to institute proceedings or to issue an

order with regard to the combination in restraint of trade charged in
Count I.   Marquette then argues that since the fact allegations of
Count I are the chief reliance for the charge in Count II, this latter
count also must be interpreted as charging a violation of the Sherman
Act.   Assuming, without deciding, that the conduct charged in each
count constitutes a violation of the Sherman Act, we hold that the
Commission does have jurisdiction to conclude that such conduct may
also be an unfair method of competition and hence constitute a violation of § 5 of the Federal Trade Commission Act.

* * *

The Multiple Basing Point Delivered Price System.—Since the
multiple basing point delivered price system of fixing prices and terms
of cement sales is the nub of this controversy, it will be helpful at this
preliminary stage to point out in general what it is and how it works.
A brief reference to the distinctive characteristics of "factory" or
"mill prices" and "delivered prices" is of importance to an understanding of the basing point delivered price system here involved.

Goods may be sold and delivered to customers at the seller's mill
or warehouse door or may be sold free on board (f. o. b.) trucks or
railroad cars immediately adjacent to the seller's mill or warehouse.
In either event the actual cost of the goods to the purchaser is, broadly speaking, the seller's "mill price" plus the purchaser's cost of transportation.   However, if the seller fixes a price at which he undertakes to deliver goods to the purchaser where they are to be used, the
cost to the purchaser is the "delivered price."   A seller who makes the
"mill price" identical for all purchasers of like amount and quality
simply delivers his goods at the same place (his mill) and for the same
price (price at the mill).   He thus receives for all f. o. b. mill sales an
identical net amount of money for like goods from all customers.   But
a "delivered price" system creates complications which may result in
a seller's receiving different net returns from the sale of like goods.
The cost of transporting 500 miles is almost always more than the cost
of transporting 100 miles.   Consequently if customers 100 and 500
miles away pay the same "delivered price," the seller's net return is
less from the more distant customer.   This difference in the producer's net return from sales to customers in different localities under a "delivered price" system is an important element in the charge
under Count I of the complaint and is the crux of Count II.

The best known early example of a basing point price system was
called "Pittsburgh plus."   It related to the price of steel.   The Pittsburgh price was the base price, Pittsburgh being therefore called a
price basing point.   In order for the system to work, sales had to be
made only at delivered prices.   Under this system the delivered price
of steel from anywhere in the United States to a point of delivery anywhere in the United States was in general the Pittsburgh price plus
the railroad freight rate from Pittsburgh to the point of delivery.
Take Chicago, Illinois, as an illustration of the operation and consequences of the system.   A Chicago steel producer was not free to sell

his steel at cost plus a reasonable profit. He must sell it at the Pittsburgh price plus the railroad freight rate from Pittsburgh to the point of delivery. Chicago steel customers were by this pricing plan thus arbitrarily required to pay for Chicago produced steel the Pittsburgh base price plus what it would have cost to ship the steel by rail from Pittsburgh to Chicago had it been shipped. The theoretical cost of this fictitious shipment became known as "phantom freight." But had it been economically possible under this plan for a Chicago producer to ship his steel to Pittsburgh, his "delivered price" would have been merely the Pittsburgh price, although he actually would have been required to pay the freight from Chicago to Pittsburgh. Thus the "delivered price" under these latter circumstances required a Chicago (non-basing point) producer to "absorb" freight costs. That is, such a seller's net returns became smaller and smaller as his deliveries approached closer and closer to the basing point.

Several results obviously flow from use of a single basing point system such as "Pittsburgh plus" originally was. One is that the "delivered prices" of all producers in every locality where deliveries are made are always the same regardless of the producers' different freight costs. Another is that sales made by a non-base mill for delivery at different localities result in net receipts to the seller which vary in amounts equivalent to the "phantom freight" included in, or the "freight absorption" taken from the "delivered price."

As commonly employed by respondents, the basing point system is not single but multiple. That is, instead of one basing point, like that in "Pittsburgh plus," a number of basing point localities are used. In the multiple basing point system, just as in the single basing point system, freight absorption or phantom freight is an element of the delivered price on all sales not governed by a basing point actually located at the seller's mill. And all sellers quote identical delivered prices in any given locality regardless of their different costs of production and their different freight expenses. Thus the multiple and single systems function in the same general manner and produce the same consequences—identity of prices and diversity of net returns. Such differences as there are in matters here pertinent are therefore differences of degree only.

*   *   *

There is no warrant in the Act for reaching a conclusion which would thus frustrate its purposes. If the Commission's opinions expressed in congressionally required reports would bar its members from acting in unfair trade proceedings, it would appear that opinions expressed in the first basing point unfair trade proceeding would similarly disqualify them from ever passing on another. See Morgan v. United States, 313 U.S. 409, 421. Thus experience acquired from their work as commissioners would be a handicap instead of an advantage. Such was not the intendment of Congress. For Congress acted on a committe report stating: "It is manifestly desirable that the terms of the commissioners shall be long enough to give them an opportunity to acquire the expertness in dealing with these special questions concerning industry that comes from experience." Report of Committee on Interstate Commerce, No. 597, June 13, 1914, 63d Cong., 2d Sess. 10–11.

* * *

The Old Cement Case.—This Court's opinion in Cement Mfrs.' Protective Ass'n v. United States, 268 U.S. 588, known as the Old Cement case, is relied on by the respondents in almost every contention they present. We think it has little relevance, if any at all, to the issues in this case.

In that case the United States brought an action in the District Court to enjoin an alleged combination to violate § 1 of the Sherman Act. The respondents were the Cement Manufacturers Protective Association, four of its officers, and nineteen cement manufacturers. The District Court held hearings, made findings of fact, and issued an injunction against those respondents. This Court, with three justices dissenting, reversed upon a review of the evidence. It did so because the Government did not charge and the record did not show "any agreement or understanding between the defendants placing limitations on either prices or production," or any agreement to utilize the basing point system as a means of fixing prices. The Court said "But here the government does not rely upon agreement or understanding, and this record wholly fails to establish, either directly or by inference, any concerted action other than that involved in the gathering and dissemination of pertinent information with respect to the sale and distribution of cement to which we have referred, and it fails to show any effect on price and production except such as would naturally flow from the dissemination of that information in the trade and its natural influence on individual action." Id., at page 606, of 268 U.S. In the Old Cement case and in Maple Flooring Mfrs.' Ass'n v. United States, 268 U.S. 563, decided the same day, the Court's attention was focused on the rights of a trade association, despite the Sherman Act, openly to gather and disseminate statistics and information as to production costs, output, past prices, merchandise on hand, specific job contracts, freight rates, etc., so long as the Association did these things without attempts to foster agreements or concerted action with reference to prices, production, or terms of sale. Such associations were declared guiltless of violating the Sherman Act, because "in fact, no prohibited concert of action was found." Corn Products Refining Co. v. Federal Trade Commission, 324 U.S. 726, 735.

The Court's holding in the Old Cement case would not have been inconsistent with a judgment sustaining the Commission's order here, even had the two cases been before this Court the same day. The issues in the present Commission proceedings are quite different from those in the Old Cement case, although many of the trade practices shown here were also shown there. In the first place, unlike the Old Cement case the Commission does here specifically charge a combination to utilize the basing point system as a means to bring about uniform prices and terms of sale. And here the Commission has focused attention on this issue, having introduced evidence on the issue which covers thousands of pages. Furthermore, unlike the trial court in the Old Cement case, the Commission has specifically found the existence of a combination among respondents to employ the basing point system for the purpose of selling at identical prices.

In the second place, individual conduct, or concerted conduct, which falls short of being a Sherman Act violation may as a matter of law constitute an "unfair method of competition" prohibited by the Trade Commission Act. A major purpose of that Act, as we have frequently said, was to enable the Commission to restrain practices as "unfair" which, although not yet having grown into Sherman Act dimensions, would most likely do so if left unrestrained. The Commission and the courts were to determine what conduct, even though it might then be short of a Sherman Act violation, was an "unfair method of competition." This general language was deliberately left to the "Commission and the courts" for definition because it was thought that "There is no limit to human inventiveness in this field"; that consequently, a definition that fitted practices known to lead towards an unlawful restraint of trade today would not fit tomorrow's new inventions in the field; and that for Congress to try to keep its precise definitions abreast of this course of conduct would be an "endless task." See Federal Trade Commission v. R. F. Keppel & Bro., 291 U.S. 304, 310–312, and congressional committee reports there quoted.

These marked differences between what a court must decide in a Sherman Act proceeding and the duty of the Commission in determining whether conduct is to be classified as an unfair method of competition are enough in and of themselves to make the Old Cement decision wholly inapplicable to our problem in reviewing the findings in this case. That basic problem is whether the Commission made findings of concerted action, whether those findings are supported by evidence, and if so whether the findings are adequate as a matter of law to sustain the Commission's conclusion that the multiple basing point system as practiced constitutes an "unfair method of competition," because it either restrains free competition or is an incipient menace to it.

Findings and Evidence.—It is strongly urged that the Commission failed to find, as charged in both counts of the complaint, that the respondents had by combination, agreements, or understandings among themselves utilized the multiple basing point delivered price system as a restraint to accomplish uniform prices and terms of sale. A subsidiary contention is that assuming the Commission did so find, there is no substantial evidence to support such a finding. We think that adequate findings of combination were made and that the findings have support in the evidence.

The Commission's findings of fact set out at great length and with painstaking detail numerous concerted activities carried on in order to make the multiple basing point system work in such way that competition in quality, price and terms of sale of cement would be nonexistent, and that uniform prices, job contracts, discounts, and terms of sale would be continuously maintained. The Commission found that many of these activities were carried on by the Cement Institute, the industry's unincorporated trade association, and that in other instances the activities were under the immediate control of groups of respondents. Among the collective methods used to accomplish these purposes, according to the findings, were boycotts; discharge of uncooperative employees; organized opposition to the erection of new cement plants; selling cement in a recalcitrant price cutter's sales territory at a price so low that the recalcitrant was forced to adhere to the established basing point prices; discouraging the shipment of cement by truck or barge; and preparing and distributing freight rate books which provided respondents with similar figures to use as actual or "phantom" freight factors, thus guaranteeing that their delivered prices (base prices plus freight factors) would be identical on all sales whether made to individual purchasers under open bids or to governmental agencies under sealed bids. These are but a few of the many activities of respondents which the Commission found to have been done in combination to reduce or destroy price competition in cement. After having made these detailed findings of concerted action, the Commission followed them by a general finding that "the capacity, tendency, and effect of the combination maintained by the respondents herein in the manner aforesaid is to * * * promote and maintain their multiple basing point delivered-price system and obstruct and defeat any form of competition which threatens or tends to threaten the continued use and maintenance of said system and the uniformity of prices created and maintained by its use." The Commission then concluded that "The aforesaid combination and acts and practices of respondents pursuant thereto and in connection therewith, as hereinabove found, under the conditions and circumstances set forth, constitute unfair methods of competition in commerce within the intent and meaning of the Federal Trade Commission Act." And the Commission's cease and desist order prohibited respondents "from entering into, continuing, cooperating in, or carrying out any planned common course of action, understanding, agreement, combination, or conspiracy between and among any two or more of said respondents * * *" to do certain things there enumerated.

Thus we have a complaint which charged collective action by respondents designed to maintain a sales technique that restrained competition, detailed findings of collective activities by groups of respondents to achieve that end, then a general finding that respondents maintained the combination, and finally an order prohibiting the continuance of the combination. It seems impossible to conceive that anyone reading these findings in their entirety could doubt that the Commission found that respondents, collectively maintained a multiple basing point delivered price system for the purpose of suppressing competition in cement sales. The findings are sufficient. The contention that they were not is without substance.

* * *

Although there is much more evidence to which reference could be made, we think that the following facts shown by evidence in the record, some of which are in dispute, are sufficient to warrant the Commission's finding of concerted action.

When the Commission rendered its decision there were about 80 cement manufacturing companies in the United States operating about 150 mills. Ten companies controlled more than half of the mills and there were substantial corporate affiliations among many of the others. This concentration of productive capacity made concerted action far less difficult than it would otherwise have been. The belief is prevalent in the industry that because of the standardized nature of cement, among other reasons, price competition is wholly unsuited to it. That belief is historic. It has resulted in concerted activities to devise means and measures to do away with competition in the industry. Out of those activities came the multiple basing point delivered price system. Evidence shows it to be a handy instrument to bring about elimination of any kind of price competition. The use of the multiple basing point delivered price system by the cement producers has been coincident with a situation whereby for many years, with rare exceptions, cement has been offered for sale in every given locality at identical prices and terms by all producers. Thousands of secret sealed bids have been received by public agencies which corresponded in prices of cement down to a fractional part of a penny.[2]

Occasionally foreign cement has been imported, and cement dealers have sold it below the delivered price of the domestic product. Dealers who persisted in selling foreign cement were boycotted by the domestic producers. Officers of the Institute took the lead in securing pledges by producers not to permit sales f. o. b. mill to purchasers who furnished their own trucks, a practice regarded as seriously disruptive of the entire delivered price structure of the industry.

During the depression in the 1930's, slow business prompted some producers to deviate from the prices fixed by the delivered price system. Meetings were held by other producers; an effective plan was

---

2. The following is one among many of the Commission's findings as to the identity of sealed bids:

An abstract of the bids for 6,000 barrels of cement to the United States Engineer Office at Tucumcari, New Mexico, opened April 23, 1936, shows the following:

Name of Bidder	Price per Bbl.
Monarch	$3.286854
Ash Grove	3.286854
Oklahoma	3.286854
Consolidated	3.286854
Lehigh	3.286854
Southwestern	3.286854
U. S. Portland Cement Co.	3.286854
Trinity	3.286854
Lone Star	3.286854
Universal	3.286854
Colorado	3.286854

All bids subject to 10¢ per barrel discount for payment in 15 days. (Com. Ex. 175-A). See 157 F.2d at page 576.

[Court's footnote 15.]

devised to punish the recalcitrants and bring them into line. The plan was simple but successful. Other producers made the recalcitrant's plant an involuntary base point. The base price was driven down with relatively insignificant losses to the producers who imposed the punitive basing point, but with heavy losses to the recalcitrant who had to make all its sales on this basis. In one instance where a producer had made a low public bid, a punitive base point price was put on its plant and cement was reduced 10¢ per barrel; further reductions quickly followed until the base price at which this recalcitrant had to sell its cement dropped to 75¢ per barrel, scarcely one-half of its former base price of $1.45. Within six weeks after the base price hit 75¢ capitulation occurred and the recalcitrant joined a Portland cement association. Cement in that locality then bounced back to $1.15, later to $1.35, and finally to $1.75.

The foregoing are but illustrations of the practices shown to have been utilized to maintain the basing point price system. Respondents offered testimony that cement is a standardized product, that "cement is cement," that no differences existed in quality or usefulness, and that purchasers demanded delivered price quotations because of the high cost of transportation from mill to dealer. There was evidence, however, that the Institute and its members had, in the interest of eliminating competition, suppressed information as to the variations in quality that sometimes exist in different cements. Respondents introduced the testimony of economists to the effect that competition alone could lead to the evolution of a multiple basing point system of uniform delivered prices and terms of sale for an industry with a standardized product and with relatively high freight costs. These economists testified that for the above reasons no inferences of collusion, agreement, or understanding could be drawn from the admitted fact that cement prices of all United States producers had for many years almost invariably been the same in every given locality in the country. There was also considerable testimony by other economic experts that the multiple basing point system of delivered prices as employed by respondents contravened accepted economic principles and could only have been maintained through collusion.

The Commission did not adopt the views of the economists produced by the respondents. It decided that even though competition might tend to drive the price of standardized products to a uniform level, such a tendency alone could not account for the almost perfect identity in prices, discounts, and cement containers which had prevailed for so long a time in the cement industry. The Commission held that the uniformity and absence of competition in the industry were the results of understandings or agreements entered into or carried out by concert of the Institute and the other respondents. It may possibly be true, as respondents' economists testified, that cement producers will, without agreement express or implied and without understanding explicit or tacit, always and at all times (for such has been substantially the case here) charge for their cement precisely, to the fractional part of a penny, the price their competitors charge. Certainly it runs counter to what many people have believed, namely, that without agreement, prices will vary—that the desire to sell will sometimes be so strong that a seller will be willing to lower his prices and take his chances. We therefore hold that the Commission was not compelled to accept the views of respondents' economist-witnesses that active competition was bound to produce uniform cement prices. The Commission was authorized to find understanding, express or implied, from evidence that the industry's Institute actively worked, in cooperation with various of its members, to maintain the multiple basing point delivered price system; that this pricing system is calculated to produce, and has produced, uniform prices and terms of sale throughout the country; and that all of the respondents have sold their cement substantially in accord with the pattern required by the multiple basing point system.

＊　＊　＊

Unfair Methods of Competition.—We sustain the Commission's holding that concerted maintenance of the basing point delivered price system is an unfair method of competition prohibited by the Federal Trade Commission Act. In so doing we give great weight to the Commission's conclusion, as this Court has done in other cases. Federal Trade Commission v. R. F. Keppel & Bro., 291 U.S. 304, 314, Federal Trade Commission v. Pacific States Paper Trade Ass'n, 273 U.S. 52, 63. In the Keppel case the Court called attention to the express intention of Congress to create an agency whose membership would at all times be experienced, so that its conclusions would be the result of an expertness coming from experience. We are persuaded that the Commission's long and close examination of the questions it here decided has provided it with precisely the experience that fits it for performance of its statutory duty. The kind of specialized knowledge Congress wanted its agency to have was an expertness that would fit it to stop at the threshold every unfair trade practice—that kind of practice, which if left alone, "destroys competition and establishes monopoly." Federal Trade Commission v. Raladam Co., 283 U.S. 643, 647, 650 ＊　＊　＊.

We cannot say that the Commission is wrong in concluding that the delivered-price system as here used provides an effective instrument which, if left free for use of the respondents, would result in complete destruction of competition and the establishment of monopoly in the cement industry. That the basing point price system may lend itself to industry-wide anti-competitive practices is illustrated in the following among other cases: United States v. United States Gypsum Co. et al., 333 U.S. 364. ＊　＊　＊ We uphold the Commission's conclusion that the basing point delivered price system employed by respondents is an unfair trade practice which the Trade Commission may suppress.

The Price Discrimination Charge in Count Two.—The Commission found that respondents' combination to use the multiple basing point delivered price system had effected systematic price discrimination in violation of § 2 of the Clayton Act as amended by the Robinson-Patman Act, 15 U.S.C.A. § 13.   Section 2(a) of that Act declares it to "be unlawful for any person engaged in commerce * * * either directly or indirectly, to discriminate in price between different purchasers of commodities of like grade and quality * * * where the effect of such discrimination may be substantially to lessen competition or tend to create a monopoly in any line of commerce, or to injure, destroy, or prevent competition with any person who either grants or knowingly receives the benefit of such discrimination, or with customers of either of them * * *"   Section 2(b) provides that proof of discrimination in price (selling the same kind of goods cheaper to one purchaser than to another), makes out a prima facie case of violation, but permits the seller to rebut "the prima facie case thus made by showing that his lower price * * * was made in good faith to meet an equally low price of a competitor * * *."

The Commission held that the varying mill nets received by respondents on sales between customers in different localities constituted a "discrimination in price between different purchasers" within the prohibition of § 2(a), and that the effect of this discrimination was the substantial lessening of competition between respondents. The Circuit Court of Appeals reversed the Commission on this count. It agreed that respondents' prices were unlawful insofar as they involved the collection of phantom freight, but it held that prices involving only freight absorption came within the "good faith" proviso of § 2(b).

The respondents contend that the differences in their net returns from sales in different localities which result from use of the multiple basing point delivered price system are not price discriminations within the meaning of § 2(a).   If held that these net return differences are price discriminations prohibited by § 2(a), they contend that the discriminations were justified under § 2(b) because "made in good faith to meet an equally low price of a competitor."   Practically all the arguments presented by respondents in support of their contentions were considered by this Court and rejected in 1945 in Corn Products Co. v. Federal Trade Commission, 324 U.S. 726, and in the related case of Federal Trade Commission v. A. E. Staley Mfg. Co., 324 U.S. 746.   As stated in the Corn Products opinion at page 730, of 324 U.S., certiorari was granted in those two cases because the "questions involved" were "of importance in the administration of the Clayton Act in view of the widespread use of basing point price systems."   For this reason the questions there raised were given thorough consideration.   Consequently, we see no reason for again reviewing the questions that were there decided.

In the Corn Products case the Court, in holding illegal a single basing point system, specifically reserved decision upon the legality under the Clayton Act of a multiple basing point price system, but only in view of the "good faith" proviso of § 2(b), and referred at that point to the companion Staley opinion. 324 U.S. at page 735. The latter case held that a seller could not justify the adoption of a competitor's basing point price system under § 2(b) as a good faith attempt to meet the latter's equally low price. Thus the combined effect of the two cases was to forbid the adoption for sales purposes of any basing point pricing system. It is true that the Commission's complaint in the Corn Products and Staley cases simply charged the individual respondents with discrimination in price through use of a basing point price system, and did not, as here, allege a conspiracy or combination to use that system. But the holdings in those two cases that § 2 forbids a basing point price system are equally controlling here, where the use of such a system is found to have been the result of a combination.

* * *

We hold that the Commission properly concluded that respondents' pricing system results in price discriminations. Its findings that the discriminations substantially lessened competition between respondents and that they were not made in good faith to meet a competitor's price are supported by evidence. Accordingly, the Commission was justified in issuing a cease and desist order against a continuation of the unlawful discriminatory pricing system.

The Order.—There are several objections to the Commission's cease and desist order. We consider the objections, having in mind that the language of its prohibitions should be clear and precise in order that they may be understood by those against whom they are directed. See Illinois Commerce Commission v. Thomson, 318 U.S. 675, 685. But we also have in mind that the Commission has a wide discretion generally in the choice of remedies to cope with trade problems entrusted to it by the Commission Act. Jacob Siegel Co. v. Federal Trade Commission, 327 U.S. 608, 611–613.

There is a special reason, however, why courts should not lightly modify the Commission's orders made in efforts to safeguard a competitive economy. Congress when it passed the Trade Commission Act felt that courts needed the assistance of men trained to combat monopolistic practices in the framing of judicial decrees in antitrust litigation. Congress envisioned a commission trained in this type of work by experience in carrying out the functions imposed upon it. To this end it provided in § 7 of the Act, 15 U.S.C. § 47, that courts might, if it should be concluded that the Government was entitled to a decree in an antitrust case, refer that case "to the commission, as a master in chancery, to ascertain and report an appropriate form of decree therein." The Court could then adopt or reject such a report.

In the present proceeding the Commission has exhibited the familiarity with the competitive problems before it which Congress originally anticipated the Commission would achieve from its experience. The order it has prepared is we think clear and comprehensive. At the same time the prohibitions in the order forbid no activities except those which if continued would directly aid in perpetuating the same old unlawful practices. Nor do we find merit to the charges of surplusage in the order's terms.

Most of the objections to the order appear to rest on the premise that its terms will bar an individual cement producer from selling cement at delivered prices such that its net return from one customer will be less than from another, even if the particular sale be made in good faith to meet the lower price of a competitor. The Commission disclaims that the order can possibly be so understood. Nor do we so understand it. As we read the order, all of its separate prohibiting paragraphs and sub-paragraphs, which need not here be set out, are modified and limited by a preamble. This preamble directs that all of the respondents "do forthwith cease and desist from entering into, continuing, cooperating in, or carrying out any planned common course of action, understanding or agreement, combination or conspiracy, between and among any two or more of said respondents, or between any one or more of said respondents and others not parties hereto, to do or perform any of the following things. * * *" Then follow the prohibitory sentences. It is thus apparent that the order by its terms is directed solely at concerted, not individual activity on the part of the respondents.

       *   *   *

The Commission's order should not have been set aside by the Circuit Court of Appeals. Its judgment is reversed and the cause is remanded to that court with directions to enforce the order. It is so ordered.

Reversed and remanded.

Mr. Justice DOUGLAS and Mr. Justice JACKSON took no part in the consideration or decision of these cases.

Mr. Justice BURTON dissented.

ELECTROLUX CORPORATION v. VAL–WORTH, INC.

Court of Appeals of New York, 1959.
6 N.Y.2d 556, 190 N.Y.S.2d 977, 161 N.E.2d 197.

CONWAY, Chief Judge. The plaintiff is the manufacturer of the widely known "Electrolux" vacuum cleaner. The defendants-respondents are Solomon Sacks, who does business as "Famous Vacuum Shops" and "Famous Appliance Shops," and Vacuum Cleaner Conservation Company, Inc., of which Sacks is the president and principal stockholder.

It appears that respondents have been purchasing used "Model XII" Electrolux vacuum cleaners from plaintiff and others since 1948 for prices ranging from $3.00 to $7.50 each. Respondents would then disassemble the machines, clean and rebuild them, and, when necessary, supply new parts and accessories some of which were not manufactured by the plaintiff. The result would then be sold and advertised as "rebuilt Electrolux" vacuum cleaners (trade-mark "Electrolux" displayed prominently). However, a small label and a decalcomania transfer which recite that the machine was reconditioned by Famous Vacuum Shops were attached to the machine.

In 1949 plaintiff requested by letter that respondents make it clear that the machines have been rebuilt by "Famous" rather than by Electrolux. Since then, respondents have continued to buy thousands of used machines from plaintiff, rebuild them and advertise them as rebuilt by Famous Vacuum Shops, or Famous Appliance Shops with the full knowledge and acquiescence of plaintiff until January of 1953. However, the plaintiff, though it sold many used machines which it had acquired as "trade-ins" to dealers such as respondents, refused at all times to sell them new parts and accessories.

In 1952 respondents arranged for television advertising with a television promoter. They agreed that the commercials would furnish telephone numbers for prospective inquirers and that telephone responses would be turned over to respondents for $2 to $3 each. During the commercials which were broadcast over four television channels, the actor or salesman exhibited a "rebuilt Electrolux," described it as such in glowing terms and offered it for $14.95. Telephone numbers were also furnished for prospective inquirers.

The record further discloses that Adler, an investigator hired by the plaintiff, called one of the telephone numbers furnished during the commercial and requested a demonstration. Subsequently, one Forde, a salesman, arrived at Adler's home where he demonstrated and sold to him a rebuilt machine. But then he attempted to sell a new machine not manufactured by the plaintiff which he claimed was a better machine. However, the investigator refused to make any further purchase and subsequently turned the rebuilt machine over to plaintiff's engineers who examined it. Although the motor and body were manufactured by Electrolux, some of the accessories were not.

The proof also demonstrates that respondents sold new machines manufactured by several of plaintiff's competitors but that respondents did not mention these machines on the commercials. Rather, they offered the rebuilt machines at $14.95 for the purpose of attracting prospects to whom more expensive new machines not manufactured by plaintiff might be sold. Furthermore, respondents' salesmen were not compensated for selling the "rebuilt Electrolux" but rather their compensation depended on sales of the other machines.

In June of 1953 Electrolux brought an action seeking injunctive relief, as well as damages, against Sacks, Vacuum Cleaner Conservation Company and others who are not parties to this appeal. After trial before the court sitting without a jury, Special Term rendered a decision with specific findings of fact, including those set forth above, and conclusions of law.

In addition to the facts already stated, Special Term found that the procedure was to endeavor to sell the "rebuilt Electrolux" and then to "switch" the transaction to the new machine by calling the "rebuilt Electrolux" "just a lot of junk", and by saying that it looked "silly" and by disparaging it generally. Furthermore, respondents would give a salesman the names and addresses of four telephone inquirers, four new machines but only one "rebuilt Electrolux." Moreover, the salesman would be instructed not to permit the rebuilt machine to leave his hands but rather to disparage it and to try to sell the new machine instead. In addition the rebuilt machine could not be sold profitably for $14.95 for the initial cost and business expenses compelled respondents to rely on the sale of the higher priced machines in order to make the operation a paying one. In short, the court found that the telecasts were calculated to give the impression that a used Electrolux with Electrolux parts, which retained the quality associated in the public mind with plaintiff's products, was obtainable at a low price whereas respondent's actual purpose was to discourage the purchase of the advertised machines and induce the public to buy costly machines of makes other than Electrolux.

Special Term also found that some of the non-Electrolux parts were functionally inferior to the corresponding parts manufactured by the plaintiff. Moreover, it was further found that Sacks instructed the television promoter to telecast that the machines were rebuilt by the famous vacuum cleaner company (meaning Electrolux, a famous company). This use of the word "famous" was held to be deceptive whether used as an adjective or a noun. However, the court also found that since January 12, 1953, when Electrolux made its first complaint in this regard, there has been no advertising using the word "famous", the reference having been changed to Parsons Appliance Corporation.

Special Term concluded, in substance, that it was actionably deceptive to advertise the rebuilt machines with the Electrolux name when they contained non-Electrolux parts and that it was also actionable to use the name without stating that the reconditioning was actually performed by Vacuum Cleaner Conservation Company. The court also held that respondents' sales practices constituted "bait advertising" and that, as such, it was unfair to the public as well as the plaintiff owner of the advertised trade name. In addition, the court took the view that plaintiff was entitled to damages attributable to defendants' acts of unfair competition, in an amount to be determined by a court-appointed Referee.

* * *

It readily appears from the foregoing that three types of conduct are here involved. The first two which form the essence of the first cause of action in the complaint fall into that category of unfair competition wherein it is charged that defendants have "palmed off" their goods as those of the plaintiff. They are (a) the use of the Electrolux trade name on a machine which contains non-Electrolux parts and accessories, and (b) the use of the word "famous" on the telecast. The third is respondents' use of the rebuilt machine as a lure to sell other nonadvertised machines which is alleged in the complaint as the second cause of action and which shall be treated last.

* * * The Appellate Division and the Special Term are in essential agreement on the facts as to the prior dealings between plaintiff and respondents in which plaintiff sold the old machines with knowledge and acquiescence in the fact that the machines would be reconditioned and sold as rebuilt Electrolux vacuum cleaners. In brief, plaintiff knew what was happening to the machines and, yet, continued to sell old vacuum cleaners to respondents although at the same time refusing any new parts and accessories with which to repair them.

The Appellate Division held that plaintiff was estopped from enjoining a course of business of which it not only presumably had knowledge, but in which it actively participated. We agree in this conclusion. For, as we have said in Rothschild v. Title Guarantee & Trust Co., 1912, 204 N.Y. 458, "Where a person wronged is silent under a duty to speak, or by an act or declaration recognizes the wrong as an existing and valid transaction, and in some degree, at least, gives it effect so as to benefit himself or so as to affect the rights or relations created by it between the wrongdoer and a third person, he acquiesces in and assents to it and is equitably estopped from impeaching it." Assuming that it was actionable to use foreign parts in the "rebuilt Electrolux", plaintiff profited by continuing sales of trade-in machines while at the same time refusing to sell genuine Electrolux parts to respondents. "One cannot knowingly sanction business methods adopted by a rival, much less invite his competitor to engage in a business and later recover damages for the alleged losses to his business by means which he encouraged." William H. Keller, Inc., v. Chicago Pneumatic Tool Co., 7 Cir., 1923, 298 F. 52, certiorari denied 1924, 265 U.S. 593 * * *. Furthermore, inasmuch as plaintiff is so estopped from complaining of respondents' use of the trade name Electrolux on old Electrolux machines which had been rebuilt with parts and accessories not manufactured by plaintiff, we do not consider whether any of the non-Electrolux parts are inferior. Nor do we need decide whether under other circumstances the use of those parts in the reconditioning and sale of used Electrolux vacuum cleaners would be an actionable act of unfair competition.

The second question results from the use of the word "famous" in the telecasts prior to January 12, 1953. Even if we assume that both courts deemed it misleading, we observe that there is no question but that this practice was discontinued on television after protest by plaintiff about six months prior to the commencement of the action. The Appellate Division took the view that this discontinuance six months prior to the commencement of the action and the absence of any indication in the record that defendants intend to resume the practice render an injunction unnecessary and inappropriate. We are in accord with this result, for the extraordinary relief of an injunction is protection for the future and is not proper unless the injury is imminent.   *   *   *   In addition, the written use of the word "famous" in connection with "Famous Appliance Shops" does not seem to be in question, especially since, in 1949, plaintiff merely insisted that future radio broadcasts make it clear that the machines had been rebuilt by "Famous".   Also, we agree that that part of the injunction which restrained respondents from offering machines which were rebuilt by Vacuum Cleaner Conservation Company without stating that the reconstruction was the work of that particular company was error.   Representations that the machines were rebuilt by Parsons Appliance Corporation, Famous Vacuum Shops or Famous Appliance Shops would have no effect on plaintiff unless they tended to impute the work to Electrolux.   Therefore, Electrolux is not entitled to have such representations enjoined.

*   *   *

Thus, there remains only the second cause of action.   The issue there is whether respondents' sales activities which have been characterized by the Special Term as "bait advertising" are actionable and whether an injunction will lie.

The Appellate Division agreed with Special Term that respondents were using the rebuilt machines as a lure to sell a more costly machine not made by plaintiff.   However, they reversed those findings of fact which spelled out a sales program lacking any bona fide intent to sell the rebuilt machines but instead planning to disparage it in order to "switch" the transaction to other machines at the expense of plaintiff's reputation and good name.   Most of the evidence on those issues was based on the testimony of (a) Adler, the investigator, (b) Forde, the salesman who testified for the plaintiff, and (c) of defendant Sacks.   There was a sharp conflict of testimony, particularly between Forde and Sacks.   That raised an issue of credibility which was primarily in the hands of the original trier of the facts. *   *   *   In addition, Forde's testimony was corroborated by Sack's own admissions as to the extent of his expenses for selling a $14.95 machine and his admission that he did not pay any compensation to any of his salesmen if and when they sold a "rebuilt Electrolux" machine.   Accordingly, on the basis of the whole record, we conclude that those findings of the trial court on this issue which were reversed by the Appellate Division are supported by the weight of the credible evidence and should not have been reversed.

Thus, the facts disclose a sales promotion with the following steps:

1.   Advertising a "rebuilt Electrolux" at a very attractive price in order to invite inquiry.

2.   Gaining admittance to people's homes under the guise of answering the inquiries, but really for the purpose of selling a much more expensive new machine in competition with Electrolux.

3.   "Switching" the transaction by "knocking" or disparaging the "rebuilt Electrolux" and introducing the new machine.

As we have already indicated, we hold that plaintiff may be deemed to have allowed its trade name and mark to be employed by defendant in the sale of "rebuilt Electrolux" vacuum cleaners. But this is not to say that plaintiff has consented that its name and mark be used as a lure in a "bait and switch" promotion scheme to sell new vacuum cleaners in direct competition with itself.

Unfair competition was thought at one time to consist generally in "palming off", i. e., " * * * the sale of the goods of one manufacturer * * * for those of another." Elgin Nat. Watch Co. v. Illinois Watch Case Co., 1901, 179 U.S. 665. * * * Protection from "palming off" has been extended in our courts to situations where the parties are not even in competition. See, e. g., Cornell University v. Messing Bakeries, 1955, 309 N.Y. 722. * * * Moreover, in 1918 the Supreme Court of the United States refused to limit relief from unfair competition to cases of "palming off" in International News Service v. Associated Press, 1918, 248 U.S. 215, where defendant news gathering service was pirating news gathered and reported by plaintiff to eastern newspapers and then transmitting it, as its own product, to western newspapers in time for publication in the west. The Supreme Court commenting that defendant is "endeavoring to reap where it has not sown", 248 U.S. 239, held that plaintiff had property rights in the freshly gathered news which might not be misappropriated by defendant. The principle that one may not misappropriate the results of the skill, expenditures and labors of a competitor has since often been implemented in our courts. * * *

The growth of the protection against such "parasitism" reflects the requirement that the courts and the law keep pace with the mushrooming increases in business complexity and the concomitant opportunities afforded thereby for chicanery. As the Appellate Division, First Department has said: "Unfair competition is a form of unlawful business injury. * * * The incalculable variety of illegal commercial practices denominated as unfair competition is proportionate to the unlimited ingenuity that overreaching entrepreneurs and trade pirates put to use." Ronson Art Metal Works, Inc. v. Gibson Lighter Mfg. Co., 159 N.Y.S.2d 606. There is no question that this case involves an ingenious scheme put forth by unscrupulous entrepreneurs. But whether it may be enjoined as unfair competition is a difficult problem. Although there are a number of cases in other jurisdictions which have touched on the problem * * * our research has not disclosed any cases where the issue has been squarely presented and decided.

It is true that a manufacturer may not sue " * * * as a vicarious avenger of the defendant's customers" (Ely-Norris Safe Co. v. Mosler Safe Co., 2 Cir., 1925, 7 F.2d 603). But if defendants' methods are deceitful and run contrary to accepted business ethics, the public policy of the State is relevant, though perhaps not decisive, in evaluating a claim of unfair competition. Judge Duer observed over a century ago: "To protect him * * * [the owner of the trademark] is not only the evident duty of a court as an act of justice, but the interests of the public, as well as of individuals, require that the necessary protection shall be given." Amoskeag Mfg. Co. v. Spear & Ripley, 1849, 4 Super. 599, 605. We are in accord with these sentiments and take the view that it is relevant that activities of the nature of "bait and switch" advertising are deceptive and harmful to the public interest. * * *

The majority of the Appellate Division took the view that an injunction here would impinge upon "loss leader" selling where a merchant offers goods at a loss in order to attract customers to whom he can make other more profitable sales. But this is not a situation where a person comes into a store attracted by a bargain and buys other items as well. See Sunbeam Corp. v. Payless Drug Stores, D.C.N.D.Cal.1953, 113 F.Supp. 31. Here, the customer, who is, as indicated by the dissenting Justice below, trapped in his own home, is faced with a choice between the rebuilt machine as to which only he made inquiry and the new machine, with the salesman using all of his talents to effectuate the "switch". Furthermore, it is not common for the average consumer to purchase two vacuum cleaners at one time, which demonstrates how this scheme uses plaintiff's good name as a weapon against itself in a highly competitive market. Finally, one cannot say that it is normal business ethics for a merchant to discourage sales of items which he has advertised in glowing terms in order to sell different *unadvertised* goods. Thus, it is difficult to see how an injunction on these facts would impinge upon ordinary "cut-rate" or "loss-leader" selling practices.

It is easy to understand the natural outrage which would be experienced by the management of a reputable firm upon learning that its name and mark have been employed in a disreputable scheme to gain admission to people's homes. Aside from the pain caused by possible exposure to the ire of those of the public who would feel cheated as soon as the salesman revealed his true purpose, there is the pain of having one's good will employed as a weapon in direct competition against one's self. Furthermore, there are substantial legal damages caused thereby, the continuance of which equity is empowered to prevent. Respondents' salesmen, as they disparage the rebuilt machine in order to effectuate the "switch", are not likely to attribute any malfunctioning or inferiority to the reconditioning work of their employer rather than to Electrolux. Thus, the public is made susceptible to a jaundiced view of basic Electrolux design or structure. In fact, whether or not the rebuilt machine is a "piece of junk" or "silly", the purchasing public is likely to lose confidence in the name and mark of Electrolux. Disparagement or "knocking" is essential to this scheme and it results in real damage to Electrolux. This is further exaggerated by the fact that the advertisement, which sets up the opportunity to "knock" the product, makes profuse use of the name "Electrolux" in glowing terms. Thus, it is clear that those persons to whom respondents send their salesmen are conditioned by the advertising to think in terms of Electrolux, and the disappointment inevitably caused by the "switch" or attempted "switch" is bound to be damaging. Similar sentiments were expressed in Bourjois, Inc., v. Park

Drug Co., 8 Cir., 1936, 82 F.2d 468, where defendant was accused of using falsehoods to divert customers from plaintiff's nationally known brand of cosmetics to its own brand. The court commented that defamation or false representations concerning another's product " * * * when proven to have been made by the clerks of a mercantile corporation as a part of a selling plan or system, constitute unfair competition which may be enjoined at the instance of the person whose good will is injured thereby" 82 F.2d at page 470. * * *

In respect to the damages, however, the provision for an accounting was improper. * * * There is nothing here to indicate that the purchasers of the rival machines thought that they were doing business with Electrolux. Plaintiff urges upon us the case of Warren, Inc. v. Turner's Gowns, Ltd., 1941, 285 N.Y. 62, where we said that " * * * equity will treat the wrongdoer as a trustee for the plaintiff so far as the former has realized profits from its acts" (285 N.Y. at page 68). But there, the defendant was giving the impression that it was a branch store of the plaintiff. The damage in the instant case is chiefly to the good will and reputation of plaintiff corporation. Thus, it would seem that the measure of damages would be any loss in business which can be traced directly to respondents' disparagement of the "rebuilt Electrolux." * * * This will no doubt be most difficult to prove, due to the widespread and shifting nature of the injury which is, of course, one of the reasons dictating injunctive relief. But if the plaintiff is able to prove such damages, it should be given the opportunity to do so. * * *

Accordingly, the judgment of the Appellate Division is modified (1) to reinstate the judgment of the Special Term insofar as it provides that defendants be enjoined from offering any vacuum cleaner under the trade name Electrolux at an attractive price for the purpose of luring prospects with the object of diverting them from the advertised article by disparagement or other like conduct and for the purpose of inducing them to purchase a product or products not manufactured by the plaintiff, and (2) to reinstate that part of the judgment which provides for a reference on the issue of damages but not including defendants' profits, with costs.

DESMOND, DYE, FROESSEL, VAN VOORHIS and BURKE, JJ., concur with CONWAY, C. J.

FULD, J., dissents and votes to affirm.

Judgment modified in accordance with the opinion herein and, as so modified, affirmed, with costs to appellant.

4. UNFAIR AND DECEPTIVE ADVERTISING

Reference has been made to Section 5 of the Federal Trade Commission Act, 15 U.S.C.A. § 45, which proscribes "[u]nfair or deceptive acts or practices in commerce * * *". The effect of this provision is that the Federal Trade Commission Act extends to all unfair acts whether or not they are methods of competition. The statutory language is exceedingly vague, perhaps necessarily so, and thus the Commission is the primary body which through its own activities and policies determines the meaning of the statute. It appears that Congress intended that the Commission and its staff of experts be the persons to do this. As a consequence the courts have been reluctant to substitute their judgment for that of the Commission, and it is rather unusual for an order of the Commission to be overturned completely by a court, although some aspects of an order may be remanded to the Commission for modification or further hearings.

The case which follows is an example of the work of the Commission in this respect and the manner of determining what is an "unfair and deceptive" trade practice.

FEDERAL TRADE COMMISSION v. COLGATE–PALMOLIVE CO.

Supreme Court of the United States, 1965.
380 U.S. 374, 85 S.Ct. 1035, 13 L.Ed.2d 904.

Mr. Chief Justice WARREN delivered the opinion of the Court.

The basic question before us is whether it is a deceptive trade practice, prohibited by § 5 of the Federal Trade Commission Act, to represent falsely that a televised test, experiment, or demonstration provides a viewer with visual proof of a product claim, regardless of whether the product claim is itself true.

The case arises out of an attempt by respondent Colgate-Palmolive Company to prove to the television public that its shaving cream, "Rapid Shave," outshaves them all. Respondent Ted Bates & Company, Inc., an advertising agency, prepared for Colgate three one-minute commercials designed to show that Rapid Shave could soften even the toughness of sandpaper. Each of the commercials contained the same "sandpaper test." The announcer informed the audience that, "To prove Rapid Shave's super-moisturizing power, we put it right from the can onto this tough, dry sandpaper. It was apply * * * soak * * * and off in a stroke." While the announcer was speaking, Rapid Shave was applied to a substance that appeared to be sandpaper, and immediately thereafter a razor was shown shaving the substance clean.

The Federal Trade Commission issued a complaint against respondents Colgate and Bates charging that the commercials were false and deceptive. The evidence before the hearing examiner disclosed that sandpaper of the type depicted in the commercials could not be shaved immediately following the application of Rapid Shave, but required a substantial soaking period of approximately 80 minutes. The evidence also showed that the substance resembling sandpaper was in fact a simulated prop, or "mock-up," made of plexiglass to which sand had been applied. However, the examiner found that Rapid Shave could shave sandpaper, even though not in the short time represented by the commercials, and that if real sandpaper had been used in the commercials the inadequacies of television transmission would have made it appear to viewers to be nothing more than plain, colored paper. The examiner dismissed the complaint because neither misrepresentation—concerning the actual moistening time or the identity of the shaved substance—was in his opinion a material one that would mislead the public.

The Commission, in an opinion dated December 29, 1961, reversed the hearing examiner. It found that since Rapid Shave could not shave sandpaper within the time depicted in the commercials, respondents had misrepresented the product's moisturizing power. Moreover, the Commission found that the undisclosed use of a plexiglass substitute for sandpaper was an additional material misrepresentation that was a deceptive act separate and distinct from the misrepresentation concerning Rapid Shave's underlying qualities. Even if the sandpaper could be shaved just as depicted in the commercials, the Commission found that viewers had been misled into believing they had seen it done with their own eyes. As a result of these findings the Commission entered a cease-and-desist order against the respondents.

An appeal was taken to the Court of Appeals for the First Circuit which rendered an opinion on November 20, 1962, 310 F.2d 89. That court sustained the Commission's conclusion that respondents had misrepresented the qualities of Rapid Shave, but it would not accept the Commission's order forbidding the future use of undisclosed simulations in television commercials. It set aside the Commission's order and directed that a new order be entered. On May 7, 1963, the Commission, over the protest of respondents, issued a new order narrowing and clarifying its original order to comply with the court's mandate. The Court of Appeals again found unsatisfactory that portion of the order dealing with simulated props and refused to enforce it, 326 F.2d 517. We granted certiorari, 377 U.S. 942, to consider this aspect of the case and do not have before us any question concerning the misrepresentation that Rapid Shave could shave sandpaper immediately after application, that being conceded.

I.

A threshold question presented is whether the petition for certiorari was filed within 90 days after the entry of the judgment below as required by 28 U.S.C. § 2101(c) (1958 ed.). Respondents claim that the failure of the Commission to seek certiorari from the judgment of the Court of Appeals rendered on November 20, 1962, barred a subsequent order prohibiting the use of simulated props in commercials that offer visual proof of a product claim.

* * * At the least the court's second opinion resolved a genuine ambiguity in the first, and the time within which certiorari had to be requested dates from the second judgment. See Federal Trade Comm. v. Minneapolis-Honeywell Regulator Co., 344 U.S. 206, 211.

II.

In reviewing the substantive issues in the case, it is well to remember the respective roles of the Commission and the courts in the administration of the Federal Trade Commission Act. When the Commission was created by Congress in 1914, it was directed by § 5 to prevent "[u]nfair methods of competition in commerce." Congress amended the Act in 1938 to extend the Commission's jurisdiction to include "unfair or deceptive acts or practices in commerce"[1]—a significant amendment showing Congress' concern for consumers as well as for competitors. It is important to note the generality of these standards of illegality; the proscriptions in § 5 are flexible, "to be defined with particularity by the myriad of cases from the field of business." Federal Trade Comm. v. Motion Picture Advertising Service Co., 344 U.S. 392, 394.

This statutory scheme necessarily gives the Commission an influential role in interpreting § 5 and in applying it to the facts of particular cases arising out of unprecedented situations. Moreover, as an administrative agency which deals continually with cases in the area, the Commission is often in a better position than are courts to determine when a practice is "deceptive" within the meaning of the Act. This Court has frequently stated that the Commission's judgment is to be given great weight by reviewing courts. This admonition is especially true with respect to allegedly deceptive advertising since the finding of a § 5 violation in this field rests so heavily on inference and pragmatic judgment. Nevertheless, while informed judicial determination is dependent upon enlightenment gained from administrative experience, in the last analysis the words "deceptive practices" set forth a legal standard and they must get their final meaning from judicial construction. Cf. Federal Trade Comm. v. R. F. Keppel & Bro., Inc., 291 U.S. 304.

We are not concerned in this case with the clear misrepresentation in the commercials concerning the speed with which Rapid Shave could shave sandpaper, since the Court of Appeals upheld the Commission's finding on that matter and the respondents have not challenged the finding here. We granted certiorari to consider the Commission's conclusion that even if an advertiser has himself conducted

1. 15 U.S.C.A. § 45(a)(1). (Court's Footnote 12.)

a test, experiment or demonstration which he honestly believes will prove a certain product claim, he may not convey to television viewers the false impression that they are seeing the test, experiment or demonstration for themselves, when they are not because of the undisclosed use of mock-ups.

We accept the Commission's determination that the commercials involved in this case contained three representations to the public: (1) that sandpaper could be shaved by Rapid Shave; (2) that an experiment had been conducted which verified this claim; and (3) that the viewer was seeing this experiment for himself. Respondents admit that the first two representations were made, but deny that the third was. The Commission, however, found to the contrary, and, since this is a matter of fact resting on an inference that could reasonably be drawn from the commercials themselves, the Commission's finding should be sustained. For the purposes of our review, we can assume that the first two representations were true; the focus of our consideration is on the third which was clearly false. The parties agree that § 5 prohibits the intentional misrepresentation of any fact which would constitute a material factor in a purchaser's decision whether to buy. They differ, however, in their conception of what "facts" constitute a "material factor" in a purchaser's decision to buy. Respondents submit, in effect, that the only material facts are those which deal with the substantive qualities of a product. The Commission, on the other hand, submits that the misrepresentation of *any* fact so long as it materially induces a purchaser's decision to buy is a deception prohibited by § 5.

The Commission's interpretation of what is a deceptive practice seems more in line with the decided cases than that of respondents. This Court said in Federal Trade Comm. v. Algoma Lumber Co., 291 U.S. 67: "[T]he public is entitled to get what it chooses, though the choice may be dictated by caprice or by fashion or perhaps by ignorance." It has long been considered a deceptive practice to state falsely that a product ordinarily sells for an inflated price but that it is being offered at a special reduced price, even if the offered price represents the actual value of the product and the purchaser is receiving his money's worth. Applying respondents' arguments to these cases, it would appear that so long as buyers paid no more than the product was actually worth and the product contained the qualities advertised, the misstatement of an inflated original price was immaterial.

It has also been held a violation of § 5 for a seller to misrepresent to the public that he is in a certain line of business, even though the misstatement in no way affects the qualities of the product. As was said in Federal Trade Comm. v. Royal Milling Co., 288 U.S. 212:

"If consumers or dealers prefer to purchase a given article because it was made by a particular manufacturer or class of manufacturers, they have a right to do so, and this right cannot be satisfied by imposing upon them an exactly similar article, or one equally as good, but having a different origin."

The courts of appeals have applied this reasoning to the merchandising of reprocessed products that are as good as new, without a disclosure that they are in fact reprocessed. And it has also been held that it is a deceptive practice to misappropriate the trade name of another.

Respondents claim that all these cases are irrelevant to our decision because they involve misrepresentations related to the product itself and not merely to the manner in which an advertising message is communicated. This distinction misses the mark for two reasons. In the first place, the present case is not concerned with a mode of communication, but with a misrepresentation that viewers have objective proof of a seller's product claim over and above the seller's word. Secondly, all of the above cases, like the present case, deal with methods designed to get a consumer to purchase a product, not with whether the product, when purchased, will perform up to expectations. We find an especially strong similarity between the present case and those cases in which a seller induces the public to purchase an arguably good product by misrepresenting his line of business, by concealing the fact that the product is reprocessed, or by misappropriating another's trademark. In each the seller has used a misrepresentation to break down what he regards to be an annoying or irrational habit of the buying public—the preference for particular manufacturers or known brands regardless of a product's actual qualities, the prejudice against reprocessed goods, and the desire for verification of a product claim. In each case the seller reasons that when the habit is broken the buyer will be satisfied with the performance of the product he receives. Yet, a misrepresentation has been used to break the habit and, as was stated in Algoma Lumber, a misrepresentation for such an end is not permitted.

We need not limit ourselves to the cases already mentioned because there are other situations which also illustrate the correctness of the Commission's finding in the present case. It is generally accepted that it is a deceptive practice to state falsely that a product has received a testimonial from a respected source. In addition, the Commission has consistently acted to prevent sellers from falsely stating that their product claims have been "certified." We find these situations to be indistinguishable from the present case. We can assume that in each the underlying product claim is true and in each the seller actually conducted an experiment sufficient to prove to himself the truth of the claim. But in each the seller has told the public that it could rely on something other than his word concerning both the truth of the claim and the validity of his experiment. We find it an immaterial difference that in one case the viewer is told to rely on the word of a celebrity or authority he respects, in another on the word of a testing agency, and in the present case on his own perception of an undisclosed simulation.

Respondents again insist that the present case is not like any of the above, but is more like a case in which a celebrity or independent testing agency has in fact submitted a written verification of an experiment actually observed, but, because of the inability of the camera to transmit accurately an impression of the paper on which the testimonial is written, the seller reproduces it on another substance so that it can be seen by the viewing audience. This analogy ignores the finding of the Commission that in the present case the seller misrepresented to the public that it was being given objective proof of a product claim. In respondents' hypothetical the objective proof of the product claim that is offered, the word of the celebrity or agency that the experiment was actually conducted, does exist; while in the case before us the objective proof offered, the viewer's own perception of an actual experiment, does not exist. Thus, in respondents' hypothetical, unlike the present case, the use of the undisclosed mock-up does not conflict with the seller's claim that there is objective proof.

We agree with the Commission, therefore, that the undisclosed use of plexiglass in the present commercials was a material deceptive practice, independent and separate from the other misrepresentation found. We find unpersuasive respondents' other objections to this conclusion. Respondents claim that it will be impractical to inform the viewing public that it is not seeing an actual test, experiment or demonstration, but we think it inconceivable that the ingenious advertising world will be unable, if it so desires, to conform to the Commission's insistence that the public be not misinformed. If, however, it becomes impossible or impractical to show simulated demonstrations on television in a truthful manner, this indicates that television is not a medium that lends itself to this type of commercial, not that the commercial must survive at all costs. Similarly unpersuasive is respondents' objection that the Commission's decision discriminates against sellers whose product claims cannot be "verified" on television without the use of simulations. All methods of advertising do not equally favor every seller. If the inherent limitations of a method do not permit its use in the way a seller desires, the seller cannot by material misrepresentation compensate for those limitations.

Respondents also claim that the Commission reached out to decide a question not properly before it and has presented this Court with an abstract question. They argue that since the commercials in the present case misrepresented the time element involved in shaving sandpaper, this Court should not consider the additional misrepresentation that the public had objective proof of the seller's claim. As we have already said, these misrepresentations are separate and distinct, and we fail to see why respondents should be sheltered from a cease-and-desist order with respect to one deceptive practice merely because they also engaged in another.

* * *

III.

We turn our attention now to the order issued by the Commission. It has been repeatedly held that the Commission has wide discretion in determining the type of order that is necessary to cope with the unfair practices found, e. g., Jacob Siegel Co. v. Federal Trade Comm., 327 U.S. 608, and that Congress has placed the primary responsibility for fashioning orders upon the Commission, Federal Trade Comm. v. National Lead Co., 352 U.S. 419. For these reasons the courts should not "lightly modify" the Commission's orders. Federal Trade Comm. v. Cement Institute, 333 U.S. 683. However, this Court has also warned that an order's prohibitions "should be clear and precise in order that they may be understood by those against whom they are directed," Federal Trade Comm. v. Cement Institute, supra, at 726, and that "[t]he severity of possible penalties prescribed * * * for violations of orders which have become final underlines the necessity for fashioning orders which are, at the outset, sufficiently clear and precise to avoid raising serious questions as to their meaning and application." Federal Trade Comm. v. Henry Broch & Co., 368 U.S. 360.

The Court of Appeals has criticized the reference in the Commission's order to "test, experiment or demonstration" as not capable of practical interpretation. It could find no difference between the Rapid Shave commercial and a commercial which extolled the goodness of ice cream while giving viewers a picture of a scoop of mashed potatoes appearing to be ice cream. We do not understand this difficulty. In the ice cream case the mashed potato prop is not being used for additional proof of the product claim, while the purpose of the Rapid Shave commercial is to give the viewer objective proof of the claims made. If in the ice cream hypothetical the focus of the commercial becomes the undisclosed potato prop and the viewer is invited, explicitly or by implication, to see for himself the truth of the claims about the ice cream's rich texture and full color, and perhaps compare it to a "rival product," then the commercial has become similar to the one now before us. Clearly, however, a commercial which depicts happy actors delightedly eating ice cream that is in fact mashed potatoes or drinking a product appearing to be coffee but which is in fact some other substance is not covered by the present order.

The crucial terms of the present order—"test, experiment or demonstration * * * represented * * * as actual proof of a claim"—are as specific as the circumstances will permit. If respondents in their subsequent commercials attempt to come as close to the line of misrepresentation as the Commission's order permits, they may without specifically intending to do so cross into the area proscribed by this order. However, it does not seem "unfair to require that one who deliberately goes perilously close to an area of proscribed conduct shall take the risk that he may cross the line." Boyce Motor Lines, Inc. v. United States, 342 U.S. 337. In commercials where the emphasis is on the seller's word, and not on the viewer's own perception, the respondents need not fear that an undisclosed use of props is prohibited by the present order. On the other hand, when the commercial not only makes a claim, but also invites the viewer to rely on his own perception, for demonstrative proof of the claim, the respondents will be aware that the use of undisclosed props in strategic places might be a material deception. We believe that respondents will have no difficulty applying the Commission's order to the vast majority of their contemplated future commercials. If, however, a situation arises in which respondents are sincerely unable to determine whether a proposed course of action would violate the present order, they can, by complying with the Commission's rules, oblige the Commission to give them definitive advice as to whether their proposed action, if pursued, would constitute compliance with the order.

Finally, we find no defect in the provision of the order which prohibits respondents from engaging in similar practices with respect to "any product" they advertise. The propriety of a broad order depends upon the specific circumstances of the case, but the courts will not interfere except where the remedy selected has no reasonable relation to the unlawful practices found to exist. In this case the respondents produced three different commercials which employed the same deceptive practice. This we believe gave the Commission a sufficient basis for believing that the respondents would be inclined to use similar commercials with respect to the other products they advertise. We think it reasonable for the Commission to frame its order broadly enough to prevent respondents from engaging in similarly illegal practices in future advertisements. As was said in Federal Trade Comm. v. Ruberoid Co., 343 U.S. 470: "[T]he Commission is not limited to prohibiting the illegal practice in the precise form in which it is found to have existed in the past." Having been caught violating the Act, respondents "must expect some fencing in." Federal Trade Comm. v. National Lead Co., 352 U.S. 419.

The judgment of the Court of Appeals is reversed and the case remanded for the entry of a judgment enforcing the Commission's order.

Reversed and remanded.

Mr. Justice HARLAN, whom Mr. Justice STEWART joined, dissented in part.

QUESTIONS

1. Suppose that we did not have the Sherman Act, or that the Supreme Court for one reason or another had held that the Sherman Act was invalid or did not apply to the Standard Oil Trust, what kind of an economy would we have today? Would each kind of eco-

nomic activity be controlled by a separate group of trustees or a separate board of directors? Would the steel industry, the automobile industry, the chemical industry, the transportation industry, the communications industry, and so on and on and on, each be controlled by a trust? Or would the law have reacted in some other fashion? For example, would we have a complete extension of the system used to regulate public utilities applied to each separate industry? How would all prices be determined? If this were to be done by a regulatory body, what standards would that body use in determining the price of the product or service? Would every industry be guaranteed a profitable operation? How would the regulatory body determine that a given product should be distributed in a specific area? Who would determine the design of each product or service? By what standards? Do the mechanism of the free market and the profit system do this for us now? Do we have a free market now?

2. Do we really have free competition in our major industries? Is oligopolistic competition really any different from monopoly? How much competition is there among the three major automobile manufacturers? Do they compete on some basis other than price? Style? Comfort? Safety? Is there any real price competition in the steel industry? If these industries operate in restraint of trade, are their restraints reasonable or unreasonable? Is the theory of the Sherman Act outmoded in the latter half of the twentieth century? Is governmental price-fixing the answer? Is the theory of Section 5 of the Federal Trade Commission Act, prohibiting unfair competition and unfair or deceptive trade practices (without reference to any combination), a more effective tool in maintaining a free market? Do we want a free market? Do we want the laws necessary to maintain a free market? If not, is governmental price-fixing the answer? If not, what would we have to replace the system? What new laws?

3. Is a conglomerate by its nature a combination in restraint of trade? Is it an "unreasonable" restraint of trade? Is the acquisition of a financial institution with great sums of money to invest in corporate bonds and preferred stocks, where the acquisition is made by a combination of companies engaged in a wide variety of industries needing capital for expansion, itself a combination in restraint of trade? Is it an unfair method of competition insofar as the other components in the combination have ready access to capital which their competitors do not? That the financial institution has an assured outlet for its invested funds which its competitors do not? Suppose the financial institution is regulated in the manner in which it can make its investments, would this make any difference? Would the government (national or state) which has established the regulatory body make any difference? Would the major concern of the regulations, for example safety of the investment rather than any inquiry into the competitive effect on the entire economy, make any difference? If so, should a new regulatory body, or new regulations, be adopted? If so, by whom? Would these regulations serve the

public satisfactorily? Should every business unit be confined to its primary business activity? Should all conglomerates be required to divest themselves of every business unit different from a single business? By sale? By a spin-off to its shareholders? What would this do to our traditional freedom of contract and freedom to acquire or transfer property? Are, or should, these freedoms be unlimited?

4. Should all violations of the anti-trust laws which are now called "per se violations" be subject to the "rule of reason"? Is it correct that one cannot demonstrate that a price is reasonable? Is it correct that it would be impossible to administer a system where some governmental agency would be involved in reviewing the reasonableness of prices? What was the experience in World War II with price stabilization agencies? What is the current experience with establishing ceilings on certain prices? Has the market place satisfactorily served its function? If not, what should be done in its place? Should not the manufacturer of any product be able to show that it has a reasonable distribution program when it combines with its chosen distributors to market its products? Is this any different from the so-called "franchise" system? If a manufacturer can control the minimum resale price of his commodity (allowed by statute on the premise, correct or incorrect, that resale price maintenance is necessary to protect his goodwill in his tradename and to protect the small retailer from the giant), could he not use the same premises to choose his exclusive distributors?

5. If we did not have the standards of Section 3 of the Clayton Act and Section 5 of the Federal Trade Commission Act relating to fair trade practices, what system would we have in place of them? Is it more efficient for the manufacturer of a product to design the product in such manner so that only he can provide replacement parts? If done through this kind of design, why do we attempt to prohibit by law a contract which would require the distributors of this manufacturer's products to buy replacement parts only from him? Do we allow technological tie-ins but prohibit contractual ones? What would happen if a statute were to provide that, similar to tires or batteries as to which there is no legal compulsion, most parts on automobiles had to be standard on all manufacturer's automobiles? Would replacement parts be less expensive? Who would determine the standards? Would safety or style be paramount? Who would make these determinations? Does the market, does freedom of contract, make them now?

6. Suppose that our national marketing system had no more restrictions imposed on it than are observed in an oriental bazaar, would we have achieved the same volume of production and distribution of goods and services? Is *caveat emptor*, let the buyer beware, a satisfactory marketing system? Why don't we allow misrepresentation and deceit? Why don't we encourage sellers and buyers to cheat each other? Why don't we adhere entirely to the system of freedom of contract? What has occurred or is occurring, that has

given rise to private groups and individuals advocating "consumerism"? Has the law fallen behind the necessities of the times? Is our national marketing system, so dependent on advertising, only a short step beyond the oriental bazaar? Should we require advertisers to disclose the *whole* truth, instead of selected truths? Has the common law system of individual suits by persons who have been cheated in the market place been adequate to the consumer problems of the twentieth century? Have class actions been adequate? Have governmental agencies charged with the responsibility of enforcing these laws performed satisfactorily? Do we need new laws? New agencies? Public or private? A greater number of dedicated Davids to take on the Goliaths? Is the government itself a Goliath in this context?

Suggested Reference Sources

Texts and Treatises

Callmann, *The Law of Unfair Competition and Trademarks,* Callaghan & Company, Mundelein, Illinois.

Kaysen & Turner, *Anti-Trust Policy: An Economic and Legal Analysis,* Harvard University Press, Cambridge, Massachusetts.

Rowe, *Price Discrimination Under the Robinson-Patman Act,* Little, Brown & Co., Boston, Massachusetts.

Loose-Leaf Services

Bureau of National Affairs (BNA), Anti-Trust and Trade Regulation Report, Washington, D. C.

Commerce Clearing House, Trade Regulation Reporter, Chicago, Illinois.

Topic Headings in the Index to Legal Periodicals

Anti-Trust Law

Prices

Restraint of Trade

Unfair Competition

Anti-Trust Law: Mergers

Fair Trade

Advertising

Chapter VIII

ADMINISTRATIVE AGENCIES

A. INTRODUCTORY NOTE

The materials in this chapter are concerned with that aspect of governmental activity ordinarily referred to as administrative regulation. An extensive compendium of judicial and administrative decisions might be provided so that, by a process of induction, one might develop a picture of what the administrative process is. However, because of the many different types of administrative agencies present within the governmental scheme, confusion might result from such an exercise in that one might discern a pattern evolving from either cases concerning one type of agency or cases dealing with similar types of actions taken by an agency which pattern may be insignificant or even specious. Further, because one will more than likely have need for exposure to both state as well as federal administrative activity (with the former frequently reflecting a level of sophistication and complexity quite different from that of the latter), the cases contained in this chapter will merely be demonstrative of (1) the subject matter jurisdiction of which administrative regulation takes cognizance, and (2) some procedures administrative agencies use in carrying out their assigned tasks.

Looking, for a moment, at the federal government, nowhere within the four corners of the Constitution and its Amendments is there to be found any reference, direct or indirect, to that configuration of government that we call today the administrative agency (cf. the executive, the legislative, the judiciary). Since a fundamental precept of American constitutional law is that the federal government is a government of limited and designated powers defined with reference to the Constitution, the existence of the administrative agency seems to pose a constitutional anomaly. Moreover, since administrative regulation bears heavily upon the daily activities of most American business, how then can our ethic of freedom of action within known boundaries (which stands at the center of the notion of due process) comport with the existence of a scheme of governmental activity unknown to the Constitution? This anomaly is further "aggravated" by the fact that the totality of administrative agencies frequently is referred to as the fourth branch of government.

The administrative agency was born out of the economic and political history of the last decades of the 19th Century, particularly the activities of railroad empires which mushroomed into vast agglommerations of land, labor and capital. Farmers, businessmen and others who sought to avail themselves of market access and other advantages the railroads brought were forced by the concentration of economic (and political) power by the railroads to accept terms and conditions of use that bordered on the unconscionable. Acquisition by the railroads, moreover, of control over the manifold services coextensive with rail transportation further placed potential customers in the position of having to deal with the railroads exclusively, without any equivalence of bargaining power, without any alternative. In a word, no competition existed and the pound of flesh that was exacted came at a severely high cost. Remedying this state of affairs posed a significant legal as well as political obstacle for the philosophy that prevailed at this time was an exaltation of free enterprise and laissez faire. The common law concept of one plaintiff suing one defendant for a redress of his grievances was demonstrably inadequate, particularly where the defendant was so much more powerful than the plaintiff and frequently dominated or controlled the courts and legislatures. Discontent and antagonism festered in those who felt that they had been taken advantage of by the railroads. Finally, the rumblings on the Plains reached the halls of Congress and the "how" of coping with the situation was perceived by Congress to be not a matter of mechanics but rather the "by what authority" within the context of prevailing philosophy. Feeling the results of growing uneasiness with existing conditions, Congress was finally moved to see in its power to legislate respecting interstate commerce the authority for coping with the railroad "situation". It saw its job to be implementing a control over the railroads' ability unilaterally to set rates and determine the terms and conditions of service.

Figuratively taking the railroad by its caboose, Congress enacted the Interstate Commerce Act and created the Interstate Commerce Commission (ICC) to effect regulatory and control activities over the railroads with a specific mandate to bring into some semblance of equilibrium the respective positions of the railroads and their customers. Through the offices of the ICC, rates were to be established and operations were to be reviewed with the twin objectives of protecting the new railroad industry while providing for its use economically and efficiently.

It was the industrial revolution in the United States that gave birth to the fourth branch of government and not the disparity per se of the respective economic positions of the railroads and their customers. The latter seems only to have been a manifestation of specialization, increasing concentration of resources and resultant pressures on diverse interests within the economic system. Existing patterns of governmental activity were not capable of responding to these changes and new methods and adaptations had to be found. We must remember that for the first 100 years of this country's existence and growth we were basically an agrarian community located on the Eastern seaboard; a community where local population groups were essentially self-sufficient and capable within themselves of resolving most economic problems that arose. The power relationships that existed within these communities were perceived as acceptable and an inherent characteristic of the community. But with the burgeoning of the frontier, the amassing of vast amounts of resource control and the transformation of the homogeneous interactive group to an heterogeneous one, political and legal designs had to respond accordingly.

A by-product of the congressional experience in creating the ICC was the recognition that through its committees and other existing processes Congress could not realistically maintain a continuing, sophisticated or effective regulatory mechanism to deal with narrow subject matter activities. Congress could, however, delegate its constitutional authority to statutorily created special purpose agencies which could act administratively in these areas. And, although the ICC experience itself was not without disappointments to both the customers of the railroads and the railroads, it did serve to show both Congress and the general populace that regulatory authority delegated to such an agency was efficacious and that other such agencies could be created in other special subject matter areas.

What then is the administrative agency? A congressional creation cut loose from direct congressional control, born to deal with a specific subject. But the defining of the administrative agency in terms of its genesis really tells us nothing as would, for example, the defining of the agency in terms of its subject matter jurisdiction. However, it might be of equal significance to define the agency according to its powers, i. e., the manner in which it is authorized to deal with its special subject matter. Therefore, what the administrative agency is must be related in terms both of subject matter jurisdiction and powers with the characteristic of how and why the agency came into existence; within this context the other descriptive characteristics are articulated.

One additional characteristic of the administrative agency must be noted even though its significance lies almost exclusively in the realm of political science analysis. The vast majority of federal administrative agencies are organizationally classified as independent agencies, i. e., organs of government existing and operating independently of any of the other branches of government (save, of course, for the budgetary aspect of their existence). However, there are a number of administrative agencies some of which were created initially as independent agencies and others of which were not whose present existence occurs organizationally within one or another of the executive departments, i. e., cabinet level organizations. These too are nonetheless administrative agencies in the same sense as those which are independent; they function similarly and vary most in the manner in which appointments are made and staffing patterns are arranged.

Finally, it must be noted that the executive departments themselves exercise jurisdiction over many specific subject matters frequently in a manner that subjects them to constitutional, statutory and procedural tests exactly the same as those applied to the administrative agencies.   (Herein of the Administrative Procedures Act, more of which will be dealt with later.)

Since the creation of the ICC, Congress has brought into existence more than 50 administrative agencies whose subject matter jurisdiction is as varied as the characteristics of economic endeavor, political action and social demands.

INDEPENDENT AGENCIES

ACTION
Administrative Conference of the United States
Advisory Commission on Intergovernmental Relations
American Battle Monuments Commission
Appalachian Regional Commission
Atomic Energy Commission
Canal Zone Government
Civil Aeronautics Board
Civil Service Commission
Commission on Civil Rights
Commission on Fine Arts
Delaware River Basin Commission
District of Columbia Government
District of Columbia Redevelopment Land Agency
Environmental Protection Agency
Equal Employment Opportunity Commission
Export-Import Bank of the United States
Farm Credit Administration
Federal Coal Mine Safety Board of Review
Federal Communications Commission
Federal Deposit Insurance Corporation
Federal Home Loan Bank Board
Federal Maritime Commission
Federal Mediation and Conciliation Service
Federal Power Commission
Federal Reserve System
Federal Trade Commission
Foreign Claims Settlement Commission
General Services Administration
Indian Claims Commission
Inter-American Social Development Institute
Interstate Commerce Commission
National Aeronautics and Space Administration
National Capital Housing Authority
National Capital Planning Commission
National Credit Union Administration
National Foundation on the Arts and Humanities
National Labor Relations Board
National Mediation Board
National Science Foundation
Occupational Safety and Health Review Commission

Overseas Private Investment Corporation
Panama Canal Company
Postal Rate Commission
Railroad Retirement Board
Renegotiation Board
Securities and Exchange Commission
Selective Service System
Small Business Administration
Smithsonian Institution
Subversives Activities Control Board
Tariff Commission of the United States
Tax Court of the United States
Tennessee Valley Authority
United States Arms Control and Disarmament Agency
United States Information Agency
United States Postal Services
Veterans' Administration

Agencies Within Executive Departments (selected)

Internal Revenue Service (Treasury)
Agency for International Development (State)
Community Relations Service (Justice)
Federal Bureau of Investigation (Justice)
Bonneville Power Administration (Interior)
Southeastern Power Administration (Interior)
Southwestern Power Administration (Interior)
Alaska Power Administration (Interior)
Rural Electrification Administration (Agriculture)
Commodity Credit Corporation (Agriculture)
Economic Development Administration (Commerce)
Maritime Administration (Commerce)
Food and Drug Administration (HEW)
Social Security Administration (HEW)
United States Coast Guard (Transportation)
Federal Aviation Administration (Transportation)
Federal Highway Administration (Transportation)
Federal Railroad Administration (Transportation)
National Transportation Safety Board (Transportation)

Subject matter jurisdiction, however, is not to be viewed as the determinant of independence of action by any of the above even though, theoretically, each agency was established to exercise its jurisdiction independently of any other governmental organ. Several recent cases in point demonstrate that an inevitable overlap will occur.

Upon its own initiative, the Equal Employment Opportunity Commission (EEOC) undertook to inquire into the minority group employment practices of companies in the public utility and broadcasting industries. In addition to the filing of complaints against several employers for allegedly having violated Title VII of the Civil Rights Act of 1964, EEOC brought its findings to the attention both of the Federal Power Commission (FPC) and the Federal Communications Commission (FCC) urging upon these agencies that within the context of their respective jurisdictions (rate-making and licensing) they read an equal employment opportunity standard into their requirements and sanction their regulatees accordingly. Moreover, whether the activity in question be one of employment practices, profit structure, manufacturing process or product performance, the proliferation of government activity almost ensures that every dimension of economic behavior will be subject to the jurisdiction of at least one agency with the result being more than likely that a given business company will have to deal not only with more than one federal agency but also with state counterparts.

Having been established legislatively to exercise jurisdiction over specific subject matter areas, the administrative agency's powers might reflect the totality of government activity in a microcosm. A given agency might possess any one or combination of investigative, legislative or adjudicative powers. Should the agency be empowered to act in more than one of these ways it is more than likely that activity in one such area will lead to activity in the other(s).

The power to conduct investigations, without more, ordinarily is contained within a congressional mandate to make recommendations for legislative action, advise for executive action or educate for public information. In this respect, therefore, agencies exercising only investigative powers rarely deal with matters for the purpose of providing an individual a remedy for action taken (against him) by another individual or a government body. (This is not to say, however, that the results of such an agency's investigation may not ultimately be used for such a purpose in another forum.)

In the conduct of its investigative activities, the agency's authority to proceed may include the power to compel testimony and the production of evidence, the making of a verbatim record, the examination and cross-examination of witnesses, or any one or more of the elements more frequently associated with judicial proceedings. On the other hand, however, any or all of such powers may be lacking and the agency's investigative activities then would be predicated upon the use of material and information either voluntarily produced or already extant.

Although it is not inaccurate to speak of the administrative agency as possessing legislative powers, it must clearly be understood that in the hierarchy of government it is only the legislature (Congress, at the federal level) that possesses plenary legislative jurisdiction. As noted above, the administrative agency is a creature of the legislature and the legislative powers exercised by the agency are derived from the legislature. The statutory mandate given the agency by the legislature, therefore, serves as the reference point from which the agency's own legislative authority emanates. The agency, through the exercise of its legislative authority administers the legislature's statutory mandate.

The nature of the agency's legislative authority is usually said to be of two general types: rule making and rate making.

In the exercise of rule-making authority, the agency ordinarily promulgates the rules and regulations, procedures, by which it has determined to conduct its affairs. Rule-making authority, therefore, refers to the standards by which the agency itself will be bound in its dealings with regulatees. Conversely, however, this also means that regulatees also will be held to these same standards in their dealings with the agency.

Rate-making, on the other hand, refers to the standards that the agency sets according to which regulatees must conduct their affairs.

Insofar as there is a definitive distinction between rule-making and rate-making it lies not just in the direction of the thrust of such legislative efforts but also in the process by which such legislation can validly be brought into existence. Since the rule-making effort is essentially "inner-directed", traditional notions of due process as such may relate to the involvement of regulatees in that decision-making process ordinarily do not obtain; whereas, since the essential thrust of rate-making is "outer-directed", i. e., designed to regulate regulatees, traditional notions of due process are said to obtain and require the participation of regulatees in the decision-making process. A major area of controversy, however, does exist respecting a clear definition in all cases of when rule-making truly is rule-making as compared with those situations when rule-making is more like rate-making.

Even though in most situations the results of the rule-making effort may not become effective immediately but must be published and effectuated only after regulatees are given a reasonable time to become acquainted with such, and even though, upon occasion, regulatees will be allowed the opportunity to influence the "true" rule-making effort, these factors do not rise to the level of participation that characterizes the notion of due process as is required in the rate-making situations. The formalities, timing and nature and extent of regulatee participation characteristic of the respective decision-making process of rule-making and rate-making constitute an area of such significance that frequently the substance of the legislative effort is overshadowed by these procedural considerations. It must be remembered that the congressional delegation of power is of an administrative character and when the agency effort moves from the "procedural" (i. e. administrative) side of the line over to the "substantive" (i. e. legislative) side of the line the agency must then act differently—in a sense more like the legislature and involve the concerned public in its decision-making.

The most common examples of rule-making might be the timing of agency meetings, what procedures will govern such meetings and what kinds of documents in what form will be required to be presented to the agency before formal recognition of a matter will be accorded. Rate-making can be exemplified by those levels of charges common carriers, for example, will be allowed to charge customers, what routes may be traversed, what level of capital investment will be required of a regulatee and how much competition and by whom will be allowed in any given endeavor.

"True" rule-making activities will involve only the agency staff who will prepare, develop and produce for acceptance by the agency's policy-making center the rules and regulations desired. Such rules and regulations will result most frequently when the agency undertakes new and different activities or when changes in existing standards are called for because of statutory changes or because of changes in circumstances or conditions upon which existing activities are predicated.

With the completion within the agency of the rules to be proposed for adoption, the agency then must give notice of these rules to the public and allow for comment before they become final. Unless it can be shown that proposed rules may be arbitrary, capricious or in some other way definitely detrimental to the interest of the public or regulatees, they will become effective after the proper period of time subsequent to announcement has elapsed.

The rate-making function, however, is more complex and usually takes a much longer period of time than the making of rules. When it has been decided that rate-making is desirable—either because of the kinds of changes indicated with reference to rule-making or because the agency itself or a regulatee can show presumptively that such may be desirable—the agency must publicize to those regulatees who may be potentially affected by such rate changes (or introductions) that rate-making will occur, the nature of the legislation to be promulgated and the type of information it would be desirable for the regulatees to furnish to the agency. Recently, additionally, the public has been allowed to participate in this decision-making process and the agency hearings conducted to develop the informational base for its decision have approached the tenor of trials between adversaries although it is quite clear both in law and in fact that this is not the nature of such hearings. The hearings, in a manner of speaking, are investigative in nature.

Since the hearings conducted by the agency to develop the informational base upon which to proceed with rate-making will be participated in by all persons desiring to affect the decision-making process, including the agency's staff presenting its position, subsequent to the conclusion of the hearings and sufficient additional time to allow written information to be introduced into the record that might have been inconvenient for the hearings, the agency policy makers then will retire to digest the material presented and to produce the legislation to be proposed. These proposals in turn will be publicized and become effective after sufficient time is given for dissemination subject to further modification because of challenge or additional pertinent information—in which case publication and delay is once again required.

Administrative agency adjudicative functions ordinarily occur with respect to the resolution of complaints against regulatees brought to the attention of the agency by some member of the public or upon the initiative of the agency itself. Such a complaint may concern an alleged departure from specifically promulgated standards, a general concern that in some respect the regulatee has acted "improperly" or even an attempt to establish through indirection a new standard as a result of action or inaction that has somehow disadvantaged some other. The multifariousness of complaints knows no bounds save the ingenuity of man and frequently administrative agencies are on the receiving end of "complaints" that rise to a level of being nothing more than disgruntlements or disappointments. However, at the time such a complaint is lodged with the agency no decision can be made as to its validity and, therefore, some staff investigation is required.

Subsequent to the "docketing" of the matter, a member of the agency's investigative staff is assigned the responsibility of documenting the facts and circumstances that have given rise to the complaint. These initial investigations usually are performed under the jurisdiction of a regional operation the geographical choice being determined by the situs of the alleged delict. Depending upon the nature and complexity of the matter, such investigations can be concluded easily within weeks or can take varying amounts of time extending into years. But, upon the conclusion of such an investigation an administrative decision then must be made as to whether the facts and circumstances so disclosed indicate that "there is reason to believe" or that there is "probable cause" that the regulatee has engaged in the conduct complained of and that such conduct is violative of the standard of law applicable. This level of decision is necessary for the agency must be able to know whether the matter should be dismissed or processed further (and more formally).

Should the matter present a situation justifying further processing, i. e., that it should not be dismissed, usual procedure then is to formalize the matter further, initiate attempts to "conciliate" and, if conciliation efforts are "successful", dispose of the matter administratively without prejudice to the regulatee.

Throughout the administrative processing of a complaint to the point of conciliation or non-conciliation, technically speaking prejudice to the regulatee has not attached. This is merely to say that procedural safeguards of due process (in the strict judicial sense) are not required. However, should a matter be neither dismissed nor conciliated and the agency does not close it administratively for other reasons but determines to attempt to sanction the regulatee, at the time this formal decision is embodied in a notice of hearing or formal complaint (cf. the nature of the document entered into the file from which the agency first took cognizance of the matter), the agency's formal judicial process begins, prejudice attaches and the regulatee now is entitled to the protections of due process (modified in some measures to account for the fact that the agency judicial process is not quite that of a court's, i. e., it is quasi-judicial). At the conclusion of the agency's hearing of the matter it will either dismiss it or render a finding that a violation has occurred and enter an order requiring the regulatee to cease such unlawful activities. From any such adverse order the regulatee may then appeal to the courts.

With the tremendous variety of subject matters dealt with by the large number of federal administrative agencies, it is no surprise to find that their organizational arrangements are equally as multifarious. But notwithstanding the great diversity in organizational arrangements, there are elements of commonality. And, by and large, that which is organizationally common from one agency to another tends to be a function of whether the agency is an "enforcement" agency or one without enforcement powers. The organizational arrangements of the two agencies included herein can be considered exemplary.

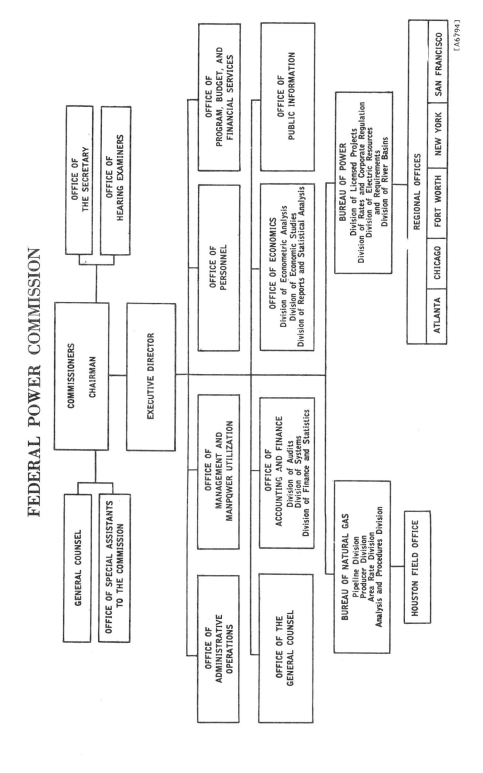

FEDERAL POWER COMMISSION

[A6794]

[A67951]

INTERSTATE COMMERCE COMMISSION

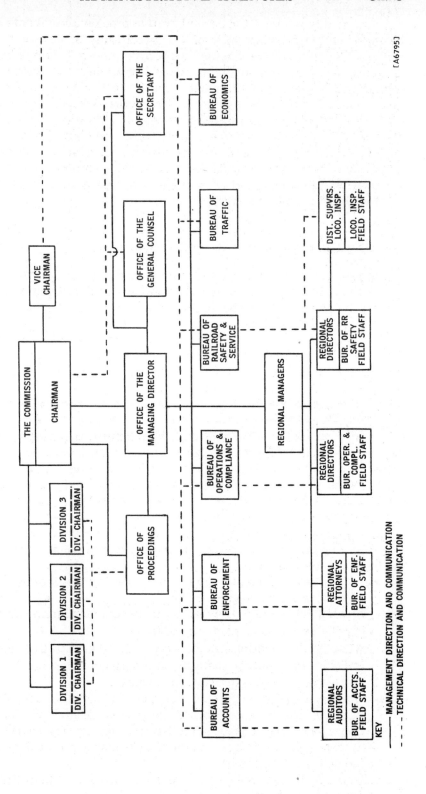

KEY
——— MANAGEMENT DIRECTION AND COMMUNICATION
- - - - TECHNICAL DIRECTION AND COMMUNICATION

In any discussion of the administrative process, special note must be made of the growing body of law specifically applicable to this process. Administrative law, as this body of law is known, concerns virtually every dimension of activity an administrative agency can engage in, the nature of the agency itself and the relationships that must obtain between the agency and the other branches of government and the public. Most of the doctrines of administrative law have evolved as common law but are in many places reinforced by and supplemented with special statutory provisions. Insofar as federal administrative law is concerned, the most notable contribution of statute law has been the Administrative Procedures Act (a counterpart of which exists in many states).

Answers to the following types of questions are furnished by reference (in part) to doctrines of administrative law:

—whether and to what extent the legislature can delegate to an administrative agency jurisdiction respecting a specific subject

—how must and to what extent may an administrative agency inquire into a particular matter

—if authorized, how must the administrative agency pursue its rule-making authority, its rate-making authority

—when does the requirement of the opportunity to be heard obtain

—if authorized, how must the administrative agency pursue its adjudicatory process

—to what extent, if at all, may the administrative agency delegate its authority to another

—who must make decisions for the administrative agency

—under what circumstances and when must individual administrative agency personnel disqualify themselves from participating in agency activities, decisions

—how must the administrative agency's investigative, legislative and adjudicative functions be insulated from each other so as not to allow for taint

—what rules of evidence should obtain during the various stages of administrative agency action

—in what form and with what completeness must administrative agency decisions be communicated

—what is the relationship between one administrative agency decision and another, between the decision of an administrative agency and a court (and vice-versa)

—what is the relationship between the jurisdiction of one administrative agency and another, between a federal administrative agency and a state administrative agency (or court)

—at what point in time in administrative agency proceedings may judicial intervention occur

—who are the proper parties to be involved in administrative agency consideration of a matter

—in what way is judicial intervention capable of being sought

—what kinds of administrative agency actions are not subject to judicial review

—if administrative agency action is judicially reviewable, to what extent will there be a review.

It is clear that with the expanding concerns and activities of government in all sectors of economic, social and technical endeavor there has come a proliferation of governmental bodies. Bureaucratic tentacles have spread throughout the warp and woof of Everyman's existence. It is for the reader to judge whether such should be evaluated morally. Whatever judgment may be made it cannot be gainsaid that increasing governmental activity has called for the creation of entities suited to act in such matters effectively and efficiently. American jurisprudence seems to have, for the time being, at least, identified the administrative agency with all of its manifold forms and characteristics as that governmental form to be used. Whether this will continue to be the case will, of course, be a matter for determination as those times arrive when specific issues challenge us to question existing institutions. But at this time in our history the administrative process as manifest by the administrative agency is not only a fact but a force that has truly risen to the level of being the fourth branch of government.

HANNAH v. LARCHE

Supreme Court of the United States, 1960.
363 U.S. 420, 80 S.Ct. 1502, 4 L.Ed.2d 1307.

Mr. Chief Justice WARREN delivered the opinion of the Court.

These cases involve the validity of certain Rules of Procedure adopted by the Commission on Civil Rights * * *. They arise out of the Commission's investigation of alleged Negro voting deprivations in the State of Louisiana. * * * The specific rules challenged are those which provide that the identity of persons submitting complaints to the Commission need not be disclosed, and that those summoned to testify before the Commission, including persons against whom complaints have been filed, may not cross-examine other witnesses called by the Commission. * * * The specific questions which we must decide are (1) whether the Commission was authorized by Congress to adopt the Rules of Procedure challenged by the respondents, and (2) if so, whether those procedures violate the Due Process Clause of the Fifth Amendment.

* * * The Commission had received some sixty-seven complaints from individual Negroes who alleged that they had been discriminatorily deprived of their right to vote. * * * The Commission began its investigation into the Louisiana voting situation by making several *ex parte* attempts to acquire information. * * *

* * * Interrogatories requested very detailed and specific information * * *. The voting registrars refused to answer the interrogatories. * * *

* * * [B]ecause the Commission's attempts to obtain information *ex parte* had been frustrated, the Commission * * * decided to hold the Shreveport hearing commencing on July 13, 1959.

Notice of the scheduled hearing was sent * * * subpoenas *duces tecum* were served on the respondents * * * ordering them to appear at the hearing and to bring with them various voting and registration records within their custody and control. * * *

Two days later * * * the respondents * * * filed two separate complaints in the District Court for the Western District of Louisiana. Both complaints alleged that the respondents would suffer irreparable harm by virtue of the Commission's refusal to furnish the names of persons who had filed allegations of voting deprivations, as well as the contents of the allegations, and by its further refusal to permit the respondents to confront and cross-examine the persons making such allegations. In addition, both complaints alleged that the Commission's refusal not only violated numerous provisions of the Federal Constitution, but also constituted "ultra vires" acts not authorized either by Congress or the Chief Executive. * * *

On October 7, 1959, a divided three-judge District Court * * * held that the Civil Rights Act of 1957 was constitutional since it "very definitely constitutes appropriate legislation" authorized by the Fourteenth and Fifteenth Amendments and Article I, Section 2, of the Federal Constitution. The court then held that since the respondents' allegations with regard to apprisal, confrontation, and cross-examination raised a "serious constitutional issue," this Court's decision in Greene v. McElroy, 360 U.S. 474, required a preliminary determination as to whether Congress specifically authorized the Commission "to adopt rules for investigations * * * which would deprive parties investigated of their rights of confrontation and cross-examination and their right to be apprised of the charges against them." 177 F.Supp. at page 822. The court found that Congress had not so authorized the Commission, and an injunction was therefore issued. * * *

After thoroughly analyzing the Rules of Procedure contained in the Civil Rights Act of 1957 and the legislative history which led to the adoption of that Act, we are of the opinion that the court below erred in its conclusion and that Congress did authorize the Commission to adopt the procedures here in question.

It could not be said that Congress ignored the procedures which the Commission was to follow in conducting its hearings. Section 102 of the Civil Rights Act of 1957 lists a number of procedural rights intended to safeguard witnesses from potential abuses. Briefly summarized, the relevant subdivisions of Section 102 provide that the Chairman shall make an opening statement as to the subject of the hearing; that a copy of the Commission's rules shall be made available to witnesses; that witnesses "may be accompanied by their own counsel for the purpose of advising them concerning their constitutional rights"; that potentially defamatory, degrading, or incriminating testimony shall be received in executive session, and that any person defamed, degraded, or incriminated by such testimony shall have an opportunity to appear voluntarily as a witness and to request the Commission to subpoena additional witnesses; that testimony taken in executive session shall be released only upon the consent of the Commission; and that witnesses may submit brief and pertinent sworn statements in writing for inclusion in the record.

The absence of any reference to apprisal, confrontation, and cross-examination, in addition to the fact that counsel's role is specifically limited to advising witnesses of their constitutional rights, creates a presumption that Congress did not intend witnesses appearing before the Commission to have the rights claimed by respondents. * * *

The legislative background of the Civil Rights Act not only provides evidence of congressional authorization, but it also distinguishes these cases from Greene v. McElroy, supra, upon which the court below relied so heavily. * * * Here, we have substantially more than the mere acquiescence upon which the Government relied in Greene. There was a conscious, intentional selection by Congress of one bill, providing for none of the procedures demanded by respondents, over another bill, which provided for all of those procedures. We have no doubt that Congress' consideration and rejection of the procedures here at issue constituted an authorization to the Commission to conduct its hearings according to the Rules of Procedure it has adopted, and to deny to witnesses the rights of apprisal, confrontation, and cross-examination.

The existence of authorization inevitably requires us to determine whether the Commission's Rules of Procedure are consistent with the Due Process Clause of the Fifth Amendment.

* * * The requirements of due process frequently vary with the type of proceeding involved * * *.

"Due process" is an elusive concept. Its exact boundaries are undefinable, and its content varies according to specific factual contexts. Thus, when governmental agencies adjudicate or make binding determinations which directly affect the legal rights of individuals, it is imperative that those agencies use the procedures which have traditionally been associated with the judicial process. On the other hand, when governmental action does not partake of an adjudication, as for example, when a general fact-finding investigation is being conducted, it is not necessary that the full panoply of judicial procedures be used. Therefore, as a generalization, it can be said that due process embodies the differing rules of fair play, which through the years, have become associated with differing types of proceedings. Whether the Constitution requires that a particular right obtain in a specific proceeding depends upon a complexity of factors. The nature of the alleged right involved, the nature of the proceeding, and the possible burden on that proceeding, are all considerations which must be taken into account. An analysis of these factors demonstrates why it is that the particular rights claimed by the respondents need not be conferred upon those appearing before purely investigative agencies, of which the Commission on Civil Rights is one.

It is probably sufficient merely to indicate that the rights claimed by respondents are normally associated only with adjudicatory proceedings, and that since the Commission does not adjudicate it need not be bound by adjudicatory procedures. Yet, the respondents contend and the court below implied, that such procedures are required since the Commission's proceedings might irreparably harm those being investigated by subjecting them to public opprobrium and scorn, the distinct likelihood of losing their jobs, and the possibility of criminal prosecutions. That any of these consequences will result is purely conjectural. There is nothing in the record to indicate that such will be the case or that past Commission hearings have had any harmful effects upon witnesses appearing before the Commission. However, even if such collateral consequences were to flow from the Commission's investigations, they would not be the result of any affirmative determinations made by the Commission, and they would not affect the legitimacy of the Commission's investigative function.

On the other hand, the investigative process could be completely disrupted if investigative hearings were transformed into trial-like proceedings, and if persons who might be indirectly affected by an investigation were given an absolute right to cross-examine every witness called to testify. * * *

In addition to these persuasive considerations, we think it is highly significant that the Commission's procedures are not historically foreign to other forms of investigation under our system. Far from being unique, the Rules of Procedure adopted by the Commission are similar to those which * * * have traditionally governed the proceedings of the vast majority of governmental investigating agencies.

* * *

The history of investigations conducted by the executive branch of the Government is also marked by a decided absence of those procedures here in issue. The best example is provided by the administrative regulatory agencies. Although these agencies normally make determinations of a quasi-judicial nature, they also frequently conduct purely fact-finding investigations. When doing the former, they are governed by the Administrative Procedure Act, 5 U.S.C.A. §§ 1001, 1011, and the parties to the adjudication are accorded the traditional safeguards of a trial. However, when these agencies are conducting nonadjudicative, fact-finding investigations, rights such as appraisal, confrontation, and cross-examination generally do not obtain.

A typical agency is the Federal Trade Commission. Its rules draw a clear distinction between adjudicative proceedings and investigative proceedings. * * * Although the latter are frequently initiated by complaints from undisclosed informants * * * and although the Commission may use the information obtained during investigations to initiate adjudicative proceedings, * * * nevertheless, persons summoned to appear before investigative proceedings are entitled only to a general notice of "the purpose and scope of the investigation," * * * and while they may have the advice of counsel, "counsel may not, as a matter of right, otherwise participate in the investigation." * * * The reason for these rules is obvious. The Federal Trade Commission could not conduct an efficient investigation if persons being investigated were permitted to convert the investigation into a trial. We have found no authorities suggesting that the rules governing Federal Trade Commission investigations violate the Constitution, and this is understandable since any person investigated by the Federal Trade Commission will be accorded all the traditional judicial safeguards at a subsequent adjudicative proceeding, just as any person investigated by the Civil Rights Commission will have all of these safeguards, should some type of adjudicative proceeding subsequently be instituted.

Another regulatory agency which distinguishes between adjudicative and investigative proceedings is the Securities and Exchange Commission. This Commission conducts numerous investigations, many of which are initiated by complaints from private parties. * * * Although the Commission's Rules provide that parties to adjudicative proceedings shall be given detailed notice of the matters to be determined * * * and a right to cross-examine witnesses appearing at the hearing, * * * those provisions of the Rules are made specifically inapplicable to investigations, * * * even though the Commission is required to initiate civil or criminal proceedings if an investigation discloses violations of law. * * *

We think it is fairly clear from this survey of various phases of governmental investigation that witnesses appearing before investigating agencies, whether legislative, executive, or judicial, have generally not been accorded the rights of apprisal, confrontation, or cross-examination. * * * The logic behind this historical practice was recognized and described by Mr. Justice Cardozo's landmark opinion in Norwegian Nitrogen Products Co. v. United States, 288 U.S. 294. In that case, the Court was concerned with the type of hearing that the Tariff Commission was required to hold when conducting its investigations. Specifically, the Court was asked to decide whether the Tariff Act of 1922, 42 Stat. 858, gave witnesses appearing before the Commission the right to examine confidential information in the Commission files and to cross-examine other witnesses testifying at Commission hearings. Although the Court did not phrase its holding in terms of due process, we think that the following language from Mr. Justice Cardozo's opinion is significant:

"The Tariff Commission advises; these others ordain. There is indeed this common bond that all alike are instruments in a governmental process which according to the accepted classification is legislative, not judicial. * * * Whatever the appropriate label, the kind of order that emerges from a hearing before a body with power to ordain is one that impinges upon legal rights in a very different way from the report of a commission which merely investigates and advises. The traditionary forms of hearing appropriate to the one body are unknown to the other. What issues from the Tariff Commission as a report and recommendation to the President, may be accepted, modified, or rejected. If it happens to be accepted, it does not bear fruit in anything that trenches upon legal rights." 288 U.S., at page 318.

And in referring to the traditional practice of investigating bodies, Mr. Justice Cardozo had this to say:

"[W]ithin the meaning of this act the 'hearing' assured to one affected by a change of duty does not include a privilege to ransack the records of the Commission, and to subject its confidential agents to an examination as to all that they have learned. *There was no thought to revolutionize the practice of investigating bodies generally, and of this one in particular.*" Id., 288 U.S. at page 319. (Emphasis supplied.)

Thus, the purely investigative nature of the Commission's proceedings, the burden that the claimed rights would place upon those proceedings, and the traditional procedure of investigating agencies in general, leads us to conclude that the Commission's Rules of Procedure comport with the requirements of due process.

* * *

Reversed and remanded.

* * *

Mr. Justice DOUGLAS, with whom Mr. Justice BLACK concurs, dissenting.

With great deference to my Brethren I dissent from a reversal of these judgments.

* * *

Complaints have been filed with the Commission charging respondents, who are registrars of voters in Louisiana, with depriving persons of their voting rights by reason of their color. If these charges are true and if the registrars acted willfully * * * the registrars are criminally responsible under a federal statute which subjects to fine and imprisonment anyone who willfully deprives a citizen of any right under the Constitution "by reason of his color, or race." 18 U.S.C.A. § 242.

The investigation and hearing by the Commission are therefore necessarily aimed at determining if this criminal law has been violated. The serious and incriminating nature of the charge and the disclosure of facts concerning it are recognized by the Congress, for the Act requires certain protective procedures to be adopted where defamatory, degrading, or incriminating evidence may be adduced.

"If the Commission determines that evidence or testimony at any hearing may tend to defame, degrade, or incriminate any person, it shall (1) receive such evidence or testimony in executive session; (2) afford such person an opportunity voluntarily to appear as a witness; and (3) receive and dispose of requests from such person to subpena additional witnesses." 42 U.S.C.A. § 1975a(c).

Yet these safeguards, given as a matter of grace, do not in my judgment dispose of the constitutional difficulty. First, it is the Commission's judgment, not the suspect's, that determines whether the hearing shall be secret or public.   *   *   *   The secrecy of the inquisition only underlines its inherent vices: "Secret inquisitions are dangerous things justly feared by free men everywhere. They are the breeding place for arbitrary misuse of official power. They are often the beginning of tyranny as well as indispensable instruments for its survival. Modern as well as ancient history bears witness that both innocent and guilty have been seized by officers of the state and whisked away for secret interrogation or worse until the groundwork has been securely laid for their inevitable conviction.   *   *   *   [S]ecretly compelled testimony does not lose its highly dangerous potentialities merely because" it is taken in preliminary proceedings. Second, the procedure seems to me patently unconstitutional whether the hearing is public or secret. Under the Commission's rules the accused is deprived of the right to notice of the charges against him and the opportunity of cross-examination. This statutory provision, fashioned to protect witnesses as such rather than a prospective defendant, permits the Commission to exclude the accused entirely from the hearing and deny him the opportunity even to observe the testimony of his accusers. And even if the Commission were inclined in a particular case to protect the accused from the opprobrium likely to flow from the testimony of individual witnesses against him by holding secret sessions, this would be little comfort after the Commission's findings, based on such untested evidence, were publicized across the Nation.

      *   *   *

The grand jury is the accusatory body in federal law as provided by the Fifth Amendment.   *   *   *   Thomas Erskine stated the matter accurately and eloquently in Jones v. Shipley, 21 How.St.Tr. 847.

"[I]t is unnecessary to remind your lordships, that, in a civil case, the party who conceives himself aggrieved, states his complaint to the court,—avails himself at his own pleasure of its process,—compels an answer from the defendant by its authority, —or taking the charge *pro confesso* against him on his default, is entitled to final judgment and execution for his debt, without any interposition of a jury. But in criminal cases it is otherwise; the court has no cognizance of them, without leave from the people forming a grand inquest. If a man were to commit a capital offense in the face of all the judges of England, their united authority could not put him upon his trial:—they could file no complaint against him, even upon the records of the supreme criminal court, but could only commit him for safe custody, which is equally competent to every common justice of the peace:—the grand jury alone could arraign him, and in their discretion might likewise finally discharge him, by throwing out the bill, with the names of all your lordships as witnesses on the back of it. If it shall be said, that this exclusive power of the grand jury does not extend to lesser misdemeanors, which may be prosecuted by information; I answer, that for that very reason it becomes doubly necessary to preserve the power of the other jury which is left."

This idea, though uttered in 1783, is modern and relevant here.
* * *

This Commission has no such guarantee of fairness. * * * The members cannot be as independent as grand juries because they meet not for one occasion only; they do a continuing job for the executive and, if history is a guide, tend to acquire a vested interest in that role.

The grand jury, adopted as a safeguard against "hasty, malicious, and oppressive" action by the Federal Government * * * stands as an important safeguard to the citizen against open and public accusations of crime. * * *

Grand juries have their defects. They do not always return a true bill, for while the prejudices of the community may radiate through them, they also have the saving quality of being familiar with the people involved. They are the only accusatory body in the Federal Government that is recognized by the Constitution. I would allow no other engine of government, either executive or legislative, to take their place—at least when the right of confrontation and cross-examination are denied the accused as is done in these cases.
* * *

The Civil Rights Commission, it is true, returns no indictment. Yet in a real sense the hearings on charges that a registrar has committed a federal offense are a trial. Moreover, these hearings before the Commission may be televised or broadcast on the radio. * * * This is in reality a trial in which the whole Nation sits as a jury. Their verdict does not send men to prison. But it often condemns men or produces evidence to convict and even saturates the Nation with prejudice against an accused so that a fair trial may be impossible. As stated in 37 A.B.A.J. 392 (1951), "If several million television viewers see and hear a politician, a businessman or a movie actor subjected to searching interrogation, without ever having an opportunity to cross-examine his accusers or offer evidence in his own support, that man will stand convicted, or at least seriously compromised, in the public mind, whatever the later formal findings may be." The use of this procedure puts in jeopardy our traditional concept of the way men should be tried and replaces it with "a new concept of guilt based on inquisitorial devices." Note, 26 Temp.L.Q. 70, 73.

* * *

* * * If the hearings are to be without the safeguards which due process requires of all trials—civil and criminal—there is only one way I know by which the Federal Government may proceed and that is by grand jury. If these trials before the Commission are to be held on charges that these respondents are criminals, the least we can do is to allow them to know what they are being tried for, and to confront their accusers and to cross-examine them. * * * Confrontation and cross-examination are so basic to our concept of due process * * * that no proceeding by an administrative agency is a fair one that denies these rights.

References are made to federal statutes governing numerous administrative agencies such as the Federal Trade Commission and the Securities and Exchange Commission; and the inference is that what is done in this case can be done there. * * * No effort was ever made, so far as I am aware, to compel a person, charged with violating a federal law, to run the gantlet (sic) of a hearing over his objection. No objection based either on the ground now advanced nor on the Fifth Amendment was, so far as I know, ever overruled. Investigations were made; and they were searching. Such evidence of law violations as was obtained was turned over to the Department of Justice. But never before, I believe, has a federal executive agency attempted, over the objections of an accused, to force him through a hearing to determine whether he has violated a federal law. If it did, the action was lawless and courts should have granted relief.

* * *

APPENDIX TO OPINION OF THE COURT [1]

[Footnotes at end of table]

Agency	Scope of agency's investigative authority	Extent of agency's subpoena power in investigative proceedings	The type of notice required to be given in investigative proceedings [3]	The right, if any, of persons affected by an investigation to cross-examine others testifying at investigative proceedings [4]	Miscellaneous comments
Executive and Administrative Agencies [2] Atomic Energy Commission.	The Commission is authorized to "make such studies and investigations, * * * and hold such meetings or hearings as [it] may deem necessary or proper to assist it in exercising" any of its statutory functions. 42 U.S.C.A. § 2201(c).	The Commission may subpoena any person to appear and testify or produce documents "at any designated place." 42 U.S.C.A. § 2201 (c).	This is not specified by statute. The Commission's Rules of Practice provide that "[t]he procedure to be followed in informal hearings shall be such as will best serve the purpose of the hearing." 10 CFR § 2.720. The Rules of Practice do not require any specific type of notice to be given in informal hearings. Ibid.	This is not specified by statute. The Commission's Rules of Practice do not require that those summoned to appear before informal hearings be given the right to cross-examine other witnesses. Rather, the Commission is given the discretion to adopt those procedures which "will best serve the purpose of the hearing." 10 CFR § 2.720.	The Commission's Rules of Practice draw a sharp distinction between informal and formal hearings. Formal hearings are used only in "cases of adjudication," 10 CFR § 2.708, and parties to the hearings are given detailed notice of the subject of the hearing, id., § 2.735, as well as the right to cross-examine witnesses, id., § 2.747. Informal hearings are used in investigations "for the purposes of obtaining necessary or useful information, and affording participation by interested persons, in the formulation, amendment, or rescission of rules and regulations." Id., § 2.708. The safeguards which are accorded in the formal, adjudicative hearings are not mentioned in the Commission's Rule relating to informal hearings. Id., § 2.720.

Agency	Scope of agency's investigative authority	Extent of agency's subpoena power in investigative proceedings	The type of notice required to be given in investigative proceedings [3]	The right, if any, of persons affected by an investigation to cross-examine others testifying at investigative proceedings [4]	Miscellaneous comments
Federal Communications Commission.	(1) The Commission is authorized to investigate any matters contained in a complaint "in such manner and by such means as it shall deem proper." 47 U.S.C.A. § 208. (2) The Federal Communications Commission was also authorized to conduct a special investigation of the American Telephone and Telegraph Company, and to obtain information concerning the company's history and structure, the services rendered by it, its failure for monopolistic control on the company, the methods of competition engaged in by the company, and the company's attempts to influence public opinion by the use of propaganda. 49 Stat. 43.	(1) The Commission may "subpena the attendance and testimony of witnesses and the production of all books, papers, schedules of charges, contracts, agreements, and documents, relating to any matter under investigation." 47 U.S.C.A. § 409(e). (2) The Commission was also given the subpoena power by the statute authorizing the investigation of the American Telephone and Telegraph Company. 49 Stat. 45.	This is not specified by statute. The Commission's Rules of Practice do not specify the type of notice to be given in investigative proceedings. However, the Rules do provide that the "[p]rocedures to be followed by the Commission shall, unless specifically prescribed * * * [in the Rules], be such as in the opinion of the Commission will best serve the purposes of * * * [any investigative] proceeding." 47 CFR § 1.10.	This is not specified by statute. Nor do the Commission's Rules of Practice refer to cross-examination in investigative proceedings. Therefore, whether persons appearing at an investigation have the privilege of cross-examining witnesses apparently depends upon whether the Commission is of the opinion that cross-examination "will best serve the purposes of such proceeding." 47 CFR § 1.10. It should also be noted that even in that portion of the Commission's Rules relating to adjudicative proceedings, there is no specific provision relating to cross-examination. Id., §§ 1.101-1.193.	It should be noted that the Commission's Report on the Telephone Investigation made no mention of the type of notice, if any, given to those summoned to appear at the investigation. Nor was there any reference to cross-examination. The Commission did permit the Company "to submit statements in writing pointing out any inaccuracies in factual data or statistics in the reports introduced in the hearings or in any testimony in connection therewith, provided that such statements were confined to the presentation of facts and that no attempt would be made therein to draw conclusions therefrom." H. R. Doc. No. 340, 76th Cong., 1st Sess. xviii.
Federal Trade Commission.	(1) The Commission is authorized to investigate "the organization, business, conduct, practices, and management of any	(1) The Commission may "subpoena the attendance and testimony of witnesses	(1) This is not specified by statute. The Commission's Rules of Practice provide that	(1) This is not specified by statute. The Commission's Rules of Practice provide that	(1) It is interesting to note that the Commission's Rules of Practice draw an ex-

[A6797]

Agency	Scope of agency's investigative authority	Extent of agency's subpoena power in investigative proceedings	The type of notice required to be given in investigative proceedings [3]	The right, if any, of persons affected by an investigation to cross-examine others testifying at investigative proceedings [4]	Miscellaneous comments
Federal Trade Commission— Continued.	corporation engaged in commerce"; to make an investigation of the manner in which antitrust decrees are being carried out; to investigate and report the facts relating to any alleged violations of the antitrust Acts by any corporation; and "to investigate * * * trade conditions in and with foreign countries where associations, combinations, or practices of manufacturers, merchants, or traders, or other conditions, may affect the foreign trade of the United States. 15 U.S.C.A. § 46. (2) The Commission was also authorized to conduct a special investigation of the motor vehicle industry to determine (a) "the extent of concentration of control and of monopoly in the manufacturing, warehousing, distribution, and sale of automobiles, accessories, and parts, including methods and devices used by manufacturers for obtaining and maintaining their control or monopoly * * * and the extent, if any, to which fraudulent, dishonest, unfair, and injurious methods [were] employed, including combinations, monopolies, price fixing, or unfair trade practices"; and	and the production of all such documentary evidence relating to any matter under investigation." 15 U.S.C.A. § 49. (2) The Commission was also given the subpoena power under the statute authorizing the investigation of the motor vehicle industry. 52 Stat. 218.	"[a]ny party under investigation compelled to furnish information or documentary evidence shall be advised with respect to the purpose and scope of the investigation." 16 CFR, 1959 Supp., § 1.33. (2) The Commission's Report on the Motor Vehicle Industry did not indicate what type of notice, if any, was given to those summoned to testify at the investigation. H. R. Doc. No. 468, 76th Cong., 1st Sess. Presumably, the Commission's regular Rules of Practice obtained.	a person required to testify in an investigative proceeding "may be accompanied and advised by counsel, but counsel may not, as a matter of right, otherwise participate in the investigation." 16 CFR, 1959 Supp., § 1.40. Moreover, while the Rules of Practice make no mention of the right to cross-examine witnesses in investigative proceedings, see id., § 1.31–1.42, such a right is specifically given to parties in an adjudicative proceeding. Id., § 3.16. (2) The Commission's Report on the Motor Vehicle Industry did not refer to cross-examination. H.R. Doc. No. 468, 76th Cong., 1st Sess.	press and sharp distinction between investigative and adjudicative proceedings, and that the Commission's Rules relating to notice and cross-examination in investigative proceedings are very similar to those adopted by the Civil Rights Commission. (2) It should also be observed that FTC investigations may be initiated "upon complaint by members of the consuming public, businessmen, or the concerns aggrieved by unfair practices," 16 CFR, 1959 Supp., § 1.11, and that complaints received by the Commission may charge "any violation of law over which the Commission has jurisdiction." Id., § 1.12. (3) Also relevant to our inquiry is the fact that the Commission does not "publish or divulge the name of an applicant or com-

Agency	Scope of agency's investigative authority	Extent of agency's subpoena power in investigative proceedings	The type of notice required to be given in investigative proceedings [3]	The right, if any, of persons affected by an investigation to cross-examine others testifying at investigative proceedings [4]	Miscellaneous comments
Federal Trade Commission—Continued.	(b) "the extent to which any of the antitrust laws of the United States [were] being violated." 52 Stat. 218.				plaining party." Id., § 1.15. (4) Finally, it is important to observe that the FTC, unlike the Civil Rights Commission, has the authority to commence adjudicative proceedings based upon the material obtained by means of investigative proceedings. Id., § 1.42.
National Labor Relations Board.	Under the National Labor Relations Act, the Board is given the power to investigate petitions and charges submitted to it relating to union representation and unfair labor practices. 29 U.S.C.A. §§ 159(c), 160(l).	"For the purpose of all hearings and investigations * * * the Board [may] * * * copy any evidence of any person being investigated or proceeded against that relates to any matter under investigation," and it may also issue subpoenas requiring the attendance and testimony of witnesses in any proceeding or investigation. 29 U.S.C.A. § 161.	This is not specified by statute. The Board's Statements of Procedure and Rules and Regulations provide for the preliminary investigation of all petitions and charges received by the Board. Although a copy of the initial charge may be served upon an alleged violator, there is no specific rule requiring the Board to give notice of the preliminary investigation. See 29 CFR, 1960 Supp., §§ 101.4, 101.18, 101.22, 101.27,	This is not specified by statute. The Board's Statements of Procedure and Rules and Regulations provide for the right to cross-examine witnesses at formal, adjudicative hearings, 29 CFR, 1960 Supp., §§ 101.10, 102.38, 102.66, 102.86, 102.90, but there is no such provision with regard to preliminary investigations. Id., §§ 101.4, 101.18, 101.22, 101.27, 101.32, 102.63, 102.77, 102.85.	It should be noted that the National Labor Relations Board may use the information collected during preliminary investigations to initiate adjudicative proceedings. 29 U.S.C.A. § 160(l). The Commission on Civil Rights has no such power. Moreover, the Board, unlike the Civil Rights Commission, may use the information obtained by it through investigations to petition the federal courts for appropriate injunctive

Agency	Scope of agency's investigative authority	Extent of agency's subpoena power in investigative proceedings	The type of notice required to be given in investigative proceedings [3]	The right, if any, of persons affected by an investigation to cross-examine others testifying at investigative proceedings [4]	Miscellaneous comments
National Labor Relations Board—Con.			101.32, 102.63, 102.77, 102.85.		relief. 29 U.S.C.A. § 160(l).
Securities and Exchange Commission.	(1) Under the Securities Act of 1933, as amended, the Commission is authorized to conduct "all investigations which, * * * are necessary and proper for the enforcement of" the Act. 15 U.S.C.A. § 77s(b). (2) The Securities Exchange Act of 1934 authorizes the Commission to "make such investigations as it deems necessary to determine whether any person has violated or is about to violate any provisions of [the Act] or any rule or regulation thereunder." 15 U.S.C.A. § 78u (a). (3) The Public Utility Holding Company Act of 1935 empowers the Commission to "investigate any facts, conditions, practices, or matters which it may deem necessary or appropriate to determine whether any person has violated or is about to violate any provision of [the Act] or any rule or regulation thereunder, or to aid in the enforcement of the provisions of [the	All of the Acts which authorize the Commission to conduct investigations also bestow upon it the power to subpoena witnesses, compel their attendance, and require the production of any books, correspondence, memoranda, contracts, agreements, and other records which are relevant to the investigation. Securities Act of 1933, 15 U.S.C.A. § 77c (b); Securities Exchange Act of 1934, 15 U.S.C.A. § 78u (b); Public Utility Holding Company Act of 1935, 15 U.S.C.A. § 78r (c); Trust Indenture Act of 1939, 15 U.S.C.A. § 77uuu (a); Investment Company Act of 1940, 15 U.S.C.A. § 80a–41(b); Investment Advisers Act	This is not specified by statute. Nor do the Commission's Rules of Practice relating to formal investigations make any mention of the type of notice which must be given in such proceedings. 17 CFR § 202.4. The Commission's Rules do provide for the giving of notice in adjudicative proceedings, id., § 201.3, 1950 Supp. ings., id., 1950 Supp. § 201.3, but this provision is made specifically inapplicable to investigative proceedings. Id., § 201.20.	This is not specified by statute. The Commission's Rules of Practice make no mention of the right to cross-examine witnesses in investigative proceedings. 17 CFR § 202.4. Parties are given the right to cross-examine witnesses in adjudicative proceedings, id., § 201.5, but this provision is made specifically inapplicable to investigative proceedings. Id., § 201.20.	The Securities and Exchange Commission's procedures for investigative proceedings are very similar to those of the Civil Rights Commission. Investigations may be initiated upon complaints received from members of the public, and these complaints may contain specific charges of illegal conduct. 17 CFR § 202.4. It should be noted, however, that the Securities and Exchange Commission, unlike the Civil Rights Commission, is an adjudicatory body, and it may use the information gathered through investigative proceedings to initiate "administrative proceedings looking to the imposition of remedial sanctions, * * * (or) injunction proceedings

[A6800]

Agency	Scope of agency's investigative authority	Extent of agency's subpoena power in investigative proceedings	The type of notice required to be given in investigative proceedings 3	The right, if any, of persons affected by an investigation to cross-examine others testifying at investigative proceedings 4	Miscellaneous comments
Securities and Exchange Commission—Con.	Act], in the prescribing of rules and regulations thereunder, or in obtaining information, to serve as further legislation concerning the matters to which [the Act] relates." 15 U.S.C.A. § 79r (a). (4) The Trust Indenture Act of 1939 authorizes the Commission to conduct "any investigation * * * which * * * is necessary and proper for the enforcement of" the Act. 15 U.S.C.A. § 77uuu (a). (5) The Investment Company Act of 1940 gives the Commission the power to "make such investigations as it deems necessary to determine whether any person has violated or is about to violate any provision of * * * [the Act] or of any rule, regulation, or order thereunder, or to determine whether any action in any court or any proceeding before the Commission shall be instituted under * * * [the Act] against a particular person or persons, or with respect to a particular person or persons, or with respect to a particular transaction or transactions." 15 U.S.C.A. § 80a–41(a). (6) Finally, under the Investment Advisers Act of 1940, the Commission is authorized to determine by investigation whether "the provisions of * * * [the Act] or of any rule or regulation prescribed under the authority thereof, have been or are about to be violated by any person." 15 U.S.C.A. § 80b–9(a).	of 1940, 15 U.S.C.A. § 80b–9(b).			in the courts, and, in the case of a wilful violation," it may refer the "matter to the Department of Justice for criminal prosecution," Ibid. See also Securities Act of 1933, 15 U.S.C.A. § 77t (b); Securities Exchange Act of 1934, 15 U.S.C.A. § 78u (e); Public Utility Holding Company Act of 1935, 15 U.S.C.A. § 79r (f); Investment Company Act of 1940, 15 U.S. C.A. § 80a–41(e); Investment Advisers Act of 1940, 15 U.S.C.A. § 80b–9(e).

[A68011]

Agency	Scope of agency's investigative authority	Extent of agency's subpoena power in investigative proceedings	The type of notice required to be given in investigative proceedings 3	The right, if any, of persons affected by an investigation to cross-examine others testifying at investigative proceedings 4	Miscellaneous comments
The Department of Agriculture.	(1) Under the Perishable Agricultural Commodities Act of 1930, the Department is authorized to investigate any complaint filed with the Secretary alleging that someone has violated the Act. 7 U.S.C.A. § 499f (c). (2) The Department also enforces the Packers and Stockyards Act of 1921, which, for the purposes of that Act, gives the Secretary the investigative and other enforcement powers possessed by the Federal Trade Commission, 7 U.S.C.A. § 222. The Department's Rules of Practice also provide that investigations shall be conducted when informal complaints charging a violation of the Act are received by the Secretary. 9 CFR § 202.23.	(1) The Perishable Agricultural Commodities Act of 1930 authorizes the Secretary to "require by subpoena the attendance and testimony of witnesses and the production of such accounts, records, and memoranda, as may be material for the determination of any complaint under" the Act. 7 U.S.C.A. § 499m(b). (2) The Packers and Stockyards Act of 1921 gives to the Secretary those powers conferred upon the Federal Trade Commission by "sections 46 and 48-50 of Title 15." Among those powers is the authority to subpoena witnesses. 7 U.S.C.A. § 222.	This is not specified by statute. The Department's Rules of Practice adopted pursuant to the Perishable Agricultural Commodities Act and the Packers and Stockyards Act do not refer to the type of notice, if any, which must be given in investigative proceedings, 7 CFR § 47.3; 9 CFR § 202.3, although a specific right to notice is given in adjudicative proceedings. 7 CFR §§ 47.6, 47.27; 9 CFR §§ 202.6, 202.23, 202.39.	This is not specified by statute. The Department's Rules of Practice adopted pursuant to the Perishable Agricultural Commodities Act and the Packers and Stockyards Act contain no reference to cross - examination during investigative proceedings, 7 CFR § 47.3; 9 CFR § 202.3, although such a right is given in the formal adjudicative stage of the proceedings. 7 CFR §§ 47.15, 47.32; 9 CFR §§ 202.11, 202.29, 202.48.	(1) The Department of Agriculture, unlike the Civil Rights Commission, may use the information obtained through investigations in its subsequent adjudicative proceedings under the Perishable Agricultural Commodities Act. 7 CFR § 47.7. (2) It is also of interest that investigation proceedings under both the Perishable Agricultural Commodities Act and the Packers and Stockyards Act are commenced by the filing of complaints from private individuals. 7 CFR § 47.3; 9 CFR § 202.3. (3) Finally, it should be noted that the Department of Agriculture administers the Federal Seed Act, 7 U.S.C.A. §§ 1551-1610, which makes it unlawful to engage in certain practices relating to the labelling and importation of seeds, and a statute regulating export standards for apples and pears, 7 U.S.C.A. §§ 581-589. The Rules of Practice adopted by the Secretary pursuant to statutory authorization provide that proceedings under these statutes shall be initiated by an investigation of the charges contained in

Agency	Scope of agency's investigative authority	Extent of agency's subpoena power in investigative proceedings	The type of notice required to be given in investigative proceedings 3	The right, if any, of persons affected by an investigation to cross-examine others testifying at investigative proceedings 4	Miscellaneous comments
The Department of Agriculture—Continued					any complaint received by the Secretary. These Rules make no mention of the type of notice, if any, given to those being investigated; nor is there any reference to cross-examination during the investigative stage of the proceedings. 7 CFR §§ 201.151, 33.17.
Food and Drug Administration (Department of Health, Education and Welfare).	The Regulations adopted pursuant to the Federal Caustic Poison Act, 15 U.S.C.A. §§ 401–411, authorize the Administration to conduct investigations, 21 CFR § 285.15, and to hold preliminary hearings "whenever it appears * * * that the provisions of section 3 or 6 of the Caustic Poison Act * * * have been violated and criminal proceedings are contemplated." Id., § 285.17.	The Act makes no provision for compelling testimony.	This is not specified by statute. The Administration's Regulations make no reference to notice of investigative proceedings, but they do require that general notice be given to those against whom prosecution is contemplated. 21 CFR § 285.17.	This is not specified by statute. The Administration's regulations make no mention of the right to cross-examine witnesses appearing at investigative proceedings or preliminary hearings. 21 CFR § 285.17.	It should be noted that the Administration investigates specific instances of possible unlawful activity, and that, unlike the Civil Rights Commission, the Secretary (acting through the Administration) is required to refer possible violations to the proper United States Attorney. 15 U.S.C.A. § 409(b).

1. This Appendix describes the Rules of Procedure governing the authorized investigative proceedings of a representative group of administrative agencies, executive departments, presidential commissions, and congressional committees. The Appendix does not purport to be a complete enumeration of the hundreds of agencies which have conducted investigations during the course of this country's history. Rather, it is designed to demonstrate that the procedures adopted by the Civil Rights Commission are similar to those which have traditionally been used by investigating agencies in both the executive and legislative branches of our Government. (Court's footnote 1.)

2. We have found many other administrative agencies and presidential commissions empowered to conduct investigations and to subpoena witnesses. Those agencies are not listed in the body of this Appendix because we were unable to find an adequate description of the rules of procedure governing their investigative proceedings. However, it is significant that the statutes creating these agencies made no reference to appraisal or cross-examination in investigative proceedings. Among the agencies in this category are: (1) Bureau of Corporations in the Department of Commerce and Labor, 32 Stat. 827; (2) Commission on Industrial Relations, 37 Stat. 415; (3) the Railroad Labor Board, 41 Stat. 469; (4) the United States Coal Commission, 42 Stat. 1023; (5) the Investigation Commission established by the Railroad Retirement Act of 1935, 49 Stat. 972, 45 U.S.C.A. §§ 215–228 note; (6) National Bituminous Coal Commission, 49 Stat. 992; (7) Wage and Hour Division of the Department of Labor, 29 U.S.C.A. § 204; (8) Board of Investigation to Investigate Various Modes of Transportation, 49 U.S.C.A. note preceding section 1; (9) Commission on Organization of the Executive Branch of the Government, 5 U.S.C.A. §§ 133a–133h note; (10) Commission on Intergovernmental Relations, 5 U.S.C.A. §§ 133a–133h] note. (Court's footnote 2.)

3. If the relevant statute makes no reference to notice, this fact will be mentioned. The negative inference which may be drawn from the absence of any statutory requirement that notice be given is supported by the fact that, in a few instances, Congress has made specific provision for the giving of notice in investigative proceedings. * * * (Court's footnote 3.)

4. If the relevant statute makes no reference to cross-examination, that fact will be mentioned because of the inference which may be drawn therefrom that Congress did not intend persons appearing at investigative hearings to cross-examine other witnesses. This inference is strengthened by the fact that in a relatively few instances Congress has, for one reason or another, required that persons being investigated by a commission or agency be given the right to cross-examine other witnesses. See, e. g. 46 U.S.C.A. § 239, which authorized the Secretary of Commerce to appoint special boards to investigate the causes of marine casualties. (Court's footnote 4.)

[A68031]

CITIZENS COMMITTEE v. FEDERAL COMMUNICATIONS COMMISSION

United States Court of Appeals, D.C. Circuit, 1970.
436 F.2d 263.

McGOWAN, Circuit Judge. This proceeding to review an order of the Federal Communications Commission was initiated by a voluntary association of citizens of Atlanta, Georgia. Their concern is with a substantial alteration in the program format incident to a change in ownership of a licensee—a concern which they requested the Commission to explore in an evidentiary hearing before giving its final approval to the transfer. The Commission denied that request, and it is the propriety of that action alone which is presently before us. For the reasons hereinafter appearing, we do not think the omission of a hearing in this instance was compatible with the applicable statutory standards.

* * * Strauss Broadcasting Company of Atlanta * * * filed with the Commission an application for transfer of the operating rights of the Atlanta Stations WGKA–AM and WGKA–FM * * * from Glenkaren Associates, Inc. Under Glenkaren, the stations had for many years maintained a classical music format. * * * Strauss proposed a format comprised of a "blend of popular favorites, Broadway hits, musical standards, and light classics." * *

Publication of notice of the transfer application provoked a public outcry against the change in format, including adverse comment in the columns of a leading Atlanta newspaper. More than 2000 persons, by individual letters and group petitions, informally protested the change to the Commission. Subsequently, Strauss filed two amendments to its transfer application. The first, on April 22, 1968, dealt largely with the "newspaper campaign," which was alleged to be responsible for the protests addressed to the Commission. * * *

A second amendment was filed June 3, 1968. It transmitted summaries of interviews with 13 prominent citizens which purported to reflect favorable views of the proposed new format. * * *

* * *.

On September 4, 1968, the Commission, without a hearing, granted the transfer application. The Commission recited as a fact that the necessity for the transfer was that the existing owner could not supply adequate capital for needed improvements. It also noted that opposition to the change was provoked by the newspaper comments, whereas interviews with community leaders had apparently evoked "nothing but support" for Strauss's proposals. The Commission concluded that the proposed programming was established by the surveys to be one that served the public interest, and that the "informal objections" raised no substantial question requiring a hearing. * * *

On September 25, 1968, appellant filed a petition for reconsideration * * *. Appellant challenged the significance of Strauss's surveys of 13 community leaders, questioning the representative na-

ture of this sampling, and comparing it with the large number of protests actually received by the Commission before its approval order
was entered.   Perhaps the greatest stress was laid on the fact that of
Atlanta's many AM and FM stations, only one (WGKA) was classical.

Strauss countered, on October 9, 1968, with an opposition to the
petition, alleging lack of standing on appellant's part * * *.

In subsequent months voluminous papers were filed by both sides.
* * *

On March 4, 1969, the Commission requested Strauss to "undertake further efforts to ascertain by a more comprehensive survey"
the tastes and needs of the community.   In response, Strauss filed on
April 30, 1969 a statistical survey of "program preferences" in
Atlanta * * *.

Out of 640 people asked, 73% preferred * * * [popular music]
and 16% preferred * * * [classical music].   Four [per cent]
gave no reply, and the remainder preferred neither. * * *

At this point, another factor entered the controversy, namely,
the existence of a daytime-only 500 watt AM classical station in
Decatur, Georgia, (WOMN), some 10 miles from Atlanta.   Strauss
asserted that this station adequately served the daytime needs of
WGKA's former audience.   Appellant responded that WOMN's signal
reached few Atlanta listeners at an acceptable level of signal quality.

On August 25, 1969, the Commission entered a Memorandum
Opinion and Order. * * * "[T]he case here comes down to a
choice of program formats—a choice which in the circumstances is
one for the judgment of the licensee." * * *

In dissent, Commissioner Cox asserted that a hearing was required. * * * He did not see how the requisite public interest
finding could be made short of the illumination afforded by a hearing.

* * * We think the substantial issue presented is that of the
necessity for a hearing. * * * The Federal Communications Act
provides that no license may be transferred "except upon application
to the Commission and upon finding by the Commission that the public interest, convenience, and necessity will be served thereby."   47
U.S.C.A. § 310(b).   An application of this kind is directed to be disposed of as if the transferees were making application for the license
* * * in the first instance * * *.   [And,] if, in the case of
any such application, "a substantial and material question of fact is
presented," or the Commission is for any reason unable to make the
prescribed finding, "it shall formally designate the application for
hearing * * *."

* * * [C]ounsel for the Commission has asserted principally
the proposition that the Commission has a discretion in these matters
which is not to be disturbed unless it is palpably abused. * * *

The Commission's point of departure seems to be that, if the
programming contemplated * * * is shown to be favored by a
significant number of the residents of Atlanta, then a determination

to use that format is a judgment for the broadcaster to make, and not the Commission. * * *

* * * [T]here are some 20 * * * channels, all owned by the people as a whole * * *. * * * [I]t is surely in the public interest * * * for all major aspects of contemporary culture to be accommodated by the commonly-owned public resources whenever that is technically and economically feasible.

* * * The Commission's judgmental function does not end simply upon a showing that a numerical majority prefer the Beatles to Beethoven, impressive as that fact may be in the eyes of the advertisers.

The Commission's response in this instance to the 16% figure was to abdicate. * * *

In the first place, there is the key assumption by the Commission that transfer of the station licenses was made necessary by the financial necessities of Glenkaren arising from the unprofitability of the existing operation. * * *

* * * We, of course, do not presume to know what a hearing might ultimately reveal with respect to Glenkaren's financial situation, but the Commission's flat assumptions about it need a closer look than they have yet had.

A second area of factual inquiry clamoring for the clarifying influence of direct testimony subject to cross-examination is that of the interviews of prominent citizens. * * * Appellant, as a supplement to its petition for reconsideration, filed the affidavits of a number of the interviewees, which give a different picture of their position than do the summaries prepared by intervenor. This in turn prompted intervenor to secure and file unsworn letters from the original interviewees which purported to adopt the summaries as correct.

But these last do not in all instances resolve the ambiguities inevitable in this way of trying to establish what a witness said and what his position really was. * * *

The truth is most likely to be refined and discovered in the crucible of an evidentiary hearing; and it is precisely a situation like the one revealed by this record which motivated the Congress to stress the availability to the Commission of the hearing procedure. * * *

A third important issue which appears to be in dispute is the degree to which daytime listeners in Atlanta are provided with classical music from a non-Atlanta source. This is the question of the scope of the coverage of Atlanta by WOMN, the station located in Decatur, Georgia. The Commission disposed of this matter by saying in a footnote that "a large portion" of the City of Atlanta is reached by this station. Commissioner Cox in his dissent refers to WOMN as providing Atlanta with "some service." * * * At the oral argument before us no one appeared to be familiar with the contour charts which would be highly relevant to a reasoned disposition of this question. Since the Commission appears to justify its action in some considerable part by the asserted availability to Atlanta listeners of at least a daytime classical format it is obviously important that this dispute of fact be explored and resolved.

It is, of course, true that a licensee has considerable latitude in the matter of programming; and it is not for the Commission arbitrarily to dictate what the programming content shall be. * * * But it is not true that the Commission is devoid of any responsibility whatsoever for programming, or that its concern with it stops whenever 51% of the people in the area are shown to favor a particular format. * * *

The order denying reconsideration is vacated and the matter is remanded for an evidentiary hearing.

SUN OIL COMPANY v. FEDERAL POWER COMMISSION

United States Court of Appeals, District of Columbia Circuit, 1971.
445 F.2d 764.

TAMM, Circuit Judge.   The primary issue involved in this case is whether a rate of return allowed Florida Gas Transmission Company (hereinafter "Florida Gas") by the Federal Power Commission (hereinafter "the Commission") is invalid because the Commission did not make adequate findings to support its decision.   After consideration of this issue and all others presented, we hold that the findings given in support of the rate determination are inadequate and remand the case to the Commission for further proceedings.

I.   History of the Case

* * * As part of its operations, Florida Gas transports gas produced in Texas and Louisiana by Sun Oil Company (hereinafter "Sun Oil" or "Sun") to Florida Power Corporation (hereinafter "Florida Power") and Florida Power and Light Company (hereinafter "Florida P & L").   The rates charged for this transportation are set forth in FPC Rate Schedules T–1 (for Florida Power) and T–2 (for Florida P & L).   Sun Oil has entered into contracts with Florida Power and Florida P & L whereby the price it receives for gas sold to these companies is tied to Florida Gas' transportation rates. * * *

On August 14, 1965, in what was later designated FPC Docket No. RP66–4, Florida Gas filed to increase its T–1 rate from 14.6 cents to 17.9 cents per MM Btu and its T–2 rate from 18.5 cents to 21.9 cents per MM Btu. * * * These new rates became effective, subject to refund, on November 1, 1965.

Early in 1967 hearings were held before one of the Commission's Hearing Examiners to determine whether Sun Oil was entitled to a refund under the new rates.   In the meantime Florida Gas received authorization from the Commission for a major expansion of its pipeline capacity. * * *   In this separate proceeding Florida Gas had offered to make certain rate reductions and the Commission in its opinion conditioned the company's expansion upon its adoption of these lower rates. * * * The Commission also stated that a rate investigation * * * would be held to determine whether the new rates were reasonable in light of Florida Gas' expanded operation. * * * On March 31, 1967, in what later became Docket RP68-1, Florida Gas made the rate reduction filing required by the Commission. Shortly thereafter Sun Oil moved for consolidation of this docket with the RP66-4 rate proceedings. The Commission granted this motion and later allowed yet another rate proceeding, Docket RP69-2, to be consolidated with the earlier two dockets.

The reduced T-1 and T-2 rates involved in Docket RP68-1 went into effect on June 10, 1968. Docket RP66-4, the only proceeding at issue here, therefore relates only to the "locked in" period from November 1, 1965 to June 9, 1968. * * *

The consolidated cases were then "phased," that is, the Commission first determined the rates of return, leaving the other issues involving cost of service and rate design to be resolved at a later date. In the proceedings before the Commission's Hearing Examiner in the first "phase," the primary issue presented as to Docket RP66-4 was whether Florida Gas was estopped from claiming a rate of return greater than 6.5 per cent. The rates it requested in its original filing in 1965 were designed to generate this return, and the Commission's Staff felt the company was bound by this figure. * * * Since the rates in effect during the "locked in" period of this docket had in fact generated a return of 6.98 per cent, the Staff felt Sun Oil was entitled to a refund.

The Examiner rejected this argument, holding that Florida Gas was not bound by the rate of return utilized in its original filing. * * * He could not determine from the record before him what would be a fair and reasonable rate of return * * *, apparently because "no one cross-examined the principal rate of return evidence put in the record by Florida Gas [or] * * * put in an answering case or evidence of any kind on the subject." * * * The Examiner did feel, however, that Florida Gas had established a prima facie case for the 6.98 per cent actually earned. * * * To provide "fairness to all sides" * * * the Examiner allowed Sun Oil and the Commission's Staff thirty days after the issuance of his opinion in which to present new evidence. * * *

Neither Sun Oil nor the Commission's Staff took advantage of this opportunity to contest the merits of the 6.98 figure before the Examiner. Instead, they appealed his decisions in all three dockets to the Commission * * *. With regard to Docket RP66-4, the Commission agreed with the Examiner that Florida Gas was not limited by its filing to a 6.5 per cent rate of return. * * * It held that a fair and reasonable rate of return for the "locked in" period involved in this docket would be 7 per cent, which allowed Florida Gas a return on equity of 9.36 per cent. * * * For the later two dockets the Commission allowed a rate of return of 7.25 per cent, which would result in a return on equity of 9.9 per cent. * * * Sun applied for a rehearing, contesting only the rate of return allowed in Docket RP66–4. It alleged that this rate was not supported by substantial evidence or adequate findings and that the Examiner, by in effect requesting Sun Oil to come forward with additional evidence, unlawfully shifted the burden of proof from Florida Gas to Sun Oil. The Commission denied Sun's application and this appeal followed.

* * *

In the leading case of Bluefield Waterworks and Improvement Co. v. Public Service Comm., 262 U.S. 679, the Supreme Court set forth guidelines as to what constitutes a proper return on equity, return on equity being the critical factor involved in determining rate of return. There the court said:

A public utility is entitled to such rates as will permit it to earn a return on the value of the property which it employs for the convenience of the public equal to that generally being made at the same time and in the same general part of the country on investments in other business undertakings which are attended by corresponding risks, and uncertainties; but it has no constitutional right to profits such as are realized or anticipated in highly profitable enterprises or speculative ventures. The return should be reasonably sufficient to assure confidence in the financial soundness of the utility and should be adequate, under efficient and economical management, to maintain and support its credit and enable it to raise the money necessary for the proper discharge of its public duties.

* * * Judgments made under these guidelines are obviously qualitative, and, since the Commission is acknowledged to have expertise in this complex field, its decisions are entitled to great weight. It is, however, required under the Administrative Procedure Act, 5 U.S.C.A. § 1001 et seq. (1964), to include in each of its decisions "a statement of * * * findings and conclusions, as well as the reasons or basis therefor, upon all the material issues of fact, law or discretion presented on the record * * *" 5 U.S.C.A. § 1007(b) (1964). These findings and conclusions must be sufficient to demonstrate that the Commission has considered "all relevant facts" * * * and that it has "exercised its practical, expert judgment." * * *

In the Docket RP66–4 portion of its opinion the Commission first summarized briefly the testimony of Dr. Dorau, Florida Gas' witness, who had "presented evidence of comparable earnings, cost of debt capital and the return needed for capital attraction" and had concluded that a rate of return of 6.88 per cent would not be excessive. * * * The Commission then gave the equity and debt ratios and the cost of embedded debt for Florida Gas for the period in question and stated that it had reviewed the other economic evidence in the record. * * * Finally, the Commission reviewed the rates of return and returns on equity actually earned by other natural gas companies and by companies in the Bell System and indicated that it used these comparative earnings as a basis in determining that Florida Gas' rate of return should be seven per cent.   *   *   *

After reviewing several earlier rate of return cases, the Eighth Circuit concluded [in State Corp. Com'n of Kansas v. FPC, 206 F.2d 690 (1953), concerning the Northern Natural Gas Company] that "much broader discussions and considerations were gone into in other cases than are to be found in the Commission's opinion in the case under review."   *   *   *   Although the court agreed that comparative yields on common stocks were relevant in determining rates, it did not believe they were so all important as to obviate the need for consideration of such matters as the financial history and position of Northern.   *   *   *   Moreover, it felt the Commission's study of comparative yields was of questionable validity because the Commission had not first weighed Northern's risks against those of the other companies whose yields were compared with Northern's.   *   *   *   Finally, the court said that the Commission's statement that it had examined all the evidence in the record was not sufficient to show "that the conclusion of the Commission as to the rate of return is the result of the application of the Commission's expertise and judgment   *   *   *."   *   *   *

*   *   *   [C]omparative earnings, like comparative yields, cannot be applied directly to determine the rate of return for a given company; more intensive economic analysis of the company is required. Thus, in Natural Gas Pipeline Co. of America, 40 F.P.C. 81, 90 (1968), it was held that actual earnings of other utility companies could be used only to set a ceiling on the rate of return to be allowed.   There the Commission said that these earnings "[are] not amenable to a direct translation into a rate of return allowance" because the companies being used for purposes of comparison might have different risks than the company under consideration, might be regulated by agencies with different standards than the Commission, and might have earnings from activities not regulated by any agency.   *   *   *

Even   *   *   *   the Commission recognized the dangers involved in using comparative earnings in rate of return determinations.   In criticizing Dr. Dorau's testimony as to the proper rate to be allowed in Dockets RP68–1 and RP69–2 it stated:

> Dr. Dorau's conclusion is a manifestation of the doctrine that actual earnings of other companies are fair return, which in turn becomes the standard against which lesser returns are to be deemed less than a fair return.   But actual earnings of other companies by reason of being earned are not thereby converted into fair return.   Among the many difficulties and complexities entailed in comparing earnings in addition to varying capital structures and operational problems, is, in many instances, the necessity to adjust for the upward bias due to the impact of non-utility

* * * The Commission thus seems to have ignored its own better judgment and to have relied heavily on the evidence of actual earnings of other utility companies in setting the RP66–4 rate of return.

Even if the Commission did use these rates only to set a ceiling this portion of its opinion, standing alone, would be defective because the other findings and conclusions contained therein are not sufficient to support the Commission's rate of return determination. We must, therefore, consider whether the findings and conclusions * * * provide adequate support for the RP66–4 rate determination.

* * *

The Commission consolidated its discussion of the factors bearing upon the rates of return to be allowed in Dockets RP68–1 and RP69–2. In this discussion it first analyzed the risks involved in Florida Gas' operation and concluded that the company was "no more of a risk than other mature pipelines." * * * It then stated that in setting the rates of return for Dockets RP68–1 and RP69–2 it gave full consideration to the fact that Florida Gas' cost of embedded debt for the period covered by these dockets was a high 6.21 per cent. * * * Next, the Commission quoted figures which showed that the rate of return on equity allowed Florida Gas was in the lower range of equity allowances given in contested rate of return cases since 1960. * * * Finally, the Commission noted with approval that Florida Gas had increased the percentage of debt in its capital structure.

The factors given above are those the Commission normally considers in making rate of return determinations. However, there is no indication that the Commission considered these factors in setting the RP66–4 rates; in fact, all indications are to the contrary. * * *

The Commission's statement * * * to the effect that actual earnings of other utility companies establish a basis for setting rates of return * * * seems to indicate that the Commission based this determination in large part upon its analysis of these comparative earnings. The statement thus lends credence to the premise that the Commission ignored many of the factors mentioned later in its opinion in setting the RP66–4 rate of return.

Finally, * * * [t]he Examiner did not make specific findings on the evidence presented as to this docket. Moreover, he made the revealing comment "that the final answer [as to what is a fair rate of return] is not yet available from this record." * * * The Examiner's failure to make findings and his criticism of the record do not of themselves render the Commission's rate of return determination invalid. They do, however, provide yet another indication that the evidence Florida Gas presented as to Docket RP66–4 was at no point subjected to intensive analysis by the Commission.

* * *

Reversed and remanded for proceedings consistent with this opinion.

J. SKELLY WRIGHT, Circuit Judge (dissenting):
* * *

The classic statement of the standard to be applied in determining a fair return on equity is found in *Hope Natural Gas, supra,* 320 U.S. at 603, 64 S.Ct. at 288: " * * * [T]he return to the equity owner should be commensurate with returns on investments in other enterprises having corresponding risks. That return, however, should be sufficient to assure confidence in the financial integrity of the enterprise, so as to maintain its credit and to attract capital." * * *

In any event, the record here fully supports the Commission's findings which, though lacking in detail, are completely adequate when taken with those of the examiner adopted by the Commission. In allowing Florida Gas 9.36 per cent return on equity, the Commission followed the same pattern of decision as in all its pipeline rate of return cases since 1960. As the Commission indicated, in about three fourths of the contested cases during that time, the equity return allowed was 9.5 per cent or more. The Commission issued three rate of return decisions within the year prior to the issuance of its opinion on review and one within six months thereafter. All of these decisions are completely consistent with the one here, not only as to rate of return on equity, but on the type of evidence produced and the findings made. In fact, in all of them the allowance for equity holders was in excess of 9.36 per cent.

The Commission also found that 9.36 per cent equity return is consistent, not only with the return allowed other pipelines, but with the return allowed electric utilities and the Bell System. The record before the Commission also included complete equity return data on six principal industry groups outlined and explained as it relates to this case by a witness admittedly expert in the field. Thus the record as a whole completely supports the Commission's findings and decision. Fortified with the pertinent economic and financial facts bearing on equity return on investments in similar enterprises having corresponding risks and guided by the *Hope Natural Gas* standards, the Commission has made its findings and rendered its decision in this case. * * *

We should remember the basic teaching of *Hope Natural Gas:*

" * * * If the total effect of the rate order cannot be said to be unjust and unreasonable, judicial inquiry under the Act is at an end. The fact that the method employed to reach that result may contain infirmities is not then important. Moreover, the Commission's order does not become suspect by reason of the fact that it is challenged. It is the product of expert judgment which carries a presumption of validity. And he who would upset the rate order under the Act carries the heavy burden of making a convincing showing that it is invalid because it is unjust and unreasonable in its consequences. * * * "

320 U.S. at 602, 64 S.Ct. at 288. Sending this case back to the Commission, in my opinion, is an exercise in wheel-spinning. There is no

real possibility that Sun Oil will get the $1,000,000 it claims. The record in this case and the result in almost every other pipeline case before the Commission support the Commission's order under review. Moreover, on remand the Commission in good conscience could not set a return on equity lower than the 9.36 per cent in this case when in the same proceeding between the same parties, involving the same gas, albeit for a slightly later period, the Commission has set a return on equity of 9.9 per cent which is not even contested on review.

I respectfully dissent.

NOR–AM AGRICULTURAL PRODUCTS, INC. v. HARDIN

United States Court of Appeals, Seventh Circuit, 1970.
435 F.2d 1151.

CUMMINGS, Circuit Judge. This is an appeal from a preliminary injunction granted by the district court which effectually restrains the Secretary of Agriculture * * * from continuing the suspension of the registration of 17 Panogenic compounds as "economic poisons" under the Federal Insecticide, Fungicide and Rodenticide Act. 7 U.S. C.A. § 135 et seq. * * *

Plaintiff Morton International, Inc. manufactures seventeen types of cyano (methylmercuri) guanadine known as Panogens. Plaintiff Nor-Am Agricultural Products, Inc. distributes Morton's Panogens. These mercury compounds are used as fungicides in treating seeds intended for planting. They were duly registered as "economic poisons" with the Secretary of Agriculture, as required * * *.

* * * [O]n February 18, 1970, the Department of Agriculture telegraphed plaintiff Nor-Am that its Panogen registrations had been suspended "in view of the recent accident involving the ingestion of pork from hog feed seed treated with cyano (methylmercuri) guanadine." * * * [T]he registration of the 17 Panogens was suspended "[t]o prevent an imminent hazard to the public from the use of cyano (methylmercuri) guanadine as a seed treatment." * * * [T]hree New Mexico children had been hospitalized in a comatose condition because they had eaten pork from hogs fed screenings and sweepings from seed previously treated with a fungicide product containing cyano (methylmercuri) guanadine. * * * [O]ther incidents had been reported showing that mercury treated seed screenings and sweepings had been fed to livestock or "disposed of in a manner that results in wildlife feeding on them." Finally, * * * ingestion of cyano (methylmercuri) guanadine reportedly caused irreversible injury to the central nervous system.

* * *

Administrative review of the Secretary's order was initiated on March 27, 1970, when Nor-Am requested an expedited administrative hearing * * *. Instead of awaiting such a hearing, however, plaintiffs filed this suit on April 9, 1970, and quickly sought a preliminary injunction. Thereupon defendants moved to dismiss the proceeding. They claimed that the district court lacked jurisdiction to review the suspension order in advance of the hearing established by the statute; that plaintiffs had not exhausted the administrative procedures established by the Act; that the Secretary's order was a non-reviewable, discretionary act; and that the Secretary had not acted arbitrarily or capriciously. * * *

At the hearing on the motion for the preliminary injunction, two Nor-Am employees and the general manager of a seed improvement association testified that Panogen products had been marketed for 20 years as a very useful fungicide seed treatment. Nothing as economical or efficacious is available as a satisfactory substitute for liquid methylmercury seed treatment products. Plaintiffs added a red dye to their products in order to prevent misuse of treated seed as human or animal feed. Warning labels were also prepared by plaintiffs for use on their products and on the treated seed containers. Plaintiffs' witnesses knew of no "permanent" injuries caused by Panogens.

* * *

* * * The district judge determined that unless preliminary injunctive relief were granted, plaintiffs would suffer irreparable harm for which they had no adequate administrative or legal remedy, although they were "likely to prevail on the merits." The judge further concluded that preliminary relief was "consistent with the public interest." Accordingly, he held the suspension of the Panogen registrations to have been arbitrary, capricious, and contrary to law, and defendants were enjoined from taking action against plaintiffs or the Panogens in reliance on the suspension order. * * * Finally, the preliminary injunction permitted defendants to issue notices of cancellation of the registrations of these "economic poisons" effective only after * * * public hearing * * *. Upon consideration of this cause * * *, we are of the opinion that the district court lacked power to grant this relief because the plaintiffs have not exhausted their administrative remedy.

The fundamental provisions regulating judicial review of administrative actions are contained in the 1946 Administrative Procedure Act. * * *

"Agency action made reviewable by statute and final agency action for which there is no other adequate remedy in a court are subject to judicial review. A preliminary, procedural, or intermediate agency action or ruling not directly reviewable is subject to review on the review of the final agency action. * * *" * * *

In determining the status of the instant suspension in the light of the Administrative Procedure Act, we must turn first to the pertinent provisions of the Federal Insecticide, Fungicide and Rodenticide Act. * * *

* * * Congress provided for emergency action by permitting immediate suspension of registration in the face of "an imminent haz-

ard to the public." 7 U.S.C.A. § 135b(c). In almost the same breath, however, Congress recognized the need for prompt determination of the accuracy of the Secretary's judgment and provided that in the wake of an emergency suspension the Secretary should "give the registrant prompt notice of such action and afford the registrant the opportunity to have the matter submitted to an advisory committee and for an expedited hearing under this section."

The 1964 Amendments also added special provisions for judicial review of agency actions directed toward denial, suspension, or cancellation of the registration of "economic poisons." * * *

"[f]inal orders of the Secretary under this section shall be subject to judicial review, in accordance with the provisions of subsection d. * * *" 7 U.S.C.A. § 135b(c).

* * *

[T]hese statutory provisions do not expressly or impliedly contemplate immediate review of emergency suspensions. * * *. Implicit * * * is the limitation on judicial review resulting from the specific extension on review * * * only to "final orders of the Secretary." * * *

Equally unacceptable is the contention that an emergency suspension order is a "final order" of the Secretary * * *. That limitation on judicial review serves to avoid delay and interference with agency proceedings by confining review to orders effectively terminating administrative adjudication. * * * By its very nature * * * the emergency suspension of registration represents a tentative, temporary measure. This interlocutory character is unaltered by the inclusion of the customary prerequisite that the hazard be "imminent." It is preliminary to more thorough administrative consideration of the hazardous condition of the "poisons." The statute expressly contemplates special proceedings to follow suspension posthaste. These include the informal submission of the disputed matters to an advisory committee of experts whose report and recommendations become part of the record for consideration at the expedited hearing and * * * on judicial review. The emergency suspension becomes final only if unopposed or affirmed, in whole or in part, by subsequent decision based upon a full and formal consideration.

The provisions for judicial review * * * also compel the inference that the emergency action of the Secretary by no means culminates administrative proceedings on the matters of registration of an "economic poison." Review is not "de novo" in a trial court; rather, it is based on the substantiality of the evidence in the administrative record and is before the appropriate court of appeals. Such provisions with respect to judicial review are classic indications that Congress intended administrative adjudications to proceed to conclusion prior to judicial scrutiny.

We conclude that Congress intended to confine judicial review of registration disputes * * * to final orders of the Secretary culminating administrative adjudication. Under this Act, the emergency suspension of registration   *   *   *   does not constitute such a final order   *   *   *.

Plaintiffs contend that this order should nevertheless entitle them to review under the "final agency action" provision of Section 10(c) of the Administrative Procedure Act. They argue that suspension of registration by the Secretary possesses sufficient "finality" as an administrative action to warrant immediate recourse to the courts despite its status as a preliminary act within the framework * * * of the Federal Insecticide, Fungicide and Rodenticide Act. Suspension, they urge, immediately and drastically affects their rights and interests as greatly as formally finalized cancellation. * * * Unless they are permitted this exceptional remedy, they claim that the Secretary's findings amount to autonomous discretion.

      *   *   *

The function of the Secretary's emergency power, as well as the practical exigencies of coordinating administrative and judicial machinery, militates against avoiding the prescribed procedures. The emergency suspension of registration of an economic poison * * * involves highly discretionary administrative action with deeply rooted antecedents in the realm of public health and safety. * * * Where, as here, Congress follows discretionary preliminary or interlocutory agency action with specially fashioned adjudicative machinery, strict observance of the prescribed procedure prior to judicial intervention is compellingly indicated.

Precipitous judicial review * * * strains administrative resources at a stage in the process which is most delicate * * *. The administrative process is interrupted before issues have been crystalized and narrowed and without affording opportunity for application of technical expertise and informed judgment. * * * At the very least, however, the agency must postpone its further proceedings (even if it plans ultimately to expedite them) pending the outcome of judicial review. Not only may this aggravate the harm suffered by the innocent registrant by prolonging litigation, but it unnecessarily encumbers governmental efforts and may have the adverse effect of coloring further agency actions.

      *   *   *   [H]ere, judicial review is sought of the factual basis supporting an emergency order which itself initiates clearly defined adjudicatory proceedings within the agency. These distinctions were expressly recognized by the Court in *Abbott Laboratories* when it distinguished Ewing v. Mytinger & Casselberry, Inc., 339 U.S. 594, by pointing out that the

> "drug manufacturer in *Ewing* was quite obviously seeking an unheard-of form of relief which, if allowed, would have permitted interference in the early stages of an administrative determination as to specific facts, and would have prevented the regular operation of the seizure procedures established by the Act." 387 U.S. at p. 148.

Similarly, we find distinguishable and inapplicable the holding in Environmental Defense Fund, Incorporated v. Hardin, 428 F.2d 1093 (D.C.Cir.1970) * * *. There the Secretary of Agriculture refused to issue notices of emergency suspension or cancellation for DDT and the Court concluded that due to his inaction there were no further administrative proceedings available to the interested parties under the Federal Insecticide, Fungicide and Rodenticide Act. In contrast, issuance of a notice of emergency suspension under Section 4(c) of the present Act specifically results in further formal agency proceedings.
* * *

* * * Here the plaintiffs have not yet exhausted their statutorily prescribed administrative remedies and there has as yet been no "final agency action" within Section 10(c) of the Administrative Procedure Act.

* * * [P]laintiffs urge that the equity powers of the court have been properly invoked to prevent irreparable injury caused by the suspension order.

The circumvention of clearly prescribed administrative procedures by awarding equitable relief is an exceptional practice. As explained in Aircraft & Diesel Equipment Corp. v. Hirsch, 331 U.S. 752, the rule that administrative remedies may occasionally be by-passed to protect strong private interests from irreparable harm

"is not one of mere convenience or ready application. * * * [A] strong showing is required, both of inadequacy of the prescribed procedure and of impending harm, to permit shortcircuiting the administrative process. * * *"

Plaintiffs have failed to establish such an irremediable threat to sufficiently strong interests to warrant equitable intercession at this juncture.

* * * Nothing in the nature of the objections raised by plaintiffs here suggests that exhaustion of agency remedies would be an exercise in futility. * * * The administrative agency has shown no incapacity or unwillingness to correct a demonstrably false suspension without advice from the courts. * * * Finally, failure of the courts to entertain a complaint at this time does not foreclose judicial review entirely. * * *

The primary interests threatened in this case are not public but private. They are interests of property rather than of life or liberty.
* * *

We do not demean plaintiffs' possible losses when noting moreover, that the temporary suspension affects business profits * * *. Where public health and safety demand emergency removal of a commodity from the market, even unrecoverable financial losses incurred *pendente lite* must be deemed an expense of the litigation itself.
* * *

Congress was not bound to supply the optimal protection to registrants affected by emergency suspensions. Congress balanced the public and private interests when it fashioned not only the Secretary's discretionary power but also the administrative procedures to follow exercise of that power. The Court's conclusion in Ewing v. Mytinger & Casselberry, Inc., 339 U.S. 594, is applicable to this case with equal force:

> "The purpose of the * * * provision is plain. It is to arrest the distribution of an article that is dangerous, or whose labeling is fraudulent or misleading, pending a determination of the issue of adulteration or misbranding. The public therefore has a stake in the jurisdictional issue before us. If the District Court can step in, stay the institution of [suspensions], and bring the administrative regulation to a halt until it hears the case, the public will be denied the speedy protection which Congress provided by [suspension]. * * * Congress weighed the potential injury to the public from misbranded articles against the injury to the purveyor of the article from a temporary interference with its distribution and decided in favor of the speedy, preventive device of [suspension]. We would impair or destroy the effectiveness of that device if we sanctioned the interference which a grant of jurisdiction to the District Court would entail."

* * * In reaching this conclusion, we express no opinion on the merits of the controversy between these parties concerning the registration of Panogens.

The preliminary injunction is dissolved and the case is remanded to the district court with instructions to dismiss the complaint.

Reversed.

PELL, Circuit Judge (dissenting).

* * *

The crucial and basic question here involved, * * * in my opinion, is whether judicial intervention is permissible in the event of arbitrary and capricious administrative action. I do not find in the present majority opinion confrontation with this issue. The record before us cries out that the governmental suspension of Panogen as an economic poison was bottomed on the emotional impact of a single incident, one which was tragic and yet one which there was no reason for thinking would be repeated. When a product has been successfully used on the market for more than twenty years and is essential for agriculture, and when there has been no other recorded incident that the use of the product has been detrimental to the public health, I can reach no conclusion other than that the suspension was, in the technical and legal sense, an arbitrary and capricious one.

* * *

* * * [O]n the evening of February 17, 1970 there was a national television broadcast on the Huntley-Brinkley newscast which discussed and portrayed the Alamogordo, New Mexico tragic incident. On the very next day, the registration was suspended. It takes no particular application of judicial knowledge to be aware of the nationwide coverage achieved by the particular television program. It takes no

great perception in reading the record to conceive the emotional impact involved when three young children are rendered virtually vegetables.

*   *   *

As this dissent was being prepared, the Nobel Peace Prize was awarded to an American agricultural scientist for studies that developed wheat strains giving bigger yields in older types, thereby helping the world's hunger problems. The scientist had pioneered in breeding new varieties of disease-resistant wheat plants. Disease resistance was the purpose of Panogen's development. Such research highlights the belief of many informed individuals that three or four more decades will bring upon us a real crisis in feeding the world's population. Whether, as might be argued, the minimal dangers to a few people through misuse of a valuable agricultural product is less important than the overall threat of eventual failure to be able to feed the world is not a problem to which this court need address itself. It is a problem, however, to which in my opinion the administrative agency should have addressed itself, and in depth, prior to exercising its extraordinary power of immediate suspension.

At the hearing in the district court on a motion for the preliminary injunction, the evidence, which was not contradicted, reflected that no product as economical nor as efficacious was available as a satisfactory substitute for liquid methylmercuri seed treatment.

*   *   *

*   *   * The government testimony reflected that the only permanent human injuries to the knowledge of the department were to the three Alamogordo children. Hogs owned by the children's father had died, but they had been fed poisoned feed as a result of a misuse of the treated seed which was never intended for feed purposes. *   * Next, the testimony indicated that the effects had been observed in pheasant, quail and other wildlife *   *   *. The scientific community, according to the testimony, has discovered no effective antidote for alkylmercury compounds. In varying degrees, this is no doubt true of many poisonous substances, but they are tolerated if in their proper use they serve a worthwhile purpose. *   *   *

In this country I dare say there are very few barns, medicine chests or even kitchen cupboards which do not have products contained therein which would be extremely detrimental to people if misused. In the case on appeal the evidence amply supports a misuse of the product in the Alamogordo situation. The fact that misuse may result in damage does not in my opinion make a product imminently hazardous in the absence of an evidentiary showing that such misuse is frequent or was reasonably likely to occur.

The doctrine of exhaustion of administrative remedies is pragmatic in origin. It wears no constitutional halo. I can conceive no valid justification for its wooden and mechanistic application where the expertise which the rationale of the rule seeks to protect is so singularly not exercised, as in the case before us. Nor does the prac-

ticality of the doctrine in the overall scheme of governmental operation necessarily require slavish homage to it.

* * *

* * * [W]ith regard to the Alamogordo incident, which apparently was the real basis of the secretary's order of suspension, this
was not an established fact but was assumed for the purpose of the
case to have been caused by the Panogen. As the district judge stated
on the assumption basis, "the record establishes a unique combination of circumstances which are unlikely to recur, including diversion
of treated material to animal feed, disregard of label cautions and
warnings, slaughter of a hog after it showed signs of illness, and continued eating by a single family of contaminated food from a slaugh-
tered hog after twelve of the same pen of hogs had died and two had
become blind."

* * *

Another significant aspect in the present case is that the plaintiffs and the other distributors and manufacturers were not required
to recall existing stocks from customers. While it is true that problems of disposition presented themselves, these have been surmounted
where a real and hazardous situation existed of significant proportions * * *. If Panogen were of the caliber of imminent hazard
to the public requiring a suspension order, certainly it would seem that
an absolute recall would have been necessary.

* * *

The present majority opinion also states that the plaintiff's direct
and immediate concern is the impact of suspension on their business
rather than the claimed danger to farmers and consumers from removal of their product. No doubt this is true although the profit motive is not a dishonorable one in our country. Even if it is true, this
makes the detriment of the elimination of the product no less real to
the farmers and consumers.

* * *

UNITED STATES v. MORTON SALT CO.

Supreme Court of the United States, 1950.
338 U.S. 632, 70 S.Ct. 357, 94 L.Ed. 401.

Mr. Justice JACKSON delivered the opinion of the Court.

* * *

Proceedings under § 5 of the Federal Trade Commission Act culminated in a Commission order requiring respondents Morton Salt
Company and International Salt Company, together with eighteen
other salt producers and a trade association, to cease and desist from
stated practices in connection with the pricing, producing and marketing of salt. The Court of Appeals for the Seventh Circuit affirmed
the order. * * * The decree directed that reports of the manner
of compliance be filed with the Commission within ninety days, but

it reserved jurisdiction "to enter such further orders herein from time to time as may become necessary effectively to enforce compliance in every respect with this decree and to prevent evasion thereof." * * * The reports of compliance were subsequently filed and accepted, and there the matter appears to have rested for a little upwards of four years.

On September 2, 1947, the Commission ordered additional and highly particularized reports to show continuing compliance with the decree. * * * The new order recited that it was issued on the Commission's own motion pursuant to its published Rule of Practice No. XXVI * * *. It ordered * * * "additional reports showing in detail the manner and form in which they have been, and are now, complying with said modified order to cease and desist and said decree." It demanded of each producer a "complete statement" of the "prices, terms, and conditions of sale of salt, together with books or compilations of freight rates used in calculating delivered prices, price lists and price announcements distributed, published or employed in marketing salt from and after January 1, 1944." * * * The Association and some of the producers reported satisfactorily. These two respondents did not. * * *

The Commission next gave respondents notices asserting their default * * *. Neither respondent asked any hearing on the notice of default. These suits were then commenced in the name of the United States in District Court * * * asking mandatory injunctions commanding respondents to report as directed * * *. The court found no dispute as to material facts and dismissed the complaints for want of jurisdiction. * * * The Court of Appeals * * * affirmed. * * * We granted certiorari * * *.

The Government's suits and the Commission's order are challenged upon a variety of grounds * * *. [T]hat (1) the order constitutes an interference with the decree and an invasion of the powers of the Court of Appeals; (2) the Commission's Rule XXVI is *ultra vires* and violates the Federal Administrative Procedure Act, 5 U.S. C.A. § 1001 et seq.; (3) the procedure is unauthorized by those sections of the Act on which it is based; (4) it is novel and arbitrary and violates the Fourth and Fifth Amendments to the Constitution. * * * [W]e reject each of these contentions.

　　　* * *

It seems conceded * * * that some power or duty, independently of the decree, must still have resided in the Commission. Certainly entry of the court decree did not wholly relieve the Commission of responsibility for its enforcement. The decree recognized that. It left to the Commission the right and hence the responsibility "to initiate contempt proceedings for the violation of this decree." This must have contemplated that the Commission could obtain accurate information from time to time on which to base a responsible conclusion that there was or was not cause for such a proceeding. * * * In addition, the Trade Commission has a continuing duty to prevent unfair methods of competition and unfair or deceptive acts or practices in commerce. That responsibility as to all within the coverage of the Act is not suspended or exhausted as to any violator whose guilt is once established.

* * *

* * * May not the Commission, in view of its residual duty of enforcement affirmatively satisfy itself that the decree is being observed? Whether this usurps the courts' own function is, we think, answered by consideration of the fundamental relationship between the courts and administrative bodies.

The Trade Commission Act is one of several in which Congress, to make its policy effective, has relied upon the initiative of administrative officials and the flexibility of the administrative process. Its agencies are provided with staffs to institute proceedings and to follow up decrees and police their obedience. While that process at times is adversary, it also at times is inquisitorial. These agencies are expected to ascertain when and against whom proceedings should be set in motion and to take the lead in following through to effective results.

* * *

* * * Courts are not expected to start wheels moving or to follow up judgments. Courts neither have, nor need, sleuths to dig up evidence, staffs to analyze reports, or personnel to prepare prosecutions for contempts. * * *

The court in this case advisedly left it to the Commission to receive the report of compliance and to institute any contempt proceedings. * * * In the case before us, it is true that the Commission's cease and desist order was merged in the court's decree; but the court neither assumed to itself nor denied to the Commission that agency's duty to inform itself and protect commerce against continued or renewed unlawful practice.

This case illustrates the difference between the judicial function and the function the Commission is attempting to perform. * * * Federal judicial power itself extends only to adjudication of cases and controversies and it is natural that its investigative powers should be jealously confined to these ends. * * *

* * * Because judicial power is reluctant if not unable to summon evidence until it is shown to be relevant to issues in litigation, it does not follow that an administrative agency charged with seeing that the laws are enforced may not have and exercise powers of original inquiry. It has a power of inquisition, if one chooses to call it that, which is not derived from the judicial function. * * * When investigative and accusatory duties are delegated by statute to an administrative body, it * * * may take steps to inform itself as to whether there is probable violation of the law.

Of course, the Commission cannot intrude upon or usurp the court's function of adjudication. * * * What the Commission has done, however, is not to modify but to follow up this decree. It has not asked this report in the name of the court, or in reliance upon judicial powers, but in reliance upon its own law-enforcing powers.

* * *   Congress obviously deemed it a function of the Commission, rather than of the courts, to probe compliance with such decrees * * *.

* * * Our * * * concern * * * is whether the Commission's order infringes prerogatives of the court. We hold it does not.

* * *

The Administrative Procedure Act was framed against a background of rapid expansion of the administrative process as a check upon administrators whose zeal might otherwise have carried them to excesses not contemplated in legislation creating their offices. It created safeguards even narrower than the constitutional ones, against arbitrary official encroachment on private rights.

Thus § 3(a) of the Act requires every agency to which it applies, which includes the Federal Trade Commission, to publish in the Federal Register certain statements of its rules, organization and procedure * * *. In addition § 6(b) proscribes any requirement of a report or other investigative demand "in any manner or for any purpose except as authorized by law."

Principally on the basis of these two sections respondents contend that the current order cannot be enforced except in violation of the Administrative Procedure Act. * * *

* * * [T]he Federal Trade Commission published in the Federal Register its Rules * * *. The Commission's Rule XXVI * * * sets the time limit for filing initial reports of compliance with Commission orders and asserts the Commission's right to require, within its sound discretion, the filing of further compliance reports thereafter. * * *

We conclude that the Commission's published Rule XXVI announced the right it claims in this case to demand of a party against whom an enforcement decree has been entered that it "file with the Commission, from time to time thereafter, further reports in writing, setting forth in detail the manner and form in which they are complying with said order * * *." * * *

Respondents hardly challenge this conclusion. Theirs is the more subtle argument that requirement of supplemental reports following court enforcement of a Commission order is unauthorized by statute * * * so that no valid notice * * * had been or could be given * * *. This leads to the question of statutory authority for the order to report * * *.

The Court of Appeals found the Commission to be without statutory authority to require additional reports as to compliance. * * * Respondents also say that the present use of the asserted power is novel and unprecedented in Commission practice and introduces a new method of investigating compliance. * * *

The Commission's organic Act, § 5, comprehensively provides substantive and procedural rules for checking unfair methods of competition. The procedure is complete from complaint and service of process through final order, court review, and enforcement proceedings to recover penalties * * *.

Section 6, on which the Commission relies, * * * adds the power "to investigate from time to time the organization, business, conduct, practices, and management of any corporation engaged in commerce, * * * and its relation to other corporations and to individuals, associations, and partnerships." It also authorizes the Commission "to require, by general or special orders, corporations engaged in commerce * * * to file with the commission in such form as the commission may prescribe, annual or special, or both annual and special, reports or answers in writing to specific questions, furnishing to the commission such information as it may require as to the organization, business, conduct, practices, management, and relation to other corporations, partnerships, and individuals of the respective corporations filing such reports or answers in writing."

* * * Respondents are in the class subject to inquiry, the call is for what appears to be a special report and the matter to be reported would seem to be as to business conduct and practices about which the Commission is authorized to inquire. * * *

* * * The information was such as the Commission was authorized to obtain and we think it could be required for use in determining whether there had been proper compliance with the court's decree * * *.

* * * An annual report of a corporation is a recurrent and relatively standardized affair. The special report was used to enable the Commission to elicit any information beyond the ordinary data of a routine annual report. If the report asked here is not a special report, we would be hard put to define one.

* * *

We conclude that the authority of the Commission under § 6 to require special reports of corporations includes special reports of the manner in which they are complying with decrees enforcing § 5 cease and desist orders.

* * *

The Commission's order is criticized upon grounds that the order transgresses the Fourth Amendment's proscription of unreasonable searches and seizures and the Fifth Amendment's due process of law clause.

* * * [N]either incorporated nor unincorporated associations can plead an unqualified right to conduct their affairs in secret.
* * *

While they may and should have protection from unlawful demands made in the name of public investigation * * * corporations can claim no equality with individuals in the enjoyment of a right to privacy. * * * They are endowed with public attributes.

They have a collective impact upon society, from which they derive the privilege of acting as artificial entities. The Federal Government allows them the privilege of engaging in interstate commerce. * * * Even if one were to regard the request for information in this case as caused by nothing more than official curiosity, nevertheless law-enforcing agencies have a legitimate right to satisfy themselves that corporate behavior is consistent with the law and the public interest.

Of course a governmental investigation into corporate matters may be of such a sweeping nature and so unrelated to the matter properly under inquiry as to exceed the investigatory power. * * * But it is sufficient if the inquiry is within the authority of the agency, the demand is not too indefinite and the information sought is reasonably relevant. * * * Nothing on the face of the Commission's order transgressed these bounds.

* * * Before the courts will hold an order seeking information reports to be arbitrarily excessive, they may expect the supplicant to have made reasonable efforts before the Commission itself to obtain reasonable conditions. Neither respondent raised objection to the order's sweep, nor asked any modification, clarification or interpretation of it. Both challenged, instead, power to issue it. Their position was that the Commission had no more authority to issue a reasonable order than an unreasonable one. * * *

Of course, there are limits to what, in the name of reports, the Commission may demand. Just what these limits are we do not attempt to define in the abstract. * * *

* * * [I]n upholding this order upon this record, we are not to be understood as holding such orders exempt from judicial examination or as extending a license to exact as reports what would not reasonably be comprehended within that term as used by Congress in the context of this Act.

The judgment accordingly is reversed.

PHARMACEUTICAL MANUFACTURERS ASSOCIATION v. FINCH

United States District Court, D.Delaware, 1970.
307 F.Supp. 858.

LATCHUM, D. J. * * * [T]he Pharmaceutical Manufacturers Association ("PMA"), on behalf of its members, seeks a preliminary injunction restraining the Secretary of Health, Education and Welfare ("the Secretary") and the Commissioner of Food and Drugs ("the Commissioner") from taking any action in reliance upon the regulations contained in the Commission's Order of September 19, 1969 ("the September regulations"), 34 Fed.Reg. 14596. The September regulations promulgated new standards of evidence necessary to demonstrate the effectiveness of drug products and applied those standards retroactively so as to place in jeopardy the continued marketing of thousands of drug products introduced before 1962 with Food and Drug Administration ("FDA") approval and the effectiveness of which FDA has not yet challenged. Specifically, the regulations detail criteria for "adequate and well-controlled clinical investigations" that will be deemed by the Commissioner to constitute "substantial evidence" of effectiveness and excludes as irrelevant other clinical tests and documented clinical experience. The regulations further provide that when the Commissioner seeks to remove a product from the market for lack of substantial evidence of effectiveness, the affected drug company will be entitled to a hearing only if it demonstrates to the Commissioner an ability to produce substantial evidence before a hearing is held, and convinces the Commissioner that the efficacy of the drug in question is, in fact, supported by adequate and well controlled clinical investigation of the kind described in the regulations.

 * * * The vast majority of prescription drugs manufactured by plaintiff's member companies (aside from antibiotics) were "new drugs" when first developed and marketed * * *. Antibiotic drugs are marketed under a separate statutory scheme * * *.

From 1938, when the Act was first enacted, until 1962, there was no requirement that the effectiveness of a "new drug" be demonstrated * * * only the safety of the drug had to be established. * * *

In 1962, Congress amended Section 505 to require that new drugs be shown to be effective as well as safe before applications for marketing of such drugs are approved. Claims of "effectiveness" for a drug were required to be supported by "substantial evidence," * * * substantial evidence to mean—

> "evidence consisting of adequate and well-controlled investigations, including clinical investigations, by experts qualified by scientific training and experience to evaluate the effectiveness of the drug involved, on the basis of which it could fairly and responsibly be concluded by such experts that the drug will have the effect it purports or is represented to have under the conditions of use prescribed, recommended, or suggested in the labeling or proposed labeling thereof."

A separate but similar procedure * * * for the certification of antibiotic drugs has contained a requirement of efficacy as well as safety since its original enactment in 1945. * * *

Pursuant to the 1962 amendments, the FDA determined to undertake a review of the effectiveness of drugs that had been approved for marketing between 1938 and 1962. Thus, in 1966 the Agency entered into a contract with the National Academy of Sciences-National Research Council ("NAS–NRC") for the conduct of this effectiveness review * * *. Panels of physicians selected by the NAS–NRC * * * reviewed the claims for effectiveness of some 2800 drug products, and prepared reports for the FDA containing conclusions as to the effectiveness of these drugs. * * * In several instances, on the basis of conclusions of NAS–NRC panels, the FDA has initiated action to remove products from the market on the ground of lack of substantial evidence of effectiveness.

In two instances involving antibiotic combination drugs, the FDA (before issuing the September regulations) sought, on the basis of NAS–NRC reports * * * to require their removal from the market—before providing a hearing or before acting on objections filed by affected parties requesting a hearing. In both cases, the district court involved issued a preliminary injunction prohibiting the FDA from making effective any order removing the product from the market until thirty days after acting on objections filed by the parties—i. e., ruling as to whether "reasonable grounds" for a hearing had been stated by the affected party in its objection. * * * [B]oth Courts questioned (1) the correctness of the FDA's refusal to consider as relevant on the issue of effectiveness documented clinical experience and clinial tests other than those that meet the criteria of "adequate and well-controlled" and (2) FDA's theory that "reasonable grounds" for a hearing exist only when the Commissioner determines that the evidence presented to him does, in fact, constitute "substantial evidence" of effectiveness. Apparently, the questioned theories of the FDA in those two cases gave rise to the September regulations at issue in this case. These regulations, for the first time, set forth FDA's interpretation of the nature of the evidence required to provide substantial evidence of effectiveness under the Act. * * *

* * * PMA contends that the Commissioner exceeded his authority in substantially restricting the evidence which may be offered to establish the effectiveness of a drug product. Second, even assuming that the Commissioner has authority to promulgate the definition of substantial evidence set forth in the September regulations, PMA asserts that to apply the new requirements, without the Commissioner indicating the drugs whose effectiveness are in question and without affording an adequate period to carry out the testing required by the regulations before removing the drugs from the market, amounts to arbitrary and capricious administrative action. Third, PMA claims that the Commissioner, by requiring the presentafion of substantial evidence of a drug's effectiveness as a *condition* for obtaining a hearing, has impermissibly restricted the statutory right to a hearing to challenge the removal of a drug product. Finally, PMA contends that the regulations are invalid because they were issued without notice and opportunity for comment in violation of the requirements of Section 4 of the Administrative Procedure Act, 5 U.S.C.A. § 553.

* * * PMA's fourth contention is well taken and determinative of the present controversy * * *.

Section 4 of the Administrative Procedure Act, 5 U.S.C.A. § 553, requires that rule-making by an agency be preceded by "general notice of proposed rule-making" in the Federal Register at least thirty days before the effective date of the proposed rule, and further requires that the agency afford interested persons "an opportunity to participate in the rule making through submission of written data, views or arguments with or without opportunity for oral presentation." That procedure was not followed in this case. The September regulations were made effective by the Commissioner upon their publication in the Federal Register without prior notice or an opportunity for submission of comments by interested parties.

Exempt from the general requirements of notice and opportunity for comment are "interpretative rules, general statements of policy, or rules of agency organization, procedure, or practice." 5 U.S.C.A. § 553 (b) (A). The Commissioner has characterized the September regulations as "procedural and interpretative" * * *. But the label placed on the September rules by the Commissioner does not determine whether the notice and comment provisions are applicable. As the Supreme Court has emphasized, * * * "[T]he particular label placed upon it by the Commission is not necessarily conclusive, for it is the substance of what the Commission has purported to do and has done which is decisive." * * *

* * * [W]hether the regulations here involved are subject to the notice and comment provisions of Section 4 of the Administrative Procedure Act * * * must be made in the light of the basic purpose of those statutory requirements, * * * that when a proposed regulation of general applicability has a substantial impact on the regulated industry, or an important class of the members or the products of that industry, notice and opportunity for comment should first be provided.

* * *

The September regulations, which prescribe in specific detail, for the first time, the kinds of clinical investigations that will be deemed necessary to establish the effectiveness of existing and future drug products and which require that such evidence be submitted as a condition to avoiding summary removal from the market, are pervasive in their scope and have an immediate and substantial impact on the way PMA's members subject to FDA regulation, conduct their everyday business. The regulations apply to more than 2000 drug products first marketed between 1938 and 1962 with FDA approval and place all of them in jeopardy, subject to summary removal by order of FDA.

The all pervasive and substantial impact which the September regulations have upon the drug industry and in turn upon prescribing physicians and their patients, makes it imperative that the Commissioner comply with the notice and comment provisions of Section 4 before such regulations become effective.

* * * [T]he Commissioner argues that the testing standards of the September regulations are not new and that any burden imposed by them is the direct result of the "substantial evidence" of effectiveness requirements embodied in the 1962 amendments to the Act. Thus, the Commission concludes that the only effect of the September regulations was to "particularize" the statutory standard.

Despite this argument, the record is clear that the administrative practice applying the statutory standard to drugs marketed before 1962 has not uniformly insisted on evidence produced in accordance with the carefully controlled testing requirements of the September regulations. * * *

* * * [A]t conferences held with representatives of the drug industry between 1963 and 1964, FDA officials gave assurances that well-documented clinical experiences * * * would be considered by the Commissioner in determining the effectiveness of drugs approved for marketing between 1938 and 1962.

* * * [T]he guidelines established by * * * the NAS–NRC for the effectiveness review specifically contemplated that information freely available in scientific literature as well as "the informed judgment and experience of the members of the panels" would be relied upon in reaching judgments as to the relative effectiveness of the drug products evaluated. * * *

* * * [T]he final report of the NAS–NRC Panels clearly shows that evidence produced through other than the well-controlled tests required by the September regulations was relied on by the Panel members in evaluating the effectiveness of the drug products.

In light of the administrative practice outlined above, the Commissioner is incorrect in asserting that before September 1969 there was a uniform understanding concerning the range of evidence which could be offered to support a claim of drug effectiveness for a drug marketed before 1962. * * * [T]he September regulations did effect a material narrowing of the range of evidence which previously had been considered relevant in evaluating a drug's efficacy. * * *

* * * Many of the important issues now raised by PMA in this Court are matters which require thorough and expert consideration by the Commissioner. For example, PMA asserts that it would be difficult, if not impossible, to employ sufficient research investigators to perform the extensive testing required by the September regulations for all drug products currently marketed * * *. Claims concerning the scarcity of testing resources, and their proper allocation among competing uses are, of course, matters requiring the special expertise and judgment of the Secretary and the Commissioner. * * * If a drug has been found effective by a panel of the NAS–NRC, then a determination by the Commissioner that immediate further testing was required for this drug would necessarily tend to displace testing resources from the development of new drugs for important and presently unfulfilled therapeutic needs. * * * The existence of such important questions, however, certainly suggests that the Commissioner has the responsibility to fully inform himself concerning these and other important implications of the September regulations

The relationship of the NAS–NRC Panel studies to the standards and procedures of the FDA for judging the efficacy of drug products has, unfortunately, never been fully clarified. * * * [T]he guidelines established for the NAS–NRC Panels * * * were not limited to evidence produced by strictly controlled tests as now required by the September regulations.

* * *

PMA points out that because of the flexible guidelines followed by the NAS–NRC Panels a rating of "effective" may have been assigned to a particular drug based on a substantial concensus of medical experience and usage even though substantial evidence of the kind required by the September regulations was not relied on in reaching this conclusion. * * *

The Court is not suggesting that the Commissioner must, or even should consider the particular problems stated above, and the Court certainly does not presume to tell the Commissioner the kind of balance he should strike in considering these various, competing interests. These problems are pointed out simply to illustrate the necessity of giving notice and opportunity for comment before a regulation of such pervasive impact as here involved is finally issued. Because the minimal procedural rights of notice and opportunity for comment were not afforded in the present case, the promulgation of the September regulations was invalid and a preliminary injunction will be granted.

* * *

PHARMACEUTICAL MANUFACTURERS ASSOCIATION v. RICHARDSON

United States District Court, D.Delaware, 1970.
318 F.Supp. 301.

LATCHUM, D. J. * * * [T]he Pharmaceutical Manufacturers Association ("PMA"), on behalf of its members, seeks a preliminary injunction restraining the Secretary of Health, Education and Welfare ("the Secretary") and the Commissioner of Food and Drugs ("the Commissioner") from taking any action in reliance upon the regulations promulgated in the Commissioner's Order of May 8, 1970 ("the May regulations") * * *.

The May regulations establish standards of evidence necessary to demonstrate the effectiveness of drug products by defining the scientific content of adequate and well-controlled clinical investigations and also set forth the procedural requirements for obtaining an evidentiary hearing in any proceeding to amend the antibiotic certification regulations or to withdraw approval of a new drug application on the ground of lack of substantial evidence of effectiveness. The May regulations are a direct outgrowth of regulations previously issued by the Commissioner on September 19, 1969 ("the September regulations") * * *.

Two purely legal questions are raised by the present action: (1) May the Commissioner validly establish criteria for adequate and well-controlled clinical investigations necessary to demonstrate the effectiveness of drug products already on the market and (2) does the summary procedure specified in the May regulations comport with the Act and the requirements of due process?

* * *

In response to the decision in Pharmaceutical Manufacturers Association v. Finch, [307 F.Supp. 858], the Commissioner on February 17, 1970 published proposed regulations ("the February proposals") for comment by interested parties. Reg. 3073. The February proposals were similar in material content to the September regulations. * * * The comments of PMA to the FDA appeared to agree that the criteria for adequate and well-controlled clinical investigations were scientifically sound for entirely new drugs, but argued that the regulations should state these principles in the form of guidelines applicable to current and future clinical investigations. Four other objections to the February proposals were also made: (1) that a lesser standard of proof based on clinical experience and investigation not made in conformity with the proposed regulations should be accepted for drugs approved for marketing before 1962; (2) that firms should be given additional time to conduct definitive tests which meet the proposed requirements before proceedings are initiated to withdraw pre-1962 drugs from the market; (3) that testing most pre-1962 drugs is wasteful of testing resources and could not be carried out because of a shortage of clinical investigators [sic] and (4) that the proposed hearing regulations violated due process of law.

On May 8, 1970, the Commissioner published an Order in the Federal Register discussing and disposing of the comments of PMA and other parties, and issued final regulations which were made effective on publication. 35 Fed.Reg. 7250; codified in 21 CFR, Parts 130 and 146.

The Issue Of Substantial Evidence

PMA first challenges the May regulations on the ground that they arbitrarily define "adequate and well-controlled clinical investigations" so narrowly and rigidly as to be incompatible with the statutory definitions of "substantial evidence of effectiveness" as elucidated by the legislative history of the 1962 Drug Amendments. Its argument runs that Congress, in adding the new tests of effectiveness, intended no rigid and narrow standard as to the nature of the evidence necessary to establish effectiveness and that the very concept of "substantial evidence" was designed to reflect and accommodate the fact that clinical experts often disagree as to the effectiveness of a drug. Hence, it is contended that the statutory standard was designed to insure that any drug "believed by a substantial number of experts" to be effective could be marketed even if the view of the majority of experts was that the drug was ineffective. The Court is unable to agree with this contention.

First, the legislative history of the drug amendments of 1962 does not support PMA's view. The 1962 amendments were the culmination of an investigation into administered prices in the drug industry by the Subcommittee on Antitrust and Monopoly, Senate Committee on the Judiciary, under the Chairmanship of Senator Kefauver. Beginning in 1960, the Subcommittee heard a succession of witnesses respecting the testing of all drugs.

* * *

Summarizing this kind of testimony, the Subcommittee noted that "[t]he experts emphasized the imperative need for an objective determination of efficacy of the drug products placed on the market," and it was against this background that the "substantial evidence" rule emerged from the Senate Committee. * * * An amendment to section 505 of the Act authorized the suspension of a new drug application "upon a finding that there is a lack of substantial evidence * * * that it will have the effect claimed for it."

* * *

Among the changes adopted by the Judiciary Committee was the requirement "that all claims for effectiveness, whether made initially in a new-drug application or at any time thereafter, must be supported by 'substantial evidence' * * *." The Committee also reported that the bill had been amended to set forth a new test of effectiveness. * * *

This legislative history compels the conclusion that the substantial evidence requirement of the Act was to be applied not only to new drugs coming on the market after 1962 but was to be applied also to the drugs approved for marketing between 1938 and 1962; Congress intended no double standard for determining the effectiveness of drug claims. Further, substantial evidence was defined to mean adequate and well-controlled clinical investigations, i. e., an investigation which was as scientifically sound and objective as it was humanly possible to make.

* * *

In order to clarify the type of evidence required to support a claim of effectiveness, the May regulations were issued. They definitively spell out the criteria which have developed and been generally recognized by the scientific community, as essentials of adequate and well-controlled clinical investigations.

Turning to the criteria set forth in the May regulations, the first requirement provides that "a clear statement of the objectives of the study" be given. It is simply self-evident that in any study the investigator and evaluator must know what is being studied. * * *

The second requirement provides that (i) the patients selected for study are suitable based on diagnostic criteria of the condition to be treated and, where appropriate, confirmed by laboratory tests; (ii) the subjects are assigned to test groups in such a way as to minimize bias; and (iii) that pertinent variables, such as age, sex, severity, or duration of disease and drugs used are comparable between test groups. * * *

Requirement three provides that the study contain an explanation of "the methods of observation and recording of results * * * and the steps taken to minimize bias on the part of subject and observer."

The fourth requirement provides that the study be comparative with one of four listed known methods of comparison so as to permit quantitative evaluation of the results of the treatment.

The fifth and final criterion requires "a summary of the methods of analysis and evaluation of the data derived from the study."

These criteria * * * provide wide areas of choice for the investigator, and, contrary to PMA's contention, are in no sense unduly rigid and narrow. The regulations appear to be completely reasonable in describing the scientific content of a well-controlled and adequate investigation. * * * While conformity with the regulations will not necessarily assure scientific acceptability, the criteria must be observed to give the study a chance to yield meaningful results.

* * * Such required studies are designed to afford a greater assurance of objective results and are in contra-distinction to the subjective tests of testimonial, random observations and clinical impressions of physicians which have been relied upon in the past to support claims of efficacy for marketed drugs.

The Court concludes that the criteria of the May regulations are not arbitrarily rigid. * * * These criteria appear wholly reasonable and certainly are within the Commissioner's power to issue * * *.

Moreover, the May regulations contain some flexibility. * * * Further, the May regulations concede that other clinical experience may be offered as corroborating evidence of a drug's efficacy but that such type of evidence, standing alone, will not be acceptable. Finally, the regulations provide an administrative procedure to obtain a waiver of some of the criteria if the Director of the Bureau of Drugs finds that such criteria are not reasonably applicable to the investigation and that alternative procedures have been or can be followed which would yield results that can be accepted as substantial evidence of the drug's effectiveness.

Consequently, this Court holds that the Commissioner was authorized to issue the May regulations * * * and that the criteria therein set forth reasonably carry out the Congressional mandate that all claims of efficacy for marketed drugs must be supported by substantial evidence.

* * *

PMA's second major challenge of the May regulations is based on the contention that they deny hearing rights guaranteed by the Act and the Constitution. * * *

* * * PMA concludes that the provisions of the May regulations which require a showing of "reasonable grounds" in order to obtain a hearing before denial or withdrawal of a new drug application are contrary to the literal language of section 505(d) and (e).

This contention, however, lacks merit. The "opportunity for a hearing" provided in section 505(d) and (e) does not mean that an evidentiary hearing must be held in every case, even in the absence of genuine factual issues in dispute. It is an established principle of law that an administrative agency, such as the FDA, may by general regulations condition the holding of an evidentiary hearing upon an applicant's preliminary showing that "reasonable grounds" exist therefor * * *. The Court thus concludes that the FDA as a part of its general rule making power was authorized to require a showing of reasonable grounds as a prerequisite to an evidentiary hearing provided in section 505(d) and (e).

Second, PMA claims that the May regulations * * * amount to an impermissible "rule requiring a party to prove his case as a condition to getting a hearing or even to demonstrate that there is a substantial likelihood that he will prevail on the merits." PMA has misconceived the import of these procedural regulations. On the contrary, the May regulations simply provide that a request for an evidentiary hearing will be denied when it clearly appears that the medical documentation, which the hearing applicant is required to submit, shows on its face that there is no genuine and substantial issue of fact * * *.

If no adequate and well-controlled studies exist to support the applicant's claim of effectiveness as required by the Act and regulations, an evidentiary hearing would be a futile exercise and a waste of time. * * *

The Supreme Court in Federal Power Commission v. Texaco, 377 U.S. 33 (1964) upheld similar regulations of the FPC. * * *

Of course, if a given request for an evidentiary hearing were to raise an issue of genuine fact within the regulations, and the Commissioner were to misapply the rules, that would be subject to correction by the Courts. * * *

The Court therefore holds that the hearing procedures of the May regulations are reasonable and valid procedures and that it was within the power of the Commissioner to require that a genuine and substantial issue of fact be raised as a condition for granting an evidentiary hearing—that is a drug firm be required to demonstrate that it had conducted and identified adequate and well-controlled investigations meeting the statutory definition of substantial evidence, in support of its claim for the effectiveness of its drugs.

* * *

An order will be entered in accordance with this opinion.

B. NOTE ON STATE ADMINISTRATIVE AGENCIES

Because most of the principles discussed above with respect to federal administrative agencies will also be applicable to the administrative process at the state level it will not be necessary to go through an extended repetition. However, the nature of constitutional doctrine does differ as between the states and Federal government insofar as scope of authority is concerned. "The powers not delegated to the United States by the Constitution, nor prohibited by it to the states are reserved to the states respectively, or to the People." This language, the Tenth Amendment to the Constitution of the United States, sets limits both to Federal and State governments' scopes of authority.

Usually couched in terms of health, safety and welfare, these powers of the States comprehend matters of economic, social and political consequence touching on virtually every aspect of individual and corporate behavior and existence. And, except insofar as a particular area of concern may fall within the scope of authority of the Federal government to the exclusion of the States or may have been preempted by federal action, states are free to act with respect to such matters and exercise these powers as they determine circumscribed only by political and constitutional considerations and have implemented powers in these areas through the establishment of executive and/or administrative agencies just as at the federal level. There are, however, three major areas wherein significant differences between state and federal principles may occur: (1) the nature of the existence of state administrative agencies as a function of constitutional principles; (2) the nature of the relationship between state administrative agencies and other organs of state government; and, (3) the nature of the procedures governing state administrative agencies' activities.

We have stated that nowhere within the four corners of the federal constitution is there to be found any reference to administrative agencies. It was for Congress to develop the administrative agency through a delegation to such an entity of powers Congress itself was authorized to exercise. Although this may be the case insofar as many of the states are concerned (the same principles of constitutional law applying thereto), there have, however, been many states which have provided for the administrative process in their constitutions. To the extent that this latter is the case, many of the problems that revolve around determining whether and to what extent an administrative agency may exercise certain powers do not exist.

Having constitutionally provided for the administrative process, the form in which such process may be undertaken may likewise vary from that at the federal level. A state may have provided organizationally for the exercise of administrative functions in the form that we would normally associate with the executive level department in the federal scheme.

The evolution and growth of the federal administrative structure has occurred somewhat "Topsy-like." Engrafted upon a constitutional framework that made no reference to the administrative agency, the federal government has provided for intergovernmental and intragovernmental relationships which include the administrative agency within the context of specific substantive legislation. For example, the respective roles of the Federal Trade Commission and the Department of Justice relating to the enforcement of anti-trust legislation are provided for in those statutes dealing with anti-trust matters. So too the states may have provided for such interrelationships.

But, because the states' development of administrative activity has not been tied to a constitutional limitation of the same nature as the federal government's, such interrelationships may be dealt with at the constitutional level or in statutes designed to deal specifically and only with such.

Just as the subject matter jurisdiction of the federal administrative agency and its type of powers will determine the nature of the procedures it must adhere to, so too will it be the case at the state level. But in the case of the state agencies there has been a tendency to provide for operating procedures that may vary significantly even as between agencies with similar types of subject matter jurisdiction and powers.

QUESTIONS

1. At considerable expense, your company has become the sole licensee in the United States of the rights to produce for American consumption a food product heretofore known and found only in the Middle East. It is produced there by processing certain natural organic substances which are not to be found elsewhere; also, they are very perishable if any attempt is made to transport them for any distance. Therefore, your company has decided to develop the product from synthetics, one of which they wish to use and which would probably be essential has been ordered by the Food and Drug Administration to be withdrawn from all uses because its prior use as a drug proved to produce deleterious side-effects. This synthetic never has been used or considered for use in the way in which your company proposes and, therefore, there is no documentation as to its efficacy for the purpose. How would you propose dealing with the Food and Drug Administration? Of what significance is the argument you might make that your company has a large investment at stake? In this situation, what do you suppose ought to be the government's main concerns? Is there or should there be an alternative course of action other than having to go to the Food and Drug Administration? What might it be?

2. America's industrial giants consider themselves to be productive and efficient, these qualities being measurable and controllable as elements of profit-maximization. Bureaucracy within government agencies often is considered to be the antithesis of efficiency and productivity. Is it nonetheless measurable and controllable? What might account for the difference between business and government herein? How might this difference be reconciled? Should it be? Of what concern should this be to business?

3. Is there any alternative to the administrative agency within our political and governmental system today? Is the administrative

agency as we see it in the United States purely an American phenomenon? By its nature must it be? If it is, what is there about our system that enables such an entity to exist?

4. In the *Hannah* case the court articulates a functional due process test. A la Gertrude Stein, isn't an administrative investigation an investigation an investigation? Is the cutting edge of the due process argument really a functional one in light of the (theoretically) universal application of the Administrative Procedure Act to all federal administrative agencies?

5. Would it be a proper assertion that the fourth branch of government is really a cover-up for central economic planning? How much freedom is really left to the private entrepreneur? Professor Milton Friedman argues cogently within the context of classicial economic theory that administrative regulation is the grossest impediment to free enterprise, competition, efficiency, consumer orientation. Is he right, wrong? Why?

6. There are many areas of economic activity regulated concurrently by federal and state administrative agencies; water pollution control, fair employment practices, food quality, motor vehicle safety, to name but a few. Is this regulatory effort duplicative? If so, is it wasteful? Assuming that some regulatory effort is desirable, at which level of government do you feel it should occur? Why? Given the continued existence of both federal and state jurisdiction in many of these subject areas, does this phenomenon reflect adversely upon our governmental scheme? Have we come to accept a "vested interest" theory of government regulation of economic activity?

7. Apart from the fact that the court said it was addressing a procedural issue in the *Citizen's Committee* case, was it in effect reprimanding the FCC for failing to be sensitive to community interest? A major statutory standard in the allocation of radio frequencies is public interest and necessity. Assume that this standard or its equivalent is the *raison d'etre* for all administrative agencies; does the independence of the agency militate against adhering to such a standard? Should the formality of the Administrative Procedure Act be the only vehicle for translating public sentiment into administratively cognizable positions? Is there a valid argument to be made for making policy-makers in administrative agencies more directly responsive to public sentiment?

8. A further argument made in justification of the administrative agency and of its independence is that it has an opportunity to become expert in smaller highly sophisticated areas of economic activity. Is our political system most effectively perpetuated by experts, specialists, or "is war too important to be left to the generals alone?" Does specialization inbreed itself establishing a false adversary system where the agency itself becomes a pro/antagonist?

Suggested Reference Sources

Texts and Treatises

Cooper, *State Administrative Law.* Bobbs-Merrill Co., Indianapolis, Indiana.

Davis, *Administrative Law Treatise.* West Publishing Co., St. Paul, Minnesota.

Pike & Fischer, *Administrative Law.* Washington, D. C.

Topic Headings in the Index to Legal Periodicals

Administrative Agencies

Administrative Law

Administrative Procedure

Chapter IX

RELATIONS WITH EMPLOYEES

A. COLLECTIVE BARGAINING AND FAIR
EMPLOYMENT PRACTICES

---

1. INTRODUCTORY NOTE

The work of the world remains to be done. Men living in organized societies have developed advanced needs and desires and with them specialized skills in fulfilling them. The least skilled man has infinitely more ability than the best trained beast of burden and the most sophisticated machine. Lower animals and machines are moved about in our economy as needed or at least as purchased. But matching up men and their skills with the work to be performed is another matter entirely. For more than a century for all men, and for many centuries for white men, we have had a legal system of freedom of contract, of freedom of choice, in arranging for the distribution of employment in our economy. Every society must have a system to accomplish this; it could be done by a governmental agency requiring forced labor, that is a universal system of conscription for all employment, not just for military service, or by a system of slavery or peonage where one favored group would have the legal right to compel men to perform services for them, or any number of various combinations of these systems. Or we could let men seek their own employment—such jobs, from such employers, in such places as they choose or as their skills permit for such compensation, for such hours and conditions of employment as might be agreed upon by them and their employers. We have chosen the latter system although we have yet to make it available to all men and women.

An employment system which is based upon freedom of contract as a matter of law, at least, allows employees to choose their employers, and allows employers to a large extent to choose their employees. The limitations on these choices are a major part of the problems discussed in this Chapter. In the most simplified form of the system, which admittedly has not existed in any except the smallest enterprises for more than a century, a person seeking employment could choose his employer and between them they could choose the wages to be paid, the hours to be worked, and the other conditions of the employment. The elements of this system still exist but now we have to a large extent collectivised employers in the form of a corporation and collectivised employees in the form of their union. That is, we have no legal restraints on seeking employment across town or across the country by either employee or employer, and except for the requirements of legislation relating to minimum wages and maximum hours, there are no limitations on wages, hours, or other conditions of employment. Unquestionably, economic limitations such as the cost of travelling 3,000 miles to find a job are restraints on this process; the point is, however, that there are no *legal* restraints. There is no governmental agency directing people to work for any employer (except persons drafted for military service), no governmental agency directing employers to hire specified persons for the performance of services for them, no governmental agency fixing the hourly rate of compensation to be paid nor even the number of hours to be worked except to the extent that the Fair Labor Standards Act (sometimes called the Wage and Hour Act), 29 U.S.C.A. § 201 et seq., requires the payment of a minimum wage or of compensation equal to one and a half times the normal hourly rate for hours worked in excess of 40 per week. So far as our legal system is concerned if a man desires to be employed in any manner he chooses, he may do so; there is no law or governmental agency which directs him to perform services in any specified occupation. He may be prohibited by law from engaging in certain of the learned professions until he demonstrates a minimum competency, but the government at no time compels him to enter any of such professions.

But these rights are not unlimited. The concentration of economic power which resulted from the collective ownership of a business enterprise in the form of a corporation impinged upon the freedom of contract of the employee to seek employment and to bargain for his wages, hours, and other conditions of employment. This development began to accelerate in the nineteenth century, and except for the rise of labor unions and the legislation discussed in this chapter, continued unimpeded into the twentieth century. The rise of the modern corporation from the viewpoint of an employee in many respects has been a throwback to the feudal system, because as a practical matter the individual employee has no freedom of contract in negotiating the terms of his employment. In more recent times labor unions have changed this. Collectivised employers in the form of one corporation or in the form of many corporations assembled in an employer association have been met by collectivised employees in the form of local and international unions. At first employers were able to maintain their dominant position in the bargaining process by seeking the aid of the law in having labor unions declared unlawful (or even by having legally constituted authorities permit employers to use such physical force as they desired to destroy labor unions and their representatives). This, predictably, resulted in the use of similar amounts of force on the part of unions and their supporters to seek either redress or a restoration of the balance in the bargaining process.

Organized society could not tolerate this kind of private warfare for any length of time. Further, when the Great Depression of the 1930's disclosed serious dislocations in the economy with vast numbers of employable men unemployed and great numbers of industrial plants either closed down or operating at a fraction of their capacity, the unlimited right of an employer to make such employment contracts as he chose became restricted. This led to the adoption in 1935 of the Wagner Act, which was amended by the Taft-Hartley Act in 1947 and is now formally called the Labor Management Relations Act (herein called the Labor Act). Section 1 of the Act, 29 U.S.C.A. § 151, reported infra in NLRB v. Jones & Laughlin Steel Corp., 301 U.S. 1, 57 S.Ct. 615, 81 L.Ed. 893 (1936) contains a statement of congressional policy in this respect. (There are some interesting references in this Section to the "flow of commerce", the "instrumentalities of commerce", and the "channels of commerce", all of which were of great significance in the Constitutional debates of the 1930's, but today seem rather quaint and even stilted.)

Compulsory collective bargaining has become the new legal system; employers as a matter of law are obligated to bargain with the representatives of their employees and to fix the wages, hours, and other conditions of employment in a collective bargaining agreement. But the new order has still preserved the fundamentals of freedom of contract because all contractual disputes are to be resolved by the parties themselves through collective bargaining. No government agency, whether it be a court or an administrative agency, is empowered to adjudicate the disputes between employers and employees concerning the amount of wages to be paid, the number of hours to be worked, or what fringe benefits, if any, are to be provided. The activity of the National Labor Relations Board is limited to providing for the establishment and maintenance of collective bargaining within the system. We have no Court of Wage and Hour Disputes, nor do the United States District Courts nor the courts of any of the states entertain any kind of litigation concerning the hourly rate to be paid to employees, or any other term or condition of employment. We have intentionally steered away from the adjudicatory process as a means of resolving these disputes in recognition of the fact that the employers and the employees are best able to determine what are fair and reasonable wages to be paid within a given industry or within a single employment unit rather than having this done by some government bureau or as the result of a verdict in a jury trial. Just the thought of this is ludicrous to anyone who has participated in this process, yet the suggestion is made from time to time by well-intentioned but uninformed people. Collective bargaining is the method we have chosen.

One of the functions of the Labor Act was to establish new rules to be observed by both parties in collective bargaining. The need for the restoration of a balance between employers and unions had been clearly demonstrated by several decades of history leading up to the Great Depression. Experience has shown that the free and uncontrolled selection of employee representatives is necessary for this purpose. Thus Section 7 of the Labor Act, 29 U.S.C.A. § 157, guarantees the rights of employees to form unions, to bargain collectively, and to engage in other concerted activities. (See NLRB v. Jones & Laughlin Steel Corp., referred to supra and reported infra.) Sec. 7 is the Magna Carta of organized labor; all other provisions of the Labor Act really stem from it. Section 8 of the Act, 29 U.S.C.A. § 158 (as originally adopted) lists certain kinds of employer activities which are called "unfair labor practices." These include interference with any of the rights guaranteed by Sec. 7 of the Act, encouraging or discouraging union membership by discriminating in favor of or against union members in hiring or conditions of employment. Twelve years after the original Act, it was amended by the Taft-Hartley Act which added somewhat similar restraints upon a union. Section 8(b), 29 U.S.C.A. § 158(b) provides that discrimination by a union in favor of or against union members in hiring or conditions of employment, or causing or attempting to cause an employer to do the same is also an unfair labor practice. Other provisions of the Act relate to the rights and methods of employees in selecting their union, methods of conducting elections, "certification" of a union as the collective bargaining representative of the employees and provisions for the administration of the Act by the National Labor Relations Board (the NLRB).

The NLRB, as noted above, is not concerned with adjudicating disputes between employers and employees relating to the conditions of the employment. If a union charges an employer with an unfair labor practice, taken from Section 8 of the Labor Act, for example interfering with the rights of the employees to organize and join the union, it will file an unfair labor practice charge with the NLRB, and then the agency becomes involved in the matter. This is done on a rather simple printed form and is not nearly as complicated as a Complaint filed in court by a plaintiff who is initiating a law suit. The NLRB will send one of its employees to the industrial plant to investigate the charge and frequently this is enough to bring about a settlement of the dispute. If not, the investigator makes his report to his superiors who review the matter and if it is determined that a violation of the Labor Act has occurred, then a formal unfair labor practice charge will be filed against the employer with the Board. Again an effort will be made to settle the dispute. Again, if not settled, a hearing will be scheduled upon adequate notice to both the employer and the union, and a Trial Examiner will appear at a designated time and place to hear the evidence to be submitted by both the union and the employer. A stenographic record of the hearing will be made and after it is completed, the Trial Examiner will study it and make a report to the NLRB. The Trial Examiner's report will then be reviewed by the General Counsel's office, and if it is then determined that an unfair labor practice has occurred, the matter will be referred to the full NLRB which, after hearing the arguments of the employer and the union will either sustain or dismiss the charge. If sustained it will then issue an order to the employer to restore employees to their jobs, sometimes with back pay, or to cease and desist from a specified activity. If the employer does not comply, then the Board is empowered to go into a Court of Appeals to seek an order from the court requiring the employer to comply with the order of the Board; the employer is given an opportunity to defend the legal matters involved in the proceedings in court. If the employer fails to observe the order of the court, then he is subject to being held in contempt of court, which can include substantial monetary fines or even imprisonment until there is compliance with the order of the court. Since unions may be the subject of unfair labor practice charges, the same procedure would be followed upon the filing of a complaint by an employer or employee. It is interesting to note that no court becomes involved in this process until an administrative agency has issued its order, and then an appellate court rather than a United States District Court which is the court which has original jurisdiction of nearly all legal disputes under the Federal court system; in one sense, the National Labor Relations Board is placed in a position equal to that of a United States District Court.

Employers and unions have developed a means of adjusting disputes which they cannot settle by their grievance procedure by referring the matter to arbitration. This generally occurs as a result of a provision in the collective bargaining agreement. Generally the grievance procedure will move disputes through a hierarchical organization of the employer and a corresponding organization of the union; that is, a shop foreman and his opposite number, a shop steward (an active employee selected by his fellow employees for this purpose), will attempt to settle the dispute and in this manner most disputes are settled. But if not settled, then the dispute proceeds through one or more steps of middle management and a business agent or some officer of the local union, and again most disputes referred to them are settled. But if not, then the top management officer in charge of labor relations (or in an association of a number of employers, its association officer charged with this function) and a regional or national representative of the union will attempt to dispose of the matter. Of course, there are an infinite variety of grievance procedures depending on the industry or on the size of the employment unit. But only when a dispute has not been settled according to the grievance procedure will it be referred to arbitration. In a few industries there will be a full time impartial umpire or arbitrator who will adjudicate these disputes; in most instances a single arbitrator will be selected who is known to both the employer and the union as being a fair and experienced arbitrator; in other instances a panel of three arbitrators, one chosen by each of the contesting parties and the third chosen by those two, will adjudicate the dispute. It should be noted, however, that in all cases the actual person or persons settling the dispute are persons chosen by the disputants and not some forum such as a court thrust on them by some outside agency such as the government.

In any event, under Sec. 301 of the Labor Act, 29 U.S.C.A. § 185, provisions in a collective bargaining agreement requiring binding arbitration of a grievance are enforceable in a United States District Court. It should be noted that what is referred to the court is not the fundamental grievance or dispute between the employer and employee; this remains to be settled outside the courts. What is referred to the courts for adjudication is the issue of the right under the contract which one of the parties has to compel arbitration of the fundamental dispute. This is well illustrated by the case of The Boys Markets Inc. v. Retail Clerks Union, Local 770, 398 U.S. 235, 90 S.Ct. 1583, 26 L.Ed.2d 199 (1970) reported infra.

Nearly all the legal limitations on the freedom to make such employment contracts as the parties may desire are limitations on the employer. As noted above an employer may not refuse to bargain collectively, he may not discriminate in hiring or other conditions of employment because of union activity, or because of race, color, sex, religion, or national origin. Further, he may not require his employees to work more than forty hours per week, without paying them one and a half times their hourly rate for the extra hours of employment, Fair Labor Standards Act, 29 U.S.C.A. § 201 et seq. Also, under the Walsh-Healy Act of 1938, 41 U.S.C.A. § 35, if the employer is engaged in any government contract he must pay "the prevailing wage" within the area in which he is operating; the prevailing wage is determined by a division of the United States Department of Labor and in practice generally is equal to the wage rates negotiated under collective bargaining agreements in the area. The practical effect of this Act is generally to require employers to pay the union scale of wages for services performed in the production of government contracts.

Employers are also obligated under state law to provide workmen's compensation benefits for employees who are injured by an accident in the course of their employment. The scale of benefits to be paid to injured employees varies according to the state statute, and in many instances these benefits are grossly inadequate. Except for the very large employers which operate their own programs for this purpose, most employers carry insurance to cover this liability. This has resulted in the shifting of the obligation in this area from the employer to an insurance company; in the past this has resulted in a wide range of performance of this obligation. Insurance companies in the operation of their business were intent on keeping their costs as low as possible and thus frequently would deny claims and litigate the question of whether or not the employee was injured by an "accident" or whether it occurred in "the course of his employment", all without regard to the preferences of the employer. Some employers with humanitarian instincts and interested in the economic welfare of their injured employees, frequently found themselves frustrated by the provisions of their workmen's compensation insurance contracts. But not all insurance companies are to be criticized for their actions in this field; some have maintained a physical rehabilitation program for injured employees seeking to assist them in their recovery and early return to work; others have not. In recent years there has been a gradual improvement in the administration of workmen's compensation benefit programs. The improvement has come about largely because of the activity of labor unions in providing guidance and assistance to employees in processing their claims under the various statutes, and in some cases in providing them with legal representation. Also, the legal expenses which the insurance companies have incurred in litigating these questions have risen, so that more and more benefits are paid without much dispute (an unintended contribution of the legal profession to the workmen's compensation program). Many problems still exist in this area; one of the most important is how to gear the amount of benefits to the rising cost of living without encouraging malingering. Since inflation seems to be a way of life in the American economy this problem will probably be with us as long as we have inflation.

These programs are required by law; they are different from the basic concept of freedom of contract. In many industries (probably all except motor transportation) employers and unions have reached agreements requiring payment of premium wages for hours worked in excess of eight per day and in some cases for work performed on Saturdays, Sundays and holidays. Also, by contract (and in this case not excepting motor transportation) additional benefits in excess of the statutory benefits for injuries to workmen are paid. Thus in this part of the economy certain programs directing employers to do specific things have been enacted into law, but the fundamental relationship is still based on the democratic concept of freedom of contract.

———

2. DUTY TO BARGAIN

NATIONAL LABOR RELATIONS BOARD v. JONES & LAUGHLIN STEEL CORPORATION

Supreme Court of the United States, 1937.
301 U.S. 1, 57 S.Ct. 615, 81 L.Ed. 893.

Mr. Chief Justice HUGHES delivered the opinion of the Court.

In a proceeding under the National Labor Relations Act of 1935 the National Labor Relations Board found that the respondent, Jones & Laughlin Steel Corporation, had violated the act by engaging in unfair labor practices affecting commerce. The proceeding was instituted by the Beaver Valley Lodge No. 200, affiliated with the Amalgamated Association of Iron, Steel and Tin Workers of America, a labor organization. The unfair labor practices charged were that the corporation was discriminating against members of the union with regard to hire and tenure of employment, and was coercing and intimidating its employees in order to interfere with their self-organization. The discriminatory and coercive action alleged was the discharge of certain employees.

The National Labor Relations Board, sustaining the charge, ordered the corporation to cease and desist from such discrimination and coercion, to offer reinstatement to ten of the employees named, to make good their losses in pay, and to post for thirty days notices that the corporation would not discharge or discriminate against members, or those desiring to become members, of the labor union. As the corporation failed to comply, the Board petitioned the Circuit Court of Appeals to enforce the order. The court denied the petition holding that the order lay beyond the range of federal power. 83 F.2d 998. We granted certiorari. 299 U.S. 534.

The scheme of the National Labor Relations Act—which is too long to be quoted in full—may be briefly stated. The first section (29 U.S.C.A. § 151) sets forth findings with respect to the injury to commerce resulting from the denial by employers of the right of employees to organize and from the refusal of employers to accept the procedure of collective bargaining. There follows a declaration that it is the policy of the United States to eliminate these causes of obstruction to the free flow of commerce.[1] The act then defines the terms it uses, including the terms "commerce" and "affecting commerce." Section 2 (29 U.S.C.A. § 152). It creates the National Labor Relations Board and prescribes its organization. Sections 3–6 (29 U.S.C.A. §§ 153–156). It sets forth the right of employees to self-organization and to bargain collectively through representatives of their own choosing. Section 7 (29 U.S.C.A. § 157). It defines "unfair labor practices." Section 8 (29 U.S.C.A. § 158). It lays down rules as to the representation of employees for the purpose of collective

1. This section is as follows:
"Section 1. The denial by employers of the right of employees to organize and the refusal by employers to accept the procedure of collective bargaining lead to strikes and other forms of industrial strife or unrest, which have the intent or the necessary effect of burdening or obstructing commerce by (a) impairing the efficiency, safety, or operation of the instrumentalities of commerce; (b) occurring in the current of commerce; (c) materially affecting, restraining, or controlling the flow of raw materials or manufactured or processed goods from or into the channels of commerce, or the prices of such materials or goods in commerce; or (d) causing diminution of employment and wages in such volume as substantially to impair or disrupt the market for goods flowing from or into the channels of commerce.
"The inequality of bargaining power between employees who do not possess full freedom of association or actual liberty of contract, and employers who are organized in the corporate or other forms of ownership association substantially burdens and affects the flow of commerce, and tends to aggravate recurrent business depressions, by depressing wage rates and the purchasing power of wage earners in in-

dustry and by preventing the stabilization of competitive wage rates and working conditions within and between industries.
"Experience has proved that protection by law of the right of employees to organize and bargain collectively safeguards commerce from injury, impairment, or interruption, and promotes the flow of commerce by removing certain recognized sources of industrial strife and unrest, by encouraging practices fundamental to the friendly adjustment of industrial disputes arising out of differences as to wages, hours, or other working conditions, and by restoring equality of bargaining power between employers and employees.
"It is hereby declared to be the policy of the United States to eliminate the causes of certain substantial obstructions to the free flow of commerce and to mitigate and eliminate these obstructions when they have occurred by encouraging the practice and procedure of collective bargaining and by protecting the exercise by workers of full freedom of association, self-organization, and designation of representatives of their own choosing, for the purpose of negotiating the terms and conditions of their employment or other mutual aid or protection." 29 U.S.C.A. § 151. (Court's footnote 2.)

bargaining. Section 9 (29 U.S.C.A. § 159). The Board is empowered to prevent the described unfair labor practices affecting commerce and the act prescribes the procedure to that end. The Board is authorized to petition designated courts to secure the enforcement of its order. The findings of the Board as to the facts, if supported by evidence, are to be conclusive. If either party on application to the court shows that additional evidence is material and that there were reasonable grounds for the failure to adduce such evidence in the hearings before the Board, the court may order the additional evidence to be taken. Any person aggrieved by a final order of the Board may obtain a review in the designated courts with the same procedure as in the case of an application by the Board for the enforcement of its order. Section 10 (29 U.S.C.A. § 160). The Board has broad powers of investigation. Section 11 (29 U.S.C.A. § 161). Interference with members of the Board or its agents in the performance of their duties is punishable by fine and imprisonment. Section 12 (29 U.S.C.A. § 162). Nothing in the act is to be construed to interfere with the right to strike. Section 13 (29 U.S.C.A. § 163). There is a separability clause to the effect that, if any provision of the act or its application to any person or circumstances shall be held invalid, the remainder of the act or its application to other persons or circumstances shall not be affected. Section 15 (29 U.S.C.A. § 165). * * *

The procedure in the instant case followed the statute. * * *

Contesting the ruling of the Board, the respondent argues (1) that the act is in reality a regulation of labor relations and not of interstate commerce; (2) that the act can have no application to the respondent's relations with its production employees because they are not subject to regulation by the federal government; and (3) that the provisions of the act violate section 2 of article 3 and the Fifth and Seventh Amendments of the Constitution of the United States.

The facts as to the nature and scope of the business of the Jones & Laughlin Steel Corporation have been found by the Labor Board, and, so far as they are essential to the determination of this controversy, they are not in dispute. The Labor Board has found: The corporation is organized under the laws of Pennsylvania and has its principal office at Pittsburgh. It is engaged in the business of manufacturing iron and steel in plants situated in Pittsburgh and nearby Aliquippa, Pa. It manufactures and distributes a widely diversified line of steel and pig iron, being the fourth largest producer of steel in the United States. With its subsidiaries—nineteen in number—it is a completely integrated enterprise, owning and operating ore, coal and limestone properties, lake and river transportation facilities and terminal railroads located at its manufacturing plants. It owns or controls mines in Michigan and Minnesota. It operates four ore steamships on the Great Lakes, used in the transportation of ore to its factories. It owns coal mines in Pennsylvania. It operates towboats and steam barges used in carrying coal to its factories. It owns limestone properties in various places in Pennsylvania and West Virginia. It owns the Monongahela connecting railroad which connects the plants of the Pittsburgh works and forms an interconnection with the Pennsylvania, New York Central and Baltimore & Ohio Railroad systems. It owns the Aliquippa & Southern Railroad Company, which connects the Aliquippa works with the Pittsburgh & Lake Erie, part of the New York Central system. Much of its product is shipped to its warehouses in Chicago, Detroit, Cincinnati and Memphis,—to the last two places by means of its own barges and transportation equipment. In Long Island City, New York, and in New Orleans it operates structural steel fabricating shops in connection with the warehousing of semifinished materials sent from its works. Through one of its wholly-owned subsidiaries it owns, leases, and operates stores, warehouses, and yards for the distribution of equipment and supplies for drilling and operating oil and gas wells and for pipe lines, refineries and pumping stations. It has sales offices in twenty cities in the United States and a wholly-owned subsidiary which is devoted exclusively to distributing its product in Canada. Approximately 75 per cent. of its product is shipped out of Pennsylvania.

Summarizing these operations, the Labor Board concluded that the works in Pittsburgh and Aliquippa "might be likened to the heart of a self-contained, highly integrated body. They draw in the raw materials from Michigan, Minnesota, West Virginia, Pennsylvania in part through arteries and by means controlled by the respondent; they transform the materials and then pump them out to all parts of the nation through the vast mechanism which the respondent has elaborated."

To carry on the activities of the entire steel industry, 33,000 men mine ore, 44,000 men mine coal, 4,000 men quarry limestone, 16,000 men manufacture coke, 343,000 men manufacture steel, and 83,000 men transport its product. Respondent has about 10,000 employees in its Aliquippa plant, which is located in a community of about 30,000 persons.

Respondent points to evidence that the Aliquippa plant, in which the discharged men were employed, contains complete facilities for the production of finished and semifinished iron and steel products from raw materials; that its works consist primarily of a by-product coke plant for the production of coke; blast furnaces for the production of pig iron; open hearth furnaces and Bessemer converters for the production of steel; blooming mills for the reduction of steel ingots into smaller shapes; and a number of finishing mills such as structural mills, rod mills, wire mills, and the like. In addition, there are other buildings, structures and equipment, storage yards, docks and an intraplant storage system. Respondent's operations at these works are carried on in two distinct stages, the first being the conversion of raw materials into pig iron and the second being the manufacture of semifinished and finished iron and steel products; and in both cases the operations result in substantially changing the character, utility and value of the materials wrought upon, which is apparent from the nature and extent of the processes to which they are subjected and which respondent fully describes. Respondent also directs attention to the fact that the iron ore which is procured from mines in Minnesota and Michigan and transported to respondent's plant is stored in stock piles for future use, the amount of ore in storage varying with the season but usually being enough to maintain operations from nine to ten months; that the coal which is procured from the mines of a subsidiary located in Pennsylvania and taken to the plant at Aliquippa is there, like ore, stored for future use, approximately two to three months' supply of coal being always on hand; and that the limestone which is obtained in Pennsylvania and West Virginia is also stored in amounts usually adequate to run the blast furnaces for a few weeks. Various details of operation, transportation, and distribution are also mentioned which for the present purpose it is not necessary to detail.

Practically all the factual evidence in the case, except that which dealt with the nature of respondent's business, concerned its relations with the employees in the Aliquippa plant whose discharge was the subject of the complaint. These employees were active leaders in the labor union. Several were officers and others were leaders of particular groups. Two of the employees were motor inspectors; one was a tractor driver; three were crane operators; one was a washer in the coke plant; and three were laborers. Three other employees were mentioned in the complaint but it was withdrawn as to one of them and no evidence was heard on the action taken with respect to the other two.

While respondent criticizes the evidence and the attitude of the Board, which is described as being hostile toward employers and particularly toward those who insisted upon their constitutional rights, respondent did not take advantage of its opportunity to present evidence to refute that which was offered to show discrimination and coercion. In this situation, the record presents no ground for setting aside the order of the Board so far as the facts pertaining to the circumstances and purpose of the discharge of the employees are concerned. Upon that point it is sufficient to say that the evidence supports the findings of the Board that respondent discharged these men "because of their union activity and for the purpose of discouraging membership in the union." We turn to the questions of law which respondent urges in contesting the validity and application of the act.

* * *

Second. *The Unfair Labor Practices in Question.*—The unfair labor practices found by the Board are those defined in section 8, subdivisions (1) and (3). These provide:

"Sec. 8. It shall be an unfair labor practice for an employer—

"(1) To interfere with, restrain, or coerce employees in the exercise of the rights guaranteed in section 7 [section 157 of this title].
* * *

"(3) By discrimination in regard to hire or tenure of employment or any term or condition of employment to encourage or discourage membership in any labor organization."

Section 8, subdivision (1), refers to section 7, which is as follows:

"Section 7. Employees shall have the right to self-organization, to form, join, or assist labor organizations, to bargain collectively through representatives of their own choosing, and to engage in concerted activities, for the purpose of collective bargaining or other mutual aid or protection."

Thus, in its present application, the statute goes no further than to safeguard the right of employees to self-organization and to select representatives of their own choosing for collective bargaining or other mutual protection without restraint or coercion by their employer.

That is a fundamental right. Employees have as clear a right to organize and select their representatives for lawful purposes as the respondent has to organize its business and select its own officers and agents. Discrimination and coercion to prevent the free exercise of the right of employees to self-organization and representation is a proper subject for condemnation by competent legislative authority. Long ago we stated the reason for labor organizations. We said that they were organized out of the necessities of the situation; that a single employee was helpless in dealing with an employer; that he was dependent ordinarily on his daily wage for the maintenance of himself and family; that, if the employer refused to pay him the wages that he thought fair, he was nevertheless unable to leave the employ and resist arbitrary and unfair treatment; that union was essential to give laborers opportunity to deal on an equality with their employer. American Steel Foundries v. Tri-City Central Trades Council, 257 U.S. 184, 209. We reiterated these views when we had under consideration the Railway Labor Act of 1926, 44 Stat. 577. Fully recognizing the legality of collective action on the part of employees in order to safeguard their proper interests, we said that Congress was not required to ignore this right but could safeguard it. Congress could seek to make appropriate collective action of employees an instrument of peace rather than of strife. We said that such collective action would be a mockery if representation were made futile by interference with freedom of choice. Hence the prohibition by Congress of interference with the selection of representatives for the purpose of negotiation and conference between employers and employees, "instead of being an invasion of the constitutional right of either, was based on the recognition of the rights of both." Texas & N. O. R. Co. v. Railway & S. S. Clerks [281 U.S. 548]. We have reasserted the same principle in sustaining the application of the Railway Labor Act as amended in 1934 (45 U.S.C.A. § 151 et seq.). Virginian Railway Co. v. System Federation, No. 40, supra.

Third.   The Application of the Act to Employees Engaged in Production.—The Principle Involved.—Respondent says that, whatever may be said of employees engaged in interstate commerce, the industrial relations and activities in the manufacturing department of respondent's enterprise are not subject to federal regulation.   The argument rests upon the proposition that manufacturing in itself is not commerce.   * * *

The government distinguishes these cases.   The various parts of respondent's enterprise are described as interdependent and as thus involving "a great movement of iron ore, coal and limestone along well-defined paths to the steel mills, thence through them, and thence in the form of steel products into the consuming centers of the country—a definite and well-understood course of business."   It is urged that these activities constitute a "stream" or "flow" of commerce, of which the Aliquippa manufacturing plant is the focal point, and that industrial strife at that point would cripple the entire movement.   Reference is made to our decision sustaining the Packers and Stockyards Act.   Stafford v. Wallace, 258 U.S. 495.   The Court found that the stockyards were but a "throat" through which the current of commerce flowed and the transactions which there occurred could not be separated from that movement.   Hence the sales at the stockyards were not regarded as merely local transactions, for, while they created "a local change of title," they did not "stop the flow," but merely changed the private interests in the subject of the current.   Distinguishing the cases which upheld the power of the state to impose a nondiscriminatory tax upon property which the owner intended to transport to another state, but which was not in actual transit and was held within the state subject to the disposition of the owner, the Court remarked: "The question, it should be observed, is not with respect to the extent of the power of Congress to regulate interstate commerce, but whether a particular exercise of state power in view of its nature and operation must be deemed to be in conflict with this paramount authority."   Id., 258 U.S. 495.   See Minnesota v. Blasius, 290 U.S. 1.   Applying the doctrine of Stafford v. Wallace, supra, the Court sustained the Grain Futures Act of 1922 with respect to transactions on the Chicago Board of Trade, although these transactions were "not in and of themselves interstate commerce."   Congress had found that they had become "a constantly recurring burden and obstruction to that commerce."   Board of Trade of City of Chicago v. Olsen, 262 U.S. 1, 32.   * * *

Respondent contends that the instant case presents material distinctions.   Respondent says that the Aliquippa plant is extensive in size and represents a large investment in buildings, machinery and equipment.   The raw materials which are brought to the plant are delayed for long periods and, after being subjected to manufacturing processes "are changed substantially as to character, utility and value."   The finished products which emerge "are to a large extent manufactured without reference to pre-existing orders and contracts and are entirely different from the raw materials which enter at the other

end."   Hence respondent argues that, "If importation and exporta-
tion in interstate commerce do not singly transfer purely local activities into the field of congressional regulation, it should follow that
their combination would not alter the local situation."   Arkadelphia
Milling Co. v. St. Louis, Southwestern R. Co., 249 U.S. 134, 151.   * *

We do not find it necessary to determine whether these features
of defendant's business dispose of the asserted analogy to the "stream
of commerce" cases.   The instances in which that metaphor has been
used are but particular, and not exclusive, illustrations of the protective power which the government invokes in support of the present
act.   The congressional authority to protect interstate commerce
from burdens and obstructions is not limited to transactions which
can be deemed to be an essential part of a "flow" of interstate or foreign commerce.   Burdens and obstructions may be due to injurious
action springing from other sources.   The fundamental principle is
that the power to regulate commerce is the power to enact "all appropriate legislation" for its "protection or advancement" (The
Daniel Ball, 10 Wall. 557); to adopt measures "to promote its growth
and insure its safety" (County of Mobile v. Kimball, 102 U.S. 691);
"to foster, protect, control, and restrain." (Second Employers' Liability Cases, 223 U.S. 1).   See Texas & N. O. R. Co. v. Railway & S.
S. Clerks, supra.   That power is plenary and may be exerted to protect interstate commerce "no matter what the source of the dangers
which threaten it."   Second Employers' Liability Cases, 223 U.S. 1;
Schechter Corporation v. United States, supra.   Although activities
may be intrastate in character when separately considered, if they
have such a close and substantial relation to interstate commerce
that their control is essential or appropriate to protect that commerce
from burdens and obstructions, Congress cannot be denied the power
to exercise that control.   * * *   Undoubtedly the scope of this power must be considered in the light of our dual system of government
and may not be extended so as to embrace effects upon interstate
commerce so indirect and remote that to embrace them, in view of
our complex society, would effectually obliterate the distinction between what is national and what is local and create a completely centralized government.   Id.   The question is necessarily one of degree.
As the Court said in Board of Trade of City of Chicago v. Olsen, 262
U.S. 1, repeating what had been said in Stafford v. Wallace, supra:
"Whatever amounts to more or less constant practice, and threatens
to obstruct or unduly to burden the freedom of interstate commerce
is within the regulatory power of Congress under the commerce
clause, and it is primarily for Congress to consider and decide the fact
of the danger and to meet it."

That intrastate activities, by reason of close and intimate relation to interstate commerce, may fall within federal control is demonstrated in the case of carriers who are engaged in both interstate
and intrastate transportation.   There federal control has been found
essential to secure the freedom of interstate traffic from interference
or unjust discrimination and to promote the efficiency of the inter-

state service. The Shreveport Case (Houston, E. & W. T. R. Co. v. United States), 234 U.S. 342; Railroad Commission of Wisconsin v. Chicago, B. & Q. R. Co., 257 U.S. 563. It is manifest that intrastate rates deal *primarily* with a local activity. But in rate making they bear such a close relation to interstate rates that effective control of the one must embrace some control over the other. Id. Under the Transportation Act, 1920, Congress went so far as to authorize the Interstate Commerce Commission to establish a statewide level of intrastate rates in order to prevent an unjust discrimination against interstate commerce. Railroad Commission of Wisconsin v. Chicago, B. & Q. R. R. Co., supra. * * *

The close and intimate effect which brings the subject within the reach of federal power may be due to activities in relation to productive industry although the industry when separately viewed is local. This has been abundantly illustrated in the application of the Federal Anti-Trust Act (15 U.S.C.A. §§ 1–7). * * *

It is thus apparent that the fact that the employees here concerned were engaged in production is not determinative. The question remains as to the effect upon interstate commerce of the labor practice involved. In the Schechter Case, supra, we found that the effect there was so remote as to be beyond the federal power. To find "immediacy or directness" there was to find it "almost everywhere," a result inconsistent with the maintenance of our federal system. In the Carter Case, supra, the Court was of the opinion that the provisions of the statute relating to production were invalid upon several grounds,—that there was improper delegation of legislative power, and that the requirements not only went beyond any sustainable measure of protection of interstate commerce but were also inconsistent with due process. These cases are not controlling here.

Fourth. Effects of the Unfair Labor Practice in Respondent's Enterprise.—Giving full weight to respondent's contention with respect to a break in the complete continuity of the "stream of commerce" by reason of respondent's manufacturing operations, the fact remains that the stoppage of those operations by industrial strife would have a most serious effect upon interstate commerce. In view of respondent's far-flung activities, it is idle to say that the effect would be indirect or remote. It is obvious that it would be immediate and might be catastrophic. We are asked to shut our eyes to the plainest facts of our national life and to deal with the question of direct and indirect effects in an intellectual vacuum. Because there may be but indirect and remote effects upon interstate commerce in connection with a host of local enterprises throughout the country, it does not follow that other industrial activities do not have such a close and intimate relation to interstate commerce as to make the presence of industrial strife a matter of the most urgent national concern. When industries organize themselves on a national scale, making their relation to interstate commerce the dominant factor in their activities, how can it be maintained that their industrial labor relations constitute a forbidden field into which Congress may not enter when it is necessary to protect interstate commerce from the paralyzing consequences of industrial war? We have often said that interstate commerce itself is a practical conception. It is equally true that interferences with that commerce must be appraised by a judgment that does not ignore actual experience.

Experience has abundantly demonstrated that the recognition of the right of employees to self-organization and to have representatives of their own choosing for the purpose of collective bargaining is often an essential condition of industrial peace. Refusal to confer and negotiate has been one of the most prolific causes of strife. This is such an outstanding fact in the history of labor disturbances that it is a proper subject of judicial notice and requires no citation of instances. The opinion in the case of Virginian Railway Co. v. System Federation No. 40, supra, points out that, in the case of carriers, experience has shown that before the amendment, of 1934, of the Railway Labor Act, "when there was no dispute as to the organizations authorized to represent the employees, and when there was willingness of the employer to meet such representative for a discussion of their grievances, amicable adjustment of differences had generally followed and strikes had been avoided." That, on the other hand, "a prolific source of dispute had been the maintenance by the railroads of company unions and the denial by railway management of the authority of representatives chosen by their employees." The opinion in that case also points to the large measure of success of the labor policy embodied in the Railway Labor Act. But, with respect to the appropriateness of the recognition of self-organization and representation in the promotion of peace, the question is not essentially different in the case of employees in industries of such a character that interstate commerce is put in jeopardy from the case of employees of transportation companies. And of what avail is it to protect the facility of transportation, if interstate commerce is throttled with respect to the commodities to be transported!

These questions have frequently engaged the attention of Congress and have been the subject of many inquiries. The steel industry is one of the great basic industries of the United States, with ramifying activities affecting interstate commerce at every point. The Government aptly refers to the steel strike of 1919–1920 with its far-reaching consequences. The fact that there appears to have been no major disturbance in that industry in the more recent period did not dispose of the possibilities of future and like dangers to interstate commerce which Congress was entitled to foresee and to exercise its protective power to forestall. It is not necessary again to detail the facts as to respondent's enterprise. Instead of being beyond the pale, we think that it presents in a most striking way the close and intimate relation which a manufacturing industry may have to interstate commerce and we have no doubt that Congress had constitutional authority to safeguard the right of respondent's employees to self-organization and freedom in the choice of representatives for collective bargaining.

Fifth. The Means Which the Act Employs.—Questions under the Due Process Clause and Other Constitutional Restrictions.—Respondent asserts its right to conduct its business in an orderly manner without being subjected to arbitrary restraints. What we have said points to the fallacy in the argument. Employees have their correlative right to organize for the purpose of securing the redress of grievances and to promote agreements with employers relating to rates of pay and conditions of work. Texas & N. O. R. Co. v. Railway S. S. Clerks, supra; Virginian Railway Co. v. System Federation No. 40. Restraint for the purpose of preventing an unjust interference with that right cannot be considered arbitrary or capricious. The provision of section 9(a) that representatives, for the purpose of collective bargaining, of the majority of the employees in an appropriate unit shall be the exclusive representatives of all the employees in that unit, imposes upon the respondent only the duty of conferring and negotiating with the authorized representatives of its employees for the purpose of settling a labor dispute. This provision has its analogue in section 2, Ninth, of the Railway Labor Act, as amended (45 U.S.C.A. § 152, subd. 9), which was under consideration in Virginian Railway Co. v. System Federation No. 40, supra. The decree which we affirmed in that case required the railway company to treat with the representative chosen by the employees and also to refrain from entering into collective labor agreements with any one other than their true representative as ascertained in accordance with the provisions of the act. We said that the obligation to treat with the true representative was exclusive and hence imposed the negative duty to treat with no other. We also pointed out that, as conceded by the government, the injunction against the company's entering into any contract concerning rules, rates of pay and working conditions except with a chosen representative was "designed only to prevent collective bargaining with any one purporting to represent employees" other than the representative they had selected. It was taken "to prohibit the negotiation of labor contracts, generally applicable to employees" in the described unit with any other representative than the one so chosen, "but not as precluding such individual contracts" as the company might "elect to make directly with individual employees." We think this construction also applies to section 9(a) of the National Labor Relations Act (29 U.S.C.A. § 159(a).

The act does not compel agreements between employers and employees. It does not compel any agreement whatever. It does not prevent the employer "from refusing to make a collective contract and hiring individuals on whatever terms" the employer "may by unilateral action determine." The act expressly provides in section 9(a) that any individual employee or a group of employees shall have the right at any time to present grievances to their employer. The theory of the act is that free opportunity for negotiation with accredited representatives of employees is likely to promote industrial peace and may bring about the adjustments and agreements which the act in itself does not attempt to compel. * * * The act does not interfere with the normal exercise of the right of the employer to select its employees or to discharge them. The employer may not, under cover of that right, intimidate or coerce its employees with respect to their self-organization and representation, and, on the other hand, the Board is not entitled to make its authority a pretext for interference with the right of discharge when that right is exercised for other reasons than such intimidation and coercion. The true purpose is the subject of investigation with full opportunity to show the facts. It would seem that when employers freely recognize the right of their employees to their own organizations and their unrestricted right of representation there will be much less occasion for controversy in respect to the free and appropriate exercise of the right of selection and discharge.

The act has been criticized as one-sided in its application; that it subjects the employer to supervision and restraint and leaves untouched the abuses for which employees may be responsible; that it fails to provide a more comprehensive plan,—with better assurances of fairness to both sides and with increased chances of success in bringing about, if not compelling, equitable solutions of industrial disputes affecting interstate commerce. But we are dealing with the power of Congress, not with a particular policy or with the extent to which policy should go. We have frequently said that the legislative authority, exerted within its proper field, need not embrace all the evils within its reach. The Constitution does not forbid "cautious advance, step by step," in dealing with the evils which are exhibited in activities within the range of legislative power. * * * The question in such cases is whether the Legislature, in what it does prescribe, has gone beyond constitutional limits.

The procedural provisions of the act are assailed. But these provisions, as we construe them, do not offend against the constitutional requirements governing the creation and action of administrative bodies. See Interstate Commerce Commission v. Louisville & Nashville R. Co., 227 U.S. 88. The act establishes standards to which the Board must conform. There must be complaint, notice and hearing. The Board must receive evidence and make findings. The findings as to the facts are to be conclusive, but only if supported by evidence. The order of the Board is subject to review by the designated court, and only when sustained by the court may the order be enforced. Upon that review all questions of the jurisdiction of the Board and the regularity of its proceedings, all questions of constitutional right or statutory authority are open to examination by the court. We construe the procedural provisions as affording adequate opportunity to secure judicial protection against arbitrary action in accordance with the well-settled rules applicable to administrative agencies set up by Congress to aid in the enforcement of valid legislation. It is not necessary to repeat these rules which have frequently been declared. None of them appears to have been transgressed in the instant case. Respondent was notified and heard. It had opportunity to meet the charge of unfair labor practices upon the merits, and by withdrawing from the hearing it declined to avail itself of that opportunity. The facts found by the Board support its order and the evidence supports the findings. Respondent has no just ground for complaint on this score.

The order of the Board required the reinstatement of the employees who were found to have been discharged because of their "union activity" and for the purpose of "discouraging membership in the union." That requirement was authorized by the act. Section 10(c), 29 U.S.C.A. § 160(c). In Texas & N. O. R. Co. v. Railway & S. S. Clerks, supra, a similar order for restoration to service was made by the court in contempt proceedings for the violation of an injunction issued by the court to restrain an interference with the right of employees as guaranteed by the Railway Labor Act of 1926. The requirement of restoration to service of employees discharged in violation of the provisions of that act was thus a sanction imposed in the enforcement of a judicial decree. We do not doubt that Congress could impose a like sanction for the enforcement of its valid regulation. The fact that in the one case it was a judicial sanction, and in the other a legislative one, is not an essential difference in determining its propriety.

Respondent complains that the Board not only ordered reinstatement but directed the payment of wages for the time lost by the discharge, less amounts earned by the employee during that period. This part of the order was also authorized by the act. Section 10(c). It is argued that the requirement is equivalent to a money judgment and hence contravenes the Seventh Amendment with respect to trial by jury. The Seventh Amendment provides that "In suits at common law, where the value in controversy shall exceed twenty dollars; the right of trial by jury shall be preserved." The amendment thus preserves the right which existed under the common law when the amendment was adopted. * * * Thus it has no application to cases where recovery of money damages is an incident to equitable relief even though damages might have been recovered in an action at law. * * * It does not apply where the proceeding is not in the nature of a suit at common law. Guthrie National Bank v. Guthrie, 173 U.S. 528.

The instant case is not a suit at common law or in the nature of such a suit. The proceeding is one unknown to the common law. It is a statutory proceeding. Reinstatement of the employee and payment for time lost are requirements imposed for violation of the statute and are remedies appropriate to its enforcement. The contention under the Seventh Amendment is without merit.

Our conclusion is that the order of the Board was within its competency and that the act is valid as here applied. The judgment of the Circuit Court of Appeals is reversed and the cause is remanded for further proceedings in conformity with this opinion. It is so ordered.

Reversed and remanded.

Mr. Justice McREYNOLDS dissented.

NATIONAL LABOR RELATIONS BOARD v.
GISSEL PACKING CO.

Supreme Court of the United States, 1969.
395 U.S. 575, 89 S.Ct. 1918, 23 L.Ed.2d 547.

Mr. Chief Justice WARREN delivered the opinion of the Court.

These cases involve the extent of an employer's duty under the National Labor Relations Act to recognize a union that bases its claim to representative status solely on the possession of union authorization cards, and the steps an employer may take, particularly with regard to the scope and content of statements he may make, in legitimately resisting such card-based recognition. * * *

I.

Of the four cases before us, three—*Gissel Packing Co., Heck's Inc.*, and *General Steel Products, Inc.*—were consolidated following separate decisions in the Court of Appeals for the Fourth Circuit and brought here by the National Labor Relations Board in No. 573. Food Store Employees Union, Local No. 347, the petitioning Union in *Gissel*, brought that case here in a separate petition in No. 691. All three cases present the same legal issues in similar, uncomplicated factual settings that can be briefly described together. The fourth case, No. 585 (*Sinclair Company*), brought here from the Court of Appeals for the First Circuit and argued separately, presents many of the same questions and will thus be disposed of in this opinion; but because the validity of some of the Board's factual findings are under attack on First Amendment grounds, detailed attention must be paid to the factual setting of that case.

Nos. 573 and 691.
[Gissel]

In each of the cases from the Fourth Circuit, the course of action followed by the Union and the employer and the Board's response were similar. In each case, the Union waged an organizational campaign, obtained authorization cards from a majority of employees in the appropriate bargaining unit, and then, on the basis of the cards, demanded recognition by the employer. All three employers refused to bargain on the ground that authorization cards were inherently unreliable indicators of employee desires; and they either embarked on, or continued, vigorous antiunion campaigns that gave rise to numerous unfair labor practice charges. In *Gissel*, where the employer's campaign began almost at the outset of the Union's organizational drive, the Union (petitioner in No. 691), did not seek an election, but instead filed three unfair labor practice charges against the employer, for refusing to bargain in violation of § 8(a) (5), for coercion and intimidation of employees in violation of § 8(a) (1),

and for discharge of Union adherents in violation of § 8(a) (3).[1]
In *Heck's* an election sought by the Union was never held because of
nearly identical unfair labor practice charges later filed by the Union
as a result of the employer's antiunion campaign, initiated after the
Union's recognition demand.[2] And in *General Steel*, an election petitioned for by the Union and won by the employer was set aside by
the Board because of the unfair labor practices committed by the
employer in the pre-election period.[3]

1. At the outset of the Union campaign, the Company vice president informed two employees, later discharged, that if they were caught talking to Union men, "you God-damned things will go." Subsequently, the Union presented oral and written demands for recognition, claiming possession of authorization cards from 31 of the 47 employees in the appropriate unit. Rejecting the bargaining demand, the Company began to interrogate employees as to their Union activities; to promise them better benefits than the Union could offer; and to warn them that if the "union got in, [the vice president] would just take his money and let the union run the place," that the Union was not going to get in, and that it would have to "fight" the Company first. Further, when the Company learned of an impending Union meeting, it arranged, so the Board later found, to have an agent present to report the identity of the Union's adherents. On the first day following the meeting, the vice president told the two employees referred to above that he knew they had gone to the meeting and that their work hours were henceforth reduced to half a day. Three hours later, the two employees were discharged. (Court's footnote 1.)

2. The organizing drive was initiated by the employees themselves at Heck's Charleston warehouses. The Union first demanded recognition on the basis of 13 cards from 26 employees of the Company's three Charleston warehouses. After responding "No comment" to the Union's repeated requests for recognition, the president assembled the employees and told them of his shock at their selection of the Union; he singled out one of the employees to ask if he had signed an authorization card. The next day the Union obtained the additional card necessary to establish a majority. That same day, the leading Union supporter (the employee who had first established contacts with the Union and had solicited a large number of the cards) was discharged, and another employee was interrogated as to his Union activities, encouraged to withdraw his authorization, and warned that a Union victory could result in reduced hours, fewer raises, and withdrawal of bonuses. A second demand for recognition was made two days later, and thereafter the president summoned two known Union supporters to his office and offered them new jobs at higher pay if they would use their influence to "break up the union."

The same pattern was repeated a year later at the Company's Ashland, Kentucky, store, where the Union obtained cards from 21 of the 38 employees by October 5, 1965. The next day, the assistant store manager told an employee that he knew that the Union had acquired majority status. When the Union requested recognition on October 8, however, the Company refused on the ground that it was not sure whether department heads were included in the bargaining unit—even though the cards represented a majority with or without the department heads. After a second request for recognition and an offer to submit the cards to the employer for verification, respondent again refused, on grounds of uncertainty about the definition of the unit and because a poll taken by the Company showed that a majority of the employees did not want Union representation. Meanwhile, the Company told the employees that an employee of another company store had been fired on the spot for signing a card, warned employees that the Company knew which ones had signed cards, and polled employees about their desire for Union representation without giving them assurances against reprisals. (Court's footnote 2.)

3. Throughout the Union's six-month organizational campaign—both before and after its demand for recognition based on possession of cards from 120 of the 207 employees in the appropri-

In each case, the Board's primary response was an order to bargain directed at the employers, despite the absence of an election in *Gissel* and *Heck's* and the employer's victory in *General Steel*. More specifically, the Board found in each case (1) that the Union had obtained valid authorization cards [4] from a majority of the employees in the bargaining unit and was thus entitled to represent the employees for collective bargaining purposes; and (2) that the employer's refusal to bargain with the Union in violation of § 8(a)(5) was motivated, not by a "good faith" doubt of the Union's majority status, but by a desire to gain time to dissipate that status. The Board based its conclusion as to the lack of good faith doubt on the fact that the employers had committed substantial unfair labor practices during their antiunion campaign efforts to resist recognition. Thus, the Board found that all three employers had engaged in restraint and coercion of employees in violation of § 8(a)(1). * * *

Consequently, the Board ordered the companies to cease and desist from their unfair labor practices, to offer reinstatement and back pay to the employees who had been discriminatorily discharged, to bargain with the Unions on request, and to post the appropriate notices.

On appeal, the Court of Appeals for the Fourth Circuit, in *per curiam* opinions in each of the three cases (398 F.2d 336), sustained the Board's findings as to the §§ 8(a)(1) and (3) violations, but rejected the Board's findings that the employers' refusal to bargain violated § 8(a)(5) and declined to enforce those portions of the Board's orders directing the respondent companies to bargain in good faith. * * *

No. 585.

[Sinclair]

In No. 585, the factual pattern was quite similar. The petitioner, a producer of mill rolls, wire, and related products at two

ate unit—the Company's foremen and supervisors interrogated employees about their Union involvement; threatened them with discharge for engaging in Union activities or voting for the Union; suggested that unionization might hurt business and make new jobs more difficult to obtain; warned that strikes and other dire economic consequences would result (a supervisor informed a group of employees that if the Union came in, "a nigger would be the head of it," and that when the Company put in 10 new machines, "the niggers would be the operators of them"); and asserted that, although the Company would have to negotiate with the Union, it could negotiate endlessly and would not have to sign anything. (Court's footnote 3.)

4. The cards used in all four campaigns in Nos. 573 and 691 and in the one drive in No. 585 unambiguously authorized the Union to represent the signing employee for collective bargaining purposes; there was no reference to elections. Typical of the cards was the one used in the Charleston campaign in *Heck's*, and it stated in relevant part:
"Desiring to become a member of the above Union of the International Brotherhood of Teamsters, Chauffeurs, Warehousemen and Helpers of America, I hereby make application for admission to membership. I hereby authorize you, your agents or representatives to act for me as collective bargaining agent on all matters pertaining to rates of pay, hours, or any other conditions of employment." (Court's footnote 4.)

plants in Holyoke, Massachusetts, was shut down for some three months in 1952 as the result of a strike over contract negotiations with the American Wire Weavers Protective Association, the representative of petitioner's journeymen and apprentice wire weavers from 1933 to 1952. The Company subsequently reopened without a union contract, and its employees remained unrepresented through 1964, when the Company was acquired by an Ohio corporation, with the Company's former president continuing as head of the Holyoke, Massachusetts, division. In July 1965, the International Brotherhood of Teamsters, Local Union No. 404, began an organizing campaign among petitioner's Holyoke employees and by the end of the summer had obtained authorization cards from 11 of the Company's 14 journeymen wire weavers choosing the Union as their bargaining agent. On September 20, the Union notified petitioner that it represented a majority of its wire weavers, requested that the Company bargain with it, and offered to submit the signed cards to a neutral third party for authentication. After petitioner's president declined the Union's request a week later, claiming, *inter alia*, that he had a good faith doubt of majority status because of the cards' inherent unreliability, the Union petitioned, on November 8, for an election that was ultimately set for December 9.

When petitioner's president first learned of the Union's drive in July, he talked with all of his employees in an effort to dissuade them from joining a union. He particularly emphasized the results of the long 1952 strike, which he claimed "almost put our company out of business," and expressed worry that the employees were forgetting the "lessons of the past." He emphasized, secondly, that the Company was still on "thin ice" financially, that the Union's "only weapon is to strike," and that a strike "could lead to the closing of the plant," since the parent company had ample manufacturing facilities elsewhere. He noted, thirdly, that because of their age and the limited usefulness of their skills outside their craft, the employees might not be able to find re-employment if they lost their jobs as a result of a strike. Finally, he warned those who did not believe that the plant could go out of business to "look around Holyoke and see a lot of them out of business." The president sent letters to the same effect to the employees in early November, emphasizing that the parent company had no reason to stay in Massachusetts if profits went down.

During the two or three weeks immediately prior to the election on December 9, the president sent the employees a pamphlet captioned: "Do you want another 13-week strike?" stating, *inter alia,* that: "We have no doubt that the Teamsters Union can again close the Wire Weaving Department and the entire plant by a strike. We have no hopes that the Teamsters Union Bosses will not call a strike. * * * The Teamsters Union is a strike happy outfit." Similar communications followed in late November, including one stressing the Teamsters' "hoodlum control." Two days before the election, the Company sent out another pamphlet that was entitled: "Let's Look at the Record," and that purported to be an obituary of companies in the Holyoke-Springfield, Massachusetts, area that had allegedly gone out of business because of union demands, eliminating some 3,500 jobs; the first page carried a large cartoon showing the preparation of a grave for the Sinclair Company and other headstones containing the names of other plants allegedly victimized by the unions. Finally, on the day before the election, the president made another personal appeal to his employees to reject the Union. He repeated that the Company's financial condition was precarious; that a possible strike would jeopardize the continued operation of the plant; and that age and lack of education would make re-employment difficult. The Union lost the election 7–6, and then filed both objections to the election and unfair labor practice charges which were consolidated for hearing before the trial examiner. * * *

The Board found that under the "totality of the circumstances" petitioner's activities constituted a violation of § 8(a) (1) of the Act. The Board further agreed with the trial examiner that petitioner's activities, because they "also interfered with the exercise of a free and untrammeled choice in the election," and "tended to foreclose the possibility" of holding a fair election, required that the election be set aside. The Board also found that the Union had a valid card majority (the unambiguous cards, see n. 4, *supra,* went unchallenged) when it demanded recognition initially and that the Company declined recognition, not because of a good faith doubt as to the majority status, but, as the § 8(a) (1) violations indicated, in order to gain time to dissipate that status—in violation of § 8(a) (5). Consequently, the Board set the election aside, entered a cease-and-desist order, and ordered the Company to bargain on request.

On appeal, the Court of Appeals for the First Circuit sustained the Board's findings and conclusions and enforced its order in full. * * *

II.

In urging us to reverse the Fourth Circuit and to affirm the First Circuit, the National Labor Relations Board contends that we should approve its interpretation and administration of the duties and obligations imposed by the Act in authorization card cases. * * *

The traditional approach utilized by the Board for many years has been known as the *Joy Silk* doctrine. Joy Silk Mills, Inc., 85 N.L. R.B. 1263 (1949), enforced, 185 F.2d 732 (1950). Under that rule, an employer could lawfully refuse to bargain with a union claiming representative status through possession of authorization cards if he had a "good faith doubt" as to the union's majority status; instead of bargaining, he could insist that the union seek an election in order to show bad faith and that an employer "will not be held to have vio-faith doubt and enter a bargaining order in one of two ways. It could find (1) that the employer's independent unfair labor practices were evidence of bad faith, showing that the employer was seeking time to dissipate the union's majority. Or the Board could find (2) that the employer had come forward with no reasons for entertaining any doubt and therefore that he must have rejected the bargaining demand in bad faith.   An example of the second category was Snow & Sons, 134 N.L.R.B. 709 (1961), enforced, 308 F.2d 687 (C.A.9th Cir. 1962), where the employer reneged on his agreement to bargain after a third party checked the validity of the card signatures and insisted on an election because he doubted that the employees truly desired representation.   The Board entered a bargaining order with very broad language to the effect that an employer could not refuse a bargaining demand and seek an election instead "without a valid ground therefor."   *   *   *

The leading case codifying modifications to the *Joy Silk* doctrine was Aaron Brothers, 158 N.L.R.B. 1077 (1966).   There the Board made it clear that it had shifted the burden to the General Counsel to show bad faith and that an employer "will not be held to have violated his bargaining obligation   *   *   *   simply because he refuses to rely upon cards, rather than an election, as the method for determining the union's majority."   158 N.L.R.B., at 1078.   Two significant consequences were emphasized.   The Board noted (1) that not every unfair labor practice would automatically result in a finding of bad faith and therefore a bargaining order; the Board implied that it would find bad faith only if the unfair labor practice was serious enough to have the tendency to dissipate the union's majority.   The Board noted (2) that an employer no longer needed to come forward with reasons for rejecting a bargaining demand.   The Board pointed out, however, that a bargaining order would issue if it could prove that an employer's "course of conduct" gave indications as to the employer's bad faith.   *   *   *   the Board announced at oral argument that it had virtually abandoned the *Joy Silk* doctrine altogether.   Under the Board's current practice, an employer's good faith doubt is largely irrelevant, and the key to the issuance of a bargaining order is the commission of serious unfair labor practices that interfere with the election processes and tend to preclude the holding of a fair election.   Thus, an employer can insist that a union go to an election, regardless of his subjective motivation, so long as he is not guilty of misconduct; he need give no affirmative reasons for rejecting a recognition request, and he can demand an election with a simple "no comment" to the union.   The Board pointed out, however, (1) that an employer could not refuse to bargain if he *knew,* through a personal poll for instance, that a majority of his employees supported the union, and (2) that an employer could not refuse recognition initially because of questions as to the appropriateness of the unit and then later claim, as an afterthought, that he doubted the union's strength.

*   *   *

III.

A.

The first issue facing us is whether a union can establish a bargaining obligation by means other than a Board election and whether the validity of alternate routes to majority status, such as cards, was affected by the 1947 Taft-Hartley amendments. The most commonly traveled route for a union to obtain recognition as the exclusive bargaining representative of an unorganized group of employees is through the Board's election and certification procedures under § 9(c) of the Act (29 U.S.C.A. § 159(c)); it is also, from the Board's point of view, the preferred route. A union is not limited to a Board election, however, for, in addition to § 9, the present Act provides in § 8 (a) (5) (29 U.S.C.A. § 158(a) (5)), as did the Wagner Act in § 8(5), that "[i]t shall be an unfair labor practice for an employer * * * to refuse to bargain collectively with the representatives of his employees, subject to the provisions of section 9(a)." Since § 9(a), in both the Wagner Act and the present Act, refers to the representative as the one "designated or selected" by a majority of the employees without specifying precisely how that representative is to be chosen, it was early recognized that an employer had a duty to bargain whenever the union representative presented "convincing evidence of majority support." Almost from the inception of the Act, then, it was recognized that a union did not have to be certified as the winner of a Board election to invoke a bargaining obligation; it could establish majority status by other means under the unfair labor practice provision of § 8(a) (5)—by showing convincing support, for instance, by a union-called strike or strike vote, or, as here, by possession of cards signed by a majority of the employees authorizing the union to represent them for collective bargaining purposes.

We have consistently accepted this interpretation of the Wagner Act and the present Act, particularly as to the use of authorization cards. * * * We * * * pointed out in United Mine Workers v. Arkansas Flooring Co., 351 U.S. 62 (1956), * * * where the union had obtained signed authorization cards from a majority of the employees, that "[i]n the absence of any bona fide dispute as to the existence of the required majority of eligible employees, the employer's denial of recognition of the union would have violated § 8(a) (5) of the Act." * * *

In short, we hold that the 1947 amendments did not restrict an employer's duty to bargain under § 8(a) (5) solely to those unions whose representative status is certified after a Board election.

B.

We next consider the question whether authorization cards are such inherently unreliable indicators of employee desires that, whatever the validity of other alternate routes to representative status, the cards themselves may never be used to determine a union's majority and to support an order to bargain. In this context, the employers urge us to take the step the 1947 amendments and their legislative history indicate Congress did not take, namely, to rule out completely the use of cards in the bargaining arena. Even if we do not unhesitatingly accept the Fourth Circuit's view in the matter, the employers argue, at the very least we should * * * establish stricter controls over the solicitation of the cards by union representatives.

The objections to the use of cards voiced by the employers and the Fourth Circuit boil down to two contentions. (1) that, as contrasted with the election procedure, the cards cannot accurately reflect an employee's wishes, either because an employer has not had a chance to present his views and thus a chance to insure that the employee choice was an informed one, or because the choice was the result of group pressures and not individual decision made in the privacy of a voting booth; and (2) that quite apart from the election comparison, the cards are too often obtained through misrepresentation and coercion which compound the cards' inherent inferiority to the election process. Neither contention is persuasive, and each proves too much. The Board itself has recognized, and continues to do so here, that secret elections are generally the most satisfactory—indeed the preferred—method of ascertaining whether a union has majority support. The acknowledged superiority of the election process, however, does not mean that cards are thereby rendered totally invalid, for where an employer engages in conduct disruptive of the election process, cards may be the most effective—perhaps the only—way of assuring employee choice. As for misrepresentation, in any specific case of alleged irregularity in the solicitation of the cards, the proper course is to apply the Board's customary standards * * * and rule that there was no majority if the standards were not satisfied. It does not follow that because there are some instances of irregularity, the cards can never be used; otherwise, an employer could put off his bargaining obligation indefinitely through continuing interference with elections.

* * *

The employers' second complaint, that the cards are too often obtained through misrepresentation and coercion, must be rejected also in view of the Board's present rules for controlling card solicitation, which we view as adequate to the task where the cards involved state their purpose clearly and unambiguously on their face. We would be closing our eyes to obvious difficulties, of course, if we did not recognize that there have been abuses, primarily arising out of misrepresentations by union organizers as to whether the effect of signing a card was to designate the union to represent the employee for collective bargaining purposes or merely to authorize it to seek an election to determine that issue. And we would be equally blind if we did not recognize that various courts of appeals and commentators have differed significantly as to the effectiveness of the Board's *Cumberland Shoe* doctrine * * * to cure such abuses.

* * *

We need make no decision as to the conflicting approaches used with regard to dual-purpose cards, for in each of the five organization campaigns in the four cases before us the cards used were single-purpose cards, stating clearly and unambiguously on their face that the signer designated the union as his representative. And even the view forcefully voiced by the Fourth Circuit below that unambiguous cards as well present too many opportunities for misrepresentation comes before us somewhat weakened in view of the fact that there were no allegations of irregularities in four of those five campaigns (*Gissel*, the two *Heck's* campaigns, and *Sinclair*). Only in *General Steel* did the employer challenge the cards on the basis of misrepresentations. There, the trial examiner, after hearing testimony from over 100 employees and applying the traditional Board approach * * *, concluded that "all of these employees not only intended, but were fully aware, that they were thereby designating the Union as their representative." Thus, the sole question before us, raised in only one of the four cases here, is whether the *Cumberland Shoe* doctrine is an adequate rule under the Act for assuring employee free choice.

In resolving the conflict among the circuits in favor of approving the Board's *Cumberland* rule, we think it sufficient to point out that employees should be bound by the clear language of what they sign unless that language is deliberately and clearly canceled by a union adherent with words calculated to direct the signer to disregard and forget the language above his signature. There is nothing inconsistent in handing an employee a card that says the signer authorizes the union to represent him and then telling him that the card will probably be used first to get an election. Elections have been, after all, and will continue to be, held in the vast majority of cases; the union will still have to have the signatures of 30% of the employees when an employer rejects a bargaining demand and insists that the union seek an election. We cannot agree with the employers here that employees as a rule are too unsophisticated to be bound by what they sign unless expressly told that their act of signing represents something else. In addition to approving the use of cards, of course, Congress has expressly authorized reliance on employee signatures alone in other areas of labor relations, * * *

We agree, however, with the Board's own warnings in Levi Strauss & Co., 172 N.L.R.B. No. 57, 68 L.R.R.M. 1338, 1341, and n. 7 (1968), that in hearing testimony concerning a card challenge, trial examiners should not neglect their obligation to ensure employee free choice by a too easy mechanical application of the *Cumberland* rule. We also accept the observation that employees are more likely than not, many months after a card drive and in response to questions by company counsel, to give testimony damaging to the union, particularly where company officials have previously threatened reprisals for union activity in violation of § 8(a) (1). We therefore reject any rule that requires a probe of an employee's subjective motivations as involving an endless and unreliable inquiry. * * * And we reiterate that nothing we say here indicates our approval of the *Cumberland Shoe* rule when applied to ambiguous, dual-purpose cards.

The employers argue as a final reason for rejecting the use of the cards that they are faced with a Hobson's choice under current Board rules and will almost inevitably come out the loser. They contend that if they do not make an immediate, personal investigation into possible solicitation irregularities to determine whether in fact the union represents an uncoerced majority, they will have unlawfully refused to bargain for failure to have a good faith doubt of the union's majority; and if they do make such an investigation, their efforts at polling and interrogation will constitute an unfair labor practice in violation of § 8(a) (1) and they will again be ordered to bargain. As we have pointed out, however, an employer is not obligated to accept a card check as proof of majority status, under the Board's current practice, and he is not required to justify his insistence on an election by making his own investigation of employee sentiment and showing affirmative reasons for doubting the majority status. See Aaron Brothers, 158 N.L.R.B. 1077, 1078. If he does make an investigation, the Board's recent cases indicate that reasonable polling in this regard will not always be termed violative of § 8 (a) (1). * * * And even if an employer's limited interrogation is found violative of the Act, it might not be serious enough to call for a bargaining order. * * *

IV.

We consider finally petitioner Sinclair's First Amendment challenge to the holding of the Board and the Court of Appeals for the First Circuit. At the outset we note that the question raised here most often arises in the context of a nascent union organizational drive, where employers must be careful in waging their antiunion campaign. As to conduct generally, the above-noted gradations of unfair labor practices, with their varying consequences, create certain hazards for employers when they seek to estimate or resist unionization efforts. But so long as the differences involve conduct easily avoided, such as discharge, surveillance, and coercive interrogation, we do not think that employers can complain that the distinctions are unreasonably difficult to follow. Where an employer's antiunion efforts consist of speech alone, however, the difficulties raised are not so easily resolved. The Board has eliminated some of the problem areas by no longer requiring an employer to show affirmative reasons for insisting on an election and by permitting him to make reasonable inquiries. We do not decide, of course, whether these allowances are mandatory. But we do note that an employer's free speech right to communicate his views to his employees is firmly established and cannot be infringed by a union or the Board. Thus, § 8(c) (29 U.S.C.A. § 158(c)) merely implements the First Amendment by requiring that the expression of "any views, argument, or opinion" shall not be "evidence of an unfair labor practice," so long as such expression contains "no threat of reprisal or force or promise of benefit" in violation of § 8(a) (1). Section 8(a) (1), in turn, prohibits interference, restraint or coercion of employees in the exercise of their right to self-organization.

Any assessment of the precise scope of employer expression, of course, must be made in the context of its labor relations setting. Thus, an employer's rights cannot outweigh the equal rights of the employees to associate freely, as those rights are embodied in § 7 and protected by § 8(a) (1) and the proviso to § 8(c). And any balancing of those rights must take into account the economic dependence of the employees on their employers, and the necessary tendency of the former, because of that relationship, to pick up intended implications of the latter that might be more readily dismissed by a more disinterested ear. Stating these obvious principles is but another way of recognizing that what is basically at stake is the establishment of a nonpermanent, limited relationship between the employer, his economically dependent employee and his union agent, not the election of legislators or the enactment of legislation whereby that relationship is ultimately defined and where the independent voter may be freer to listen more objectively and employers as a class freer to talk. Cf. New York Times Co. v. Sullivan, 376 U.S. 254 (1964).

    * * * Thus, an employer is free to communicate to his employees any of his general views about unionism or any of his specific views about a particular union, so long as the communications do not contain a "threat of reprisal or force or promise of benefit." He may even make a prediction as to the precise effects he believes unionization will have on his company. In such a case, however, the prediction must be carefully phrased on the basis of objective fact to convey an employer's belief as to demonstrably probable consequences beyond his control or to convey a management decision already arrived at to close the plant in case of unionization. See Textile Workers v. Darlington Mfg. Co., 380 U.S. 263 (1965). If there is any implication that an employer may or may not take action solely on his own initiative for reasons unrelated to economic necessities and known only to him, the statement is no longer a reasonable prediction based on available facts but a threat of retaliation based on misrepresentation and coercion, and as such without the protection of the First Amendment. We therefore agree with the court below that "[c]onveyance of the employer's belief, even though sincere, that unionization will or may result in the closing of the plant is not a statement of fact unless, which is most improbable, the eventuality of closing is capable of proof." 397 F.2d 157. As stated elsewhere, an employer is free only to tell "what he reasonably believes will be the likely economic consequences of unionization that are outside his control," and not "threats of economic reprisal to be taken solely on his own volition." NLRB v. River Togs, Inc., 382 F.2d 198 (C.A.2d Cir. 1967).

    Equally valid was the finding by the court and the Board that petitioner's statements and communications were not cast as a prediction of "demonstrable 'economic consequences,' " 397 F.2d, at 160, but rather as a threat of retaliatory action. The Board found that petitioner's speeches, pamphlets, leaflets, and letters conveyed the following message: that the company was in a precarious financial condition; that the "strike-happy" union would in all likelihood have to obtain its potentially unreasonable demands by striking, the probable result of which would be a plant shutdown, as the past history of labor relations in the area indicated; and that the employees in such a case would have great difficulty finding employment elsewhere. In carrying out its duty to focus on the question: "[W]hat did the speaker intend and the listener understand?" (A. Cox, Law and the National Labor Policy 44 (1960)), the Board could reasonably conclude that the intended and understood import of that message was not to predict that unionization would inevitably cause the plant to close but to threaten to throw employees out of work regardless of the economic realities. In this connection, we need go no further than to point out (1) that petitioner had no support for its basic assumption that the union, which had not yet even presented any demands, would have to strike to be heard, and that it admitted at the hearing that it had no basis for attributing other plant closings in the area to unionism; and (2) that the Board has often found that employees, who are particularly sensitive to rumors of plant closings, take such hints as coercive threats rather than honest forecasts.

* * *

* * * But an employer, who has control over that relationship and therefore knows it best, cannot be heard to complain that he is without an adequate guide for his behavior. * * * At the least he can avoid coercive speech simply by avoiding conscious overstatements he has reason to believe will mislead his employees.

For the foregoing reasons, we affirm the judgment of the Court of Appeals for the First Circuit in No. 585, and we reverse the judgments of the Court of Appeals for the Fourth Circuit in Nos. 573 and 691 insofar as they decline enforcement of the Board's orders to bargain and remand those cases to that court with directions to remand to the Board for further proceedings in conformity with this opinion.

It is so ordered.

---

3. UNORGANIZED EMPLOYEES

NATIONAL LABOR RELATIONS BOARD v. WASHINGTON ALUMINUM COMPANY

Supreme Court of the United States, 1962.
370 U.S. 9, 82 S.Ct. 1099, 8 L.Ed.2d 298.

Mr. Justice BLACK delivered the opinion of the Court.

The Court of Appeals for the Fourth Circuit, with Chief Judge Sobeloff dissenting, refused to enforce an order of the National Labor Relations Board directing the respondent Washington Aluminum Company to reinstate and make whole seven employees whom the company had discharged for leaving their work in the machine shop without permission on claims that the shop was too cold to work in. Because that decision raises important questions affecting the proper administration of the National Labor Relations Act, we granted certiorari.

The Board's order, as shown by the record and its findings, rested upon these facts and circumstances. The respondent company is engaged in the fabrication of aluminum products in Baltimore, Maryland, a business having interstate aspects that subject it to regulation under the National Labor Relations Act. The machine shop in which the seven discharged employees worked was not insulated and had a number of doors to the outside that had to be opened frequently. An oil furnace located in an adjoining building was the chief source of heat for the shop, although there were two gas-fired space heaters that contributed heat to a lesser extent. The heat produced by these units was not always satisfactory and, even prior to the day of the walkout involved here, several of the eight machinists who made up the day shift at the shop had complained from time to time to the company's foreman "over the cold working conditions."

January 5, 1959, was an extraordinarily cold day for Baltimore, with unusually high winds and a low temperature of 11 degrees followed by a high of 22. When the employees on the day shift came to work that morning, they found the shop bitterly cold, due not only to the unusually harsh weather, but also to the fact that the large oil furnace had broken down the night before and had not as yet been put back into operation. As the workers gathered in the shop just before the starting hour of 7:30, one of them, a Mr. Caron, went into the office of Mr. Jarvis, the foreman, hoping to warm himself but, instead, found the foreman's quarters as uncomfortable as the rest of the shop. As Caron and Jarvis sat in Jarvis' office discussing how bitingly cold the building was, some of the other machinists walked by the office window "huddled" together in a fashion that caused Jarvis to exclaim that "[i]f those fellows had any guts at all, they would go home." When the starting buzzer sounded a few moments later, Caron walked back to his working place in the shop and found all the other machinists "huddled there, shaking a little, cold." Caron then said to these workers, " * * * Dave [Jarvis] told me if we had any guts, we would go home. * * * I am going home, it is too damned cold to work." Caron asked the other workers what they were going to do and, after some discussion among themselves, they decided to leave with him. One of these workers, testifying before the Board, summarized their entire discussion this way: "And we had all got together and thought it would be a good idea to go home; maybe we could get some heat brought into the plant that way." As they started to leave, Jarvis approached and persuaded one of the workers to remain at the job. But Caron and the other six workers on the day shift left practically in a body in a matter of minutes after the 7:30 buzzer.

When the company's general foreman arrived between 7:45 and 8 that morning, Jarvis promptly informed him that all but one of the employees had left because the shop was too cold. The company's president came in at approximately 8:20 a. m. and, upon learning of the walkout, immediately said to the foreman, " * * * if they have all gone, we are going to terminate them." After discussion "at great length" between the general foreman and the company president as to what might be the effect of the walkout on employee discipline and plant production, the president formalized his discharge of the workers who had walked out by giving orders at 9 a. m. that the affected workers should be notified about their discharge immediately, either by telephone, telegram or personally. This was done.

On these facts the Board found that the conduct of the workers was a concerted activity to protest the company's failure to supply adequate heat in its machine shop, that such conduct is protected under the provision of § 7 of the National Labor Relations Act which guarantees that "Employees shall have the right * * * to engage in * * * concerted activities for the purpose of collective bargaining or other mutual aid or protection," and that the discharge of these workers by the company amounted to an unfair labor practice under § 8(a) (1) of the Act, which forbids employers "to interfere with, restrain, or coerce employees in the exercise of the rights guaranteed in section 7." Acting under the authority of § 10(c) of the Act, which provides that when an employer has been guilty of an unfair labor practice the Board can "take such affirmative action including reinstatement of employees with or without back pay, as will effectuate the policies of this Act," the Board then ordered the company to reinstate the discharged workers to their previous positions and to make them whole for losses resulting from what the Board found to have been the unlawful termination of their employment.

In denying enforcement of this order, the majority of the Court of Appeals took the position that because the workers simply "summarily left their place of employment" without affording the company an "opportunity to avoid the work stoppage by granting a concession to a demand," their walkout did not amount to a concerted activity protected by § 7 of the Act. On this basis, they held that there was no justification for the conduct of the workers in violating the established rules of the plant by leaving their jobs without permission and that the Board had therefore exceeded its power in issuing the order involved here because § 10(c) declares that the Board shall not require reinstatement or back pay for an employee whom an employer has suspended or discharged "for cause."

We cannot agree that employees necessarily lose their right to engage in concerted activities under § 7 merely because they do not present a specific demand upon their employer to remedy a condition they find objectionable. The language of § 7 is broad enough to protect concerted activities whether they take place before, after, or at the same time such a demand is made. To compel the Board to interpret and apply that language in the restricted fashion suggested by the respondent here would only tend to frustrate the policy of the Act to protect the right of workers to act together to better their working conditions. Indeed, as indicated by this very case, such an interpretation of § 7 might place burdens upon employees so great that it would effectively nullify the right to engage in concerted activities which that section protects. The seven employees here were part of a small group of employees who were wholly unorganized. They had no bargaining representative and, in fact, no representative of any kind to present their grievances to their employer. Under these circumstances, they had to speak for themselves as best they could. As pointed out above, prior to the day they left the shop, several of them had repeatedly complained to company officials about the cold working conditions in the shop. These had been more or less spontaneous individual pleas, unsupported by any threat of concerted protest, to which the company apparently gave little consideration and which it now says the Board should have treated as nothing more than "the same sort of gripes as the gripes made about the heat in the summertime." The bitter cold of January 5, however, finally brought these workers' individual complaints into concert so that some more effective action could be considered. Having no bargaining representative and no established procedure by which they could take full advantage of their unanimity of opinion in negotiations with the company, the men took the most direct course to let the company know that they wanted a warmer place in which to work. So, after talking among themselves, they walked out together in the hope that this action might spotlight their complaint and bring about some improvement in what they considered to be the "miserable" conditions of their employment. This we think was enough to justify the Board's holding that they were not required to make any more specific demand than they did to be entitled to the protection of § 7.

Although the company contends to the contrary, we think that the walkout involved here did grow out of a "labor dispute" within the plain meaning of the definition of that term in § 2(9) of the Act, which declares that it includes "any controversy concerning terms, tenure or *conditions of employment* * * *." The findings of the Board, which are supported by substantial evidence and which were not disturbed below, show a running dispute between the machine shop employees and the company over the heating of the shop on cold days—a dispute which culminated in the decision of the employees to act concertedly in an effort to force the company to improve that condition of their employment. The fact that the company was already making every effort to repair the furnace and bring heat into the shop that morning does not change the nature of the controversy that caused the walkout. At the very most, that fact might tend to indicate that the conduct of the men in leaving was unnecessary and unwise, and it has long been settled that the reasonableness of workers' decisions to engage in concerted activity is irrelevant to the determination of whether a labor dispute exists or not. Moreover, the evidence here shows that the conduct of these workers was far from unjustified under the circumstances. The company's own foreman expressed the opinion that the shop was so cold that the men should go home. This statement by the foreman but emphasizes the obvious—that is, that the conditions of coldness about which complaint had been made before had been so aggravated on the day of the walkout that the concerted action of the men in leaving their jobs seemed like a perfectly natural and reasonable thing to do.

Nor can we accept the company's contention that because it admittedly had an established plant rule which forbade employees to leave their work without permission of the foreman, there was justifiable "cause" for discharging these employees, wholly separate and apart from any concerted activities in which they engaged in protest against the poorly heated plant. Section 10(c) of the Act does authorize an employer to discharge employees for "cause" and our cases have long recognized this right on the part of an employer. But this, of course, cannot mean that an employer is at liberty to punish a man by discharging him for engaging in concerted activities which § 7 of the Act protects. And the plant rule in question here purports to permit the company to do just that for it would prohibit even the most plainly protected kinds of concerted work stoppages until and unless the permission of the company's foreman was obtained.

It is of course true that § 7 does not protect all concerted activities, but that aspect of the section is not involved in this case. The activities engaged in here do not fall within the normal categories of unprotected concerted activities such as those that are unlawful, violent or in breach of contract. Nor can they be brought under this Court's more recent pronouncement which denied the protection of § 7 to activities characterized as "indefensible" because they were there found to show a disloyalty to the workers' employer which this Court deemed unnecessary to carry on the workers' legitimate concerted activities. The activities of these seven employees cannot be classified as "indefensible" by any recognized standard of conduct. Indeed, concerted activities by employees for the purpose of trying to protect themselves from working conditions as uncomfortable as the testimony and Board findings showed them to be in this case are unquestionably activities to correct conditions which modern labor-management legislation treats as too bad to have to be tolerated in a humane and civilized society like ours.

We hold therefore that the Board correctly interpreted and applied the Act to the circumstances of this case and it was error for the Court of Appeals to refuse to enforce its order. The judgment of the Court of Appeals is reversed and the cause is remanded to that court with directions to enforce the order in its entirety.

Reversed and remanded.

Mr. Justice FRANKFURTER and Mr. Justice WHITE took no part in the consideration or decision of this case.

4. ENFORCEMENT PROBLEMS

THE BOYS MARKETS, INC. v. RETAIL CLERK'S UNION, LOCAL 770

Supreme Court of the United States, 1970.
398 U.S. 235, 90 S.Ct. 1583, 26 L.Ed.2d 199.

Mr. Justice BRENNAN delivered the opinion of the Court.

In this case we re-examine the holding of Sinclair Refining Co. v. Atkinson, 370 U.S. 195 (1962), that the anti-injunction provisions of the Norris-LaGuardia Act[1] preclude a federal district court from enjoining a strike in breach of a no-strike obligation under a collective-bargaining agreement, even though that agreement contains provisions, enforceable under § 301(a) of the Labor Management Relations Act, 1947,[2] for binding arbitration of the grievance dispute concerning which the strike was called. The Court of Appeals for the Ninth Circuit, considering itself bound by *Sinclair* reversed the grant by the District Court for the Central District of California of petitioner's prayer for injunctive relief. 416 F.2d 368 (1969). We granted certiorari. 396 U.S. 1000 (1970). Having concluded that *Sinclair* was erroneously decided and that subsequent events have undermined its continuing validity, we overrule that decision and reverse the judgment of the Court of Appeals.

I

In February 1969, at the time of the incidents that produced this litigation, petitioner and respondent were parties to a collective-bargaining agreement which provided, *inter alia,* that all controversies concerning its interpretation or application should be resolved by adjustment and arbitration procedures set forth therein and that, during the life of the contract, there should be "no cessation or stop-

[1]. "No court of the United States shall have jurisdiction to issue any restraining order or temporary or permanent injunction in any case involving or growing out of any labor dispute to prohibit any person or persons participating or interested in such dispute (as these terms are herein defined) from doing, whether singly or in concert, any of the following acts:
"(a) Ceasing or refusing to perform any work or to remain in any relation of employment;

* * * * * *

"(e) Giving publicity to the existence of, or the facts involved in, any labor dispute, whether by advertising, speaking, patrolling, or by any other method not involving fraud or violence;
"(f) Assembling peaceably to act or to organize to act in promotion of their interests in a labor dispute;

* * * * * *

"(i) Advising, urging, or otherwise causing or inducing without fraud or violence the acts heretofore specified * * *." 29 U.S.C.A. § 104.
(Court's footnote 1.)

[2]. "Suits for violation of contracts between an employer and a labor organization representing employees in an industry affecting commerce as defined in this chapter, or between any such labor organizations, may be brought in any district court of the United States having jurisdiction of the parties, without respect to the amount in controversy or without regard to the citizenship of the parties." 29 U.S.C.A. § 185(a).
(Court's footnote 2.)

page of work, lock-out, picketing or boycotts   *   *   *.'"   The dispute arose when petitioner's frozen foods supervisor and certain members of his crew who were not members of the bargaining unit began to rearrange merchandise in the frozen food cases of one of petitioner's supermarkets.   A union representative insisted that the food cases be stripped of all merchandise and be restocked by union personnel.   When petitioner did not accede to the union's demand, a strike was called and the union began to picket petitioner's establishment.   Thereupon petitioner demanded that the union cease the work stoppage and picketing and sought to invoke the grievance and arbitration procedures specified in the contract.

The following day, since the strike had not been terminated, petitioner filed a complaint in California Superior Court seeking a temporary restraining order, a preliminary and permanent injunction, and specific performance of the contractual arbitration provision. The state court issued a temporary restraining order forbidding continuation of the strike and also an order to show cause why a preliminary injunction should not be granted.   Shortly thereafter, the union removed the case to the Federal District Court and there made a motion to quash the state court's temporary restraining order.   In opposition, petitioner moved for an order compelling arbitration and enjoining continuation of the strike.   Concluding that the dispute was subject to arbitration under the collective-bargaining agreement and that the strike was in violation of the contract, the District Court ordered the parties to arbitrate the underlying dispute and simultaneously enjoined the strike, all picketing in the vicinity of petitioner's supermarket, and any attempts by the union to induce the employees to strike or to refuse to perform their services.

II

At the outset, we are met with respondent's contention that *Sinclair* ought not to be disturbed because the decision turned on a question of statutory construction which Congress can alter at any time. Since Congress has not modified our conclusions in *Sinclair*, even though it has been urged to do so, respondent argues that principles of *stare decisis* should govern the present case.

We do not agree that the doctrine of *stare decisis* bars a re-examination of *Sinclair* in the circumstances of this case.   We fully recognize that important policy considerations militate in favor of continuity and predictability in the law.   Nevertheless, as Mr. Justice Frankfurter wrote for the Court, "[S]*tare decisis* is a principle of policy and not a mechanical formula of adherence to the latest decision, however recent and questionable, when such adherence involves collision with a prior doctrine more embracing in its scope, intrinsically sounder, and verified by experience."   Helvering v. Hallock, 309 U.S. 106   *   *   *   It is precisely because *Sinclair* stands as a significant departure from our otherwise consistent emphasis upon the congressional policy to promote the peaceful settlement of labor disputes through arbitration and our efforts to accommodate and harmonize this policy with those underlying the anti-injunction provisions of the Norris-LaGuardia Act that we believe *Sinclair* should be reconsidered. Furthermore, in light of developments subsequent to *Sinclair*, in particular our decision in Avco Corp. v. Aero Lodge 735, 390 U.S. 557 (1968), it has become clear that the *Sinclair* decision does not further but rather frustrates realization of an important goal of our national labor policy.

Nor can we agree that conclusive weight should be accorded to the failure of Congress to respond to *Sinclair* on the theory that congressional silence should be interpreted as acceptance of the decision. The Court has cautioned that "[i]t is at best treacherous to find in congressional silence alone the adoption of a controlling rule of law." Girouard v. United States, 328 U.S. 61 (1946). Therefore, in the absence of any persuasive circumstances evidencing a clear design that congressional inaction be taken as acceptance of *Sinclair*, the mere silence of Congress is not a sufficient reason for refusing to reconsider the decision. Helvering v. Hallock, *supra*.

III

"The substantive law to apply in suits under § 301(a) is federal law, which the courts must fashion from the policy of our national labor laws," Textile Workers Union of America v. Lincoln Mills, 353 U.S. 448 (1957), and more specifically that a union can obtain specific performance of an employer's promise to arbitrate grievances. We rejected the contention that the anti-injunction proscriptions of the Norris-LaGuardia Act prohibited this type of relief, noting that a refusal to arbitrate was not "part and parcel of the abuses against which the Act was aimed," *id.*, at 458, and that the Act itself manifests a policy determination that arbitration should be encouraged. See 29 U.S.C.A. § 108.[1] Subsequently in the *Steelworkers Trilogy* we emphasized the importance of arbitration as an instrument of federal policy for resolving disputes between labor and management and cautioned the lower courts against usurping the functions of the arbitrator.

Serious questions remained, however, concerning the role that state courts were to play in suits involving collective-bargaining agreements. Confronted with some of these problems in Charles Dowd Box Co. v. Courtney, 368 U.S. 502 (1962), we held that Congress clearly intended *not* to disturb the pre-existing jurisdiction of the state courts over suits for violations of collective-bargaining agreements. We noted that the "clear implication of the entire record of the congressional debates in both 1946 and 1947 is that the purpose of conferring jurisdiction upon the federal district courts

---

1. Section 108 provides:

"No restraining order or injunctive relief shall be granted to any complainant who has failed to comply with any obligation imposed by law which is involved in the labor dispute in question, or who has failed to make every reasonable effort to settle such dispute either by negotiation or with the aid of any available governmental machinery of mediation or voluntary arbitration."

(Court's footnote 8.)

was not to displace, but to supplement, the thoroughly considered jurisdiction of the courts of the various States over contracts made by labor organizations." *Id.*, at 511.

Shortly after the decision in *Dowd Box*, we sustained, in Local 174, Teamsters, etc. v. Lucas Flour Co., 369 U.S. 95 (1962), an award of damages by a state court to an employer for a breach by the union of a no-strike provision in its contract. While emphasizing that "in enacting § 301 Congress intended doctrines of federal labor law uniformly to prevail over inconsistent local rules," *id.*, at 104, we did not consider the applicability of the Norris-LaGuardia Act to state court proceedings because the employer's prayer for relief sought only damages and not specific performance of a no-strike obligation.

Subsequent to the decision in *Sinclair*, we held in Avco Corp. v. Aero Lodge 735, *supra*, that § 301(a) suits initially brought in state courts may be removed to the designated federal forum under the federal question removal jurisdiction delineated in 28 U.S.C.A. § 1441. In so holding, however, the Court expressly left open the questions whether state courts are bound by the anti-injunction proscriptions of the Norris-LaGuardia Act and whether federal courts, after removal of a § 301(a) action, are required to dissolve any injunctive relief previously granted by the state courts. * * * Three Justices who concurred expressed the view that *Sinclair* should be reconsidered "upon an appropriate future occasion." 390 U.S., at 562 (Stewart, J., concurring).

The decision in *Avco,* viewed in the context of *Lincoln Mills* and its progeny, has produced an anomalous situation which, in our view, makes urgent the reconsideration of *Sinclair*. The principal practical effect of *Avco* and *Sinclair* taken together is nothing less than to oust state courts of jurisdiction in § 301(a) suits where injunctive relief is sought for breach of a no-strike obligation. Union defendants can, as a matter of course, obtain removal to a federal court, and there is obviously a compelling incentive for them to do so in order to gain the advantage of the strictures upon injunctive relief which *Sinclair* imposes on federal courts. The sanctioning of this practice, however, is wholly inconsistent with our conclusion in *Dowd Box* that the congressional purpose embodied in § 301(a) was to *supplement*, and not to encroach upon, the pre-existing jurisdiction of the state courts. It is ironic indeed that the very provision that Congress clearly intended to provide additional remedies for breach of collective-bargaining agreements has been employed to displace previously existing state remedies. We are not at liberty thus to depart from the clearly expressed congressional policy to the contrary.

On the other hand, to the extent that widely disparate remedies theoretically remain available in state, as opposed to federal, courts, the federal policy of labor law uniformity elaborated in *Lucas Flour Co.*, is seriously offended. This policy, of course, could hardly require, as a practical matter, that labor law be administered identically in all courts, for undoubtedly a certain diversity exists among the state and federal systems in matters of procedural and remedial detail, a fact that Congress evidently took into account in deciding not to disturb the traditional jurisdiction of the States. The injunction, however, is so important a remedial device, particularly in the arbitration context, that its availability or non-availability in various courts will not only produce rampant forum shopping and maneuvering from one court to another but will also greatly frustrate any relative uniformity in the enforcement of arbitration agreements.

Furthermore, the existing scheme, with the injunction remedy technically available in the state courts but rendered inefficacious by the removal device, assigns to removal proceedings a totally unintended function. While the underlying purposes of Congress in providing for federal question removal jurisdiction remain somewhat obscure, there has never been a serious contention that Congress intended that the removal mechanism be utilized to foreclose completely remedies otherwise available in the state courts. Although federal question removal jurisdiction may well have been intended to provide a forum for the protection of federal rights where such protection was deemed necessary or to encourage the development of expertise by the federal courts in the interpretation of federal law, there is no indication that Congress intended by the removal mechanism to effect a wholesale dislocation in the allocation of judicial business between the state and federal courts. * * *

It is undoubtedly true that each of the foregoing objections to *Sinclair-Avco* could be remedied either by overruling *Sinclair* or by extending that decision to the States. While some commentators have suggested that the solution to the present unsatisfactory situation does lie in the extension of the *Sinclair* prohibition to state court proceedings, we agree with Chief Justice Traynor of the California Supreme Court that "whether or not Congress could deprive state courts of the power to give such [injunctive] remedies when enforcing collective bargaining agreements, it has not attempted to do so either in the Norris-LaGuardia Act or section 301." McCarroll v. Los Angeles County Dist. Council of Carpenters, 49 Cal.2d 45, 315 P.2d 322 (1957), cert. denied, 355 U.S. 932 (1958). * * *

An additional reason for not resolving the existing dilemma by extending *Sinclair* to the States is the devastating implications for the enforceability of arbitration agreements and their accompanying no-strike obligations if equitable remedies were not available. As we have previously indicated, a no-strike obligation, express or implied, is the *quid pro quo* for an undertaking by the employer to submit grievance disputes to the process of arbitration. * * * Any incentive for employers to enter into such an arrangement is necessarily dissipated if the principal and most expeditious method by which the no-strike obligation can be enforced is eliminated. While it is of course true, as respondent contends, that other avenues of redress, such as an action for damages, would remain open to an aggrieved employer, an award of damages after a dispute has been settled is no substitute for an immediate halt to an illegal strike. Furthermore, an action for damages prosecuted during or after a labor dispute would only tend to aggravate industrial strife and delay an early resolution of the difficulties between employer and union.

Even if management is not encouraged by the unavailability of the injunction remedy to resist arbitration agreements, the fact remains that the effectiveness of such agreements would be greatly reduced if injunctive relief were withheld. Indeed, the very purpose of arbitration procedures is to provide a mechanism for the expeditious settlement of industrial disputes without resort to strikes, lockouts, or other self-help measures. This basic purpose is obviously largely undercut if there is no immediate, effective remedy for those very tactics that arbitration is designed to obviate. Thus, because *Sinclair*, in the aftermath of *Avco*, casts serious doubt upon the effective enforcement of a vital element of stable labor-management relations—arbitration agreements with their attendant no-strike obligations—we conclude that *Sinclair* does not make a viable contribution to federal labor policy.

IV

* * *

The literal terms of § 4 of the Norris-LaGuardia Act must be accommodated to the subsequently enacted provisions of § 301(a) of the Labor Management Relations Act and the purposes of arbitration. Statutory interpretation requires more than concentration upon isolated words; rather, consideration must be given to the total corpus of pertinent law and the policies that inspired ostensibly inconsistent provisions. * * *

The Norris-LaGuardia Act was responsive to a situation totally different from that which exists today. In the early part of this century, the federal courts generally were regarded as allies of management in its attempt to prevent the organization and strengthening of labor unions; and in this industrial struggle the injunction became a potent weapon that was wielded against the activities of labor groups. The result was a large number of sweeping decrees, often issued *ex parte*, drawn on an *ad hoc* basis without regard to any systematic elaboration of national labor policy. * * *

In 1932 Congress attempted to bring some order out of the industrial chaos that had developed and to correct the abuses that had resulted from the interjection of the federal judiciary into union-management disputes on the behalf of management. See declaration of public policy, Norris-LaGuardia Act, § 2, 47 Stat. 70. Congress, therefore, determined initially to limit severely the power of the federal courts to issue injunctions "in any case involving or growing out of any labor dispute * * *." § 4, 47 Stat. 70. Even as initially enacted, however, the prohibition against federal injunctions was by no means absolute. See Norris-LaGuardia Act, §§ 7, 8, 9, 47 Stat. 71, 72. Shortly thereafter Congress passed the Wagner Act, designed to curb various management activities that tended to discourage employee participation in collective action.

As labor organizations grew in strength and developed toward maturity, congressional emphasis shifted from protection of the nascent labor movement to the encouragement of collective bargaining and to administrative techniques for the peaceful resolution of industrial disputes. This shift in emphasis was accomplished, however, without extensive revision of many of the older enactments, including the anti-injunction section of the Norris-LaGuardia Act. Thus it became the task of the courts to accommodate, to reconcile the older statutes with the more recent ones.

A leading example of this accommodation process is Brotherhood of Railroad Trainmen v. Chicago River & Ind. R. Co., 353 U.S. 30 (1957). There we were confronted with a peaceful strike which violated the statutory duty to arbitrate imposed by the Railway Labor Act. The Court concluded that a strike in violation of a statutory arbitration duty was not the type of situation to which the Norris-LaGuardia Act was responsive, that an important federal policy was involved in the peaceful settlement of disputes through the statutorily mandated arbitration procedure, that this important policy was imperiled if equitable remedies were not available to implement it, and hence that Norris-LaGuardia's policy of nonintervention by the federal courts should yield to the overriding interest in the successful implementation of the arbitration process.

The principles elaborated in *Chicago River* are equally applicable to the present case. To be sure, *Chicago River* involved arbitration procedures established by statute. However, we have frequently noted, in such cases as *Lincoln Mills*, the *Steelworkers Trilogy,* and *Lucas Flour*, the importance that Congress has attached generally to the voluntary settlement of labor disputes without resort to self-help and more particularly to arbitration as a means to this end. Indeed, it has been stated that *Lincoln Mills,* in its exposition of § 301 (a), "went a long way towards making arbitration the central institution in the administration of collective bargaining contracts."

The *Sinclair* decision, however, seriously undermined the effectiveness of the arbitration technique as a method peacefully to resolve industrial disputes without resort to strikes, lockouts, and similar devices. Clearly employers will be wary of assuming obligations to arbitrate specifically enforceable against them when no similarly efficacious remedy is available to enforce the concomitant undertaking of the union to refrain from striking. On the other hand, the central purpose of the Norris-LaGuardia Act to foster the growth and viability of labor organizations is hardly retarded—if anything, this goal is advanced—by a remedial device that merely enforces the obligation that the union freely undertook under a specifically enforceable agreement to submit disputes to arbitration. We conclude, therefore, that the unavailability of equitable relief in the arbitration context presents a serious impediment to the congressional policy favoring the voluntary establishment of a mechanism for the peaceful resolution of labor disputes, that the core purpose of the Norris-LaGuardia Act is not sacrificed by the limited use of equitable remedies to further this important policy, and consequently that the Norris-LaGuardia Act does not bar the granting of injunctive relief in the circumstances of the instant case.

V

Our holding in the present case is a narrow one. We do not undermine the vitality of the Norris-LaGuardia Act. We deal only with the situation in which a collective-bargaining contract contains a mandatory grievance adjustment or arbitration procedure. Nor does it follow from what we have said that injunctive relief is appropriate as a matter of course in every case of a strike over an arbitrable grievance. The dissenting opinion in *Sinclair* suggested the following principles for the guidance of the district courts in determining whether to grant injunctive relief—principles that we now adopt:

"A District Court entertaining an action under § 301 may not grant injunctive relief against concerted activity unless and until it decides that the case is one in which an injunction would be appropriate despite the Norris-LaGuardia Act. When a strike is sought to be enjoined because it is over a grievance which both parties are contractually bound to arbitrate, the District Court may issue no injunctive order until it first holds that the contract *does* have that effect; and the employer should be ordered to arbitrate, as a condition of his obtaining an injunction against the strike. Beyond this, the District Court must, of course, consider whether issuance of an injunction would be warranted under ordinary principles of equity— whether breaches are occurring and will continue, or have been threatened and will be committed; whether they have caused or will cause irreparable injury to the employer; and whether the employer will suffer more from the denial of an injunction than will the union from its issuance." 370 U.S., at 228. (Emphasis in original.)

In the present case there is no dispute that the grievance in question was subject to adjustment and arbitration under the collective-bargaining agreement and that the petitioner was ready to proceed with arbitration at the time an injunction against the strike was sought and obtained. The District Court also concluded that, by reason of respondent's violations of its no-strike obligation, petitioner "has suffered irreparable injury and will continue to suffer irreparable injury." Since we now overrule *Sinclair*, the holding of the Court of Appeals in reliance on *Sinclair* must be reversed. Accordingly, we reverse the judgment of the Court of Appeals and remand the case with directions to enter a judgment affirming the order of the District Court.

It is so ordered.

Judgment of Court of Appeals reversed and case remanded with directions.

Mr. Justice MARSHALL took no part in the decision of this case.

Mr. Justice STEWART, concurring.

When Sinclair Refining Co. v. Atkinson, 370 U.S. 195, was decided in 1962, I subscribed to the opinion of the Court. Before six years had passed I had reached the conclusion that the Sinclair holding should be reconsidered, and said so in Avco Corp. v. Aero Lodge No. 735, 390 U.S. 557, at 562, (concurring opinion). Today I join the Court in concluding "that *Sinclair* was erroneously decided and that subsequent events have undermined its continuing validity   *   *   *."

In these circumstances the temptation is strong to embark upon a lengthy personal *apologia*. But since Mr. Justice BRENNAN has so clearly stated my present views in his opinion for the Court today, I simply join in that opinion and in the Court's judgment. An aphorism of Mr. Justice FRANKFURTER provides me refuge: "Wisdom too often never comes, and so one ought not to reject it merely because it comes late." Henslee v. Union Planters Bank, 335 U.S. 595, at 600 (dissenting opinion).

Mr. Justice BLACK, dissenting.

     *   *   *

Although Congress has been urged to overrule our holding in *Sinclair,* it has steadfastly refused to do so. Nothing in the language or history of the two Acts has changed. Nothing at all has changed, in fact, except the membership of the Court and the personal views of one Justice. I remain of the opinion that *Sinclair* was correctly decided, and, moreover, that the prohibition of the Norris-LaGuardia Act is close to the heart of the entire federal system of labor regulation. In my view *Sinclair* should control the disposition of this case.

Even if the majority were correct, however, in saying that *Sinclair* misinterpreted the Taft-Hartley and Norris-LaGuardia Acts, I should be compelled to dissent. I believe that both the making and the changing of laws which affect the substantial rights of the people are primarily for Congress, not this Court. Most especially is this so when the laws involved are the focus of strongly held views of powerful but antagonistic political and economic interests. The Court's function in the application and interpretation of such laws must be carefully limited to avoid encroaching on the power of Congress to determine policies and make laws to carry them out.

When the Court implies that the doctrine called *stare decisis* rests solely on "important policy considerations   *   *   * in favor of continuity and predictability in the law," it does not tell the whole story. Such considerations are present and, in a field as delicate as labor relations, extremely important. Justice Brandeis said, dissenting in Burnet v. Coronado Oil & Gas Co., 285 U.S. 393, 406, 52 S.Ct. 443, 447, 76 L.Ed. 815 (1932):

"*Stare decisis* is usually the wise policy, because in most matters it is more important that the applicable rule of law be settled than that it be settled right."

In the ordinary case, considerations of certainty and the equal treatment of similarly situated litigants will provide a strong incentive to adhere to precedent.

When this Court is interpreting a statute, however, an additional factor must be weighed in the balance. It is the deference that this Court owes to the primary responsibility of the legislature in the making of laws. Of course, when this Court first interprets a statute, then the statute becomes what this court has said it is. See Gulf, C. & S. F. R. Co. v. Moser, 275 U.S. 133, 136, 48 S.Ct. 49, 50, 72 L.Ed. 200 (1927). Such an initial interpretation is proper, and unavoidable, in any system in which courts have the task of applying general statutes in a multitude of situations. B. Cardozo, The Nature of the Judicial Process 112–115 (1921). The Court undertakes the task of interpretation, however, not because the Court has any special ability to fathom the intent of Congress, but rather because interpretation is unavoidable in the decision of the case before it. When the law has been settled by an earlier case then any subsequent "reinterpretation" of the statute is gratuitous and neither more nor less than an amendment: it is no different in effect from a judicial alteration of language that Congress itself placed in the statute.

Altering the important provisions of a statute is a legislative function. And the Constitution states simply and unequivocally: "All legislative Powers herein granted shall be vested in a Congress of the United States * * *." U.S.Const. Art. I. It is the Congress, not this Court, that responds to the pressures of political groups, pressures entirely proper in a free society. It is Congress, not this Court, that has the capacity to investigate the divergent considerations involved in the management of a complex national labor policy. And it is Congress, not this Court, that is elected by the people. This Court should, therefore, interject itself as little as possible into the law-making and law-changing process. Having given our view on the meaning of a statute, our task is concluded, absent extraordinary circumstances. When the Court changes its mind years later, simply because the judges have changed, in my judgment, it takes upon itself the function of the legislature.

The legislative effect of the Court's reversal is especially clear here. In *Sinclair* the Court invited Congress to act if it should be displeased with the judicial interpretation of the statute. We said, 370 U.S., at 214–215:

"Strong arguments are made to us that it is highly desirable that the Norris-LaGuardia Act be changed in the public interest. If that is so, Congress itself might see fit to change that law and repeal the anti-injunction provisions of the Act insofar as suits for violation of collective agreements are concerned, as the House bill under consideration originally provided. It might, on the other hand, decide that if injunctions are necessary, the whole idea of enforcement of these agreements by private suits should be discarded in favor of enforcement through the administrative machinery of the Labor Board, as Senator Taft provided in his Senate bill. Or it might decide that neither of these methods is entirely satisfactory and turn instead to a completely new approach. The question of what change, if any, should be made in the existing law is one of legislative policy properly within the exclusive domain of Congress—it is a question for lawmakers, not law interpreters."

Commentators on our holding found this invitation to legislative action clear, and judicial self-restraint proper. See Dunau, Three Problems in Labor Arbitration, 55 Va.L.Rev. 427, 464–465 (1969); Wellington & Albert, Statutory Interpretation and the Political Process: A Comment on Sinclair v. Atkinson, 72 Yale L.J. 1547, 1565–1566 (1963). Bills were introduced in Congress seeking to effect a legislative change. S. 3132, 89th Cong., 1st Sess. (1965); H.R. 9059, 89th Cong., 1st Sess. (1965). Congress, however, did not act, thus indicating at least a willingness to leave the law as *Sinclair* had construed it. It seems to me highly inappropriate for this Court now, eight years later, in effect to enact the amendment that Congress has refused to adopt. * * *

I do not believe that the principle of *stare decisis* forecloses all reconsiderations of earlier decisions. In the area of constitutional law, for example, where the only alternative to action by this Court is the laborious process of constitutional amendment and where the ultimate responsibility rests with this Court, I believe reconsideration is always proper. * * * Even on statutory questions the appearance of new facts or changes in circumstances might warrant re-examination of past decisions in exceptional cases under exceptional circumstances. In the present situation there are no such circumstances. Congress has taken no action inconsistent with our decision in *Sinclair*. * * *

---

5. THE RIGHT TO STRIKE

The legal basis of the right to strike is somewhat hazy; the legal validity of a court decree enjoining a strike, that is the concerted activity of employees in refusing to work, is even hazier. The XIIIth Amendment provides, "[N]either slavery nor involuntary servitude * * * shall exist within the United States, or any place subject to their jurisdiction." The First Amendment provides, in part, that the right of the people peaceably to assemble may not be abridged by law. While there have been other historical bases which have prevented an employer from compelling an employee to perform services, these two Constitutional provisions make it clear that an employee may not be compelled to work if he chooses not to do so, either individually or collectively with other members of his union. Thus a court decree enjoining a strike may not compel an employee to work; he may not be ordered to return to his job threatened with being held in contempt of court if he refuses.

In a strike employees attempt to do two basic things, one to withhold their services, a fundamental right in a free society, and the other to prevent the employer from obtaining the services of other persons to perform the jobs which the employees think of as being theirs. It is this second part of the strike activity which is the only part which can be reached by the law. In practice, however, this nearly always means that once the strike is broken by an injunction that the employees return to work rather than expose themselves to the hazard of being permanently displaced by a newly recruited employee. Strikers picket, and in this manner attempt to prevent other persons from performing the services which they themselves are intent upon withholding. Picketing, both peaceful and violent, has had an interesting legal history in the last several decades. It is picketing, either mass picketing or violent picketing, that is most frequently enjoined and in this manner the strike is broken.

There is a tremendous amount of emotionalism in connection with strikes and strike injunctions. In 1947 when Congress adopted the Taft-Hartley Act, amending the Labor Act, it sought through Section 208, 29 U.S.C.A. § 178, to provide a system for dealing with strikes affecting an entire industry which would "[imperil] the national health or safety." The principal features of the Act are discussed in United Steel Workers v. United States of America, 361 U.S. 39, 80 S. Ct. 1, 4 L.Ed.2d 12 (1959) which is reported below. A major departure from prior practice, which is not discussed in the case, was that the injunction could be sought only by the Attorney General of the United States, rather than by private employers. This rather severe limitation on the right to strike thus was not to be available to employers unless the government intervened on their behalf; while the Act permits the government to seek an injunction in the event of a lockout (in effect a strike by the employer against the employees in a labor dispute) the Act has yet to be used in this fashion.

UNITED STEELWORKERS OF AMERICA v. UNITED STATES

Supreme Court of the United States, 1959.
361 U.S. 39, 80 S.Ct. 1, 4 L.Ed.2d 12.

PER CURIAM.

The Attorney General sought and obtained in the District Court for the Western District of Pennsylvania an injunction against the continuation of an industry-wide strike of workers in the basic steel industry pursuant to § 208 of the Labor Management Relations Act, 1947, 61 Stat. 155, 29 U.S.C.A. § 178. We granted certiorari, 361 U.S. 878, to review the judgment of the Court of Appeals for the Third Circuit, 271 F.2d 676, affirming the District Court, 178 F.Supp. 297. In pertinent part, § 208 provides that if the District Court—

"finds that * * * [a] threatened or actual strike or lockout—

"(i) affects an entire industry or a substantial part thereof engaged in trade, commerce, transportation, transmission, or communication among the several States or with foreign nations, or engaged in the production of goods for commerce; and

"(ii) if permitted to occur or to continue, will imperil the national health or safety, it shall have jurisdiction to enjoin any such strike or lockout, or the continuing thereof, and to make such other orders as may be appropriate."

The arguments of the parties here and in the lower courts have addressed themselves in considerable part to the propriety of the District Court's exercising its equitable jurisdiction to enjoin the strike in question once the findings set forth above had been made. These arguments have ranged widely into broad issues of national labor policy, the availability of other remedies to the Executive, the effect of a labor injunction on the collective bargaining process, consideration of the conduct of the parties to the labor dispute in their negotiations, and conjecture as to the course of those negotiations in the future. We do not believe that Congress in passing the statute intended that the issuance of injunctions should depend upon judicial inquiries of this nature. Congress was not concerned with the merits of the parties' positions or the conduct of their negotiations. Its basic purpose seems to have been to see that vital production should be resumed or continued for a time while further efforts were made to settle the dispute. To carry out its purposes, Congress carefully surrounded the injunction proceedings with detailed procedural devices and limitations. The public report of a board of inquiry, the exercise of political and executive responsibility personally by the President in directing the commencement of injunction proceedings, the statutory provisions looking toward an adjustment of the dispute during the injunction's pendency, and the limited duration of the injunction, represent a congressional determination of policy factors involved in the difficult problem of national emergency strikes. This congressional determination of the policy factors is of course binding on the courts.

The statute imposes upon the courts the duty of finding, upon the evidence adduced, whether a strike or lockout meets the statutory conditions of breadth of involvement and peril to the national health or safety. We have accordingly reviewed the concurrent findings of the two lower courts. Petitioner here contests the findings that the continuation of the strike would imperil the national health and safety. The parties dispute the meaning of the statutory term "national health"; the Government insists that the term comprehends the country's general well-being, its economic health; petitioner urges that simply the physical health of the citizenry is meant. We need not resolve this question, for we think the judgment below is amply supported on the ground that the strike imperils the national safety. Here we rely upon the evidence of the strike's effect on specific defense projects; we need not pass on the Government's contention that "national safety" in this context should be given a broader construction and application.

The petitioner suggests that a selective reopening of some of the steel mills would suffice to fulfill specific defense needs. The statute was designed to provide a public remedy in times of emergency; we cannot construe it to require that the United States either formulate a reorganization of the affected industry to satisfy its defense needs without the complete reopening of closed facilities, or demonstrate in court the unfeasibility of such a reorganization. There is no room in the statute for this requirement which the petitioner seeks to impose on the Government.

We are of opinion that the provision in question as applied here is not violative of the constitutional limitation prohibiting courts from exercising powers of a legislative or executive nature, powers not capable of being conferred upon a court exercising solely "the judicial power of the United States." Keller v. Potomac Elec. Power Co., 261 U.S. 428; Federal Radio Comm. v. General Elec. Co., 281 U.S. 464. Petitioner contends that the statute is constitutionally invalid because it does not set up any standard of lawful or unlawful conduct on the part of labor or management. But the statute does recognize certain rights in the public to have unimpeded for a time production in industries vital to the national health or safety. It makes the United States the guardian of these rights in litigation. Cf. United States v. American Bell Tel. Co., 128 U.S. 315. * * * The availability of relief, in the common judicial form of an injunction, depends on findings of fact, to be judicially made. Of the matters decided judicially, there is no review by other agencies of the Government. Cf. Gordon v. United States, 2 Wall. 561, 117 U.S. 697. We conclude that the statute entrusts the courts only with the determination of a "case or controversy," on which the judicial power can operate, not containing any element capable of only legislative or executive determination. We do not find that the termination of the injunction after a specified time, or the machinery established in an attempt to obtain a peaceful settlement of the underlying dispute during the injunction's pendency, detracts from this conclusion.

The result is that the judgment of the Court of Appeals for the Third Circuit, affirming that of the District Court, is affirmed. Our mandate shall issue forthwith.

It is so ordered.

Mr. Justice FRANKFURTER and Mr. Justice HARLAN: In joining the Court's opinion we note our intention to file in due course an amplification of our views upon the issues involved which could not be prepared within the time limitations imposed by the necessity of a prompt adjudication in this case. See 80 S.Ct. 177.

Mr. Justice DOUGLAS, dissenting.

Great cases, like this one, are so charged with importance and feeling that, as Mr. Justice Holmes once remarked (Northern Securities Co. v. United States, 193 U.S. 197, 400–401, 24 S.Ct. 436, 468, 48 L.Ed. 679, dissenting opinion), they are apt to generate bad law. We need, therefore, to stick closely to the letter of the law we enforce in order to keep this controversy from being shaped by the intense interest which the public rightfully has in it. The statute, which Congress had authority to pass, speaks in narrow and guarded terms. Section 206 of the Labor Management Relations Act 1947, 61 Stat. 155, 29 U.S. C.A. § 176, gives the President power to invoke the aid of a board of inquiry whenever he is of the opinion that a strike or lockout will imperil "the national health or safety." The President, in appointing the board of inquiry in this case, stated:

"The strike has closed 85 percent of the nation's steel mills, shutting off practically all new supplies of steel. Over 500,000 steel workers and about 200,000 workers in related industries, together with their families, have been deprived of their usual means of support. Present steel supplies are low and the resumption of full-scale production will require some weeks. If production is not quickly resumed, severe effects upon the economy will endanger the economic health of the nation."

It is plain that the President construed the word "health" to include the material well-being or public welfare of the Nation. When the Attorney General moved under § 208 for an injunction in the District Court based on the opinion of the President and the conclusions of the board of inquiry, the union challenged the conclusion that "the national health or safety" was imperiled, as those words are used in the Act. The District Court found otherwise, stating five ways in which the strike would, if permitted to continue, imperil "the national health and safety":

"(a) Certain items of steel required in top priority military missile programs of the United States are not made by any mill now operating, nor available from any inventory or from imports. Any further delay in resumption of steel production would result in an irretrievable loss of time in the supply of weapons systems essential to the national defense plans of the United States and its allies.

"(b) The planned program of space activities under the direction of the National Aeronautics and Space Administration has been delayed by the strike and will be further delayed if it is continued. Specifically, project MERCURY, the nation's manned satellite program, which has the highest national priority, has been delayed by reason of delay in construction of buildings essential to its operation. This program is important to the security of the nation. Other planned space programs will be delayed or threatened with delay by a continuation of the strike.

"(c) Nuclear Submarines and the naval shipbuilding program other than submarines, including new construction, modernization, and conversion, have been affected by reason of the inability to secure boilers, compressors, and other component parts requiring steel. Products of the steel industry are indispensable to the manufacture of such items and delay in their production will irreparably injure national defense and imperil the national safety.

"(d) Exported steel products are vital to the support of the United States bases overseas and for the use of NATO allies and similar collective security groups. The steel strike, if permitted to continue, will seriously impair these programs, thus imperiling the national safety.

"(e) A continuation of the strike will have the ultimate effect of adversely affecting millions of small business enterprises, almost all of which are directly or indirectly dependent upon steel products and most of which lack the resources to stock large inventories. In addition, it will have the effect of idling millions of workers and a large proportion of the facilities in industries dependent upon steel for their continued operation. Manufacturing industries directly dependent on steel mill products account for the employment of approximately 6,000,000 workers and normal annual wages and salaries totalling approximately $34,000,000,000. The products of these industries are valued at over $125,000,000,000. The national health will be imperiled if the strike is permitted to continue."

Here again it is obvious that "national health" was construed to include the economic well-being or general welfare of the country. The Court of Appeals, in sustaining the injunction, was apparently of the same view. This seems to me to be an assumption that is unwarranted. I think that Congress, when it used the words "national health," was safeguarding the heating of homes, the delivery of milk, the protection of hospitals, and the like. The coal industry, closely identified with physical health of people, was the industry paramount in the debates on this measure. The coal industry is indeed cited on the Senate side in illustration of the need for the measure. S.Rep. No. 105, 80th Cong., 1st Sess., p. 14. There were those in the Senate who wanted to go so far as to outlaw strikes "in utilities and key Nationwide industries" in order to protect the "public welfare." 93 Cong.Rec. A1035. Reference was, indeed, made to strikes in industries "like coal or steel" among those to be barred in "the public interest." Ibid. But the Senate did not go that far. The Senate bill reached only situations where there was peril to the "national health or safety." The House bill went further and included cases where there was peril to "the public health, safety, or interest." The Senate view prevailed, its version being adopted by the Conference. Some light is thrown on the wide difference between those two standards— if words are to be taken in their usual sense—by the following colloquy on the floor of the House:

"Mr. KENNEDY. I believe that this country should certainly be in a position to combat a strike that affects the health and safety of the people. Therefore, I feel that the President must have the power to step in and stop those strikes. I am not in the position of opposing everything in this bill, but there are certain things in the bill that are wrong. I do not see how the President is going to have the power to stop strikes that will affect the health and safety of the people under the procedure listed in section 203. I think he must have that power.

"I agree with you that any bill providing for an injunction should carefully consider the position of the striking union and make sure that their rights are protected. I think that in those cases Federal seizure until the dispute is settled would perhaps equalize the burden in the fairest possible manner.

"Mr. OWENS. Will not the gentleman admit that we have a third word in there? It is 'interest.' Could we not better use the word 'welfare' instead of 'interest,' because the word 'welfare' occurs in the Constitution? It is just as broad as the word 'interest' and more practical.

"Mr. KENNEDY. The proposal embraces two separate things, health and safety. Because the remedy is drastic these two, in my opinion, are sufficient. I believe we should apply this remedy when the strike affects health or safety, but not the welfare and interest, which may mean anything. I would not interfere in an automobile strike because while perhaps that affects national interest, it does not affect health and safety.

Mr. OWENS. Does not the gentleman agree that 'welfare' is the stronger and in line with the President's idea?

"Mr. KENNEDY. No. Both 'welfare' and 'interest' are too indefinite. They could cover anything. I would not have the law apply except in cases where the strike affected health and safety."

To read "welfare" into "health" gives that word such a vast reach that we should do it only under the most compelling necessity. We must be mindful of the history behind this legislation. In re Debs, 158 U.S. 564, stands as ominous precedent for the easy use of the injunction in labor disputes. Freewheeling Attorneys General used compelling public demands to obtain the help of courts in stilling the protests of labor. The revulsion against that practice was deep, and it led ultimately to the enactment of the Norris-LaGuardia Act, 47 Stat. 70, 29 U.S.C.A. § 101. We deal, of course, with a later Congress and an Act that by § 208(b) sets aside *pro tanto* the earlier Act. What Congress has created Congress can refashion. But we should hesitate to conclude that Congress meant to restore the use of the injunction in labor disputes whenever that broad and all-inclusive concept of the public welfare is impaired. The words used—"national health or safety"—are much narrower.

* * *

It is a fact of which we can take judicial notice that steel production in its broadest reach may have a great impact on "national health." Machinery for processing food is needed; hospitals require surgical instruments; refrigeration is dependent on steel; and so on. Whether there are such shortages that imperil the "national health" is not shown by this record. But unless these particularized findings are made no case can be made out for founding the injunction on impending peril to the "national health."

* * * Section 208(a) gives the District Court "jurisdiction to enjoin" the strike. There is no command that it *shall* enjoin 100% of the strikers when only 1% or 5% or 10% of them are engaged in acts that imperil the national "safety." We are dealing here with equity practice which has several hundred years of history behind it. We cannot lightly assume that Congress intended to make the federal judiciary a rubber stamp for the President. His findings are entitled to great weight, and I along with my Brethren accept them insofar as national "safety" is concerned. But it is the court, not the President, that is entrusted by Article III of the Constitution to shape and fashion the decree. If a federal court is to do it, it must act in its traditional manner, not as a military commander ordering people to work willy-nilly, nor as the President's Administrative Assistant. If the federal court is to be merely an automaton stamping the papers an Attorney General presents, the judicial function rises to no higher level than an IBM machine. Those who grew up with equity and know its great history should never tolerate that mechanical conception.

  * * * We should hesitate long before we conclude that Congress intended an injunction to issue against 500,000 workers when the inactivity of only 5,000 or 10,000 of the total imperils the national "safety."

  Plainly there is authority in the District Court to protect the national "safety" by issuance of an injunction. But there is nothing in this record to sustain the conclusion that it is necessary to send 500,000 men back to work to give the defense department all the steel it needs for the Nation's "safety." If more men are sent back to work than are necessary to fill the defense needs of the country, other objectives are being served than those specified in the statute. What are these other objectives? What right do courts have in serving them? What authority do we have to place the great weight of this injunction on the backs of labor, when the great bulk of those affected by it have nothing to do with production of goods necessary for the Nation's "safety" in the military sense of that word? Labor injunctions were long used as cudgels—so broad in scope, so indiscriminate in application as once to be dubbed "a 'scarecrow' device for curbing the economic pressure of the strike." See Frankfurter and Greene, The Labor Injunction (1930), pp. 107–108. The crop of evils that grew up during those regimes was different in some respects from those generated by this decree. The problems of vagueness, of uncertainty, of detailed judicial supervision that made police courts out of equity courts are not present here. But the same indiscriminate leveling of those within and those without the law is present. The injunction applies all the force of the Federal Government against men whose work has nothing to do with military defense as well as against those whose inactivity imperils the "national safety." It is not confined to the precise evil at which the present Act is aimed. Like the old labor injunctions that brought discredit to the federal judiciary this is a blanket injunction broad and all-inclusive, bringing within its scope men whose work has nothing whatsoever to do with the defense needs of the Nation. Being wide of the statutory standard it has, to use the words of Mr. Justice Brandeis, all the vices of the injunction which is used "to endow property with active, militant power which would make it dominant over men." See Truax v. Corrigan, 257 U.S. 312, 354, 368 (dissenting opinion). I cannot believe that Congress intended the federal courts to issue injunctions that bludgeon all workers merely because the labor of a few of them is needed in the interest of "national safety."

  * * * Collective bargaining and mediation are today the norm, except for the period of time in which an injunction is in force. By the terms of § 209, however, any injunction rendered may not continue longer than 80 days. The Act thus permits an injunction restricted in duration and narrowly confined by the requirements of the "national health or safety." When we uphold this injunction we force men back to work when their inactivity has no relation to "national health or safety." These whose inactivity produces the peril to "national health or safety" which the Act guards against and only those should be covered in the injunction. The rest—who are the vast majority of the 500,000 on strike—should be treated as the employers are treated. They should continue under the regime of collective bargaining and mediation until they settle their differences or until Congress provides different or broader remedies. When we assume that all the steelworkers are producing steel for defense when in truth only a fraction of them are, we are fulfilling the dreams of those who sponsored the House bill and failed in their efforts to have Congress legislate so broadly.

Though unlikely, it is possible that, had the District Court given the problem the consideration that it deserves, it could have found that the only way to remove the peril to national safety caused by the strike was to issue the broad, blanket injunction. It may be that it would be found impractical to send only part of the steelworkers back to work. The record in this case, however, is devoid of evidence to sustain that position. Furthermore, there is no indication that the District Court ever even considered such a possibility. I am unwilling to take judicial notice that it requires 100% of the workers to produce the steel needed for national defense when 99% of the output is devoted to purposes entirely unconnected with defense projects.

The trier of fact under our federal judicial system is the District Court—not this Court nor the Court of Appeals. No finding was made by the District Court on the feasibility of a limited reopening of the steel mills and it is not, as the concurring opinion suggests, the province of the Court of Appeals to resolve conflicts in the evidence that was before the District Court.

I would reverse this decree and remand the cause to the District Court for particularized findings as to how the steel strike imperils the "national health" and what plants need to be reopened to produce the small quantity of steel now needed for the national "safety." There would also be open for inquiry and findings any questions pertaining to "national health" in the narrow sense in which the Act uses those words.

[Justices FRANKFURTER and HARLAN filed separate opinions one month later.]

---

6. FAIR EMPLOYMENT PRACTICES

It may yet be too soon to conclude that equality of opportunity in employment has become inculcated within the fabric of business decision-making to the same extent as productivity or cost-effectiveness, but it is fair to say that significant resources have been allocated by businessmen toward recognizing the existence of problems in inter-group relations. And, although it also may be quit glib to say that traditions of business decision-making now reflect cognizance of the strident social issues of the time, a completely candid picture of contemporary business must recognize that new dimensions of a "social" nature are present. What might be said insofar as the matter of fair employment practices is concerned, is that business is coming to realize that purely economic determinants no longer stand as the only guideposts for decision-making and that as the entreprenurial endeavor is an integral facet of societal activity it should reflect more closely a broader range of social values. Or, possibly, in other words, a democratic society manifests its democracy not in discreetly identified pigeonholes of activity but throughout everyone of its constituent endeavors.

Fair employment practices, moreover, is not a new "constraint" on the businessman. In 1945 when then President Roosevelt created the Fair Employment Practices Commission to advise him in matters of the employment practices of government contractors, businessmen then were made aware that the ideal democracy required more "democratic" action in the arena of employment practices. But even then equality of opportunity still was not considered a matter of civil right.

The issue of whether "civil rights" ought to be vindicated throughout every facet of social endeavor, including employment, as against the need for the businessman to make decisions to foster "business" objectives without being "side-tracked" by such a concern is an issue that lies much closer to the center of current business concerns as compared with the more stridently articulated philosophical question of whether equality of opportunity is in fact a civil right. And, even though it might be easy to argue either side on political, social or moral grounds, for the businessman it is just as easy to incorporate fair employment practices concerns into his decision-making frame as a matter of good business.

Discrimination costs money. It is costly to deny a job to a person who may be qualified and let that job remain vacant for any additional period of time. It is costly to deny a job to a person who can be trained when looking for the "right" person may take time. These are measurable costs easily factored into the calculus of business decisions.

But there really is no need to debate the validity or propriety of the concept of equality of opportunity in employment. What has become of greater significance today is knowing and understanding what that means as a function of law and as it manifests itself in the everyday context of business decisions. (N.B. From this point forward there really is no need to appeal to "social conscience.")

At the State level fair employment practices legislation (FEP laws) has existed since 1948. And, even though the Roosevelt FEPC also was created at that time it was not until 1965 that the federal government created an agency of the same character—powers and authorities—as had the States during the period from 1948, viz., the Equal Employment Opportunity Commission (EEOC).

Generally, speaking, all of these official governmental agencies deal with matters of discrimination in employment in the same or similar ways, follow similar procedures and consider the same kinds of acts and practices to be discriminatory. The process usually begins by a complaint being lodged by one who feels that he or she has been discriminated against (or by the agency itself or an organization "representing" persons of the class the legislation was designed to "protect").

Once such a complaint has been generated, the administrative machinery cranks into operation as a preliminary investigation is conducted to determine whether there is reason to believe that if a more extensive and intensive investigation were to ensue there would be a likelihood of finding that the charges made would be verified. Should this preliminary question be determined in the affirmative, a full-scale investigation proceeds, the objective of which being *not* to seek corroboration of the charges but to determine all of the facts and circumstances surrounding the actions which have occurred. And it is the record made through such a full-scale investigation which will be used to infer whether there is reason to believe the actions were violative of the law.

Should the decision be that there is "probable cause" to believe a violation has occurred, this immediately is communicated to the respondent business which then is invited to "conciliate" the matter. If conciliation cannot be had, a quasi-judicial public hearing will be held.

The object and purpose of the public hearing is to have all of the facts and circumstances in the matter brought before a hearing officer (who may be an independent person named by the agency or a member of the agency policy-making organ not theretofore involved in any way with the case) in a formal adversary milieu so that a finding can be made which then would be the basis for any sanction or review by a court of competent jurisdiction.

During the period 1948–1968, activity by the many FEP agencies did not generate much of a corpus of jurisprudence. Whether this be for "political" or other reasons is conjecture. Since 1968, however, there has evolved a body of fair employment practices law so that it is fair to conclude that as a doctrinal phenomenon of law fair employment practices must be a consideration in business decision-making.

Title VII of the Federal Civil Rights Act of 1964, 42 U.S.C.A. § 2000(e) et seq., among other things limits the power of an employer in hiring or changing the status of an employee because of the employee's race, color, religion, sex, or national origin. The first case to reach the United States Supreme Court involving Title VII was Griggs v. Duke Power Co., 401 U.S. 424, 91 S.Ct. 849, 28 L.Ed.2d 158 (1971), reported infra. It should be noted that Title VII prohibits certain kinds of employment practices; it does not directly compel an employer to hire certain people in order to obtain a balance among his employees based on race, sex, or religion, etc. Nor does it compel employees to work in any employment unit in order to obtain such kind of balance. The Act does not promote integration of the races, sexes or religions by requiring anybody to do anything affirmative; it prohibits employers from practicing bigotry in the exercise of their freedom to make employment contracts. (There is no "busing" of employees.) Without this legislation employers would be free to continue their employment practices even though they were completely contrary to the democratic traditions of our society.

GRIGGS v. DUKE POWER COMPANY

Supreme Court of the United States, 1970.
401 U.S. 424, 91 S.Ct. 849, 28 L.Ed.2d 158.

Mr. Chief Justice BURGER delivered the opinion of the Court.

We granted the writ in this case to resolve the question whether an employer is prohibited by the Civil Rights Act of 1964, Title VII, from requiring a high school education or passing of a standardized general intelligence test as a condition of employment in or transfer to jobs when (a) neither standard is shown to be significantly related to successful job performance, (b) both requirements operate to disqualify Negroes at a substantially higher rate than white applicants, and (c) the jobs in question formerly had been filled only by white employees as part of a longstanding practice of giving preference to whites.[1]

Congress provided, in Title VII of the Civil Rights Act of 1964, for class actions for enforcement of provisions of the Act and this proceeding was brought by a group of incumbent Negro employees against Duke Power Company. All the petitioners are employed at the Company's Dan River Steam Station, a power generating facility located at Draper, North Carolina. At the time this action was instituted, the Company had 95 employees at the Dan River Station, 14 of whom were Negroes; 13 of these are petitioners here.

The District Court found that prior to July 2, 1965, the effective date of the Civil Rights Act of 1964, the Company openly discriminated on the basis of race in the hiring and assigning of employees at its

---

1. The Act provides:
"Sec. 703(a) It shall be an unlawful employment practice for an employer—

* * * * * *

"(2) to limit, segregate, or classify his employees in any way which would deprive or tend to deprive any individual of employment opportunities or otherwise adversely affect his status as an employee, because of such individual's race, color, religion, sex, or national origin.

* * * * * *

"(h) Notwithstanding any other provision of this title, it shall not be an unlawful employment practice for an employer * * * to give and to act upon the results of any professionally developed ability test provided that such test, its administration or action upon the results is not designed, intended, or used to discriminate because of race, color, religion, sex or national origin. * * *" (Court's footnote 1.)

Dan River plant. The plant was organized into five operating departments: (1) Labor, (2) Coal Handling, (3) Operations, (4) Maintenance, and (5) Laboratory and Test. Negroes were employed only in the Labor Department where the highest paying jobs paid less than the lowest paying jobs in the other four "operating" departments in which only whites were employed. Promotions were normally made within each department on the basis of job seniority. Transferees into a department usually began in the lowest position.

In 1955 the Company instituted a policy of requiring a high school education for initial assignment to any department except Labor, and for transfer from the Coal Handling to any "inside" department (Operations, Maintenance, or Laboratory). When the Company abandoned its policy of restricting Negroes to the Labor Department in 1965, completion of high school also was made a prerequisite to transfer from Labor to any other department. From the time the high school requirement was instituted to the time of trial, however, white employees hired before the time of the high school education requirement continued to perform satisfactorily and achieve promotions in the "operating" departments. Findings on this score are not challenged.

The Company added a further requirement for new employees on July 2, 1965, the date on which Title VII became effective. To qualify for placement in any but the Labor Department it became necessary to register satisfactory scores on two professionally prepared aptitude tests, as well as to have a high school education. Completion of high school alone continued to render employees eligible for transfer to the four desirable departments from which Negroes had been excluded if the incumbent had been employed prior to the time of the new requirement. In September 1965 the Company began to permit incumbent employees who lacked a high school education to qualify for transfer from Labor or Coal Handling to an "inside" job by passing two tests—the Wonderlic Personnel Test, which purports to measure general intelligence, and the Bennett Mechanical Aptitude Test. Neither was directed or intended to measure the ability to learn to perform a particular job or category of jobs. The requisite scores used for both initial hiring and transfer approximated the national median for high school graduates.

The District Court had found that while the Company previously followed a policy of overt racial discrimination in a period prior to the Act, such conduct had ceased. The District Court also concluded that Title VII was intended to be prospective only and, consequently, the impact of prior inequities was beyond the reach of corrective action authorized by the Act.

The Court of Appeals was confronted with a question of first impression, as are we, concerning the meaning of Title VII. After careful analysis a majority of that court concluded that a subjective test of the employer's intent should govern, particularly in a close case, and that in this case there was no showing of a discriminatory purpose in the adoption of the diploma and test requirements. On this basis, the Court of Appeals concluded there was no violation of the Act.

The Court of Appeals reversed the District Court in part, rejecting the holding that residual discrimination arising from prior employment practices was insulated from remedial action. The Court of Appeals noted, however, that the District Court was correct in its conclusion that there was no finding of a racial purpose of invidious intent in the adoption of the high school diploma requirement or general intelligence test and that these standards had been applied fairly to whites and Negroes alike. It held that, in the absence of a discriminatory purpose, use of such requirements was permitted by the Act. In so doing, the Court of Appeals rejected the claim that because these two requirements operated to render ineligible a markedly disproportionate number of Negroes, they were unlawful under Title VII unless shown to be job-related. We granted the writ on these claims. 399 U.S. 926.

The objective of Congress in the enactment of Title VII is plain from the language of the statute. It was to achieve equality of employment opportunities and remove barriers that have operated in the past to favor an identifiable group of white employees over other employees. Under the Act, practices, procedures, or tests neutral on their face, and even neutral in terms of intent, cannot be maintained if they operate to "freeze" the status quo of prior discriminatory employment practices.

The Court of Appeals' opinion, and the partial dissent, agreed that, on the record in the present case, "whites fare far better on the Company's alternative requirements" than Negroes. This consequence would appear to be directly traceable to race. Basic intelligence must have the means of articulation to manifest itself fairly in a testing process. Because they are Negroes, petitioners have long received inferior education in segregated schools and this Court expressly recognized these differences in Gaston County v. United States, 395 U.S. 285 (1969). * * * Congress did not intend by Title VII, however, to guarantee a job to every person regardless of qualifications. In short, the Act does not command that any person be hired simply because he was formerly the subject of discrimination, or because he is a member of a minority group. Discriminatory preference for any group, minority or majority, is precisely and only what Congress has proscribed. What is required by Congress is the removal of artificial, arbitrary, and unnecessary barriers to employment when the barriers operate invidiously to discriminate on the basis of racial or other impermissible classification.

* * * The Act proscribes not only overt discrimination but also practices that are fair in form, but discriminatory in operation. The touchstone is business necessity. If an employment practice which operates to exclude Negroes cannot be shown to be related to job performance, the practice is prohibited.

On the record before us, neither the high school completion requirement nor the general intelligence test is shown to bear a demonstrable relationship to successful performance of the jobs for which it was used. Both were adopted, as the Court of Appeals noted, without meaningful study of their relationship to job-performance ability. Rather, a vice president of the Company testified, the requirements were instituted on the Company's judgment that they generally would improve the overall quality of the work force.

The evidence, however, shows that employees who have not completed high school or taken the tests have continued to perform satisfactorily and make progress in departments for which the high school and test criteria are now used. The promotion record of present employees who would not be able to meet the new criteria thus suggests the possibility that the requirements may not be needed even for the limited purpose of preserving the avowed policy of advancement within the Company. In the context of this case, it is unnecessary to reach the question whether testing requirements that take into account capability for the next succeeding position or related future promotion might be utilized upon a showing that such long range requirements fulfill a genuine business need. In the present case the Company has made no such showing.

The Court of Appeals held that the Company had adopted the diploma and test requirements without any "intention to discriminate against Negro employees." We do not suggest that either the District Court or the Court of Appeals erred in examining the employer's intent; but good intent or absence of discriminatory intent does not redeem employment procedures or testing mechanisms that operate as "built-in headwinds" for minority groups and are unrelated to measuring job capability.

* * * Congress directed the thrust of the Act to the *consequences* of employment practices, not simply the motivation. More than that, Congress has placed on the employer the burden of showing that any given requirement must have a manifest relationship to the employment in question.

The facts of this case demonstrate the inadequacy of broad and general testing devices as well as the infirmity of using diplomas or degrees as fixed measures of capability. * * *

The Company contends that its general intelligence tests are specifically permitted by § 703(h) of the Act. That section authorizes the use of "any professionally developed ability test" that is not "designed, intended, *or used* to discriminate because of race * * *." (Emphasis added.)

* * * From the sum of the legislative history relevant in this case, the conclusion is inescapable that the EEOC's construction of § 703(h) to require that employment tests be job-related comports with congressional intent.

Nothing in the Act precludes the use of testing or measuring procedures; obviously they are useful. What Congress has forbidden is giving these devices and mechanisms controlling force unless they are demonstrably a reasonable measure of job performance. Congress has not commanded that the less qualified be preferred over the better qualified simply because of minority origins. Far from disparaging job qualifications as such, Congress has made such qualifications the controlling factor, so that race, religion, nationality, and sex become irrelevant. What Congress has commanded is that any tests used must measure the person for the job and not the person in the abstract.

The judgment of the Court of Appeals is, as to that portion of the judgment appealed from, reversed.

Mr. Justice BRENNAN took no part in the consideration or decision of this case.

B. COMPENSATION PLANS

INTRODUCTORY NOTE

People seek compensation for the services they perform for a business. Nearly everyone needs compensation in order to live, to provide the food, shelter, clothing, and a host of other things that are necessary or desirable in modern life. Even those persons who have an income from investments or from any other source, or who are supported by their families, still demand compensation for their services. (Many people willingly contribute their services to charitable or non-business enterprises, but they are generally limited to those who have some other income.) Our system (other than for a temporary emergency) permits people to bargain, either individually or collectively, for the compensation to be paid to them. Only in the government service, both civilian and military, do we have any "law" fixing the rate of compensation to persons who are providing services to any enterprise. And even in this area, limited to civilian employment, we have recently seen the rise of collective bargaining; this has been particularly true at the local government level. But absent this kind of employment our ideas about freedom of contract prevail. The hourly wage rate is negotiated by collective bargaining; the weekly, monthly, or annual salary of non-collective bargaining unit employees, or supervisory or managerial employees, is determined by individual negotiation between employee and employer; or in some cases by employer fiat; and the lower on the scale of the hierarchy of managerial employees, the less bargaining power the employees have. The system in practice means that an employee who is not part of a collective bargaining unit who does not like the scale of compensation offered to him by his employer is free to go elsewhere, and depending upon the economic prosperity of the times, he may find employment with compensation satisfactory to him; or he may stay where he is. The prospect of success of a bookkeeper employed by a large conglomerate in bargaining with his superiors for additional compensation exists only in theory; but insofar as the law is concerned he is free to go elsewhere to seek other employment with more satisfactory compensation. He is not legally an indentured servant, not legally a slave or a peon, not legally a captive employee; to the extent that these legalisms are more theoretical than real, we may need a substantial change in the system. Or the employee may join a union.

In addition to current compensation to provide for current needs, most persons are interested in providing some system for their financial security upon their retirement from active employment. The Social Security System established by the United States is a base upon which many persons desire to build for this purpose. The severe economic hardships that were placed upon elderly persons during the Great Depression clearly demonstrated the need for this legislation. While the private pension system did exist prior to the 1930's, it actually covered only a miniscule portion of our population. Retired employees living on pensions during the Great Depression were few in number indeed; their contemporaries without the benefit of a program of this kind suffered the most severe economic hardship of any group in our society. Because of their age and frequently infirm condition, they were in fact unemployable, and because the old family system of the younger productive members of a family group taking care of the elders had broken down (younger people themselves were either unemployed or underemployed), and because private charity was almost non-existent and public charity, i. e., poorhouses and poor farms, were quickly overpopulated, elderly people with no income suffered most.

Wage and salary stabilization programs which were adopted during World War II (and again in 1971) followed the policy of little or no current increases in compensation but gradually did permit the institution of various forms of deferred compensation. It was thought that if the money involved in the cost of a pension were not to be paid to employees currently but were put into a trust fund for their benefit to be paid to them at a later time, the desired effect of maintaining some stability in prices would be achieved. (Since all of these plans added to the cost of production anyone could have recognized that this increase in cost would increase prices, but this fundamental fact was either ignored or a political decision was made to forget it.)

Oddly, this new program was not dealt with directly but only indirectly by amending the Internal Revenue Code in 1942. Perhaps at the time it was thought that the most serious problem was a potential loss of governmental revenue and that this should be the focus of the new statute. There was no legislation that would have required the distribution of the funds to all persons on whose behalf a contribution had been made, or the restoration of the funds to the contributing employer when for any reason excess funds had been contributed, with a recomputation of income-taxes, nor the re-definition of fraudulent or deceptive employment practices, any one or all of which might have dealt with the problem. Also, legislation might have been enacted which would have provided incentives to employers to establish retirement plans without relying primarily upon tax benefits. Nonetheless, tax benefits were the carrot used to induce employers to adopt plans of this kind and at the same time were used to attempt to enact a new social policy. Thus we find that the Internal Revenue Code, Sections 401 through 404, and Section 501(a), contains the main body of Federal law relating to deferred compensation plans.

The scheme of the Internal Revenue Code in this regard is to establish standards for "qualified" pension, profit-sharing, and stock bonus plans in Section 401. Any plan which is established as a consequence of collective bargaining will almost undoubtedly meet all of the requirements of Section 401 so that there is little concern among persons who negotiate these plans about meeting the requirements of this Section. But there are a multitude of plans adopted for noncollective bargaining unit employes, or in employment units where there is no union, which must meet all of the intricate requirements of this Section. The principal difficulty arises when an employer desires to have a plan of this kind benefit less than all of his employees. If 70% or more of all the employees will be eligible to benefit under the plan, and if 80% or more of this group actually benefit, there is no problem with "qualification." It can be seen that in most industries this standard will be sufficient to qualify a union-negotiated plan. But if less than the above percentages of employees are to benefit from the plan, and this happens many, many times, then a plan will be qualified "[if] the contributions or benefits provided under the plan do not discriminate in favor of employees who are officers, shareholders, persons whose principal duties consist in supervising the work of other employees, or highly compensated employees." The case of Commissioner v. Pepsi-Cola Niagara Bottling Corp., 399 F.2d 390 (2d Cir. 1968), reported below, deals with this problem. Incidentally, as the Court stated in a foot-note to its opinion in that case, there is a "[s]parcity of reported cases" dealing with pension plans because of the general practice of obtaining determination letters (advance rulings) from the Internal Revenue Service stating that the plan meets the requirements of the Internal Revenue Code.

Section 401 of the Internal Revenue Code, 26 U.S.C.A. § 401, sets forth the statutory requirements for a "qualified" pension, profit-sharing, or stock-bonus plan. More than fifty pages of fine print are involved in regulations which have been adopted by the Internal Revenue Service relating to these plans, only a small portion of which are reported below. Section 1.401–(c), reported infra, admittedly the most complex section of the regulation, is one which almost defies comprehension. Section 402 of the Code, 26 U.S.C.A. § 402, provides for the taxability of beneficiaries of employees' trusts. This generally provides that no tax is paid by an employee on the contribution as it is made to the trust for his benefit. Later he is required to pay a tax only on the amount actually distributed or made available to him, that is normally at his retirement, when presumably he will be in a lower income tax bracket than during the years of his employment.

Section 403 deals with the taxation of employee annuities, a system which is not widely used. Section 404 provides in effect that an employer may have a current income tax deduction for a contribution to a qualified employee's trust in the year in which the contribution is made. This Section is also supplemented by detailed regulations of more than thirty pages of fine print. Section 501(a) provides that a trust fund which is described in Section 401(a) that is a "qualified" trust forming a part of a pension, profit-sharing or stock bonus plan as described above, is exempt from taxation. (The same section in one brief sentence also exempts charitable trusts from taxation.) This permits the pension trust fund to grow on a tax-free basis and thus substantially to reduce the cost of a retirement benefit; over a working period of thirty years in which annual contributions are made the accumulated income can reduce this cost by more than half. The sections of the Internal Revenue Code noted above, and the Regulations, are supplemented by more than 150 Revenue Rulings. From time to time the Internal Revenue Service publishes a comprehensive up-dated guide relating to the qualification of these plans. The most recent one of this kind was Revenue Ruling (usually abbreviated Rev. Rul.) 69–421, published on August 11, 1969. Approximately one third of this Revenue Ruling is reported below; a comparison of the readability of it with Regulations Section 1.401(c) is easily noted.

Among the amendments added to the Labor Management Relations Act, 29 U.S.C.A. § 141 et seq., added by the Taft-Hartley Act in 1947 was Section 302, 29 U.S.C.A. § 168. Sub-section (a) provides that it shall be unlawful for an employer to pay money to a representative of his employees; sub-section (b) provides that it shall be unlawful for the representative to receive the money; and sub-section (c) provides a number of exceptions to (a) and (b), the fifth of which makes it possible for employers to make contributions to a trust fund established either for a pension plan or for a health and welfare plan (they must be separate trust funds). Section 302(c) (5) in one long paragraph, contains the entire body of Federal law regulating pension funds and health and welfare funds. The provisions of the Internal Revenue Code relating to these matters relate only to taxation; while it may be impractical to suggest that one could establish one of these plans without the tax benefits, yet if one wants to establish a pension plan without reference to the Internal Revenue Code he may do so without any concern about violating the law, although he would have to pay the taxes involved. Not so with Section 302(c) (5) of the Labor Act; if an employer is to make contributions to a pension or health and welfare fund established by representatives of the employees (by them alone or jointly with an employer through collective bargaining) he must comply with the terms of the Act. The Welfare and Pension Plans Disclosure Act, 29 U.S.C.A. § 301 et seq. is not a regulatory Act; it requires only that annual detailed reports about the plans be sent to a Washington bureau where they are filed and are available for inspection by the public. But disclosure and filing are not regulation. No administrative agency is charged with regulating these plans or overseeing their practices or determining the eligibility of employees to participate in the plans or to receive any benefits; the only method of enforcement of any rights under the written agreements establishing these trust funds is by a suit in a common law court.

Two cases are reported below which deal with some of the problems under Section 302(c) (5) of the Labor Act. Moglia v. Geoghegan, 403 F.2d 110 (2d Cir. 1968), with its seemingly harsh result, points up the necessity for full compliance with the provisions of the Act. Blassie v. Kroger Co., 345 F.2d 58 (8th Cir. 1965), deals with some of the problems which may arise because trustees of these plans fail to comprehend their proper role, or are poorly advised. The report of this case is substantially condensed (the original is quite lengthy) because many of the facts which led to the litigation were peculiar to the parties themselves. Also, the case is not well-known for the excerpts which have been printed, but it is believed that in the years to come these parts of the opinion will be referred to frequently. As then Circuit Judge Blackmun, later Justice Blackmun of the United States Supreme Court, commented, "[T]his is a trust, with all the implications which that term possesses" (at p. 76). This is a concept of the greatest importance, one which assuredly will be litigated, perhaps extensively, in the future. Trust funds of this kind in the aggregate hold assets in excess of $150,000,000,000 and it is anticipated they will hold assets of $250,000,000,000 by 1980. Already they are the largest single pool of investment capital in the American economy. They have been established to provide benefits for a large part of the employed people in the United States. The trust funds vary in size from one established for a single employee with a few thousand dollars of assets to trust funds with more than 200,000 participants and more than $1,000,000,000 in assets. Their area of operation varies from a single community to all fifty states. To the extent that there is any law governing the administration of these trust funds it is trust law, which is state law and not Federal law. It is the same trust law which governs the family trust which has been established under a will or under an inter vivos trust agreement because, after all, these trust funds have been established under an inter vivos trust agreement. Probate Courts, Surrogates Courts, Orphans' Courts, etc., with their concepts and procedures for handling a trust fund with one or a half dozen beneficiaries at present are the only courts established to supervise the administration of any trust, including these employee benefit plan trusts. The simple fact is that these trusts do not often get into court, not at the state level, so that the capacity of our existing body of trust law to supervise the administration of a multi-million dollar trust fund with hundreds of thousands of beneficiaries scattered over the United States has only recently been questioned. Legislation has been introduced in Congress, the Fiduciary Responsibility Act, but it remains to be seen whether it will be adopted, and if adopted whether it will apply to the hundreds of thousands of small employee benefit plans operating entirely within one state. Also, the Act does not take into account that these plans are, and perhaps should be operated as a business and not as a family trust.

———

INCOME TAX REGULATIONS

* * *

§ 1.401–1 Qualified pension, profit-sharing and stock bonus plans

(a) Introduction. (1) Sections 401 through 405 relate to pension, profit-sharing, stock bonus, and annuity plans, compensation paid under a deferred-payment plan and bond purchase plans. Section 401(a) prescribes the requirements which must be met for qualification of a trust forming part of a pension, profit-sharing, or stock bonus plan.

(2) A qualified pension, profit-sharing, or stock bonus plan is a definite written program and arrangement which is communicated to the employees and which is established and maintained by an employer—

(i) In the case of a pension plan, to provide for the livelihood of the employees or their beneficiaries after the retirement of such employees through the payment of benefits determined without regard to profits (see paragraph (b) (1) (i) of this section);

(ii) In the case of a profit-sharing plan, to enable employees or their beneficiaries to participate in the profits of the employer's trade or business, or in the profits of an affiliated employer who is entitled to deduct his contributions to the plan under section 404(a)(3)(B), pursuant to a definite formula for allocating the contributions and for distributing the funds accumulated under the plan (see paragraph (b)(1)(ii) of this section); and

(iii) In the case of a stock bonus plan, to provide employees or their beneficiaries benefits similar to those of profit-sharing plans, except that such benefits are distributable in stock of the employer, and that the contributions by the employer are not necessarily dependent upon profits. If the employer's contributions are dependent upon profits, the plan may enable employees or their beneficiaries to participate not only in the profits of the employer, but also in the profits of an affiliated employer who is entitled to deduct his contributions to the plan under section 404(a)(3) (B) (see paragraph (b)(1)(iii) of this section).

(3) In order for a trust forming part of a pension, profit-sharing, or stock bonus plan to constitute a qualified trust under section 401(a), the following tests must be met:

(i) It must be created or organized in the United States, as defined in section 7701(a)(9), and it must be maintained at all times as a domestic trust in the United States;

(ii) It must be part of a pension, profit-sharing, or stock bonus plan established by an employer for the exclusive benefit of his employees or their beneficiaries (see paragraph (b)(2) through (5) of this section);

(iii) It must be formed or availed of for the purpose of distributing to the employees or their beneficiaries the corpus and income of the fund accumulated by the trust in accordance with the plan; and, in the case of a plan which covers (as defined in paragraph (a)(2) of § 1.401–10) any self-employed individual, the time and method of such distribution must satisfy the requirements of section 401(a)(9) with respect to each employee covered by the plan (see paragraph (e) of § 1.401–11) ;

(iv) It must be impossible under the trust instrument at any time before the satisfaction of all liabilities with respect to employees and their beneficiaries under the trust, for any part of the corpus or income to be used for, or diverted to, purposes other than for the exclusive benefit of the employees or their beneficiaries (see § 1.401–2) ;

(v) It must be part of a plan which benefits prescribed percentages of the employees, or which benefits such employees as qualify under a classification set up by the employer and found by the Commissioner not to be discriminatory in favor of certain specified classes of employees (see § 1.401–3 and, in addition, see § 1.401–12 for special rules as to plans covering owner-employees) ;

(vi) It must be part of a plan under which contributions or benefits do not discriminate in favor of certain specified classes of employees (see § 1.401–4) ;

(vii) It must be part of a plan which provides the nonforfeitable rights described in section 401(a) (7) (see § 1.401–6) ;

(viii) If the trust forms part of a pension plan, the plan must provide that forfeitures must not be applied to increase the benefits any employee would receive under such plan (see § 1.401–7) ;

(ix) It must, if the plan benefits any self-employed individual who is an owner-employee, satisfy the additional requirements for qualification contained in section 401(a) (10) and (d).

(4) For taxable years beginning after December 31, 1962, self-employed individuals may be included in qualified plans. See §§ 1.401–10 through 1.401–13.

(b) General rules. (1)(i) A pension plan within the meaning of section 401(a) is a plan established and maintained by an employer primarily to provide systematically for the payment of definitely determinable benefits to his employees over a period of years, usually for life, after retirement. Retirement benefits generally are measured by, and based on, such factors as years of service and compensation received by the employees. The determination of the amount of retirement benefits and the contributions to provide such benefits are not dependent upon profits. Benefits are not definitely determinable if funds arising from forfeitures on termination of service, or any other reason, may be used to provide increased benefits for the remaining participants (see § 1.401–7, relating to the treatment of forfeitures under a qualified pension plan). A plan designed to provide benefits for employees or their beneficiaries to be paid upon retirement or over a period of years after retirement will, for the purposes of section 401(a), be considered a pension plan if the employer contributions under the plan can be determined actuarially on the basis of definitely determinable benefits, or, as in the case of money purchase pension plans, such contributions are fixed without being geared to profits. A pension plan may provide for the payment of a pension due to disability and may also provide for the payment of incidental death benefits through insurance or otherwise. However, a plan is not a pension plan if it provides for the payment of benefits not customarily included in a pension plan such as layoff benefits or benefits for sickness, accident, hospitalization, or medical expenses (except medical benefits described in section 401(h) as defined in paragraph (a) of § 1.401–14).

(ii) A profit-sharing plan is a plan established and maintained by an employer to provide for the participation in his profits by his employees or their beneficiaries. The plan must provide a definite predetermined formula for allocating the contributions made to the plan among the participants and for distributing the funds accumulated under the plan after a fixed number of years, the attainment of a stated age, or upon the prior occurrence of some event such as layoff, illness, disability, retirement, death, or severance of employment. A formula for allocating the contributions among the participants is definite if, for example, it provides for an allocation in proportion to the basic compensation of each participant. A plan (whether or not it contains a definite predetermined formula for determining the profits to be shared with the employees) does not qualify under section 401 (a) if the contributions to the plan are made at such times or in such amounts that the plan in operation discriminates in favor of officers, shareholders, persons whose principal duties consist in supervising the work of other employees, or highly compensated employees. For the rules with respect to discrimination, see §§ 1.401–3 and 1.401–4. A profit-sharing plan within the meaning of section 401 is primarily a plan of deferred compensation, but the amounts allocated to the account of a participant may be used to provide for him or his family incidental life or accident or health insurance.

(iii) A stock bonus plan is a plan established and maintained by an employer to provide benefits similar to those of a profit-sharing plan, except that the contributions by the employer are not necessarily dependent upon profits and the benefits are distributable in stock of the employer company. For the purpose of allocating and distributing the stock of the employer which is to be shared among his employees or their beneficiaries, such a plan is subject to the same requirements as a profit-sharing plan.

(iv) As to inclusion of full-time life insurance salesmen within the class of persons considered to be employees, see section 7701(a) (20).

(2) The term "plan" implies a permanent as distinguished from a temporary program. Thus, although the employer may reserve the right to change or terminate the plan, and to discontinue contributions thereunder, the abandonment of the plan for any reason other than business necessity within a few years after it has taken effect will be evidence that the plan from its inception was not a bona fide program for the exclusive benefit of employees in general. Especially will this be true if, for example, a pension plan is abandoned soon after pensions have been fully funded for persons in favor of whom discrimination is prohibited under section 401(a). The permanency of the plan will be indicated by all of the surrounding facts and circumstances, including the likelihood of the employer's ability to continue contributions as provided under the plan. In the case of a profit-sharing plan, other than a profit-sharing plan which covers employees and owner-employees (see section 401(d)(2)(B)), it is not necessary that the employer contribute every year or that he contribute the same amount or contribute in accordance with the same ratio every year. However, merely making a single or occasional contribution out of profits for employees does not establish a plan of profit-sharing. To be a profit-sharing plan, there must be recurring and substantial contributions out of profits for the employees. In the event a plan is abandoned, the employer should promptly notify the district director, stating the circumstances which led to the discontinuance of the plan.

(3) If the plan is so designed as to amount to a subterfuge for the distribution of profits to shareholders, it will not qualify as a plan for the exclusive benefit of employees even though other employees who are not shareholders are also included under the plan. The plan must benefit the employees in general, although it need not provide benefits for all of the employees. Among the employees to be benefited may be persons who are officers and shareholders. However, a plan is not for the exclusive benefit of employees in general if, by any device whatever, it discriminates either in eligibility requirements, contributions, or benefits in favor of employees who are officers, shareholders, persons whose principal duties consist in supervising the work of other employees, or the highly compensated employees. See section 401(a)(3), (4), and (5). Similarly, a stock bonus or profit-sharing plan is not a plan for the exclusive benefit of employees in general if the funds therein may be used to relieve the employer from contributing to a pension plan operating concurrently and covering the same employees. All of the surrounding and attendant circumstances and the details of the plan will be indicative of whether it is a bona fide stock bonus, pension, or profit-sharing plan for the exclusive benefit of employees in general. The law is concerned not only with the form of a plan but also with its effects in operation. For example, section 401(a)(5) specifies certain provisions which of themselves are not discriminatory. However, this does not mean that a plan containing these provisions may not be discriminatory in actual operation.

(4) A plan is for the exclusive benefit of employees or their beneficiaries even though it may cover former employees as well as present employees and employees who are temporarily on leave, as, for example, in the Armed Forces of the United States. A plan covering only former employees may qualify under section 401(a) if it complies with the provisions of section 401(a)(3)(B), with respect to coverage, and section 401(a)(4), with respect to contributions and benefits, as applied to all of the former employees. The term "beneficiaries" of an employee within the meaning of section 401 includes the estate of the employee, dependents of the employee, persons who are the natural objects of the employee's bounty, and any persons designated by the employee to share in the benefits of the plan after the death of the employee.

(5) (i) No specific limitations are provided in section 401(a) with respect to investments which may be made by the trustees of a trust qualifying under section 401(a). Generally, the contributions may be used by the trustees to purchase any investments permitted by the trust agreement to the extent allowed by local law. However, such a trust will be subject to tax under section 511 with respect to any "unrelated business taxable income" (as defined in section 512) realized by it from its investments. Furthermore, the tax-exempt status of the trust will be forfeited if the investments made by the trustees constitute "prohibited transactions" within the meaning of section 503. See also the regulations under such sections.

(ii) Where the trust funds are invested in stock or securities of, or loaned to, the employer or other person described in section 503(c), full disclosure must be made of the reasons for such arrangement and the conditions under which such investments are made in order that a determination may be made whether the trust serves any purpose other than constituting part of a plan for the exclusive benefit of employees. The trustee shall report any of such investments on the return which under section 6033 it is required to file and shall with respect to any such investment furnish the information required by such return. See § 1.6033–1.

(c) Portions of years. A qualified status must be maintained throughout the entire taxable year of the trust in order for the trust to obtain any exemption for such year. But see section 401(a)(6) and § 1.401–3.

(d) Plan of several employers. A trust forming part of a plan of several employers for their employees will be qualified if all the requirements are otherwise satisfied.

(e) Determination of exemptions and returns. (1) An employees' trust may request a determination letter as to its qualification under section 401 and exemption under section 501. For the procedure for obtaining such a determination letter see paragraph (1) of § 601.201 of this chapter (Statement of Procedural Rules).

(2) A trust which qualifies under section 401(a) and which is exempt under section 501(a) must file a return in accordance with section 6033 and the regulations thereunder. See §§ 1.6033–1 and 1.6033–2(a)(2). In case such a trust realizes any unrelated business taxable income, as defined in section 512, such trust is also required to file a return with respect to such income. See paragraph (e) of § 1.6012–2 and paragraph (a) (5) of § 1.6012–3 for requirements with respect to such returns. For information required to be furnished periodically by an employer with respect to the qualification of a plan, see §§ 1.404(a)–2, 1.404(a)–2A, and 1.6033–2(a) (2)(ii)(*i*).

§ 1.401–2   Impossibility of diversion under the trust instrument

(a) In general. (1) Under section 401(a)(2) a trust is not qualified unless under the trust instrument it is impossible (in the taxable year and at any time thereafter before the satisfaction of all liabilities to employees or their beneficiaries covered by the trust) for any part of the trust corpus or income to be used for, or diverted to, purposes other than for the exclusive benefit of such employees or their beneficiaries. This section does not apply to funds of the trust which are allocated to provide medical benefits described in section 401(h) as defined in paragraph (a) of § 1.401–14. For the rules prohibiting diversion of such funds and the requirement of reversion to the employer after satisfaction of all liabilities under the medical benefits account, see paragraph (c) (4) and (5) of § 1.401–14.

(2) As used in section 401(a)(2), the phrase "if under the trust instrument it is impossible" means that the trust instrument must definitely and affirmatively make it impossible for the nonexempt diversion or use to occur, whether by operation or natural termination of the trust, by power of revocation or amendment, by the happening of a contingency, by collateral arrangement, or by any other means. Although it is not essential that the employer relinquish all power to modify or terminate the rights of certain employees covered by the trust, it must be impossible for the trust funds to be used or diverted for purposes other than for the exclusive benefit of his employees or their beneficiaries.

(3) As used in section 401(a)(2), the phrase "purposes other than for the exclusive benefit of his employees or their beneficiaries" includes all objects or aims not solely designed for the proper satisfaction of all liabilities to employees or their beneficiaries covered by the trust.

(b) Meaning of "liabilities". (1) The intent and purpose in section 401(a)(2) of the phrase "prior to the satisfaction of all liabilities with respect to employees and their beneficiaries under the trust" is to permit the employer to reserve the right to recover at the termination of the trust, and only at such termination, any balance remaining in the trust which is due to erroneous actuarial computations during the previous life of the trust. A balance due to an "erroneous actuarial computation" is the surplus arising because actual requirements differ from the expected requirements even though the latter were based upon previous actuarial valuations of liabilities or determinations of costs of providing pension benefits under the plan and were made by a person competent to make such determinations in accordance with reasonable assumptions as to mortality, interest, etc., and correct procedures relating to the method of funding. For example, a trust has accumulated assets of $1,000,000 at the time of liquidation, determined by acceptable actuarial procedures using reasonable assumptions as to interest, mortality, etc., as being necessary to provide the benefits in accordance with the provisions of the plan. Upon such liquidation it is found that $950,000 will satisfy all of the liabilities under the plan. The surplus of $50,000 arises, therefore, because of the difference between the amounts actuarially determined and the amounts actually required to satisfy the liabilities. This $50,000, therefore, is the amount which may be returned to the employer as the result of an erroneous actuarial computation. If, however, the surplus of $50,000 had been accumulated as a result of a change in the benefit provisions or in the eligibility requirements of the plan, the $50,000 could not revert to the employer because such surplus would not be the result of an erroneous actuarial computation.

(2) The term "liabilities" as used in section 401(a)(2) includes both fixed and contingent obligations to employees. For example, if 1,000 employees are covered by a trust forming part of a pension plan, 300 of whom have satisfied all the requirements for a monthly pension, while the remaining 700 employees have not yet completed the required period of service, contingent obligations to such 700 employees have nevertheless arisen which constitute "liabilities" within the meaning of that term. It must be impossible for the employer (or other nonemployee) to recover any amounts other than such amounts as remain in the trust because of "erroneous actuarial computations" after the satisfaction of all fixed and contingent obligations. Furthermore, the trust instrument must contain a definite affirmative provision to this effect, irrespective of whether the obligations to employees have their source in the trust instrument itself, in the plan of which the trust forms a part, or in some collateral instrument or arrangement forming a part of such plan, and regardless of whether such obligations are, technically speaking, liabilities of the employer, of the trust, or of some other person forming a part of the plan or connected with it.

§ 1.401–3 Requirements as to coverage

(a) (1) In order to insure that stock bonus, pension, and profit-sharing plans are utilized for the welfare of employees in general, and to prevent the trust device from being used for the principal benefit of shareholders, officers, persons whose principal duties consist in supervising the work of other employees, or highly paid employees, or as a means of tax avoidance, a trust will not be qualified unless it is part of a plan which satisfies the coverage requirements of section 401(a)(3). However, if the plan covers any individual who is an owner-employee, as defined in section 401(c)(3), the requirements of section 401(a)(3) and this section are not applicable to such plan, but the plan must satisfy the requirements of section 401(d) (see § 1.401–12).

(2) The percentage requirements in section 401(a)(3)(A) refer to a percentage of all the active employees, including employees temporarily on leave, such as those in the Armed Forces of the United States, if such employees are eligible under the plan.

(3) The application of section 401(a)(3)(A) may be illustrated by the following example:

Example. A corporation adopts a plan at a time when it has 1,000 employees. The plan provides that all full-time employees who have been employed for a period of two years and have reached the age of 30 shall be eligible to participate. The plan also requires participating employees to contribute 3 percent of their monthly pay. At the time the plan is made effective 100 of the 1,000 employees had not been employed for a period of two years. Fifty of the employees were seasonal employees whose customary employment did not exceed five months in any calendar year. Twenty-five of the employees were part-time employees whose customary employment did not exceed 20 hours in any one week. One hundred and fifty of the full-time employees who had been employed for two years or more had not yet reached age 30. The requirements of section 401(a)(3) (A) will be met if 540 employees are covered by the plan, as shown by the following computation:

(i) Total employees with respect to whom the percentage requirements are applicable (1,000 minus 175 (100 plus 50 plus 25)) 825

(ii) Employees not eligible to participate because of age requirements 150

(iii) Total employees eligible to participate 675

(iv) Percentage of employees in item (i) eligible to participate .... 81+%

(v) Minimum number of participating employees to qualify the plan (80 percent of 675) 540

If only 70 percent, or 578, of the 825 employees satisfied the age and service requirements, then 462 (80 percent of 578) participating employees would satisfy the percentage requirements.

(b) If a plan fails to qualify under the percentage requirements of section 401(a)(3)(A), it may still qualify under section 401(a)(3)(B) provided always that (as required by section 401(a)(3) and (4)) the plan's eligibility conditions, benefits, and contributions do not discriminate in favor of employees who are officers, shareholders, persons whose principal duties consist in supervising the work of other employees, or the highly compensated employees.

(c) Since, for the purpose of section 401, a profit-sharing plan is a plan which provides for distributing the funds accumulated under the plan after a fixed number of years, the attainment of a stated age, or upon the prior occurrence of some event such as illness, disability, retirement, death, layoff, or severance of employment, employees who receive the amounts allocated to their accounts before the expiration of such a period of time or the occurrence of such a contingency shall not be considered covered by a profit-sharing plan in determining whether the plan meets the coverage requirements of section 401(a)(3)(A) and (B). Thus, in case a plan permits employees to receive immediately the amounts allocated to their accounts, or to have such amounts paid to a profit-sharing plan for them, the employees who receive the shares immediately shall not, for the purpose of section 401, be considered covered by a profit-sharing plan.

(d) Section 401(a)(5) sets out certain classifications that will not in themselves be considered discriminatory. However, those so designated are not intended to be exclusive. Thus, plans may qualify under section 401 (a)(3)(B) even though coverage thereunder is limited to employees who have either reached a designated age or have been employed for a designated number of years, or who are employed in certain designated departments or are in other classifications, provided the effect of covering only such employees does not discriminate in favor of officers, shareholders, employees whose principal duties consist in supervising the work of other employees, or highly compensated employees. For example, if there are 1,000 employees, and the plan is written for only salaried employees, and consequently only 500 employees are covered, that fact alone will not justify the conclusion that the plan does not meet the coverage requirements of section 401 (a)(3)(B). Conversely, if a contributory plan is offered to all of the employees but the contributions required of the employee participants are so burdensome as to make the plan acceptable only to the highly paid employees, the classification will be considered discriminatory in favor of such highly paid employees.

(e) (1) Section 401(a)(5) contains a provision to the effect that a classification shall not be considered discriminatory within the meaning of section 401(a)(3)(B) merely because all employees whose entire annual remuneration constitutes "wages" under section 3121(a)(1) (for purposes of the Federal Insurance Contributions Act, Chapter 21 of the Code) are excluded from the plan. A reference to section 3121(a)(1) for years after 1954 shall be deemed a reference to section 1426(a)(1) of the Internal Revenue Code of 1939 for years before 1955. This provision, in conjunction with section 401(a)(3)(B), is intended to permit the qualification of plans which supplement the old-age, survivors, and disability insurance benefits under the Social Security Act. (42 U.S.C.A. ch. 7). Thus, a classification which excludes all employees whose entire remuneration constitutes "wages" under section 3121(a)(1), will not be considered discriminatory merely because of such exclusion. Similarly, a plan which includes all employees will not be considered discriminatory solely because the contributions or benefits based on that part of their remuneration which is excluded from wages under section 3121(a)(1) differ from the contributions or benefits based on that part of their remuneration which is not so excluded. However, in making his determination with respect to discrimination in classification under section 401(a)(3)(B), the Commissioner will consider whether the total benefits resulting to each employee under the plan and under the Social Security Act, or under the Social Security Act only, establish an integrated and correlated retirement system satisfying the tests of section 401(a). If, therefore, a classification of employees under a plan results in relatively or proportionately greater benefits for employees earning above any specified salary amount or rate than for those below any such salary amount or rate, it may be found to be discriminatory within the meaning of section 401(a)(3)(B). If, however, the relative or proportionate differences in benefits which result from such classification are approximately offset by the old-age survivors, and disability insurance benefits which are provided by the Social Security Act and which are not attributable to employee contributions under the Federal Insurance Contributions Act, the plan will be considered to be properly integrated with the Social Security Act and will, therefore, not be considered discriminatory.

(2) (i) For purposes of determining whether a plan is properly integrated with the Social Security Act, the amount of old-age, survivors, and disability insurance benefits which may be considered as attributable to employer contributions under the Federal Insurance Contributions Act is computed on the basis of the following:

(a) The rate at which the maximum monthly old-age insurance benefit is provided under the Social Security Act is considered to be the average of (1) the rate at which the maximum benefit currently payable under the Act (i. e., in 1971) is provided to an employee retiring at age 65, and (2) the rate at which the maximum benefit ultimately payable under the Act (i. e., in 2010) is provided to an employee retiring at age 65. The resulting figure is 43 percent of the average monthly wage on which such benefit is computed.

(b) The total old-age, survivors and disability insurance benefits with respect to an employee is considered to be 162 percent of the employee's old-age insurance benefits. The resulting figure is 70 percent of the average monthly wage on which it is computed.

(c) In view of the fact that social security benefits are funded through equal contributions by the employer and employee, 50 percent of such benefits is considered attributable to employer contributions. The resulting figure is 35 percent of the average monthly wage on which the benefit is computed.

Under these assumptions, the maximum old-age, survivors, and disability insurance benefits which may be attributed to employer contributions under the Federal Insurance Contributions Act is an amount equal to 35 percent of the earnings on which they are computed. These computations take into account all amendments to the Social Security Act through the Social Security Amendments of 1971 (85 Stat. 6). It is recognized, however, that subsequent amendments to this Act may increase the percentages described in (a) or (b) of this subdivision (i), or both. If this occurs, the method used in this subparagraph for determining the integration formula may result in a figure under (c) of this subdivision (i), which is greater than 35 percent and a plan could be amended to adopt such greater figure in its benefit formula. In order to minimize future plan amendments of this nature, an employer may anticipate future changes in the Social Security Act by immediately utilizing such a higher figure, but not in excess of 37½ percent, in developing its benefit formula.

(ii) Under the rules provided in this subparagraph, a classification of employees under a noncontributory pension of annuity plan which limits coverage to employees whose compensation exceeds the applicable integration level under the plan, will not be considered discriminatory within the meaning of section 401(a)(3)(B), where:

(a) The integration level applicable to an employee is his covered compensation, or is (1) in the case of an active employee, a stated dollar amount uniformly applicable to all active employees which is not greater than the covered compensation of any active employee, and (2) in the case of a retired employee, an amount which is not greater than his covered compensation. (For rules relating to determination of an employee's covered compensation, see subdivision (iv) of this subparagraph.)

(b) The rate at which normal annual retirement benefits are provided for any employee with respect to his average annual compensation in excess of the plan's integration level applicable to him does not exceed 37½ percent.

(c) Average annual compensation is defined to mean the average annual compensation over the highest 5 consecutive years.

(d) There are no benefits payable in case of death before retirement.

(e) The normal form of retirement benefits is a straight life annuity, and if there are optional forms, the benefit payments under each optional form are actuarially equivalent to benefit payments under the normal form.

(f) In the case of any employee who reaches normal retirement age before completion of 15 years of service with the employer, the rate at which normal annual retirement benefits are provided for him with respect to his average annual compensation in excess of the plan's integration level applicable to him does not exceed 2½ percent for each year of service.

(g) Normal retirement age is not lower than age 65.

(h) Benefits payable in case of retirement or severance of employment before normal retirement age cannot exceed the actuarial equivalent of the maximum normal retirement benefits, which might be provided in accordance with (a) through (g) of this subdivision (ii), multiplied by a fraction, the numerator of which is the actual number of years of service of the employee at retirement or severance, and the denominator of which is the total number of years of service he would have had if he had remained in service until normal retirement age. A special disabled life mortality table shall not be used in determining the actuarial equivalent in the case of severance due to disability.

(iii) (a) If a plan was properly integrated with old-age and survivors insurance benefits on July 5, 1968 (hereinafter referred to as an "existing plan"), then, notwithstanding the fact that such plan does not satisfy the requirements of subdivision (ii) of this subparagraph, it will continue to be considered properly integrated with such benefits until January 1, 1972. Such plan will be considered properly integrated after December 31, 1971, so long as the benefits provided under the plan for each employee equal the sum of—

(1) The benefits to which he would be entitled under a plan which, on July 5, 1968, would have been considered properly integrated with old-age and survivors insurance benefits, and under which benefits are provided at the same (or a lesser) rate with respect to the same portion of compensation with respect to which benefits are provided under the existing plan, multiplied by the percentage of his total service with the employer performed before a specified date not later than January 1, 1972; and

(2) The benefits to which he would be entitled under a plan satisfying the requirements of subdivision (ii) of this subparagraph, multiplied by the percentage of his total service with the employer performed on and after such specified date.

(b) A plan which, on July 5, 1968, was properly integrated with old-age and survivors insurance benefits will not be considered not to be properly integrated with such benefits thereafter merely because such plan provides a minimum benefit for each employee (other than an employee who owns, directly or indirectly, stock possessing more than 10 percent of the total combined voting power or value of all classes of stock of the employer corporation) equal to the benefit to which he would be entitled under the plan as in effect on July 5, 1968, if he continued to earn annually until retirement the same amount of compensation as he earned in 1967.

(c) If a plan was properly integrated with old-age and survivors insurance benefits on May 17, 1971, notwithstanding the fact that such plan does not satisfy the requirements of subdivision (ii) of this subparagraph, it will continue to be considered properly integrated with such benefits until January 1, 1972.

(iv) (a) For purposes of this subparagraph, an employee's covered compensation is the amount of compensation with respect to which old-age insurance benefits would be provided for him under the Social Security Act (as in effect at any uniformly applicable date occurring before the employee's separation from the service) if for each year until he reaches age 65 his annual compensation is at least equal to the maximum amount of earnings subject to tax in each such year under the Federal Insurance Contributions Act. A plan may provide that an employee's covered compensation is the amount determined under the preceding sentence rounded to the nearest whole multiple of a stated dollar amount which does not exceed $600.

(b) The age brackets referred to in (a) of this subdivision under the Social Security Act as amended by the Social Security Amendments of 1967 are as follows:

If the employee reaches age 65—	His covered compensation is—
Before 1969	$4,800
After 1968 but before 1972	5,400
After 1971 but before 1979	6,000
After 1978 but before 1994	6,600
After 1993 but before 2001	7,200
After 2000	7,800

(v) In the case of an integrated plan providing benefits different from those described in subdivision (ii) or (iii) (whichever is applicable) of this subparagraph, or providing benefits related to years of service, or providing benefits purchasable by stated employer contributions, or under the terms of which the employees contribute, or providing a combination of any of the foregoing variations, the plan will be considered to be properly integrated only if, as determined by the Commissioner, the benefits provided thereunder by employer contributions cannot exceed in value the benefits described in subdivision (ii) or (iii) (whichever is applicable) of this subparagraph. Similar principles will govern in determining whether a plan is properly integrated if participation therein is limited to employees earning in excess of amounts other than those specified in subdivision (iv) of this subparagraph, or if it bases benefits or contributions on compensation in excess of such amounts, or if it provides for an offset of benefits otherwise payable under the plan on account of old-age survivors, and disability insurance benefits. Similar principles will govern in determining whether a profit-sharing or stock bonus plan is properly integrated with the Social Security Act.

(3) A plan supplementing the Social Security Act and excluding all employees whose entire annual remuneration constitutes "wages" under section 3121(a)(1) will not, however, be deemed discriminatory merely because, for administrative convenience, it provides a reasonable minimum benefit not to exceed $20 a month.

(4) Similar considerations, to the extent applicable in any case, will govern classifications under a plan supplementing the benefits provided by other Federal or State laws. See section 401(a)(5).

(5) If a plan provides contributions or benefits for a self-employed individual, the rules relating to the integration of such a plan with the contributions or benefits under the Social Security Act are set forth in paragraph (c) of § 1.401–1 and paragraph (h) of § 1.401–12.

(f) An employer may designate several trusts or a trust or trusts and an annuity plan or plans as constituting one plan which is intended to qualify under section 401(a)(3), in which case all of such trusts and plans taken as a whole may meet the requirements of such section. The fact that such combination of trusts and plans fails to qualify as one plan does not prevent such of the trusts and plans as qualify from meeting the requirements of section 401(a).

(g) It is provided in section 401(a)(6) that a plan will satisfy the requirements of section 401(a)(3), if on at least one day in each quarter of the taxable year of the plan it satisfies such requirements. This makes it possible for a new plan requiring contributions from employees to qualify if by the end of the quarter-year in which the plan is adopted it secures sufficient contributing participants to meet the requirements of section 401(a)(3). It also affords a period of time in which new participants may be secured to replace former participants, so as to meet the requirements of either subparagraph (A) or (B) of section 401(a)(3).

§ 1.401–4 Discrimination as to contributions or benefits

(a)(1)(i) In order to qualify under section 401(a), a trust must not only meet the coverage requirements of section 401(a)(3), but, as provided in section 401(a)(4), it must also be part of a plan under which there is no discrimination in contributions or benefits in favor of officers, shareholders, employees whose principal duties consist in supervising the work of other employees, or highly compensated employees as against other employees whether within or without the plan.

(ii) Since, for the purpose of section 401, a profit-sharing plan is a plan which provides for distributing the funds accumulated under the plan after a fixed number of years, the attainment of a stated age, or upon the prior occurrence of some event such as illness, disability, retirement, death, layoff, or severance of employment, any amount allocated to an employee which is withdrawn before the expiration of such a period of time or the occurrence of such a contingency shall not be considered in determining whether the contributions under the plan discriminate in favor of officers, shareholders, employees whose principal duties consist in supervising the work of other employees, or highly compensated employees. Thus, in case a plan permits employees to receive immediately the whole or any part of the amounts allocated to their accounts, or to have the whole or any part of such amounts paid to a profit-sharing plan for them, any amounts which are received immediately shall not, for the purpose of section 401, be considered contributed to a profit-sharing plan.

(iii) Funds in a stock bonus or profit-sharing plan arising from forfeitures on termination of service, or other reason, must not be allocated to the remaining participants in such a manner as will effect the prohibited discrimination. With respect to forfeitures in a pension plan, see § 1.401–7.

(2)(i) Section 401(a)(5) sets out certain provisions which will not in and of themselves be discriminatory within the meaning of section 401(a) (3) or (4). See § 1.401–3. Thus, a plan will not be considered discriminatory merely because the contributions or benefits bear a uniform relationship to total compensation or to the basic or regular rate of compensation, or merely because the contributions or benefits based on that part of the annual compensation of employees which is subject to the Federal Insurance Contributions Act (chapter 21 of the Code) differ from the contributions or benefits based on any excess of such annual compensation over such part. With regard to the application of the rules of section 401(a) (5) in the case of a plan which benefits a self-employed individual, see paragraph (c) of § 1.401–11.

(ii) The exceptions specified in section 401(a)(5) are not an exclusive enumeration, but are merely a recital of provisions frequently encountered which will not of themselves constitute forbidden discrimination in contributions or benefits.

(iii) Variations in contributions or benefits may be provided so long as the plan, viewed as a whole for the benefit of employees in general, with all its attendant circumstances, does not discriminate in favor of employees within the enumerations with respect to which discrimination is prohibited. Thus, benefits in a stock bonus or profit-sharing plan which vary by reason of an allocation formula which takes into consideration years of service, or other factors, are not prohibited unless they discriminate in favor of such employees.

(b) A plan which excludes all employees whose entire remuneration constitutes wages under section 3121(a)(1) (relating to the Federal Insurance Contributions Act), or a plan under which the contributions or benefits based on that part of an employee's remuneration which is excluded from "wages" under such Act differs from the contributions or benefits based on that part of the employee's remuneration which is not so excluded, or a plan under which the contributions or benefits differ because of any retirement benefit created under State or Federal law, will not be discriminatory because of such exclusion or difference, provided the total benefits resulting under the plan and under such law establish an integrated and correlated retirement system satisfying the tests of section 401(a).

(c)(1) Although a qualified plan may provide for termination at will by the employer or discontinuance of contributions thereunder, this will not of itself prevent a trust from being a qualified trust. However, a qualified pension plan must expressly incorporate provisions which comply with the restrictions contained in subparagraph (2) of this paragraph at the time the plan is established, unless (i) it is reasonably certain at the inception of the plan that such restrictions would not affect the amount of contributions which may be used for the benefit of any employee, or (ii) the Commissioner determines that such provisions are not necessary to prevent the prohibited discrimination that may occur in the event of any early termination of the plan. Although these provisions are the only provisions required to be incorporated in the plan to prevent the discrimination that may arise because of an early termination of the plan, the plan may in operation result in the discrimination prohibited by section 401(a)(4), unless other provisions are later incorporated in the plan.

(2)(i) If employer contributions under a qualified pension plan may be used for the benefit of an employee who is among the 25 highest paid employees of the employer at the time the plan is established and whose anticipated annual pension under the plan exceeds $1,500, such plan must provide that upon the occurrence of the conditions described in subdivision (ii) of this subparagraph, the employer contributions which are used for the benefit of any such employee are restricted in accordance with subdivision (ii) of this subparagraph.

(ii) The restrictions described in subdivision (iii) of this subparagraph become applicable if—

(a) The plan is terminated within 10 years after its establishment,

(b) The benefits of an employee described in subdivision (i) of this subparagraph become payable within 10 years after the establishment of the plan, or

(c) The benefits of an employee described in subdivision (i) of this subparagraph became payable after the plan had been in effect for 10 years, and the full current costs of the plan for the first 10 years have not been funded.

In the case of an employee described in (b) of this subdivision, the restrictions will remain applicable until the plan has been in effect for 10 years, but if at that time the full current costs have been funded the restrictions will no longer apply to the benefits payable to such an employee. In the case of an employee described in (b) or (c) of this subdivision, if at the end of the first 10 years the full current costs are not met, the restrictions will continue to apply until the full current costs are funded for the first time.

(iii) The restrictions required under subdivision (i) of this subparagraph must provide that the employer contributions which may be used for the benefit of an employee described in such subdivision shall not exceed the greater of $20,000, or 20 percent of the first $50,000 of the annual compensation of such employee multiplied by the number of years between the date of the establishment of the plan and—

(a) The date of the termination of the plan,

(b) In the case of an employee described in subdivision (ii)(b) of this subparagraph, the date the benefit of the employee becomes payable, if before the date of the termination of the plan, or

(c) In the case of an employee described in subdivision (ii)(c) of this subparagraph, the date of the failure to meet the full current costs of the plan.

However, if the full current costs of the plan have not been met on the date described in (a) or (b) of this subdivision, whichever is applicable, then the date of the failure to meet such full current costs shall be substituted for the date referred to in (a) or (b) of this subdivision. For purposes of determining the contributions which may be used for the benefit of an employee when (b) of this subdivision applies, the number of years taken into account may be recomputed for each year if the full current costs of the plan are met for such year.

(iv) For purposes of this subparagraph, the employer contributions which, at a given time, may be used for the benefits of an employee include any unallocated funds which would be used for his benefits if the plan were then terminated or the employee were then to withdraw from the plan, as well as all contributions allocated up to that time exclusively for his benefits.

(v) The provisions of this subparagraph apply to a former or retired employee of the employer, as well as to an employee still in the employer's service.

(vi) The following terms are defined for purposes of this subparagraph—

(a) The term "benefits" includes any periodic income, any withdrawal values payable to a living employee, and the cost of any death benefits which may be payable after retirement on behalf of an employee, but does not include the cost of any death benefits with respect to an employee before retirement nor the amount of any death benefits actually payable after the death of an employee whether such death occurs before or after retirement.

(b) The term "full current costs" means the normal cost, as defined in § 1.404(a)–6, for all years since the effective date of the plan, plus interest on any unfunded liability during such period.

(c) The term "annual compensation" of an employee means either such employee's average regular annual compensation, or such average compensation over the last five years, or such employee's last annual compensation if such compensation is reasonably similar to his average regular annual compensation for the five preceding years.

(3) The amount of the employer contributions which can be used for the benefit of a restricted employee may be limited either by limiting the annual amount of the employer contributions for the designated employee during the period affected by the limitation, or by limiting the amount of funds under the plan which can be used for the benefit of such employee, regardless of the amount of employer contributions.

(4) The restrictions contained in subparagraph (2) of this paragraph may be exceeded for the purpose of making current retirement income benefit payments to retired employees who would otherwise be subject to such restrictions, if—

(i) The employer contributions which may be used for any such employee in accordance with the restrictions contained in subparagraph (2) of this paragraph are applied either (a) to provide level amounts of annuity in the basic form of benefit provided for under the plan for such employee at retirement (or, if he has already retired, beginning immediately), or (b) to provide level amounts of annuity in an optional form of benefit provided under the plan if the level amount of annuity under such optional form of benefit is not greater than the level amount of annuity under the basic form of benefit provided under the plan;

(ii) The annuity thus provided is supplemented, to the extent necessary to provide the full retirement income benefits in the basic form called for under the plan, by current payments to such employee as such benefits come due; and

(iii) Such supplemental payments are made at any time only if the full current costs of the plan have then been met, or the aggregate of such supplemental payments for all such employees does not exceed the aggregate employer contributions already made under the plan in the year then current.

If disability income benefits are provided under the plan, the plan may contain like provisions with respect to the current payment of such benefits.

(5) If a plan has been changed so as to increase substantially the extent of possible discrimination as to contributions and as to benefits

actually payable in event of the subsequent termination of the plan or the subsequent discontinuance of contributions thereunder, then the provisions of this paragraph shall be applied to the plan as so changed as if it were a new plan established on the date of such change. However, the provision in subparagraph (2)(iii) of this paragraph that the unrestricted amount of employer contributions on behalf of any employee is at least $20,000 is applicable to the aggregate amount contributed by the employer on behalf of such employee from the date of establishment of the original plan, and, for purposes of determining if the employee's anticipated annual pension exceeds $1,500, both the employer contributions on the employee's behalf prior to the date of the change in the plan and those expected to be made on his behalf subsequent to the date of the change (based on the employee's rate of compensation on the date of the change) are to be taken into account.

(6) This paragraph shall apply to taxable years of a qualified plan commencing after September 30, 1963. In the case of an early termination of a qualified pension plan during any such taxable year, the employer contributions which may be used for the benefit of any employee must conform to the requirements of this paragraph. However, any pension plan which is qualified on September 30, 1963, will not be disqualified merely because it does not expressly include the provisions prescribed in this paragraph.

* * *

REVENUE RULING

Section 401.—Qualified Pension, Profit-Sharing, and Stock Bonus Plans
26 CFR 1.401–1: Qualified pension, profit-sharing and stock bonus plans.

Updated guides relative to the qualification of employees' pension, annuity, profit-sharing and stock bonus plans under section 401 of the Code.

Rev.Rul. 69–421

* * *

PART 2.—QUALIFIED PENSION, ANNUITY, PROFIT-SHARING,
AND STOCK BONUS PLANS

Section 401(a) of the Internal Revenue Code of 1954—Regulations Section 1.401–1

(a) APPLICABLE PLANS.—The provisions of section 401(a) of the Code are applicable only to qualified trusteed pension, profit-sharing, and stock bonus plans. A custodial account, as defined in section 401(f) of the Code is treated as a qualified trust and is subject to the same requirements that apply to a trust. Nontrusteed annuity plans under which tax deferment and capital gains are provided for in section 403(a) of the Code and deductions for employer contributions are allowable under section 404(a) (2), and qualified bond purchase plans as defined in section 405(a), are subject to some of the requirements of section 401(a) and section 401(d). Paragraphs (3) through (8) of section 401(a) are applicable to all such annuity and bond purchase plans. In addition, if such annuity and bond purchase plans cover self-employed individuals as defined in section 401(c) (1) of the Code, they must also meet the requirements of section 401(a)(9).

Furthermore, if any of the self-employed individuals are owner-employees as defined in section 401(c)(3) of the Code, the plans must also satisfy the requirements of sections 401(a)(10) and 401(d), except section 401(d)(1) (bank trustee), but, in the case of bond purchase plans, sections 401(d)(5)(B) (limited contributions) and 401(d)(8) (excess contributions), are not applicable. See section 405(a)(1) of the Code. For definitions of the applicable plans, see the Income Tax Regulations: Section 1.401–1(b)(1)(i) for pension plans, section 1.401–1(b)(1)(ii) for profit-sharing plans, section 1.401–1(b)(1)(iii) for stock bonus plans, section 1.404(a)–3(a) for annuity plans, section 1.401–9 for face-amount certificates treated as annuity contracts, and section 1.405–1(b) for bond purchase plans. Section 1.401–8 describes custodial accounts.

(b) FUNDED PLANS.—A qualified plan must be a funded plan. Contributions may be made to a trust or under a custodial account, or may be used to pay premiums on insurance contracts, or to purchase face-amount certificates or used to buy retirement bonds. A qualified plan does not provide for direct payments by an employer to his employees, as in the case of a pay-as-you-go pension plan. However, employer contributions to or under a recognized funding medium may, under appropriate circumstances, be delayed pursuant to an established funding method. Thus, a qualified pension plan may provide that current contributions be made by employees only, but that the employer is obligated to pay the full amount of the stipulated benefits to each retired employee-participant after the funds in the trust forming a part of such plan have been fully exhausted. See Rev. Rul. 54–152, C.B. 1954–1, 149. The employer may also make contributions in any year to substitute for the otherwise required employee contributions. Rev.Rul. 68–25, C.B. 1968–1, 151. It should be observed, however, that minimum funding requirements must be maintained even if contributions are made by employees only. See part 6(d) hereof.

(c) PLAN OF DEFERRED COMPENSATION.—A qualified plan is a plan of deferred compensation. A pension plan provides systematically for the payment of definitely determinable benefits to employees over a period of years, usually for life, after retirement. See section 1.401–1(b)(1)(i) of the regulations. A plan does not qualify as a pension plan under section 401(a) of the Code where all compensation is deferred and paid after retirement in the form of benefits under the plan. See Rev.Rul. 69–230, I.R.B. 1969–19, 10. A profit-sharing plan must provide a definite predetermined formula for allocating contributions among participants and for distributing the accumulated funds after a fixed number of years, the attainment of a stated age, or upon the prior occurrence of some event such as layoff, illness, disability, retirement, death, or severance of employment. See section 1.401–1(b)(1)(ii) of the regulations. The term "fixed number of years" is considered to mean at least two years. See Rev.Rul. 54–231, C.B. 1954–1, 150. A specified period, such as the completion of 60 months of participation under the plan is an event on the occurrence of which distributions may be made. See Rev.Rul. 68–24, C.B. 1968–1, 150. A stock bonus plan is similar to a profit-sharing plan except that the contributions by the employer are not necessarily dependent upon profits and the benefits are distributable in stock of the employer company. See section 1.401–1 (b)(1)(iii) of the regulations. A qualified bond purchase plan is established and maintained solely to purchase for and distribute to employees or their beneficiaries U. S. retirement plan bonds. See section 1.405–1(b) of the regulations.

(d) DOMESTIC TRUST.—A qualified employees' trust must be organized or created in the United States and maintained at all times as a domestic trust. See section 1.401–1(a)(3)(i) of the regulations. If, however, a foreign situs trust meets the requirements of section 401(a) of the Code in all other respects, employers making contributions thereunder are allowed deductions within the applicable limits, as provided in section 404(a)(4). Beneficiaries are granted the same tax treatment, in accordance with section 402(c), as is applicable to beneficiaries of a domestic trust. It should be noted, however, that unless a nonresident alien beneficiary is engaged in a trade or business in the United States, or provision is otherwise made by treaty, the long-term capital gain treatment does not apply to distributions to such beneficiary and withholding of tax applies to the distributions, regardless of whether the trust is foreign or domestic. See sections 871 and 1441 of the Code and corresponding regulations.

(e) PLAN AND TRUST OF MULTIPLE EMPLOYERS.—A single plan and trust may be maintained by two or more employers, regardless of their affiliation, but each must meet all applicable requirements. See section 1.401–1(d) of the regulations and Rev.Rul. 69–250, I.R.B. 1969–20, 9.

(1) *Pooled Funds.*—Where, under specified conditions, separate qualified and exempt trusts pool their funds in a group trust created to provide diversification of investments, the group trust may also be exempt and the status for exemption of the separate trusts will not be adversely affected. See Rev.Rul. 56–267, C.B. 1956–1, 206, and Rev.Rul. 66–297, C.B. 1966–2, 234.

(2) *Corporate Participation in Joint Ventures.*—Once an employer-employee relationship is established between a partnership or joint venture and the individuals rendering services to the partnership or joint venture, the relationship is also established between those individuals and each partner or joint venturer for purposes of section 401(a) of the Code. Accordingly, a corporation that participates in a joint venture is required to take the employees of the joint venture into account in determining whether its employees' plan meets the requirements of section 401(a) of the Code. See Rev.Rul. 68–370, C.B. 1968–2, 174.

(f) WRITTEN PROGRAM.—A qualified plan must be a definite written program setting forth all provisions essential for qualification. See section 1.401–1(a)(2) of the regulations. In the case of a trusteed plan, there must be a valid existing trust, complete in all respects and recognized as such under the applicable local law, pursuant to a plan in effect. However, in establishing a trust under a plan of an employer on the accrual basis, if only the trust corpus is lacking at the close of the first taxable year, the trust is deemed to be in effect for such taxable year if the corpus is furnished no later than the due date of the employer's return, plus extensions of time in which to file. See Rev.Rul. 57–419, C.B. 1957–2, 264. The trust must be evidenced by an executed written document setting forth the terms thereof. See Rev.Rul. 56–673, C.B. 1956–2, 281, and Rev.Rul. 69–231, I.R.B. 1969–19, 11. In the case of a nontrusteed annuity plan evidenced only by contracts with an insurance company, the plan is not in effect until such contracts are executed and issued. Where, however, the plan is separate and apart from a group annuity contract, or annuity contracts, the plan may be in effect before the close of the first taxable year if (1) appropriate steps are taken to establish the plan in such year by applying for the insurance contracts pursuant to authorization by the employer's board of directors or acknowledgment in the case of an unincorporated employer, setting forth a definite plan for the purchase of retirement annuities under annuity contracts, under which liability is created to provide the intended benefits, (2) the application has been accepted by the insurance company, the contracts or abstracts have been prepared in sufficient detail setting forth all terms, and at least a part payment of the premiums due has been irrevocably made, and (3) the plan has been communicated to the employees. See Rev.Rul. 59–402, C.B. 1959–2, 122.

(g) Source of Contributions.—Contributions to a qualified trust are made by the employer, or employees, or both, or, in the case of a profit-sharing plan or stock bonus plan in which contributions are determined with reference to profits of a group of affiliated corporations, contributions on behalf of employees of a loss member may be made up by the profit-making corporations. See sections 401(a) and 404(a)(3)(B) of the Code. Also, as provided in section 406 of the Code, a domestic corporation may include in its qualified plan, and make contributions on behalf of, employees of a foreign subsidiary who are citizens of the United States and covered for social security benefits in this country, and, in accordance with section 407, a domestic parent corporation may similarly include in its qualified plan, and make contributions on behalf of, employees of a domestic subsidiary who are citizens of the United States engaged in foreign service. Although a qualified plan must provide for contributions by one or more of the parties mentioned above, contributions by others are not precluded. See Rev.Rul. 69–35, I.R.B. 1969–5, 19. Thus, for example, the past service liability under a pension plan may be funded in whole or in part by a transfer to the pension trust of a portion of the corpus of a fund created by a former director of the employer-bank to provide welfare benefits for employees of the bank, and the current service cost may be funded by the earnings of the balance of the fund, supplemented by contributions from the employer, when necessary, provided that such funding is done on a uniform basis on behalf of all participants. See Rev.Rul. 63–46, C.B. 1963–1, 85. Also, funds may be transferred from a non-exempt welfare fund to an exempt pension trust. See Rev.Rul. 68–223, C.B. 1968–1, 154. Since a profit-sharing plan must provide for participation in the employer's profits, the qualification of such a plan will be adversely affected by an amendment to permit employees to make voluntary contributions prior to the time they become eligible to share in the employer's profits. See Rev.Rul. 68–651, C.B. 1968–2, 167. However, a plan will not fail to qualify as a profit-sharing plan merely because it provides that employer contributions shall be made from current profits or accumulated earned surplus, as determined under generally accepted accounting principles and practices without regard to whether the employer has current or accumulated earnings and profits for Federal income tax purposes. See Rev.Rul. 66–174, C.B. 1966–1, 81.

(h) Permanency.—A qualified plan is a permanent and continuing program. A plan that is abandoned without a valid business reason within a few years after it is set up does not satisfy this requirement. Also, if the plan is discontinued before ample provision is made for comparable benefits for employees other than those in whose favor discrimination is prohibited, it will be deemed not to have been a bona fide program for the exclusive benefit of employees in general from its inception. This is especially true in the case of a pension plan under which benefits are funded at a higher rate for employees in whose favor discrimination is prohibited than for other employees. In the case of a profit-sharing plan, merely making a single or occasional contribution out of profits for employees does not satisfy the requirement for permanency. There must be recurring and substantial contributions. See section 1.401–1(b)(2) of the regulations. For a more detailed discussion of the applicable principles and illustrative cases, see Rev.Rul. 55–60, C.B. 1955–1, 37, Rev.Rul. 69–24, I.R.B. 1969–4, 9, and Rev.Rul. 69–25, I.R.B. 1969–4, 14. See also section 4.04 of Rev.Proc. 69–4, I.R.B. 1969–1, 19, at 21, for information to be filed for a determination as to the effect of a curtailment or termination on the prior qualification of a plan; Rev.Rul. 69–252, I.R.B. 1969–20, 10, as to notice by the trustee on termination of a plan; Rev.Rul. 56–596, C.B. 1956–2, 288, as to the effect of a suspension of contributions; Rev.Rul. 69–157, I.R.B. 1969–14, 13, as to continued qualification of the plan and exemption of the trust where contributions are discontinued for a valid business reason but the trust is retained to make distributions in accordance with the original terms of the plan; and Rev.Rul. 55–681, C.B. 1955–2, 585, and Rev.Rul. 69–159, I.R.B. 1969–14, 14, as to union negotiated plans. A qualified profit-sharing plan may, under appropriate circumstances, provide that an employee may elect each year to participate in the trust forming a part of such plan or to accept his share in cash. See, however, parts 4(d) and 5(a) as to meeting the requirements for coverage and nondiscrimination in contributions or benefits. A profit-sharing plan that does not contain a definite contribution formula may qualify if all other applicable requirements are met. See section 1.401–1(b)(1)(ii) of the regulations and Rev.Proc. 56–22, C.B. 1956–2, 1380.

(i) COMMUNICATIONS TO EMPLOYEES.—The employees are to be apprised of the establishment of a qualified plan and the salient provisions thereof. The most effective way of doing so is to furnish each employee with a copy of the plan. Where this is not feasible, however, various substitutes may be used. It will be sufficient that a booklet summarizing the plan in all its essential features be furnished the employees, or that a notice be posted on the company's bulletin board, which must be in conspicuous view, stating that a plan has been established, setting forth the type thereof, specifying the eligibility requirements, containing a synopsis of all benefits provided thereunder, indicating whether employees are to contribute and, if so, the amount or rate of contributions, defining the provisions for vesting, and, in the case of a profit-sharing or stock bonus plan, setting forth the employer contribution formula, if any. In all cases where substitutes are used for furnishing employees with copies of the plan, the medium used must clearly state that a copy of the complete plan may be inspected at a designated place on the company's premises during reasonable times which must be stated.

(j) EMPLOYEE PARTICIPANTS.—A qualified plan must benefit employees or their beneficiaries exclusively. See section 1.401–1(a)(3)(ii) of the regulations. However, a plan is for the exclusive benefit of the employees or their beneficiaries even though it may cover former employees or employees who are temporarily on leave. See section 1.401–1(b)(4) of the regulations. See also, Revenue Ruling 66–175, C.B. 1966–1, 82, which holds that a union-negotiated industry wide pension plan will not fail to qualify merely because it permits certain former employees of participating employers to make voluntary contributions to the trust fund. A self-employed individual who derives earned income from self-employment after December 31, 1962, is considered an employee and may participate in a qualified plan to a limited extent. See section 401(c)(1) of the Code. The term "employee" does not include a self-employed individual when the term "common-law" employee is used or when the context otherwise requires that the term "employee" does not include a self-employed individual. See section 1.401–10(b) (3) of the regulations. A qualified plan cannot be maintained where there are no employees, active or retired, who are covered thereunder. See Rev.Rul. 55–629, C.B. 1955–2, 588. An arrangement does not qualify as a plan under section 401(a) of the Code if the benefits that it provides are not payable to an employee but only to his beneficiary upon his death. See Rev.Rul. 56–656, C.B. 1956–2, 280.

(1) *Partners and Sole Proprietors.*—Except to the limited extent applicable to the participation of self-employed individuals after December 31, 1962, partners and sole proprietors are not employees and therefore are not eligible to participate in a qualified plan. Neither are they to be credited for services as partners or sole proprietors prior to becoming employees in a successor corporation, either for prior service benefits or for meeting eligibility requirements. See Rev.Rul. 69–144, I.R.B. 1969–13, 9.

(2) *Associates.*—Where an organization is classified as an association taxable as a corporation, and an employer-employee relationship exists between the association and the persons who are associated therein, such associates, if otherwise eligible, may be included in a plan that is intended to qualify under section 401(a) of the Code. The fact that an organization establishes a plan under section 401(a) of the Code is not determinative of whether such organization will be classified as a partnership or as an association taxable as a corporation. See Rev.Rul. 57–546, C.B. 1957–2, 886, modifying Rev.Rul. 56–23, C.B. 1956–1, 598. Guides for determining whether an organization is a trust, a partnership, or an association taxable as a corporation are set forth in the Regulations on Procedure and Administration pertaining to section 7701 of the Code, Revenue Procedure 65–27, C.B. 1965–2, 1017, and Revenue Ruling 66–92, C.B. 1966–1, 77, contain the procedures and guides for resolving issues connected with the tax classification of professional service organizations and deferred compensation plans established by such organizations.

(3) *Stockholder Participants.*—Stockholders who are bona fide employees of a corporation may participate in the corporation's plan to the same extent as other employees. See section 1.401–1(b)(3) of the regulations. This is true even though the corporation is an electing small business corporation as defined in section 1371 of the Code. See Rev.Rul. 66–218, C.B. 1966–2, 120. If, however, the plan is designed as a subterfuge for the distribution of profits to stockholders, it will not qualify as a plan for the exclusive benefit of employees. The plan must not be weighted in favor of stockholder-employees with respect to meeting the eligibility requirements or the requirements as to nondiscrimination in contributions or benefits. See section 1.401–1(b)(3) of the regulations. For example, where the coverage requirements of a plan are limited so as to preclude employees other than the company's sole stockholder from participating, the plan does not qualify. See Rev.Rul. 63–108, C.B. 1963–1, 87. For the rules regarding professional service corporations see section 301.7701–2 of the Regulations on Procedure and Administration.

(4) *Attorneys and Other Practitioners.*—An attorney or other professional person may be a bona fide employee and, as such, eligible to participate in a qualified plan. The mere fact that a professional person has an independent income from the practice of his profession will not necessarily preclude him from participating in such a plan. He must, however, be an

employee for all purposes, including coverage for social security or a similar public program, if applicable to other employees, and for income tax withholding purposes. If his actual employment for such purposes commences as of a certain date, he is not to be credited for services prior thereto, such as, for example, meeting the years-of-service requirements to be eligible to participate in the plan or to obtain benefits based on past services. An individual, however, may be treated as a self-employed person with respect to one activity and yet be a common-law employee regarding another. For example, an attorney may be a common law employee of a corporation and maintain an office for his independent practice of law in the evenings.

(5) *Insurance Agents.*—Section 7701(a)(20) of the Code provides that for the purpose of contributions to, and distributions from, a pension, profit-sharing, or stock bonus trust, or under an annuity plan, the term "employee" shall include a full-time life insurance salesman who is considered an employee for the purpose of the Federal Insurance Contribution Act or, in the case of services performed before January 1, 1951, would be considered an employee if his services were performed during 1951. Thus, the same rules apply in determining the eligibility for inclusion of full-time life insurance salesmen in a qualified plan as are applicable in determining their tax status for old age and survivors disability insurance purposes. Also, such full-time salesmen are treated as "common-law" employees for participation in a plan which includes self-employed individuals. Insurance brokers and others who are not full-time life insurance salesmen within the purview of section 3121(d)(3)(B) of the Code, however, may not be included in a qualified plan except as self-employed individuals.

(k) INVESTMENT OF TRUST FUNDS.—Investments of an exempt employees' trust are subject to the following provisions and requirements: (1) as a function of a trust which under section 401(a) of the Code is part of a plan of an employer for the exclusive benefit of his employees or their beneficiaries, the investments must be consistent with such purpose; (2) the investments must not constitute prohibited transactions, as defined in section 503(c), or section 503(j) if owner-employees are included in the plan; (3) investments that result in unrelated business taxable income subject the trust to tax under section 511 on such income; and (4) the investments must not be used to operate a feeder organization.

(1) *Exclusive Benefit Requirement.*—The primary purpose of benefiting employees or their beneficiaries must be maintained with respect to investments of the trust funds as well as with respect to other activities of the trust. This requirement, however, does not prevent others from also deriving some benefit from a transaction with the trust. For example, a sale of securities at a profit benefits the seller, but if the purchase price is not in excess of the fair market value of the securities at the time of sale and the applicable investment requisites set forth below have been met, the investment is consistent with the exclusive-benefit-of-employees requirement. The requisites are: (1) The cost must not exceed fair market value at time of purchase; (2) a fair return commensurate with the prevailing rate must be provided; (3) sufficient liquidity must be maintained to permit distributions in accordance with the terms of the plan; and (4) the safeguards and diversity that a prudent investor would adhere to must be present. However, the requirement set forth in item (2) with respect to a fair return is not applicable to obligatory investments in employer securities in the case of a stock bonus plan. See Rev.Rul. 69–65, I.R.B. 1969–7, 9. Upon compliance with these requisites, if the trust instrument and local

law permit investments in the stock or securities of the employer, such investments are not deemed to be inconsistent with the purposes of section 401(a) of the Code. The District Director of Internal Revenue, however is to be notified if trust funds are invested in stock or securities of, or loaned to, the employer or related or controlled interests so that a determination may be made whether the trust serves any purpose other than constituting part of a plan for the exclusive benefit of employees. See section 1.401–1 (b)(5)(ii) of the regulations. Such notification is to be made as part of the annual information return, Form 990–P, unless an advance determination letter is requested and, if so, at the time of making a request to the appropriate District Director for such letter. The notification is to include the information called for in section 4.05 of Revenue Procedure 69–4, I.R.B. 1969–1, 19, and be certified by the accounting or other responsible officer.

(2) *Prohibited Transactions.*—Exemption will be denied to an employees' trust that engages in a prohibited transaction within the purview of section 503(c) of the Code, or section 503(j) if owner-employees are included in the plan. Special rules, however, apply to the requirement for adequate security in the case of obligations acquired by the trust under the conditions of section 503(h) of the Code and, pursuant to section 503 (i), in the case of loans to unincorporated employers engaged in the stock brokerage business.

(3) *Unrelated Business Taxable Income.*—An exempt employees' trust is taxable under section 511 of the Code on its unrelated business taxable income, as defined in section 512, which is derived from any unrelated trade or business, as defined in section 513. Special rules are set forth in section 514 of the Code with respect to business leases. If business lease indebtedness is incurred, rental income is includible in gross income in the ratio that the business lease indebtedness, at the close of the taxable year, bears to the adjusted basis of the property at such time.

(4) *Feeder Organizations.*—An employees' trust that is operated for the primary purpose of carrying on a trade or business for profit is denied exemption under section 502 of the Code, even though all of its profits are payable to one or more exempt organizations.

(5) *Common Trust Funds.*—The exempt status of an employees' trust will not be adversely affected merely because the trustee, a bank, invests the funds of the trust in a common trust fund maintained by the bank and exempt under section 584 of the Code. See Rev.Rul. 67–301, C.B. 1967–2, 146.

(*l*) DESIGNATION OF BENEFICIARIES.—Beneficiaries of employees under a qualified plan may be designated by the respective participants without restriction, or they may be restricted under the plan to specified persons or to a group of persons, who are the natural objects of the employee's bounty, his estate, or his dependents. See Rev.Rul. 54–398, C.B. 1954–2, 239.

(m) DEFINITELY DETERMINABLE BENEFITS.—Benefits under a qualified pension plan must be definitely determinable. Benefits are not definitely determinable if funds arising from forfeitures on termination of service, or other reason, may be used to provide increased benefits for the remaining participants instead of being used as soon as possible to reduce the amount of contributions by the employer. See section 1.401–1(b)(1)(i) of the regulations. However, a qualified pension plan may anticipate the effect of forfeitures in determining the costs under the plan. A determination of the amount of forfeitures under such a plan must be made at least once during each taxable year of the employer. See section 1.401–7 of the regulations and part 7(a) hereof. The requirement regarding the application of forfeitures is equally applicable to pension plans of the money-purchase type. See Rev.Rul. 109, C.B. 1953–1, 288, and Rev.Rul. 60–73, C.B. 1960–1, 155. Benefits that vary with the increase or decrease in the market value of the assets from which such benefits are payable or that vary with the fluctuation of a specified and generally recognized cost-of-living index, are consistent with a plan providing for definitely determinable benefits. See Rev.Rul. 185, C.B. 1953–2, 202, and Rev.Rul. 68–116, C.B. 1968–1, 177. In a stock bonus or profit-sharing plan provision may also be made that forfeitures be used to reduce the employer contributions that otherwise would be required under the contribution formula, but such application of forfeitures is not mandatory in plans of these types. See part 7(b) hereof. It should be observed, however, that whatever provision is made for absorbing forfeitures, discrimination in favor of employees who are officers, shareholders, supervisors, or highly compensated must not result.

(n) INCIDENTAL BENEFITS.—Primarily qualified plans provide the benefits that pertain to the respective types. Thus, a qualified pension plan does not provide for the payment of benefits not customarily included in that type of plan, such as layoff benefits or benefits for sickness, accident, hospitalization, or medical expenses, except hospitalization and medical expenses for retired employees as provided for in section 401(h) of the Code. See sections 1.401–1(b)(1)(i) and 1.401–14 of the regulations. Neither may such a plan provide only such benefits as are furnished through the purchase of ordinary life insurance contracts that may be converted to life annuities at the normal retirement date. See Rev.Rul. 54–67, C.B. 1954–1, 149, and Rev.Rul. 65–25, C.B. 1965–1, 173. However, a provision in a pension plan permitting a retired employee to authorize the trustee to deduct and pay union dues from his monthly pension benefit will not cause the plan to fail to qualify. See Rev.Rul. 68–159, C.B. 1968–1, 153. Furthermore, the annuity portion of an insurance contract by means of which an employees' nontrusteed annuity plan is funded may, if otherwise satisfactory, qualify even though the contract also provides separate term life insurance and accident and health insurance. See Rev.Rul. 56–633, C.B. 1956–2, 279. If life insurance benefits are applied to reduce employer contributions under a pension plan, amounts contributed by the employer for such insurance constitute advance funding and are not currently deductible. See Rev.Rul. 55–748, C.B. 1955–2, 234. Where the life or accident and health insurance features are incidental to the primary benefit of a qualified plan, they may be included in such plan to a limited extent. See section 1.401–1(b)(1)(i) and section 1.401–14 of the regulations.

(1) *Life Insurance Under Pension and Annuity Plans.*—In a pension or annuity plan funded with insurance contracts, the life insurance benefit is deemed to be incidental where it provides a pre-retirement death benefit no greater than 100 times the monthly annuity, that is, $1,000 of life insurance for each $10 of monthly annuity. See Rev.Rul. 60–83, C.B. 1960–1, 157. This is true even though the pension plan involved is of the money purchase type. However, a money purchase plan may, in the alternative, incorporate the limitation applicable to the incidental use of trust funds to purchase ordinary life insurance contracts under a qualified profit-sharing plan. See Rev.Rul. 66–143, C.B. 1966–1, 79, as clarified by Rev.Rul. 68–31, C.B. 1968–1, 151. The death benefit is similarly incidental in a plan providing

a post retirement death benefit equal to 50 percent of base salary in effect in the year preceding retirement, requiring less than 10 percent of the cost of the plan exclusive of the death benefit. See Rev.Rul. 60–59, C.B. 1960–1, 154. Also, the death benefit payable under a qualified pension plan to the widow of an employee who died prior to attaining normal retirement age may be regarded as incidental where the value of such benefit does not exceed the death benefit that would have been payable had the benefit been funded under a typical retirement income contract. See Rev.Rul. 61–121, C.B. 1961–2, 65. Where the plan is funded by ordinary life insurance contracts plus an auxiliary fund, it may permit a pre-retirement death benefit equal to the greater of (a) the proceeds of the ordinary life insurance contracts, or (b) the sum of (i) the reserve under the life insurance contracts and (ii) the employees account in the auxiliary fund. On the other hand, a death benefit equal to the sum of the proceeds of the ordinary life insurance contracts and the amount of the employee's account in the auxiliary fund would exceed the death benefit under a typical level premium retirement income contract with a face amount of 100 times the anticipated monthly retirement benefit, and would preclude the plan from qualifying. See Rev.Rul. 68–453, C.B. 1968–2, 163.

(2) *Life Insurance Under Profit-Sharing Plans.*—In the case of a profit-sharing plan that provides for the use of trust funds that have not been accumulated for at least two years, to purchase and pay premiums on ordinary life insurance contracts, the insurance feature is deemed to be incidental if: (1) The aggregate life insurance premiums for each participant is less than one-half of the aggregate of the contributions allocated to the credit of the participant at any particular time, and (2) the plan requires the trustee to convert the entire value of the life insurance contract at or before retirement into cash, or to provide periodic income so that no portion of such value may be used to continue life insurance protection beyond retirement, or to distribute the contract to the participant. See Rev.Rul. 54–51, C.B. 1954–1, 147, as amplified by Rev.Rul. 57–213, C.B. 1957–1, 157, and Rev.Rul. 60–84, C.B. 1960–1, 159.

(3) *Accident and Health Insurance Under Profit-Sharing Plans.*— Where profit-sharing funds have not been accumulated for at least two years, distributions therefrom to pay premiums for accident and health insurance are treated as incidental if the aggregate of such distributions does not exceed 25 percent of the funds allocated to the account of the participant for whom the insurance is acquired. If such funds are used to purchase both ordinary life and accident and health insurance, the amount expended for accident and health insurance, plus one-half of the premiums paid for ordinary life insurance, may not in the aggregate exceed 25 percent of the funds allocated to an employee's account. See Rev.Rul. 61–164, C.B. 1961–2, 99.

(o) EMPLOYEE WITHDRAWALS UNDER A PENSION PLAN.—A qualified pension plan may provide for the payment, prior to normal retirement, of a pension due to disability and for incidental death benefits through insurance or from the accumulated funds. It may also provide hospitalization and medical benefits for retired employees in accordance with section 401 (h) of the Code. Withdrawals of funds by employees for other purposes, however, whether in times of financial need or otherwise, are subject to restrictions.

(2) *Funds Consisting of Employer Contributions or Increments.*—A pension plan must not permit participants, prior to any severance of em-

ployment or the termination of the plan, to withdraw all or a part of the funds accumulated on their behalf which consist of employer contributions or fund increments. See Rev.Rul. 69–277, I.R.B. 1969–22, 12. However, a profit-sharing plan may permit such withdrawals under appropriate circumstances. See Rev.Rul. 60–323, C.B. 1960–2, 148, modifying Rev.Rul. 56–693, C.B. 1956–2, 282.

(2) *Discontinuance of Participation.*—Upon discontinuance of participation in a pension plan, an employee may be permitted to withdraw his own contributions together with an amount that represents the increments actually earned thereon, but not in excess of such increments. See Rev.Rul. 60–281, C.B. 1960–2, 146.

(3) *Employee Voluntary Contributions.*—A pension plan may provide for withdrawals by participants of their voluntary contributions which are made in addition to compulsory contributions, where such withdrawals do not affect an employee's participation in the plan, the employer's past or future contributions on behalf of such employee, or the basic benefits provided by both the participant's and employer's nonwithdrawable contributions. See Rev.Rul. 60–323.

(4) *Conversion of Contributory to Noncontributory Plan.*—Where a contributory pension plan is amended to provide for employer contributions only, provision may be made for a refund of employee contributions if discrimination does not result in favor of employees who are officers, shareholders, supervisors, or highly compensated. See Rev.Rul. 61–79, C.B. 1961–1, 138.

(5) *Increments on Employee Contributions.*—The recognition of an employee's right to withdraw his own contributions carries with it the right to receive any increments actually earned thereon. See Rev.Rul. 60–281 and Rev.Rul. 67–340, C.B. 1967–2, 147. Thus, a qualified pension plan that permits an employee to withdraw his voluntary contributions may permit the employee to withdraw any increments of the withdrawn contributions. See Rev.Rul. 69–277.

(p) PROFIT-SHARING AND STOCK BONUS PLANS OF AFFILIATED COMPANIES.—In the case of a profit-sharing plan, or stock bonus plan in which contributions are determined with reference to profits, of an affiliated group of corporations within the purview of section 1504 of the Code, contributions made by other members of the group for the benefit of employees of a corporation that is prevented from making a contribution because it lacks current or accumulated earnings or profits may be deducted only to the extent and in the manner provided in section 404(a)(3)(B) of the Code and section 1.404(a)–10 of the regulations. See Rev.Rul. 69–35, I.R.B. 1969–5, 19.

(q) FEEDER PLAN.—A stock bonus or profit-sharing plan that provides that the funds therein may be used to meet the costs of a pension or annuity plan operated concurrently and covering the same employees, if and when the employer suspends contributions to the latter plan, is generally called a "feeder" plan. Such a plan does not qualify because it relieves the employer from contributing to the pension or annuity plan and, therefore, is not for the exclusive benefit of employees or their beneficiaries. See section 1.401–1(b)(3) of the regulations. An employee who has a vested right under a stock bonus or profit-sharing plan, however, may, if the plan so provides, authorize a transfer of all or a part of his vested interest in order to make up a deficiency in the employer's contribution under the pension or annuity plan. In such a case, the amount transferred is includible in the employee's gross income to the same extent as if such interest had been distributed. See Rev.Rul. 69–295, I.R.B. 1969–23, 11. It should be observed that a "feeder plan" differs from a "feeder organization," as to which see paragraph (k) (4) hereof and section 502 of the Code which denies exemption under section 501 to an organization that is operated for the primary purpose of carrying on a trade or business for profit even though all of its profits are payable to one or more organizations exempt under section 501.

(r) CONTINGENCY OR SURPLUS RESERVES.—The practice of contributing the full amount of annual premiums under an insured pension plan, without reduction for accumulated dividends and regardless of the amount of the allowable deduction limitation, would result in the creation of a contingency or surplus reserve. If a significant part of a trust fund consists of such a reserve, the plan's qualification could be adversely affected. If the advance funding, however, is minor in relation to the actuarial liability under the plan, if there is no possibility of the reversion of a substantial amount to the employer on termination of the plan, and if the advance funding is exclusively for the benefit of the employees or their beneficiaries, such advance funding would not adversely affect the qualification of the plan. Advance funding does not give rise to a current deduction. Accordingly, the deduction otherwise allowable under section 404(a) of the Code, for any taxable year, to the employer must be reduced by the amount of dividends earned, and interest credited on accumulations thereof, in the current or next preceding taxable year. See Rev.Rul. 60–33, C.B. 1960–1, 152.

(s) VALUATION OF SECURITIES ON INVENTORY DATE.—Any type of qualified plan that provides for distributions in accordance with amounts stated or ascertainable and credited to participants, as in profit-sharing, stock bonus, and trusteed pension plans of the money-purchase type, must provide for a valuation of securities held by the trust, at least once a year, on a specified inventory date, in accordance with a method consistently followed and uniformly applied. The fair market value on the inventory date is to be used for this purpose. The respective accounts of participants are to be adjusted in accordance with the valuation. If, for example, as a result of a valuation on the inventory date, John Doe's account, which previously showed a balance of $1,000, is to be increased by one-tenth of 1 percent of the increase in the value of the trust assets, and such increase is $50,000, his interest is to be increased by $50.

(t) ALLOCATION OF STOCK BONUS AND PROFIT-SHARING FUNDS.—All funds in an exempt stock bonus or profit-sharing trust must be allocated to participants in accordance with a definite formula. Thus, no reserves are to be established by withholding allocations from participants. If suspense accounts are maintained, provision is to be made for ascertaining the respective shares of participants in such accounts and such shares are to be included in the distribution.

(u) PLANS PROVIDING FOR LUMP-SUM DISTRIBUTIONS ONLY.—A plan that provides for lump-sum distributions only, but does not contain the basic requisites of a profit-sharing or stock bonus plan, is not a qualified plan under section 401(a) of the Code. A pension plan provides systematically for the payment of definitely determinable benefits to employees over a period of years, usually for life, after retirement. A profit-sharing plan provides for participation in the employer's profits by his employees or their beneficiaries. A stock bonus plan provides benefits similar to those of a profit-sharing plan, except that the contributions by the employer are not necessarily dependent upon profits and the benefits are distributable in stock of the employer corporation. See section 1.401–1(b)(1)(iii) of the regulations. Where, however, a plan provides for employee contributions up to 10 percent of earnings and for employer contributions whether or not it has profits equal to the amounts contributed by the employees, and benefits are paid only in the form of lump-sum cash distributions on retirement or separation from the service for other reasons, the plan is not one within the purview of section 401(a) and, therefore, does not qualify under such section. See Rev.Rul. 62–195, C.B. 1962–2, 125.

* * *

COMMISSIONER OF INTERNAL REVENUE v. PEPSI–COLA NIAGARA BOTTLING CORPORATION

United States Court of Appeals, Second Circuit, 1968.
399 F.2d 390.

FRIENDLY, Circuit Judge. This petition by the Commissioner of Internal Revenue to review a decision of the Tax Court, 48 T.C. 75, annulling his determination of deficiencies in the income tax of Pepsi-Cola Niagara Bottling Corporation for 1961, 1962 and 1963, raises a nice, though narrow, question of the interpretation of § 401(a) of the Internal Revenue Code defining what pension, profit-sharing and stock bonus plans qualify for deduction of contributions as provided in § 404. The statute, so far as here relevant, is set out in the margin.[1]

In November 1960 the Bottling Corporation, an enterprise of moderate size, established a profit-sharing and retirement plan for its salaried employees and a trust to receive contributions thereunder.

1. § 401(a) *Requirements for qualification.*—
A trust created or organized in the United States and forming a part of a stock bonus, pension, or profit-sharing plan of an employer for the exclusive benefit of his employees or their beneficiaries shall constitute a qualified trust under this section—

* * * * * *

(3) if the trust, or two or more trusts, or the trust or trusts and annuity plan or plans are designated by the employer as constituting parts of a plan intended to qualify under this subsection which benefits either—
(A) 70 percent or more of all the employees, or 80 percent or more of all the employees who are eligible to benefit under the plan if 70 percent or more of all the employees are eligible to benefit under the plan, excluding in each case employees who have been employed not more than a minimum period prescribed by the plan, not exceeding 5 years, em-

ployees whose customary employment is for not more than 20 hours in any one week, and employees whose customary employment is for not more than 5 months in any calendar year, or
(B) such employees as qualify under a classification set up by the employer and found by the Secretary or his delegate not to be discriminatory in favor of employees who are officers, shareholders, persons whose principal duties consist in supervising the work of other employees, or highly compensated employees;
and
(4) if the contributions or benefits provided under the plan do not discriminate in favor of employees who are officers, shareholders, persons whose principal duties consist in supervising the work of other employees, or highly compensated employees. (Court's footnote 1.)

The Corporation was to contribute 40% of its annual net profits in excess of $4,000 but not exceeding 15% of the compensation of all participants. Eligibility was limited to all regular salaried employees who had completed three years of continuous service on December 31, 1961, or any anniversary date of the plan. Benefits were distributed on the basis of a formula which credited each covered employee with one unit for each $100 of compensation and one unit for each year of continuous employment; no deduction was made for the portion of compensation, $4800 in the years in question, constituting "wages" for which social security contributions were made, 26 U.S.C.A. § 3121(a) (1).[2] Omitting temporary and seasonal employees on an hourly wage basis whose exclusion is not claimed by the Commissioner to disqualify the plan, the Corporation had six salaried employees who were covered and eight hourly wage employees who were not; their names and compensation are shown in the margin.[3]

The Corporation did not seek a determination of the plan's qualification until December 1963; the District Director of Internal Revenue denied this on the ground that the plan was discriminatory in favor of "highly paid" employees within the meaning of § 401(a) (3) (B) and (4). The Chief of the Pension Trust Branch sustained this, the Corporation then amended the plan as of January 1, 1965, to make all permanent employees eligible for coverage, and the District Director accepted the plan as so amended. Consistently with these rulings of his subordinates, the Commissioner determined income tax deficiencies for 1961, 1962 and 1963 based on disallowance of contributions of $5,831, $5,381 and $8,080, respectively. The Tax Court an-

---

2. Other features of the plan, not significant as to the issue here presented, are set forth in the Tax Court's opinion. (Court's footnote 2.)

3. A. SALARIED EMPLOYEES COVERED UNDER PLAN.

NAME	SALARIES		
	1961	*1962*	*1963*
Harry G. Winter	$28,000.00	$28,000.00	$30,000.00
Peter P. Seereiter	10,710.00	11,180.00	11,813.41
Joseph A. Guaetta	9,410.00	9,620.00	9,880.00
Ray W. Lambrecht	8,515.50	8,880.00	9,223.50
Bernard J. Riggs	7,595.40	8,060.00	8,580.00
Kenneth Rowland	5,615.00*	5,720.00	2,990.00
P. Robert Cahill	n.e.**	n.e.**	3,430.00*

B. PERMANENT HOURLY PAID EMPLOYEES NOT COVERED UNDER PLAN.

NAME	WAGES		
	1961	*1962*	*1963*
Raymond J. Mitchell	$ 6,626.02	$ 7,128.93	$ 7,342.94
Herbert Holt	6,452.27	6,745.47	7,071.47
Roger Roth	5,255.01	5,662.86	5,812.61
Randy Riggs	1,110.99	5,601.81	6,060.14
Arlie Grose	5,405.80	5,544.50	5,604.28
Jane M. Berhalter	4,823.83	5,287.93	5,509.87
Mabel Bowers	4,715.12	5,240.47	5,553.81
Helen Kendall	3,968.96	4,160.00	4,420.00

* Not eligible under three-year requirement
** Not employed

(Court's footnote 3.)

nulled this determination on the basis that persons receiving the modest compensation of all the participants save the president of the Corporation could not rationally be regarded as "highly paid," particularly when the differential between them and the uncovered employees was so small, see fn. 3.

We can readily agree that a plan like the Bottling Corporation's was untypical of the "mischief and defect," Heydon's Case, 3 Co. 72 (1584), for which the Revenue Code's pension trust sections had failed to provide until 1942 when they were placed in substantially their present form, 56 Stat. 798, 862–63. We do not, however, accept the Tax Court's result; a legislature seeking to catch a particular abuse may find it necessary to cast a wider net.

The movement for reform of the deduction for pension, profit-sharing and bonus plans had begun with a message to Congress from President Roosevelt on June 1, 1937. This incorporated a letter from the Secretary of the Treasury stating that the exemption "has been twisted into a means of tax avoidance by the creation of pension trusts which include as beneficiaries only small groups of officers and directors who are in the high income tax brackets." 81 Cong.Rec. 5125, 75th Cong., 1st Sess. After investigating and deciding that correction was indeed in order, Congress had to determine in what manner to move from the agreed general purpose to legislation that could be practically applied to the thousands of varying situations with which the Internal Revenue Service would be faced. Congress adopted a two-fold approach. Plans would qualify if a sufficient proportion of the firm's employees were eligible or participated. If, however, a plan's coverage provisions were not so broad as to include the minimum percentage of employees prescribed in § 401(a) (3) (A), they were to be subjected to a more intensive scrutiny by the Treasury Department whose nature the legislature could prescribe only in a more generalized way. Restrictive plans were to qualify only if the Secretary or his delegate were to find that the eligibility requirements were not "discriminatory" in favor of officers, shareholders, supervisors, or "highly paid employees." The legislative history suggests that Congress did not believe itself equipped to give more content to the two phrases we have quoted. The original House Bill sought to define more precisely the characteristics of plans that discriminated in favor of the "highly paid," at least with regard to a companion provision, § 401(a) (4), which guarded against the danger that highly paid employees would gain a disproportionate share of pension benefits despite the fact that eligibility requirements were not found discriminatory under § 401(a) (3). It stated that the "benefits or contributions" required under the plan shall "not have the effect of discriminating in favor of *any* employee whose compensation is greater than that of *other* employees." H.R. 7378, § 144(a) (4), 77th Cong., 2d Sess. (1942) (emphasis supplied). A literal reading of this provision would unequivocally have made fairness to the lowest paid employee covered by the plan the test of qualification. This formulation, however, was apparently believed to be unduly rigid, for when the tax bill was returned from the Ways and Means Committee to which it had been referred for reconsideration, § 401(a) (4) had been amended to correspond with the more general language of § 401(a) (3) (B), simply banning discrimination in favor of the "highly paid."

The Commissioner found himself confronted with problems in administering the statute similar to those that Congress had encountered in drafting it. While there are attractions in the idea that a plan can be rejected under §§ 401(a) (3) and (4) only if it discriminates in favor of employees who would generally be regarded as "highly paid," it poses difficulties of administration which the Tax Court did nothing to resolve. Words like "high" and "highly" clamor for a referent. A 500 foot hill would look high in Central Park but not among the Grand Tetons or even at Lake Placid. Apparently the Tax Court regarded the president of the Bottling Corporation with a $28,000–$30,000 salary as "highly paid," and we assume he would be so considered in Niagara Falls, but he hardly would be in Hollywood. More to the point, while we would not regard Bernard J. Riggs, with a salary of $7595–$8580 from the Bottling Corporation as "highly paid," that might not be the view of Helen Kendall whose wages ranged from $3969 to $4420 in the same period, see fn. 3. Considerations such as these led the Commissioner to rule in 1956:

> In order for the plan to meet the coverage requirements, there must be sufficient participation by the lower paid employees to demonstrate that in practice the plan does not discriminate in favor of the high paid employees. * * * The terms "highly compensated" and "lower compensated" are relative, and the distinction between them must be based upon the circumstances of each case. Rev.Rul. 56–497, 1956–2 Cum.Bull. 284, 286.

We cannot say that in thus reading "highly" as "more highly" and taking the compensation of noncovered employees as the standard, the Commissioner went beyond the powers Congress conferred upon him by § 401(a) (3). When Congress has used a general term and has empowered an administrator to define it, the courts must respect his construction if this is within the range of reason. Gray v. Powell, 314 U.S. 402, 411–413 (1941); NLRB v. Hearst Publications, Inc., 322 U.S. 111, 130–132, 64 S.Ct. 851, 88 L.Ed. 1170 (1944). That requirement was met here and it was not for the Tax Court to substitute its reading for that of the administrator on the firing line.[4]

The Tax Court's decision likewise cannot be sustained on the basis that, given the Commissioner's reading of the statute, the facts did not fairly support his determination of non-compliance. While use of the phrase "found by the Commissioner," § 401(a) (3) (A), does not preclude meaningful judicial review, it does suggest an intention that the Commissioner's finding be given a shade more than its usual substantial weight. Compare Grenada Industries, Inc. v. C. I. R.,

4. We were told at the argument that the sparsity of reported cases dealing with the problem here considered is due to the general practice of obtaining advance clearance of plans. (Court's footnote 5.)

17 T.C. 231, 255, aff'd, 202 F.2d 873 (5 Cir.), cert. denied, 346 U.S. 819 (1953).   In two of the three years every one of the covered eligible employees received higher compensation than any of the noncovered employees, although the differential between the lowest of the covered group and the highest of the uncovered group was only in the neighborhood of $1000; and even in 1962 only one noncovered employee received more than one covered employee.   The median salary of the covered group was around $9000; the median wage of the noncovered group was less than $6000.   Averages would produce a larger discrepancy.   Just how high a penetration of the covered group by the uncovered group would require the Commissioner to find the taint removed is an issue not here before us.

We add only that the Corporation's case is not aided by § 401(a) (5).   While that subsection says that a plan shall not be considered discriminatory "merely because it is limited to salaried or clerical employees," this is quite different from saying that no plan covering all salaried employees can be discriminatory.   See Fleitz v. C. I. R., 50 T.C. No. 35 (1968).

The judgment is reversed, with directions to the Tax Court to sustain the Commissioner's determination.

WATERMAN, Circuit Judge (dissenting).   I must respectfully dissent from my distinguished brethren.   I would affirm the Tax Court on its opinion, reported at 48 T.C. 75.   I would hold, with that court, that taxpayer's employees' profit-sharing plan in effect in the calendar years 1961, 1962, and 1963, was not discriminatory in favor of a prohibited group of employees within the meaning of Sections 401(a) (3) and 401(a) (4) of the Internal Revenue Code quoted in footnote 1 of the majority opinion.

The case is before us because the Commissioner disallowed the deductions taxpayer took in calendar 1961, 1962, and 1963, for its contributions to the trust that was established to manage the fund provided for by the plan, and he appeals from the decision of the Tax Court, adverse to him, which allowed them.   Upon disallowing these deductions the Commissioner determined income tax deficiencies for the three years of $1,749.34, $1,614.46, and $2,327.03, respectively. The Commissioner's ground for holding that taxpayer's plan resulted in prohibited discrimination and therefore did not qualify under § 401 (a) was that the plan discriminated in favor of taxpayer's salaried employees and discriminated against its hourly rated employees, the position of the Internal Revenue Service, quoted in the Tax Court's opinion, 48 T.C. 75, at 80, being that: "While a classification limited to salaried employees may be nondiscriminatory, the facts in the instant case show that such classification results in coverage of the officers, shareholders, supervisors and highly compensated employees and exclusion of the hourly rated employees, who are comparatively low paid."

All pertinent facts were stipulated before the Tax Court, and a summary of the plan's provisions is set forth in the Tax Court's opinion. The Tax Court, and my brothers in footnote 3 of their majority opinion, recite the compensation the six covered salaried employees and the eight hourly paid employees received during each of the three years.

It is obvious that the Tax Court's analysis, 48 T.C. 75 at 84–85, of the compensation received by each of the fourteen permanent employees of taxpayer demonstrates that the Commissioner had not related the statutory term "highly compensated employees" to the compensation standards designed to prevent rather substantial tax avoidance that Congress had in mind when the statutory sections were passed. Indeed, as pointed out by the Tax Court, the Commissioner's argument advanced to that court and reiterated by him to us is that this taxpayer's plan should not be looked at with reference to whether it effects the substantial tax avoidance that Congress had in mind and desired to proscribe. The Commissioner's position is that, irrespective of its effect upon the quantum of tax receipts involved, a plan may not be approved by him if in its operation favoritism is shown to "highly compensated employees," which term is not to be applied in an absolute sense, but vis-a-vis the excluded employees.

My brothers appear to accept this argument. As expository of Congressional intent, I doubt its validity, but, assuming the argument to be generally a sound one, it is surely inapplicable here. A glance at the 1962 pay schedule [5] for all employees except possibly Winter, the owner of the business, demonstrates that in an absolute sense the salaries of the salaried employees did not make them "highly compensated," in that the salaries made them high-bracket taxpayers; and that, in a relative sense vis-a-vis the excluded employees, two of the excluded hourly-compensated employees were more "highly compensated" (also in an absolute sense, but whether looked at absolutely or relatively, in terms of efficacy at the supermarket, having more funds to spend) than salaried employee Rowland, and that all but one of the eight excluded employees received an averaged gross weekly pay check within $10 a week of Rowland's $110, the average weekly pay of the seventh lowest paid excluded employee being $100.88. On this set of facts, though the plan is limited to salaried employees, I am not left with a definite and firm conviction that the Tax Court erred in holding that this limited coverage did not discriminate in favor of the "highly compensated employees" of taxpayer.

The issue of discrimination is basically an issue of fact, an issue determinable case by case. Here I do not find the factual findings of the Tax Court to be unsupported, see 26 U.S.C.A. § 7482(a), Fed.R. Civ.P. 52(a), or that the inferences which that court drew from its examination of the stipulated facts and agreed-upon exhibits to be implausible, C.I.R. v. Duberstein, 363 U.S. 278, 289–291 (1960) or that the court has overlooked pertinent facts, see Schley v. C.I.R., 2 Cir., 375 F.2d 747, 757 (dissenting opinion). Therefore I am not of the

5. The last full year in which Rowland was employed, and the year in which he became eligible under the Plan. (Dissent footnote 1.)

opinion that the Tax Court's finding that the operation of taxpayer's plan does not discriminate is a clearly erroneous finding.

Nevertheless, the Commissioner suggests that, if we are to consider ourselves bound in any way by factual findings made below we are bound, unless his findings are arbitrary, by his, the Commissioner's findings and by his unreviewed exercise of his technically motivated judgment; and we ought not to be bound by the factual determinations of the Tax Court sitting in review over him. Despite this rather extraordinary argument, I am sure that the Tax Court has justified and will continue to justify its existence as an impartial adjudicator between taxpayer and tax collector, and I, for one, despite the Commissioner's express wish in the premises, do not intend to by-pass it here.

In a case decided by the Tax Court later than this case now before us, the Tax Court, distinguishing Pepsi-Cola Niagara Bottling Co., followed the Commissioner, held that he acted properly in not qualifying the plan under § 401(a) which was then before it, and agreed with him that "his determination should not be set aside unless it is found to be arbitrary or an abuse of discretion." Ed and Jim Fleitz, Inc. et al. v. Commissioner, 50 T.C. No. 35 (1968). Applying this standard the Tax Court reaffirmed the result my brothers would reverse here, and therefore impliedly found that here the Commissioner did act arbitrarily. This case-by-case development in the area seems to me to be quite praiseworthy and to indicate that the Tax Court is properly applying proper standards of review.

I would affirm.

MOGLIA v. GEOGHEGAN

United States Court of Appeals, Second Circuit, 1968.
403 F.2d 110, cert. denied 394 U.S. 919, 1969.

WATERMAN, Circuit Judge. This is an appeal from a judgment of the United States District Court for the Southern District of New York, dismissing plaintiff-appellant's complaint. Appellant sought a declaratory judgment pursuant to 28 U.S.C.A. § 2201 and Rule 57, Fed. R.Civ.P., declaring her to be entitled to receive payments under the Pension Plan of Local 282-Pension Trust Fund of $200.00 per month for a period of thirty-six months commencing May 1, 1965; directing appellees, as trustees of said Fund, to make such payments; and awarding her any reasonable attorney's fees incurred by her in enforcing the trust. Jurisdiction in the district court was founded on the existence of a question arising under a statute of the United States regulating interstate commerce, the Labor-Management Relations Act of 1947, § 302, 29 U.S.C.A. § 186, making the action one of which the district court had original jurisdiction pursuant to 28 U.S. C.A. § 1337. Appellees moved for summary judgment on the ground that appellant was not entitled to the relief she sought. Appellant also moved for summary judgment. Appellant's motion was denied and appellees' motion was granted. The learned district judge explained the result he reached in a reasoned opinion which contained the detailed facts involved. His opinion is reported at 267 F.Supp. 641 (D.C. 1967). We affirm the result reached below.

Appellant is the widow of John J. Moglia (Moglia) who died on August 7, 1966. At all times relevant to this case Moglia had been a member in good standing of the International Brotherhood of Teamsters, Chauffeurs, Warehousemen and Helpers of America, Local 282 (Local 282), a labor organization representing employees of employers within the meaning of Section 302(a) (2), Labor-Management Relations Act of 1947; 29 U.S.C.A. § 186(a) (2).

Appellees are the Trustees (Trustees) of the Local 282-Pension Trust Fund (Fund) which was established in 1955 by Local 282 and various employers who had entered into collective bargaining agreements with the Local. The Fund was the successor of other trust funds in which the Local had theretofore participated and was created by execution of an agreement and declaration of trust (trust agreement).

The trust agreement authorized the Trustees to receive payments from employers who signed collective bargaining agreements with the Local requiring such payments. The trust agreement specified that the Fund be used to provide retirement benefits for employees of contributing employers pursuant to a Pension Plan to be formulated by the Trustees.

The Fund was supposed to be maintained in strict conformity with Section 302(a) and (b) and with Section 302(c) (5) of the Labor-Management Act of 1947. Section 302(a) and (b) provide as follows:

(a) It shall be unlawful for any employer or association of employers or any person who acts as a labor relations expert, adviser, or consultant to an employer or who acts in the interest of an employer to pay, lend or deliver, or agree to pay, lend, or deliver, any money or other thing of value—

(1) to any representative of any of his employees who are employed in an industry affecting commerce; or

(2) to any labor organization, or any officer or employee thereof, which represents, seeks to represent, or would admit to membership, any of the employees of such employer who are employed in an industry affecting commerce;

*   *   *   *   *   *   *   *   *   *

(b) (1) It shall be unlawful for any person to request, demand, receive, or accept, or agree to receive or accept, any payment, loan, or delivery of any money or other thing of value prohibited by subsection (a) of this section.

Violations of Section 302 are punishable by criminal penalties. Section 302(d) provides:

(d) Any person who willfully violates any of the provisions of this section shall, upon conviction thereof, be guilty of a misdemeanor and be subject to a fine of not more than $10,000 or to imprisonment for not more than one year, or both.

Section 302(c) (5) establishes *limited* exceptions to subsections (a) and (b) for payments to trust funds which meet *specified* requirements. The statutory requirements are that the employer's payments be made

* * * to a trust fund established by such representative, for the sole and exclusive benefit of the employees of such employer, and their families and dependents (or of such employees, families, and dependents jointly with the employees of other employers making similar payments, and their families and dependents): *Provided,* that (A) such payments are held in trust for the purpose of paying, either from principal or income or both, for the benefit of employees, their families and dependents, for medical or hospital care, pensions on retirement or death of employees, compensation for injuries or illness resulting from occupational activity or insurance to provide any of the foregoing, or unemployment benefits or life insurance, disability and sickness insurance, or accident insurance; (B) the detailed basis on which such payments are to be made is specified in a written agreement with the employer, and employees and employers are equally represented in the administration of such fund, together with such neutral persons as the representatives of the employers and the representatives of employees may agree upon and in the event the employer and employee groups deadlock on the administration of such fund and there are no neutral persons empowered to break such deadlock, such agreement provides that the two groups shall agree on an impartial umpire to decide such dispute, or in event of their failure to agree within a reasonable length of time, an impartial umpire to decide such dispute shall, on petition of either group, be appointed by the district court of the United States for the district where the trust fund has its principal office, and shall also contain provisions for an annual audit of the trust fund, a statement of the results of which shall be available for inspection by interested persons at the principal office of the trust fund and at such other places as may be designated in such written agreement; and (C) such payments as are intended to be used for the purpose of providing pensions or annuities for employees are made to a separate trust which provides that the funds held therein cannot be used for any purpose other than paying such pensions or annuities; * * *.

The trust agreement was written to conform with the statutory mandate and spelled out limitations upon payments into and out of the Fund. It is uncontroverted that the trust agreement at all times contained the limitations required by Section 302.

From July 1, 1953, through March 31, 1965, Moglia's employer for twenty-eight years, Elmhurst Contracting Co., Inc., or its successor (Elmhurst), made payments into the Fund on behalf of Moglia and other employees and such payments were received and accepted by the

Fund. During this period, the books of Elmhurst were regularly audited by auditors for the Fund to assure that the payments being made were in the proper amounts.

On April 15, 1965, listing Elmhurst as his only employer, Moglia filed an application for a pension with the Fund. It is uncontroverted that Moglia's age, length of service, and other qualifications for benefits under the Pension Plan of the Fund at the time of the filing of his application for a pension, and up to the time of his death, were such that, if he were entitled to benefits under the Pension Plan, he would have been entitled to payments for life commencing May 1, 1965, at the rate of $200.00 per month. If Moglia was entitled to these payments and he did not receive them during his lifetime, appellant, as his widow, would be entitled, pursuant to the provisions of the Pension Plan, to receive them for a period of thirty-six months, commencing May 1, 1965.

For some reason, the Fund does not investigate pension eligibility until after an application for pension benefits has been filed, and, after Moglia applied, an investigation of Elmhurst's status with the Fund revealed that Elmhurst had never entered into a collective bargaining agreement or a pension trust agreement with the Local although the Local had often requested it to do so.

The facts surrounding Moglia's application were reported to the Trustees at a meeting on June 15, 1965, but action on the application was deferred until the Trustees had an opportunity to consult with counsel. They were advised by counsel that payment to Moglia was prohibited by the Labor-Management Relations Act of 1947 and by the trust agreement, and that Moglia's application must be denied. They were also advised that the Labor-Management Relations Act of 1947 and the trust agreement prohibited them from accepting Elmhurst's payments. Accordingly, Moglia's application was rejected by the Trustees, and all the Elmhurst payments were refunded to Elmhurst. Elmhurst refused to accept the refund pending termination of the present litigation, and its payments are now being held apart from the rest of the Fund to be disposed of in accordance with the final determination of this action.

The question presented to us by appellant is whether she is entitled to receive pension benefit payments from the Local 282-Pension Trust Fund notwithstanding the fact that there never has been a written collective bargaining agreement or any other written agreement between Elmhurst and Local 282 detailing the basis upon which payments were to be made by Elmhurst, on behalf of its employees, into the Trust Fund. The answer to this question involves a construction of the relevant language of Section 302 of the Labor-Management Relations Act of 1947.

Appellant first contends that the written agreement requirement contained in subsection 302(c) (5) (B) applies only to payments made by employers into the Fund and not to payments made by the Trustees out of the Fund to employees, and, therefore, the Trustees would not be violating Section 302 by making payments to appellant. However, we hold that, inasmuch as both Elmhurst's payments into the Fund and the Trustees' receipt of said payments were prohibited by Section 302 in the absence of a written agreement as required by subsection 302(c) (5) (B), appellant was not a person who could, under Section 302, lawfully be paid pension benefit payments from the Trust Fund.

Section 302 was originally passed as part of the Taft-Hartley Act of 1947. The Section's purpose was to curb the abuses, discovered by Congress after extensive investigation, which seemed to be inherent in funds created and maintained by contributions exacted from employers but which were administered by union officials without any obligation to account to the contributors or to the union membership. See, e. g., 92 Cong.Rec., Part 4, 79th Cong., 2d Sess.1946, p. 4893 (Senator Byrd), p. 4897 (Senator Knowland), p. 4894 (Senator Ball); S.Rep. No. 105, 80th Cong., 1st Sess., 52 (1947); 93 Cong.Rec., Part 4, 80th Cong., 1st Sess.1947, p. 4678 (Senator Ball), p. 4678 (Senator Byrd), pp. 4746 and 4747 (Senator Taft). In 1959, Section 302 was amended to include within its ambit conduct which had been held to be outside Section 302 but conduct that Congress felt was of the type Section 302 was originally aimed at prohibiting. 1959 U.S.Code Cong. & Ad.News, 2326–30, 2360–70. A reading of the legislative history of Section 302 shows that Congress intended to prohibit the establishment of any union funds by means of employer payments unless the funds conformed in all respects with the specific dictates of Section 302(c). E.g., 92 Cong.Rec., Part 4, 79th Cong., 2d Sess.1946, supra; 93 Cong.Rec., Part 4, 80th Cong., 1st Sess.1947, supra; 1959 U.S.Code Cong. & Ad.News, supra; see International Longshoremen's Ass'n v. Seatrain Lines, Inc., 326 F.2d 916, 919–920 (2 Cir. 1964); Bey v. Muldoon, 217 F.Supp. 401 (E.D.Pa.1962).

Under Section 302, *any* payment made by an employer to an employee representative, and this includes trustees administering a pension trust fund, see, e. g., United States v. Ryan, 350 U.S. 299 (1956) * * *, and the receipt of such payments by an employee representative are absolutely forbidden unless there is a written agreement between the employer and the union specifying the basis upon which the payments are made. Thus, in the case of a legally established union pension trust fund, the only employer contributions which may be accepted by the trustees administering the fund are those contributions from employers who have a written agreement with the union as required by subsection 302(c) (5) (B). Absent the written agreement, there is no valid Section 302 trust as to those employer contributions; the parties making and accepting such contributions are violating Section 302, and the intended beneficiary of the illegal employer contributions has no legal right under Section 302 to the benefits normally derived from employer contributions to the trust fund. Only employees and former employees of employers who are lawfully contributing to a union pension trust fund may qualify as beneficiaries of a Section 302 trust. Rittenberry v. Lewis, 238 F.Supp.

506 (E.D.Tenn.1965); Bolgar v. Lewis, 238 F.Supp. 595 (W.D.Pa. 1960).

Appellant makes an appealing argument that Congress intended to encourage and foster the creation and extension of union welfare funds and therefore that this court should not construe Section 302 so as to deny appellants the benefits of this welfare fund. As pointed out by the court below, acceptance of appellant's argument would not necessarily implement the congressional intention although it would provide benefits for the appellant. The reason for the rigid structure of Section 302 is to insure that employer contributions are only for a proper purpose and to insure that the benefits from the established fund reach only the proper parties. Schwartz v. Associated Musicians of Greater N. Y., Local 802, 340 F.2d 228, 233–234 (2 Cir. 1964). Any erosion of the strict requirements of this section could provide an unintended loophole for the unscrupulous, and could result in a diversion of funds away from the proper parties as had occurred before Section 302 was enacted. See Arroyo v. United States, 359 U.S. 419, 423–427 (1959); cf. International Longshoremen's Ass'n v. Seatrain Lines, Inc., supra, 326 F.2d at 920.

Our construction of Section 302 may work a hardship in the instant case, especially as neither appellant nor her deceased husband appear to have engaged in any wrongful conduct; but we consider the construction of the statute that we have adopted is the only acceptable one in light of the congressional history and intent. Of course this does not preclude appellant from pursuing any other remedies that may be available to her.

Appellant also asks the court to invoke the theory of equitable estoppel as a basis for allowing pension benefits from the Trust Fund. Appellant argues that the Trustees, having accepted Elmhurst's contributions into the Fund for twelve years, and having regularly audited Elmhurst's books in order to assure that payments were being made in the proper amounts, are estopped from denying pension benefits to appellant on the ground that there was no written agreement between the Local and Elmhurst. Whatever merit this argument may have if directed to the appellee trustees' invocation of the terms of the trust agreement to deny appellant at this late date any pension benefits, a matter we need not decide, the equitable estoppel argument cannot supply the essential element of the written agreement Congress required by subsection 302(c) (5) (B).

The statutory requirement of a written agreement is not a minor technicality which may be dispensed with when, there being no written agreement, the acts of one party may be said to estop him from defending on that ground. A written agreement is necessary before payments may be made under the section. As compelling and as appealing as appellant's case is, the structure of the section and the Congressional intent underlying the section preclude any judicial inroads into its rigid, specific requirements.

Appellant conceded in the district court that at no time relevant to the cause of action asserted in her complaint there was a collective bargaining agreement or any other written agreement, as such, between Elmhurst and the Local. Appellant, now, without intending to qualify her concession, argues that the written agreement requirement of subsection 302(c) (5) (B) was, in fact, satisfied in the instant case. Appellant contends that subsection 302(c) (5) (B) only requires a written agreement and not a signed, written agreement, William Dunbar Co. v. Painters & Glaziers District Council, 129 F.Supp. 417 (D.D.C.1955), and such an agreement in fact existed in the form of the unsigned collective bargaining agreement which was attached to the unsigned trust agreement governing the Fund. According to appellant, Elmhurst's conduct and action in observing the terms of the collective bargaining agreement attached to the trust agreement by paying uniform union scale wages and by making contributions to the trust fund were tantamount to ratification and adoption of a written agreement by Elmhurst even though it had not signed it. We do not agree with appellant's analysis.

In the first place, the *Dunbar* case involved a situation where employers were disputing their obligation to contribute to a union trust fund in the absence of a signed, written trust agreement. The district court in *Dunbar* found *as a fact* that, at one time previously, there had been in existence a valid, formal, written trust agreement, and that the original signed copy of this agreement had disappeared and only an unsigned copy remained. The question before the court in *Dunbar* was whether the employers could be compelled to contribute to the trust fund on the basis of the duplicate written agreement bearing no signatures. On these facts the district court held that subsection 302(c) (5) (B) only required a written and not a signed agreement. *Dunbar* is clearly factually distinguishable from the instant case.

In the second place, ratification and adoption are only forms of acceptance of a contract and must conform to the general principles governing the formation of contracts. Two essential elements of a contract formation are mutuality of agreement and mutuality of obligation. See, generally, 17 C.J.S. Contracts § 1(1) (1962). Both of these elements are missing in this case. The union demanded the acceptance of a complete collective bargaining agreement along with the trust agreement. Elmhurst did not appear to be willing to accept these terms at any time. In such a situation it would be ridiculous to assert that there was agreement between the parties and a mutuality of obligation. Therefore, on the record as made, we hold that there was no ratification of, or any adoption of, the collective bargaining agreement by Elmhurst.

Appellant has raised a number of questions relating to the possible abuse of discretion on the part of the trustees in so construing the trust agreement as to prevent them from paying benefits to the appellant. As we are holding that it would be illegal for the trustees to retain the contributions of Elmhurst or to pay benefits to appellant, it is not necessary to discuss these contentions for they relate only to the proper interpretation of the trust agreement or to the power of the Trustees under the agreement to deny pension benefits to the appellant.

We realize that other claimants to union welfare funds and perhaps even other claimants to this very pension trust may find themselves in the position of appellant. Nevertheless, the proper remedy for such a regrettable situation is not the enforcement of a claimant's rights under the trust because that would allow evasion of a carefully drafted statute. The congressional scheme, if properly enforced by government attorneys, is designed to prevent this unfortunate situation from ever arising. Employing Plasterers' Association of Chicago v. Journeymen Plasterers' Protective and Benevolent Society of Chicago, Local No. 5, 279 F.2d 92, 97–98 (7 Cir. 1960). If the sanctions provided by Section 302(d) had ever been invoked here, neither the Trustees of this particular fund nor the trustees of any other similarly situated fund would ever permit the state of affairs to reach this deplorable condition.[1]

Affirmed.

BLASSIE v. KROGER COMPANY

United States Court of Appeals, Eighth Circuit, 1965.
345 F.2d 58.

BLACKMUN, Circuit Judge. The plaintiffs, The Kroger Co., The Great Atlantic & Pacific Tea Co., Inc., and National Food Stores, Inc., are three retail chain employers which have stores in the Saint Louis area and which, with many other employers, make contributions on behalf of employees to the "Local 88 Meat & Related Industries Welfare Fund Trust".

By this action, begun in January 1962 against the five then trustees (two union, two employer and one public) of the Trust, the three plaintiffs seek to enjoin alleged violations of § 302 of the Labor Management Relations Act, 1947, as amended, 29 U.S.C.A. § 186. Section 302(e) provides jurisdiction. The union is Meat Cutters Local No. 88. Its international affiliate is Amalgamated Meat Cutters & Butcher Workmen of North America, AFL–CIO.

The plaintiffs were generally successful at the trial, for the district court, after filing its memorandum opinion, Kroger Co. v. Blassie, 225 F.Supp. 300 (E.D.Mo.1964), entered a judgment and decree on January 24, 1964.

*　*　*

---

1. At 267 F.Supp. 641, 643, 648, the district judge appears to indicate by dicta that a present execution by the employer of the collective bargaining and trust agreements could validate the 36 months of pension payments appellant claims were payable to her month by month from May 1, 1965 to April 1, 1968, and could legalize the abortive payments by Elmhurst to the Fund. Though we approach the resolution of the dispute between the parties by the same route taken by the district judge we point out that we are not adopting this dicta. (Court's footnote 8.)

Former union trustees Blassie and Etzel have taken a general appeal. Present employee trustees Harry R. Poole and Frank X. Davis appeal from [a] portion of the court's judgment and decree. * * * Defendants Edward J. Schnuck, Albert Wagenfuehr, and the Right Reverend Monsignor John W. Miller, who are also present trustees, and Mathews, have not appealed. The plaintiffs have effected no cross appeal.

The issues here, in general terms, are: * * * (e) the propriety of the court's order directing the sale of the Jefferson County land and improvements; (f) the availability of the pharmacy to persons other than beneficiaries of the Trust; and (g) the propriety of the court's order directing the removal of the Trust's offices. These seven issues all obviously have to do with the propriety, under § 302 (c) and the trust agreement, of trust expenditures and activities. * * *

The Statute. Section 302, being a part of the Labor Management Relations Act, came into being in 1947. It was amended, after this Trust was already in existence, by § 505 of the Labor-Management Reporting and Disclosure Act of 1959, Pub.L. 86–257, 73 Stat. 537. The latter Act's amendments, although applicable to the Trust, do not affect the present issues.

The statute by § 302(a), makes it unlawful for an employer to make any payment to any "representative" of any of its employees who are employed in an industry affecting commerce, or to any labor organization, or officer or employee thereof, which represents any of the employees. Correspondingly, by § 302(b), the demand for or receipt of any such payment is also made unlawful.

Section 302(c), however, provides exceptions to this declaration of unlawfulness. These are (1) compensation for an employee's service; (2) the payment of a judgment or proper award; (3) a purchase at the prevailing market price in the regular course of business; (4) check-off of union dues; (5) certain payments to a welfare trust fund; and (6), as added in 1959, payments to a trust fund "for the purpose of pooled vacation, holiday, severance or similar benefits, or defraying costs of apprenticeship or other training programs", provided that the trust has the same protective provisions specified by § 302(c) (5) (B).

The fifth exception [1] is the one which is vital here. It relates to payments made to a trust established "for the sole and exclusive ben-

1. Section 302(c).
"The provisions of this section shall not be applicable * * * (5) with respect to money or other thing of value paid to a trust fund established by such representative for the sole and exclusive benefit of the employees of such employer, and their families and dependents (or of such employees, families, and dependents jointly with the employees of other employers making similar payments, and their families

and dependents): *Provided,* That (A) such payments are held in trust for the purpose of paying, either from principal or income or both, for the benefit of employees, their families and dependents, for medical or hospital care, pensions on retirement or death of employees, compensation for injuries or illness resulting from occupational activity or insurance to provide any of the foregoing, or unemployment benefits or life insurance, disability and efit of the employees * * * and their families and dependents (or of such * * * jointly with the employees of other employers making similar payments, and their families and dependents)". But it contains provisos that (A) the payments are held for the purpose of paying "for the benefit of employees, their families and dependents, for medical or hospital care, pensions on retirement or death of employees" or other stated benefits; (B) the basis on which the payments are to be made is specified in a written agreement with the employer; the employees and employers are equally represented in the administration of the trust together with such neutral persons as may be agreed upon; and provisions are present for an annual audit the results of which shall be available for inspection by interested persons; and (C) payments intended for pensions or annuities for employees "are made to a separate trust which provides that the funds held therein cannot be used for any purpose other than paying such pensions or annuities".

By § 302(d) a willful violation of the section is a misdemeanor.

General Facts. 1. The plaintiffs' Saint Louis area stores have separate meat departments. Employees in those departments are members of the union. For some years a collective bargaining relationship has existed between the union and meat industry employers. This resulted in a series of labor agreements and the establishment of the Trust in January 1953. After the Trust was expanded to include employees of retailers the plaintiffs by contract became contributing employers.

2. Defendant Blassie was one of the original union trustees. He was also an officer and business agent of the union. Defendant Etzel was the other union trustee and was so designated in 1957. He too, was an officer of the union. Defendant Mathews was president of the union when the suit was instituted and an alternate union trustee. Defendant Schnuck is an employer trustee. Defendant Wagenfuehr is the other employer trustee but was not accepted as such by Blassie and Etzel; his status was finally recognized shortly before trial. Defendant Miller is the public trustee.

3. The president of the International on May 13, 1963, while the suit was pending, removed Blassie and Etzel as trustees and replaced them with Poole and Davis. Although the trial took place after this removal and substitution, Poole and Davis were not joined as

sickness insurance, or accident insurance; (B) the detailed basis on which such payments are to be made is specified in a written agreement with the employer, and employees and employers are equally represented in the administration of such fund, together with such neutral persons as the representatives of the employers and the representatives of employees may agree upon * * * and shall also contain provisions for an annual audit of the trust fund, a statement of the results of which shall be available for inspection by interested persons at the principal office of the trust fund and at such other places as may be designated in such written agreement; and (C) such payments as are intended to be used for the purpose of providing pensions or annuities for employees are made to a separate trust which provides that the funds held therein cannot be used for any purpose other than paying such pensions or annuities * * *."

parties defendant and did not formally come into the case until they were permitted to intervene, pursuant to Rule 24, F.R.Civ.P., after trial and immediately prior to judgment. Blassie and Etzel actively participated in the trial.

* * *

6. At the time of the trial a contributing employer paid $31.70 per month for each covered employee who averaged 23 or more hours of work per week for the month. The three plaintiffs were contributing more than $200,000 annually. This figure was more than one-fourth of the total contributions to the Trust.

7. The Trust has three primary fields of operation: the group insurance program, the Medical Institute, and the Jefferson County land.

(a) The insurance program is supervised by a salaried administrator. His office receives the contributions from participating employers and pays the premiums for group and other insurance carried by the Trust.

(b) The Trust in 1958 completed the construction of a building in Saint Louis for its Medical Institute. The Institute has a medical staff and administrative personnel.

(c) The Jefferson County land. This consists of approximately 586 acres acquired in late 1958. Although described as a "Retreat for Convalescing and Geriatrics Treatment", and although there was some evidence presented that the property was regarded as part of a long term program to provide medical and health benefits, and was not intended to be limited to recreation, the trial court found that it was acquired for recreational purposes and that up to the time of trial had not been used for any other purpose.

8. Pension benefits have never been provided by the Trust.

Matters not in issue on the appeal. Because the plaintiffs have effected no cross-appeal, some items in the complaint and in the prayer for relief are not at issue here. We refer to them only so that we may be sure to set to one side these presently nonsignificant but originally controversial aspects of the case. Among these are the plaintiffs' suggestions as to inequality in representation among the trustees and as to differences in the methods of removing union trustees and employer trustees. The May 27, 1963, amendment may have resolved both these problems. Another, and the warmest issue, was misconduct of the union trustees, particularly Blassie. The range of the allegations and proof as to this is largely evident from the trial court's opinion and from the court's characterization of Blassie's activity on p. 306 of 225 F.Supp. This provides a colorful and unsavory background for the case but we need not repeat it here. The trial court went on to hold that control of day-to-day administration of the Trust is a matter for the state courts and that jurisdiction is granted to federal courts to enjoin violations rather than to provide a remedy for abuses already perpetrated.

We note in passing that it has been said that a trust of this kind (or at least the union trustees thereof) qualifies as a "representative" of the employees under § 302(a) and is thus within the basic prohibition of the statute. Local No. 2 of Operative Plasterers, etc. v. Paramount Plastering, Inc., 310 F.2d 179, 182, 185–186 (9 Cir. 1962), cert. denied 372 U.S. 944, 83 S.Ct. 935, 9 L.Ed.2d 969; Mechanical Contractors Ass'n of Philadelphia, Inc. v. Local Union 420, 265 F.2d 607, 611 (3 Cir. 1959).

The Statute's Purposes. These have been clearly recognized by the Supreme Court in Arroyo v. United States, 359 U.S. 419, 425–426, 79 S.Ct. 864, 868–869, 3 L.Ed.2d 915 (1959):

> "The provision [§ 302] was enacted as part of a comprehensive revision of federal labor policy in the light of experience acquired during the years following passage of the Wagner Act * * *, and was aimed at practices which Congress considered inimical to the integrity of the collective bargaining process. * * * Those members of Congress who supported the amendment were concerned with corruption of collective bargaining through bribery of employee representatives by employers, with extortion by employee representatives, and with the possible abuse by union officers of the power which they might achieve if welfare funds were left to their sole control.

> * * *

> "Congress believed that if welfare funds were established which did not define with specificity the benefits payable thereunder, a substantial danger existed that such funds might be employed to perpetuate control of union officers, for political purposes, or even for personal gain. * * * To remove these dangers, specific standards were established to assure that welfare funds would be established only for purposes which Congress considered proper and expended only for the purposes for which they were established." [2]

> * * *

The Jefferson County land and recreational activity. Blassie and Etzel appeal with respect to this issue. * * *

The district court noted, pp. 310–311 of 225 F.Supp., the expenditure of a substantial amount of trust funds in the purchase and development of this land acquired from a corporation owned and controlled by Blassie and Etzel; its limited seasonal use; its being made available to persons and groups having no connection with the union or the Trust; and its planning and domination by Blassie. The court found, p. 310, that "the area was acquired for recreational purposes and it has never been used in any respect for any other purpose". The evidence adequately supports this finding of fact and it is not our privilege to disturb it.

---

2. Much of the Opinion is omitted at this point.

This takes us to the statute. If the acquisition and maintenance of a facility solely for recreation is within the intendment of § 302 (c), it must be so because of the protection of either § 302(c) (5) (A) and the reference there to "medical or hospital care", or, perhaps, the protection of § 302(c) (6) and the reference there to "pooled vacation, holiday, severance or similar benefits".

We, as was the district court, are not yet ready to construe the term "medical or hospital care" to include "any type of recreational facility or program instituted wholly for recreational purposes". Recreation is not one of the carefully listed exceptions to the statute's prohibition of an employer's payments. While the old adage about all work and no play may make sense, and while some recreation may be desirable for the development of a more fit and complete person, this is not the text of the statute which confronts us. The circumstances under which the statute came into existence, see   *   *   * Arroyo v. United States, supra, pp. 424–426 of 359 U.S., Arroyo's emphasis, p. 426, upon Congress' concern "with specificity" of benefits and its having established "specific standards"; the origin of § 302 in an amendment to the Case bill, H.R. 4908, 79th Cong., 2d Sess., 92 Cong.Rec. 4809, 5521–22, see Arroyo v. United States, supra, footnote 6 on p. 425 of 359 U.S., a presidential veto of which was sustained; that amendment's second draft's reference to "health, welfare, or other benefits", 92 Cong.Rec. 5041; the later elimination of the words, "or other benefits", in the bill as passed, 92 Cong.Rec. 5499; the detailed listing of the exceptions; and the fact that Congress might have specified recreation had it been an intended purpose, are all factors which convince us (despite the use of general terms in the debates) that "medical or hospital care" does not reach out to include pure recreation and purely recreational facilities.

We reach a like conclusion as to the language of § 302(c) (6). This, adopted in 1959, carefully spells out, as an amendment to such a statute should, a then desired broadening of the stated exceptions. This was to remove doubts theretofore existing as to apprenticeship and training programs and as to vacation, holiday, severance or similar benefits. H.Rep.No.741, 2 U.S.Code Cong. & Ad.News, 86th Cong., 1st Sess., 1959, pp. 2424, 2445–2456 and 2469–2470. If one is to relate "or similar benefits" solely to the statute's preceding word "severance", this, of course, lends no assistance to Blassie and Etzel. If one is to relate the phrase also to "pooled vacation" and "holiday", we are still not persuaded. We are faced here with a carefully drawn and restricted statute and we believe it right and proper to leave any expansion to pure recreation to the Congress rather than to presume to accomplish that end by a judicial determination which rests on a dubious foundation.

      *   *   *

It may well be that circumstances will arise sometime, or even are present today, where a particular facility with recreational attributes nevertheless has, in the light of developing medical knowledge and advice, a direct relationship to medical care and would be permissible under the statute. This would have to be determined for each case. We agree with the district court here that the over-ambitious, expensive, wholly recreational program revealed by this record for the Jefferson County land, despite its claimed justification as a part of an alleged plan for the far future, is not that case.

The Teamsters amicus expresses deep concern that the district court's reported opinion is more sweeping in its condemnation of rec-reation as a trust purpose than is the language of its unreported de-cree directed only to "any type of recreational facility or program in-stituted wholly for recreational purposes". We may be understood, in our affirmance of the district court on this point, as reading that court's opinion in line with the decree it entered.

The pharmacy and its availability to outsiders. Only Blassie and Etzel appeal as to this. The Trust's Saint Louis building which houses its Medical Institute contains space for a pharmacy. The Trust leased this space and fixtures to two brothers. The lessees operate the pharmacy but are obligated to make drugs available to trust beneficiaries on a cost plus basis. This effects a substantial savings for the customer. The favorable patronage, however, has not been restricted to beneficiaries of the Trust. Instead, it has been made available to members of three other unions and perhaps other persons not connected with the Trust.

The district court held that the Trust is one solely for the benefit of the trust beneficiaries and that the pharmacy's availability to out-siders violates the statute.

Blassie and Etzel argue that the Trust does not operate the phar-macy; that trust funds are not used to buy and sell drugs; that the Trust merely arranged that the lessees would sell to trust beneficiaries at reduced prices; that the Trust has no authority to limit the les-sees' class of customers; and that sales to outsiders create volume which probably makes it possible to sell drugs favorably to benefi-ciaries.

We agree with the reasoning of the district court. The Trust and its assets are solely for the benefit of its beneficiaries. We see nothing violative of § 302(c) or of the trust agreement in the trus-tees' insistence that the lessees furnish drugs to trust beneficiaries at a reduced price. At the same time, we see nothing legal in a direc-tion by the trustees, through contract or otherwise, that this favor-able arrangement be extended and made available for non-benefi-ciaries, such as union members who are not covered employees, mem-bers of other unions, or an outsider of any kind. The pharmacy is not a facility for the union man as such. It is one for the trust ben-eficiary. The evidence does not reveal the pharmacy lease as an in-vestment asset of the Trust. Instead, it shows it to be a service fa-cility in a service building, complementing the medical and surgical care available there and actually comprising a part of that care. Any suggestion that it is not for a landlord to dictate the details of a les-see's business operations cannot be applicable here. The pharmacy facility is no more available to an outsider than the Medical Institute itself is or should be.

We realize that there will be difficulties in enforcement here and that there are easy ways for a beneficiary or a pharmacist, or others, to get around the restriction. Nevertheless, the principle exists. This is a trust, with all the implications which that term possesses. The trustees may not, directly or indirectly or through the lessees, by contract, rebate, insufficient rent, dictation, pressure, or in any other manner, afford benefits to outsiders which belong exclusively to the beneficiaries.

The location of the trust offices. The administrative office for the trust's insurance program has been located for some years in a Saint Louis building owned by the union's Benevolent Society. The same building contains offices of the Society, of the union itself, of the union's credit union, of the union's insurance agency, and of another union. The district court ordered relocation removed from any union activities. Blassie and Etzel appeal as to this and they are joined in protest by the eastern amici.

Here, again, the Act and the trust agreement are silent. Nevertheless, we do not disturb the district court's decree as to this issue.

We are not to be understood as holding that the statute or any legal principle inflexibly prohibits the location of the office of a § 302(c) trust in a building owned by the union or by one of its agencies or, for that matter, by a contributing employer. See Ware v. Adams, 53 LRRM 2290 (S.D.Cal.1963). There might be an element of convenience for the trust beneficiaries in such a location or an element of financial savings to the trust. There is, however, no obligation for the trust so to locate, with consequent benefit to a landlord who is also an interested party. We incline to the belief that it is better judgment for trustees to locate trust offices in quarters which have no connection with any of the parties to the trust agreement. This is more in keeping with the fiduciary personality of the trust and its presumed independent character. While the choice of location may well be, ordinarily, a matter for the discretion of the trustees and not one to be determined anew by a court, the gist of the district court's holding here is that this discretion was abused, that this abuse was a violation of the Act, and that its perpetuation may be enjoined under § 302(e). We cannot say that, on this record, this was error. Precedent is afforded by American Bakeries Co. v. Barrick, 162 F.Supp. 882 (N.D.Ohio, 1958), aff'd 285 F.2d 426 (6 Cir. 1960).

In summary, therefore, we find ourselves in general accord with those portions of the district court's judgment and decree relating to the Jefferson County land, to the non-use of trust assets for a recreational facility or program instituted wholly for recreational purposes, and to the removal of the trust office (Paragraphs II, III, and V), * * * and to the pharmacy (Paragraph IV) when its availability is extended to the broadened class of beneficiaries contemplated by this opinion. * * *

We observe, perhaps gratuitously, that we attempt by this opinion to lay down general guidelines for trusts of this kind. This, of course gives no assurance that the functioning of any particular trust will be free of difficulty. We suspect fewer problems will arise if this Trust, in contrast to its past, is administered by its trustees in an atmosphere of true joint administration and free from individual domination and manipulation. This is the intendment of the Congress and of the statute which it produced. There is really no reason why the Trust cannot be made to function in a businesslike, impartial and fair manner and in full compliance with the provisions of the trust agreement. Thereby it will fulfill the purposes for which it was created.

The district court's judgment and decree is vacated and the case is remanded for the entry of a new judgment and decree in conformance with the views herein expressed.

NOTE ON VESTED BENEFITS

From time to time in the past there have been reports of serious hardships being imposed upon employees, both active as well as those retired, because the pension plan which they were depending upon for the payment of their retirement benefits was inadequately funded. One of the best known reports is related to an automobile manufacturer which discontinued business; the assets of the pension fund which had previously been established were not sufficient to continue paying benefits in full to employees already retired and as a consequence there were no funds to pay any pensions to active employees regardless of their age or the period of time that they had been participating in the pension plan. Many examples of these hardships have come to light and these in turn have led to demands for legislation. Several bills have been introduced into Congress seeking to correct these situations but so far no legislation has been adopted. Usually what is proposed is that employees be granted a "vested" interest in their pension benefits on an increasing scale starting after few years and becoming fully vested after ten to twenty years of participation in the plan. This would mean that an employee with a fully vested interest would be assured that his pension trust fund would be sufficiently funded (have enough assets) to pay him his full pension at retirement; and with less than a fully vested interest he would be assured of a proportionally smaller pension. This situation would apply regardless of the financial condition of his employer or the termination of the pension fund for any reason.

Most of the persons who make these proposals are well meaning, but most fail to understand the manner in which the lack of vesting in a pension plan occurs. No benefits can be paid out of a pension plan until contributions have been made, which are then invested and increase through investment income and gains. The amount available as benefits is limited by the amount of the contributions in the first place, and the income and gains from the invested funds. Upon the establishment of a pension plan there is a great demand for pension benefits to employees who are past 50 years of age and who claim either that they have been the ones who were instrumental in building up their union to the point where it could bargain for these benefits, or that they have been the employees who have been working for their company for many years and have contributed to its success to the point where it can pay these benefits, or both. This group of employees will insist upon pension benefits which cannot possibly be paid to them by the amount of contributions which will be made to the pension fund on their behalf through the remaining years of their employment. Since the money must come from some place the prevailing practice is to take it from the contributions being made on behalf of the younger employees, and the cost of "past service" (employment with the employer prior to their entry into the pension plan) of the older employees must be amortized from the contributions to be made over a period of years on behalf of younger employees. Whether these demands of the older employees are agreed to for humane reasons, or because they have substantial political power within their union, the fact is that the pension benefits which they will receive for approximately one generation will have to be paid long after they have retired from the contributions of active employees.

Thus, up to now, the style of benefit which is to be paid from a pension plan has been a matter of freedom of contract where the peculiarities of any given industry or unit within an industry have been dealt with by a matter of bargaining rather than by legislative mandate. Because employees have not been informed of this situation, and probably because employers and unions alike have not been sufficiently aware of the fundamental economics of a pension plan, benefits to be paid have not been vested in many plans. Also, on many occasions a conscious decision has been made to establish a higher retirement benefit than would be available if the benefit were to be vested. Further, an increase in the yield from investments, over the amount assumed in designing the benefit program, could well provide for the cost of vesting. For example, if the cost of vesting were to amount to 10% of the benefits, i. e. fully vested benefits would amount to 90% of the benefits available without vesting, an increase in the assumed yield on investments of approximately $\frac{1}{2}$% to 1% would provide sufficient funds to pay for vested benefits. Thus a more aggressive investment program could also be the method of dealing with the problem. This fact alone could solve the vesting problem in many pension plans if the parties to the plan, union, employers, and trustees, were to agree to invest the pension funds in securities with a higher investment yield or potential gain (and still be prudent investments) than in securities or government bonds with the greatest safety.

There is a wide variety of employment experience within different industries. While there is greater mobility of labor within our society in the latter part of the twentieth century than was known before World War II, and thus there are more frequent changes of jobs by employees, there are still many industries where turnover of employees is substantially less than in others. Also, the mortality of employees in some industries is much greater than in others, mortality both prior to retirement and after retirement, and these factors can make a substantial difference in the cost and the design of a pension plan. In those industries in which turnover is relatively high, providing a vested benefit will substantially increase the cost of the plan; conversely, in those industries where turnover is low the cost of a vested benefit will be low. In those industries where the physical demands of the job are such that mortality is higher than the general average, the cost of pensions will be lower and providing a vested benefit will be less costly; or, instead of vesting in these industries it may be decided to provide larger or earlier retirement benefits. Or, without reference to any other factors or problems, it may be determined to establish an industry-wide or area-wide pension fund, and assume that most employees upon terminating their employment with one employer will obtain employment with another who is participating in the fund; it is planned that these employees will then carry their benefits with them so long as they remain employed by any employer who is participating in the fund. These plans are very common and are the largest in the country.

Bargaining for these matters is still the way we deal with these problems. If legislation is to come, as seems quite probable, it ought to contemplate these realities, rather than be a response to the emotions which can quite properly be generated for elderly employees whose pension promise has turned out to be hollow. So far there has been no litigation directly relating to the failure to design a vested benefit in a pension plan.

QUESTIONS

1. Is the system of freedom of contract in determining the wages, hours, and other conditions of employment really a valid system for this purpose in a free society? Suppose that either employer or union has substantially greater bargaining power, does a fair contract evolve? In considering this, review the situation of the unorganized employee employed by the only industry in a small town. Or, the large union with the financial strength of dues contributed by more than a million members dealing with a sole proprietor who employs five people. Does the law make any provision for economic assistance to the employee in the first instance or the employer in the second instance in finding a new job or new employees? But what system would we use in our society if not freedom of contract? Would we have a free society without freedom of contract? What other laws would we have?

2.   Is a system of conscription for private employment (slavery or peonage) a valid system in a free society?   Obviously not, but how can we get persons with the necessary aptitudes into socially useful employment if we rely entirely on freedom of contract?   How can we get a sufficient number of physicians and other medical personnel, for example, to provide the necessary medical services to rural, economically depressed people?   Or is there some other system beside freedom of contract and conscription that would accomplish this?   How within the traditions of a free society and the 13th Amendment?   Is the wage and profit system, parts of the system of freedom of contract, working in this regard?   If we conscript people for employment ought we not to consider conscripting business property for the same purpose?   And fix interest rates and profits?   Is the problem of matching appropriately skilled employees with employers also the problem of matching employers with those employees?   Aside from freedom of contract do we have any provision in our legal system to accomplish this?   Should we?

3.   In industries where collective bargaining is now the accepted method of determining wages, hours, and other conditions of employment, who bargains for the public?   In an oligopolistic industry where one union bargains with the few producers, on a collective basis, is there any limit to the wages and salaries upon which they can agree?   If labor and capital get together and recognize that there is no limit to the amount of wages to be paid, and if all producers in the industry are to be paying the same wages, who will protect the buyers of the products of that industry who do not have this same advantage?   If big labor and big industry combine in this regard who will stop them?   An Economic Stabilization Agency?   A Price Commission?   A Pay Board?   A Cost of Living Council?   A "jaw-boning" politician?   If free competition existed, instead of oligopolistic competition, would this make any difference?

4.   Should we have some kind of adjudicatory machinery to settle labor disputes?   Is a labor dispute like other disputes which can be settled in common law courts?   Is there any similarity or difference between the dispute, on the one hand, of a plaintiff and a defendant involved in an automobile accident suit, and an employer and a union disputing the amount of wages on the other?   Does the necessity of developing an on-going relationship which exists both prior to and after a dispute between an employer and a union make it difficult or impossible to have an outside agency of any kind adjudicate the dispute?   Is compulsory arbitration of all disputes between employer and union which they cannot settle themselves a valid substitute for a strike?   Would it be fair when an anti-strike injunction is issued to require the employer to meet the demands of the union until a new collective bargaining agreement has been established?   Does the existing system of labor injunctions result in a return to work on the employer's terms?   If so, is this fair in a free society?   If so, should we lend the force of government always to one party to any dispute without regard to the merits of the dispute?   Who would determine the merits of the dispute?   By what standards?

5. Should the trustees of an employee benefit plan, such as a pension plan, be permitted to operate the pension plan by exercising sound business judgment? If so, may they exercise this kind of judgment under the prevailing rules of state trust laws? Ought the trustees of these plans be permitted to settle a disputed claim, or establish investment policy, on some basis other than on the basis established by the law which relates to protecting widows and orphans from the maladministration of a trust established by a deceased husband or father? Is not the operation of a large pension plan much more like the operation of an insurance company than the operation of a trust fund established for a widow or a grandson? If the law is to be changed in this regard, what standard should be enacted for the protection of the employee beneficiaries of these trust funds? The same, generally, as exists for stockholders of corporations? Ought the trustees of these plans be required to observe the same standards of care as the directors of a corporation? Or is their function different? How?

6. Should the Federal Social Security system be changed to permit optional participation by employees over and above the present mandated level of participation? That is, should all private pension funds be "covered into" the Social Security system to provide greater benefits for the participants over and above those presently provided by statute? Should the private pension system be required to adhere to certain minimum standards of operation, of eligibility, and of benefits with the privilege of building upon this with additional contributions? Or should the present system of freedom of contract in determining the amount of contributions to a plan, and the benefits to be derived from them, continue with no governmental mandates with reference to them? Can a system of adequate operational controls be devised which does not cross into the areas of contributions and benefits? If the operational controls were to cost more money would not this affect contributions or benefits? Should the trustees of a pension plan be permitted to design the benefits of their plan on the assumption that their invested funds will earn 4% when top quality, long-term investments are yielding $7\frac{1}{2}\%$? Would a government requirement that a higher rate of return on investments be assumed so that the cost to the plan of government regulation be a fair way of dealing with this problem? If so, should the government then guarantee this rate of return on investments? If so, what standards if any, should the government prescribe with reference to investments? Would this then get the government involved in the investment policies and practices of pension funds? Should this be done in all events since pension funds are the largest single pool of investment capital in the American economy? If so, what would happen to the freedom to design a pension plan to meet the peculiarities of a given employment unit or industry? What would happen to the investment industry? What would happen to freedom of contract?

Suggested Reference Sources

Texts and Treatises

Gregory, *Labor And The Law,* Norton Press, New York City.

Sovern, *Legal Restraints On Racial Discrimination in Employment.* Twentieth Century Fund, New York City.

Loose-Leaf Services

Bureau of National Affairs, (BNA) Collective Bargaining, Negotiations and Contracts, Washington, D. C.

Bureau of National Affairs, (BNA) Labor Relations Reporter, Washington, D. C.

Commerce Clearing House, Employment Practices Guide, Chicago, Illinois.

Prentice-Hall, Pension And Profit Sharing, Englewood Heights, N. J.

Topic Headings in the Index to Legal Periodicals

Labor Law

Boycotts and Strikes

Collective Bargaining

Discrimination

Picketing

Unions

Wages

Labor Management Relations

Chapter X

DEALING WITH LOCAL GOVERNMENT

A. INTRODUCTORY NOTE

Because, as we have seen, the business decision where to locate is, in our economic system, by and large, left exclusively to the businessman and not dictated by government, the determinants of locating in a particular place (at a particular time) will be judged by their effect upon the business itself as measured by whatever standards management sets. Matters such as proximity to markets, availability of resources, transportation, etc., all figure into the calculus. Additionally, governmental activity also will be included in this business decision-making process as we saw when we considered the subjects of state laws concerning securities and incorporation, for example. Frequently this same consideration must be given to the potential impact local government activity may have. For, unlike federal activity which most likely will be uniform throughout the United States, local government activity may vary significantly not only from region to region or from State to State but from place to place within a single State. And local government activity may reflect the kinds of considerations which conduce to the activities of business in general or a particular type of business or which may be translated into deterrents specifically erected to inhibit the carrying on of business in general or a particular type of business.

When we speak of local government, the ready reference for most persons is the city or the county. But these types of local government represent only two of the many forms in which governmental authority is distributed at the municipal level, i. e., at the tertiary level of government in our federal system where the initial level is federal and the secondary level is the State. Frequently the nature of municipal government authority is distributed so that local government below the State level is multi-layered with sometimes as many as two, three or four levels of local government intervening between the State government and the lowest level of local government.

In our political system in the United States the Constitution of the United States is the basic reference for determining the distribution of governmental authority. Pursuant to the Xth Amendment of the Constitution, all authority not specifically delegated to the Federal government or specifically denied to the States is reserved to the States (and to the people); therefore, all residual governmental authority in the United States reposes with the States and it is the States which determine the manner in which this residual authority is disbursed and exercised through their own constitutional and statutory schemes.

There are many variations of how governmental authority is distributed as between the States. Generally speaking, however, whatever lesser governmental entities may be established they are delegated specific governmental authority with the State reserving to itself all residual authority. But there are many States which often provide for a sharing of such authority with lesser governmental entities. And, generally speaking, again, most States provide for the creation of lesser governmental authorities known as cities and counties with specific authority distributed between these governments. But, here too, there are many variations and in recent years, it is almost universal to find the variations of kinds of lesser governmental entities being the rule rather than the exception. However, no matter what the nature of the lesser governmental entity, common to all such entities is the fact that (1) they are created pursuant to a State constitutional or statutory scheme, (2) they are creatures of specifically defined powers, and (3) they are all local governments exercising authority which is State authority specifically delegated.

Lesser governmental entities exist in many forms in addition to the city and the county. Depending upon whether the State scheme of lesser governmental entities allows such entity when created to determine for itself the extent to which it will exercise a broad range of authority, a distinction may be made between "governmental" entities and "quasi-governmental" entities. But, this distinction notwithstanding, if the entity created exercises authority derivatively from the State's authority it is nonetheless an entity of local government. To "de-confuse" this, such entities often are referred to collectively as *municipal corporations*. This label helps to avoid creating the image that a quasi-governmental entity is in fact the same kind of animal as the governmental entity. Moreover, the collective designation "municipal corporation" allows for classifying together many local governmental entities whose individual characteristics may be quite dissimilar but which nevertheless came into existence according to the tests set out before.

Municipal corporations frequently are structured somewhat along the lines of the business corporation and frequently possess many of the same characteristics. But they are corporations more accurately in another sense of the word. These municipal corporations act as a collective body for the benefit of the collective public.

In addition to the city and the county, other examples of municipal corporations are: township, borough, school district, water district, fire district, toll road authority, state university or community college, etc., to name but a few. The major area of classification among municipal corporations is that based upon the nature of the subject matter over which the entity has jurisdiction. The distinction here is as between the entity which is authorized to act, more or less generally, with respect to matters of health, safety, and welfare;

to exercise general police powers jurisdiction as compared with the entity which is single-function oriented.

The growth during the decades following the Second World War of the single function oriented municipal corporation was provoked almost exclusively because of limitations in State constitutions and statutes on the ability of municipal corporations to borrow public funds for the financing of endeavors they wished to pursue. For example, if a city found that it had borrowed its statutory limit to provide the services it already was providing but also found that it needed additional funds for an expansion of its water treatment facility, it might seek to have a water district established which then could borrow the money unencumbered by the fact that the city had already reached its borrowing limits. The city then after the creation of the district, might transfer to the district its interests in the facilities already controlled by it thereby leaving to the district sole responsibility for the water operations occurring within the city.

Frequently, however, municipal corporations of single function orientation are created when the geographical area to be served cuts across traditional political boundaries. In this way an independent governmental entity can act to provide services where no other existing entity might. Such activity occurs when the service area is logically larger than a city or a county, or includes parts of one other local government and parts of another and the ability to provide such service would be non-existent if traditional political boundaries had to be respected. The jurisdictional boundaries for the new municipal corporation then become those of its service area.

Both governmental and quasi-governmental entities exist throughout the United States having been created to satisfy the needs of localities and the requirements of State law. Needs and requirements of this nature are to be found in all of the states with, of course, many variations reflecting the individual State differences. However, such differences also may exist within a single state. The state may recognize that because of differences in concentrations of population, for example, the governmental needs as between these different areas of population concentration will be different and that the municipal corporations that may come into existence to serve the people may have to be reflective of these population differences. The most common example of this phenomenon is the distinction made between classes of cities where cities of different classes are enabled to do more, or less, depending upon the class. Cities of the first class may be allowed to create their own police departments where cities of the third class may not be allowed to. Cities of the second class may be empowered to coordinate their fire-fighting efforts with any other second or third-class city in fairly close proximity where cities of the first class may not be. (Frequently, however, the population basis for distinguishing between cities within the State is a function of State legislatures dominated by rural legislators wishing to ensure that large urban centers within the State do not share pro rata in

State finances which if allowed would have the effect of leaving very little for rural areas.)

Our concern with the activities of municipal corporations as they bear upon business location and operation, however, does not require conversance with all of the varieties of and distinctions between municipal corporations which could exist within a State or with all of the different types of activities in which these entities may or could be engaged. For, as a rule, activities of these municipal corporations are quite similar from state to state and whatever the nature of the characteristic which may distinguish one such entity from another all exercise "police powers" of the State in providing for the general health, safety or welfare of the citizens of the community.

There are, however, activities of these municipal corporations (1) which have the effect of making it either more or less advantageous to locate and operate a business in a specific locality, and (2) which although of generalized applicability have a more particularly direct and decisive affect upon business. These activities are to be distinguished from those which are the product of a special and concerted decision to treat business "specially", be it advantageously or disadvantageously, which also may be extant.

Municipal corporations are not peculiar to the American political or legal experience; they are found, many in exactly the same form, throughout the world. They have, however, tended to proliferate more extensively in the United States, not only for the reason given before but more so because of the American ethic of distrust of concentrations of political power. If we superimpose upon that ethic the prevalent political theory that people generally wish to focus governmental power at that geographic level which is proximate to the level at which their daily concerns operate, we will find that an extensive network of municipal corporations creates the potential for more numerous legal problems. Moreover, legal problems may be created that do not exist elsewhere and which would not exist but for the coincidence of these phenomena.

In testing the constitutionality of local regulations, for example, if the frame of reference for them were to be a community standard borne out of a larger geographic area many such regulations might be too restrictive; whereas, given the smaller population reference, the more homogeneous value system likely to be found therein, such regulations then can be observed to impact more uniformly, less discriminatorily and, therefore, less subject to constitutional attack. If we then go back to the reference of the Xth Amendment to the Constitution we may see both the rationale for it and the thrust of it.

The result of such an inquiry will be to find at the local level, under the aegis of health, safety and welfare, the existence of a plethora of regulations controlling and constraining business activity. Running a gamut which could begin with adulterated milk and end with zoning, municipal corporations have entered the regulatory field so as to affect virtually every aspect and dimension of the business effort. Moreover, justified by the health, safety and welfare rubric, municipal corporations have extended their activity to the actual undertaking of efforts not traditionally included within what traditionally would be called the governmental definition, i. e., they have begun to engage in what otherwise might be called proprietary efforts.

The cases in this chapter are only exemplary of the range of local matters with which business must be concerned. But just as significantly it must be recognized that but for our political perspectives and value concerns such matters either might not exist at all, might exist at some other level of government or might exist in some form heretofore not expressed.

But our perceptions of the role of local government have not remained static. As our population concentrations have enlarged, relocated themselves and become more heterogeneous we have come to recognize that the nature and form of local government has had to accommodate. These accommodations, in turn, have caused the legal consequences running therefrom to vary from those that ran from the status quo ante. Just what typology is most accurate in establishing points of reference for legal problems of concern to the businessman at the local level when local government itself continues to metamorphose may be the height of conjecture. Our legal system always has, in a sense, been a reactive one and, therefore, it might be best to look first to the character of the business activity; it may be from that frame of reference that insofar as business activity is concerned local government, whatever its nature or form, will (continue to) direct its attention.

B.   LOCAL TAXATION

NORTHWESTERN STATES PORTLAND CEMENT CO. v. BOARD OF REVIEW OF CITY OF MASON CITY

Supreme Court of Iowa, 1953.
244 Iowa 720, 58 N.W.2d 15.

BLISS, Justice. We will refer to the Cement Company as the plaintiff and to the Board of Review as the defendant. The plaintiff operates a large plant in Mason City, Iowa, to manufacture Portland Cement. It owns a substantial amount of land underlaid with both limestone and clay which it quarries and excavates for use in the manufacture of cement in the plant located on this land.

On or about May 31st, 1951, the Assessor of Mason City, as of January 1st of that year, made an assessment for taxes against certain personal property of plaintiff, in which, with other kinds of property, all taxable as personal property, was a quantity of finished cement assessed in the sum of $22,173, and a quantity of raw material in the factory, in the process of being made into cement, which was assessed at $3,387, all as shown in Assessment Roll No. 2351.

At this time an assessment was also made against other personal property of plaintiff consisting of new machinery and equipment which it had installed in its main manufacturing plant or factory during the years 1949 and 1950, but which had not been assessed in either of those years. While it was personal property, under Code section hereinafter set out, it was required to be, and was, for the purposes of taxation, regarded as, and assessed as, real estate. As shown by Assessment Roll No. 2160, this new machinery and equipment was assessed at $297,344.

On June 18, 1951, plaintiff filed with the defendant Board a separate written protest against each assessment. As noted above, the first-mentioned assessment totaled $25,560. In its protest plaintiff stated that the assessment should have been $8,840, and that the over-assessment was $16,720. * * *

In its protest against the assessment of the new machinery and equipment, there was no claim made that it was excessive, but it asked that it be cancelled as illegal and void, for the reason that, since under the statute the machinery used in a manufacturing establishment must be regarded as real estate for taxation purposes, the "machinery and equipment referred to in said Assessment Roll No. 2160 was non-assessable for the year 1951 for the reason that the year 1951 was not a year in which real estate was listed and valued for taxation, and the same (machinery and equipment) neither constituted omitted real estate nor buildings erected since the previous assessment on real estate, as provided and defined by law". The protest contained no other ground or objection.

The Board of Review denied each of the protests, and confirmed each of the challenged assessments. Plaintiff duly appealed to the district court from the ruling on each protest. * * * It is alleged that: the assessment of $25,560 was 60% of the 100% valuation of $42,602 made by the assessor; the items of the finished cement, 184,-780 barrels, clinker, 22,466 barrels, limestone, 16,105 tons, and clay, 29,391 tons; the assessor in his 1951 assessment valued the average inventories of plaintiff's finished cement and clinker each at twenty cents a barrel, the limestone at sixty cents a ton, and the clay in storage at forty cents a ton; the assessor arrived at these valuations by estimating the value of the clay and limestone entering into the finished cement and the goods in process at the time the same entered the primary crusher at plaintiff's manufacturing plant; that all such limestone and clay was acquired by plaintiff and was quarried and removed from the land which it had purchased in the vicinity of the plant, and was conveyed to the primary crushers by the plaintiff with its machinery and equipment, which was included in plaintiff's manufacturing machinery and equipment for the purpose of assessment for taxation and constituted a part of its manufacturing establishment; the average full and fair value of all such limestone and clay before the same was quarried, dug and removed from plaintiff's land was 5.42 cents per ton for the limestone, and 8.42 cents per ton for the clay, and that based on these values the average full and fair value of the clay and limestone which entered into plaintiff's average 1950 clinker inventory was 1.84 cents a barrel, and which entered into the average 1950 inventory of finished cement was 5.94 cents a barrel; the plaintiff acquired all of this land with its clay and limestone for the purpose of manufacturing cement; the plaintiff's process of manufacturing, for all purposes incident to the valuation and assessment of its personal property for taxation, commences with the digging and removing of the limestone and clay from its quarries and fields; the plaintiff's average inventories of finished cement and goods in process of manufacturing should be valued for assessment purposes under the laws of Iowa upon the basis of the value of the limestone and clay entering into such inventories before the same were quarried and removed by plaintiff from its limestone and clay fields, that is upon the basis of 5.42 cents per ton for limestone and 8.42 cents per ton for clay.

Based upon valuations determined in this way, plaintiff alleged in its petition that the barrels and tons of limestone, clay, and clinker, listed above were of a taxable or assessed value of but $8,840, instead of $25,560, the 60% valuation fixed by the assessor. * * *

Section 428.4, Code 1950, I.C.A., provides: "Property shall be taxed each year, and personal property shall be listed and assessed each year in the name of the owner thereof on the first day of January. Real estate shall be listed and valued in 1933 and every four years thereafter, *and in each year in which real estate is not regularly assessed, the assessor shall list and assess any real property not included in the previous assessment,* and also any buildings erected since the previous assessment, * * *." (Italics ours.)

Section 428.20, Code 1950, I.C.A., is: " 'Manufacturer' defined— duty to list. Any person, firm, or corporation who purchases, receives, or holds personal property of any description for the purpose of adding to the value thereof by any process of manufacturing, refining, purifying, combining of different materials, or by the packing of meats, with a view to selling the same for gain or profit, shall be deemed a manufacturer for the purposes of this title (Taxation), and shall list such property for taxation."

Section 428.21, Code 1950, I.C.A., is: "Assessment—how made. Such personal property, whether in a finished or unfinished state, shall be assessed at the same ratio as provided in section 441.13 of its average value estimated upon those materials only which enter into the combination, manufacture, or pack, such average to be ascertained as in section 428.17."

Section 428.22, Code 1950, I.C.A., is: "Machinery deemed real estate. Machinery used in manufacturing establishments shall, for the purpose of taxation, be regarded as real estate."

* * * This new machinery and equipment costing approximately a million dollars was installed in 1949 after January 1st, and in 1950. For the purpose of taxation it was regarded as real estate, as provid-

ed in section 428.22, supra.   These matters are conceded by both parties.

The year 1949 was the year for assessing real estate. Since the new machinery and equipment was not in the plant "as of January 1st", no part of it was assessed as real estate in 1949. The installation was completed in 1950 but none of this property was assessed in that year.   In 1951, since this new machinery and new equipment was deemed real estate for taxation, it was assessed as provided in the italicized lines in the copy of section 428.4, supra, as "any real property not included in the previous assessment".   It was the position of the plaintiff before the Board and the trial court, and is on this appeal, that this property was assessable only in the years in which real estate was regularly assessed, and that it could not be assessed in any other year, since it was not in fact, "real property".   For this reason plaintiff insists that the assessment in 1951 be cancelled, in its entirety, as invalid.

* * *

* * * Peter Andersen, Secretary-Treasurer and a Director of plaintiff, who had previously testified for it, was recalled by it, and asked to state what the books of plaintiff showed was the total cost of the new machinery and equipment which was added to the plant of the plaintiff during the years 1949 and 1950. His answer was $1,-022,343.01. * * * [H]e was asked to state what portion of this amount was to replace worn-out machinery and equipment, and what portion was to install machinery and equipment for a new use or function.   Accepting his testimony as given—and it would have been difficult to refute it—the amounts spent for the last-stated purpose, were $10,768.45 for new additions to the plant water system; $87,734.36 for air separators, "which did not replace machinery and equipment which was formerly in the plant.   These air separators performed a new and different function from any machinery and equipment in the plant at the time they were installed."   Continuing, the witness said: "The next item are [sic] the dust collectors for $77,733.31.   These dust collectors did not replace machinery and equipment which were in the Mason City plant. * * * The next item is for a truck-turn-around at the crusher building for $15,567.40.   This truck-turn-around did not replace machinery and equipment which was formerly in the plant."   These items of new machinery and equipment which had never been in the plant until 1949 and 1950, and which replaced no old or used machinery and equipment cost the plaintiff $191,803.52. The trial court found the amount of this new and additional machinery and equipment to be $51,402.70, but gave no figures to justify it. We find no evidence in the record to sustain such finding.

Mr. William Clemenshaw, an appraisal expert whose company has its headquarters in Cleveland, Ohio, and who had been employed by the three taxing bodies of Mason City to appraise the taxable real estate in 1949, and the taxable personal property in 1950, for the 1951 assessment year, was a witness for defendant after the reopening of the case. He testified that in 1949 and 1950 he had discussed with

Mr. Andersen the appraisal of plaintiff's property, and the latter had given him audits of the company for those years, and that he made typewritten notes from these audits to aid him in the appraisal. These notes, Exhibit No. 20, were received in evidence. The total of the items of expenditures for new machinery and equipment as shown in these notes was $1,144,711.98, but after rechecking the various items and eliminating some that he thought should not be considered, he testified that: "I came to the conclusion that the total additions in the years 1949 and 1950 was a total of $991,116.19. That was the total cost of the additions." His familiarity with the old machinery and equipment was not sufficient to enable him to know what part of the new installations replaced old machinery and what part was newly added, so that he gave no testimony in that respect. He did not discuss this matter with Mr. Andersen. It is apparent that neither Mr. Andersen nor Mr. Clemenshaw gave any consideration to the trial court's theory.

Mr. Clemenshaw testified as to how he arrived at the figure of $297,334, which he recommended to the assessor, as the proper 1951 assessment for the new machinery and equipment that was installed in 1949 and 1950. He took into consideration that "the cost trend of machinery and new equipment averaged about 100 per cent higher than the values that were used in these appraisals at the time they were made in 1948." He was also asked whether he made an adjustment on the basis that some of this machinery was replacing old machinery. He answered: "Yes. * * * As I said before we did not make a piece meal inventory of each item of machinery and equipment because time did not permit * * *; but it was generally known that much of the machinery and equipment of the cement plant was very inadequate and antiquated and in our opinion had probably been written off the books many years ago. Most of it was living on borrowed time, and it was now being replaced with something new, and it was undepreciated * * *." Taking into consideration the higher trend in prices and the worn-out and obsolescent condition of the old equipment and machinery and its depreciated value because thereof, as evidenced in the 1949 assessment of real property, he testified he reduced his total figure of $991,116.19 by 50 per cent, thus reducing it to $45,558.09, and then took 60% thereof to arrive at the taxable valuation of $297,334.85, which he recommended to the assessor.

I. The plaintiff does not question the fairness of the amount of this assessment, but it contends that since it is regarded as real estate for the purpose of taxation, it could be assessed and taxed only in the regular, every-fourth, year, in which real estate property is assessed and taxed, and that the assessment of it in the year 1951, which was not a regular year for taxing real estate, was therefore illegal and void.

Code section 428.22, I.C.A., supra, provides that machinery used in manufacturing establishments shall be regarded as real estate for taxation purposes. The property assessed in 1951 was of that description. It must be deemed real estate, or regarded as such, in its assessment and taxation. It was real estate within the purview and purpose of Code, section 428.4, I.C.A., supra. It had never been assessed until the year 1951, so that for the purpose of taxation—and that is the only purpose of said section 428.4—it was "any real property not included in the previous assessment", as provided in said section. In the assessment of 1951, it was to be considered and assessed for taxation just the same as any land, improved or unimproved, "not included in the previous assessment" in 1949. Such a construction or interpretation is clearly and fairly applicable to the quoted language of the section, and such an intent on the part of the Legislature is plainly and reasonably expressed therein. Unless excepted or exempted it is the established law of this state that all property is to be taxed. Cherry v. Board of Review, 238 Iowa 189. It is to be presumed that in enacting tax laws, the Legislature so intended, if the language used fairly expresses such intention. Assuredly, it must not be presumed that any legislature intended to enact laws permitting the nullification of such recognized rule of law. In the instant case the plaintiff installed the new machinery in 1949 to the approximate value of $769,-000, and in 1950, of $220,169. If the contention of the plaintiff is the law of this state, then the state will be deprived of taxes on the machinery installed in 1949, for the years 1950, 1951 and 1952 and for that installed in 1950, for the years 1951 and 1952. Under such statutory construction as the plaintiff urges upon the court, manufacturers will confine their installation of new machinery to the regular year for assessing real estate, so as to avoid the largest possible tax burden. It is our conclusion that the Legislature did not so intend and did not so enact that such an enormous escape from taxes should be permitted to manufacturers.

  * * * In support of the construction contended for by defendant, Louis H. Cook was a witness in its behalf. For thirteen years he had been Director of Research for the Iowa State Tax Commission, and before that he was Chairman of the original Iowa State Tax Commission, beginning in 1929. He has devoted his adult life to the study of tax problems. He was familiar with the tax laws of Iowa and to [sic] interpretations placed upon them by the Tax Commission and by tax officers. The Tax Commission has supervision over all matters relating to tax assessments and collections in Iowa. He testified that it has been the interpretation of the Commission and of himself that new machinery installed in a manufacturing plant in some year other than a year for the regular assessment of real estate, shall be listed and assessed by the assessor or by the Board of Review as real estate not previously listed and assessed in a regular year for the assessment of real estate. Plaintiff offered no evidence to the contrary.

It is the contention of plaintiff that it is not liable for any taxes under the assessment of $297,334 for new machinery, because such assessment is illegal and void. The trial court decreed that $245,931.-50 of said assessment was improper because new machinery in that amount was purchased and installed to replace worn-out and obsolete machinery which theretofore had been valued and assessed for the purposes of taxation, and the sum of $51,402.70, of the assessment represented new machinery added to the plant to perform functions not theretofore performed. The court held the latter amount was a properly assessed valuation.

It was the court's expressed reasoning that the assessment of the machinery in 1949 would carry forward for four years and its deterioration and obsolescence would probably substantially balance the replacement of new machinery. It does not appear to this court probable that the old machinery would depreciate from 1949 to 1950, both inclusive, to the extent of almost a million dollars, the approximate cost of the new additions.

The court also said: "Also, since old machines in plaintiff's plant in 1949 were included in the valuation of plaintiff's machinery for the next succeeding four years, to add a new machine replacing such old machine during the four year period, and also adding the taxable value of the new machine in the year following its installation, would result in the plaintiff being taxed upon the old machine which had been removed from the plant, and also the new machine at the same time, thereby resulting in double taxation of the plaintiff."

We cannot follow the able trial court all the way. Double taxation is twice taxing the same identical property. The assessor and the Board did not do that. In 1949 they assessed, as real estate, worn out and obsolescent machines—some installed in 1920. That assessment was placed against machinery of a greatly depreciated value— much of it charged off on the books of plaintiff in years past. But in 1951 the valuation and assessment was on different machinery— neither old, inadequate, nor antiquated—but on new, up-to-date machinery and equipment, purchased at high prices. The assessment on machinery of that high value ought not be offset and obliterated almost entirely as was done by the trial court. It allowed an assessment of $51,402.70 on machinery which was not replacement, which amount we find should have been $191,803.52, were we to follow the trial court's theory with respect to non-replacement machinery. But we do concede that the value of a new machine in the 1951 assessment should not be added to the 1949 assessment of the old machine, but that the 1951 assessment should replace the 1949 assessment of the old machine. In other words, that the latter assessment should be deducted from the 1951 assessment. That is just what Mr. Clemenshaw effected in arriving at the assessment on this new machinery, which he recommended to the assessor. He considered that the new machinery was bought at appreciated prices, 100% above what was paid for the old machinery, and that most of the old machinery "was living on borrowed time", and of greatly depreciated value. He made a compromise adjustment between the two to arrive at a 60% assessed, or taxable, valuation of $297,344 on this new machinery. It is our conclusion that the trial court erred in confirming but $51,402.70 of this assessment and that the entire assessment of $297,344, as fixed by the assessor and sustained by the Board, should have been confirmed by the district court.

We here note that the district court, in confirming the assessment in the amount of $51,402.70, agreed with the defendant, that new machinery regarded as real estate, not assessed in a previous year, could be assessed in a year other than a regular year for assessing real estate, as provided in Code section 428.4, I.C.A., supra. Such is the conclusion of this court.

* * *

II. We return now to the first protest—the one against the assessment of the finished cement and the material in process of manufacture. The assessor assessed the personal property, and the Board sustained it, on the basis of the limestone broken to pieces five-inches wide or less, delivered from the quarries to the primary stone crusher at the manufacturing plant, and on the value of the clay as it is delivered to the plant from the clay pits. Limestone, clay, and gypsum are the component parts of cement. Plaintiff has no gypsum and buys it F. O. B. Fort Dodge, and pays the freight on it delivered to its plant. We note here that in its estimated values of the component parts of manufactured cement, it did not include the value of the gypsum.

Plaintiff insists that the limestone and clay should not be valued as these products are delivered at the mill, after the limestone has been dynamited out of the place where Nature or other Higher Power placed it or it was formed, and it has been broken into small pieces and loaded into dummy railroad cars, or into motor trucks and conveyed to the plant; and that the clay should not be valued after it has been excavated from the pits and loaded and conveyed to the plant in like manner, to the limestone.

Plaintiff contends that this raw material should not be valued as "personal property" as stated in Code section 428.21, I.C.A., supra, after its value has been increased by the application of dynamite, tools, machinery, for quarrying, loading, conveyance to the mill, and the labors of men, all of which were required to make it available for the actual manufacture of cement, but that this value for the determination of the cost and value of the finished cement, or of ingredients in the process of manufacture, should be made of them, not as personal property, but in their natural condition as parts of the earth. In other words, as real estate or land, unchanged by artificial means.

Mr. Cook, hereinbefore referred to, testified that he was familiar with Code sections 428.20 and 428.21 of the 1950 Code, I.C.A., dealing with the assessment of materials of manufacturers; and that the Tax Commission and he have interpreted those sections to require the valuations of materials going into the manufacture of finished products and material in process, to be made at the point immediately prior to the first manufacturing operation; and that the word "material" as so interpreted means usable material immediately prior to the first manufacturing operation; that "material" does not necessarily mean the absolutely raw or crude product, but it may and often does include such products after their value has been increased by labor and machinery or other artificial change. Such interpretation had been employed by the Tax Commission for a period of over twenty years. Andrew S. St. Regis, Chief Deputy Assessor for Des Moines gave similar testimony. He testified that he had so valued and assessed materials of various kinds in the manufacture of different kinds of finished products, including cement. No testimony was offered to the contrary by the plaintiff.

Testimony of the kind given by these witnesses of defendant is entitled to much weight by courts, and where the administrative interpretation of a statute is of long standing it will not be lightly discarded. * * *

The fact that labor may have increased the value or form of the original raw matter is not material. The hide of the animal is raw material to the tanner, but leather is raw material to the manufacturer of shoes or other leather goods. * * *

The gypsum which plaintiff uses in the manufacture of its cement is purchased by it at Fort Dodge and shipped to Mason City. Of course, plaintiff pays for the cost of its production and conveyance to its plant, and all elements of its costs are factors in determining the value of the finished cement. Likewise the cost of getting its limestone and clay to its crushers, is increased by the labor in getting it there, and that labor of man and machine is a factor in determining the assessed value of the finished or unfinished product. The quarrying of the stone and the digging of the clay, and conveying it to the cement mill is merely making this material available for its manufacturing process at its factory. It is no more a part of the manufacture than the procuring of the gypsum from Fort Dodge. But whether it be limestone or clay made available by the labor of its own employees and machines, and other equipment, or it be gypsum which it buys from another, the cost of getting all of it to the entrance of its mill is a proper factor in determining its assessed value, and the assessed value of the cement.

The trial court sustained the Board in denying plaintiff's protest against the assessment of this material, and its conclusions of law, saying: "In so far as the valuation of the material entering into the manufacture of the finished product, for instance cement, is concerned it would not make any difference whether the clay or limestone was purchased from others, dug from plaintiff's own clay pit or from its own limestone quarry, or were given to the plaintiff without charge. In all three instances these materials should be valued on the ground ready to be placed in the primary crusher. The statutes in question are taxation statutes and should be uniformly applied, regardless of the source or method of acquiring such materials."

The decree of the court in sustaining the assessment of the finished cement, and the materials in process of manufacture, as fixed by the assessor and sustained by the Board of Review, in the sum of $25,560 is affirmed, and the cause is remanded to the District Court for judgment and decree in conformity herewith on each protest of plaintiff, to the end that the assessment of $25,560 noted just above, and the assessment of $297,344 are each sustained.

* * *

The judgment and decree is

Reversed in part and affirmed in part.

All Justices concur.

C. CONDEMNATION OF PROPERTY

CITY OF HOUSTON v. BIGGERS

Court of Civil Appeals of Texas, 1964.
380 S.W.2d 700, cert. denied, 380 U.S. 962.

BELL, Chief Justice. This is an appeal from a judgment in a condemnation case awarding appellant title to 128,520 square feet of land in the City of Houston and giving appellees recovery against appellant for $1,157,615.00 which was the value of the land as determined by a jury.

Appellant complains that the trial court erred in not granting its motion to dismiss the case which motion was made after verdict but prior to the rendition of judgment. The position of appellees is that because of the acts on the part of appellant hereinafter noticed there had been "a taking" of the property before the motion to dismiss was made and the point of no return had therefore been reached by appellant.

On April 3, 1962, the Judge of the court, in response to a petition filed by appellant, appointed commissioners to determine the value of appellees' property. The property was to be acquired by appellant as a part of the "Civic Center." After hearing, the commissioners, on June 22, 1962, made their award and it was filed with the judge July 6, 1962. On the same day appellees filed their objections to the award. Trial of the case in court commenced March 25, 1963. The jury returned its verdict March 29, 1963. On April 3, 1963, the City Council passed a motion authorizing the City Attorney to dismiss the case and directing him to prepare an ordinance eliminating appellees' property from the "Civic Center." On April 4 the motion to dismiss the case was filed. It recited the action of the Council in determining not to purchase the property at the value assessed and to exclude the property from the Civic Center and authorizing dismissal of the case.

On April 19 appellees filed an answer to the motion to dismiss and made a motion for judgment on the verdict. The basis of the opposition was that because of the appellant's acts with regard to the property, which we will specifically notice when we review the evidence given on the motion, appellees would be prejudiced by dismissal.

On April 19 appellant filed an amended motion to dismiss which attached a copy of an ordinance passed April 17 purporting to exclude the property from the Civic Center.

A hearing was commenced on the motion to dismiss on April 19, at which evidence was introduced, but it was not completed and was recessed until April 26. However, the court rendered judgment on the verdict April 19. At that time, as evidenced by the judgment signed by the court, appellant excepted to the judgment, and it was also recited therein that the motion to dismiss had been filed.

On April 26 the hearing on the motion to dismiss was resumed and at that time appellant filed what it denominated "Motion to Set Aside Judgment and Enter Judgment of Dismissal." It added an ordinance of April 24 passed by the City Council which definitely excluded appellees' land from the Civic Center. After further evidence was introduced the motion to dismiss was overruled.

The evidence on the motion to dismiss reflected without dispute that appellant had never taken physical possession of the property or any part thereof and that no deposit of the amount of the award made by the commissioners had ever been made so as to give appellant the right to possession. It showed that September 23, 1958, the City Council passed an ordinance determining that "Public necessity and convenience required the designation and protection of the Civic Center." The Civic Center was then designated as covering a defined area including appellees' land. It further provided that within the area no new structures would be permitted to be built and no repairs to existing structures would be permitted where the cost of the repairs in one calendar year exceeded 25% of the value of the structure repaired. The Director of Public Works and Engineering was directed to refuse any permit to build new structures or to make repairs contrary to the ordinance.

Mr. Ross Biggers, one of the appellees, testified that since the passage of the ordinance appellees had made repairs to the existing structure by putting on a new roof. He had made no application for any permit for a new structure. There is no evidence that appellees contemplated any new structure or additions to the existing structure. Appellee operated a printing business on the property. The operations, including the use of the building and parking facilities, utilized an estimated 5% of the property. Appellees at no time sought amendment of the ordinance to exclude their property. It appears that prior to 1961 the City assessed the property for taxes at a relatively small amount ,and beginning in 1961 raised the valuation from $6,950.00 to $217,000.00. Mr. Biggers made it clear that all values for tax purposes, both before and including the increase, were those fixed by the City and not appellees. The owners did not render the property nor was there any appeal to the Board of Equalization. In 1961, when there was this great increase Mr. Biggers appeared before the City Council to protest the increase when he could not utilize the property further because of the ordinance and increase his revenue. He did not, he testified, appear to protest that the amount of the increase exceeded what was a fair value for tax purposes. At that time someone on the Council told him not to worry, the City was going to take the property.

The evidence showed that at times after the passage of the ordinance of September, 1958, appellees had had various people who were interested in negotiating for purchase of the property but ended negotiations when it was learned the property was under threat of condemnation. It should be stated that appellant had the ordinance creating the Civic Center filed in the Deed Records of Harris County. The ordinance in fact directed the City Secretary to file a certified copy with the County Clerk. One advertiser wanted to lease space from appellees for a sign at $500.00 per month but lost interest when he learned of the threat of condemnation. It does not appear just when this interest was shown but the letters introduced in evidence are dated in 1961 and 1962.

As above stated, the City Council, by motion, on April 3, 1963, directed dismissal of the suit and the preparation of an ordinance excluding this property. An ordinance, which is numbered 63–544, was passed April 17, 1963. In the ordinance it was found by the Council that the value as found by the jury exceeded the benefit that would result to the public from acquisition of the property. Section 2 of the ordinance recites that the Council finds and determines that the ordinance of September 23, 1958 (Ordinance No. 58–1033) should be amended so as to exclude this property. It directed the City Secretary to file a certified copy for record with the County Clerk. It was purportedly passed as an emergency measure. Appellees contend this ordinance did not take effect immediately because not shown [sic] to have been supported by the proper number of Councilmen. Also, they contend, it merely declares the land should be excluded but does not specifically enact that it is thereby excluded. On April 24 the Council passed Ordinance No. 63–560, which definitely excluded appellees' land.

In testifying as to value in the condemnation hearing before the jury, Mr. Ross Biggers, one of the appellees, testified the property had a market value of $1,285,200.00, or $10.00 per square foot. One of appellees' experts testified the same and another testified to $1,250,-000.00. Mr. Jungman, one of appellees' experts, testified for several years there had been a rising market and gave as his opinion that the property in the area was increasing at about 16% per annum. Mr. Biggers testified he would rather have the property than get $10.00 per square foot for it.

Appellees' position is that because of the facts detailed the court was correct in overruling the motion to dismiss. The foundation for such is their contention as follows:

1. The passage of Ordinance No. 58–1033 and its continuance in force until the ordinance of April 24, 1963 effected a "taking" of the property.

2. They would be prejudiced because they had been unable to negotiate for the sale or additional use of the property that might entail additional structures.

3. They had been put to expense in connection with the proceedings.

4. Appellant could, after dismissing the suit, refile and possibly get a lower award. In this connection they seem to assert this is the real purpose in seeking to dismiss. In other words, they challenge the good faith of appellant.

We are of the view that the court was in error in not sustaining the appellant's motion to dismiss.

The rule is well settled in Texas that a condemnor may elect to dismiss a condemnation proceeding at any time prior to judgment if there has been no taking of possession of the property under and by virtue of acquiring the right to possession under an order in a condemnation proceeding or under an agreement with the condemnee pending the proceedings. Brazos River Conservation and Reclamation Dist. v. Allen, 141 Tex. 208, 171 S.W.2d 842 * * *.

In many of the cited cases the expression is used that there may be dismissal where the landowner "will not be prejudiced." It was then held there was no legal prejudice in any of them except those where prior to attempted dismissal there was actual physical possession under and by virtue of condemnation proceedings, or, possession by agreement pending condemnation and at the time of attempted dismissal possession had not been returned or offered to be returned.

In this case it is undisputed that appellant at no time had possession of the land or any part thereof.

The passage of the ordinance including the land in what was contemplated as a Civic Center did not, as appellees contend, constitute a taking. The act was purely legislative and could be changed at any time. Even though it might have, as a practical matter, interfered with the marketability of the property, it would cause but an incidental damage which is not compensable. The fact that at some future time land might be taken under eminent domain, even where the threatened taking is imminent, is but one of the conditions on which an owner holds property.

In the case of State v. Vaughan, 319 S.W.2d 349 (Tex.C.C.A.), no writ history, the State of Texas sued to condemn residence property that was used by the owners to lease to tenants. The property was within the area that had been designated under authority of statute, by the State Building Commission, as the area where property would be acquired for the construction of State buildings. The Executive Director wrote the owners a letter notifying them of the intent to condemn the property. Tenants, knowing of this, began to move. In the case the owners sought to recover as an element of damage the loss of rental caused by the threat of condemnation. The court denied recovery, holding the action occasioning the vacation by tenants did not constitute a "taking" because there was no physical invasion by the condemnor.

* * *

Appellees urge they were prejudiced because the threat of condemnation by virtue of the ordinance prevented negotiations for sale and prevented their effective use of the property except for about 5% of the area. This would be but an incidental damage that is not compensable. In this connection, however, it is noticed that the evidence shows such repairs as appellees wished to make on their property they were permitted to make. They apparently did not wish to make any additional improvements because they made no application for a permit to build. Mr. Biggers did testify they took the Council at its word that no permit for building would be issued. We have no doubt that had appellees desired to build but did not do so because they felt they could not get a permit, Mr. Biggers would have so testified. If appellees had desired to do so they had their remedy, in spite of the ordinance, by mandamus. Kirschke v. City of Houston, 330 S.W.2d 629 (Tex.C.C.A.), ref., n. r. e. It would be purely speculative to say that appellees were deprived of any sale by interference with the right to negotiate. There is nothing to suggest an agreement would have probably been reached between appellees and a prospective purchaser. In the absence of such we are unable to see how any damage could be shown with any certainty. Too, it is noted the evidence shows there was a rising market in the area where appellees' property is located. They still have their property and Mr. Ross Biggers testified he had [sic] rather have the property than the $1,285,200.00 that he testified it was worth. The award was less than this.

* * *

Finally, appellees seem to challenge the good faith of the City in contending the City can refile the suit and they suggest the purpose of the City in dismissing was to avoid the high award of the jury and then to refile suit. There is no evidence to support such a suggestion. As related above, the City Council immediately after the verdict directed dismissal of the suit and preparation of an ordinance eliminating the area from the Civic Center. Then they, on April 17 passed an ordinance declaring it should be eliminated. We need not discuss whether it was in form sufficient to actually accomplish abandonment because it certainly evidences the Council's intention to abandon. Then when its sufficiency for that purpose was challenged, on April 24 an ordinance certainly sufficient was passed. It is true that the court excluded this ordinance, and we think erroneously, on the ground it was passed after the hearing on the motion to dismiss had commenced. However, it was passed prior to the completion of the hearing. It is true also that it was passed after judgment had been rendered on the verdict. However, the motion to dismiss was pending when the judgment was rendered and was being actively prosecuted by appellant. Too, the judgment was rendered before completion of the hearing on the motion to dismiss over appellant's objection as evidenced by its exception contained in the judgment and at a time when the court recessed the hearing on the motion to dismiss. We think this evidences rendition of the judgment without prejudice to appellant's motion to dismiss.

The judgment of the trial court is reversed with directions to the trial court to enter an order dismissing the case.

D. ZONING

VILLAGE OF EUCLID, OHIO v. AMBLER REALTY CO.

Supreme Court of the United States, 1926.
272 U.S. 365, 47 S.Ct. 114, 71 L.Ed. 307.

Mr. Justice SUTHERLAND delivered the opinion of the Court.

* * *

Appellee is the owner of a tract of land containing 68 acres, situated in the westerly end of the village, abutting on Euclid avenue to the south and the Nickel Plate Railroad to the north. Adjoining this tract, both on the east and on the west, there have been laid out restricted residential plats upon which residences have been erected.

On November 13, 1922, an ordinance was adopted by the village council, establishing a comprehensive zoning plan for regulating and restricting the location of trades, industries, apartment houses, two-family houses, single family houses, etc., the lot area to be built upon, the size and height of buildings, etc.

The entire area of the village is divided by the ordinance into six classes of use districts, denominated U–1 to U–6, inclusive; three classes of height districts, denominated H–1 to H–3, inclusive; and four classes of area districts, denominated A–1 to A–4, inclusive. The use districts are classified in respect of the buildings which may be erected within their respective limits, as follows: U–1 is restricted to single family dwellings, public parks, water towers and reservoirs, suburban and interurban electric railway passenger stations and rights of way, and farming, noncommercial greenhouse nurseries, and truck gardening; U–2 is extended to include two-family dwellings; U–3 is further extended to include apartment houses, hotels, churches, schools, public libraries, museums, private clubs, community center buildings, hospitals, sanitariums, public playgrounds, and recreation buildings, and a city hall and courthouse; U–4 is further extended to include banks, offices, studios, telephone exchanges, fire and police stations, restaurants, theaters and moving picture shows, retail stores and shops, sales offices, sample rooms, wholesale stores for hardware, drugs, and groceries, stations for gasoline and oil (not exceeding 1,000 gallons storage) and for ice delivery, skating rinks and dance halls, electric substations, job and newspaper printing, public garages for motor vehicles, stables and wagon sheds (not exceeding five horses, wagons or motor trucks), and distributing stations for central store and commercial enterprises; U–5 is further extended to include billboards and advertising signs (if permitted), warehouses, ice and ice cream manufacturing and cold storage plants, bottling works, milk bottling and central distribution stations, laundries, carpet cleaning, dry cleaning, and dyeing establishments, blacksmith, horseshoeing, wagon and motor vehicle repair shops, freight stations, street car barns, stables and wagon sheds (for more than five horses, wagons or motor trucks), and wholesale produce markets and salesrooms; U–6 is further extended to include plants for sewage disposal and for producing gas, garbage and refuse incineration, scrap iron, junk, scrap paper, and rag storage, aviation fields, cemeteries, crematories, penal and correctional institutions, insane and feeble-minded institutions, storage of oil and gasoline (not to exceed 25,000 gallons), and manufacturing and industrial operations of any kind other than, and any public utility not included in, a class U–1, U–2, U–3, U–4, or U–5 use. There is a seventh class of uses which is prohibited altogether.

Class U–1 is the only district in which buildings are restricted to those enumerated. In the other classes the uses are cumulative— that is to say, uses in class U–2 include those enumerated in the preceding class U–1; class U–3 includes uses enumerated in the preceding classes, U–2 and U–1; and so on. In addition to the enumerated uses, the ordinance provides for accessory uses; that is, for uses customarily incident to the principal use, such as private garrages. Many regulations are provided in respect of such accessory uses.

The height districts are classified as follows: In class H–1, buildings are limited to a height of 2½ stories, or 35 feet; in class H–2, to 4 stories, or 50 feet; in class H–3, to 80 feet. To all of these, certain exceptions are made, as in the case of church spires, water tanks, etc.

The classification of area districts is: In A–1 districts, dwellings or apartment houses to accommodate more than one family must have at least 5,000 square feet for interior lots and at least 4,000 square feet for corner lots; in A–2 districts, the area must be at least 2,500 square feet for interior lots, and 2,000 square feet for corner lots; in A–3 districts, the limits are 1,250 and 1,000 square feet, respectively; in A–4 districts, the limits are 900 and 700 square feet, respectively. The ordinance contains, in great variety and detail, provisions in respect of width of lots, front, side, and rear yards, and other matters, including restrictions and regulations as to the use of billboards, signboards, and advertising signs.

* * *

Appellee's tract of land comes under U–2, U–3 and U–6. The first strip of 620 feet immediately north of Euclid avenue falls in class U–2, the next 130 feet to the north, in U–3, and the remainder in U–6. The uses of the first 620 feet, therefore, do not include apartment houses, hotels, churches, schools, or other public and semipublic buildings, or other uses enumerated in respect of U–3 to U–6, inclusive. The uses of the next 130 feet include all of these, but exclude industries, theaters, banks, shops, and the various other uses set forth in respect of U–4 to U–6, inclusive.

* * *

The ordinance is assailed on the grounds that it is in derogation of section 1 of the Fourteenth Amendment to the federal Constitution in that it deprives appellee of liberty and property without due process of law and denies it the equal protection of the law, and that it offends against certain provisions of the Constitution of the state of Ohio. The prayer of the bill is for an injunction restraining the enforcement of the ordinance and all attempts to impose or maintain as to appellee's property any of the restrictions, limitations or conditions. The court below held the ordinance to be unconstitutional and void, and enjoined its enforcement. 297 F. 307.

Before proceeding to a consideration of the case, it is necessary to determine the scope of the inquiry. The bill alleges that the tract of land in question is vacant and has been held for years for the purpose of selling and developing it for industrial uses, for which it is especially adapted, being immediately in the path of progressive industrial development; that for such uses it has a market value of about $10,000 per acre, but if the use be limited to residential purposes the market value is not in excess of $2,500 per acre; that the first 200 feet of the parcel back from Euclid avenue, if unrestricted in respect of use, has a value of $150 per front foot, but if limited to residential uses, and ordinary mercantile business be excluded therefrom, its value is not in excess of $50 per front foot.

It is specifically averred that the ordinance attempts to restrict and control the lawful uses of appellee's land, so as to confiscate and destroy a great part of its value; that it is being enforced in accordance with its terms; that prospective buyers of land for industrial, commercial, and residential uses in the metropolitan district of Cleveland are deterred from buying any part of this land because of the existence of the ordinance and the necessity thereby entailed of conducting burdensome and expensive litigation in order to vindicate the right to use the land for lawful and legitimate purposes; that the ordinance constitutes a cloud upon the land, reduces and destroys its value, and has the effect of diverting the normal industrial, commercial, and residential development thereof to other and less favorable locations.

The record goes no farther than to show, as the lower court found, that the normal and reasonably to be expected use and development of that part of appellee's land adjoining Euclid avenue is for general trade and commercial purposes, particularly retail stores and like establishments, and that the normal and reasonably to be expected use and development of the residue of the land is for industrial and trade purposes. Whatever injury is inflicted by the mere existence and threatened enforcement of the ordinance is due to restrictions in respect of these and similar uses, to which perhaps should be added—if not included in the foregoing—restrictions in respect of apartment houses. Specifically there is nothing in the record to suggest that any damage results from the presence in the ordinance of those restrictions relating to churches, schools, libraries, and other public and semipublic buildings. It is neither alleged nor proved that there is or may be a demand for any part of appellee's land for any of the last-named uses, and we cannot assume the existence of facts which would justify an injunction upon this record in respect to this class of restrictions. For present purposes the provisions of the ordinance in respect of these uses may therefore be put aside as unnecessary to be considered. It is also unnecessary to consider the effect of the restrictions in respect of U–1 districts, since none of appellee's land falls within that class.

We proceed, then, to a consideration of those provisions of the ordinance to which the case as it is made relates, first disposing of a preliminary matter.

A motion was made in the court below to dismiss the bill on the ground that, because complainant (appellee) had made no effort to obtain a building permit or apply to the zoning board of appeals for relief, as it might have done under the terms of the ordinance, the suit was premature. The motion was properly overruled, the effect of the allegations of the bill is that the ordinance of its own force operates greatly to reduce the value of appellee's lands and destroy their marketability for industrial, commercial and residential uses, and the attack is directed, not against any specific provision or provisions, but against the ordinance as an entirety. Assuming the premises, the existence and maintenance of the ordinance in effect constitutes a present invasion of appellee's property rights and a threat to continue it. Under these circumstances, the equitable jurisdiction is clear. See Terrace v. Thompson, 263 U.S. 197; Pierce v. Society of Sisters, 268 U.S. 510.

* * * The question is * * * as stated by appellee: Is the ordinance invalid, in that it violates the constitutional protection "to the right of property in the appellee by attempted regulations under the guise of the police power, which are unreasonable and confiscatory"?

Building zone laws are of modern origin. They began in this country about 25 years ago. Until recent years, urban life was comparatively simple; but, with the great increase and concentration of population, problems have developed, and constantly are developing, which require, and will continue to require, additional restrictions in respect of the use and occupation of private lands in urban communities. Regulations, the wisdom, necessity, and validity of which, as applied to existing conditions, are so apparent that they are now uniformly sustained, a century ago, or even half a century ago, probably would have been rejected as arbitrary and oppressive. Such regulations are sustained, under the complex conditions of our day, for reasons analogous to those which justify traffic regulations, which, before the advent of automobiles and rapid transit street railways, would have been condemned as fatally arbitrary and unreasonable. And in this there is no inconsistency, for, while the meaning of constitutional guaranties never varies, the scope of their application must expand or contract to meet the new and different conditions which are constantly coming within the field of their operation. In a changing world it is impossible that it should be otherwise. But although a degree of elasticity is thus imparted, not to the *meaning,* but to the *application* of constitutional principles, statutes and ordinances, which, after giving due weight to the new conditions, are found clearly not to conform to the Constitution, of course, must fall.

The ordinance now under review, and all similar laws and regulations, must find their justification in some aspect of the police power, asserted for the public welfare. The line which in this field separates the legitimate from the illegitimate assumption of power is not capable of precise delimitation. It varies with circumstances and conditions. A regulatory zoning ordinance, which would be clearly valid as applied to the great cities, might be clearly invalid as applied to rural communities. * * * Thus the question whether the power exists to forbid the erection of a building of a particular kind or for a particular use, like the question whether a particular thing is a nuisance, is to be determined, not by an abstract consideration of the building or of the thing considered apart, but by considering it in connection with the circumstances and the locality. Sturgis v. Bridgeman, L.R. 11 Ch. 852. A nuisance may be merely a right thing in the wrong place, like a pig in the parlor instead of the barnyard. If the validity of the legislative classification for zoning purposes be fairly debatable, the legislative judgment must be allowed to control. Radice v. New York, 264 U.S. 292.

There is no serious difference of opinion in respect of the validity of laws and regulations fixing the height of buildings within reasonable limits, the character of materials and methods of construction, and the adjoining area which must be left open, in order to minimize the danger of fire or collapse, the evils of overcrowding and the like, and excluding from residential sections offensive trades, industries and structures likely to create nuisances. See Welch v. Swasey, 214 U.S. 91 * * *.

Here, however, the exclusion is in general terms of all industrial establishments, and it may thereby happen that not only offensive or dangerous industries will be excluded, but those which are neither offensive nor dangerous will share the same fate. But this is no more than happens in respect of many practice-forbidding laws which this court has upheld, although drawn in general terms so as to include individual cases that may turn out to be innocuous in themselves. * * * The inclusion of a reasonable margin, to insure effective enforcement, will not put upon a law, otherwise valid, the stamp of invalidity. Such laws may also find their justification in the fact that, in some fields, the bad fades into the good by such insensible degrees that the two are not capable of being readily distinguished and separated in terms of legislation. In the light of these considerations, we are not prepared to say that the end in view was not sufficient to justify the general rule of the ordinance, although some industries of an innocent character might fall within the proscribed class. It cannot be said that the ordinance in this respect "passes the bounds of reason and assumes the character of a merely arbitrary fiat." Purity Extract Co. v. Lynch, 226 U.S. 192. Moreover, the restrictive provisions of the ordinance in this particular may be sustained upon the principles applicable to the broader exclusion from residential districts of all business and trade structures, presently to be discussed.

It is said that the village of Euclid is a mere suburb of the city of Cleveland; that the industrial development of that city has now reached and in some degree extended into the village, and in the obvious course of things will soon absorb the entire area for industrial enterprises; that the effect of the ordinance is to divert this natural development elsewhere, with the consequent loss of increased values to the owners of the lands within the village borders. But the village, though physically a suburb of Cleveland, is politically a separate municipality, with powers of its own and authority to govern itself as it sees fit, within the limits of the organic law of its creation and the state and federal Constitutions. Its governing authorities, presumably representing a majority of its inhabitants and voicing their will, have determined, not that industrial development shall cease at its boundaries, but that the course of such development shall proceed within definitely fixed lines. If it be a proper exercise of the police power to relegate industrial establishments to localities separated from residential sections, it is not easy to find a sufficient reason for denying the power because the effect of its exercise is to divert an industrial flow from the course which it would follow, to the injury of the residential public, if left alone, to another course where such injury will be obviated. It is not meant by this, however, to exclude the possibility of cases where the general public interest would so far outweigh the interest of the municipality that the municipality would not be allowed to stand in the way.

* * *

The Supreme Court of Illinois * * * in sustaining a comprehensive building zone ordinance dividing the city into eight districts, including exclusive residential districts for one and two-family dwellings, churches, educational institutions, and schools, said:

"The constantly increasing density of our urban populations, the multiplying forms of industry and the growing complexity of our civilization make it necessary for the state, either directly or through some public agency by its sanction, to limit individual activities to a greater extent than formerly. With the growth and development of the state the police power necessarily develops, within reasonable bounds, to meet the changing conditions.
* * *

" * * * The harmless may sometimes be brought within the regulation or prohibition in order to abate or destroy the harmful. The segregation of industries, commercial pursuits, and dwellings to particular districts in a city, when exercised reasonably, may bear a rational relation to the health, morals, safety, and general welfare of the community. The establishment of such districts or zones may, among other things, prevent congestion of population, secure quiet residence districts, expedite local transportation, and facilitate the suppression of disorder, the extinguishment of fires, and the enforcement of traffic and sanitary regulations. The danger of fire and the risk of contagion are often lessened by the exclusion of stores and factories from areas devoted to residences, and, in consequence, the safety and health of the community may be promoted. * * *

" * * * The exclusion of places of business from residential districts is not a declaration that such places are nuisances or that they are to be suppressed as such, but it is a part of the general plan by which the city's territory is allotted to different uses, in order to prevent, or at least to reduce, the congestion, disorder, and dangers which often inhere in unregulated municipal development."

The Supreme Court of Louisiana * * * said:

"In the first place, the exclusion of business establishments from residence districts might enable the municipal government to give better police protection. Patrolmen's beats are larger, and therefore fewer, in residence neighborhoods than in business neighborhoods. A place of business in a residence neighborhood furnishes an excuse for any criminal to go into the neighborhood, where, otherwise, a stranger would be under the ban of suspicion. Besides, open shops invite loiterers and idlers to congregate; and the places of such congregations need police protection. In the second place, the zoning of a city into residence districts and commercial districts is a matter of economy in street paving. Heavy trucks, hauling freight to and from places of business in residence districts, require the city to maintain the same costly pavement in such districts that is required for business districts; whereas, in the residence districts, where business establishments are excluded, a cheaper pavement serves the purpose. * * *

"Aside from considerations of economic administration, in the matter of police and fire protection, street paving, etc., any business establishment is likely to be a genuine nuisance in a neighborhood of residences. Places of business are noisy; they are apt to be disturbing at night; some of them are malodorous; some are unsightly; some are apt to breed rats, mice, roaches, flies, ants, etc. * * *

"If the municipal council deemed any of the reasons which have been suggested, or any other substantial reason, a sufficient reason for adopting the ordinance in question, it is not the province of the courts to take issue with the council. We have nothing to do with the question of the wisdom or good policy of municipal ordinances. If they are not satisfying to a majority of the citizens, their recourse is to the ballot—not the courts."

The matter of zoning has received much attention at the hands of commissions and experts, and the results of their investigations have been set forth in comprehensive reports. These reports, which bear every evidence of painstaking consideration, concur in the view that the segregation of residential, business and industrial buildings will make it easier to provide fire apparatus suitable for the character and intensity of the development in each section; that it will increase the safety and security of home life, greatly tend to prevent street accidents, especially to children, by reducing the traffic and resulting confusion in residential sections, decrease noise and other conditions which produce or intensify nervous disorders, preserve a more favorable environment in which to rear children, etc. With particular reference to apartment houses, it is pointed out that the development of detached house sections is greatly retarded by the coming of apartment houses, which has sometimes resulted in destroying the entire section for private house purposes; that in such sections very often the apartment house is a mere parasite, constructed in order to take advantage of the open spaces and attractive surroundings created by the residential character of the district. Moreover, the coming of one apartment house is followed by others, interfering by their height and bulk with the free circulation of air and monopolizing the rays of the sun which otherwise would fall upon the smaller homes, and bringing, as their necessary accompaniments, the disturbing noises incident to increased traffic and business, and the occupation, by means of moving and parked automobiles, of larger portions of the streets, thus detracting from their safety and depriving children of the privilege of quiet and open spaces for play, enjoyed by those in more favored localities—until, finally, the residential character of the neighborhood and its desirability as a place of detached residences are utterly destroyed. Under these circumstances, apartment houses, which in a different environment would be not only entirely unobjectionable but highly desirable, come very near to being nuisances.

If these reasons, thus summarized, do not demonstrate the wisdom or sound policy in all respects of those restrictions which we have indicated as pertinent to the inquiry, at least, the reasons are sufficiently cogent to preclude us from saying, as it must be said before the ordinance can be declared unconstitutional, that such provisions are clearly arbitrary and unreasonable, having no substantial relation to the public health, safety, morals, or general welfare. * * *

 * * * [W]here the equitable remedy of injunction is sought, as it is here, not upon the ground of a present infringement or denial of a specific right, or of a particular injury in process of actual execution, but upon the broad ground that the mere existence and threat-

ened enforcement of the ordinance, by materially and adversely affecting values and curtailing the opportunities of the market, constitute a present and irreparable injury, the court will not scrutinize its provisions, sentence by sentence, to ascertain by a process of piecemeal dissection whether there may be, here and there, provisions of a minor character, or relating to matters of administration, or not shown to contribute to the injury complained of, which, if attacked separately, might not withstand the test of constitutionality. In respect of such provisions, of which specific complaint is not made, it cannot be said that the landowner has suffered or is threatened with an injury which entitles him to challenge their constitutionality. * * *

The relief sought here is * * * an injunction against the enforcement of any of the restrictions, limitations, or conditions of the ordinance. And the gravamen of the complaint is that a portion of the land of the appellee cannot be sold for certain enumerated uses because of the general and broad restraints of the ordinance. What would be the effect of a restraint imposed by one or more or [sic] the innumerable provisions of the ordinance, considered apart, upon the value or marketability of the lands, is neither disclosed by the bill nor by the evidence, and we are afforded no basis, apart from mere speculation, upon which to rest a conclusion that it or they would have any appreciable effect upon those matters. Under these circumstances, therefore, it is enough for us to determine, as we do, that the ordinance in its general scope and dominant features, so far as its provisions are here involved, is a valid exercise of authority, leaving other provisions to be dealt with as cases arise directly involving them.

And this is in accordance with the traditional policy of this court. In the realm of constitutional law, especially, this court has perceived the embarrassment which is likely to result from an attempt to formulate rules or decide questions beyond the necessities of the immediate issue. It has preferred to follow the method of a gradual approach to the general by a systematically guarded application and extension of constitutional principles to particular cases as they arise, rather than by out of hand attempts to establish general rules to which future cases must be fitted. This process applies with peculiar force to the solution of questions arising under the due process clause of the Constitution as applied to the exercise of the flexible powers of police, with which we are here concerned.

Decree reversed.

Mr. Justice VAN DEVANTER, Mr. Justice McREYNOLDS, and Mr. Justice BUTLER dissent.

CITY AND COUNTY OF SAN FRANCISCO v. SAFEWAY STORES

California District Court of Appeal, 1957.
150 Cal.App.2d 327, 310 P.2d 68.

BRAY, Justice.   Plaintiff sued to have defendant's use of a certain traffic easement for ingress to and egress from its property upon which its store is located, by its customers and others, declared a public nuisance and enjoined.   Defendant appeals from a judgment in plaintiff's favor.

Questions Presented.

1.   Is the use of a traffic easement in a residential zone for purposes of ingress and egress to a parking lot on mercantile store premises by the general public, delivery trucks, etc., a violation of the zoning restrictions?

2.   Is such a violation a public nuisance?

Facts.

There is no conflict in the evidence, the facts having been mostly stipulated.   The Stonesons prior to and on March 13, 1940, owned a tract of land in San Francisco, bounded by 19th Avenue, Ocean Avenue, Eucalyptus Avenue and a municipal right of way. It was divided into lots.   Lots 9 to 16, both inclusive, front on 19th Avenue.   On March 13, 1940, they were zoned by a San Francisco ordinance as first residential zone.   Lots 8, 17 and 18 constitute the easterly portion of said tract.   By said ordinance lots 17 and 18 were zoned as commercial zone.   In 1948 most of lot 8 was so zoned "with stipulations" limiting it to use for parking only. Defendant maintains its store on lot 18, with an extension thereof on a portion of lot 8 which portion was zoned "commercial" for that purpose in 1950.   March 15, 1940, the Stonesons recorded a "Declaration of Easement," which after reciting that they were the owners of the above entire tract, described a portion of said tract and then stated: "Now Therefore, the undersigned, Henry Stoneson and Ellis L. Stoneson, do hereby create and declare and there is hereby created and there shall hereafter exist a traffic easement upon and over that portion of said property herein lastly described, and which said easement shall be kept open and unobstructed at all times."

Lots 9 to 16, both inclusive, are held in separate ownerships. Lots 8, 17 and 18 belong to defendant.   Prior to May, 1953, the line between the easement and defendant's property was fenced, thus preventing access from the easement to that property.   In that month defendant removed a portion of the fence near Eucalyptus Avenue, thereby connecting the parking lot with the traffic easement.   While there is an "exit" sign at this point, it is ignored as cars go both in and out of the parking lot there.   Moreover, some drivers now use the easement as a cutoff, coming off 19th Avenue into Eucalyptus, thence through the easement into the parking lot and on to Ocean

Avenue. Defendant's customers desiring to go from the parking lot to Ocean Avenue use the driveway of the residents on the easement in order to make the turn. In so doing they damage property. Trucks and suppliers of service to Safeway frequently use the easement for both ingress and egress. Since defendant's property was opened for parking through the easement, the traffic has increased immensely. The easement is now used as a thoroughfare.

1. Commercial Use.

Defendant contends that the use of the easement for entry into and exit from the parking area adjoining its store is not an integral or essential part of its commercial operation, and therefore is not a commercial use or a violation of the ordinance. This question has never been directly passed upon in California. The decisions in other jurisdictions are not uniform. Ones supporting the action of the trial court here are City of Yonkers v. Rentways, Inc., 1952, 304 N.Y. 499; Village of Great Neck Estates v. Bemak & Lehman, 1928, 248 N.Y. 651; Town of Brookline v. Co-Ray Realty Co., 1950, 326 Mass. 206.

In the City of Yonkers case it was held, based upon prior decisions of that state, that the use of a lot in a residential zone for ingress to and egress from an adjoining public garage in a business zone, was a business use and violative of the residential zoning ordinance. " * * * it can hardly be denied that the day in, day out moving of vehicles across private land from a public street to the shelter of a garage building is part of the business of garaging vehicles." 109 N.E.2d at page 599.

The Village of Great Neck case involved the same type of question. It was held that the use of the property as a driveway to the public garage was a public use, although there apparently was some use of the driveway for the storage and repair of automobiles. The court stated in 218 N.Y.S. at page 360: "The interesting question involved is as to whether the owner of a garage located entirely outside the village may be restrained from permitting his customers to drive into his garage and out of it, over a driveway connected with a private residence in a zone within the village, which is restricted to residence uses."

In the Town of Brookline case the defendant owned a tract of land partly in the City of Boston and partly in the Town of Brookline. It proposed to construct an apartment house on the Boston portion and to use the Brookline portion as a rear yard and service entrance. The Brookline portion was in a "single residence district." The proposed use was held to be a violation of the single residence zoning ordinance.

Cited as opposing this doctrine is Borough of Prospect Park v. McClaskey, 1943, 151 Pa.Super. 467, where it was held that the use of a driveway in a commercial zone to take supplies into the yard of a brick manufactory in an industrial zone and to haul bricks out was not such an accessory use to the industry as to violate an ordinance. The reason is expressed as follows, 30 A.2d at page 181: "A driveway for the purpose of affording means of passage to trucks is equally advantageous and suitable for commercial as for industrial purposes." It is significant that the court also said: " * * * it is conceivable that the public use of a private driveway lying within a residential district in connection with a public garage located in an adjoining commercial district may so change the character of the driveway as to render its public use prohibitive as 'a commercial use' * * *".

In State ex rel. Szodomka v. Gruber, 1942, 201 La. 1068, also cited by defendant, it was held that the use of a 100 foot lot and a 75 foot driveway thereto in a residential zone for parking and entrance to a restaurant in an adjoining commercial zone was not a use which could be considered as a part of the restaurant business, and hence was not a violation of the residential zoning ordinance. It is significant, however, that the court stated that the only one complaining was a person residing more than 100 feet away, and that "The fact that the municipal authorities, the city attorney and other officials who are entrusted with the enforcement of the municipal ordinances, are not complaining or contending that the" use objected to was a violation of the zoning ordinance, confirmed the court's opinion that there was no violation. It then said: "If the municipal authorities should construe the ordinance as forbidding such use * * * the municipality would either stop this use of the property or lift the ban against it."

In Faulkner v. City of Keene, 1931, 85 N.H. 147, cited by defendant, the plaintiffs sought a declaratory judgment holding among other matters that the proposed use of a 25 foot lot in a residential zone adjacent to a proposed filling station in a commercial zone was not a commercial use or a violation of the residential zone ordinance. The case is of no value to us for the reason that as the court points out, no one contended that the use of the lot as an approach to the filling station was a violation of the ordinance. The defendants were contending that the real purpose was to use the lot for servicing cars. The court then held that such was not the intended use.

Another case cited by defendant is Sudduth v. Snyder, 1938, 120 W.Va. 746, which dealt with the following situation: The plaintiff sought to compel the city of Bluefield to issue to him a permit to construct a filling station and approaches thereto, on his property. The proposed filling station proper was within a zone permitting filling stations. However, the balance of the plaintiff's property upon which he proposed to construct the approaches to the filling station was within a zone prohibiting such stations. The position of the city was that the filling station proper and its approaches thereto were one project. The court held that the ordinance controlling the location of filling stations was based on the theory of protection against fire, and was intended to apply to the station proper, as distinguished from the approaches thereto, and that the right to construct a filling station carries with it the right to such approaches as are reasonably necessary to its use. Such approaches being essential to that use, and not being in conflict with the purposes of the ordinance respecting fire protection, the construction and use thereof cannot be prohibited. The court was careful to point out that there was no contention that the use of the property would constitute a public nuisance, thus indicating that a different decision might have been reached if the use were a public nuisance.

Mercantile stores surrounded by large parking areas are a modern development. The success of such stores depends greatly upon the parking facilities provided. Foot patronage is minimum. Most of the shoppers come in automobiles which must be parked on the store grounds. To hold otherwise would be neither factual nor realistic. Such parking is an essential and integral part of the store's business. A large number of trucks daily visit such stores bringing fresh supplies. Thus the use of property zoned for residence for the vast amount of public ingress and egress necessarily connected with a store of the Safeway type, is a violation of a residential zoning ordinance.

Defendant seems to contend that the use of a traffic easement in connection with its store business and parking facilities cannot be a commercial use, thereby implying that the right to pass over the easement is superior to the right to zone that easement. In effect, defendant is contending that property held in fee may be zoned for a particular use but that a lesser interest, such as an easement, cannot be zoned. The fallacy of this argument is that it is the property itself which is zoned and not any particular interest in it as such. Obviously, if a parcel of land is zoned the particular interest therein of any individual is subject to that zoning.

This is not a case, as defendant seems to consider it, of a question of the rights of the owner of a dominant tenement over the owners of servient tenements. There is no question of defendant's ownership of an interest in the traffic easement, any more than its ownership of the parking and store area. The question here is concerning defendant's right to use its interest in violation of a zoning ordinance. The trial court properly held that defendant had no right to do so.

2. Public Nuisance.

Plaintiff brought this action and the court made its findings upon the premise that the violation of the ordinance constituted a public nuisance and was injurious to the general public and not only to individuals in their private rights.

The evidence showed that automobiles patronizing defendant's store, and the trucks supplying it, go in and out over the easement; that trucks servicing the store spill swill on the easement; that trucks, by reason of their size, have blocked traffic; that the traffic on the easement has increased "immensely" in connection with the Safeway store; that accident hazards have been created; that children playing on the property adjoining the easement have been endangered; that the patrons of the store back their cars on and injure private property. Defendant offered no evidence to controvert any of the foregoing, nor to show that the actions of their patrons in this respect were without its knowledge or approval. This evidence plus the fact that by stipulation of the parties, the trial judge visited the scene, amply supports the court's findings to the effect that the use of the easement by defendant injuriously affects the real and personal property and personal enjoyment and health of the residents in the vicinity and neighborhood of said easement and that such commercial use of the easement was a public nuisance.

The judgment is affirmed.

E. LIMITATIONS IN DEALING WITH LOCAL OFFICIALS

CITY OF LINCOLN v. FIRST NAT. BANK OF LINCOLN

Supreme Court of Nebraska, 1945.
146 Neb. 221, 19 N.W.2d 156.

CHAPPELL, Justice.   The city of Lincoln sought a declaratory judgment in the district court for Lancaster county to determine whether it was legal to continue the deposit of its funds in the defendant First National Bank of Lincoln, Nebraska, while a member of the city council was a stockholder, director or officer of the bank. The question arose by reason of identical provisions contained in section 3, article VII, home rule charter, City of Lincoln, 1917, and section 15–603, R.S.1943, applicable to cities of that class. The charter and the statute each provide in part: "No officer of the city shall be interested directly or indirectly in any contract to which the city, or anyone for its benefit, is a party; and such interest in any contract shall avoid the obligation thereof on the part of the city. * * * Nor shall any officer receive any pay or perquisite from the city other than his salary * * *."

* * *

The matters presented for decision involve only questions of law. There is no dispute concerning the facts. On August 8, 1938, the city council by resolution authorized and empowered the city treasurer, their appointee, to deposit city funds in any one bank within the city of Lincoln in an amount up to the paid-up capital and surplus of the bank, not to exceed ninety per cent of the value of securities to be pledged to secure such deposits. The resolution also designated classes of securities permitted to be used by the bank. On May 15, 1939, the council adopted a resolution designating certain banks, including defendant, as sole and only depositories for city funds.

By arrangement with the city treasurer since 1938, division as to time and amount of deposits has been upon a basis of 15 months in proportion to capital and surplus, four months of which were allotted to the Continental National Bank, four to the National Bank of Commerce and seven to defendant bank. At the time of trial defendant bank was being used for a depository and would continue to be so used for approximately seven months. Deposits are made daily, recorded in a regular bank book and withdrawn by check. Suburban banks have water and light department moneys on deposit but do not have active checking accounts.

Stanley Maly, a stockholder, director and vice-president of defendant bank, was elected and qualified as a member of the city council on May 12, 1941, for a four year term. Subsequently the city treasurer has deposited city funds in defendant bank and it has accepted them claiming it was legally entitled to do so. At the time of the trial there was on deposit with defendant approximately $1,250,-000 of city funds and deposits will continue to be made in the future if legal to do so. To secure the city funds defendant has placed in escrow with the Federal Reserve Bank of Kansas City, Missouri, $1,-000,000 in United States Treasury bonds at 2¾ per cent, due December 15, 1965.

The evidence offered by defendant consists of a stipulation received subject to the objection that it was immaterial and irrelevant. This evidence is that from 1911 to 1913, from 1917 to 1921 and from 1929 to 1931 certain mayors of the city were stockholders and directors of banks, including defendant, in which city funds were deposited during that period. In this connection the position of defendant is that this evidence discloses an administrative interpretation of the statute involved contrary to the city's contentions both before and after the adoption of the home rule charter which should be considered by the court in giving the provisions involved their true construction.

At the outset it should be said that the resolutions authorizing the city treasurer to deposit city funds in any one bank upon certain conditions of security and the later designation of defendant bank as one of the sole depositories for city funds were passed by the city council long before Stanley Maly became a councilman. The sole question presented here is whether the First National Bank, of which Stanley Maly is admittedly a stockholder, director and officer, is prohibited from receiving deposits of city funds because he is now a member of the city council.

* * *

We turn then to decision of the important question, whether a bank deposit constitutes a contract within the prohibitions of the charter and statute. It seems clear under the circumstances that if a deposit in a bank is a contract and an officer of the city has an interest therein that such a contract comes squarely within the charter and statute. If a deposit is a contract it is one made by volition of the parties as distinguished from one that is ministerial, and it is not one of common benefit or privilege open to all citizens upon the same terms or standard rates such as water or electricity furnished by the city. The electors and Legislature had a right to include the provisions here involved in the charter and statutes which should not and cannot be voided in a proper case by judicial construction.

We find that the question presented must be answered affirmatively. It is said in 7 Am.Jur., sec. 405, p. 286: "The term 'deposit,' when used in connection with a banking transaction, denotes a contractual relationship ensuing from the delivery, by one known as the 'depositor,' of moneys, funds, or things into the possession of the bank, which receives the same upon the agreement to pay, repay, or return, upon the order or demand of the depositor, the moneys, funds, or equivalent amount, or things, received; this agreement on the part of the bank is usually a tacit one and implied *   *   *." Also in 9 C.J.S., Banks and Banking, § 267b, p. 545: "The relation of banker and depositor is created by contract." This court has held that the relation of banker and depositor can only be created by contract express or implied. *   *   *

The resolution of the council giving the city treasurer authority to deposit and the designation by the council of defendant bank and others as the sole and only depositories are only resolutions of the council. Such a resolution standing alone is not a contract. The former was simply a grant of authority to the treasurer, and the latter a limitation of his authority naming and designating certain banks of which defendant was only one. The actual deposit of city funds as authorized in a designated bank creates the contractual relationship between the city and the particular bank in which the deposits are made. In this connection each daily deposit gives rise to a new and continuous contractual relationship between the city and the bank until the undertaking of the bank to pay upon proper demand by check according to general usage in such cases or according to special stipulation with the city is fully performed. *   *   *

Manifestly the defendant is deriving a benefit or profit from the deposits of the city funds. The defendant in its answer so admitted. As a business institution it could not ordinarily be expected to receive and disburse so large an account without prospect of profit commensurate with the service required. Naturally, any person who was a stockholder, director or officer thereof would be both directly and indirectly financially interested in any contractual arrangement which returned a profit to his corporation. However, we call attention to the fact that if the contract is of a kind prohibited by law it is immaterial whether the officer of the city actually profited from the contract or whether he was actually influenced by his interest. The question is whether there was any contract to which the city or anyone for its benefit is a party in which the officer of the city was interested directly or indirectly by virtue of an opportunity to benefit or profit therefrom.

In People ex rel. Schenectady Illuminating Co. v. Board of Sup'rs of Schenectady County, 151 N.Y.S. 830, it was said: "The contract is unenforceable, not because a public officer has failed in his duty, but because he has some interest in conflict with his duty. The interest referred to is not necessarily a money interest, nor is it an interest sufficiently large to induce a man generally honest to disregard his duty. It may be indirect. It is such an interest as is covered by the moral rule: No man can serve two masters whose interests conflict. Smith v. City of Albany, supra [61 N.Y. 444]. Too great refinement of reasoning must not be indulged to uphold a contract against this provision of the law on the ground that the interest is so little or so indirect."

In Neisius v. Henry, 142 Neb. 29, we had occasion to examine a statutory provision which uses language almost identical with the city charter and statute involved. That statute, now section 17–611, R.S. 1943, provides in part: "No officer of any city or village shall be interested, directly or indirectly, in any contract to which the corporation, or any one for its benefit, is a party; and any such interest in any such contract shall avoid the obligation thereof on the part of such corporation, nor shall any officer receive any pay or perquisites from the city other than his salary * * *." In the opinion last above cited it was said: "It is argued by defendants that this statute does not by its terms, or by implication, render the contract void, but that on the contrary it is carefully worded so as to make it voidable only. If the contract be voidable only under this statute, some affirmative act on the part of a city would be required to terminate liability. We think the statute clearly expresses a contrary meaning. The use of the words 'and any such interest in any such contract shall avoid the obligation thereof on the part of such corporation' does not import any affirmative action on the part of the city to avoid the obligation of the contract. The interest of the officer in the contract avoids ipso facto the obligation thereof on the part of the city." We therein also quoted from and followed the construction placed upon the same statute in Village of Bellevue v. Sterba, 140 Neb. 744, wherein it was said: "Where a statute prohibits an officer of a village from having an interest in any contract with the village, and avoids the obligation of any such contract so made, it is void for all purposes, and any funds paid out because of such purported contract may be recovered back at the suit of the village or of a taxpayer suing in its behalf." In Neisius v. Henry, supra, we also disapproved the reasoning in Call Publishing Co. v. City of Lincoln, 29 Neb. 149, in the following language: "The reasoning indulged in fails to give effect to the words 'and any such interest in any such contract shall avoid the obligation thereof on the part of such corporation.' To 'avoid the obligation' is plain language and clearly implies relief from all liability, not only as to unperformed portions of the contract, but from the whole transaction from its very inception."

In Hobbs, Wall & Co. v. Moran, 109 Cal.App. 316, it is said: "Such transactions are held to be void whether they arise from the relationship of an agency which is public, quasi-public, or private in its nature. The theory of the law is that a councilman or other officer of a city sustains the same fiduciary relationship toward the citizens of his community that a trustee bears to his cestui que trust * * *."

The statement is made in 44 C.J., sec. 2176, p. 93: "Cases are numerous wherein a municipality was brought into contractual relation with firms or companies, of which a councilman or other city officer was a member, stockholder or employee, and the courts have usually applied the general doctrines to the undoing of such contracts, just as though the officers were individually interested." As stated in 37 Am.Jur., sec. 274, p. 897, "A charter or statutory provision which prohibits a municipal officer from being directly or indirectly interested in a contract with the municipality has been held to extend to contracts beween the municipality and a corporation of which a municipal officer is a stockholder or stockholder and officer. Such a contract is void and incapable of ratification even though the municipal officer has no official connecton with the contract and no knowledge of its existence." * * *

As said in Hardy v. City of Gainesville, 121 Ga. 327: "A stockholder in a private corporation clearly has an interest in its contracts, and, if the city cannot make a contract with the officer himself, it cannot make it with a corporation in which such officer is a stockholder." In Dillon, Municipal Corporations, vol. 2, (5th ed.) sec. 773, p. 1143, it is stated in somewhat different language: "At common law and generally under statutory enactments, it is now established beyond question that a contract made by an officer of a municipality with himself, or in which he is interested, is contrary to public policy and tainted with illegality; and this rule applies whether such officer acts alone on behalf of the municipality, or as a member of the board of council. * * * The fact that the interest of the offending officer in the invalid contract is indirect and is very small is immaterial." See, also, James v. City of Hamburg, 174 Iowa 301.

We can only conclude that the deposits of the City of Lincoln in defendant bank are prohibited by virtue of section 3, article VII of the home rule charter and section 15–603, R.S.1943, while a member of the city council or officer of the city is a stockholder, director or officer of the bank. In arriving at this conclusion we have not overlooked the former executive or administrative construction of the charter and statute presented by defendant. We find that it is immaterial and of no effect under the circumstances presented. * * *

For the reasons heretofore stated the judgment of the district court is reversed and remanded with directions that the trial court enter a judgment finding and adjudging that the deposit of city funds in defendant bank is illegal and void while an officer of the city is either a stockholder, officer or director of defendant bank. An injunction will not be granted since deposits by the city may be discontinued at any time and we assume, as a matter of course, that both the city and the bank will abide by the final decision of the court.

Reversed with directions.

F. LOCAL GOVERNMENT AS BUSINESS

———

MITCHELL v. NORTH CAROLINA INDUSTRIAL DEVELOP-MENT FINANCING AUTHORITY

Supreme Court of North Carolina, 1968.
273 N.C. 137, 159 S.E.2d 745.

SHARP, Justice. This case, brought to test the constitutionality of the North Carolina Industrial Development Financing Act, does not call into question the actual operation of Authority nor does it involve the validity or tax status of any bond issue, for no bonds have been issued. * * * The question for decision is whether an initial appropriation of $37,062.00 of tax money from the State's Contingency and Emergency Fund may be made to enable Authority to organize and commence its operations.

N.C.Const. art. V, § 3 provides: "The power of taxation shall be exercised in a just and equitable manner, *for public purposes only*, and shall never be surrendered, suspended, or contracted away." (Emphasis added.) This limitation of taxing power was contained in the Constitution of 1868 and reaffirmed by the vote of the people in 1962 when Article V, § 3 of the Constitution was revised. The power to appropriate money *from* the public treasury is no greater than the power to levy the tax which put the money in the treasury. Both powers are subject to the constitutional proscription that tax revenues may not be used for private individuals or corporations, no matter how benevolent. Horner v. Chamber of Commerce, 231 N.C. 440. The crucial question, therefore, is whether Authority was created for a public purpose. If so, it may be activated by the questioned appropriation of tax funds; otherwise not. Britt v. City of Wilmington, 236 N.C. 446.

The initial responsibility for determining what is and what is not a public purpose rests with the legislature, and its findings with reference thereto are entitled to great weight. If, however, an enactment is in fact for a private purpose, and therefore unconstitutional, it cannot be saved by legislative declarations to the contrary. * * * The State's Constitution is a restriction of powers; those powers not surrendered are reserved to the people to be exercised through their representatives in the General Assembly. Therefore, so long as an act is not forbidden, the wisdom of the enactment is exclusively a legislative decision. * * * If the use is public, the expediency or necessity for establishing it is exclusively for the legislature. * * *

A slide-rule definition to determine public purpose for all time cannot be formulated; the concept expands with the population, economy, scientific knowledge, and changing conditions. As people are brought closer together in congested areas, the public welfare requires governmental operation of facilities which were once considered exclusively private enterprises, Fawcett v. Mt. Airy, 134 N.C.

125, and necessitates the expenditure of tax funds for purposes which, in an earlier day, were not classified as public. Keeter v. Town of Lake Lure, 264 N.C. 252. Often public and private interests are so comingled that it is difficult to determine which predominates. It is clear, however, that for a use to be public its benefits must be in common and not for particular persons, interests, or estates; the ultimate net gain or advantage must be the public's as contradistinguished from that of an individual or private entity. Briggs v. City of Raleigh, 195 N.C. 223.

"It has been said that the term 'public purpose' is merely a classification distinguishing objects for which the government is to provide from those which are left to private inclination, interest, or liberality. A private enterprise, on the other hand, is one which is ordinarily pursued by individuals in cultivating the soil, manufacturing articles for sale, dealing in merchandise, and the various and numerous other activities which enlist individual energy in a complex and advancing civilization. * * * The term 'public purpose,' as used in a constitutional provision that taxes shall be levied for public purposes only, is synonymous with 'governmental purpose' in the broad connotation given the latter term under the modern concept of government and the relation between government and society." 51 Am. Jur. Taxation § 326 (1944).

* * *

In the interstate competition for industry, an overwhelming majority of the states now authorize the use of industrial development bonds. Although the plans vary in detail, they are basically the same. Local governmental units, or some agency of the state created for this specific purpose, pay for a site and construct a plant with funds derived from the issuance of revenue bonds. The facility is then leased to a manufacturer whose rental payments are used to retire the bonds. When the bonds are paid, the industry, if it so desires, may exercise an option to buy the facility or it may continue to lease it, depending upon its agreement with the lessor. This arrangement enables the manufacturer to expand or relocate without a heavy investment of its own capital. * * *

At the time the General Assembly passed the Act, it declared in Resolution No. 52, that it considered the Act bad public policy. It explained that it felt compelled to authorize industrial revenue bonds in order to compete for industry with neighboring states which use them. * * *

Section 103(a) (1) of the Internal Revenue Code of 1954 provides that gross income does not include interest on the obligations of a state, a territory, or a possession of the United States, or of any political subdivision of the foregoing. Under revenue rulings, income from revenue bonds which are obligations of a political subdivision is excluded "notwithstanding the fact that the bonds were issued to finance the construction of industrial plants for lease to private concerns," with payment to be made from the revenues of the lease rather than the general revenues of the municipality. * * *

Since the tax advantage is the primary appeal which these industrial bonds make to purchasers, the elimination of this status would curtail their use to finance private business expansion—as the General Assembly recognized in Resolution 52. The Supreme Court of Wyoming also noted this fact when it passed upon the constitutionality of the Wyoming Industrial Development Project Act in Uhls v. State, 429 P.2d 74. It said: "Such financing (industrial revenue bonds) has been resorted to because municipal bonds are exempt from Federal taxation, and small communities have been able to use this tax-exempt status to encourage local industrial development. No doubt it is only a matter of time until Congress will see fit to remove tax exemptions for municipal revenue bonds." * * *

According to an item in Newsweek, January 29, 1968, p. 59: "The Treasury Department and the Securities and Exchange Commission will campaign this year for a crackdown on the growing use of tax exempt industrial revenue bonds to finance private business expansion. During 1967, the worth of such bonds issued by state and local governments exceeded $1 billion." The National League of Cities and the North Carolina League of Municipalities say that tax-free revenue bonds pose a growing threat to the financial stability of city government; that they amount to a subsidy to "blue ribbon" industry; that they compete with general-purpose municipal bonds, thereby reducing the market and raising the interest rates on such bonds; and that they endanger the entire tax-exempt status accorded income from governmental bonds. * * *

Whatever may be the ultimate fate of governmental industrial revenue bonds, our research indicates that at least forty-two states (not counting North Carolina) have held that governmental financing for industrial development serves a public purpose. The courts of * * * twenty-one jurisdictions * * * have, without constitutional amendments, upheld the validity of legislation authorizing governmental industrial aid bonds or other types of financial assistance. They have either assumed the public purpose of such acts or reasoned as follows: An inadequate number of jobs means an oversupply of labor, which results in low wages. Unemployment and low wages lead to hunger, ill health, and crime. The continued existence of an established industry and the establishment of new industry provide jobs, measurably increase the resources of the community, promote the economy of the state, and thereby contribute to the welfare of its people. The stimulation of the economy is, therefore, an essential public and governmental purpose. The fact that a private interest incidentally benefits from such governmental aid is not fatal if substantial public benefits also result. See generally, Note, The "Public Purpose" of Municipal Financing for Industrial Development, 70 Yale L.J. 789 (1961) * * *.[1]

---

1. At this point the court discusses the status of the problem of using public funds to finance private industrial development in 22 states.

* * * The financing of private enterprise with public funds contravenes the fundamental concept of North Carolina's Constitution.

Ours is still an expanding economy. According to the stipulations, in 1961, the Commissioner of Revenue collected 456.2 million dollars in taxes; in 1967, 801.3 million. In each of the intervening years there was an increase in collections. In 1963, new and expanded plant investments in North Carolina amounted to $386,929,000; in 1966, $613,581,000. For the first half of 1967, industrial investments amounted to $313,850,000. There is no suggestion in the record, and the Court judicially notices, that our social order is not threatened by widespread unemployment such as confronted the entire nation during the depression years, which began in 1929. No drastic "pump-priming" legislation is presently required to save the economy. The State is not losing population because of the lack of job opportunities. * * *

The rule in North Carolina is that it is not the function of government to engage in private business. Nash v. Town of Tarboro, 227 N.C. 283 (1947), was an action to enjoin the Town of Tarboro from issuing bonds (which the legislature had authorized and the electorate had approved) for the construction of a hotel. The Town had no adequate hotel facilities. Notwithstanding, this Court held that the cost of constructing and maintaining a hotel was not a public purpose within the meaning of N.C.Const. art. V, § 3 and that the act of the legislature authorizing the expenditure was unconstitutional. In writing the opinion, Denny, J. (later C. J.), said:

"It may be desirable for the Town of Tarboro to have additional hotel accommodations. Such facilities would, no doubt, serve a useful purpose and tend to enhance the value of property generally, as well as to promote the commercial life of the community, but ordinarily such benefits will be considered too incidental to justify the expenditure of public funds. * * * Every legitimate business in a community promotes the public good. * * * But 'It may be safely stated that no decision can be found sustaining taxation by a municipality, where its principal object is to promote the trade and business interests of the municipality, and the benefit to the inhabitants is merely indirect and incidental.' * * * 'Many objects may be public in the general sense that their attainment will confer a public benefit or promote the public convenience, but not be public in the sense that the taxing power of the State may be used to accomplish them.' * * *" Id. at 289–290.

The opinion quoted with approval the following statement from Citizens' Savings & Loan Ass'n v. City of Topeka, 87 U.S. 655:

"'* * * If it be said that a benefit results to the local public of a town by establishing manufacturers, the same may be said of any other business or pursuit which employs capital or labor. The merchant, the mechanic, the innkeeper, the banker, the builder, the steamboat owner are equally promoters of the public good, and equally deserving the aid of the citizens by forced contributions. No line can be drawn in favor of the manufacturer which would not open the coffers of the public treasury to the importunities of two thirds of the businessmen of the city or town.' "

* * *

The State does not engage in a private enterprise when it undertakes a project of slum clearance. Wells v. Housing Authority, 213 N.C. 744 (1938). Slums are a serious menace to society; they breed both disease and crime. As Seawell, J., pointed out in Wells v. Housing Authority, supra, the State can combat these two evils in overcrowded areas only by "the removal of physical surroundings conducive to these conditions." Id. at 748. The existence of a slum area proves the impotency or unwillingness of private enterprise to cope with the problem, and "where community initiative has failed and authority alone can prevail," government must deal with the emergency created. Id. at 748. If slums are to be cleared, an Authority with the power of eminent domain is necessary to eliminate them. That power is greater than the power "which might be given by the Legislature in aid of any private enterprise." Id. at 750.

In Dennis v. City of Raleigh, 253 N.C. 400 (1960), it was held that an appropriation of $2,500 by the City (made under statutory authority) to advertise the advantages of Raleigh was for a public purpose albeit not a necessary expense. As the opinion pointed out, the purpose of the contemplated advertising was to promote the public interest and general welfare of the City, not a private business or property interest. Appropriations for such advertising, therefore, could be made from any surplus funds not derived from taxation.

* * * [T]he North Carolina Department of Conservation and Development annually expends approximately $750,000 in advertising and industry hunting. However, such efforts by the State and its subdivision are to induce industries to locate here "on their own"—a far cry from providing a site and plant, built to specifications, to induce a particular industry to locate here.

In passing upon the validity of an act, this Court must consider the consequences of its decision. Were we to hold that Authority serves a public purpose when it acquires a site, constructs a manufacturing plant, and leases it to a private enterprise, we would thereby authorize the legislature to give Authority the power to condemn private property as a site for any project which it undertook. "For the most part the term 'public purposes' is employed in the same sense in the law of taxation and in the law of eminent domain." 1 Cooley, Taxation § 176 (4th Ed. 1924).

That the legislature may grant the power of eminent domain to any state agency which needs to acquire property for a public purpose or use was clearly enunciated by Parker, J. (now C. J.), in Redevelopment Commission of Greensboro v. Security National Bank, 252 N.C.

595 (1960): "In the exercise of the power of eminent domain, private property can be taken only for a public purpose, or more properly speaking a public use, and upon the payment of just compensation." If, however, a project is for a public use, the grant of the power of eminent domain "is a clear and valid exercise of legislative power, for the power of eminent domain is merely the means to the end." Id. at 603.

Prescott, Judge, dissenting in City of Frostburg v. Jenkins, 215 Md. 9, pointed out the possibilities inherent in holding an act such as the one we consider here to be for a public purpose:

"* * * Suppose A owns a parcel of land in Frostburg and desires to erect thereon a manufactory to make shoes. B is interested in conducting a shirt manufactory and the desirable location therefor is A's parcel of ground. Are there many persons who would consider that B's undertaking is such a 'public purpose' as would entitle the City of Frostburg to condemn A's property in order to erect an establishment for B, paying both for the property and the erection of the building from the proceeds of the bonds issued in pursuance of the act being considered? I think not; yet the majority opinion holds that the bonds to be issued are for a 'public purpose'." Id. at 27.

That the power of eminent domain should or could ever be used in behalf of a private interest is a concept foreign to North Carolina, and it transcends our Constitution. If public purpose is now to include State or municipal ownership and operation of the means of production—even on an interim basis; if we are to bait corporations which refuse to become industrial citizens of North Carolina unless the State gives them a subsidy, the people themselves must so declare. Such fundamental departures from well established constitutional principles can be accomplished in this State only by a constitutional amendment.

We hold that Authority's primary function, to acquire sites and to construct and equip facilities for private industry, is not for a public use or purpose; that it may not expend the challenged appropriation of tax funds for its organization; and that the Act which purports to authorize the expenditure violates Article V, § 3 of the Constitution. This ruling makes it unnecessary for us to consider the other questions debated in the briefs.

The judgment of the court below is reversed and the case remanded to the Superior Court for the entry of judgment in accordance with plaintiff's prayer for relief.

Reversed and remanded.

QUESTIONS

1. Businesses are free to locate, generally speaking, wherever they wish and for whatever reason they wish. Is this desirable? Why? If this freedom should be curtailed, what machinery would

be necessary to enforce such a curtailment? What should the nature of the standards be that would be necessary to determine the fact of curtailment, the extent to which such would be desirable? What role, if any, should localities play in any governmental scheme which might be created to curtail freedom of movement?

2. Frequently localities undertake special economic development programs designed to lure business away from other locations. Concessions often are given through rent-free facilities, exemption from local taxes, etc. Are such programs consistent with considerations of anti-trust policy? Does the local government, in effect, combine with an incoming business to grant it an unfair advantage over its competitors? Suppose the local government should decline to give an incoming business these advantages because there already is a similar business on the local scene, would this be an unreasonable restraint of trade? Are these programs consistent with traditional values of minimizing governmental intervention in business decision-making? If site-selection is to become a competition between localities, should this activity itself be subject to federal control? What recourse, if any, should be allowed to the locality that loses its prime or a major economic base?

3. Social awareness on the part of businessmen has become a matter of significant concern to top management in companies throughout the United States in recent years. This has translated itself into programs conducted by business in many communities where executives are given time off to work with community service projects, employees being urged to participate in civic projects and to join civic groups, and community relations offices being established in businesses to assist local projects and provide a vehicle for involving business personnel generally. Do these efforts have the potential of causing the values business holds to be assumed by these "non-business" activities? Should business be allowed to affect local activities to the extent it could because of its providing such a broad range of assistance (and thereby further influencing the value and direction of such activities)? Is there a need for some degree of isolation between business and civic activity? It is possible that these concerns may exist only within smaller communities where the diversity of resources available in larger communities does not exist. But what if it is discovered that business planning calculates into its resource allocation such civic engagements, and communities of all sizes show that civic activities are dominated by persons from business and industry. What might this say for the direction and thrust of civic programs? For the diversion of such resources from strictly business endeavors?

4. Except in the larger cities in the United States, most elected local officials are part-time officials and part-time in whatever else they do. If it can be shown that the vast majority or a substantial number of such officials are drawn from business and industry—presumably because such time off can be planned for and budgeted as compared with professionals and others whose time off from work means loss of income—what might this say about the character of

local political decisions?   Is there a possible constitutional question of equal protection which could be raised respecting business' ability to endure this loss of productive time vis-a-vis the inability of non-business personnel?   Might this also be considered an unconstitutional underwriting of government affairs by private business?

5.   When it is said that local government provides for the general health, safety and welfare, how can it be said with confidence that there is in fact a weighing of the competing interests of all within the local community?   Take, for example, the problem raised in the *Safeway Stores* case; does zoning have the same impact on large economic units as it might have on the individual homeowner?   Is the mechanism of zoning adequate to effectuate the policies which seem to underlie it?   What do you think those policies are?   What alternative mechanisms do you think might be implemented if (a) the results to be achieved are the same and (b) we wish to have greater confidence that the general health, safety and welfare are being provided for and protected?   Would your answer be the same if either or both of those assumptions is modified?   How might it change?

6.   Zoning is considered to be but one dimension of the overall concern of land-use planning.   American political thought has generally eschewed central governmental planning.   However, does local governmental activity produce a result which closely resembles central planning?   Is this desirable?   At the local level, what, if any, alternatives are there?   Further, land-use planning today is also said to incorporate considerations of environmental control.   Insofar as industrial activity is concerned, are such considerations best dealt with at the local level?   How do such considerations fit into the calculus of providing for the general health, safety and welfare?   Consider the last question again by including as a criterion for corrective action by industry the two concepts of "best control technology available"   *   *   *   "best control technology practicable."

7.   The *Mitchell* case reflects a growing involvement by local governments in activities that theretofore traditionally were undertaken by business.   One such area where this involvement is becoming even more common is that of the ownership and operation of mass transit systems.   Does this governmental action provide for the general health, safety and welfare?   What considerations are there which would support the argument that (a) local government should engage in such activities, and (b) local government should not engage in such activities?   Would your answer change if the activity were not mass transit but the operation of (a) a hospital, (b) a water treatment plant, or (c) a produce market?   Why (not)?

8.   Population shifts and technological change, among other things, have not respected local governmental boundaries.   Providing for the general health, safety and welfare frequently justifies the consideration of activities which might cut across these political boundaries.   Whether for reasons of economics of scale or logic, is

there a "logical" list of activities which should be undertaken by local government without respect for such boundaries? If so, what should be the determinant for service area or jurisdiction? Should these areas be coextensive with political boundaries? Should political boundaries be altered to conform to service areas? Should the political boundaries or service areas be the same for all purposes or should they differ according to activity? Which activities? Who should determine which activities should go beyond traditional political boundaries and who should determine what the new areas should be?

9. Questions of local public administration have in the past most frequently been answered on an *ad hoc* basis. If planning and programming does become prospective, does the businessman *qua* businessman have a role therein or should his input be merely as just another citizen?

––––––––

Suggested Reference Sources

Texts and Treatises

Anderson, *American Law of Zoning*. Lawyers Cooperative Publishing Co., Rochester, N. Y.

McQuillin, *Law of Municipal Corporations*. Callaghan & Company, Mundelein, Illinois.

Loose-Leaf Services

Commerce Clearing House, Urban Affairs Reporter, Chicago, Illinois.

Topic Headings in the Index to Legal Periodicals

Municipal Corporations

Zoning

Eminent Domain

Chapter XI

THE BUSINESS IN FINANCIAL DIFFICULTY

A. INTRODUCTORY NOTE

Even though a particular business may never find itself in financial difficulty, all business enterprises sooner or later will have to deal with some other business in financial difficulty. As will be seen below, "insolvency" is a word with many meanings, but for the time being "financial difficulty" and "insolvency" will be used to mean approximately the same thing. Many business enterprises in financial difficulty will be able to make some kind of adjustment with their creditors without going into a formal bankruptcy, and the creditors will be satisfied with this adjustment. Nonetheless, the legal problems involved in an insolvency are always projected against the background of a possible bankruptcy and the exercise of the various rights and the performance of the various liabilities are considered either as though the insolvent business were already adjudicated a bankrupt or could be so adjudicated.

Many businessmen adhere to the concept that "the first loss is the smallest loss." While this aphorism is not very precise, what is generally meant is that when a business in financial difficulty proposes to settle with all its creditors at something less than the full amount due, the acceptance of this offer by the creditor will result in his receiving more money than if the debtor goes into bankruptcy. This is not always true and sometimes a thorough examination of the affairs of the insolvent company will result in uncovering transactions embarrassing to the debtor or in finding other assets which can be made available to the creditors. This happens much more frequently in a bankruptcy proceeding than it does in an informal insolvency proceeding, but there is a well settled attitude that in the end the creditors will not receive any more on account of the money due them whether or not a formal bankruptcy occurs. And this attitude exists even among those creditors who hold security for the money owed them. Some banks are advised to charge their reserve for uncollectible accounts for the amount owed them by any creditor who goes into bankruptcy even though the bank may hold a mortgage to secure its claim. This is unfortunate, because any system of law which results in widespread dissatisfaction with the achievement of the fundamental purpose of the law is bound to result in contempt and disrespect for the law, an attitude hardly to be desired in a democratic society. But not all creditors view insolvency proceedings in this manner.

The United States Constitution in Article I, Section 8 grants to Congress the power to establish "[u]niform Laws on the subject of

Bankruptcies throughout the United States;　*　*　*　". Prior to 1898 when Congress exercised this power most of the insolvency proceedings were handled under the laws of the several states. These were called "assignments for the benefit of creditors" and the laws provided for a scheme for the distribution of the assets of an insolvent debtor. But in 1898 the first comprehensive National Bankruptcy Act was established and this was thoroughly amended in 1938 by the Chandler Act. Today all bankruptcies, as such, are administered under the provisions of the National Bankruptcy Act, 11 U.S.C.A. § 1, et seq.

Nearly any debtor may be adjudicated a bankrupt. Section 4 of the Bankruptcy Act, which is reported below, states who may become a voluntary or an involuntary bankrupt. Obviously, the distinction between voluntary and involuntary is the choice of the debtor; one cannot become an involuntary bankrupt unless three of his creditors file a petition seeking to have a United States District Court adjudicate him a bankrupt. Any person having the right to become a bankrupt may obtain a decree of the Court adjudicating him a bankrupt; however, only those persons who have committed an act of bankruptcy, as set forth in Section 3 of the Act, 11 U.S.C.A. § 21, may be adjudicated involuntary bankrupts. The most frequent complaint about a debtor, leading to his bankruptcy, is the second act of bankruptcy, that is, that while he was insolvent he preferred one or more of his creditors over others. As a practical matter, any business in financial difficulty will start to pay one general creditor (discussed below) in preference to other general creditors because the former will have been more demanding for the payment of his claim than the latter, and most persons in financial difficulty find it difficult to resist these vigorous demands.

A bankruptcy proceeding commences with a petition in bankruptcy filed with the United States District Court in the District in which the debtor maintains his principal place of business. If it is a voluntary petition, it will almost without exception be granted, and the business enterprise will then have become a bankrupt. If it is an involuntary petition, the business enterprise whose creditors seek to put it into bankruptcy will be given an opportunity to defend the petition and to show either that it was not insolvent in the bankruptcy sense or that it did not commit any of the acts of bankruptcy. While this rarely occurs, it is not unknown. Most enterprises when faced with the hostility of a petition in bankruptcy filed by its creditors will concede the point and permit the bankruptcy to proceed.

At the time of filing the petition in bankruptcy, whether it be voluntary or involuntary, one or more creditors may also petition the court for the appointment of a Receiver. In a voluntary bankruptcy it is no secret that this frequently occurs because the debtor will have informed one or more of his creditors that he plans to file a petition, and it is not entirely a coincidence that the creditors are present in the courthouse at the time that the voluntary petition in bankruptcy is filed with the clerk. These creditors are then prepared with their own petition seeking the appointment of a Receiver. In an involuntary proceeding, the creditor seeking the bankruptcy also nearly always asks the court to appoint a Receiver immediately on the ground that unless one is so appointed the assets of the insolvent enterprise will be wrongfully diminished or concealed. Because of the press of other business and the knowledge that most debtors will not resist, Federal Courts frequently do not examine into the merits of these petitions and appoint a Receiver in nearly every application. This also is unfortunate. The Receiver is charged with assuming custody and control of the assets of the debtor. He may not operate the debtor's business without specific order of the court. His function is merely a holding function until the bankruptcy proceeding can be organized in its normal course which eventually results in the election of a Trustee by the general creditors of the debtor; the Trustee will then replace him.

Upon the adjudication of bankruptcy, as a matter of course, the case is referred to a Referee in bankruptcy. A Referee is an official of the court who sits as a judge of the bankruptcy court and has all the powers of a United States District Judge except the power to hold persons in contempt of court. His function is to supervise the administration of the bankruptcy proceedings under the terms of the Bankruptcy Act. He will send notices to all of the creditors whose names appear on the "Schedule" of creditors presented to him and will notify them of a date and place for the first meeting of the creditors.

At the first meeting of the creditors the Referee will examine the bankrupt, and if it is a corporation he will examine its president and other officers, about the affairs of the insolvent business. The Receiver and any creditor who so desires may also participate in this examination. At this meeting the creditors will elect a Trustee in bankruptcy who will be elected by a majority of the creditors (with creditors voting the dollar amount of their claims). Frequently there is little contest for this job and the Referee will have to cast about to find someone who is interested in the estate of the debtor to serve as Trustee. The Trustee will have to post a bond with corporate surety in a fair sum fixed by the Referee. He will engage an attorney, but may do so only upon an order of the Referee granting him permission to do so.

The Trustee is charged with taking custody of the assets from the Receiver if one has been appointed (and frequently the person who has been serving as a Receiver is elected the Trustee) and to make an inventory and obtain an appraisal of the value of the assets of the debtor's estate; he will also be charged with assembling all of these, and according to the procedures established in the Bankruptcy Act, selling them and reducing them to cash. He is required to settle claims and disputes between the debtor and his creditors or between the bankrupt estate and persons who owe money to it, and under established procedures to pay secured creditors or to allow them to reclaim their security in satisfaction of the obligations of the debtor held by them. He may disburse money only with the permission of the Referee who will countersign all checks drawn by the Trustee. At the conclusion of the administration of the bankruptcy he must prepare and file an account, and thereafter a meeting of all the creditors will be held and he will then submit a report of his administration. His compensation is fixed by statute at a very minimum amount. Both the Trustee and his attorney (who is frequently much better paid than the Trustee) must petition the Referee for their compensation.

In concluding the administration of the bankrupt estate the money on hand is distributed to the creditors in a strict order of priority. Secured creditors are paid in full to the extent that their securities when sold produce enough cash for this purpose. Any surplus from the sale of assets which were pledged or mortgaged as security, and the proceeds of the sale of all other unencumbered assets of the debtor will then be used to pay priority creditors. The various classes of priority creditors are set forth in Section 64 of the Bankruptcy Act, 11 U.S.C.A. § 104, which is reported below. Each priority is paid in full before anything is paid to the next lower priority, etc. After all priority creditors are paid in full, and not until then, any balance remaining will be distributed to the general creditors. These are the creditors who get a pro rata distribution on the amounts of their claims, and frequently they wind up with either a very minor amount or nothing on account of their claims.

With the adoption of the Uniform Commercial Code and with the ease of perfecting a security interest under the provisions of Article IX of the Commercial Code, more and more business enterprises become bankrupt with none of their assets unsecured. When the business gets into financial difficulty, it will raise additional money through granting security interests in its accounts receivable, inventory, machinery and equipment, etc. There is a whole class of lenders who are experienced in making loans of this kind; they will prepare the necessary written documents and do the necessary filing in public offices in order to perfect their security interest. This frequently means that when the business enterprise goes into bankruptcy none of its assets is available to pay even the expenses of administration of the bankrupt (under Section 64 of the Bankruptcy Act, reported infra, the first priority is the cost and expenses of administration) so that more and more no one is willing to undertake to serve as Trustee or counsel for the Trustee in a bankruptcy proceeding. However, where there is a good prospect of raising a substantial sum of money available for the payment of administration expenses and other claims with a lower priority, there is frequently an unholy scramble to seek to be appointed Receiver, then Trustee, and counsel for either or both those persons.

There is a substantial segment of the legal profession which devotes most of its time to the administration of the affairs of bankrupt companies. Because they frequently will have performed their services with little or no compensation, and because the opportunity of being paid well does not often arise, there is frequently much subtle, if not unethical, solicitation of claims of creditors looking to the engagement as counsel by the Receiver or Trustee. It is not uncommon to hear businessmen complain that it appears to them that the bankruptcy procedure exists for the benefit of the lawyers and not for the creditors.

Yet in spite of all this the Bankruptcy Act does provide two important functions in a democratic society. In a system where the government owns all business or where there is no private property, no one can fail in business and thus no one goes into bankruptcy. However, in a system where the distribution of resources is accomplished by freedom of contract and a system of free choice, and not by any governmental agency or fiat, some method of distribution of the property of a bankrupt must be available. This is accomplished by the Bankruptcy Act. Equally important is the concept of the rehabilitation of a debtor; when this is a corporation, no real problem exists because the corporation just passes into limbo in nearly every case. However, the individual debtors involved in a bankruptcy are given the opportunity to start over again, that is, an opportunity for rehabilitation. Whether this is done in the expectation that the debtor will once more become a productive member of society, or is done as a consequence of morals or ethics, it can be readily seen that in a democratic society this is a useful procedure.

The Bankruptcy Act provides for an orderly distribution of the property of an insolvent enterprise. We do not permit self-help, strong-arm methods, or hired brigands as the method of distributing the assets of an insolvent debtor. Equality of distribution of assets is an important purpose of the Act and this is demonstrated by Sampsell v. Imperial Paper & Color Corp., 313 U.S. 215, 61 S.Ct. 904, 85 L.Ed. 1293 (1941) which is reported below. An additional function of great importance is the rehabilitation of a debtor. This is accomplished by a "discharge" in bankruptcy which is what a debtor seeks either in a voluntary or involuntary bankruptcy; when a debtor is discharged of his obligations he no longer owes them. Section 14 of the Bankruptcy Act, 11 U.S.C.A. § 32, lists the situations in which a discharge in bankruptcy will be granted. Two cases, Perez v. Campbell, 402 U.S. 637, 91 S.Ct. 1704, 29 L.Ed.2d 233 (1971) and In re Biscoe, 45 F.Supp. 422 (1942) illustrate some of the consequences and problems relating to discharges; the latter case also illustrates the policy of the law of expediting the administration of bankruptcies (although this is frequently not achieved).

Some of the problems involved in equality of distribution, and preferences and fraudulent transfers are illustrated by two cases, Onondaga Litholite Co. et al. v. Receiver of Salt Springs National Bank, 218 F.2d 671 (2nd Cir. 1955), and In the Matter of Simon, 197 F.Supp. 301 (E.D.N.Y.1961), both reported below.

These cases should be read in reference to the selected sections of the Bankruptcy Act which are reported below. Section 3 of the Act, 11 U.S.C.A. § 21, lists those incidents which can lead to a bankruptcy; Sec. 14, 11 U.S.C.A. § 32, lists the circumstances under which a discharge in bankruptcy may or may not be granted; Section 17, 11 U.S.C.A. § 35 lists those debts which are not discharged by a bankruptcy; Section 60, 11 U.S.C.A. § 96, lists the kinds of transactions which are deemed to be preferences and which can be set aside during the administration of a bankruptcy; Section 63, 11 U.S.C.A. § 103, contains a list of the debts or claims against the bankrupt which may be proved in the proceeding and thus become entitled to a distribution; Section 64, 11 U.S.C.A. § 104, referred to above, lists the debts which have priority of payment in distribution; and Section 68, 11 U.S.C.A. § 108, provides that mutual debts between the claimant and the bankrupt estate may be set off against each other. All of these are important in understanding the legal problems relating to a business in financial difficulty. Obviously this is only a cursory examination of these problems, but the provisions of the Bankruptcy Act noted above and the cases reported are necessary to an understanding of the fundamentals of the legal problems in this area.

B.　ORDINARY BANKRUPTCY

1.　SELECTED SECTIONS OF CHAPTERS III AND IV OF THE BANKRUPTCY ACT

TITLE 11　UNITED STATES CODE

BANKRUPTCY

§ 21.　Acts of bankruptcy

(a) Acts of bankruptcy by a person shall consist of his having (1) concealed, removed, or permitted to be concealed or removed any part of his property, with intent to hinder, delay, or defraud his creditors or any of them, or made or suffered a transfer of any of his property, fraudulent under the provisions of section 107 or 110 of this title; or (2) made or suffered a preferential transfer, as defined in subdivision a of section 96 of this title; or (3) suffered or permitted, while insolvent, any creditor to obtain a lien upon any of his property through legal proceedings or distraint and not having vacated or discharged such lien within thirty days from the date thereof or at least five days before the date set for any sale or other disposition of such property; or (4) made a general assignment for the benefit of his creditors; or (5) while insolvent or unable to pay his debts as they mature, procured, permitted, or suffered voluntarily or involuntarily the appointment of a receiver or trustee to take charge of his property; or (6) admitted in writing his ability to pay his debts and his willingness to be adjudged a bankrupt.

(b) A petition may be filed against a person within four months after the commission of an act of bankruptcy. Such time with respect to the third act of bankruptcy shall expire four months after the date the lien through legal proceedings or distraint was obtained and, with respect to the first or fourth act of bankruptcy, such time shall not expire until four months after the date when the transfer or assignment became so far perfected that no bona fide purchaser from the debtor could thereafter have acquired any rights in the property so transferred or assigned superior to the rights of the transferee or assignee therein, and such time with respect to the second act of bankruptcy shall not expire until four months after the date when the transfer became perfected as described in subdivision a of section 96 of this title. For the purposes of this section, it is sufficient if intent to hinder, delay or defraud under the first act of bankruptcy, where such intent is an element of such act, or if insolvency under the second act of bankruptcy, exists either at the time when the transfer was made or at the time when it became perfected, as hereinabove provided.

(c) It shall be a complete defense to any proceedings under the first act of bankruptcy to allege and prove that the party proceeded against was not insolvent as defined in this title at the time of the filing of the petition against him. If solvency at such date is proved by the alleged bankrupt, the proceedings shall be dismissed. In such proceedings the burden of proving solvency shall be on the alleged bankrupt.

(d) Whenever a person against whom a petition has been filed alleging the commission of the second, third, or fifth act of bankruptcy takes issue with and denies the allegation of his insolvency or his inability to pay his debts as they mature, he shall appear in court on the hearing, and prior thereto if ordered by the court, with his books, papers, and accounts, and submit to an examination and give testimony as to all matters tending to establish solvency or insolvency or ability or inability to pay his debts as they mature and, in case of his failure so to do, the burden of proving solvency or ability to pay his debts as they mature shall rest upon him. July 1, 1898, c. 541, § 3, 30 Stat. 546; Feb. 5, 1903, c. 487, § 2, 32 Stat. 797; May 27, 1926, c. 406, § 3, 44 Stat. 662; June 22, 1938, c. 575, § 1, 52 Stat. 844; July 7, 1952, c. 579, § 3, 66 Stat. 421.

§ 22. Who may become bankrupts

(a) Any person, except a municipal, railroad, insurance, or banking corporation or a building and loan association, shall be entitled to the benefits of this title as a voluntary bankrupt.

(b) Any natural person, except a wage earner or farmer, and any moneyed, business, or commercial corporation, except a building and loan association, a municipal, railroad, insurance, or banking corporation, owing debts to the amount of $1,000 or over, may be adjudged an involuntary bankrupt upon default or an impartial trial and shall be subject to the provisions and entitled to the benefits of this title. The bankruptcy of a corporation shall not release its officers, the members of its board of directors or trustees or of other similar controlling bodies, or its stockholders or members, as such, from any liability under the laws of a State or of the United States. The status of an alleged bankrupt as a wage earner or farmer shall be determined as of the time of the commission of the act of bankruptcy. July 1, 1898, c. 541, § 4, 30 Stat. 547; Feb. 5, 1903, c. 487, § 3, 32 Stat. 797; June 25, 1910, c. 412, §§ 3, 4, 36 Stat. 839; Feb. 11, 1932, c. 38, 47 Stat. 47; May 15, 1935, c. 114, § 1, 49 Stat. 246; June 22, 1938, c. 575, § 1, 52 Stat. 845.

§ 32. Discharges, when granted

(a) The adjudication of any person, except a corporation, shall operate as an application for a discharge: *Provided,* That the bankrupt may, before the hearing on such application, waive by writing, filed with the court, his right to a discharge. A corporation may, within six months after its adjudication, file an application for a discharge in the court in which the proceedings are pending.

(b)(1) The court shall make an order fixing a time for the filing of objections to the bankrupt's discharge and a time for the filing of applications pursuant to section 35(c)(2) of this title to determine the dischargeability of debts, which time or times shall be not less than thirty days nor more than ninety days after the first date set for the first meeting of creditors. Notice of such order shall be given to all parties in interest as provided in section 94(b) of this title. The Court may, upon its own motion or, for cause shown, upon motion of any party in interest, extend the time or times for filing such objections or applications.

(2) Upon the expiration of the time fixed in the order for filing objections or of any extension of such time granted by the court, the court shall discharge the bankrupt if no objection has been filed and if the filing fees required to be paid by this title have been paid in full; otherwise, the court shall hear such proofs and pleas as may be made in opposition to the discharge, by the trustee, creditors, the United States attorney, or such other attorney as the Attorney General may designate, at such time as will give the bankrupt and the objecting parties a reasonable opportunity to be fully heard.

(c) The court shall grant the discharge unless satisfied that the bankrupt has (1) committed an offense punishable by imprisonment as provided under section 152 of Title 18; or (2) destroyed, mutilated, falsified, concealed, or failed to keep or preserve books of account or records, from which his financial condition and business transactions might be ascertained, unless the court deem such acts or failure to have been justified under all the circumstances of the case; or (3) while engaged in business as a sole proprietor, partnership, or as an executive of a corporation, obtained for such business money or property on credit or as an extension or renewal of credit by making or publishing or causing to be made or published in any manner whatsoever a materially false statement in writing respecting his financial condition or the financial condition of such partnership or corporation; or (4) at any time subsequent to the first day of the twelve months immediately preceding the filing of the petition in bankruptcy, transferred, removed, destroyed, or concealed, or permitted to be removed, destroyed, or concealed, any of his property with intent to hinder, delay, or defraud his creditors; or (5) in a proceeding under this title commenced within six years prior to the date of the filing of the petition in bankruptcy has been granted a discharge, or had a composition or an arrangement by way of composition or a wage earner's plan by way of composition confirmed under this title; or (6) in the course of a proceeding under this title refused to obey any lawful order of, or to answer any material question approved by, the court; or (7) has failed to explain satisfactorily any losses of assets or deficiency of assets to meet his liabilities; or (8) has failed to pay the filing fees required to be paid by this title in full: *Provided,* That if, upon the hearing of an objection to a discharge, the objector shall show to the satisfaction of the court that there are reasonable grounds for believing that the bankrupt has committed any of the acts which, under this subdivision, would prevent his discharge in bankruptcy, then the burden of proving that he has not committed any of such acts shall be upon the bankrupt.

(d) When requested by the court, the United States attorney, located in the judicial district in which the bankruptcy proceeding is pending, or such other attorney as the Attorney General may designate, shall examine into the acts and conduct of the bankrupt and, if satisfied that probable grounds exist for the denial of the discharge and that the public interest so warrants, he shall oppose the discharge of such bankrupt in like manner as provided in the case of a trustee.

(e) If the bankrupt fails to appear at the hearing upon the objections to his application for a discharge, or having appeared refuses to submit himself to examination, or if the court finds after hearing upon notice that the bankrupt has failed without sufficient excuse to appear and submit himself to examination at the first meeting of creditors or at any meeting specially called for his examination, he shall be deemed to have waived his right to a discharge, and the court shall enter an order to that effect.

(f) An order of discharge shall—

(1) declare that any judgment theretofore or thereafter obtained in any other court is null and void as a determination of the personal liability of the bankrupt with respect to any of the following: (a) debts not excepted from the discharge under subdivision (a) of section 35 of this title; (b) debts discharged under paragraph (2) of subdivision (c) of section 35 of this title; and (c) debts determined to be discharged under paragraph (3) of subdivision (c) of section 35 of this title; and

(2) enjoin all creditors whose debts are discharged from thereafter instituting or continuing any action or employing any process to collect such debts as personal liabilities of the bankrupt.

(g) An order of discharge which has become final may be registered in any other district by filing therein a certified copy of such order and when so registered shall have the same effect as an order of the bankruptcy court of the district where registered and may be enforced in like manner.

(h) Within forty-five days after the order of discharge becomes final the court shall give notice of the entry thereof to all parties in interest as specified in subdivision (b) of section 94 of this title. Such notice shall also specify the debts, if any, theretofore determined by the court to be nondischargeable, the debts, if any, as to which applications to determine dischargeability are pending, and those contents of the order of discharge required by subdivision (f) of this section.

As amended Sept. 2, 1957, Pub.L. 85–275, § 1, 71 Stat. 599; July 12, 1960, Pub.L. 86–621, § 1, 74 Stat. 408; Sept. 2, 1965, Pub.L. 89–166, 79 Stat. 646; Oct. 19, 1970, Pub.L. 91–467, §§ 2, 3, 84 Stat. 990, 991.

§ 35. Dischargeability of debts—Debts not affected by discharge

(a) A discharge in bankruptcy shall release a bankrupt from all of his provable debts, whether allowable in full or in part, except such as (1) are taxes which became legally due and owing by the bankrupt to the United States or to any State or any subdivision thereof within three years preceding bankruptcy: *Provided, however,* That a discharge in bankruptcy shall not release a bankrupt from any taxes (a) which were not assessed in any case in which the bankrupt failed to make a return required by law, (b) which were assessed within one year preceding bankruptcy in any case in which the bankrupt failed to make a return required by law, (c) which were not reported on a return made by the bankrupt and which were not assessed prior to bankruptcy by reason of a prohibition on assessment pending the exhaustion of administrative or judicial remedies available to the bankrupt, (d) with respect to which the bankrupt made a false or fraudulent return, or willfully attempted in any manner to evade or defeat, or (e) which the bankrupt has collected or withheld from others as required by the laws of the United States or any State or political subdivision thereof, but has not paid over; but a discharge shall not be a bar to any remedies available under applicable law to the United States or to any State or any subdivision thereof, against the exemption of the bankrupt allowed by law and duly set apart to him under this title: *And provided further*, That a discharge in bankruptcy shall not release or affect any tax lien; (2) are liabilities for obtaining money or property by false pretenses or false representations, or for obtaining money or property on credit or obtaining an extension or renewal of credit in reliance upon a materially false statement in writing respecting his financial condition made or published or caused to be made or published in any manner whatsoever with intent to deceive, or for willful and malicious conversion of the property of another; (3) have not been duly scheduled in time for proof and allowance, with the name of the creditor if known to the bankrupt, unless such creditor had notice or actual knowledge of the proceedings in bankruptcy; (4) were created by his fraud, embezzlement, misappropriation or defalcation while acting as an officer or in any fiduciary capacity; (5) are for wages and commissions to the extent they are entitled to priority under subdivision (a) of section 104 of this title; (6) are due for moneys of an employee received or retained by his employer to secure the faithful performance by such employee of the terms of a contract of employment; (7) are for alimony due or to become due, or for maintenance or support of wife or child, or for seduction of an unmarried female or for breach of promise of marriage accompanied by seduction, or for criminal conversation; or (8) are liabilities for willful and malicious injuries to the person or property of another other than conversion as excepted under clause (2) of this subdivision.

Proceedings for debts dischargeable

(b) The failure of a bankrupt or debtor to obtain a discharge in a prior proceeding under this title for any of the following reasons shall not bar the release by discharge in a subsequent proceeding under the title of debts that were dischargeable under subdivision (a) of this section in the prior proceeding: (1) discharge was denied in the prior proceeding solely under clause (5) or clause (8) of subdivision (c) of section 32 of this title; (2) the prior proceeding was dismissed without prejudice for failure to pay filing fees or to secure costs. If a bankrupt or debtor fails to obtain a discharge in a proceeding under this title by reason of a waiver filed pursuant to section 32(a) of this title or by reason of a denial on any ground under section 32(c) of this title other than clause (5) or clause (8) thereof, the debts provable in such proceeding shall not be released by a discharge granted in any subsequent proceeding under this title. A debt not released by a discharge in a proceeding under this title by reason of clause (3) of subdivision (a) of this section may nevertheless be dischargeable in a subsequent bankruptcy proceeding.

Procedure

(c)(1) The bankrupt or any creditor may file an application with the court for the determination of the dischargeability of any debt.

(2) A creditor who contends that his debt is not discharged under clause (2), (4), or (8) of subdivision (a) of this section must file an application for a determination of dischargeability within the time fixed by the court pursuant to paragraph (1) of subdivision (b) of section 32 of this title and, unless an application is timely filed, the debt shall be discharged.

Notwithstanding the preceding sentence, no application need be filed for a debt excepted by clause (8) if a right to trial by jury exists and any party to a pending action on such debt has timely demanded a trial by jury or if either the bankrupt or a creditor submits a signed statement of an intention to do so.

(3) After hearing upon notice, the court shall determine the dischargeability of any debt for which an application for such determination has been filed, shall make such orders as are necessary to protect or effectuate a determination that any debt is dischargeable and, if any debt is determined to be nondischargeable, shall determine the remaining issues, render judgment, and make all orders necessary for the enforcement thereof. A creditor who files such application does not submit himself to the jurisdiction of the court for any purposes other than those specified in this subdivision.

(4) The provisions of this subdivision shall apply whether or not an action on a debt is then pending in another court and any party may be enjoined from instituting or continuing such action prior to or during the pendency of a proceeding to determine its dischargeability under this subdivision.

(5) Nothing in this subdivision shall be deemed to affect the right of any party, upon timely demand, to a trial by jury where such right exists.

(6) If a bankruptcy case is reopened for the purpose of obtaining the orders and judgments authorized by this subdivision, no additional filing fee shall be required.

As amended July 12, 1960, Pub.L. 86–621, § 2, 74 Stat. 409; July 5, 1966, Pub.L. 89–496, § 2, 80 Stat. 270; Oct. 19, 1970, Pub.L. 91–467, §§ 5–7, 84 Stat. 992.

§ 91. Meetings of creditors

(a) The court shall cause the first meeting of the creditors of a bankrupt to be held not less than ten nor more than thirty day after the adjudication, at the place or at one of the places designated by the conference pursuant to paragraph (1) of subdivision (b) of section 65 of this title as a place at which court shall be held within the judicial district in which the proceeding is pending or if that place would be unreasonably inconvenient as a place of meeting for the parties in interest, the court shall fix a place for the meeting within said judicial district which is not unreasonably inconvenient for the parties in interest. If such meeting should by any mischance not be held within such time, the court shall fix the date as soon as may be thereafter, when it shall be held.

(b) At the first meeting of creditors, the judge or referee shall preside and, before proceeding with other business, may allow or disallow the claims of creditors there presented, and shall publicly examine the bankrupt or cause him to be examined, and may permit creditors to examine him.

(c) The creditors shall at each meeting take such steps as may be pertinent and necessary for the promotion of the best interests of the estate and the enforcement of this title.

(d) The court shall call a meeting of creditors whenever one-fourth or more in number of those who have proved their claims shall file a written request to that effect; if such request is signed by a majority of such creditors, which number represents a majority in amount of such claims, and contains a request for such meeting to be held at a designated place, the court shall call such meeting at such place within thirty days after the date of the filing of the request.

(e) Whenever the affairs of the estate are ready to be closed a final meeting of creditors shall be ordered: *Provided, however,* That a no-asset case may be closed without ordering such final meeting.   July 1, 1898, c. 541, § 55, 30 Stat. 559; June 22, 1938, c. 575, § 1, 52 Stat. 865; May 16, 1951, c. 82, 65 Stat. 42.

§ 96.   Preferred creditors

(a)(1) A preference is a transfer, as defined in this title, of any of the property of a debtor to or for the benefit of a creditor for or on account of an antecedent debt, made or suffered by such debtor while insolvent and within four months before the filing by or against him of the petition initiating a proceeding under this title, the effect of which transfer will be to enable such creditor to obtain a greater percentage of his debt than some other creditor of the same class.

(2) For the purposes of subdivisions (a) and (b) of this section, a transfer of property other than real property shall be deemed to have been made or suffered at the time when it became so far perfected that no subsequent lien upon such property obtainable by legal or equitable proceedings on a simple contract could become superior to the rights of the transferee. A transfer of real property shall be deemed to have been made or suffered when it became so far perfected that no subsequent bona fide purchase from the debtor could create rights in such property superior to the rights of the transferee.   If any transfer of real property is not so perfected against a bona fide purchase, or if any transfer of other property is not so perfected against such liens by legal or ·equitable proceedings prior to the filing of a petition initiating a proceeding under this title, it shall be deemed to have been made immediately before the filing of the petition.

(3) The provisions of paragraph (2) of this subdivision shall apply whether or not there are or were creditors who might have obtained such liens upon the property other than real property transferred and whether or not there are or were persons who might have become bona fide purchasers of such real property.

(4) A lien obtainable by legal or equitable proceedings upon a simple contract within the meaning of paragraph (2) of this subdivision is a lien arising in ordinary course of such proceedings upon the entry or docketing of a judgment or decree, or upon attachment, garnishment, execution, or like process, whether before, upon, or after judgment or decree and whether before or upon levy.   It does not include liens which under applicable law are given a special priority over other liens which are prior in time.

(5) A lien obtainable by legal or equitable proceedings could become superior to the rights of a transferee or a purchase could create rights superior to the rights of a transferee within the meaning of paragraph (2) of this subdivision, if such consequences would follow only from the lien or purchase itself, or from such lien or purchase followed by any step wholly within the control of the respective lien holder or purchaser, with or without the aid of ministerial action by public officials.   Such a lien could not, however, become so superior and such a purchase could not create such superior rights for the purposes of paragraph (2) of this subdivision through any acts subsequent to the obtaining of such a lien or subsequent to such a purchase which require the agreement or concurrence of any third party or which require any further judicial action, or ruling.

(6) The recognition of equitable liens where available means of perfecting legal liens have not been employed is declared to be contrary to the policy of this section. If a transfer is for security and if (A) applicable law requires a signed and delivered writing, or a delivery of possession, or a filing or recording, or other like overt action as a condition to its full validity against third persons other than a buyer in the ordinary course of trade claiming through or under the transferor and (B) such overt action has not been taken, and (C) such transfer results in the acquisition of only an equitable lien, then such transfer is not perfected within the meaning of paragraph (2) of this subdivision. Notwithstanding the first sentence of paragraph (2) of this subdivision, it shall not suffice to perfect a transfer which creates an equitable lien such as is described in the first sentence of this paragraph, that it is made for a valuable consideration and that both parties intend to perfect it and that they take action sufficient to effect a transfer as against liens by legal or equitable proceedings on a simple contract: *Provided, however,* That where the debtor's own interest is only equitable, he can perfect a transfer thereof by any means appropriate fully to transfer an interest of that character: *And provided further,* That nothing in this paragraph shall be construed to be contrary to the provisions of paragraph (7) of this subdivision.

(7) Any provision in this subdivision (a) to the contrary notwithstanding if the applicable law requires a transfer of property other than real property for or on account of a new and contemporaneous consideration to be perfected by recording, delivery, or otherwise, in order that no lien described in paragraph (2) of this subdivision could become superior to the rights of the transferee therein, or if the applicable law requires a transfer of real property for such a consideration to be so perfected in order that no bona fide purchase from the debtor could create rights in such property superior to the rights of the transferee, the time of transfer shall be determined by the following rules:

I. Where (A) the applicable law specifies a stated period of time of not more than twenty-one days after the transfer within which recording, delivery, or some other act is required, and compliance therewith is had within such stated period of time; or where (B) the applicable law specifies no such stated period of time or where such stated period of time is more than twenty-one days, and compliance therewith is had within twenty-one days after the transfer, the transfer shall be deemed to be made or suffered at the time of the transfer.

II. Where compliance with the law applicable to the transfer is not had in accordance with the provisions of subparagraph I of this paragraph, the transfer shall be deemed to be made or suffered at the time of compliance therewith, and if such compliance is not had prior to the filing of the petition initiating a proceeding under this title, such transfer shall be deemed to have been made or suffered immediately before the filing of such petition.

(8) If no such requirement of applicable law specified in paragraph (7) of this subdivision exists, a transfer wholly or in part, for or on account of a new and contemporaneous consideration shall, to the extent of such consideration and interest thereon and the other obligations of the transferor connected therewith, be deemed to be made or suffered at the time of the transfer. A transfer to secure a future loan, if such a loan is actually made, or a transfer which becomes security for a future loan, shall

have the same effect as a transfer for or on account of a new and contemporaneous consideration.

(b) Any such preference may be avoided by the trustee if the creditor receiving it or to be benefited thereby or his agent acting with reference thereto has, at the time when the transfer is made, reasonable cause to believe that the debtor is insolvent. Where the preference is voidable, the trustee may recover the property or, if it has been converted, its value from any person who has received or converted such property, except a bonafide purchaser from or lienor of the debtor's transferee for a present fair equivalent value: *Provided, however,* That where such purchaser or lienor has given less than such value, he shall nevertheless have a lien upon such property, but only to the extent of the consideration actually given by him. Where a preference by way of lien or security title is voidable, the court may on due notice order such lien or title to be preserved for the benefit of the estate, in which event such lien or title shall pass to the trustee. For the purpose of any recovery or avoidance under this section, where plenary proceedings are necessary, any State court which would have had jurisdiction if bankruptcy had not intervened and any court of bankruptcy shall have concurrent jurisdiction.

(c) If a creditor has been preferred, and afterward in good faith gives the debtor further credit without security of any kind for property which becomes a part of the debtor's estate, the amount of such new credit remaining unpaid at the time of the adjudication in bankruptcy may be set off against the amount which would otherwise be recoverable from him.

(d) If a debtor shall, directly or indirectly, in contemplation of the filing of a petition by or against him, pay money or transfer property to an attorney at law, for services rendered or to be rendered, the transaction may be examined by the court on its own motion or shall be examined by the court on petition of the trustee or any creditor and shall be held valid only to the extent of a reasonable amount to be determined by the court, and the excess may be recovered by the trustee for the benefit of the estate.

If, whether before or after filing, a debtor shall agree orally or in writing to pay money or transfer property to an attorney at law after the filing, the transaction may be examined by the court on its own motion or shall be examined by the court on petition of the bankrupt made prior to discharge and shall be held valid only to the extent of a reasonable amount to be determined by the court, and any excess obligation shall be canceled, or if excess payment or transfer has been made, returned to the bankrupt.

(e)(1) Where the bankrupt is a stockbroker, the following definitions and provisions of this subdivision shall apply: "Property" shall include cash, securities, whether or not negotiable, and all other property of similar character; "customers" of a stockbroker shall include persons who have claims on account of securities received, acquired, or held by the stockbroker from or for the account of such persons (a) for safekeeping, or (b) with a view to sale, or (c) to cover consummated sales, or (d) pursuant to purchases, or (e) as collateral security, or (f) by way of loans of securities by such persons to the stockbroker, and shall include persons who have claims against the stockbroker arising out of sales or conversions of such securities; "cash customers" shall mean customers entitled to immediate possession of such securities without the payment of any sum to the stockbroker; the same person may be a cash customer with reference to certain securities and not a cash customer with reference to other securities; the "net equity" of a customer's account shall be determined by excluding any specifically identifiable securities reclaimable by the customer and by subtracting the indebtedness of the customer to the stockbroker from the sum which would have been owing by the stockbroker to the customer had the stockbroker liquidated, by sale or purchase on the date of bankruptcy, the remaining securities or security commitments of the customer.

(2) All property at any time received, acquired, or held by a stockbroker from or for the account of customers, except cash customers who are able to identify specifically their property in the manner prescribed in paragraph (4) of this subdivision and the proceeds of all customers' property rightfully transferred or unlawfully converted by the stockbroker, shall constitute a single and separate fund; and all customers except such cash customers shall constitute a single and separate class of creditors, entitled to share ratably in such fund on the basis of their respective net equities as of the date of bankruptcy: *Provided, however,* That such fund shall to the extent approved by the court be subject to the priority of payment of the costs and expenses enumerated in clauses (1) and (2) of subdivision (a) of section 104 of this title. If such fund shall not be sufficient to pay in full the claims of such class of creditors, such creditors shall be entitled, to the extent only of their respective unpaid balances, to share in the general estate with the general creditors.

(3) Any property remaining after the liquidation of a pledge made by a stockbroker shall be apportioned between his general estate and such single and separate fund in the proportion in which the general property of the stockbroker and the property of his customers contributed to such pledge.

(4) No cash received by a stockbroker from or for the account of a customer for the purchase or sale of securities, and no securities or similar property received by a stockbroker from or for the account of a cash customer for sale and remittance or pursuant to purchase or as collateral security, or for safekeeping, or any substitutes therefor or the proceeds thereof, shall for the purposes of this subdivision (e) be deemed to be specifically identified, unless such property remained in its identical form in the stockbroker's possession until the date of bankruptcy, or unless such property or any substitutes therefor or the proceeds thereof were, more than four months before bankruptcy or at a time while the stockbroker was solvent, allocated to or physically set aside for such customer, and remained so allocated or set aside at the date of bankruptcy.

(5) Where such single and separate fund is not sufficient to pay in full the claims of such single and separate class of creditors, a transfer by a stockbroker of any property which, except for such transfer, would have been a part of such fund may be recovered by the trustee for the benefit of such fund, if such transfer is voidable or void under the provisions of this title. For the purpose of such recovery, the property so transferred shall be deemed to have been the property of the stockbroker and, if such transfer was made to a customer or for his benefit, such customer shall be deemed to have been a creditor, the laws of any State to the contrary notwithstanding. If any securities received or acquired by a stockbroker from a cash customer are transferred by the stockbroker, such customer shall not have any specific interest in or specific right to any securities of like kind on hand at the time of bankruptcy, but such securities of like kind or the proceeds thereof shall become part of such single and separate

fund: *Provided, however,* That a customer shall have a specific title to securities (a) which have been physically set aside by a stockbroker, more than four months before his bankruptcy or while solvent, in safekeeping for such customer, and so retained until the date of bankruptcy, regardless of the name in which such securities are registered, or (b) which a stockbroker, more than four months before his bankruptcy or while solvent, caused to be registered in the name of such customer. July 1, 1898, c. 541, § 60, 30 Stat. 562; Feb. 5, 1903, c. 487, § 13, 32 Stat. 799; June 25, 1910, c. 412, § 11, 36 Stat. 842; May 27, 1926, c. 406, § 14, 44 Stat. 666; June 22, 1938, c. 575, § 1, 52 Stat. 869; Mar. 18, 1950, c. 70, § 1, 64 Stat. 24; May 8, 1963, Pub.L. 88–17, 77 Stat. 14.

§ 103. Debts which may be proved

(a) Debts of the bankrupt may be proved and allowed against his estate which are founded upon (1) a fixed liability, as evidenced by a judgment or an instrument in writing, absolutely owing at the time of the filing of the petition by or against him, whether then payable or not, with any interest thereon which would have been recoverable at that date or with a rebate of interest upon such as were not then payable and did not bear interest; (2) costs taxable against a bankrupt who was at the time of the filing of the petition by or against him plaintiff in a cause of action which would pass to the trustee and which the trustee declines to prosecute after notice; (3) a claim for taxable costs incurred in good faith by a creditor before the filing of the petition in an action to recover a probable [1] debt; (4) an open account, or a contract express or implied; (5) provable debts reduced to judgments after the filing of the petition and before the consideration of the bankrupt's application for a discharge, less costs incurred and interest accrued after the filing of the petition and up to the time of the entry of such judgments; (6) an award of an industrial-accident commission, body, or officer of any State having jurisdiction to make awards of workmen's compensation in case of injury or death from injury, if such injury occurred prior to adjudication; (7) the right to recover damages in any action for negligence instituted prior to and pending at the time of the filing of the petition in bankruptcy; (8) contingent debts and contingent contractual liabilities; or (9) claims for anticipatory breach of contracts, executory in whole or in part, including unexpired leases of real or personal property: *Provided, however,* That the claim of a landlord for damages for injury resulting from the rejection of an unexpired lease of real estate or for damages or indemnity under a covenant contained in such lease shall in no event be allowed in an amount exceeding the rent reserved by the lease, without acceleration, for the year next succeeding the date of the surrender of the premises to the landlord or the date of reentry of the landlord, whichever first occurs, whether before or after bankruptcy, plus an amount equal to the unpaid rent accrued, without acceleration, up to such date: *And provided further,* That in the case of an assignment of any such claim for damages, the court shall, in determining the amount thereof, examine the circumstances of the assignment and the consideration paid or to be paid therefor, and may allow the claim of the assignee in such amount, subject to the provisions of the foregoing proviso of this clause, as will be fair and equitable.

(b) In the interval after the filing of an involuntary petition and before the appointment of a receiver or the adjudication, whichever first oc-

1. So in original. Probably should read "provable".

curs, a claim arising in favor of a creditor by reason of property transferred or services rendered by the creditor to the bankrupt for the benefit of the estate shall be provable to the extent of the value of such property or services.

(c) Notwithstanding any State law to the contrary, the rejection of an executory contract or unexpired lease, as provided in this title, shall constitute a breach of such contract or lease as of the date of the filing of the petition initiating a proceeding under this title.

(d) Where any contingent or unliquidated claim has been proved, but, as provided in subdivision (d) of section 93 of this title, has not been allowed, such claim shall not be deemed provable under this title.   July 1, 1898, c. 541, § 63, 30 Stat. 562; June 7, 1934, c. 424, § 4(a), 48 Stat. 923; June 18, 1934, c. 580, 48 Stat. 991; June 5, 1936, c. 512, § 1, 49 Stat. 1475; June 22, 1938, c. 575, § 1, 52 Stat. 873; July 7, 1952, c. 579, § 18, 66 Stat. 426.

§ 104. Debts which have priority

(a) The debts to have priority, in advance of the payment of dividends to creditors, and to be paid in full out of bankrupt estates, and the order of payment, shall be (1) the costs and expenses of administration, including the actual and necessary costs and expenses of preserving the estate subsequent to filing the petition; the fees for the referees' salary and expense fund; the filing fees paid by creditors in involuntary cases or by persons other than the bankrupts in voluntary cases; where property of the bankrupt, transferred or concealed by him either before or after the filing of the petition, is recovered for the benefit of the estate of the bankrupt by the efforts and at the cost and expense of one or more creditors, the reasonable costs and expenses of such recovery; the trustee's expenses in opposing the bankrupt's discharge or in connection with the criminal prosecution of an offense punishable under chapter 9 of Title 18, or an offense concerning the business or property of the bankrupt punishable under other laws, Federal or State; the fees and mileage payable to witnesses as now or hereafter provided by the laws of the United States, and one reasonable attorney's fee, for the professional services actually rendered, irrespective of the number of attorneys employed, to the bankrupt in voluntary and involuntary cases, and to the petitioning creditors in involuntary cases, and if the court adjudges the debtor bankrupt over the debtor's objection or pursuant to a voluntary petition filed by the debtor during the pendency of an involuntary proceeding, for the reasonable costs and expenses incurred, or the reasonable disbursements made, by them, including but not limited to compensation of accountants and appraisers employed by them, in such amount as the court may allow.   Where an order is entered in a proceeding under any chapter of this title directing that bankruptcy be proceeded with, the costs and expenses of administration incurred in the ensuing bankruptcy proceeding, including expenses necessarily incurred by a debtor in possession, receiver, or trustee in preparing the schedule and statement required to be filed by section 638, 778, or 883 of this title, shall have priority in advance of payment of the unpaid costs and expenses of administration, including the allowances provided for in such chapter, incurred in the superseded proceeding and in the suspended bankruptcy proceeding, if any; (2) wages and commissions, not to exceed $600 to each claimant, which have been earned within three months before the date of the commencement of the proceeding, due to workmen, servants, clerks, or traveling, or city salesmen on salary or commission basis, whole or part time, whether or not selling exclusively for the bankrupt; and for the purposes of this clause, the term "traveling or city salesman" shall include all such salesmen, whether or not they are independent contractors selling the products or services of the bankrupt on a commission basis, with or without a drawing account or formal contract; (3) where the confirmation of an arrangement or wage earner plan or the bankrupt's discharge has been refused, revoked, or set aside upon the objection and through the efforts and at the cost and expense of one or more creditors, or, where through the efforts and at the cost and expense of one or more creditors, evidence shall have been adduced resulting in the conviction of any person of an offense under chapter 9 of Title 18, the reasonable costs and expenses of such creditors in obtaining such refusal, revocation, or setting aside, or in adducing such evidence; (4) taxes which became legally due and owing by the bankrupt to the United States or to any State or any subdivision thereof which are not released by a discharge in bankruptcy: *Provided, however*, That no priority over general unsecured claims shall pertain to taxes not included in the foregoing priority: *And provided further*, That no order shall be made for the payment of a tax assessed against any property of the bankrupt in excess of the value of the interest of the bankrupt estate therein as determined by the court; and (5) debts other than for taxes owing to any person, including the United States, who by the laws of the United States is entitled to priority, and rent owing to a landlord who is entitled to priority by applicable State law or who is entitled to priority by paragraph (2) of subdivision c of section 107 of this title: *Provided, however*, That such priority for rent to a landlord shall be restricted to the rent which is legally due and owing for the actual use and occupancy of the premises affected, and which accrued within three months before the date of bankruptcy.

As amended July 30, 1956, c. 784, § 1, 70 Stat. 725; July 28, 1959, Pub.L. 86–110, § 3, 73 Stat. 260; Sept. 25, 1962, Pub.L. 87–681, § 8, 76 Stat. 571; July 5, 1966, Pub.L. 89–495, § 2, 80 Stat. 268; July 5, 1966, Pub.L. 89–496, § 3, 80 Stat. 271; Nov. 28, 1967, Pub.L. 90–157, § 1, 81 Stat. 511.

§ 108. Set-offs and counterclaims

a. In all cases of mutual debts or mutual credits between the estate of a bankrupt and a creditor the account shall be stated and one debt shall be set off against the other, and the balance only shall be allowed or paid.

b. A set-off or counterclaim shall not be allowed in favor of any debtor of the bankrupt which (1) is not provable against the estate and allowable under subdivision g of section 93 of this title; or (2) was purchased by or transferred to him after the filing of the petition or within four months before such filing, with a view to such use and with knowledge or notice that such bankrupt was insolvent or had committed an act of bankruptcy. July 1, 1898, c. 541, § 68, 30 Stat. 565; June 22, 1938, c. 575, § 1, 52 Stat. 878.

2. EQUALITY OF DISTRIBUTION OF ASSETS

SAMPSELL v. IMPERIAL PAPER & COLOR CORPORATION

Supreme Court of the United States, 1941.
313 U.S. 215, 61 S.Ct. 904, 85 L.Ed. 1293.

Mr. Justice DOUGLAS delivered the opinion of the Court.

One Downey was adjudged a voluntary bankrupt in November, 1938. Prior to June, 1936, Downey had been engaged in business, unincorporated, and had incurred a debt to the predecessor of Standard Coated Products Corporation of approximately $104,000. In that month he formed a corporation, Downey Wallpaper & Paint Co., under the laws of California. Downey, his wife and his son were the sole stockholders, directors and officers. Downey's stock of goods was transferred to the corporation on credit, which was extended from time to time. He leased space in the store building occupied by him to the corporation, which continued business at the old stand. Except for qualifying shares, neither he nor the other members of his family paid cash for the stock which was issued to them but received most of those shares a few months prior to bankruptcy in satisfaction of the balance of the obligation owed to him by the corporation. Respondent extended credit to the corporation. At the time of Downey's bankruptcy respondent's claim amounted to about $5,400 and was unsecured.

On petition of the trustee in bankruptcy, the referee issued an order to show cause directed to the corporation, Downey, his wife and son why the assets of the corporation should not be marshalled for the benefit of the creditors of the bankrupt estate and administered by the trustee. Downey answered. There was a hearing. The referee found, inter alia, that the transfer of the property to the corporation was not in good faith but was made for the purpose of placing the property beyond the reach of Downey's creditors and of retaining for Downey and his family all of the beneficial interest therein; that the stock was issued in satisfaction of Downey's claim against the corporation, when Downey was hopelessly insolvent, to prevent Downey's creditors from reaching the assets so transferred; that the corporation was "nothing but a sham and a cloak" devised by Downey "for the purpose of preserving and conserving his assets" for the benefit of himself and his family; and that the corporation was formed for the purpose of hindering, delaying and defrauding his creditors. The referee accordingly ordered that the property of the corporation was property of the bankrupt estate and that it be administered for the benefit of the creditors of the estate. That order was entered on April 7, 1939. No appeal from that order was taken.

Respondent, who was not a party to that proceeding, later filed its claim stating that as a creditor of the corporation it had a prior right to distribution of the funds in the hands of the trustee received from the liquidation of the assets of the corporation. It secured an order to show cause why the trustee should not so apply such funds. The trustee objected to the allowance of the claim as a prior claim and contended that it should be allowed only as a general unsecured claim. There was a hearing. The referee found that respondent with knowledge of Downey's indebtedness was instrumental in getting him to form the corporation and had full knowledge of its fraudulent character. He disallowed respondent's claim as a prior claim but allowed it as a general unsecured claim. That order was confirmed. On appeal, the Circuit Court of Appeals reversed, holding that respondent's claim should be accorded priority against the funds realized from the liquidation of the corporation's property. * * * We granted the petition for certiorari, * * * because of the importance in administration of the bankruptcy act of the questions raised.

We think the Circuit Court of Appeals was in error.

* * *

Mere legal paraphernalia will not suffice to transform into a substantial adverse claimant a corporation whose affairs are so closely assimilated to the affairs of the dominant stockholder that in substance it is little more than his corporate pocket. Whatever the full reach of that rule may be, it is clear that a family corporation's adverse claim is merely colorable where, as in this case, the corporation is formed in order to continue the bankrupt's business, where the bankrupt remains in control, and where the effect of the transfer is to hinder, delay or defraud his creditors. In re Schoenberg, 2 Cir., 70 F.2d 321; In re Berkowitz, D.C., 173 F. 1013. And see Glenn, Liquidation, §§ 30–32. Cf. Shapiro v. Wilgus, 287 U.S. 348, 53 S.Ct. 142, 77 L.Ed. 355, 85 A.L.R. 128. Hence Downey's corporation was in no position to assert against Downey's trustee that it was so separate and insulated from Downey's other business affairs as to stand in an independent and adverse position. * * *

That conclusion, of course, does not mean that the order consolidating the estates did, or in the absence of the respondent as a party, could determine what priority, if any, it had to the corporate assets. In re Foley, 9 Cir., 4 F.2d 154. All questions of fraudulent conveyance aside, creditors of the corporation normally would be entitled to satisfy their claims out of corporate assets prior to any participation by the creditors of the stockholder. In re Smith, 2 Cir., 36 F.2d 697. Such priority, however, would be denied if the corporation's creditors were parties to a fraudulent transfer of the stockholder's assets to the corporation. Furthermore, where the transfer was fraudulent or where the relationship between the stockholder and the corporation was such as to justify the use of summary proceedings to absorb the corporate assets into the bankruptcy estate of the stockholder, the corporation's unsecured creditors would have the burden of showing that their equity was paramount in order to obtain priority as respects the corporate assets. Cf. New York Trust Co. v. Island Oil & Transport Corp., 2 Cir., 56 F.2d 580. The power of the bankruptcy court to subordinate claims or to adjudicate equities arising out of the relationship between the several creditors is complete. * * * But the theme of the Bankruptcy Act is equality of distribution. § 65, sub. a, 11 U.S.C.A. § 105, sub. a; Moore v. Bay, 284 U.S. 4. To bring himself outside of that rule an unsecured creditor carries a burden of showing by clear and convincing evidence that its application to his case so as to deny him priority would work an injustice. Such burden has been sustained by creditors of the affiliated corporation and their paramount equity has been established where there was no fraud in the transfer, where the transferor remained solvent, and where the creditors had extended credit to the transferee, Commerce Trust Co. v. Woodbury [77 F.2d 478].

But in this case there was a fraudulent transfer. The saving clause in 13 Eliz. which protected innocent purchasers for value was not broad enough to protect mere unsecured creditors of the fraudulent transferee. * * * To be sure, creditors of a fraudulent transferee have at times been accorded priority over the creditors of the transferor where they have "taken the property into their own custody". 1 Glenn, Fraudulent Conveyances and Preferences, 1940, § 238. * * * The same result obtains in case of bona fide lien creditors of the fraudulent transferee. * * * And estoppel or other equitable considerations might well result in the award of priority even to unsecured creditors of the transferee, the conveyance being good between the parties. * * * Yet none of these considerations is applicable here.

The facts do not justify the invocation of estoppel against Downey's individual creditors. Respondent is neither a lien creditor nor an innocent grantee for value. At best it is in no more favorable position than a judgment creditor who has not levied execution. Furthermore, respondent had at least some knowledge as to the fraudulent character of Downey's corporation. * * * And title to the property fraudulently conveyed has vested in the bankruptcy trustee of the grantor. We have not been referred to any state law or any equitable considerations which under these circumstances would accord respondent the priority which it seeks. It therefore is entitled only to pari passu participation with Downey's individual creditors. Buffum v. Barceloux Co., 289 U.S. 227.

The judgment of the Circuit Court of Appeals is reversed and that of the District Court affirmed.

It is so ordered.

Reversed.

3. REHABILITATION OF A DEBTOR (DISCHARGE FROM HIS LIABILITIES)

PEREZ v. CAMPBELL

Supreme Court of the United States, 1971.
402 U.S. 637, 91 S.Ct. 1704, 29 L.Ed.2d 233.

Mr. Justice WHITE delivered the opinion of the Court.

This case raises an important issue concerning the construction of the Supremacy Clause of the Constitution—whether Ariz.Rev. Stat. § 28–1163(B), which is part of Arizona's Motor Vehicle Safety Responsibility Act, is invalid under that clause as being in conflict with the mandate of § 17 of the Bankruptcy Act, 11 U.S.C.A. § 35, providing that receipt of a discharge in bankruptcy fully discharges all but certain specified judgments. The courts below, concluding that this case was controlled by Kesler v. Department of Public Safety, 369 U.S. 153 (1962), and Reitz v. Mealey, 314 U.S. 33 (1941), two earlier opinions of this Court dealing with alleged conflicts between the Bankruptcy Act and state financial responsibility laws, ruled against the claim of conflict and upheld the Arizona statute.

On July 8, 1965, petitioner Adolfo Perez, driving a car registered in his name, was involved in an automobile accident in Tucson, Arizona. The Perez automobile was not covered by liability insurance at the time of the collision. The driver of the second car was the minor daughter of Leonard Pinkerton, and in September 1966 the Pinkertons sued Mr. and Mrs. Perez in state court for personal injuries and property damage sustained in the accident. On October 31, 1967, the petitioners confessed judgment in this suit, and a judgment order was entered against them on November 8, 1967, for $2,425.98 plus court costs.

Mr. and Mrs. Perez each filed a voluntary petition in bankruptcy in Federal District Court on November 6, 1967. Each of them duly scheduled the judgment debt to the Pinkertons. The District Court entered orders on July 8, 1968, discharging both Mr. and Mrs. Perez from all debts and claims provable against their estates, including the Pinkerton judgment. 11 U.S.C.A. § 35; * * *

During the pendency of the bankruptcy proceedings, the provisions of the Arizona Motor Vehicle Safety Responsibility Act came into play. * * *

Article 4 of the Arizona Act, which includes the only provision at issue here, deals with suspension of licenses and registrations for nonpayment of judgments. Interestingly, it is only when the judgment debtor in an automobile accident lawsuit—usually an owner-operator like Mr. Perez—fails to respond to a judgment entered against him that he must overcome two hurdles in order to regain his driving privileges. Section 28–1161, the first section of Article 4, requires the state court clerk or judge, when a judgment has remained unsatisfied for 60 days after entry, to forward a certified copy of the judgment to the superintendent. This was done in the present case, and on March 13, 1968, Mr. and Mrs. Perez were served with notice that their driver's licenses and registration were suspended pursuant to § 28–1162(A). Under other provisions of Article 4, such suspension is to continue until the judgment is paid, and § 28–1163(B) specifically provides that "[a] discharge in bankruptcy following the rendering of any such judgment shall not relieve the judgment debtor from any of the requirements of this article." In addition to requiring satisfaction of the judgment debt, § 28–1163(A) provides that the license and registration "shall remain suspended and shall not be renewed, nor shall any license or registration be thereafter issued in the name of the person, * * * until the person gives proof of financial responsibility" for a future period. Again, the validity of this limited requirement that some drivers post evidence of financial responsibility for the future in order to regain driving privileges is not questioned here. Nor is the broader issue of whether a State may require proof of financial responsibility as a precondition for granting driving privileges to anyone before us for decision. What is at issue here is the power of a State to include as part of this comprehensive enactment designed to secure compensation for automobile accident victims a section providing that a discharge in bankruptcy of the automobile accident tort judgment shall have no effect on the judgment debtor's obligation to repay the judgment creditor, at least insofar as such repayment may be enforced by the withholding of driving privileges by the State. It was that question among others, which petitioners raised after suspension of their licenses and registration by filing a complaint in Federal District Court seeking declaratory and injunctive relief and requesting a three-judge court. They asserted several constitutional violations, and also alleged that § 28–1163(B) was in direct conflict with the Bankruptcy Act and was thus violative of the Supremacy Clause of the Constitution. In support of their complaint, Mr. and Mrs. Perez filed affidavits stating that the suspension of their licenses and registration worked both physical and financial hardship upon them and their children. The District Judge granted the petitioners leave to proceed *in forma pauperis,* but thereafter granted the respondents' motion to dismiss the complaint for failure to state a claim upon which relief could be granted, citing *Kesler* and *Reitz.* The Court of Appeals affirmed, relying on the same two decisions. * * *

I

Deciding whether a state statute is in conflict with a federal statute and hence invalid under the Supremacy Clause is essentially a two-step process of first ascertaining the construction of the two statutes and then determining the constitutional question whether they are in conflict. In the present case, both statutes have been authoritatively construed. In Schecter v. Killingsworth, 93 Ariz. 273, (1963), the Supreme Court of Arizona held that "[t]he Financial Responsibility Act has for its principal purpose the protection of the public using the highways from financial hardship which may result from the use of automobiles by financially irresponsible persons." The Arizona court has consistently adhered to this construction of its legislation, * * * and we are bound by its rulings. See, *e. g.,* General Trading Co. v. State Tax Comm'n, 322 U.S. 335, 337 (1944).

* * *

Turning to the federal statute, the construction of the Bankruptcy Act is similarly clear. This Court on numerous occasions has stated that "[o]ne of the primary purposes of the Bankruptcy Act" is to give debtors "a new opportunity in life and a clear field for future effort, unhampered by the pressure and discouragement of pre-existing debt." Local Loan Co. v. Hunt, 292 U.S. 234 (1934). * * * There can be no doubt, * * * that Congress intended this "new opportunity" to include freedom from most kinds of pre-existing tort judgments.

II

With the construction of both statutes clearly established, we proceed immediately to the constitutional question whether a state statute that protects judgment creditors from "financially irresponsible persons" is in conflict with a federal statute that gives discharged debtors a new start "unhampered by the pressure and discouragement of preexisting debt." As early as Gibbons v. Ogden, 9 Wheat. 1, 6 L.Ed. 23 (1824), Chief Justice Marshall stated the governing principle—that "acts of the State Legislatures * * *, [which] *interfere with,* or are contrary to the laws of Congress, made in pursuance of the constitution," are invalid under the Supremacy Clause. Id., at 211 (emphasis added). Three decades ago Mr. Justice Black, after reviewing the precedents, wrote in a similar vein that, while "[t]his Court, in considering the validity of state laws in the light of treaties or federal laws touching the same subject, ha[d] made use of the following expressions: conflicting; contrary to; occupying the field; repugnance; difference; irreconcilability; inconsistency; violation; curtailment; and interference[,] * * * [i]n the final analysis," our function is to determine whether a challenged state statute "stands as an obstacle to the accomplishment and execution of the full purposes and objectives of Congress." Hines v. Davidowitz, 312 U.S. 52 (1941). Since *Hines* the Court has frequently adhered to this articulation of the meaning of the Supremacy Clause.

* * *

Both *Kesler* and *Reitz,* however, ignored this controlling principle. The Court in *Kesler* conceded that Utah's financial responsibility law left "the bankrupt to some extent burdened by the discharged debt," * * * made "it more probable that the debt will be paid despite the discharge," * * * and thereby made "some inroad * * * on the consequences of bankruptcy. * * *" Utah's statute, in short, frustrated Congress' policy of giving discharged debtors a new start. But the *Kesler* majority was not concerned by this frustration. In upholding the statute, the majority opinion looked not to the effect of the legislation but simply asserted that the statute was "not an Act for the Relief of Mulcted Creditors," * * * and was "not designed to aid collection of debts but to enforce a policy against irresponsible driving. * * *" The majority, that is, looked to the purpose of the state legislation and upheld it because the purpose was not to circumvent the Bankruptcy Act but to promote highway safety; those in dissent, however, were concerned that, whatever the purpose of the Utah Act, its "plain and inevitable effect * * * [was] to create a powerful weapon for collection of a debt from which [the] bankrupt [had] been released by federal law." Such a result, they argued, left "the States free * * * to impair * * * an important and historic policy of this Nation * * * embodied in its bankruptcy laws."

The opinion of the Court in *Reitz* was similarly concerned not with the fact that New York's financial responsibility law frustrated the operation of the Bankruptcy Act, but with the purpose of the law, which was divined as the promotion of highway safety.

* * *

The dissenting opinion written by Mr. Justice Douglas for himself and three others noted that the New York legislation put "the bankrupt * * * at the creditor's mercy," with the results that "[i]n practical effect the bankrupt may be in as bad, or even worse, a position than if the State had made it possible for a creditor to attach his future wages" and that "[b]ankruptcy * * * [was not] the sanctuary for hapless debtors which Congress intended."

We can no longer adhere to the aberrational doctrine of *Kesler* and *Reitz* that state law may frustrate the operation of federal law as long as the state legislature in passing its law had some purpose in mind other than one of frustration. Apart from the fact that it is at odds with the approach taken in nearly all our Supremacy Clause cases, such a doctrine would enable state legislatures to nullify nearly all unwanted federal legislation by simply publishing a legislative committee report articulating some state interest or policy—other than frustration of the federal objective—that would be tangentially furthered by the proposed state law. In view of the consequences, we certainly would not apply the *Kesler* doctrine in all Supremacy Clause cases. Although it is possible to argue that *Kesler* and *Reitz* are somehow confined to cases involving either bankruptcy or highway safety, analysis discloses no reason why the States should have broader power to nullify federal law in these fields than in others. Thus, we conclude that *Kesler* and *Reitz* can have no authoritative effect to the extent they are inconsistent with the controlling principle that any state legislation which frustrates the full effectiveness of federal law is rendered invalid by the Supremacy Clause. Section 28–1163(B) thus may not stand.

* * *

From the foregoing, we think it clear that § 28–1163(B) of the Arizona Financial Responsibility Act is constitutionally invalid. The judgment of the Court of Appeals is reversed and the case is remanded for further proceedings consistent with this opinion.

It is so ordered.

Reversed and remanded.

Mr. Justice BLACKMUN, joined by THE CHIEF JUSTICE, Mr. Justice HARLAN, and Mr. Justice STEWART.

I concur in the result as to petitioner Emma Perez and dissent as to petitioner Adolfo Perez.

I

The slaughter on the highways of this Nation exceeds the death toll of all our wars.[1] The country is fragmented about the current conflict in Southeast Asia, but I detect little genuine public concern about what takes place in our very midst and on our daily travel routes. * * *

This being so, it is a matter of deep concern to me that today the Court lightly brushes aside and overrules two case where it had upheld a representative attempt by the States to regulate traffic and where the Court had considered and rejected the very Supremacy Clause argument that it now discovers to be so persuasive.

II

I think it is desirable to stress certain factual details. The facts, of course, are only alleged, but for purposes of the motion to dismiss, we are to accept them as true. Cooper v. Pate, 378 U.S. 546, 84 S.Ct. 1733, 12 L.Ed.2d 1030 (1964).

Arizona is a community property state. Adolfo and Emma Perez are husband and wife. They were resident citizens of Arizona at the time of the accident in Tucson in July 1965. Mr. Perez was driving an automobile registered in his name. He was alone. Mrs. Perez was not with him and had nothing to do with her husband's operation of the car on that day. The automobile, however, was the property of the marital community.

Accompanying, and supposedly supportive of, the Perez complaint in the present suit, were affidavits of Mr. and Mrs. Perez. These affidavits asserted that the Perezes had four minor children ages 6 to 17; that Emma is a housewife and not otherwise gainfully employed; that Emma's inability to drive has required their two older children, aged 17 and 14, to walk one and a half miles to high school and the third child, aged 9, one mile to elementary school, with consequent nose-bleeding; that Emma's inability to drive has caused inconvenience and financial injury; and that Adolfo's inability to drive has caused inconvenience because he must rely on others for transportation or use public facilities or walk.

* * *

---

1. See Appendix to this opinion.

IV

Adolfo Perez

Inasmuch as the case is before us on the defendants' motion to dismiss the Perez complaint that alleged Adolfo's driving alone, the collision, and the judgment in favor of the Pinkertons, it is established, for present purposes, that the Pinkerton judgment was based on Adolfo's negligence in driving the Perez vehicle.

Adolfo emphasizes, and I recognize, that under Article I, § 8, cl. 4 of the Constitution, Congress has possessed the power to establish "uniform Laws on the subject of Bankruptcies throughout the United States"; that, of course, this power, when exercised, as it has been since 1898, is "exclusive," New Lamp Chimney Co. v. Ansonia Brass and Copper Co., 91 U.S. 656 (1875), and "unrestricted and paramount," International Shoe Co. v. Pinkus, 278 U.S. 261 (1929); that one of the purposes of the Bankruptcy Act is to "relieve the honest debtor from the weight of oppressive indebtedness and to permit him to start afresh * * *," * * * and that a bankrupt by his discharge receives "a new opportunity in life and a clear field for future effort, unhampered by the pressure and discouragement of pre-existing debts," Local Loan Co. v. Hunt, 292 U.S. 234 (1934).

From these general and accepted principles it is argued that § 28–1163.B, with its insistence upon post-discharge payment as a condition for license and registration restoration, is violative of the Bankruptcy Act and, thus, of the Supremacy Clause.

As Mr. Perez acknowledges in his brief here, the argument is not new. It was raised with respect to a New York statute in Reitz v. Mealey, 314 U.S. 33 (1941), and was rejected there by a five-to-four vote:

" * * * The use of the public highways by motor vehicles, with its consequent dangers, renders the reasonableness and necessity of regulation apparent. The universal practice is to register ownership of automobiles and to license their drivers. Any appropriate means adopted by the states to insure competence and care on the part of its licensees and to protect others using the highway is consonant with due process. * * * "

* * *

Nine years ago, the same argument again was advanced, this time with respect to Utah's Motor Vehicle Safety Responsibility Act, and again was rejected. Kesler v. Department of Public Safety, 369 U.S. 153 (1962). * * *

The Perezes in their brief, p. 7, acknowledge that the Arizona statutes challenged here "are not unlike the Utah ones discussed in Kesler." Accordingly, Adolfo Perez is forced to urge that *Reitz* and the remaining portion of *Kesler* that bears upon the subject be overruled. The Court bows to that argument.

I am not prepared to overrule those two cases and to undermine their control over Adolfo Perez' posture here. I would adhere to the rulings and I would hold that the States have an appropriate and legitimate concern with highway safety; that the means Arizona has adopted with respect to one in Adolfo's position (that is, the driver whose negligence has caused harm to others and whose judgment debt based on that negligence remains unsatisfied) in its attempt to assure driving competence and care on the part of its licensees, as well as to protect others, is appropriate state legislation; and that the Arizona statute, like its Utah counterpart, despite the tangential effect upon bankruptcy, does not operate in derogation of the Bankruptcy Act or conflict with it to the extent it may rightly be said to violate the Supremacy Clause.

* * * Here is a serious and conscientious attempt by a State to legislate and do something about the problem that, in terms of death and bodily injury and adverse civilian effect, is so alarming. Here is a statute widely adopted by the several States and legitimately assumed by the lawmakers of those States to be consistent with the Bankruptcy Act, an assumption rooted in positive, albeit divided, decision by this Court, not once, but twice. And here is a statute the Congress itself, the very author of the Bankruptcy Act, obviously considered consistent therewith. I fear that the Court today makes *stare decisis* meaningless and downgrades it to the level of a tool to be used or cast aside as convenience dictates. I doubt if Justices Roberts, Stone, Reed, Frankfurter, Murphy, Warren, Clark, Harlan, Brennan, and Stewart, who constituted the respective majorities on the merits in *Reitz* and *Kesler,* were all that wrong.

* * *

Emma Perez

Emma Perez' posture is entirely different. Except for possible emotional strain resulting from her husband's predicament, she was in no way involved in the Pinkerton accident. She was not present when it occurred and no negligence or nonfeasance on her part contributed to it. Emma thus finds herself in a position where, having done no wrong, she nevertheless is deprived of her operator's license. This comes about because the Perez vehicle concededly was community property under § 25–211.A, and because, for some reason, the judgment was confessed as to her as well as against her husband. As one *amicus* brief describes it, Emma, a fault-free driver, "is without her license solely because she is the impecunious wife of an impecunious, negligent driver in a community property state."

* * *

I conclude that the reasoning of the Court of Appeals, in its application to Emma Perez and her operator's license, does not comport with the purpose and policy of the Bankruptcy Act and that it effects a result at odds with the Supremacy Clause. Emma's subordinate position with respect to the community's personal property, and her complete lack of connection with the Pinkerton accident and with the negligence that occasioned it, are strange accompaniments for the deprival of her operator's license. * * *

I therefore would hold that under these circumstances the State's action, under § 28–1163.B, in withholding from Emma her operator's license is not, within the language of *Reitz,* an appropriate means for Arizona "to insure competence and care on the part of [Emma] and to protect others" using the highways, 314 U.S., at 36, 62 S.Ct., at 26, and that it interferes with the paramount federal interest in her bankruptcy discharge and violates the Supremacy Clause.

APPENDIX

MOTOR-VEHICLE DEATHS AND WAR DEATHS

From 1900 through 1969, motor-vehicle deaths in the U.S. totalled nearly 1,800,000. Deaths of U.S. military personnel in all wars are shown below. In making comparisons, it must be kept in mind that nearly everyone is exposed to motor-vehicle accidents but relatively few are exposed to war deaths.

U. S. Military Casualties is Principal Wars

| War | Deaths | | | Nonfatal |
	Total	Battle	Others*	Wounds
Total	† 1,146,000	643,052	† 503,200	§ 1,540,000
Revolutionary War (1775–83)	4,435	4,435	N.A.	6,188
War of 1812 (1812–15)	2,260	2,260	N.A.	4,505
Mexican War (1846–48)	13,283	1,733	11,550	4,152
Civil War (1861–65)				
Union Forces	364,511	140,414	224,097	281,881
Confederate Forces	133,821	74,524	59,297	N.A.
Spanish-American War (1898)	2,446	385	2,061	1,662
World War I (1917–18)	116,708	53,513	63,195	204,002
World War II (1941–45)	407,316	292,131	115,185	670,846
Korean War (1950–53)	54,246	33,629	20,617	103,284
Viet Nam War (1961–69)	47,251	40,028	7,223	262,799

Source: Office of Secretary of Defense.   * Includes deaths from disease, accidents, etc.
† Rounded.   § Incomplete and rounded. N.A. Not available.

Accident Facts (1970 ed.), p. 63, published by the National Safety Council.

The same publication, page 59, discloses that the annual death toll for motor vehicle accidents in the United States has exceeded 52,000 in each of the last five calendar years. Thus, the *annual* motor vehicle carnage approximates the *total* number of lives lost during the entire Vietnam conflict beginning in 1961.

IN RE BISCOE

District Court, D. Massachusetts, 1942.
45 F.Supp. 422.

WYZANSKI, District Judge. Watts is a creditor of the bankrupt Biscoe. He claims Biscoe borrowed money by making a false representation of his assets and liabilities. Now, in the course of Biscoe's bankruptcy and with no proceeding pending in any other court involving the same claim, Watts petitions this court to determine that Biscoe is liable to him for obtaining money by false pretenses and that the liability is non-dischargeable under Section 17, sub. a(2) of the Bankruptcy Act, U.S.C.A. Title 11, § 35, sub. a(2).

The bankruptcy statutes do not direct the bankruptcy court to determine whether a particular debt is dischargeable. And the official forms in current use do not specify which debts are discharged, but merely provide that the bankrupt is "discharged from all debts and claims which are made provable by said Act against his estate, except such debts as are, by said Act, excepted from the operation of a discharge in bankruptcy". Official Form No. 45, 11 U.S.C.A. following section 53 (the decree).

But although the statutes do not specifically require the bankruptcy court to make the determination, it is clear that the bankruptcy court has the power, at least upon an ancillary bill, to hear and decide whether a particular debt is discharged. Local Loan Co. v. Hunt, 292 U.S. 234. * * *

However, the power of the bankruptcy court to determine during the bankruptcy proceedings whether a particular debt will be discharged has not been customarily exercised either in this district, In re Mussey, D.C.D.Mass., 99 F. 71, or elsewhere, In re Colao, D.C.S.D.N.Y., 10 F.Supp. 406. See Collier on Bankruptcy, 14th Ed., vol. 1, § 17.28 note 2. In recent days only one District Judge sitting in bankruptcy has said he would undertake to determine during the course of the bankruptcy proceeding whether a particular debt was dischargeable. Hisey v. Lewis-Gale Hospital, D.C.W.D.Va., 27 F.Supp. 20, 25, and that judge admits his course would differ from what he understands to be the universal practice in other districts.

The usual practice is to leave the claimant if he regards his claim as undischarged to sue upon it in any appropriate forum, and to allow the discharged bankrupt there to plead his discharge. Such defence is one that the state or any other court is bound to consider, and if error is committed in failing to accord to the discharge its due weight, the way is open to the Supreme Court of the United States. In re Devereaux, 2 Cir., 76 F.2d 522, 524.

There are good reasons for continuing this practice.

The primary purpose of the Bankruptcy Act is equitably, promptly, and economically to collect the bankrupt's assets, convert them into cash and distribute them among creditors and then to permit the bankrupt to start afresh free from obligations and responsibilities consequent upon business misfortune. Williams et al. v. United States Fidelity Co., 236 U.S. 549. If, on the petition of a creditor, the bankruptcy court stops to adjudicate questions like the one at bar, then the completion of a bankruptcy case will be delayed and the proceedings made more burdensome for the estate at the ultimate expense of creditors not directly involved.

Equally important, the proposal that the bankruptcy court should hear the creditor's claim of fraud is an ingenious device for depriving the bankrupt of a jury trial on the issue of whether he committed the fraud. Such a change in the procedural remedy is almost the equivalent of a change in the substantive law. Congress was slow to except from discharges liabilities for obtaining money by false pretenses as distinguished from judgments for such liabilities, compare Section 17, sub. a(2) of the Act of July 1, 1898, c. 541, 30 Stat. 550 with Section 5 of the Act of February 5, 1903, c. 487, 32 Stat. 798 and subsequent statutes now compiled in the U.S.C. Title 11, § 35, sub. a(2); and it might well have refused ever to have made the additional exception if it had supposed that referees and judges rather than juries were to be the tribunals for determining the issue of fraud.

Finally, it may not be irrelevant to recall the caveat of the Supreme Court of the United States in Local Loan Co. v. Hunt, 292 U.S. 234. That warning may have been primarily directed at the impropriety of a bankruptcy court restraining a creditor from suing the bankrupt after his discharge save in most unusual circumstances. But the opinion also indicates that a bankruptcy court should be reluctant to bring into its forum questions which may be equally well solved elsewhere.

Petition denied.

---

4. PREFERENCES & FRAUDULENT TRANSFERS

ONONDAGA LITHOLITE COMPANY v. RECEIVER OF SALT SPRINGS NATIONAL BANK

United States Court of Appeals, Second Circuit, 1955.
218 F.2d 671.

HINCKS, Circuit Judge. This appeal is brought by the First Trust and Deposit Company, a creditor of the bankrupt Onondaga Litholite Company, from an order of the Bankruptcy Court subordinating its claim to those of all other creditors. The trustee in bankruptcy and certain creditors are the appellees.

The facts are as follows: the appellant had loaned the Onondaga, prior to its adjudication, a substantial sum much needed by Onondaga as working capital. Thereafter, when Onondaga was unable to meet this and other obligations, the appellant and another bank became voting trustees of Onondaga. The appellant also owned $18,900 in face amount of Onondaga's first mortgage bonds which were in default and, when convinced that Onondaga could no longer operate with profit, through a wholly controlled dummy, Domark, caused a foreclosure of the mortgage and on a foreclosure sale bought in all the mortgaged property for $25,000.

Upon the adjudication of Onondaga the appellant had a claim of undisputed validity in the amount of $616,233.23. The trustee in bankruptcy brought an action in the New York State Supreme Court against the appellant based upon a claim that its acquisition, through the foreclosure sale, of Onondaga's mortgaged property constituted an illegal preference and a fraudulent conveyance. The trial court dismissed his complaint on motion, and its judgment was affirmed by the Appellate Division. The New York Court of Appeals, however, reversed on the ground that there was enough evidence in the case to afford an inference that acquisition by the appellant of the bankrupt's assets constituted an illegal preference or a fraudulent transfer. The trustee prevailed in the trial court on the second run. The Appellate Division affirmed the judgment of the trial court except as to damages: it directed a judgment in favor of the trustee in the amount of $55,000 which it found to represent the full market value of the transferred assets ($54,850), less the amount paid by appellant at the foreclosure proceeding ($25,000), plus interest on the difference ($21,551.-70), plus costs of $1,946.95, the judgment also providing for additional interest to be computed to date of payment. Langan v. First Trust & Deposit Co., 277 App.Div. 1090, 101 N.Y.S.2d 36. This judgment was affirmed by the New York Court of Appeals, 302 N.Y. 932, 100 N.E.2d 189, and was promptly paid to the trustee by the appellant.

The question presented is whether the appellant is entitled in the Bankruptcy Court to share on a parity with other unsecured creditors in a fund made available for distribution only after a successful showing by the trustee in the state-court action that the appellant was the recipient of an illegal preference or fraudulent transfer of the bankrupt's property.

The referee and the court below held that a bankruptcy court is a court of equity with the power to subordinate claims in cases of this type. Appellant's claim was subordinated on the theory that as a transferee of a fraudulent conveyance it is not entitled to share equally with other creditors on general equitable principles.

We think that Section 57, sub. g, of the Bankruptcy Act, 11 U.S. C.A. § 93, sub. g, applies here. Under that section, "the claims of creditors who have received or acquired preferences, liens, conveyances, transfers, assignments or encumbrances, void or voidable under this Act, shall not be allowed unless such creditor shall surrender such preferences" etc.

We hold that the Bankruptcy Court was without power in the circumstances of this case, to order the subordination of the appellant's claim. Section 57, sub. g was designed to insure equality of distribution of the bankrupt's assets, not exempted under the Act, amongst its creditors: it was not designed to punish a creditor who had sought to withhold the debtor's assets from the bankruptcy estate. If a creditor having a valid common claim free from equitable infirmities, in an effort to obtain satisfaction of his claim or security therefor, accepts a conveyance of assets of his debtor—later the bankrupt—with actual intent thereby to defraud the debtor's other creditors, nevertheless, if after adjudication he surrenders the assets thus acquired to the court, he may share on a parity with other creditors. And it makes no difference that the surrender is the result of a successful action instituted by the trustee against the creditor: Section 57, sub. g *does not distinguish between voluntary and involuntary surrender.* Keppel v. Tiffin Savings Bank, 197 U.S. 356. * * * In the Keppel case the Court, so far as here relevant, was faced with the same language as is found in the present Section 57, sub. g, and its doctrine has been frequently followed. * * *

We do not think it of any consequence that the state-court action as originally instituted purported to be brought solely for creditors other than appellant and that the judgment in the state court was for money damages instead of recovery of the bankrupt's assets in kind. The trustee's power is determined under the Bankruptcy Act. As so measured, the trustee, in seeking to recover assets of the estate, acts for all creditors and lacks power to exclude any from the benefit of a successful endeavor. Certainly the thrust of Section 57, sub. g may not be avoided by a misconception on the part of a trustee as to his duties and powers. The case would be different if the trustee in the state-court action had not fully recovered the assets or the value thereof from the transferee-creditor. This is not such a case.

Reversed.

IN THE MATTER OF SIMON

United States District Court, E. D. New York, 1961.
197 F.Supp. 301.

BARTELS, District Judge. This is a petition to review the findings of fact and conclusions of the Referee in Bankruptcy made on March 28, 1961 in overruling the objections by the objecting creditor to the bankrupt's discharge. A similar review was sought of a prior decision of the same Referee dated November 6, 1957 and was granted on January 30, 1958 by Judge Byers directing the Referee to hold a further hearing and to take further evidence with regard to certain specific issues set forth in his order dated February 26, 1958. In substance, the basis for the objections is that the bankrupt who owned 50 of the 100 issued and outstanding shares of Domestic Employment Center, Inc., transferred said shares to the other stockholder, one Abraham Fine, for $1 with intent to hinder, delay and defraud his creditors, thus barring his discharge under Section 14 of the Bankruptcy Act. The transfer of said stock occurred on July 14, 1955, within a year of the petition, and was made, according to the bankrupt, pursuant to a restrictive covenant agreement between the bankrupt and Fine dated March 24, 1953, providing, among other things, for cross-options to the two stockholders of this closed corporation upon certain contingencies. A voluntary petition in bankruptcy was filed on March 22, 1956 and the order granting the discharge was dated November 14, 1957.

After approximately 600 pages of additional testimony, numerous additional exhibits, voluminous briefs and protracted proceedings, the Referee has made further findings of fact and conclusions of law and has again overruled the objections and specifications of the objecting creditor. The record is long and the proceeding is unnecessarily voluminous and tedious. An outline of the issues appears in Judge Byers' opinion and also in the Referee's decision and it will be unnecessary for this Court to burden the record with a further summary of the facts.

The Referee has again found, *inter alia*, that the bankrupt was bound by the terms of the stockholders' agreement, that the transfer of the bankrupt's shares was pursuant to the stockholders' agreement, that Fine's right to purchase had not expired on July 14, 1955, that in making the transfer the bankrupt relied in good faith upon the valuation of the shares set forth in accountant Sperber's letter of July 12, 1955, that the bankrupt believed the shares to have "a negative value", that he did not know of "any hidden value of the shares at that time", that the bankrupt believed he was bound by the stockholders' agreement and was so advised by his attorney Stein, that the transfer was made in good faith and that there was no obligation on the part of Fine to pay any value in excess of the book value of the shares in accordance with the formula in the stockholders' agreement and further, that there was no agreement or option between Fine and the bankrupt for the return of the stock. In computing the book value of the stock in accordance with the formula the Referee relied upon the accounting theories of two expert accountants, one the bankrupt's accountant associated with Alfred Sperber and the other, an accountant retained by the bankrupt for the purpose of testifying as an expert witness. The positions taken by these accountants were opposed by the accountant on behalf of the objecting creditor, who incidentally had rendered accounting services to Domestic well after July 14, 1955 and whose theories produced a higher valuation.

After examination of the record the Court has concluded that the paramount issue here is the intent or good faith of the bankrupt in making the transfer. Whether or not the agreement was valid or the transfer was made pursuant to the agreement or the computation of the value of the stock was in accordance with the formula therein described, becomes unimportant if in fact the bankrupt in making the transfer acted in good faith without intent to defraud creditors. Much evidence has been adduced with respect to the value of the stock and various accounting theories employed in computing this value upon the theory that if the stock had value the transfer was invalid. A question has also been raised as to the existence of Fine's right to purchase the stock on July 14, 1955 under the terms of the agreement. The Referee found that the stock had no value under the agreement formula and that there was not an iota of proof which indicated that the bankrupt knew that the stock had value or that he had any reason to know that accountant Sperber's letter stating a negative value was untrue. The Referee concluded that at least as between the bankrupt and Fine the agreement was binding and that the bankrupt believed he was bound by the terms thereof when he made the transfer.

Most of the arguments attacking the Referee's findings are based upon an attack upon the credibility of the witnesses and upon suspicion and inferences which the Court is asked to draw from the various relationships of the parties. The objecting creditor also asserts that the Referee's interpretation of the agreement is erroneous as a matter of law. If the findings of fact of the Referee are accurate the interpretation of the agreement becomes immaterial. As indicated in Margolis v. Nazareth Fair Grounds & Farmers Market, 2 Cir., 1957, 249 F.2d 221, 223, the "clearly erroneous" rule is strictly enforced in this circuit, the Court stating:

"The findings of fact of a referee in bankruptcy will not be disturbed unless they are 'clearly erroneous.' General Order in Bankruptcy, 47, 11 U.S.C.A. following § 53. This requirement of Order 47 'has been strictly enforced in this circuit, especially where credibility is a key factor.' In Matter of Nemerov, D.C.S.D.N.Y.1955, 134 F. Supp. 678, 681. Here the facts were in dispute and the findings of the referee based in part on his judgment of the credibility of the witnesses who testified before him must be given great weight. See Rasmussen v. Gresly, 8 Cir., 1935, 77 F.2d 252, 254, wherein Judge Sanborn said, 'A different rule would virtually make * * * a trial de novo.' "

The basis of the objection to the discharge is that the bankrupt has violated the proscription of Section 14, sub. c(4) of the Bankruptcy Act, 11 U.S.C.A. § 32 sub. c(4), in that he transferred or concealed his property "with intent to hinder, delay, or defraud his creditors". In explaining the requirements of this bar the court said in In re Pioch, 3 Cir., 1956, 235 F.2d 903, at pages 905–906:

"To bar the bankrupt's discharge there must be an actual fraudulent intent on the part of the bankrupt to hinder, delay or defraud his creditors and constructive intent is not sufficient; the reasons for denying a discharge to a bankrupt must be real and substantial, not merely technical and conjectural; speculation cannot be substituted for proof and the requirement is for probative facts capable of supporting, with reason, the conclusions of the trier of fact; the burden of proof is on the objecting creditor to prevent the bankrupt's discharge, otherwise stated, the objecting creditor must make out a prima facie case; * * * and 'it is not so much the acts of the bankrupt that will prevent his discharge, as it is the intent with which he acts.' "

* * *

Here the Referee had an opportunity to hear and see the witnesses and his findings must be accepted unless it clearly appears that he has been mistaken. This is particularly true when the motive and intent of the bankrupt becomes material. In re Slocum, 2 Cir., 1927, 22 F.2d 282. * * * In the present case the Court is asked to substitute speculation and suspicion for evidence and proof. There is nothing in this record which would enable the Court to state that the finding of the Referee on the crucial point of good faith and lack of intent to defraud is clearly erroneous. Under the circumstances the Court adopts and confirms the Referee's findings, overrules the objections thereto, and directs the entry of an order accordingly.

C.   ARRANGEMENTS

1.   INTRODUCTORY NOTE

Not all proceedings under the Bankruptcy Act end in the termination of the business of the insolvent debtor. Reorganizations of insolvent corporations under the provisions of Chapter X are a highly specialized kind of legal problem and as a consequence are not dealt with in this volume. This does not mean that they have little or no importance; to the contrary they are of greatest importance because Chapter X is resorted to for the relief of the problems of the very largest insolvent corporations. (Sometimes medium size and small corporations also seek relief under Chapter X.) One characteristic of a proceeding under Chapter X which differs from other provisions of the Bankruptcy Act is that the rights of secured creditors, generally those holding bonds secured by mortgages or other security, can be dealt with in relation to other creditors and stockholders. Every effort is made to keep the enterprise in operation rather than to liquidate it, although the contractual rights of the various security holders cannot be changed so as to favor one class whose rights are subordinate to the rights of another class. For the most part, the business creditor of a corporation pursuing relief under Chapter X will encounter the same difficulties as those under a normal bankruptcy or under Chapter XI, which is discussed below.

Only a debtor may seek relief under Chapter XI of the Bankruptcy Act, 11 U.S.C.A. §§ 701–709. None of his creditors may file a petition to compel him to do this (as may be done under Chapter X), although a debtor who does petition for relief under Chapter XI must admit his insolvency (Section 323, 11 U.S.C.A. § 723) and if he is not successful in obtaining the relief available under Chapter XI, then a straight bankruptcy will result.

Chapter XI provides for an "Arrangement" to be made between a debtor and his creditors. (The personal pronoun "his" will be used in this section to make it clear that an individual as well as a corporation may seek relief under Chapter XI while only a corporation can do so under Chapter X). An Arrangement is a debtor's plan, and only his plan, for the compromise of his debts, either by paying less than the full amount due, or paying the debts at some later time than their due date, or some combination of the two. If he is successful in achieving this, he can continue to operate his business and if he performs all the provisions of the Arrangement, he can then be discharged of all his unsecured debts and liabilities covered by the Arrangement. No secured claims can be dealt with in a proceeding under Chapter XI; the debtor must obtain the consent of his secured creditors to a separate proposal which he makes to them and they cannot be compelled to accept the terms of the arrangement as general creditors can be as noted below.

A proceeding under Chapter XI is initiated by a debtor by filing his petition, which may, and frequently does, result in the appointment of a receiver at the request of some of his creditors. Either at the time of filing his petition or shortly thereafter he must file his proposed Arrangement which will then be considered by his creditors at a meeting called for that purpose. The meeting of the creditors proceeds in much the same manner as a proceeding in a normal bankruptcy. If the Arrangement has been accepted in writing by all the creditors affected thereby it will be confirmed by the Referee (Section 361, 11 U.S.C.A. § 761). If the arrangement has not been accepted by all of the creditors, then the Referee either at the first meeting of the creditors or a subsequent meeting will confirm the Arrangement if it has been accepted in writing by a majority in number and amount of all the creditors affected by the plan. In both cases, however, the Referee will confirm the Arrangement only if he is satisfied that the requirements of Section 366, 11 U.S.C.A. § 766, have been met, the principal one of which is that the Arrangement is "[f]or the best interest of the creditors and is feasible; * * *." As a practical matter a Referee is reluctant not to confirm an Arrangement which has been accepted by a substantial majority in number and amount of the creditors but he must exercise his independent judgment and find that the Arrangement is for the best interests of the creditors and that it is feasible; occasionally a Referee because of his vast experience in matters of this kind will refuse to confirm an Arrangement because it is not feasible for the debtor to perform all of its terms.

If the Referee refuses to confirm the Arrangement, or if it is not accepted in writing by a majority in number and amount of the creditors affected by the Arrangement, then the Referee will adjudicate the petitioner a bankrupt, and a normal bankruptcy will ensue. If, however, the Arrangement is accepted by the creditors and is confirmed by the Referee, then the Referee will order the distribution of the money or notes that the Arrangement calls for and his confirmation will operate as a discharge of all of the unsecured debts and liabilities of the debtor provided for in the Arrangement. (See Sections 361 to 371 of the Bankruptcy Act, 11 U.S.C.A. §§ 761–771.)

The Arrangement of Ajax Bus Co., Inc. which is reported below is an actual Arrangement, although the name of the debtor and various other parties contained in the Arrangement have been changed. This Arrangement is more complex than most, and is unusual in that it gives unsecured creditors an option to receive 30% of their debts in cash in full settlement or to receive 100% payable in installments over five years. Few debtors in proposing an Arrangement are so generous with their creditors. The Arrangement contains all of the provisions required by Sections 356 and 357 of the Bankruptcy Act, 11 U.S.C.A. §§ 756, 757; many Arrangements which are filed are much briefer and fail to contain all the provisions required by the statute. It is difficult to gauge whether any Arrangement has been successful, because it can reasonably be argued that the continuation of a business enterprise for another one or two years was made possible through the proceeding under Chapter XI which otherwise would not have been possible. However, a purely subjective observation of a number of Arrangements has been that many times they have been proceedings which have just prolonged the agony of both the debtor and his creditors. The Arrangement executed by Ajax Bus Co., Inc. must be considered a resounding success because all of the obligations undertaken under the Arrangement were performed in full and on time, and the business expanded considerably and became a prosperous enterprise. It was a corporation which had already been adjudicated a bankrupt, and after bankruptcy proceedings had commenced it filed a petition for this Arrangement under the provisions of Sec. 321 of the Bankruptcy Act, 11 U.S.C.A. § 721. It undoubtedly would have been liquidated had the Arrangement not been proposed, accepted, confirmed, and fully performed. The Arrangement in full is reported below.

---

2. ARRANGEMENT OF AJAX BUS CO., INC.

IN THE DISTRICT COURT OF THE UNITED STATES FOR THE EASTERN DISTRICT OF ———

IN THE MATTER OF:
AJAX BUS CO., INC.
                    Debtor

In Proceedings for an Arrangement

No. 76543

ARRANGEMENT

AJAX BUS CO., INC., the above-named Debtor proposes the following Arrangement with its creditors, subject to the approval of its secured creditors:

ARTICLE I

PROVISIONS MODIFYING OR ALTERING THE RIGHTS OF UNSECURED CREDITORS

A. The unsecured debts of the Debtor are to be treated as follows:

1. All debts which have priority under the provisions of the Act of Congress relating to Bankruptcy are to be paid in cash in full within ten (10) days after confirmation.

2. All other debts of the Debtor, which are unsecured, shall be settled and satisfied by either of the two following methods, any one of which may be elected by any unsecured creditor as he may choose:

(a) Thirty (30%) per cent of their respective debts to be paid in cash in full settlement within ten (10) days after confirmation; or

(b) One Hundred (100%) per cent of their respective debts payable in twenty equal quarterly installments, the first installment to be paid on the first day of the fourth month following the last day of the month in which the Arrangement has been confirmed by the delivery of twenty equal promissory notes signed by the Debtor as maker, successively due each quarter commencing with the first installment as specified above; said notes shall be payable at City Trust Company, New York, New York; or such other place as the unsecured creditors shall direct;

each of said notes shall state that it is one of a series of twenty notes, and that upon default in the payment of any one of the notes, and the continuation of such default for ten days, the remaining notes of the series shall at the option of the holder of said notes immediately become due and payable without notice; said notes will be deposited for distribution with such person or persons as the Court may designate within ten days after confirmation of the Arrangement; and the rights of such unsecured creditors shall be modified and altered accordingly. In the alternative, providing the same is satisfactory to the unsecured creditors, the debtor will deliver only twenty notes in the total amount aggregating the amount due to the holders of the unsecured claims electing to participate on the installment basis, to such nominee as the unsecured creditors shall designate, and payments on account of said notes shall be made to said nominee who shall distribute the same as the unsecured creditors shall direct.

(c) In the event that any unsecured creditor fails to elect the provisions of either subsection (a) or subsection (b) above, within ten (10) days after confirmation, such creditor shall be paid thirty (30%) per cent of its debt in cash in full settlement on the tenth day after confirmation.

ARTICLE II

PROVISIONS IN REGARD TO EXECUTORY CONTRACTS

The only executory contract upon which the Debtor is obligated is a certain lease for its garage and terminal facilities at 1234 N. 700th Street, New York, New York. The owner of said premises, the Lessor, is Ajax Realty and Contracting Co., Inc., which holds as security for the rent to be paid thereon, a security interest in the Certificate of Public Convenience granted to the Debtor by the Department of Transportation of the State of New York, and an assignment of all of its accounts receivable in the total amount of Fifty-four Thousand ($54,000.00) Dollars as of September 1, 1972. The Debtor proposes to continue said lease, not to reject it, and not to alter the right of its Lessor, except that subject to confirmation of the Arrangement it will procure the release of the security interest held by said creditor in all of the accounts receivable of the Debtor.

ARTICLE III

UNDERTAKINGS OF DEBTOR

A. Within ten (10) days after confirmation of the Debtor's plan it proposes to pay to the secured creditors holding security in the buses and other vehicles owned by the Debtor the appraised value of their security, providing such appraised value does not exceed Twenty-one Thousand ($21,000.00) Dollars. Any deficiency which may result on account of the claims of the secured creditors as a result of such payment will thus become unsecured claims, and the holders thereof may have the rights and privileges extended to unsecured creditors, as provided in Article I above.

B.   Within ten (10) days after confirmation of the Arrangement, the Debtor will pay to those unsecured creditors who have elected the thirty (30%) per cent cash payment set forth in Article I above, and whose claims have either been proved, or admitted to be due by the debtor, the cash due pursuant to the Arrangement.   As to any unsecured creditors whose claims are disputed, or not admitted to be due, and not proved to be due, the Debtor will pay to such holders of such disputed claims who have elected a cash payment, thirty (30%) per cent of the amount admitted to be due, and within ten days after the disputed claim has been finally adjudicated or admitted to be due, the Debtor will pay the holder of such claim the remaining amount then found to be due; as to the holders of disputed claims who elect to receive payment in full in twenty installments outlined above, the Debtor will deliver its notes pursuant to the provisions of Article I above in the amount that the Debtor admits to be due, and upon the final adjudication or admission of the amount to be due on such disputed claims, the Debtor will deliver its note for the additional amount found to be due, as well as pay in full the installments which otherwise would have been paid had the amount been proved at the time that the first installment was due on said note.

C.   Within ten days after confirmation of the Arrangement the Debtor will deliver to such creditors as elect to receive payments in installments as set forth in Article I above, or to the nominee of the unsecured creditors, the notes to be delivered as set forth in Article I above.

D.   Upon payment of the sum set forth above or delivery of the notes set forth above, all creditors, both secured and unsecured, shall release and satisfy all claims due to such creditors, satisfy any liens or encumbrances held by them on any of the assets or property of the Debtor, excepting only the notes provided for in Article I above.

ARTICLE IV

PROVISIONS FOR CONTINUATION OF DEBTOR'S BUSINESS

The Debtor shall remain in possession and operation of its business without restraint by any of its creditors, or any Court presently having jurisdiction of the within matter, and shall so continue so long as the Debtor continues to meet the obligations imposed upon it by the within plan, except that the Debtor agrees that until the notes mentioned in Article I above have been paid in full the Debtor will not increase the salaries of John Smith and William Jones more than twenty (20%) per cent.

ARTICLE V

PROVISIONS FOR DEBTS INCURRED DURING PENDENCY OF ARRANGEMENT

All debts incurred after the filing of the Petition and prior to the confirmation of the Arrangement shall be paid in cash in full on or before confirmation, except that the time of payment of all or any part of such debts may be extended by agreement with the creditors to whom such debts are due, and such extended debts shall, when due, have priority and payment over the debts affected by this Arrangement.

ARTICLE VI

PAYMENT OF EXPENSES

The Debtor will pay the expenses incurred in connection with filing the original Petition under Chapter XI of the Act of Congress relating to Bankruptcy, and the expenses of the Referee in Bankruptcy, but all other costs and expenses of the proceeding shall be paid by the creditors as the Referee in Bankruptcy shall direct, notwithstanding the provision of Article I above relating to the payment of priority debts in cash in full; and specifically, the expenses of any trustee, receiver, or nominee for the creditors shall be borne by the creditors.

ARTICLE VII

ISSUANCE OF NEW OBLIGATIONS

The Debtor proposes to borrow such sum or sums of money as may be necessary to finance the provisions of this Arrangement, and to grant a security interest and/or lien upon any and all of its assets, including but not limited to its buses and other motor vehicles, its aforesaid Certificate of Public Convenience, its garage machinery, equipment and fixtures, its office equipment and fixtures, its accounts receivable and any and all other assets or property of any kind or nature whatsoever, upon such terms, conditions, maturity dates, and interest rate as the officers and directors of the Debtor may negotiate. Such written security instruments as may be necessary to accomplish the foregoing shall be delivered simultaneously with the deposit of any such sums of money as may be necessary to finance the provisions of this Arrangement and as the Court or Referee in Bankruptcy may direct.

ARTICLE VIII

CONSENT OF SECURED CREDITORS

White Equipment Co., Inc., a New Jersey corporation, with its principal office at 456 Broad Street, Camden, New Jersey, presently holds a garageman's lien on three certain buses, property of the Debtor, and described by the Debtor as vehicles Nos. 101, 397 and 426; said garageman's lien being in the amount of Twenty Thousand Six Hundred Sixty ($20,660.00) Dollars, as well as a security interest in the aforesaid Certificate of Public Convenience, and as well as a security interest in the accounts receivable of the Debtor. Said White Equipment Co., Inc., by its consent, indicated in writing below, to the provisions of this Arrangement, has agreed to postpone in payment any amounts due it on account of said indebtedness of Twenty Thousand Six Hundred Sixty ($20,660.00) Dollars, providing the creditors of the Debtor agree to the within Arrangement. In consideration of the said postponement in payment, White Equipment Co., Inc. is to be granted a lien upon the said three buses described above, and agrees not to enforce any of its right as a secured creditor so long as the payments are being made upon the notes described in Article I hereof, but in the event of the acceleration of the amounts due on account of said notes, White Equipment Co., Inc. is to be permitted to enforce any rights it may have as a secured creditor upon any property of the Debtor in which it holds a security interest.

AJAX BUS CO.

By: _____

John Smith, President

Dated: September 1, 1972.

CONSENT

White Equipment Co., Inc. hereby consents to the Arrangement above.

WHITE EQUIPMENT CO., INC.

By: _____

Charles Brown, President

Attest:

_____

Robert Jackson, Secretary

QUESTIONS

1. Should we have public administrators of bankruptcies? That is, should we have court appointed officers who will perform the functions now performed by trustees and receivers, in supervising the liquidation of an insolvent enterprise? Does the public have a sufficient interest in this to have these persons paid at public expense? Would the persons who are charged with administering the estates of bankrupt enterprises be more skilled and more diligent if they were assured of regular compensation? Do the rights of creditors of bankrupt enterprises get the full protection to which they are entitled now? Particularly in a bankruptcy in which there is very little or no money to pay the receiver and trustee for their services?

2. Should the statutory order of priority of distribution of money in a bankruptcy be changed? Should all creditors, whether they

hold security for their claims, or are granted priority by the statute, be treated as the general creditors, that is, should all creditors be treated equally? If a lender could not obtain security for his loan, how would the business which is a high credit risk obtain additional credit? What would happen to the interest rate for business enterprises of this kind? Do we really want to take away the priority for unpaid wages which is now established by the Act? Should the amount of the wage priority claim be increased from $600 to a larger amount? In the twentieth century is it necessary that the "sovereign" be paid all taxes and other debts due to it ahead of most other creditors?

3. Why should we have a bankruptcy system at all? Why should the complete insolvency of a business, insofar as paying creditors is concerned, be treated any differently from the manner in which creditors are paid in a non-bankrupt but financially shaky business? Should we not permit the most diligent creditors to seek payment of their claims in full and let the less diligent take what they can get? Does not most of the law relating to the business system reward initiative? Is a bankruptcy system some attempt to establish order in a process which otherwise would reward those creditors who exert the most power without regard to the relative merit of their claims? Does the bankruptcy system eliminate rewarding those creditors who are willing to resort to violence if necessary to collect their claims?

4. Since rehabilitation of the debtor is one of the two major policies of the Bankruptcy Act, why don't we also grant a discharge to the fraudulent debtor? Are we legislating some kind of morality when the statute denies him a discharge? Are we seeking some form of revenge? Will the creditors get any more payment on their claims from the fraudulent debtor if all of his property has already been taken away from him in the bankruptcy? Why do we insist on having him owe the money for the rest of his life until it is paid? Are there not other means of his conducting a business enterprise (for example, "in his wife's name") to circumvent the existing limitations? What, if anything, could the business system do to protect itself against fraud? Is the denial of a discharge in bankruptcy a sufficient means of doing this now?

5. Is the theory of an Arrangement, as provided in Chapter XI of the Bankruptcy Act, a sound theory? That is, should there be more, or less, emphasis on the rehabilitation of a debtor in the sense that the business enterprise should not be terminated but efforts should be made to continue it in operation? How often have Arrangements under Chapter XI been successful? If they have not been successful often enough, should the system be abandoned or should some efforts be made to improve the system? What changes in either event? Should the shareholders of a corporation which has proposed an Arrangement under Chapter XI be required to defer any benefits to them as shareholders until all creditors of the corporation have been paid in full? If the shareholders are to continue to have an economic interest in the corporation, should they be required to transfer

all of their rights as shareholders to the creditors of the company? Is an Arrangement which has been approved for a corporation, insofar as the shareholders are concerned, any different from rehabilitating an individual person who has been adjudicated a bankrupt?

6. Why should a democratic society be concerned about those business enterprises which have failed? Why do we need a system of law to deal with business failures? How many non-business plans of mankind fail, yet go unnoticed in society at large as well as by the legal system? What is there about the failure of a business enterprise that merits the special recognition we accord to it? Is there something peculiar about the democratic system which grants special attention to a business in financial difficulty? Are we inordinately concerned with property rights? Compare the bankruptcy system with the response which the law makes to the human derelict; are we missing something? Should we abandon the bankruptcy system? Or should we be more responsive to human values?

Suggested Reference Sources

Texts and Treatises

Collier, *Collier On Bankruptcy,* Matthew Bender & Company, Albany, N. Y.

Remington, *Treatise On the Bankruptcy Law Of The United States,* Lawyers Cooperative Publishing Co., Rochester, N. Y.

Topic Headings in the Index to Legal Periodicals

Bankruptcy

Insolvency

Corporate Reorganizations

Bankruptcy: Discharge

Bankruptcy: Assets

Bankruptcy: Claims

Bankruptcy: Preferences

Fraudulent Conveyances

*

INDEX